THE ENCYCLICALS OF JOHN PAUL II

EDITED WITH INTRODUCTIONS BY J. MICHAEL MILLER, C.S.B.

Our Sunday Visitor Publishing Division
Our Sunday Visitor, Inc.
Huntington, Indiana 46750

International Standard Book Number: 0-87973-726-3
Library of Congress Catalog Card Number: 96-68285

Cover design by Monica Watts; photo by Dean Curtis

PRINTED IN THE UNITED STATES OF AMERICA

726

Abbreviations of the Books of the Bible

Acts	Acts of the Apostles	Lk	Luke
Bar	Baruch	1 Mac	1 Maccabees
1 Chron	1 Chronicles	2 Mac	2 Maccabees
2 Chron	2 Chronicles	Mic	Micah
Col	Colossians	Mk	Mark
1 Cor	1 Corinthians	Mt	Matthew
2 Cor	2 Corinthians	Neh	Nehemiah
Dan	Daniel	Num	Numbers
Dt	Deuteronomy	1 Pet	1 Peter
Eccles	Ecclesiastes	2 Pet	2 Peter
Eph	Ephesians	Phil	Philippians
Ex	Exodus	Philem	Philemon
Ezek	Ezekiel	Prov	Proverbs
Gal	Galatians	Ps	Psalms
Gen	Genesis	Rev	Revelation
Heb	Hebrews	Rom	Romans
Hos	Hosea	1 Sam	1 Samuel
Is	Isaiah	2 Sam	2 Samuel
Jas	James	Sir	Sirach
Jer	Jeremiah	1 Thess	1 Thessalonians
Jn	John	2 Thess	2 Thessalonians
1Jn	1 John	1 Tim	1 Timothy
2 Jn	2 John	2 Tim	2 Timothy
Jon	Jonah	Tit	Titus
Jos	Joshua	Tob	Tobit
Judg	Judges	Wis	Wisdom
Lam	Lamentations	Zech	Zechariah
Lev	Leviticus	Zeph	Zephaniah

Other Abbreviations

AAS   *Acta Apostolicae Sedis.* Rome, 1909—.

CCL   *Corpus Christianorum. Series Latina.* Turnhout, 1953—.

CSCO   *Corpus Scriptorum Christianorum Orientalium.* Paris-Louvain, 1903—.

CSEL   *Corpus Scriptorum Ecclesiasticorum Latinorum.* Vienna, 1866—.

DS   Denziger-Schönmetzer. Henry Denziger and Adolf Schönmetzer, eds., *Enchiridion Symbolorum, Definitionum et Declarationum de Rebus Fidei et Morum.* 33rd ed. Freiburg im Breisgau, 1964.

PG   *Patrologia Graeca.* J. P. Migne, ed. Paris, 1857-1866. 162 volumes.

PL   *Patrologia Latina.* J. P. Migne, ed. Paris, 1844-1864. 221 volumes.

SCh   *Sources Chrétiennes.* Paris, 1941—.

Contents

Preface

The twelve encyclicals issued by Pope John Paul II between 1979 and 1995 are among the outstanding contributions of his pontificate to the Church and the world. Intent on confronting the great challenges which face humanity on the threshold of the third Christian millennium, the Pope has undertaken to admonish, inspire, and encourage men and women as they cross "the threshold of hope." His letters focus on Jesus Christ as the answer to the deep-seated questions of his contemporaries.

Since no single compilation of these texts has hitherto been available, this book is designed to meet such a need. It is meant to facilitate access to a wide readership of the Pope's compelling vision of the world, the Church, and the human person. The collection is intended not only for preachers, theologians, religious educators, and students of theology, but also, and especially, for all those who wish to have first-hand contact with the major writings which embody the mind, heart, and will of John Paul II in such a profound and original manner.

Because of their rich theological, pastoral, and spiritual content, these documents deserve careful and meditative study; this volume is organized in order to meet that objective. It begins with a chapter which treats papal encyclicals in general and those of John Paul in particular. Each encyclical is then introduced by a summary of its content and an analysis of its central themes. A selected bibliography of articles and books readily available in English is also included for every encyclical. The frequent references to *L'Osservatore Romano* are to the weekly English edition of this Vatican publication.

The index of biblical citations and subject index are especially helpful to homilists and students of particular aspects of John Paul's teaching. The biblical index lists the direct quotations and references to Sacred Scripture which I judged to be significant, either because they contribute to the development of the Pope's argument in a given encyclical or because he uses them in an original way. The subject index is designed to assist those who wish to penetrate John Paul's thought more deeply in a specific area. Not generated by an automatic word search, the subject index selects themes central to the Pope's world view. Consequently, not every reference to a word or idea is included, but only those which I considered to be sufficiently important or developed to warrant inclusion in a comprehensive index. In both indexes the order of the references in each entry is chronological, according to the date of the encyclical's publication.

The definitive texts of papal encyclicals appear, in Latin, in the *Acta Apostolicae Sedis*, the Holy See's monthly journal which publishes the official documents of the Pope and the Roman Curia. The translations in this collection were prepared by the Secretariat of State and published by the Vatican Press. The only changes I have inserted are those which adapt the original translation to the conventions of American spelling, capitalization, and punctuation. In a very few instances, authoritatively approved editorial corrections were made after the document's initial publication; these modifications have been incorporated into the translations in this volume. Furthermore, some changes in formatting have been made for the sake of consistency, adapting the earlier documents to the style used in the more recently published encyclicals. With the same view to consistency, the footnotes have likewise been edited.

In order to make the indexes as "reader friendly" as possible, each individual paragraph of the various encyclicals is numbered. Where there is more than one paragraph within a section of the official text, each paragraph within that section has been numbered sequentially. For example, if the original version has a section numbered 8, which itself contains four paragraphs, then the enumeration is 8.1, 8.2, 8.3, and 8.4. In every case, however, the enumeration of the sections of the Latin original and official English translation has been retained; only the subdivision into numbered paragraph units has been added.

Heartfelt thanks are due to many friends for their help in seeing this collection of John Paul II's encyclicals into print. I would especially like to mention the following colleagues who painstakingly read the manuscript and offered invaluable suggestions: Sister Anne Clare Keeler, F.S.E., of the Press Office of the Holy See; James Manney and Henry O'Brien of Our Sunday Visitor; Monsignor Alan McCormack, former Chancellor of the Archdiocese of Toronto; Father Joseph McLaughlin, S.S.E., of Saint Michael's College in Winooski, Vermont; Father P. Wallace Platt, C.S.B., of the Cardinal Flahiff Basilian Centre in Toronto; Father Richard J. Schiefen, C.S.B., of the University of Saint Thomas in Houston; and Father William Sheehan, C.S.B., of the Vatican Apostolic Library. Their unfailing encouragement for this project and their deep love for the Church were a constant source of inspiration, and I happily acknowledge my profound debt of gratitude to them.

Introduction to the Papal Encyclicals

Christ has entrusted the Pope with a teaching authority whose purpose is to foster the unity of faith, safeguard the understanding of truth, and build up ecclesial communion. When he carries out this ministry, the Bishop of Rome enjoys a specific charism as the Church's preeminent teacher and the principal guarantor of her obedience to divine revelation. Since the eighteenth century, one of the chief ways in which he has exercised this office of teaching has been through the publication of encyclical letters.[1]

Pope Paul VI defined an encyclical as "a document in the form of a letter sent by the Pope to the Bishops of the entire world; 'encyclical' means circular. It is a very ancient form of ecclesiastical correspondence that characteristically denotes the communion of faith and charity that exists among the various 'Churches,' that is, among the various communities that make up the Church."[2]

Origin and history

While no Old Testament book takes the form of a letter, the New Testament contains twenty-one epistles. The first Christian leaders frequently used letters to keep in contact with far-flung communities of believers. The New Testament also bears witness to the practice of a circular letter sent by its author to more than one local church. The First Letter of Peter, for example, was addressed to "the Dispersion in Pontus, Galatia, Cappadocia, Asia, and Bithynia" (1:1). Because many ancient manuscripts omit any reference to specific recipients, the Letter to the Ephesians is often regarded as a letter destined to all the churches in Asia Minor. This convention of writing a single letter to more than one community continued in the post-apostolic age. In the

---

[1] Encyclicals are one type of authoritative papal document currently in use. The following list ranks them in decreasing order of formal authority: apostolic constitutions, encyclical letters, encyclical epistles, apostolic exhortations, apostolic letters, letters, and messages. The *ex cathedra* definitions of Mary's Immaculate Conception and Assumption were, for example, promulgated by an apostolic letter and an apostolic constitution: respectively, Pius IX's *Ineffabilis Deus* (1854) and Pius XII's *Munificentissimus Deus* (1950). John Paul II has declared, as a teaching to be definitively held, that the Church has no authority to ordain women to the ministerial priesthood. He made this statement in the apostolic letter *Ordinatio Sacerdotalis* (1994). At least on formal grounds, it is a less authoritative document than an encyclical. See Francis G. Morrisey, "Papal and Curial Pronouncements: Their Canonical Significance in Light of the 1983 Code of Canon Law," *The Jurist*, 50 (1990), 102-125.

[2] Paul VI, General Audience, August 5, 1964, *The Pope Speaks*, 10 (1965), 249.

second century, for instance, a letter known as *The Martyrdom of Polycarp* was directed, as the introduction tells us, "to the church of God which sojourns in Philomelium, and all dioceses of the holy and Catholic Church in every place."

Following the example of this early practice, bishops of the first centuries frequently sent letters to one another, and sometimes to the faithful, as a way of promoting unity in faith and discipline. These letters, meant to foster communion among the various churches, contained information about doctrine, feast-day celebrations, and liturgical calendars. At the center of this network of epistolary interchange was the Roman See, the hub of ecclesial communion. The Bishop of Rome received innumerable letters from bishops throughout the world and, in turn, circulated them among the other churches. He also addressed epistles of his own to bishops and other individuals.[3] Commenting on the custom of the Pope's receiving and writing letters, Optatus of Milevis (†370) wrote: "Thanks to an exchange of official letters, the entire universe agrees and becomes one with the Bishop of Rome in a society of communion."[4]

When the collegial bonds among bishops began to weaken in the early Middle Ages, papal letters then concentrated on the affairs of individual local churches. Correspondence between diocesan bishops and the Holy See became bilateral, and the practice of sending a common letter to all bishops waned.

Benedict XIV (1740-1758) is credited with reviving the ancient tradition of the Pope writing a common letter either to a specific group of bishops or to the episcopate as a whole. Not long after his election, Pope Benedict sent out the circular letter *Ubi Primum* (1740) to all members of the college of bishops. Because of this gesture, collections of papal encyclicals now routinely begin with his pontificate. Gregory XVI (1831-1846) called these papal letters "encyclicals" and, during his papacy, this term passed into general use.[5] For many papal documents published before the mid-nineteenth century, however, scholars fail to agree on which ones can properly be classified as encyclicals. Only for those issued after the First Vatican Council (1870) is there a

---

[3] In the first eight centuries four types of papal documents can be distinguished: epistles, the ordinary correspondence addressed to Bishops and others; decrees, letters promulgating decisions made by the Pope on his own authority; decretals, decisions made by the Roman See in response to questions on discipline and administration; and rescripts, pronouncements granting favors sought from the Holy See. See Claudia Carlen, *Papal Pronouncements — A Guide: 1740-1978*, vol. 1 (Ann Arbor: The Pierian Press, 1990), xi.

[4] Optatus of Milevis, *The Schism of the Donatists*, 2.3.

[5] Joaquín Salaverri, "Encyclicals," in *Sacramentum Mundi*, ed. Karl Rahner, vol. 2 (New York: Herder and Herder, 1969), 229.

consensus about the attribution of this designation to specific papal writings. Claudia Carlen's five-volume edition of the papal encyclicals in English, for example, lists 277 encyclicals from the pontificate of Benedict XIV up to that of John Paul I (1978).[6]

Pius IX (1846-1878) continued the practice of writing circular letters adopted by his predecessor Gregory XVI, and Leo XIII (1878-1903) solidified it, writing more than seventy-five encyclicals. Whereas until the First Vatican Council the tone of encyclicals had been chiefly admonitory, Leo often wrote circular letters to respond to new problems, including those concerning the social order. His innovative approach did much to popularize encyclicals as points of reference for Catholic doctrine and apostolic activity.

In the pontificates of the twentieth century, the number of encyclicals published by each Pope has varied considerably: sixteen were written by Pius X (1903-1914), twelve by Benedict XV (1914-1922), thirty by Pius XI (1922-1939), forty-one by Pius XII (1939-1958), eight by John XXIII (1958-1963), seven by Paul VI (1963-1978), and twelve between 1978 and 1996 by John Paul II.

Audience

Encyclicals are normally, but not always, written for the universal Church: for bishops and faithful throughout the world. Until very recently, those intended for the whole Church bore the salutation: "To Our Venerable Brethren, Patriarchs, Primates, Archbishops, Bishops, and Other Local Ordinaries Enjoying Peace and Communion with the Holy See." During the pontificate of John Paul II, however, the salutation has been simplified. Most encyclicals are now addressed "To the Bishops, Priests and Deacons, Men and Women Religious, and Lay Faithful."

Sometimes, however, the Popes have directed encyclicals to bishops of a particular nation and, even more occasionally, to a country's Catholic citizens as well. In 1791, for example, Pius VI wrote *Charitas*, an encyclical on the Civil Constitution of the Clergy, to "Our Beloved Children the Capitulars, Clergy and People of the Kingdom of France." Leo XIII, in particular, frequently wrote just to bishops of a specific country or region.[7]

---

[6] See Claudia Carlen, *The Papal Encyclicals: 1740-1981*, 5 vols. (Ann Arbor: The Pierian Press, 1981).

[7] During the course of his twenty-five year pontificate, Leo XIII wrote encyclicals to the bishops of the Americas, Austria, Bavaria, Belgium, Bohemia, Brazil, Canada, England, France, Germany, Greece, Hungary, Ireland, Italy, Latin America, Moravia, Peru, Poland, Portugal, Prussia, Scotland, Spain, Switzerland, and the United States.

While traditionally bishops have been the recipients of encyclicals, the Popes sometimes addressed their letters to other groups or to all the faithful.[8] For example, encyclicals have been sent to bishops of various non-Latin Catholic churches, to heads of religious orders, and to priests. When Benedict XV wished to mark the sixth centenary of Dante's death in 1921, he wrote the encyclical *In Praeclara Summorum* to "Professors and Students of Literature and Learning in the Catholic World." With John Paul II, the practice of including the lay faithful in the salutation of encyclicals, a custom which began under John XXIII and continued under Paul VI, has become standard. *Veritatis Splendor* (1993), which was addressed only to bishops, and *Ut Unum Sint* (1995), which has no salutation, are John Paul II's only exceptions to this new convention.

A further modern development is the frequent inclusion of "all men [and women] of good will" in an encyclical's salutation, when it deals with social and moral questions of concern to all humanity. John XXIII began this usage in *Pacem in Terris* (1963), and his successors continued it. Paul VI's *Ecclesiam Suam* (1964), *Populorum Progressio* (1967), and *Humanae Vitae* (1968) were directed to everyone. John Paul II's encyclicals which treat social questions likewise mention "all people of good will" in their opening greeting. These include *Redemptor Hominis* (1979), *Laborem Exercens* (1981), *Sollicitudo Rei Socialis* (1987), *Centesimus Annus* (1991), and *Evangelium Vitae* (1995).

Encyclical Letters and Encyclical Epistles

Since Pius XI, the Popes have distinguished between encyclical "letters" and encyclical "epistles." The latter treat a question of interest either to a restricted group or to the bishops of a specific country or region of the Church. In theory, because encyclical epistles are not addressed to the whole Church, they are considered less solemn and therefore enjoy less formal authority than encyclical letters.

Many encyclicals published by Popes before Pius XI can, in fact, be counted as encyclical "epistles," even though the official version does not title them in this way. Unlike Leo XIII, his successors Pius X, Benedict XV, and Pius XI addressed few encyclicals to the bishops of a particular country. Pius XII was

---

[8] The first encyclical directed to all Catholics was Clement XIV's *Salutis Nostrae* (1774), which proclaimed the Jubilee of 1775. This practice, however, failed to become common. Later, Pius XI addressed *Quadragesimo Anno* (1931) to "all the faithful of the Catholic world." Pius XII never included the lay faithful in the salutation of an encyclical, whereas John XXIII addressed the laity in his first encyclical, *Ad Petri Cathedram* (1959), and again later in *Mater et Magistra* (1961) and *Pacem in Terris* (1963). Paul VI directed some encyclicals only to bishops, and others to bishops and all the faithful.

the last Pope to write encyclicals to a restricted sector of the hierarchy, issuing four of them.[9]

Numerous questions previously taken up in encyclicals are now covered in the Pope's *ad limina* talks to bishops. He addresses them as a group when they come to Rome at five-year intervals to receive his encouragement and give him an account of their ministry.[10] Furthermore, the Bishop of Rome also uses other types of documents, such as papal messages or letters, when he wishes to address a particular sector of the hierarchy or an episcopal conference.

From the Second Vatican Council (1962-1965) onward, encyclical epistles are rare. John Paul II has written one encyclical epistle, *Slavorum Apostoli* (1985), to commemorate the eleven hundredth centenary of the evangelizing work of Saints Cyril and Methodius among the Slavs. In fact, contemporary theologians regularly overlook the distinction, using the term "encyclical" to refer to both encyclical epistles and encyclical letters.[11]

Kinds

According to the subject matter treated, encyclicals (letters and epistles) can be conveniently divided into three major categories: doctrinal, social, and exhortatory.

Doctrinal encyclicals

Two kinds of doctrinal encyclicals can be distinguished. First are those which deal with particular points of Catholic doctrine in a general way. While undoubtedly conditioned by the theological climate of their age, these encyclicals are primarily aimed at a serene exposition of Church teaching. Leo XIII's *Divinum Illud Munus* (1897), on the Holy Spirit, Pius XII's *Mystici Corporis* (1943), on the mystical Body of Christ, and his *Sempiternus Rex* (1951), on the Christology of the Council of Chalcedon, and Paul VI's *Ecclesiam Suam* (1964), on the Church and dialogue, are examples of this kind of doctrinal encyclical. The Trinitarian cycle of John Paul II also falls into this category:

---

[9] See *Ecclesiae Fastos* (1954), on Saint Boniface, to the bishops of Great Britain, Germany, Austria, France, Belgium, and Holland; *Ad Sinarum Gentem* (1954), on the supranationality of the Church, and *Ad Apostolorum Principis* (1958), on Communism and the Church in China, to the Chinese bishops; and *Le pèlerinage a Lourdes* (1958), on the centenary of the Marian apparitions at Lourdes, to the French bishops.

[10] See J. Michael Miller, *The Shepherd and the Rock: Origins, Development, and Mission of the Papacy* (Huntington: Our Sunday Visitor, 1995), 248-250.

[11] This confusion in terminology is reflected even in magisterial documents. In the apostolic letter *Orientale Lumen* (1995), *Slavorum Apostoli* is mistakenly referred to as an "encyclical letter" (§7.1).

Redemptor Hominis (1979), *Dives in Misericordia* (1980), and *Dominum et Vivificantem* (1986).

Second are those doctrinal encyclicals which more explicitly involve the Pope's responsibility to safeguard the integrity of the apostolic deposit of faith. They are chiefly concerned with presenting Catholic teaching which is in some way under attack. If the Church's unity of faith is threatened, the Bishop of Rome uses his apostolic authority to judge questions of doctrine and, if necessary, to correct views contrary to the Church's faith. When Christians are faced with conflicting voices and never-ending theological disputes, papal teaching helps to give them surety about what the Church believes. Through his interventions, the Pope is "defending the right of the people of God to receive the message of the Church in its purity and integrity and not be disturbed by a particular dangerous opinion."[12]

This second kind of doctrinal encyclical includes Pius IX's *Quanta Cura* (1864), to which was attached the *Syllabus of Errors*, Leo XIII's *Satis Cognitum* (1896), on the unity of the Church, Pius X's *Pascendi Dominici Gregis* (1907), on the condemnation of modernism, Pius XI's *Mortalium Animos* (1928), on Catholic participation in the ecumenical movement, and *Casti Connubii* (1930), on contraception and Christian marriage, Pius XII's *Humani Generis* (1950), on false opinions threatening to undermine Catholic doctrine, and Paul VI's *Humanae Vitae* (1968), on the regulation of birth. *Veritatis Splendor* (1993) and *Evangelium Vitae* (1995) are doctrinal encyclicals in which John Paul II uses his authority to judge questions touching the deposit of faith. *Veritatis Splendor* deals with fundamental questions of moral theology; it warns, for example, of the dangers posed by the ethical theories of consequentialism and proportionalism. To combat these views, the Pope reasserts the Church's tradition that some acts are in themselves intrinsically evil. *Evangelium Vitae* contains authoritative doctrinal statements on the inviolability of innocent human life, and on the grave moral evil of abortion and euthanasia.

Social encyclicals

Social encyclicals "treat more directly economic, political, and cultural issues, action, and problems which militate against the common welfare of people in society and which affect the dignity of human persons, families, communities, and nations."[13] Many social encyclicals have dealt with weighty issues, particularly in the last hundred years, but others have treated questions of

---

[12] Congregation for the Doctrine of the Faith, Instruction on the Ecclesial Vocation of the Theologian, *Donum Veritatis* (1990), §37.

[13] Charles D. Skok, "Encyclicals, Social," in *The Modern Catholic Encyclopedia*, ed. Michael Glazier and Monika K. Hellwig (Collegeville: Liturgical Press, 1994), 281.

less lasting significance. In this latter group can be included Leo XIII's encyclical condemning dueling,[14] Benedict XV's encyclical on the peace conference following World War I,[15] and Pius XI's encyclical on motion pictures.[16]

Since Leo XIII's *Rerum Novarum* (1891), on the relation between capital and labor, many Popes have used encyclicals to formulate and foster a social doctrine which has enriched Catholic teaching and significantly influenced Church life. Among the most notable are Pius XI's *Quadragesimo Anno* (1931), on the reconstruction of the social order, John XXIII's *Mater et Magistra* (1961), on Christianity and social progress, and *Pacem in Terris* (1963), on establishing world peace, and Paul VI's *Populorum Progressio* (1967), on the development of peoples. John Paul II has published three social encyclicals: *Laborem Exercens* (1981), on human work, *Sollicitudo Rei Socialis* (1987), on social concerns, and *Centesimus Annus* (1991), on the hundredth anniversary of *Rerum Novarum*.

Exhortatory encyclicals

A third category of encyclicals includes those primarily aimed at encouraging a particular attitude, devotional practice, or course of action among Catholics. The innumerable encyclicals which commemorate the anniversaries of saints,[17] and those dedicated to encouraging devotion to the rosary[18] or the Sacred Heart of Jesus[19] fall into this exhortatory category. So, too, do encyclicals whose purpose is to inspire Catholics to take action in a certain field. Pius IX, for example, wrote an encyclical on urging aid for Ireland during the

[14] *Pastoralis Officii* (1891).

[15] *Quod Iam Diu* (1918).

[16] *Vigilanti Cura* (1936).

[17] Among the more well known are *Grande Munus* (1880), on Saints Cyril and Methodius; *Auspicato Concessum* (1882), on Saint Francis of Assisi; *Militantis Ecclesiae* (1897), on Saint Peter Canisius; *Iucunda Sane* (1904), on Pope Saint Gregory the Great; *Communium Rerum* (1909), on Saint Anselm of Aosta; *Editae Saepe* (1910), on Saint Charles Borromeo; *Spiritus Paraclitus* (1920), on Saint Jerome; *Principi Apostolorum Petro* (1920), on Saint Ephrem the Syrian; *Fausto Appentente Die* (1921), on Saint Dominic; *Studiorum Ducem* (1923), on Saint Thomas Aquinas; *Rite Expiatis* (1926), on Saint Francis of Assisi; *Ad Salutem* (1930), on Saint Augustine; *Orientalis Ecclesiae* (1944), on Saint Cyril of Alexandria; *Fulgens Radiatur* (1947), on Saint Benedict; *Doctor Mellifluus* (1953), on Saint Bernard of Clairvaux; *Ecclesiae Fastos* (1954), on Saint Boniface; *Invicti Athletae* (1957), on Saint Andrew Bobola; *Sacerdotii Nostri Primordia* (1959), on Saint John Vianney; and *Aeterna Dei Sapientia* (1961), on Pope Saint Leo the Great.

[18] Leo XIII dedicated nine encyclicals specifically to the rosary, while Pius XI, Pius XII, and John XXIII each wrote one encyclical on this Marian devotion.

[19] See Leo XIII's *Annum Sacrum* (1899), on consecration to the Sacred Heart, and Pius XI's *Miserentissimus Redemptor* (1928), on reparation to the Sacred Heart. Pius XII's *Haurietis Aquas* (1956) treats the theme of devotion to the Sacred Heart from a theological and biblical perspective.

potato famine of the 1840s,[20] Benedict XV one on the plight of children in central Europe after World War I,[21] and Pius XII one on encouraging prayers for peace and freedom during the Hungarian Revolution of 1956.[22] Among the exhortatory encyclicals of John Paul II three deserve mention: *Slavorum Apostoli* (1985), which commemorates Saints Cyril and Methodius as the evangelizers of the Slavs; *Redemptoris Missio* (1990), which reaffirms the permanent value of the Church's commitment to evangelization and encourages greater missionary activity; and *Ut Unum Sint* (1995), which appeals to all churches and ecclesial communities to make greater efforts to foster the full, visible unity of Christians.

Structure, preparation, and style

Like other papal and Vatican documents, encyclicals are commonly known by the first two or three words of their Latin title. Occasionally, when the official version is issued in a language other than Latin, they are referred to by the opening words of the vernacular original. This is the case, for example, for two well-known encyclicals of Pius XI: *Non abbiamo bisogno* (1931), on fascism and Catholic Action in Italy, and *Mit brennender Sorge* (1937), on the Church and the German Reich.

The authoritative version of an encyclical is published in the Vatican's official organ, the *Acta Apostolicae Sedis*.[23] Nearly always it is in Latin.[24] A few encyclicals, however, have no official Latin translation.[25] Other languages that have been used for encyclicals include French, German, Italian, and Spanish. Even though some have been addressed to the bishops of an English-speaking country, no encyclical has ever been released officially in English. While

[20] *Praedecessores Nostros* (1847).

[21] *Paterno Iam Diu* (1919).

[22] *Luctuosissimi Eventus* (1956).

[23] Since 1909, the *Acta Apostolicae Sedis*, which contains all the official acts of the Pope and the Roman Curia, has been published monthly. It was preceded by the non-official but authoritative *Acta Sanctae Sedis*, also published monthly, from 1865 to 1908.

[24] Even though the Latin text of an encyclical is now first released in the daily Italian edition of *L'Osservatore Romano*, the Latin version published in this newspaper is not the official one. On occasion, slight corrections have been introduced between an encyclical's first appearance and its later official publication in the *Acta Apostolicae Sedis*. This occurred, for example, with *Divini Illius Magistri* (1931) and *Evangelium Vitae* (1995).

[25] Examples of such encyclicals are *Dall'alto dell Apostolico Seggio* (1890), on freemasonry in Italy; *Non abbiamo bisogno* (1931), on fascism and Catholic Action in Italy; and *Mit brennender Sorge* (1937), on the Church and the German Reich. Others, while sent to the bishops in their own language, are published in the *Acta Apostolicae Sedis* in both the vernacular and Latin; see, for example, *No es muy conocida* (1937), on the persecution of the Church in Mexico.

many Popes have written in Latin, others have composed in Italian or, as with John Paul II, in Polish. At present, the various language sections of the Secretariat of State of the Holy See are responsible for preparing approved translations from an Italian draft, though the official text remains the Latin version.[26]

An encyclical's date of publication is frequently linked to a liturgical feast which sheds light on its subject matter. Paul VI's *Ecclesiam Suam* (1964), on the Church and dialogue, and John Paul II's *Veritatis Splendor* (1993), on fundamental moral questions, for example, were both published on August 6, the feast of the Transfiguration. John Paul's *Redemptoris Mater* (1987), on Mary, and *Evangelium Vitae* (1995), on human life, bear the significant date, March 25, the solemnity of the Annunciation. Encyclicals which commemorate earlier documents often carry the same date as the original. Pius XI's *Quadragesimo Anno* (1931) and John XXIII's *Mater et Magistra* (1961) were both released on May 15, the date of the publication of Leo XIII's *Rerum Novarum* (1891). John Paul II, however, chose to publish his anniversary commemorations of Leo's landmark encyclical, *Laborem Exercens* (1981) and *Centesimus Annus* (1991), on May 1, the memorial of Saint Joseph the Worker.

The closing of encyclicals is stylized. It indicates the place of publication, usually "in Rome, at Saint Peter's," as well as the calendar date and the year of the present Pope's pontificate. Frequently the closing paragraph also refers to the liturgical feast celebrated on the day of publication.

Popes often consult theologians, experts, and bishops when they are preparing an encyclical. For this reason many encyclicals, such as *Humanae Vitae* (1968) and *Veritatis Splendor* (1993) were several years in the making. Though the individuals consulted are bound to the strictest secrecy, a close scrutiny of the documents provides some clues about which theologians had a hand in their preparation. For many years, the Jesuits at Roman institutions of higher learning were the primary consultants to the Popes. Pius XII's *Mystici Corporis* (1943) reflects the views of Sebastian Tromp, as *Divino Afflante Spiritu* (1943) shows the influence of Augustin Bea.[27]

Until recently, the fact that the Pope sought advice from theologians, officials of the Roman Curia, and other bishops was not publicly acknowledged. John Paul II, however, has openly stated that he consulted his brother bishops in preparing *Evangelium Vitae* (1995). In its introduction he wrote that he asked them, "in the spirit of episcopal collegiality, to offer me their coopera-

---

[26] Approved Vatican translations appear in Dutch, English, French, German, Italian, Polish, Portuguese, and Spanish.

[27] Ladislas Örsy, *The Church: Learning and Teaching* (Wilmington: Michael Glazier, 1987), 50.

tion in drawing up a specific document." He then added: "I am deeply grateful to all the Bishops who replied and provided me with valuable facts, suggestions and proposals" (§5.2). Regardless of the help the Pope receives in composing an encyclical, when he approves its publication, he does so with the authority of the Successor of Peter. Its content is officially proposed as his own teaching, not that of any collaborator who may have contributed to planning or editing the document.

As for the length of encyclicals, it has varied significantly over the years: from Leo XIII's 248-word *Quod Votis* (1902), on the founding of a Catholic university in Eastern Europe, to John Paul II's *Evangelium Vitae* (1995), the longest to date, of nearly 50,000 words.

No special literary style, except the use of a formal salutation and closing, characterizes papal encyclicals. Until John Paul II, papal rhetoric was, at least by today's standards, unfailingly formal and sometimes stilted. Popes used the formal first person plural "we" when referring to themselves. From his first encyclical onward, John Paul has adopted a far more personal voice, abandoning the plural of majesty, and sometimes including bits of autobiographical material.[28] Like all writings, encyclicals reflect the literary talents of their authors. A comparison of the encyclicals of John Paul II with those of Paul VI shows that the former are less rigorously organized, more discursive and repetitive, and more homiletic in tone.

Authority

Encyclicals are a privileged way in which the Bishop of Rome, with the special assistance of Christ, fulfills his Petrine ministry of teaching. He may clarify the meaning of revelation, recall the importance of a particular teaching in the deposit of faith, guard against ideas incompatible with Church doctrine, or apply the Gospel to new questions that have arisen. While no canonical or theological reason would prevent the Successor of Peter from making an *ex cathedra* pronouncement in an encyclical, no Pope has solemnly defined a dogma of faith in this way.[29] In other words, "the contents of an encyclical are presumed to belong to the ordinary magisterium unless the opposite is clearly manifested."[30]

---

[28] See, for example, his remarks on his election to the papacy (*Redemptor Hominis*, §2) and his comments on ecumenical meetings with other Christian leaders (*Ut Unum Sint*, §§24, 72).

[29] Francis A. Sullivan, "The Doctrinal Weight of *Evangelium Vitae*," *Theological Studies*, 56 (1995), 563.

[30] G. K. Malone, "Encyclical," in *New Catholic Encyclopedia*, vol. 5 (New York: McGraw-Hill Book Company, 1967), 332.

While the Pope exercises his ordinary magisterium whenever he issues an encyclical, he engages it in varying degrees. Some exhortatory encyclicals, for example, contain large amounts of biographical material on saints, and the social encyclicals routinely include analyses of particular economic and political situations. Since the Pope does not intend to teach on such matters, these hagiographic or analytic details engage his ordinary teaching authority only in a very limited way. In the case of the social encyclicals, the extended analyses are included either to support the Pope's more authoritative affirmations or to make more understandable his recommendations about how to implement the doctrinal principles he has outlined.

In papal encyclicals, therefore, a distinction exists between what is intended to be merely explanatory or exhortatory and what is taught as a matter of faith or morals. Consequently, an accurate assessment of the authority of specific statements of an encyclical is determined both by an examination of the particular matter dealt with and by the way in which the Pope proposes it. When, for example, the Successor of Peter introduces a pronouncement with "I confirm that"[31] or "I declare that,"[32] he is indicating that he is invoking his Petrine authority. In this regard John Paul II has said:

> In the Encyclicals *Veritatis Splendor* and *Evangelium Vitae* . . . I wished once again to set forth the constant doctrine of the Church's faith with an act confirming truths which are clearly witnessed to by Scripture, the apostolic Tradition and the unanimous teaching of the Pastors. These declarations, by virtue of the authority handed down to the Successor of Peter to "confirm the brethren" (Lk 22:32), thus express the common certitude present in the life and teaching of the Church.[33]

By his own admission, John Paul II has used the encyclical form for declaring or confirming a teaching already proposed by the universal ordinary magisterium of the episcopal college.

The authority of an encyclical does not depend on the reasons the Pope gives for his teaching. If reasonable arguments determined a document's authority, observes Francis Sullivan, "papal teaching would have no more claim

---

[31] See, for example, *Evangelium Vitae* (1995), with reference to the confirmation of the Church's teaching on the inviolability of innocent human life (§57.4) and the condemnation of euthanasia (§65.4).

[32] See *Evangelium Vitae* (1995), §62.3, with reference to the condemnation of direct abortion.

[33] Address to the Plenary Assembly of the Congregation for the Doctrine of the Faith, November 24, 1995, *L'Osservatore Romano*, 48 (1995), 3.

on the assent of Catholics than it does on the assent of anyone else who might happen to read an encyclical."[34] When the Successor of Peter publishes an encyclical, he teaches in Christ's name and is guided by the Holy Spirit. He is not acting as a theologian whose authority depends on the strength of the arguments adduced in order to uphold a certain judgment. Because of the divine assistance promised to Peter and his successors (cf. Mt 16:18-19; Lk 22:31-32; Jn 21:15-17), the teaching of the Bishop of Rome enjoys an authority that goes beyond the force of his argumentation.

The kind of assent to be given to an encyclical varies according to the Pope's express intention.[35] In order to assess precisely the degree of assent called for in a specific instance, the hermeneutical principles applied to the study of all magisterial documents must be used. This can be a painstaking task, one which requires a thorough knowledge of the principles of interpretation.[36] At the same time, what Pius XII asserted about the authority of papal encyclicals also remains valid:

> The teaching contained in encyclical letters cannot be dismissed on the pretext that the Popes do not exercise in them the supreme power of their teaching authority. Rather, such teachings belong to the ordinary magisterium, of which it is true to say: "He who hears you, hears me" (Lk 10:16); for the most part, too, what is expounded and inculcated in encyclical letters already appertains to Catholic doctrine for other reasons.[37]

When the Pope exercises his ordinary magisterium in an encyclical, the assent that Catholics are expected to give is what Vatican II refers to as the

---

[34] Francis A. Sullivan, *Magisterium: Teaching Authority in the Catholic Church* (New York: Paulist Press, 1983), 165-166.

[35] See Miller, *The Shepherd and the Rock*, 180-182, 200-201.

[36] See the now classic formulation, published by the Congregation for the Doctrine of the Faith, of some of the principles to be borne in mind in such an investigation: "The meaning of the pronouncements of faith depends partly upon the expressive power of the language used at a certain point in time and in particular circumstances. Moreover, it sometimes happens that some dogmatic truth is first expressed incompletely (but not falsely), and at a later date, when considered in a broader context of faith or human knowledge, it receives a fuller and more perfect expression. In addition, when the Church makes new pronouncements she intends to confirm or clarify what is in some way contained in Sacred Scripture or in previous expressions of Tradition; but at the same time she usually has the intention of solving certain questions or removing certain errors. All these things have to be taken into account in order that these pronouncements may be properly interpreted" (Declaration in Defense of Catholic Doctrine on the Church against Certain Errors of the Present Day, *Mysterium Ecclesiae* [1973], §5).

[37] *Humani Generis* (1950), §20.

"religious submission of will and of mind [which] must be shown, in a special way, to the authentic teaching of the Roman Pontiff, even when he is not speaking *ex cathedra*."[38] The kind of response called for by this exercise of the ordinary papal magisterium "must be understood within the logic of faith and under the impulse of obedience to the faith."[39]

Such assent is called "religious" submission because it is rooted in a person's love of God and trust in his care for the Church. This confidence includes the belief that God has given the Pope a special charism which makes his ordinary magisterium a reliable guide in matters of Christian faith and living. An individual's assent, therefore, does not depend on purely rational motives, such as being convinced by the persuasive force of an encyclical's argumentation. As religious "submission," the assent to be given requires an attitude of docility to papal teaching, a sincere adherence to the doctrine expressed.

Influence on Church Life

Most of the 289 encyclicals published since 1740 have long been forgotten. There is good reason for this. An encyclical to the bishops of Albania on the use of Islamic names by Christians,[40] to the bishops of France on the Law of Separation,[41] or to the American bishops thanking them for their good wishes on the Pope's anniversary[42] are of no continuing theological or pastoral interest. Perhaps ten percent of the encyclicals published before the pontificate of John Paul II are still studied by theologians.[43] But this ten percent is extraordinarily significant. It is impossible to imagine the development of the Church's social teaching, for example, without referring to the principles set out in *Rerum Novarum* (1891), *Quadragesimo Anno* (1931), *Mater et Magistra* (1961), *Pacem in Terris* (1963), or *Populorum Progressio* (1967). Nor can one under-

---

[38] *Lumen Gentium*, §25; cf. Code of Canon Law (1983), canon 752.

[39] Congregation for the Doctrine of the Faith, Instruction of the Ecclesial Vocation of the Theologian, *Donum Veritatis* (1990), §23.

[40] Benedict XIV, *Quod Provinciale* (1754).

[41] Pius X, *Vehementer Nos* (1906).

[42] Leo XIII, *In Amplissimo* (1902).

[43] This percentage increases for more recent Popes, although they too have written encyclicals which have quietly fallen into oblivion. Of Pius XII's forty-one encyclicals, perhaps ten are significant — a remarkable achievement. For John XXIII, two of his eight encyclicals have made a lasting contribution to Church life: *Mater et Magistra* (1961) and *Pacem in Terris* (1963). Even Paul VI's small corpus of seven encyclicals, truncated with *Humanae Vitae* (1968), which was published ten years before the end of his pontificate, contains two long-forgotten Marian encyclicals, *Mense Maio* (1965) and *Christi Matri* (1966). In fact, his major document on Mary was issued as an apostolic exhortation, *Marialis Cultus* (1974).

estimate the contribution made to the renewal of philosophy and theology in light of Saint Thomas by *Aeterni Patris* (1879), to biblical studies by *Divino Afflante Spiritu* (1943), to ecclesiology by *Mystici Corporis* (1943), to the liturgy by *Mediator Dei* (1947), or to world peace by *Pacem in Terris* (1963).

Somewhat surprisingly, the *Catechism of the Catholic Church* (1992) cites papal encyclicals rather sparingly. In total, the *Catechism* contains forty-five direct quotations and seventy-eight references to papal encyclicals. John Paul's encyclicals are cited directly or indirectly seventy-five times, thirty-six of which are to *Centesimus Annus* (1991). More than half of the *Catechism's* total references to encyclicals are to the various social encyclicals.[44]

During the papal ministry of recent Popes, the publication of encyclical letters has often been a major event in ecclesial and secular circles and has sometimes provoked controversy. Pius XII's *Humani Generis* (1950) and especially Paul VI's *Humanae Vitae* (1968) fall into this category. In fact, *Humanae Vitae* is commonly judged to mark a watershed in the life of the Church after the Second Vatican Council. Of John Paul II's encyclicals, *Centesimus Annus* (1991), *Veritatis Splendor* (1993), and *Evangelium Vitae* (1995) have given rise to the most commentary in the public press. As the bibliography shows, these three encyclicals have also stimulated a great deal of theological reflection, above all *Veritatis Splendor*. Others, however, such as *Dives in Misericordia* (1980) and *Slavorum Apostoli* (1985), caused ripples only in the narrowest circles. Indeed, some papal documents, which are published with less formal authority, receive far more attention from theologians and the public at large. For example, Paul VI's apostolic exhortation, *Evangelii Nuntiandi* (1975), on evangelization in the modern world, and John Paul II's apostolic letter *Mulieris Dignitatem* (1988), on the dignity and vocation of women, have both had an impact on Church life which far exceeds that of many encyclicals. For the most part, both scholars and the media pay a great deal more attention to encyclicals that deal with social or moral issues than to those that treat strictly theological questions.

Papal encyclicals remain a vital teaching instrument in the hands of the Bishop of Rome. For more than two hundred years Popes have used them as a principal way of exercising their teaching ministry. In recent years, beginning with John XXIII, three trends can be discerned regarding the role of encyclicals in the Church's life. First, encyclicals have been increasingly re-

---

[44] The following list first gives the number of direct quotes and then the number of indirect citations ("cf.") to the encyclicals of the various Popes mentioned in the *Catechism of the Catholic Church:* Pius IX (0-1), Leo XIII (2-4), Pius XI (1-4), Pius XII (12-6), John XXIII (4-1), Paul VI (8-5), John Paul II (18-57).

stricted to matters of primary doctrinal or moral importance to the universal Church. Second, they are now usually addressed to all Catholics and, frequently, to all people of good will. Third, modern Popes take great pains to present the teaching of their encyclicals in a way which is persuasive and convincing for their readers.

John Paul II's Encyclicals

Because of the divinely established office that he exercises and the personal charism that he possesses, Pope John Paul II commands world-wide attention when he publishes an encyclical. Several of them, especially *Centesimus Annus* (1991), *Veritatis Splendor* (1993), and *Evangelium Vitae* (1995), have evoked widespread comment in the media: both high praise and harsh criticism. Encyclicals are an instrument which the Pope uses to impress his own stamp upon the Church as Peter's 263rd Successor.

Vision

John Paul II has a clear and comprehensive vision for bringing the Church into the third Christian millennium.[45] His inspiring perspective stems from the conviction that the Church is called to serve every person and the whole world by preaching "the unsearchable riches of Christ" (Eph 3:8). For this undertaking to be successful, he believes that the Church must be energized, awakened to an ever deeper conversion and awareness of the freshness of the Gospel as the answer to humanity's deepest yearnings. In the twelve encyclicals issued between 1979 and 1996, the Pope places his intellectual and spiritual resources at the service of this goal.

Certainly it is difficult, if not impossible, to summarize John Paul's thought under a single rubric. It is too complex, sophisticated, and wide-ranging for such an undertaking. Nonetheless, the reading of his encyclicals allows us to discern a unique vision. Before exploring this vision, we must first clarify his

[45] Among the studies of John Paul's life and vision are the following: Paul Johnson, *Pope John Paul II and the Catholic Restoration* (London: Weidenfeld & Nicolson, 1982); John M. McDermott, ed., *The Thought of Pope John Paul II* (Rome: Gregorian University Press, 1993); John Saward, *Christ Is the Answer: The Christ-Centered Teaching of Pope John Paul II* (Edinburgh: T&T Clark, 1995); Kenneth L. Schmitz, *At the Center of the Human Drama: The Philosophical Anthropology of Karol Wojtyla/John Paul II* (Washington: Catholic University of America Press, 1993); Tad Szulc, *Pope John Paul II: The Biography* (New York: Scribner, 1995); Michael Walsh, *John Paul II: A Biography* (London: HarperCollins, 1994); George A. Weigel, *The Final Revolution: The Resistance Church and the Collapse of Communism* (New York: Oxford University Press, 1992); and George Hunston Williams, *The Mind of John Paul II: Origins of His Thought and Action* (New York: Seabury Press, 1981).

understanding of the present historical moment. After considering his interpretation of the signs of the times, we can then describe the path he marks
out in order to meet today's challenge of evangelization.

In many of his encyclicals, the Pope describes the evils confronting contemporary men and women. At the present time, he thinks that civilization is
in crisis, especially in the scientifically developed and technologically advanced
West. More and more this civilization, which is rooted in Christianity, is becoming interiorly and spiritually impoverished. According to Joyce Little, "John
Paul II sees in the modern world an active, willful displacement of God by
man and believes that this displacement of God, more than any other single
factor, explains the human catastrophes of the twentieth century."[46] Post-
modern society does not so much deny God as keep him at a distance. This
secularist attitude severs the Gospel from culture, enclosing religion in the
totally private sphere, and it thwarts Christianity's power of being a "sign of
contradiction" to the world. According to John Paul, secularism expresses
itself in a materialist and consumerist view of life. In turn, this perspective is
buttressed by a false idea of freedom—one which is untethered from the truth.
Thus ethical relativism takes hold and the moral underpinnings of society are
shaken to the roots.

John Paul neither cavalierly condemns nor uncritically accepts modernity. Rather, with the light of the Gospel as handed down and lived in the
Church, he patiently sifts and judges the fruits that modernity has brought
forth. On the positive side, he extols the progress made regarding the rights of
workers, as in *Laborem Exercens* (1981). On the negative side, he sternly re-
bukes moral permissiveness in *Veritatis Splendor* (1993) and laments the "culture of death" in *Evangelium Vitae* (1995). There is, he believes, a struggle for
the world's soul taking place, a struggle between good and evil, between light
and darkness. In the balance, however, the encyclicals of John Paul bear
witness to his profound hope in the Triune God who is bringing his saving
design to fulfillment.

At the center of the Pope's vision is Christ's work of Redemption. He includes reference to this mystery in the title of three of his encyclicals: *Redemptor
Hominis* (1979), *Redemptoris Mater* (1987), and *Redemptoris Missio* (1990).
But his Christocentrism shines through each and every encyclical. It is the
redemptive Incarnation of the Man-God who fully reveals the dignity of the
person: *Ecce homo!* This is the window which John Paul opens in his encycli-

---

[46] Joyce Little, *The Church and the Culture War: Secular Anarchy or Sacred Order* (San
Francisco: Ignatius Press, 1995), 67.

cals, the key which unlocks the intertwined mysteries of God and man, the light which illumines the future path of humanity.

The Pope is just as much at ease with the theocentrism of *Dominum et Vivificantem* (1986), the piety of *Redemptoris Mater* (1987), and the praise of Saints Cyril and Methodius in *Slavorum Apostoli* (1985) as he is with his discussion of the causes of underdevelopment in *Sollicitudo Rei Socialis* (1987) and the reasons for the collapse of Communism in *Centesimus Annus* (1991). In his social encyclicals, John Paul affirms the unique and specific contribution that the Church makes to resolving human problems. It is from the perspective of an anthropocentrism enlightened by Christ, for example, that he criticizes Marxism in *Redemptor Hominis* (1979), *Laborem Exercens* (1981), and *Centesimus Annus*. Throughout his writings the Pope insists that there is no contradiction between theocentrism and anthropocentrism; rather, in Christ and because of Christ, there is a profound link. Acknowledgement of God's sovereignty in no way diminishes the dignity and freedom of human persons but ennobles them and reveals their lofty calling to the fullness of life (cf. Jn 10:10).

Plan

In John Paul's corpus of twelve encyclicals, there is an evident pattern in his choice of subjects and in the order of their publication. *Redemptor Hominis* (1979), *Dives in Misericordia* (1980), and *Dominum et Vivificantem* (1986) form a well-planned Trinitarian trilogy. The Pope begins with Christ the Redeemer, the way to the Father, who is rich in mercy, and ends with the Holy Spirit, the Lord and giver of life. John Paul has said that his inspiration for this order comes from the salutation of Saint Paul: "The grace of the Lord Jesus Christ and the love of God and the fellowship of the Holy Spirit be with you all" (2 Cor 13:13).[47] This Trinitarian series is completed by *Redemptoris Mater* (1987), his encyclical on Mary, the first fruit of Redemption.

The Pope's three social encyclicals also form a kind of trilogy. Each was written to commemorate the anniversary of a previous encyclical: the ninetieth anniversary of *Rerum Novarum* (1891) for *Laborem Exercens* (1981), the centenary of the same encyclical for *Centesimus Annus* (1991), and the twentieth anniversary of *Populorum Progressio* (1967) for *Sollicitudo Rei Socialis* (1987). Likewise, the order of the two encyclicals on moral questions stems from a deliberate design. His treatment of fundamental moral issues in *Veritatis Splendor* (1993) is followed by specific applications to questions of human life in *Evangelium Vitae* (1995). On the other hand, *Slavorum Apostoli* (1985), *Redemptoris Missio* (1990), and *Ut Unum Sint* (1995) reflect John Paul's pasto-

---

[47] See *Dominum et Vivificantem*, §2.3.

ral priorities for the Church but show no concern for relating them to one another.

Use of Sacred Scripture

Following the example set by the documents of the Second Vatican Council, John Paul liberally quotes or refers to the Bible in his encyclicals. The total number of direct scriptural citations and references varies from more than three hundred in *Evangelium Vitae* (1995), to only twenty in *Centesimus Annus* (1991). Within each encyclical the proportion of biblical quotations and references compared with those from other sources differs greatly: from ninety percent in *Dives in Misericordia* (1980) to fifteen percent in *Centesimus Annus*.[48]

While John Paul cites from a broad range of scriptural texts, he also shows a preference for certain authors and books. In the New Testament corpus, he favors Saint John, with his emphasis on the Incarnation, among the evangelists, and Romans among the Pauline letters.[49] Overall, the Old Testament accounts for less than ten percent of the total number of his biblical quotations and references. By far the most widely cited Old Testament texts are those from Genesis 1-4.[50]

Without denying the importance of historical-critical exegesis, the Pope normally makes little use of the methods of contemporary biblical scholarship in his encyclicals. For example, when citing the Gospels, he treats "freely the episodes in each Gospel as historical without the slightest qualification."[51]

---

[48] The following statistics demonstrate the Pope's frequent use of Scripture. The first figure in parentheses refers to the number of direct scriptural quotes in the encyclical; the second refers to the number of notes with biblical references ("cf."): *Redemptor Hominis* (83-55), *Laborem Exercens* (39-32), *Dives in Misericordia* (71-55), *Slavorum Apostoli* (7-6), *Dominum et Vivificantem* (122-102), *Redemptoris Mater* (86-66), *Sollicitudo Rei Socialis* (30-13), *Redemptoris Missio* (86-70), *Centesimus Annus* (7-13), *Veritatis Splendor* (157-145), *Evangelium Vitae* (195-111), and *Ut Unum Sint* (29-17).

[49] For the Pope's twelve encyclicals, the number of direct quotations and indirect references to the New Testament are, approximately, as follows: Matthew (223), Mark (62), Luke (193), and John (318), Acts (100), Romans (135), 1 Corinthians (60), 2 Corinthians (30), Galatians (61), Ephesians (73), Philippians (20), Colossians (29), 1 Thessalonians (5), 2 Thessalonians (7), 1 Timothy (11), 2 Timothy (6), Titus (4), Philemon (1), Hebrews (30), James (8), 1 Peter (15), 2 Peter (10), 1 John (48), 2 John (0), 3 John (0), Jude (0), and Revelation (30).

[50] Significant use of these three chapters is found in *Laborem Exercens* (1981), *Dominum et Vivificantem* (1986), *Sollicitudo Rei Socialis* (1987), *Centesimus Annus* (1991), *Veritatis Splendor* (1993), and *Evangelium Vitae* (1995).

[51] Terrence Prendergast, " 'A Vision of Wholeness': A Reflection on the Use of Scripture in a Cross-Section of Papal Writings," in *The Thought of Pope John Paul II*, ed. John M. McDermott (Rome: Gregorian University Press, 1993), 81.

Moreover, he does not draw out the distinctive theology of the different authors or stages of the tradition. The meaning of the text as it now stands, not how it came to be written, governs his approach to the Bible. Occasionally, when the results of research shed light on a particular interpretation, he includes exegetical notes. His long explanation of the expression "fullness of time" in Galatians 4:4[52] and even longer one of "mercy" (*hesed* and *rahamim*) in the Old Testament[53] illustrate his use of technical exegetical excursions. Usually, however, the Pope avoids scholarly explanations in his writings.

The Second Vatican Council teaches that "holy Scripture should be read in the light of the same Spirit by whom it was written."[54] This "reading" opens the way for interpreting Scripture within the whole history of salvation, including the time of the Church. To expound Scripture "in the Spirit" is to reach its depths: what the Church Fathers called its "interior intelligibility."[55] This is the method that John Paul follows in his encyclicals. He provides his readers with the fruits of his *lectio divina*, which is based on a prayerful reading of the biblical texts. The Pope stresses the Scriptures' spiritual sense, painting with broad and intuitive strokes which convey his sense of the Bible's unity and coherence as a witness to the Tradition. This method is borne out, for example in his approach to Genesis 1-3 in *Laborem Exercens* (1981), John 14-17 in *Dominum et Vivificantem* (1986), Luke 2 in *Redemptoris Mater* (1987), Matthew 19 in *Veritatis Splendor* (1993), and Genesis 4 in *Evangelium Vitae* (1995).

John Paul's primary interest is to make Scripture come alive for contemporary readers: to kindle their devotion and their practice of the faith. For example, in *Redemptor Hominis* (1979), after quoting sections from the portrayal of the last judgment in Matthew 25:31-46, he comments: "This eschatological scene must always be 'applied' to man's history; it must always be made the 'measure' for human acts as an essential outline for an examination of conscience by each and every one" (§16.10). In *Veritatis Splendor* (1993), Jesus' encounter with the young man, described in Matthew 19:16-25, is presented as the dialogue of every person who is seeking eternal life.

---

[52] *Redemptoris Mater*, note 2.

[53] *Dives et Misericordia*, note 52.

[54] *Dei Verbum*, §12.

[55] See J. Michael Miller, "Interior Intelligibility: The Use of Scripture in Papal and Conciliar Documents," *The Canadian Catholic Review*, 11 (September 1993), 9-18.

Use of philosophy and theology

In their encyclicals, the Popes wish to avoid committing the Church to a particular school of philosophy or theology. They deliberately leave open questions still legitimately debated among theologians. Despite this desire to remain impartial, the papal magisterium "takes over the terminology, thought-categories, and theories of theologians, insofar as these can be made to bear and convey the Christian faith."[56] In this sense, John Paul II engages in theology when writing his encyclicals. His teaching frequently contains insights stemming from his own theological and philosophical studies. The convincing power of the Pope's teaching is due, at least in part, to his intellectual and spiritual formation.

It is readily apparent that John Paul's encyclicals reflect his philosophical background in phenomenology. Phenomenology focuses on the correlation between subject and object: not on either the subject alone, as in much modern philosophy, or on the object alone, as is common in some kinds of scholasticism. The Pope favors the use of the phenomenological *method* of exhaustive description of "things in themselves." But, with regard to content, he remains solidly grounded in the philosophical realism of Aristotle and Saint Thomas Aquinas. While scholars debate the relationship between phenomenology and Thomism in John Paul's thought, in his encyclicals he writes as a Thomist who uses the method of phenomenology.[57]

According to Avery Dulles, the Pope develops an "original anthropology which owes something to classical Thomism and something to modern personalist phenomenology, especially as represented by Max Scheler. . . . John Paul prefers to begin with action. 'I act, therefore I am' might fairly characterize his starting point. . . . By my free actions, he asserts, I make myself what I am."[58] The view that individuals manifest themselves through their actions is especially evident in the Pope's analysis of the moral act in *Veritatis Splendor* (1993).

An examination of the sources cited in John Paul's encyclicals shows that besides his heavy reliance on Scripture, he also frequently refers to the Church Fathers, particularly to Saint Augustine, Saint Thomas Aquinas and other

---

[56] Avery Dulles, *A Church to Believe In* (New York: Crossroad Publishing Company, 1982), 127.

[57] See, for example, Robert F. Harvanek, "The Philosophical Foundations of the Thought of John Paul II," and Gerald A. McCool, "The Theology of John Paul II" in *The Thought of Pope John Paul II*, ed. John M. McDermott (Rome: Gregorian University Press, 1993), 1-21 and 29-53.

[58] Avery Dulles, "The Prophetic Humanism of John Paul II," *America*, 169 (1993), 7.

Doctors of the Church, and to previous statements of the papal and conciliar magisterium. Especially evident is his constant appeal to the documents of the Second Vatican Council, above all *Lumen Gentium* and *Gaudium
et Spes*.[59] This is in keeping with his conviction, first expressed in *Redemptor
Hominis* (1979), that the Council was a providential event whose directives
he is committed to implementing. References to canon law, on the other
hand, are remarkably few. And, because he wishes to remain above the
fray of contemporary debate, the Pope quotes no living theologian in his
encyclicals.

Those who collaborate in drafting encyclicals bring their own theological viewpoints to the process. Despite this assistance given to the Pope,
after comparing the style and substance of Karol Wojtyla's writings with
those of his encyclicals, Dulles concludes that "several of his encyclicals
are so personal in tone that it seems safe to attribute them to himself, even
though he presumably had assistants in the final process of editing."[60]

Style

John Paul's use of the method common to phenomenological analysis
at least partially accounts for the unique style of his encyclicals. Phenomenology places a premium on the careful, detailed description of whatever
is observed or analyzed. In his encyclicals, the Pope often approaches the
same question from several angles, sometimes even citing identical sources
twice or more in a single document. When examining an issue, he brings
to bear as many different perspectives as possible to the question at hand
and freely integrates insights drawn from theology, philosophy, and other
disciplines to make his point. John Paul's encyclicals thus testify to the
interrelationship of the mysteries of faith, and to his concern for the integrity of saving truth.

For those accustomed to the more scholastic approach found in the encyclicals of Pius XII and Paul VI, John Paul II's style of writing may seem mean-
dering. He does not set out with a clear proposition for which he then adduces
persuasive arguments. Nor does he use the two-step method of neo-scholasti-
cism which has marked many encyclicals, especially those dealing with social
issues. He does not study questions first from the viewpoint of natural reason
and then from that of revelation. Rather, the Pope "intertwines the philosophical and theological perspectives in a study of problems rooted in the funda-

---

[59] His twelve encyclicals contain about 170 citations and references to *Lumen Gentium* and
about 130 to *Gaudium et Spes*.

[60] Dulles, "Prophetic Humanism of John Paul II," 6.

mental framework of anthropology."[61] John Paul describes, thinks, and judges, and then often repeats the cycle with only a slight variation. Until readers become familiar with the Wojtylan style, they can experience a certain disorientation when studying the Pope's encyclicals. One recognizes his insights, but sometimes finds it hard to follow the logical development of his argument. Despite these difficulties, John Paul's encyclicals are accessible to a wide public. That *Evangelium Vitae* (1995) became a best-seller is a case in point.

Papal encyclicals are not mere declarations of doctrine, discipline, or policy but letters which aim to convince their readers about a certain point of Church teaching, devotion, or way of acting. Especially today the Pope tries to furnish persuasive reasons for what he teaches. John Paul wishes to present Catholic doctrine to the faithful in a convincing and understandable way. When his pastoral concern and meditative approach are combined with use of the phenomenological method, encyclicals that are much longer than those of his predecessors are the inevitable result.[62]

A study of Pope John Paul II's encyclicals reveals the vision and strategy of his pontificate. It is a vision which at once recalls the central mysteries of faith and appeals to all men and women of good will to build the future on a firm spiritual and ethical foundation. In applying the Pope's vision to contemporary problems the encyclicals shed light on Church teaching, often in a fresh and creative way. To read the twelve encyclicals of John Paul II is to undertake an intellectual and spiritual pilgrimage which explores the mystery of the redemptive Incarnation in all its depth, vitality, power, and fascination.

---

[61] John J. Conley, "The Philosophical Foundations of the Thought of John Paul II: A Response," in *The Thought of Pope John Paul II*, ed. John M. McDermott (Rome: Gregorian University Press, 1993), 25-26.

[62] The number of pages in the official Latin versions published in the *Acta Apostolicae Sedis* are as follows: *Redemptor Hominis* (68), *Dives in Misericordia* (56), *Laborem Exercens* (71), *Slavorum Apostoli* (35), *Dominum et Vivificantem* (92), *Redemptoris Mater* (73), *Sollicitudo Rei Socialis* (74), *Redemptoris Missio* (92), *Centesimus Annus* (75), *Veritatis Splendor* (96), *Evangelium Vitae* (122), and *Ut Unum Sint* (62).

Redemptor Hominis

Editor's Introduction

Within six months of assuming the papal ministry, John Paul II signed his first encyclical, *Redemptor Hominis,* on March 4, 1979.[1] In announcing its publication at an Angelus address, he explained his purpose:

> I tried to express in it what has animated and continually animates my thoughts and my heart since the beginning of the pontificate. . . . The Encyclical contains those thoughts which then, at the beginning of this new life, were pressing with particular forcefulness in my mind and which, certainly, had already been maturing in me previously, during the years of my service as a priest, and then as a bishop. I am of the opinion that, if Christ called me in this way, with such thoughts. . . , with such sentiments, it was because he wanted these calls of the intellect and of the heart, these expressions of faith, hope, and charity, to ring out in my new and universal ministry, right from its beginning. Therefore as I see and feel the relationship between the Mystery of the Redemption in Christ Jesus and the dignity of man, so I would like so much to unite the mission of the Church with service of man in his impenetrable mystery. I see in that the central task of my new ecclesial service.[2]

An even more remarkable admission of the long gestation of this encyclical in the thought of Karol Wojtyla appeared many years later in his book *Crossing the Threshold of Hope.* When commenting on the publication of *Redemptor Hominis* so soon after his election as Pope, John Paul wrote: "This means that I was actually carrying its contents within me. I had only to 'copy' from memory and experience what I had already been living on the threshold of the papacy. I emphasize this because the encyclical represents a confirmation, on the one hand, of the tradition of the schools from which I came and, on the other hand, of the pastoral style, reflected in the encyclical. . . . The encyclical aims to be a great hymn of joy for the fact that man has been redeemed through Christ — redeemed in spirit and in body."[3] *Redemptor Hominis* is the fruit of personal reflection, written in John Paul II's own hand.

The first encyclical of a new Pope is rightly interpreted as a kind of programmatic statement of the inspiration which will guide his pontificate. John XXIII's *Ad Petri Cathedram* (1959), for example, focused on truth, unity, and

---

[1] *Acta Apostolicae Sedis,* 71 (1979), 257-324.
[2] Angelus, March 11, 1979, *L'Osservatore Romano,* 12 (March 19, 1979), 2.
[3] *Crossing the Threshold of Hope* (New York: Random House, 1994), 48-49.

peace in a spirit of charity, while Paul VI wrote about dialogue in the Church in *Ecclesiam Suam* (1964). In *Redemptor Hominis* John Paul II lays out the principal themes which later emerge in his teaching with greater emphasis. The encyclical begins to flesh out the appeal made at the Mass celebrated to mark the beginning of his Petrine ministry: "Do not be afraid. Open wide the doors for Christ. To his saving power open the boundaries of States, economic and political systems, the vast fields of culture, civilization and development. Do not be afraid."[4] In the encyclical the Pope furnishes principles which will guide his papacy in the period of expectation called "this new advent of the Church connected with the approaching end of the second millennium" (§7.1).

Abandoning the plural of majesty, the "we" that characterized previous papal encyclicals, the Pope's style is personal. He is also innovative in his choice of vocabulary, using a terminology which is less narrowly ecclesiastical and more culturally resonant than that of his predecessors. Following the example of Saint Peter's great confession of faith (cf. Mt 16:16), he writes as one who bears witness to faith in Christ, especially the mysteries of the Incarnation and Redemption. By his own admission, John Paul intends to share the thoughts and sentiments which he had long pondered in his mind and heart, all of them organized around a principal theme announced at the outset: "The Redeemer of man, Jesus Christ, is the center of the universe and of history" (§1.1). For the first time, Redemption emerges as the primary theological idea of a pontificate. According to John Paul, all questions and problems receive light from this essential truth. Christ occupies the central place in human thought and life: "We must constantly aim at him 'who is the head,' 'through whom are all things and through whom we exist,' who is both 'the way, and the truth' and 'the resurrection and the life' " (§7.3). Jesus Christ is the center of the Church's faith, teaching, theology, and life.

In the encyclical itself the Pope does not spell out the reasons motivating his choice of Christ the Redeemer as the subject of his first major document. This theme, however, stems from his conviction that Christianity is a soteriological religion centered on mankind's salvation. For John Paul, a baleful heritage of the Enlightenment is that many contemporary men and women act as if God were not interested in the world, as if he did not exist. But, the Pope affirms, the world is not self-sufficient; it needs to be redeemed. Hence, the frequent use in *Redemptor Hominis*, and in so many of his writings, of his favorite biblical quotation: "God so loved the world that he gave his only Son, so that every one who believes in him might not perish but have eternal life" (Jn 3:16).

---

[4] Homily, October 22, 1979, *L'Osservatore Romano*, 44 (1979), 12.

Summary

While the encyclical undoubtedly concentrates on the mystery of Redemption, it also touches upon many other topics and themes. *Redemptor Hominis* is divided into four main chapters. In chapter one, "Inheritance" (§§1-6), the Pope situates his pontificate within the perspective of the Second Vatican Council and the coming of the year 2000. Chapter two, "The Mystery of the Redemption" (§§7-12), is a reflection on Christ the Redeemer and the divine and human dimensions of his saving act. Chapter three, "Redeemed Man and His Situation in the Modern World" (§§13-17), takes up the fears of modern men and women and recalls how Christ's union with each person is the source of hope. Lastly, in chapter four, "The Church's Mission and Man's Destiny" (§§18-22), John Paul discusses the Church's vocation to be priest, prophet, and king in the world. The repetition in the treatment of some themes and several pastoral and theological asides convey a certain conversational tone. Even so, the opening words "Redeemer" and "man" are like the two foci of an ellipse which reveal the heart of the Pope's thought. God turns toward humanity in his Son's redemptive Incarnation: God as Redeemer and the person as redeemed are the two principal themes of the theological vision outlined in his first encyclical.

Paul VI, Vatican II, and the Pontificate of John Paul II

John Paul begins *Redemptor Hominis* by situating his ministry in the present time of the Church: the approach of the "great Jubilee" of the year 2000. After describing the events surrounding his own election as Pope, he expresses his gratitude for "the rich inheritance of the recent Pontificates" (§3.1), especially those of John XXIII and Paul VI, and for the gift of the Second Vatican Council. John Paul particularly praises Paul VI, because "he knew how to preserve a providential tranquillity and balance even in the most critical moments, when the Church seemed to be shaken from within, and he always maintained unhesitating hope in the Church's solidity" (§3.1). Together the Popes and the Council "set in motion this new surge of life for the Church, a movement that is much stronger than the symptoms of doubt, collapse and crisis" (§5.4).

The Pope also confirms his esteem for episcopal collegiality, expressed in synods and episcopal conferences. Thanks to them the Church is united in the fellowship of service and in her apostolic endeavors. "The principle of collegiality," he writes, "showed itself particularly relevant in the difficult post-conciliar period, when the shared unanimous position of the College of the Bishops . . . helped to dissipate doubts and at the same time indicated the correct ways for renewing the Church in her universal dimension" (§5.2).

Before concluding his opening chapter, John Paul makes two points. First, he pledges himself to pursue Christian unity: "In the present historical situation of Christianity and the world the only possibility we see of fulfilling the Church's universal mission, with regard to ecumenical questions, is that of seeking sincerely, perseveringly, humbly and also courageously the ways of drawing closer and of union" (§6.1). True ecumenical activity, he says, means openness, willingness to dialogue and a shared investigation of the truth, without "giving up or in any way diminishing the treasures of divine truth that the Church has constantly confessed and taught" (§6.2). Second, the Pope wishes to draw closer to non-Christian religions. This is accomplished "through dialogue, contacts, prayer in common, investigation of the treasures of human spirituality" (§6.3). The foundation of this interreligious dialogue is the conviction that "it is a noble thing to have a predisposition for understanding every person, analyzing every system and recognizing what is right" (§6.3). Both themes are treated at much greater length in later encyclicals: Christian unity in *Ut Unum Sint* (1995) and interreligious dialogue in *Redemptoris Missio* (1990).

Theology of Redemption

In chapter two, the Pope begins his sustained doctrinal reflection on Redemption, "this tremendous mystery of love in which creation is renewed" (§9.1). He recalls that Christ, the Son of the living God, speaks to people as one who is himself a man: "It is his life that speaks, his humanity, his fidelity to the truth, his all-embracing love" (§7.4). Christ addresses the profound yearnings of every human heart.

Moreover, through the Incarnation and Redemption creation is restored, recovering again "its original link with the divine source of Wisdom and Love" (§8.1). In Christ, human nature is raised to an incomparable dignity, and its deepest meaning is fully revealed.

John Paul then discusses the mystery of Redemption from two different perspectives: his two foci of the divine and the human. First, from God's side, so to speak, the Redemption reveals the love and holiness of the three divine Persons. Certainly the Redemption is accomplished by Christ's saving act accomplished on the Cross. At Golgotha the sinless Son fully responds to the Father's love, revealing a love that is greater than sin. Consequently, "he it was, and he alone, who satisfied the Father's eternal love" (§9.1). But the Cross is also "a fresh manifestation of the eternal fatherhood of God, who in him draws near again to humanity, to each human being, giving him the thrice holy 'Spirit of truth'" (§9.1). In the Paschal Mystery the Triune God of creation is revealed as the Triune God of Redemption.

Second, the Pope considers the "human dimension" of the Redemption, which "marked the high point of the history of man within God's loving plan" (§1.2). Because of the Redemption, the human person is newly created, restored to the dignity lost because of sin, and made an heir of immeasurable greatness. Thus, he can draw near to Christ, appropriating and assimilating "the whole of the reality of the Incarnation and Redemption in order to find himself" (§10.1). Individuals can plumb the depths of their identity in light of their creation in God's image and likeness (cf. Gen 1:26-27), but most especially in light of their redemption by Christ's blood. This journey of self-discovery ends not in oneself, but in Christ.

After establishing the absolute priority of Christ in God's plan, the Pope then turns to the mission of the Church. Her "fundamental function in every age and particularly in ours" is to direct man's gaze toward Christ, to help humanity "to be familiar with the profundity of the Redemption taking place in Christ Jesus" (§10.3). According to John Paul, the Church must recognize that individuals take different routes in their quest for God, a quest which also involves the search "for the full meaning of human life" (§11.2). Even more, the Church must proclaim that it is in and through Christ that God has definitively drawn close to people, making them aware of the inner truth of humanity ennobled by the grace of divine adoption. Consequently, the Church's mission is "helping each person to find himself in Christ" (§11.5). Aware of her responsibility to the truth which she must share with the world as a gift, the Church accomplishes her mission by proclaiming Christ "who brings man freedom based on truth" (§12.3). The mystery of Christ shines forth within the mystery of his Body, the Church.

Redeemed humanity's situation in the modern world

Before discussing in detail redeemed humanity's situation in the modern world, chapter three describes the Church's specific task of bringing Christ to all people. She is to foster union between Christ and every individual, not just between Christ and Christians. Indeed, the human person is "the primary route that the Church must travel in fulfilling her mission: *he is the primary and fundamental way for the Church*, the way traced out by Christ himself, the way that leads invariably through the mystery of the Incarnation and the Redemption" (§14.1). The Church looks to man in order to bring him the truth about God and about himself.

For the fruitful accomplishment of her mission, the Church must be aware of the present-day threats to the humanity to which she ministers. The world, "subjected to futility" (Rom 8:20), needs to be redeemed. Because the world is not the source of salvation, it cannot save man from evil, suffering, and death. The fullness of life that the human spirit yearns for so restlessly cannot be satisfied by the world. Among the "signs of the times," John Paul sees that people are more and more living in fear. They are afraid, he says, that part of what they produce from their creativity and genius "can become the means and instrument for an unimaginable self-destruction, compared with which all the cataclysms and catastrophes of history known to us seem to fade away" (§15.2). Whether they are aware of it or not, people need redemption.

Modern developments in science and technology have not been accompanied by a similar advancement in morals and ethics. Despite the marvels of progress, disquiet still reigns. The Pope asks whether man "is becoming truly better, that is to say more mature spiritually, more aware of the dignity of his humanity, more responsible, more open to others" (§15.4). These achievements are the gauges of true progress.

As a result of his analysis John Paul concludes that today's world situation "seems indeed to be far removed from the objective demands of the moral order, from the requirements of justice, and even more of social love" (§16.1). All too often the dignity conferred on people by the mysteries of the Incarnation and Redemption is squandered. Consumerism, misguided freedom, the unjust distribution of wealth, lack of solidarity, the arms race, the conflict between East and West, the trampling of inviolable human rights, especially that of religious freedom, all of these challenge the Church. The Pope's judgment of the twentieth century is somber: "This century has so far been a century of great calamities for man, of great devastations, not only material ones but also moral ones, indeed, perhaps above all, moral ones" (§17.1).

The Church's mission as priest, prophet, and king

After his review of contemporary life, John Paul returns in chapter four to a discussion of Christ and the Church. Through the Cross, Christ united himself to the Church. Thus, if every person is to share in the mystery of Redemption, "the Church must be strongly united with each man" (§18.1). Her vocation is to foster every person's vocation in Christ.

The Church, which lives by Christ and for Christ, shares in his threefold mission to the world as prophet, priest, and king. The Pope deals with her prophetic mission under the rubric of "the Church as responsible for truth" (§19), with her priestly mission in the section on the sacraments of the Eucharist and Penance (§20), and with her prophetic mission in the section entitled "the Christian vocation to service and kingship" (§21).

Every person is "the way for the Church" (§14.4). The Church is mindful of the problems of contemporary society, each of which can be illumined by the Gospel. Thus, she "cannot remain insensible to whatever serves man's true welfare, any more than she can remain indifferent to what threatens it" (§13.2). Attentive to the assaults on human dignity, the Church must constantly reaffirm that dignity. She is interested in social, economic, and political affairs because of the Gospel's concern for ethical, spiritual, and religious values. In light of the signs of the times and the demands of changing situations, human problems must be considered from the perspective of Christ's redemptive death and Resurrection.

Every individual — Pope, bishop, religious, and lay person — is united to Christ in his Body, the Church, and in a differentiated way shares in his threefold mission as prophet, priest, and king, a theme well developed by Vatican II. In the mystery of Redemption, the Church finds "the light and strength that are indispensable for her mission" (§18.4).

As "the social subject of responsibility for divine truth" (§19.1), says the Pope, the Church shares in Christ's prophetic mission. For Christians this entails always professing the truth of the Gospel with complete fidelity. But above all, with respect to the truth, it means "loving it and seeking the most exact understanding of it, in order to bring it closer to ourselves and others in all its saving power, its splendor and its profundity joined with simplicity" (§19.2). This prophetic mission belongs primarily to the bishops, but also in a special way to theologians who must "seek to serve the Magisterium" (§19.2). Besides bishops and theologians, the whole People of God is responsible for truth, a duty which is "one of the fundamental demands determining man's vocation in the community of the Church" (§19.6). All Christians must cultivate a love for truth, "whatever field it may belong to, while educating others in truth and teaching them to mature in love and justice" (§19.6).

According to John Paul, the Church's priestly mission is primarily carried out by celebration of the sacraments, "through which each Christian receives the saving power of the Redemption" (§20.1). The fruits of Redemption are available through a personal encounter with God's love in the sacraments. They are the principal means by which humanity and the world are restored to the Father. In a special way the Eucharist unites people to the redeeming act of Christ's sacrifice and thereby builds up the community. John Paul also points out the close link between the Eucharist and Penance, recalling the profoundly intimate nature of conversion and the need for individual sacramental confession. He stresses everyone's right to a personal encounter with the forgiving Christ. "By guarding the sacrament of Penance," the Pope writes, "the Church expressly affirms her faith in the mystery of the Redemption as a living and life-giving reality that fits in with man's inward truth, with human guilt and also with the desires of the human conscience" (§20.6).

John Paul describes the Christian's mission to kingship, which is realized by putting into practice the dignity of one's unique vocation. Everyone is invited to take part in "the drama of present-day human existence" (§15.2), the "great drama that can leave nobody indifferent" (§16.5). Human beings can enter into the drama of salvation because they are united to Christ, whose Incarnation is its central act. Betraying his familiarity with, and love for, the theater, the Pope says in this regard: "God entered the history of humanity and, as a man, became an actor in that history, one of the thousands of millions of human beings but at the same time Unique!" (§1.2).

Each individual has a mission and is given a "singular, unique and unrepeatable grace" for building up the Church (§21.3). Faithfulness to one's vocation, whatever it happens to be, is readiness for "kingly service," after the example of Christ who "came not to be served but to serve" (Mt 20:28). Every Christian's vocation of kingship is fulfilled in service: " 'being a king' is truly possible only by 'being a servant' " (§21.1). Here the Pope recalls the great gift of freedom, which is not an end in itself or simply the ability to do as one pleases. Rather, he says: "Christ teaches us that the best use of freedom is charity, which takes concrete form in self-giving and in sacrifice" (§21.5). True freedom is the capacity to fulfill one's deepest aspirations by choosing what is true and good: "The full truth about human freedom is indelibly inscribed on the mystery of the Redemption" (§21.5).

The encyclical closes with what will become a typical pattern: a meditation on Mary's relationship to the particular subject matter of the encyclical and a prayer to her. According to the Pope, Mary is the one who can best introduce us into the divine and human dimensions of the mystery of the Redemption, since this mystery "took shape beneath the heart of the Virgin of Nazareth when she pronounced her 'fiat' " (§22.4). In Mary, God is exceptionally close to each individual; consequently, "Mary must be on all the ways for the Church's daily life" (§22.5). Through her maternal presence, Mary assures the Church that "she is living the mystery of the Redemption in all its life-giving profundity and fullness" (§22.5).

Key Themes

There is little doubt that *Redemptor Hominis* furnishes the first threads of a theological tapestry that the Pope carefully weaves in subsequent encyclicals. Here I would like to emphasize two themes which testify to the Christocentric focus of his thought: the links which he establishes between the truth about Christ and the person, and between the Church and the person. John Paul's inaugural encyclical outlines a theological anthropology based on a vision that is Christological and ecclesiological. This anthropological perspective pervades the whole encyclical and, indeed, the writings of his entire pontificate.

Christ and the person

In his second encyclical, *Dives et Misericordia* (1980), the Pope writes that his first encyclical is devoted "to the truth about man, a truth that is revealed to us in its fullness and depth in Christ" (§1.2). John Paul's anthropology is firmly rooted in the truth about Christ the Redeemer. Jesus reveals not only who God is, but who the human person is, and how he or she ought to live in harmony with this twofold truth. To discover his own personhood, every individual must first turn to Christ who, in revealing himself to humanity, thereby reveals the mystery of the human person. Because of the light shed by the Incarnation and the Redemption, the mystery, dignity, and vocation of the person can be truly understood. The redemptive Incarnation restores people to the dignity that God intended them to have from the beginning, before their life was obscured by sin.

Besides his strong sense of each person's precariousness before suffering and death, John Paul also recognizes the never-ending restlessness of his spirit. In *Redemptor Hominis,* as he does frequently in his writings, the Pope cites Saint Augustine's exclamation in the *Confessions:* "You have made us for yourself, Lord, and our heart is restless until it rests in you." Christ alone meets the deepest longings of the human heart for truth, freedom, fullness of life, and community. Christ alone answers the fundamental questions of human existence. Thus the Pope can say of himself, but speaking on behalf of all humanity: "Our spirit is set in one direction, the only direction for our intellect, will and heart is — toward Christ our Redeemer, toward Christ the Redeemer of man. We wish to look toward him — because there is salvation in no one else but him, the Son of God" (§7.2).

At the heart of John Paul's Christocentric anthropology is the teaching contained in *Gaudium et Spes,* a passage to which he returns for inspiration repeatedly throughout his ministry: "Christ the new Adam, in the very revelation of the mystery of the Father and of his love, fully reveals man to himself and brings to light his most high calling. . . . Human nature, by the very fact that it was assumed, not absorbed, in him, has been raised in us also to a dignity beyond compare. For, by his Incarnation, he, the Son, in a certain way united himself with each man" (§22; cf. *Redemptor Hominis*, §§8.2, 13.1, 18.1).

Christ has penetrated the mystery of the person, entering into his "heart." He not only reveals God to individuals, but he reveals them to themselves. In Christ they grasp the hidden mystery of their humanity.

With the Redemption won through the Paschal Mystery, human dignity, tarnished by sin, is restored: "In Christ and through Christ man has acquired full awareness of his dignity, of the heights to which he is raised, of the surpassing worth of his own humanity, and of the meaning of his existence" (§11.3). For people to discover their true identity, they must "assimilate the whole of the reality of the Incarnation and Redemption" (§10.1). Christology establishes anthropology on a solid footing. Life's deepest meaning is found only in union with Christ, a union which provides the basis for the person's true worth.

Drawing upon the patristic and scholastic tradition of Christ's headship, John Paul very frequently affirms that Christ is the Redeemer of all people and of each person individually. His concern is not "the 'abstract' man, but the real, 'concrete,' 'historical' man. We are dealing with 'each' man, for each one is included in the mystery of the Redemption and with each one Christ has united himself forever through this mystery" (§13.3). The Church walks with man because "every man without any exception whatever — has been redeemed by Christ, and because with man — with each man without any exception whatever — Christ is united, even when man is unaware of it" (§14.3). The sinful fragmentation of humanity is ended by Christ, who draws all into union with himself, the Father, and the Holy Spirit.

John Paul uses a striking image to depict the mystery of reconciliation effected by the Redemption. He compares it to soldering the link of a chain, "broken in the man Adam, so in the Man Christ it was reforged" (§8.1). Jesus is the New Adam, the link reuniting God with all creation. This restored dignity has been "bought with a price" (1 Cor 6:20): Christ's sacrificial offering on the Cross. The reforging accomplished by the Redemption fulfills the individual's need for love which his nature demands. Without love, divine love, "he remains a being that is incomprehensible for himself" (§10.1). People must encounter this love, experience it, and make it their own. Being loved by God — the proof of which shines forth in the Redemption — allows a person to find again "the greatness, dignity and value that belong to his humanity" (§10.1).

The Redemption is the true basis for optimism about humanity's destiny. In its light the fears which endanger contemporary men and women, despite progress in many spheres, can be soberly faced: the sense of alienation from themselves, from the fruits of their labor, and from nature. The Pope recalls that the "situation in the modern world seems indeed to be far removed from the objective demands of the social order, from the requirements of justice, and even more of social love" (§16.1). By revealing people's dignity and their transcendent destiny, Christ alone opens the way to freedom from this moral chaos.

A moralistic condemnation of humanity's woes is not the Pope's intention. Instead, he wishes to show the desperate situation from which people can be saved. John Paul insists that Christ is the one who brings "freedom based on truth" (§12.3), freeing people from everything that diminishes authentic freedom. Armed with this insight and the power of grace, they can discern the way of authentic liberation. True freedom consists "in the priority of ethics over technology, in the primacy of the person over things, and in the superiority of spirit over matter" (§16.1).

The Church and the person

Like Christ, the Church is at the service of the human person. She reveals Christ to the world, helping people to discover themselves in him. The Church always does so from "within the sphere of the mystery of the Redemption, which has become the fundamental principle of her life and mission" (§7.4). John Paul writes: "Inspired by eschatological faith, the Church considers an essential, unbreakably united element of her mission this solicitude for man, for his humanity, for the future of men on earth and therefore also for the course set for the whole of development and progress" (§15.6). This maternal care of the Church derives from the mystery of Redemption. "Her solicitude," writes the Pope, "is about the whole man and is focused on him in an altogether special manner. The object of her care is man in his unique unrepeatable human reality" (§13.3).

Entrusted with care for the "treasure of humanity," the Church seeks to see people with "the eyes of Christ himself" (§18.3). The more she serves man, the more she serves Christ. While the Church is essential to God's saving plan, she is not its focus: that belongs to Christ alone. She "lives his mystery, draws unwearyingly from it and continually seeks ways of bringing this mystery of her Master and Lord to humanity — to the peoples, the nations, the succeeding generations, and every individual human being" (§7.4). John Paul's ecclesiology is radically Christological. The Church is subordinate to Christ; he is the reason for her existence and the source of her vitality.

The Church's mission is to penetrate and foster Christ's saving relationship with every individual person: "Indeed, precisely because Christ united himself with her in the mystery of Redemption, the Church must be strongly united with each man" (§18.1). Her goal is not her own glorification. Rather, "the Church wishes to serve this single end: that each person may be able to find Christ, in order that Christ may walk with each person the path of life, with the power of the truth about man and the world that is contained in the mystery of the Incarnation and Redemption and with the power of the love that is radiated by that truth" (§13.1).

The Church, then, is passionately involved with humanity, with whatever serves people's true spiritual and temporal welfare. Man is "the primary route that the Church must travel in fulfilling her mission: *he is the primary and fundamental way for the Church*, the way traced out by Christ himself, the way that leads inevitably through the mystery of the Incarnation and Redemption" (§14.1). The Church is divinely commissioned to be the advocate of authentic humanity, promoting the inviolable dignity of every human person, because each and every one has been redeemed by Christ.

In *Redemptor Hominis,* John Paul II lays the foundation for the Christocentric vision which unfolds throughout his pontificate. Through the Incarnation and Redemption of the Man-God, every person is introduced into the sphere of salvation. According to the Pope, human beings need the Incarnate Son in order to decipher the mystery of their own humanity: "The man who wishes to understand himself thoroughly — and not just in accordance with the immediate, partial, often superficial, and even illusory standards and measures of his being — he must with his unrest, uncertainty, and even his weakness and sinfulness, with his life and death, draw near to Christ" (§10.1). Only Christ's incarnate and divine humanity can give meaning to human life and reveal the noble vocation of each individual. Beginning with passionate fervor in his first encyclical, John Paul will never tire of proclaiming the great mystery at the heart of the Church's mission: "In Christ and through Christ God has revealed himself fully to mankind and has definitively drawn close to it" (§11.3).

* * *

Selected Bibliography

"All Ways Lead to Man." Editorial. *America,* 140 (1979), 249.

Baum, Gregory. "The First Papal Encyclical." *The Ecumenist,* 17 (1979), 55-59.

Galichon, Alain. "The First Encyclical." *L'Osservatore Romano,* 33 (1979), 6-7.

Gawronski, Raymond T. "*Redemptor Hominis.*" In *The Thought of Pope John Paul II.* Edited by John M. McDermott. Rome: Gregorian University Press, 1993. 221-230.

Honoré, Jean. "Christ the Redeemer, Core of John Paul II's Teaching." In *John*

Paul II: A Panorama of His Teachings. Preface by Joseph Bernardin. New York: New City Press, 1989. 12-26.

McCabe, Herbert. "*Redemptor Hominis.*" *New Blackfriars,* 60 (1979), 146-147.

McDonagh, Edna. "*Redemptor Hominis* and Ireland." *The Furrow,* 30 (1979), 624-640.

Morneau, Robert. "*Redemptor Hominis:* Themes and Theses." *Review for Religious,* 39 (1980), 247-262.

Richards, Michael. "Mankind Redeemed." *Clergy Review,* 64 (1979), 194-195.

Schall, James. "*Redemptor Hominis:* The Amazement of God." *Homiletic and Pastoral Review,* 80 (October 1979), 11-19.

Stevens, M. "*Redemptor Hominis.*" In *The New Dictionary of Catholic Social Thought.* Edited by Judith A. Dwyer. Collegeville: Liturgical Press, 1994. 817-822.

Williams, George Hunston. *The Mind of John Paul II: Origins of His Thought and Action.* New York: Seabury Press, 1981. 305-311.

ENCYCLICAL LETTER

REDEMPTOR HOMINIS

ADDRESSED BY THE SUPREME PONTIFF

JOHN PAUL II

TO HIS VENERABLE BROTHERS

IN THE EPISCOPATE

THE PRIESTS

THE RELIGIOUS FAMILIES

THE SONS AND DAUGHTERS

OF THE CHURCH

AND TO ALL MEN AND WOMEN

OF GOOD WILL

AT THE BEGINNING

OF HIS PAPAL MINISTRY

Redemptor Hominis

Venerable Brothers and
Dear Sons and Daughters,
Greetings and the Apostolic Blessing!

I

Inheritance

At the close of the second millennium

1.1 The Redeemer of man, Jesus Christ, is the center of the universe and of history. To him go my thoughts and my heart in this solemn moment of the world that the Church and the whole family of present-day humanity are now living. In fact, this time, in which God in his hidden design has entrusted to me, after my beloved Predecessor John Paul I, the universal service connected with the Chair of Saint Peter in Rome, is already very close to the year 2000. At this moment it is difficult to say what mark that year will leave on the face of human history or what it will bring to each people, nation, country and continent, in spite of the efforts already being made to foresee some events. For the Church, the People of God spread, although unevenly, to the most distant limits of the earth, it will be the year of a great Jubilee. We are already approaching that date, which, without prejudice to all the corrections imposed by chronological exactitude, will recall and reawaken in us in a special way our awareness of the key truth of faith which Saint John expressed at the beginning of his Gospel: "The Word became flesh and dwelt among us,"[1] and elsewhere: "God so loved the world that he gave his only Son, that whoever believes in him should not perish but have eternal life."[2]

1.2 We also are in a certain way in a season of a new Advent, a season of expectation: "In many and various ways God spoke of old to our fathers by the prophets; but in these last days he has spoken to us by a Son. . . ,"[3] by the Son, his Word, who became man and was born of the Virgin Mary. This act of Redemption marked the high point of the history of man within God's loving plan. God entered the history of humanity and, as a man, became an actor in that history, one of the thousands of millions of human beings but at the

[1] Jn 1:14.
[2] Jn 3:16.
[3] Heb 1:1-2.

same time Unique! Through the Incarnation God gave human life the dimension that he intended man to have from his first beginning; he has granted that dimension definitively — in the way that is peculiar to him alone, in keeping with his eternal love and mercy, with the full freedom of God — and he has granted it also with the bounty that enables us, in considering the original sin and the whole history of the sins of humanity, and in considering the errors of the human intellect, will and heart, to repeat with amazement the words of the sacred liturgy: "O happy fault . . . which gained us so great a Redeemer!"[4]

The first words of the new Pontificate

2.1 It was to Christ the Redeemer that my feelings and my thoughts were directed on October 16 of last year, when, after the canonical election, I was asked: "Do you accept?" I then replied: "With obedience in faith to Christ, my Lord, and with trust in the Mother of Christ and of the Church, in spite of the great difficulties, I accept." Today I wish to make that reply known publicly to all without exception, thus showing that there is a link between the first fundamental truth of the Incarnation, already mentioned, and the ministry that, with my acceptance of my election as Bishop of Rome and Successor of the Apostle Peter, has become my specific duty in his See.

2.2 I chose the same names that were chosen by my beloved Predecessor John Paul I. Indeed, as soon as he announced to the Sacred College on August 26, 1978, that he wished to be called John Paul — such a double name being unprecedented in the history of the papacy — I saw in it a clear presage of grace for the new Pontificate. Since that Pontificate lasted barely 33 days, it falls to me not only to continue it but in a certain sense to take it up again at the same starting point. This is confirmed by my choice of these two names. By following the example of my venerable Predecessor in choosing them, I wish like him to express my love for the unique inheritance left to the Church by Popes John XXIII and Paul VI and my personal readiness to develop that inheritance with God's help.

2.3 Through these two names and two Pontificates I am linked with the whole tradition of the Apostolic See and with all my Predecessors in the expanse of the twentieth century and of the preceding centuries. I am connected, through one after another of the various ages back to the most remote, with the line of the mission and ministry that confers on Peter's See an altogether special place in the Church. John XXIII and Paul VI are a stage to which I wish to refer directly as a threshold from which I intend to continue, in a

---

[4] *Exsultet* at the Easter Vigil.

certain sense together with John Paul I, into the future, letting myself be guided by unlimited trust in and obedience to the Spirit that Christ promised and sent to his Church. On the night before he suffered he said to his Apostles: "It is to your advantage that I go away, for if I do not go away, the Counselor will not come to you; but if I go, I will send him to you."[5] "When the Counselor comes, whom I shall send to you from the Father, even the Spirit of truth, who proceeds from the Father, he will bear witness to me; and you also are witnesses, because you have been with me from the beginning."[6] "When the Spirit of truth comes, he will guide you into all the truth; for he will not speak on his own authority, but whatever he hears he will speak, and he will declare to you the things that are to come."[7]

Trust in the Spirit of truth and of love

3.1 Entrusting myself fully to the Spirit of truth, therefore, I am entering into the rich inheritance of the recent Pontificates. This inheritance has struck deep roots in the awareness of the Church in an utterly new way, quite unknown previously, thanks to the Second Vatican Council, which John XXIII convened and opened and which was later successfully concluded and perseveringly put into effect by Paul VI, whose activity I was myself able to watch from close at hand. I was constantly amazed at his profound wisdom and his courage and also by his constancy and patience in the difficult postconciliar period of his Pontificate. As helmsman of the Church, the bark of Peter, he knew how to preserve a providential tranquillity and balance even in the most critical moments, when the Church seemed to be shaken from within, and he always maintained unhesitating hope in the Church's solidity. What the Spirit said to the Church through the Council of our time, what the Spirit says in this Church to all the Churches[8] cannot lead to anything else — in spite of momentary uneasiness — but still more mature solidity of the whole People of God, aware of their salvific mission.

3.2 Paul VI selected this present-day consciousness of the Church as the first theme in his fundamental Encyclical beginning with the words *Ecclesiam Suam*. Let me refer first of all to this Encyclical and link myself with it in this first document that, so to speak, inaugurates the present Pontificate. The Church's consciousness, enlightened and supported by the Holy Spirit and fathoming more and more deeply both her divine mystery and her human

[5] Jn 16:7.
[6] Jn 15:26-27.
[7] Jn 16:13.
[8] Cf. Rev 2:7.

mission, and even her human weaknesses — this consciousness is and must remain the first source of the Church's love, as love in turn helps to strengthen and deepen her consciousness. Paul VI left us a witness of such an extremely acute consciousness of the Church. Through the many things, often causing suffering, that went to make up his Pontificate he taught us intrepid love for the Church, which is, as the Council states, a "sacrament or sign and means of intimate union with God, and of the unity of all mankind."[9]

Reference to Paul VI's first Encyclical

4.1 Precisely for this reason, the Church's consciousness must go with universal openness, in order that all may be able to find in her "the unsearchable riches of Christ"[10] spoken of by the Apostle of the Gentiles. Such openness, organically joined with the awareness of her own nature and certainty of her own truth, of which Christ said: "The word which you hear is not mine but the Father's who sent me,"[11] is what gives the Church her apostolic, or in other words her missionary, dynamism, professing and proclaiming in its integrity the whole of the truth transmitted by Christ. At the same time she must carry on the dialogue that Paul VI, in his Encyclical *Ecclesiam Suam* called "the dialogue of salvation," distinguishing with precision the various circles within which it was to be carried on.[12] In referring today to this document that gave the program of Paul VI's Pontificate, I keep thanking God that this great Predecessor of mine, who was also truly my father, knew how to display *ad extra*, externally, the true countenance of the Church, in spite of the various internal weaknesses that affected her in the postconciliar period. In this way much of the human family has become, it seems, more aware, in all humanity's various spheres of existence, of how really necessary the Church of Christ, her mission and her service are to humanity. At times this awareness has proved stronger than the various critical attitudes attacking *ab intra*, internally, the Church, her institutions and structures, and ecclesiastics and their activities. This growing criticism was certainly due to various causes and we are furthermore sure that it was not always without sincere love for the Church. Undoubtedly one of the tendencies it displayed was to overcome what has been called triumphalism, about which there was frequent discussion during the Council. While it is right that, in accordance with the example of her

---

[9] Second Vatican Ecumenical Council, Dogmatic Constitution on the Church *Lumen Gentium*, 1: *AAS* 57 (1965), 5.

[10] Eph 3:8.

[11] Jn 14:24.

[12] Paul VI, Encyclical Letter *Ecclesiam Suam* (August 6, 1964): *AAS* 56 (1964), 650ff.

Master, who is "humble in heart,"[13] the Church also should have humility as her foundation, that she should have a critical sense with regard to all that goes to make up her human character and activity, and that she should always be very demanding on herself, nevertheless criticism too should have its just limits. Otherwise it ceases to be constructive and does not reveal truth, love and thankfulness for the grace in which we become sharers principally and fully in and through the Church. Furthermore such criticism does not express an attitude of service but rather a wish to direct the opinion of others in accordance with one's own, which is at times spread abroad in too thoughtless a manner.

4.2 Gratitude is due to Paul VI because, while respecting every particle of truth contained in the various human opinions, he preserved at the same time the providential balance of the bark's helmsman.[14] The Church that I — through John Paul I — have had entrusted to me almost immediately after him is admittedly not free of internal difficulties and tension. At the same time, however, she is internally more strengthened against the excesses of self-criticism: she can be said to be more critical with regard to the various thoughtless criticisms, more resistant with respect to the various "novelties," more mature in her spirit of discerning, better able to bring out of her everlasting treasure "what is new and what is old,"[15] more intent on her own mystery, and because of all that more serviceable for her mission of salvation for all: God "desires all men to be saved and to come to the knowledge of the truth."[16]

Collegiality and apostolate

5.1 In spite of all appearances, the Church is now more united in the fellowship of service and in the awareness of apostolate. This unity springs

---

[13] Mt 11:29.

[14] Mention must be made here of the salient documents of the Pontificate of Paul VI, some of which were spoken of by himself in his homily during Mass on the Solemnity of the Holy Apostles Peter and Paul (June 29, 1978): Encyclical Letter *Ecclesiam Suam* (August 6, 1964): *AAS* 56 (1964), 609-650; Apostolic Letter *Investigabiles Divitias Christi* (February 6, 1965): *AAS* 57 (1965), 298-301; Encyclical Letter *Sacerdotalis Caelibatus* (June 24, 1967): *AAS* 59 (1967), 657-697; Solemn Profession of Faith (June 30, 1968): *AAS* 60 (1968), 433-445; Encyclical Letter *Humanae Vitae* (July 25, 1968): *AAS* 60 (1968), 481-503; Apostolic Exhortation *Quinque Iam Anni* (December 8, 1970): *AAS* 63 (1971), 97-106; Apostolic Exhortation *Evangelica Testificatio* (June 29, 1971): *AAS* 63 (1971), 497-535; Apostolic Exhortation *Paterna cum Benevolentia* (December 8, 1974): *AAS* 67 (1975), 5-23; Apostolic Exhortation *Gaudete in Domino* (May 9, 1975): *AAS* 67 (1975), 289-322; Apostolic Exhortation *Evangelii Nuntiandi* (December 8, 1975): *AAS* 68 (1976), 5-76.

[15] Mt 13:52.

[16] 1 Tim 2:4.

from the principle of collegiality, mentioned by the Second Vatican Council. Christ himself made this principle a living part of the Apostolic College of the Twelve with Peter at their head, and he is continuously renewing it in the College of the Bishops, which is growing more and more over all the earth, remaining united with and under the guidance of the Successor of Saint Peter. The Council did more than mention the principle of collegiality: it gave it immense new life, by — among other things — expressing the wish for a permanent organ of collegiality, which Paul VI founded by setting up the Synod of the Bishops, whose activity not only gave a new dimension to his Pontificate but was also later clearly reflected in the Pontificate of John Paul I and that of his unworthy Successor from the day they began.

5.2 The principle of collegiality showed itself particularly relevant in the difficult postconciliar period, when the shared unanimous position of the College of the Bishops — which displayed, chiefly through the Synod, its union with Peter's Successor — helped to dissipate doubts and at the same time indicated the correct ways for renewing the Church in her universal dimension. Indeed, the Synod was the source, among other things, of that essential momentum for evangelization that found expression in the Apostolic Exhortation *Evangelii Nuntiandi,*[17] which was so joyously welcomed as a program for renewal which was both apostolic and also pastoral. The same line was followed in the work of the last ordinary session of the Synod of the Bishops, held about a year before the death of Pope Paul VI and dedicated, as is known, to catechesis. The results of this work have still to be arranged and enunciated by the Apostolic See.

5.3 As we are dealing with the evident development of the forms in which episcopal collegiality is expressed, mention must be made at least of the process of consolidation of National Episcopal Conferences throughout the Church and of other collegial structures of an international or continental character. Referring also to the centuries-old tradition of the Church, attention should be directed to the activity of the various diocesan, provincial and national Synods. It was the Council's idea, an idea consistently put into practice by Paul VI, that structures of this kind, with their centuries of trial by the Church, and the other forms of collegial collaboration by Bishops, such as the metropolitan structure — not to mention each individual Diocese — should pulsate in full awareness of their own identity and, at the same time, of their own originality within the universal unity of the Church. The same spirit of collaboration and shared responsibility is spreading among priests also, as is

---

[17] Paul VI, Apostolic Exhortation *Evangelii Nuntiandi* (December 8, 1975): *AAS* 68 (1976), 5-76.

confirmed by the many Councils of Priests that have sprung up since the Council. That spirit has extended also among the laity, not only strengthening the already existing organizations for lay apostolate but also creating new ones that often have a different outline and excellent dynamism. Furthermore, lay people conscious of their responsibility for the Church have willingly committed themselves to collaborating with the Pastors and with the representatives of the Institutes of Consecrated Life, in the spheres of the diocesan synods and of the pastoral councils in the parishes and Dioceses.

5.4 I must keep all this in mind at the beginning of my Pontificate as a reason for giving thanks to God, for warmly encouraging all my brothers and sisters and for recalling with heartfelt gratitude the work of the Second Vatican Council and my great predecessors, who set in motion this new surge of life for the Church, a movement that is much stronger than the symptoms of doubt, collapse and crisis.

The road to Christian unity

6.1 What shall I say of all the initiatives that have sprung from the new ecumenical orientation? The unforgettable Pope John XXIII set out the problem of Christian unity with evangelical clarity as a simple consequence of the will of Jesus Christ himself, our Master, the will that Jesus stated on several occasions but to which he gave expression in a special way in his prayer in the Upper Room the night before he died: "I pray . . . Father . . . that they may all be one."[18] The Second Vatican Council responded concisely to this requirement with its Decree on Ecumenism. Pope Paul VI, availing himself of the activities of the Secretariat for Promoting Christian Unity, began the first difficult steps on the road to the attainment of that unity. Have we gone far along that road? Without wishing to give a detailed reply, we can say that we have made real and important advances. And one thing is certain: we have worked with perseverance and consistency, and the representatives of other Christian Churches and Communities have also committed themselves together with us, for which we are heartily grateful to them. It is also certain that in the present historical situation of Christianity and the world the only possibility we see of fulfilling the Church's universal mission, with regard to ecumenical questions, is that of seeking sincerely, perseveringly, humbly and also courageously the ways of drawing closer and of union. Pope Paul VI gave us his personal example for this. We must therefore seek unity without being discouraged at the

[18] Jn 17:21; cf. 17:11, 22-23; 10:16; Lk 9:49, 50, 54.

difficulties that can appear or accumulate along that road; otherwise we would be unfaithful to the word of Christ, we would fail to accomplish his testament. Have we the right to run this risk?

6.2 There are people who in the face of the difficulties or because they consider that the first ecumenical endeavors have brought negative results would have liked to turn back. Some even express the opinion that these efforts are harmful to the cause of the Gospel, are leading to a further rupture in the Church, are causing confusion of ideas in questions of faith and morals and are ending up with a specific indifferentism. It is perhaps a good thing that the spokesmen for these opinions should express their fears. However, in this respect also, correct limits must be maintained. It is obvious that this new stage in the Church's life demands of us a faith that is particularly aware, profound and responsible. True ecumenical activity means openness, drawing closer, availability for dialogue, and a shared investigation of the truth in the full evangelical and Christian sense; but in no way does it or can it mean giving up or in any way diminishing the treasures of divine truth that the Church has constantly confessed and taught. To all who, for whatever motive, would wish to dissuade the Church from seeking the universal unity of Christians the question must once again be put: Have we the right not to do it? Can we fail to have trust — in spite of all human weakness and all the faults of past centuries — in our Lord's grace as revealed recently through what the Holy Spirit said and we heard during the Council? If we were to do so, we would deny the truth concerning ourselves that was so eloquently expressed by the Apostle: "By the grace of God I am what I am, and his grace toward me was not in vain."[19]

6.3 What we have just said must also be applied — although in another way and with the due differences — to activity for coming closer together with the representatives of the non-Christian religions, an activity expressed through dialogue, contacts, prayer in common, investigation of the treasures of human spirituality, in which, as we know well, the members of these religions also are not lacking. Does it not sometimes happen that the firm belief of the followers of the non-Christian religions — a belief that is also an effect of the Spirit of truth operating outside the visible confines of the Mystical Body — can make Christians ashamed at being often themselves so disposed to doubt concerning the truths revealed by God and proclaimed by the Church and so prone to relax moral principles and open the way to ethical permissiveness? It is a noble thing to have a predisposition for understanding every person, analyzing every system and recognizing what is right; this does not at all mean

---

[19] 1 Cor 15:10.

losing certitude about one's own faith[20] or weakening the principles of morality, the lack of which will soon make itself felt in the life of whole societies, with deplorable consequences besides.

II

The Mystery of the Redemption

Within the mystery of Christ

7.1 While the ways on which the Council of this century has set the Church going, ways indicated by the late Pope Paul VI in his first Encyclical, will continue to be for a long time the ways that all of us must follow, we can at the same time rightly ask at this new stage: How, in what manner should we continue? What should we do, in order that this new Advent of the Church connected with the approaching end of the second millennium may bring us closer to him whom Sacred Scripture calls "Everlasting Father," *Pater futuri saeculi?*[21] This is the fundamental question that the new Pope must put to himself on accepting in a spirit of obedience in faith the call corresponding to the command that Christ gave Peter several times: "Feed my lambs,"[22] meaning: Be the shepherd of my sheepfold, and again: "And when you have turned again, strengthen your brethren."[23]

7.2 To this question, dear Brothers, sons and daughters, a fundamental and essential response must be given. Our response must be: Our spirit is set in one direction, the only direction for our intellect, will and heart is — toward Christ our Redeemer, toward Christ, the Redeemer of man. We wish to look toward him — because there is salvation in no one else but him, the Son of God — repeating what Peter said: "Lord, to whom shall we go? You have the words of eternal life."[24]

7.3 Through the Church's consciousness, which the Council considerably developed, through all levels of this self-awareness, and through all the fields of activity in which the Church expresses, finds and confirms herself, we must constantly aim at him "who is the head,"[25] through whom are all things and

[20] Cf. First Vatican Ecumenical Council, Dogmatic Constitution on the Catholic Faith *Dei Filius*, Chapter 3, *De Fide*, Canon 6: *Conciliorum Oecumenicorum Decreta*, Ed. Istituto per le Scienze Religiose, 3rd ed., Bologna, 1973, 811.

[21] Is 9:6.

[22] Jn 21:15.

[23] Lk 22:32.

[24] Jn 6:68; cf. Acts 4:8-12.

[25] Cf. Eph 1:10, 22; 4:25; Col 1:18.

through whom we exist,"[26] who is both "the way, and the truth"[27] and "the resurrection and the life,"[28] seeing whom, we see the Father,[29] and who had to go away from us[30] — that is, by his death on the Cross and then by his Ascension into heaven — in order that the Counselor should come to us and should keep coming to us as the Spirit of truth.[31] In him are "all the treasures of wisdom and knowledge,"[32] and the Church is his Body.[33] "By her relationship with Christ, the Church is a kind of sacrament or sign and means of intimate union with God, and of the unity of all mankind,"[34] and the source of this is he, he himself, he the Redeemer.

7.4 The Church does not cease to listen to his words. She rereads them continually. With the greatest devotion she reconstructs every detail of his life. These words are listened to also by non-Christians. The life of Christ speaks, also, to many who are not capable of repeating with Peter: "You are the Christ, the Son of the living God."[35] He, the Son of the living God, speaks to people also as Man: it is his life that speaks, his humanity, his fidelity to the truth, his all-embracing love. Furthermore, his death on the Cross speaks — that is to say the inscrutable depth of his suffering and abandonment. The Church never ceases to relive his death on the Cross and his Resurrection, which constitute the content of the Church's daily life. Indeed, it is by the command of Christ himself, her Master, that the Church unceasingly celebrates the Eucharist, finding in it the "fountain of life and holiness,"[36] the efficacious sign of grace and reconciliation with God, and the pledge of eternal life. The Church lives his mystery, draws unwearyingly from it and continually seeks ways of bringing this mystery of her Master and Lord to humanity — to the peoples, the nations, the succeeding generations, and every individual human being — as if she were ever repeating, as the Apostle did: "For I decided to know nothing among you except Jesus Christ and him crucified."[37]

---

[26] 1 Cor 8:6; cf. Col 1:17.

[27] Jn 14:6.

[28] Jn 11:25.

[29] Cf. Jn 14:9.

[30] Cf. Jn 16:7.

[31] Cf. Jn 16:7, 13.

[32] Col 2:3.

[33] Cf. Rom 12:5; 1 Cor 6:15; 10:17; 12:12, 27; Eph 1:23; 2:16; 4:4; Col 1:24; 3:15.

[34] Second Vatican Ecumenical Council, Dogmatic Constitution on the Church *Lumen Gentium*, 1: *AAS* 57 (1965), 5.

[35] Mt 16:16.

[36] Cf. Litany of the Sacred Heart.

[37] 1 Cor 2:2.

The Church stays within the sphere of the mystery of the Redemption, which has become the fundamental principle of her life and mission.

Redemption as a new creation

8.1 The Redeemer of the world! In him has been revealed in a new and more wonderful way the fundamental truth concerning creation to which the Book of Genesis gives witness when it repeats several times: "God saw that it was good."[38] The good has its source in Wisdom and Love. In Jesus Christ the visible world which God created for man[39] — the world that, when sin entered, "was subjected to futility"[40] — recovers again its original link with the divine source of Wisdom and Love. Indeed, "God so loved the world that he gave his only Son."[41] As this link was broken in the man Adam, so in the Man Christ it was reforged.[42] Are we of the twentieth century not convinced of the overpoweringly eloquent words of the Apostle of the Gentiles concerning the "creation (that) has been groaning in travail together until now"[43] and "waits with eager longing for the revelation of the sons of God,"[44] the creation that "was subjected to futility"? Does not the previously unknown immense progress — which has taken place especially in the course of this century — in the field of man's dominion over the world itself reveal — to a previously unknown degree — that manifold subjection "to futility"? It is enough to recall certain phenomena, such as the threat of pollution of the natural environment in areas of rapid industrialization, or the armed conflicts continually breaking out over and over again, or the prospectives of self-destruction through the use of atomic, hydrogen, neutron, and similar weapons, or the lack of respect for the life of the unborn. The world of the new age, the world of space flights, the world of the previously unattained conquests of science and technology — is it not also the world "groaning in travail"[45] that "waits with eager longing for the revealing of the sons of God"?[46]

8.2 In its penetrating analysis of "the modern world," the Second Vatican Council reached that most important point of the visible world that is man, by penetrating like Christ the depth of human consciousness and by making contact

[38] Cf. Gen 1 *passim.*
[39] Cf. Gen 1:26-30.
[40] Rom 8:20, cf. 8:19-22; Second Vatican Ecumenical Council, Pastoral Constitution on the Church in the Modern World *Gaudium et Spes,* 2, 13: *AAS* 58 (1966), 1026, 1034-1035.
[41] Jn 3:16.
[42] Cf. Rom 5:12-21.
[43] Rom 8:22.
[44] Rom 8:19.
[45] Rom 8:22.
[46] Rom 8:19.

with the inward mystery of man, which in biblical and non-biblical language is expressed by the word "heart." Christ, the Redeemer of the world, is the one who penetrated in a unique, unrepeatable way into the mystery of man and entered his "heart." Rightly therefore does the Second Vatican Council teach: "The truth is that only in the mystery of the Incarnate Word does the mystery of man take on light. For Adam, the first man, was a type of him who was to come (Rom 5.14), Christ the Lord. Christ, the new Adam, in the very revelation of the mystery of the Father and of his love, *fully reveals man to himself* and brings to light his most high calling." And the Council continues: "He who is the 'image of the invisible God' (Col 1:15), is himself the perfect man who has restored in the children of Adam that likeness to God which had been disfigured ever since the first sin. Human nature, by the very fact that it was assumed, not absorbed, in him, has been raised in us also to a dignity beyond compare. For, by his Incarnation, he, the Son of God, *in a certain way united himself with each man.* He worked with human hands, he thought with a human mind. He acted with a human will, and with a human heart he loved. Born of the Virgin Mary, he has truly been made one of us, like to us in all things except sin,"[47] he, the Redeemer of man.

The divine dimension of the mystery of the Redemption

9.1 As we reflect again on this stupendous text from the Council's teaching, we do not forget even for a moment that Jesus Christ, the Son of the living God, became our reconciliation with the Father.[48] He it was, and he alone, who satisfied the Father's eternal love, that fatherhood that from the beginning found expression in creating the world, giving man all the riches of creation, and making him "little less than God,"[49] in that he was created "in the image and after the likeness of God."[50] He and he alone also satisfied that fatherhood of God and that love which man in a way rejected by breaking the first Covenant[51] and the later covenants that God "again and again offered to man."[52] The Redemption of the world — this tremendous mystery of love in which creation is renewed[53] — is, at its deepest root, the fullness of justice in

---

[47] Second Vatican Ecumenical Council, Pastoral Constitution on the Church in the Modern World *Gaudium et Spes*, 22: *AAS* 58 (1966), 1042-1043.

[48] Rom 5:11; Col 1:20.

[49] Ps 8:5.

[50] Cf. Gen 1:26.

[51] Cf. Gen 3:6-13.

[52] Cf. Eucharistic Prayer IV.

[53] Cf. Second Vatican Ecumenical Council, Pastoral Constitution on the Church in the Modern World *Gaudium et Spes*, 37: *AAS* 58 (1966), 1054-1055; Dogmatic Constitution on the Church *Lumen Gentium*, 48: *AAS* 57 (1965), 53-54.

a human heart — the heart of the firstborn Son — in order that it may become justice in the hearts of many human beings, predestined from eternity in the First-born Son to be children of God[54] and called to grace, called to love. The Cross on Calvary, through which Jesus Christ — a Man, the Son of the Virgin Mary, thought to be the son of Joseph of Nazareth — "leaves" this world, is also a fresh manifestation of the eternal fatherhood of God, who in him draws near again to humanity, to each human being, giving him the thrice holy "Spirit of truth."[55]

9.2 This revelation of the Father and outpouring of the Holy Spirit, which stamp an indelible seal on the mystery of the Redemption, explain the meaning of the Cross and death of Christ. The God of creation is revealed as the God of Redemption, as the God who is "faithful to himself,"[56] and faithful to his love for man and the world, which he revealed on the day of creation. His is a love that does not draw back before anything that justice requires in him. Therefore "for our sake (God) made him (the Son) to be sin who knew no sin."[57] If he "made to be sin" him who was without any sin whatever, it was to reveal the love that is always greater than the whole of creation, the love that is he himself, since "God is love."[58] Above all, love is greater than sin, than weakness, than the "futility of creation";[59] it is stronger than death; it is a love always ready to raise up and forgive, always ready to go to meet the prodigal son,[60] always looking for "the revealing of the sons of God,"[61] who are called "to the glory that is to be revealed."[62] This revelation of love is also described as mercy;[63] and in man's history this revelation of love and mercy has taken a form and a name: that of Jesus Christ.

The human dimension of the mystery of the Redemption

10.1 Man cannot live without love. He remains a being that is incomprehensible for himself, his life is senseless, if love is not revealed to him, if he does not encounter love, if he does not experience it and make it his own, if he does not participate intimately in it. This, as has already been

---

[54] Cf. Rom 8:29-30; Eph 1:8.
[55] Cf. Jn 16:13.
[56] Cf. 1 Thess 5:24.
[57] 2 Cor 5:21; cf. Gal 3:13.
[58] 1 Jn 4:8, 16.
[59] Cf. Rom 8:20.
[60] Cf. Lk 15:11-32.
[61] Rom 8:19.
[62] Cf. Rom 8:18.
[63] Cf. Saint Thomas Aquinas, *Summa Theologiae*, III, q. 46, a. 1, ad 3.

said, is why Christ the Redeemer "fully reveals man to himself." If we may use the expression, this is the human dimension of the mystery of the Redemption. In this dimension man finds again the greatness, dignity and value that belong to his humanity. In the mystery of the Redemption man becomes newly "expressed" and, in a way, is newly created. He is newly created! "There is neither Jew nor Greek, there is neither slave nor free, there is neither male nor female; for you are all one in Christ Jesus."[64] The man who wishes to understand himself thoroughly — and not just in accordance with immediate, partial, often superficial, and even illusory standards and measures of his being — he must with his unrest, uncertainty and even his weakness and sinfulness, with his life and death, draw near to Christ. He must, so to speak, enter into him with all his own self, he must "appropriate" and assimilate the whole of the reality of the Incarnation and Redemption in order to find himself. If this profound process takes place within him, he then bears fruit not only of adoration of God but also of deep wonder at himself. How precious must man be in the eyes of the Creator, if he "gained so great a Redeemer,"[65] and if God "gave his only Son" in order that man "should not perish but have eternal life."[66]

10.2 In reality, the name for that deep amazement at man's worth and dignity is the Gospel, that is to say: the Good News. It is also called Christianity. This amazement determines the Church's mission in the world and, perhaps even more so, "in the modern world." This amazement, which is also a conviction and a certitude — at its deepest root it is the certainty of faith, but in a hidden and mysterious way it vivifies every aspect of authentic humanism — is closely connected with Christ. It also fixes Christ's place — so to speak, his particular right of citizenship — in the history of man and mankind. Unceasingly contemplating the whole of Christ's mystery, the Church knows with all the certainty of faith that the Redemption that took place through the Cross has definitively restored his dignity to man and given back meaning to his life in the world, a meaning that was lost to a considerable extent because of sin. And for that reason, the Redemption was accomplished in the Paschal Mystery, leading through the Cross and death to Resurrection.

10.3 The Church's fundamental function in every age and particularly in ours is to direct man's gaze, to point the awareness and experience of the whole of humanity toward the mystery of Christ, to help all men to be familiar with the profundity of the Redemption taking place in Christ Jesus. At the

---

[64] Gal 3:28.
[65] *Exsultet* at the Easter Vigil.
[66] Cf. Jn 3:16.

same time man's deepest sphere is involved — we mean the sphere of human hearts, consciences and events.

The mystery of Christ as the basis of the Church's mission and of Christianity

11.1 The Second Vatican Council did immense work to form that full and universal awareness by the Church of which Pope Paul VI wrote in his first Encyclical. This awareness — or rather self-awareness — by the Church is formed "in dialogue"; and before this dialogue becomes a conversation, attention must be directed to "the other," that is to say: the person with whom we wish to speak. The Ecumenical Council gave a fundamental impulse to forming the Church's self-awareness by so adequately and competently presenting to us a view of the terrestrial globe as a map of various religions. It showed furthermore that this map of the world's religions has superimposed on it, in previously unknown layers typical of our time, the phenomenon of atheism in its various forms, beginning with the atheism that is programmed, organized and structured as a political system.

11.2 With regard to religion, what is dealt with is in the first place religion as a universal phenomenon linked with man's history from the beginning, then the various non-Christian religions, and finally Christianity itself. The Council document on non-Christian religions, in particular, is filled with deep esteem for the great spiritual values, indeed for the primacy of the spiritual, which in the life of mankind finds expression in religion and then in morality, with direct effects on the whole of culture. The Fathers of the Church rightly saw in the various religions as it were so many reflections of the one truth, "seeds of the Word,"[67] attesting that, though the routes taken may be different, there is but a single goal to which is directed the deepest aspiration of the human spirit as expressed in its quest for God and also in its quest, through its tending toward God, for the full dimension of its humanity, or in other words for the full meaning of human life. The Council gave particular attention to the Jewish religion, recalling the great spiritual heritage common to Christians and Jews. It also expressed its esteem for the believers of Islam, whose faith also looks to Abraham.[68]

---

[67] Cf. Saint Justin, *Apologia*, I, 46, 1-4; *Apologia*, II, 7 (8), 1-4; 10, 1-3; 13, 3-4: *Florilegium Patristicum*, II, 2nd ed., Bonn, 1911, 81, 125, 129, 133; Clement of Alexandria, *Stromata*, I, 19, 91 and 94: *SCh* 30, 117-118, 119-120; Second Vatican Ecumenical Council, Decree on the Church's Missionary Activity *Ad Gentes*, 11: *AAS* 58 (1966), 960; Dogmatic Constitution on the Church *Lumen Gentium*, 17: *AAS* 57 (1965), 21.

[68] Cf. Second Vatican Ecumenical Council, Declaration on the Relationship of the Church to Non-Christian Religions *Nostra Aetate*, 3-4: *AAS* 58 (1966), 741-743.

11.3 The opening made by the Second Vatican Council has enabled the Church and all Christians to reach a more complete awareness of the mystery of Christ, "the mystery hidden for ages"[69] in God, to be revealed in time in the Man Jesus Christ, and to be revealed continually in every time. In Christ and through Christ God has revealed himself fully to mankind and has definitively drawn close to it; at the same time, in Christ and through Christ man has acquired full awareness of his dignity, of the heights to which he is raised, of the surpassing worth of his own humanity, and of the meaning of his existence.

11.4 All of us who are Christ's followers must therefore meet and unite around him. This unity in the various fields of the life, tradition, structures and discipline of the individual Christian Churches and Ecclesial Communities cannot be brought about without effective work aimed at getting to know each other and removing the obstacles blocking the way to perfect unity. However, we can and must immediately reach and display to the world our unity in proclaiming the mystery of Christ, in revealing the divine dimension and also the human dimension of the Redemption, and in struggling with unwearying perseverance for the dignity that each human being has reached and can continually reach in Christ, namely the dignity of both the grace of divine adoption and the inner truth of humanity, a truth which — if in the common awareness of the modern world it has been given such fundamental importance — for us is still clearer in the light of the reality that is Jesus Christ.

11.5 Jesus Christ is the stable principle and fixed center of the mission that God himself has entrusted to man. We must all share in this mission and concentrate all our forces on it, since it is more necessary than ever for modern mankind. If this mission seems to encounter greater opposition nowadays than ever before, this shows that today it is more necessary than ever and, in spite of the opposition, more awaited than ever. Here we touch indirectly on the mystery of the divine "economy" which linked salvation and grace with the Cross. It was not without reason that Christ said that "the Kingdom of heaven has suffered violence, and men of violence take it by force"[70] and moreover that "the children of this world are more astute . . . than are the children of light."[71] We gladly accept this rebuke, that we may be like those "violent people of God" that we have so often seen in the history of the Church and still see today, and that we may consciously join in the great mission of revealing

---

[69] Col 1:26.
[70] Mt 11:12.
[71] Lk 16:8.

Christ to the world, helping each person to find himself in Christ, and helping the contemporary generations of our brothers and sisters, the peoples, nations, States, mankind, developing countries and countries of opulence — in short, helping everyone to get to know "the unsearchable riches of Christ,"[72] since these riches are for every individual and are everybody's property.

The Church's mission and human freedom

12.1 In this unity in mission, which is decided principally by Christ himself, all Christians must find what already unites them, even before their full communion is achieved. This is apostolic and missionary unity, missionary and apostolic unity. Thanks to this unity we can together come close to the magnificent heritage of the human spirit that has been manifested in all religions, as the Second Vatican Council's Declaration *Nostra Aetate* says.[73] It also enables us to approach all cultures, all ideological concepts, all people of good will. We approach them with the esteem, respect and discernment that since the time of the Apostles has marked the *missionary* attitude, the attitude *of the missionary.* Suffice it to mention Saint Paul and, for instance, his address in the Areopagus at Athens.[74] The *missionary* attitude always begins with a feeling of deep esteem for "what is in man,"[75] for what man has himself worked out in the depths of his spirit concerning the most profound and important problems. It is a question of respecting everything that has been brought about in him by the Spirit, which "blows where it wills."[76] The mission is never destruction, but instead is a taking up and fresh building, even if in practice there has not always been full correspondence with this high ideal. And we know well that the conversion that is begun by the mission is a work of grace, in which man must fully find himself again.

12.2 For this reason the Church in our time attaches great importance to all that is stated by the Second Vatican Council in its *Declaration on Religious Freedom,* both the first and the second part of the document.[77] We perceive intimately that the truth revealed to us by God imposes on us an obligation. We have, in particular, a great sense of responsibility for this truth. By Christ's institution the Church is its guardian and teacher, having been endowed with a unique assistance of the Holy Spirit in order to guard and teach it in its most

[72] Eph 3:8.
[73] Cf. Second Vatican Ecumenical Council, Declaration on the Relationship of the Church to Non-Christian Religions *Nostra Aetate*, 1-2: *AAS* 58 (1966), 740-741.
[74] Acts 17:22-31.
[75] Jn 2:25.
[76] Jn 3:8.
[77] Cf. *AAS* 58 (1966), 929-946.

exact integrity.[78] In fulfilling this mission, we look toward Christ himself, the first evangelizer,[79] and also toward his Apostles, martyrs and confessors. The *Declaration on Religious Freedom* shows us convincingly that, when Christ and, after him, his Apostles proclaimed the truth that comes not from men but from God ("My teaching is not mine, but his who sent me,"[80] that is, the Father's), they preserved, while acting with their full force of spirit, a deep esteem for man, for his intellect, his will, his conscience and his freedom.[81] Thus the human person's dignity itself becomes part of the content of that proclamation, being included not necessarily in words but by an attitude toward it. This attitude seems to fit the special needs of our times. Since man's true freedom is not found in everything that the various systems and individuals see and propagate as freedom, the Church, because of her divine mission, becomes all the more the guardian of this freedom, which is the condition and basis for the human person's true dignity.

12.3 Jesus Christ meets the man of every age, including our own, with the same words: "You will know the truth, and the truth will make you free."[82] These words contain both a fundamental requirement and a warning: the requirement of an honest relationship with regard to truth as a condition for authentic freedom, and the warning to avoid every kind of illusory freedom, every superficial unilateral freedom, every freedom that fails to enter into the whole truth about man and the world. Today also, even after two thousand years, we see Christ as the one who brings man freedom based on truth, frees man from what curtails, diminishes and as it were breaks off this freedom at its root, in man's soul, his heart and his conscience. What a stupendous confirmation of this has been given and is still being given by those who, thanks to Christ and in Christ, have reached true freedom and have manifested it even in situations of external constraint!

12.4 When Jesus Christ himself appeared as a prisoner before Pilate's tribunal and was interrogated by him about the accusation made against him by the representatives of the Sanhedrin, did he not answer: "For this I was born, and for this I have come into the world, to bear witness to the truth"?[83] It was as if with these words spoken before the judge at the decisive moment he was once more confirming what he had said earlier: "You will know the

---

[78] Cf. Jn 14:26.

[79] Paul VI, Apostolic Exhortation *Evangelii Nuntiandi* (December 8, 1975), 6: *AAS* 68 (1976), 9.

[80] Jn 7:16.

[81] Cf. *AAS* 58 (1966), 936-938.

[82] Jn 8:32.

[83] Jn 18:37.

truth, and the truth will make you free." In the course of so many centuries, of so many generations, from the time of the Apostles on, is it not often Jesus Christ himself that has made an appearance at the side of people judged for the sake of the truth? And has he not gone to death with people condemned for the sake of the truth? Does he ever cease to be the continuous spokesman and advocate for the person who lives "in spirit and truth"?[84] Just as he does not cease to be it before the Father, he is it also with regard to the history of man. And in her turn the Church, in spite of all the weaknesses that are part of her human history, does not cease to follow him who said: "The hour is coming, and now is, when the true worshipers will worship the Father in spirit and truth, for such the Father seeks to worship him. God is spirit, and those who worship him must worship in spirit and truth."[85]

III

Redeemed Man and His Situation in the Modern World

Christ united himself with each man

13.1 When we penetrate by means of the continually and rapidly increasing experience of the human family into the mystery of Jesus Christ, we understand with greater clarity that there is at the basis of all these ways that the Church of our time must follow, in accordance with the wisdom of Pope Paul VI,[86] one single way: it is the way that has stood the test of centuries and it is also the way of the future. Christ the Lord indicated this way especially, when, as the Council teaches, "by his Incarnation, he, the Son of God, in a certain way *united himself with each man.*"[87] The Church therefore sees its fundamental task in enabling that union to be brought about and renewed continually. The Church wishes to serve this single end: that each person may be able to find Christ, in order that Christ may walk with each person the path of life, with the power of the truth about man and the world that is contained in the mystery of the Incarnation and the Redemption and with the power of the love that is radiated by that truth. Against a background of the ever increasing historical processes, which seem at the present time to have results

---

[84] Cf. Jn 4:23.

[85] Jn 4:23-24.

[86] Cf. Paul VI, Encyclical Letter *Ecclesiam Suam* (August 6, 1964): *AAS* 56 (1964), 609-659.

[87] Second Vatican Ecumenical Council, Pastoral Constitution on the Church in the Modern World *Gaudium et Spes*, 22: *AAS* 58 (1966), 1042.

especially within the spheres of various systems, ideological concepts of the world and regimes, Jesus Christ becomes, in a way, newly present, in spite of all his apparent absences, in spite of all the limitations of the presence and of the institutional activity of the Church. Jesus Christ becomes present with the power of the truth and the love that are expressed in him with unique, unrepeatable fullness in spite of the shortness of his life on earth and the even greater shortness of his public activity.

13.2 Jesus Christ is the chief way for the Church. He himself is our way "to the Father's house"[88] and is the way to each man. On this way leading from Christ to man, on this way on which Christ unites himself with each man, nobody can halt the Church. This is an exigency of man's temporal welfare and of his eternal welfare. Out of regard for Christ and in view of the mystery that constitutes the Church's own life, the Church cannot remain insensible to whatever serves man's true welfare, any more than she can remain indifferent to what threatens it. In various passages in its documents the Second Vatican Council has expressed the Church's fundamental solicitude that life in "the world should conform more to man's surpassing dignity"[89] in all its aspects, so as to make that life "ever more human."[90] This is the solicitude of Christ himself, the Good Shepherd of all men. In the name of this solicitude, as we read in the Council's Pastoral Constitution, "the Church must in no way be confused with the political community, nor bound to any political system. She is at once a sign and a safeguard of the transcendence of the human person."[91]

13.3 Accordingly, what is in question here is man in all his truth, in his full magnitude. We are not dealing with the "abstract" man, but the real, "concrete," "historical" man. We are dealing with "each" man, for each one is included in the mystery of the Redemption and with each one Christ has united himself forever through this mystery. Every man comes into the world through being conceived in his mother's womb and being born of his mother, and precisely on account of the mystery of the Redemption is entrusted to the solicitude of the Church. Her solicitude is about the whole man and is focused on him in an altogether special manner. The object of her care is man in his unique unrepeatable human reality, which keeps intact the image and likeness of God himself.[92] The Council points out this very fact when, speaking of

---

[88] Cf. Jn 14:1ff.

[89] Second Vatican Ecumenical Council, Pastoral Constitution on the Church in the Modern World *Gaudium et Spes*, 91: *AAS* 58 (1966), 1113.

[90] Ibid., 38: loc. cit., 1056.

[91] Ibid., 76: loc. cit., 1099.

[92] Cf. Gen 1:26.

that likeness, it recalls that "man is the only creature on earth that God willed for itself."[93] Man as "willed" by God, as "chosen" by him from eternity and called, destined for grace and glory — this is "each" man, "the most concrete" man, "the most real"; this is man in all the fullness of the mystery in which he has become a sharer in Jesus Christ, the mystery in which each one of the four thousand million human beings living on our planet has become a sharer from the moment he is conceived beneath the heart of his mother.

For the Church all ways lead to man

14.1 The Church cannot abandon man, for his "destiny," that is to say his election, calling, birth and death, salvation or perdition, is so closely and unbreakably linked with Christ. We are speaking precisely of each man on this planet, this earth that the Creator gave to the first man, saying to the man and the woman: "subdue it and have dominion."[94] Each man in all the unrepeatable reality of what he is and what he does, of his intellect and will, of his conscience and heart. Man who in his reality has, because he is a "person," a history of his life that is his own and, most important, a history of his soul that is his own. Man who, in keeping with the openness of his spirit within and also with the many diverse needs of his body and his existence in time, writes this personal history of his through numerous bonds, contacts, situations, and social structures linking him with other men, beginning to do so from the first moment of his existence on earth, from the moment of his conception and birth. Man in the full truth of his existence, of his personal being and also of his community and social being — in the sphere of his own family, in the sphere of society and very diverse contexts, in the sphere of his own nation or people (perhaps still only that of his clan or tribe), and in the sphere of the whole of mankind — this man is the primary route that the Church must travel in fulfilling her mission: *he is the primary and fundamental way for the Church,* the way traced out by Christ himself, the way that leads invariably through the mystery of the Incarnation and the Redemption.

14.2 It was precisely this man in all the truth of his life, in his conscience, in his continual inclination to sin and at the same time in his continual aspiration to truth, the good, the beautiful, justice and love that the Second Vatican Council had before its eyes when, in outlining his situation in the modern world, it always passed from the external elements of this situation to the truth within humanity: "In man himself many elements wrestle with one an-

---

[93] Second Vatican Ecumenical Council, Pastoral Constitution on the Church in the Modern World *Gaudium et Spes,* 24: *AAS* 58 (1966), 1045.

[94] Gen 1:28.

other. Thus, on the one hand, as a creature he experiences his limitations in a multitude of ways. On the other, he feels himself to be boundless in his desires and summoned to a higher life. Pulled by manifold attractions, he is constantly forced to choose among them and to renounce some. Indeed, as a weak and sinful being, he often does what he would not, and fails to do what he would. Hence he suffers from internal divisions, and from these flow so many and such great discords in society."[95]

14.3 This man is the way for the Church — a way that, in a sense, is the basis of all the other ways that the Church must walk — because man — every man without any exception whatever — has been redeemed by Christ, and because with man — with each man without any exception whatever — Christ is in a way united, even when man is unaware of it: "Christ, who died and was raised up for all, provides man" — each man and every man — "with the light and the strength to measure up to his supreme calling."[96]

14.4 Since this man is the way for the Church, the way for her daily life and experience, for her mission and toil, the Church of today must be aware in an always new manner of man's "situation." That means that she must be aware of his possibilities, which keep returning to their proper bearings and thus revealing themselves. She must likewise be aware of the threats to man and of all that seems to oppose the endeavor "to make human life ever more human"[97] and make every element of this life correspond to man's true dignity — in a word, she must be aware of *all that is opposed* to that process.

What modern man is afraid of

15.1 Accordingly, while keeping alive in our memory the picture that was so perspicaciously and authoritatively traced by the Second Vatican Council, we shall try once more to adapt it to the "signs of the times," and to the demands of the situation, which is continually changing and evolving in certain directions.

15.2 The man of today seems ever to be under threat from what he produces, that is to say from the result of the work of his hands and, even more so, of the work of his intellect and the tendencies of his will. All too soon, and often in an unforeseeable way, what this manifold activity of man yields is not only subjected to "alienation," in the sense that it is simply taken away from the person who produces it, but rather it turns against man himself, at least in

---

[95] Second Vatican Ecumenical Council, Pastoral Constitution on the Church in the Modern World *Gaudium et Spes*, 10: *AAS* 58 (1966), 1032.

[96] Ibid., 10: loc. cit., 1033.

[97] Ibid., 38: loc. cit., 1056; cf. Paul VI, Encyclical Letter *Populorum Progressio* (March 26, 1967), 21: *AAS* 59 (1967), 267-268.

part, through the indirect consequences of its effects returning on himself. It is or can be directed against him. This seems to make up the main chapter of the drama of present-day human existence in its broadest and universal dimension. Man therefore lives increasingly in fear. He is afraid that what he produces — not all of it, of course, or even most of it, but part of it and precisely that part that contains a special share of his genius and initiative — can radically turn against himself; he is afraid that it can become the means and instrument for an unimaginable self-destruction, compared with which all the cataclysms and catastrophes of history known to us seem to fade away. This gives rise to a question: Why is it that the power given to man from the beginning by which he was to subdue the earth[98] turns against himself, producing an understandable state of disquiet, of conscious or unconscious fear and of menace, which in various ways is being communicated to the whole of the present-day human family and is manifesting itself under various aspects?

15.3 This state of menace for man from what he produces shows itself in various directions and various degrees of intensity. We seem to be increasingly aware of the fact that the exploitation of the earth, the planet on which we are living, demands rational and honest planning. At the same time, exploitation of the earth not only for industrial but also for military purposes and the uncontrolled development of technology outside the framework of a long-range authentically humanistic plan often bring with them a threat to man's natural environment, alienate him in his relations with nature and remove him from nature. Man often seems to see no other meaning in his natural environment than what serves for immediate use and consumption. Yet it was the Creator's will that man should communicate with nature as an intelligent and noble "master" and "guardian," and not as a heedless "exploiter" and "destroyer."

15.4 The development of technology and the development of contemporary civilization, which is marked by the ascendancy of technology, demand a proportional development of morals and ethics. For the present, this last development seems unfortunately to be always left behind. Accordingly, in spite of the marvel of this progress, in which it is difficult not to see also authentic signs of man's greatness, signs that in their creative seeds were revealed to us in the pages of the Book of Genesis, as early as where it describes man's creation,[99] this progress cannot fail to give rise to disquiet on many counts. The first reason for disquiet concerns the essential and fundamental question: Does this progress, which has man for its author and promoter, make human life on earth "more human" in every aspect of that life? Does it make it more "worthy of man"? There

[98] Cf. Gen 1:28.
[99] Cf. Gen 1-2.

can be no doubt that in various aspects it does. But the question keeps coming back with regard to what is most essential: whether in the context of this progress man, as man, is becoming truly better, that is to say more mature spiritually, more aware of the dignity of his humanity, more responsible, more open to others, especially the neediest and the weakest, and readier to give and to aid all.

15.5 This question must be put by Christians, precisely because Jesus Christ has made them so universally sensitive about the problem of man. The same question must be asked by all men, especially those belonging to the social groups that are dedicating themselves actively to development and progress today. As we observe and take part in these processes we cannot let ourselves be taken over merely by euphoria or be carried away by one-sided enthusiasm for our conquests, but we must all ask ourselves, with absolute honesty, objectivity and a sense of moral responsibility, the essential questions concerning man's situation today and in the future. Do all the conquests attained until now and those projected for the future for technology accord with man's moral and spiritual progress? In this context is man, as man, developing and progressing or is he regressing and being degraded in his humanity? In men and "in man's world," which in itself is a world of moral good and evil, does good prevail over evil? In men and among men is there a growth of social love, of respect for the rights of others — for every man, nation and people — or on the contrary is there an increase of various degrees of selfishness, exaggerated nationalism instead of authentic love of country, and also the propensity to dominate others beyond the limits of one's legitimate rights and merits and the propensity to exploit the whole of material progress and that in the technology of production for the exclusive purpose of dominating others or of favoring this or that imperialism?

15.6 These are the essential questions that the Church is bound to ask herself, since they are being asked with greater or less explicitness by the thousands of millions of people now living in the world. The subject of development and progress is on everybody's lips and appears in the columns of all the newspapers and other publications in all the languages of the modern world. Let us not forget, however, that this subject contains not only affirmations and certainties but also questions and points of anguished disquiet. The latter are no less important than the former. They fit in with the dialectical nature of human knowledge and even more with the fundamental need for solicitude by man for man, for his humanity, and for the future of people on earth. Inspired by eschatological faith, the Church considers an essential, unbreakably united element of her mission this solicitude for man, for his humanity, for the future of men on earth, and therefore also for the course set for the whole of development and progress. She finds the principle of this solicitude in Jesus Christ himself, as the Gospels witness. This is why she wishes to make it grow continually through her relationship with Christ, reading man's situation in the modern world in accordance with the most important signs of our time.

Progress or threat

16.1 If, therefore, our time, the time of our generation, the time that is approaching the end of the second millennium of the Christian era, shows itself a time of great progress, it is also seen as a time of threat in many forms for man. The Church must speak of this threat to all people of good will and must always carry on a dialogue with them about it. Man's situation in the modern world seems indeed to be far removed from the objective demands of the moral order, from the requirements of justice, and even more of social love. We are dealing here only with that which found expression in the Creator's first message to man at the moment in which he was giving him the earth, to "subdue" it.[100] This first message was confirmed by Christ the Lord in the mystery of the Redemption. This is expressed by the Second Vatican Council in those beautiful chapters of its teaching that concern man's "kingship," that is to say his call to share in the kingly function — the *munus regale* — of Christ himself.[101] The essential meaning of this "kingship" and "dominion" of man over the visible world, which the Creator himself gave man for his task, consists in the priority of ethics over technology, in the primacy of the person over things, and in the superiority of spirit over matter.

16.2 This is why all phases of present-day progress must be followed attentively. Each stage of that progress must, so to speak, be x-rayed from this point of view. What is in question is the advancement of persons, not just the multiplying of things that people can use. It is a matter — as a contemporary philosopher has said and as the Council has stated — not so much of "having more" as of "being more."[102] Indeed there is already a real perceptible danger that, while man's dominion over the world of things is making enormous advances, he should lose the essential threads of his dominion and in various ways let his humanity be subjected to the world and become

---

[100] Gen 1:28; cf. Second Vatican Ecumenical Council, Decree on the Instruments of Social Communication *Inter Mirifica*, 6: *AAS* 56 (1964), 147; Pastoral Constitution on the Church in the Modern World *Gaudium et Spes*, 74, 78: *AAS* 58 (1966), 1095-1096, 1101-1102.

[101] Cf. Second Vatican Ecumenical Council, Dogmatic Constitution on the Church *Lumen Gentium*, 10, 36: *AAS* 57 (1965), 14-15, 41-42.

[102] Cf. Second Vatican Ecumenical Council, Pastoral Constitution on the Church in the Modern World *Gaudium et Spes*, 35: *AAS* 58 (1966), 1053; Paul VI, Address to the Diplomatic Corps (January 7, 1965): *AAS* 57 (1965), 232; Encyclical Letter *Populorum Progressio* (March 26, 1967), 14: *AAS* 59 (1967), 264.

himself something subject to manipulation in many ways — even if the manipulation is often not perceptible directly — through the whole of the organization of community life, through the production system and through pressure from the means of social communication. Man cannot relinquish himself or the place in the visible world that belongs to him; he cannot become the slave of things, the slave of economic systems, the slave of production, the slave of his own products. A civilization purely materialistic in outline condemns man to such slavery, even if at times, no doubt, this occurs contrary to the intentions and the very premises of its pioneers. The present solicitude for man certainly has at its root this problem. It is not a matter here merely of giving an abstract answer to the question: Who is man? It is a matter of the whole of the dynamism of life and civilization. It is a matter of the meaningfulness of the various initiatives of everyday life and also of the premises for many civilization programs, political programs, economic ones, social ones, State ones, and many others.

16.3 If we make bold to describe man's situation in the modern world as far removed from the objective demands of the moral order, from the exigencies of justice, and still more from social love, we do so because this is confirmed by the well-known facts and comparisons that have already on various occasions found an echo in the pages of statements by the Popes, the Council and the Synod.[103] Man's situation today is certainly not uniform but marked with numerous differences. These differences have causes in history, but they

---

[103] Cf. Pius XII, Radio Message for the Fiftieth Anniversary of the Encyclical Letter *Rerum Novarum* (June 1, 1941): *AAS* 33 (1941), 195-205; Christmas Radio Message (December 24, 1941): *AAS* 34 (1942), 10-21; Christmas Radio Message (December 24, 1942): *AAS* 35 (1943), 9-24; Christmas Radio Message (December 24, 1943): *AAS* 36 (1944), 11-24; Christmas Radio Message (December 24, 1944): *AAS* 37 (1945), 10-23; Address to the Cardinals (December 24, 1945): *AAS* 38 (1946), 15-25; Address to the Cardinals (December 24, 1946): *AAS* 39 (1947), 7-17; Christmas Radio Message (December 24, 1947): *AAS* 40 (1948), 8-16; John XXIII, Encyclical Letter *Mater et Magistra* (May 15, 1961): *AAS* 53 (1961), 401-464; Encyclical Letter *Pacem in Terris* (April 11, 1963): *AAS* 55 (1963), 257-304; Paul VI, Encyclical Letter *Ecclesiam Suam* (August 6, 1964): *AAS* 56 (1964), 609-659; Address to the General Assembly of the United Nations (October 4, 1965): *AAS* 57 (1965), 877-885; Encyclical Letter *Populorum Progressio* (March 26, 1967): *AAS* 59 (1967), 257-299; Address to the Campesinos of Colombia (August 23, 1968): *AAS* 60 (1968), 619-623; Address to the General Assembly of the Latin American Episcopate (August 24, 1968): *AAS* 60 (1968), 639-649; Address to the Conference of FAO (November 16, 1970): *AAS* 62 (1970), 830-838; Apostolic Letter *Octogesima Adveniens* (May 14, 1971): *AAS* 63 (1971), 401-441; Address to the Cardinals (June 23, 1972): *AAS* 64 (1972), 496-505; Address at the Opening of the Third General Conference of the Latin American Bishops (January 28, 1979): *AAS* 71 (1979), 187-205; Address to Indians, Cuilipan (January 29, 1979): *AAS* 71 (1979), 207-210; Address to Workers, Guadalajara (January 30, 1979): *AAS* 71 (1979), 221-224; Address to Workers, Monterrey (January 31, 1979): *AAS* 71 (1979), 240-242; Second Vatican Ecumenical Council, Declaration on Religious Freedom *Dignitatis Humanae: AAS* 58 (1966), 1025-1115; Synod of Bishops, Justice in the World *De Iustitia in Mundo: AAS* 63 (1971), 923-941.

also have strong ethical effects. Indeed everyone is familiar with the picture of the consumer civilization, which consists in a certain surplus of goods necessary for man and for entire societies — and we are dealing precisely with the rich, highly developed societies — while the remaining societies — at least broad sectors of them — are suffering from hunger, with many people dying each day of starvation and malnutrition. Hand in hand go a certain abuse of freedom by one group — an abuse linked precisely with a consumer attitude uncontrolled by ethics — and a limitation by it of the freedom of the others, that is to say those suffering marked shortages and being driven to conditions of even worse misery and destitution.

16.4 This pattern, which is familiar to all, and the contrast referred to, in the documents giving their teaching, by the Popes of this century, most recently by John XXIII and by Paul VI,[104] represent, as it were, the gigantic development of the parable in the Bible of the rich banqueter and the poor man Lazarus.[105] So widespread is the phenomenon that it brings into question the financial, monetary, production and commercial mechanisms that, resting on various political pressures, support the world economy. These are proving incapable either of remedying the unjust social situations inherited from the past or of dealing with the urgent challenges and ethical demands of the present. By submitting man to tensions created by himself, dilapidating at an accelerated pace material and energy resources, and compromising the geophysical environment, these structures unceasingly make the areas of misery spread, accompanied by anguish, frustration and bitterness.[106]

16.5 We have before us here a great drama that can leave nobody indifferent. The person who, on the one hand, is trying to draw the maximum profit and, on the other hand, is paying the price in damage and injury is always man. The drama is made still worse by the presence close at hand of the privileged social classes and of the rich countries, which accumulate goods to an excessive degree and the misuse of whose riches very often becomes the cause of various ills. Add to this the fever of inflation and the plague of unemployment: these are further symptoms of the moral disorder that is being

---

[104] Cf. John XXIII, Encyclical Letter *Mater et Magistra* (May 15, 1961), II: *AAS* 53 (1961), 418ff.; Encyclical Letter *Pacem in Terris* (April 11, 1963): *AAS* 55 (1963), 289ff.; Paul VI, Encyclical Letter *Populorum Progressio* (March 26, 1967): *AAS* 59 (1967), 257-299.

[105] Cf. Lk 16:19-31.

[106] Cf. John Paul II, Homily, Santo Domingo (January 25, 1979), 3: *AAS* 71 (1979), 157-158; Address to Indians and Campesinos, Oaxaca (January 30, 1979), 2: *AAS* 71 (1979), 207-208; Address to Workers, Monterrey (January 31, 1979), 4: *AAS* 71 (1979), 242.

noticed in the world situation and therefore requires daring creative resolves in keeping with man's authentic dignity.[107]

16.6 Such a task is not an impossible one. The principle of solidarity, in a wide sense, must inspire the effective search for appropriate institutions and mechanisms, whether in the sector of trade, where the laws of healthy competition must be allowed to lead the way, or on the level of a wider and more immediate redistribution of riches and of control over them, in order that the economically developing peoples may be able not only to satisfy their essential needs but also to advance gradually and effectively.

16.7 This difficult road of the indispensable transformation of the structures of economic life is one on which it will not be easy to go forward without the intervention of a true conversion of mind, will and heart. The task requires resolute commitment by individuals and peoples that are free and linked in solidarity. All too often freedom is confused with the instinct for individual or collective interest or with the instinct for combat and domination, whatever be the ideological colors with which they are covered. Obviously these instincts exist and are operative, but no truly human economy will be possible unless they are taken up, directed and dominated by the deepest powers in man, which decide the true culture of peoples. These are the very sources for the effort which will express man's true freedom and which will be capable of ensuring it in the economic field also. Economic development, with every factor in its adequate functioning, must be constantly programmed and realized within a perspective of universal joint development of each individual and people, as was convincingly recalled by my Predecessor Paul VI in *Populorum Progressio*. Otherwise, the category of "economic progress" becomes in isolation a superior category subordinating the whole of human existence to its partial demands, suffocating man, breaking up society, and ending by entangling itself in its own tensions and excesses.

16.8 It is possible to undertake this duty. This is testified by the certain facts and the results, which it would be difficult to mention more analytically here. However, one thing is certain: at the basis of this gigantic sector it is necessary to establish, accept and deepen the sense of moral responsibility, which man must undertake. Again and always man.

16.9 This responsibility becomes especially evident for us Christians when we recall — and we should always recall it — the scene of the last judgment according to the words of Christ related in Matthew's Gospel.[108]

[107] Cf. Paul VI, Apostolic Letter *Octogesima Adveniens* (May 14, 1971), 42: *AAS* 63 (1971), 431.
[108] Cf. Mt 25:31-46.

16.10 This eschatological scene must always be "applied" to man's history; it must always be made the "measure" for human acts as an essential outline for an examination of conscience by each and every one: "I was hungry and you gave me no food . . . naked and you did not clothe me . . . in prison and you did not visit me."[109] These words become charged with even stronger warning, when we think that, instead of bread and cultural aid, the new States and nations awakening to independent life are being offered, sometimes in abundance, modern weapons and means of destruction placed at the service of armed conflicts and wars that are not so much a requirement for defending their just rights and their sovereignty but rather a form of chauvinism, imperialism, and neocolonialism of one kind or another. We all know well that the areas of misery and hunger on our globe could have been made fertile in a short time, if the gigantic investments for armaments at the service of war and destruction had been changed into investments for food at the service of life.

16.11 This consideration will perhaps remain in part an "abstract" one. It will perhaps offer both "sides" an occasion for mutual accusation, each forgetting its own faults. It will perhaps provoke new accusations against the Church. The Church, however, which has no weapons at her disposal apart from those of the spirit, of the word and of love, cannot renounce her proclamation of "the word . . . in season and out of season."[110] For this reason she does not cease to implore each side of the two and to beg everybody in the name of God and in the name of man: Do not kill! Do not prepare destruction and extermination for men! Think of your brothers and sisters who are suffering hunger and misery! Respect each one's dignity and freedom!

Human rights: "letter" or "spirit"

17.1 This century has so far been a century of great calamities for man, of great devastations, not only material ones but also moral ones, indeed, perhaps above all, moral ones. Admittedly, it is not easy to compare one age or one century with another under this aspect, since that depends also on changing historical standards. Nevertheless, without applying these comparisons, one still cannot fail to see that this century has so far been one in which people have provided many injustices and sufferings for themselves. Has this process been decisively curbed? In any case, we cannot fail to recall at this point, with esteem and profound hope for the future, the magnificent effort made to give life to the United Nations Organization, an effort conducive to the definition and establishment of man's objective and inviolable rights, with the member

[109] Mt 25:42, 43.
[110] 2 Tim 4:2.

States obliging each other to observe them rigorously. This commitment has been accepted and ratified by almost all present-day States, and this should constitute a guarantee that human rights will become throughout the world a fundamental principle of work for man's welfare.

17.2 There is no need for the Church to confirm how closely this problem is linked with her mission in the modern world. Indeed it is at the very basis of social and international peace, as has been declared by John XXIII, the Second Vatican Council, and later Paul VI, in detailed documents. After all, peace comes down to respect for man's inviolable rights — *opus iustitiae pax* — while war springs from the violation of these rights and brings with it still graver violations of them. If human rights are violated in time of peace, this is particularly painful and from the point of view of progress it represents an incomprehensible manifestation of activity directed against man, which can in no way be reconciled with any program that describes itself as "humanistic." And what social, economic, political or cultural program could renounce this description? We are firmly convinced that there is no program in today's world in which man is not invariably brought to the fore, even when the platforms of the programs are made up of conflicting ideologies concerning the way of conceiving the world.

17.3 If, in spite of these premises, human rights are being violated in various ways, if in practice we see before us concentration camps, violence, torture, terrorism, and discrimination in many forms, this must then be the consequence of the other premises, undermining and often almost annihilating the effectiveness of the humanistic premises of these modern programs and systems. This necessarily imposes the duty to submit these programs to continual revision from the point of view of the objective and inviolable rights of man.

17.4 The Declaration of Human Rights linked with the setting up of the United Nations Organization certainly had as its aim not only to depart from the horrible experiences of the last World War but also to create the basis for continual revision of programs, systems and regimes precisely from this single fundamental point of view, namely the welfare of man — or, let us say, of the person in the community — which must, as a fundamental factor in the common good, constitute the essential criterion for all programs, systems and regimes. If the opposite happens, human life is, even in time of peace, condemned to various sufferings and, along with these sufferings, there is a development of various forms of domination, totalitarianism, neocolonialism and imperialism, which are a threat also to the harmonious living together of the nations. Indeed, it is a significant fact, repeatedly confirmed by the experiences of history, that violation of the rights of man goes hand in hand with violation of the rights of the nation, with which man is united by organic links as with a larger family.

17.5 Already in the first half of this century, when various State totalitarianisms were developing, which, as is well known, led to the horrible catastrophe of war, the Church clearly outlined her position with regard to these regimes that to all appearances were acting for a higher good, namely the good of the State, while history was to show instead that the good in question was only that of a certain party, which had been identified with the State.[111] In reality, those regimes had restricted the rights of the citizens, denying them recognition precisely of those inviolable human rights that have reached formulation on the international level in the middle of our century. While sharing the joy of all people of good will, of all people who truly love justice and peace, at this conquest, the Church, aware that the "letter" on its own can kill, while only "the spirit gives life,"[112] must continually ask, together with these people of good will, whether the Declaration of Human Rights and the acceptance of their "letter" mean everywhere also the actualization of their "spirit." Indeed, well-founded fears arise that very often we are still far from this actualization and that at times the spirit of social and public life is painfully opposed to the declared "letter" of human rights. This state of things, which is burdensome for the societies concerned, would place special responsibility toward these societies and the history of man on those contributing to its establishment.

17.6 The essential sense of the State, as a political community, consists in the fact that the society and people composing it are master and sovereign of their own destiny. This sense remains unrealized if, instead of the exercise of power with the moral participation of the society or people, what we see is the imposition of power by a certain group upon all the other members of the society. This is essential in the present age, with its enormous increase in people's social awareness and the accompanying need for the citizens to have a right share in the political life of the community, while taking account of the real conditions of each people and the necessary vigor of public authority.[113] These therefore are questions of pri-

---

[111] Pius XI, Encyclical Letter *Quadragesimo Anno* (May 15, 1931), III: *AAS* 23 (1931), 213; Encyclical Letter *Non abbiamo bisogno* (June 29, 1931): *AAS* 23 (1931), 285-312; Encyclical Letter *Divini Redemptoris* (March 19, 1937): *AAS* 29 (1937), 65-106; Encyclical Letter *Mit brennender Sorge* (March 14, 1937): *AAS* 29 (1937), 145-147; Pius XII, Encyclical Letter *Summi Pontificatus* (October 20, 1939): *AAS* 31 (1939), 413-453.

[112] Cf. 2 Cor 3:6.

[113] Cf. Second Vatican Ecumenical Council, Pastoral Constitution on the Church in the Modern World *Gaudium et Spes*, 31: *AAS* 58 (1966), 1050.

mary importance from the point of view of the progress of man himself and the overall development of his humanity.

17.7 The Church has always taught the duty to act for the common good and, in so doing, has likewise educated good citizens for each State. Furthermore, she has always taught that the fundamental duty of power is solicitude for the common good of society; this is what gives power its fundamental rights. Precisely in the name of these premises of the objective ethical order, the rights of power can only be understood on the basis of respect for the objective and inviolable rights of man. The common good that authority in the State serves is brought to full realization only when all the citizens are sure of their rights. The lack of this leads to the dissolution of society, opposition by citizens to authority, or a situation of oppression, intimidation, violence, and terrorism, of which many examples have been provided by the totalitarianisms of this century. Thus the principle of human rights is of profound concern to the area of social justice and is the measure by which it can be tested in the life of political bodies.

17.8 These rights are rightly reckoned to include the right to religious freedom together with the right to freedom of conscience. The Second Vatican Council considered especially necessary the preparation of a fairly long declaration on this subject. This is the document called *Dignitatis Humanae*,[114] in which is expressed not only the theological concept of the question but also the concept reached from the point of view of natural law, that is to say from the "purely human" position, on the basis of the premises given by man's own experience, his reason and his sense of human dignity. Certainly the curtailment of the religious freedom of individuals and communities is not only a painful experience but it is above all an attack on man's very dignity, independently of the religion professed or of the concept of the world which these individuals and communities have. The curtailment and violation of religious freedom are in contrast with man's dignity and his objective rights. The Council document mentioned above states clearly enough what that curtailment or violation of religious freedom is. In this case we are undoubtedly confronted with a radical injustice with regard to what is particularly deep within man, what is authentically human. Indeed, even the phenomenon of unbelief, a-religiousness and atheism, as a human phenomenon, is understood only in relation to the phenomenon of religion and faith. It is therefore difficult, even from a "purely human" point of view, to accept a position that gives only atheism the right of citizenship in public and social life, while believers are, as though by principle, barely tolerated or are treated as second-class citizens or

[114] Cf. *AAS* 58 (1966), 929-946.

are even — and this has already happened — entirely deprived of the rights of citizenship.

17.9 Even if briefly, this subject must also be dealt with, because it too enters into the complex of man's situations in the present-day world and because it too gives evidence of the degree to which this situation is overburdened by prejudices and injustices of various kinds. If we refrain from entering into details in this field in which we would have a special right and duty to do so, it is above all because, together with all those who are suffering the torments of discrimination and persecution for the name of God, we are guided by faith in the redeeming power of the Cross of Christ. However, because of my office, I appeal in the name of all believers throughout the world to those on whom the organization of social and public life in some way depends, earnestly requesting them to respect the rights of religion and of the Church's activity. No privilege is asked for, but only respect for an elementary right. Actuation of this right is one of the fundamental tests of man's authentic progress in any regime, in any society, system or milieu.

IV

The Church's Mission and Man's Destiny

The Church as concerned for man's vocation in Christ

18.1 This necessarily brief look at man's situation in the modern world makes us direct our thoughts and our hearts to Jesus Christ, and to the mystery of the Redemption, in which the question of man is inscribed with a special vigor of truth and love. If Christ "united himself with each man,"[115] the Church lives more profoundly her own nature and mission by penetrating into the depths of this mystery and into its rich universal language. It was not without reason that the Apostle speaks of Christ's Body, the Church.[116] If this Mystical Body of Christ is God's People — as the Second Vatican Council was to say later, on the basis of the whole of the biblical and patristic tradition — this means that in it each man receives within himself that breath of life that comes from Christ. In this way, turning to man and his real problems, his hopes and sufferings, his achievements and falls — this too also makes the Church as a body, an organism, a social unit perceive the same divine influ-

---

[115] Second Vatican Ecumenical Council, Pastoral Constitution on the Church in the Modern World *Gaudium et Spes*, 22: AAS 58 (1966), 1042.

[116] Cf. 1 Cor 6:15, 11:3, 12:12-13; Eph 1:22-23, 2:15-16, 4:4-6, 5:30; Col 1:18, 3:15; Rom 12:4-5; Gal 3:28.

ences, the light and strength of the Spirit that come from the crucified and risen Christ, and it is for this very reason that she lives her life. The Church has only one life: that which is given her by her Spouse and Lord. Indeed, precisely because Christ united himself with her in his mystery of Redemption, the Church must be strongly united with each man.

18.2 This union of Christ with man is in itself a mystery. From the mystery is born "the new man," called to become a partaker of God's life,[117] and newly created in Christ for the fullness of grace and truth.[118] Christ's union with man is power and the source of power, as Saint John stated so incisively in the prologue of his Gospel: "(The Word) gave power to become children of God."[119] Man is transformed inwardly by this power as the source of a new life that does not disappear and pass away but lasts to eternal life.[120] This life, which the Father has promised and offered to each man in Jesus Christ, his eternal and only Son, who, "when the time had fully come,"[121] became incarnate and was born of the Virgin Mary, is the final fulfillment of man's vocation. It is in a way the fulfillment of the "destiny" that God has prepared for him from eternity. This "divine destiny" is advancing, in spite of all the enigmas, the unsolved riddles, the twists and turns of "human destiny" in the world of time. Indeed, while all this, in spite of all the riches of life in time, necessarily and inevitably leads to the frontier of death and the goal of the destruction of the human body, beyond that goal we see Christ. "I am the resurrection and the life; he who believes in me . . . shall never die."[122] In Jesus Christ, who was crucified and laid in the tomb and then rose again, "our hope of resurrection dawned . . . the bright promise of immortality,"[123] on the way to which man, through the death of the body, shares with the whole of visible creation the necessity to which matter is subject. We intend and are trying to fathom ever more deeply the language of the truth that man's Redeemer enshrined in the phrase "It is the spirit that gives life, the flesh is of no avail."[124] In spite of appearances, these words express the highest affirmation of man — the affirmation of the body given life by the Spirit.

18.3 The Church lives these realities; she lives by this truth about man, which enables him to go beyond the bounds of temporariness and at the same

[117] 2 Pet 1:4.
[118] Cf. Eph 2:10; Jn 1:14, 16.
[119] Jn 1:12.
[120] Cf. Jn 4:14.
[121] Gal 4:4.
[122] Jn 11:25-26.
[123] Preface of Christian Death I.
[124] Jn 6:63.

time to think with particular love and solicitude of everything within the dimensions of this temporariness that affect man's life and the life of the human spirit, in which is expressed that never-ending restlessness referred to in the words of Saint Augustine: "You made us for yourself, Lord, and our heart is restless until it rests in you."[125] In this creative restlessness beats and pulsates what is most deeply human — the search for truth, the insatiable need for the good, hunger for freedom, nostalgia for the beautiful, and the voice of conscience. Seeking to see man as it were with "the eyes of Christ himself," the Church becomes more and more aware that she is the guardian of a great treasure, which she may not waste but must continually increase. Indeed, the Lord Jesus said: "He who does not gather with me scatters."[126] This treasure of humanity enriched by the inexpressible mystery of divine filiation[127] and by the grace of "adoption as sons"[128] in the only Son of God, through whom we call God "Abba, Father"[129] is also a powerful force unifying the Church above all inwardly and giving meaning to all her activity. Through this force the Church is united with the Spirit of Christ, that Holy Spirit promised and continually communicated by the Redeemer and whose descent, which was revealed on the day of Pentecost, endures for ever. Thus the powers of the Spirit,[130] the gifts of the Spirit,[131] and the fruits of the Holy Spirit[132] are revealed in men. The present-day Church seems to repeat with ever greater fervor and with holy insistence: "Come, Holy Spirit!" Come! Come! "Heal our wounds, our strength renew; On our dryness pour your dew; Wash the stains of guilt away; Bend the stubborn heart and will; Melt the frozen, warm the chill; Guide the steps that go astray."[133]

18.4 This appeal to the Spirit, intended precisely to obtain the Spirit, is the answer to all the "materialisms" of our age. It is these materialisms that give birth to so many forms of insatiability in the human heart. This appeal is making itself heard on various sides and seems to be bearing fruit also in different ways. Can it be said that the Church is not alone in making this appeal? Yes, it can, because the "need" for what is spiritual is expressed also by people who are outside the visible confines of the Church.[134] Is not this

[125] *Confessiones*, I, 1: *CSEL* 33, 1.
[126] Mt 12:30.
[127] Cf. Jn 1:12.
[128] Gal 4:5.
[129] Gal 4:6; Rom 8:15.
[130] Cf. Rom 15:13; 1 Cor 1:24.
[131] Cf. Is 11:2-3; Acts 2:38.
[132] Cf. Gal 5:22-23.
[133] Sequence for Pentecost.
[134] Cf. Second Vatican Ecumenical Council, Dogmatic Constitution on the Church *Lumen Gentium*, 16: *AAS* 57 (1965), 20.

confirmed by the truth concerning the Church that the recent Council so acutely emphasized at the point in the Dogmatic Constitution *Lumen Gentium* where it teaches that the Church is a "sacrament or sign and means of intimate union with God, and of the unity of all mankind"?[135] This invocation addressed to the Spirit to obtain the Spirit is really a constant self-insertion into the full magnitude of the mystery of the Redemption, in which Christ, united with the Father and with each man, continually communicates to us the Spirit who places within us the sentiments of the Son and directs us toward the Father.[136] This is why the Church of our time — a time particularly hungry for the Spirit, because it is hungry for justice, peace, love, goodness, fortitude, responsibility, and human dignity — must concentrate and gather around that Mystery, finding in it the light and the strength that are indispensable for her mission. For if, as was already said, man is the way for the Church's daily life, the Church must be always aware of the dignity of the divine adoption received by man in Christ through the grace of the Holy Spirit[137] and of his destination to grace and glory.[138] By reflecting ever anew on all this, and by accepting it with a faith that is more and more aware and a love that is more and more firm, the Church also makes herself better fitted for the service to man to which Christ the Lord calls her when he says: "The Son of man came not to be served but to serve."[139] The Church performs this ministry by sharing in the "triple office" belonging to her Master and Redeemer. This teaching, with its biblical foundation, was brought fully to the fore by the Second Vatican Council, to the great advantage of the Church's life. For when we become aware that we share in Christ's triple mission, his triple office as priest, as prophet and as king,[140] we also become more aware of what must receive service from the whole of the Church as the society and community of the People of God on earth, and we likewise understand how each one of us must share in this mission and service.

The Church as responsible for truth

19.1 In the light of the sacred teaching of the Second Vatican Council, the Church thus appears before us as the social subject of responsibility for divine truth. With deep emotion we hear Christ himself saying: "The word which

---

[135] Ibid., 1: loc. cit., 5.

[136] Cf. Rom 8:15; Gal 4:6.

[137] Cf. Rom 8:15.

[138] Cf. Rom 8:30.

[139] Mt 20:28.

[140] Second Vatican Ecumenical Council, Dogmatic Constitution on the Church *Lumen Gentium*, 31-36: *AAS* 57 (1965), 37-42.

you hear is not mine but the Father's who sent me."[141] In this affirmation by our Master do we not notice responsibility for the revealed truth, which is the "property" of God himself, since even he, "the only Son," who lives "in the bosom of the Father,"[142] when transmitting that truth as a prophet and teacher, feels the need to stress that he is acting in full fidelity to its divine source? The same fidelity must be a constitutive quality of the Church's faith, both when she is teaching it and when she is professing it. Faith as a specific supernatural virtue infused into the human spirit makes us sharers in knowledge of God as a response to his revealed Word. Therefore, it is required, when the Church professes and teaches the faith, that she should adhere strictly to divine truth,[143] and should translate it into living attitudes of "obedience in harmony with reason."[144] Christ himself, concerned for this fidelity to divine truth, promised the Church the special assistance of the Spirit of truth, gave the gift of infallibility[145] to those whom he entrusted with the mandate of transmitting and teaching that truth[146] — as has besides been clearly defined by the First Vatican Council[147] and has then been repeated by the Second Vatican Council[148] — and he furthermore endowed the whole of the People of God with a special sense of the faith.[149]

19.2 Consequently, we have become sharers in this mission of the prophet Christ, and in virtue of that mission we together with him are serving divine truth in the Church. Being responsible for that truth also means loving it and seeking the most exact understanding of it, in order to bring it closer to ourselves and others in all its saving power, its splendor and its profundity joined

---

[141] Jn 14:24.

[142] Jn 1:18.

[143] Cf. Second Vatican Ecumenical Council, Dogmatic Constitution on Divine Revelation *Dei Verbum*, 5, 10, 21: *AAS* 58 (1966), 819, 822, 827-828.

[144] Cf. First Vatican Ecumenical Council, Dogmatic Constitution on the Catholic Faith *Dei Filius*, Chapter 3: *Conciliorum Oecumenicorum Decreta*, Ed. Istituto per le Scienze Religiose, 3rd ed., Bologna, 1973, 807.

[145] Cf. First Vatican Ecumenical Council, Dogmatic Constitution on the Church of Christ *Pastor Aeternus: Conciliorum Oecumenicorum Decreta*, Ed. Istituto per le Scienze Religiose, 3rd ed., Bologna, 1973, 811-816; Second Vatican Ecumenical Council, Dogmatic Constitution on the Church *Lumen Gentium*, 25: *AAS* 57 (1965), 30-31.

[146] Cf. Mt 28:19.

[147] Cf. First Vatican Ecumenical Council, Dogmatic Constitution on the Church of Christ *Pastor Aeternus: Conciliorum Oecumenicorum Decreta*, Ed. Istituto per le Scienze Religiose, 3rd ed., Bologna, 1973, 811-816.

[148] Cf. Second Vatican Ecumenical Council, Dogmatic Constitution on the Church *Lumen Gentium*, 18-27: *AAS* 57 (1965), 21-33.

[149] Cf. ibid., 12, 35: loc. cit., 16-17, 40-41.

with simplicity. This love and this aspiration to understand the truth must go hand in hand, as is confirmed by the histories of the saints in the Church. These received most brightly the authentic light that illuminates divine truth and brings close God's very reality, because they approached this truth with veneration and love — love in the first place for Christ, the living Word of divine truth, and then love for his human expression in the Gospel, Tradition and theology. Today we still need above all that understanding and interpretation of God's Word; we need that theology. Theology has always had and continues to have great importance for the Church, the People of God, to be able to share creatively and fruitfully in Christ's mission as prophet. Therefore, when theologians, as servants of divine truth, dedicate their studies and labors to ever deeper understanding of that truth, they can never lose sight of the meaning of their service in the Church, which is enshrined in the concept *intellectus fidei*. This concept has, so to speak, a two-way function, in line with Saint Augustine's expression: *intellege, ut credas — crede, ut intellegas*,[150] and it functions correctly when they seek to serve the Magisterium, which in the Church is entrusted to the Bishops joined by the bond of hierarchical communion with Peter's Successor, when they place themselves at the service of their solicitude in teaching and giving pastoral care, and when they place themselves at the service of the apostolic commitments of the whole of the People of God.

19.3 As in preceding ages, and perhaps more than in preceding ages, theologians and all men of learning in the Church are today called to unite faith with learning and wisdom, in order to help them to combine with each other, as we read in the prayer in the liturgy of the memorial of Saint Albert, Doctor of the Church. This task has grown enormously today because of the advance of human learning, its methodology, and the achievements in knowledge of the world and of man. This concerns both the exact sciences and the human sciences, as well as philosophy, which, as the Second Vatican Council recalled is closely linked with theology.[151]

19.4 In this field of human knowledge, which is continually being broadened and yet differentiated, faith too must be investigated deeply, manifesting the magnitude of revealed mystery and tending toward an understanding of truth, which has in God its one supreme source. If it is permissible and even desirable that the enormous work to be done in this direction should take into

---

[150] Cf. Saint Augustine, *Sermo* 43, 7-9: *PL* 38, 257-258.

[151] Cf. Second Vatican Ecumenical Council, Pastoral Constitution on the Church in the Modern World *Gaudium et Spes*, 44, 57, 59, 62: *AAS* 58 (1966), 1064-1065, 1077-1079, 1079-1080, 1082-1084; Decree on Priestly Formation *Optatam Totius*, 15: *AAS* 58 (1966), 722.

consideration a certain pluralism of methodology, the work cannot however depart from the fundamental unity in the teaching of faith and morals which is that work's end. Accordingly, close collaboration by theology with the Magisterium is indispensable. Every theologian must be particularly aware of what Christ himself stated when he said: "The word which you hear is not mine but the Father's who sent me."[152] Nobody, therefore, can make of theology as it were a simple collection of his own personal ideas, but everybody must be aware of being in close union with the mission of teaching truth for which the Church is responsible.

19.5 The sharing in the prophetic office of Christ himself shapes the life of the whole of the Church in her fundamental dimension. A particular share in this office belongs to the Pastors of the Church, who teach and continually and in various ways proclaim and transmit the doctrine concerning the Christian faith and morals. This teaching, both in its missionary and its ordinary aspect, helps to assemble the People of God around Christ, prepares for participation in the Eucharist and points out the ways for sacramental life. In 1977 the Synod of the Bishops dedicated special attention to catechesis in the modern world, and the mature results of its deliberations, experiences and suggestions will shortly find expression — in keeping with the proposal made by the participants in the Synod — in a special papal document. Catechesis certainly constitutes a permanent and also fundamental form of activity by the Church, one in which her prophetic charism is manifested: witnessing and teaching go hand in hand. And although here we are speaking in the first place of priests, it is however impossible not to mention also the great number of men and women religious dedicating themselves to catechetical activity for love of the divine Master. Finally, it would be difficult not to mention the many lay people who find expression in this activity for their faith and their apostolic responsibility.

19.6 Furthermore, increasing care must be taken that the various forms of catechesis and its various fields — beginning with the fundamental field, family catechesis, that is the catechesis by parents of their children — should give evidence of the universal sharing by the whole of the People of God in the prophetic office of Christ himself. Linked with this fact, the Church's responsibility for divine truth must be increasingly shared in various ways by all. What shall we say at this point with regard to the specialists in the various disciplines, those who represent the natural sciences and letters, doctors, jurists, artists and technicians, teachers at various levels and with different specializations? As members of the People of God, they all have their own part

[152] Jn 14:24.

to play in Christ's prophetic mission and service of divine truth, among other ways by an honest attitude toward truth, whatever field it may belong to, while educating others in truth and teaching them to mature in love and justice. Thus, a sense of responsibility for truth is one of the fundamental points of encounter between the Church and each man and also one of the fundamental demands determining man's vocation in the community of the Church. The present-day Church, guided by a sense of responsibility for truth, must persevere in fidelity to her own nature, which involves the prophetic mission that comes from Christ himself: "As the Father has sent me, even so I send you. . . . Receive the Holy Spirit."[153]

Eucharist and Penance

20.1 In the mystery of the Redemption, that is to say in Jesus Christ's saving work, the Church not only shares in the Gospel of her Master through fidelity to the word and service of truth, but she also shares, through a submission filled with hope and love, in the power of his redeeming action expressed and enshrined by him in a sacramental form, especially in the Eucharist.[154] The Eucharist is the center and summit of the whole of sacramental life, through which each Christian receives the saving power of the Redemption, beginning with the mystery of Baptism, in which we are buried into the death of Christ, in order to become sharers in his Resurrection,[155] as the Apostle teaches. In the light of this teaching, we see still more clearly the reason why the entire sacramental life of the Church and of each Christian reaches its summit and fullness in the Eucharist. For by Christ's will there is in this sacrament a continual renewing of the mystery of the sacrifice of himself that Christ offered to the Father on the altar of the Cross, a sacrifice that the Father accepted, giving, in return for this total self-giving by his Son, who "became obedient unto death,"[156] his own paternal gift, that is to say the grant of new immortal life in the Resurrection, since the Father is the first source and the giver of life from the beginning. That new life, which involves the bodily glorification of the crucified Christ, became an efficacious sign of the new gift granted to humanity, the gift that is the Holy Spirit, through whom the divine life that the Father has in himself and gives to his Son[157] is communicated to all men who are united with Christ.

---

[153] Jn 20:21-22.

[154] Cf. Second Vatican Ecumenical Council, Constitution on the Sacred Liturgy *Sacrosanctum Concilium*, 10: *AAS* 56 (1964), 102.

[155] Cf. Rom 6:3-5.

[156] Phil 2:8.

[157] Cf. Jn 5:26; 1 Jn 5:11.

20.2 The Eucharist is the most perfect sacrament of this union. By celebrating and also partaking of the Eucharist we unite ourselves with Christ on earth and in heaven who intercedes for us with the Father[158] but we always do so through the redeeming act of his sacrifice, through which he has redeemed us, so that we have been "bought with a price."[159] The "price" of our Redemption is likewise a further proof of the value that God himself sets on man and of our dignity in Christ. For by becoming "children of God,"[160] adopted sons,[161] we also become in his likeness "a kingdom and priests" and obtain "a royal priesthood,"[162] that is to say we share in that unique and irreversible restoration of man and the world to the Father that was carried out once for all by him, who is both the eternal Son[163] and also true Man. The Eucharist is the sacrament in which our new being is most completely expressed and in which Christ himself unceasingly and in an ever new manner "bears witness" in the Holy Spirit to our spirit[164] that each of us, as a sharer in the mystery of the Redemption, has access to the fruits of the filial reconciliation with God[165] that he himself actuated and continually actuates among us by means of the Church's ministry.

20.3 It is an essential truth, not only of doctrine but also of life, that the Eucharist builds the Church,[166] building it as the authentic community of the People of God, as the assembly of the faithful, bearing the same mark of unity that was shared by the Apostles and the first disciples of the Lord. The Eucharist builds ever anew this community and unity, ever building and regenerating it on the basis of the Sacrifice of Christ, since it commemorates his death on the Cross,[167] the price by which he redeemed us. Accordingly, in the Eucharist we touch in a way the very mystery of the Body and Blood of the Lord, as is attested by the very words used at its institution, the words that, because of that institution, have become the

---

[158] Heb 9:24; 1 Jn 2:1.

[159] 1 Cor 6:20.

[160] Jn 1:12.

[161] Cf. Rom 8:23.

[162] Rev 5:10; 1 Pet 2:9.

[163] Cf. Jn 1:1-4, 18; Mt 3:17, 11:27, 17:5; Mk 1:11; Lk 1:32, 35; 3:22; Rom 1:4; 2 Cor 1:19; 1 Jn 5:5, 20; 2 Pet 1:17; Heb 1:2.

[164] Cf. 1 Jn 5:5-11.

[165] Cf. Rom 5:10, 11; 2 Cor 5:18-19; Col 1:20, 22.

[166] Cf. Second Vatican Ecumenical Council, Dogmatic Constitution on the Church *Lumen Gentium*, 11: *AAS* 57 (1965), 15-16; Paul VI, Address at General Audience (September 15, 1965): *Insegnamenti* III (1965), 1036.

[167] Cf. Second Vatican Ecumenical Council, Constitution on the Sacred Liturgy *Sacrosanctum Concilium*, 47: *AAS* 56 (1964), 113.

words with which those called to this ministry in the Church unceasingly celebrate the Eucharist.

20.4 The Church lives by the Eucharist, by the fullness of this sacrament, the stupendous content and meaning of which have often been expressed in the Church's Magisterium from the most distant times down to our own days.[168] However, we can say with certainty that, although this teaching is sustained by the acuteness of theologians, by men of deep faith and prayer, and by ascetics and mystics, in complete fidelity to the Eucharistic mystery, it still reaches no more than the threshold, since it is incapable of grasping and translating into words what the Eucharist is in all its fullness, what is expressed by it and what is actuated by it. Indeed, the Eucharist is the ineffable sacrament! The essential commitment and, above all, the visible grace and source of supernatural strength for the Church as the People of God is to persevere and advance constantly in Eucharistic life and Eucharistic piety and to develop spiritually in the climate of the Eucharist. With all the greater reason, then, it is not permissible for us, in thought, life or action, to take away from this truly most holy Sacrament its full magnitude and its essential meaning. It is at one and the same time a Sacrifice-Sacrament, a Communion-Sacrament, and a Presence-Sacrament. And, although it is true that the Eucharist always was and must continue to be the most profound revelation of the human brotherhood of Christ's disciples and confessors, it cannot be treated merely as an "occasion" for manifesting this brotherhood. When celebrating the Sacrament of the Body and Blood of the Lord, the full magnitude of the divine mystery must be respected, as must the full meaning of this sacramental sign in which Christ is really present and is received, the soul is filled with grace and the pledge of future glory is given.[169] This is the source of the duty to carry out rigorously the liturgical rules and everything that is a manifestation of community worship offered to God himself, all the more so because in this sacramental sign he entrusts himself to us with limitless trust, as if not taking into consideration our human weakness, our unworthiness, the force of habit, routine, or even the possibility of insult. Every member of the Church, especially Bishops and priests, must be vigilant in seeing that this Sacrament of love shall be at the center of the life of the People of God, so that through all the manifestations of worship due to it Christ shall be given back "love for love" and truly become "the life of our souls."[170] Nor can we, on

---

[168] Cf. Paul VI, Encyclical Letter *Mysterium Fidei* (September 3, 1965): *AAS* 57 (1965), 553-574.

[169] Cf. Second Vatican Ecumenical Council, Constitution on the Sacred Liturgy *Sacrosanctum Concilium*, 47: *AAS* 56 (1964), 113.

[170] Cf. Jn 6:51, 57; 14:6; Gal 2:20.

the other hand, ever forget the following words of Saint Paul: "Let a man examine himself, and so eat of the bread and drink of the cup."[171]

20.5 This call by the Apostle indicates at least indirectly the close link between the Eucharist and Penance. Indeed, if the first word of Christ's teaching, the first phrase of the Gospel Good News, was "Repent, and believe in the Gospel" (*metanoeite*),[172] the Sacrament of the Passion, Cross and Resurrection seems to strengthen and consolidate in an altogether special way this call in our souls. The Eucharist and Penance thus become in a sense two closely connected dimensions of authentic life in accordance with the spirit of the Gospel, of truly Christian life. The Christ who calls to the Eucharistic banquet is always the same Christ who exhorts us to penance and repeats his "Repent."[173] Without this constant ever renewed endeavor for conversion, partaking of the Eucharist would lack its full redeeming effectiveness and there would be a loss or at least a weakening of the special readiness to offer God the spiritual sacrifice[174] in which our sharing in the priesthood of Christ is expressed in an essential and universal manner. In Christ, priesthood is linked with his sacrifice, his self-giving to the Father; and, precisely because it is without limit, that self-giving gives rise in us human beings subject to numerous limitations to the need to turn to God in an ever more mature way and with a constant, ever more profound conversion.

20.6 In the last years much has been done to highlight in the Church's practice — in conformity with the most ancient Tradition of the Church — the community aspect of penance and especially of the Sacrament of Penance. We cannot however forget that conversion is a particularly profound inward act in which the individual cannot be replaced by others and cannot make the community be a substitute for him. Although the participation by the fraternal community of the faithful in the penitential celebration is a great help for the act of personal conversion, nevertheless, in the final analysis, it is necessary that in this act there should be a pronouncement by the individual himself with the whole depth of his conscience and with the whole of his sense of guilt and of trust in God, placing himself like the Psalmist before God to confess: "Against you . . . have I sinned."[175] In faithfully observing the centuries-old practice of the Sacrament of Penance — the practice of individual confession with a personal act of sorrow and the intention to amend and make satisfaction — the Church is therefore defending the human soul's individual right: man's right to a more personal encounter with the crucified forgiving Christ, with Christ saying, through the

[171] 1 Cor 11:28.
[172] Mk 1:15.
[173] Mk 1:15.
[174] Cf. 1 Pet 2:5.
[175] Ps 51:6.

minister of the Sacrament of Reconciliation: "Your sins are forgiven";[176] "Go, and do not sin again."[177] As is evident, this is also a right on Christ's part with regard to every human being redeemed by him: his right to meet each one of us in that key moment in the soul's life constituted by the moment of conversion and for-giveness. By guarding the Sacrament of Penance, the Church expressly affirms her faith in the mystery of the Redemption as a living and life-giving reality that fits in with man's inward truth, with human guilt and also with the desires of the human conscience. "Blessed are those who hunger and thirst for righteousness, for they shall be satisfied."[178] The Sacrament of Penance is the means to satisfy man with the righteousness that comes from the Redeemer himself.

20.7 In the Church, gathering particularly today in a special way around the Eucharist and desiring that the authentic Eucharistic community should become a sign of the gradually maturing unity of all Christians, there must be a lively-felt need for penance, both in its sacramental aspect,[179] and in what concerns penance as a virtue. This second aspect was expressed by Paul VI in the Apostolic Constitution *Paenitemini*.[180] One of the Church's tasks is to put into practice the teaching *Paenitemini* contains; this subject must be investi-gated more deeply by us in common reflection, and many more decisions must be made about it in a spirit of pastoral collegiality and with respect for the different traditions in this regard and the different circumstances of the lives of the people of today. Nevertheless, it is certain that the Church of the new Advent, the Church that is continually preparing for the new coming of the Lord, must be the Church of the Eucharist and of Penance. Only when viewed in this spiritual aspect of her life and activity is she seen to be the Church of the divine mission, the Church *in statu missionis*, as the Second Vatican Council has shown her to be.

The Christian vocation to service and kingship

21.1 In building up from the very foundations the picture of the Church as the People of God — by showing the threefold mission of Christ himself, through participation in which we become truly God's People — the Second Vatican

---

[176] Mk 2:5.

[177] Jn 8:11.

[178] Mt 5:6.

[179] Cf. Sacred Congregation for the Doctrine of the Faith, *Normae Pastorales circa Absolutionem Sacramentalem Generali Modo Impertiendam* (June 16, 1972): AAS 64 (1972), 510-514; Paul VI, Address to a Group of Bishops from the United States of America on Their *ad Limina* Visit (April 20, 1978): AAS 71 (1979), 328-332; John Paul II, Address to a Group of Canadian Bishops on Their *ad Limina* Visit (November 17, 1978): AAS 71 (1979), 32-36.

[180] Cf. AAS 58 (1966), 177-198.

Council highlighted, among other characteristics of the Christian vocation, the one that can be described as "kingly." To present all the riches of the Council's teaching we would here have to make reference to numerous chapters and paragraphs of the Constitution *Lumen Gentium* and of many other documents by the Council. However, one element seems to stand out in the midst of all these riches: the sharing in Christ's kingly mission, that is to say the fact of rediscovering in oneself and others the special dignity of our vocation that can be described as "kingship." This dignity is expressed in readiness to serve, in keeping with the example of Christ, who "came not to be served but to serve."[181] If, in the light of this attitude of Christ's, "being a king" is truly possible only by "being a servant," then "being a servant" also demands so much spiritual maturity that it must really be described as "being a king." In order to be able to serve others worthily and effectively we must be able to master ourselves, possess the virtues that make this mastery possible. Our sharing in Christ's kingly mission — his "kingly function" (*munus*) — is closely linked with every sphere of both Christian and human morality.

21.2 In presenting the complete picture of the People of God and recalling the place among that people held not only by priests but also by the laity, not only by the representatives of the Hierarchy but also by those of the Institutes of Consecrated Life, the Second Vatican Council did not deduce this picture merely from a sociological premise. The Church as a human society can of course be examined and described according to the categories used by the sciences with regard to any human society. But these categories are not enough. For the whole of the community of the People of God and for each member of it what is in question is not just a specific "social membership"; rather, for each and every one what is essential is a particular "vocation." Indeed, the Church as the People of God is also — according to the teaching of Saint Paul mentioned above, of which Pius XII reminded us in wonderful terms — "Christ's Mystical Body."[182] Membership in that body has for its source a particular call, united with the saving action of grace. Therefore, if we wish to keep in mind this community of the People of God, which is so vast and so extremely differentiated, we must see first and foremost Christ saying in a way to each member of the community: "Follow me."[183] It is the community of the disciples, each of whom in a different way — at times very consciously and consistently, at other times not very consciously and very inconsistently — is following Christ. This shows also the deeply "personal" aspect and dimension

[181] Mt 20:28.
[182] Pius XII, Encyclical Letter *Mystici Corporis* (June 29, 1943): *AAS* 35 (1943), 193-248.
[183] Jn 1:43.

of this society, which, in spite of all the deficiencies of its community life — in the human meaning of this word — is a community precisely because all its members form it together with Christ himself, at least because they bear in their souls the indelible mark of a Christian.

21.3 The Second Vatican Council devoted very special attention to show-ing how this "ontological" community of disciples and confessors must in-creasingly become, even from the "human" point of view, a community aware of its own life and activity. The initiatives taken by the Council in this field have been followed up by the many further initiatives of a synodal, apostolic and organizational kind. We must, however, always keep in mind the truth that every initiative serves true renewal in the Church and helps to bring the authentic light that is Christ[184] insofar as the initiative is based on adequate awareness of the individual Christian's vocation and of responsibility for this singular, unique and unrepeatable grace by which each Christian in the com-munity of the People of God builds up the Body of Christ. This principle, the key rule for the whole of Christian practice — apostolic and pastoral practice, practice of interior and of social life — must with due proportion be applied to the whole of humanity and to each human being. The Pope, too, and every Bishop must apply this principle to himself. Priests and religious must be faithful to this principle. It is the basis on which their lives must be built by married people, parents, and women and men of different conditions and professions, from those who occupy the highest posts in society to those who perform the simplest tasks. It is precisely the principle of the "kingly service" that imposes on each one of us, in imitation of Christ's example, the duty to demand of himself exactly what we have been called to, what we have person-ally obliged ourselves to by God's grace, in order to respond to our vocation. This fidelity to the vocation received from God through Christ involves the joint responsibility for the Church for which the Second Vatican Council wishes to educate all Christians. Indeed, in the Church as the community of the People of God under the guidance of the Holy Spirit's working, each member has "his own special gift," as Saint Paul teaches.[185] Although this "gift" is a personal vocation and a form of participation in the Church's saving work, it also serves others, builds the Church and the fraternal communities in the various spheres of human life on earth.

21.4 Fidelity to one's vocation, that is to say persevering readiness for "kingly service," has particular significance for these many forms of building,

---

[184] Cf. Second Vatican Ecumenical Council, Dogmatic Constitution on the Church *Lumen Gentium*, 1: *AAS* 57 (1965), 5.

[185] 1 Cor 7:7, cf. 12:7, 27; Rom 12:6; Eph 4:7.

especially with regard to the more exigent tasks, which have more influence on the life of our neighbor and of the whole of society. Married people must be distinguished for fidelity to their vocation, as is demanded by the indissoluble nature of the sacramental institution of marriage. Priests must be distinguished for a similar fidelity to their vocation, in view of the indelible character that the Sacrament of Orders stamps on their souls. In receiving this sacrament, we in the Latin Church knowingly and freely commit ourselves to live in celibacy, and each one of us must therefore do all he can, with God's grace, to be thankful for this gift and faithful to the bond that he has accepted forever. He must do so as married people must, for they must endeavor with all their strength to persevere in their matrimonial union, building up the family community through this witness of love and educating new generations of men and women, capable in their turn of dedicating the whole of their lives to their vocation, that is to say to the "kingly service" of which Jesus Christ has offered us the example and most beautiful model. His Church, made up of all of us, is "for men" in the sense that, by basing ourselves on Christ's example[186] and collaborating with the grace that he has gained for us, we are able to attain to "being kings," that is to say we are able to produce a mature humanity in each one of us. Mature humanity means full use of the gift of freedom received from the Creator when he called to existence the man made "in his image, after his likeness." This gift finds its full realization in the unreserved giving of the whole of one's human person, in a spirit of the love of a spouse, to Christ and, with Christ, to all those to whom he sends men and women totally consecrated to him in accordance with the evangelical counsels. This is the ideal of the religious life, which has been undertaken by the Orders and Congregations both ancient and recent, and by the Secular Institutes.

21.5 Nowadays it is sometimes held, though wrongly, that freedom is an end in itself, that each human being is free when he makes use of freedom as he wishes, and that this must be our aim in the lives of individuals and societies. In reality, freedom is a great gift only when we know how to use it consciously for everything that is our true good. Christ teaches us that the best use of freedom is charity, which takes concrete form in self-giving and in service. For this "freedom Christ has set us free"[187] and ever continues to set us free. The Church draws from this source the unceasing inspiration, the call and the drive for her mission and her service among all mankind. The full truth about human freedom is indelibly inscribed on the mystery of the Re-

[186] Cf. Second Vatican Ecumenical Council, Dogmatic Constitution on the Church *Lumen Gentium,* 36: *AAS* 57 (1965), 41-42.
[187] Gal 5:1, cf. 5:13.

demption. The Church truly serves mankind when she guards this truth with untiring attention, fervent love and mature commitment and when in the whole of her own community she transmits it and gives it concrete form in human life through each Christian's fidelity to his vocation. This confirms what we have already referred to, namely that man is and always becomes the "way" for the Church's daily life.

The Mother in whom we trust

22.1 When, therefore, at the beginning of the new Pontificate I turn my thoughts and my heart to the Redeemer of man, I thereby wish to enter and penetrate into the deepest rhythm of the Church's life. Indeed, if the Church lives her life, she does so because she draws it from Christ, and he always wishes but one thing, namely that we should have life and have it abundantly.[188] This fullness of life in him is at the same time for man. Therefore the Church, uniting herself with all the riches of the mystery of the Redemption, becomes the Church of living people, living because given life from within by the working of "the Spirit of truth"[189] and visited by the love that the Holy Spirit has poured into our hearts.[190] The aim of any service in the Church, whether the service is apostolic, pastoral, priestly or episcopal, is to keep up this dynamic link between the mystery of the Redemption and every man.

22.2 If we are aware of this task, then we seem to understand better what it means to say that the Church is a mother[191] and also what it means to say that the Church always, and particularly at our time, has need of a Mother. We owe a debt of special gratitude to the Fathers of the Second Vatican Council, who expressed this truth in the Constitution *Lumen Gentium* with the rich Mariological doctrine contained in it.[192] Since Paul VI, inspired by that teaching, proclaimed the Mother of Christ "Mother of the Church,"[193] and that title has become known far and wide, may it be permitted to his unworthy Successor to turn to Mary as Mother of the Church at the close of these reflections which it was opportune to make at the beginning of his papal service. Mary is Mother of the Church because, on account of the Eternal Father's ineffable

[188] Cf. Jn 10:10.

[189] Jn 16:13.

[190] Cf. Rom 5:5.

[191] Cf. Second Vatican Ecumenical Council, Dogmatic Constitution on the Church *Lumen Gentium*, 63-64: *AAS* 57 (1965), 64.

[192] Cf. ibid., 52-69: loc. cit., 58-67.

[193] Paul VI, Address at the Closing of the Third Session of the Second Vatican Ecumenical Council (November 21, 1964): *AAS* 56 (1964), 1015.

choice[194] and due to the Spirit of Love's special action,[195] she gave human life to the Son of God, "for whom and by whom all things exist"[196] and from whom the whole of the People of God receives the grace and dignity of election. Her Son explicitly extended his Mother's maternity in a way that could easily be understood by every soul and every heart by designating, when he was raised on the Cross, his beloved disciple as her son.[197] The Holy Spirit inspired her to remain in the Upper Room, after our Lord's Ascension, recollected in prayer and expectation, together with the Apostles, until the day of Pentecost, when the Church was to be born in visible form, coming forth from darkness.[198] Later, all the generations of disciples, of those who confess and love Christ, like the Apostle John, spiritually took this Mother to their own homes,[199] and she was thus included in the history of salvation and in the Church's mission from the very beginning, that is from the moment of the Annunciation. Accordingly, we who form today's generation of disciples of Christ all wish to unite ourselves with her in a special way. We do so with all our attachment to our ancient tradition and also with full respect and love for the members of all the Christian Communities.

22.3 We do so at the urging of the deep need of faith, hope and charity. For if we feel a special need, in this difficult and responsible phase of the history of the Church and of mankind, to turn to Christ, who is Lord of the Church and Lord of man's history on account of the mystery of the Redemption, we believe that nobody else can bring us as Mary can into the divine and human dimension of this mystery. Nobody has been brought into it by God himself as Mary has. It is in this that the exceptional character of the grace of the divine motherhood consists. Not only is the dignity of this motherhood unique and unrepeatable in the history of the human race, but Mary's participation, due to this maternity, in God's plan for man's salvation through the mystery of the Redemption is also unique in profundity and range of action.

22.4 We can say that the mystery of the Redemption took shape beneath the heart of the Virgin of Nazareth when she pronounced her "fiat." From then on, under the special influence of the Holy Spirit, this heart, the heart of both a virgin and a mother, has always followed the work of her Son and has gone out to all those whom Christ has embraced and continues to embrace with

---

[194] Cf. Second Vatican Ecumenical Council, Dogmatic Constitution on the Church *Lumen Gentium*, 56: *AAS* 57 (1965), 60.

[195] Ibid.

[196] Heb 2:10.

[197] Cf. Jn 19:26.

[198] Cf. Acts 1:14, 2.

[199] Cf. Jn 19:27.

inexhaustible love. For that reason her heart must also have the inexhaust- ibility of a mother. The special characteristic of the motherly love that the Mother of God inserts in the mystery of the Redemption and the life of the Church finds expression in its exceptional closeness to man and all that hap- pens to him. It is in this that the mystery of the Mother consists. The Church, which looks to her with altogether special love and hope, wishes to make this mystery her own in an ever deeper manner. For in this the Church also recog- nizes the way for her daily life, which is each person.

22.5 The Father's eternal love, which has been manifested in the his- tory of mankind through the Son whom the Father gave, "that whoever believes in him should not perish but have eternal life,"[200] comes close to each of us through this Mother and thus takes on tokens that are of more easy understanding and access by each person. Consequently, Mary must be on all the ways for the Church's daily life. Through her maternal pres- ence the Church acquires certainty that she is truly living the life of her Master and Lord and that she is living the mystery of the Redemption in all its life-giving profundity and fullness. Likewise the Church, which has struck root in many varied fields of the life of the whole of present-day humanity, also acquires the certainty and, one could say, the experience of being close to man, to each person, of being each person's Church, the Church of the People of God.

22.6 Faced with these tasks that appear along the ways for the Church, those ways that Pope Paul VI clearly indicated in the first Encyclical of his Pontificate, and aware of the absolute necessity of all these ways and also of the difficulties thronging them, we feel all the more our need for a profound link with Christ. We hear within us, as a resounding echo, the words that he spoke: "Apart from me you can do nothing."[201] We feel not only the need but even a categorical imperative for great, intense and growing prayer by all the Church. Only prayer can prevent all these great succeeding tasks and diffi- culties from becoming a source of crisis and make them instead the occasion and, as it were, the foundation for ever more mature achievements on the People of God's march toward the Promised Land in this stage of history ap- proaching the end of the second millennium. Accordingly, as I end this medi- tation with a warm and humble call to prayer, I wish the Church to devote herself to this prayer, together with Mary the Mother of Jesus,[202] as the Apostles and disciples of the Lord did in the Upper Room in Jerusalem after his Ascen-

---

[200] Jn 3:16.
[201] Jn 15:5.
[202] Cf. Acts 1:14.

sion.[203] Above all, I implore Mary, the heavenly Mother of the Church, to be so good as to devote herself to this prayer of humanity's new Advent, together with us who make up the Church, that is to say the Mystical Body of her only Son. I hope that through this prayer we shall be able to receive the Holy Spirit coming upon us[204] and thus become Christ's witnesses "to the end of the earth"[205] like those who went forth from the Upper Room in Jerusalem on the day of Pentecost.

22.7 With the Apostolic Blessing.

Given at Rome, at Saint Peter's, on the fourth of March, the first Sunday of Lent, in the year 1979, the first year of my Pontificate.

[203] Cf. Acts 1:13.
[204] Cf. Acts 1:8.
[205] Ibid.

Dives in Misericordia

Editor's Introduction

On the First Sunday of Advent in 1980, Pope John Paul II announced the reason for the publication of his second encyclical, *Dives in Misericordia*,[1] on the mercy of God: "Its main purpose is to recall the Father's love, revealed in the whole messianic mission of Christ, beginning with his coming into the world up to the Paschal Mystery of his Cross and Resurrection."[2] After discussing the truth about the person in *Redemptor Hominis* (1979), the Pope now turns to the Father who is "rich in mercy" (Eph 2:4). He is convinced that the Church and the world need mercy, a mercy expressing a love that is stronger than sin and death. The core of the Gospel is simple: God the Father, in his Son, is close to sinners, loving and saving them through the mercy given through the power of the Holy Spirit.

Dives in Misericordia, the second panel of John Paul's Trinitarian triptych, is intimately linked to his anthropological and Christological vision outlined in *Redemptor Hominis*. Christ is again in the foreground. He is presented as the incarnation of the Father's mercy, the one in whom and through whom the mystery of the Father's love becomes visible for humanity. Christ is the revealer and the sacrament of divine mercy through his preaching, works and, above all, through his Paschal Mystery. People need this revelation to grasp their true worth: "Man cannot be manifested in the full dignity of his nature without reference — not only on the level of concepts but also in an integrally existential way — to God" (§1.2).

While *Redemptor Hominis* concentrated on John Paul's Christian anthropology, *Dives in Misericordia* is more theological, more immediately God-centered. But they are closely connected. According to the Pope, anthropology and theology are complementary: "The more the Church's mission is centered upon man — the more it is, so to speak, anthropocentric — the more it must be confirmed and actualized theocentrically, that is to say, be directed in Jesus Christ to the Father" (§1.4). *Redemptor Hominis* and *Dives in Misericordia*, inspired by the same anthropological concern, can be considered as one encyclical in two installments. In John Paul's words: "The mystery of Christ, which reveals to us the great vocation of man and which led me to emphasize in the Encyclical *Redemptor Hominis* his incomparable dignity, also obliges

---

[1] *Acta Apostolicae Sedis*, 72 (1980), 1177-1232.
[2] Angelus, November 30, 1980, *L'Osservatore Romano*, 49 (1980), 2.

me to proclaim mercy as God's merciful love, revealed in that same mystery of Christ" (§15.5).

Currents of thought which try to separate anthropocentrism from theocentrism, the Pope believes, violate a fundamental teaching of the Second Vatican Council. Following Christ, the Church "seeks to link them up in human history, in a deep and organic way" (§1.4). In order to know what it means to be fully human, it is necessary to know God, especially as he has revealed himself in Jesus: "Man and man's lofty calling are revealed in Christ *through* the revelation of the Father and his love" (§1.2). Indeed, Christ reveals individuals to themselves by revealing to them the love of the Father. Divine love and human dignity are the foundation of an authentic humanism on which a civilization of love can be built. True humanism must be open to God, as true justice must be open to love.

Dives in Misericordia received much less attention in the media and in theological commentaries than the more programmatic *Redemptor Hominis*. Perhaps this lack of attention is due to the encyclical's greater dependence on Sacred Scripture and its more contemplative, even spiritual, tone. While it is more sharply focused than John Paul's inaugural encyclical, it too bears the marks of his personal style: the refrain-like way in which he returns to certain themes and his tendency to pile scriptural quotations one upon the other. Almost all the Pope's references in this document are to the Bible, with only very few to magisterial documents. The encyclical pays some attention to the threats and dangers facing contemporary men and women, but dwells less on them than did *Redemptor Hominis*. *Dives in Misericordia* contains an innovative and inspiring theology of divine mercy which establishes a solid underpinning in the Gospel for the Pope's teaching in his later social encyclicals.

Summary

Dives in Misericordia unfolds in eight chapters around the theme of divine mercy. Chapter one, "He Who Sees Me Sees the Father (cf. Jn 14.9)" (§§1-2), deals with the revelation of the Father's mercy in Christ, and chapter two, "The Messianic Message" (§3), with Jesus' preaching of the Gospel of mercy. In chapter three, "The Old Testament" (§4), the Pope describes God's mercy already at work in the history of the people of Israel. In chapter four, "The Parable of the Prodigal Son" (§§5-6), he explains the true nature of mercy and stresses the dignity conferred on human beings by God's merciful love. Chapter five, "The Paschal Mystery" (§§7-9), considers Jesus' death and Resurrection as the fullest revelation of divine mercy, a mercy stronger than sin and death; Mary, the Mother of Mercy, is its foremost recipient. Chapter six, " 'Mercy

. . . from Generation to Generation' (Lk 1:50)" (§§10-12), takes up the contemporary situation of humanity in light of its need for a mercy which goes beyond justice. In chapter seven, "The Mercy of God in the Mission of the Church" (§§13-14), the Pope explores the Church's program of mercy: her duty to proclaim and practice it. The encyclical concludes with chapter eight, "The Prayer of the Church in Our Times" (§15), in which John Paul urges everyone to implore God's mercy on humanity. Viewed schematically, *Dives in Misericordia* first deals with mercy as revealed in Scripture, then with contemporary humanity's need for mercy, and finally with the Church's mission with respect to mercy.

Revelation of mercy

While the revelation of God's merciful and saving love has its beginning "in *the very mystery of creation*" (§4.12), it was greatly clarified by the people of the Old Covenant. Both as individuals and as a community the Jewish people had "*a special experience of the mercy of God*" (§4.1). They knew this mercy as an interior personal experience when they endured the suffering and misfortune of physical and moral evil. But they also knew it as a people. Through saving deeds and prophetic words, God revealed his mercy to the people he chose for himself.

Despite Israel's transgressions, God remained faithful to the Covenant. According to John Paul, especially in the prophets' preaching, "*mercy* signifies *a special power of love*, which *prevails over the sin and infidelity* of the chosen people" (§4.3). The people's intimacy with God depended on mercy; it was "the content of their dialogue with him" (§4.9). While the Old Testament never doubts the perfection of God's justice, it also reveals that "love is 'greater' than justice: greater in the sense that it is primary and fundamental" (§4.11).

The Pope maintains that a kind of quantum leap in divine revelation takes place as a result of the Incarnation. The whole Old Testament tradition about God's mercy receives from Christ its "definitive meaning" (§2.2). Jesus embodies the Father's "philanthropy," his love for humanity, especially for those who are suffering or threatened in any way. The Messiah is "a particularly clear sign of God who is love, a sign of the Father" (§3.1). Beginning in the synagogue at Nazareth, Christ makes divine mercy a principal theme of his preaching. Through "his lifestyle and through his actions, Jesus revealed that love is *present in the world*" (§3.2). In the biblical tradition, God's tender love for weak and sinful humanity is called "mercy."

John Paul dwells at length on the parable of the prodigal son (cf. Lk 15:14-

32), a parable which synthesizes the biblical understanding of mercy. While Jesus does not use the word "mercy" in his story, "it nevertheless expresses the essence of the divine mercy in a particularly clear way" (§5.2). In keeping with his desire to link theology and anthropology, the Pope also uses the parable to illustrate how divine love confirms human dignity. Indeed, the son "in a certain sense is the man of every period, beginning with the one [Adam] who was the first to lose the inheritance of grace and original justice" (§5.3). The son's tragedy is "the awareness of squandered sonship," that is, of his lost dignity (§5.4). But the father, faithful to his own fatherhood, is passionately concerned with his son's dignity and restores it. The elder son appears to represent the rejection of God's love as merciful, eliminating his need to receive and offer mercy, and preferring instead "a world of cold and unfeeling justice, in the name of which each person would claim his or her own rights vis-à-vis others" (§14.8).

In the Pope's words, "love is transformed into mercy when it is necessary to go beyond the precise norm of justice" (§5.6). This correction or tempering of justice by love enables the recipient of another's mercy to be confirmed in his dignity, to return to the truth about himself. Mercy has the power to transform human situations and hearts. "Mercy is manifested in its true and proper aspect," writes John Paul, "when it restores to value, promotes and *draws good from all the forms of evil* existing in the world and in man" (§6.5).

As the model of merciful love for others, Christ, by his way of life and his actions, makes the Father present *"as love and mercy"* (§3.4). Jesus' life of mercy is especially evident in his reaching out to those who are suffering from pain, injustice, or poverty — to the whole of humanity afflicted by physical and moral evil. The Incarnate Son, therefore, personifies mercy and enfleshes it in the situations of everyday life. At the same time, Jesus demands that those who are beneficiaries of divine mercy must "be guided in their lives by love and mercy" (§3.6). Christ's messianic program of mercy points out the path which the Church and humanity must follow.

The biblical revelation of mercy culminates in the Paschal Mystery of Christ's Passion, death, and Resurrection, "the summit of the revelation of the inscrutable mystery of God" (§8.6). Jesus, who more than any other human being deserved mercy, did not receive it during the torments of his Passion. Despite the appeals in Gethsemane to his Father, the Father does not spare his own Son (cf. Rom 8:32). Christ's redemptive act carried out for humanity's salvation fulfills the demands of divine justice. But this justice, writes the Pope, is "to God's measure"; it springs "completely from love: from the love of the Father and of the Son, and completely bears fruit in love" (§7.3). It is *"a radical revelation of mercy"* (§8.1). On Calvary the revelation of divine love as merciful reaches its apex. Eternal love touches the most painful wounds of humanity, showing love to be more powerful than sin.

In *Dives in Misericordia,* the Pope returns to the theme of Redemption which he developed in *Redemptor Hominis.* In its "divine dimension," the Paschal Mystery fully reveals the holiness of God, "the depth of that love which does not recoil before the extraordinary sacrifice of the Son in order to satisfy the fidelity of the Creator and Father toward all human beings" (§7.1). Through this mystery God grants people a participation in his own Triune life. In its "human dimension," the Redemption "reveals the unheard-of greatness of man" (§7.1).

By raising Jesus from the dead the Father again manifests his merciful love. Like sin, death, too, kneels before divine mercy. In the Resurrection, Christ "experienced in a radical way mercy shown to himself, that is to say the love of the Father which is *more powerful than death*" (§8.7). Moreover, through his Resurrection, "Christ has revealed the God of merciful love, precisely because *he accepted the Cross as the way to the Resurrection*" (§8.6). The glorified Son is both the living embodiment of mercy received from the Father and its inexhaustible source for humanity. According to John Paul, "Christ's messianic program, the program of mercy, becomes the program of his people, the program of the Church" (§8.3).

As the one who sang that "his mercy is . . . from generation to generation" (Lk 1:50), Mary is the human person who *"has the deepest knowledge of the mystery of God's mercy"* (§9.3). She welcomes mercy in an exceptional way, has the deepest knowledge of it, and experiences its price at the foot of the Cross. In her and through her, God's merciful love continues to be poured forth upon the Church and the world. Considered in its depth and sublimity, mercy sums up the content of divine revelation.

Humanity's need of mercy

Chapter six examines the present generation's need of divine mercy in the light of Scripture and Tradition. Contemporary men and women are aware of the profound changes brought about in recent decades: in science and technology, and in social and cultural life. In many ways this progress has placed the current generation "in a privileged position" (§10.2).

Yet, despite the countless possibilities opened up by this progress, there also exist "unease and a sense of powerlessness" (§10.3), a "feeling of being under threat" (§11.1). John Paul realistically describes the fears pressing upon humanity: the danger of mass destruction by nuclear arms, the primacy attributed to things rather than persons, totalitarianism, the loss of interior freedom, environmental destruction, feelings of remorse, the ever increasing gap between rich and poor individuals and nations, and consumerism. These situations of physical and moral evil produce a "moral uneasiness" which "is destined to become even more acute" (§11.4). The world is entangled in contradictions and tensions that threaten human freedom, conscience, and religion. According to the encyclical, it is obvious that "a fundamental defect, or rather a series of defects, indeed a defective machinery is at the root of contemporary economics and materialistic civilization" (§11.4).

The Pope points to "the ethical character of the tensions and struggles pervading the world" (§12.1). The Church shares the uneasiness of many people about the increase in moral permissiveness and the decline of fundamental values. Among the values being threatened are those of respect for human life from the moment of conception, of regard for the indissoluble unity of marriage, of esteem for family stability, and of truth in human relationships. To overcome this crisis, the Pope asks: Is justice enough?

On the one hand, John Paul notes that a sense of justice has been reawakened in the modern world. The Church, he writes, shares "this profound and ardent desire for a life which is just in every respect" (§12.2). This fact is confirmed by her social doctrine, which has greatly developed in the course of the last century. On the other hand, the Pope observes that, in practice, the pursuit of justice is often thwarted and distorted: "negative forces have gained the upper hand over justice, such as spite, hatred and even cruelty" (§12.3). From his analysis of the contemporary world, John Paul draws the same conclusion that he did from his biblical and theological reflection. "Justice alone is not enough," he writes, "*if that deeper power, which is love*, is not allowed to shape human life in its various dimensions" (§12.3). The present generation, therefore, has a particular need of mercy; it must open justice to love. Mercy, not merely justice, provides the solid foundation of a society which can truly meet human aspirations.

Mercy and the Church's mission

In Chapters seven and eight, the Pope discusses the pastoral ramifications for the Church's mission which are inspired by his meditation and analysis. Her mission is to direct people to gaze upon the Cross, thereby responding to the Father's invitation *"to have 'mercy' on his only Son, the Crucified One"* (§8.3). The Church must teach the meaning of mercy to the faithful. Believers learn about mercy and experience it in their lives when they let Christ into their hearts, when they see him in the "least of the brethren" (cf. Mt 25:31-46). Whenever people offer mercy to one another, they receive Mercy himself.

John Paul recommends that pastoral initiatives be undertaken simultaneously on three fronts, so that the Church will bear effective witness to God's mercy. First, she is to proclaim this mercy; second, she must help people to embody it in their lives; and third, she must ardently plead for mercy by her unceasing prayer.

By following the messianic program of her Lord, the Church professes and lives by the mercy of God. She directs herself to the contemplation of the Heart of Christ, drawing close to the sources of the Savior's mercy. Her proclamation of mercy entails constant meditation on the word of God and "above all conscious and mature participation *in the Eucharist* and in the *Sacrament of Penance*" (§13.3). While the Eucharist draws believers into the merciful love which is more powerful than death, Reconciliation makes possible a personal experience of divine mercy which is more powerful than sin. The Church constantly preaches that conversion to God "always consists *in discovering his mercy*" (§13.6). Conversion, writes the Pope, is "the most concrete expression of the working of love and of the presence of mercy present in the human world" (§6.5).

Second, besides the Church's commitment to profess and receive God's mercy, she is called to put mercy into practice. She must be committed to implementing a program of mercy that will foster authentic human dignity in personal relationships and social life. Merciful love "is supremely indispensable between those who are closest to one another: between husbands and wives, between parents and children, between friends; and it is indispensable in education and in pastoral work" (§14.6). The Church's mission includes the task of making the world more human. This will come about, the Pope maintains, only if social relationships are governed not only by justice but also by "that 'merciful love' which constitutes the messianic message of the Gospel" (§14.7). The practice of forgiveness is essential if the world is to radiate a love which is more powerful than sin. Society will become more human, he writes, "only when we introduce into all the mutual relationships which form its moral aspect the moment of forgiveness" (§14.8). According to John Paul, the Church has the task of introducing the mystery of mercy revealed in Christ into all spheres of personal and social life.

Dives in Misericordia closes with a reminder that the Church's fundamental duty is to raise "*a cry for the mercy of God* amid the many forms of evil which weigh upon humanity and threaten it" (§15.1). Love for humanity impels the Pope to implore God's mercy. From the heart of the Church he prays that there should well up a cry which begs God to manifest his merciful love to the men and women of this generation.

Key Themes

While in this encyclical the Pope turns his attention especially to the Father who is "rich in mercy" (Eph 2:4), he nonetheless does so in a typically Christological way. It is in Christ that people have the possibility of discovering the Father's merciful love, and it is in him that the revelation of mercy is enfleshed and definitive. Through Jesus Christ, "every path to man . . . is simultaneously an approach to the Father and his love" (§1.3).

Among the encyclical's different themes, two are particularly profound and merit further comment: first, the relation between mercy and human dignity; and second, the connection between love, mercy, and justice.

Divine mercy and human dignity

John Paul thinks that many people today are uncomfortable with the idea of God's mercy. They tend to "exclude from life and to remove from the human heart the very idea of mercy" (§2.3). The mastery of science and technology feeds a sense of dominion over the world that belittles mercy as weakness. The exaltation of toughness, on the one hand, and victimization, on the other, leave little room for mercy.

The Pope suggests several reasons for this contemporary loss of the sense of mercy. First, for many people the idea of mercy implies a relationship of inequality between the one offering mercy and the one receiving it. They think that the recipient of mercy is humiliated. When mercy is confused with pity, it is resented. To be an object of someone's pity is to be stripped of one's dignity. Whenever this attitude takes hold, writes the Pope, "we are quick to deduce that mercy belittles the receiver, that it offends the dignity of man" (§6.4). In this sense, mercy is understood in a unilateral way, exclusively as a good done to others, almost an indulgence which preserves the distance between the parties involved.

Second, others think that the practice of mercy is a kind of shield used to cover up ignoring the demands of justice. All in all, contemporary men and women seem to be more comfortable with the idea of regulated justice than with that of gratuitous mercy. They prefer to build social relationships on justice, not mercy. In order to enlighten people with the truth about mercy, the Pope tackles these faulty attitudes.

In the parable of the prodigal son, John Paul presents the father as "*faithful to his fatherhood, faithful to the love* that he had always lavished on his son" (§6.1). The father himself is "prodigal" in his love. Joy at his son's return is prompted by his awareness that "a fundamental good has been saved: the good of his son's humanity" (§6.2). Two goods are involved in this situation:

one that remained intact, and another that was lost and found again. Despite his waywardness, the son never stopped being his father's son. The reality of fatherhood itself — which never ceases, even in the face of his son's squandering — obliged the father to be concerned about his lost son's dignity. Indeed, the father, by running to meet him, "loses" his own dignity.

Paternal love takes the form of mercy. Because it is forgiving, merciful love does not belittle the son. It is not a demeaning pity. Rather, the relationship of mercy involves both father and son in sharing the common experience of the son's restored dignity: he has returned to the truth about himself. Similarly, divine mercy in no way compromises human dignity but restores it to its full value. The dignity of every individual is anchored in God's faithful and merciful love for him.

The Pope also notes that the practice of mercy among persons is based on a shared encounter. There is an exchange of mercy. Both its giver and its recipient meet in the experience of the dignity proper to the individual. "In reciprocal relationships between persons," writes John Paul, "merciful love is never a unilateral act or process" (§14.2). The mutuality of mercy is at work even in the Redemption. Christ is not only the merciful Redeemer, but also "the one who stands at the door and knocks at the door of every man" (§8.4). As such, he seeks people's love, manifesting the desire for a kind of solidarity in mercy.

Appearances to the contrary notwithstanding, a person who practices mercy is as well a beneficiary of mercy. Anyone who performs a true act of merciful love knows that he is receiving mercy from the one who accepts it. Both giver and recipient serve "the great cause of the dignity of the person; and this contributes to uniting people in a more profound manner" (§14.5). Those who practice mercy discover their own humanity more deeply because they recognize the human dignity of the other. Those who receive mercy discover their own dignity because it is valued and, at the same time, they are inspired to be merciful to others. The giver and the recipient of mercy meet "at an essential point, namely the dignity or essential value of the person" (§14.11). Mercy establishes relationships based on human dignity and loving respect for the person. For the Pope, a fellowship of mercy is more profoundly human than a society of justice.

Love, mercy, and justice

In Sacred Scripture God's love is merciful to sinners. It is a forgiving love which prevails over people's sin and infidelity. The Father's eternal love is a merciful love. By it he "gave his only Son" (Jn 3:16) in the sacrifice of the

Cross. According to John Paul, to believe in this love is to believe in mercy. "For mercy is an indispensable dimension of love; it is as it were love's second name and, at the same time, the specific manner in which love is revealed and effected vis-à-vis the reality of the evil that is in the world, affecting and besieging man" (§7.6). During the present stage of salvation history, in which sin continues to exist, divine love is revealed as mercy. "God, 'who is love,' " writes the Pope, "*cannot reveal himself otherwise* than as mercy" (§13.4). Divine mercy is that love which is more powerful than sin and death, lifting people up when they fall into the abyss.

The Pope's treatment of the relation between justice and merciful love is fascinating. On the one hand, he praises the modern concern which seeks to establish justice among individuals, peoples, and nations. The pursuit of justice is a good which the Church should foster. On the other hand, he is convinced that, because the practice of justice is open to deviations, it needs to be completed by mercy.

No doubt John Paul has totalitarian systems in mind when he writes that "very often *programs which start from the idea of justice* and which ought to assist its fulfillment among individuals, groups and human societies, *in practice suffer from distortions*" (§12.3). When spite, hatred, or cruelty gain the upper hand, deviations from justice commonly occur. Experience proves, the Pope believes, that "justice alone is not enough, that it can even lead to the negation and destruction of itself, if that *deeper power, which is love*, is not allowed to shape human life in its various dimensions" (§12.3). Setting up programs and organizing activities whose goal is justice is insufficient. Justice must be complemented by merciful love. This mercy, as we have seen, promotes justice precisely because it embodies "equality" between the giver and the recipient. "*Mercy* that is truly Christian," writes John Paul, "is also, in a certain sense, *the most perfect incarnation* of 'equality' between people, and therefore also the most perfect incarnation of *justice* as well" (§14.5).

The parable of the prodigal son shows just how inadequate it is to establish relations according to the exact and strict norms of justice. The father's attitude to his wayward son points to the need of going beyond justice to the practice of merciful love. Love becomes mercy precisely when it exceeds a kind of justice that is narrowly conceived. Is this not perhaps what the elder son failed to understand? Revelation tells us that mercy is both more powerful and more profound than justice. The order is crucial. Love conditions justice, and justice serves love. This relationship between love and justice is clearly manifested in Christ's redemptive act. Here divine justice is satisfied, but it is a justice "to God's measure" (§7.3); that is, it has its source in love and bears its fruit in love. Thus, the Pope concludes, "the primacy and supe-riority of love vis-à-vis justice . . . are *revealed precisely through mercy*" (§4.11). Justice imbued with love sets mercy in motion.

Does John Paul imply that mercy should replace justice in social relation-ships? Not at all. "Mercy differs from justice," he says, *"but is not in opposition to it"* (§4.11). Justice remains integral to the social order. The Pope's concern is to link justice with mercy. He wishes to emphasize "the need to draw from the powers of the spirit which condition the very order of justice, powers which are still more profound" (§12.3). The order of justice has its roots in merciful love. *"True mercy is, so to speak, the most profound source of justice"* (§14.4). While justice can arbitrate between people concerning the equitable distribu-tion of goods, only merciful love can fully restore the fundamental value of lost human dignity. The equality which justice effects "is limited to the realm of objective and extrinsic goods, while love and mercy bring it about that people meet one another in that value which is man himself, with the dignity that is proper to him" (§14.5). Always, for John Paul, it is the dignity of the human person that is to the fore.

Only the attitude and practice of merciful love can guarantee a truly hu-man society. Furthermore, this merciful love requires that forgiveness, too, should be an integral aspect of social relationships. In this way justice is enlarged by love. A society which tries to eliminate forgiveness would be noth-ing but "a world of cold and unfeeling justice, in the name of which each person would claim his or her own rights vis-à-vis others" (§14.8).

The willingness to forgive, which is inextricably bound up with merciful love, *"does not cancel out* the objective *requirements of justice*. . . . In no pas-sage of the Gospel does forgiveness, or mercy as its source, mean indulgence toward evil, toward scandals, toward injury or insult" (§14.10). In forgiveness, then, mercy gives justice a richer content than the equitable distribution of goods or fair compensation. Mercy is "an indispensable element for *shaping* mutual relationships between people, in a spirit of deepest respect for what is human, and in a spirit of mutual brotherhood. It is impossible to establish this bond between people, if they wish to regulate their mutual relationships solely according to the measure of justice" (§14.6). Justice is the first step of merciful love, which alone can satisfy the dignity of the person and serve as the foundation of a truly human society.

The Father is the source of mercy; the Son, the way of mercy; the Holy Spirit, the life of mercy. "In the name of Jesus Christ crucified and risen, in the spirit of his messianic mission, enduring in the history of humanity, *we raise our voices and pray* that the Love which is in the Father may once again be revealed at this stage of history, and that, through the work of the Son and Holy Spirit, it may be shown to be present in our modern world and to be more powerful than evil: more powerful than sin and death" (§15.6).

* * *

Selected Bibliography

"Encyclical: *Dives in Misericordia*." Editorial. *The Tablet*, 234 (1980), 1210.

Ferraro, Giuseppe. "The Pneumatological Dimension." *L'Osservatore Romano*, 37 (1981), 5.

Lapide, Pinchas. "*Dives in Misericordia:* An Encyclical for Christians and Jews." *Journal of Ecumenical Studies*, 18 (1981), 140-142.

Martin, Ralph. "Rich in Mercy." *New Covenant*, 11 (July 1981), 20-22.

Mondin, Battista. "A Monumental Comment on *Dives in Misericordia*." *L'Osservatore Romano*, 36 (1981), 5.

Morneau, Robert F. "*Dives in Misericordia:* Themes and Theses." *Review for Religious*, 40 (1981), 670-683.

O'Hare, Joseph. "Mercy Appears." *America*, 143 (1980), 402.

ENCYCLICAL LETTER

DIVES IN MISERICORDIA

OF THE SUPREME PONTIFF

JOHN PAUL II

ON THE MERCY OF GOD

Dives in Misericordia

Venerable Brothers and
Dear Sons and Daughters,
Greetings and the Apostolic Blessing!

I

He Who Sees Me Sees the Father
(cf. Jn 14:9)

The revelation of mercy

1.1 It is "God, who is rich in mercy"[1] whom Jesus Christ has revealed to us as Father: it is his very Son who, in himself, has manifested him and made him known to us.[2] Memorable in this regard is the moment when Philip, one of the twelve Apostles, turned to Christ and said: "Lord, show us the Father, and we shall be satisfied"; and Jesus replied: "Have I been with you so long, and yet you do not know me. . . ? He who has seen me has seen the Father."[3] These words were spoken during the farewell discourse at the end of the paschal supper, which was followed by the events of those holy days during which confirmation was to be given once and for all of the fact that "God, who is rich in mercy, out of the great love with which he loved us, even when we were dead through our trespasses, made us alive together with Christ."[4]

1.2 Following the teaching of the Second Vatican Council and paying close attention to the special needs of our times, I devoted the Encyclical *Redemptor Hominis* to the truth about man, a truth that is revealed to us in its fullness and depth in Christ. A no less important need in these critical and difficult times impels me to draw attention once again in Christ to the countenance of the "Father of mercies and God of all comfort."[5] We read in the Constitution *Gaudium et Spes*: "Christ the new Adam . . . fully reveals man to himself and brings to light his lofty calling," and does it "in

---

[1] Eph 2:4.
[2] Cf. Jn 1:18; Heb 1:1-2.
[3] Jn 14:8-9.
[4] Eph 2:4-5.
[5] 2 Cor 1:3.

the very *revelation of the mystery of the Father and of his love.*"[6] The words that I have quoted are clear testimony to the fact that man cannot be manifested in the full dignity of his nature without reference — not only on the level of concepts but also in an integrally existential way — to God. Man and man's lofty calling are revealed in Christ through the revelation of the mystery of the Father and his love.

1.3 For this reason it is now fitting to reflect on this mystery. It is called for by the varied experiences of the Church and of contemporary man. It is also demanded by the pleas of many human hearts, their sufferings and hopes, their anxieties and expectations. While it is true that every individual human being is, as I said in my Encyclical *Redemptor Hominis*, the way for the Church, at the same time the Gospel and the whole of Tradition constantly show us that we must travel *this way* with every individual *just as Christ traced it out* by revealing in himself the Father and his love.[7] In Jesus Christ, every path to man, as it has been assigned once and for all to the Church in the changing context of the times, is simultaneously an approach to the Father and his love. The Second Vatican Council has confirmed this truth for our time.

1.4 The more the Church's mission is centered upon man — the more it is, so to speak, anthropocentric — the more it must be confirmed and actualized theocentrically, that is to say, be directed in Jesus Christ to the Father. While the various currents of human thought both in the past and at the present have tended and still tend to separate theocentrism and anthropocentrism, and even to set them in opposition to each other, the Church, following Christ, seeks to link them up in human history, in a deep and organic way. And this is also one of the basic principles, perhaps the most important one, of the teaching of the last Council. Since, therefore, in the present phase of the Church's history we put before ourselves as our primary task *the implementation of the doctrine* of the great *Council,* we must act upon this principle with faith, with an open mind and with all our heart. In the Encyclical already referred to, I have tried to show that the deepening and the many-faceted enrichment of the Church's consciousness resulting from the Council must open our minds and our hearts more widely to Christ. Today I wish to say that openness to Christ, who as the Redeemer of the world fully "reveals man to himself," can only be achieved through an ever more mature reference to the Father and his love.

---

[6] Pastoral Constitution on the Church in the Modern World *Gaudium et Spes*, 22: *AAS* 58 (1966), 1042.

[7] Cf. ibid.

The incarnation of mercy

2.1 Although God "dwells in unapproachable light,"[8] he speaks to man by means of the whole of the universe: "ever since the creation of the world his invisible nature, namely, his eternal power and deity, has been clearly perceived in the things that have been made."[9] This indirect and imperfect knowledge, achieved by the intellect seeking God by means of creatures through the visible world, falls short of "vision of the Father." "No one has ever seen God," writes Saint John, in order to stress the truth that "the only Son, who is in the bosom of the Father, he has made him known."[10] This "making known" reveals God in the most profound mystery of his being, one and three, surrounded by "unapproachable light."[11] Nevertheless, through this "making known" by Christ we know God above all in his relationship of love for man: in his "philanthropy."[12] It is precisely here that "his invisible nature" becomes in a special way "visible," incomparably more visible than through all the other "things that have been made": it becomes *visible in Christ and through Christ*, through his actions and his words, and finally through his death on the Cross and his Resurrection.

2.2 In this way, in Christ and through Christ, God also becomes especially visible in his mercy; that is to say, there is emphasized that attribute of the divinity which the Old Testament, using various concepts and terms, already defined as "mercy." Christ confers on the whole of the Old Testament tradition about God's mercy a definitive meaning. Not only does he speak of it and explain it by the use of comparisons and parables, but above all *he himself makes it incarnate* and personifies it. *He himself, in a certain sense, is mercy.* To the person who sees it in him — and finds it in him — God becomes "visible" in a particular way as the Father "who is rich in mercy."[13]

2.3 The present-day mentality, more perhaps than that of people in the past, seems opposed to a God of mercy, and in fact tends to exclude from life and to remove from the human heart the very idea of mercy. The word and the concept of "mercy" seem to cause uneasiness in man, who, thanks to the enormous development of science and technology, never before known in history, has become the master of the earth and has subdued and dominated it.[14] This dominion over the earth, sometimes understood in a one-sided and superficial way,

---

[8] 1 Tim 6:16.
[9] Rom 1:20.
[10] Jn 1:18.
[11] 1 Tim 6:16.
[12] Tit 3:4.
[13] Eph 2:4.
[14] Cf. Gen 1:28.

seems to have no room for mercy. However, in this regard we can profitably refer to the picture of "man's situation in the world today" as described at the beginning of the Constitution *Gaudium et Spes*. Here we read the following sentences: "In the light of the foregoing factors there appears the dichotomy of a world that is at once powerful and weak, capable of doing what is noble and what is base, disposed to freedom and slavery, progress and decline, brotherhood and hatred. Man is growing conscious that the forces he has unleashed are in his own hands and that it is up to him to control them or be enslaved by them."[15]

2.4 The situation of the world today not only displays transformations that give grounds for hope in *a better future for man on earth*, but also reveals a multitude of *threats*, far surpassing those known up till now. Without ceasing to point out these threats on various occasions (as in addresses at UNO, to UNESCO, to FAO and elsewhere), the Church must at the same time examine them in the light of the truth received from God.

2.5 The truth, revealed in Christ, about God the "Father of mercies,"[16] enables us to "see" him as particularly close to man especially when man is suffering, when he is under threat at the very heart of his existence and dignity. And this is why, in the situation of the Church and the world today, many individuals and groups guided by a lively sense of faith are turning, I would say almost spontaneously, to the mercy of God. They are certainly being moved to do this by Christ himself, who through his Spirit works within human hearts. For the mystery of God the "Father of mercies" revealed by Christ becomes, in the context of today's threats to man, as it were a unique appeal addressed to the Church.

2.6 In the present Encyclical I wish to accept this appeal; I wish to draw from the eternal and at the same time — for its simplicity and depth — incomparable language of revelation and faith, in order through this same language to express once more before God and before humanity the major anxieties of our time.

2.7 In fact, revelation and faith teach us not only to meditate in the abstract upon the mystery of God as "Father of mercies," but also to have recourse to that mercy in the name of Christ and in union with him. Did not Christ say that our Father, who "sees in secret,"[17] is always waiting for us to have recourse to him in every need and always waiting for us to study his mystery: the mystery of the Father and his love?[18]

---

[15] Pastoral Constitution on the Church in the Modern World *Gaudium et Spes*, 9: *AAS* 58 (1966), 1032.

[16] 2 Cor 1:3.

[17] Mt 6:4, 6, 18.

[18] Cf. Eph 3:18; also Lk 11:5-13.

2.8 I therefore wish these considerations to bring this mystery closer to everyone. At the same time I wish them to be a heartfelt appeal by the Church to mercy, which humanity and the modern world need so much. And they need mercy even though they often do not realize it.

II

The Messianic Message

When Christ began to do and to teach

3.1 Before his own townspeople, in Nazareth, Christ refers to the words of the Prophet Isaiah: "The Spirit of the Lord is upon me, because he has anointed me to preach good news to the poor. He has sent me to proclaim release to the captives and recovering of sight to the blind, to set at liberty those who are oppressed, to proclaim the acceptable year of the Lord."[19] These phrases, according to Luke, are *his first messianic declaration.* They are followed by the actions and words known through the Gospel. By these actions and words Christ makes the Father present among men. It is very significant that the people in question are especially the poor, those without means of subsistence, those deprived of their freedom, the blind who cannot see the beauty of creation, those living with broken hearts, or suffering from social injustice, and finally sinners. It is especially for these last that the Messiah becomes a particularly clear sign of God who is love, a sign of the Father. In this visible sign the people of our own time, just like the people then, can see the Father.

3.2 It is significant that, when the messengers sent by John the Baptist came to Jesus to ask him: "Are you he who is to come, or shall we look for another?",[20] he answered by referring to the same testimony with which he had begun his teaching at Nazareth: "Go and tell John what it is that you have seen and heard: the blind receive their sight, the lame walk, lepers are cleansed, and the deaf hear, the dead are raised up, the poor have good news preached to them." He then ended with the words: "And blessed is he who takes no offense at me."[21]

3.3 Especially through his lifestyle and through his actions, Jesus revealed that *love is present in the world* in which we live, an effective love, a love that addresses itself to man and embraces everything that makes up his humanity. This love makes itself particularly noticed in contact with suffering, injus-

---

[19] Lk 4:18-19.
[20] Lk 7:19.
[21] Lk 7:22-23.

tice and poverty, in contact with the whole historical "human condition," which in various ways manifests man's limitation and frailty, both physical and moral. It is precisely the mode and sphere in which love manifests itself that in biblical language is called "mercy."

3.4 Christ, then, reveals God who is Father, who is "love," as Saint John will express it in his first letter;[22] Christ reveals God as "rich in mercy," as we read in Saint Paul.[23] This truth is not just the subject of a teaching; it is a reality made present to us by Christ. *Making the Father present as love and mercy* is, in Christ's own consciousness, the fundamental touchstone of his mission as the Messiah; this is confirmed by the words that he uttered first in the synagogue at Nazareth and later in the presence of his disciples and of John the Baptist's messengers.

3.5 On the basis of this way of manifesting the presence of God who is Father, love and mercy, Jesus makes mercy one of the principal *themes* of his *preaching*. As is his custom, he first teaches "in parables," since these express better the very essence of things. It is sufficient to recall the parable of the Prodigal Son,[24] or the parable of the Good Samaritan,[25] but also — by contrast — the parable of the merciless servant.[26] There are many passages in the teaching of Christ that manifest love-mercy under some ever-fresh aspect. We need only consider the Good Shepherd who goes in search of the lost sheep,[27] or the woman who sweeps the house in search of the lost coin.[28] The Gospel writer who particularly treats of these themes in Christ's teaching is Luke, whose Gospel has earned the title of "the Gospel of mercy."

3.6 When one speaks of preaching, one encounters a problem of major importance with reference to the meaning of terms and the content of concepts, especially the content of *the concept of "mercy" (in relationship to the concept of "love")*. A grasp of the content of these concepts is the key to understanding the very reality of mercy. And this is what is most important for us. However, before devoting a further part of our considerations to this subject, that is to say, to establishing the meaning of the vocabulary and the content proper to the concept of "mercy," we must note that Christ, in revealing the love-mercy of God, at the same time *demanded from people* that they also should be guided in their lives by love and mercy. This requirement forms

[22] 1 Jn 4:16.
[23] Eph 2:4.
[24] Lk 15:11-32.
[25] Lk 10:30-37.
[26] Mt 18:23-35.
[27] Mt 18:12-14; Lk 15:3-7.
[28] Lk 15:8-10.

part of the very essence of the messianic message, and constitutes the heart of the Gospel *ethos*. The Teacher expresses this both through the medium of the commandment which he describes as "the greatest,"[29] and also in the form of a blessing, when in the Sermon on the Mount he proclaims: "Blessed are the merciful, for they shall obtain mercy."[30]

3.7 In this way, the messianic message about mercy preserves a particular divine-human dimension. Christ — the very fulfillment of the messianic prophecy — by becoming the incarnation of the love that is manifested with particular force with regard to the suffering, the unfortunate and sinners, makes present and thus more fully reveals the Father, who is God "rich in mercy." At the same time, by becoming for people a model of merciful love for others, Christ proclaims by his actions even more than by his words that call to mercy which is one of the essential elements of the Gospel *ethos*. In this instance it is not just a case of fulfilling a commandment or an obligation of an ethical nature; it is also a case of satisfying a condition of major importance for God to reveal himself in his mercy to man: "The merciful . . . shall obtain mercy."

III

The Old Testament

4.1 The concept of "mercy" in the Old Testament has a long and rich history. We have to refer back to it in order that the mercy revealed by Christ may shine forth more clearly. By revealing that mercy both through his actions and through his teaching, Christ addressed himself to people who not only knew the concept of mercy, but who also, as *the People of God of the Old Covenant*, had drawn from their age-long history *a special experience of the mercy of God*. This experience was social and communal, as well as individual and interior.

4.2 Israel was, in fact, the people of the Covenant with God, a Covenant that it broke many times. Whenever it became aware of its infidelity — and in the history of Israel there was no lack of Prophets and others who awakened this awareness — it appealed to mercy. In this regard, the books of the Old Testament give us very many examples. Among the events and texts of greater importance one may recall: the beginning of the history of the Judges,[31] the prayer of Solomon at the inauguration of the Temple,[32] part of the prophetic

---

[29] Mt 22:38.
[30] Mt 5:7.
[31] Cf. Judg 3:7-9.
[32] Cf. 1 Kings 8:22-53.

work of Micah,[33] the consoling assurances given by Isaiah,[34] the cry of the Jews in exile,[35] and the renewal of the Covenant after the return from exile.[36]

4.3 It is significant that in their preaching the Prophets link mercy, which they often refer to because of the people's sins, with the incisive image of love on God's part. The Lord loves Israel with the love of a special choosing, much like the love of a spouse,[37] and for this reason he pardons its sins and even its infidelities and betrayals. When he finds repentance and true conversion, he brings his people back to grace.[38] In the preaching of the Prophets, *mercy* signifies *a special power of love*, which *prevails over the sin and infidelity* of the chosen people.

4.4 In this broad "social" context, mercy appears as a correlative to the interior experience of individuals languishing in a state of guilt or enduring every kind of suffering and misfortune. *Both physical evil and moral evil, namely sin*, cause the sons and daughters of Israel to turn to the Lord and beseech his mercy. In this way David turns to him, conscious of the seriousness of his guilt;[39] Job too, after his rebellion, turns to him in his tremendous misfortune;[40] so also does Esther, knowing the mortal threat to her own people.[41] And we find still other examples in the books of the Old Testament.[42]

4.5 At the root of this many-sided conviction, which is both communal and personal, and which is demonstrated by the whole of the Old Testament down the centuries, is the basic experience of the chosen people at the Exodus: the Lord saw the affliction of his people reduced to slavery, heard their cry, knew their sufferings and decided to deliver them.[43] In this act of salvation by the Lord, the Prophet perceived his love and compassion.[44] This is precisely the grounds upon which the people and each of its members based their certainty of the mercy of God, which can be invoked whenever tragedy strikes.

4.6 Added to this is the fact that sin too constitutes man's misery. The

---

[33] Cf. Mic 7:18-20.
[34] Cf. Is 1:18, 51:4-16.
[35] Cf. Bar 2:11-3, 8.
[36] Cf. Neh 9.
[37] Cf., for example, Hos 2:21-25; Is 54:6-8.
[38] Cf. Jer 31:20; Ezek 39:25-29.
[39] Cf. 2 Sam 11; 12; 24:10.
[40] Job *passim*.
[41] Esther 4:17ff.
[42] Cf., for example, Neh 9:30-32; Tob 3:2-3, 11-12; 8:16-17; 1 Mac 4:24.
[43] Cf. Ex 3:7-8.
[44] Cf. Is 63:9.

people of the Old Covenant experienced this misery from the time of the Exodus, when they set up the golden calf. The Lord himself triumphed over this act of breaking the Covenant when he solemnly declared to Moses that he was a "God merciful and gracious, slow to anger, and abounding in steadfast love and faithfulness."[45] It is in this central revelation that the chosen people, and each of its members, will find, every time that they have sinned, the strength and the motive for turning to the Lord to remind him of what he had exactly revealed about himself[46] and to beseech his forgiveness.

4.7 Thus, in deeds and in words, the Lord revealed his mercy from the very beginnings of the people which he chose for himself; and, in the course of its history, this people continually entrusted itself, both when stricken with misfortune and when it became aware of its sin, to the God of mercies. All the subtleties of love become manifest in the Lord's mercy toward those who are his own: he is their Father,[47] for Israel is his firstborn son;[48] the Lord is also the bridegroom of her whose new name the Prophet proclaims: *Ruhamah*, "Beloved" or "she has obtained pity."[49]

4.8 Even when the Lord is exasperated by the infidelity of his people and thinks of finishing with it, it is still his tenderness and generous love for those who are his own which overcomes his anger.[50] Thus it is easy to understand why the psalmists, when they desire to sing the highest praises of the Lord, break forth into hymns to the God of love, tenderness, mercy and fidelity.[51]

4.9 From all this it follows that mercy does not pertain only to the notion of God, but it is something that characterizes the life of the whole people of Israel and each of its sons and daughters: *mercy is the content of intimacy with their Lord*, the content of their dialogue with him. Under precisely this aspect, mercy is presented in the individual books of the Old Testament with a great richness of expression. It may be difficult to find in these books a purely theoretical answer to the question of what mercy is in itself. Nevertheless, the *terminology* that is used is in itself able to tell us much about this subject.[52]

---

[45] Ex 34:6.

[46] Cf. Num 14:18; 2 Chron 30:9; Neh 9:17; Ps 86; Wis 15:1; Sir 2:11; Joel 2:13.

[47] Cf. Is 63:16.

[48] Cf. Ex 4:22.

[49] Cf. Hos 2:3.

[50] Cf. Hos 11:7-9; Jer 31:20; Is 54:7-8.

[51] Cf. Ps 103 and 145.

[52] In describing mercy, the books of the Old Testament use two expressions in particular, each having a different semantic nuance. First there is the term *hesed*, which indicates a profound attitude of "goodness." When this is established between two individuals, they do not just wish each other well; they are also faithful to each other by virtue of an interior commit-

4.10 The Old Testament proclaims the mercy of the Lord by the use of many terms with related meanings; they are differentiated by their particular content, but *it could be said that they all converge from different directions on one single fundamental content,* to express its surpassing richness and at the same time to bring it close to man under different aspects. The Old Testament encourages people suffering from misfortune, especially those weighed down by sin — as also the whole of Israel, which had entered into the Covenant with God — *to appeal for mercy,* and enables them to count upon it: it reminds them of his mercy in times of failure and loss of trust. Subsequently, the Old Testament *gives thanks and glory* for mercy every time that mercy is made manifest in the life of the people or in the lives of individuals.

ment, and therefore also *by virtue of a faithfulness to themselves.* Since *hesed* also means "grace" or "love," this occurs precisely on the basis of this fidelity. The fact that the commitment in question has not only a moral character but almost a juridical one makes no difference. When in the Old Testament the word *hesed* is used of the Lord, this always occurs in connection with the covenant that God established with Israel. This covenant was, on God's part, a gift and a grace for Israel. Nevertheless, since, in harmony with the covenant entered into, God had made a commitment to respect it, *hesed* also acquired in a certain sense a legal content. The juridical commitment on God's part ceased to oblige whenever Israel broke the covenant and did not respect its conditions. But precisely at this point, *hesed,* in ceasing to be a juridical obligation, revealed its deeper aspect: it showed itself as what it was at the beginning, that is, as love that gives, love more powerful than betrayal, grace stronger than sin.

This fidelity vis-à-vis the unfaithful "daughter of my people" (cf. Lam 4:3, 6) is, in brief, *on God's part, fidelity to himself.* This becomes obvious in the frequent recurrence together of the two terms *hesed we'emet* (grace and fidelity), which could be considered a case of hendiadys (cf., for example, Ex 34:6; 2 Sam 2:6, 15:20; Ps 25:10, 40:11-12, 85:11, 138:2; Mic 7:20). "It is not for your sake, O house of Israel, that I am about to act, but for the sake of my holy name" (Ezek 36:22). Therefore Israel, although burdened with guilt for having broken the covenant, cannot lay claim to God's *hesed* on the basis of (legal) justice; yet it can and must go on hoping and trusting to obtain it, since the God of the covenant is really "responsible for his love." The fruits of this love are forgiveness and restoration to grace, the reestablishment of the interior covenant.

The second word which in the terminology of the Old Testament serves to define mercy is *rahamim.* This has a different nuance from that of *hesed.* While *hesed* highlights the marks of fidelity to self and of "responsibility for one's own love" (which are in a certain sense masculine characteristics), *rahamim,* in its very root, *denotes the love of a mother* (rehem = mother's womb). From the deep and original bond — indeed the unity — that links a mother to her child there springs a particular relationship to the child, a particular love. Of this love one can say that it is completely gratuitous, not merited, and that in this aspect it constitutes an interior necessity: an exigency of the heart. It is, as it were, a "feminine" variation of the masculine fidelity to self expressed by *hesed.* Against this psychological background, *rahamim* generates a whole range of feelings, including goodness and tenderness, patience and understanding, that is, readiness to forgive.

The Old Testament attributes to the Lord precisely these characteristics, when it uses the

4.11 In this way, mercy is in a certain sense contrasted with God's justice, and in many cases is shown to be not only more powerful than that justice but also more profound. Even the Old Testament teaches that, although justice is an authentic virtue in man, and in God signifies transcendent perfection, nevertheless love is "greater" than justice: greater in the sense that it is primary and fundamental. Love, so to speak, conditions justice and, in the final analysis, justice serves love. The primacy and superiority of love vis-à-vis justice — this is a mark of the whole of revelation — are *revealed precisely through mercy.* This seemed so obvious to the Psalmists and Prophets that the very term justice ended up by meaning the salvation accomplished by the Lord and his mercy.[53] *Mercy differs from justice, but is not in opposition to it,* if

term *rahamim* in speaking of him. We read in Isaiah: "Can a woman forget her sucking child, that she should have no compassion on the son of her womb? *Even these may forget, yet I will not forget you*" (Is 49:15). This love, faithful and invincible thanks to the mysterious power of motherhood, is expressed in the Old Testament texts in various ways: as salvation from dangers, especially from enemies; also as forgiveness of sins — of individuals and also of the whole of Israel; and finally in readiness to fulfill the (eschatological) promise and hope, in spite of human infidelity, as we read in Hosea: "I will heal their faithlessness, I will love them freely" (Hos 14:5).

In the terminology of the Old Testament we also find other expressions, referring in different ways to the same basic content. But the two terms mentioned above deserve special attention. They clearly show their *original anthropomorphic aspect:* in describing God's mercy, the biblical authors use terms that correspond to the consciousness and experience of their contemporaries. The Greek terminology in the Septuagint translation does not show as great a wealth as the Hebrew: therefore it does not offer all the semantic nuances proper to the original text. At any rate, the New Testament builds upon the wealth and depth that already marked the Old.

In this way, we have inherited from the Old Testament — as it were in a special synthesis — not only the wealth of expressions used by those books in order to define God's mercy, but also a specific and obviously anthropomorphic "psychology" of God: *the image of his anxious love,* which in contact with evil, and in particular with the sin of the individual and of the people, *is manifested as mercy.* This image is made up not only of the rather general content of the verb *hanan* but also of the content of *hesed* and *rahamim.* The term *hanan* expresses a wider concept: it means in fact the manifestation of grace, which involves, so to speak, a constant predisposition to be generous, benevolent and merciful.

In addition to these basic semantic elements, the Old Testament concept of mercy is also made up of what is included in the verb *hamal,* which literally means "to spare" (a defeated enemy) but also "to show mercy and compassion," and in consequence forgiveness and remission of guilt. There is also the term *hus,* which expresses pity and compassion, but especially in the affective sense. These terms appear more rarely in the biblical texts to denote mercy. In addition, one must note the word *'emet,* already mentioned: it means primarily "solidity, security" (in the Greek of the Septuagint: "truth") and then "fidelity," and in this way it seems to link up with the semantic content proper to the term *hesed.*

[53] Ps 40:11, 98:2-3; Is 45:21, 51:5, 8; 56:1.

we admit in the history of man — as the Old Testament precisely does — the presence of God, who already as Creator has linked himself to his creature with a particular love. Love, by its very nature, excludes hatred and ill-will toward the one to whom he once gave the gift of himself: *Nihil odisti eorum quae fecisti,* "you hold nothing of what you have made in abhorrence."[54] These words indicate the profound basis of the relationship between justice and mercy in God, in his relations with man and the world. They tell us that we must seek the life-giving roots and intimate reasons for this relationship by going back to "the beginning," *in the very mystery of creation.* They foreshadow in the context of the Old Covenant the full revelation of God, who is "love."[55]

4.12 Connected with the mystery of creation is the *mystery of the election,* which in a special way shaped the history of the people whose spiritual father is Abraham by virtue of his faith. Nevertheless, through this people which journeys forward through the history both of the Old Covenant and of the New, that mystery of election refers to every man and woman, to the whole great human family. "I have loved you with an everlasting love, therefore I have continued my faithfulness to you."[56] "For the mountains may depart . . . my steadfast love shall not depart from you, and my covenant of peace shall not be removed."[57] This truth, once proclaimed to Israel, involves a *perspective* of the whole history of man, a perspective both *temporal* and *eschatological.*[58] Christ reveals the Father within the framework of the same perspective and on ground already prepared, as many pages of the Old Testament writings demonstrate. At the end of this revelation, on the night before he dies, he says to the Apostle Philip these memorable words: "Have I been with you so long, and yet you do not know me. . . ? He who has seen me has seen the Father."[59]

IV

The Parable of the Prodigal Son

An analogy

5.1 At the very beginning of the New Testament, two voices resound in Saint Luke's Gospel in unique harmony concerning the mercy of God, a har-

---

[54] Wis 11:24.
[55] 1 Jn 4:16.
[56] Jer 31:3.
[57] Is 54:10.
[58] Jon 4:2, 11; Ps 145:9; Sir 18:8-14; Wis 11:23-12:1.
[59] Jn 14:9.

mony which forcefully echoes the whole Old Testament tradition. They express the semantic elements linked to the differentiated terminology of the ancient books. *Mary,* entering the house of Zechariah, *magnifies* the Lord with all her soul for "his *mercy,*" which *"from generation to generation"* is bestowed on those who fear him. A little later, as she recalls the election of Israel, she proclaims the mercy which he who has chosen her holds "in remembrance" from all time.[60] Afterwards, in the same house, when John the Baptist is born, his father *Zechariah* blesses the God of Israel and glorifies him for performing the mercy promised to our fathers and for *remembering his holy Covenant.*[61]

5.2 *In the teaching of Christ himself,* this image inherited from the Old Testament becomes at the same time *simpler and more profound.* This is perhaps most evident in the parable of the prodigal son.[62] Although the word "mercy" does not appear, it nevertheless expresses the essence of the divine mercy in a particularly clear way. This is due not so much to the terminology, as in the Old Testament books, as to the analogy that enables us to understand more fully the very mystery of mercy, as a profound drama played out between the father's love and the prodigality and sin of the son.

5.3 That son, who receives from the father the portion of the inheritance that is due to him and leaves home to squander it in a far country "in loose living," in a certain sense is the man of every period, beginning with the one who was the first to lose the inheritance of grace and original justice. The analogy at this point is very wide-ranging. The parable indirectly touches upon every breach of the covenant of love, every loss of grace, every sin. In this analogy there is less emphasis than in the prophetic tradition on the unfaithfulness of the whole people of Israel, although the *analogy of the prodigal son* may extend to this also. "When he had spent everything," the son "began to be in need," especially as "a great famine arose in that country" to which he had gone after leaving his father's house. And in this situation "he would gladly have fed on" anything, even "the pods that the swine ate," the swine that he herded for "one of the citizens of that country." But even this was refused him.

5.4 The analogy turns clearly toward man's interior. The inheritance that

---

[60] In both places it is a case of *hesed,* that is, the fidelity that God manifests to his own love for the people, fidelity to the promises that will find their definitive fulfillment precisely in the motherhood of the Mother of God (cf. Lk 1:49-54).

[61] Cf. Lk 1:72. Here too it is a case of mercy in the meaning of *hesed,* insofar as in the following sentences, in which Zechariah speaks of the "tender mercy of our God," there is clearly expressed the second meaning, namely, *rahamim* (Latin translation: *viscera misericordiae*), which rather identifies God's mercy with a mother's love.

[62] Cf. Lk 15:11-32.

the son had received from his father was a quantity of material goods, but more important than these goods was *his dignity as a son in his father's house.* The situation in which he found himself when he lost the material goods should have made him aware of the loss of that dignity. He had not thought about it previously, when he had asked his father to give him the part of the inheritance that was due to him, in order to go away. He seems not to be conscious of it even now, when he says to himself: "How many of my father's hired servants have bread enough and to spare, but I perish here with hunger." He measures himself by the standard of the goods that he has lost, that he no longer "possesses," while the hired servants of his father's house "possess" them. These words express above all his attitude to material goods; nevertheless under their surface is concealed the tragedy of lost dignity, the awareness of squandered sonship.

5.5 It is at this point that he makes the decision: "I will arise and *go to my father, and I will say to him, 'Father, I have sinned* against heaven and before you; I am no longer worthy to be called your son. Treat me as one of your hired servants.' "[63] These are words that reveal more deeply the essential problem. Through the complex material situation in which the prodigal son found himself because of his folly, because of sin, the sense of lost dignity had matured. When he decides to return to his father's house, to ask his father to be received — no longer by virtue of his right as a son, but as an employee — at first sight he seems to be acting by reason of the hunger and poverty that he had fallen into; this motive, however, is permeated by an awareness of a deeper loss: to be *a hired servant in his own father's house* is certainly a great humiliation and source of shame. Nevertheless, the prodigal son is ready to undergo that humiliation and shame. He realizes that he no longer has any right except to be an employee in his father's house. His decision is taken in full consciousness of what he has deserved and of what he can still have a right to in accordance with the norms of justice. Precisely this reasoning demonstrates that, at the center of the prodigal son's consciousness, the sense of lost dignity is emerging, the sense of that dignity that springs from the relationship of the son with the father. And it is with this decision that he sets out.

5.6 In the parable of the prodigal son, the term "justice" is not used even once; just as in the original text the term "mercy" is not used either. *Nevertheless, the relationship between justice and love, that is manifested as mercy,* is inscribed with great exactness in the content of the Gospel parable. It becomes more evident that love is transformed into mercy when it is necessary to go beyond the precise norm of justice — precise and often too narrow. The

---

[63] Lk 15:18-19.

prodigal son, having wasted the property he received from his father, deserves — after his return — to earn his living by working in his father's house as a hired servant and possibly, little by little, to build up a certain provision of material goods, though perhaps never as much as the amount he had squandered. This would be demanded by the order of justice, especially as the son had not only squandered the part of the inheritance belonging to him but *had also hurt and offended his father* by his whole conduct. Since this conduct had in his own eyes deprived him of his dignity as a son, it could not be a matter of indifference to his father. It was bound to make him suffer. It was also bound to implicate him in some way. And yet, after all, it was his own son who was involved, and such a relationship could never be altered or destroyed by any sort of behavior. The prodigal son is aware of this and it is precisely this awareness that shows him clearly the dignity which he has lost and which makes him honestly evaluate the position that he could still expect in his father's house.

Particular concentration on human dignity

6.1 This *exact picture of the prodigal son's state of mind enables us to understand* exactly *what the mercy of God consists in.* There is no doubt that in this simple but penetrating analogy the figure of the father reveals to us God as Father. The conduct of the father in the parable and his whole behavior, which manifests his internal attitude, enables us to rediscover the individual threads of the Old Testament vision of mercy in a synthesis which is totally new, full of simplicity and depth. The father of the prodigal son *is faithful to his fatherhood, faithful to the love* that he had always lavished on his son. This fidelity is expressed in the parable not only by his immediate readiness to welcome him home when he returns after having squandered his inheritance; it is expressed even more fully by that joy, that merrymaking for the squanderer after his return, merrymaking which is so generous that it provokes the opposition and hatred of the elder brother, who had never gone far away from his father and had never abandoned the home.

6.2 The father's fidelity to himself — a trait already known by the Old Testament term *hesed* — is at the same time expressed in a manner particularly charged with affection. We read, in fact, that when the father saw the prodigal son returning home "he had *compassion,* ran to meet him, threw his arms around his neck and kissed him."[64] He certainly does this under the influence of a deep affection, and this also explains his generosity toward his son, that generosity which so angers the elder son. Nevertheless, the causes

---

[64] Lk 15:20.

of this emotion are to be sought at a deeper level. Notice, the father is aware that a fundamental good has been saved: the good of his son's humanity. Although the son has squandered the inheritance, *nevertheless his humanity is saved.* Indeed, *it has been,* in a way, *found again.* The father's words to the elder son reveal this: "It was fitting to make merry and be glad, for this your brother was dead and is alive; he was lost and is found."[65] In the same chapter fifteen of Luke's Gospel, we read the parable of the sheep that was found[66] and then the parable of the coin that was found.[67] Each time there is an emphasis on the same joy that is present in the case of the prodigal son. The father's fidelity to himself is totally concentrated upon the humanity of the lost son, upon his dignity. This explains above all his joyous emotion at the moment of the son's return home.

6.3 Going on, one can therefore say that the love for the son, the love that springs from the very essence of fatherhood, in a way obliges the father to be concerned about his son's dignity. This concern is the measure of his love, the love of which Saint Paul was to write: "Love is patient and kind . . . love does not insist on its own way; it is not irritable or resentful . . . but rejoices in the right . . . hopes all things, endures all things" and "love never ends."[68] Mercy — as Christ has presented it in the parable of the prodigal son — has *the interior form of the love* that in the New Testament is called *agape.* This love is able to reach down to every prodigal son, to every human misery, and above all to every form of moral misery, to sin. When this happens, the person who is the object of mercy does not feel humiliated, but rather found again and "restored to value." The father first and foremost expresses to him his joy that he has been "found again" and that he has "returned to life. This joy indicates a good that has remained intact: even if he is prodigal, a son does not cease to be truly his father's son; it also indicates a good that has been found again, which in the case of the prodigal son was his return to the truth about himself.

6.4 What took place in the relationship between the father and the son in Christ's parable is not to be evaluated "from the outside." Our prejudices about mercy are mostly the result of appraising them only from the outside. At times it happens that by following this method of evaluation *we see in mercy* above all a *relationship of inequality* between the one offering it and the one receiving it. And, in consequence, we are quick to deduce that mercy

---

[65] Lk 15:32.
[66] Cf. Lk 15:3-6.
[67] Cf. Lk 15:8-9.
[68] 1 Cor 13:4-8.

belittles the receiver, that it offends the dignity of man. The parable of the prodigal son shows that the reality *is different:* the relationship of mercy is based on the common experience of that good which is man, on the common experience of the dignity that is proper to him. This common experience makes the prodigal son begin to see himself and his actions in their full truth (this vision in truth is a genuine form of humility); on the other hand, for this very reason he becomes a particular good for his father: the father sees so clearly the good which has been achieved thanks to a mysterious radiation of truth and love, that he seems to forget all the evil which the son had committed.

6.5 The parable of the prodigal son expresses in a simple but profound way *the reality of conversion.* Conversion is the most concrete expression of the working of love and of the presence of mercy in the human world. The true and proper meaning of mercy does not consist only in looking, however penetratingly and compassionately, at moral, physical or material evil: mercy is manifested in its true and proper aspect when it restores to value, promotes and *draws good from all the forms of evil* existing in the world and in man. Understood in this way, mercy constitutes the fundamental content of the messianic message of Christ and the constitutive power of his mission. His disciples and followers understood and practiced mercy in the same way. Mercy never ceased to reveal itself, in their hearts and in their actions, as an especially creative proof of the love which does not allow itself to be "conquered by evil," but overcomes "evil with good."[69] The genuine face of mercy has to be ever revealed anew. In spite of many prejudices, mercy seems particularly necessary for our times.

V

The Paschal Mystery

Mercy revealed in the Cross and Resurrection

7.1 The messianic message of Christ and his activity among people end with the Cross and Resurrection. We have to penetrate deeply into this final event — which especially in the language of the Council is defined as the *mysterium paschale* — if we wish to express in depth the truth about mercy, as it has been revealed in depth in the history of our salvation. At this point of our considerations, we shall have to draw closer still to the content of the Encyclical *Redemptor Hominis.* If, in fact, the reality of the Redemption, in its human dimension, reveals the unheard-of greatness of man, *qui talem ac*

---

[69] Cf. Rom 12:21.

tantum meruit habere Redemptorem,[70] at the same time *the divine dimension of the Redemption* enables us, I would say, in the most empirical and "historical" way, to uncover the depth of that love which does not recoil before the extraordinary sacrifice of the Son, in order to satisfy the fidelity of the Creator and Father toward human beings, created in his image and chosen from "the beginning," in this Son, for grace and glory.

7.2 The events of Good Friday and, even before that, in prayer in Gethsemane, introduce a fundamental change into the whole course of the revelation of love and mercy in the messianic mission of Christ. The one who "went about doing good and healing"[71] and "curing every sickness and disease"[72] now himself seems to merit the greatest mercy and to *appeal for mercy,* when he is arrested, abused, condemned, scourged, crowned with thorns, when he is nailed to the Cross and dies amidst agonizing torments.[73] It is then that he particularly deserves mercy from the people to whom he has done good, and he does not receive it. Even those who are closest to him cannot protect him and snatch him from the hands of his oppressors. At this final stage of his messianic activity the words which the Prophets, especially Isaiah, uttered concerning the Servant of Yahweh are fulfilled in Christ: "Through his stripes we are healed."[74]

7.3 Christ, as the man who suffers really and in a terrible way in the Garden of Olives and on Calvary, addresses himself to the Father — that Father whose love he has preached to people, to whose mercy he has borne witness through all of his activity. But he is not spared — not even he — the terrible suffering of death on the Cross: *"For our sake God made him to be sin who knew no sin,"*[75] Saint Paul will write, summing up in a few words the whole depth of the Cross and at the same time the divine dimension of the reality of the Redemption. Indeed this Redemption is the ultimate and definitive revelation of the holiness of God, who is the absolute fullness of perfection: fullness of justice and of love, since justice is based on love, flows from it and tends toward it. In the Passion and death of Christ — in the fact that the Father did not spare his own Son, but "for our sake made him sin"[76] — absolute justice is expressed, for Christ undergoes the Passion and Cross because of the sins of humanity. This constitutes even a "superabundance" of justice,

[70] Cf. *Exsultet* at the Easter Vigil.
[71] Acts 10:38.
[72] Mt 9:35.
[73] Cf. Mk 15:37; Jn 19:30.
[74] Is 53:5.
[75] 2 Cor 5:21.
[76] 2 Cor 5:21.

for the sins of man are "compensated for" by the sacrifice of the Man-God. Nevertheless, this justice, which is properly justice "to God's measure," springs completely from love: from the love of the Father and of the Son, and completely bears fruit in love. Precisely for this reason the divine justice revealed in the Cross of Christ is "to God's measure," because it springs from love and is accomplished in love, producing fruits of salvation. *The divine dimension of the Redemption* is put into effect not only by bringing justice to bear upon sin, but also by restoring to love that creative power in man thanks to which he once more has access to the fullness of life and holiness that come from God. In this way, Redemption involves the revelation of mercy in its fullness.

7.4 The Paschal Mystery is the culmination of this revealing and effecting of mercy, which is able to justify man, to restore justice in the sense of that salvific order which God willed from the beginning in man and, through man, in the world. The suffering Christ speaks in a special way to man, and not only to the believer. The non-believer also will be able to discover in him the eloquence of solidarity with the human lot, as also the harmonious fullness of a disinterested dedication to the cause of man, to truth and to love. And yet the divine dimension of the Paschal Mystery goes still deeper. *The Cross* on Calvary, the Cross upon which Christ conducts his final dialogue with the Father, *emerges from the very heart of the love* that man, created in the image and likeness of God, has been given as a gift, according to God's eternal plan. God, as Christ has revealed him, does not merely remain closely linked with the world as the Creator and the ultimate source of existence. He is also Father: he is linked to man, whom he called to existence in the visible world, by a bond still more intimate than that of creation. It is love which not only creates the good but also grants participation in the very life of God: Father, Son and Holy Spirit. For he who loves desires to give himself.

7.5 The Cross of Christ on Calvary stands *beside the path* of that *admirabile commercium,* of that *wonderful self-communication of God to man,* which also includes the call to man to share in the divine life by giving himself, and with himself the whole visible world, to God, and like an adopted son to become a sharer in the truth and love which is in God and proceeds from God. It is precisely beside the path of man's eternal election to the dignity of being an adopted child of God that there stands in history the Cross of Christ, the only-begotten Son, who, as "light from light, true God from true God,"[77] came to give the final witness to the wonderful *covenant of God with humanity, of God with man* — every human being. This covenant, as old as man — it goes back to the very mystery of creation — and afterwards many times renewed with

[77] Nicene-Constantinopolitan Creed.

one single chosen people, is equally the new and definitive Covenant, which was established there on Calvary, and is not limited to a single people, to Israel, but is open to each and every individual.

7.6 What else, then, does the Cross of Christ say to us, the Cross that in a sense is the final word of his messianic message and mission? And yet this is not yet the word of the God of the Covenant: that will be pronounced at the dawn when first the women and then the Apostles come to the tomb of the crucified Christ, see the tomb empty and for the first time hear the message "He is risen." They will repeat this message to the others and will be witnesses to the risen Christ. Yet, even in this glorification of the Son of God, the Cross remains, that Cross which — through all the messianic testimony of the Man, the Son, who suffered death upon it — *speaks and never ceases to speak of God the Father, who is absolutely faithful to his eternal love for man,* since he "so loved the world" — therefore man in the world — that "he gave his only Son, that whoever believes in him should not perish but have eternal life."[78] Believing in the crucified Son means "seeing the Father,"[79] means believing that love is present in the world and that this love is more powerful than any kind of evil in which individuals, humanity, or the world are involved. Believing in this love means *believing in mercy.* For mercy is an indispensable dimension of love; it is as it were love's second name and, at the same time, the specific manner in which love is revealed and effected vis-à-vis the reality of the evil that is in the world, affecting and besieging man, insinuating itself even into his heart and capable of causing him to "perish in Gehenna."[80]

Love more powerful than death, more powerful than sin

8.1 The Cross of Christ on Calvary is also a witness to the strength of evil against the very Son of God, against the one who, alone among all the sons of men, was by his nature absolutely innocent and free from sin, and whose coming into the world was untainted by the disobedience of Adam and the inheritance of original sin. And here, precisely in him, in Christ, justice is done to sin at the price of his sacrifice, of his obedience "even to death."[81] He who was without sin, "God made him sin for our sake."[82] Justice is also brought to bear upon death, which from the beginning of man's history had been allied to sin. Death has justice done to it at the price of the death of the one who was without sin and who alone was able — by means of his own death — to inflict

[78] Jn 3:16.
[79] Cf. Jn 14:9.
[80] Mt 10:28.
[81] Phil 2:8.
[82] 2 Cor 5:21.

death upon death.[83] In this way *the Cross of Christ,* on which the Son, consubstantial with the Father, *renders full justice to God,* is also *a radical revelation of mercy,* or rather of the love that goes against what constitutes the very root of evil in the history of man: against sin and death.

8.2 The Cross is the most profound condescension of God to man and to what man — especially in difficult and painful moments — looks on as his unhappy destiny. The Cross is like a touch of eternal love upon the most painful wounds of man's earthly existence; it is the total fulfillment of the messianic program that Christ once formulated in the synagogue at Nazareth[84] and then repeated to the messengers sent by John the Baptist.[85] According to the words once written in the prophecy of Isaiah,[86] this program consisted in the revelation of merciful love for the poor, the suffering and prisoners, for the blind, the oppressed and sinners. In the Paschal Mystery the limits of the many-sided evil in which man becomes a sharer during his earthly existence are surpassed: the Cross of Christ, in fact, makes us understand the deepest roots of evil, which are fixed in sin and death; thus the Cross becomes an eschatological sign. Only in the eschatological fulfillment and definitive renewal of the world *will love conquer, in all the elect, the deepest sources of evil,* bringing as its fully mature fruit the kingdom of life and holiness and glorious immortality. The foundation of this eschatological fulfillment is already contained in the Cross of Christ and in his death. The fact that Christ "was raised the third day"[87] constitutes the final sign of the messianic mission, a sign that perfects the entire revelation of merciful love in a world that is subject to evil. At the same time it constitutes the sign that foretells "a new heaven and a new earth,"[88] when God "will wipe away every tear from their eyes, there will be no more death, or mourning, no crying or pain, for the former things have passed away."[89]

8.3 In the eschatological fulfillment mercy will be revealed as love, while in the temporal phase, in human history, which is at the same time the history of sin and death, love must be revealed above all as mercy and must also be actualized as mercy. Christ's messianic program, the program of mercy, becomes the program of his people, the program of the Church. At its very center there is always the Cross, for it is in the Cross that the revelation of merciful

[83] Cf. 1 Cor 15:54-55.
[84] Cf. Lk 4:18-21.
[85] Cf. Lk 7:20-23.
[86] Cf. Is 35:5, 61:1-3.
[87] 1 Cor 15:4.
[88] Rev 21:1.
[89] Rev 21:4.

love attains its culmination. Until "the former things pass away,"[90] the Cross will remain the point of reference for other words too of the Revelation of John: "Behold, I stand at the door and knock; if anyone hears my voice and opens the door, I will come in and eat with him and he with me."[91] In a special way, God also reveals his mercy when he *invites man to have "mercy" on his only Son, the Crucified One.*

8.4 Christ, precisely as the Crucified One, is the Word that does not pass away,[92] and he is the one who stands at the door and knocks at the heart of every man,[93] without restricting his freedom, but instead seeking to draw from this very freedom love, which is not only an act of solidarity with the suffering Son of man, but also a kind of "mercy" shown by each one of us to the Son of the eternal Father. In the whole of this messianic program of Christ, in the whole revelation of mercy through the Cross, could man's dignity be more highly respected and ennobled, for, in obtaining mercy, he is in a sense the one who at the same time "shows mercy"?

8.5 In a word, is not this the position of Christ with regard to man when he says: "As you did it to one of the least of these . . . you did it to me"?[94] Do not the words of the Sermon on the Mount: "Blessed are the merciful, for they shall obtain mercy,"[95] constitute, in a certain sense, a synthesis of the whole of the Good News, of the whole of the "wonderful exchange" (*admirabile commercium*) contained therein? This exchange is a law of *the very plan of salvation,* a law which is simple, strong and at the same time "easy." Demonstrating from the very start what the "human heart" is capable of ("to be merciful"), do not these words from the Sermon on the Mount reveal in the same perspective the deep mystery of God: that inscrutable unity of Father, Son and Holy Spirit, in which love, containing justice, sets in motion mercy, which in its turn reveals the perfection of justice?

8.6 The Paschal Mystery is Christ at the summit of the revelation of the inscrutable mystery of God. It is precisely then that the words pronounced in the Upper Room are completely fulfilled: "He who has seen me has seen the Father."[96] In fact, Christ, whom the Father "did not spare"[97] for the sake of man and who in his Passion and in the torment of the Cross did not obtain

[90] Cf. Rev 21:4.
[91] Rev 3:20.
[92] Cf. Mt 24:35.
[93] Cf. Rev 3:20.
[94] Mt 25:40.
[95] Mt 5:7.
[96] Jn 14:9.
[97] Rom 8:32.

human mercy, has revealed in his Resurrection the fullness of the love that the Father has for him and, in him, for all people. "He is not God of the dead, but of the living."[98] In his Resurrection Christ *has revealed the God of merciful love,* precisely because *he accepted the Cross as the way to the Resurrection.* And it is for this reason that — when we recall the Cross of Christ, his Passion and death — our faith and hope are centered on the Risen One: on that Christ who "on the evening of that day, the first day of the week, . . . stood among them" in the Upper Room, "where the disciples were, . . . breathed on them, and said to them: 'Receive the Holy Spirit. If you forgive the sins of any, they are forgiven; if you retain the sins of any, they are retained.' "[99]

8.7 Here is the Son of God, who in his Resurrection experienced in a radical way mercy shown to himself, that is to say the love of the Father which is *more powerful than death.* And it is also the same Christ, the Son of God, who at the end of his messianic mission — and, in a certain sense, even beyond the end — reveals himself as the inexhaustible source of mercy, of the same love that, in a subsequent perspective of the history of salvation in the Church, is to be everlastingly confirmed as *more powerful than sin.* The paschal Christ is the definitive incarnation of mercy, its living sign in salvation history and in eschatology. In the same spirit, the liturgy of Eastertide places on our lips the words of the Psalm: *Misericordias Domini in aeternum cantabo.*[100]

Mother of Mercy

9.1 These words of the Church at Easter reecho in the fullness of their prophetic content the words that Mary uttered during her visit to Elizabeth, the wife of Zechariah: "His mercy is . . . from generation to generation."[101] At the very moment of the Incarnation, these words open up a new perspective of salvation history. After the Resurrection of Christ, this perspective is new on both the historical and the eschatological level. From that time onward there is a succession of new generations of individuals in the immense human family, in ever-increasing dimensions; there is also a succession of new generations of the People of God, marked with the sign of the Cross and of the Resurrection and "sealed"[102] with the sign of the Paschal Mystery of Christ, the absolute revelation of the mercy that Mary proclaimed on the threshold of her kinswoman's house: "His mercy is . . . from generation to generation."[103]

[98] Mk 12:27.
[99] Jn 20:19-23.
[100] Cf. Ps 89:1.
[101] Lk 1:50.
[102] Cf. 2 Cor 1:21-22.
[103] Lk 1:50.

9.2 Mary is also the one who obtained mercy in a particular and exceptional way, as no other person has. At the same time, still in an exceptional way, she made possible with the sacrifice of her heart her own sharing in revealing God's mercy. This sacrifice is intimately linked with the Cross of her Son, at the foot of which she was to stand on Calvary. Her sacrifice is a unique sharing in the revelation of mercy, that is, a sharing in the absolute fidelity of God to his own love, to the covenant that he willed from eternity and that he entered into in time with man, with the people, with humanity; it is a sharing in that revelation that was definitively fulfilled through the Cross. *No one has experienced, to the same degree as the Mother of the Crucified One,* the mystery of the Cross, the overwhelming encounter of divine transcendent justice with love: that "kiss" given by mercy to justice.[104] No one has received into his heart, as much as Mary did, that mystery, that truly divine dimension of the redemption effected on Calvary by means of the death of the Son, together with the sacrifice of her maternal heart, together with her definitive "fiat."

9.3 Mary, then, is the one who *has the deepest knowledge of the mystery of God's mercy.* She knows its price, she knows how great it is. In this sense, we call her the *Mother of Mercy:* our Lady of Mercy, or Mother of Divine Mercy; in each one of these titles there is a deep theological meaning, for they express the special preparation of her soul, of her whole personality, so that she was able to perceive, through the complex events, first of Israel, then of every individual and of the whole of humanity, that mercy of which "from generation to generation"[105] people become sharers according to the eternal design of the Most Holy Trinity.

9.4 The above titles which we attribute to the Mother of God speak of her principally, however, as the Mother of the Crucified and Risen One; as *the one who, having obtained mercy in an exceptional way,* in an equally exceptional way *"merits" that mercy* throughout her earthly life and, particularly, at the foot of the Cross of her Son; and finally as the one who, through her hidden and at the same time incomparable sharing in the messianic mission of her Son, was called in a special way to bring close to people that love which he had come to reveal: the love that finds its most concrete expression vis-à-vis the suffering, the poor, those deprived of their own freedom, the blind, the oppressed and sinners, just as Christ spoke of them in the words of the prophecy of Isaiah, first in the synagogue at Nazareth[106] and then in response to the question of the messengers of John the Baptist.[107]

---

[104] Cf. Ps 85:10.
[105] Lk 1:50.
[106] Cf. Lk 4:18.
[107] Cf. Lk 7:22.

9.5 It was precisely this "merciful" love, which is manifested above all in contact with moral and physical evil, that the heart of her who was the Mother of the Crucified and Risen One shared in singularly and exceptionally — that Mary shared in. In her and through her, this love continues to be revealed in the history of the Church and of humanity. This revelation is especially fruitful because in the Mother of God it is based upon the unique tact of her maternal heart, on her particular sensitivity, on her particular fitness to reach all those *who most easily accept the merciful love of a mother*. This is one of the great life-giving mysteries of Christianity, a mystery intimately connected with the mystery of the Incarnation.

9.6 "The motherhood of Mary in the order of grace," as the Second Vatican Council explains, "lasts without interruption from the consent which she faithfully gave at the Annunciation and which she sustained without hesitation under the Cross, until the eternal fulfillment of all the elect. In fact, being assumed into heaven she has not laid aside this office of salvation but by her manifold intercession she continues to obtain for us the graces of eternal salvation. By her maternal charity, she takes care of the brethren of her Son who still journey on earth surrounded by dangers and difficulties, until they are led into their blessed home."[108]

VI

"Mercy . . . from Generation to Generation" (Lk 1:50)

An image of our generation

10.1 We have every right to believe that our generation too was included in the words of the Mother of God when she glorified that mercy shared in "from generation to generation" by those who allow themselves to be guided by the fear of God. The words of Mary's *Magnificat* have a prophetic content that concerns not only the past of Israel but also the whole future of the People of God on earth. In fact, all of us now living on earth are *the generation* that is aware of the approach of the third millennium and that profoundly *feels the change* that is occurring in history.

10.2 The present generation knows that it is in a privileged position: progress provides it with countless possibilities that only a few decades ago were undreamed of. Man's creative activity, his intelligence and his work, have brought

---

[108] Dogmatic Constitution on the Church *Lumen Gentium*, 62: *AAS* 57 (1965), 63.

about profound changes both in the field of science and technology and in that of social and cultural life. Man has extended his power over nature and has acquired deeper knowledge of the laws of social behavior. He has seen the obstacles and distances between individuals and nations dissolve or shrink through an increased sense of what is universal, through a clearer awareness of the unity of the human race, through the acceptance of mutual dependence in authentic solidarity, and through the desire and possibility of making contact with one's brothers and sisters beyond artificial geographical divisions and national or racial limits. Today's young people, especially, know that the progress of science and technology can produce not only new material goods but also a wider sharing in knowledge. The extraordinary progress made in the field of information and data processing, for instance, will increase man's creative capacity and provide access to the intellectual and cultural riches of other peoples. New communications techniques will encourage greater participation in events and a wider exchange of ideas. The achievements of biological, psychological and social science will help man to understand better the riches of his own being. It is true that too often this progress is still the privilege of the industrialized countries, but it cannot be denied that the prospect of enabling every people and every country to benefit from it has long ceased to be a mere utopia when there is a real political desire for it.

10.3 But side by side with all this, or rather as part of it, there are also the difficulties that appear whenever there is growth. There is unease and a sense of powerlessness regarding the profound response that man knows that he must give. The picture of the world today also contains shadows and imbalances that are not always merely superficial. The Pastoral Constitution *Gaudium et Spes* of the Second Vatican Council is certainly not the only document that deals with the life of this generation, but it is a document of particular importance. "The dichotomy affecting the modern world," we read in it, "is, in fact, a symptom of *a deeper dichotomy* that is *in man himself*. He is the meeting point of many conflicting forces. In his condition as a created being he is subject to a thousand shortcomings, but feels untrammeled in his inclinations and destined for a higher form of life. Torn by a welter of anxieties he is compelled to choose between them and repudiate some among them. Worse still, feeble and sinful as he is, he often does the very thing he hates and does not do what he wants. And so he feels himself divided, and the result is a host of discords in social life."[109]

10.4 Toward the end of the introductory exposition we read: ". . . in the

[109] Pastoral Constitution on the Church in the Modern World *Gaudium et Spes*, 10: *AAS* 58 (1966), 1032.

face of modern developments there is a growing body of men who are asking the most fundamental of all questions or are glimpsing them with a keener insight: What is man? *What is the meaning of suffering, evil, death, which have not been eliminated* by all this progress? What is the purpose of these achievements, purchased at so high a price?"[110]

10.5 In the span of the fifteen years since the end of the Second Vatican Council, has this picture of tensions and threats that mark our epoch become less disquieting? It seems not. On the contrary, the tensions and threats that in the Council document seem only to be outlined and not to manifest in depth all the dangers hidden within them have revealed themselves more clearly in the space of these years; they have in a different way confirmed that danger, and do not permit us to cherish the illusions of the past.

Sources of uneasiness

11.1 Thus, in our world the feeling of being under threat is increasing. There is an increase of that existential fear connected especially, as I said in the Encyclical *Redemptor Hominis*, with the prospect of a conflict that in view of today's atomic stockpiles could mean the partial self-destruction of humanity. But the threat does not merely concern what human beings can do to human beings through the means provided by military technology; it also concerns many other dangers produced by a materialistic society which — in spite of "humanistic" declarations — accepts the primacy of things over persons. Contemporary man, therefore, fears that by the use of the means invented by this type of society, *individuals* and the environment, communities, societies and nations *can fall victim to the abuse of power by other* individuals, environments and societies. The history of our century offers many examples of this. In spite of all the declarations on the rights of man in his integral dimension, that is to say in his bodily and spiritual existence, we cannot say that these examples belong only to the past.

11.2 Man rightly fears falling victim to an oppression that will deprive him of his interior freedom, of the possibility of expressing the truth of which he is convinced, of the faith that he professes, of the ability to obey the voice of conscience that tells him the right path to follow. The technical means at the disposal of modern society conceal within themselves not only the possibility of self-destruction through military conflict, but also *the possibility* of a "peaceful" *subjugation of individuals, of environments*, of entire societies and of nations, that for one reason or another might prove inconvenient for those who possess the necessary means and are ready to use them without scruple. An

---

[110] Ibid.

instance is the continued existence of torture, systematically used by authority as a means of domination and political oppression and practiced by subordinates with impunity.

11.3 Together with awareness of the biological threat, therefore, there is a growing awareness of yet another threat, even more destructive of what is essentially human, what is intimately bound up with the dignity of the person and his or her right to truth and freedom.

11.4 All this is happening *against the background of the gigantic remorse* caused by the fact that, side by side with wealthy and surfeited people and societies, living in plenty and ruled by consumerism and pleasure, the same human family contains individuals and groups *that are suffering from hunger.* There are babies dying of hunger under their mothers' eyes. In various parts of the world, in various socioeconomic systems, there exist entire areas of poverty, shortage and underdevelopment. This fact is universally known. *The state of inequality* between individuals and between nations not only still exists; it is increasing. It still happens that side by side with those who are wealthy and living in plenty there exist those who are living in want, suffering misery and often actually dying of hunger; and their number reaches tens, even hundreds of millions. This is why moral uneasiness is destined to become even more acute. It is obvious that a fundamental defect, or rather a series of defects, indeed a defective machinery is at the root of contemporary economics and materialistic civilization, which does not allow the human family to break free from such radically unjust situations.

11.5 This picture of today's world in which there is so much evil both physical and moral, so as to make of it a world entangled in contradictions and tensions, and at the same time full of threats to human freedom, conscience and religion — this picture explains the uneasiness felt by contemporary man. This uneasiness is experienced not only by those who are disadvantaged or oppressed, but also by those who possess the privileges of wealth, progress and power. And, although there is no lack of people trying to understand the causes of this uneasiness, or trying to react against it with the temporary means offered by technology, wealth or power, still in the very depth of the human spirit *this uneasiness is stronger than all temporary means.* This uneasiness concerns — as the analyses of the Second Vatican Council rightly pointed out — the fundamental problems of all human existence. It is linked with the very sense of man's existence in the world, and is an uneasiness for the future of man and all humanity; it demands decisive solutions, which now seem to be forcing themselves upon the human race.

Is justice enough?

12.1 It is not difficult to see that in the modern world *the sense of justice* has been reawakening on a vast scale; and without doubt this emphasizes that which goes against justice in relationships between individuals, social groups and "classes," between individual peoples and States, and finally between whole political systems, indeed between what are called "worlds." This deep and varied trend, at the basis of which the contemporary human conscience has placed justice, gives proof of the ethical character of the tensions and struggles pervading the world.

12.2 *The Church shares with the people of our time* this profound and ardent desire for a life which is just in every aspect, nor does she fail to examine the various aspects of the sort of justice that the life of people and society demands. This is confirmed by the field of Catholic social doctrine, greatly developed in the course of the last century. On the lines of this teaching proceed the education and formation of human consciences in the spirit of justice, and also individual undertakings, especially in the sphere of the apostolate of the laity, which are developing in precisely this spirit.

12.3 And yet, it would be difficult not to notice that very often *programs which start from the idea of justice* and which ought to assist its fulfillment among individuals, groups and human societies, *in practice suffer from distortions.* Although they continue to appeal to the idea of justice, nevertheless experience shows that other negative forces have gained the upper hand over justice, such as spite, hatred and even cruelty. In such cases, the desire to annihilate the enemy, limit his freedom, or even force him into total dependence, becomes the fundamental motive for action; and this contrasts with the essence of justice, which by its nature tends to establish equality and harmony between the parties in conflict. This kind of abuse of the idea of justice and the practical distortion of it show how far human action can *deviate from justice itself,* even when it is being undertaken in the name of justice. Not in vain did Christ challenge his listeners, faithful to the doctrine of the Old Testament, for their attitude which was manifested in the words: "An eye for an eye and a tooth for a tooth."[111] This was the form of distortion of justice at that time; and today's forms continue to be modeled on it. It is obvious, in fact, that in the name of an alleged justice (for example, historical justice or class justice) the neighbor is sometimes destroyed, killed, deprived of liberty or stripped of fundamental human rights. The experience of the past and of our own time demonstrates that justice alone is not enough, that it can even lead to the negation and destruction of itself, if *that deeper power, which is*

---

[111] Mt 5:38.

love, is not allowed to shape human life in its various dimensions. It has been precisely historical experience that, among other things, has led to the formulation of the saying: *summum ius, summa iniuria*. This statement does not detract from the value of justice and does not minimize the significance of the order that is based upon it; it only indicates, under another aspect, the need to draw from the powers of the spirit which condition the very order of justice, powers which are still more profound.

12.4 *The Church*, having before her eyes the picture of the generation to which we belong, *shares the uneasiness of so many of the people of our time.* Moreover, one cannot fail to be worried by *the decline of many fundamental values,* which constitute an unquestionable good not only for Christian morality but simply *for human morality, for moral culture:* these values include respect for human life from the moment of conception, respect for marriage in its indissoluble unity, and respect for the stability of the family. Moral permissiveness strikes especially at this most sensitive sphere of life and society. Hand in hand with this go the crisis of truth in human relationships, lack of responsibility for what one says, the purely utilitarian relationship between individual and individual, the loss of a sense of the authentic common good and the ease with which this good is alienated. Finally, there is the "desacralization" that often turns into "dehumanization": the individual and the society for whom nothing is "sacred" suffer moral decay, in spite of appearances.

VII

The Mercy of God in the Mission of the Church

In connection with this picture of our generation, a picture which cannot fail to cause profound anxiety, there come to mind once more those words which, by reason of the Incarnation of the Son of God, resounded in Mary's *Magnificat*, and which sing of "mercy from generation to generation." The Church of our time, constantly pondering the eloquence of these inspired words, and applying them to the sufferings of the great human family, must become more particularly and profoundly conscious of the need to *bear witness in her whole mission to God's mercy*, following in the footsteps of the tradition of the Old and the New Covenant, and above all of Jesus Christ himself and his Apostles. The Church must bear witness to the mercy of God revealed in Christ, in the whole of his mission as Messiah, *professing it* in the first place as a salvific truth of faith and as necessary for a life in harmony with faith, and then *seeking to introduce it and to make it incarnate in the lives* both of her faithful and as far as possible in the lives of all people of good will. Finally, the Church — professing mercy and remaining always faithful to it — has the right and the duty to call upon the mercy of God, *imploring it* in the face of all the manifestations of physical and moral evil, before all the threats that cloud the whole horizon of the life of humanity today.

The Church professes the mercy of God and proclaims it

13.1 The Church must *profess and proclaim God's mercy in all its truth,* as it has been handed down to us by revelation. We have sought, in the foregoing pages of the present document, to give at least an outline of this truth, which finds such rich expression in the whole of Sacred Scripture and in Sacred Tradition. In the daily life of the Church the truth about the mercy of God, expressed in the Bible, resounds as a perennial echo through the many readings of the Sacred Liturgy. The authentic sense of faith of the People of God perceives this truth, as is shown by various expressions of personal and community piety. It would of course be difficult to give a list or summary of them all, since most of them are vividly inscribed in the depths of people's hearts and minds. Some theologians affirm that mercy is the greatest of the attributes and perfections of God, and the Bible, Tradition and the whole faith life of the People of God provide particular proofs of this. It is not a question here of the perfection of the inscrutable essence of God in the mystery of the divinity itself, but of the perfection and attribute whereby man, in the intimate truth of his existence, encounters the living God particularly closely and particularly often. In harmony with Christ's words to Philip,[112] the "vision of the Father" — a vision of God through faith — finds precisely in the encounter with his mercy a unique moment of interior simplicity and truth, similar to that which we discover in the parable of the prodigal son.

13.2 "He who has seen me has seen the Father."[113] The Church professes the mercy of God, the Church lives by it in her wide experience of faith and also in her teaching, constantly contemplating Christ, concentrating on him, on his life and on his Gospel, on his Cross and Resurrection, on his whole mystery. Everything that forms the "vision" of Christ in the Church's living faith and teaching brings us nearer to the "vision of the Father" in the holiness of his mercy. The Church seems in a particular way to profess the mercy of God and to venerate it when she directs herself to the Heart of Christ. In fact, it is precisely this drawing close to Christ in the mystery of his Heart which

[112] Cf. Jn 14:9-10.
[113] Jn 14:9.

enables us to dwell on this point — a point in a sense central and also most accessible on the human level — of the revelation of the merciful love of the Father, a revelation which constituted the central content of the messianic mission of the Son of Man.

13.3 *The Church* lives an authentic life when she *professes and proclaims mercy* — the most stupendous attribute of the Creator and of the Redeemer — and when she brings people close to the sources of the Savior's mercy, of which she is the trustee and dispenser. Of great significance in this area is constant meditation on the word of God, and above all conscious and mature participation in *the Eucharist* and *in the Sacrament of Penance or Reconciliation.* The Eucharist brings us ever nearer to that *love* which is more powerful than death: "For as often as we eat this bread and drink this cup," we proclaim not only the death of the Redeemer but also his Resurrection, "until he comes" in glory.[114] The same Eucharistic rite, celebrated in memory of him who in his messianic mission revealed the Father to us by means of his words and his Cross, attests to the inexhaustible *love* by virtue of which he desires always to be united with us and present in our midst, coming to meet every human heart. It is the Sacrament of Penance or Reconciliation that prepares the way for each individual, even those weighed down with great faults. In this sacrament each person can experience mercy in a unique way, that is, the love which is more powerful than sin. This has already been spoken of in the Encyclical *Redemptor Hominis;* but it will be fitting to return once more to this fundamental theme.

13.4 It is precisely because sin exists in the world, which "God so loved . . . that he gave his only Son,"[115] that God, who "is love,"[116] *cannot reveal himself otherwise* than as mercy. This corresponds not only to the most profound truth of that love which God is, but also to the whole interior truth of man and of the world which is man's temporary homeland.

13.5 Mercy in itself, as a perfection of the infinite God, is also infinite. Also infinite therefore and inexhaustible is the Father's readiness to receive the prodigal children who return to his home. *Infinite are the readiness and power of forgiveness* which flow continually from the marvelous value of the sacrifice of the Son. No human sin can prevail over this power or even limit it. On the part of man only a lack of good will can limit it, a lack of readiness to be converted and to repent, in other words persistence in obstinacy, opposing grace and truth, especially in the face of the witness of the Cross and Resurrection of Christ.

---

[114] Cf. 1 Cor 11:26; acclamation in the Roman Missal.
[115] Jn 3:16.
[116] 1 Jn 4:8.

13.6 Therefore, the Church professes and proclaims conversion. Conversion to God always consists in *discovering his mercy*, that is, in discovering that love which is patient and kind[117] as only the Creator and Father can be; the love to which the "God and Father of our Lord Jesus Christ"[118] is faithful to the uttermost consequences in the history of his covenant with man; even to the Cross and to the death and Resurrection of the Son. Conversion to God is always the fruit of the "rediscovery" of this Father, who is rich in mercy.

13.7 Authentic knowledge of the God of mercy, the God of tender love, is a constant and inexhaustible source of conversion, not only as a momentary interior act but also as a permanent attitude, as a state of mind. Those who come to know God in this way, who "see" him in this way, can live only in a state of being continually converted to him. They live, therefore, *in statu conversionis;* and it is this state of conversion which marks out the most profound element of the pilgrimage of every man and woman on earth *in statu viatoris*. It is obvious that the Church professes the mercy of God, revealed in the crucified and risen Christ, not only by the word of her teaching but above all through the deepest pulsation of the life of the whole People of God. By means of this testimony of life, the Church fulfills the mission proper to the People of God, the mission which is a sharing in and, in a sense, a continuation of the messianic mission of Christ himself.

13.8 The contemporary Church is profoundly conscious that only on the basis of the mercy of God will she be able to carry out the tasks that derive from the teaching of the Second Vatican Council, and, in the first place, the ecumenical task which aims at uniting all those who confess Christ. As she makes many efforts in this direction, the Church confesses with humility that only that *love* which is more powerful than the weakness of human divisions *can definitively bring about that unity* which Christ implored from the Father and which the Spirit never ceases to beseech for us "with sighs too deep for words."[119]

The Church seeks to put mercy into practice

14.1 Jesus Christ taught that man not only receives and experiences the mercy of God, but that he is also called "to practice mercy" toward others: "Blessed are the merciful, for they shall obtain mercy."[120] The Church sees in these words a call to action, and she tries to practice mercy. All the Beatitudes of the Sermon on the Mount indicate the way of conversion and of reform of

[117] Cf. 1 Cor 13:4.
[118] 2 Cor 1:3.
[119] Rom 8:26.
[120] Mt 5:7.

life, but the one referring to those who are merciful is particularly eloquent in this regard. Man attains to the merciful love of God, his mercy, to the extent that he himself is interiorly transformed in the spirit of that love toward his neighbor.

14.2 This authentically evangelical process is not just a spiritual transformation realized once and for all: it is a whole lifestyle, an essential and continuous characteristic of the Christian vocation. It consists in the constant discovery and persevering practice of *love as a unifying and also elevating power* despite all difficulties of a psychological or social nature: it is a question, in fact, of a *merciful love* which, by its essence, is a creative love. In reciprocal relationships between persons merciful love is never a unilateral act or process. Even in the cases in which everything would seem to indicate that only one party is giving and offering, and the other only receiving and taking (for example, in the case of a physician giving treatment, a teacher teaching, parents supporting and bringing up their children, a benefactor helping the needy), in reality the one who gives is always also a beneficiary. In any case, he too can easily find himself in the position of the one who receives, who obtains a benefit, who experiences merciful love; he too can find himself the object of mercy.

14.3 In this sense *Christ* crucified is for us the loftiest model, inspiration and encouragement. When we base ourselves on this *disquieting model,* we are able with all humility to show mercy to others, knowing that Christ accepts it as if it were shown to himself.[121] On the basis of this model, we must also continually purify all our actions and all our intentions in which mercy is understood and practiced in a unilateral way, as a good done to others. An act of merciful love is only really such when we are deeply convinced at the moment that we perform it that we are at the same time receiving mercy from the people who are accepting it from us. If this bilateral and reciprocal quality is absent, our actions are not yet true acts of mercy, nor has there yet been fully completed in us that conversion to which Christ has shown us the way by his words and example, even to the Cross, nor are we yet sharing fully in the *magnificent source of merciful love* that has been revealed to us by him.

14.4 Thus, the way which Christ showed to us in the Sermon on the Mount with the Beatitude regarding those who are merciful is much richer than what we sometimes find in ordinary human opinions about mercy. These opinions see mercy as a unilateral act or process, presupposing and maintaining a certain distance between the one practicing mercy and the one benefitting from it, between the one who does good and the one who receives it. Hence the

---

[121] Cf. Mt 25:34-40.

attempt to free interpersonal and social relationships from mercy and to base them solely on justice. However, such opinions about mercy fail to see the fundamental link between mercy and justice spoken of by the whole biblical tradition, and above all by the messianic mission of Jesus Christ. *True mercy is, so to speak, the most profound source of justice.* If justice is in itself suitable for "arbitration" between people concerning the reciprocal distribution of objective goods in an equitable manner, love and only love (including that kindly love that we call "mercy") is capable of restoring man to himself.

14.5 *Mercy* that is truly Christian is also, in a certain sense, *the most perfect incarnation* of "equality" between people, and therefore also the most perfect incarnation of *justice* as well, insofar as justice aims at the same result in its own sphere. However, the equality brought by justice is limited to the realm of objective and extrinsic goods, while love and mercy bring it about that people meet one another in that value which is man himself, with the dignity that is proper to him. At the same time, "equality" of people through "patient and kind" love[122] does not take away differences: the person who gives becomes more generous when he feels at the same time benefitted by the person accepting his gift; and vice versa, the person who accepts the gift with the awareness that, in accepting it, he too is doing good is in his own way serving the great cause of the dignity of the person; and this contributes to uniting people in a more profound manner.

14.6 Thus, mercy becomes an indispensable element for *shaping* mutual relationships between people, in a spirit of deepest respect for what is human, and in a spirit of mutual brotherhood. It is impossible to establish this bond between people, if they wish to regulate their mutual relationships solely according to the measure of justice. In every sphere of interpersonal relationships justice must, *so to speak, be "corrected" to a considerable extent* by that love which, as Saint Paul proclaims, "is patient and kind" or, in other words, possesses the characteristics of that *merciful love* which is so much of the essence of the Gospel and Christianity. Let us remember, furthermore, that *merciful love* also means the cordial *tenderness and sensitivity* so eloquently spoken of in the parable of the prodigal son,[123] and also in the parables of the lost sheep and the lost coin.[124] Consequently, merciful love is supremely indispensable between those who are closest to one another: between husbands and wives, between parents and children, between friends; and it is indispensable in education and in pastoral work.

[122] Cf. 1 Cor 13:4.
[123] Cf. Lk 15:11-32.
[124] Cf. Lk 15:1-10.

14.7 Its sphere of action, however, is not limited to this. If Paul VI more than once indicated the "civilization of love"[125] as the goal toward which all efforts in the cultural and social fields as well as in the economic and political fields should tend, it must be added that this good will never be reached if in our thinking and acting concerning the vast and complex spheres of human society we stop at the criterion of "an eye for an eye, a tooth for a tooth"[126] and do not try to transform it in its essence, by complementing it with another spirit. Certainly, the Second Vatican Council also leads us in this direction, when it speaks repeatedly of the need *to make the world more human*,[127] and says that the realization of this task is precisely the mission of the Church in the modern world. Society can become ever more human only if we introduce into the many-sided setting of interpersonal and social relationships, not merely justice, but also that "merciful love" which constitutes the messianic message of the Gospel.

14.8 Society can become "ever more human" only when we introduce into all the mutual relationships which form its moral aspect the moment of forgiveness, which is so much of the essence of the Gospel. Forgiveness demonstrates the presence in the world of *the love which is more powerful than sin.* Forgiveness is also the fundamental condition for reconciliation, not only in the relationship of God with man, but also in relationships between people. A world from which forgiveness was eliminated would be nothing but a world of cold and unfeeling justice, in the name of which each person would claim his or her own rights vis-à-vis others; the various kinds of selfishness latent in man would transform life and human society into a system of oppression of the weak by the strong, or into an arena of permanent strife between one group and another.

14.9 For this reason, the Church must consider it one of her principal duties — at every stage of history and especially in our modern age — *to proclaim and to introduce into life* the mystery of mercy, supremely revealed in Jesus Christ. Not only for the Church herself as the community of believers but also in a certain sense for all humanity, this mystery is the *source* of a life different from the life which can be built by man, who is exposed to the oppressive forces of the threefold concupiscence active within him.[128] It is pre-

---

[125] Cf. Homily for the Closing of the Holy Year (December 25, 1975): *Insegnamenti* XIII (1975), 1568.

[126] Mt 5:38.

[127] Cf. Pastoral Constitution on the Church in the Modern World *Gaudium et Spes*, 40: *AAS* 58 (1966), 1057-1059; Paul VI, Apostolic Exhortation *Paterna cum Benevolentia* (December 8, 1974), in particular, 1, 6: *AAS* 67 (1975), 7-9, 17-23.

[128] Cf. 1 Jn 2:16.

cisely in the name of this mystery that Christ teaches us to forgive always. How often we repeat the words of the prayer which he himself taught us, asking "*forgive us* our trespasses *as we forgive* those who trespass against us," which means those who are guilty of something in our regard![129] It is indeed difficult to express the profound value of the attitude which these words describe and inculcate. How many things these words say to every individual about others and also about himself! The consciousness of being trespassers against each other goes hand in hand with the call to fraternal solidarity, which Saint Paul expressed in his concise exhortation to "forbear one another in love."[130] What a lesson of humility is to be found here with regard to man, with regard both to one's neighbor and to oneself! What a school of good will for daily living, in the various conditions of our existence! If we were to ignore this lesson, what would remain of any "humanist" program of life and education?

14.10 Christ emphasizes so insistently the need to forgive others that when Peter asked him how many times he should forgive his neighbor he answered with the symbolic number of "seventy times seven,"[131] meaning that he must be able to forgive everyone every time. It is obvious that such a generous requirement of *forgiveness does not cancel out* the objective *requirements of justice*. Properly understood, justice constitutes, so to speak, the goal of forgiveness. In no passage of the Gospel message does forgiveness, or mercy as its source, mean indulgence toward evil, toward scandals, toward injury or insult. In any case, reparation for evil and scandal, compensation for injury, and satisfaction for insult are conditions for forgiveness.

14.11 Thus the fundamental structure of justice always enters into the sphere of mercy. Mercy, however, has the power to confer on justice a new content, which is expressed most simply and fully in forgiveness. Forgiveness, in fact, shows that, over and above the process of "compensation" and "truce" which is specific to justice, love is necessary, so that man may affirm himself as man. Fulfillment of the conditions of justice is especially indispensable in order that love may reveal its own nature. In analyzing the parable of the prodigal son, we have already called attention to the fact that *he who forgives and he who is forgiven* encounter one another at an essential point, namely the dignity or essential value of the person, a point which cannot be lost and the affirmation of which, or its rediscovery, is a source of the greatest joy.[132]

---

[129] Mt 6:12.
[130] Eph 4:2; cf. Gal 6:2.
[131] Mt 18:22.
[132] Cf. Lk 15:32.

14.12 The Church rightly considers it her duty and the purpose of her mission *to guard the authenticity of forgiveness*, both in life and behavior and in educational and pastoral work. She protects it simply by guarding its *source*, which is the mystery of the mercy of God himself as revealed in Jesus Christ.

14.13 The basis of the Church's mission, in all the spheres spoken of in the numerous pronouncements of the most recent Council and in the centuries-old experience of the apostolate, is none other than "drawing from the wells of the Savior":[133] this is what provides many guidelines for the mission of the Church in the lives of individual Christians, of individual communities, and also of the whole People of God. This "drawing from the wells of the Savior" can be done only in the spirit of that poverty to which we are called by the words and example of the Lord: "You received without pay, give without pay."[134] Thus, in all the ways of the Church's life and ministry — through the evangelical poverty of her ministers and stewards and of the whole people which bears witness to "the mighty works" of its Lord — the God who is "rich in mercy" has been made still more clearly manifest.

VIII

The Prayer of the Church in Our Times

The Church appeals to the mercy of God

15.1 The Church proclaims the truth of God's mercy revealed in the crucified and risen Christ, and she professes it in various ways. Furthermore, she seeks to practice mercy toward people through people, and she sees in this an indispensable condition for solicitude for a better and "more human" world, today and tomorrow. However, at no time and in no historical period — especially at a moment as critical as our own — can the Church forget *the prayer that is a cry for the mercy of God* amid the many forms of evil which weigh upon humanity and threaten it. Precisely this is the fundamental right and duty of the Church in Christ Jesus, her right and duty toward God and toward humanity. The more the human conscience succumbs to secularization, loses its sense of the very meaning of the word "mercy," moves away from God and distances itself from the mystery of mercy, the more *the Church has the right and the duty* to appeal to the God of mercy "with loud cries."[135] These

---

[133] Cf. Is 12:3.
[134] Mt 10:8.
[135] Cf. Heb 5:7.

"loud cries" should be the mark of the Church of our times, cries uttered to God to implore his mercy, the certain manifestation of which she professes and proclaims as having already come in Jesus crucified and risen, that is, in the Paschal Mystery. It is this mystery which bears within itself the most complete revelation of mercy, that is, of that love which is more powerful than death, more powerful than sin and every evil, the love which lifts man up when he falls into the abyss and frees him from the greatest threats.

15.2 Modern man feels these threats. What has been said above in this regard is only a rough outline. Modern man often anxiously wonders about the solution to the terrible tensions which have built up in the world and which entangle humanity. And if at times he *lacks the courage to utter the word "mercy,"* or if in his conscience empty of religious content he does not find the equivalent, *so much greater is the need for the Church to utter this word,* not only in her own name but also in the name of all the men and women of our time.

15.3 Everything that I have said in the present document on mercy should therefore *be continually transformed into an ardent prayer:* into a cry that implores mercy according to the needs of man in the modern world. *May this cry be full of that truth about mercy* which has found such rich expression in Sacred Scripture and in Tradition, as also in the authentic life of faith of countless generations of the People of God. With this cry let us, like the sacred writers, call upon the God who cannot despise anything that he has made,[136] the God who is faithful to himself, to his fatherhood and his love. And, like the Prophets, let us appeal to that love which has maternal characteristics and which, like a mother, follows each of her children, each lost sheep, even if they should number millions, even if in the world evil should prevail over goodness, even if contemporary humanity should deserve a new "flood" on account of its sins, as once the generation of Noah did. Let us have recourse to that fatherly love revealed to us by Christ in his messianic mission, a love which reached its culmination in his Cross, in his death and Resurrection. Let us have recourse to God through Christ, mindful of the words of Mary's *Magnificat,* which proclaim mercy "from generation to generation." Let us implore God's mercy for the present generation. May the Church which, following the example of Mary, also seeks to be the spiritual mother of mankind, express in this prayer her maternal solicitude and at the same time her confident love, that love from which is born the most burning need for prayer.

15.4 Let us offer up our *petitions, directed by the faith, by the hope, and by*

---

[136] Cf. Wis 11:24; Ps 145:9; Gen 1:31.

the charity which Christ has planted in our hearts. This attitude is likewise love of God, whom modern man has sometimes separated far from himself, made extraneous to himself, proclaiming in various ways that God is "superfluous." This is, therefore, *love of God,* the insulting rejection of whom by modern man we feel profoundly, and we are ready to cry out with Christ on the Cross: "Father, forgive them; for they know not what they do."[137] At the same time it is *love of people,* of all men and women without any exception or division: without difference of race, culture, language, or world outlook, without distinction between friends and enemies. This is love for people — it desires every true good for each individual and for every human community, every family, every nation, every social group, for young people, adults, parents, the elderly — a love for everyone, without exception. This is love, or rather an anxious solicitude to ensure for each individual every true good and to remove and drive away every sort of evil.

15.5 And, if any of our contemporaries do not share the faith and hope which lead me, as a servant of Christ and steward of the mysteries of God,[138] to implore God's mercy for humanity in this hour of history, let them at least try to understand *the reason for my concern. It is dictated by love for man,* for all that is human and which, according to the intuitions of many of our contemporaries, is threatened by an immense danger. The mystery of Christ, which reveals to us the great vocation of man and which led me to emphasize in the Encyclical *Redemptor Hominis* his incomparable dignity, also obliges me to proclaim mercy as God's merciful love, revealed in that same mystery of Christ. It likewise obliges me to have recourse to that mercy and to beg for it at this difficult, critical phase of the history of the Church and of the world, as we approach the end of the second millennium.

15.6 In the name of Jesus Christ crucified and risen, in the spirit of his messianic mission, enduring in the history of humanity, *we raise our voices and pray* that the Love which is in the Father may once again be revealed at this stage of history, and that, through the work of the Son and Holy Spirit, it may be shown to be present in our modern world and to be more powerful than evil: more powerful than sin and death. We pray for this through the intercession of her who does not cease to proclaim "mercy . . . from generation to generation," and also through the intercession of those for whom there have been completely fulfilled the words of the Sermon on the Mount: "Blessed are the merciful, for they shall obtain mercy."[139]

[137] Lk 23:34.
[138] Cf. 1 Cor 4:1.
[139] Mt 5:7.

* * *

15.7 In continuing the great task of implementing the Second Vatican Council, in which we can rightly see a new phase of the self-realization of the Church — in keeping with the epoch in which it has been our destiny to live — the *Church* herself must be constantly guided by the full consciousness that in this work it is not permissible for her, for any reason, to withdraw into herself. *The reason* for her *existence* is, in fact, *to reveal God,* that Father who allows us to "see" him in Christ.[140] No matter how strong the resistance of human history may be, no matter how marked the diversity of contemporary civilization, no matter how great the denial of God in the human world, so much the greater must be the Church's closeness to that mystery which, hidden for centuries in God, was then truly shared with man, in time, through Jesus Christ.

15.8 With my Apostolic Blessing.

Given in Rome, at Saint Peter's, on the thirtieth day of November, the First Sunday of Advent, in the year 1980, the third of the Pontificate.

[140] Cf. Jn 14:9.

Laborem Exercens

Editor's Introduction

Fascinated as he is by commemorative events, Pope John Paul II marked the ninetieth anniversary of Leo XIII's *Rerum Novarum* (1891) by publishing his first social encyclical, *Laborem Exercens*, on September 14, 1981.[1] Before him, Pius XI in *Quadragesimo Anno* (1931), John XXIII in *Mater et Magistra* (1961), and Paul VI in *Octogesima Adveniens* (1971) had observed the anniversary of Leo's ground-breaking encyclical with documents of their own.

Laborem Exercens is a very personal document. The encyclical has solid roots in the Pope's own experience as a worker. It reflects his familiarity with various worlds of work: in mines and factories, in artistic and literary production, in scholarship and pastoral ministry. More particularly, *Laborem Exercens* has its origins in the long debate carried on by the Archbishop of Kracow with Marxist intellectuals. The topics chosen, which include the struggle between capital and labor, ownership of the means of production, and solidarity, as well as the terminology of the encyclical, bear ample witness to this background of controversy. Here, however, he is less concerned with economic systems than with the human person as a "worker." Furthermore, John Paul intended his letter to encourage the Solidarity union movement, which in the early 1980s was the primary motor for effecting social and political change in a Poland under a totalitarian regime.

The style of encyclical is distinctively Wojtylan. It reveals the Pope's preference for combining a phenomenological description of experience with philosophical-theological meditation. While he cites the Second Vatican Council's *Gaudium et Spes*, John Paul never directly quotes from any previous social encyclical, not even from *Rerum Novarum*. The encyclical's footnotes are almost entirely biblical, indicating that its primary inspiration is Sacred Scripture. As in his two previous encyclicals, *Redemptor Hominis* (1979) and *Dives in Misericordia* (1980), the Pope relies heavily upon the plastic and descriptive language of the Bible, especially from the opening chapters of Genesis, to develop his theme. The encyclical unfolds the meaning of the human vocation to work in light of the biblical text on "subduing the earth" (cf. Gen 1:28). This call to exercise dominion is to be carried out by those created "in the image of God" (Gen 1:27) through their work, which the Pope qualifies as *"one of the characteristics that distinguish* man from the rest of creatures" (preface).

[1] *Acta Apostolicae Sedis*, 73 (1981), 577-647.

Unlike earlier social encyclicals which dealt with a wide range of different questions, *Laborem Exercens* is sharply focused. John Paul chooses a very specific theme — the dignity and role of human work — and explores its many ramifications: "Through work man must earn his daily bread and contribute to the continual advance of science and technology and, above all, to elevating unceasingly the cultural and moral level of the society within which he lives in community with those who belong to the same family" (preface). At the present moment, he believes, the world is faced with important choices. It is "on the eve of new developments in technological, economic, and political conditions which, according to many experts, will influence the world of work and production no less than the industrial revolution of the last century" (§1.3).

A crisis in the meaning of human work is a crucial factor contributing to society's current plight. "Work, as human issue, is at the very center of the 'social question'" (§2.1). Moreover, the Pope adds, "human work is *a key*, probably *the essential key*, to the whole social question" (§3.2). It is a problem with ramifications which extend beyond the so-called "working class"; the dimensions of the crisis are universal. Therefore he does not confine his encyclical to a reflection on the work only of industrial or agricultural workers. Instead, he extends it to encompass the work done by every sector of society: management, white-collar workers, scientists, intellectuals, artists, women in the home. "Each and every individual, to the proper extent and in an incalculable number of ways, takes part in the giant process whereby man 'subdues the earth' through his work" (§4.4). To use a favorite expression of the Pope's, the world's "workbench" includes all those who labor for their daily bread — all men and women.

As in his two previous encyclicals, John Paul takes up the "way" of the human person, this time with regard to his fundamental activity of work. *Laborem Exercens* is yet another chapter in the Pope's book on Christian anthropology. Moreover, since work is a great gift and good for humanity, his tone throughout the encyclical is constructive and exhortatory.

Summary

The encyclical straightforwardly develops the Pope's "Gospel of work" in five chapters. The "Introduction" (§§1-3) gives the reasons for writing the encyclical and situates *Rerum Novarum* within the developing tradition of Catholic social doctrine. Chapter two, "Work and Man" (§§4-10), discusses the meaning of work by drawing on biblical teaching and describes the consequences of understanding work in a "subjective" sense. In chapter three, "Conflict between Labor and Capital in the Present Phase of History" (§§11-15), John Paul explains why the worker has priority over capital, and in chapter four, "Rights of Workers" (§§16-23), he outlines the human rights which work must foster and guarantee. Chapter five, "Elements for a Spirituality of Work" (§§24-27), relates how work enters into God's saving design for human beings who through it share in the activity of the Creator and Redeemer.

The introduction situates the encyclical's theme in the light of the ninetieth anniversary of *Rerum Novarum,* but the Pope makes it clear that his document is neither a commentary nor a contemporary updating of Leo XIII's teaching. John Paul mentions "the fresh questions and problems" which call into question the dignity of work (§1.2). Whereas earlier Church teaching concentrated on the "worker question" within individual nations, today the issue at stake is more fundamental, touching basic questions of Christian anthropology. This new situation "calls for the discovery of the *new meanings of human work*" (§2.1). The Pope concludes that the gradual solution to the social question must be sought in efforts to "make life more human." In this framework, "the key, namely human work, acquires fundamental and decisive importance" (§3.2).

Dignity of the worker

Chapter two contains the encyclical's most theologically dense and intellectually challenging section. It describes the theological and anthropological foundations of the dignity of work and of the worker.

The Church's conviction that "work is a fundamental dimension of man's existence on earth" (§4.1) stems from *"the very first pages of the Book of Genesis"* (§4.2). In the original covenant which God established with humanity at creation, he called man and woman to share in "subduing the earth" (cf. Gen 1:28). Created in the image of God, they express their dignity and liberty through work: "In carrying out this mandate, man, every human being, reflects the very action of the Creator of the universe" (§4.2). The Pope says in a later section that "man ought to imitate God, his Creator, in working, because man alone has the unique characteristic of likeness to God" (§25.3).

John Paul introduces a distinction between the "objective" and "subjective" meaning of work, a distinction which he employs throughout the encyclical. In its "objective" sense, work refers to the multiple activities, resources, and instruments which people use to produce the "objects" of their work: from agricultural and manufactured goods, to artistic and scientific productions, to services. All of these constitute the "objective" work that is done.

In its "subjective" sense, work refers to *who* does it, to workers themselves. Crucial to the Pope's theology of work is his affirmation that *"as a person, man is therefore the subject of work*. As a person he works, he performs various actions belonging to the work process; independently of their objective content, these actions must all serve to realize his humanity, to fulfill the calling to be a person that is his by reason of his very humanity" (§6.2). At the center of John Paul's thought is the dignity of the worker. Work, therefore, has an intrinsic value because it has man or woman as its subject.

For this reason work is also a spiritual activity that has consequences for a person's interior life. The ethical dimensions of work are "linked to the fact that the one who carries it out is a person" (§6.3). Individuals are the "subject" of work. This subjectivity is what gives all work its true value. "Work is 'for man,'" says the Pope succinctly, "and not man 'for work'" (§6.6). The primacy of the person, of the worker over work, can never be compromised.

John Paul then describes the abuses which occur when the priority due to the subjective meaning of work is ignored. Any socioeconomic system which regards work "as a special kind of 'merchandise,' or as an impersonal 'force' needed for production" (§7.2), reverses the order decreed by God. Whether capitalist or collectivist, a society which accords primary importance to the objective sense of work undermines an authentic anthropology. Such a society fails to recognize that the person "ought to be treated as the effective subject of work and its true maker and creator" (§7.3), independently of the work done. In the last century, industrialization produced *"the degradation of man as the subject of work"* (§8.2). This situation led to worker solidarity as a way of protecting the dignity and rights of labor. The twentieth century has not fared much better. Different ideological systems, the Pope says, *"have allowed flagrant injustices to persist or have created new ones"* (§8.4).

Because work has this profound subjective meaning, it is closely linked to personal and social moral values. Despite its arduousness, work manifests and expands human dignity. Work is good not only because it transforms nature but even more because it is the means by which a person *"achieves fulfillment* as a human being and indeed, in a sense, becomes 'more a human being'"* (§9.3). Besides working for themselves, people also ought to work because of their concern for others. Work provides the "foundation for the formation of family life" (§10.1) and enriches society and culture, adding "to the heritage of the whole human family, of all the people living in the world" (§10.3).

Priority of labor

In chapter three of *Laborem Exercens*, John Paul takes up the classical problem of the conflict between labor and capital. He describes the historical origins of this conflict and the ideological struggle between Marxism and liberalism to which it gave birth. Then he interprets the conflict in ethical terms, recalling "a principle that has always been taught by the Church: *the principle of the priority of labor over capital*" (§12.1). Why does labor enjoy this priority? In the process of production the Pope sees labor — the worker — always as a "primary *efficient cause*, while capital, the whole collection of the means of production, remains a mere *instrument* or instrumental cause" (§12.1, cf. §12.5). Capital is "the result of work and bears the signs of human labor" (§12.5). As the objective dimension of work, capital is meant to serve the subjective dimension: the worker. This way of describing the relationship between capital and labor restates and applies the principle of "the primacy of man in the production process, *the primacy of man over things*" (§12.6).

From this truth, "which is part of the abiding heritage of the Church's teaching" (§12.6), John Paul draws several conclusions. First, capital should not be opposed to labor, nor labor to capital. Unfortunately, recent history reflects just such an opposition. With the advent of industrialization, labor was separated from capital and treated as an objective commodity. The Pope calls this separation the error of economism, that is, "considering human labor solely according to its economic purpose" (§13.3). Whenever work is objectified in this way, the error of materialism, whether theoretical or practical, takes hold. Whatever its form, materialism disregards the Church's conviction of "the primacy of the person over things, and of *human labor over capital*" (§13.5).

According to the encyclical, the priority of labor over capital also has ramifications for how the ownership of property is to be understood. The Pope reaffirms classical Church teaching on the person's right to private property, a teaching which diverges from the collectivism of Marxism and the capitalism of liberalism. He adds, however, that the "Christian tradition has never upheld this right as absolute and untouchable. On the contrary, it has always understood this right within the broader context of the right common to all to use the goods of the whole of creation: *the right to private property is subordinated to the right to common use*, to the fact that goods are meant for everyone" (§14.2). Property, including the means of production which comprise capital, is acquired through work and is meant to serve work in the "subjective" sense. The purpose of property is to foster individual freedom and creativity.

Whether individuals, groups, or even the State own the means of production is less important than the principle that ownership is to promote the subjective dimension of work. Property should be at the service of persons. The worker ought to take part in the productive process "as a sharer in responsibility and creativity at the workbench to which he applies himself" (§15.1). The priority of labor over capital as "a postulate of the order of social morality" (§15.1) can only be realized in an economic system that recognizes the subjectivity of workers. A system implements this principle by encouraging participation in decision-making and a just sharing in the goods produced. Consequently, an economic system is judged ethically according to the extent to which it recognizes and fosters the primacy of the subjective over the objective dimension of work.

Workers' rights

Chapter four deals with work as a source of several specific human rights. Within the broad framework of human rights, work is "a source of rights on the part of the *worker*" (§16.1).

In order to clarify the precise rights of workers, John Paul introduces a distinction between the "direct" and the "indirect" employer. He describes the direct employer as "the person or institution with whom the worker enters directly into a work contract in accordance with definite conditions" (§16.5). The Pope, however, directs most of his attention to the indirect employer; that is, to the "many different factors . . . that exercise a determining influence on the shaping both of the work contract and, consequently, of just or unjust relationships in the field of human labor" (§16.5). This latter category includes the people, institutions, and principles of conduct which in any way affect workers and working conditions. As a primary instrument in formulating labor policy, the State is a key indirect employer. But so, too, are multinational organizations and the many international bodies which have an impact on both the direct employer and the worker. While the duties of direct employers to workers are readily admitted, the Pope wishes to raise the awareness of indirect employers to their responsibilities. They too have duties to workers, precisely because of their decisive role in shaping "just or unjust relationships in the field of human labor" (§16.5). The responsibilities of an indirect employer entail "respect for the objective rights of the worker . . . [which] must constitute *the adequate and fundamental criterion* for shaping the whole economy" (§17.4).

The Pope then describes certain fundamental rights of workers, including the right to employment, just remuneration, social benefits, free association, and the right to strike.

A person's obligation to work, which derives from the created order, also entails the right to do so. Since work is intimately related to human dignity, John Paul pays special attention to the issue of the *"suitable employment for all who are capable of it"* (§18.1). He exhorts indirect employers to take two practical steps: *"to act against unemployment,* which in all cases is an evil"; and to provide unemployment benefits, which is "a duty springing from the fundamental principle of the moral order in this sphere, namely the principle of the common use of goods or, to put it in another and still simpler way, the right to life and subsistence" (§18.1). Making employment available safeguards the individual's inalienable right to work. The obligation to provide employment is not limited to individual countries but now must be broadened to include indirect employers at the world-wide level. Only by means of international collaboration can the "scourge of unemployment" be overcome (§8.6).

Laborem Exercens also mentions that "a just wage is the concrete means of *verifying the justice* of the whole socioeconomic system" (§19.2). It is the way of carrying out in practice "the first principle of the whole ethical and social order, namely, *the principle of the common use of goods"* (§19.2). Here the encyclical also states that workers have the right to a family wage, social benefits, which include health care, regular weekly rest comprising at least Sunday, and an annual vacation.

John Paul next defends the right of workers to form associations, "movements of solidarity in the sphere of work" (§8.5). The purpose of such groups is to protect the just rights of labor. These organizations, which are not restricted to industrial workers, are *"a mouthpiece for the struggle for social justice"* (§20.3). In other words, they aim to foster the subjective sense of work, so that "workers will not only *have* more" but will also "realize their humanity more fully in every respect" (§20.6).

Movements of workers should be open to dialogue and cooperation with others. They are not agents of class struggle, "against others"; instead, their vocation is to promote justice in the workplace. The Pope insists, moreover, that work is a force which unites people. Its contribution to society consists in its "power to build a community" (§20.3), a community of work and solidarity. Consequently, the right to form unions is not a right to group or class egoism or to "play politics." The specific role of these associations must always be respected: "to secure the just rights of workers within the framework of the common good of the whole of society" (§20.5). Within just limits, the right to strike is a legitimate, if extreme, means for workers to defend and further their rights. This right, however, must not be abused, especially for political purposes.

In his discussion of workers' rights, John Paul also turns his attention to certain groups of people who are more at risk in today's society. First, he considers women. Mothers should not be forced to work outside the home so as to make the family's ends meet. Moreover, if women choose to work, they "should be able to fulfill their tasks *in accordance with their own nature*. . . . The *true advancement of women* requires that labor should be structured in such a way that women do not have to pay for their advancement by abandoning what is specific to them and at the expense of the family" (§19.5). John Paul also recalls the dignity of agricultural workers, and urges that disabled persons be offered work according to their capabilities (cf. §22.2) and that migrant workers and emigrants "should not be *placed at a disadvantage*" with regard to other workers (§23.3). Respect for the dignity of the human person requires that the subjective dimension of work always be given priority over its objective dimension. Human beings are never to be reduced to being instruments, whether of production, property, capital, or scientific research.

Spirituality of work

The encyclical concludes with a presentation of a specifically Christian spirituality of work. Far from being merely an appendix, chapter five contains the most inspiring pages of *Laborem Exercens*. Here the Pope explains his neologism "the Gospel of work." He describes the transcendent significance of work in three sections: first, as a share in God's creative activity; second, as ennobled by Christ; and third, as a way of sharing in the Paschal Mystery.

The Gospel sheds light on the dignity of people's work. It leads them to see *"the meaning which it has in the eyes of God"* and the way in which "work enters into the salvation process" (§24.1). Through work people are to come closer "to God, the Creator and Redeemer, to participate in his salvific plan for man and the world and to deepen their friendship with Christ" (§24.2). Created in God's image, "man ought to imitate God, his Creator, in working" (§25.3). By means of work each person shares in the wonder of creation, continuing to develop and perfect the created world.

It is due to the redemptive Incarnation, however, that the full "truth" about the dignity of workers is most clearly revealed. Jesus not only teaches the value of human work but manifests this through his life as "a man of work." Indeed, John Paul says that Christ *"looks with love upon human work"* (§26.1), appreciating and respecting it.

The spirituality of work reaches its most profound level in the Paschal Mystery of Christ's Passion, death, and Resurrection. Through embracing the toil and suffering inevitably involved in work, people can be intimately associated with the crucified and risen Lord. "By enduring the trial of work in union with Christ crucified for us, man in a way collaborates with the Son of God for the redemption of humanity" (§27.3). Like the Paschal Mystery, work is penetrated by the mystery of Jesus' Resurrection. Work, too, says the Pope, has a role "not only in *earthly progress* but also in *the development of the Kingdom of God*" (§27.7).

Key Themes

In this first of his social encyclicals John Paul lays the foundation for his particular contribution to the developing tradition of the Church's social doctrine. Later he will explore other themes, but in *Laborem Exercens* he sets his course. Three teachings stand out. First, the Church's unique contribution to questions of social justice, the Pope believes, rests primarily on the treasures she can bring forth from the word of God. Her contribution derives from her specifically religious and ethical vision. Second, the encyclical forcefully asserts the transcendent dignity of the human person as the foundation of all social doctrine. Third, John Paul is convinced that the Church's teaching on justice must be rooted in Christ the Redeemer, for he alone is the key who unlocks the mystery of the human person.

Religious-ethical vision

While he is persuaded of the unique contribution to the human family that can be made by the Church's social teaching, the Pope is careful never to confuse this teaching with an economic or political ideology. The religious and political-economic spheres have different competencies. That is why the Church cannot offer technical solutions to the problems to which she directs her attention as an "expert in humanity." Instead of offering scientific expertise, she seeks to form consciences. The Pope holds that it is the responsibility of the laity to put the Magisterium's principles into practice by carrying out the necessary specialized analysis of social questions and by proposing concrete solutions to them.

In *Laborem Exercens*, John Paul II follows a rigorously ethical-religious perspective in presenting the "Gospel of work." Although he describes certain historical, social, and ideological dimensions which condition the situation of workers, the Pope is not primarily concerned with this analysis. Rather, he affirms that "the Church considers it her task always to call attention to the dignity and rights of those who work, to condemn situations in which that dignity and those rights are violated, and to help to guide" changes which will "ensure authentic progress by man and society" (§1.4). The Church speaks out in the defense of work from her own viewpoint, that of fostering "its human value and of the moral order to which it belongs" (§24.2). Essential to the Church's vocation to evangelize the world is the formation and proclamation of a spirituality of work.

Even though John Paul addresses his encyclical to all workers, whether Catholic or not, nonetheless from beginning to end he draws his teaching principally from divine revelation. The source of the Church's teaching, he says, "is above all the revealed word of God, and therefore what is a conviction of the intellect is also a conviction of faith. . . . Relating herself to man, she seeks *to express* the eternal *designs* and transcendent *destiny* which *the living God*, the Creator and Redeemer, has linked with him" (§4.1). From this lofty perspective, the Pope sometimes makes precise suggestions which would put the Church's social teaching into practice.

In *Laborem Exercens* he mentions, for instance, proposals regarding the joint ownership of the means of production and the sharing by workers in management and/or profits. But, in keeping with the specificity of the Church's contribution to the world of work, he is careful *not* to endorse any particular way of guaranteeing the dignity of workers, when it is a question of the concrete application of principles. Instead, he states: "Whether these various proposals can or cannot be applied concretely, it is clear that recognition of the proper position of labor and the worker in the production process demands various adaptations in the sphere of the right to ownership of the means of production" (§14.5). According to the Pope, the Church's teaching concerning the "truth" about work derives from the revelation faithfully transmitted through Tradition and interpreted by the Magisterium.

Primacy of the person

The absolute primacy of the person over things, the priority of the worker over the work done, is the guiding thesis of *Laborem Exercens*. "We must emphasize and give prominence to the primacy of man in the production process," writes John Paul, *"the primacy of man over things"* (§12.6). The major principle of his social teaching is an anthropological truth: the dignity of the human person created in God's image and likeness and redeemed by Christ's sacrifice (cf. §§4.2, 6.2, 9.2, 25.2). At the very beginning of the encyclical, the Pope recalls what he said in *Redemptor Hominis* (1979): the person "is the primary and fundamental way for the Church" (§1.1). By exploring how the worker is this "way," *Laborem Exercens* offers another building block for the edifice of John Paul's Christian anthropology.

In spite of the heavy toil involved in work, it is good for people. Work is intended to be a means of achieving personal fulfillment, of "becoming more human" (cf. §9.3). According to the Pope, the dignity of work is eloquently confirmed by the Son of God who "devoted most of the years of his life on earth to *manual work* at the carpenter's bench" (§6.5).

Drawing on his belief that the person must be treated as "the effective subject of work and its true maker and creator" (§7.3), John Paul judges socioeconomic systems in light of the value they attribute to work's subjective dimension. Materialistic societies are those which overturn the divine order, giving — in different ways — primary importance to the objective dimension of work. No interpretation of the relationship between capital and labor that is anchored in either practical or theoretical materialism can ever provide an adequate understanding of human work and the dignity of the worker. No materialist view, whether collectivist or capitalist, can sufficiently guarantee "man's character as *a subject* in social life and, especially, in the dynamic *structure of the whole economic process*" (§14.4). The dignity of the human person requires that in every dimension of life, including work, he or she always be respected as an "end" of activity and never as a "means."

Work and Redemption

John Paul's theological focus on the mystery of Redemption — the golden thread of his Magisterium — is concretely verified in *Laborem Exercens*. Through work people draw close to God, participating in Christ's "threefold mission as priest, prophet and king, as the Second Vatican Council so eloquently teaches" (§24.2). By sharing in this mission of Jesus, workers are directly taken up into God's saving plan.

According to Genesis, besides being a "blessing," work is also a "curse" as the result of original sin. The Pope recalls that Saint Thomas Aquinas called work a *bonum arduum,* an "arduous good" (cf. §9.3). It requires great personal effort in the midst of tensions, conflicts, and crises: "In the sweat of your face you shall eat bread" (Gen 3:19). This toil, says John Paul, "*is familiar to all workers,* and, since work is a universal calling, it is familiar to everyone" (§9.2). Moreover, this onerous dimension of work contains "*an announcement of death*" (§27.1). If work's inevitable drudgery is not merely wasted, what is its meaning in God's plan?

John Paul links the "sweat and toil" of work to discipleship. It serves to open a window to the transcendent. Work presents Christians "with the possibility of sharing lovingly in the work Christ came to do" (§27.3). This "work" of Christ was the Redemption, accomplished through his suffering, death, and Resurrection. Thus, Christians can find in their work "a small part of the Cross of Christ" and can accept it "in the same spirit of redemption in which Christ accepted his Cross for us" (§27.5). Work associates believers with the Paschal Mystery. The Cross gives a new and profound meaning to human labor.

Work is also related to the Lord's Resurrection. "In work, thanks to the light that penetrates from the Resurrection of Christ," writes the Pope, "we always find a *glimmer* of new life, of the *new good*, as if it were an announcement of 'the new heavens and the new earth' in which man and the world participate precisely through the toil that goes with work" (§27.5). Work not only contributes to earthly progress but also to "*the development of the Kingdom of God*, to which we are all called through the power of the Holy Spirit and through the word of the Gospel" (§27.7).

* * *

Selected Bibliography

Barta, Russell. "Work: In Search of New Meanings." *Chicago Studies*, 23 (August 1984), 155-168.

Baum, Gregory. "*Laborem Exercens*." In *The New Dictionary of Catholic Social Thought*. Edited by Judith A. Dwyer. Collegeville: Liturgical Press, 1994. 527-535.

Baum, Gregory. *The Priority of Labor: A Commentary on "Laborem Exercens."* New York: Paulist Press, 1982.

Bedoyere, Quentin de la. "Man and His Work." *The Tablet*, 235 (1981), 1192-1194.

Charrier, Fernando. "Labour and Capital." *L'Osservatore Romano*, 42 (1981), 8.

Desto, Robert A. "*Laborem Exercens*." In *A Century of Catholic Social Thought*. Edited by George Weigel and Robert Royal. Lanham: University Press of America, 1991. 145-161.

Dorr, Donal. "The New Social Encyclical." *The Furrow*, 32 (1981), 700-712.

Duncan, Roger. "On Reading *Laborem Exercens*," *Homiletic and Pastoral Review*, 86 (July 1986), 11-19.

Faulhaber, Robert William. "The Church and Culture — John Paul II's 'On Human Work.'" *Listening*, 18 (1983), 103-118.

Fiore, Benjamin. "*Laborem Exercens*." In *The Thought of Pope John Paul II: A Collection of Essays and Studies*. Edited by John M. McDermott. Rome: Gregorian University Press, 1993. 231-236.

Gini, Al. "Meaningful Work and the Rights of the Worker: A Commentary on *Rerum Novarum* and *Laborem Exercens*." *Thought*, 67 (1992), 225-239.

Ginsburg, Helen. "Teachings of John Paul II on Work and the Rights of Workers." *Social Thought*, 13 (Spring-Summer 1987), 46-59.

Glemp, Jozef. "Human Work in the Teaching of Our Holy Father John Paul II."

In *John Paul II: A Panorama of His Teachings.* Preface by Joseph Bernardin. New York: New City Press, 1989. 144-160.

Haas, Richard. "The Market Place." *Living Prayer,* 27 (July/August 1994), 10-11.

Heckel, Roger. "Continuity and Renewal." *L'Osservatore Romano,* 40 (1981), 4-5.

Hehir, J. Bryan. "Challenge to a Tradition." *Commonweal,* 108 (1981), 522.

Hennelly, Alfred T. "Pope John Paul's Spirituality of Work." *America,* 146 (1982), 31-33.

Kelley, John J. "The Silence about Subsidiarity." *America,* 145 (1981), 382-383.

Morneau, Robert F. *Themes and Theses of Six Recent Papal Documents: A Commentary.* New York: Alba House, 1985. 111-135.

Preston, Ronald H. "Pope John Paul II on Work." *Theology,* 86 (January 1983), 19-24.

Roos, Lothar. "On a Theology and Ethics of Work." *Communio,* 11 (1984), 136-144.

Schotte, Jan. "The Social Teaching of the Church: *Laborem Exercens,* A New Challenge." *Review of Social Economy,* 40 (1982), 340-357.

Sorge, Bartolomeo. "*Laborem Exercens:* Toward a New Solidarity." In *Official Catholic Social Teaching: Readings in Moral Theology.* Edited by Charles Curran and Richard McCormick. Vol. 5. New York: Paulist Press, 1986. 241-246.

Spiazzi, Raimondo. "Gospel of Work and the Dignity of Man." *L'Osservatore Romano,* 41 (1981), 9-10.

Traffas, John R. "The Spirit of Community and the Spirituality of Work: A Note on *Laborem Exercens.*" *Communio,* 10 (1983), 407-411.

Volf, Miroslav. "On Human Work: An Evaluation of the Key Ideas of the Encyclical *Laborem Exercens.*" *Scottish Journal of Theology,* 37 (1984), 65-79.

ENCYCLICAL LETTER

LABOREM EXERCENS

ADDRESSED BY THE SUPREME PONTIFF

JOHN PAUL II

TO HIS VENERABLE BROTHERS

IN THE EPISCOPATE

TO THE PRIESTS

TO THE RELIGIOUS FAMILIES

TO THE SONS AND DAUGHTERS

OF THE CHURCH

AND TO ALL MEN AND WOMEN

OF GOOD WILL

ON HUMAN WORK

ON THE NINETIETH ANNIVERSARY

OF *RERUM NOVARUM*

Laborem Exercens

Venerable Brothers and
Dear Sons and Daughters,
Greetings and the Apostolic Blessing!

Through work man must earn his daily bread[1] and contribute to the continual advance of science and technology and, above all, to elevating unceasingly the cultural and moral level of the society within which he lives in community with those who belong to the same family. And work means any activity by man, whether manual or intellectual, whatever its nature or circumstances; it means any human activity that can and must be recognized as work, in the midst of all the many activities of which man is capable and to which he is predisposed by his very nature, by virtue of humanity itself. Man is made to be in the visible universe an image and likeness of God himself,[2] and he is placed in it in order to subdue the earth.[3] From the beginning therefore he is *called to work. Work is one of the characteristics that distinguish* man from the rest of creatures, whose activity for sustaining their lives cannot be called work. Only man is capable of work, and only man works, at the same time by work occupying his existence on earth. Thus work bears a particular mark of man and of humanity, the mark of a person operating within a community of persons. And this mark decides its interior characteristics; in a sense it constitutes its very nature.

I

Introduction

Human work on the nintieth anniversary of Rerum Novarum

1.1 Since May 15 of the present year was the *ninetieth anniversary* of the publication by the great Pope of the "social question," Leo XIII, of the decisively important Encyclical which begins with the words *Rerum Novarum,* I wish to devote this document to *human work* and, even more, to *man* in the vast context of the reality of work. As I said in the Encyclical *Redemptor Hominis,*

---

[1] Cf. Ps 128:2; cf. also Gen 3:17-19; Prov 10:22; Ex 1:8-14; Jer 22:13.
[2] Cf. Gen 1:26.
[3] Cf. Gen 1:28.

published at the beginning of my service in the See of Saint Peter in Rome, man "is the primary and fundamental way for the Church,"[4] precisely because of the inscrutable mystery of Redemption in Christ; and so it is necessary to return constantly to this way and to follow it ever anew in the various aspects in which it shows us all the wealth and at the same time all the toil of human existence on earth.

1.2 Work is one of these aspects, a perennial and fundamental one, one that is always relevant and constantly demands renewed attention and decisive witness. Because fresh *questions* and *problems* are always arising, there are always fresh hopes, but also fresh fears and threats, connected with this basic dimension of human existence: man's life is built up every day from work, from work it derives its specific dignity, but at the same time work contains the unceasing measure of human toil and suffering, and also of the harm and injustice which penetrate deeply into social life within individual nations and on the international level. While it is true that man eats the bread produced by the work of his hands[5] — and this means not only the daily bread by which his body keeps alive but also the bread of science and progress, civilization and culture — it is also a perennial truth that he eats this bread by *"the sweat of his face,"*[6] that is to say, not only by personal effort and toil but also in the midst of many tensions, conflicts and crises, which, in relationship with the reality of work, disturb the life of individual societies and also of all humanity.

1.3 We are celebrating the ninetieth anniversary of the Encyclical *Rerum Novarum* on the eve of new developments in technological, economic and political conditions which, according to many experts, will influence the world of work and production no less than the industrial revolution of the last century. There are many factors of a general nature: the widespread introduction of automation into many spheres of production, the increase in the cost of energy and raw materials, the growing realization that the heritage of nature is limited and that it is being intolerably polluted, and the emergence on the political scene of peoples who, after centuries of subjection, are demanding their rightful place among the nations and in international decision-making. These new conditions and demands will require a reordering and adjustment of the structures of the modern economy and of the distribution of work. Unfortunately, for millions of skilled workers these changes may perhaps mean unemployment, at least for a time, or the need for retraining. They will very probably involve a reduction or a less rapid increase in material well-being for

---

[4] Encyclical Letter *Redemptor Hominis* (March 4, 1979), 14: *AAS* 71 (1979), 284.

[5] Cf. Ps 128:2.

[6] Gen 3:19.

the more developed countries. But they can also bring relief and hope to the millions who today live in conditions of shameful and unworthy poverty.

1.4 It is not for the Church to analyze scientifically the consequences that these changes may have on human society. But the Church considers it her task always to call attention to the dignity and rights of those who work, to condemn situations in which that dignity and those rights are violated, and to help to guide the above-mentioned changes so as to ensure authentic progress by man and society.

In the organic development of the Church's social action and teaching

2.1 It is certainly true that work, as a human issue, is at the very center of the "social question" to which, for almost a hundred years, since the publication of the above-mentioned Encyclical, the Church's teaching and the many undertakings connected with her apostolic mission have been especially directed. The present reflections on work are not intended to follow a different line, but rather to be in organic connection with the whole tradition of this teaching and activity. At the same time, however, I am making them, according to the indication in the Gospel, in order to bring out *from the heritage of the Gospel "what is new and what is old."*[7] Certainly, work is part of "what is old" — as old as man and his life on earth. Nevertheless, the general situation of man in the modern world, studied and analyzed in its various aspects of geography, culture and civilization, calls for the discovery of the *new meanings of human work*. It likewise calls for the formulation of the *new tasks* that in this sector face each individual, the family, each country, the whole human race, and, finally, the Church herself.

2.2 During the years that separate us from the publication of the Encyclical *Rerum Novarum*, the social question has not ceased to engage the Church's attention. Evidence of this are the many documents of the Magisterium issued by the Popes and by the Second Vatican Council, pronouncements by individual Episcopates, and the activity of the various centers of thought and of practical apostolic initiatives, both on the international level and at the level of the local Churches. It is difficult to list here in detail all the manifestations of the commitment of the Church and of Christians in the social question, for they are too numerous. As a result of the Council, the main coordinating center in this field is the *Pontifical Commission Justice and Peace*, which has corresponding bodies within the individual Bishops' Conferences. The name of this institution is very significant. It indicates that the social question must be dealt with in its whole

---

[7] Cf. Mt 13:52.

complex dimension. Commitment to justice must be closely linked with commitment to peace in the modern world. This twofold commitment is certainly supported by the painful experience of the two great world wars which in the course of the last ninety years have convulsed many European countries and, at least partially, countries in other continents. It is supported, especially since the Second World War, by the permanent threat of a nuclear war and the prospect of the terrible self-destruction that emerges from it.

2.3 If we follow the *main line of development of the documents* of the supreme Magisterium of the Church, we find in them an explicit confirmation of precisely such a statement of the question. The key position, as regards the question of world peace, is that of John XXIII's Encyclical *Pacem in Terris*. However, if one studies the development of the question of social justice, one cannot fail to note that, whereas during the period between *Rerum Novarum* and Pius XI's *Quadragesimo Anno* the Church's teaching concentrates mainly on the just solution of the "labor question" within individual nations, in the next period the Church's teaching widens its horizon to take in the whole world. The disproportionate distribution of wealth and poverty and the existence of some countries and continents that are developed and of others that are not call for a leveling out and for a search for ways to ensure just development for all. This is the direction of the teaching in John XXIII's Encyclical *Mater et Magistra*, in the Pastoral Constitution *Gaudium et Spes* of the Second Vatican Council, and in Paul VI's Encyclical *Populorum Progressio*.

2.4 This trend of development of the Church's teaching and commitment in the social question exactly corresponds to the objective recognition of the state of affairs. While in the past *the "class" question* was especially highlighted as the center of this issue, in more recent times it is *the "world" question* that is emphasized. Thus, not only the sphere of class is taken into consideration but also the world sphere of inequality and injustice, and, as a consequence, not only the class dimension but also the world dimension of the tasks involved in the path toward the achievement of justice in the modern world. A complete analysis of the situation of the world today shows in an even deeper and fuller way the meaning of the previous analysis of social injustices; and it is the meaning that must be given today to efforts to build justice on earth, not concealing thereby unjust structures but demanding that they be examined and transformed on a more universal scale.

The question of work, the key to the social question

3.1 In the midst of all these processes — those of the diagnosis of objective social reality and also those of the Church's teaching in the sphere of the

complex and many-sided social question — *the question of human work* naturally appears many times. This issue is, in a way, a *constant factor* both of
social life and of the Church's teaching. Furthermore, in this teaching, attention to the question goes back much further than the last ninety years. In fact
the Church's social teaching finds its source in Sacred Scripture, beginning
with the Book of Genesis and especially in the Gospel and the writings of the
Apostles. From the beginning it was part of the Church's teaching, her concept of man and life in society, and, especially, the social morality which she
worked out according to the needs of the different ages. This traditional patrimony was then inherited and developed by the teaching of the Popes on the
modern "social question," beginning with the Encyclical *Rerum Novarum*. In
this context, study of the question of work, as we have seen, has continually
been brought up to date while maintaining that Christian basis of truth which
can be called ageless.

3.2 While in the present document we return to this question once more —
without, however, any intention of touching on all the topics that concern it —
this is not merely in order to gather together and repeat what is already contained in the Church's teaching. It is rather in order to highlight — perhaps
more than has been done before — the fact that human work is *a key*, probably *the essential key*, to the whole social question, if we try to see that question really from the point of view of man's good. And if the solution — or rather
the gradual solution — of the social question, which keeps coming up and
becomes ever more complex, must be sought in the direction of "making life
more human,"[8] then the key, namely human work, acquires fundamental and
decisive importance.

II

Work and Man

In the Book of Genesis
4.1 The Church is convinced that work is a fundamental dimension of
man's existence on earth. She is confirmed in this conviction by considering
the whole heritage of the many sciences devoted to man: anthropology, pale-
ontology, history, sociology, psychology and so on; they all seem to bear witness to this reality in an irrefutable way. But the source of the Church's conviction is above all the revealed word of God, and therefore what is *a convic-*

---

[8] Second Vatican Ecumenical Council, Pastoral Constitution on the Church in the Modern
World *Gaudium et Spes*, 38: *AAS* 58 (1966), 1055.

tion of the intellect is also *a conviction of faith.* The reason is that the Church — and it is worthwhile stating it at this point — believes in man: she *thinks of man* and addresses herself to him *not only* in the light of historical experience, not only with the aid of the many methods of scientific knowledge, but in the first place in the light of the revealed word of the living God. Relating herself to man, she seeks *to express* the eternal *designs* and transcendent *destiny* which *the living God,* the Creator and Redeemer, has linked with him.

4.2 The Church finds *in the very first pages of the Book of Genesis* the source of her conviction that work is a fundamental dimension of human existence on earth. An analysis of these texts makes us aware that they express — sometimes in an archaic way of manifesting thought — the fundamental truths about man, in the context of the mystery of creation itself. These truths are decisive for man from the very beginning, and at the same time they trace out the main lines of his earthly existence, both in the state of original justice and also after the breaking, caused by sin, of the Creator's original covenant with creation in man. When man, who had been created "in the image of God . . . male and female,"[9] hears the words: "Be fruitful and *multiply, and fill the earth and subdue it,*"[10] even though these words do not refer directly and explicitly to work, beyond any doubt they indirectly indicate it as an activity for man to carry out in the world. Indeed, they show its very deepest essence. Man is the image of God partly through the mandate received from his Creator to subdue, to dominate, the earth. In carrying out this mandate, man, every human being, reflects the very action of the Creator of the universe.

4.3 Work understood as a "transitive" activity, that is to say an activity beginning in the human subject and directed toward an external object, presupposes a specific dominion by man over "the earth," and in its turn it confirms and develops this dominion. It is clear that the term "the earth" of which the biblical text speaks is to be understood in the first place as that fragment of the visible universe that man inhabits. By extension, however, it can be understood as the whole of the visible world insofar as it comes within the range of man's influence and of his striving to satisfy his needs. The expression "subdue the earth" has an immense range. It means all the resources that the earth (and indirectly the visible world) contains and which, through the conscious activity of man, can be discovered and used for his ends. And so these words, placed at the beginning of the Bible, *never cease to be relevant.* They embrace equally the past ages of civilization and economy, as also

[9] Gen 1:27.
[10] Gen 1:28.

the whole of modern reality and future phases of development, which are perhaps already to some extent beginning to take shape, though for the most part they are still almost unknown to man and hidden from him.

4.4 While people sometimes speak of periods of "acceleration" in the economic life and civilization of humanity or of individual nations, linking these periods to the progress of science and technology and especially to discoveries which are decisive for social and economic life, at the same time it can be said that none of these phenomena of "acceleration" exceeds the essential content of what was said in that most ancient of biblical texts. As man, through his work, becomes more and more the master of the earth, and as he confirms his dominion over the visible world, again through his work, he nevertheless remains in every case and at every phase of this process within the Creator's original ordering. And this ordering remains necessarily and indissolubly linked with the fact that man was created, as male and female, "in the image of God." This *process* is, at the same time, *universal:* it embraces all human beings, every generation, every phase of economic and cultural development, and *at the same time* it is a process that takes place *within each human being,* in each conscious human subject. Each and every individual is at the same time embraced by it. Each and every individual, to the proper extent and in an incalculable number of ways, takes part in the giant process whereby man "subdues the earth" through his work.

Work in the objective sense: technology

5.1 This universality and, at the same time, this multiplicity of the process of "subduing the earth" throw light upon human work, because man's dominion over the earth is achieved in and by means of work. There thus emerges the meaning of *work in an objective sense,* which finds expression in the various epochs of culture and civilization. Man dominates the earth by the very fact of domesticating animals, rearing them and obtaining from them the food and clothing he needs, and by the fact of being able to extract various natural resources from the earth and the seas. But man "subdues the earth" much more when he begins to cultivate it and then to transform its products, adapting them to his own use. Thus agriculture constitutes through human work a primary field of economic activity and an indispensable factor of production. Industry in its turn will always consist in linking the earth's riches — whether nature's living resources, or the products of agriculture, or the mineral or chemical resources — with man's work, whether physical or intellectual. This is also in a sense true in the sphere of what are called service industries, and also in the sphere of research, pure or applied.

5.2 In industry and agriculture man's work has today in many cases ceased to be mainly manual, for the toil of human hands and muscles is aided by *more and more highly perfected machinery.* Not only in industry but also in agriculture we are witnessing the transformations made possible by the gradual development of science and technology. Historically speaking, this, taken as a whole, has caused great changes in civilization, from the beginning of the "industrial era" to the successive phases of development through new technologies, such as the electronics and the microprocessor technology in recent years.

5.3 While it may seem that in the industrial process it is the machine that "works" and man merely supervises it, making it function and keeping it going in various ways, it is also true that for this very reason industrial development provides grounds for reproposing in new ways the question of human work. Both the original industrialization that gave rise to what is called the worker question and the subsequent industrial and post-industrial changes show in an eloquent manner that, even in the age of ever more mechanized "work," *the proper subject of work continues to be man.*

5.4 The development of industry and of the various sectors connected with it, even the most modern electronics technology, especially in the fields of miniaturization, communications and telecommunications and so forth, shows how vast is the role of technology, that ally of work that human thought has produced, in the interaction between the subject and object of work (in the widest sense of the word). Understood in this case not as a capacity or aptitude for work, but rather as *a whole set of instruments* which man uses in his work, technology is undoubtedly man's ally. It facilitates his work, perfects, accelerates and augments it. It leads to an increase in the quantity of things produced by work, and in many cases improves their quality. However, it is also a fact that, in some instances, technology can cease to be man's ally and become almost his enemy, as when the mechanization of work "supplants" him, taking away all personal satisfaction and the incentive to creativity and responsibility, when it deprives many workers of their previous employment, or when, through exalting the machine, it reduces man to the status of its slave.

5.5 If the biblical words "subdue the earth" addressed to man from the very beginning are understood in the context of the whole modern age, industrial and post-industrial, then they undoubtedly include also *a relationship with technology,* with the world of machinery which is the fruit of the work of the human intellect and a historical confirmation of man's dominion over nature.

5.6 The recent stage of human history, especially that of certain societies, brings a correct affirmation of technology as a basic coefficient of economic progress; but, at the same time, this affirmation has been accompanied by and continues to be accompanied by the raising of essential questions concerning human work in relationship to its subject, which is man. These questions are particularly charged with *content and tension of an ethical and social character*. They therefore constitute a continual challenge for institutions of many kinds, for States and governments, for systems and international organizations; they also constitute a challenge for the Church.

Work in the subjective sense: man as the subject of work

6.1 In order to continue our analysis of work, an analysis linked with the word of the Bible telling man that he is to subdue the earth, we must concentrate our attention on *work in the subjective sense*, much more than we did on the objective significance, barely touching upon the vast range of problems known intimately and in detail to scholars in various fields and also, according to their specializations, to those who work. If the words of the Book of Genesis to which we refer in this analysis of ours speak of work in the objective sense in an indirect way, they also speak only indirectly of the subject of work; but what they say is very eloquent and is full of great significance.

6.2 Man has to subdue the earth and dominate it, because as the "image of God" he is a person, that is to say, a subjective being capable of acting in a planned and rational way, capable of deciding about himself, and with a tendency to self-realization. *As a person, man is therefore the subject of work*. As a person he works, he performs various actions belonging to the work process; independently of their objective content, these actions must all serve to realize his humanity, to fulfill the calling to be a person that is his by reason of his very humanity. The principal truths concerning this theme were recently recalled by the Second Vatican Council in the Constitution *Gaudium et Spes*, especially in chapter one, which is devoted to man's calling.

6.3 And so this "dominion" spoken of in the biblical text being meditated upon here refers not only to the objective dimension of work but at the same time introduces us to an understanding of its subjective dimension. Understood as a process whereby man and the human race subdue the earth, work corresponds to this basic biblical concept only when throughout the process man manifests himself and confirms himself *as the one who "dominates."* This dominion, in a certain sense, refers to the subjective dimension even more than to the objective one: this dimension conditions *the very ethical nature of work*. In fact there is no doubt that human work has an ethical value of its own, which clearly and directly remains linked to the fact that the one who carries it out is a person, a conscious and free subject, that is to say, a subject that decides about himself.

6.4 This truth, which in a sense constitutes the fundamental and perennial heart of Christian teaching on human work, has had and continues to have primary significance for the formulation of the important social problems characterizing whole ages.

6.5 *The ancient world* introduced its own typical differentiation of people into classes according to the type of work done. Work which demanded from the worker the exercise of physical strength, the work of muscles and hands, was considered unworthy of free men, and was therefore given to slaves. By broadening certain aspects that already belonged to the Old Testament, Christianity brought about a fundamental change of ideas in this field, taking the whole content of the Gospel message as its point of departure, especially the fact that the one who, while *being God, became like us in all things*[11] devoted most of the years of his life on earth to *manual work* at the carpenter's bench. This circumstance constitutes in itself the most eloquent "Gospel of work," showing that the basis for determining the value of human work is not primarily the kind of work being done but the fact that the one who is doing it is a person. The sources of the dignity of work are to be sought primarily in the subjective dimension, not in the objective one.

6.6 Such a concept practically does away with the very basis of the ancient differentiation of people into classes according to the kind of work done. This does not mean that, from the objective point of view, human work cannot and must not be rated and qualified in any way. It only means that *the primary basis of the value of work is man himself*, who is its subject. This leads immediately to a very important conclusion of an ethical nature: however true it may be that man is destined for work and called to it, in the first place work is "for man" and not man "for work." Through this conclusion one rightly comes to recognize the preeminence of the subjective meaning of work over the objective one. Given this way of understanding things, and presupposing that different sorts of work that people do can have greater or lesser objective value, let us try nevertheless to show that each sort is judged above all by *the measure of the dignity* of the subject of work, that is to say the person, *the individual who carries it out*. On the other hand, independently of the work that every man does, and presupposing that this work constitutes a purpose — at times a very demanding one —- of his activity, this purpose does not possess a definitive meaning in itself. In fact, in the final analysis it is always

[11] Cf. Heb 2:17; Phil 2:5-8.

man who is *the purpose of the work*, whatever work it is that is done by man — even if the common scale of values rates it as the merest "service," as the most monotonous, even the most alienating work.

A threat to the right order of values

7.1 It is precisely these fundamental affirmations about work that always emerged from the wealth of Christian truth, especially from the very message of the "Gospel of work," thus creating the basis for a new way of thinking, judging and acting. In the modern period, from the beginning of the industrial age, the Christian truth about work had to oppose the various trends of *materialistic and economistic* thought.

7.2 For certain supporters of such ideas, work was understood and treated as a sort of "merchandise" that the worker — especially the industrial worker — sells to the employer, who at the same time is the possessor of the capital, that is to say, of all the working tools and means that make production possible. This way of looking at work was widespread especially in the first half of the nineteenth century. Since then, explicit expressions of this sort have almost disappeared, and have given way to more human ways of thinking about work and evaluating it. The interaction between the worker and the tools and means of production has given rise to the development of various forms of capitalism — parallel with various forms of collectivism — into which other socioeconomic elements have entered as a consequence of new concrete circumstances, of the activity of workers' associations and public authorities, and of the emergence of large transnational enterprises. Nevertheless, the *danger* of treating work as a special kind of "merchandise," or as an impersonal "force" needed for production (the expression "work force" is, in fact, in common use), *always exists*, especially when the whole way of looking at the question of economics is marked by the premises of materialistic economism.

7.3 A systematic opportunity for thinking and evaluating in this way, and in a certain sense a stimulus for doing so, is provided by the quickening process of the development of a one-sidedly materialistic civilization, which gives prime importance to the objective dimension of work, while the subjective dimension — everything in direct or indirect relationship with the subject of work — remains on a secondary level. In all cases of this sort, in every social situation of this type, there is a confusion or even a reversal of the order laid down from the beginning by the words of the Book of Genesis: *man is treated as an instrument of production*,[12] whereas he — he alone, independently of the work he does — ought to be treated as the effective subject of

---

[12] Cf. Pius XI, Encyclical Letter *Quadragesimo Anno* (May 15, 1931), III: *AAS* 23 (1931), 221.

work and its true maker and creator. Precisely this reversal of order, whatever the program or name under which it occurs, should rightly be called "capitalism" — in the sense more fully explained below. Everybody knows that capitalism has a definite historical meaning as a system, an economic and social system, opposed to "socialism" or "communism." But in the light of the analysis of the fundamental reality of the whole economic process — first and foremost of the production structure that work is — it should be recognized that the error of early capitalism can be repeated wherever man is in a way treated on the same level as the whole complex of the material means of production, as an instrument and not in accordance with the true dignity of his work — that is to say, where he is not treated as subject and maker, and for this very reason as the true purpose of the whole process of production.

7.4 This explains why the analysis of human work in the light of the words concerning man's "dominion" over the earth goes to the very heart of the ethical and social question. This concept should also find *a central place* in the whole *sphere of social and economic policy*, both within individual countries and in the wider field of international and intercontinental relationships, particularly with reference to the tensions making themselves felt in the world not only between East and West but also between North and South. Both John XXIII in the Encyclical *Mater et Magistra* and Paul VI in the Encyclical *Populorum Progressio* gave special attention to these dimensions of the modern ethical and social question.

Worker solidarity

8.1 When dealing with human work in the fundamental dimension of its subject, that is to say, the human person doing the work, one must make at least a summary evaluation of developments during the ninety years since *Rerum Novarum* in relation to the subjective dimension of work. Although the subject of work is always the same, that is to say man, nevertheless wide-ranging changes take place in the objective aspect. While one can say that, by reason of its subject, *work is one single thing* (one and unrepeatable every time), yet when one takes into consideration its objective directions one is forced to admit that *there exist many works,* many different sorts of work. The development of human civilization brings continual enrichment in this field. But at the same time, one cannot fail to note that in the process of this development not only do new forms of work appear but also others disappear. Even if one accepts that on the whole this is a normal phenomenon, it must still be seen whether certain ethically and socially dangerous irregularities creep in, and to what extent.

8.2 It was precisely one such *wide-ranging anomaly* that gave rise in the last century to what has been called "the worker question," sometimes described as "the proletariat question." This question and the problems connected with it gave rise to a just social reaction and caused the impetuous emergence of a great burst of solidarity between workers, first and foremost industrial workers. The call to solidarity and common action addressed to the workers — especially to those engaged in narrowly specialized, monotonous and depersonalized work in industrial plants, when the machine tends to dominate man — was important and eloquent from the point of view of social ethics. It was the reaction *against the degradation of man as the subject of work,* and against the unheard-of accompanying exploitation in the field of wages, working conditions and social security for the worker. This reaction united the working world in a community marked by great solidarity.

8.3 Following the lines laid down by the Encyclical *Rerum Novarum* and many later documents of the Church's Magisterium, it must be frankly recognized that the reaction against the system of injustice and harm that cried to heaven for vengeance[13] and that weighed heavily upon workers in that period of rapid industrialization was justified *from the point of view of social morality.* This state of affairs was favored by the liberal sociopolitical system, which, in accordance with its "economistic" premises, strengthened and safeguarded economic initiative by the possessors of capital alone, but did not pay sufficient attention to the rights of the workers, on the grounds that human work is solely an instrument of production, and that capital is the basis, efficient factor and purpose of production.

8.4 From that time, worker solidarity, together with a clearer and more committed realization by others of workers' rights, has in many cases brought about profound changes. Various forms of neo-capitalism or collectivism have developed. Various new systems have been thought out. Workers can often share in running businesses and in controlling their productivity, and in fact do so. Through appropriate associations, they exercise influence over conditions of work and pay, and also over social legislation. But at the same time various ideological or power systems, and new relationships which have arisen at various levels of society, *have allowed flagrant injustices to persist or have created new ones.* On the world level, the development of civilization and of communications has made possible a more complete diagnosis of the living and working conditions of man globally, but it has also revealed other forms of injustice, much more extensive than those which in the last century stimulated unity between workers for particular solidarity in the working world. This is true in countries which have completed a certain process of industrial

---

[13] Dt 24:15; Jas 5:4; and also Gen 4:10.

revolution. It is also true in countries where the main working milieu continues to be *agriculture* or other similar occupations.

8.5 Movements of solidarity in the sphere of work — a solidarity that must never mean being closed to dialogue and collaboration with others — can be necessary also with reference to the condition of social groups that were not previously included in such movements but which, in changing social systems and conditions of living, are undergoing *what is in effect "proletarianization"* or which actually already find themselves in a "proletariat" situation, one which, even if not yet given that name, in fact deserves it. This can be true of certain categories or groups of the working "intelligentsia," especially when ever wider access to education and an ever increasing number of people with degrees or diplomas in the fields of their cultural preparation are accompanied by a drop in demand for their labor. This *unemployment of intellectuals* occurs or increases when the education available is not oriented toward the types of employment or service required by the true needs of society, or when there is less demand for work which requires education, at least professional education, than for manual labor, or when it is less well paid. Of course, education in itself is always valuable and an important enrichment of the human person; but in spite of that, "proletarianization" processes remain possible.

8.6 For this reason, *there must be continued study of the subject of work* and of the subject's living conditions. In order to achieve social justice in the various parts of the world, in the various countries, and in the relationships between them, there is a need for ever new *movements of solidarity of* the workers and *with* the workers. This solidarity must be present whenever it is called for by the social degrading of the subject of work, by exploitation of the workers, and by the growing areas of poverty and even hunger. The Church is firmly committed to this cause, for she considers it her mission, her service, a proof of her fidelity to Christ, so that she can truly be the "Church of the poor." And the "poor" appear under various forms; they appear in various places and at various times; in many cases they appear as a *result of the violation of the dignity of human work:* either because the opportunities for human work are limited as a result of the scourge of unemployment, or because a low value is put on work and the rights that flow from it, especially the right to a just wage and to the personal security of the worker and his or her family.

Work and personal dignity

9.1 Remaining within the context of man as the subject of work, it is now appropriate to touch upon, at least in a summary way, certain problems that *more closely define the dignity of human work,* in that they make it possible to characterize more fully its specific moral value. In doing this we must always keep in mind the biblical calling to "subdue the earth,"[14] in which is expressed the will of the Creator that work should enable man to achieve that "dominion" in the visible world that is proper to him.

9.2 God's fundamental and original intention with regard to man, whom he created in his image and after his likeness,[15] was not withdrawn or canceled out even when man, having broken the original covenant with God, heard the words: "In the sweat of your face you shall eat bread."[16] These words refer to *the sometimes heavy toil* that from then onward has accompanied human work; but they do not alter the fact that work is the means whereby man *achieves that "dominion"* which is proper to him over the visible world, by "subjecting" the earth. Toil is something that is universally known, for it is universally experienced. It is familiar to those doing physical work under sometimes exceptionally laborious conditions. It is familiar not only to agricultural workers, who spend long days working the land, which sometimes "bears thorns and thistles,"[17] but also to those who work in mines and quarries, to steelworkers at their blast-furnaces, to those who work in builders' yards and in construction work, often in danger of injury or death. It is likewise familiar to those at an intellectual workbench; to scientists; to those who bear the burden of grave responsibility for decisions that will have a vast impact on society. It is familiar to doctors and nurses, who spend days and nights at their patients' bedsides. It is familiar to women, who, sometimes without proper recognition on the part of society and even of their own families, bear the daily burden and responsibility for their homes and the upbringing of their children. *It is familiar to all workers,* and, since work is a universal calling, it is familiar to everyone.

9.3 And yet, in spite of all this toil — perhaps, in a sense, because of it — work is a good thing for man. Even though it bears the mark of *a bonum arduum,* in the terminology of Saint Thomas,[18] this does not take away the fact that, as such, it is a good thing for man. It is not only good in the sense that it is useful or something to enjoy; it is also good as being something worthy, that is to say, something that corresponds to man's dignity, that expresses this dignity and increases it. If one wishes to define more clearly the ethical meaning of work, it is this truth that one must particularly keep in mind. Work is a good thing for man — a good thing for his humanity — because through work man *not only transforms nature,* adapting it to his own

---

[14] Cf. Gen 1:28.
[15] Cf. Gen 1:25-27.
[16] Gen 3:19.
[17] Heb 6:8, cf. Gen 3:18.
[18] Cf. *Summa Theologiae*, I-II, q. 40, a. 1; I-II, q. 34, a. 2, ad 1.

needs, but he also *achieves fulfillment* as a human being and indeed, in a sense, becomes "more a human being."

9.4 Without this consideration it is impossible to understand the meaning of the virtue of industriousness, and more particularly it is impossible to understand why industriousness should be a virtue: for virtue, as a moral habit, is something whereby man becomes good as man.[19] This fact in no way alters our justifiable anxiety that in work, whereby *matter* gains in *nobility, man* himself should not experience a *lowering* of his own dignity.[20] Again, it is well known that it is possible to use work in various ways *against man*, that it is possible to punish man with the system of forced labor in concentration camps, that work can be made into a means for oppressing man, and that in various ways it is possible to exploit human labor, that is to say the worker. All this pleads in favor of the moral obligation to link industriousness as a virtue with *the social order of work,* which will enable man to become, in work, "more a human being" and not be degraded by it, not only because of the wearing out of his physical strength (which, at least up to a certain point, is inevitable), but especially through damage to the dignity and subjectivity that are proper to him.

Work and society: family and nation

10.1 Having thus confirmed the personal dimension of human work, we must go on to the second *sphere of values* which is necessarily linked to work. Work constitutes a foundation for the formation of *family life,* which is a natural right and something that man is called to. These two spheres of values — one linked to work and the other consequent on the family nature of human life — must be properly united and must properly permeate each other. In a way, work is a condition for making it possible to found a family, since the family requires the means of subsistence which man normally gains through work. Work and industriousness also influence the whole *process of education* in the family, for the very reason that everyone "becomes a human being" through, among other things, work, and becoming a human being is precisely the main purpose of the whole process of education. Obviously, two aspects of work in a sense come into play here: the one making family life and its upkeep possible, and the other making possible the achievement of the purposes of the family, especially education. Nevertheless, these two aspects of work are linked to one another and are mutually complementary in various points.

---

[19] Cf. *Summa Theologiae,* I-II, q. 56, a. 3.

[20] Cf. Pius XI, Encyclical Letter *Quadragesimo Anno* (May 15, 1931), III: *AAS* 23 (1931), 221-222.

10.2 It must be remembered and affirmed that the family constitutes one of the most important terms of reference for shaping the social and ethical order of human work. The teaching of the Church has always devoted special attention to this question, and in the present document we shall have to return to it. In fact, the family is simultaneously a *community made possible by work* and the first *school of work,* within the home, for every person.

10.3 The third sphere of values that emerges from this point of view — that of the subject of work — concerns the *great society* to which man belongs on the basis of particular cultural and historical links. This society — even when it has not yet taken on the mature form of a nation — is not only the great "educator" of every man, even though an indirect one (because each individual absorbs within the family the contents and values that go to make up the culture of a given nation); it is also a great historical and social incarnation of the work of all generations. All of this brings it about that man combines his deepest human identity with membership of a nation, and intends his work also to increase the common good developed together with his compatriots, thus realizing that in this way work serves to add to the heritage of the whole human family, of all the people living in the world.

10.4 These three spheres are always *important for human work* in its subjective dimension. And this dimension, that is to say, the concrete reality of the worker, takes precedence over the objective dimension. In the subjective dimension there is realized, first of all, that "dominion" over the world of nature to which man is called from the beginning according to the words of the Book of Genesis. The very process of "subduing the earth," that is to say work, is marked in the course of history, and especially in recent centuries, by an immense development of technological means. This is an advantageous and positive phenomenon, on condition that the objective dimension of work does not gain the upper hand over the subjective dimension, depriving man of his dignity and inalienable rights or reducing them.

III

Conflict between Labor and Capital in the Present Phase of History

Dimensions of the conflict

11.1 The sketch of the basic problems of work outlined above draws inspiration from the texts at the beginning of the Bible and in a sense forms the very framework of the Church's teaching, which has remained unchanged throughout the centuries within the context of different historical experiences. However, the experiences preceding and following the publication of the Encyclical *Rerum Novarum* form a background that endows that teaching with particular expressiveness and the eloquence of living relevance. In this analysis, work is seen as a great reality with a fundamental influence on the shaping in a human way of the world that the Creator has entrusted to man; it is a reality closely linked with man as the subject of work and with man's rational activity. In the normal course of events this reality fills human life and strongly affects its value and meaning. Even when it is accompanied by toil and effort, work is still something good, and so man develops through love for work. This entirely *positive and creative, educational and meritorious character of man's work* must be the basis for the judgments and decisions being made today in its regard in spheres that include *human rights,* as is evidenced by the international *declarations* on work and the many *labor codes* prepared either by the competent legislative institutions in the various countries or by organizations devoting their social, or scientific and social, activity to the problems of work. One organization fostering such initiatives on the international level is the International Labor Organization, the oldest specialized agency of the United Nations Organization.

11.2 In the following part of these considerations I intend to return in greater detail to these important questions, recalling at least the basic elements of the Church's teaching on the matter. I must however first touch on a very important field of questions in which her teaching has taken shape in this latest period, the one marked and in a sense symbolized by the publication of the Encyclical *Rerum Novarum.*

11.3 Throughout this period, which is by no means yet over, the issue of work has of course been posed on the basis of the great *conflict* that in the age of, and together with, industrial development emerged *between "capital" and "labor,"* that is to say between the small but highly influential group of entrepreneurs, owners or holders of the means of production, and the broader multitude of people who lacked these means and who shared in the process of production solely by their labor. The conflict originated in the fact that the workers put their powers at the disposal of the entrepreneurs, and these, following the principle of maximum profit, tried to establish the lowest possible wages for the work done by the employees. In addition there were other elements of exploitation, connected with the lack of safety at work and of safeguards regarding the health and living conditions of the workers and their families.

11.4 This conflict, interpreted by some as a socioeconomic *class conflict,* found expression in the *ideological conflict* between liberalism, understood as the ideology of capitalism, and Marxism, understood as the ideology of scientific socialism and communism, which professes to act as the spokesman for the working class and the worldwide proletariat. Thus the real conflict between labor and capital was transformed into a *systematic class struggle,* conducted not only by ideological means but also and chiefly by political means. We are familiar with the history of this conflict and with the demands of both sides. The Marxist program, based on the philosophy of Marx and Engels, sees in class struggle the only way to eliminate class injustices in society and to eliminate the classes themselves. Putting this program into practice presupposes *the collectivization of the means of production* so that, through the transfer of these means from private hands to the collectivity, human labor will be preserved from exploitation.

11.5 This is the goal of the struggle carried on by political as well as ideological means. In accordance with the principle of "the dictatorship of the proletariat," the groups that as political parties follow the guidance of Marxist ideology aim, by the use of various kinds of influence, including revolutionary pressure, to win *a monopoly of power in each society,* in order to introduce the collectivist system into it by eliminating private ownership of the means of production. According to the principal ideologists and leaders of this broad international movement, the purpose of this program of action is to achieve the social revolution and to introduce socialism and, finally, the communist system throughout the world.

11.6 As we touch on this extremely important field of issues, which constitute not only a theory but a whole fabric of socioeconomic, political, and international life in our age, we cannot *go into the details,* nor is this necessary, for they are known both from the vast literature on the subject and by experience. Instead, we must leave the context of these issues and go back to the fundamental issue of human work, which is the main subject of the considerations in this document. It is clear, indeed, that this issue, which is of such importance for man — it constitutes one of the fundamental dimensions of his earthly existence and of his vocation — can also be explained only by taking into account the full context of the contemporary situation.

The priority of labor

12.1 The structure of the present-day situation is deeply marked by many conflicts caused by man, and the technological means produced by human work play a primary role in it. We should also consider here the prospect of worldwide catastrophe in the case of a nuclear war, which would have almost unimaginable possibilities of destruction. In view of this situation we must first of all recall a principle that has always been taught by the Church: *the principle of the priority of labor over capital.* This principle directly concerns the process of production: in this process labor is always a primary *efficient cause,* while capital, the whole collection of means of production, remains a mere *instrument* or instrumental cause. This principle is an evident truth that emerges from the whole of man's historical experience.

12.2 When we read in the first chapter of the Bible that man is to subdue the earth, we know that these words refer to all the resources contained in the visible world and placed at man's disposal. However, these resources *can serve man only through work.* From the beginning there is also linked with work the question of ownership, for the only means that man has for causing the resources hidden in nature to serve himself and others is his work. And to be able through his work to make these resources bear fruit, man takes over ownership of small parts of the various riches of nature: those beneath the ground, those in the sea, on land, or in space. He takes all these things over by making them his workbench. He takes them over through work and for work.

12.3 The same principle applies in the successive phases of this process, in which *the first phase* always remains the relationship of man with *the resources and riches of nature.* The whole of the effort to acquire knowledge with the aim of discovering these riches and specifying the various ways in which they can be used by man and for man teaches us that everything that comes from man throughout the whole process of economic production, whether labor or the whole collection of means of production and the technology connected with these means (meaning the capability to use them in work), presupposes these riches and resources of the visible world, riches and resources *that man finds* and does not create. In a sense man finds them already prepared, ready for him to discover them and to use them correctly in the productive process. In every phase of the development of his work, man comes up against the leading role of *the gift made* by "nature," that is to say, in the final analysis, *by the Creator.* At the beginning of man's work is the mystery of creation. This affirmation, already indicated as my starting point, is the guiding thread of this document, and will be further developed in the last part of these reflections.

12.4 Further consideration of this question should confirm our conviction of *the priority of human labor over* what in the course of time we have grown accustomed to calling *capital.* Since the concept of capital includes not only the natural resources placed at man's disposal but also the whole collection of means by which man appropriates natural resources and transforms them in accordance with his needs (and thus in a sense humanizes them), it must immediately be noted *that all these means are the result of the historical heritage of human labor.* All the means of production, from the most primitive to the ultramodern ones — it is man that has gradually developed them: man's experience and intellect. In this way there have appeared not only the simplest instruments for cultivating the earth but also, through adequate progress in science and technology, the more modern and complex ones: machines, factories, laboratories and computers. Thus *everything that is at the service of work,* everything that in the present state of technology constitutes its ever more highly perfected "instrument," *is the result of work.*

12.5 This gigantic and powerful instrument — the whole collection of means of production that in a sense are considered synonymous with "capital" — is the result of work and bears the signs of human labor. At the present stage of technological advance, when man, who is the subject of work, wishes to make use of this collection of modern instruments, the means of production, he must first assimilate cognitively the result of the work of the people who invented those instruments, who planned them, built them and perfected them, and who continue to do so. *Capacity for work* — that is to say, for sharing efficiently in the modern production process — demands greater and greater *preparation* and, before all else, proper *training.* Obviously, it remains clear that every human being sharing in the production process, even if he or she is only doing the kind of work for which no special training or qualifications are required, is the real efficient subject in this production process, while the whole collection of instruments, no matter how perfect they may be in themselves, is only a mere instrument subordinate to human labor.

12.6 This truth, which is part of the abiding heritage of the Church's teaching, must always be emphasized with reference to the question of the labor system and with regard to the whole socioeconomic system. We must emphasize and give prominence to the primacy of man in the production process, *the primacy of man over things.* Everything contained in the concept of capital in the strict sense is only a collection of things. Man, as the subject of work, and independently of the work that he does — man alone is a person. This truth has important and decisive consequences.

Economism and materialism

13.1 In the light of the above truth we see clearly, first of all, that capital cannot be separated from labor; in no way can labor be opposed to capital or capital to labor, and still less can the actual people behind these concepts be opposed to each other, as will be explained later. A labor system can be right, in the sense of being in conformity with the very essence of the issue, and in the sense of being intrinsically true and also morally legitimate, if in its very basis *it overcomes the opposition between labor and capital* through an effort at being shaped in accordance with the principle put forward above: the principle of the substantial and real priority of labor, of the subjectivity of human labor and its effective participation in the whole production process, independently of the nature of the services provided by the worker.

13.2 Opposition between labor and capital does not spring from the structure of the production process or from the structure of the economic process. In general the latter process demonstrates that labor and what we are accustomed to call capital are intermingled; it shows that they are inseparably linked. Working at any workbench, whether a relatively primitive or an ultramodern one, a man can easily see that *through his work he enters into two inheritances:* the inheritance of what is given to the whole of humanity in the resources of nature, and the inheritance of what others have already developed on the basis of those resources, primarily by developing technology, that is to say, by producing a whole collection of increasingly perfect instruments for work. In working, man also "enters into the labor of others."[21] Guided both by our intelligence and by the faith that draws light from the word of God, we have no difficulty in accepting this image of the sphere and process of man's labor. It is *a consistent image, one that is humanistic as well as theological.* In it man is the master of the creatures placed at his disposal in the visible world. If some dependence is discovered in the work process, it is dependence on the Giver of all the resources of creation, and also on other human beings, those to whose work and initiative we owe the perfected and increased possibilities of our own work. All that we can say of everything in the production process which constitutes a whole collection of "things," the instruments, the capital, is that it *conditions* man's work; we cannot assert that it constitutes as it were an impersonal "subject" *putting* man and man's work *into a position of dependence.*

13.3 This *consistent image,* in which the principle of the primacy of person over things is strictly preserved, *was broken up in human thought,* sometimes after a long period of incubation in practical living. The break occurred in such a way that labor was separated from capital and set in opposition to it, and capital was set in opposition to labor, as though they were two impersonal forces, two production factors juxtaposed in the same "economistic" perspective. This way of stating the issue contained a fundamental error, what

---

[21] Cf. Jn 4:38.

we can call *the error of economism,* that of considering human labor solely according to its economic purpose. This fundamental error of thought can and must be called *an error of materialism,* in that economism directly or indirectly includes a conviction of the primacy and superiority of the material, and directly or indirectly places the spiritual and the personal (man's activity, moral values and such matters) in a position of subordination to material reality. This is still not *theoretical materialism* in the full sense of the term, but it is certainly *practical materialism,* a materialism judged capable of satisfying man's needs, not so much on the grounds of premises derived from materialist theory, as on the grounds of a particular way of evaluating things, and so on the grounds of a certain hierarchy of goods based on the greater immediate attractiveness of what is material.

13.4 The error of thinking in the categories of economism went hand in hand with the formation of a materialist philosophy, as this philosophy developed from the most elementary and common phase (also called common materialism, because it professes to reduce spiritual reality to a superfluous phenomenon) to the phase of what is called dialectical materialism. However, within the framework of the present consideration, it seems that *economism had a decisive importance* for the fundamental issue of human work, in particular for the separation of labor and capital and for setting them up in opposition as two production factors viewed in the above-mentioned economistic perspective; and it seems that economism influenced this non-humanistic way of stating the issue before the materialist philosophical system did. Nevertheless it is obvious that materialism, including its dialectical form, is incapable of providing sufficient and definitive bases for thinking about human work, in order that the primacy of man over the capital instrument, the primacy of the person over things, may find in it adequate and irrefutable *confirmation and support.* In dialectical materialism too man is not first and foremost the subject of work and the efficient cause of the production process, but continues to be understood and treated, in dependence on what is material, as a kind of "resultant" of the economic or production relations prevailing at a given period.

13.5 Obviously, the antinomy between labor and capital under consideration here — *the antinomy* in which *labor was separated from capital and set up in opposition to it,* in a certain sense on the ontic level, as if it were just an element like any other in the economic process — did not originate merely in the philosophy and economic theories of the eighteenth century; rather it originated in the whole of the *economic and social practice* of that time, the time of the birth and rapid development of industrialization, in which what was mainly seen was the possibility of vastly increasing material wealth, means, while the end, that is to say, man, who should be served by the means, was ignored. It was this practical error that *struck a blow* first and foremost against human labor, against *the working man,* and caused the ethically just social reaction already spoken of above. The same error, which is now part of history, and which was connected with the period of primitive capitalism and liberalism, can nevertheless be repeated in other circumstances of time and place, if people's thinking starts from the same theoretical or practical premises. The only chance there seems to be for radically overcoming this error is through adequate changes both in theory and in practice, changes *in line with* the definite *conviction of the primacy* of the person over things, and of human *labor over capital* as a whole collection of means of production.

Work and ownership

14.1 The historical process briefly presented here has certainly gone beyond its initial phase, but it is still taking place and indeed is spreading in the relationships between nations and continents. It needs to be specified further from another point of view. It is obvious that, when we speak of opposition between labor and capital, we are not dealing only with abstract concepts or "impersonal forces" operating in economic production. Behind both concepts there are people, living, actual people: on the one side are those who do the work without being the owners of the means of production, and on the other side those who act as entrepreneurs and who own these means or represent the owners. Thus *the issue of ownership or property* enters from the beginning into the whole of this difficult historical process. The Encyclical *Rerum Novarum,* which has the social question as its theme, stresses this issue also, recalling and confirming the Church's teaching on ownership, on the right to private property even when it is a question of the means of production. The Encyclical *Mater et Magistra* did the same.

14.2 The above principle, as it was then stated and as it is still taught by the Church, *diverges* radically from the program of *collectivism* as proclaimed by Marxism and put into practice in various countries in the decades following the time of Leo XIII's Encyclical. At the same time it differs from the program of *capitalism* practiced by liberalism and by the political systems inspired by it. In the latter case, the difference consists in the way the right to ownership or property is understood. Christian tradition has never upheld this right as absolute and untouchable. On the contrary, it has always understood this right within the broader context of the right common to all to use the goods of the whole of creation: *the right to private property is subordinated to the right to common use,* to the fact that goods are meant for everyone.

14.3 Furthermore, in the Church's teaching, ownership has never been understood in a way that could constitute grounds for social conflict in labor. As mentioned above, property is acquired first of all through work in order that it may serve work. This concerns in a special way ownership of the means of production. Isolating these means as a separate property in order to set it up in the form of "capital" in opposition to "labor" — and even to practice exploitation of labor — is contrary to the very nature of these means and their possession. They cannot be *possessed against labor,* they cannot even be *possessed for possession's sake,* because the only legitimate title to their possession — whether in the form of private ownership or in the form of public or collective ownership — is *that they should serve labor,* and thus, by serving labor, that they should make possible the achievement of the first principle of this order, namely, the universal destination of goods and the right to common use of them. From this point of view, therefore, in consideration of human labor and of common access to the goods meant for man, one cannot exclude the *socialization,* in suitable conditions, of certain means of production. In the course of the decades since the publication of the Encyclical *Rerum Novarum,* the Church's teaching has always recalled all these principles, going back to the arguments formulated in a much older tradition, for example, the well-known arguments of the *Summa Theologiae* of Saint Thomas Aquinas.[22]

14.4 In the present document, which has human work as its main theme, it is right to confirm all the effort with which the Church's teaching has striven and continues to strive always to ensure the priority of work and, thereby, man's character as a *subject* in social life and, especially, in the dynamic *structure of the whole economic process.* From this point of view the position of "rigid" capitalism continues to remain unacceptable, namely the position that defends the exclusive right to private ownership of the means of production as an untouchable "dogma" of economic life. The principle of respect for work demands that this right should undergo a constructive revision, both in theory and in practice. If it is true that capital, as the whole of the means of production, is at the same time the product of the work of generations, it is equally true that capital is being unceasingly created through the work done with the help of all these means of production, and these means can be seen as a great workbench at which the present generation of workers is working day after day. Obviously we are dealing here with different kinds of work, not only so-

---

[22] On the right to property see *Summa Theologiae,* II-II, q. 66, aa. 2 and 6; *De Regimine Principum,* Book 1, Chapters 15 and 17. On the social function of property see *Summa Theologiae,* II-II, q. 134, a. 1, ad 3.

called manual labor but also the many forms of intellectual work, including white-collar work and management.

14.5 In the light of the above, the many proposals put forward by experts in Catholic social teaching and by the highest Magisterium of the Church take on special significance:[23] *proposals for joint ownership of the means of work,* sharing by the workers in the management and/or profits of business, so-called shareholding by labor, etc. Whether these various proposals can or cannot be applied concretely, it is clear that recognition of the proper position of labor and the worker in the production process demands various adaptations in the sphere of the right to ownership of the means of production. This is so not only in view of older situations but also, first and foremost, in view of the whole of the situation and the problems in the second half of the present century with regard to the so-called Third World and the various new independent countries that have arisen, especially in Africa but elsewhere as well, in place of the colonial territories of the past.

14.6 Therefore, while the position of "rigid" capitalism must undergo continual revision, in order to be reformed from the point of view of human rights, both human rights in the widest sense and those linked with man's work, it must be stated that, from the same point of view, these many deeply desired reforms cannot be achieved by an *a priori elimination of private ownership of the means of production.* For it must be noted that merely taking these means of production (capital) out of the hands of their private owners is not enough to ensure their satisfactory socialization. They cease to be the property of a certain social group, namely the private owners, and become the property of organized society, coming under the administration and direct control of another group of people, namely those who, though not owning them, from the fact of exercising power in society *manage* them on the level of the whole national or the local economy.

14.7 This group in authority may carry out its task satisfactorily from the point of view of the priority of labor; but it may also carry it out badly by claiming for itself *a monopoly of the administration and disposal* of the means of production and not refraining even from offending basic human rights. Thus, merely converting the means of production into State property in the collectivist system is by no means equivalent to "socializing" that property. We can speak of socializing only when the subject character of society is ensured, that is to say, when on the basis of his work each person is fully entitled to

---

[23] Cf. Pius XI, Encyclical Letter *Quadragesimo Anno* (May 15, 1931), II: *AAS* 23 (1931), 199; Second Vatican Ecumenical Council, Pastoral Constitution on the Church in the Modern World *Gaudium et Spes,* 68: *AAS* 58 (1966), 1089-1090.

consider himself a part-owner of the great workbench at which he is working with every one else. A way toward that goal could be found by associating labor with the ownership of capital, as far as possible, and by producing a wide range of intermediate bodies with economic, social and cultural purposes; they would be bodies enjoying real autonomy with regard to the public powers, pursuing their specific aims in honest collaboration with each other and in subordination to the demands of the common good, and they would be living communities both in form and in substance, in the sense that the members of each body would be looked upon and treated as persons and encouraged to take an active part in the life of the body.[24]

The "personalist" argument

15.1 Thus, *the principle of the priority of labor* over capital is a postulate of the order of social morality. It has key importance both in the system built on the principle of private ownership of the means of production and also in the system in which private ownership of these means has been limited even in a radical way. Labor is in a sense inseparable from capital; in no way does it accept the antinomy, that is to say, the separation and opposition with regard to the means of production that has weighed upon human life in recent centuries as a result of merely economic premises. When man works, using all the means of production, he also wishes the fruit of this work to be used by himself and others, and he wishes to be able to take part in the very work process as a sharer in responsibility and creativity at the workbench to which he applies himself.

15.2 From this spring certain specific rights of workers, corresponding to the obligation of work. They will be discussed later. But here it must be emphasized, in general terms, that the person who works desires *not only* due *remuneration* for his work; he also wishes that, within the production process, provision be made for him to be able to *know* that in his work, even on something that is owned in common, he is working *"for himself."* This awareness is extinguished within him in a system of excessive bureaucratic centralization, which makes the worker feel that he is just a cog in a huge machine moved from above, that he is for more reasons than one a mere production instrument rather than a true subject of work with an initiative of his own. The Church's teaching has always expressed the strong and deep conviction that man's work concerns not only the economy but also, and especially, personal values. The economic system itself and the production process benefit precisely when these personal values are fully respected. In the mind of Saint

---

[24] Cf. John XXIII, Encyclical Letter *Mater et Magistra* (May 15, 1961), II: *AAS* 53 (1961), 419.

Thomas Aquinas,[25] this is the principal reason in favor of private ownership of the means of production. While we accept that for certain well-founded reasons exceptions can be made to the principle of private ownership — in our own time we even see that the system of "socialized ownership" has been introduced — nevertheless the personalist *argument still holds good* both on the level of principles and *on the practical level.* If it is to be rational and fruitful, any socialization of the means of production must take this argument into consideration. Every effort must be made to ensure that in this kind of system also the human person can preserve his awareness of working "for himself." If this is not done, incalculable damage is inevitably done throughout the economic process, not only economic damage but first and foremost damage to man.

IV

Rights of Workers

Within the broad context of human rights

16.1 While work, in all its many senses, is an obligation, that is to say a duty, it is also a source of rights on the part of the *worker.* These rights must be examined in the broad *context of human rights as a whole,* which are connatural with man, and many of which are proclaimed by various international organizations and increasingly guaranteed by the individual States for their citizens. Respect for this broad range of human rights constitutes the fundamental condition for peace in the modern world: peace both within individual countries and societies and in international relations, as the Church's Magisterium has several times noted, especially since the Encyclical *Pacem in Terris.* The *human rights that flow from work* are part of the broader context of those fundamental rights of the person.

16.2 However, within this context they have a specific character corresponding to the specific nature of human work as outlined above. It is in keeping with this character that we must view them. Work is, as has been said, *an obligation,* that is to say, *a duty, on the part of man.* This is true *in all the many meanings of the word.* Man must work, both because the Creator has commanded it and because of his own humanity, which requires work in order to be maintained and developed. Man must work out of regard for others, especially his own family, but also for the society he belongs to, the country of which he is a child, and the whole human family of which he is a member, since he is the heir to the work of generations and at the same time a

---

[25] Cf. *Summa Theologiae,* II-II, q. 65, a. 2.

sharer in building the future of those who will come after him in the succession of history. All this constitutes the moral obligation of work, understood in its wide sense. When we have to consider the moral rights, corresponding to this obligation, of every person with regard to work, we must always keep before our eyes the whole vast range of points of reference in which the labor of every working subject is manifested.

16.3 For when we speak of the obligation of work and of the rights of the worker that correspond to this obligation, we think in the first place of the relationship between *the employer, direct or indirect, and the worker.*

16.4 The distinction between the direct and the indirect employer is seen to be very important when one considers both the way in which labor is actually organized and the possibility of the formation of just or unjust relationships in the field of labor.

16.5 Since *the direct employer* is the person or institution with whom the worker enters directly into a work contract in accordance with definite conditions, we must understand as *the indirect* employer many different factors, other than the direct employer, that exercise a determining influence on the shaping both of the work contract and, consequently, of just or unjust relationships in the field of human labor.

Direct and indirect employer

17.1 The concept of indirect employer includes both persons and institutions of various kinds, and also collective labor contracts and the *principles* of conduct which are laid down by these persons and institutions and which determine the whole socioeconomic *system* or are its result. The concept of "indirect employer" thus refers to many different elements. The responsibility of the indirect employer differs from that of the direct employer — the term itself indicates that the responsibility is less direct — but it remains a true responsibility: the indirect employer substantially determines one or other facet of the labor relationship, thus conditioning the conduct of the direct employer when the latter determines in concrete terms the actual work contract and labor relations. This is not to absolve the direct employer from his own responsibility, but only to draw attention to the whole network of influences that condition his conduct. When it is a question of establishing *an ethically correct labor policy,* all these influences must be kept in mind. A policy is correct when the objective rights of the worker are fully respected.

17.2 The concept of indirect employer is applicable to every society, and in the first place to the State. For it is the State that must conduct a just labor policy. However, it is common knowledge that in the present system of economic relations in the world there are numerous *links between* individual *States,* links that find expression, for instance, in the import and export process, that is to say, in the mutual exchange of economic goods, whether raw materials, semi-manufactured goods, or finished industrial products. These links also create mutual *dependence,* and as a result it would be difficult to speak, in the case of any State, even the economically most powerful, of complete self-sufficiency or autarky.

17.3 Such a system of mutual dependence is in itself normal. However, it can easily become an occasion for various forms of exploitation or injustice and as a result influence the labor policy of individual States; and finally it can influence the individual worker, who is the proper subject of labor. For instance the *highly industrialized countries,* and even more the businesses that direct on a large scale the means of industrial production (the companies referred to as multinational or transnational), fix the highest possible prices for their products, while trying at the same time to fix the lowest possible prices for raw materials or semi-manufactured goods. This is one of the causes of an ever-increasing disproportion between national incomes. The gap between most of the richest countries and the poorest ones is not diminishing or being stabilized but is increasing more and more, to the detriment, obviously, of the poor countries. Evidently this must have an effect on local labor policy and on the worker's situation in the economically disadvantaged societies. Finding himself in a system thus conditioned, the direct employer fixes working conditions below the objective requirements of the workers, especially if he himself wishes to obtain the highest possible profits from the business which he runs (or from the businesses which he runs, in the case of a situation of "socialized" ownership of the means of production).

17.4 It is easy to see that this framework of forms of dependence linked with the concept of the indirect employer is enormously extensive and complicated. It is determined, in a sense, by *all* the elements that are decisive for economic life *within a given society and State,* but also by much wider links and forms of dependence. The attainment of the worker's rights cannot, however, be doomed to be merely a result of economic systems which on a larger or smaller scale are guided chiefly by the criterion of maximum profit. On the contrary, it is respect for the objective rights of the worker — every kind of worker: manual or intellectual, industrial or agricultural, etc.— that must constitute *the adequate and fundamental criterion* for shaping the whole economy, both on the level of the individual society and State and within the whole of the world economic policy and of the systems of international relationships that derive from it.

17.5 Influence in this direction should be exercised by all *the International Organizations* whose concern it is, beginning with the United Nations Organization. It appears that the International Labor Organization and the Food and Agriculture Organization of the United Nations and other bodies too have fresh contributions to offer on this point in particular. Within the individual States there are ministries or *public departments* and also various *social institutions* set up for this purpose. All of this effectively indicates the importance of the indirect employer — as has been said above — in achieving full respect for the worker's rights, since the rights of the human person are the key element in the whole of the social moral order.

The employment issue

18.1 When we consider the rights of workers in relation to the "indirect employer," that is to say, all the agents at the national and international level that are responsible for the whole orientation of labor policy, we must first direct our attention to *a fundamental issue:* the question of finding work, or, in other words, the issue of *suitable employment for all who are capable of it.* The opposite of a just and right situation in this field is unemployment, that is to say the lack of work for those who are capable of it. It can be a question of general unemployment or of unemployment in certain sectors of work. The role of the agents included under the title of indirect employer is *to act against unemployment,* which in all cases is an evil, and which, when it reaches a certain level, can become a real social disaster. It is particularly painful when it especially affects young people, who after appropriate cultural, technical and professional preparation fail to find work, and see their sincere wish to work and their readiness to take on their own responsibility for the economic and social development of the community sadly frustrated. The obligation to provide unemployment benefits, that is to say, the duty to make suitable grants indispensable for the subsistence of unemployed workers and their families, is a duty springing from the fundamental principle of the moral order in this sphere, namely the principle of the common use of goods or, to put it in another and still simpler way, the right to life and subsistence.

18.2 In order to meet the danger of unemployment and to ensure employment for all, the agents defined here as "indirect employer" must make provision for *overall planning* with regard to the different kinds of work by which not only the economic life but also the cultural life of a given society is shaped; they must also give attention to organizing that work in a correct and rational way. In the final analysis this overall concern weighs on the shoulders of the State, but it cannot mean one-sided centralization by the public authorities.

Instead, what is in question is a just and rational *coordination*, within the framework of which the *initiative* of individuals, free groups and local work centers and complexes must be *safeguarded*, keeping in mind what has been said above with regard to the subject character of human labor.

18.3 The fact of the mutual dependence of societies and States and the need to collaborate in various areas mean that, while preserving the sovereign rights of each society and State in the field of planning and organizing labor in its own society, action in this important area must also be taken in the dimension of *international collaboration* by means of the necessary treaties and agreements. Here too the criterion for these pacts and agreements must more and more be the criterion of human work considered as a fundamental right of all human beings, work which gives similar rights to all those who work, in such a way that the living standard of the workers in the different societies will *less and less show those disturbing differences* which are unjust and are apt to provoke even violent reactions. The International Organizations have an enormous part to play in this area. They must let themselves be guided by an exact diagnosis of the complex situations and of the influence exercised by natural, historical, civil and other such circumstances. They must also be more highly operative with regard to plans for action jointly decided on, that is to say, they must be more effective in carrying them out.

18.4 In this direction it is possible to actuate a plan for universal and proportionate progress by all, in accordance with the guidelines of Paul VI's Encyclical *Populorum Progressio*. It must be stressed that the constitutive element in this *progress* and also the most adequate *way to verify it* in a spirit of justice and peace, which the Church proclaims and for which she does not cease to pray to the Father of all individuals and of all peoples, is *the continual reappraisal of man's work*, both in the aspect of its objective finality and in the aspect of the dignity of the subject of all work, that is to say, man. The progress in question must be made through man and for man and it must produce its fruit in man. A test of this progress will be the increasingly mature recognition of the purpose of work and increasingly universal respect for the rights inherent in work in conformity with the dignity of man, the subject of work.

18.5 Rational planning and the proper organization of human labor in keeping with individual societies and States should also facilitate the discovery of the right proportions between the different kinds of employment: work on the land, in industry, in the various services, white-collar work and scientific or artistic work, in accordance with the capacities of individuals and for the common good of each society and of the whole of mankind. The organization of human life in accordance with the many possibilities of labor should be matched by a suitable *system of instruction* and education, aimed first of all at developing mature human beings, but also aimed at preparing people specifically for assuming to good advantage an appropriate place in the vast and socially differentiated world of work.

18.6 As we view the whole human family throughout the world, we cannot fail to be struck by *a disconcerting fact* of immense proportions: the fact that, while conspicuous natural resources remain unused, there are huge numbers of people who are unemployed or underemployed and countless multitudes of people suffering from hunger. This is a fact that without any doubt demonstrates that both within the individual political communities and in their relationships on the continental and world level there is something wrong with the organization of work and employment, precisely at the most critical and socially most important points.

Wages and other social benefits

19.1 After outlining the important role that concern for providing employment for all workers plays in safeguarding respect for the inalienable rights of man in view of his work, it is worthwhile taking a closer look at these rights, which in the final analysis are formed within the relationship *between worker and direct employer*. All that has been said above on the subject of the indirect employer is aimed at defining these relationships more exactly, by showing the many forms of conditioning within which these relationships are indirectly formed. This consideration does not however have a purely descriptive purpose; it is not a brief treatise on economics or politics. It is a matter of highlighting the *deontological and moral aspect*. The key problem of social ethics in this case is that of *just remuneration* for work done. In the context of the present there is no more important way for securing a just relationship between the worker and the employer than that constituted by remuneration for work. Whether the work is done in a system of private ownership of the means of production or in a system where ownership has undergone a certain "socialization," the relationship between the employer (first and foremost the direct employer) and the worker is resolved on the basis of the wage, that is, through just remuneration for work done.

19.2 It should also be noted that the justice of a socioeconomic system and, in each case, its just functioning, deserve in the final analysis to be evaluated by the way in which man's work is properly remunerated in the system. Here we return once more to the first principle of the whole ethical and social order, namely, *the principle of the common use of goods*. In every system, regardless of the fundamental relationships within it between capital and labor, wages, that is to say *remuneration for work,* are still a *practical means* whereby the vast majority of people can have access to those goods which are intended for common use: both the goods of nature and manufactured goods. Both kinds of goods become accessible to the worker through the wage which he receives as remuneration for his work. Hence, in every case, a just wage is the concrete means of *verifying the justice* of the whole socioeconomic system and, in any case, of checking that it is functioning justly. It is not the only means of checking, but it is a particularly important one and, in a sense, the key means.

19.3 This means of checking concerns above all the family. Just remuneration for the work of an adult who is responsible for a family means remuneration which will suffice for establishing and properly maintaining a family and for providing security for its future. Such remuneration can be given either through what is called *a family wage* — that is, a single salary given to the head of the family for his work, sufficient for the needs of the family without the other spouse having to take up gainful employment outside the home — or through *other social measures* such as family allowances or grants to mothers devoting themselves exclusively to their families. These grants should correspond to the actual needs, that is, to the number of dependents for as long as they are not in a position to assume proper responsibility for their own lives.

19.4 Experience confirms that there must be *a social reevaluation of the mother's role,* of the toil connected with it, and of the need that children have for care, love and affection in order that they may develop into responsible, morally and religiously mature and psychologically stable persons. It will redound to the credit of society to make it possible for a mother — without inhibiting her freedom, without psychological or practical discrimination, and without penalizing her as compared with other women — to devote herself to taking care of her children and educating them in accordance with their needs, which vary with age. Having to abandon these tasks in order to take up paid work outside the home is wrong from the point of view of the good of society and of the family when it contradicts or hinders these primary goals of the mission of a mother.[26]

19.5 In this context it should be emphasized that, on a more general level, the whole labor process must be organized and adapted in such a way as to respect the requirements of the person and his or her forms of life, above all life in the home, taking into account the individual's age and sex. It is a fact that in many societies women work in nearly every sector of life. But it is

---

[26] Second Vatican Ecumenical Council, Pastoral Constitution on the Church in the Modern World *Gaudium et Spes,* 67: AAS 58 (1966), 1089.

fitting that they should be able to fulfill their tasks *in accordance with their own nature*, without being discriminated against and without being excluded from jobs for which they are capable, but also without lack of respect for their family aspirations and for their specific role in contributing, together with men, to the good of society. The *true advancement of women* requires that labor should be structured in such a way that women do not have to pay for their advancement by abandoning what is specific to them and at the expense of the family, in which women as mothers have an irreplaceable role.

19.6 Besides wages, various *social benefits* intended to ensure the life and health of workers and their families play a part here. The expenses involved in health care, especially in the case of accidents at work, demand that medical assistance should be easily available for workers, and that as far as possible it should be cheap or even free of charge. Another sector regarding benefits is the sector associated with the *right to rest*. In the first place this involves a regular weekly rest comprising at least Sunday, and also a longer period of rest, namely the holiday or vacation taken once a year or possibly in several shorter periods during the year. A third sector concerns the right to a pension and to insurance for old age and in case of accidents at work. Within the sphere of these principal rights, there develops a whole system of particular rights which, together with remuneration for work, determine the correct relationship between worker and employer. Among these rights there should never be overlooked the right to a working environment and to manufacturing processes which are not harmful to the workers' physical health or to their moral integrity.

Importance of unions

20.1 All these rights, together with the need for the workers themselves to secure them, give rise to yet another right: the *right of association,* that is to form associations for the purpose of defending the vital interests of those employed in the various professions. These associations are called *labor or trade unions.* The vital interests of the workers are to a certain extent common for all of them; at the same time however each type of work, each profession, has its own specific character which should find a particular reflection in these organizations.

20.2 In a sense, unions go back to the medieval guilds of artisans, insofar as those organizations brought together people belonging to the same craft and thus *on the basis of their work.* However, unions differ from the guilds on this essential point: the modern unions grew up from the struggle of the workers — workers in general but especially the industrial workers — to protect their *just rights* vis-à-vis the entrepreneurs and the owners of the means of production. Their task is to defend the existential interests of workers in all sectors in which their rights are concerned. The experience of history teaches that organizations of this type are an indispensable *element of social life*, especially in modern industrialized societies. Obviously, this does not mean that only industrial workers can set up associations of this type. Representatives of every profession can use them to ensure their own rights. Thus there are unions of agricultural workers and of white-collar workers; there are also employers' associations. All, as has been said above, are further divided into groups or subgroups according to particular professional specializations.

20.3 Catholic social teaching does not hold that unions are no more than a reflection of the "class" structure of society and that they are a mouthpiece for a class struggle which inevitably governs social life. They are indeed *a mouthpiece for the struggle for social justice*, for the just rights of working people in accordance with their individual professions. However, this struggle should be seen as a normal endeavor "for" the just good: in the present case, for the good which corresponds to the needs and merits of working people associated by profession; but it *is not a struggle "against" others*. Even if in controversial questions the struggle takes on a character of opposition toward others, this is because it aims at the good of social justice, not for the sake of "struggle" or in order to eliminate the opponent. It is characteristic of work that it first and foremost unites people. In this consists its social power: the power to build a community. In the final analysis, both those who work and those who manage the means of production or who own them must in some way be united in this community. *In the light of this fundamental structure* of all work — in the light of the fact that, in the final analysis, labor and capital are indispensable components of the process of production in any social system — it is clear that, even if it is because of their work needs that people unite to secure their rights, their union remains a constructive factor of *social order* and *solidarity*, and it is impossible to ignore it.

20.4 Just efforts to secure the rights of workers who are united by the same profession should always take into account the limitations imposed by the general economic situation of the country. Union demands cannot be turned into a kind of *group or class "egoism,"* although they can and should also aim at correcting — with a view to the common good of the whole of society — everything defective in the system of ownership of the means of production or in the way these are managed. Social and socioeconomic life is certainly like a system of "connected vessels," and every social activity directed toward safeguarding the rights of particular groups should adapt itself to this system.

20.5 In this sense, union activity undoubtedly enters the field of *politics,* understood as *prudent concern for the common good*. However, the role of unions is not to "play politics" in the sense that the expression is commonly under-stood today. Unions do not have the character of political parties struggling for power; they should not be subjected to the decision of political parties or have too close links with them. In fact, in such a situation they easily lose contact with their specific role, which is to secure the just rights of workers within the framework of the common good of the whole of society; instead they become *an instrument used for other purposes*.

20.6 Speaking of the protection of the just rights of workers according to their individual professions, we must of course always keep in mind that which deter-mines the subjective character of work in each profession, but at the same time, indeed before all else, we must keep in mind that which conditions the specific dignity of the subject of the work. The activity of union organizations opens up many possibilities in this respect, including their *efforts to instruct and educate* the workers and to *foster their self-education*. Praise is due to the work of the schools, what are known as workers' or people's universities and the training programs and courses which have developed and are still developing this field of activity. It is always to be hoped that, thanks to the work of their unions, workers will not only *have* more, but above all *be* more: in other words, that they will realize their humanity more fully in every respect.

20.7 *One method* used by unions in pursuing the just rights of their mem-bers is *the strike* or work stoppage, as a kind of ultimatum to the competent bodies, especially the employers. This method is recognized by Catholic social teaching as legitimate under the proper conditions and within just limits. In this connection workers should be assured the *right to strike*, without being subjected to personal penal sanctions for taking part in a strike. While admit-ting that it is a legitimate means, we must at the same time emphasize that a strike remains, in a sense, an extreme means. *It must not be abused;* it must not be abused especially for "political" purposes. Furthermore it must never be forgotten that, when essential community services are in question, they must in every case be ensured, if necessary by means of appropriate legisla-tion. Abuse of the strike weapon can lead to the paralysis of the whole of socioeconomic life, and this is contrary to the requirements of the common good of society, which also corresponds to the properly understood nature of work itself.

Dignity of agricultural work

21.1 All that has been said thus far on the dignity of work, on the objective and subjective dimension of human work, can be directly applied to the question of agricultural work and to the situation of the person who cultivates the earth by toiling in the fields. This is a vast sector of work on our planet, a sector not restricted to one or another continent, nor limited to the societies which have already attained a certain level of development and progress. The world of agriculture, which provides society with the goods it needs for its daily sustenance, is of *fundamental importance*. The conditions of the rural population and of agricultural work vary from place to place, and the social position of agricultural workers differs from country to country. This depends not only on the level of development of agricultural technology but also, and perhaps more, on the recognition of the just rights of agricultural workers and, finally, on the level of awareness regarding the social ethics of work.

21.2 Agricultural work involves considerable difficulties, including unremitting and sometimes exhausting physical effort and a lack of appreciation on the part of society, to the point of making agricultural people feel that they are social outcasts and of speeding up the phenomenon of their mass exodus from the countryside to the cities and unfortunately to still more dehumanizing living conditions. Added to this are the lack of adequate professional training and of proper equipment, the spread of a certain individualism, and also *objectively unjust situations*. In certain developing countries, millions of people are forced to cultivate the land belonging to others and are exploited by the big landowners, without any hope of ever being able to gain possession of even a small piece of land of their own. There is a lack of forms of legal protection for the agricultural workers themselves and for their families in case of old age, sickness or unemployment. Long days of hard physical work are paid miserably. Land which could be cultivated is left abandoned by the owners. Legal titles to possession of a small portion of land that someone has personally cultivated for years are disregarded or left defenseless against the "land hunger" of more powerful individuals or groups. But even in the economically developed countries, where scientific research, technological achievements and State policy have brought agriculture to a very advanced level, the right to work can be infringed when the farm workers are denied the possibility of sharing in decisions concerning their services, or when they are denied the right to free association with a view to their just advancement socially, culturally and economically.

21.3 In many situations radical and urgent changes are therefore needed in order to restore to agriculture — and to rural people — their just value *as the basis for a healthy economy*, within the social community's development as a whole. Thus it is necessary to proclaim and promote the dignity of work, of all work but especially of agricultural work, in which man so eloquently "subdues" the earth he has received as a gift from God and affirms his "dominion" in the visible world.

The disabled person and work

22.1 Recently, national communities and International Organizations have turned their attention to another question connected with work, one full of implications: the question of disabled people. They too are fully human subjects with corresponding innate, sacred and inviolable rights, and, in spite of the limitations and sufferings affecting their bodies and faculties, they point up more clearly the dignity and greatness of man. Since disabled people are subjects with all their rights, they should be helped to participate in the life of society in all its aspects and at all the levels accessible to their capacities. The disabled person is one of us and participates fully in the same humanity that we possess. It would be radically unworthy of man, and a denial of our common humanity, to admit to the life of the community, and thus admit to work, only those who are fully functional. To do so would be to practice *a serious form of discrimination*, that of the strong and healthy against the weak and sick. Work in the objective sense should be subordinated, in this circumstance too, to the dignity of man, to the subject of work and not to economic advantage.

22.2 The various bodies involved in the world of labor, both the direct and the indirect employer, should therefore by means of effective and appropriate measures foster the right of disabled people to professional training and work, so that they can be given a productive activity suited to them. Many practical problems arise at this point, as well as legal and economic ones; but the community, that is to say, the public authorities, associations and intermediate groups, business enterprises and the disabled themselves should pool their ideas and resources so as to attain this goal that must not be shirked: *that disabled people may be offered work according to their capabilities*, for this is demanded by their dignity as persons and as subjects of work. Each community will be able to set up suitable structures for finding or creating jobs for such people both in the usual public or private enterprises, by offering them ordinary or suitably adapted jobs, and in what are called "protected" enterprises and surroundings.

22.3 Careful attention must be devoted to the physical and psychological working conditions of disabled people — as for all workers — to their just remuneration, to the possibility of their promotion, and to the elimination of various obstacles. Without hiding the fact that this is a complex and difficult task, it is to be hoped that *a correct concept of labor in the subjective sense* will produce a situation which will make it possible for disabled people to feel that they are not cut off from the working world or dependent upon society, but that they are full-scale subjects of work, useful, respected for their human dignity and called to contribute to the progress and welfare of their families and of the community according to their particular capacities.

Work and the emigration question

23.1 Finally, we must say at least a few words on the subject of *emigration in search of work*. This is an age-old phenomenon which nevertheless continues to be repeated and is still today very widespread as a result of the complexities of modern life. Man has the right to leave his native land for various motives — and also the right to return — in order to seek better conditions of life in another country. This fact is certainly not without difficulties of various kinds. Above all it generally constitutes a loss for the country which is left behind. It is the departure of a person who is also a member of a great community united by history, tradition and culture; and that person must begin life in the midst of another society united by a different culture and very often by a different language. In this case, it is the loss of *a subject of work,* whose efforts of mind and body could contribute to the common good of his own country, but these efforts, this contribution, are instead offered to another society which in a sense has less right to them than the person's country of origin.

23.2 Nevertheless, even if emigration is in some aspects an evil, in certain circumstances it is, as the phrase goes, a necessary evil. Everything should be done — and certainly much is being done to this end — to prevent this material evil from causing greater *moral harm;* indeed every possible effort should be made to ensure that it may bring benefit to the emigrant's personal, family and social life, both for the country to which he goes and the country which he leaves. In this area much depends on just legislation, in particular with regard to the rights of workers. It is obvious that the question of just legislation enters into the context of the present considerations, especially from the point of view of these rights.

23.3 The most important thing is that the person working away from his native land, whether as a permanent emigrant or as a seasonal worker, should not be *placed at a disadvantage* in comparison with the other workers in that society in the matter of working rights. Emigration in search of work must in no way become an opportunity for financial or social exploitation. As regards the work relationship, the same criteria should be applied to immigrant workers as to all other workers in the society concerned. The value of work should be measured by the same standard and not according to the difference in nationality, religion or race. For even greater reason *the situation of constraint* in which the emigrant may find himself *should not be exploited.* All these circumstances should categorically give way, after special qualifications have of course been taken into consideration, to the fundamental value of work, which is bound up with the dignity of the human person. Once more the fundamental principle must be repeated: the hierarchy of values and the profound meaning of work itself require that capital should be at the service of labor and not labor at the service of capital.

V

Elements for a Spirituality of Work

A particular task for the Church

24.1 It is right to devote the last part of these reflections about human work, on the occasion of the ninetieth anniversary of the Encyclical *Rerum Novarum,* to the spirituality of work in the Christian sense. Since work in its subjective aspect is always a personal action, *an actus personae,* it follows that *the whole person, body and spirit,* participates in it, whether it is manual or intellectual work. It is also to the whole person that the word of the living God is directed, the evangelical message of salvation, in which we find many points which concern human work and which throw particular light on it. These points need to be properly assimilated: an inner effort on the part of the human spirit, guided by faith, hope and charity, is needed in order that through these points the *work* of the individual human being may *be given the meaning which it has in the eyes of God* and by means of which work enters into the salvation process on a par with the other ordinary yet particularly important components of its texture.

24.2 The Church considers it her duty to speak out on work from the viewpoint of its human value and of the moral order to which it belongs, and she sees this as one of her important tasks within the service that she renders to the evangelical message as a whole. At the same time she sees it as her particular duty *to form a spirituality of work* which will help all people to come closer, through work, to God, the Creator and Redeemer, to participate in his salvific plan for man and the world and to deepen their friendship with Christ in their lives by accepting, through faith, a living participation in his threefold mission as priest, prophet and king, as the Second Vatican Council so eloquently teaches.

Work as a sharing in the activity of the Creator

25.1 As the Second Vatican Council says, "throughout the course of the centuries, men have labored to better the circumstances of their lives through a monumental amount of individual and collective effort. To believers, this point is settled: considered in itself, such human activity accords with God's will. For man, created to God's image, received a mandate to subject to himself the earth and all that it contains, and to govern the world with justice and holiness; a mandate to relate himself and the totality of things to him who was to be acknowledged as the Lord and Creator of all. Thus, by the subjection of all things to man, the name of God would be wonderful in all the earth."[27]

25.2 The word of God's revelation is profoundly marked by the fundamental truth that *man, created in the image of God, shares by his work in the activity of the Creator* and that, within the limits of his own human capabilities, man in a sense continues to develop that activity, and perfects it as he advances further and further in the discovery of the resources and values contained in the whole of creation. We find this truth at the very beginning of Sacred Scripture, in the Book of Genesis, where the creation activity itself is presented in the form of "work" done by God during "six days,"[28] "resting" on the seventh day.[29] Besides, the last book of Sacred Scripture echoes the same respect for what God has done through his creative "work" when it proclaims: "Great and wonderful are your deeds, O Lord God the Almighty";[30] this is similar to the Book of Genesis, which concludes the description of each day of creation with the statement: "And God saw that it was good."[31]

25.3 This description of creation, which we find in the very first chapter of the Book of Genesis, is also *in a sense the first "gospel of work."* For it shows what the dignity of work consists of: it teaches that man ought to imitate God, his Creator, in working, because man alone has the unique characteristic of likeness to God. Man ought to imitate God both in working and also in resting, since God himself wished to present his own creative activity under the form of *work and rest.* This activity by God in the world always continues, as the words of Christ attest: "My Father is working still. . .":[32] he works with creative power by sustaining in existence the world that he called into being

---

[27] Second Vatican Ecumenical Council, Pastoral Constitution on the Church in the Modern World *Gaudium et Spes*, 34: *AAS* 58 (1966), 1052-1053.

[28] Cf. Gen 2:2; Ex 20:8, 11; Dt 5:12-14.

[29] Cf. Gen 2:3.

[30] Rev 15:3.

[31] Gen 1:4, 10, 12, 18, 21, 25, 31.

[32] Jn 5:17.

from nothing, and he works with salvific power in the hearts of those whom from the beginning he has destined for "rest"[33] in union with himself in his "Father's house."[34] Therefore man's work too not only requires a rest every "seventh day,"[35] but also cannot consist in the mere exercise of human strength in external action; it must leave room for man to prepare himself, by becoming more and more what in the will of God he ought to be, for the *"rest" that the Lord reserves for his servants and friends.*[36]

25.4 Awareness that man's work is a participation in God's activity ought to permeate, as the Council teaches, even "*the most ordinary everyday activities.* For, while providing the substance of life for themselves and their families, men and women are performing their activities in a way which appropriately benefits society. They can justly consider that by their labor they are unfolding the Creator's work, consulting the advantages of their brothers and sisters, and contributing by their personal industry to the realization in history of the divine plan."[37]

25.5 This Christian spirituality of work should be a heritage shared by all. Especially in the modern age, the *spirituality* of work should show the *maturity* called for by the tensions and restlessness of mind and heart. "Far from thinking that works produced by man's own talent and energy are in opposition to God's power, and that the rational creature exists as a kind of rival to the Creator, Christians are convinced that the triumphs of the human race are a sign of God's greatness and the flowering of his own mysterious design. For the greater man's power becomes, the farther his individual and community responsibility extends. . . . People are not deterred by *the Christian message* from building up the world, or impelled to neglect the welfare of their fellows. They are, rather, more stringently bound to do these very things."[38]

25.6 The knowledge that by means of work man shares in the work of creation constitutes the most profound *motive* for undertaking it in various sectors. "The faithful, therefore," we read in the Constitution *Lumen Gentium,* "must learn the deepest meaning and the value of all creation, and its orientation to the praise of God. Even by their secular activity they must assist one another to live holier lives. In this way the world will be permeated by the spirit of Christ and more effectively achieve its purpose in justice, charity and

---

[33] Cf. Heb 4:1, 9-10.

[34] Jn 14:2.

[35] Cf. Dt 5:12-14; Ex 20:8-12.

[36] Cf. Mt 25:21.

[37] Second Vatican Ecumenical Council, Pastoral Constitution on the Church in the Modern World *Gaudium et Spes,* 34: *AAS* 58 (1966), 1052-1053.

[38] Ibid.

peace. . . . Therefore, by their competence in secular fields and by their personal activity, elevated from within by the grace of Christ, let them work vigorously so that by human labor, technical skill, and civil culture created goods may be perfected according to the design of the Creator and the light of his Word."[39]

Christ, the man of work

26.1 The truth that by means of work man participates in the activity of God himself, his Creator, was *given particular prominence by Jesus Christ —* the Jesus at whom many of his first listeners in Nazareth "were astonished, saying, 'Where did this man get all this? What is the wisdom given to him? . . . Is not this the carpenter?' "[40] For Jesus not only proclaimed but first and foremost fulfilled by his deeds the "gospel," the word of eternal Wisdom, that had been entrusted to him. Therefore this was also "the gospel of work," because *he who proclaimed it was himself a man of work,* a craftsman like Joseph of Nazareth.[41] And if we do not find in his words a special command to work — but rather on one occasion a prohibition against too much anxiety about work and life[42] — at the same time the eloquence of the life of Christ is unequivocal: he belongs to the "working world," he has appreciation and respect for human work. It can indeed be said that *he looks with love upon human work* and the different forms that it takes, seeing in each one of these forms a particular facet of man's likeness with God, the Creator and Father. Is it not he who says, "My Father is the vinedresser,"[43] and in various ways puts *into his teaching* the fundamental truth about work which is already expressed in the whole tradition of the Old Testament, beginning with the Book of Genesis?

26.2 *The books of the Old Testament* contain many references to human work and to the individual professions exercised by man: for example, the doctor,[44] the pharmacist,[45] the craftsman or artist,[46] the blacksmith[47] — we could apply these words to today's foundry-workers — the potter,[48] the farmer,[49]

---

[39] Second Vatican Ecumenical Council, Dogmatic Constitution on the Church *Lumen Gentium,* 36: *AAS* 57 (1965), 41.

[40] Mk 6:2-3.

[41] Cf. Mt 13:55.

[42] Cf. Mt 6:25-34.

[43] Jn 15:1.

[44] Cf. Sir 38:1-3.

[45] Cf. Sir 38:4-8.

[46] Cf. Ex 31:1-5; Sir 38:27.

[47] Cf. Gen 4:22; Is 44:12.

[48] Cf. Jer 18:3-4; Sir 38:29-30.

[49] Cf. Gen 9:20; Is 5:1-2.

the scholar,[50] the sailor,[51] the builder,[52] the musician,[53] the shepherd,[54] and the fisherman.[55] The words of praise for the work of women are well known.[56] *In his parables on the Kingdom* of God, Jesus Christ constantly refers to human work: that of the shepherd,[57] the farmer,[58] the doctor,[59] the sower,[60] the householder,[61] the servant,[62] the steward,[63] the fisherman,[64] the merchant,[65] the laborer.[66] He also speaks of the various forms of women's work.[67] He compares the apostolate to the manual work of harvesters[68] or fishermen.[69] He refers to the work of scholars too.[70]

26.3 This teaching of Christ on work, based on the example of his life during his years in Nazareth, finds a particularly lively echo *in the teaching of the Apostle Paul.* Paul boasts of working at his trade (he was probably a tentmaker),[71] and thanks to that work he was able even as an Apostle to earn his own bread.[72] "With toil and labor we worked night and day, that we might not burden any of you."[73] Hence his instructions, in the form of *exhortation and command,* on the subject of work: "Now such persons we command and exhort in the Lord Jesus Christ to do their work in quietness and to earn their own living," he writes to the Thessalonians.[74] In fact, noting that some "are

[50] Cf. Eccles 12:9-12; Sir 39:1-8.

[51] Cf. Ps 107:23-30; Wis 14:2-3a.

[52] Cf. Gen 11:3; 2 Kings 12:12-13, 22:5-6.

[53] Cf. Gen 4:21.

[54] Cf. Gen 4:2, 37:2; Ex 3:1; 1 Sam 16:11, and *passim.*

[55] Cf. Ezek 47:10.

[56] Cf. Prov 31:10-27.

[57] For example, Jn 10:1-16.

[58] Cf. Mk 12:1-12.

[59] Cf. Lk 4:23.

[60] Cf. Mk 4:1-9.

[61] Cf. Mt 13:52.

[62] Cf. Mt 24:45; Lk 12:42-48.

[63] Cf. Lk 16:1-8.

[64] Cf. Mt 13:47-50.

[65] Cf. Mt 13:45-46.

[66] Cf. Mt 20:1-16.

[67] Cf. Mt 13:33; Lk 15:8-9.

[68] Cf. Mt 9:37; Jn 4:35-38.

[69] Cf. Mt 4:19.

[70] Cf. Mt 13:52.

[71] Cf. Acts 18:3.

[72] Cf. Acts 20:34-35.

[73] 2 Thess 3:8. Saint Paul recognizes that missionaries have a right to their keep: 1 Cor 9:6-14; Gal 6:6; 2 Thess 3:9; cf. Lk 10:7.

[74] 2 Thess 3:12.

living in idleness . . . not doing any work,"[75] the Apostle does not hesitate to say in the same context: "If any one will not work, let him not eat."[76] In another passage *he encourages* his readers: "Whatever your task, work heartily, as serving the Lord and not men, knowing that from the Lord you will receive the inheritance as your reward."[77]

26.4 The teachings of the Apostle of the Gentiles obviously have key importance for the morality and spirituality of human work. They are an important complement to the great though discreet gospel of work that we find in the life and parables of Christ, in what Jesus "did and taught."[78]

26.5 On the basis of these illuminations emanating from the Source himself, the Church has always proclaimed what we find *expressed in modern terms* in the teaching of the Second Vatican Council: "Just as human activity proceeds from man, so it is ordered toward man. For when a man works he not only alters things and society, he develops himself as well. He learns much, he cultivates his resources, he goes outside of himself and beyond himself. Rightly understood, this kind of growth is of greater value than any external riches which can be garnered. . . . Hence, the norm of human activity is this: that in accord with the divine plan and will, it should harmonize with the genuine good of the human race, and allow people as individuals and as members of society to pursue their total vocation and fulfill it."[79]

26.6 Such a *vision of the values of human work,* or in other words such a spirituality of work, fully explains what we read in the same section of the Council's Pastoral Constitution with regard to the right *meaning of progress:* "A person is more precious for what he is than for what he has. Similarly, all that people do to obtain greater justice, wider brotherhood, and a more humane ordering of social relationships has greater worth than technical advances. For these advances can supply the material for human progress, but of themselves alone they can never actually bring it about."[80]

26.7 This teaching on the question of progress and development — a subject that dominates present-day thought — can be understood only as the fruit of a tested spirituality of human work; and it is *only on the basis of such a spirituality* that it can be realized and put into practice. This is the teaching, and also the program, that has its roots in "the gospel of work."

---

[75] 2 Thess 3:11.

[76] 2 Thess 3:10.

[77] Col 3:23-24.

[78] Cf. Acts 1:1.

[79] Second Vatican Ecumenical Council, Pastoral Constitution on the Church in the Modern World *Gaudium et Spes,* 35: *AAS* 58 (1966), 1053.

[80] Ibid.

Human work in the light of the Cross and the Resurrection of Christ

27.1 There is yet another aspect of human work, an essential dimension of it, that is profoundly imbued with the spirituality based on the Gospel. All *work*, whether manual or intellectual, is inevitably linked with *toil*. The Book of Genesis expresses it in a truly penetrating manner: the original *blessing* of work contained in the very mystery of creation and connected with man's elevation as the image of God is contrasted with the *curse* that *sin* brought with it: "Cursed is the ground because of you; in toil you shall eat of it all the days of your life."[81] This toil connected with work marks the way of human life on earth and constitutes *an announcement of death:* "In the sweat of your face you shall eat bread till you return to the ground, for out of it you were taken."[82] Almost as an echo of these words, the author of one of the Wisdom books says: "Then I considered all that my hands had done and the toil I had spent in doing it."[83] There is no one on earth who could not apply these words to himself.

27.2 In a sense, the final word of the Gospel on this matter as on others is found in the Paschal Mystery of Jesus Christ. It is here that we must seek an answer to these problems so important for the spirituality of human work. *The Paschal Mystery* contains *the Cross* of Christ and his obedience unto death, which the Apostle contrasts with the disobedience which from the beginning has burdened man's history on earth.[84] It also contains *the elevation* of Christ, who by means of death on a Cross returns to his disciples in *the Resurrection* with the power of the Holy Spirit.

27.3 Sweat and toil, which work necessarily involves in the present condition of the human race, present the Christian and everyone who is called to follow Christ with the possibility of sharing lovingly in the work that Christ came to do.[85] This work of salvation came about through suffering and death on a Cross. By enduring the toil of work in union with Christ crucified for us, man in a way collaborates with the Son of God for the redemption of humanity. He shows himself a true disciple of Christ by carrying the cross in his turn every day[86] in the activity that he is called upon to perform.

27.4 Christ, "undergoing death itself for all of us sinners, taught us by example that we too must shoulder that cross which the world and the flesh

---

[81] Gen 3:17.
[82] Gen 3:19.
[83] Eccles 2:11.
[84] Cf. Rom 5:19.
[85] Cf. Jn 17:4.
[86] Cf. Lk 9:23.

inflict upon those who pursue peace and justice"; but also, at the same time, "appointed Lord *by his Resurrection* and given all authority in heaven and on earth, Christ is now at work in people's hearts through the power of his Spirit. . . . He animates, purifies, and strengthens those noble longings too by which the human family strives *to make its life more human* and to render the whole earth submissive to this goal."[87]

27.5 The Christian finds in human work a small part of the Cross of Christ and accepts it in the same spirit of redemption in which Christ accepted his Cross for us. In work, thanks to the light that penetrates us from the Resurrection of Christ, we always find a *glimmer* of new life, of the *new good,* as if it were an announcement of "the new heavens and the new earth"[88] in which man and the world participate precisely through the toil that goes with work. Through toil — and never without it. On the one hand this confirms the indispensability of the Cross in the spirituality of human work; on the other hand the Cross which this toil constitutes reveals a new good springing from work itself, from work understood in depth and in all its aspects and never apart from work.

27.6 Is this *new good* — the fruit of human work — already a small part of that "new earth" where justice dwells?[89] If it is true that the many forms of toil that go with man's work are a small part of the Cross of Christ, what is the relationship of this new good to *the Resurrection of Christ?* The Council seeks to reply to this question also, drawing light from the very sources of the revealed word: "Therefore, while we are warned that it profits a man nothing if he gains the whole world and loses himself (cf. Lk 9:25), the expectation of a new earth must not weaken but rather stimulate our concern for cultivating this one. For here grows the body of a new human family, a body which even now is able to give some kind of foreshadowing of the new age. Earthly progress must be carefully distinguished from the growth of Christ's Kingdom. Nevertheless, to the extent that the former can contribute to the better ordering of human society, it is of vital concern to the Kingdom of God."[90]

27.7 In these present reflections devoted to human work we have tried to emphasize everything that seemed essential to it, since it is through man's labor that not only "the fruits of our activity" but also "human dignity, broth-

---

[87] Second Vatican Ecumenical Council, Pastoral Constitution on the Church in the Modern World *Gaudium et Spes,* 38: *AAS* 58 (1966), 1055-1056.

[88] Cf. 2 Pet 3:13; Rev 21:1.

[89] Cf. 2 Pet 3:13.

[90] Second Vatican Ecumenical Council, Pastoral Constitution on the Church in the Modern World *Gaudium et Spes,* 39: *AAS* 58 (1966), 1057.

erhood and freedom" must increase on earth.[91] Let the Christian who listens to the word of the living God, uniting work with prayer, know the place that his work has not only in *earthly progress* but also in *the development of the Kingdom of God*, to which we are all called through the power of the Holy Spirit and through the word of the Gospel.

27.8 In concluding these reflections, I gladly impart the Apostolic Blessing to all of you, Venerable Brothers and beloved sons and daughters.

27.9 I prepared this document for publication on last May 15, on the ninetieth anniversary of the Encyclical *Rerum Novarum*, but it is only after my stay in the hospital that I have been able to revise it definitively.

Given at Castel Gandolfo, on the fourteenth day of September, the Feast of the Triumph of the Cross, in the year 1981, the third of the Pontificate.

[91] Ibid.

Slavorum Apostoli

Editor's Introduction

On the solemnity of the Most Holy Trinity, June 2, 1985, Pope John Paul II signed *Slavorum Apostoli*.[1] His fourth encyclical, entitled "the Apostles to the Slavs," marks the eleven-hundredth anniversary of the evangelization of the Slavs by Saints Cyril and Methodius. In a later address the Pope expressed why he wrote this encyclical epistle: "I endeavored to portray the admirable charism and work of the two great evangelizers, convinced as I was that the entire Church, and especially those involved in evangelization today, can draw great profit from the example of their life, of their ecclesial sense, and of their apostolic method."[2] As the first Pope from a Slav nation, a fact which he mentions three times in the encyclical (cf. §§3.3, 28, 31.2), John Paul wishes to commemorate the "apostolic merits" (§3.1) of the two brothers from Salonika.

The Pope first showed his fraternal affection for the two Saints in his apostolic letter *Egregiae Virtutis* (1980), which commemorated the centenary of Leo XIII's encyclical epistle *Grande Munus* (1880). In *Egregiae Virtutis* John Paul declared Saints Cyril and Methodius co-patrons of Europe, alongside Saint Benedict. But why an encyclical on the two Saints now? In 1985, the Church celebrated the eleventh centenary of Methodius' death, although the festivities honored the memory of both brothers. For the Pope, the publication of an encyclical was a fitting way to recall their contribution to the spiritual and cultural formation of Europe. Furthermore, recent years have witnessed a revival of religious, historical, and cultural interest in Cyril and Methodius, an interest in harmony with the Second Vatican Council's concern for the Church's missionary activity. In the light of these signs of the times, the Pope wished to retell the brothers' story: to "read in their lives and apostolic activity the elements that the wisdom of divine Providence placed in them, so that *they might be revealed with fresh fullness in our own age and might bear new fruit*" (§3.4).

Slavorum Apostoli, besides being John Paul's shortest encyclical, is distinguished from his other letters in four respects. First, it is his only encyclical "epistle"; that is, its subject matter is less doctrinal than that in encyclical

---

[1] *Acta Apostolicae Sedis,* 77 (1985), 779-813.
[2] Address to the European Ecumenical Symposium, October 12, 1985, *L'Osservatore Romano,* 43 (1985), 5.

letters. Unlike the encyclical epistles of previous Popes, however, it is directed to the whole Church. Second, the epistle contains a great deal of biographical material on the lives of Cyril and Methodius. In many ways it is a work of hagiography. Third, *Slavorum Apostoli* uses a wider range of sources than is found in John Paul's other encyclicals. Most citations and references come from the 1969 critical edition of the *Life of Constantine* and the *Life of Methodius: Constantinus et Methodius Thessalonicenses: Fontes* (Zagreb, 1960). Furthermore, the encyclical cites Sacred Scripture infrequently and without commentary, and refers to the Second Vatican Council only five times. Fourth, with its numerous references to the Trinity (cf. §§18.3, 20, 30, 31.1), the encyclical echoes the theological writings of the Church Fathers, particularly those from the East.

While John Paul uses a warm and devotional tone, he engages not merely in pious exhortation but also in pastoral theology. In an adroit manner, the Pope mixes historical facts and situations from the ninth century with reflections on their present-day significance. He follows this method because he believes that God assigns each people and nation a specific role in his plan. In light of this divine design, the encyclical describes the Slavs' "destined place in the Church" (§20). Cyril and Methodius, the Apostles of the Slavs, are relevant today because of their original approach to evangelization; they paid very close attention to the role played by inculturation, ecclesial communion, and culture. Their message is therefore "clearly of great importance for our own age" (§26.1).

Summary

Slavorum Apostoli is divided, without any subheadings, into eight chapters, which include the introduction and conclusion. The introduction (§§1-3) explains the occasion for writing the encyclical and provides reasons why the story of Cyril and Methodius merits retelling at this time. In chapter two, "Biographical Sketch" (§§4-7), the Pope gives a brief account of the Saints' lives, while in chapter three, "Heralds of the Gospel" (§§8-11), he presents them as exemplary evangelizers. Chapter four, "They Planted the Church of God" (§§12-15), outlines how the brothers founded new local churches among the Slavs, and chapter five, "Catholic Sense of the Church" (§§16-20), describes the success of their efforts to inculturate the Gospel. John Paul treats the contribution of Cyril and Methodius to the development of Slavic culture in chapter six, "The Gospel and Culture" (§§21-22), and chapter seven, "The Significance and Influence of the Christian Millennium in the Slav World" (§§23-27). The conclusion (§§28-32) deals primarily with the question of Europe as the homeland of a Christianity which embraces the traditions of both East and West.

Biographical sketch

While the date of the encyclical coincides with the anniversary of the death of Methodius in 885, it pays almost equal attention to his younger brother Cyril. Greeks by birth and Byzantine in culture, the two brothers Constantine (Cyril) and Michael (Methodius) led active lives before retiring to the monastic life. Their love for the contemplative life was, however, interrupted. When Prince Rastislav of Greater Moravia requested Emperor Michael III of Byzantium to send him missionaries, who could explain "the true Christian faith in their own language" (§5.1, cf. §9.1), Cyril and Methodius were chosen for the mission among the Slavs. Because of the language barrier, previous missionaries had met with little success among the Slavs. In 863, the brothers began their evangelization of central and southern Europe, a task to which they devoted the rest of their lives. During a visit to Rome, Cyril died on February 14, 865.

After his brother's death, Methodius was consecrated archbishop and named papal legate for the Slavs of Greater Moravia. His apostolic activity there was hampered, however, by political and religious disputes. Methodius' orthodoxy was called into question and his translation of the liturgy into Slavonic was contested. In 880, however, he presented his case to Pope John VIII (†882) and was cleared of the charges levelled against him. Methodius then went to Constantinople, where he received similar approval from Patriarch Photius and the Emperor. Until his death in 885, Methodius dedicated his time chiefly to making further translations of the Bible, liturgical texts, the Church Fathers, and ecclesiastical and Byzantine civil law.

Heralds of the Gospel

The biographical portraits of chapter two provide the foundation for the Pope's weightier comments on the Saints' lasting significance as evangelizers. Cyril and Methodius made their greatest contribution "in the specific area of missionary activity" (§26.2). John Paul commends their "pastoral attitude of concern to bring the revealed truth to new peoples — while respecting their cultural originality" (§7.3). He considers them as models of contemporary evangelization for several reasons: their spirit of availability and adaptability, their innovative way of preaching the Gospel, their passion for the Church's unity and catholicity, and their appreciation of the culture of the peoples whom they were evangelizing.

John Paul draws attention to the brothers' readiness to leave their homeland, comparing them to Abraham and Saint Paul. Following the example of these fathers in faith, Cyril and Methodius abandoned "the refined culture of Byzantium, imbued with Christian principles" (§8.3) and went to preach the Gospel among less sophisticated peoples. While remaining men of Hellenistic culture and Byzantine formation, the brothers became "Slavs at heart" (§12.1). With energy, prudence, zeal, and charity, they adopted a specific strategy in their missionary work: "they desired to become similar in every aspect to those to whom they were bringing the Gospel; they wished to become part of those peoples and to share their lot in everything" (§9.3).

Cyril and Methodius were proud of the cultural and theological richness of Greco-Byzantine culture. Nonetheless, they never sought "to impose on the peoples assigned to their preaching either the undeniable superiority of the Greek language and Byzantine culture, or the customs and way of life of the more advanced society in which they had grown up and which necessarily remained familiar and dear to them" (§13.1).

The missionary genius of the Apostles of the Slavs lies in their willingness to make use of a language and culture other than their own in proclaiming the faith. They courageously searched for "new forms of living and effective ways of bringing the Good News to the Slav nations which were then forming" (§10.1). With a genuine missionary zeal, the brothers made heroic efforts to learn the language, to understand the mentality, and "to assimilate and identify themselves with all the needs and expectations of the Slav peoples" (§11.2). In applying this "new method of catechesis" (§11.1), Cyril and Methodius succeeded "in maintaining perfect orthodoxy and consistent attention both to the deposit of Tradition and to the new elements in the lives of the peoples being evangelized" (§10.1). By means of their original catechetical and pastoral methods, the saintly brothers initiated the inculturation of the Gospel among the Slavs. This strategy bore fruit not only in Moravia but later in the Balkans, Bulgaria, Poland, Romania, and Russia.

Mentors of unity and catholicity

In *Slavorum Apostoli*, John Paul emphasizes that Cyril and Methodius carried out their evangelizing mission with profound concern for the Church's unity and catholicity. They expressed this solicitude by assiduously fostering the bonds of communion between the churches established among the Slavs and the sees of Rome and Constantinople.

Especially important to the Pope is the trust in the Apostolic See shown by the holy brothers. Together they answered the invitation of Nicholas I (†867) to go to Rome. Pope Nicholas wanted to compare "the doctrine being taught by the Brothers in Greater Moravia with that which the holy Apostles Peter and Paul had passed down" (§11.1). According to John Paul, the brothers visited Rome because "they considered it their duty to give an account of their missionary work to the Roman Pontiff" (§13.1). Once in Rome, besides the endorsement of Hadrian II (†872), they also sought priestly ordination for their missionary companions. Cyril and Methodius "submitted to his judgment, in order to obtain his approval, the doctrine which they professed and taught, the liturgical books which they had written in the Slavonic language, and the methods which they were using in evangelizing those peoples" (§13.1). Above all, they wanted their mission to be confirmed by "the Apostolic See of Rome, the visible center of the Church's unity" (§13.2). Concern for the unity of the universal Church, expressed by profound devotion to the See of Peter, characterized their evangelizing work.

The Apostles of the Slavs desired to remain in full communion not only with the church at Rome but also with their patriarchal church at Constantinople. Under the aegis of the Patriarch of Constantinople, they began their mission in Greater Moravia "imbued with all the wealth of tradition and religious experience which marked Eastern Christianity" (§12.3). According to John Paul, a great merit of Cyril and Methodius was their concern "to preserve unity of faith and love between the Churches of which they were members, namely, between the Church of Constantinople and the Church of Rome on the one hand, and the Churches which arose in the lands of the Slavs on the other" (§14.2). "It can be said of the two evangelizers," the Pope goes on to say, "that characteristic of them was their love for the communion of the universal Church both in the East and in the West, and, within the universal Church, love for the particular Church that was coming into being in the Slav nations" (§26.1). Despite the emerging conflict between the eastern and western Churches, the Slav churches succeeded in remaining in full communion with both the Pope and the Patriarch.

Thanks to the brothers' preaching, duly approved by the Bishops of Rome and the Patriarchs of Constantinople, "the Slavs were able to feel that they too, together with the other nations of the earth, were descendants and heirs of the promise made by God to Abraham" (§20). Through the efforts of Cyril and Methodius, new peoples became aware of their vocation to take an active part in the history of salvation. According to John Paul, each nation and people, and not merely each individual, has such a particular role in God's plan. Far from fostering an arrogant or intolerant nationalism, this respect for the rights of nations and peoples recognizes the dignity of every culture, a respect which establishes peaceful coexistence on a solid foundation.

Love for the Church's unity led the two Saints to an equally intense love for her catholicity, a love praised by John Paul. They believed that the young Slav churches had a specific contribution to make to the universal Church: "each local Church is called to enrich with its own endowments the Catholic 'pleroma' " (§13.3). According to the Pope, the theological and pastoral vision of Cyril and Methodius was at once traditional and up-to-date: it promoted the use of the vernacular in the liturgy and in the Bible, and it accepted whatever was truly good in native cultures. For them, catholicity was like "a melodious chorus sustained by the voices of unnumbered multitudes, rising in countless modulations, tones and harmonies for the praise of God from every part of the globe, at every moment of history" (§17.1). In support of this vision Methodius defended "in particular the liturgy in the Old Slavonic language and the fundamental ecclesiastical rights proper to the Churches in the various nations" (§15.1). "For full catholicity," writes John Paul, "every nation, every culture has its own part to play in the universal plan of salvation" (§27.1). He later concludes: "We desire to accept in its entirety everything original and valid which the Slav nations have brought and continue to bring to the spiritual patrimony of the Church and of humanity" (§31.2).

Contribution to culture

While the Pope sprinkles the encyclical with numerous references to the Saints' contributions to Slavic culture, he does so at greatest length in chapters six and seven, where he examines the relationship between the Gospel and culture in the Slav world. From very early on, the Slavs regarded Cyril and Methodius "as the fathers of both their Christianity and their culture" (§25.1). By their efforts to incarnate the Gospel among the Slav peoples they formed and developed the culture of many nations.

The Saints' greatest cultural achievement was undoubtedly linguistic and literary. Even before setting out on his first mission to Greater Moravia, Cyril, whose studies had prepared him to be "a religious and cultural expert" (§4.4), composed a new alphabet perfectly adapted to the sounds of Old Slavonic. Even today this alphabet is called "Cyrillic." John Paul praises the brothers' "original and ingenious creation of an alphabet for the Slavonic language . . . [which] made a fundamental contribution to the culture and literature of all the Slav nations" (§21.2).

The primary instruments through which Cyril and Methodius exerted their influence were their Old Slavonic translations of the liturgy and the Bible. Aware that many churches of the East used the vernacular in their liturgies, they were not afraid "to make it into an effective instrument for bringing the divine truths to those who spoke it" (§12.5). Moreover, the brothers knew that speaking the language of the people was not enough. They also decided to consign the word of God to writing, so that its listeners could better remember, meditate, and transmit it to others. Their literary achievements conferred "a capacity and cultural dignity upon the Old Slavonic liturgical language, which became for many hundreds of years not only the ecclesiastical but also the official and literary language, and even the common language of the more educated classes of the greater part of the Slav nations" (§21.3).

Because Cyril and Methodius believed that the " 'fullness of time' [had] arrived for these peoples and nations" (§30.2), they left a precious cultural heritage. Their translations of the liturgy and the Scriptures remain fundamental reference points in the history of Slavic literature. The brothers' initiatives forged a literary language which was decisive in the development of the culture, identity, and spiritual strength of many Slav nations. Expressing his admiration for their accomplishments, the Pope writes: "These merits vis-à-vis the culture of all the Slav peoples and nations make the work of evangelization carried out by Saints Cyril and Methodius in a certain sense constantly present in the history and in the life of these peoples and nations" (§22.2).

Key Themes

Slavorum Apostoli has been widely overlooked, I believe, because many fail to see the doctrinal underpinnings of the Pope's paean of praise for the holy brothers. Beneath the hagiographic account, of interest chiefly to Slavs, there is a solid core of pastoral theology. In the encyclical John Paul develops three ideas dear to his theological vision: the importance of inculturating the Gospel among all peoples, the need to restore full communion between the churches of the East and the West, and the unique role of Christian Europe in God's plan. He returns to the first two themes in later encyclicals: *Redemptoris Missio* (1990) and *Ut Unum Sint* (1995) respectively. And in 1991 he convoked the Special Assembly for Europe of the Synod of Bishops on the theme "Christianity and Culture in Europe: Memory, Awareness, and Planning."

Inculturation

The commemoration of Cyril and Methodius affords the Pope an opportunity, at one and the same time, to hold up the Saints as models for contemporary men and women, to recall the urgent need for evangelization *ad gentes* and for the new evangelization of cultures with Christian roots, and to describe the relationship between the Gospel and culture. These three motifs meet in his treatment of inculturation, a topic dealt with for the first time in a papal encyclical. The Gospel must be inculturated so that those being evangelized will understand the message more easily, live it more deeply, and be able to explain it more persuasively. Furthermore, inculturation guarantees and fosters the Church's catholicity. The Saints from Salonika recognized that the Christian faith reaches people in the particular human community where they live: in their concrete linguistic, intellectual, cultural, and historical situation.

In the words of John Paul, the evangelization carried out by the Apostles of the Slavs contains "a model of what today is called 'inculturation' — the incarnation of the Gospel in native cultures" (§21.1). Their work to inculturate the Gospel, novel in its day, foreshadows the teaching of the Second Vatican Council. Due to their philosophical and cultural formation, the brothers were well prepared to bring Christianity to the Slavs "in an understandable way" (§9.1). They carried out this program despite the hostility of some, especially in the West, who regarded their work "as a threat to a still incomplete unity" (§12.6). Moreover, the Pope attributes to Cyril and Methodius an idea which is also very much his own: "all nations, cultures and civilizations have their own part to play and their own place in God's mysterious plan and in the universal history of salvation" (§19.2). In proposing Cyril and Methodius as models of how to inculturate the Gospel, he praises their personal gifts, their attitude to the peoples and cultures being evangelized, and their catechetical pedagogy.

Missionaries must be ready to abandon the security, and even the nobility, of their own culture in order to bring the Gospel to others. They must also be willing to identify with others' needs and expectations, proposing the Good News as Cyril and Methodius did: "without any spirit of superiority or domination, but out of love of justice and with a clear apostolic zeal for peoples" (§12.5). In their missionary activity the saintly brothers expressed the perfect communion in love which "preserves the Church from all forms of particularism, ethnic exclusivism or racial prejudice, and from any nationalistic arrogance" (§11.3).

The Gospel's inculturation demands from the missionary an effort "to gain a good grasp of the interior world" of those to be evangelized (§11.1). Such is the example of Cyril and Methodius: "They set themselves to understanding and penetrating the language, customs and traditions of the Slav peoples, faithfully interpreting the aspirations and human values which were present and expressed therein" (§10.2). Their method entailed esteem for peoples' values and aspirations, and a spirit of dialogue which excluded any imposition of the truth by force. Because of the respect that they showed, the brothers were successful in shedding the light of the Gospel on these values.

Following this example, evangelizers today are likewise to carry out their mission "with full respect for the culture already existing" in a given place (§26.2). They, too, must always be ready to praise "every real human value" (§19.1). The Pope insists that missionaries should approach pre-Christian cultures with reverence. He writes: "The Gospel does not lead to the impoverishment or extinction of those things which every individual, people and nation and every culture throughout history recognizes and brings into being as goodness, truth and beauty" (§18.2).

John Paul does not suggest that non-Christian cultures can simply be baptized in every respect. Inculturation is a two-way street: the Gospel must enter a people's culture, but at the same time that culture needs to be changed by the Gospel. In the meeting between Christianity and culture, the Gospel both assimilates and develops the positive values found in a specific culture: it perfects them "by the mysterious and ennobling light of Revelation" (§18.2). This divine light forms and develops the cultures it encounters. When a culture is purified and enlightened by the Gospel, it both enriches the Church's catholicity and is empowered to bring forth new cultural fruits. Thus the Pope maintains that "all the cultures of the Slav nations owe their 'beginning' or development to the work of the Brothers from Salonika" (§21.2).

Successful inculturation of the Gospel also requires maintaining "a resolute and vigilant fidelity to right doctrine and to the tradition of the perfectly united Church" (§14.3). Simultaneously, evangelization must be "adapted to the concrete historical situation" (§20). Cyril and Methodius admirably accomplished this arduous balancing act. They realized, the Pope writes, "that an essential condition of the success of their missionary activity was correctly to transpose biblical notions and Greek theological concepts into a very different context of thought and historical experience" (§11.1). Their new catechetical technique entailed proclaiming the Gospel to the Slavs "in images and concepts that would sound familiar to them" (§11.1). Adaptation, not assimilation, to the mentality and customs of new peoples is essential. For John Paul, the saintly brothers are ideal evangelizers because they preached the eternal truths of the Gospel to peoples "in a way that completely fitted their own mentality and respected the actual conditions of their own life" (§16.1).

Prophets of ecumenism

In the mind of John Paul II, the need to restore full, visible communion between the Orthodox churches and the Catholic Church is a duty deriving from Christ's will. To achieve this goal, he looks first of all to the structures of unity which existed between them in the first millennium. He refers, for example, to the ecclesial situation of the ninth century: Constantinople was in "full communion with Rome" (§6.2) and the churches of the East and the West coexisted "in the bosom of the one Church" (§25.3). Each church had its own theological, disciplinary, and liturgical traditions, but there was one "perfectly united Church" (§14.3).

Besides referring to the unity of the Church in the first millennium, the Pope also mentions the increasing tension that was then developing between East and West. Already in the time of Cyril and Methodius "certain differences between Constantinople and Rome had begun to appear as pretexts for disunity, even though the deplorable split between the two parts of the same Christian world was still in the distant future" (§12.3). The brothers were personally involved in the situations of growing "uncertain and painful complexity" (§10.1). These difficulties notwithstanding, the Saints faithfully and resolutely preserved their young churches in communion with both Constantinople and Rome. While controversies raged around them, Cyril and Methodius remained "in full spiritual and canonical unity with the Church of Rome, with the Church of Constantinople and with the new Churches which they had founded among the Slav peoples" (§14.3).

According to the Pope, the brothers' apostolic activity possesses "an ecumenical appeal: it is an invitation to restore, in the peace of reconciliation, the unity that was gravely damaged after the time of Cyril and Methodius, and, first and foremost, the unity between East and West" (§13.2). In fact, he asserts that they are "the authentic precursors of ecumenism" (§14.1). They worked for unity to such an extent, says John Paul, "that Jesus' priestly prayer — *ut unum sint* — is their missionary motto" (§13.2). Throughout their lives the brothers struggled to eliminate all division in the Church.

Because the Saints from Salonika maintained their churches in communion with both Constantinople and Rome, the Pope regards them as "the connecting links or spiritual bridge between the Eastern and Western traditions, which *both* come together in the *one* great Tradition of the universal Church" (§27.1). Throughout the encyclical John Paul balances their love for, and obligation to, the churches of the East and the West by carefully pointing out their loyalty to both ecclesial traditions.

Within less than two hundred years after their death, the Church's unity was fractured. The Slavs, who entered Christianity by way of both the East and the West, directly experienced the tragic effects of the later Schism. Because of the love of Cyril and Methodius for the Tradition of the united Church, the Pope looks to them as "the patrons of the ecumenical endeavor of the sister Churches of East and West." They are, he says, "figures that awaken in all Christians a great 'longing for union' and for unity between the two sister Churches of East and West" (§27.1). Coming from the East and welcomed by the West, the saintly brothers are models of how to recover "visible unity in perfect and total communion" (§27.1) between Orthodox and Catholics.

Europe's Christian vocation

John Paul II is convinced that because of Europe's Christian origins, it is meant to be united. He praises the Apostles of the Slavs for their "outstanding contribution to the formation of the common Christian roots of Europe" (§25.2). Europe, for the Pope, is not simply the West; it also embraces the nations of central and eastern Europe. The continent therefore encompasses two currents of religious tradition and culture. More than a collection of States, Europe is an assembly of peoples or nations, each of which has its own providential destiny. The charism of Cyril and Methodius reminds the West that Europe is not only Roman and Latin but also Greek and Byzantine. Europe enjoys a dual heritage which the Saints acknowledged and fostered. Even more, the Slavs are especially poised within Europe to build peace and unity, and to stimulate the continent's "hoped-for spiritual renewal" (§25.3).

For the Pope, in spite of Europe's present division into political, economic and culture blocs, it is called to manifest its common spiritual and cultural heritage more clearly. Though now divided, Europe is destined to be united. He writes enthusiastically of the "unity of Europe" (§2.1) and of "the unity of the Continent" (§25.2). But this unity exists in diversity; it is meant to show the complementarity of the eastern and western traditions, the two "lungs" of a single body. Consequently, John Paul hopes that Europe will gradually overcome "everything that divides Churches, nations and peoples" (§2.2). In bringing about this unity, the Church, which is "the universal sign and sacrament of salvation and of the unity of the human race" (§27.3), wishes to cooperate. She looks to Saints Cyril and Methodius to inspire people from the East and the West to live together in harmony and peace.

If eastern and western Europe are to come together, unity must replace division. John Paul writes: "Being Christians in our day means being builders of communion in the Church and in society" (§27.2). Models of this spiritual and social communion, which is open to religious and cultural diversity, are the brothers from Salonika. In their day, Cyril and Methodius played a unique role in promoting unity in diversity. Thus their message is "of great relevance for our own age, which, precisely by reason of the many complex problems of religious, cultural, civil and international nature, is seeking a vital unity in the real communion of its various elements" (§26.1). Because the brothers evangelized "at the crossroads of the mutual influences between East and West" (§5.2), they form a lasting spiritual and cultural bridge between Greeks and Latins.

At the end of the encyclical the Pope prays to the Holy Trinity, that Europe, religiously and culturally united, will once more be an example for the world:

> Grant to the whole of Europe, O Most Holy Trinity, that through the intercession of the two holy Brothers it may feel ever more strongly the need for religious and Christian unity and for a brotherly communion of all its peoples, so that when incomprehension and mutual distrust have been overcome and when ideological conflicts have been conquered in the common awareness of the truth, it may be for the whole world an example of just and peaceful coexistence in mutual respect and inviolate liberty (§30.5).

* * *

Selected Bibliography

Every, George. "*Slavorum Apostoli:* A Note." *One in Christ,* 21 (1985), 271-273.

Kalvoda, Josef. "The Cyrilo-Methodian Idea." *The Priest,* 42 (February 1986), 18-19.

Loya, Joseph A. "John Paul II's Encyclical *Slavorum Apostoli:* An Ecumenical Assessment." *Ecumenical Trends,* 14 (1985), 167-168.

ENCYCLICAL EPISTLE

SLAVORUM APOSTOLI

OF HIS HOLINESS

JOHN PAUL II

TO THE BISHOPS, PRIESTS

AND RELIGIOUS FAMILIES

AND TO ALL THE CHRISTIAN FAITHFUL

IN COMMEMORATION

OF THE ELEVENTH CENTENARY

OF THE EVANGELIZING WORK

OF SAINTS CYRIL AND METHODIUS

Slavorum Apostoli

I

Introduction

1.1 The Apostles of the Slavs, *Saints Cyril and Methodius*, are remembered by the Church together with the great work of evangelization which they carried out. Indeed it can be said that their memory is particularly vivid and relevant to our day.

1.2 Considering the grateful veneration enjoyed for centuries by the holy Brothers from Salonika (the ancient *Thessalonica*), especially *among the Slav nations,* and mindful of their incalculable contribution to the work of proclaiming the Gospel among those peoples; mindful too of the cause of reconciliation, friendly coexistence, human development and respect for the intrinsic dignity of every nation, by my Apostolic Letter *Egregiae Virtutis*[1] of December 31, 1980, I proclaimed Saints Cyril and Methodius Co-Patrons of Europe. In this way I followed the path already traced out by my Predecessors, and notably by Leo XIII, who over a hundred years ago, on September 30, 1880, extended the cult of the two Saints to the whole Church, with the Encyclical Epistle *Grande Munus*,[2] and by Paul VI, who, with the Apostolic Letter *Pacis Nuntius*[3] of October 24,1964, proclaimed Saint Benedict Patron of Europe.

2.1 The purpose of the document of five years ago was to remind people of these solemn acts of the Church and to call the attention of Christians and of all people of good will who have at heart the welfare, harmony and unity of Europe to the ever-living relevance of the eminent figures of Benedict, Cyril and Methodius, as concrete models and spiritual aids for the Christians of today, and especially for the nations of the continent of Europe, which, espe-

---

[1] John Paul II, Apostolic Letter *Egregiae Virtutis* (December 31, 1980): *AAS* 73 (1981), 258-262.

[2] Leo XIII, Encyclical Epistle *Grande Munus* (September 30, 1880): *Leonis XIII P. M. Acta*, II, Rome, 1882, 125-137; cf. also Pius IX, Letter to the Archbishops and Bishops of the Kingdom of the Serbs-Croats-Slovenes and of the Czechoslovakian Republic *Quod S. Cyrillum* (February 13, 1927): *AAS* 19 (1927), 93-96; John XXIII, Apostolic Letter to the Prelates of the Slav Nations *Magnifici Eventus* (May 11, 1963): *AAS* 55 (1963), 434-439; Paul VI, Apostolic Letter for the Eleventh Centenary of the Death of Saint Cyril *Antiquae Nobilitatis* (February 2, 1969): *AAS* 61 (1969), 137-149.

[3] Paul VI, Apostolic Letter *Pacis Nuntius* (October 24, 1964): *AAS* 56 (1964), 965-967.

cially through the prayers and work of these Saints, have long been consciously and originally rooted in the Church and in Christian tradition.

2.2 The publication of my Apostolic Letter in 1980, which was dictated by the firm hope of a gradual overcoming in Europe and the world of everything that divides the Churches, nations and peoples, was linked to *three circumstances* that were the subject of my prayer and reflection. The first was the eleventh centenary of the Pontifical Letter *Industriae Tuae*,[4] whereby Pope John VIII in the year 880 approved the use of the Old Slavonic language in the liturgy translated by the two holy Brothers. The second circumstance was the first centenary of the above-mentioned Encyclical Epistle *Grande Munus*. The third was the beginning, precisely in 1980, of the happy and promising theological dialogue between the Catholic Church and the Orthodox Churches on the Island of Patmos.

3.1 In the present document I wish to make particular reference to the Epistle *Grande Munus*, by which Pope Leo XIII intended to remind the Church and the world of the apostolic merits of both the Brothers — not only of Methodius, who, according to tradition, ended his days at Velehrad in Greater Moravia in the year 885, but also of Cyril, whom death separated from his brother in 869, when he was in Rome, the city which received and which still preserves his relics with profound veneration in the Basilica of Saint Clement.

3.2 Recalling the holy lives and apostolic merits of the two *Brothers from Salonika*, Pope Leo XIII fixed their annual liturgical feast on July 7. After the Second Vatican Council, as a result of the liturgical reform, the feast was transferred to February 14, which from the historical point of view is the date of the heavenly birthday of Saint Cyril.[5]

3.3 At a distance of over a hundred years from Pope Leo's Epistle, *the new circumstances* in which it so happens that there falls the eleventh centenary of the death of Saint Methodius encourage us to give renewed expression to the Church's memory of this important anniversary. And a particular obligation to do so is felt by the first Pope called to the See of Peter from Poland, and thus from the midst of the *Slav nations*.

3.4 The events of the last hundred years and especially of the last decades have helped to revive in the Church not only the religious memory of the two holy Brothers but also a historical and cultural interest in them. Their special charisms have become still better understood in the light of the situations and experiences of our own times. A contribution to this has been made by many

[4] Cf. *Magnae Moraviae Fontes Historici*, vol. III, Brno, 1969, 197-208.
[5] Only in a few Slav nations is the feast still celebrated on July 7.

events which belong, as true signs of the times, to the history of the twentieth century; the first of these is that great event which took place in the life of the Church: *the Second Vatican Council.* In the light of the magisterium and pastoral orientation of that Council we can look in a new way — a more mature and profound way — at these two holy figures, now separated from us by eleven centuries. And we can read in their lives and apostolic activity the elements that the wisdom of divine Providence placed in them, so that *they might be revealed with fresh fullness in our own age and might bear new fruits.*

II

Biographical Sketch

4.1 Following the example offered by the Epistle *Grande Munus,* I wish to recall the life of Saint Methodius, without, however, thereby ignoring the life — so closely like it — of his brother Saint Cyril. This I will do in general terms, leaving to historical research the detailed discussion of individual points.

4.2 The city which saw the birth of the two holy Brothers is the modern Salonika, which in the ninth century was an important center of commercial and political life in the Byzantine Empire, and occupied a notable position in the intellectual and social life of that part of the Balkans. Being situated on the frontier of the Slav territories, it also certainly had a Slav name: Solun.

4.3 Methodius was the elder brother and his baptismal name was probably Michael. He was born between 815 and 820. His younger brother Constantine, who came to be better known by his religious name Cyril, was born in 827 or 828. Their father was a senior official of the imperial administration. The family's social position made possible for the two Brothers a similar career, which in fact Methodius did take up, reaching the rank of Archon or Prefect in one of the frontier Provinces where many Slavs lived. However, toward the year 840 he interrupted his career and retired to one of the monasteries at the foot of Mount Olympus in Bithynia, then known as the Holy Mountain.

4.4 His brother Cyril studied with great success in Byzantium, where he received Holy Orders, after having resolutely refused a brilliant political future. By reason of his exceptional intellectual and religious talents and knowledge, there were entrusted to him while he has still a young man delicate ecclesiastical appointments, such as that of Librarian of the Archive attached to the great Church of Holy Wisdom in Constantinople, and, simultaneously, the prestigious position of Secretary to the Patriarch of that city. However, he very soon made it known that he wished to be relieved of these posts, in order to be able to devote himself to study and the contemplative life, far from the pursuit of ambition. Thus he retired secretly to a monastery on the Black Sea coast. He was discovered six months later, and was persuaded to accept the task of teaching philosophy in the School of higher learning in Constantinople, where by reason of the excellence of his knowledge he gained the epithet of *The Philosopher* by which he is still known. Later on he was sent by the Emperor and the Patriarch on a mission to the Saracens. On the completion of this task he retired from public life in order to join his elder brother Methodius and share with him the monastic life. But once again, together with Methodius, he was included in a Byzantine delegation sent to the Khazars, acting as a religious and cultural expert. While staying in the Crimea at Kherson, they identified what they believed to be the church in which had been buried Saint Clement, Pope of Rome and martyr, who had been exiled to that distant region. They recovered his relics and took them with them.[6] These relics later accompanied the two holy Brothers on their missionary journey to the West, until they were able to bring them solemnly to Rome and present them to Pope Hadrian II.

5.1 The event which was to determine the whole of the rest of their lives was the request made by Prince Rastislav of Greater Moravia to the Emperor Michael III, to send to his peoples "a Bishop and teacher . . . able to explain to them the true Christian faith in their own language."[7]

5.2 Those chosen were Saints Cyril and Methodius, who readily accepted, set out and, probably by the year 863, reached Greater Moravia — a State then including various Slav peoples of Central Europe, at the crossroads of the mutual influences between East and West. They undertook among these peoples that mission to which both of them devoted the rest of their lives, spent amidst journeys, privations, sufferings, hostility and persecution, which for Methodius included even a period of cruel imprisonment. All of this they bore with strong faith and indomitable hope in God. They had in fact prepared well for the task entrusted to them: they took with them the texts of the Sacred Scriptures needed for celebrating the Sacred Liturgy, which they had prepared and translated into the Old Slavonic language and written in a new alphabet, devised by Constantine the Philosopher and perfectly adapted to

---

[6] Cf. *Vita Constantini* VIII, 16-18: *Constantinus et Methodius Thessalonicenses, Fontes*, recensuerunt et illustraverunt Fr. Grivec et Fr. Tomši (Radovi Staroslavenskog Instituta, Knjiga 4, Zagreb, 1960), 184.

[7] Cf. *Vita Constantini* XIV, 2-4: loc. cit., 199-200.

the sounds of that language. The missionary activity of the two Brothers was accompanied by notable success, but also by the understandable difficulties which the preceding initial Christianization, carried out by the neighboring Latin Churches, placed in the way of the new missionaries.

5.3 About three years later, while traveling to Rome, they stopped in Pannonia where the Slav Prince Kocel, who had fled from the important civil and religious center of Nitra, gave them a hospitable reception. From here, after some months, they set out again for Rome together with their followers, for whom they desired to obtain Holy Orders. Their route passed through Venice, where the innovating elements of the mission they were carrying out were subjected to a public discussion. In Rome Pope Hadrian II, who had in the meantime succeeded Nicholas I, received them very cordially. He approved the Slavonic liturgical books, which he ordered to be solemnly placed on the altar in the Church of Saint Mary *ad Praesepe*, today known as Saint Mary Major, and recommended that their followers be ordained priests. This phase of their efforts concluded in a most favorable manner. Methodius however had to carry out the next stages by himself, because his younger brother, now gravely ill, scarcely had time to take religious vows and put on the monastic habit before he died shortly afterwards, on February 14, 869, in Rome.

6.1 Saint Methodius remained faithful to the words which Cyril had said to him on his deathbed: "Behold, my brother, we have shared the same destiny, plowing the same furrow; I now fall in the field at the end of my day. I know that you greatly love your Mountain; but do not for the sake of the Mountain give up your work of teaching. For where better can you find salvation?"[8]

6.2 Consecrated Archbishop for the territory of the ancient Diocese of Pannonia, and named Papal Legate "ad gentes" (for the Slav peoples), he assumed the ecclesiastical title of the reestablished episcopal See of Sirmium. However, Methodius' apostolic activity was cut short as the result of political and religious complications which culminated in his imprisonment for two years, on the charge of having invaded the episcopal jurisdiction of another. He was set free only on the personal intervention of Pope John VIII. The new sovereign of Greater Moravia, Prince Svatopluk, also subsequently showed hostility to the work of Methodius. He opposed the Slavonic liturgy and spread doubts in Rome about the new Archbishop's orthodoxy. In the year 880 Methodius was called *ad limina Apostolorum*, to present once more the whole

---

[8] *Vita Methodii* VI, 2-3: loc. cit., 225.

question personally to John VIII. In Rome, absolved of all the accusations, he obtained from the Pope the publication of the Bull *Industriae Tuae*,[9] which, at least in substance, restored the prerogatives granted to the liturgy in Slavonic by Pope John's Predecessor Hadrian II. When in 881 or 882 Methodius went to Constantinople, he received a similar recognition of perfect legitimacy and orthodoxy also from the Byzantine Emperor and the Patriarch Photius, who at that time was in full communion with Rome. He devoted the last years of his life principally to making further translations of the Sacred Scriptures, the liturgical books, the works of the Fathers of the Church and also the collection of ecclesiastical and Byzantine civil laws called the *Nomocanon*. Concerned for the survival of the work which he had begun, he named as his successor his disciple Gorazd. He died on April 6, 885, in the service of the Church established among the Slav peoples.

7.1 His far-seeing work, his profound and orthodox doctrine, his balance, loyalty, apostolic zeal and intrepid magnanimity gained Methodius the recognition and trust of Roman Pontiffs, of Patriarchs of Constantinople, of Byzantine Emperors and of various Princes of the young Slav peoples. Thus he became the guide and legitimate Pastor of the Church which in that age became established in the midst of those nations. He is unanimously venerated, together with his brother Constantine, as the preacher of the Gospel and teacher "from God and the holy Apostle Peter,"[10] and as the foundation of full unity between the Churches of recent foundation and the more ancient ones.

7.2 For this reason, "men and women, humble and powerful, rich and poor, free men and slaves, widows and orphans, foreigners and local people, the healthy and the sick"[11] made up the throng that amid tears and songs accompanied to his burial place the good Teacher and Pastor who had become "all things to all men, that I might by all means save some."[12]

7.3 To tell the truth, after the death of Methodius the work of the holy Brothers suffered a grave crisis, and persecution of their followers grew so severe that the latter were forced to abandon their missionary field. Nonetheless, their sowing of the Gospel seed did not cease to bear fruit, and their pastoral attitude of concern to bring the revealed truth to new peoples while respecting their cultural originality remains a living model for the Church and for the missionaries of all ages.

[9] Cf. *Magnae Moraviae Fontes Historici*, vol. III, Brno, 1969, 197-208.
[10] Cf. *Vita Methodii* VIII, 1-2: loc. cit., 225.
[11] Cf. *Vita Methodii* XVII, 13: loc. cit., 237.
[12] Cf. ibid.; cf. also 1 Cor 9:22.

III
Heralds of the Gospel

8.1 Byzantine in culture, the brothers Cyril and Methodius succeeded in becoming apostles of the Slavs in the full sense of the word. Separation from one's homeland, which God sometimes requires of those he has chosen, when accepted with faith in his promise is always a mysterious and fertile precondition for the development and growth of the People of God on earth. The Lord said to Abraham: "Go from your country and your kindred and your father's house to the land that I will show you. And I will make of you a great nation, and I will bless you, and make your name great, so that you will be a blessing."[13]

8.2 In the dream which Saint Paul had at Troas in Asia Minor, a Macedonian, therefore an inhabitant of the European continent, came before him and implored him to come to his country to proclaim there the Word of God: "Come over to Macedonia and help us."[14]

8.3 Divine Providence, which for the two holy Brothers expressed itself through the voice and authority of the Emperor of Byzantium and of the Patriarch of the Church of Constantinople, addressed to them a similar exhortation, when it asked them to go as missionaries among the Slavs. For them, this task meant giving up not only a position of honor but also the contemplative life. It meant leaving the area of the Byzantine Empire and undertaking a long pilgrimage in the service of the Gospel among peoples that, in many aspects, were still very alien to the system of civil society based on the advanced organization of the State and the refined culture of Byzantium, imbued with Christian principles. A similar request was addressed three times to Methodius by the Roman Pontiff, when he sent him as Bishop among the Slavs of Greater Moravia, in the ecclesiastical regions of the ancient Diocese of Pannonia.

9.1 The Slavonic *Life of Methodius* reports in the following words the request made by the Prince Rastislav to the Emperor Michael III through his envoys: "Many Christian teachers have reached us from Italy, from Greece and from Germany, who instruct us in different ways. But we Slavs . . . have no one to direct us toward the truth and instruct us in an understandable way."[15] It was then that Constantine and Methodius were invited to go there.

---

[13] Gen 12:1-2.
[14] Acts 16:9.
[15] *Vita Methodii* V, 2: loc. cit., 223.

Their profoundly Christian response to the invitation in this circumstance and on all similar occasions is admirably expressed by the words of Constantine to the Emperor: "However tired and physically worn out I am, I will go with joy to that land";[16] "with joy I depart for the sake of the Christian faith."[17]

9.2 The truth and the power of their missionary mandate came from the depths of the mystery of the Redemption, and their evangelizing work among the Slav peoples was to constitute an important link in the mission entrusted by the Savior to the Church until the end of time. It was a fulfillment — in time and in concrete circumstances — of the words of Christ, who in the power of his Cross and Resurrection told the Apostles: "Preach the Gospel to the whole creation";[18] "Go therefore and make disciples of all nations."[19] In so doing, the preachers and teachers of the Slav peoples let themselves be guided by the apostolic ideal of Saint Paul: "For in Christ Jesus you are all children of God, through faith. For as many of you as were baptized into Christ have put on Christ. There is neither Jew nor Greek, there is neither slave nor free, there is neither male nor female; for you are all one in Christ Jesus."[20]

9.3 Together with a great respect for persons and a disinterested concern for their true good, the two holy Brothers had the resources of energy, prudence, zeal and charity needed for bringing the light to the future believers, and at the same time for showing them what is good and offering concrete help for attaining it. For this purpose they desired to become similar in every aspect to those to whom they were bringing the Gospel; they wished to become part of those peoples and to share their lot in everything.

10.1 Precisely for this reason they found it natural to take a clear position in all the conflicts which were disturbing the societies as they became organized. They took as their own the difficulties and problems inevitable for peoples who were defending their own identity against the military and cultural pressure of the new Romano-Germanic Empire, and who were attempting to resist forms of life which they felt to be foreign. It was also the beginning of wider divergences, which were unfortunately destined to increase, between Eastern and Western Christianity, and the two holy missionaries found themselves personally involved in this. But they always succeeded in maintaining perfect orthodoxy and consistent attention both to the deposit of Tradition and to the new elements in the lives of the peoples being evangelized. Situations of oppo-

---

[16] *Vita Constantini* XIV, 9: loc. cit., 200.
[17] *Vita Constantini* VI, 7: loc. cit., 179.
[18] Mk 16:15.
[19] Mt 28:19.
[20] Gal 3:26-28.

sition often weighed upon them in all their uncertain and painful complexity. But this did not cause Constantine and Methodius to try to withdraw from the trial. Misunderstanding, overt bad faith and even, for Saint Methodius, imprisonment accepted for love of Christ, did not deflect either of them from their tenacious resolve to help and to serve the good of the Slav peoples and the unity of the universal Church. This was the price which they had to pay for the spreading of the Gospel, the missionary enterprise, the courageous search for new forms of living and effective ways of bringing the Good News to the Slav nations which were then forming.

10.2 For the purposes of evangelization, the two holy Brothers — as their biographies indicate — undertook the difficult task of translating the texts of the Sacred Scriptures, which they knew in Greek, into the language of the Slav population which had settled along the borders of their own region and native city. Making use of their own Greek language and culture for this arduous and unusual enterprise, they set themselves to understanding and penetrating the language, customs and traditions of the Slav peoples, faithfully interpreting the aspirations and human values which were present and expressed therein.

11.1 In order to translate the truths of the Gospel into a new language, they had to make an effort to gain a good grasp of the interior world of those to whom they intended to proclaim the word of God in images and concepts that would sound familiar to them. They realized that an essential condition of the success of their missionary activity was to transpose correctly biblical notions and Greek theological concepts into a very different context of thought and historical experience. It was a question of a new method of catechesis. To defend its legitimacy and prove its value, Saint Methodius, at first together with his brother and then alone, did not hesitate to answer with docility the invitations to come to Rome, invitations received first from Pope Nicholas I in 867 and then from Pope John VIII in 879. Both Popes wished to compare the doctrine being taught by the Brothers in Greater Moravia with that which the holy Apostles Peter and Paul had passed down, together with the glorious trophy of their holy relics, to the Church's chief episcopal See.

11.2 Previously, Constantine and his fellow workers had been engaged in creating a new alphabet, so that the truths to be proclaimed and explained could be written in Old Slavonic and would thus be fully comprehended and grasped by their hearers. The effort to learn the language and to understand the mentality of the new peoples to whom they wished to bring the faith was truly worthy of the missionary spirit. Exemplary too was their determination to assimilate and identify themselves with all the needs and expectations of the Slav peoples. Their generous decision to identify themselves with those peoples' life and traditions, once having purified and enlightened them by revelation, make Cyril and Methodius true models for all the missionaries who in every period have accepted Saint Paul's invitation to become all things to all people in order to redeem all. And in particular for the missionaries who, from ancient times until the present day, from Europe to Asia and today in every continent, have labored to translate the Bible and the texts of the liturgy into the living languages of the various peoples, so as to bring them the one word of God, thus made accessible in each civilization's own forms of expression.

11.3 Perfect communion in love preserves the Church from all forms of particularism, ethnic exclusivism or racial prejudice, and from any nationalistic arrogance. This communion must elevate and sublimate every purely natural legitimate sentiment of the human heart.

IV

They Planted the Church of God

12.1 But the characteristic of the approach adopted by the Apostles of the Slavs Cyril and Methodius which I especially wish to emphasize is the *peaceful* way in which they built up the Church, guided as they were by their vision of the Church as one, holy and universal.

12.2 Even though Slav Christians, more than others, tend to think of the holy Brothers as "Slavs at heart," the latter nevertheless remain men of Hellenic culture and Byzantine training. In other words, men who fully belonged to the civil and ecclesiastical tradition of the Christian East.

12.3 Already in their time certain differences between Constantinople and Rome had begun to appear as pretexts for disunity, even though the deplorable split between the two parts of the same Christian world was still in the distant future. The evangelizers and teachers of the Slavs set out for Greater Moravia imbued with all the wealth of tradition and religious experience which marked Eastern Christianity and which was particularly evident in theological teaching and in the celebration of the Sacred Liturgy.

12.4 The sacred rites in all the Churches within the borders of the Byzantine Empire had long been celebrated in Greek. However, the traditions of many national Churches of the East, such as the Georgian and Syriac, which used the language of the people in their liturgies, were well known to the advanced cultural milieu of Constantinople. They were especially well known to Constantine the Philosopher, as a result of his studies and of his many contacts with Christians belonging to those Churches, both in the capital and in the course of his journeys.

12.5 Both the Brothers were aware of the antiquity and legitimacy of these traditions, and were therefore not afraid to use the Slavonic language in the liturgy and to make it into an effective instrument for bringing the divine truths to those who spoke it. This they did without any spirit of superiority or domination, but out of love of justice and with a clear apostolic zeal for peoples then developing.

12.6 Western Christianity, after the migrations of the new peoples, had amalgamated the newly arrived ethnic groups with the Latin-speaking population already living there, and had extended to all, in order to unite them, the Latin language, liturgy and culture which had been transmitted by the Church of Rome. The uniformity thus achieved gave relatively young and rapidly expanding societies a sense of strength and compactness, which contributed to a closer unity among them and a more forceful affirmation in Europe. It is understandable that in such a situation differences sometimes came to be regarded as a threat to a still incomplete unity. One can also understand how strongly the temptation was felt to eliminate such differences, even by using forms of coercion.

13.1 At this point it is an unusual and admirable thing that the holy Brothers, working in such complex and precarious situations, did not seek to impose on the peoples assigned to their preaching either the undeniable superiority of the Greek language and Byzantine culture, or the customs and way of life of the more advanced society in which they had grown up and which necessarily remained familiar and dear to them. Inspired by the ideal of uniting in Christ the new believers, they adapted to the Slavonic language the rich and refined texts of the Byzantine liturgy and likewise adapted to the mentality and customs of the new peoples the subtle and complex elaborations of Greco-Roman law. In following this program of harmony and peace, Cyril and Methodius were ever respectful of the obligations of their mission. They acknowledged the traditional prerogatives and ecclesiastical rights laid down by conciliar canons. Thus, though subjects of the Eastern Empire and believers subject to the Patriarchate of Constantinople, they considered it their duty to give an account of their missionary work to the Roman Pontiff. They likewise submitted to his judgment, in order to obtain his approval, the doctrine which they professed and taught, the liturgical books which they had written in the

Slavonic language, and the methods which they were using in evangelizing those peoples.

13.2 Having undertaken their mission under orders from Constantinople, they then in a sense sought to have it confirmed by approaching the Apostolic See of Rome, the visible center of the Church's unity.[21] Thus they established the Church with an awareness of her universality as one, holy, catholic and apostolic. This is clearly and explicitly seen in their whole way of acting. It can be said that Jesus' priestly prayer — *ut unum sint*[22] — is their missionary motto in accordance with the Psalmist's words: "Praise the Lord, all nations! Extol him, all peoples."[23] For us today their apostolate also possesses the eloquence of an ecumenical appeal: it is an invitation to restore, in the peace of reconciliation, the unity that was gravely damaged after the time of Cyril and Methodius, and, first and foremost, the unity between East and West.

13.3 The conviction held by the holy Brothers from Salonika, namely that each local Church is called to enrich with its own endowments the Catholic "pleroma," was in perfect harmony with their evangelical insight that the different conditions of life of the individual Christian Churches can never justify discord, disagreement and divisions in the profession of the one faith and in the exercise of charity.

14.1 As we know, according to the teaching of the Second Vatican Council "the 'ecumenical movement' means those activities and enterprises which, according to various needs of the Church and as opportunities offer, are initiated and organized to promote Christian unity."[24] Thus it seems in no way anachronistic to see Saints Cyril and Methodius as the authentic precursors of ecumenism, inasmuch as they wished to eliminate effectively or to reduce any divisions, real or only apparent, between the individual communities belonging to the same Church. For the division which unfortunately occurred in the course of the Church's history and which sadly still persists "not only openly contradicts the will of Christ, (but) provides a stumbling block to the

---

[21] The successors of Pope Nicholas I, even though they were concerned at conflicting reports regarding the teaching and activity of Cyril and Methodius, expressed their full agreement when they had a direct meeting with the Brothers. Prohibitions or limitations in the use of the new liturgy are to be attributed more than anything else to the pressures of the moment, to changing political alliances, and to the need to maintain harmony.

[22] Cf. Jn 17:21-22.

[23] Ps 117:1.

[24] Decree on Ecumenism *Unitatis Redintegratio*, 4.

world, and inflicts damage on the most holy cause of proclaiming the Gospel to every creature."[25]

14.2 The fervent solicitude shown by both Brothers and especially by Methodius by reason of his episcopal responsibility, to preserve unity of faith and love between the Churches of which they were members, namely, between the Church of Constantinople and the Church of Rome on the one hand, and the Churches which arose in the lands of the Slavs on the other, was and will always remain their great merit. This merit is all the greater if one takes into account the fact that their mission was exercised in the years 863-885, thus in the critical years when there emerged and began to grow more serious the fatal discord and bitter controversy between the Churches of the East and the West. The division was accentuated by the question of where Bulgaria, which had just officially accepted Christianity, canonically belonged.

14.3 In this stormy period, which was also marked by armed conflicts between neighboring Christian peoples, the holy Brothers from Salonika preserved a resolute and vigilant fidelity to right doctrine and to the tradition of the perfectly united Church, and in particular to the "divine teachings" and "ecclesiastical teachings"[26] on which, in accordance with the Canons of the ancient Councils, her structure and organization were founded. This fidelity enabled them to complete their great missionary tasks and to remain in full spiritual and canonical unity with the Church of Rome, with the Church of Constantinople and with the new Churches which they had founded among the Slav peoples.

15.1 Methodius especially did not hesitate to face misunderstandings, conflicts and even slanders and physical persecution, rather than fall short of his exemplary ecclesial fidelity, and in order to remain faithful to his duties as a Christian and a Bishop and to the obligations which he had assumed vis-à-vis the Church of Byzantium which had begotten him and sent him out as a missionary together with Cyril. Then there were his obligations to the Church of Rome, thanks to which he fulfilled his charge as Archbishop in "the territory of Saint Peter";[27] likewise his obligations to that Church growing in the lands of the Slavs, which he accepted as his own and successfully defended — convinced of his just right — before the ecclesiastical and civil authorities, protecting in particular the liturgy in the Old Slavonic language and the fundamental ecclesiastical rights proper to the Churches in the various nations.

[25] Second Vatican Ecumenical Council, Decree on Ecumenism *Unitatis Redintegratio*, 1.
[26] Cf. *Vita Methodii* IX, 3; VIII, 16: loc. cit., 229; 228.
[27] Cf. *Vita Methodii* IX, 2: loc. cit., 229.

15.2 By thus acting, he always resorted, as did Constantine the Philosopher, to dialogue with those who opposed his ideas or his pastoral initiatives and who cast doubt on their legitimacy. Thus he would always remain a teacher for all those who, in whatever age, seek to eliminate discord by respecting the manifold fullness of the Church, which, conforming to the will of its Founder Jesus Christ, must be always one, holy, catholic and apostolic. This task was perfectly reflected in the Creed of the 150 Fathers of the First Ecumenical Council of Constantinople, which is the unalterable profession of faith of all Christians.

V

Catholic Sense of the Church

16.1 It is not only the evangelical content of the doctrine proclaimed by Saints Cyril and Methodius that merits particular emphasis. Also very expressive and instructive for the Church today is the catechetical and pastoral method that they applied in their apostolic activity among the peoples who had not yet heard the Sacred Mysteries celebrated in their native language, nor heard the word of God proclaimed in a way that completely fitted their own mentality and respected the actual conditions of their own life.

16.2 We know that the Second Vatican Council, twenty years ago, had as one of its principal tasks that of reawakening the self-awareness of the Church and, through her interior renewal, of impressing upon her a fresh missionary impulse for the proclamation of the eternal message of salvation, peace and mutual concord among peoples and nations, beyond all the frontiers that yet divide our planet, which is intended by the will of God the Creator and Redeemer to be the common dwelling for all humanity. The dangers that in our times are accumulating over our world cannot make us forget the prophetic insight of Pope John XXIII, who convoked the Council with the intent and the conviction that it would be capable of preparing and initiating a period of springtime and rebirth in the life of the Church.

16.3 And, among its statements on the subject of universality, the same Council included the following: "All men are called to belong to the new People of God. Wherefore this People, while remaining one and unique, is to be spread throughout the whole world and must exist in all ages, so that the purpose of God's will may be fulfilled. In the beginning God made human nature one. After his children were scattered, he decreed that they should at length be unified again (cf. Jn 11:52). . . . The Church or People of God takes nothing away from the temporal welfare of any people by establishing that Kingdom. Rather does she foster and take to herself, insofar as they are good, the abilities, resources, and customs of each people. Taking them to herself she purifies, strengthens, and ennobles them. . . . This characteristic of universality which adorns the People of God is a gift from the Lord himself. . . . In virtue of this catholicity each individual part of the Church contributes through its special gifts to the good of the other parts and of the whole Church. Thus through the common sharing of gifts and through the common effort to attain fullness in unity, the whole and each of its parts receive increase."[28]

17.1 We can say without fear of contradiction that such a traditional and at the same time extremely up-to-date vision of the catholicity of the Church — like a symphony of the various liturgies in all the world's languages united in one single liturgy, or a melodious chorus sustained by the voices of unnumbered multitudes, rising in countless modulations, tones and harmonies for the praise of God from every part of the globe, at every moment of history — this vision corresponds in a particular way to the theological and pastoral vision which inspired the apostolic and missionary work of Constantine the Philosopher and of Methodius, and which sustained their mission among the Slav nations.

17.2 In Venice, before the representatives of the ecclesiastical world, who held a rather narrow idea of the Church and were opposed to this vision, Saint Cyril defended it with courage. He showed that many peoples had already in the past introduced and now possessed a liturgy written and celebrated in their own language, such as "the Armenians, the Persians, the Abasgians, the Georgians, the Sogdians, the Goths, the Avars, the Tirsians, the Khazars, the Arabs, the Copts, the Syrians and many others."[29]

17.3 Reminding them that God causes the sun to rise and the rain to fall on all people without exception,[30] he said: "Do not all breathe the air in the same way? And you are not ashamed to decree only three languages (Hebrew, Greek and Latin), deciding that all other peoples and races should remain blind and deaf! Tell me: do you hold this because you consider God is so weak that he cannot grant it, or so envious that he does not wish it?"[31] To the historical and logical arguments which they brought against him, Cyril re-

---

[28] Second Vatican Ecumenical Council, Dogmatic Constitution on the Church *Lumen Gentium*, 13.

[29] *Vita Constantini* XVI, 8: loc. cit., 205.

[30] Cf. Mt 5:45.

[31] *Vita Constantini* XVI, 4-6: loc. cit., 205.

plied by referring to the inspired basis of Sacred Scripture: "Let every tongue confess that Jesus Christ is Lord, to the glory of God the Father."[32] "All the earth worships you; they sing praises to you, sing praises to your name."[33] "Praise the Lord, all nations! Extol him, all peoples!"[34]

18.1 The Church is catholic also because she is able to present in every human context the revealed truth, preserved by her intact in its divine content, in such a way as to bring it into contact with the lofty thoughts and just expectations of every individual and every people. Moreover, the entire patrimony of good which every generation transmits to posterity, together with the priceless gift of life, forms as it were an immense and many-colored collection of tesserae that together make up the living mosaic of the Pantocrator, who will manifest himself in his total splendor only at the moment of the Parousia.

18.2 The Gospel does not lead to the impoverishment or extinction of those things which every individual, people and nation and every culture throughout history recognizes and brings into being as goodness, truth and beauty. On the contrary, it strives to assimilate and to develop all these values: to live them with magnanimity and joy and to perfect them by the mysterious and ennobling light of revelation.

18.3 The concrete dimension of catholicity, inscribed by Christ the Lord in the very make-up of the Church, is not something static, outside history and flatly uniform. In a certain sense it wells up and develops every day as something new from the unanimous faith of all those who believe in God, One and Three, revealed by Jesus Christ and preached by the Church through the power of the Holy Spirit. This dimension issues quite spontaneously from mutual respect — proper to fraternal love — for every person and every nation, great or small, and from the honest acknowledgment of the qualities and rights of brethren in the faith.

19.1 The catholicity of the Church is manifested in the active joint responsibility and generous cooperation of all for the sake of the common good. The Church everywhere effects her universality by accepting, uniting and exalting in the way that is properly hers, with motherly care, every real human value. At the same time, she strives in every clime and every historical situation to win for God each and every human person, in order to unite them with one another and with him in his truth and his love.

---

[32] *Vita Constantini* XVI, 58: loc. cit., 208; cf. Phil 2:11.
[33] *Vita Constantini* XVI, 12: loc. cit., 206; cf. Ps 66:4.
[34] *Vita Constantini* XVI, 13: loc. cit., 206; cf. Ps 117:1.

19.2 All individuals, all nations, cultures and civilizations have their own part to play and their own place in God's mysterious plan and in the universal history of salvation. This was the thought of the two holy Brothers: God "merciful and kind,"[35] "waiting for all people to repent, that all may be saved and come to the knowledge of the Truth,[36] . . . does not allow the human race to succumb to weakness and perish, and to fall into the temptation of the enemy. But year by year and at every time he does not cease to lavish on us a manifold grace, from the beginning until today in the same way: first, through the Patriarchs and Fathers, and after them through the Prophets; and again through the Apostles and Martyrs, the just men and the Doctors whom he chooses in the midst of this stormy life."[37]

20 The message of the Gospel which Saints Cyril and Methodius translated for the Slav peoples, drawing with wisdom from the treasury of the Church "things old and new,"[38] was transmitted through preaching and instruction in accordance with the eternal truths, at the same time being adapted to the concrete historical situation. Thanks to the missionary efforts of both Saints, the Slav peoples were able for the first time to realize their own vocation to share in the eternal design of the Most Holy Trinity, in the universal plan for the salvation of the world. At the same time, they can recognized their role at the service of the whole history of the humanity created by God the Father, redeemed by the Son our Savior and enlightened by the Holy Spirit. Thanks to this preaching, duly approved by the authorities of the Church — the Bishops of Rome and the Patriarchs of Constantinople — the Slavs were able to feel that they too, together with the other nations of the earth, were descendants and heirs of the promise made by God to Abraham.[39] In this way, thanks to the ecclesiastical organization created by Saint Methodius and thanks to their awareness of their own Christian identity, the Slavs took their destined place in the Church which had now arisen also in that part of Europe. For this reason, their modern descendants keep in grateful and everlasting remembrance the one who became the link that binds them to the chain of the great heralds of the divine revelation of the Old and New Testaments: "After all of these, the merciful God, in our own time, raised up for the good work, for the sake of our own people, for whom nobody had ever cared, our teacher, the

---

[35] Cf. Ps 111:4; Joel 2:13.
[36] Cf. 1 Tim 2:4.
[37] *Vita Constantini* I, 1: loc. cit., 169.
[38] Cf. Mt 13:52.
[39] Cf. Gen 15:1-21.

holy Methodius, whose virtues and struggles we unblushingly compare, one by one, to those of these men pleasing to God."[40]

VI

The Gospel and Culture

21.1 The Brothers from Salonika were not only heirs of the faith but also heirs of the culture of Ancient Greece, continued by Byzantium. Everyone knows how important this heritage is for the whole of European culture and, directly or indirectly, for the culture of the entire world. The work of evangelization which they carried out — as pioneers in territory inhabited by Slav peoples — contains both a model of what today is called "inculturation" — the incarnation of the Gospel in native cultures — and also the introduction of these cultures into the life of the Church.

21.2 By incarnating the Gospel in the native culture of the peoples which they were evangelizing, Saints Cyril and Methodius were especially meritorious for the formation and development of that same culture, or rather of many cultures. Indeed all the cultures of the Slav nations owe their "beginning" or development to the work of the Brothers from Salonika. For by their original and ingenious creation of an alphabet for the Slavonic language the Brothers made a fundamental contribution to the culture and literature of all the Slav nations.

21.3 Furthermore, the translation of the sacred books, carried out by Cyril and Methodius together with their pupils, conferred a capacity and cultural dignity upon the Old Slavonic liturgical language, which became for many hundreds of years not only the ecclesiastical but also the official and literary language, and even the common language of the more educated classes of the greater part of the Slav nations, and in particular of all the Slavs of the Eastern Rite. It was also used in the Church of the Holy Cross in Cracow, where the Slav Benedictines had established themselves. Here were published the first liturgical books printed in this language. Up to the present day this is the language used in the Byzantine liturgy of the Slavonic Eastern Churches of the Rite of Constantinople, both Catholic and Orthodox, in Eastern and South Eastern Europe, as well as in various countries of Western Europe. It is also used in the Roman liturgy of the Catholics of Croatia.

22.1 In the historical development of the Slavs of Eastern Rite, this language played a role equal to that of the Latin language in the West. It also

---

[40] *Vita Methodii* II, 1: loc. cit., 220-221.

lasted longer than Latin — in part until the nineteenth century — and exercised a much more direct influence on the formation of the local literary languages, thanks to its close kinship with them.

22.2 These merits vis-à-vis the culture of all the Slav peoples and nations make the work of evangelization carried out by Saints Cyril and Methodius in a certain sense constantly present in the history and in the life of these peoples and nations.

VII

The Significance and Influence of the Christian Millennium in the Slav World

23.1 The apostolic and missionary activity of Saints Cyril and Methodius, which belongs to the second half of the ninth century, can be considered the first effective evangelization of the Slavs.

23.2 This activity involved the individual territories in varying degrees, and was mainly concentrated in the territories of the then existing State of Greater Moravia. It principally included the regions belonging to the metropolis of which Methodius was Pastor, namely Moravia, Slovakia and Pannonia, the last being a part of modern Hungary. Included in the sphere of the wider influence exercised by this apostolic activity, especially that of the missionaries trained by Methodius, were the other groups of Western Slavs, particularly those of Bohemia. The first historical Prince of Bohemia of the dynasty of the Premyslids, Bozyvoj (Borivoj), was probably baptized according to the Slavonic Rite. Later this influence reached the Sorbo-Lusatian tribes, and the territories of southern Poland. However, from the time of the fall of Greater Moravia in about 905-906, the Latin Rite took the place of the Slav Rite, and Bohemia was assigned ecclesiastically to the Bishop of Regensburg and the metropolis of Salzburg. However, it is worthy of note that about the middle of the tenth century, at the time of Saint Wenceslaus, there was still a strong intermingling of the elements of both rites, and an advanced coexistence of both languages in the liturgy: Slavonic and Latin. Moreover, the Christianization of the people was not possible without using the native language. And only upon such a foundation could the development of the Christian terminology in Bohemia take place, and from here, subsequently, the development and consolidation of ecclesiastical terminology in Poland. Information about the Prince of the Vislits in the *Life of Methodius* is the most ancient historical reference to one of the Polish tribes.[41] Insufficient data exist for it to be possible

---

[41] Cf. *Vita Methodii* XI, 2-3: loc. cit., 231.

to link this item of information with the institution in the Polish territories of a Slav Rite ecclesiastical organization.

24.1 The Baptism of Poland in 966, in the person of the first historical sovereign, Mieszko, who married the Bohemian princess Dubravka, took place principally through the Bohemian Church, and by this route Christianity reached Poland from Rome in the Latin form. But the fact remains that the beginnings of Christianity in Poland are in a way linked with the work of the Brothers who set out from distant Salonika.

24.2 Among the Slavs of the Balkan peninsula the efforts of the holy Brothers bore fruit in an even more visible way. Thanks to their apostolate the Christianity which had already for some time been established in Croatia was consolidated.

24.3 Principally through their disciples, who had been expelled from the area where they had originally worked, the mission of Cyril and Methodius was confirmed and developed wonderfully in Bulgaria. Here, thanks to Saint Clement of Okhrid, dynamic centers of monastic life arose, and here particularly the Cyrillic alphabet developed. From here too Christianity moved to other territories, until it passed through neighboring Romania and reached the ancient Rus' of Kiev, and then spread from Moscow eastward. In a few years, in 1988 to be exact, the millennium of the Baptism of Saint Vladimir, Grand Duke of Kiev, will be celebrated.

25.1 Rightly therefore, Saints Cyril and Methodius were at an early date recognized by the family of Slav peoples as the fathers of both their Christianity and their culture. In many of the territories mentioned above, although there had been various missionaries, the majority of the Slav population in the ninth century still retained pagan customs and beliefs. Only in the land cultivated by our Saints, or at least prepared by them for cultivation, did Christianity definitively enter the history of the Slavs during the following century.

25.2 Their work is an outstanding contribution to the formation of the common Christian roots of Europe, roots which by their strength and vitality are one of the most solid points of reference, which no serious attempt to reconstruct in a new and relevant way the unity of the Continent can ignore.

25.3 After eleven centuries of Christianity among the Slavs, we clearly see that the heritage of the Brothers from Salonika is and remains for the Slavs deeper and stronger than any division. Both Christian traditions — the Eastern deriving from Constantinople and the Western deriving from Rome — arose in the bosom of the one Church, even though against the background of different cultures and of a different approach to the same problems. This diversity, when its origin is properly understood and when its value and meaning are properly considered, can only enrich the culture of Europe and its religious tradition, and likewise become an adequate foundation for its hoped-for spiritual renewal.

26.1 Ever since the ninth century, when in Christian Europe a new organization was emerging, Saints Cyril and Methodius have held out to us a message clearly of great relevance for our own age, which precisely by reason of the many complex problems of a religious, cultural, civil and international nature, is seeking a vital unity in the real communion of its various elements. It can be said of the two evangelizers that characteristic of them was their love for the communion of the universal Church both in the East and in the West, and, within the universal Church, love for the particular Church that was coming into being in the Slav nations. From them also comes for the Christians and people of our time the invitation *to build communion together*.

26.2 But it is in the specific area of missionary activity that the example of Cyril and Methodius is of even greater value. For this activity is an essential task of the Church, and is urgent today in the already mentioned form of "inculturation." The two Brothers not only carried out their mission with full respect for the culture already existing among the Slav peoples, but together with religion they eminently and unceasingly promoted and extended that culture. By analogy, today the Churches of ancient origin can and must help the young Churches and peoples to mature in their own identity and progress in it.[42]

27.1 Cyril and Methodius are as it were the connecting links or spiritual bridge between the Eastern and Western traditions, which *both* come together in the *one* great Tradition of the universal Church. For us they are the champions and also the patrons of the ecumenical endeavor of the sister Churches of East and West, for the rediscovery through prayer and dialogue of visible unity in perfect and total communion, "the unity which," as I said on the occasion of my visit to Bari, "is neither absorption nor fusion."[43] Unity is a meeting in truth and love, granted to us by the Spirit. Cyril and Methodius, in

[42] Cf. Second Vatican Ecumenical Council, Decree on the Church's Missionary Activity *Ad Gentes*, 38.

[43] John Paul II, Address at the Ecumenical Meeting in the Basilica of Saint Nicholas, Bari (February 26, 1984), 2: *Insegnamenti* VII/1 (1984), 532.

their personality and their work, are figures that awaken in all Christians a great "longing for union" and for unity between the two sister Churches of East and West.[44] For full catholicity, every nation, every culture has its own part to play in the universal plan of salvation. Every particular tradition, every local Church must remain open and alert to the other Churches and traditions and, at the same time, to universal and catholic communion; were it to remain closed in on itself, it too would run the risk of becoming impoverished.

27.2 By exercising their own charism, Cyril and Methodius made a decisive contribution to the building of Europe not only in Christian religious communion but also to its civil and cultural union. Not even today does there exist any other way of overcoming tensions and repairing the divisions and antagonisms both in Europe and in the world which threaten to cause a frightful destruction of lives and values. Being Christians in our day means being builders of communion in the Church and in society. This calls for openness to others, mutual understanding, and readiness to cooperate through the generous exchange of cultural and spiritual resources.

27.3 One of the fundamental aspirations of humanity today is to rediscover unity and communion for a life truly worthy of man on the worldwide level. The Church, conscious of being the universal sign and sacrament of salvation and of the unity of the human race, declares her readiness to accomplish this duty of hers, to which "the conditions of this age lend special urgency so that all people joined more closely today by various social, technical, and cultural bonds can achieve as well full unity in Christ."[45]

VIII

Conclusion

28 It is fitting, then, that the Church should celebrate with solemnity and joy the eleven centuries that have elapsed since the close of the apostolic work of the first Archbishop, ordained in Rome for the Slav peoples, Methodius, and of his brother Cyril, and that she should thus commemorate the entry of these peoples on to the scene of the history of salvation and into the list of European nations which during the preceding centuries had already accepted the Gospel message. Everyone will understand with what profound happiness I will share in this celebration as the first son of the Slav race to be called,

[44] Ibid., 1: loc. cit., 531.
[45] Second Vatican Ecumenical Council, Dogmatic Constitution on the Church *Lumen Gentium*, 1.

after nearly two millennia, to occupy the episcopal See that once belonged to Peter in this city of Rome.

29.1 *"Into thy hands I commend my spirit"*: we salute the eleventh centenary of Saint Methodius' death with the very words which — as his *Life* in Old Slavonic recounts[46] — he uttered before he died, when he was about to join his fathers in faith, hope and charity: the Patriarchs, Prophets, Apostles, Doctors and Martyrs. By the testimony of his words and life, sustained by the charism of the Spirit, he gave an example of a vocation fruitful not only for the century in which he lived but also for the centuries which followed, and in a special way for our own times.

29.2 His blessed "passing" in the spring of the year 885 after the Incarnation of Christ (and according to the Byzantine calculation of time, in the year 6393 since the creation of the world) took place at a time when disquieting clouds were gathering above Constantinople and hostile tensions were increasingly threatening the peace and life of the nations, and even threatening the sacred bonds of Christian brotherhood and communion linking the Churches of the East and West.

29.3 In his Cathedral, filled with the faithful of different races, the disciples of Saint Methodius paid solemn homage to their dead Pastor for the message of salvation, peace and reconciliation which he had brought and to which he had devoted his life: "They celebrated a sacred office in Latin, Greek and Slavonic,"[47] adoring God and venerating the first Archbishop of the Church which he established among the Slavs, to whom he and his brother had proclaimed the Gospel in their own language. This Church grew even stronger when through the explicit consent of the Pope it received a native hierarchy, rooted in the apostolic succession and remaining in unity of faith and love both with the Church of Rome and with that of Constantinople, from which the Slav mission had begun.

29.4 Now that eleven centuries have passed since his death, I desire to be present at least spiritually *in Velehrad*, where — it seems — Providence enabled Methodius to end his apostolic life:

— I desire also to pause in the *Basilica of Saint Clement in Rome*, in the place where Saint Cyril was buried;

— and at the Tombs of both these Brothers, the Apostles of the Slavs, I desire *to recommend to the Most Blessed Trinity their spiritual heritage* with a special prayer.

---

[46] Cf. *Vita Methodii* XVII, 9-10: loc. cit., 237; Lk 23:46; Ps 31:6.
[47] *Vita Methodii* XVII, 11: loc. cit., 237.

30.1 *"Into your hands I commend . . ."*

O great God, One in Trinity, I entrust to you the heritage of faith of the Slav nations; preserve and bless this work of yours!

30.2 Remember, O Almighty Father, the moment when, in accordance with your will, the "fullness of time" arrived for these peoples and nations, and the holy Missionaries from Salonika faithfully fulfilled the command that your Son Jesus Christ had entrusted to his Apostles; following in their footsteps and in those of their successors, they brought into the lands inhabited by the Slavs the light of the Gospel, the Good News of salvation and, in their presence, bore testimony

— that you are the Creator of man, that you are our Father and that in you we are all brethren;

— that through the Son, your eternal Word, you have given existence to all things, and have called human beings to share in your life without end;

— that you have so loved the world as to grant it the gift of your only-begotten Son, who for us men and for our salvation came down from heaven and by the power of the Holy Spirit became incarnate in the womb of the Virgin Mary and was made man;

— and that finally you have sent the Spirit of power and consolation so that every human being, redeemed by Christ, may in him receive the dignity of a child and become a co-heir of the unfailing promises which you have made to humanity!

30.3 Your plan of creation, O Father, culminating in the Redemption, touches the living man and embraces his entire life and the history of all peoples.

30.4 Grant, O Father, what the whole Church today implores from you and grant also that the *people and the nations* which, thanks to the apostolic mission of the holy Brothers from Salonika, have known and accepted you, the true God, and through Baptism have entered into the holy community of your children, may still continue, without hindrance, to accept with enthusiasm and trust this evangelical program and continue to realize all their human possibilities on the foundation of their teachings!

— May they follow, in conformity with their own conscience, the voice of your call along the paths shown to them for the first time eleven centuries ago!

— May their membership of the Kingdom of your Son never be considered by anyone to be contrary to the good of their earthly homeland!

— May they render to you due praise in private and in public life!

— May they live in truth, charity, justice and in the enjoyment of the messianic peace which enfolds human hearts, communities, the earth and the entire universe!

— Aware of their dignity as human beings and children of God, may they have the strength to overcome all hatred and to conquer evil with good!

30.5 But also grant to the whole of Europe, O Most Holy Trinity, that through the intercession of the two holy Brothers it may feel ever more strongly the need for religious and Christian unity and for a brotherly communion of all its peoples, so that when incomprehension and mutual distrust have been overcome and when ideological conflicts have been conquered in the common awareness of the truth, it may be for the whole world an example of just and peaceful coexistence in mutual respect and inviolate liberty.

31.1 To you, therefore, God the Father Almighty, God the Son who have redeemed the world, God the Spirit who are the sustainer and teacher of all holiness, I desire to entrust the whole Church of yesterday, today and tomorrow, the Church both in Europe and throughout the earth. Into your hands I commit this singular wealth, made up of so many different gifts, ancient and new, placed in the common treasury by so many different sons and daughters.

31.2 The whole Church thanks you, who called the Slav nations into the communion of the faith, for this heritage and for the contribution made by them to the universal patrimony. The Pope of Slav origin in a special way thanks you for this. May this contribution never cease to enrich the Church, the Continent of Europe and the whole world! May it never fail in Europe and in the world of today! May it never fade from the memories of our contemporaries! We desire to accept in its entirety everything original and valid which the Slav nations have brought and continue to bring to the spiritual patrimony of the Church and of humanity. The whole Church, aware of this common treasure, professes her spiritual solidarity with them and reaffirms her own responsibility toward the Gospel, for the work of salvation which she is called upon to accomplish also today in the whole world, unto the ends of the earth. It is essential to go back to the past in order to understand, in the light of the past, the present reality and in order to discern tomorrow. For the mission of the Church is always oriented and directed with unfailing hope toward the future.

32.1 The future! However much it may humanly speaking seem filled with threats and uncertainties, we trustfully place it in your hands, Heavenly Father, invoking upon it the intercession of the Mother of your Son and Mother of the Church, the intercession of your Apostles Peter and Paul, and of Saints Benedict, Cyril and Methodius, of Augustine and Boniface and all the other evangelizers of Europe who, strong in faith, hope and charity, proclaimed to our fathers your salvation and your peace, and amid the toils of the spiritual sowing began to build *the civilization of love* and the new order based on your holy law and the help of your grace, which at the end of the age will give life to all things and all people in the heavenly Jerusalem. Amen!

32.2 To you, dear brothers and sisters, my Apostolic Blessing.

Given in Rome, at Saint Peter's, on June 2, the Solemnity of the Most Holy Trinity, in the year 1985, the seventh of my Pontificate.

Dominum et Vivificantem

Editor's Introduction

Pope John Paul II published the last encyclical of his Trinitarian trilogy on Pentecost Sunday, May 18, 1986.[1] *Dominum et Vivificantem* completes his prolonged meditation on Saint Paul's exhortation: "The grace of our Lord Jesus Christ [*Redemptor Hominis*] and the love of God [*Dives in Misericordia*] and the fellowship of the Holy Spirit be with you all" (2 Cor 13:13). As the third millennium draws near, the Pope wishes to awaken in the Church the time of a new Advent of preparation for the "event which should recall to everyone and as it were make present anew the coming of the Word in the fullness of time" (§61.1). In this Advent of expectation, the Holy Spirit is "at the center of the Christian faith and is the source and dynamic power of the Church's renewal" (§2.3).

Two contemporary ecclesial events furnish the particular stimulus for the encyclical. First, John Paul is responding to the call of the Second Vatican Council which emphasized "the need for a new study of the doctrine of the Holy Spirit" (§2.1), a point later reiterated by Paul VI. Second, he wishes to commemorate the sixteenth centenary of the First Council of Constantinople, whose anniversary had been celebrated in 1981. By recalling the doctrine on the Holy Spirit defined at Constantinople, the Pope points to the important role that the Third Person of the Trinity can play in drawing East and West closer together on the threshold of the year 2000.

Dominum et Vivificantem is by far the longest treatment of the Holy Spirit, indeed of the mystery of the Trinity, in the papal Magisterium of any age. Yet the encyclical is not a full or systematic discussion of Church teaching on the Holy Spirit. John Paul imposes certain limits on himself. He intends neither "to explore exhaustively the extremely rich doctrine on the Holy Spirit, nor to favor any particular solution of questions which are still open" (§2.6). The Pope uses the literary form of an exhortation rather than that of a theological treatise. He wishes to rekindle believers' trust in the Spirit's life-giving power to effect renewal in the Church and in society.

John Paul declares that his reflections have been drawn "*from the heart of the heritage of the Council.* For the conciliar texts, thanks to their teaching on the Church in herself and the Church in the world, move us to penetrate ever

---

[1] *Acta Apostolicae Sedis*, 78 (1986), 809-900.

deeper into the Trinitarian mystery of God himself" (§2.3). He takes pains to note that, while the Second Vatican Council is especially concerned with ecclesiology, "the teaching of this Council is essentially 'pneumatological': it is *permeated by the truth about the Holy Spirit*, as the soul of the Church" (§26.1). To prove his point, he frequently cites from conciliar documents, especially *Lumen Gentium* and, above all, *Gaudium et Spes*.

At the same time, the Pope admits to being "helped and stimulated also by the heritage we share with *the Oriental Churches*, which have jealously guarded the extraordinary riches of the teachings of the Fathers [of the Church] on the Holy Spirit" (§2.2). However, in order to present his teaching on the Holy Spirit, the Pope depends above all on Sacred Scripture. More than eighty percent of the encyclical's footnotes are to the Bible. In particular, he relies on the Last Supper discourse in John, chapters 14-17. While rooted profoundly in the sources of Scripture and Tradition, the encyclical's tone still reflects the Pope's meditative style.

Summary

Dominum et Vivificantem is divided into an introduction, three principal chapters, and a conclusion. In chapter one, "The Spirit of the Father and of the Son, Given to the Church" (§§3-26), the Pope recalls the various ways and the gradual stages by which the Holy Spirit is revealed to the Church and to the world. Chapter two, "The Spirit Who Convinces the World concerning Sin" (§§27-48), deals with how the Holy Spirit awakens in human beings a sense of their sinfulness in order to prepare the way for conversion and living in the truth. Chapter three, "The Spirit Who Gives Life" (§§49-56), explains the reasons for the Jubilee and discusses how the Spirit is vitally active in the life of individuals, the Church, and the world. The order of these chapters follows the unfolding movement of the Spirit's role in salvation history: he was promised by Jesus and given to the Church (§§1-26); at the present time, the Spirit stirs up a sense of sinfulness as a prerequisite for salvation (§§27-48); as the life-giving Spirit, he is the Church's source of hope, leading her to the Lord who is coming (§§49-67).

All the Pope's reflections in this encyclical take as their point of departure the Trinitarian communion among the three divine Persons. "*The Triune God*, who 'exists' in himself as a transcendent reality of interpersonal gift, *giving himself in the Holy Spirit as gift to man*," John Paul writes, "*transforms the human world from within*, from inside hearts and minds" (§59.2). This saving presence and life-giving action of the Spirit are the principal themes developed in *Dominum et Vivificantem*.

Farewell discourse

The Pope structures chapter one around his reading of Saint John's account of the farewell discourse in which Jesus promises and reveals the Spirit-Paraclete. Here John Paul distinguishes three different ways in which Jesus promises that the Spirit would give himself to humanity. As the other Paraclete, following upon Christ who is the first Paraclete, the Spirit continues "in the world, through the Church, the work of *the Good News of salvation*" (§3.2). First, the Spirit of truth inspires the spread of the same Gospel proclaimed by Jesus, ensuring its continuity and identity in history; he helps "people to understand the correct meaning of the content of Christ's message" (§4). Second, the Spirit bears witness to Christ (cf. Jn 15:26) by supporting and confirming the human testimony of the Apostles. The Paraclete "inspires, guarantees and convalidates the faithful transmission of this revelation in the preaching and writing of the Apostles" (§5.3). Third, as the Paraclete-Advocate, the Holy Spirit is "man's supreme guide and the light of the human spirit" (§6.3), defending the faith of believers. He "unceasingly continues the historical presence on earth of the Redeemer and his saving work" (§7.1).

This *"new salvific self-giving of God, in the Holy Spirit"* (§11), marks a fresh beginning in salvation history, going beyond God's initial self-giving in creation. After the Fall, the self-communication of the Triune God in the Holy Spirit is brought about through the work of Christ the Redeemer. The Pope describes this gift of the Spirit in relation to Christ, who receives the Spirit and gives him to the Apostles. Here John Paul turns to the historical manifestations of the Spirit in salvation history: from the first signs of his activity in the Old Testament to his continuing mission in the Church manifested on Pentecost, the culmination of the Paschal Mystery.

The Spirit in the Old and New Covenant

In his presentation of the Spirit's activity in the Old Testament, the Pope begins with Isaiah 11:1-3, which refers to the "Spirit of the Lord" given to the Messiah. This text, he says, "constitutes a kind of bridge between the ancient biblical concept of 'spirit,' understood primarily as a 'charismatic breath of wind,' and the *'Spirit' as a person and as a gift, a gift for the person*" (§15.3). In the Old Covenant, the Messiah is portrayed as "the one who possesses *the fullness of this Spirit in himself* and at the same time *for others*" (§16.7). Isaiah's prophecy begins "the path toward the full revelation of the Holy Spirit in the unity of the Trinitarian mystery" (§15.3). The Old Testament prophetic texts, however, reveal no distinction of divine Persons within the one God. Only when these passages are read in the light of the definitive revelation of Christ can they be interpreted as referring to the Holy Spirit.

It is the New Testament that reveals the Holy Spirit as a distinct divine Person and his nature as gift. From the very outset of their narratives, the Gospel writers emphasize the uniqueness of the Holy Spirit. "The conception and birth of Jesus Christ," writes the Pope, "are in fact the greatest work accomplished by the Holy Spirit in the history of creation and salvation: the supreme grace — the 'grace of union,' the source of every other grace, as Saint Thomas explains" (§50.2). At the Jordan, during Jesus' baptism, a *"Trinitarian theophany"* (§19.4) reveals Jesus as the Messiah, the One "anointed" with the Holy Spirit. His public ministry "is carried out in the active presence of the Holy Spirit" (§20.1). Indeed, the Pope writes that the Spirit not only accompanies Jesus' ministry "from outside," so to speak, but also "from within." Everything that Jesus says and does flows "from that *fullness of the Spirit* which is in him, which fills his heart, pervades his own 'I,' inspires and enlivens his actions from the depths" (§21.1).

During Christ's farewell discourse in the Upper Room, the Holy Spirit is revealed in a newer and fuller way. Jesus discloses that the Spirit is not only a gift to the person of the Messiah, but is also himself "a Person-gift" (§22.3). The Paschal Mystery of Jesus' Passion, death, and Resurrection is "the *time of the new coming* of the Holy Spirit, as the Paraclete and Spirit of truth" (§23). This is the moment of the Spirit's definitive revelation as "a Person who is the gift" (§23). Through Christ's redemptive action, his self-offering to the One who "gave his only Son" (Jn 3:16), the Holy Spirit is conferred on the Church in a new way. The Spirit comes "after" Jesus' departure through the Cross and "at the price of" that departure (§30.2). The fruit of Christ's Passion is God's gift of his Spirit.

This divine gift is definitively expressed by the Resurrection. Whereas before his glorification Jesus had been a recipient of the Spirit, with the Resurrection he becomes the active dispenser of the same Spirit (cf. Jn 20:22-23). Having received in himself the fullness of the gift of the Spirit, the risen Lord on Easter evening gives the Apostles the Spirit "through the wounds of his crucifixion" (§24.3). He sends the Paraclete "to transform us into his own risen image" (§24.1). Later, on Pentecost, what had taken place inside the Upper Room is manifested outside, to the whole world. With this descent of the Holy Spirit "*the promises and predictions* that so explicitly referred to the Counselor, the Spirit of truth, began to be fulfilled in complete power and clarity upon the Apostles, thus determining the birth of the Church" (§25.4).

The Spirit is the gift of the glorified Christ to the Apostles, who were thus enabled to fulfill the mission that Jesus had entrusted to them.

Convincing the world concerning sin

Chapter two of *Dominum et Vivificantem* is a dense, original, and often difficult treatment of Jesus' words at the Last Supper: "And when he [the Counselor] comes, he will convince the world concerning sin and righteousness and judgment: concerning sin, because they do not believe in me; concerning righteousness, because I go to the Father, and you will see me no more; concerning judgment, because the ruler of this world is judged" (Jn 16:8-11). Using this passage from John's Gospel, the Pope examines at length the relationship of the Holy Spirit to sin, "showing the evil that sin contains" (§39.1). John Paul's explanation of the cosmic dimensions of sin leads him to a discussion of the Spirit's universal saving action.

The extent of humanity's sinfulness can come to light only through the action of the Spirit. He "searches everything, even the depths of God" (1 Cor 2:10) — a text cited ten times in the encyclical. Only the Spirit of truth can unmask the depths of human sin and reveal how that sin is related to the Cross of Christ. John Paul believes that this revelation about sin made by the Spirit "must be given *the widest possible meaning*, insofar as it includes all the sin in the history of humanity" (§29.3). It is the Spirit himself who undertakes to disclose the meaning of evil in the world. First, the Pope describes Pentecost as the beginning of the Spirit's work of "convincing" humanity of its sinfulness. He follows this with a novel analysis of original sin, of the Spirit's role in Christ's redemptive sacrifice and in enlightening human consciences, and of the sin against the Holy Spirit.

Pentecost

Just as the Holy Spirit was given to the Eleven on Easter (Jn 21:22-23), after Christ's "departure" in death, so too is he given on Pentecost, after his second "departure" at the Ascension. Saint Peter's discourse on Pentecost fulfills Jesus' prophecy that the Spirit will convince the world of its sinfulness: "Repent, and be baptized every one of you in the name of Jesus Christ for the forgiveness of your sins; and you shall receive the gift of the Holy Spirit" (Acts 2:38). This convincing of sin involves accusing the world because it crucified the Messiah, but it is also "a convincing *concerning the remission of sins*, in the power of the Holy Spirit" (§31.2).

The Holy Spirit, who "searches even the depths of God" (1 Cor 2:10), reveals that all sin is related to the Cross of Christ. In some sense every sin is one of unbelief: "concerning sin, because they do not believe in me" (Jn 16:9). By opening people to an understanding of the depths of their sinfulness, the Spirit prepares the way for their conversion. Consequently, "convincing the world concerning sin" rightly belongs to the Church's preaching of the Gospel of salvation. It is a proclamation to the world of the existence of sin, and creates the necessary condition for receiving the grace of Redemption. With the Spirit's help, people's consciences can recognize sin *"in the entire dimension of evil* proper to it" (§32.2).

Original sin

Dominum et Vivificantem contains the longest treatment of original sin in any of John Paul's documents. Included in that sin about which the world must be "convinced," original sin opens mankind to its need for a Redeemer. The Pope points out that the sin of the first parents is the original sin which is *"the principle and root of all the others"* (§33.1). Original sin, too, is a sin of non-belief; it is the rejection or *"turning away from the truth contained in the Word of God*, who creates the world" (§33.2). In the divine plan, the gift of the Spirit, bestowed on those created in God's image and likeness, involved a call to friendship. Original sin was the refusal of this call. *"The sin of the human beginning,"* the Pope says, *"consists in untruthfulness and in the rejection of the gift and the love* which determine the beginning of the world and of man" (§35.2). Far from being merely a past occurrence, the consequences of this first sin continue to afflict humanity down to the present day.

John Paul further describes original sin as a sin of disobedience, a transgression of the limit set by God on our first parents. Original sin expresses man's desire "to decide by himself what is good and what is evil" (§36.2). It attempts to appropriate a decision which belongs to God alone, who is "the one definitive source of the moral order in the world created by him" (§36.2). The disobedience of Adam and Eve, like that entailed in every sin, involves a rejection of creaturehood. It falsifies who God is, and who the person is. Satan, the "father of lies" (Jn 8:44), persuades man that God is *"an enemy* of his own creature," even a threat to his freedom (§38.1). Throughout the course of history, the devil continues to exert *"a constant pressure on man to reject God,* even to the point of hating him" (§38.2).

"Light of consciences"

After his excursus on original sin, the Pope turns to a consideration of God's response to humanity's fallenness, concentrating on the particular role played by the Paraclete in the mystery of Redemption. Through the Paschal

Mystery the Spirit enters the world "with a new outpouring of love" (§39.3). This love is manifested in the work of "convincing concerning sin"; that is, "the gift of the truth of conscience and the gift of the certainty of Redemption" (§31.2). The Paraclete is "the one who is now to continue the salvific work rooted in the sacrifice of the Cross" (§42.1); "he brings to completion in human souls the work of the Redemption accomplished by Christ, and distributes its fruits" (§46.4, cf. §§53.1, 67.2).

Because of the Paschal Mystery, the door into a person's inmost being, the sanctuary of human conscience, is now open to the Spirit. According to John Paul, the Spirit "*makes man realize his own evil* and at the same time *directs him toward what is good*" (§42.2). The Paraclete purifies consciences, ensuring that they can fulfill their function of enabling people "*to call evil and good by their proper name*" (§43.3). Thus, through the Counselor, the process of conversion begins, that initial step which is indispensable for the forgiveness of sins. When he acts as the voice of conscience, the Spirit of truth carries out his role of "convincing the world concerning sin."

In the sanctuary of conscience, the Spirit reveals to people that they are created beings, "and therefore in complete ontological and ethical dependence upon the Creator" (§44.3). He is "the light of consciences," as the Church prays in the Sequence for Pentecost. The Holy Spirit enables people to recognize evil, turn away from it, and open themselves to the gift of reconciliation. According to the Pope, the Spirit "comes in *each concrete case of conversion-forgiveness*, by virtue of the sacrifice of the Cross" (§45.2).

Sin against the Holy Spirit

John Paul closes chapter two with a discussion of blasphemy against the Holy Spirit, the sin which "will not be forgiven" (cf. Mt 12.31-32; Mk 3:28-29; Lk 12:10). This sin involves the rejection of the "convincing concerning sin" stirred up by the Spirit, the stifling of God's voice in the conscience. It is, says the Pope, "*the refusal to accept the salvation which God offers to man through the Holy Spirit*" (§46.3). The sin against the Spirit is a person's freely willed refusal to repent of his sin, the definitive rejection of divine forgiveness. Blasphemy against the Holy Spirit is "the sin committed by the person who claims to have a '*right*' *to persist in evil* — in any sin at all — and who thus rejects Redemption" (§46.4). What Scripture refers to as "hardness of heart," an interior resistance to conversion, the Pope equates with "*the loss of the sense of sin*" in the contemporary world (§47.1). Blasphemy against the Holy Spirit is a denial of the truth concerning forgiveness, a spurning of his action in the heart of conscience.

The Jubilee of the year 2000

Although already mentioned in *Redemptor Hominis,* in this encyclical the Pope discusses at greater length a theme which will emerge with increasing frequency in his writings: the Jubilee of the year 2000. Above all, the Jubilee has a Christological aspect, referring to the commemoration of the "fullness of time" (Gal 4:4) when the redemptive Incarnation took place in the womb of the Virgin Mary. But it also has a pronounced pneumatological dimension, since the mystery of the hypostatic union was accomplished in Mary "by the power of the Holy Spirit." Besides recalling a historical event, the Jubilee will provide an occasion for reflection on the salvific work of the Holy Spirit. This Spirit is, as the Creed says, the "Giver of life," who bestows on people the new life of divine filiation.

Unfortunately, however, the life-giving Spirit "*meets with resistance and opposition* in our human reality" (§55.1). As in most encyclicals, in *Dominum et Vivificantem* John Paul furnishes an analysis of the contemporary situation in the light of the subject he is pondering. Here he views the world through the prism of Saint Paul's teaching on the conflict between "flesh" and "spirit" (cf. Gal 5:16-17), between "death" and "life." On the one hand, this conflict is waged within each individual: between openness to the Spirit's action and resistance to him. On the other hand, this struggle also has an external dimension: between the "desires against the spirit" and the "desires against the flesh" which collide in contemporary society. Today's anti-religious materialism, both theoretical and practical, is "the systematic and logical development of that 'resistance' and opposition" to the Spirit condemned by Saint Paul (§56.3). Humanity is threatened by the decadence and indifferentism of those who live as if God did not exist. "Desires against the spirit" mark modern society, where "*the signs and symptoms* of death have become particularly present and frequent" (§57.2). Among the signs of death he mentions specifically are the arms race and threat of nuclear destruction, death-dealing poverty and famine, abortion and euthanasia, wars and terrorism.

In spite of the increasing signs of death in society, a theme which the Pope develops in more detail in *Evangelium Vitae* (1995), the Church confidently preaches that the Spirit is the Giver of life: "She proclaims him and cooperates with him in giving life" (§58.1). The Spirit continually brings people into the sphere of divine life, enabling them to discover the full meaning of their humanity. He leads them to penetrate the "divine dimension of their being and life, both as individuals and as a community" (§60.1), and frees them from whatever ensnares them in deceit.

At the end of chapter three, John Paul turns his attention to the Church, where the Spirit's "coming" in history is constantly being brought about. The

Pope refers to the Church as "the sign and instrument of the presence and action of the life-giving Spirit" (§64.2). Through the power of the Spirit, Christ's continuing presence and action are mediated by the sacraments. By means of them the Spirit gives eternal life. It is above all through the Eucharist that the Spirit strengthens people and teaches them to discover "the divine sense of human life" (§62.1).

The Pope concludes his encyclical with an appeal to the Holy Spirit as "*the guardian of hope* in the human heart" (§67.1). As the uncreated gift, he convinces the world concerning sin "in order to restore what is good in man and in the world: in order to 'renew the face of the earth' " (§67.3).

Key Themes

For all its richness, the pneumatology of John Paul II is not a complete or systematic presentation of Church doctrine on the Holy Spirit. He says, for instance, very little about the internal procession of the Spirit within the Trinity, and he ignores the controversy with the Orthodox Churches concerning the *filioque*.

Undoubtedly the most original section of *Dominum et Vivificantem* is the Pope's meditative exegesis of John's passage (16:8-11) on "convincing the world concerning sin and righteousness and judgment," a text that we have already examined. But he also develops other fresh theological perspectives: first, in examining the relationship between Christ and the Holy Spirit; and second, in describing the Spirit's mission to the individual, the Church, and the world.

The Son and the Spirit

In keeping with his Christocentric vision of reality, John Paul II pays particular attention to the relation of the Incarnate Son to the Holy Spirit. Pneumatology and Christology are interdependent. The Pope repeatedly mentions that the Spirit is the gift which Christ gave through his Cross. While Jesus is the first Paraclete (cf. 1 Jn 2:1), the Spirit continues the Son's saving mission in the Church. John Paul draws attention to the *causal* relationship of interdependence between the two divine Persons: "The Holy Spirit will come insofar as Christ will depart through the Cross: he will come not only *afterward*, but *because of* the Redemption accomplished by Christ, through the will and action of the Father" (§8.2, cf. §§3.2, 13, 14.2, 22.1, 30.2). God's new self-communication to human beings is inseparably linked to Christ's redemptive work, which the Spirit prolongs in history. The Son's "departure" at Calvary is the price paid for the Spirit's "coming" in the Upper Room at Pentecost. "The mission of the Son, in a certain sense, finds its 'fulfillment' in the Redemption. The mission of the Holy Spirit 'draws from' the Redemption" (§24.4). Whereas the Son accomplished the Redemption in the power of the Spirit, the "other Paraclete" carries it out in time.

According to God's plan, the sending of the Son and the sending of the Spirit are necessarily connected. "There is no sending of the Holy Spirit (after original sin)," writes the Pope, "without the Cross and the Resurrection" (§24.4). The missions of the two divine Persons are linked: the Son fulfills his mission in the act of Redemption, and the Spirit constantly "draws from" the Redemption. The Spirit precedes Christ's coming into the world and, when he departs through the Cross, the Spirit succeeds him.

In a novel way John Paul expresses the presence and activity of the Spirit in the Son's redemptive sacrifice on the altar of the Cross. He uses a passage from the Letter to the Hebrews to make his point: "How much more shall the blood of Christ, who through the eternal Spirit offered himself without blemish to God, purify your conscience from dead works to serve the living God?" (9:14). According to the Pope, "on the way to his 'departure' through Gethsemane and Golgotha, the same *Christ Jesus* in his own humanity *opened himself totally* to this *action of the Spirit-Paraclete*, who from suffering enables eternal salvific love to spring forth" (§40.3). It was on the Cross that Jesus fully opened the innermost depths of his humanity to the Paraclete's action.

On Calvary Christ allowed the Spirit "*to transform that humanity into a perfect sacrifice* through the act of his death as the victim of love" (§40.4). Just as in the Old Testament "fire from heaven" burnt the oblations, so by analogy is the Holy Spirit the " *'fire from heaven' which works in the depth of the mystery of the Cross*" (§41.1). As the fire of love, the Paraclete enters the heart of the Redemption, "bringing it into the *divine reality of the Trinitarian communion*" (§41.1). The Holy Spirit is present in the Paschal Mystery, says the Pope, "*in all his divine subjectivity:* as the one who is now to continue the salvific work rooted in the sacrifice of the Cross" (§42.1). Christ, by means of his priestly offering, "receives" the Spirit to whom, in his humanity, he totally opened himself. Thus, as risen Lord, he can "give" him to the Apostles, the Church, and humanity. The Cross and Resurrection are the necessary condition for the bestowal of the new gift of the Spirit which God makes in the everlasting Covenant.

Mission to the person, the Church, and the world

The Pope anchors the universality of the offer of salvation in the close relation which exists between the order of creation and the order of redemption. The role of the Holy Spirit is crucial in establishing the bond between these two orders. He is "the eternal source of every gift that comes from God in the order of creation, the direct principle and, in a certain sense, the subject of God's self-communication in the order of grace" (§50.1). God's self-giving in the Spirit began with creation itself: "He was already at work from the beginning in the mystery of creation and throughout the history of the Old Covenant" (§42.1, cf. §52.3).

In fact, there is only one vocation for every individual: the elevation to divine grace, communion with the Triune God. This new life comes to people when the Father sends the Spirit of his Son into their hearts (cf. Gal 4:4). "The divine filiation planted in the human soul through sanctifying grace is the work of the Holy Spirit" (§52.2). He is the uncreated Gift who gives human beings a share in his life, granting them the created gift whereby they become partakers of the divine nature (cf. 2 Pet 1:4). "Through the gift of grace, which comes from the Holy Spirit," writes John Paul, "man enters a *new life,*' is brought into the supernatural reality of the divine life itself and becomes a 'dwelling-place in the Holy Spirit,' a living temple of God" (§58.3).

The Paraclete is active in the world from its origins, but because of original sin and the subsequent history of actual sin, a fresh start was necessary. This was accomplished through the Paschal Mystery; it ushered in "the time of the 'new beginning' of the self-communication of the Triune God to humanity in the Holy Spirit through the work of Christ the Redeemer" (§23). Just as sin alienates everyone from God, so too Redemption unites everyone to God. As the Pope says, the work of salvation is "constantly carried out in human hearts and minds — in the history of the world — by the Holy Spirit" (§24.4).

John Paul takes up the mission of the Holy Spirit to the individual in light of the importance which he attributes to the dignity of the human person. Individual personal fulfillment is found in divine filiation. As the Giver of life, the Spirit "*communicates himself to human beings*, constituting in them the source of eternal life" (§1.3). He establishes an intimate interpersonal communion between each individual and the Triune God. The gift of the Spirit, the Pope writes, "ultimately means *a call to friendship*, in which the transcendent 'depths of God' become in some way opened to participation on the part of man" (§34). In people's souls the Spirit brings to completion the Redemption accomplished by Christ.

Rebirth, or becoming children of God, takes place "*when God the Father 'sends the Spirit of his Son into our hearts'* [cf. Gal 4:6; Rom 5:5; 2 Cor 1:22]. . . . Sanctifying grace is the principle and source of man's new life: divine, supernatural life" (§52.2). As the uncreated Gift, the Spirit gives human beings the created gift of new life. Through him the Trinity comes to dwell in them (cf. Jn

14:23) and raises people's "living area" to a sharing in the divine life itself. Now, says the Pope, "*man lives in God and by God:* he lives 'according to the Spirit' " (§58.3). The Spirit's first mission, then, is to individual human beings; he raises them to supernatural life.

Dominum et Vivificantem also deals with the Spirit's activity in the Church, which was born on Good Friday and manifested in power on Pentecost. When the Spirit descended upon the apostolic community in the Upper Room the "*era of the Church*" began (§25.4). In a real way the Church perpetuates that Pentecostal grace through time. In this encyclical, the Pope pays little attention to the hierarchical or charismatic gifts in the Church, but focuses instead on the Spirit's presence in the sacraments and prayer. "The Church," he says, "is the *visible dispenser* of the sacred signs, while the Holy Spirit acts in them as the *invisible dispenser* of the life which they signify" (§63.3).

According to John Paul, there is no doubt that the Holy Spirit is also present "*outside the visible body of the Church*" (§53.3). As the "*source of all God's salvific activity in the world*" (§54.2), he is active from the beginning through man created in the divine image and likeness (cf. Gen 1:26-27). This universal presence of the Spirit notwithstanding, John Paul still attributes a necessary role of mediation to the Church. In her, the chosen instrument of salvation, the Holy Spirit "unceasingly continues the historical presence on earth of the Redeemer and his saving work" (§7.1). It is through her that the Spirit is present in the world. Ever since Pentecost, Christ's promise to send the Spirit "is being fulfilled in human history through the Church" (§61.1, cf. §§3.2, 14.2, 23). The Church is the Spirit's bridge to the world; by means of her he reaches the hearts of people of all times and places. In the Church, but over-flowing her boundaries, "the Holy Spirit is present and at work — he who with the breath of divine life permeates man's earthly pilgrimage and causes all creation, all history, to flow together to its ultimate end, in the infinite ocean of God" (§64.4).

* * *

Selected Bibliography

Biffi, Giacomo. "The Action of the Holy Spirit in the Church and in the World." In *John Paul II: A Panorama of His Teachings.* Preface by Joseph Bernardin. New York: New City Press, 1989. 38-47.

Hamer, Jerome. Presentation at the Press Conference for the Publication of *Dominum et Vivificantem. L'Osservatore Romano,* 23 (1986), 16-17.

O'Carroll, Michael. "*Dominum et Vivificantem.*" In *Veni Creator Spiritus: A Theological Encyclopedia of the Holy Spirit.* Collegeville: Liturgical Press, 1990. 70-72.

Peeters, Paul L. "*Dominum et Vivificantem:* The Conscience and the Heart." *Communio,* 15 (1988), 148-155.

Scola, Angelo. " 'Claim' of Christ, 'Claim' of the World: On the Trinitarian Encyclicals of John Paul II." *Communio,* 18 (1991), 332-331.

ENCYCLICAL LETTER

DOMINUM ET VIVIFICANTEM

OF THE SUPREME PONTIFF

JOHN PAUL II

ON THE HOLY SPIRIT

IN THE LIFE OF THE CHURCH

AND THE WORLD

Dominum et Vivificantem

Venerable Brothers,
Beloved Sons and Daughters,
Health and the Apostolic Blessing!

Introduction

1.1 The Church professes her faith in the Holy Spirit as *"the Lord, the giver of life."* She professes this in the Creed which is called Nicene-Constantinopolitan from the name of the two Councils — of Nicaea (A.D. 325) and Constantinople (A.D. 381) — at which it was formulated or promulgated. It also contains the statement that the Holy Spirit "has spoken through the Prophets."

1.2 These are words which the Church receives from the very source of her faith, Jesus Christ. In fact, according to the Gospel of John, the Holy Spirit is given to us with the new life, as Jesus foretells and promises on the great day of the Feast of Tabernacles: "If any one thirst, let him come to me and drink. He who believes in me as the scripture has said, 'Out of his heart shall flow rivers of living water.' "[1] And the Evangelist explains: *"This he said about the Spirit,* which those who believed in him were to receive."[2] It is the same simile of water which Jesus uses in his conversation with the Samaritan woman, when he speaks of "a spring of water welling up to eternal life,"[3] and in his conversation with Nicodemus when he speaks of the need for a new *birth "of water and the Spirit"* in order to "enter the Kingdom of God."[4]

1.3 The Church, therefore, instructed by the words of Christ, and drawing on the experience of Pentecost and her own apostolic history, has proclaimed since the earliest centuries her faith in the Holy Spirit, as *the giver of life,* the one *in whom* the inscrutable *Triune God communicates himself to human beings,* constituting in them the source of eternal life.

2.1 This faith, uninterruptedly professed by the Church, needs to be constantly reawakened and deepened in the consciousness of the People of God.

---

[1] Jn 7:37-38.

[2] Jn 7:39.

[3] Jn 4:14; cf. Second Vatican Ecumenical Council, Dogmatic Constitution on the Church *Lumen Gentium,* 4.

[4] Cf. Jn 3:5.

In the course of the last hundred years this has been done several times: by *Leo XIII*, who published the Encyclical Epistle *Divinum Illud Munus* (1897) entirely devoted to the Holy Spirit; by *Pius XII*, who in the Encyclical Letter *Mystici Corporis* (1943) spoke of the Holy Spirit as the vital principle of the Church, in which he works in union with the Head of the Mystical Body, Christ;[5] at *the Second Vatican Ecumenical Council* which brought out the need for a new study of the doctrine on the Holy Spirit, as *Paul VI* emphasized: "The Christology and particularly the ecclesiology of the Council must be succeeded by a new study of and devotion to the Holy Spirit, precisely as the indispensable complement to the teaching of the Council."[6]

2.2 In our own age, then, we are *called* anew *by the ever ancient and ever new faith of the Church*, to draw near to the Holy Spirit as *the giver of life*. In this we are helped and stimulated also by the heritage we share with *the Oriental Churches*, which have jealously guarded the extraordinary riches of the teachings of the Fathers on the Holy Spirit. For this reason too we can say that one of the most important ecclesial events of recent years has been the *Sixteenth Centenary of the First Council of Constantinople*, celebrated simultaneously in Constantinople and Rome on the Solemnity of Pentecost in 1981. *The Holy Spirit* was then better seen, through a meditation on the mystery of the Church, as the one who points out the ways leading to the union of Christians, indeed as the *supreme source of this unity*, which comes from God himself and to which Saint Paul gave a particular expression in the words which are frequently used to begin the Eucharistic Liturgy: "The grace of our Lord Jesus Christ and the love of God and the fellowship of the Holy Spirit be with you all."[7]

2.3 In a certain sense, my previous Encyclicals *Redemptor Hominis* and *Dives in Misericordia* took their origin and inspiration from this exhortation, celebrating as they do the event of our salvation accomplished in the Son, sent by the Father into the world "that the world might be saved through him"[8] and "every tongue confess that Jesus Christ is Lord, to the glory of God the Father."[9] From this exhortation now comes *the present Encyclical on the Holy Spirit*, who proceeds from the Father and the Son; with the Father and the Son he is adored and glorified: a divine Person, he is at the

---

[5] Cf. Leo XIII, Encyclical Letter *Divinum Illud Munus* (May 9, 1897): *Leonis XIII P. M. Acta*, XVII, Rome, 1898, 125-148; Pius XII, Encyclical Letter *Mystici Corporis* (June 29, 1943): *AAS* 35 (1943), 193-248.

[6] Address at General Audience (June 6, 1973): *Insegnamenti* XI (1973), 477.

[7] Roman Missal; cf. 2 Cor 13:13.

[8] Jn 3:17.

[9] Phil 2:11.

center of the Christian faith and is the source and dynamic power of the Church's renewal.[10] The Encyclical has been drawn *from the heart of the heritage of the Council.* For the conciliar texts, thanks to their teaching on the Church in herself and the Church in the world, move us to penetrate ever deeper into the Trinitarian mystery of God himself, through the Gospels, the Fathers and the liturgy: to the Father, through Christ, in the Holy Spirit.

2.4 In this way the Church is also responding to certain deep desires which she believes she can discern in people's hearts today: a fresh discovery of God in his transcendent reality as the infinite Spirit, just as Jesus presents him to the Samaritan woman; the need to adore him "in spirit and truth";[11] the hope of finding in him the secret of love and the power of a "new creation":[12] yes, precisely *the giver of life.*

2.5 The Church feels herself called to this mission of proclaiming the Spirit, while together with the human family she approaches *the end of the second millennium after Christ.* Against the background of a heaven and earth which will "pass away," she knows well that "the words which will not pass away"[13] acquire a particular eloquence. They are the words of Christ about the Holy Spirit, the inexhaustible source of the "water welling up to eternal life,"[14] as truth and saving grace. Upon these words she wishes to reflect, to these words she wishes to call the attention of believers and of all people, as she prepares to celebrate — as will be said later on — the great Jubilee which will mark the passage from the second to the third Christian millennium.

2.6 Naturally, the considerations that follow do not aim to explore exhaustively the extremely rich doctrine on the Holy Spirit, nor to favor any particular solution of questions which are still open. Their main purpose is to develop in the Church the awareness that "she is compelled by the Holy Spirit to do her part toward the full realization of the will of God, who has established Christ as the source of salvation for the whole world."[15]

---

[10] Cf. Second Ecumenical Vatican Council, Dogmatic Constitution on the Church *Lumen Gentium,* 4; John Paul II, Address to Those Taking Part in the International Congress on Pneumatology (March 26, 1982), 1: *Insegnamenti* V/1 (1982), 1004.

[11] Cf. Jn 4:24.

[12] Cf. Rom 8:22; Gal 6:15.

[13] Cf. Mt 24:35.

[14] Jn 4:14.

[15] Second Vatican Ecumenical Council, Dogmatic Constitution on the Church *Lumen Gentium,* 17.

I

The Spirit of the Father and of the Son, Given to the Church

Jesus' promise and revelation at the Last Supper

3.1 When the time for Jesus to leave this world had almost come, he told the Apostles of "another Counselor."[16] The evangelist John, who was present, writes that, during the Last Supper before the day of his Passion and death, Jesus addressed the Apostles with these words: "Whatever you ask in my name, I will do it, that the Father may be glorified in the Son. . . . I will pray the Father, and he will give you another Counselor, to be with you forever, even the Spirit of truth."[17]

3.2 It is precisely this Spirit of truth whom Jesus calls the Paraclete — and *parakletos* means "counselor," and also "intercessor," or "advocate." And he says that the Paraclete is "another" Counselor, the second one, since he, Jesus himself, is the first Counselor,[18] being the first bearer and giver of the Good News. The Holy Spirit comes after him and because of him, in order to continue in the world, through the Church, the work of *the Good News of salvation.* Concerning this continuation of his own work by the Holy Spirit Jesus speaks more than once during the same farewell discourse, preparing the Apostles gathered in the Upper Room for his departure, namely for his Passion and death on the Cross.

3.3 The words to which we will make reference here are found in *the Gospel of John.* Each one adds a new element to that prediction and promise. And at the same time they are intimately interwoven, not only from the viewpoint of the events themselves but also from the viewpoint of the mystery of the Father, Son and Holy Spirit, which perhaps in no passage of Sacred Scripture finds so emphatic an expression as here.

4 A little while after the prediction just mentioned Jesus adds: "But the *Counselor,* the Holy Spirit, whom the Father will send in my name, he *will teach you* all things, and *bring to your remembrance* all that I have said to you."[19] The Holy Spirit will be the Counselor of the Apostles and the Church,

---

[16] *Allon parakleton:* Jn 14:16.
[17] Jn 14:13, 16-17.
[18] Cf. 1 Jn 2:1.
[19] Jn 14:26.

always present in their midst — even though invisible — as the teacher of the same Good News that Christ proclaimed. The words "he will teach" and "bring to remembrance" mean not only that he, in his own particular way, will continue to inspire the spreading of the Gospel of salvation but also that he will help people to understand the correct meaning of the content of Christ's message; they mean that he will ensure continuity and identity of understanding in the midst of changing conditions and circumstances. The Holy Spirit, then, will ensure that in the Church there will always continue *the same truth* which the Apostles heard from their Master.

5.1 In transmitting the Good News, the Apostles will be in a special way associated with the Holy Spirit. This is how Jesus goes on: "When the Counselor comes, whom I shall send to you from the Father, even the Spirit of truth, who proceeds from the Father, *he will bear witness to me;* and you also are witnesses, because you have been with me from the beginning."[20]

5.2 The Apostles were the direct eyewitnesses. They "have heard" and "have seen with their own eyes," "have looked upon" and even "touched with their hands" Christ, as the Evangelist John says in another passage.[21] This human, first-hand and "historical" witness to Christ is linked to the witness of the Holy Spirit: "He will bear witness to me." *In the witness of the Spirit of truth* the human testimony of the Apostles *will find* its strongest *support.* And subsequently it will also find therein the hidden *foundation* of its continuation among the generations of Christ's disciples and believers who succeed one another down through the ages.

5.3 The supreme and most complete revelation of God to humanity is Jesus Christ himself, and *the witness of the Spirit* inspires, guarantees and convalidates the faithful transmission of this revelation in the preaching and writing of the Apostles,[22] *while the witness of the Apostles* ensures its human expression in the Church and in the history of humanity.

6.1 This is also seen from the strict correlation of content and intention with the just-mentioned prediction and promise, a correlation found in the

---

[20] Jn 15:26-27.

[21] Cf. 1 Jn 1:1-3, 4:14.

[22] "The divinely revealed truths, which are contained and expressed in the books of the Sacred Scripture, were written through the inspiration of the Holy Spirit," and thus the same Sacred Scripture must be "read and interpreted with the help of the same Spirit by means of whom it was written": Second Vatican Ecumenical Council, Dogmatic Constitution on Divine Revelation *Dei Verbum*, 11, 12.

next words of the text of John: "I have yet many things to say to you, but you cannot bear them now. When the Spirit of truth comes, *he will guide you into all the truth;* for he will not speak on his own authority, but whatever he hears he will speak, and he will declare to you the things that are to come."[23]

6.2 In his previous words Jesus presents the *Counselor,* the Spirit of truth, as the one who "will teach" and "bring to remembrance," as the one who "will bear witness" to him. Now he says: "He will guide you into all the truth." This "guiding into all the truth," referring to what the Apostles "cannot bear now," is necessarily connected *with Christ's self-emptying* through his Passion and death on the Cross, which, when he spoke these words, was just about to happen.

6.3 Later, however, it becomes clear that this "guiding into all the truth" is connected not only with *the scandal of the Cross,* but also with everything that Christ "did and taught."[24] For the *mystery of Christ* taken as a whole demands faith, since it is faith that adequately introduces man into the reality of the revealed mystery. The "guiding into all the truth" is therefore achieved in faith and through faith: and this is the work of the Spirit of truth and the result of his action in man. Here the Holy Spirit is to be man's supreme guide and the light of the human spirit. This holds true for the Apostles, the eyewitnesses, who must now bring to all people the proclamation of what Christ did and taught, and especially the proclamation of his Cross and Resurrection. Taking a longer view, this also holds true for all the generations of disciples and confessors of the Master. Since they will have *to accept* with faith and *confess* with candor the mystery of God at work in human history, the revealed mystery which explains the definitive meaning of that history.

7.1 Between the Holy Spirit and Christ there thus subsists, in the economy of salvation, an intimate bond, whereby the Spirit works in human history as "another Counselor," permanently ensuring the transmission and spreading of the Good News revealed by Jesus of Nazareth. Thus, in the Holy Spirit-Paraclete, who in the mystery and action of the Church unceasingly continues the historical presence on earth of the Redeemer and his saving work, the glory of Christ shines forth, as the following words of John attest: "He (the Spirit of truth) will glorify me, for *he will take what is mine and declare it to you.*"[25] By these words all the preceding statements are once again confirmed: "He will teach . . . , will bring to your remembrance . . . , will bear witness."

---

[23] Jn 16:12-13.
[24] Acts 1:1.
[25] Jn 16:14.

The supreme and complete self-revelation of God, accomplished in Christ and witnessed to by the preaching of the Apostles, continues to be manifested in the Church through the mission of the invisible *Counselor*, the Spirit of truth. How intimately this mission is linked with the mission of Christ, how fully it draws from this mission of Christ, consolidating and developing in history its salvific results, is expressed by the verb "take": "He will take what is mine and declare it to you." As if to explain the words "he will take" by clearly expressing the divine and Trinitarian unity of the source, Jesus adds: "*All that the Father has is mine; therefore I said that he will take what is mine* and declare it to you."[26] By the very fact of taking what is "mine," he will draw from "what is the Father's."

7.2 In the light of these words "he will take," one can therefore also explain the other significant words about the Holy Spirit spoken by Jesus in the Upper Room before the Passover: "It is to your advantage that I go away, for if I do not go away, the Counselor will not come to you; *but if I go, I will send him to you.* And when he comes, he will convince the world concerning sin and righteousness and judgment."[27] It will be necessary to return to these words in a separate reflection.

Father, Son and Holy Spirit

8.1 It is a characteristic of the text of John that the Father, the Son and the Holy Spirit are clearly called Persons, the first distinct from the second and the third, and each of them from one another. Jesus speaks of the Spirit-Counselor, using several times the personal pronoun "he"; and at the same time, throughout the farewell discourse, he reveals the bonds which unite the Father, the Son and the Paraclete to one another. Thus "the Holy Spirit . . . proceeds from the Father"[28] and the Father "gives" the Spirit.[29] The Father "sends" the Spirit in the name of the Son,[30] the Spirit "bears witness" to the Son.[31] The Son asks the Father to send the Spirit-Counselor,[32] but likewise affirms and promises, in relation to his own "departure" through the Cross: "If I go, I will send him to you."[33] Thus, the Father sends the Holy Spirit in the power of his fatherhood, as he has sent the Son;[34] but at the same time he

[26] Jn 16:15.
[27] Jn 16:7-8.
[28] Jn 15:26.
[29] Jn 14:16.
[30] Jn 14:26.
[31] Jn 15:26.
[32] Jn 14:16.
[33] Jn 16:7.
[34] Cf. Jn 3:16-17, 34; 6:57; 17:3, 18, 23.

sends him in the power of the Redemption accomplished by Christ — and in this sense the Holy Spirit is sent also by the Son: "I will send him to you."

8.2 Here it should be noted that, while all the other promises made in the Upper Room foretold the coming of the Holy Spirit *after* Christ's departure, the one contained in the text of John 16:7-8. also includes and clearly emphasizes the relationship of interdependence which could be called *causal* between the manifestation of each: "If I go, I will send him to you." The Holy Spirit will come insofar as Christ will depart through the Cross: he will come not only *afterward,* but *because of* the Redemption accomplished by Christ, through the will and action of the Father.

9 Thus in the farewell discourse at the Last Supper, we can say that *the highest point of the revelation of the Trinity* is reached. At the same time, we are on the threshold of definitive events and final words which in the end will be translated into the great missionary mandate addressed to the Apostles and through them to the Church: "Go therefore and make disciples of all nations," a mandate which contains, in a certain sense, the Trinitarian formula of Baptism: *"baptizing them in the name of the Father and of the Son and of the Holy Spirit."*[35] The formula reflects the intimate mystery of God, of the divine life, which is the Father, the Son and the Holy Spirit, the divine unity of the Trinity. The farewell discourse can be read as a special preparation for this Trinitarian formula, in which is expressed the life-giving power of the sacrament which brings about *sharing in the life of the Triune God,* for it gives sanctifying grace as a supernatural gift to man. Through grace, man is called and made "capable" of sharing in the inscrutable life of God.

10.1 In his intimate life, God "is love,"[36] the essential love shared by the three divine Persons: personal love is the Holy Spirit as the Spirit of the Father and the Son. Therefore he "searches even the depths of God,"[37] as *uncreated Love-Gift.* It can be said that in the Holy Spirit the intimate life of the Triune God becomes totally gift, an exchange of mutual love between the divine Persons and that through the Holy Spirit God exists in the mode of gift. It is the Holy Spirit who is *the personal expression* of this self-giving, of this being-love.[38] He is Person-Love. He is Person-Gift. Here we have an inexhaustible

[35] Mt 28:19.
[36] Cf. 1 Jn 4:8, 16.
[37] Cf. 1 Cor 2:10.
[38] Cf. Saint Thomas Aquinas, *Summa Theologiae*, I, qq. 37-38.

treasure of the reality and an inexpressible deepening of the concept of *person* in God, which only divine revelation makes known to us.

10.2 At the same time, the Holy Spirit, being consubstantial with the Father and the Son in divinity, is love and uncreated gift from which derives as from its source *(fons vivus) all giving of gifts* vis-à-vis creatures (created gift): the gift of existence to all things through creation; the gift of grace to human beings through the whole economy of salvation. As the Apostle Paul writes: "God's love has been poured into our hearts through the Holy Spirit which has been given to us."[39]

The salvific self-giving of God in the Holy Spirit

11 Christ's farewell discourse at the Last Supper stands in particular reference to this "giving" and "self-giving" of the Holy Spirit. In John's Gospel we have as it were the revelation of the most profound "logic" of the saving mystery contained in God's eternal plan, as an extension of the ineffable communion of the Father, Son and Holy Spirit. This is the divine "logic" which from the mystery of the Trinity leads to the mystery of the Redemption of the world in Jesus Christ. The *Redemption accomplished by the Son* in the dimensions of the earthly history of humanity — accomplished in his "departure" through the Cross and Resurrection — is at the same time, in its entire salvific power, *transmitted to the Holy Spirit*: the one who "will take what is mine."[40] The words of the text of John indicate that, according to the divine plan, Christ's "departure" is an indispensable condition for the "sending" and the coming of the Holy Spirit, but these words also say that what begins now is *the new salvific self-giving of God, in the Holy Spirit.*

12 It is a *new beginning* in relation to *the first, original* beginning *of God's salvific self-giving,* which is identified with the mystery of creation itself. Here is what we read in the very first words of the Book of Genesis: "In the beginning God created the heavens and the earth . . . , and the Spirit of God *(ruah Elohim) was moving over the face of the waters.*"[41] This biblical concept of creation includes not only the call to existence of the very being of the cosmos, that is to say *the giving of existence,* but also the presence of the Spirit of God in creation, that is to say the beginning of God's salvific self-communication to the things he creates. This is true *first of all concerning man,* who has been created in the image and likeness

[39] Rom 5:5.
[40] Jn 16:14.
[41] Gen 1:1-2.

of God: "Let us make man in our image, after our likeness."[42] "Let us make": can one hold that the plural which the Creator uses here in speaking of himself already in some way suggests the Trinitarian mystery, the presence of the Trinity in the work of the creation of man? The Christian reader, who already knows the revelation of this mystery, can discern a reflection of it also in these words. At any rate, the context of the Book of Genesis enables us to see in the creation of man the first beginning of God's salvific self-giving commensurate with the "image and likeness" of himself which he has granted to man.

13 It seems then that even the words spoken by Jesus in the farewell discourse should be read again in the light of that "beginning," so long ago yet fundamental, which we know from Genesis. "If I do not go away, the Counselor will not come to you; but if I go, I will send him to you." Describing his "departure" *as a condition* for the "coming" of the Counselor, Christ links the new beginning of God's salvific self-communication in the Holy Spirit with the mystery of the Redemption. It is a new beginning, first of all because *between* the first beginning and the whole of human history — from the original fall onward — *sin has intervened,* sin which is in contradiction to the presence of the Spirit of God in creation, and which is above all in *contradiction to God's salvific self-communication to man.* Saint Paul writes that, precisely because of sin, "creation . . . was subjected to futility. . . , has been groaning in travail together until now" and "waits with eager longing for the revealing of the sons of God."[43]

14.1 Therefore Jesus Christ says in the Upper Room: "It is to your advantage I go away; . . . if I go, I will send him to you."[44] The "departure" of Christ through the Cross has the power of the Redemption — and this also means a new presence of the Spirit of God in creation: the new beginning of God's self-communication to man in the Holy Spirit. "And that you are children is proven by the fact that God has sent into our hearts the Spirit of his Son who cries: Abba, Father!" — as the Apostle Paul writes in *the Letter to the Galatians.*[45] The Holy Spirit is *the Spirit of the Father,* as the words of the farewell discourse in the Upper Room bear witness. At the same time he is *the Spirit of the Son: he is the Spirit of Jesus Christ,* as the Apostles and particularly Paul of Tarsus

---

[42] Gen 1:26.
[43] Rom 8:19-22.
[44] Jn 16:7.
[45] Gal 4:6; cf. Rom 8:15.

will testify.[46] With the sending of this Spirit "into our hearts," there begins the fulfillment of that for which "creation waits with eager longing," as we read in the *Letter to the Romans*.

14.2 The Holy Spirit comes *at the price* of Christ's "departure." While this "departure" caused the *Apostles to be sorrowful*"[47] and this sorrow was to reach its culmination in the Passion and death on Good Friday, "this sorrow will turn into joy."[48] For Christ will add to this redemptive "departure" the glory of his Resurrection and Ascension to the Father. Thus the sorrow with its underlying joy is, for the Apostles in the context of their Master's "departure," an "advantageous" departure, for thanks to it another "Counselor" will come.[49] At the price of the Cross which brings about the Redemption, in the power of the whole Paschal Mystery of Jesus Christ, the Holy Spirit comes in order to remain *from the day of Pentecost onward* with the Apostles, to remain with the Church and in the Church, and through her in the world.

14.3 In this way there is definitively *brought about* that *new beginning* of the self-communication of the Triune God in the Holy Spirit through the work of Jesus Christ, the Redeemer of man and of the world.

The Messiah, anointed with the Holy Spirit

15.1 There is also accomplished in its entirety the mission of the Messiah, that is to say of the One who has received the fullness of the Holy Spirit for the Chosen People of God and for the whole of humanity. "Messiah" literally means "Christ," that is, "Anointed One," and in the history of salvation it means "the one anointed with the Holy Spirit." This was the prophetic tradition of the Old Testament. Following this tradition, Simon Peter will say in the house of Cornelius: "You must have heard about the recent happenings in Judaea . . . after the baptism which John preached: how *God anointed Jesus of Nazareth with the Holy Spirit and with* power."[50]

15.2 From these words of Peter and from many similar ones,[51] one must first go back to the prophecy of *Isaiah*, sometimes called "the Fifth Gospel" or "the Gospel of the Old Testament." Alluding to the coming of a mysterious personage, which the New Testament revelation will identify with Jesus, Isaiah connects his person and mission with a particular action of the Spirit of God — the Spirit of the Lord. These are the words of the Prophet:

---

[46] Cf. Gal 4:6; Phil 1:19; Rom 8:11.
[47] Cf. Jn 16:6.
[48] Cf. Jn 16:20.
[49] Cf. Jn 16:7.
[50] Acts 10:37-38.
[51] Cf. Lk 4:16-21, 3:16, 4:14; Mk 1:10.

"There shall come forth a shoot from the stump of Jesse,
and a branch shall grow out of his roots.
And *the Spirit of the Lord shall rest upon him,*
the spirit of wisdom and understanding,
the spirit of counsel and might,
the spirit of knowledge and the fear of the Lord.
And his delight shall be the fear of the Lord."[52]

15.3 This text is important for the whole pneumatology of the Old Testament, because it constitutes a kind of bridge between the ancient biblical concept of "spirit," understood primarily as a "charismatic breath of wind," and the *"Spirit" as a person and as a gift, a gift for the person.* The Messiah of the lineage of David ("from the stump of Jesse") is precisely that person upon whom the Spirit of the Lord "shall rest." It is obvious that in this case one cannot yet speak of a revelation of the Paraclete. However, with this veiled reference to the figure of the future Messiah there begins, so to speak, the path toward the full revelation of the Holy Spirit in the unity of the Trinitarian mystery, a mystery which will finally be manifested in the New Covenant.

16.1 It is precisely the Messiah himself who is this path. In the Old Covenant, anointing had become the external symbol of the gift of the Spirit. The Messiah (more than any other anointed personage in the Old Covenant) is that single great personage *anointed by God himself.* He is the Anointed One in the sense that he possesses the fullness of the Spirit of God. He himself will also be the mediator in granting this Spirit to the whole people. Here in fact are other words of the Prophet:
"The Spirit of the Lord God is upon me,
because the Lord has anointed me
to bring good tidings to the afflicted;
he has sent me to bind up the brokenhearted,
to proclaim liberty to the captives,
and the opening of the prison to those who are bound;
to proclaim the year of the Lord's favor."[53]

16.2 The Anointed One is *also sent "with the Spirit of the Lord"*: "Now the Lord God has sent me and his Spirit."[54]

16.3 According to the Book of Isaiah, the Anointed One and the One sent

---

[52] Is 11:1-3.
[53] Is 61:1-2.
[54] Is 48:16.

together with the *Spirit of the Lord* is also the chosen *Servant of the Lord* upon whom the Spirit of God comes down:

"Behold my servant, whom I uphold,

my chosen, in whom my soul delights;

I have put my Spirit upon him."[55]

16.4 We know that the Servant of the Lord is revealed in the *Book of Isaiah* as the true Man of Sorrows: *the Messiah who suffers* for the sins of the world.[56] And at the same time it is precisely he whose mission *will bear for all humanity the true fruits of salvation:*

16.5 "He will bring forth justice to the nations . . .";[57] and he will become "a covenant to the people, a light to the nations . . .";[58] "that my salvation may reach to the end of the earth."[59]

16.6 For: "My spirit which is upon you, and my words which I have put in your mouth, shall not depart out of your mouth, or out of the mouth of your children's children, says the Lord, from this time forth and for evermore."[60]

16.7 The prophetic texts quoted here are to be read *in the light of the Gospel* — just as, in its turn, the New Testament draws a particular clarification from the marvelous light contained in these Old Testament texts. The Prophet presents the Messiah as the one who *comes in the Holy Spirit,* the one who possesses *the fullness of this Spirit in himself* and at the same time *for others,* for Israel, for all the nations, for all humanity. The fullness of the Spirit of God is accompanied by many different gifts, the treasures of salvation, destined in a particular way for the poor and suffering, for all those who open their hearts to these gifts — sometimes through the painful experience of their own existence — but first of all through that interior availability which comes from faith. The aged Simeon, the "righteous and devout man" upon whom "rested the Holy Spirit," sensed this at the moment of Jesus' presentation in the Temple, when he perceived in him the "salvation . . . prepared in the presence of all peoples" at the price of the great suffering — the Cross — which he would have to embrace together with his Mother.[61] The Virgin Mary, who "had conceived by the Holy Spirit,"[62] sensed this even more clearly, when she pon-

---

[55] Is 42:1.

[56] Cf. Is 53:5-6, 8.

[57] Is 42:1.

[58] Is 42:6.

[59] Is 49:6.

[60] Is 59:21.

[61] Cf. Lk 2:25-35.

[62] Cf. Lk 1:35.

dered in her heart the "mysteries" of the Messiah, with whom she was associated.[63]

17 Here it must be emphasized that clearly the "spirit of the Lord" who rests upon the future Messiah is above all *a gift of God for the person* of that Servant of the Lord. But the latter is not an isolated and independent person, because he acts in accordance with the will of the Lord, by virtue of the Lord's decision or choice. Even though in the light of the texts of Isaiah the salvific work of the Messiah, the Servant of the Lord, includes the action of the Spirit which is carried out through himself, nevertheless in the Old Testament context there is no suggestion of a distinction of subjects, or of the divine Persons as they subsist in the mystery of the Trinity, and as they are later revealed in the New Testament. Both in Isaiah and in the whole of the Old Testament *the personality of the Holy Spirit* is completely *hidden:* in the revelation of the one God, as also in the foretelling of the future Messiah.

18 *Jesus Christ will make reference* to this prediction *contained in the words of Isaiah* at the beginning of his messianic activity. This will happen in the same Nazareth where he had lived for thirty years in the house of Joseph the carpenter, with Mary, his Virgin Mother. When he had occasion to speak in the synagogue, he opened the *Book of Isaiah* and found the passage where it was written: "The Spirit of the Lord is upon me, because he has anointed me"; and having read this passage he said to those present: "*Today this scripture has been fulfilled* in your hearing."[64] In this way he confessed and proclaimed that he was the Messiah, the one in whom the Holy Spirit dwells as the gift of God himself, the one who possesses the fullness of this Spirit, the one who marks the "new beginning" of the gift which God makes to humanity in the Spirit.

Jesus of Nazareth, "exalted" in the Holy Spirit

19.1 Even though in his hometown of Nazareth Jesus is not accepted as the Messiah, nonetheless, at the beginning of his public activity, his messianic mission in the Holy Spirit is *revealed to the people by John the Baptist.* The latter, the son of Zechariah and Elizabeth, foretells at the Jordan the coming of the Messiah and administers the baptism of repentance. He says: "I baptize you with water; he who is mightier than I is coming, the thong of

[63] Cf. Lk 2:19, 51.
[64] Cf. Lk 4:16-21; Is 61:1-2.

whose sandals I am not worthy to untie; he will *baptize* you *with the Holy Spirit and with fire.*"[65]

19.2 John the Baptist foretells the Messiah-Christ not only as the one who "is coming" in the Holy Spirit but also as the one who *"brings"* the Holy Spirit, as Jesus will reveal more clearly in the Upper Room. Here John faithfully echoes the words of Isaiah, words which in the ancient Prophet concerned the future, while in John's teaching on the banks of the Jordan they are the immediate introduction to the new messianic reality. John is not only a prophet but also a messenger: he is the precursor of Christ. What he foretells is accomplished before the eyes of all. Jesus of Nazareth too comes to the Jordan to receive the baptism of repentance. At the sight of him arriving, John proclaims: "Behold, the Lamb of God, who takes away the sin of the world."[66] He says this through the inspiration of the Holy Spirit,[67] *bearing witness to the fulfillment of the prophecy of Isaiah.* At the same time he confesses his faith in the redeeming mission of Jesus of Nazareth. On the lips of John the Baptist, "Lamb of God" is an expression of truth about the Redeemer no less significant than the one used by Isaiah: "Servant of the Lord."

19.3 Thus, by the testimony of John at the Jordan, Jesus of Nazareth, rejected by his own fellow-citizens, is *exalted before the eyes of Israel as the Messiah,* that is to say the "One Anointed" with the Holy Spirit. And this testimony is corroborated by another testimony of a higher order, mentioned by the three Synoptics. For when all the people were baptized and as Jesus, having received baptism, was praying, "the heaven was opened, and the Holy Spirit descended upon him in bodily form, as a dove"[68] and at the same time "a voice from heaven said, 'This is my beloved Son, with whom I am well pleased.' "[69]

19.4 This is a *Trinitarian theophany* which bears witness to the exaltation of Christ on the occasion of his baptism in the Jordan. It not only confirms the testimony of John the Baptist but also reveals another more profound dimension of the truth about Jesus of Nazareth as Messiah. It is this: *the Messiah is the beloved Son of the Father.* His solemn exaltation cannot be reduced to the messianic mission of the "Servant of the Lord." In the light of the theophany at the Jordan, this exaltation touches the mystery of the very person of the Messiah. He has been raised up because he is the beloved Son in whom God is well pleased. The voice from on high says: "my Son."

[65] Lk 3:16; cf. Mt 3:11; Mk 1:7-8; Jn 1:33.
[66] Jn 1:29.
[67] Cf. Jn 1:33-34.
[68] Lk 3:21-22; cf. Mt 3:16; Mk 1:10.
[69] Mt 3:17.

20.1 The theophany at the Jordan clarifies only in a fleeting way the mystery of Jesus of Nazareth, whose entire activity will be carried out in the active presence of the Holy Spirit.[70] This mystery would be gradually revealed and confirmed by Jesus himself by means of everything that he "did and taught."[71] In the course of this teaching and of the messianic signs which Jesus performed before he came to the farewell discourse in the Upper Room, we find events and words which constitute particularly important stages of this progressive revelation. Thus the Evangelist Luke, who has already presented Jesus as "full of the Holy Spirit" and "led by the Spirit . . . in the wilderness,"[72] tells us that, after the return of the seventy-two disciples from the mission entrusted to them by the Master,[73] while they were joyfully recounting the fruits of their labors, "in that same hour *(Jesus) rejoiced in the Holy Spirit* and said: 'I thank you, Father, Lord of heaven and earth, that you have hidden these things from the wise and understanding and revealed them to babes; yea, Father, for such was your gracious will.' "[74] Jesus rejoices at the fatherhood of God: he rejoices because it has been given to him to reveal this fatherhood; he rejoices, finally, as at a particular outpouring of this divine fatherhood on the "little ones." And the Evangelist describes all this as "rejoicing in the Holy Spirit."

20.2 This "rejoicing" in a certain sense prompts Jesus to say still more. We hear: "All things have been delivered to me by my *Father*; and no one knows who the Son is except the Father, or who the Father is except *the Son* and any one to whom the Son chooses to reveal him."[75]

21.1 That which during the theophany at the Jordan came so to speak "from outside," from on high, here comes "from within," that is to say *from the depths of who Jesus is.* It is another revelation of the Father and the Son, united in the Holy Spirit. Jesus speaks only of the fatherhood of God and of his own sonship — he does not speak directly of the Spirit, who is Love and thereby the union of the Father and the Son. Nonetheless *what he says of the Father and of himself* — the Son — flows from that *fullness of the Spirit* which is in him, which fills his heart, pervades his own "I," inspires and enlivens his action from the depths. Hence that "rejoicing in the Holy Spirit." The union of

[70] Cf. Saint Basil, *De Spiritu Sancto*, XVI, 39: *PG* 32, 139.
[71] Acts 1:1.
[72] Cf. Lk 4:1.
[73] Cf. Lk 10:17-20.
[74] Lk 10:21; cf. Mt 11:25-26.
[75] Lk 10:22; cf. Mt 11:27.

Christ with the Holy Spirit, a union of which he is perfectly aware, is expressed in that "rejoicing," which in a certain way renders "perceptible" its hidden source. Thus there is a particular manifestation and rejoicing which is proper to the Son of Man, the Christ-Messiah, whose humanity belongs to the person of the Son of God, substantially one with the Holy Spirit in divinity.

21.2 In the magnificent confession of the fatherhood of God, Jesus of Nazareth also manifests himself, his divine "I": for he is the Son *"of the same substance,"* and therefore "no one knows who the Son is except the Father, or who the Father is except the Son," that Son who "for us and for our salvation" became man *by the power of the Holy Spirit* and was born of a virgin whose name was Mary.

The risen Christ says: "Receive the Holy Spirit"

22.1 It is thanks to Luke's narrative that we are brought closest to the truth contained in the discourse in the Upper Room. Jesus of Nazareth, "raised up" in the Holy Spirit, during this discourse and conversation presents himself as *the one who brings the Spirit,* as the one who is to bring him and "give" him to the Apostles and to the Church at the price of his own "departure" through the Cross.

22.2 The verb "bring" is here used to mean *first of all "reveal."* In the Old Testament, from the *Book of Genesis* onward, the Spirit of God was in some way made known, in the first place as a *"breath"* of God which gives life, as a supernatural *"living breath."* In the *Book of Isaiah,* he is presented as a *"gift"* for the person of the Messiah, as the one who comes down and rests upon him, in order to guide from within all the salvific activity of the "Anointed One." At the Jordan, Isaiah's proclamation is given a concrete form: Jesus of Nazareth is the one *who comes in the Holy Spirit* and who brings the Spirit as the gift proper to his own *Person,* in order to distribute that gift by means of this humanity: "He will baptize you with the Holy Spirit."[76] In the Gospel of Luke, this revelation of the Holy Spirit is confirmed and added to, *as the intimate source* of the life and messianic activity of Jesus Christ.

22.3 In the light of what Jesus says in the farewell discourse in the Upper Room, the Holy Spirit is revealed in a new and fuller way. He is *not only the gift to the person* (the person of the Messiah), but *is a Person-gift.* Jesus foretells his coming as that of "another *Counselor*" who, being the Spirit of truth, will lead the Apostles and the Church "into all the truth."[77] This will be accomplished by reason of the particular communion between the Holy Spirit and Christ: "He will

[76] Mt 3:11; Lk 3:16.
[77] Jn 16:13.

take what is mine and declare it to you."[78] This communion has its *original source in the Father:* "All that the Father has is mine; therefore I said that he will take what is mine and declare it to you."[79] Coming from the Father the Holy Spirit is sent by the Father.[80] The Holy Spirit is *first* sent *as a gift for the Son* who was made man, in order to fulfill the messianic prophecies. After the "departure" of Christ the Son, the Johannine text says that the Holy Spirit *"will come"* directly (it is his new mission), to complete the work of the Son. Thus it will be he who brings to fulfillment the new era of the history of salvation.

23 We find ourselves on the threshold of the Paschal events. The new, definitive revelation of the Holy Spirit as a Person who *is* the gift is accomplished at this precise moment. The *Paschal events* — the Passion, death and Resurrection of Christ — are also *the time of the new coming* of the Holy Spirit, as the Paraclete and the Spirit of truth. They are the time of the "new beginning" of the self-communication of the Triune God to humanity in the Holy Spirit through the work of Christ the Redeemer. This new beginning is the Redemption of the world: "God so loved the world that he gave his only Son."[81] Already the "giving" of the Son, *the gift of the Son,* expresses the most profound essence of God who, as Love, is the inexhaustible source of the giving of gifts. The gift *made by the Son* completes the revelation and giving of the eternal love: *the Holy Spirit,* who in the inscrutable depths of the divinity is a Person-Gift, through the work of the Son, that is to say by means of the Paschal Mystery, is given to the Apostles and to the Church in a new way, and through them is given to humanity and the whole world.

24.1 The definitive expression of this mystery is had *on the day of the Resurrection.* On this day Jesus of Nazareth "descended from David according to the flesh," as the Apostle Paul writes, is "designated Son of God in power according to the Spirit of holiness by his resurrection from the dead."[82] It can be said therefore that the messianic "raising up" of Christ in the Holy Spirit reaches its zenith in the Resurrection, in which he reveals himself also as the *Son of God,* "full of power." And this power, the sources of which gush forth in the inscrutable Trinitarian communion, is manifested, first of all, in the fact that the risen Christ does two things: on the one hand he fulfills God's prom-

[78] Jn 16:14.
[79] Jn 16:15.
[80] Cf. Jn 14:26, 15:26.
[81] Jn 3:16.
[82] Rom 1:3-4.

ise already expressed through the Prophet's words: "A new heart I will give you, and a new spirit I will put within you, . . . my spirit";[83] and on the other hand he fulfills his own promise made to the Apostles with the words: "If I go, I will send him to you."[84] It is he: the Spirit of truth, the Paraclete sent by the risen Christ to transform us into his own risen image.[85]

24.2 "On the evening of that day, the first day of the week, the doors being shut where the disciples were, for fear of the Jews, Jesus came and stood among them and said to them, 'Peace be with you.' When he had said this, he showed them his hands and his side. Then the disciples were glad when they saw the Lord. Jesus said to them again, 'Peace be with you. As the Father has sent me, even so I send you.' And when he had said this, he breathed on them, and said to them, *'Receive the Holy Spirit.'* " [86]

24.3 All the details of this key-text of John's Gospel have their own eloquence, especially if we read them in reference to the words spoken in the same Upper Room at the beginning of the Paschal events. And now these events — *the Triduum Sacrum* of Jesus whom the Father consecrated with the anointing and sent into the world — reach their fulfillment. Christ, who "gave up his spirit" *on the Cross* [87] as the Son of Man and the Lamb of God, once risen goes to the Apostles *"to breathe on them"* with that power spoken of in the *Letter to the Romans.*[88] The Lord's coming fills those present with joy: "Your sorrow will turn into joy,"[89] as he had already promised them before his Passion. And above all there is fulfilled the principal prediction of the farewell discourse: the risen Christ, as it were beginning a new creation, *"brings" to the Apostles the Holy Spirit.* He brings him at the price of his own "departure": he gives them this Spirit as it were through the wounds of his crucifixion: "He showed them his hands and his side." It is in the power of this crucifixion that he says to them: "Receive the Holy Spirit."

24.4 Thus there is established a close link between *the sending of the Son* and *the sending of the Holy Spirit.* There is no sending of the Holy Spirit (after original sin) without the Cross and the Resurrection: "If I do not go away, the *Counselor* will not come to you."[90] There is also established a close link *between the mission of the Holy Spirit and that of the Son* in the Redemption. The mission of the Son, in a certain sense, finds its "fulfillment" in the Redemption. The

[83] Ezek 36:26-27; cf. Jn 7:37-39, 19:34.
[84] Jn 16:7.
[85] Saint Cyril of Alexandria, *In Ioannis Evangelium*, Book V, Chapter II: *PG* 73, 755.
[86] Jn 20:19-22.
[87] Cf. Jn 19:30.
[88] Cf. Rom 1:4.
[89] Cf. Jn 16:20.
[90] Jn 16:7.

mission of the Holy Spirit "draws from" the Redemption: "He will take what is mine and declare it to you."[91] The *Redemption* is totally *carried out* by the Son as the Anointed One, who came and acted in the power of the Holy Spirit, offering himself finally in sacrifice on the wood of the Cross. And this Redemption is, at the same time, *constantly carried out* in human hearts and minds — in the history of the world — by the Holy Spirit, who is the "other *Counselor.*"

The Holy Spirit and the era of the Church

25.1 "Having accomplished the work that the Father had entrusted to the Son on earth (cf. Jn 17:4), *on the day of Pentecost the Holy Spirit was sent to sanctify the Church forever,* so that believers might have access to the Father through Christ in one Spirit (cf. Eph 2:18). He is the Spirit of life, the fountain of water springing up to eternal life (cf. Jn 4:14; 7:38ff.), the One through whom the Father restores life to those who are dead through sin, until one day he will raise in Christ their mortal bodies" (cf. Rom 8:10-11).[92]

25.2 In this way the Second Vatican Council speaks *of the Church's birth* on the day of Pentecost. This event constitutes the definitive manifestation of what had already been accomplished in the same Upper Room on Easter Sunday. The risen Christ came and "brought" to the Apostles the Holy Spirit. He gave him to them, saying "Receive the Holy Spirit." What had then taken place *inside the Upper Room,* "the doors being shut," later, on the day of Pentecost is manifested also outside, in public. The doors of the Upper Room are opened and the Apostles go to the inhabitants and the pilgrims who had gathered in Jerusalem on the occasion of the feast, in order to bear witness to Christ in the power of the Holy Spirit. In this way the prediction is fulfilled: "*He* will bear witness to me: and *you also* are witnesses, because you have been with me from the beginning."[93]

25.3 We read in another document of the Second Vatican Council: "Doubtless, the Holy Spirit was already at work in the world before Christ was glorified. Yet on the day of Pentecost, he came down upon the disciples to remain with them forever. On that day the Church was publicly revealed to the multitude, and the Gospel began to spread among the nations by means of preaching."[94]

25.4 The *era of the Church* began with the "coming," that is to say with the descent of the Holy Spirit on the Apostles gathered in the Upper Room in

[91] Jn 16:15.

[92] Second Vatican Ecumenical Council, Dogmatic Constitution on the Church *Lumen Gentium,* 4.

[93] Jn 15:26-27.

[94] Second Vatican Ecumenical Council, Decree on the Church's Missionary Activity *Ad Gentes,* 4.

Jerusalem, together with Mary, the Lord's Mother.[95] The time of the Church began at the moment when *the promises and predictions* that so explicitly referred to the Counselor, the Spirit of truth, began to be fulfilled in complete power and clarity upon the Apostles, thus determining the birth of the Church. The *Acts of the Apostles* speak of this at length and in many passages, which state that in the mind of the first community, whose convictions Luke expresses, *the Holy Spirit assumed the invisible* — but in a certain way "perceptible" — *guidance* of those who after the departure of the Lord Jesus felt profoundly that they had been left orphans. With the coming of the Spirit they felt capable of fulfilling the mission entrusted to them. They felt full of strength. It is precisely this that the Holy Spirit worked in them, and this is continually at work in the Church, through their successors. For the grace of the Holy Spirit which the Apostles gave to their collaborators through the imposition of hands continues to be transmitted in episcopal ordination. The Bishops in turn by the Sacrament of Orders render the sacred ministers sharers in this spiritual gift and, through the Sacrament of Confirmation, ensure that all who are reborn of water and the Holy Spirit are strengthened by this gift. And thus, in a certain way, the grace of Pentecost is perpetuated in the Church.

25.5 As the Council writes, "*the Spirit dwells in the Church* and in the hearts of the faithful as in a temple (cf. 1 Cor 3:16; 6:19). In them he prays and bears witness to the fact that they are adopted sons (cf. Gal 4:6; Rom 8:15-16:26). The *Spirit guides* the Church *into the fullness of truth* (cf. Jn 16:13) and gives her a unity of fellowship and service. He furnishes and directs her with various gifts, both hierarchical and charismatic, and adorns her with the fruits of his grace (cf Eph 4:11-12; 1 Cor 12:4; Gal 5:22). By the power of the Gospel *he makes the Church grow*, perpetually *renews* her and *leads* her to perfect union with her Spouse."[96]

---

[95] Cf. Acts 1:14.

[96] Dogmatic Constitution on the Church *Lumen Gentium*, 4. There is a whole patristic and theological tradition concerning the intimate union between the Holy Spirit and the Church, a union presented sometimes as analogous to the relation between the soul and the body in man: cf. Saint Irenaeus, *Adversus Haereses*, III, 24, 1: *SCh* 211, 470-474; Saint Augustine, *Sermo* 267, 4, 4: *PL* 38, 1231; *Sermo* 268, 2: *PL* 38, 1232; *In Iohannis Evangelium Tractatus*, 25, 13; 27, 6: *CCL* 36, 266, 272-273; Saint Gregory the Great, *In Septem Psalmos Poenitentiales Expositio*, Psalmum, V, 1: *PL* 79, 602; Didymus the Blind, *De Trinitate*, II, 1: *PG* 39, 449-450; Saint Athanasius, *Oratio III contra Arianos*, 22, 23, 24: *PG* 26, 368-369, 372-373; Saint John Chrysostom, *In Epistulam ad Ephesios*, Homily IX, 3: *PG* 62, 72-73. Saint Thomas Aquinas has synthesized the preceding patristic and theological tradition, presenting the Holy Spirit as the "heart" and the "soul" of the Church; cf. *Summa Theologiae*, III, q. 8, a. 1, ad 3; *In Symbolum Apostolorum Expositio*, a. IX; *In Tertium Librum Sententiarum*, dist. XIII, q. 2, a. 2, quaestiuncula 3.

26.1 These passages quoted from the conciliar Constitution *Lumen Gentium* tell us that the era of the Church began with the coming of the Holy Spirit. They also tell us that this era, *the era of the Church*, continues. It continues *down the centuries and generations*. In our own century, when humanity is already close to the end of the second millennium after Christ, this era of the Church expressed itself in a special way through the Second Vatican Council, as the Council of our century. For we know that it was in a special way an "ecclesiological" Council: *a Council on the theme of the Church*. At the same time, the teaching of this Council is essentially "pneumatological": it is *permeated by the truth about the Holy Spirit*, as the soul of the Church. We can say that in its rich variety of teaching the Second Vatican Council contains precisely all that "the Spirit says to the Churches"[97] with regard to the present phase of the history of salvation.

26.2 Following the guidance of the Spirit of truth and bearing witness together with him, the Council has given a special *confirmation of the presence of the Holy Spirit — the Counselor*. In a certain sense, the Council has made the Spirit newly "present" in our difficult age. In the light of this conviction one grasps more clearly the great importance of all the initiatives aimed at implementing the Second Vatican Council, its teaching and its pastoral and ecumenical thrust. In this sense also the subsequent *Assemblies of the Synod of Bishops* are to be carefully studied and evaluated, aiming as they do to ensure that the fruits of truth and love — the authentic fruits of the Holy Spirit — become a lasting treasure for the People of God in its earthly pilgrimage down the centuries. This work being done by the Church for the testing and bringing together of the salvific fruits of the Spirit bestowed in the Council is something indispensable. For this purpose one must learn how to "discern" them carefully from everything that may instead come originally from the "prince of this world."[98] This discernment in implementing the Council's work is especially necessary in view of the fact that the Council *opened itself widely to the contemporary world*, as is clearly seen from the important conciliar Constitutions *Gaudium et Spes* and *Lumen Gentium*.

26.3 We read in the Pastoral Constitution: "For theirs (that is, of the disciples of Christ) is a community composed of men. United in Christ, they are led by the Holy Spirit in their journey to the Kingdom of their Father and they have welcomed the news of salvation which is meant for every man. That is why this community realizes that it is truly and intimately *linked with man-*

[97] Cf. Rev 2:29, 3:6, 13, 22.
[98] Cf. Jn 12:31, 14:30, 16:11.

kind and its history."[99] "The Church truly knows that only God, whom she serves, meets the deepest longings of the human heart, which is never fully satisfied by what the world has to offer."[100] *"God's Spirit . . .* with a marvelous providence *directs the unfolding of time and renews the face of the earth."*[101]

II

The Spirit Who Convinces the World concerning Sin

Sin, righteousness and judgment

27.1 When Jesus during the discourse in the Upper Room foretells the coming of the Holy Spirit "at the price of" his own departure, and promises "I will send him to you," in the very same context he adds: "And when he comes, *he will convince the world concerning sin and righteousness and judgment."*[102] The same Counselor and Spirit of truth who has been promised as the one who "will teach" and "bring to remembrance, " who "will bear witness," and "guide into all the truth," in the words just quoted is foretold as the one who "will convince the world concerning sin and righteousness and judgment."

27.2 The *context* too seems significant. Jesus links this foretelling of the Holy Spirit to the words indicating his "departure" through the Cross, and indeed emphasizes the need for this departure: "It is to your advantage that I go away, for if I do not go away, the Counselor will not come to you."[103]

27.3 But what counts more is *the explanation that Jesus himself adds* to these three words: sin, righteousness, judgment. For he says this: "He will convince the world concerning sin and righteousness and judgment: concerning sin, because they do not believe in me; concerning righteousness, because I go to the Father, and you will see me no more; concerning judgment, because the ruler of the world is judged."[104] In the mind of Jesus, sin, righteousness and judgment have *a very precise meaning,* different from the meaning that one might be inclined to attribute to these words independently of the speaker's explanation. This explanation also indicates how one is to understand the "convincing the world" which is proper to the action of the Holy

---

[99] Pastoral Constitution on the Church in the Modern World *Gaudium et Spes,* 1.

[100] Ibid., 41.

[101] Ibid., 26.

[102] Jn 16:7-8.

[103] Jn 16:7.

[104] Jn 16:8-11.

Spirit. Both the meaning of the individual words and the fact that Jesus linked them together in the same phrase are important here.

27.4 *"Sin,"* in this passage, means the incredulity that Jesus encountered among "his own," beginning with the people of his own town of Nazareth. Sin means the rejection of his mission, a rejection that will cause people to condemn him to death. When he speaks next of *"righteousness,"* Jesus seems to have in mind that definitive justice, which the Father will restore to him when he grants him the glory of the Resurrection and Ascension into heaven: "I go to the Father." In its turn, and in the context of "sin" and "righteousness" thus understood, *"judgment"* means that the Spirit of truth will show the guilt of the "world" in condemning Jesus to death on the Cross. Nevertheless, Christ did not come into the world only to judge it and condemn it: *he came to save it.*[105] Convincing about sin and righteousness has as its purpose the salvation of the world, the salvation of men. Precisely this truth seems to be emphasized by the assertion that "judgment" concerns only the *"prince of this world,"* Satan, the one who from the beginning has been exploiting the work of creation against salvation, against the covenant and the union of man with God: he is "already judged" from the start. If the Spirit-Counselor is to convince the world precisely concerning judgment, it is in order to continue in the world the salvific work of Christ.

28 Here we wish to concentrate our attention principally on this mission of the Holy Spirit, which is *"to convince the world concerning sin,"* but at the same time respecting the general context of Jesus' words in the Upper Room. The Holy Spirit, who takes from the Son the work of the Redemption of the world, by this very fact takes the task of the salvific "convincing of sin." This convincing is *in permanent reference to "righteousness":* that is to say to definitive salvation in God, to the fulfillment of the economy that has as its center the crucified and glorified Christ. And this *salvific economy of God* in a certain sense removes man from *"judgment," that is from the damnation* which has been inflicted on the sin of Satan, "the prince of this world," the one who because of his sin has become "the ruler of this world of darkness."[106] And here we see that, through this reference to "judgment," vast horizons open up for understanding "sin" and also "righteousness." The Holy Spirit, by showing sin against the background of Christ's Cross in the economy of salvation (one could say "sin saved"), enables us to understand how his mission is also "to convince" of the sin that has already been definitively judged ("sin condemned").

[105] Cf. Jn 3:17, 12:47.
[106] Cf. Eph 6:12.

29.1 All the words uttered by the Redeemer in the Upper Room on the eve of his Passion *become part of the era of the Church:* first of all, the words about the Holy Spirit as the Paraclete and Spirit of truth. The words become part of it in an ever new way, in every generation, in every age. This is confirmed, as far as our own age is concerned, by the teaching of the Second Vatican Council as a whole, and especially in the Pastoral Constitution *Gaudium et Spes.* Many passages of this document indicate clearly that the Council, by opening itself to the light of the Spirit of truth, is seen to be the *authentic depositary* of the predictions and promises made by Christ to the Apostles and to the Church in the farewell discourse: in a particular way as the depositary of the predictions that the Holy Spirit would "convince the world concerning sin and righteousness and judgment."

29.2 This is already indicated by the text in which *the Council explains how it understands the "world":* "The Council focuses its attention on the world of men, the whole human family along with the sum of those realities in the midst of which that family lives. It gazes upon the world which is the theater of man's history, and carries the marks of his energies, his tragedies, and his triumphs; that world which the Christian sees as created and sustained by its Maker's love, *fallen indeed into the bondage of sin,* yet *emancipated now by Christ.* He was crucified and rose again *to break the stranglehold of personified Evil,* so that this world might be fashioned anew according to God's design and reach its fulfillment."[107] This very rich text needs to be read in conjunction with the other passages in the Constitution that seek to show *with all the realism of faith* the situation of sin in the contemporary world and that also seek to explain its essence, beginning from different points of view.[108]

29.3 When on the eve of the Passover Jesus speaks of the Holy Spirit as the one who "will convince the world concerning sin," on the one hand this statement must be given *the widest possible meaning,* insofar as it includes all the sin in the history of humanity. But on the other hand, when Jesus explains that this sin consists in the fact that "they do not believe in him," this meaning seems to *apply only* to those who rejected the messianic mission of the Son of Man and condemned him to death on the Cross. But one can hardly fail to notice that this more "limited" and historically specified meaning of sin expands, until it assumes a universal dimension *by reason of the universality of the Redemption,* accomplished through the Cross. The revelation of the mystery of the Redemption opens the way to an understanding in which *every sin* wherever and whenever committed has a reference to the Cross of

---

[107] Pastoral Constitution on the Church in the Modern World *Gaudium et Spes,* 2.
[108] Cf. ibid., 10, 13, 27, 37, 63, 73, 79, 80.

Christ — and therefore indirectly also to the sin of those who "have not believed in him," and who condemned Jesus Christ to death on the Cross.

29.4 From this point of view we must return to the event of Pentecost.

The testimony of the day of Pentecost

30.1 *Christ's prophecies* in the farewell discourse found their most exact and direct *confirmation* on the day of Pentecost, in particular the prediction which we are dealing with: "The Counselor . . . will convince the world concerning sin." On that day, the *promised Holy Spirit came down* upon the Apostles gathered in prayer together with Mary the Mother of Jesus, in the same Upper Room, as we read in the *Acts of the Apostles:* "And they were all filled with the Holy Spirit and began to speak in other tongues, as the Spirit gave them utterance,"[109] "thus bringing back to unity the scattered races and offering to the Father the first-fruits of all the nations."[110]

30.2 The connection between Christ's prediction and this event is clear. We perceive here the first and fundamental fulfillment of the promise of the Paraclete. He comes, sent by the Father, *"after" the departure of Christ,* "at the price of" that departure. This is first a departure through the Cross, and later, forty days after the Resurrection, through his Ascension into heaven. Once more, at the moment of the Ascension, Jesus orders the Apostles "not to depart from Jerusalem, but to wait for the promise of the Father"; "but before many days you shall be *baptized with the Holy Spirit*"; "but you shall receive power when the Holy Spirit has come upon you; and you shall be witnesses in Jerusalem and in all Judea and Samaria and to the end of the earth."[111]

30.3 These last words contain an echo or reminder of the prediction made in the Upper Room. And on the day of Pentecost this prediction is fulfilled with total accuracy. Acting under the influence of the Holy Spirit, who had been received by the Apostles while they were praying in the Upper Room, *Peter comes forward and speaks* before a multitude of people of different languages, gathered for the feast. He proclaims what *he* certainly *would not have had the courage to say before:* "Men of Israel, . . . Jesus of Nazareth, a man attested to you by God with mighty works and wonders and signs which God did through him in your midst . . . this Jesus, delivered up according to the definite plan and foreknowledge of God, you *crucified* and killed by the hands of lawless men. But God raised him up, having loosed the pangs of death, because it was not possible for him to be held by it."[112]

---

[109] Acts 2:4.
[110] Cf. Saint Irenaeus, *Adversus Haereses,* III, 17, 2: *SCh* 211, 330-332.
[111] Acts 1:4, 5, 8.
[112] Acts 2:22-24.

30.4 Jesus had foretold and promised: "He will bear witness to me, . . . and you also are my witnesses." In the first discourse of Peter in Jerusalem this "witness" *finds its clear beginning:* it is the witness to Christ crucified and risen — the witness of the Spirit-Paraclete and of the Apostles. And in the very content of that first witness, the Spirit of truth, through the lips of Peter, *"convinces the world concerning sin":* first of all, concerning the sin which is the rejection of Christ even to his condemnation to death, to death on the Cross on Golgotha. Similar proclamations will be repeated, according to the text of the Acts of the Apostles, on other occasions and in various places.[113]

31.1 Beginning from this initial witness at Pentecost and for all future time the action of the Spirit of truth who "convinces the world concerning the sin" of the rejection of Christ *is linked* inseparably with the witness to be borne to the Paschal Mystery: *the mystery of the Crucified and Risen One.* And in this link the same "convincing concerning sin" reveals its own salvific dimension. For it is a "convincing" that has as its purpose not merely *the accusation* of the world and still less its *condemnation.* Jesus Christ did not come into the world to judge it and condemn it but *to save it.*[114] This is emphasized in this first discourse, when Peter exclaims: "Let all the house of Israel therefore know assuredly that God has made him both Lord and Christ, this Jesus whom you crucified."[115] And then, when those present ask Peter and the Apostles: "Brethren, what shall we do?" this is Peter's answer: "*Repent,* and be baptized every one of you in the name of Jesus Christ *for the forgiveness of your sins*; and you shall receive the gift of the Holy Spirit."[116]

31.2 In this way "convincing concerning *sin*" becomes at the same time a convincing *concerning the remission of sins,* in the power of the Holy Spirit. Peter in his discourse in Jerusalem calls people to conversion, as Jesus called his listeners to conversion at the beginning of his messianic activity.[117] Conversion *requires convincing of sin;* it includes the interior judgment of the conscience, and this, being a proof of the action of the Spirit of truth in man's inmost being, becomes at the same time a new beginning of the bestowal of grace and love: "Receive the Holy Spirit."[118] Thus in this "convincing concern-

---

[113] Cf. Acts 3:14-15; 4:10, 27-28; 7:52; 10:39; 13:28-29; etc.
[114] Cf. Jn 3:17, 12:47.
[115] Acts 2:36.
[116] Acts 2:37-38.
[117] Cf. Mk 1:15.
[118] Jn 20:22.

ing sin" we discover *a double gift:* the gift of the truth of conscience and the gift of the certainty of Redemption. The Spirit of truth is the Counselor.

31.3 The convincing concerning sin, through the ministry of the *apostolic kerygma* in the early Church, is *referred* — under the impulse of the Spirit poured out at Pentecost — *to the redemptive power* of Christ crucified and risen. Thus the promise concerning the Holy Spirit made before Easter is fulfilled: "He will take what is mine and declare it to you." When therefore, during the Pentecost event, Peter speaks *of the sin of those who "have not believed"*[119] and have sent Jesus of Nazareth to an ignominious death, he bears witness to victory over sin: a victory achieved, in a certain sense, through the greatest sin that man could commit: *the killing of Jesus, the Son of God, consubstantial with the Father!* Similarly, the death of the Son of God conquers human death: "I will be your death, O death,"[120] as the sin of having crucified *the Son of God "conquers" human sin!* That sin which was committed in Jerusalem on Good Friday — and also every human sin. For the greatest sin on man's part is matched, in the heart of the Redeemer, *by the oblation of supreme love* that conquers the evil of all the sins of man. On the basis of this certainty the Church in the Roman liturgy does not hesitate to repeat every year, at the Easter Vigil, "O happy fault!" in the deacon's proclamation of the Resurrection when he sings the *"Exsultet."*

32.1 However, no one but *he himself, the Spirit of truth, can "convince the world,"* man or the human conscience of this ineffable truth. He is the Spirit who "searches even the depths of God."[121] Faced with the mystery of sin, we have to search "the depths of God" *to their very depth.* It is not enough to search the human conscience, the intimate mystery of man, but we have to penetrate the inner mystery of God, those "depths of God" that are summarized thus: to the Father — in the Son — through the Holy Spirit. It is precisely the Holy Spirit who "searches" the "depths of God," and from them draws *God's response* to man's sin. With this response there closes the process of "convincing concerning sin," as the event of Pentecost shows.

32.2 By convincing the "world" concerning the sin of Golgotha, concerning the death of the innocent Lamb, as happens on the day of Pentecost, the Holy Spirit also convinces of every sin, committed in any place and at any moment in human history: *for he demonstrates its relationship with the Cross of Christ.* The "convincing" is the demonstration of the evil of sin, of every sin, in relation

---

[119] Cf. Jn 16:9.
[120] Hos 14:14 (Vulgate); cf. 1 Cor 15:55.
[121] Cf. 1 Cor 2:10.

to the Cross of Christ. Sin, shown in this relationship, *is recognized in the entire dimension of evil* proper to it, through the *"mysterium iniquitatis"*[122] which is hidden within it. Man does not know this dimension — he is absolutely ignorant of it apart from the Cross of Christ. So he cannot be "convinced" of it except by *the Holy Spirit:* the Spirit of truth but who is also the Counselor.

32.3 For sin, shown in relation to the Cross of Christ, is at the same time *identified in the full dimension of the "mysterium pietatis,"*[123] as indicated by the Post-Synodal Apostolic Exhortation *Reconciliatio et Paenitentia.*[124] Man is also absolutely ignorant of this dimension of sin apart from the Cross of Christ. And he cannot be "convinced" of this dimension either, except *by the Holy Spirit:* the one who "searches the depths of God."

The witness concerning the beginning: the original reality of sin

33.1 This is the dimension of sin that we find in the witness concerning the beginning, commented on in the *Book of Genesis.*[125] It is the sin that according to the revealed word of God constitutes *the principle and root of all the others.* We find ourselves faced with the original reality of sin in human history and at the same time in the whole of the economy of salvation. It can be said that in this sin the *"mysterium iniquitatis"* has its beginning, but it can also be said that this is the sin concerning which the redemptive power of the *"mysterium pietatis"* becomes particularly clear and efficacious. This is expressed by Saint Paul, when he *contrasts* the *"disobedience"* of the first Adam with the *"obedience"* of Christ, the second Adam: "Obedience unto death."[126]

33.2 According to the witness concerning the beginning, sin in its original reality takes place in man's will — and conscience — first of all as "disobedience," that is, as opposition of the will of man to the will of God. This original disobedience presupposes *a rejection,* or at least *a turning away from the truth contained in the Word of God,* who creates the world. This Word is the same Word who was "in the beginning with God," who "was God," and without whom "nothing has been made of all that is," since "the world was made through him."[127] He is the Word who is also the eternal law, the source of every law which regulates the world and especially human acts. When therefore on the

---

[122] Cf. 2 Thess 2:7.

[123] Cf. 1 Tim 3:16.

[124] Cf. Post-Synodal Apostolic Exhortation *Reconciliatio et Paenitentia* (December 2, 1984), 19-22: *AAS* 77 (1985), 229-233.

[125] Cf. Gen 1-3.

[126] Cf. Rom 5:19; Phil 2:8.

[127] Cf. Jn 1:1, 2, 3, 10.

eve of his Passion Jesus Christ speaks of the sin of those who *"do not believe in him,"* in these words of his, full of sorrow, there is *as it were a distant echo of that sin* which in its original form is obscurely *inscribed* in the mystery of creation. For the one who is speaking is not only the Son of Man but the one who is also "the first-born of all creation," "for in him all things were created . . . through him and for him."[128] In the light of this truth we can understand that the "disobedience" in the mystery of the beginning presupposes in a certain sense the same "non-faith," that same *"they have not believed"* which will be repeated in the Paschal Mystery. As we have said, it is a matter of a rejection or at least a turning away from the truth contained in the Word of the Father. The rejection expresses itself in practice as "disobedience," in an act committed as an effect of the temptation which comes from the "father of lies."[129] Therefore, at the root of human sin is the lie which is a radical *rejection of the truth* contained in the Word of the Father, through whom is expressed the loving omnipotence of the Creator: the omnipotence and also the love "of God the Father, Creator of heaven and earth."

34 *"The Spirit of God,"* who according to the biblical description of creation "was moving over the face of the water,"[130] signifies the same "Spirit who searches the depths of God": *searches the depths of the Father and of the Word-Son* in the mystery of creation. Not only is he the direct witness of their mutual love from which creation derives, but he himself is this love. He himself, as love, is the eternal uncreated gift. In him is *the source and the beginning of every giving of gifts to creatures.* The witness concerning the beginning, which we find in the whole of revelation, beginning with the *Book of Genesis,* is unanimous on this point. To create means to call into existence from nothing: therefore, to create means *to give* existence. And if the visible world is created for man, therefore the world is given to man.[131] And at the same time that same man in his own humanity receives as a gift a special *"image and likeness"* to God. This means not only rationality and freedom as constitutive properties of human nature, but also, from the very beginning, the capacity of having *a personal relationship* with God, as "I" and "you," and therefore *the capacity of having a covenant,* which will take place in God's salvific communication with man. Against the background of the "image and likeness" of God, "the gift of the Spirit" ultimately means *a call to friendship,* in

---

[128] Cf. Col 1:15-18.
[129] Cf. Jn 8:44.
[130] Cf. Gen 1:2.
[131] Cf. Gen 1:26, 28, 29.

which the transcendent "depths of God" become in some way opened to participation on the part of man. The Second Vatican Council teaches: "The invisible God out of the abundance of his love speaks to men as friends and lives among them, so that he may invite and take them into fellowship with himself."[132]

35.1 The Spirit, therefore, who "searches everything, even the depths of God," knows from the beginning "the secrets of man."[133] For this reason he alone *can fully "convince concerning the sin" that happened at the beginning,* that sin which is the root of all other sins and the source of man's sinfulness on earth, a source which never ceases to be active. The Spirit of truth knows the original reality of the sin caused in the will of man by the "father of lies," he who already "has been judged."[134] The Holy Spirit therefore convinces the world of sin in connection with this "judgment," but by constantly *guiding toward the "righteousness"* that has been revealed to man together with the Cross of Christ: through "obedience unto death."[135]

35.2 Only the Holy Spirit can convince concerning the sin of the human beginning, precisely he who is the love of the Father and of the Son, he who is gift, whereas *the sin of the human beginning consists in untruthfulness and in the rejection of the gift and the love* which determine the beginning of the world and of man.

36.1 According to the witness concerning the beginning which we find in the Scriptures and in Tradition, after the first (and also more complete) description in the *Book of Genesis,* sin in its original form is understood as "disobedience," and this means simply and directly *transgression of a prohibition laid down by God.*[136] But in the light of the whole context it is also obvious that the ultimate roots of this disobedience are to be sought in the whole real situation of man. Having been called into existence, the human being — man and woman — is a creature. The "image of God," consisting in rationality and freedom, expresses the greatness and dignity of the human subject, who is a person. But this *personal subject* is also always *a creature:* in his existence and essence he depends on the Creator. According to the *Book of Genesis,* "the tree of the knowledge of good and evil" was to express and constantly remind

---

[132] Dogmatic Constitution on Divine Revelation *Dei Verbum,* 2.
[133] Cf. 1 Cor 2:10-11.
[134] Cf. Jn 16:11.
[135] Cf. Phil 2:8.
[136] Cf. Gen 2:16-17.

man of the "limit" impassable for a created being. God's prohibition is to be understood in this sense: the Creator forbids man and woman to eat of the fruit of the tree of the knowledge of good and evil. The words of the entice-ment, that is to say the temptation, as formulated in the sacred text, are an inducement to transgress this prohibition — that is to say, to *go beyond* that "limit": "When you eat of it your eyes will be opened, and you will be like God ["like gods"], knowing good and evil."[137]

36.2 "Disobedience" means precisely going beyond that limit, which re-mains impassable to the will and the freedom of man as a created being. For God the Creator is the one definitive source of the moral order in the world created by him. Man cannot decide by himself what is good and what is evil — cannot "know good and evil, like God." In the created world *God* indeed re-mains the first and sovereign source *for deciding about good and evil,* through the intimate truth of being, which is the reflection of *the Word,* the eternal Son, consubstantial with the Father. To man, created to the image of God, the Holy Spirit gives the gift of *conscience,* so that in this conscience the image may faithfully reflect its model, which is both Wisdom and eternal Law, the source of the moral order in man and in the world. "Disobedience," as the original dimension of sin, means *the rejection of this source,* through man's claim to become an independent and exclusive source for deciding about good and evil. The Spirit who "searches the depths of God," and who at the same time is for man the light of conscience and the source of the moral order, knows in all its fullness this dimension of the sin inscribed in the mystery of man's begin-ning. And the Spirit does not cease *"convincing the world of it"* in connection with the Cross of Christ on Golgotha.

37.1 According to the witness of the beginning, God in creation has re-vealed himself as omnipotence, which is love. At the same time he has re-vealed to man that, as the "image and likeness" of his Creator, he is *called to participate in truth and love.* This participation means a life in union with God, who is "eternal life."[138] But man, under the influence of the "father of lies," has separated himself from this participation. To what degree? Certainly not to the degree of the sin of a pure spirit, to the degree of the sin of Satan. The human spirit is incapable of reaching such a degree.[139] In the very description

---

[137] Gen 3:5.

[138] Cf. Gen 3:22 concerning the "tree of life"; cf. also Jn 3:36; 4:14; 5:24; 6:40, 47; 10:28; 12:50; 14:6; Acts 13:48; Rom 6:23; Gal 6:8; 1 Tim 1:16; Tit 1:2; 3:7; 1 Pet 3:22; 1 Jn 1:2; 2:25; 5:11, 13; Rev 2:7.

[139] Cf. Saint Thomas Aquinas, *Summa Theologiae,* I-II, q. 80, a. 4, ad 3.

given in *Genesis it is easy to see the difference of degree* between the "breath of evil" on the part of the one who "has sinned (or remains in sin) from the beginning"[140] and already "has been judged,"[141] and the evil of disobedience on the part of man.

37.2 Man's disobedience, nevertheless, always means a *turning away from God,* and in a certain sense *the closing up* of human freedom in his regard. It also means a certain opening of this freedom — of the human mind and will — to the one who is the "father of lies." This act of conscious choice is not only "disobedience" but also involves a *certain consent to the motivation* which was contained in the first temptation to sin and which is unceasingly renewed during the whole history of man on earth: "For God knows that when you eat of it your eyes will be opened, and you will be like God, knowing good and evil."

37.3 Here we find ourselves at the very center of what could be called the "anti-Word," that is to say the "anti-truth." For *the truth about man* becomes *falsified: who man is* and what are *the impassable limits* of his being and freedom. This "anti-truth" is possible because at the same time there is a complete *falsification* of the *truth about who God is.* God the Creator is placed in a state of suspicion, indeed of accusation, in the mind of the creature. For the first time in human history there appears the perverse "genius of suspicion." He seeks to *"falsify" Good itself, the absolute Good,* which precisely in the work of creation has manifested itself as the Good which gives in an inexpressible way: as *bonum diffusivum sui,* as *creative love.* Who can completely *"convince* concerning sin," or concerning this motivation of man's original disobedience, except the one who alone is the gift and the source of all giving of gifts, except the Spirit, who "searches the depths of God" and is the love of the Father and the Son?

38.1 For in spite of all the witness of creation and of the salvific economy inherent in it, the spirit of darkness[142] is capable of showing *God as an enemy* of his own creature, and in the first place as an enemy of man, *as a source of danger and threat to man.* In this way *Satan* manages to sow in man's soul the seed of opposition to the one who "from the beginning" would be considered as man's enemy — and not as Father. Man is challenged to become the adversary of God!

38.2 The analysis of sin in its original dimension indicates that, through

[140] 1 Jn 3:8.
[141] Jn 16:11.
[142] Cf. Eph 6:12; Lk 22:53.

the influence of the "father of lies," *throughout the history of humanity there will be a constant pressure on man to reject God,* even to the point of hating him: *"Love of self to the point of contempt for God,"* as Saint Augustine puts it.[143] Man will be inclined to see in God primarily a limitation of himself, and not the source of his own freedom and the fullness of good. We see this confirmed in the modern age, when the atheistic ideologies seek *to root out religion* on the grounds that religion causes the radical *"alienation" of man,* as if man were dispossessed of his own humanity when, accepting the idea of God, he attributes to God what belongs to man, and exclusively to man! Hence a process of thought and historico-sociological practice in which the rejection of God has reached the point of declaring his "death." An absurdity, both in concept and expression! But the ideology of the "death of God" is more a threat to *man,* as the Second Vatican Council indicates when it analyzes the question of the "independence of earthly affairs" and writes: "For without the Creator the creature would disappear . . . when God is forgotten the creature itself grows unintelligible."[144] The ideology of the "death of God" easily demonstrates in its effects that on the "theoretical and practical" levels it is the ideology of the "death of man."

The Spirit who transforms suffering into salvific love

39.1 The Spirit who searches the depths of God was called by Jesus in his discourse in the Upper Room *the Paraclete. For from the beginning the Spirit "is invoked"*[145] in order to "convince the world concerning sin." He is invoked in a definitive way through the Cross of Christ. Convincing concerning sin means showing the evil that sin contains, and this is equivalent to revealing the *mystery of iniquity.* It is not possible to grasp the evil of sin in all its sad reality without "searching the depths of God." From the very beginning, the obscure mystery of sin has appeared in the world against the background of a reference to the Creator of human freedom. Sin has appeared as an act of the will of the creature-man *contrary* to the will of God, *to the salvific will of God;* indeed, sin has appeared in opposition to the truth, on the basis of the lie which has now been definitively "judged": the lie that has placed in a state of accusation, a state of permanent suspicion, creative and salvific love itself. Man has followed the "father of lies," setting himself up in opposition to the Father of life and the Spirit of truth.

39.2 Therefore, will not "convincing concerning sin" also have to mean

---

[143] *De Civitate Dei,* XIV, 28: *CCL* 48, 451.

[144] Pastoral Constitution on the Church in the Modern World *Gaudium et Spes,* 36.

[145] In Greek the verb is *parakalein,* which means to invoke, to call to oneself.

revealing suffering? Revealing the pain, unimaginable and inexpressible, which on account of sin the Book of Genesis in its anthropomorphic vision seems to glimpse in the "depths of God" and in a certain sense in the very heart of the ineffable Trinity? The Church, taking her inspiration from revelation, believes and professes that *sin is an offense against God*. What corresponds, in the inscrutable intimacy of the Father, the Word and the Holy Spirit, to this "offense," this rejection of the Spirit who is love and gift? The concept of God as the necessarily most perfect being certainly excludes from God any pain deriving from deficiencies or wounds; but in the "depths of God" there is a Father's love that, faced with man's sin, in the language of the Bible reacts so deeply as to say: "I am sorry that I have made him."[146] "The Lord saw that the wickedness of man was great in the earth. . . . And *the Lord was sorry that he had made man on the earth. . . .* The Lord said: *'I am sorry that I have made them.'* "[147] But more often the Sacred Book speaks to us of a Father who feels compassion for man, as though sharing his pain. In a word, this inscrutable and indescribable *fatherly "pain" will bring about* above all the wonderful *economy of redemptive love* in Jesus Christ, so that through the *mysterium pietatis* love can reveal itself in the history of man as stronger than sin. So that the "gift" may prevail!

39.3 The Holy Spirit, who in the words of Jesus "convinces concerning sin," is the love of the Father and the Son, and as such is the Trinitarian gift, and at the same time the eternal source of every divine giving of gifts to creatures. Precisely in him we can picture as personified and actualized in a transcendent way that mercy which the patristic and theological tradition, following the line of the Old and New Testaments, attributes to God. In man, mercy includes sorrow and compassion for the misfortunes of one's neighbor. In God, the Spirit-Love expresses the consideration of human sin in a fresh outpouring of salvific love. From God, in the unity of the Father with the Son, the economy of salvation is born, the economy which fills the history of man with the gifts of the Redemption. Whereas sin, by rejecting love, has caused the "suffering" of man which in some way has affected the whole of creation,[148] *the Holy Spirit* will enter into human and cosmic suffering with a new outpouring of love which will redeem the world. And on the lips of Jesus the Redeemer, in whose humanity the "suffering" of God is concretized, there will be heard a word which manifests the eternal love full of mercy: *"Misereor."*[149] Thus, on the

---

[146] Cf. Gen 6:7.
[147] Gen 6:5-7.
[148] Cf. Rom 8:20-22.
[149] Cf. Mt 15:32; Mk 8:2.

part of the Holy Spirit, "convincing of sin" becomes a manifestation before creation, which is "subjected to futility," and above all in the depth of human consciences, that *sin is conquered through the sacrifice of the Lamb of God* who has become even "unto death" *the obedient servant* who, by making up for man's *disobedience*, accomplishes the Redemption of the world. In this way the spirit of truth, the Paraclete, "convinces concerning sin."

40.1 The redemptive value of Christ's sacrifice is expressed in very significant words by the author of the *Letter to the Hebrews*, who after recalling the sacrifices of the Old Covenant in which "the blood of goats and bulls . . ." purifies in "the flesh," adds: "How much more shall the blood of Christ, *who through the eternal spirit offered himself without blemish to God*, purify your conscience from dead works to serve the living God."[150] Though we are aware of other possible interpretations, our considerations on the presence of the Holy Spirit in the whole of Christ's life lead us to see this text as an invitation to reflect on the presence of the same Spirit also in the redemptive sacrifice of the Incarnate Word.

40.2 To begin with we reflect on the first words dealing with this sacrifice, and then separately on the "purification of conscience" which it accomplishes. For it is a sacrifice, offered *"through the eternal Spirit,"* that "derives" from it the power to "convince concerning sin." It is the same Holy Spirit, whom, according to the promise made in the Upper Room, *Jesus Christ* "will bring" to the Apostles on the day of his Resurrection, when he presents himself to them with the wounds of the crucifixion, and whom "he will give" them *"for the remission of sins"*: "Receive the Holy Spirit; if you forgive the sins of any, they are forgiven."[151]

40.3 We know that "God anointed Jesus of Nazareth with the Holy Spirit and with power," as Simon Peter said in the house of the centurion Cornelius.[152] We know of the Paschal Mystery of his "departure," from the *Gospel of John.* The words of the *Letter to the Hebrews* now explain to us how Christ "offered himself without blemish to God," and how he did this "through the eternal Spirit." In the sacrifice of the Son of Man the Holy Spirit is present and active just as he acted in Jesus' conception, in his coming into the world, in his hidden life and in his public ministry. According to the *Letter to the Hebrews*, on the way to his "departure" through Gethsemane and Golgotha, the same *Christ Jesus* in his own humanity *opened himself totally* to this *action of the*

---

[150] Heb 9:13-14.
[151] Jn 20:22-23.
[152] Acts 10:38.

Spirit-Paraclete, who from suffering enables eternal salvific love to spring forth. Therefore he "was heard for his godly fear. Although he was a Son, he learned obedience through what he suffered."[153] In this way *this Letter* shows how *humanity, subjected to sin*, in the descendants of the first Adam, in Jesus Christ became *perfectly subjected to God* and united to him, and at the same time full of compassion toward men. Thus there is *a new humanity*, which in Jesus Christ through the suffering of the Cross has returned to the love which was betrayed by Adam through sin. This new humanity is discovered precisely in the divine source of the original outpouring of gifts: in the Spirit, who "searches . . . the depths of God" and is himself love and gift.

40.4 The Son of God, Jesus Christ, as man, in the ardent prayer of his Passion, enabled the Holy Spirit, who had already penetrated the inmost depths of his humanity, *to transform that humanity into a perfect sacrifice* through the act of his death as the victim of love on the Cross. He made this offering by himself. As the one priest, "he offered himself without blemish to God."[154] In his humanity he was worthy to become this sacrifice, for *he alone* was "without blemish." But he offered it "through the eternal Spirit," which means that the Holy Spirit acted in a special way in this absolute self-giving of the Son of Man, in order to transform this suffering into redemptive love.

41.1 The Old Testament on several occasions speaks of "fire from heaven" which burnt the oblations presented by men.[155] By analogy one can say that the Holy Spirit is the *"fire from heaven" which works in the depth of the mystery of the Cross*. Proceeding from the Father, he directs toward the Father the sacrifice of the Son, bringing it into the *divine reality of the Trinitarian communion*. If sin caused suffering, now the pain of God in Christ crucified acquires through the Holy Spirit its full human expression. Thus there is a paradoxical mystery of love: in Christ there suffers a God who has been rejected by his own creature: "They do not believe in me!"; but at the same time, *from the depth of this suffering* — and indirectly from the depth of the very sin "of not having believed" — the Spirit *draws a new measure of the gift made to man and to creation* from the beginning. In the depth of the mystery of the Cross love is at work, that love which brings man back again to share in the life that is in God himself.

41.2 The Holy Spirit as Love and Gift *comes down, in a certain sense, into the very heart of the sacrifice* which is offered on the Cross. Referring here to

---

[153] Heb 5:7-8.
[154] Heb 9:14.
[155] Cf. Lev 9:24; 1 Kings 18:38; 2 Chron 7:1.

the biblical tradition, we can say: *he consumes this sacrifice with the fire of the love* which unites the Son with the Father in the Trinitarian communion. And since the sacrifice of the Cross is an act proper to Christ, also in this sacrifice he *"receives" the Holy Spirit*. He receives the Holy Spirit in such a way that afterwards — and he alone with God the Father — can *"give him" to the Apostles, to the Church, to humanity*. He alone "sends" the Spirit from the Father.[156] He alone presents himself before the Apostles in the Upper Room, "breathes upon them" and says: "Receive the Holy Spirit; if you forgive the sins of any, they are forgiven,"[157] as John the Baptist had foretold: "He will baptize you with the Holy Spirit and with fire."[158] With those words of Jesus, the Holy Spirit is *revealed and at the same time made present* as the Love that works in the depths of the Paschal Mystery, as the source of the salvific power of the Cross of Christ, and as the gift of new and eternal life.

41.2 This truth about the Holy Spirit finds daily *expression in the Roman liturgy*, when before Communion the priest pronounces those significant words: "Lord Jesus Christ, Son of the living God, by the will of the Father *and the work of the Holy Spirit* your death brought life to the world . . ." And in the Third Eucharistic Prayer, referring to the same salvific plan, the priest asks God that the Holy Spirit may *"make us an everlasting gift to you."*

The blood that purifies the conscience

42.1 We have said that, at the climax of the Paschal Mystery, the Holy Spirit is definitively revealed and made present in a new way. The risen Christ says to the Apostles: "Receive the Holy Spirit." Thus the Holy Spirit is *revealed*, for the words of Christ constitute the confirmation of what he had promised and foretold during the discourse in the Upper Room. And with this the Paraclete is also *made present* in a new way. In fact, he was already at work from the beginning in the mystery of creation and throughout the history of the Old Covenant of God with man. His action was fully confirmed by the sending of the Son of Man as the Messiah, who came in the power of the Holy Spirit. At the climax of Jesus' messianic mission, the Holy Spirit becomes present in the Paschal Mystery *in all his divine subjectivity:* as the one who is now to continue the salvific work rooted in the sacrifice of the Cross. Of course Jesus entrusts this work to humanity: to the Apostles, to the Church. Nevertheless, in these men and through them the Holy Spirit remains the transcendent principal agent of the accomplishment of this work in the hu-

---

[156] Cf. Jn 15:26.
[157] Jn 20:22-23.
[158] Mt 3:11.

man spirit and in the history of the world: the invisible and at the same time omnipresent Paraclete! The Spirit who "blows where he wills."[159]

42.2 The words of the risen Christ on the "first day of the week" *give particular emphasis to the presence of the Paraclete-Counselor* as the one who "convinces the world concerning sin, righteousness and judgment." For it is only in this relationship that it is possible to explain the words which Jesus directly relates to the "gift" of the Holy Spirit to the Apostles. He says: "Receive the Holy Spirit. If you forgive the sins of any, they are forgiven; if you retain the sins of any, they are retained."[160] Jesus confers on the Apostles the power to forgive sins, so that they may pass it on to their successors in the Church. But this power granted to men presupposes and includes the saving action of the Holy Spirit. By becoming "the light of hearts,"[161] that is to say the light of consciences, the Holy Spirit "convinces concerning sin," which is to say, *he makes man realize his own evil* and at the same time *directs him toward what is good.* Thanks to the multiplicity of the Spirit's gifts, by reason of which he is invoked as the "sevenfold one," every kind of human sin can be reached by God's saving power. In reality — as Saint Bonaventure says — "by virtue of the seven gifts of the Holy Spirit all evils are destroyed and all good things are produced."[162]

42.3 Thus *the conversion of the human heart,* which is an indispensable condition for the forgiveness of sins, is brought about by the influence of the Counselor. Without a true conversion, which implies inner contrition, and without a sincere and firm purpose of amendment, sins remain "unforgiven," in the words of Jesus, and with him the Tradition of the Old and New Covenants. For the first words uttered by Jesus at the beginning of his ministry, according to the *Gospel of Mark,* are these: "Repent, and believe in the Gospel."[163] A confirmation of this exhortation is the "convincing concerning sin" that the Holy Spirit undertakes in a new way by virtue of the Redemption accomplished by the blood of the Son of Man. Hence the *Letter to the Hebrews* says that this "blood purifies the conscience."[164] It therefore, so to speak, *opens to the Holy Spirit* the door into man's inmost being, namely into the sanctuary of human consciences.

---

[159] Cf. Jn 3:8.

[160] Jn 20:22-23.

[161] Cf. Sequence *Veni, Sancte Spiritus.*

[162] Saint Bonaventure, *De Septem Donis Spiritus Sancti,* Collatio II, 3: Ad Claras Aquas, V, 463.

[163] Mk 1:15.

[164] Cf. Heb 9:14.

43.1 The Second Vatican Council mentioned the Catholic teaching on conscience when it spoke about man's vocation and in particular about the dignity of the human person. It is precisely the *conscience* in particular which determines this dignity. For the conscience is "the *most secret core and sanctuary* of a man, where he is alone with God, whose voice echoes in his depths." It "can . . . speak to his heart more specifically: do this, shun that." This capacity to command what is good and to forbid evil, placed in man by the Creator, *is the main characteristic of the personal subject.* But at the same time, "in the depths of his conscience, man detects a law which he does not impose upon himself, but which holds him to obedience."[165] The conscience therefore is not an independent and exclusive capacity to decide what is good and what is evil. Rather there is profoundly imprinted upon it *a principle of obedience* vis-à-vis the *objective norm* which establishes and conditions the correspondence of its decisions with the commands and prohibitions which are at the basis of human behavior, as from the passage of the *Book of Genesis* which we have already considered.[166] Precisely in this sense the conscience is the "secret sanctuary" in which *"God's voice echoes."* The conscience is "the voice of God," even when man recognizes in it nothing more than the principle of the moral order which it is not humanly possible to doubt, even without any direct reference to the Creator. It is precisely in reference to this that the conscience always finds its foundation and justification.

43.2 The Gospel's "convincing concerning sin" under the influence of the Spirit of truth can be accomplished in man in no other way except *through the conscience.* If the conscience is upright, it serves "*to resolve according to truth* the moral problems which arise both in the life of individuals and from social relationships"; then "persons and groups turn aside from blind choice and try to be guided by the objective standards of moral conduct."[167]

43.3 A result of an upright conscience is, first of all, *to call good and evil by their proper name,* as we read in the same Pastoral Constitution: "Whatever is opposed to life itself, such as any type of murder, genocide, abortion, euthanasia, or willful self-destruction; whatever violates the integrity of the human person, such as mutilation, torments inflicted on body or mind, attempts to coerce the will itself; whatever insults human dignity, such as subhuman living conditions, arbitrary imprisonment, deportation, slavery, prostitution,

---

[165] Cf. Second Vatican Ecumenical Council, Pastoral Constitution on the Church in the Modern World *Gaudium et Spes,* 16.

[166] Cf. Gen 2:9, 17.

[167] Second Vatican Ecumenical Council, Pastoral Constitution on the Church in the Modern World *Gaudium et Spes,* 16.

the selling of women and children; as well as disgraceful working conditions, where people are treated as mere tools for profit, rather than as free and responsible persons"; and having called by name *the many different sins that are so frequent and widespread in our time*, the Constitution adds: "All these things and others of their kind are infamies indeed. They poison human society, but they do more harm to those who practice them than to those who suffer from the injury. Moreover, they are a supreme dishonor to the Creator."[168]

43.4 By calling by their proper name the sins that most dishonor man, and by showing that they are a moral evil that weighs negatively on any balance-sheet of human progress, the Council also describes all this as a stage in "a dramatic struggle between good and evil, between light and darkness," which characterizes "all of human life, whether individual or collective."[169] The 1983 Assembly of the *Synod of Bishops* on reconciliation and penance specified even more clearly the personal and social significance of human sin.[170]

44.1 In the Upper Room, on the eve of his Passion and again on the evening of Easter Day, Jesus Christ spoke of the Holy Spirit as the one who bears witness that *in human history sin continues to exist*. Yet sin has been *subjected to the saving power of the Redemption*. "Convincing the world concerning sin" does not end with the fact that sin is called by its right name and identified for what it is throughout its entire range. In convincing the world concerning sin *the Spirit of truth comes into contact with the voice of human consciences*.

44.2 By following this path we come *to a demonstration of the roots of sin*, which are to be found in man's inmost being, as described by the same Pastoral Constitution: "The truth is that the imbalances under which the modern world labors are linked with that more basic *imbalance* rooted *in the heart of man*. For in man himself many elements wrestle with one another. Thus, on the one hand, as a creature he experiences his limitations in a multitude of ways. On the other, he feels himself to be boundless in his desires and summoned to a higher life. Pulled by manifold attractions, he is constantly forced to choose among them and to renounce some. Indeed, as a weak and sinful being, *he often does what he would not, and fails to do what he would*."[171] The conciliar text is here referring to the well-known words of Saint Paul.[172]

---

[168] Ibid., 27.

[169] Cf. ibid., 13.

[170] Cf. Post-Synodal Apostolic Exhortation *Reconciliatio et Paenitentia* (December 2, 1984), 16: *AAS* 77 (1985), 213-217.

[171] Second Vatican Ecumenical Council, Pastoral Constitution on the Church in the Modern World *Gaudium et Spes*, 10.

[172] Cf. Rom 7:14-15, 19.

44.3 The "convincing concerning sin" which accompanies the human conscience in every careful reflection upon itself thus leads to the discovery of sin's roots in man, as also to the discovery of the way in which the conscience has been conditioned in the course of history. In this way we discover that original reality of sin of which we have already spoken. The *Holy Spirit "convinces concerning sin"* in relation to the mystery of man's origins, showing the fact that man is a *created being*, and therefore in complete ontological and ethical dependence upon the Creator. The Holy Spirit reminds us, at the same time, of the hereditary sinfulness of human nature. But the Holy Spirit the Counselor "convinces concerning sin" *always in relation to the Cross of Christ*. In the context of this relationship Christianity rejects any "fatalism" regarding sin. As the Council teaches: "A monumental struggle against the powers of darkness pervades the whole history of man. The battle was joined from the very origins of the world and will continue until the last day, as the Lord has attested."[173] "But *the Lord himself came to free and strengthen man*."[174] Man, therefore, far from allowing himself to be "ensnared" in his sinful condition, by relying upon the voice of his own conscience "is obliged to wrestle constantly if he is to cling to what is good. Nor can he achieve his own interior integrity without valiant efforts and *the help of God's grace*."[175] The Council rightly sees sin as *a factor of alienation* which weighs heavily on man's personal and social life. But at the same time it never tires of reminding us of the possibility of victory.

45.1 The Spirit of truth, who "convinces the world concerning sin," comes into contact with that laborious effort on the part of the human conscience which the conciliar texts speak of so graphically. This *laborious effort of conscience* also determines the paths of human conversion: turning one's back on sin, in order to restore truth and love in man's very heart. We know that recognizing evil in ourselves sometimes demands a great effort. We know that *conscience* not only commands and forbids but also *judges* in the light of interior dictates and prohibitions. It is also the *source of remorse:* man suffers interiorly because of the evil he has committed. Is not this suffering, as it were, a distant echo of that "repentance at having created man" which in anthropomorphic language the Sacred Book attributes to God? Is it not an echo of that "reprobation" which is interiorized in the "heart" of the Trinity

---

[173] Second Vatican Ecumenical Council, Pastoral Constitution on the Church in the Modern World *Gaudium et Spes*, 37.

[174] Ibid., 13.

[175] Ibid., 37.

and by virtue of the eternal love is translated into the suffering of the Cross, into Christ's obedience unto death? When the Spirit of truth permits the human conscience *to share in that suffering*, the suffering of the conscience becomes particularly profound, but also particularly salvific. Then, by means of an act of perfect contrition, the authentic conversion of the heart is accomplished: this is the evangelical "metanoia."

45.2 The laborious effort of the human heart, the laborious effort of the conscience in which this "metanoia," or conversion, takes place, is *a reflection* of that process whereby *reprobation is transformed into salvific love*, a love which is capable of suffering. The hidden giver of this saving power is the Holy Spirit: he whom the Church calls "the light of consciences" penetrates and fills "the depths of the human heart."[176] Through just such a conversion in the Holy Spirit *a person becomes open to forgiveness, to the remission of sins*. And in all this wonderful dynamism of conversion-forgiveness there is confirmed the truth of what Saint Augustine writes concerning the mystery of man, when he comments on the words of the Psalm: *"The abyss calls to the abyss."*[177] Precisely with regard to these "unfathomable depths" of man, of the human conscience, the mission of the Son and the Holy Spirit is accomplished. The *Holy Spirit "comes"* by virtue of Christ's "departure" in the Paschal Mystery: he comes in *each concrete case of conversion-forgiveness*, by virtue of the sacrifice of the Cross. For in this sacrifice "the blood of Christ . . . purifies your conscience from dead works to serve the living God."[178] Thus there are continuously fulfilled the words about the Holy Spirit as "another Counselor," the words spoken in the Upper Room to the Apostles and indirectly spoken to everyone: "You know him, for *he dwells with you* and will be in you."[179]

The sin against the Holy Spirit

46.1 Against the background of what has been said so far, certain other words of Jesus, shocking and disturbing ones, become easier to understand. We might call them *the words of "unforgiveness."* They are reported for us by the Synoptics in connection with a particular sin which is called "blasphemy against the Holy Spirit." This is how they are reported in their three versions.

[176] Cf. Sequence of Pentecost: *Reple cordis intima.*

[177] Cf. Saint Augustine, *Enarratio in Psalmum XLI*, 13: *CCL* 38, 470: "What is the abyss, and what does the abyss invoke? If abyss means depth, do we not consider that perhaps the heart of man is an abyss? What indeed is more deep than this abyss? Men can speak, can be seen through the working of their members, can be heard in conversation; but whose thought can be penetrated, whose heart can be read?"

[178] Cf. Heb 9:14.

[179] Jn 14:17.

Matthew: "Whoever says a word against the Son of Man will be forgiven but whoever speaks against the Holy Spirit will not be forgiven, either in this age or in the age to come."[180] *Mark:* "All sins will be forgiven the sons of men, and whatever blasphemies they utter; but whoever blasphemes against the Holy Spirit never has forgiveness, but is guilty of an eternal sin."[181] *Luke:* "Every one who speaks a word against the Son of Man will be forgiven; but he who blasphemes against the Holy Spirit will not be forgiven."[182]

46.2 Why is blasphemy against the Holy Spirit unforgivable? *How should this blasphemy be understood?* Saint Thomas Aquinas replies that it is a question of a sin that is "unforgivable by its very nature, insofar as it excludes the elements through which the forgiveness of sin takes place."[183]

46.3 According to such an exegesis, "blasphemy" does not properly consist in offending against the Holy Spirit in words; it consists rather *in the refusal to accept the salvation which God offers to man through the Holy Spirit,* working through the power of the Cross. If man rejects the "convincing concerning sin" which comes from the Holy Spirit and which has the power to save, he also rejects the "coming" of the Counselor — that "coming" which was accomplished in the Paschal Mystery, in union with the redemptive power of Christ's blood: the blood which "purifies the conscience from dead works."

46.4 We know that the result of such a purification is the forgiveness of sins. Therefore, whoever rejects the Spirit and the Blood remains in "dead works," in sin. And the blasphemy against the Holy Spirit consists precisely in *the radical refusal to accept this forgiveness,* of which he is the intimate giver and which presupposes the genuine conversion which he brings about in the conscience. If Jesus says that blasphemy against the Holy Spirit cannot be forgiven either in this life or in the next, it is because this *"non-forgiveness"* is linked, as to its cause, to *"non-repentance,"* in other words to the radical refusal to be converted. This means the refusal to come to the sources of Redemption, which nevertheless remain "always" open in the economy of salvation in which the mission of the Holy Spirit is accomplished. The Spirit has infinite power to draw from these sources: "he will take what is mine," Jesus said. In this way he brings to completion in human souls the work of the Redemption accomplished by Christ, and distributes its fruits. Blasphemy against the Holy Spirit, then, is the sin committed by the person who claims to

---

[180] Mt 12:31-32.

[181] Mk 3:28-29.

[182] Lk 12:10.

[183] Saint Thomas Aquinas, *Summa Theologiae,* II-II, q. 14, a. 3; cf. Saint Augustine, *Epistula* 185, 11, 48-49: *PL* 33, 814-815; Saint Bonaventure, *Commentarium in Evangelium Sancti Lucae,* Chapter XIV, 15-16: Ad Claras Aquas, VII, 314-315.

have a *"right" to persist in evil* — in any sin at all — and who thus rejects Redemption. One closes oneself up in sin, thus making impossible one's conversion, and consequently the remission of sins, which one considers not essential or not important for one's life. This is a state of spiritual ruin, because blasphemy against the Holy Spirit does not allow one to escape from one's self-imposed imprisonment and open oneself to the divine sources of the purification of consciences and of the remission of sins.

47.1 The action of the Spirit of truth, which works toward salvific "convincing concerning sin," encounters in a person in this condition an interior resistance, as it were an impenetrability of conscience, a state of mind which could be described as fixed by reason of a free choice. This is what Sacred Scripture usually calls "hardness of heart."[184] In our own time this attitude of mind and heart is perhaps reflected in *the loss of the sense of sin*, to which the Apostolic Exhortation *Reconciliatio et Paenitentia* devotes many pages.[185] Pope Pius XII had already declared that "the sin of the century is the loss of the sense of sin,"[186] and this loss goes hand in hand with the "loss of the sense of God." In the Exhortation just mentioned we read: "In fact, God is the origin and the supreme end of man, and man carries in himself a divine seed. Hence it is the reality of God that reveals and illustrates the mystery of man. It is therefore vain to hope that there will take root a sense of sin against man and against human values, if there is no sense of offense against God, namely the true sense of sin."[187]

47.2 Hence the Church constantly implores from God the grace that *integrity of human consciences* will not be lost, that their healthy *sensitivity* with regard to good and evil will not be blunted. This integrity and sensitivity are profoundly linked to the intimate action of the Spirit of truth. In this light the exhortations of Saint Paul assume particular eloquence: *"Do not quench the Spirit"; "Do not grieve the Holy Spirit."*[188] But above all the Church constantly implores with the greatest fervor that *there will be no increase* in the world of the sin that the Gospel calls "blasphemy against the Holy Spirit." Rather, she prays that it will *decrease* in human souls — and consequently in the forms

---

[184] Cf. Ps 81:12; Jer 7:24; Mk 3:5.

[185] Post-Synodal Apostolic Exhortation *Reconciliatio et Paenitentia* (December 2, 1984), 18: *AAS* 77 (1985), 224-228.

[186] Pius XII, Radio Message to the National Catechetical Congress of the United States of America in Boston (October 26, 1946): *Discorsi e Radiomessaggi* VIII (1946), 288.

[187] Post-Synodal Apostolic Exhortation *Reconciliatio et Paenitentia* (December 2, 1984), 18: *AAS* 77 (1985), 225-226.

[188] 1 Thess 5:19; Eph 4:30.

and structures of society itself — and that it will make room for that openness of conscience necessary for the saving action of the Holy Spirit. The Church prays that the dangerous sin against the Spirit will give way to a holy readiness to accept his mission as the Counselor, when he comes to "convince the world concerning sin, and righteousness and judgment."

48.1 In his farewell discourse Jesus linked these *three areas of "convincing"* as elements of the mission of the Paraclete: sin, righteousness and judgment. They mark out the area of that *mysterium pietatis* that in human history is opposed to sin, to the *mystery of iniquity.*[189] On the one hand, as Saint Augustine says, there is "love of self to the point of contempt of God"; on the other, "love of God to the point of contempt of self."[190] The Church constantly lifts up her prayer and renders her service in order that the history of consciences and the history of societies in the great human family *will not descend toward the pole of sin,* by the rejection of God's commandments "to the point of contempt of God," but rather *will rise toward the love* in which the Spirit that gives life is revealed.

48.2 Those who let themselves be "convinced concerning sin" by the Holy Spirit, also allow themselves to be convinced "concerning righteousness and judgment." The Spirit of truth who helps human beings, human consciences, to know *the truth concerning sin,* at the same time enables them to know *the truth about that righteousness* which entered human history in Jesus Christ. In this way, those who are "convinced concerning sin" and who are converted through the action of the Counselor are, in a sense, led out of the range of the "judgment": that "judgment" by which "the ruler of this world is judged."[191] In the depths of its divine-human mystery, conversion means the breaking of every fetter by which sin binds man to the whole of the *mystery of iniquity.* Those who are converted, therefore, are led by the Holy Spirit out of the range of the "judgment," and *introduced into that righteousness* which is in Christ Jesus, and is in him precisely because he receives it from the Father,[192] as a reflection of the holiness of the Trinity. This is the righteousness of the Gospel and of the Redemption, the righteousness of the Sermon on the Mount and of the Cross, which effects the purifying of the conscience through the blood of the Lamb. It is the righteousness which *the Father gives to the Son and to all those united with him in truth and in love.*

[189] Cf. Post-Synodal Apostolic Exhortation *Reconciliatio et Paenitentia* (December 2, 1984), 14-22: *AAS* 77 (1985), 211-233.

[190] Cf. Saint Augustine, *De Civitate Dei,* XIV, 28: *CCL* 48, 451.

[191] Cf. Jn 16:11.

[192] Cf. Jn 16:15.

48.3 In this righteousness the Holy Spirit, the Spirit of the Father and the Son, who "convinces the world concerning sin," reveals himself and makes himself present in man as *the Spirit of eternal life.*

III

The Spirit Who Gives Life

Reason for the Jubilee of the year 2000: Christ who was conceived of the Holy Spirit

49.1 *The Church's mind and heart turn to the Holy Spirit as this twentieth century draws to a close and the third millennium* since the coming of Jesus Christ into the world *approaches,* and as we look toward the great Jubilee with which the Church will celebrate the event. For according to the computation of time this coming is measured as an event belonging to the history of man on earth. The measurement of time in common use defines years, centuries and millennia according to whether they come *before or after* the birth of Christ. But it must also be remembered that for us Christians this event indicates, as Saint Paul says, the *"fullness of time,"*[193] because in it human history has been wholly permeated by the "measurement" of God himself: a transcendent presence of the "eternal *now.*" He "who is, who was, and who is to come"; he who is "the Alpha and the Omega, the first and the last, the beginning and the end."[194] "For *God so loved the world that he gave his only Son,* that whoever believes in him should not perish but have *eternal life.*"[195] "When the time had finally come, God sent forth his Son, born of a woman . . . so that we might receive adoption as sons."[196] And this Incarnation of the Son-Word came about *"by the power of the Holy Spirit."*

49.2 The two Evangelists to whom we owe the narrative of the birth and infancy of Jesus of Nazareth express themselves on this matter in an identical way. *According to Luke,* at the Annunciation of the birth of Jesus, Mary asks: "How shall this be, since I have no husband?" and she receives this answer: "The Holy Spirit will come upon you, and the power of the Most High will overshadow you; therefore the child to be born will be called holy, the Son of God."[197]

[193] Cf. Gal 4:4.
[194] Rev 1:8, 22:13.
[195] Jn 3:16.
[196] Gal 4:4-5.
[197] Lk 1:34-35.

49.3 *Matthew* narrates directly: "Now the birth of Jesus Christ took place in this way. When his mother Mary had been betrothed to Joseph, before they came together she was found to be with child of the Holy Spirit."[198] Disturbed by this turn of events, Joseph receives the following explanation in a dream: "Do not fear to take Mary your wife, for that which is conceived in her is of the Holy Spirit; she will bear a son, and you shall call his name Jesus, for he will save his people from their sins."[199]

49.4 Thus from the beginning the Church confesses *the mystery of the Incarnation,* this key mystery of the faith, *by making reference to the Holy Spirit.* The *Apostles' Creed* says: "He was conceived by the power of the Holy Spirit and born of the Virgin Mary." Similarly, the *Nicene-Constantinopolitan Creed* professes: "By the power of the Holy Spirit he became incarnate from the Virgin Mary, and was made man."

49.5 "By the power of the Holy Spirit" there became man he whom the Church, in the words of the same Creed, professes to be the Son, of the same substance as the Father: "*God from God,* Light from Light, true God from true God; begotten, not made." He was made man by becoming "incarnate from the Virgin Mary." This is what happened when "the fullness of time had come."

50.1 The *great Jubilee* at the close of the second millennium, for which the Church is already preparing, has a directly *Christological aspect:* for it is a celebration of the birth of Jesus Christ. At the same time it has a *pneumatological aspect,* since the mystery of the Incarnation was accomplished "by the power of the Holy Spirit." It was "brought about" by that Spirit — consubstantial with the Father and the Son — who, in the absolute mystery of the Triune God, is the Person-love, the uncreated gift, who is the eternal source of every gift that comes from God in the order of creation, the direct principle and, in a certain sense, the subject of God's self-communication in the order of grace. The *mystery of the Incarnation constitutes the climax* of this giving, this divine self-communication.

50.2 The conception and birth of Jesus Christ are in fact the greatest work accomplished by the Holy Spirit in the history of creation and salvation: the supreme grace — "the grace of union," source of every other grace, as Saint Thomas explains.[200] The great Jubilee refers to this work and also — if we penetrate its depths — to the author of this work, *to the person of the Holy Spirit.*

50.3 For the "fullness of time" is matched by a particular fullness of the

---

[198] Mt 1:18.
[199] Mt 1:20-21.
[200] Cf. Saint Thomas Aquinas, *Summa Theologiae,* III, q. 2, aa. 10-12; q. 6, a. 6; q. 7, a. 13.

self-communication of the Triune God in the Holy Spirit. "By the power of the Holy Spirit" the mystery of the *"hypostatic union"* is brought about — that is, the union of the divine nature and the human nature, of the divinity and the humanity in the one Person of the Word-Son. When at the moment of the Annunciation Mary utters her "fiat": "Be it done unto me according to your word,"[201] she conceives in a virginal way *a man,* the Son of Man, *who is the Son of God.* By means of this "humanization" of the Word-Son, the self-communication of God reaches its definitive fullness in the history of creation and salvation. This fullness acquires a special wealth and expressiveness in the text of John's Gospel: "The Word became flesh."[202] The Incarnation of God the Son signifies the taking up into unity with God not only of human nature, but in *this human nature, in a sense, of everything that is "flesh":* the whole of humanity, the entire visible and material world. The Incarnation, then, also has a cosmic significance, a cosmic dimension. The "first-born of all creation,"[203] becoming incarnate in the individual humanity of Christ, unites himself in some way with the entire reality of man, which is also "flesh"[204] — and in this reality with all "flesh," with the whole of creation.

51.1 All this is accomplished by the power of the Holy Spirit, and so is part of the great Jubilee to come. The Church cannot *prepare* for the Jubilee in any other way than *in the Holy Spirit.* What was accomplished by the power of the Holy Spirit "in the fullness of time" can only through the Spirit's power now emerge from the memory of the Church. By his power it can be made present in the new phase of man's history on earth: the year 2000 from the birth of Christ.

51.2 The Holy Spirit, who with his power overshadowed the virginal body of *Mary,* bringing about in her *the beginning of her divine motherhood,* at the same time made her heart perfectly obedient to that self-communication of God which surpassed every human idea and faculty. "Blessed is she who believed!":[205] thus Mary is greeted by her cousin Elizabeth, herself "full of the Holy Spirit."[206] In the words of greeting addressed to *her "who believed"* we seem to detect a distant (but in fact very close) contrast with all those about whom Christ will say that "they do not believe."[207] Mary entered the history of

---

[201] Lk 1:38.

[202] Jn 1:14.

[203] Col 1:15.

[204] Cf., for example, Gen 9:11; Dt 5:26; Job 34:15; Is 40:6, 42:10; Ps 145:21; Lk 3:6; 1 Pet 1:24.

[205] Lk 1:45.

[206] Cf. Lk 1:41.

[207] Cf. Jn 16:9.

the salvation of the world through the obedience of faith. And *faith*, in its deepest essence, is *the openness* of the human heart to the gift: *to God's self-communication in the Holy Spirit*. Saint Paul writes: "The Lord is the Spirit, and where the Spirit of the Lord is, there is freedom."[208] When the Triune God opens himself to man in the Holy Spirit, this opening of God reveals and also gives to the human creature the fullness of freedom. This fullness was manifested in a sublime way precisely through the faith of Mary, through the "obedience of faith":[209] truly, "Blessed is she who believed!"

Reason for the Jubilee: grace has been made manifest

52.1 In the mystery of the Incarnation the *work of the Spirit "who gives life"* reaches its highest point. It is not possible to give life, which in its fullest form is in God, except by making it the life of *a Man*, as Christ is in his humanity endowed with personhood by the Word in the hypostatic union. And at the same time, with the mystery of the Incarnation there opens in a new way *the source of this divine life in the history of mankind:* the Holy Spirit. The Word, "the first-born of all creation," becomes "the first-born of many brethren."[210] And thus he also becomes the head of the Body which is the Church, which will be born on the Cross and revealed on the day of Pentecost — and in the Church, he becomes the head of humanity: of the people of every nation, every race, every country and culture, every language and continent, all called to salvation. "The Word became flesh, (that Word in whom) *was life* and the life was the light of men . . . *to all* who received him *he gave the power to become the children of God.*"[211] But all this was accomplished and is unceasingly accomplished "by the power of the Holy Spirit."

52.2 For as Saint Paul teaches, *"all who are led by the Spirit of God"* are "children of God."[212] The filiation of divine adoption is born in man on the basis of the mystery of the Incarnation, therefore through Christ the eternal Son. But the birth, or *rebirth.* happens *when God the Father "sends the Spirit of his Son into our hearts."*[213] Then "we receive a spirit of adopted sons by which we cry 'Abba, Father!' "[214] Hence the divine filiation planted in the human soul through sanctifying grace is the work of the Holy Spirit. "It is the Spirit himself bearing witness with our spirit that we are children of God, and

---

[208] 2 Cor 3:17.
[209] Cf. Rom 1:5.
[210] Rom 8:29.
[211] Cf. Jn 1:14, 1:12-13.
[212] Cf. Rom 8:14.
[213] Cf. Gal 4:6; Rom 5:5; 2 Cor 1:22.
[214] Rom 8:15.

if children, then heirs, *heirs of God and fellow heirs with Christ.*"[215] Sanctifying grace is the principle and source of man's new life: divine, supernatural life.

52.3 The giving of this new life is as it were God's definitive answer to the Psalmist's words, which in a way echo the voice of all creatures: "When you send forth your Spirit, they shall be created; and you shall renew the face of the earth."[216] He who in the mystery of creation *gives life* to man and the cosmos in its many different forms, visible and invisible, again *renews* this life through the mystery of the Incarnation. Creation is thus completed by the Incarnation and since that moment is permeated by the powers of the Redemption, powers which fill humanity and all creation. This is what we are told by Saint Paul, whose cosmic and theological vision seems to repeat the words of the ancient Psalm: creation "waits with eager longing for *the revealing of the sons of God,*"[217] that is, those whom God has "foreknown" and whom he "has predestined to be conformed to the image of his Son."[218] Thus there is a supernatural "adoption," of which the source is the Holy Spirit, love and gift. *As such he is given to man.* And in the *superabundance of the uncreated gift there begins* in the heart of all human beings that particular *created gift* whereby they "become partakers of the divine nature."[219] Thus human life becomes permeated, through participation, by the divine life, and itself acquires a divine, supernatural dimension. There is granted the *new life,* in which as a sharer in the mystery of Incarnation "man has access to the Father in the Holy Spirit."[220] Thus there is a close relationship *between the Spirit* who gives life and *sanctifying grace* and the manifold *supernatural vitality* which derives from it in man: between the uncreated Spirit and the created human spirit.

53.1 *All this* may be said to fall within the scope of the great Jubilee mentioned above. For we must go beyond the historical dimension of the event considered in its surface value. Through the Christological content of the event we have to reach the pneumatological dimension, seeing with the eyes of faith the *two thousand years of the action of the Spirit of truth,* who down the centuries has drawn from the treasures of the Redemption achieved by Christ and given new life to human beings, bringing about in

[215] Rom 8:16-17.
[216] Cf. Ps 104:30.
[217] Rom 8:19.
[218] Rom 8:29.
[219] Cf. 2 Pet 1:4.
[220] Cf. Eph 2:18; Dogmatic Constitution on Divine Revelation *Dei Verbum,* 2.

them adoption in the only-begotten Son, sanctifying them, so that they can repeat with Saint Paul: "We have received . . . the Spirit which is from God."[221]

53.2 But as we follow this reason for the Jubilee, we cannot limit ourselves to the two thousand years which have passed since the birth of Christ. *We need to go further back*, to embrace the whole of the action of the Holy Spirit even before Christ — *from the beginning*, throughout the world, and especially in the economy of the Old Covenant. For this action has been exercised, in every place and at every time, indeed in every individual, according to the eternal plan of salvation, whereby this action was to be closely linked with the mystery of the Incarnation and Redemption, which in its turn exercised its influence on those who believed in the future coming of Christ. This is attested to especially in the *Letter to the Ephesians*.[222] Grace, therefore, bears within itself both a Christological aspect and a pneumatological one, which becomes evident above all in those who expressly accept Christ: "In him [in Christ] you . . . were sealed with the promised Holy Spirit, which is the guarantee of our inheritance, until we acquire possession of it."[223]

53.3 But, still within the perspective of the great Jubilee, we need to look further and go further afield, knowing that "the wind blows where it wills," according to the image used by Jesus in his conversation with Nicodemus.[224] The Second Vatican Council, centered primarily on the theme of the Church, reminds us of the Holy Spirit's activity also *"outside the visible body of the Church."* The Council speaks precisely of "all people of good will in whose hearts grace works in an unseen way. For, since Christ died for all, and since the ultimate vocation of man is in fact one, and divine, we ought to believe that the Holy Spirit in a manner known only to God offers to every man the possibility of being associated with this Paschal Mystery."[225]

54.1 "God is spirit, and those who worship him must worship *in spirit and truth*."[226] These words were spoken by Jesus in another conversation, the one with the Samaritan woman. The great Jubilee to be celebrated at the end of this millennium and at the beginning of the next ought to constitute a powerful call to all those who "worship God in spirit and truth." It should be for

---

[221] Cf. 1 Cor 2:12.

[222] Cf. Eph 1:3-14.

[223] Eph 1:13-14.

[224] Cf. Jn 3:8.

[225] Pastoral Constitution on the Church in the Modern World *Gaudium et Spes*, 22; cf. Dogmatic Constitution on the Church *Lumen Gentium*, 16.

[226] Jn 4:24.

everyone a special occasion for meditating on the mystery of the Triune God, who *in himself* is *wholly transcendent* with regard to the world, especially the visible world. For he is absolute Spirit, "God is spirit";[227] and also, in such a marvelous way, he is not only *close to this world* but *present* in it, and in a sense *immanent,* penetrating it and giving it life from within. This is especially true in relation to man: God is present in the intimacy of man's being, in his mind, conscience and heart: an ontological and psychological reality, in considering which Saint Augustine said of God that he was *"closer than my inmost being."*[228] These words help us to understand better the words of Jesus to the Samaritan woman: "God is spirit." Only the Spirit can be *"closer than my inmost being,"* both in my existence and in my spiritual experience. Only the Spirit can be so immanent in man and in the world, while remaining inviolable and immutable in his absolute transcendence.

54.2 But in Jesus Christ the divine presence in the world and in man has been made manifest in a new way and in visible form. In him "the grace of God has appeared indeed."[229] The love of God the Father, as a gift, infinite grace, source of life, has been made visible in Christ, and in his humanity that love has become "part" of the universe, the human family and history. This appearing of grace in human history, through Jesus Christ, has been accomplished through the power of the Holy Spirit, who is *the source of all God's salvific activity in the world:* he, the "hidden God,"[230] who as love and gift "fills the universe."[231] The Church's entire life, as will appear in the great Jubilee, means going to meet the invisible God, the hidden God: a meeting with the Spirit "who gives life."

The Holy Spirit in man's inner conflict: "For the desires of the flesh are against the Spirit, and the desires of the Spirit are against the flesh"

55.1 Unfortunately, the history of salvation shows that God's coming close and making himself present to man and the world, that marvelous "condescension" of the Spirit, *meets with resistance and opposition* in our human reality. How eloquent from this point of view are the prophetic words of the old man Simeon who, inspired by the Spirit, came to the Temple in Jerusalem, in order to foretell in the presence of the new-born Babe of Bethlehem that he "is set for the fall and rising of many in Israel, for *a sign of contradiction.*"[232]

---

[227] Jn 4:24.
[228] Cf. Saint Augustine, *Confessiones,* III, 6, 11: *CCL* 27, 33.
[229] Cf. Tit 2:11.
[230] Cf. Is 45:15.
[231] Cf. Wis 1:7.
[232] Lk 2:27, 34.

Opposition to God, who is an invisible Spirit, to a certain degree originates in the very fact of the radical difference of the world from God, that is to say in the world's "visibility" and "materiality" in contrast to him who is "invisible" and "absolute Spirit"; from the world's essential and inevitable imperfection in contrast to him, the perfect being. But this opposition becomes conflict and rebellion on the ethical plane by reason of that *sin* which takes possession of the *human heart*, wherein "the desires of the flesh are against the Spirit and the desires of the Spirit are against the flesh."[233] Concerning this sin, the Holy Spirit must "convince the world," as we have already said.

55.2 It is Saint Paul who describes in a particularly eloquent way the tension and struggle that trouble the human heart. We read in the *Letter to the Galatians:* "But I say, *walk by the Spirit, and do not gratify the desires of the flesh.* For the desires of the flesh are against the Spirit, and the desires of the Spirit are against the flesh; for these are opposed to each other, to prevent you from doing what you would."[234] There already exists in man, as *a being made up* of body and spirit, a certain tension, a certain struggle of tendencies between the "spirit" and the "flesh." But this struggle in fact belongs to the heritage of sin, is a consequence of sin and at the same time a confirmation of it. This is part of everyday experience. As the Apostle writes: "*Now the works of the flesh* are plain: fornication, impurity, licentiousness ... drunkenness, carousing and the like." These are the sins that could be called "carnal." But he also adds others: "enmity, strife, jealousy, anger, selfishness, dissension, party spirit, envy."[235] All of this constitutes the "works of the flesh."

55.3 But with these works, which are undoubtedly evil, Paul contrasts "the fruit of the Spirit," such as "love, joy, peace, patience, kindness, goodness, faithfulness, gentleness, self-control."[236] From the context it is clear that for the Apostle it is not a question of discriminating against and condemning the body, which with the spiritual soul constitutes man's nature and personal subjectivity. Rather, he is concerned with the morally *good or bad works,* or better the permanent dispositions — virtues and vices — which are the *fruit of submission to* (in the first case) or of *resistance to* (in the second case) *the saving action of the Holy Spirit.* Consequently the Apostle writes: "If we live by the Spirit, let us also walk by the Spirit."[237] And in other passages: "For those who live according to the flesh set their minds on the things of the flesh, but

---

[233] Gal 5:17.
[234] Gal 5:16-17.
[235] Cf. Gal 5:19-21.
[236] Gal 5:22-23.
[237] Gal 5:25.

those who live according to the Spirit set their minds on the things of the Spirit"; "You are in the Spirit, if in fact the Spirit of God dwells in you."[238] The contrast that Saint Paul makes between life "according to the Spirit" and life "according to the flesh" gives rise to a further contrast: *that between "life" and "death."* "To set the mind on the flesh is death, but to set the mind on the Spirit is life and peace"; hence the warning: "For if you live according to the flesh you will die, but if by the Spirit you put to death the deeds of the body you will live."[239]

55.4 Properly understood, this is *an exhortation to live in the truth,* that is, according to the dictates of an upright conscience, and at the same time it is a profession of faith in the Spirit of truth as the one who gives life. For the body is "dead because of sin, but your spirits are alive because of righteousness." "So then, brethren, we are *debtors, not to the flesh,* to live according to the flesh."[240] Rather we are debtors to *Christ,* who in the Paschal Mystery has effected our justification, obtaining for us the Holy Spirit: "Indeed, we have been bought at a great price."[241]

55.5 In the texts of Saint Paul there is a superimposing — and a mutual compenetration — of *the ontological dimension* (the flesh and the spirit), the *ethical* (moral good and evil), and the *pneumatological* (the action of the Holy Spirit in the order of grace). His words (especially in the *Letters to the Romans* and *Galatians*) enable us to know and feel vividly the strength of the tension and struggle going on in man between openness to the action of the Holy Spirit and resistance and opposition to him, to his saving gift. The terms or poles of contrast are, on man's part, his limitation and sinfulness, which are essential elements of his psychological and ethical reality; and on God's part, *the mystery of the gift,* that unceasing self-giving of divine life in the Holy Spirit. Who will win? The one who welcomes the gift.

56.1 Unfortunately, the resistance to the Holy Spirit which Saint Paul emphasizes in the *interior and subjective dimension* as tension, struggle and rebellion taking place in the human heart, finds in every period of history and especially in the modern era its *external dimension,* which takes concrete form as the content of culture and civilization, as *a philosophical system, an ideology, a program* for action and for the shaping of human behavior. It reaches its clearest expression in *materialism,* both in its theoretical form: as a system

---

[238] Cf. Rom 8:5, 9.
[239] Rom 8:6, 13.
[240] Rom 8:10, 12.
[241] Cf. 1 Cor 6:20.

of thought, and in its practical form: as a method of interpreting and evaluating facts, and likewise as a program of corresponding conduct. The system which has developed most and carried to its extreme practical consequences this form of thought, ideology and praxis is dialectical and historical materialism, which is still recognized as the essential core of Marxism.

56.2 In principle and in fact, materialism radically *excludes* the presence and action of God, who is spirit, in the world and above all in man. Fundamentally this is because it *does not accept God's existence,* being a system that is essentially and systematically atheistic. This is the striking phenomenon of our time: atheism, to which the Second Vatican Council devoted some significant pages.[242] Even though it is not possible to speak of atheism in a univocal way or to limit it exclusively to the philosophy of materialism, since there exist numerous forms of atheism and the word is perhaps often used in a wrong sense, nevertheless it is certain that *a true and proper materialism,* understood as a theory which explains reality and accepted as the key principle of personal and social action, *is characteristically atheistic. The order of values and the aims of action* which it describes are strictly bound to a reading of the whole of reality as "matter." Though it sometimes also speaks of the "spirit" and of "questions of the spirit," as for example in the fields of culture or morality, it does so only insofar as it considers certain facts as derived from matter (*epiphenomena*), since according to this system matter is the one and only form of being. It follows, according to this interpretation, that religion can only be understood as a kind of "idealistic illusion," to be fought with the most suitable means and methods according to circumstances of time and place, in order to eliminate it from society and from man's very heart.

56.3 It can be said therefore that materialism is the systematic and logical development of that "resistance" and opposition condemned by Saint Paul with the words: "The desires of *the flesh* are against the Spirit." But, as Saint Paul emphasizes in the second part of his aphorism, this antagonism is mutual: "The desires of the Spirit are against the flesh." Those who wish to live by the Spirit, accepting and corresponding to his salvific activity, cannot but reject the internal and external tendencies and claims of the "flesh," also in its ideological and historical expression as anti-religious "materialism." Against this background so characteristic of our time, in preparing for the great Jubilee we must emphasize the "desires of the Spirit," as exhortations echoing in the night of a new time of advent, at the end of which, like two thousand years ago, "every man will see the salvation of God."[243] This is a possibility and a

---

[242] Cf. Pastoral Constitution on the Church in the Modern World *Gaudium et Spes,* 19-21.
[243] Lk 3:6; cf. Is 40:5.

hope that the Church entrusts to the men and women of today. She knows that the meeting or collision between the "desires against the Spirit" *which mark so many aspects of contemporary civilization,* especially in some of its spheres, and "the desires against the flesh," with God's approach to us, his Incarnation, his constantly renewed communication of the Holy Spirit — this meeting or collision may in many cases be of a tragic nature and may perhaps lead to fresh defeats for humanity. But the Church firmly believes that on God's part there is always a salvific self-giving, a salvific coming and, in some way or other, a salvific "convincing concerning sin" by the power of the Spirit.

57.1 The Pauline contrast between the "Spirit" and the "flesh" also includes the contrast between "life" and "death." This is a serious problem, and concerning it one must say at once that materialism, as a system of thought, in all its forms, means *the acceptance of death* as the definitive *end of human existence.* Everything that is material is corruptible, and therefore the human body (insofar as it is "animal") is mortal. If man in his essence is only "flesh," death remains for him an impassable frontier and limit. Hence one can understand how it can be said that human life is nothing but an "existence in order to die."

57.2 It must be added that on the horizon of contemporary civilization — especially in the form that is most developed in the technical and scientific sense — *the signs and symptoms of death* have become particularly present and frequent. One has only to think of the arms race and of its inherent danger of nuclear self-destruction. Moreover, everyone has become more and more aware of the grave situation of vast areas of our planet marked by death-dealing poverty and famine. It is a question of problems that are not only economic but also and above all ethical. But on the horizon of our era there are gathering ever darker "signs of death": a custom has become widely established — in some places it threatens to become almost an institution — of taking the lives of human beings even before they are born, or before they reach the natural point of death. Furthermore, despite many noble efforts for peace, new wars have broken out and are taking place, wars which destroy the lives or the health of hundreds of thousands of people. And how can one fail to mention the attacks against human life by terrorism, organized even on an international scale?

57.3 Unfortunately, this is only a partial and incomplete sketch of the *picture of death* being composed in *our age* as we come ever closer to the end of the second millennium of the Christian era. Does there not rise up a new and more or less conscious plea to the life-giving Spirit from the dark shades of materialistic civilization, and especially from those increasing *signs of death* in the sociological and historical picture in which that civilization has been constructed? At any rate, even independently of the measure of human hopes or despairs, and of the illusions or deceptions deriving from the development of materialistic systems of thought and life, *there remains the Christian certainty* that the Spirit blows where he wills and that we possess "the first fruits of the Spirit," and that therefore even though we may be subjected to the sufferings of time that passes away, *"we groan inwardly as we wait for . . . the redemption of our bodies,"*[244] or of all our human essence, which is bodily and spiritual. Yes, we groan, but in an expectation filled with unflagging hope, because it is precisely this human being that God has drawn near to, God who is Spirit. God the Father, "sending his own Son in the likeness of sinful flesh and for sin, he condemned sin in the flesh."[245] At the culmination of the Paschal Mystery, the Son of God, made man and crucified for the sins of the world, appeared in the midst of his Apostles after the Resurrection, breathed on them and said, "Receive the Holy Spirit." *This "breath" continues forever,* for *"the Spirit helps us in our weakness."*[246]

The Holy Spirit strengthens the "inner man"

58.1 The mystery of the Resurrection and of Pentecost is proclaimed and lived by the Church, which has inherited and which carries on the witness of the Apostles about the Resurrection of Jesus Christ. She is the perennial witness to this victory over death which revealed the power of the Holy Spirit and determined his new coming, his new presence in people and in the world. For in Christ's Resurrection the Holy Spirit-Paraclete revealed himself especially as he who gives life: "He who raised Christ from the dead will give life to your mortal bodies also through his Spirit which dwells in you."[247] *In the name of the Resurrection of Christ the Church proclaims life,* which manifested itself beyond the limits of death, the life which is stronger than death. At the same time, she proclaims *him who gives this life:* the Spirit, *the Giver of life;* she proclaims him and cooperates with him in giving life. For "although your bodies are dead because of sin, your spirits are alive because of righteousness,"[248] the righteousness accomplished by the crucified and risen Christ. And in the name of Christ's Resurrection the Church serves the life that comes from God himself, in close union with and humble service to the Spirit.

[244] Cf. Rom 8:23.
[245] Rom 8:3.
[246] Rom 8:26.
[247] Rom 8:11.
[248] Rom 8:10.

58.2 Precisely through this service man becomes in an ever new manner the "way of the Church," as I said in the Encyclical on Christ the Redeemer[249] and as I now repeat in this present one on the Holy Spirit. United with the Spirit, the Church is supremely aware of the reality of *the inner man*, of what is deepest and most essential in man, *because it is spiritual and incorruptible.* At this level the Spirit grafts the "root of immortality,"[250] from which the new life springs. This is man's life in God, which, as a fruit of God's salvific self-communication in the Holy Spirit, can develop and flourish only by the Spirit's action. Therefore Saint Paul speaks to God on behalf of believers, to whom he declares, "I bow my knees before the Father . . . , that he may grant you . . . *to be strengthened with might through his Spirit in the inner man."*[251]

58.3 Under the influence of the Holy Spirit, this inner, "spiritual" man matures and grows strong. Thanks to the divine self-communication, the human spirit which "knows the secrets of man" meets the "Spirit who searches everything, even the depths of God."[252] *In this Spirit,* who is the eternal gift, *the Triune God opens himself to man,* to the human spirit. The hidden breath of the divine Spirit enables the human spirit to open in its turn before the saving and sanctifying self-opening of God. Through the gift of grace, which comes from the Holy Spirit, man enters a *"new life,"* is brought into the supernatural reality of the divine life itself and becomes a "dwelling-place of the Holy Spirit," a living temple of God.[253] For through the Holy Spirit, the Father and the Son come to him and take up their abode with him.[254] In the communion of grace with the Trinity, man's "living area" is broadened and raised up to the supernatural level of divine life. *Man lives in God and by God:* he lives "according to the Spirit," and "sets his mind on the things of the Spirit."

59.1 Man's intimate relationship with God in the Holy Spirit also enables him to understand himself, his own humanity, in a new way. Thus that image

---

[249] Cf. Encyclical Letter *Redemptor Hominis* (March 4, 1979), 14: *AAS* 71 (1979), 284-285.

[250] Cf. Wis 15:3.

[251] Cf. Eph 3:14-16.

[252] Cf. 1 Cor 2:10-11.

[253] Cf. Rom 8:9; 1 Cor 6:19.

[254] Cf. Jn 14:23; Saint Irenaeus, *Adversus Haereses,* V, 6, 1: *SCh* 153, 72-80; Saint Hilary, *De Trinitate*, VIII, 19, 21: *PL* 10, 250, 252; Saint Ambrose, *De Spiritu Sancto,* I, 6, 8: *PL* 16, 752-753; Saint Augustine, *Enarratio in Psalmum XLIX*, 2: *CCL* 38, 575-576; Saint Cyril of Alexandria, *In Ioannis Evangelium,* Book I: *PG* 73, 154-158; Book II: *PG* 73, 246; Book IX: *PG* 74, 262; Saint Athanasius, *Oratio III contra Arianos*, 24: *PG* 26, 374-375; *Epistula I ad Serapionem*, 24: *PG* 26, 586-587; Didymus the Blind, *De Trinitate*, II, 6-7: *PG* 39, 523-530; Saint John Chrysostom, *In Epistulam ad Romanos*, Homily XIII, 8: *PG* 60, 519; Saint Thomas Aquinas, *Summa Theologiae*, I, q. 43, aa. 1, 3-6.

and likeness of God which man is from his very beginning is fully realized.[255] This intimate truth of the human being has to be continually rediscovered in the light of Christ who is the prototype of the relationship with God. There also has to be rediscovered in Christ the reason for "full self-discovery through a sincere gift of himself" to others, as the Second Vatican Council writes: precisely by reason of this divine likeness which "shows that on earth man . . . is the only creature that God wishes for himself" in his dignity as a person, but as one open to integration and social communion.[256] The effective knowledge and full implementation of this truth of his being come about *only by the power of the Holy Spirit.* Man learns this truth from Jesus Christ and puts it into practice in his own life by the power of the Spirit, whom Jesus himself has given to us.

59.2 Along this path — the path of such an inner maturity, which includes the full discovery of the meaning of humanity — God comes close to man, and permeates more and more completely the whole human world. *The Triune God,* who "exists" in himself as a transcendent reality of interpersonal gift, *giving himself in the Holy Spirit as gift to man, transforms the human world from within,* from inside hearts and minds. Along this path the world, made to share in the divine gift, becomes — as the Council teaches — "ever more human, ever more profoundly human,"[257] while within the world, through people's hearts and minds, the Kingdom develops in which God will be definitively "all in all":[258] as gift and love. Gift and love: this is the eternal power of the opening of the Triune God to man and the world, in the Holy Spirit.

59.3 *As the year 2000* since the birth of Christ *draws near,* it is a question of ensuring that an ever greater number of people "may fully find themselves . . . through a sincere gift of self," according to the expression of the Council already quoted. Through the action of the Spirit-Paraclete, may there be accomplished in our world a process of true growth in humanity, in both individual and community life. In this regard Jesus himself "when he prayed to the Father, 'that all may be one . . . as we are one' (Jn 17:21-22) . . . *implied* a certain *likeness* between the union of the divine persons and the union *of the children of God in truth and charity.*"[259] The Council repeats this truth about man, and the Church sees in it a particularly strong and conclusive indication

---

[255] Cf. Gen 1:26-27; Saint Thomas Aquinas, *Summa Theologiae,* I, q. 93, aa. 4, 5, 8.

[256] Cf. Pastoral Constitution on the Church in the Modern World *Gaudium et Spes,* 24; cf. also 25.

[257] Cf. ibid., 38, 40.

[258] Cf. 1 Cor 15:28.

[259] Cf. Pastoral Constitution on the Church in the Modern World *Gaudium et Spes,* 24.

of her own apostolic tasks. For if man is the way of the Church, this way passes through the whole mystery of Christ, as man's divine model. Along this way the Holy Spirit, strengthening in each of us "the inner man," enables man ever more "fully to find himself through a sincere gift of self." These words of the Pastoral Constitution of the Council can be said to sum up *the whole of Christian anthropology:* that theory and practice, based on the Gospel, in which man discovers himself as belonging to Christ and discovers that in Christ he is raised to the status of a child of God, and so understands better his own dignity as man, precisely because he is the subject of God's approach and presence, the subject of the divine condescension, which contains the prospect and the very root of definitive glorification. Thus it can truly be said that "the glory of God is the living man, yet man's life is the vision of God":[260] man, living a divine life, is the glory of God, and the Holy Spirit is the hidden dispenser of this life and this glory. The Holy Spirit — says Basil the Great — "while simple in essence and manifold in his virtues . . . extends himself without undergoing any diminishing, is present in each subject capable of receiving him as if he were the only one, and gives grace which is sufficient for all."[261]

60.1 When, under the influence of the Paraclete, people discover this divine dimension of their being and life, both as individuals and as a community, they are able *to free themselves from the various determinisms* which derive mainly from the materialistic bases of thought, practice and related modes of action. In our age these factors have succeeded in penetrating into man's inmost being, into that sanctuary of the conscience where the Holy Spirit continuously radiates the light and strength of new life in the "freedom of the children of God." Man's growth in this life is hindered by the conditionings and pressures exerted upon him by dominating structures and mechanisms in the various spheres of society. It can be said that in many cases social factors, instead of fostering the development and expansion of the human spirit, ultimately deprive the human spirit of the genuine truth of its being and life — over which the Holy Spirit keeps vigil — in order to subject it to the "prince of this world."

60.2 The great Jubilee of the year 2000 thus contains a message of liberation by the power of the Spirit, who alone can help individuals and communities to free themselves from the old and new determinisms, by guiding them with the "law of the Spirit, which gives life in Christ Jesus,"[262] and thereby

[260] Cf. Saint Irenaeus, *Adversus Haereses*, IV, 20, 7: SCh 100/2, 648.
[261] Saint Basil, *De Spiritu Sancto*, IX, 22: PG 32, 110.
[262] Rom 8:2.

discovering and accomplishing the full measure of man's true freedom. For, as Saint Paul writes, "where the Spirit of the Lord is, there is freedom."[263] This revelation of freedom and hence of man's true dignity acquires a particular eloquence for Christians and for the Church in a state of persecution — both in ancient times and in the present — because the witnesses to divine Truth then become a living proof of the action of the Spirit of truth present in the hearts and minds of the faithful, and they often mark with their own death by martyrdom the supreme glorification of human dignity.

60.3 Also in the ordinary conditions of society, Christians, as *witnesses to man's authentic dignity*, by their obedience to the Holy Spirit contribute to the manifold "renewal of the face of the earth," working together with their brothers and sisters in order to achieve and put to good use everything that is good, noble and beautiful in the modern progress of civilization, culture, science, technology and the other areas of thought and human activity.[264] They do this as disciples of Christ who — as the Council writes — "appointed Lord by his Resurrection . . . is now at work in the hearts of men *through the power of his Spirit.* He arouses not only a desire for the age to come but by that very fact, he animates, purifies and strengthens those noble longings too by which the human family strives to make its life more humane and to render the earth submissive to this goal."[265] Thus they affirm still more strongly the greatness of man, made in the image and likeness of God, a greatness shown by the mystery of the Incarnation of the Son of God, who "in the fullness of time," by the power of the Holy Spirit, entered into history and manifested himself as true man, he who was begotten before every creature, "through whom are all things and through whom we exist."[266]

The Church as the sacrament of intimate union with God

61.1 As the end of the second millennium approaches, an event which should recall to everyone and as it were make present anew the coming of the Word in the fullness of time, the Church once more *means to ponder the very essence of* her *divine-human* constitution and of that *mission* which enables her to share in the messianic mission of Christ, according to the teaching and the ever valid plan of the Second Vatican Council. Following this line, we can go back to the Upper Room, where Jesus Christ reveals the Holy Spirit as the

---

[263] 2 Cor 3:17.

[264] Cf. Second Vatican Ecumenical Council, Pastoral Constitution on the Church in the Modern World *Gaudium et Spes*, 53-59.

[265] Ibid., 38.

[266] 1 Cor 8:6.

Paraclete, the Spirit of truth, and where he speaks of his own "departure" through the Cross as the necessary condition for the Spirit's "coming": "It is to your advantage that I go away, for if I do not go away, the Counselor will not come to you; but if I go, I will send him to you."[267] We have seen that this prediction first came true the evening of Easter Day and then during the celebration of Pentecost in Jerusalem, and we have seen that ever since then it is being fulfilled in human history through the Church.

61.2 In the light of that prediction, we also grasp the full meaning of *what Jesus says*, also at the Last Supper, *about his new "coming."* For it is significant that in the same farewell discourse Jesus foretells not only his "departure" but also his new "coming." His exact words are: "I will not leave you desolate; *I will come to you.*"[268] And at the moment of his final farewell before he ascends into heaven, he will repeat even more explicitly: "Lo, *I am with you*," and this "always, to the close of the age."[269] This new "coming" of Christ, this continuous coming of his, in order to be with his Apostles, with the Church, this "I am with you always, to the close of the age," does not of course change the fact of his "departure." It follows that departure, after the close of Christ's messianic activity on earth, and it occurs *in the context of the predicted sending of the Holy Spirit* and in a certain sense forms part of *his own mission.* And yet it occurs *by the power of the Holy* Spirit, who makes it possible for Christ, who has gone away, to come now and for ever in a new way. This new coming of Christ by the power of the Holy Spirit and his constant presence and action in the spiritual life are accomplished *in the sacramental reality.* In this reality, Christ, who has gone away in his visible humanity, comes, is present and acts in the Church in such an intimate way as to make it his own Body. As such, the Church lives, works and grows "to the close of the age." All this happens through the power of the Holy Spirit.

62.1 The most complete sacramental expression of the "departure" of Christ through the mystery of the Cross and Resurrection is the *Eucharist.* In every celebration of the Eucharist his coming, his salvific presence, is sacramentally realized: in the Sacrifice and in Communion. It is accomplished by the power of the Holy Spirit, as part of his own mission.[270] Through the Eucharist

---

[267] Jn 16:7.

[268] Jn 14:18.

[269] Mt 28:20.

[270] This is what the "Epiclesis" before the Consecration expresses: "Let your Spirit come upon these gifts to make them holy, so that they may become for us the Body and Blood of our Lord, Jesus Christ" (Eucharistic Prayer II).

the Holy Spirit accomplishes that *"strengthening of the inner man"* spoken of in the *Letter to the Ephesians.*[271] Through the Eucharist, individuals and communities, by the action of the Paraclete-Counselor, learn to discover the divine sense of human life, as spoken of by the Council: that sense whereby Jesus Christ "fully reveals man to man himself," suggesting "a certain likeness between *the union of the divine Persons,* and the union of God's children in truth and charity."[272] This union is expressed and made real especially through the Eucharist, in which man shares in the sacrifice of Christ which this celebration actualizes, and he also learns to "find himself . . . through a . . . gift of himself,"[273] through communion with God and with others, his brothers and sisters.

62.2 For this reason the early Christians, right from the days immediately following the coming down of the Holy Spirit, "devoted themselves to the breaking of bread and the prayers," and in this way they formed a community united by the teaching of the Apostles.[274] Thus "they recognized" that their risen Lord, who had ascended into heaven, came *into* their midst *anew in that Eucharistic community* of the Church and *by means of it.* Guided by the Holy Spirit, the Church from the beginning *expressed* and *confirmed* her identity through the Eucharist. And so it has always been, in every Christian generation, down to our own time, down to this present period when we await the end of the second Christian millennium. Of course, we unfortunately have to acknowledge the fact that the millennium which is about to end is the one in which there have occurred the great separations between Christians. All believers in Christ, therefore, following the example of the Apostles, must fervently strive to conform their thinking and action to the will of the Holy Spirit, "the principle of the Church's unity,"[275] so that all who have been baptized in the one Spirit in order to make up one body may be brethren joined in the celebration of the same Eucharist, "a sacrament of love, a sign of unity, a bond of charity!"[276]

63.1 Christ's Eucharistic presence, his sacramental "I am with you," enables the Church to *discover* ever more deeply *her own mystery,* as shown by the whole ecclesiology of the Second Vatican Council, whereby "the Church is

---

[271] Cf. Eph 3:16.

[272] Pastoral Constitution on the Church in the Modern World *Gaudium et Spes,* 24.

[273] Ibid., 24.

[274] Cf. Acts 2:42.

[275] Second Vatican Ecumenical Council, Decree on Ecumenism *Unitatis Redintegratio,* 2.

[276] Saint Augustine, *In Iohannis Evangelium Tractatus,* 26, 13: *CCL* 36, 266; cf. Second Vatican Ecumenical Council, Constitution on the Sacred Liturgy *Sacrosanctum Concilium,* 47.

in Christ as a sacrament or sign and instrument of the intimate union with God and of the unity of the whole human race."[277] *As a sacrament,* the Church is a development from the Paschal Mystery of Christ's "departure," living by his ever new "coming" by the power of the Holy Spirit, within the same mission of the Paraclete-Spirit of truth. Precisely this is the essential mystery of the Church, as the Council professes.

63.2 While it is through creation that God is he in whom we all "live and move and have our being,"[278] in its turn *the power of the Redemption* endures and develops in the history of man and the world in a double "rhythm" as it were, the source of which is found in the Eternal Father. On the one hand there is the rhythm *of the mission of the Son,* who came into the world and was born of the Virgin Mary by the power of the Holy Spirit; and on the other hand there is also the rhythm *of the mission of the Holy Spirit,* as he was revealed definitively by Christ. Through the "departure" of the Son, the Holy Spirit came and continues to come as Counselor and Spirit of truth. And in the context of his mission, as it were within the invisible presence of the Holy Spirit, the Son, who "had gone away" in the Paschal Mystery, "comes" and is continuously *present in the mystery of the Church,* at times concealing himself and at times revealing himself in her history, and always directing her steps. All of this happens in a sacramental way, through the power of the Holy Spirit, who, "drawing from the wealth of Christ's Redemption," constantly gives life. As the Church becomes ever more aware of this mystery, she sees herself more clearly, above all as a sacrament.

63.3 This also happens because, by the will of her Lord, *through the individual sacraments the Church fulfills her salvific ministry* to man. This sacramental ministry, every time it is accomplished, brings with it the mystery of the "departure" of Christ through the Cross and the Resurrection, by virtue of which the Holy Spirit comes. He comes and works: "he gives life." For the sacraments signify grace and confer grace: *they signify life and give life.* The Church is the *visible dispenser* of the sacred signs, while the Holy Spirit acts in them as the *invisible dispenser* of the life which they signify. Together with the Spirit, Christ Jesus is present and acting.

64.1 If the Church is the sacrament of intimate union with God, she is such in Jesus Christ, in whom this same union is accomplished as a *salvific reality.* She is such in Jesus Christ, through the power of the Holy Spirit. The fullness of the salvific reality, which is Christ in history, *extends* in a sacra-

---

[277] Dogmatic Constitution on the Church *Lumen Gentium,* 1.
[278] Acts 17:28.

mental way *in the power of the Spirit-Paraclete.* In this way the Holy Spirit is "another Counselor," or new Counselor, because through his action the Good News takes shape in human minds and hearts and extends through history. In all this it is the Holy Spirit who gives life.

64.2 When we use the word "sacrament" in reference to the Church, we must bear in mind that in the texts of the Council *the sacramentality of the Church* appears as distinct from the sacramentality that is proper, in the strict sense, to the sacraments. Thus we read: "The Church is . . . *in the nature of a sacrament* — a sign and instrument of communion with God." But what matters and what emerges from the analogical sense in which the word is used in the two cases is the relationship which the Church has with the power of the Holy Spirit, who alone gives life: the Church is the sign and instrument of the presence and action of the life-giving Spirit.

64.3 Vatican II adds that the Church is *"a sacrament . . . of the unity of all mankind."* Obviously it is a question of the unity which the human race — which in itself is differentiated in various ways — *has from God and in God.* This unity has its roots in the mystery of creation and acquires a new dimension in the mystery of the Redemption, which is ordered to universal salvation. Since God "wishes all men to be saved and to come to the knowledge of the truth,"[279] the Redemption includes all humanity and in a certain way all of creation. *In the same universal dimension* of Redemption the *Holy Spirit is acting,* by virtue of the "departure of Christ." Therefore the Church, rooted through her own mystery in the Trinitarian plan of salvation with good reason regards herself as the "sacrament of the unity of the whole human race." She knows that she is such through the power of the Holy Spirit, of which power she is a sign and instrument in the fulfillment of God's salvific plan.

64.4 In this way the *"condescension"* of the infinite Trinitarian Love *is brought about:* God, who is infinite Spirit, comes close to the visible world. The Triune God communicates himself to man in the Holy Spirit from the beginning through his "image and likeness." Under the action of the same Spirit, *man,* and through him *the created world,* which has been redeemed by Christ, *draw near to their ultimate destinies in God.* The Church is "a sacrament, that is sign and instrument" of this coming together of the two poles of creation and Redemption, God and man. She strives to restore and strengthen the unity at the very roots of the human race: in the relationship of communion that man has with God as his Creator, Lord and Redeemer. This is a truth which on the basis of the Council's teaching we can meditate on, explain and apply in all the fullness of its meaning in this phase of transition from the

---

[279] 1 Tim 2:4.

second to the third Christian millennium. And we rejoice to realize ever more clearly that within the work carried out by the Church in the history of salvation, which is part of the history of humanity, the Holy Spirit is present and at work — he who with the breath of divine life permeates man's earthly pilgrimage and causes all creation, all history, to flow together to its ultimate end, in the infinite ocean of God.

The Spirit and the Bride say: "Come!"

65.1 *The breath of the divine life*, the Holy Spirit, in its simplest and most common manner, expresses itself and *makes itself felt in prayer*. It is a beautiful and salutary thought that, wherever people are praying in the world, there the Holy Spirit is, the living breath of prayer. It is a beautiful and salutary thought to recognize that, if prayer is offered throughout the world, in the past, in the present and in the future, equally widespread is the presence and action of the Holy Spirit, who "breathes" prayer in the heart of man in all the endless range of the most varied situations and conditions, sometimes favorable and sometimes unfavorable to the spiritual and religious life. Many times, through the influence of the Spirit, prayer rises from the human heart in spite of prohibitions and persecutions and even official proclamations regarding the non-religious or even atheistic character of public life. Prayer always remains the voice of all those who apparently have no voice — and in this voice there always echoes *that "loud cry"* attributed to Christ by the *Letter to the Hebrews*.[280] Prayer is also *the revelation* of that *abyss* which is the heart of man: a depth which comes *from God* and *which only God can fill*, precisely *with the Holy Spirit*. We read in *Luke:* "If you then, who are evil, know how to give good gifts to your children, how much more will the heavenly Father give the Holy Spirit to those who ask him."[281]

65.2 The Holy Spirit is the gift that comes into man's heart together *with prayer*. In prayer he manifests himself first of all and above all as the gift that "helps us in our weakness." This is the magnificent thought developed by Saint Paul in the *Letter to the Romans*, when he writes: "For we do not know how to pray as we ought, but the Spirit himself intercedes for us with sighs too deep for words."[282] Therefore, the Holy Spirit not only enables us to pray, but guides us "from within" in prayer: he is present in our prayer and gives it a divine dimension.[283] Thus "*he who searches the hearts of men knows what is*

[280] Cf. Heb 5:7.
[281] Lk 11:13.
[282] Rom 8:26.
[283] Cf. Origen, *De Oratione*, 2: *PG* 11, 419-423.

the mind of the Spirit, because the Spirit intercedes for the saints according to the will of God."[284] Prayer through the power of the Holy Spirit becomes the ever more mature expression of the new man, who by means of this prayer participates in the divine life.

65.3 *Our difficult age has a special need of prayer.* In the course of history — both in the past and in the present — many men and women have borne witness to the importance of prayer by consecrating themselves to the praise of God and to the life of prayer, especially in monasteries and convents. So, too, recent years have been seeing a growth in the number of people who, in ever more widespread movements and groups, are giving first place to prayer and seeking in prayer a renewal of their spiritual life. This is a significant and comforting sign, for from this experience there is coming a real contribution to the revival of prayer among the faithful, who have been helped to gain a clearer idea of the Holy Spirit as he who inspires in hearts a profound yearning for holiness.

65.4 In many individuals and many communities there is a growing awareness that, even with all the rapid progress of technological and scientific civilization, and despite the real conquests and goals attained, *man is threatened, humanity is threatened*. In the face of this danger, and indeed already experiencing the frightful reality of man's spiritual decadence, individuals and whole communities, guided as it were by an inner sense of faith, are seeking the strength to raise man up again, to save him from himself, from his own errors and mistakes that often make harmful his very conquests. And thus they are discovering prayer, in which the "Spirit who helps us in our weakness" manifests himself. In this way the times in which we are living are bringing the Holy Spirit closer to the many who are returning to prayer. And I trust that all will find in the teaching of this Encyclical nourishment for their interior life, and that they will succeed in strengthening, under the action of the Spirit, their commitment to prayer in harmony with the Church and her Magisterium.

66.1 In the midst of the problems, disappointments and hopes, desertions and returns of these times of ours, *the Church* remains *faithful to the mystery of her birth*. While it is an historical fact that the Church came forth from the Upper Room on the day of Pentecost, in a certain sense one can say that she has never left it. Spiritually the event of Pentecost does not belong only to the past: the Church is always in the Upper Room that she bears in her heart. The Church perseveres *in prayer*, like the Apostles *together with Mary*, the Mother

---

[284] Rom 8:27.

of Christ, and with those who in Jerusalem were the first seed of the Christian community and who awaited in prayer the coming of the Holy Spirit.

66.2 The Church perseveres in prayer with Mary. This union of the praying Church with the Mother of Christ has been part of the mystery of the Church from the beginning: we see her present in this mystery as she is present in the mystery of her Son. It is the Council that says to us: *"The Blessed Virgin . . . overshadowed by the Holy Spirit . . . brought forth . . . the Son . . . , he whom God placed as the first-born among many brethren (cf. Rom 8:29), namely the faithful. In their birth and development she cooperates with a maternal love"*; she is through "her singular graces and offices . . . intimately united with the Church. . . . [She] is a model of the Church."[285] "The Church, moreover, contemplating Mary's mysterious sanctity, imitating her charity, . . . *becomes herself a mother*" and "herself is a virgin, who keeps . . . the fidelity she has pledged to her Spouse. Imitating the Mother of the Lord, and by the power of the Holy Spirit, she preserves with virginal purity an integral faith, a firm hope, and a sincere charity."[286]

66.3 Thus one can understand the profound reason why the Church, united with the Virgin Mother, prays unceasingly as the Bride to her divine Spouse, as the words of the *Book of Revelation,* quoted by the Council, attest: *"The Spirit and the Bride say to the Lord Jesus Christ: Come!"*[287] The Church's prayer is this unceasing invocation, in which "the Spirit himself intercedes for us": in a certain sense, the Spirit himself utters it *with* the Church and in the Church. For the Spirit is given to the Church in order that through his power the whole community of the People of God, however widely scattered and diverse, may persevere in hope: that hope in which "we have been saved."[288] It is *the eschatological hope*, the hope of definitive fulfillment in God, the hope of the eternal Kingdom, that is brought about by participation in the life of the Trinity. The Holy Spirit, given to the Apostles as the Counselor, *is the guardian and animator of this hope in the heart of the Church.*

66.4 In the time leading up to the third millennium after Christ, while "the Spirit and the Bride say to the Lord Jesus: Come!" this prayer of theirs is filled, as always, with an eschatological significance, which is also destined to give fullness of meaning to the celebration of the great Jubilee. It is a prayer concerned with the salvific destinies toward which the Holy Spirit by his action opens hearts throughout the history of man on earth. But at the same

---

[285] Dogmatic Constitution on the Church *Lumen Gentium,* 63.
[286] Ibid., 64.
[287] Ibid., 4; cf. Rev 22:17.
[288] Cf. Rom 8:24.

time *this prayer is directed toward a precise moment of history* which highlights the "fullness of time" marked by the year 2000. The Church wishes *to prepare* for this Jubilee *in the Holy Spirit*, just as the Virgin of Nazareth in whom the Word was made flesh was prepared by the Holy Spirit.

Conclusion

67.1 We wish to bring to a close these considerations in the heart of the Church and in the heart of man. The way of the Church passes through the heart of man, because here is the hidden *place* of the *salvific encounter with the Holy Spirit*, with the hidden God, and precisely here the Holy Spirit becomes "a spring of water welling up to eternal life."[289] He comes here as the Spirit of truth and as the Paraclete, as he was promised by Christ. From here he acts as *Counselor, Intercessor, Advocate*, especially when man, when humanity find themselves before the judgment of condemnation by that "accuser" about whom the *Book of Revelation* says that "he accuses them day and night before our God."[290] "The Holy Spirit does not cease to be *the guardian of hope* in the human heart: the hope of all human creatures, and especially of those who "have the first fruits of the Spirit" and "wait for the redemption of their bodies."[291]

67.2 The Holy Spirit, in his mysterious bond of divine communion with the Redeemer of man, is the one who brings about the continuity of his work: he takes from Christ and transmits to all, unceasingly entering into the history of the world through the heart of man. Here he becomes — as the liturgical Sequence of the Solemnity of Pentecost proclaims — the true *"father of the poor, giver of gifts, light of hearts"*; he becomes the *"sweet guest of the soul,"* whom the Church unceasingly greets on the threshold of the inmost sanctuary of every human being. For he brings "rest and relief" in the midst of toil, in the midst of the work of human hands and minds; he brings "rest" and "ease" in the midst of the heat of the day, in the midst of the anxieties, struggles and perils of every age; he brings "consolation," when the human heart grieves and is tempted to despair.

67.3 And therefore the same Sequence exclaims: "Without your aid *nothing is in man*, nothing is without fault." For only the Holy Spirit "convinces concerning sin," concerning evil, in order to restore what is good in man and in the world: in order to "renew the face of the earth." Therefore, he purifies

---

[289] Cf. Jn 4:14; Dogmatic Constitution on the Church *Lumen Gentium*, 4.
[290] Cf. Rev 12:10.
[291] Cf. Rom 8:23.

from everything that "disfigures" man, from "what is unclean"; he heals even the deepest wounds of human existence; he changes the interior dryness of souls, transforming them into the fertile fields of grace and holiness. What is "hard he softens," what is "frozen he warms," what is "wayward he sets anew" on the paths of salvation.[292]

67.4 Praying thus, the Church unceasingly professes her faith that *there exists in our created world a Spirit who is an uncreated gift.* He is the Spirit of the Father and of the Son: like the Father and the Son he is uncreated, without limit, eternal, omnipotent, God, Lord.[293] This Spirit of God "fills the universe," and all that is created recognizes in him the source of its own identity, finds in him its own transcendent expression, *turns to him* and *awaits* him, *invokes him with its own being.* Man turns to him, as to the Paraclete, the Spirit of truth and of love, *man who lives by truth and by love,* and who without the source of truth and of love *cannot live.* To him turns the Church, which is the heart of humanity, to implore for all and dispense to all those gifts of the *love* which through him "has been poured into our hearts."[294] To him turns the Church, along the intricate paths of man's pilgrimage on earth: she implores, she unceasingly implores *uprightness of human acts,* as the Spirit's work; she implores *the joy and consolation* that only he, the true Counselor, can bring by coming down into people's inmost hearts;[295] the Church implores the *grace of the virtues* that merit heavenly glory, implores *eternal salvation,* in the full communication of the divine life, to which the Father has eternally "predestined" human beings, created through love in the image and likeness of the Most Holy Trinity.

67.5 The Church with her heart which embraces all human hearts implores from the Holy Spirit that happiness which only in God has its complete realization: the joy "that *no one will be able to take away,*"[296] the joy which is *the fruit of love,* and therefore of God who is love; she implores "the righteousness, the peace and the joy of the Holy Spirit" in which, in the words of Saint Paul, consists the Kingdom of God.[297]

67.6 *Peace too is the fruit of love:* that interior peace, which weary man

[292] Cf. Sequence *Veni, Sancte Spiritus.*

[293] Cf. Creed *Quicumque: DS* 75.

[294] Cf. Rom 5:5.

[295] One should mention here the important Apostolic Exhortation *Gaudete in Domino,* published by Paul VI on May 9, in the Holy Year 1975; ever relevant is the invitation expressed there "to implore the gift of joy from the Holy Spirit," and likewise "to appreciate the properly spiritual joy that is a fruit of the Holy Spirit": *AAS* 67 (1975), 289, 302.

[296] Cf. Jn 16:22.

[297] Cf. Rom 14:17; Gal 5:22.

seeks in his inmost being; that peace besought by humanity, the human family, peoples, nations, continents, anxiously hoping to obtain it in the prospect of the transition from the second to the third Christian millennium. Since *the way of peace passes in the last analysis through love* and seeks to create the civilization of love, the Church fixes her eyes on him who is the Love of the Father and the Son, and in spite of increasing dangers she does not cease to trust, she does not cease *to invoke and to serve the peace of man on earth.* Her trust is based on him who, being the Spirit-Love, is also the *Spirit of peace* and does not cease to be present in our human world, on the horizon of minds and hearts, in order to "fill the universe" with love and peace.

67.7 Before him I kneel at the end of these considerations, and implore him, as the Spirit of the Father and the Son, to grant to all of us *the blessing and grace* which I desire to pass on, in the name of the Most Holy Trinity, to the sons and daughters of the Church and to the whole human family.

Given in Rome, at Saint Peter's, on May 18, the Solemnity of Pentecost, in the year 1986, the eighth of my Pontificate.

Redemptoris Mater

Editor's Introduction

"I have been thinking of it for a long time. I have pondered it at length in my heart."[1] With these words at a general audience, John Paul II introduced his sixth encyclical, *Redemptoris Mater*, "Mother of the Redeemer," issued on March 25, 1987.[2] Continuing his meditation on the Redemption developed in his Trinitarian trilogy, the Pope turns to Mary, whom God has called to share in this mystery in an extraordinary way. Instead of presenting Mary's singular privileges, John Paul emphasizes the dynamic mission of Mary in the "time of the Church." The encyclical is especially linked to *Redemptor Hominis*, as the title itself suggests. From the outset, the doctrinal and pastoral orientation of *Redemptoris Mater* is focused on Christ the Redeemer.

Besides this logic of the Pope's theological vision, other factors were also at work in leading him to write an encyclical on Mary. First, there is his well known Marian devotion. John Paul II's coat of arms bears a large "M" under a plain cross and carries the motto *Totus tuus*: "I am completely yours, O Mary." *Redemptoris Mater* is a personal synthesis of the Pope's Christocentric theology of Mary: her unique dignity, vocation, and mission in salvation history.

A second inspiration behind the encyclical was the upcoming celebration of the Marian Year, which was to begin on Pentecost 1987 and end on the solemnity of the Assumption 1988. Preparing for the Jubilee of the year 2000 from the beginning of his pontificate, the Pope wanted to commemorate the two thousandth anniversary of Mary's birth. This Marian Year was to provide a further step of preparation for the Jubilee, beginning a new time of "Advent" in the Church, a time of Mary. More than a mere commemoration of the past, the Marian Year was to call attention to "the *special presence* of the Mother of God in the mystery of Christ and his Church" (§48.2). By means of the encyclical he also intended to give a specific orientation to the Marian Year celebration, inviting Christians to draw inspiration and strength from Mary's example and intercession.

Third, the anniversaries of two significant ecclesial events likewise suggested the timeliness of a Marian encyclical: the twelfth centenary of the Second Council of Nicaea (787), the ecumenical council which resolved the iconoclast controversy, and the millennial celebration of the Baptism of Saint

[1] March 25, 1987, *L'Osservatore Romano*, 13 (1987), 23.
[2] *Acta Apostolicae Sedis*, 79 (1987), 361-433.

Vladimir (988), the event which began the Christianization of Russia. Lastly, *Redemptoris Mater* furnished an opportunity for the Pope to address the contemporary challenge posed by the various women's liberation movements. Women, he writes, "by looking to Mary, find in her the secret of living their femininity with dignity and of achieving their own true advancement" (§46.2). He would later develop his ideas on feminism at much greater length in *Mulieris Dignitatem* (1988) and his *Letter to Women* (1995).

Even more than his other encyclicals, *Redemptoris Mater* is a sustained reflection on Scripture. In large measure, the encyclical is a biblical meditation, an attentive listening to the inspired Word which speaks the truth about Mary. The Pope offers no historical-critical exegesis of the Marian texts; rather, he searches for the meaning which they reveal by examining the inherent relationships among them. He converses directly with the Scriptures, accepting them in their totality and unity as a testimony to God's plan of salvation for humanity and to Mary's role in that plan.

The infancy narrative of the first two chapters of Luke's Gospel and the two Marian texts of John (2:1-11, 19:25-27) are the passages that he refers to most frequently. John Paul weaves together his biblical reflections with many references to chapter eight of *Lumen Gentium* (§§52-69): "The Blessed Virgin Mary, Mother of God, in the Mystery of Christ and of the Church." This chapter, he says, offers "a clear summary of the Church's doctrine on the Mother of Christ" (§2.2). The Pope wants his encyclical "to promote a new and more careful reading of what the Council said about the Blessed Virgin Mary" (§48.3). An original synthesis results from this approach, one which, while faithful to the Council, also offers fresh insight on the mystery, call, and role of Mary.

Summary

Redemptoris Mater is more tightly structured than many of John Paul's encyclicals. While it frequently returns to the same biblical or conciliar texts, it contains fewer discursive asides and fewer references to contemporary world problems than most other papal writings. Besides its introduction and conclusion, the encyclical is divided into three main chapters. The first chapter, "Mary in the Mystery of Christ" (§§7-24), describes the various New Testament passages which deal with the Mother of Jesus. Chapter two, "The Mother of God at the Center of the Pilgrim Church" (§§25-37), is less Christological and more ecclesiological, and includes a section on ecumenism. In chapter three, "Maternal Mediation" (§§38-50), the Pope examines Mary's continuing role in salvation history and discusses the significance of the Marian Year.

Christ and Mary

As does *Lumen Gentium*, so too *Redemptoris Mater* begins with a quotation from Saint Paul: "When the time had fully come, God sent forth his Son, born of a woman" (Gal 4:4). This text sets the tone of the encyclical. "Only *in the mystery of Christ*," writes John Paul, "*is her* [Mary's] *mystery made fully clear*" (§4). In *Redemptoris Mater* the Pope applies specifically to Mary, the exceptional "daughter of the human race," the theological principle from the Second Vatican Council which he quotes repeatedly in his encyclicals: "only in the mystery of the Incarnate Word does the mystery of man take on light" (*Gaudium et Spes*, §22). In the Incarnation, the Church "encounters Christ and Mary indissolubly joined" (§1.3). For John Paul II, Christology, Mariology, and ecclesiology are intertwined as manifestations of the one mystery of salvation.

The Pope presents, though not in the chronological order of salvation history, the various scriptural texts which refer to Mary: from her eternal predestination in Christ up to her praying with the apostolic community in the Upper Room. In the encyclical, he describes the role of Mary in the history of salvation as it unfolds in God's saving design.

Referring to Ephesians 1:3-7, John Paul recalls that the divine plan of salvation is eternally linked to Christ, "who chose us in him before the foundation of the world." In this plan a special place is reserved to Mary, who is *"eternally loved in this 'beloved Son'"* (§8.5). Preserved from original sin from the first moment of her existence, "she belonged to Christ, sharing in the salvific and sanctifying grace and in that love which has its beginning in the 'Beloved,' the Son of the Eternal Father" (§10). In virtue of her Immaculate Conception, Mary, like the "Morning Star" which announces the rising of the sun, preceded "the rising of the 'Sun of Justice' in the history of the human race" (§3.2).

At the Annunciation, the angel Gabriel greeted the young Virgin as "full of grace" (Lk 1:28). He addressed her in this way "as if it were her real name" (§8.3). "Mary is 'full of grace,'" says John Paul, "because it is precisely in her that the Incarnation of the Word, the hypostatic union of the Son of God with human nature, is accomplished and fulfilled" (§9.3). Chosen to be the Mother of Christ, she receives God's grace in a unique and exceptional way. This divine choice is the reason for her singular place in the mystery of Christ: it is why "all generations will call her blessed" (cf. Lk 1:48).

In describing the Visitation, the Pope focuses on how Mary responded to the gift of this "fullness of grace." He begins his presentation of Mary's faith at this meeting of pregnant kinswomen. In greeting Mary, Elizabeth praises her cousin's faith: "And blessed is she who has believed that there would be a fulfillment of what was spoken to her from the Lord" (Lk 1:45). To be sure, Elizabeth is referring to Mary's act of faith expressed in her *fiat:* "let it be to me according to your word" (Lk 1:38). But, as the Pope notes, Mary's consent is also "the point of departure from which her whole 'journey toward God' begins" (§14.2) — a pilgrimage walked in faith from start to finish.

John Paul understands Simeon's prophecy to Mary, at the time of Jesus' presentation in the Temple, as a "second Annunciation." The God-fearing man's words tell her of "the actual historical situation in which the Son is to accomplish his mission, namely in misunderstanding and sorrow" (§16.2). Thus her pilgrimage of faith is revealed as one which will entail hardship and suffering. Throughout the hidden years at Nazareth, Mary, to whom Christ's divine sonship was revealed more profoundly than to any other person, "is in contact with the truth about her Son only in faith and through faith" (§17.2). Yet, despite Mary's exceptional knowledge, her own Son remains shrouded in the ineffable mystery of God made man.

According to the Gospels, Mary appears infrequently during Christ's public ministry. She is first seen at Cana, where "in a significant way she *contributes* to that 'beginning of the signs' which reveal the messianic power of her Son" (§21.2). This event reveals her maternal solicitude for others "as the *spokeswoman of her Son's will*" (§21.4).

Nor does John Paul ignore the more "difficult" texts of the synoptic Gospels, the passages often invoked to minimize Mary's special place in salvation history: those on Jesus' true kindred (Mt 12:46-50; Mk 3:31-35; Lk 8:19-21), and on the meaning of true blessedness (Lk 11:27-28). According to the Pope, these passages serve to divert attention "from motherhood understood only as a fleshly bond, in order to direct it toward those mysterious bonds of the spirit which develop from hearing and keeping God's word" (§20.3). This new brotherhood and motherhood which Jesus reveals to his disciples, one which involves the hearing, guarding, and living of his word, the Pope applies specifically to Mary. She is the first to hear God's word and keep it, "*the first 'disciple' of her Son*, the first to whom he seemed to say: 'Follow me' " (§20.8). More than a unique and unrepeatable biological event, Mary's motherhood is fulfilled in the listening and living of her Son's word.

At Calvary, Mary's close relationship with Jesus is most fully manifested. Through her faith, she is here *"perfectly united with Christ in his self-emptying"* act of offering himself for the world's salvation (§18.3). The Gospel of John confirms Mary's motherhood of her Son's disciples as she stood at the foot of the Cross. From the heart of the Paschal Mystery, Jesus gives her as Mother "to every single individual and all mankind" (§23.2). In the person of the beloved disciple, Christ entrusts humanity to Mary as his final testament: "Behold your mother" (Jn 19:27). Her maternity now extends beyond her Son, embracing the members of his Body. It becomes a *"gift which Christ himself makes personally to every individual"* (§45.3).

More profoundly than any other creature, Mary shares in the life and mission of the Word made flesh. From her home in Nazareth to the Upper Room in Jerusalem, she is present "as an exceptional witness to the mystery of Christ" (§27.1).

Mary and the Church

In chapter two of *Redemptoris Mater,* the Pope develops the Second Vatican Council's insight which linked Mariology with ecclesiology. "Mary, as the Mother of Christ," he writes, *"is in a particular way united with the Church"* (§5.1). John Paul is convinced that the truth about Mary is "an effective aid in exploring more deeply the truth concerning the Church" (§47.2). The Church "looks at" Mary through Jesus, just as she "looks at" Jesus through Mary (§26.4). Mary's motherhood continues in and through the Church, whose birth was manifested on Pentecost. According to John Paul, there is "a unique correspondence between the moment of the Incarnation of the Word and the moment of the birth of the Church. The person who links these two moments is Mary. . . . In both cases her discreet yet essential presence indicates the path of 'birth from the Holy Spirit' " (§24.4). As the Church makes her pilgrim journey through the world, she "proceeds along the path already trodden by the Virgin Mary" (§2.1).

In chapter three, the Pope describes Mary as the figure or model of the Church which, like "the woman" of Genesis (3:15) and Revelation (12:1), is both mother and virgin. From Mary, the Church "learns her own motherhood. . . . For, just *as Mary is at the service of the mystery of the Incarnation, so the Church is always at the service of the mystery of adoption to sonship through grace"* (§43.2). Through the nourishment of the sacraments, the Church gives a share in Christ's life to her sons and daughters. And with a mother's love Mary cooperates in the birth and development of the sons and daughters of Mother Church (cf. §44.1). As the events of the Annunciation and Pentecost reveal, both Mary and the Church have a mission of "motherhood in the Holy Spirit" (§44.1); they generate life.

Like Mary, whose motherhood is *"a result of her total self-giving to God in virginity"* (§39.1), the Church too is virginal. She remains faithful to Christ, "committed to preserving the word of God and investigating its riches with discernment and prudence, in order to bear faithful witness to it before all mankind in every age" (§43.4).

According to John Paul, Mary can be said to "precede" the Church. In a real way, Mary's Immaculate Conception marks the Church's beginning, when the saving grace of Easter was projected and "anticipated in her most noble member" (§1.3). Although she does not directly receive a share in the authority and mission of the Apostles, she is present with them at Pentecost (cf. Acts 1:13-14). In the Church, hers is a priority of grace and faith, not of office. "This heroic *faith* of hers," writes the Pope, " *'precedes'* the apostolic witness of the Church, and ever remains in the Church's heart" (§27.1). Mary's faith "represents a constant point of reference for the Church" (§6.1). She continues to go before the pilgrim People of God, guiding them until they reach the eschatological fulfillment of heaven.

The second section of chapter two deals with "the sign of ecumenism" which marks the Church's journey at the end of the second millennium. The urgent need to restore full communion among Christians leads the Pope to consider the doctrinal questions concerning Mary that emerge in ecumenical discussions. With regard to the churches and ecclesial communities of the West, he notes that there has been some progress in "finding agreement with the Catholic Church on fundamental points of Christian belief, including matters relating to the Virgin Mary" (§30.2). John Paul then asks: "Why should we not all together look to her as *our common Mother*, who prays for the unity of God's family and who 'precedes' us all at the head of the long line of witnesses of faith in the one Lord?" (§30.3). In fact, the whole thrust of *Redemptoris Mater* — a biblical portrait of Mary in the light of the Incarnation and of her obedience of faith — is an open invitation to intensify ecumenical dialogue within western Christianity.

John Paul deals with the significance and role of Mary in the Orthodox churches and the ancient churches of the East in much more detail. With them the Catholic Church feels "united by love and praise of the *Theotókos*" (§31.1). In fact, he describes the East's Mariology in the same terms he himself uses in the encyclical: "The Greek Fathers and the Byzantine tradition, contemplating the Virgin in the light of the Word made flesh, have sought to penetrate the depth of that bond which unites Mary, as the Mother of God, to Christ and the Church: the Virgin is a permanent presence in the whole reality of the salvific mystery" (§31.2). The Pope warmly recognizes the depth and beauty of the East's Marian devotion, a piety expressed in feasts, hymns, liturgy, and a rich tradition of iconography. This "wealth of praise," he says, "could help us to hasten the day when the Church can begin once more to breathe fully with her 'two lungs,' the East and the West" (§34).

The third section of chapter two is a meditation on Mary's *Magnificat*. This canticle, John Paul writes, is "*an inspired profession of her faith*, in which *her response to the revealed word* is expressed" (§36.1). Affirming that Mary's song is a bold proclamation of the "*undimmed* truth about God" (§37.1), the Pope particularly notes how the *Magnificat* aptly describes God's special love for the poor. In this prayer the Church sees her teaching confirmed: the truth about God "*cannot be separated from the manifestation of his love of preference for the poor and humble*" (§37.3).

Maternal mediation

Chapter three of *Redemptoris Mater* takes up three related themes: Mary's continuing mediation on behalf of humanity, her mission in the life of Christians and the Church, and the meaning of the Marian Year of 1987-1988.

The Church unequivocally professes that "there is one mediator between God and men, the man Christ Jesus" (1 Tim 2:5). Repeatedly the Pope declares that Mary's role of mediation is a "mediation in Christ" (§38.1). As a "shared mediation" (§38.3), it is "subordinate" to Christ's (§38.4). While everyone in the communion of saints is empowered to intercede for others before God, Mary's mediation in this regard is nonetheless "special" and "extraordinary" (§38.4). Distinguished by its specifically maternal character, hers is a loving intercession on behalf of all humanity.

When, at the Annunciation, the "handmaid of the Lord" consented to be the Mother of the Redeemer, she expressed her submission to the one mediation of Jesus. Mary consented to be not only the Mother of Christ but also his disciple and associate in the work of Redemption. By means of her *fiat* she said "yes" to sharing wholeheartedly in her Son's saving mission. "Through this fullness of grace and supernatural life she was especially predisposed to cooperation with Christ, the one Mediator of human salvation" (§39.3).

Receiving from her dying Son the motherhood of the infant community of disciples, Mary remains even now in the Church's midst, expressing her love and care by means of her maternal intercession and mediation. Just as Christ's redemptive work embraces all humanity, so too does her intercession and mediation. Assumed into heaven, the Virgin Mary continues to exercise her intercessory role for those still on their earthly pilgrimage. "Mary's motherhood continues unceasingly in the Church," says the Pope, "as the mediation which intercedes" (§40.2). This maternity of hers is in the order of grace, "for it implores the gift of the Spirit who raises up the new children of God, redeemed through the sacrifice of Christ" (§44.2).

After reflecting again on the bond uniting Mary and the Church, John Paul examines her active presence and role in the life of believers. How does she in practice show them her motherhood in the Spirit?

In his explanation of Mary's maternal mission in the Church, the Pope's preference for personalist thought comes to the fore. He recalls that in the order of nature "motherhood always establishes *a unique and unrepeatable relationship* between two people: *between mother and child* and *between child and mother*" (§45.1). The same pattern also holds true in the order of grace. Precisely for this reason, Christ's testament on Golgotha was phrased in the singular, referring to one person: "Behold your son" (Jn 19:26). From the Cross, Jesus entrusted each individual disciple, in the person of his beloved disciple, to his Mother. Mary, then, has a personal and unique bond with every Christian. But this entrusting is also mutual. Jesus confided his Mother to the beloved disciple, who "from that hour took her into his home" (cf. Jn 19:27). In fulfillment of the Lord's command, Christians are to imitate the beloved disciple. They, too, are to receive Mary into every dimension of their interior life: "Entrusting himself to Mary in a filial manner, the Christian, like the Apostle John, 'welcomes' the Mother of Christ 'into his own home' and brings her into everything that makes up his inner life" (§45.4).

With a few deft strokes the Pope notes Mary's special significance for women: "This Marian dimension of Christian life takes on special importance in relation to women and their status" (§46.2). Femininity "has a *unique relationship* with the Mother of the Redeemer." He then adds that Mary "sheds light on *womanhood as such* by the very fact that God, in the sublime event of the Incarnation, entrusted himself to the ministry, the free and active ministry, of a woman" (§46.2). Consequently, and the Pope repeats this frequently, it can be said that "women, by looking to Mary, find in her the secret of living their femininity with dignity and of achieving their own true advancement" (§46.2).

John Paul ends chapter three with some comments on his hopes for the Marian Year. First, in the light of Vatican II, he wants it to be the occasion for "a new and more careful reading" of the Council's teaching on Mary (§48.3). Even more than reaffirming doctrine, however, he wishes the Year to foster an authentic Marian spirituality. The Pope also mentions that, because the Marian Year corresponds to the millennial anniversary of the evangelization of present-day Russia, it should stimulate the cause of ecumenism. Despite the lack of full, visible communion between Catholics and Orthodox, "*in the presence of the Mother of Christ we feel that we are true brothers and sisters*" (§50.1). Lastly, the Pope sees the Year as an occasion for the whole world to look to the loving Mother of the Redeemer as its sure sign of hope.

Key Themes

Among the many themes which run through *Redemptoris Mater,* three are especially significant. Each of them sheds light not only on the Pope's Mariology but also on his fundamental Christological and anthropological vision. These themes furnish the backbone of the encyclical: Mary's faith and discipleship, her continuing presence in the Church, and her cooperation in the mystery of Redemption.

Faith and discipleship

Never before has an official Church document given such prominence to Mary's faith. In praising Mary as the preeminent model of faith, *Redemptoris Mater* elaborates an original catechesis on the meaning and role of faith in every disciple's life. In Elizabeth's greeting, "Blessed is she who believed" (Lk 1:45), the Pope sees "*a kind of 'key'* which unlocks for us the innermost reality of Mary" (§19.2). Indeed, "*she was the first to believe* . . . and followed Jesus step by step in her maternal pilgrimage of faith" (§26.5). By means of her *fiat* to the angel's greeting, Mary reveals essential truths about what it means to believe in God.

Faith is the road that all must take on their journey to God. Abraham's faith marked the beginning of the Old Covenant, and Mary's faith inaugurated the New Covenant. This is the path which everyone must tread. To prove his point, John Paul draws on Vatican II's definition of faith. "The obedience of faith," states the Council, "must be given to God who reveals, an obedience by which man entrusts his whole self freely to God" (*Dei Verbum,* §5). Such an obedience of faith is perfectly expressed in Mary. By describing the various qualities of Mary's faith, the Pope wishes to shed light on its significance for everyone's life.

"To believe," says John Paul, "means 'to abandon oneself' to the truth of the living God, knowing and humbly recognizing 'how unsearchable are his judgments and how *inscrutable his ways*' (Rom 11:33)" (§14.2). Mary is the "*first to believe*" (§26.5) and "*the first 'disciple' of her Son*" (§20.8). Referring to the teaching of the Fathers of the Church, the Pope says that Mary "conceived this Son in her mind before she conceived him in her womb: precisely in faith!" (§13.4). The Virgin lives by faith, not by vision. Like everyone, she has to walk "in the dim light of faith, accepting fully and with a ready heart everything that is decreed in the divine plan" (§14.2). Her entire life is a journey lived in obscurity. From the Annunciation to Calvary her faith matured, growing ever stronger and deeper in the face of suffering.

As lived by Mary, faith is a total, obedient, trusting, self-surrender of the mind and body to God. At the Annunciation she responds to him *"with all her human and feminine 'I' "* (§13.2). Mary's faith involves perfect cooperation and openness to the Spirit's action within her; "she entrusted herself to God without reserve" (§13.4). Hers was a perfect gift of self to God and to her brothers and sisters.

Precisely because faith is "contact with the mystery of God" (§17.2), it entails suffering. During Jesus' hidden life, Mary believes amid affliction and adversity. Drawing upon the imagery of Saint John of the Cross, a Doctor of the Church particularly dear to the Pope, John Paul affirms that during the hidden years in Nazareth Mary herself experienced *"a particular heaviness of heart,* linked with a sort of 'night of faith'." This dark night, he adds, is "a kind of 'veil' through which one has to draw near to the Invisible One and to live in intimacy with the mystery" (§17.3). Such faith is most severely tried in the face of death.

Beneath the Cross, Mary freely unites herself through the obedience of faith to her Son's oblation. She "shares through faith in the shocking mystery of this self-emptying." Using the terminology applied to Christ's humiliating death on the Cross, the Pope continues: hers is "perhaps the deepest *'kenosis' of faith* in human history" (§18.3). At Calvary, Mary's faith comes to maturity. By her faith she is united to her Son's redeeming death in a single *fiat* of wills. And here, too, she discovers and accepts her new motherhood of compassion "which was to constitute her 'part' beside her Son" (§20.8). Her motherhood of the redeemed is "generated by faith" and is *the fruit of the 'new' love* which came to definitive maturity at the foot of the Cross, through her sharing in the redemptive love of her Son" (§23.3).

Mary's faith is not an isolated or solitary treasure. It spills over into the Church's life, ever remaining "in the Church's heart. . . . All those who from generation to generation accept the apostolic witness of the Church share in that mysterious inheritance, and *in a sense share in Mary's faith*" (§27.1). The whole People of God take part in the same pilgrimage of faith as the Virgin of Nazareth. They follow her as a model and seek an increase of faith from her. According to the Pope, Mary's faith "in some way continues to become the faith of the pilgrim People of God" (§28.1).

Presence in the Church

More than the Church's exemplary model, Mary is an active presence in the life of the Church and humanity. By God's decree, the role she played in the life of Christ and the early community continues today in the Body of her Son. Again and again John Paul II stresses Mary's dynamic *personal* presence in the Church as a woman and as a mother. "Sustained by the Holy Spirit" (§38.2), she exists in glory not only as one whose virtues are to be imitated, but also as the one who is present in the interior life of believers as a mother. Her presence now, in the Spirit, is real and tangible. "Mary embraces each and every one *in* the Church, and embraces each and every one *through* the Church" (§47.2). Moreover, her presence in the community is verified by the experience of believers.

Mysteriously present in God's plan even before the creation of the world, the "Woman" who brings salvation was already promised "in the beginning" to our first parents (Gen 3:15). As "the woman clothed with the sun" (Rev 12:1), Mary accompanies the pilgrim Church until her final consummation in the glory of the heavenly Jerusalem. In the great struggle which even today is being waged against the powers of darkness, Mary takes part as a mother who watches over her children (cf. §§11, 47.3). She continues to make present for humanity the mystery of Christ, a mystery brought to life in her womb by her consent to the Incarnation. Mary's divine motherhood is ceaselessly "poured out upon the Church" (§24.2). John Paul affirms: "Mary, who from the beginning had given herself without reserve to the person and work of her Son, could not but pour out upon the Church, from the very beginning, her maternal self-giving" (§40.1).

The Church's pilgrim journey through history takes place in time and space. Mary's presence in the Church expresses itself in many different ways, not least of which is in the "specific 'geography' of faith and Marian devotion, which includes all these special places of pilgrimage where the People of God seek to meet the Mother of God . . . [for] a strengthening of their own faith" (§28.4). Despite the undeniable significance of this exterior Marian dimension, the Church's life is essentially an interior pilgrimage of faith. It is above all in the story of souls that Mary continues her mission. She has a unique and unrepeatable relationship with the heart of each of God's children. Like the beloved disciple, all Christians are to welcome her into their own home (cf. Jn 19:27), bringing her into the depths of their inner life, so that she can bring them to her Son.

God has confided to Mary the role of "introducing into the world *the Kingdom of her Son*" (§28.3). Just as Christ is present in the Church through the power of the Holy Spirit, so too is Mary. She carries out her maternal role from heaven, where she remains united with Christ in his continuing work of salvation. For Mary, to reign is to serve the disciples of her Son. As the handmaid of the Lord, "she wishes to act upon all those who entrust themselves to her as her children" (§46.1). Mary shares "in the many complicated problems which *today* beset the lives of individuals, families and nations" (§52.5). According to the Pope, she carries out her mission primarily by leading the faithful to the Eucharist; here "Christ, *his true body born of the Virgin Mary*, becomes present" (§44.3).

Mediation and intercession

John Paul's strong sense of the communion of saints, where Mary stands at the center, provides the doctrinal foundation for her continuing mission of intercession and mediation in the Church. He describes her unique role, while safeguarding it from misunderstanding. Repeatedly and scrupulously the Pope recalls that Mary's mediation is subordinate to Christ's and dependent on his; her mediation draws from the fullness of his (cf. §§22.1, 38.1, 39.3, 41.2). Never preempting Christ's role as the one Mediator, her mediation is "wholly oriented toward Christ and . . . the revelation of his salvific power" (§22.1). Yet Christ's mediation allows for participation; it is inclusive rather than exclusive. It confirms people's dignity, conferring on them the privilege and responsibility of standing before God as one Body in Christ. Especially in times of difficulty, they can intercede for one another by their prayers and sacrifices.

Only twice in *Redemptoris Mater* does John Paul refer to Mary as "mediatrix." First, when describing her role in asking Jesus to work his first "sign" at Cana, the Pope says that "*she puts herself 'in the middle,'* that is to say *she acts as a mediatrix not as an outsider, but in her position as Mother*" (§21.3). Second, he affirms that Mary has "that specifically maternal role of mediatrix of mercy *at his final coming*" (§41.2). In neither case, however, does he call her mediatrix of "all" grace. Rather, her mediation is primarily one of interceding for those entrusted to her by her Son.

Compared to the mediation of all others in the communion of saints, Mary's mediation is exceptional and unique. Her singular mediation flows from her divine motherhood. "It possesses a specifically maternal character," he writes, "which distinguishes it from the mediation of other creatures who in various and always subordinate ways share in the one mediation of Christ" (§38.3). Mary enjoys her role of mediation precisely because she is the Mother of Christ and therefore also Mother of the Church. Her motherhood, "completely pervaded by her spousal attitude as the 'handmaid of the Lord,' constitutes the first and fundamental dimension of that mediation which the Church confesses and proclaims in her regard" (§39.2). Through her mediation she expresses her maternal care for those redeemed by her Son.

While Cana was "*a sort of first announcement of Mary's maternal mediation*, wholly oriented toward Christ and tending to the revelation of his salvific power" (§22.1), only at Calvary did it come to fruition. Here, in faith, she "accomplished her maternal *cooperation* with the Savior's whole mission through her actions and sufferings" (§39.3). Thus, through this second *fiat* uttered beneath the Cross, she "*entered, in a way all her own, into the one mediation* 'between God and men' *which is the mediation of the man Christ Jesus*" (§39.3).

Even now Mary exercises her mediation, linked at the Cross to her motherhood of the Church, as a way of cooperating in the saving work of the Redeemer. She does so by interceding for her children. "In this way," writes John Paul, "Mary's motherhood continues unceasingly in the Church as the mediation which intercedes" (§40.2). Because of her motherhood, Mary's mediation has its own proper characteristics; she cares for the spiritual life of all, listening to their prayers and interceding on their behalf. Thus, the Church prays to the loving Mother of the Redeemer: "Assist your people who have fallen yet strive to rise again. To the wonderment of nature you bore your Creator!"

* * *

Selected Bibliography

Allchin, Arthur Macdonal. "*Redemptoris Mater:* An Anglican Response." *One in Christ,* 23 (1988), 324-329.

Collins, Mary Smalara. "All Generations Will Call Her Blessed." *US Catholic,* 58 (May 1993), 37-40.

Gomez, Felipe. "A New Encyclical Letter: The Mother of the Redeemer." *East Asian Pastoral Review,* 24 (1987), 108-118.

Heft, James L. "*Redemptoris Mater:* Mary's Journey of Faith." *Catechist,* 21 (September 1987), 4-5.

Mary: God's Yes to Man: John Paul's Encyclical "Redemptoris Mater." Introduction by Joseph Ratzinger. Commentary by Hans Urs von Balthasar. San Francisco: Ignatius Press, 1987. 9-40, 161-179.

Ratzinger, Joseph. Presentation at the Press Conference for the Publication of *Redemptoris Mater. L'Osservatore Romano,* 13 (1987), 21, 23.

Stahel, Thomas H. "*Redemptoris Mater.*" *America,* 156 (1987), 353-354.

Symposium on *Redemptoris Mater:* Report on the 1988 Convention. *Marian Studies,* 39 (1988), 34-162.

Taylor, Richard J. "*Redemptoris Mater:* Pope John Paul II's Encyclical for the Marian Year: Some Reflections." *Priest & People,* 2 (1988), 133-136.

ENCYCLICAL LETTER
REDEMPTORIS MATER
OF THE SUPREME PONTIFF
JOHN PAUL II
ON THE BLESSED VIRGIN MARY
IN THE LIFE
OF THE PILGRIM CHURCH

Redemptoris Mater

Venerable Brothers and
Dear Sons and Daughters,
Health and the Apostolic Blessing!

Introduction

1.1 The Mother of the Redeemer has a precise place in the plan of salvation, for "when the time had fully come, God sent forth his Son, born of woman, born under the law, to redeem those who were under the law, so that we might receive adoption as sons. And because you are sons, God has sent the Spirit of his Son into our hearts, crying, 'Abba! Father!' (Gal 4:4-6)."

1.2 With these words of the Apostle Paul, which the Second Vatican Council takes up at the beginning of its treatment of the Blessed Virgin Mary,[1] I too wish to begin my reflection on the role of Mary in the mystery of Christ and on her active and exemplary presence in the life of the Church. For they are words which celebrate together the love of the Father, the mission of the Son, the gift of the Spirit, the role of the woman from whom the Redeemer was born, and our own divine filiation, in the mystery of the "fullness of time."[2]

1.3 This "fullness" indicates the moment fixed from all eternity when the Father sent his Son "that whoever believes in him should not perish but have eternal life" (Jn 3:16). It denotes the blessed moment when the Word that "was with God . . . became flesh and dwelt among us" (Jn 1:1, 14), and made himself our brother. It marks the moment when the Holy Spirit, who had already infused the fullness of grace into Mary of Nazareth, formed in her virginal

---

[1] Cf. Second Vatican Ecumenical Council, Dogmatic Constitution on the Church *Lumen Gentium*, 52, and the whole of Chapter VIII, entitled "The Role of the Blessed Virgin Mary, Mother of God, in the Mystery of Christ and the Church."

[2] The expression "fullness of time" (*pleroma tou chronou*) is parallel with similar expressions of Judaism, both biblical (cf. Gen 29:21; 1 Sam 7:12; Tob 14:5) and extra-biblical, and especially of the New Testament (cf. Mk 1:15; Lk 21:24; Jn 7:8; Eph 1:10). From the point of view of form, it means not only the conclusion of a chronological process but also and especially the coming to maturity or completion of a particularly important period, one directed toward the fulfillment of an expectation, a coming to completion which thus takes on an eschatological dimension. According to Gal 4:4 and its context, it is the coming of the Son of God that reveals that time has, so to speak, reached its limit. That is to say, the period marked by the promise made to Abraham and by the Law mediated by Moses has now reached its climax, in the sense that Christ fulfills the divine promise and supersedes the Old Law.

womb the human nature of Christ. This "fullness" marks the moment when, with the entrance of the eternal into time, time itself is redeemed, and being filled with the mystery of Christ becomes definitively "salvation time." Finally, this "fullness" designates the hidden beginning of the Church's journey. In the liturgy the Church salutes Mary of Nazareth as the Church's own beginning,[3] for in the event of the Immaculate Conception the Church sees projected, and anticipated in her most noble member, the saving grace of Easter. And above all, in the Incarnation she encounters Christ and Mary indissolubly joined: he who is the Church's Lord and Head and she who, uttering the first *fiat* of the New Covenant, prefigures the Church's condition as spouse and mother.

2.1 Strengthened by the presence of Christ (cf. Mt 28:20), the Church journeys through time toward the consummation of the ages and goes to meet the Lord who comes. But on this journey — and I wish to make this point straightaway — she proceeds along the path already trodden by the Virgin Mary, who *"advanced in her pilgrimage of faith, and loyally persevered in her union with her Son unto the Cross."*[4]

2.2 I take these very rich and evocative words from the Constitution *Lumen Gentium*, which in its concluding part offers a clear summary of the Church's doctrine on the Mother of Christ, whom she venerates as her beloved Mother and as her model in faith, hope and charity.

2.3 Shortly after the Council, my great Predecessor Paul VI decided to speak further of the Blessed Virgin. In the Encyclical Epistle *Christi Matri* and subsequently in the Apostolic Exhortations *Signum Magnum* and *Marialis Cultus*[5] he expounded the foundations and criteria of the special veneration which the Mother of Christ receives in the Church, as well as the various forms of Marian devotion — liturgical, popular and private — which respond to the spirit of faith.

3.1 The circumstance which now moves me to take up this subject once more is *the prospect of the year 2000,* now drawing near, in which the

---

[3] Cf. Roman Missal, Preface of December 8, Immaculate Conception of the Blessed Virgin Mary; Saint Ambrose, *De Institutione Virginis*, XV, 93-94: *PL* 16, 342; Second Vatican Ecumenical Council, Dogmatic Constitution on the Church *Lumen Gentium*, 68.

[4] Second Vatican Ecumenical Council, Dogmatic Constitution on the Church *Lumen Gentium*, 58.

[5] Paul VI, Encyclical Epistle *Christi Matri* (September 15, 1966): *AAS* 58 (1966), 745-749; Apostolic Exhortation *Signum Magnum* (May 13, 1967): *AAS* 59 (1967), 465-475; Apostolic Exhortation *Marialis Cultus* (February 2, 1974): *AAS* 66 (1974), 113-168.

bimillennial Jubilee of the birth of Jesus Christ at the same time directs our gaze toward his Mother. In recent years, various opinions have been voiced suggesting that it would be fitting to precede that anniversary by a similar Jubilee in celebration of the birth of Mary.

3.2 In fact, even though it is not possible to establish an exact *chronological point* for identifying the date of Mary's birth, the Church has constantly been aware that *Mary appeared on the horizon of salvation history before Christ.*[6] It is a fact that when "the fullness of time" was definitively drawing near — the saving advent of Emmanuel — she who was from eternity destined to be his Mother already existed on earth. The fact that she "preceded" the coming of Christ is reflected every year *in the liturgy of Advent.* Therefore, if to that ancient historical expectation of the Savior we compare these years which are bringing us closer to the end of the second millennium after Christ and to the beginning of the third, it becomes fully comprehensible that in this present period we wish to turn in a special way to her, the one who in the "night" of the Advent expectation began to shine like a true "Morning Star" (*Stella Matutina*). For just as this star, together with the "dawn," precedes the rising of the sun, so Mary from the time of her Immaculate Conception preceded the coming of the Savior, the rising of the "Sun of Justice" in the history of the human race.[7]

3.3 Her presence in the midst of Israel — a presence so discreet as to pass almost unnoticed by the eyes of her contemporaries — shone very clearly before the Eternal One, who had associated this hidden "daughter of Sion" (cf. Zeph 3:14; Zech 2:10) with the plan of salvation embracing the whole history of humanity. With good reason, then, at the end of this millennium, we Christians who know that the providential plan of the Most Holy Trinity is *the central reality of revelation and of faith* feel the need to emphasize the unique presence of the Mother of Christ in history, especially during these last years leading up to the year 2000.

4 The Second Vatican Council prepares us for this by presenting in its teaching *the Mother of God in the mystery of Christ and of the Church.* If it is true, as the Council itself proclaims, that "only in the mystery of the Incarnate Word does the mystery of man take on light,"[8] then this principle must be applied in a very particular way to that exceptional "daughter of the human

---

[6] The Old Testament foretold in many different ways the mystery of Mary: cf. Saint John Damascene, *Homilia in Dormitionem*, I, 8-9: *SCh* 80, 103-107.

[7] Cf. *Insegnamenti* VI/2 (1983), 225-226; Pius IX, Apostolic Letter *Ineffabilis Deus* (December 8, 1854): *Pii IX P. M. Acta*, I, 597-599.

[8] Cf. Pastoral Constitution on the Church in the Modern World *Gaudium et Spes*, 22.

race," that extraordinary "woman" who became the Mother of Christ. Only *in the mystery of Christ is her mystery* fully *made clear*. Thus has the Church sought to interpret it from the very beginning: the mystery of the Incarnation has enabled her to penetrate and to make ever clearer the mystery of the Mother of the Incarnate Word. The Council of Ephesus (431) was of decisive importance in clarifying this, for during that Council, to the great joy of Christians, the truth of the divine motherhood of Mary was solemnly confirmed as a truth of the Church's faith. Mary *is the Mother of God* (= *Theotokos*), since by the power of the Holy Spirit she conceived in her virginal womb and brought into the world Jesus Christ, the Son of God, who is of one being with the Father.[9] "The Son of God . . . born of the Virgin Mary . . . has truly been made one of us,"[10] has been made man. Thus, through the mystery of Christ, on the horizon of the Church's faith there shines in its fullness the mystery of his Mother. In turn, the dogma of the divine motherhood of Mary was for the Council of Ephesus and is for the Church like a seal upon the dogma of the Incarnation, in which the Word truly assumes human nature into the unity of his person, without canceling out that nature.

5.1 The Second Vatican Council, by presenting Mary in the mystery of Christ, also finds the path to a deeper understanding of the mystery of the Church. Mary, as the Mother of Christ, *is in a particular way united with the Church,* "which the Lord established as his own body."[11] It is significant that the conciliar text places this truth about the Church as the Body of Christ (according to the teaching of the Pauline Letters) in close proximity to the truth that the Son of God "through the power of the Holy Spirit was born of the Virgin Mary." The reality of the Incarnation finds a sort of extension *in the mystery of the Church — the Body of Christ*. And one cannot think of the reality of the Incarnation without referring to Mary, the Mother of the Incarnate Word.

5.2 In these reflections, however, I wish to consider primarily that "pilgrimage of faith" in which "the Blessed Virgin advanced," faithfully preserving her union with Christ.[12] In this way the *"twofold bond"* which unites the Mother

---

[9] Ecumenical Council of Ephesus: *Conciliorum Oecumenicorum Decreta,* Ed. Istituto per le Scienze Religiose, 3rd ed., Bologna, 1973, 41-44, 59-61 (*DS* 250-264); cf. Ecumenical Council of Chalcedon: *Conciliorum Oecumenicorum Decreta,* Ed. Istituto per le Scienze Religiose, 3rd ed., Bologna, 1973, 84-87 (*DS* 300-303).

[10] Second Vatican Ecumenical Council, Pastoral Constitution on the Church in the Modern World *Gaudium et Spes,* 22.

[11] Dogmatic Constitution on the Church *Lumen Gentium,* 52.

[12] Cf. ibid., 58.

of God *with Christ and with the Church* takes on historical significance. Nor is it just a question of the Virgin Mother's life-story, of her personal journey of faith and "the better part" which is hers in the mystery of salvation; it is also a question of the history of the whole People of God, *of all those who take part in the same "pilgrimage of faith."*

5.3 The Council expresses this when it states in another passage that Mary "has gone before," becoming "a model of the Church in the matter of faith, charity and perfect union with Christ."[13] This *"going before" as a figure or model* is in reference to the intimate mystery of the Church, as she actuates and accomplishes her own saving mission by uniting in herself — as Mary did — the qualities *of mother and virgin.* She is a virgin who "keeps whole and pure the fidelity she has pledged to her Spouse" and "becomes herself a mother," for "she brings forth to a new and immortal life children who are conceived of the Holy Spirit and born of God."[14]

6.1 All this is accomplished in a great historical process, comparable "to a journey." *The pilgrimage of faith indicates the interior history,* that is, the story of souls. But it is also the story of all human beings, subject here on earth to transitoriness, and part of the historical dimension. In the following reflections we wish to concentrate first of all on the present, which in itself is not yet history, but which nevertheless is constantly forming it, also in the sense of the history of salvation. Here there opens up a broad prospect, within which the *Blessed Virgin Mary continues to "go before" the People of God.* Her exceptional pilgrimage of faith represents a constant point of reference for the Church, for individuals and for communities, for peoples and nations and, in a sense, for all humanity. It is indeed difficult to encompass and measure its range.

6.2 The Council emphasizes that *the Mother of God is already the eschatological fulfillment of the Church:* "In the most holy Virgin the Church has already reached that perfection whereby she exists without spot or wrinkle (cf. Eph 5:27)"; and at the same time the Council says that "the followers of Christ still strive to increase in holiness by conquering sin, and so *they raise their eyes to Mary,* who shines forth to the whole community of the elect as a model of the virtues."[15] The pilgrimage of faith no longer belongs to the Mother of the Son of God: glorified at the side of her Son in heaven, Mary has already crossed the threshold between faith and that vision which is "face to face"

---

[13] Ibid., 63; cf. Saint Ambrose, *Expositio Evangelii secundum Lucam,* II, 7: *CSEL* 32/4, 45; *De Institutione Virginis,* XIV, 88-89: *PL* 16, 341.

[14] Cf. Dogmatic Constitution on the Church *Lumen Gentium,* 64.

[15] Ibid., 65.

(1 Cor 13:12). At the same time, however, in this eschatological fulfillment, Mary does not cease to be the "Star of the Sea" (*Maris Stella*)[16] for all those who are still on the journey of faith. If they lift their eyes to her from their earthly existence, they do so because "the Son whom she brought forth is he whom God placed as the first-born among many brethren (Rom 8:29),"[17] and also because "in the birth and development" of these brothers and sisters "she cooperates with a maternal love."[18]

I

Mary in the Mystery of Christ

Full of grace

7.1 "Blessed be the God and Father of our Lord Jesus Christ, who has blessed us in Christ with every spiritual blessing in the heavenly places" (Eph 1:3). These words of the *Letter to the Ephesians* reveal the eternal design of God the Father, his plan of man's salvation in Christ. It is a universal plan, which concerns all men and women created in the image and likeness of God (cf. Gen 1:26). Just as all are included in the creative work of God "in the beginning," so all are eternally included in the divine plan of salvation, which is to be completely revealed, in the "fullness of time," with the final coming of Christ. In fact, the God who is the "Father of our Lord Jesus Christ" — these are the next words of the same *Letter* — "*chose us* in him *before the foundation of the world,* that we should be holy and blameless before him. He destined us in love to be his sons through Jesus Christ, according to the purpose of his will, to the praise of his glorious grace, which he freely bestowed on us in *the Beloved.* In him we have redemption through his blood, the forgiveness of our trespasses, according to the riches of his grace" (Eph 1:4-7).

7.2 The *divine plan of salvation* — which was fully revealed to us with the coming of Christ — is eternal. And according to the teaching contained in the *Letter* just quoted and in other Pauline Letters (cf. Col 1:12-14; Rom 3:24; Gal 3:13; 2 Cor 5:18-29), it is also *eternally linked to Christ*. It includes everyone,

---

[16] "Take away this star of the sun which illuminates the world: where does the day go? Take away Mary, this Star of the Sea, of the great and boundless sea: what is left but a vast obscurity and the shadow of death and deepest darkness?": Saint Bernard, *In Nativitate Beatae Mariae Sermo, De Aquaeductu,* 6: *Sancti Bernardi Opera,* V, 1968, 279; cf. *In Laudibus Virginis Matris Homilia,* II, 17: loc. cit., IV, 1966, 34-35.

[17] Dogmatic Constitution on the Church *Lumen Gentium,* 63.

[18] Ibid., 63.

but it reserves a special place for the *"woman"* who is the Mother of him to whom the Father has entrusted the work of salvation.[19] As the Second Vatican Council says, "she is already prophetically foreshadowed in that promise made to our first parents after their fall into sin" — according to the *Book of Genesis* (cf. 3:15). "Likewise she is the Virgin who is to conceive and bear a son, whose name will be called Emmanuel" — according to the words of Isaiah (cf. 7:14).[20] In this way the Old Testament prepares that "fullness of time" when God "sent forth his Son, born of woman . . . so that we might receive adoption as sons." The coming into the world of the Son of God is an event recorded in the first chapters of the Gospels according to Luke and Matthew.

8.1 *Mary* is definitively *introduced into the mystery of Christ through* this event: *the Annunciation* by the angel. This takes place at Nazareth, within the concrete circumstances of the history of Israel, the people which first received God's promises. The divine messenger says to the Virgin: "Hail, full of grace, the Lord is with you" (Lk 1:28). Mary "was greatly troubled at the saying, and considered in her mind what sort of greeting this might be" (Lk 1:29): what could those extraordinary words mean, and in particular the expression "full of grace" (*kecharitoméne*)?[21]

8.2 If we wish to meditate together with Mary on these words, and especially on the expression "full of grace," we can find a significant echo in the very passage from the *Letter to the Ephesians* quoted above. And if after the

---

[19] Concerning the predestination of Mary, cf. Saint John Damascene, *Homilia in Nativitatem,* 7; 10: *SCh* 80, 65; 73; *Homilia in Dormitionem,* I, 3: *SCh* 80, 85: "For it is she, who, chosen from the ancient generations, by virtue of the predestination and benevolence of the God and Father who generated you (the Word of God) outside time without coming out of himself or suffering change, it is she who gave you birth, nourished of her flesh, in the last time."

[20] Dogmatic Constitution on the Church *Lumen Gentium,* 55.

[21] In patristic tradition there is a wide and varied interpretation of this expression: cf. Origen, *In Lucam Homiliae,* VI, 7: *SCh* 87, 148; Severianus of Gabala, *In Mundi Creationem, Oratio* VI, 10: *PG* 56, 497-498; Saint John Chrysostom (Pseudo), *In Annuntiationem Deiparae et contra Arium Impium: PG* 62, 765-766; Basil of Seleucia, *Oratio* 39, *In Sanctissimae Deiparae Annuntiationem,* 5: *PG* 85, 441-446; Antipater of Bosra, *Homilia II, In Sanctissimae Deiparae Annuntiationem,* 3-11: *PG* 85, 1777-1783; Saint Sophronius of Jerusalem, *Oratio* II, *In Sanctissimae Deiparae Annuntiationem,* 17-19: *PG* 87/3, 3235-3240; Saint John Damascene, *Homilia in Dormitionem,* I, 70: *SCh* 80, 96-101; Saint Jerome, *Epistula* 65, 9: *PL* 22, 628; Saint Ambrose, *Expositio Evangelii secundum Lucam,* II, 9: *CSEL* 32/4, 45-46; Saint Augustine, *Sermo* 291, 4-6: *PL* 38, 1318-1319; *Enchiridion,* 36, 11: *PL* 40, 250; Saint Peter Chrysologus, *Sermo* 142: *PL* 52, 579-580; *Sermo* 143: *PL* 52, 583; Saint Fulgentius of Ruspe, *Epistula* 17, VI, 12: *PL* 65, 458; Saint Bernard, *In Laudibus Virginis Matris, Homilia,* III, 2-3: *Sancti Bernardi Opera,* IV, 1966, 36-38.

announcement of the heavenly messenger the Virgin of Nazareth is also called "blessed among women" (cf. Lk 1:42), it is because of that blessing with which "God the Father" has filled us "in the heavenly places, in Christ." It is a *spiritual blessing* which is meant for all people and which bears in itself fullness and universality ("every blessing"). It flows from that love which, in the Holy Spirit, unites the consubstantial Son to the Father. At the same time, it is a blessing poured out through Jesus Christ upon human history until the end: upon all people. This blessing, however, refers *to Mary in a special and exceptional degree:* for she was greeted by Elizabeth as "blessed among women."

8.3 The double greeting is due to the fact that in the soul of this "daughter of Sion" there is manifested, in a sense, all the "glory of grace," that grace which "the Father . . . has given us in his beloved Son." For the messenger greets Mary as "full of grace"; he calls her thus as if it were her real name. He does not call her by her proper earthly name: Miryam (= Mary), but *by this new name: "full of grace."* What does this name mean? Why does the archangel address the Virgin of Nazareth in this way?

8.4 In the language of the Bible "grace" means a special gift, which according to the New Testament has its source precisely in the Trinitarian life of God himself, God who is love (cf. 1 Jn 4:8). The fruit of this love is *"the election"* of which the *Letter to the Ephesians* speaks. On the part of God, this election is the eternal desire to save man through a sharing in his own life (cf. 2 Pet 1:4) in Christ: it is salvation through a sharing in supernatural life. The effect of this eternal gift, of this grace of man's election by God, is like a *seed of holiness,* or a spring which rises in the soul as a gift from God himself, who through grace gives life and holiness to those who are chosen. In this way there is fulfilled, that is to say there comes about, that "blessing" of man "with every spiritual blessing," that "being his adopted sons and daughters . . . in Christ," in him who is eternally the "beloved Son" of the Father.

8.5 When we read that the messenger addresses Mary as "full of grace," the Gospel context, which mingles revelations and ancient promises, enables us to understand that among all the "spiritual blessings in Christ" this is a special "blessing." In the mystery of Christ she is *present* even "before the creation of the world," as the one whom the Father "has chosen" *as Mother* of his Son in the Incarnation. And, what is more, together with the Father, the Son has chosen her, entrusting her eternally to the Spirit of holiness. In an entirely special and exceptional way Mary is united to Christ, and similarly she *is eternally loved in this "beloved Son,"* this Son who is of one being with the Father, in whom is concentrated all the "glory of grace." At the same time, she is and remains perfectly open to this "gift from above" (cf. Jas 1:17). As the Council teaches, Mary "stands out among the poor and humble of the Lord, who confidently await and receive salvation from him."[22]

9.1 If the greeting and the name "full of grace" say all this, in the context of the angel's announcement they refer first of all *to the election of Mary as Mother of the Son of God.* But at the same time the "fullness of grace" indicates all the supernatural munificence from which Mary benefits by being chosen and destined to be the Mother of Christ. If this election is fundamental for the accomplishment of God's salvific designs for humanity, and if the eternal choice in Christ and the vocation to the dignity of adopted children is the destiny of everyone, then the election of Mary is wholly exceptional and unique. Hence also the singularity and uniqueness of her place in the mystery of Christ.

9.2 The divine messenger says to her: "Do not be afraid, Mary, for you have found favor with God. And behold, you will conceive in your womb and bear a son, and you shall call his name Jesus. He will be great, and will be called the Son of the Most High" (Lk 1:30-32). And when the Virgin, disturbed by that extraordinary greeting, asks: "How shall this be, since I have no husband?" she receives from the angel the confirmation and explanation of the preceding words. Gabriel says to her: "*The Holy Spirit will come upon you,* and the power of the Most High will overshadow you; therefore the child to be born will be called holy, the Son of God" (Lk 1:35).

9.3 The Annunciation, therefore, is the revelation of the mystery of the Incarnation at the very beginning of its fulfillment on earth. God's salvific giving of himself and his life, in some way to all creation but directly to man, reaches *one of its high points in the mystery of the Incarnation.* This is indeed a high point among all the gifts of grace conferred in the history of man and of the universe: Mary is "full of grace," because it is precisely in her that the Incarnation of the Word, the hypostatic union of the Son of God with human nature, is accomplished and fulfilled. As the Council says, Mary is "the Mother of the Son of God. As a result she is also the favorite daughter of the Father and the temple of the Holy Spirit. Because of this gift of sublime grace, she far surpasses all other creatures, both in heaven and on earth."[23]

10 The *Letter to the Ephesians,* speaking of the "glory of grace" that "God, the Father . . . has bestowed on us in his beloved Son," adds: "In him we have redemption through his blood" (Eph 1:7). According to the belief formulated in solemn documents of the Church, this "glory of grace" is manifested in the

---

[22] Dogmatic Constitution on the Church *Lumen Gentium,* 55.
[23] Ibid., 53.

Mother of God through the fact that she has been "redeemed in a more sublime manner."[24] By virtue of the richness of the grace of the beloved Son, by reason of the redemptive merits of him who willed to become her Son, Mary was *preserved from the inheritance of original sin.*[25] In this way, from the first moment of her conception — which is to say of her existence — she belonged to Christ, sharing in the salvific and sanctifying grace and in that love which has its beginning in the "Beloved," the Son of the Eternal Father, who through the Incarnation became her own Son. Consequently, through the power of the Holy Spirit, in the order of grace, which is a participation in the divine nature, *Mary receives life from him to whom she herself,* in the order of earthly generation, *gave life* as a mother. The liturgy does not hesitate to call her "Mother of her Creator"[26] and to hail her with the words which Dante Alighieri places on the lips of Saint Bernard: "Daughter of your Son."[27] And since Mary receives this "new life" with a fullness corresponding to the Son's love for the Mother, and thus corresponding to the dignity of the divine motherhood, the angel at the Annunciation calls her "full of grace."

11.1 In the salvific design of the Most Holy Trinity, the mystery of the Incarnation constitutes the superabundant *fulfillment of the promise* made by God to man *after original sin,* after that first sin whose effects oppress the whole earthly history of man (cf. Gen 3:15). And so, there comes into the world a Son, "the seed of the woman" who will crush the evil of sin in its very origins: "he will crush the head of the serpent." As we see from the words of the Protogospel, the victory of the woman's Son will not take place without a hard struggle, a struggle that is to extend through the whole of human history. The "enmity," foretold at the beginning, is confirmed in the Apocalypse (the book of the final events of the Church and the world), in which there recurs the sign of the "woman," this time "clothed with the sun" (Rev 12:1).

11.2 Mary, Mother of the Incarnate Word, is placed *at the very center of*

---

[24] Cf. Pius XI, Apostolic Letter *Ineffabilis Deus* (December 8, 1854): *Pii IX P. M. Acta,* I, 616; Second Vatican Ecumenical Council, Dogmatic Constitution on the Church *Lumen Gentium,* 53.

[25] Cf. Saint Germanus of Constantinople, *In Annuntiationem Sanctissimae Deiparae Homilia: PG* 98, 327-328; Saint Andrew of Crete, *Canon in Beatae Mariae Natalem,* 4: *PG* 97, 1321-1322; *In Nativitatem Beatae Mariae,* I: *PG* 97, 811-812; *Homilia in Dormitionem Sanctae Mariae,* I: *PG* 97, 1067-1068.

[26] Liturgy of the Hours of August 15, Assumption of the Blessed Virgin Mary, Hymn at First and Second Vespers; Saint Peter Damian, *Carmina et Preces,* XLVII: *PL* 145, 934.

[27] *The Divine Comedy,* Paradise, XXXIII, 1; cf. Liturgy of the Hours, Memorial of the Blessed Virgin Mary on Saturday, Hymn II in the Office of Readings.

that enmity, that struggle which accompanies the history of humanity on earth and the history of salvation itself. In this central place, she who belongs to the "weak and poor of the Lord" bears in herself, like no other member of the human race, that "glory of grace" which the Father "has bestowed on us in his beloved Son," and this *grace determines the extraordinary greatness and beauty* of her whole being. Mary thus remains before God, and also before the whole of humanity, as the unchangeable and inviolable sign of God's election, spoken of in Paul's *Letter:* "in Christ . . . he chose us . . . before the foundation of the world, . . . he destined us . . . to be his sons" (Eph 1:4, 5). This election is more powerful than any experience of evil and sin, than all that "enmity" which marks the history of man. In this history Mary remains a sign of sure hope.

Blessed is she who believed

12.1 Immediately after the narration of the Annunciation, the Evangelist Luke guides us in the footsteps of the Virgin of Nazareth toward "a city of Judah" (Lk 1:39). According to scholars this city would be the modern Ain Karim, situated in the mountains, not far from Jerusalem. Mary arrived there "in haste," *to visit Elizabeth* her kinswoman. The reason for her visit is also to be found in the fact that at the Annunciation Gabriel had made special mention of Elizabeth, who in her old age had conceived a son by her husband Zechariah, through the power of God: "your kinswoman Elizabeth in her old age has also conceived a son; and this is the sixth month with her who was called barren. *For with God nothing will be impossible*" (Lk 1:36-37). The divine messenger had spoken of what had been accomplished in Elizabeth in order to answer Mary's question. "How shall this be, since I have no husband?" (Lk 1:34). It is to come to pass precisely through the "power of the Most High," just as it happened in the case of Elizabeth, and even more so.

12.2 Moved by charity, therefore, Mary goes to the house of her kinswoman. When Mary enters, Elizabeth replies to her greeting and feels the child leap in her womb, and being "filled with the Holy Spirit" she *greets Mary* with a loud cry: "Blessed are you among women, and blessed is the fruit of your womb!" (cf. Lk 1:40-42). Elizabeth's exclamation or acclamation was subsequently to become part of the *Hail Mary,* as a continuation of the angel's greeting, thus becoming one of the Church's most frequently used prayers. But still more significant are the words of Elizabeth in the question which follows: "And why is this granted me, that the mother of my Lord should come to me?" (Lk 1:43). Elizabeth bears witness to Mary: she recognizes and proclaims that before her stands the Mother of the Lord, the Mother of the Messiah. The son whom Elizabeth is carrying in her womb also shares in this witness: "The babe in my womb leaped for joy" (Lk 1:44). This child is the future John the Baptist, who at the Jordan will point out Jesus as the Messiah.

12.3 While every word of Elizabeth's greeting is filled with meaning, her final words would seem to have *fundamental importance:* "And blessed is she who believed that there would be a fulfillment of what was spoken to her from the Lord" (Lk 1:45).[28] These words can be linked with the title "full of grace" of the angel's greeting. Both of these texts reveal an essential Mariological content, namely the truth about Mary, who has become really present in the mystery of Christ precisely because she "has believed." The *fullness of grace* announced by the angel means the gift of God himself. *Mary's faith,* proclaimed by Elizabeth at the Visitation, indicates *how* the Virgin of Nazareth *responded to this gift.*

13.1 As the Council teaches, " 'The obedience of faith' (Rom 16:26; cf. Rom 1:5; 2 Cor 10:5-6) must be given to God who reveals, an obedience by which man entrusts his whole self freely to God."[29] This description of faith found perfect realization in Mary. The "decisive" moment was the Annunciation, and the very words of Elizabeth: "And blessed is she who believed" refer primarily to that very moment.[30]

13.2 Indeed, at the Annunciation Mary entrusted herself to God completely, with the "full submission of intellect and will," manifesting "the obedience of faith" to him who spoke to her through his messenger.[31] She responded, therefore, *with all her human and feminine "I,"* and this response of faith included both perfect cooperation with "the grace of God that precedes and assists" and perfect openness to the action of the Holy Spirit, who "constantly brings faith to completion by his gifts."[32]

---

[28] Cf. Saint Augustine, *De Sancta Virginitate,* III, 3: *PL* 40, 398; *Sermo* 25, 7: *PL* 46.

[29] Dogmatic Constitution on Divine Revelation *Dei Verbum,* 5.

[30] This is a classic theme, already expounded by Saint Irenaeus: "And, as by the action of the disobedient virgin, man was afflicted and, being cast down, died, so also by the action of the Virgin who obeyed the word of God, man being regenerated received, through life, life. . . . For it was meet and just . . . that Eve should be 'recapitulated' in Mary, so that the Virgin, becoming the advocate of the virgin, should dissolve and destroy the virginal disobedience by means of virginal obedience": *Expositio Doctrinae Apostolicae,* 33: *SCh* 62, 83-86; cf. *Adversus Haereses,* V, 19, 1: *SCh* 153, 248-250.

[31] Second Vatican Ecumenical Council, Dogmatic Constitution on Divine Revelation *Dei Verbum,* 5.

[32] Ibid., 5; cf. Dogmatic Constitution on the Church *Lumen Gentium,* 56.

13.3 The word of the living God, announced to Mary by the angel, referred to her: "And behold, you will conceive in your womb and bear a son" (Lk 1:31). By accepting this announcement, Mary was to become the "Mother of the Lord," and the divine mystery of the Incarnation was to be accomplished in her: "The Father of mercies willed that the consent of the predestined Mother should precede the Incarnation."[33] And Mary gives this consent, after she has heard everything the messenger has to say. She says: "Behold, I am the handmaid of the Lord; let it be to me according to your word" (Lk 1:38). This *fiat* of Mary — "let it be to me" — was decisive, on the human level, for the accomplishment of the divine mystery. There is a complete harmony with the words of the Son, who, according to the *Letter to the Hebrews*, says to the Father as he comes into the world: "Sacrifices and offering you have not desired, but *a body you have prepared for me*. . . . Lo, I have come to do your will, O God" (Heb 10:5-7). The mystery of the Incarnation was accomplished when Mary uttered her *fiat:* "Let it be to me according to your word," which made possible, as far as it depended upon her in the divine plan, the granting of her Son's desire.

13.4 Mary uttered this *fiat in faith.* In faith she entrusted herself to God without reserve and "devoted herself totally as the handmaid of the Lord to the person and work of her Son."[34] And as the Fathers of the Church teach — she conceived this Son in her mind before she conceived him in her womb: precisely in faith![35] Rightly therefore does Elizabeth praise Mary: "And blessed is she who believed *that there would be a fulfillment* of what was spoken to her from the Lord." These words have already been fulfilled: Mary of Nazareth presents herself at the threshold of Elizabeth and Zechariah's house as the Mother of the Son of God. This is Elizabeth's joyful discovery: "The mother of my Lord comes to me!"

14.1 Mary's faith can also be *compared to that of Abraham,* whom Saint Paul calls "our father in faith" (cf. Rom 4:12). In the salvific economy of God's revelation, Abraham's faith constitutes the beginning of the Old Covenant; Mary's faith at the Annunciation inaugurates the New Covenant. Just as

---

[33] Second Vatican Ecumenical Council, Dogmatic Constitution on the Church *Lumen Gentium,* 56.

[34] Ibid., 56.

[35] Cf. ibid., 53; Saint Augustine, *De Sancta Virginitate,* III, 3: *PL* 40, 398; *Sermo* 215, 4: *PL* 38, 1074; *Sermo* 196, 1: *PL* 38, 1019; *De Peccatorum Meritis et Remissione,* I, 29, 57: *PL* 44, 142; *Sermo* 25, 7: *PL* 46, 937-938; Saint Leo the Great, *Tractatus* 21, *De Natale Domini,* I: *CCL* 138, 86.

Abraham *"in hope believed against hope,* that he should become the father of many nations" (cf. Rom 4:18), so Mary, at the Annunciation, having professed her virginity ("How shall this be, since I have no husband?") *believed* that through the power of the Most High, by the power of the Holy Spirit, she would become the Mother of God's Son in accordance with the angel's revelation: "The child to be born will be called holy, the Son of God" (Lk 1:35).

14.2 However, Elizabeth's words "And blessed is she who believed" do not apply only to that particular moment of the Annunciation. Certainly the Annunciation is the culminating moment of Mary's faith in her awaiting of Christ, but it is also the point of departure from which her whole "journey toward God" begins, her whole pilgrimage of faith. And on this road, in an eminent and truly heroic manner — indeed with an ever greater heroism of faith — the "obedience" which she professes to the word of divine revelation will be fulfilled. Mary's "obedience of faith" during the whole of her pilgrimage will show surprising similarities to the faith of Abraham. Just like the Patriarch of the People of God, so too Mary, during the pilgrimage of her filial and maternal *fiat,* "in hope believed against hope." Especially during certain stages of this journey the blessing granted to her "who believed" will be revealed with particular vividness. To believe means "to abandon oneself" to the truth of the word of the living God, knowing and humbly recognizing "how unsearchable are his judgments and how *inscrutable his ways"* (Rom 11:33). Mary, who by the eternal will of the Most High stands, one may say, at the very center of those "inscrutable ways" and "unsearchable judgments" of God, conforms herself to them in the dim light of faith, accepting fully and with a ready heart everything that is decreed in the divine plan.

15.1 When at the Annunciation Mary hears of the Son whose Mother she is to become and to whom "she will give the name Jesus" (= Savior), she also learns that "the Lord God will give to him the throne of his father David," and that "he will reign over the house of Jacob for ever and of his Kingdom there will be no end" (Lk 1:32-33). The hope of the whole of Israel was directed toward this. The promised Messiah is to be "great," and the heavenly messenger also announces that *"he will be great"* — great both by bearing the name of *Son of the Most High* and by the fact that he is to assume the *inheritance of David.* He is therefore to be a king, he is to reign "over the house of Jacob." Mary had grown up in the midst of these expectations of her people: could she guess, at the moment of the Annunciation, the vital significance of the angel's words? And how is one to understand that "Kingdom" which "will have no end"?

15.2 Although through faith she may have perceived in that instant that she was the Mother of the "Messiah-King," nevertheless she replied: "*Behold, I am the handmaid of the Lord;* let it be to me according to your word" (Lk 1:38). From the first moment, Mary professed above all the "obedience of faith," abandoning herself to the meaning which was given to the words of the Annunciation by him from whom they proceeded: God himself.

16.1 Later, a little further along this way of the "obedience of faith," Mary hears *other words:* those uttered by *Simeon* in the Temple of Jerusalem. It was now forty days after the birth of Jesus when, in accordance with the precepts of the Law of Moses, Mary and Joseph "brought him up to Jerusalem to present him to the Lord" (Lk 2:22). The birth had taken place in conditions of extreme poverty. We know from Luke that when, on the occasion of the census ordered by the Roman authorities, Mary went with Joseph to Bethlehem, having found "no place in the inn," *she gave birth to her Son in a stable* and "laid him in a manger" (cf. Lk 2:7).

16.2 A just and God-fearing man, called Simeon, appears at this beginning of Mary's "journey" of faith. His words, suggested by the Holy Spirit (cf. Lk 2:25-27), confirm the truth of the Annunciation. For we read that he took up in his arms the child to whom — in accordance with the angel's command — the name Jesus was given (cf. Lk 2:21). Simeon's words match the meaning of this name, which is Savior: "God is salvation." Turning to the Lord, he says: "For my eyes have seen your *salvation* which you have prepared *in the presence of all peoples,* a light for revelation to the Gentiles, and for glory to your people Israel" (Lk 2:30-32). At the same time, however, Simeon addresses Mary with the following words: "Behold, this child is set for the fall and rising of many in Israel, and for a *sign that is spoken against,* that thoughts out of many hearts may be revealed"; and he adds with direct reference to her: "and a sword will pierce through your own soul also" (cf. Lk 2:34-35). Simeon's words cast new light on the announcement which Mary had heard from the angel: Jesus is the Savior, he is "a *light* for revelation" to mankind. Is not this what was manifested in a way on Christmas night, when the *shepherds* come to the stable (cf. Lk 2:8-20)? Is not this what was to be manifested even more clearly in the coming of the *Magi from the East* (cf. Mt 2:1-12)? But at the same time, at the very beginning of his life, the Son of Mary, and his Mother with him, will experience in themselves the truth of those other words of Simeon: "a sign that is spoken against" (Lk 2:34). Simeon's words seem like a *second Annunciation to Mary,* for they tell her of the actual historical situation in which the Son is to accomplish his mission, namely in misunderstanding and sorrow. While this announcement on the one hand confirms her faith in the accomplishment of the divine promises of salvation, on the other hand it also reveals to her that she will have to live her obedience of faith in suffering, at the side of the suffering Savior, and that her motherhood will be mysterious and sorrowful. Thus, after the visit of the Magi who came from the East, after their homage ("they fell down and worshiped him") and after they had offered gifts (cf. Mt 2:11), Mary together with the child *has to flee into Egypt* in the protective care of Joseph, for "Herod is about to search for the child, to destroy him" (cf. Mt 2:13). And until the death of Herod they will have to remain in Egypt (cf. Mt 2:15).

17.1 When the Holy Family returns to Nazareth after Herod's death, there begins the long *period of the hidden life.* She "who believed that there would be a fulfillment of what was spoken to her from the Lord" (Lk 1:45) lives the reality of these words day by day. And daily at her side is the Son to whom *"she gave the name Jesus"*; therefore in contact with him she certainly uses this name, a fact which would have surprised no one, since the name had long been in use in Israel. Nevertheless, Mary knows that he who bears the name *Jesus has been called by the angel "the Son of the Most High"* (cf. Lk 1:32). Mary knows she has conceived and given birth to him "without having a husband," by the power of the Holy Spirit, by the power of the Most High who overshadowed her (cf. Lk 1:35), just as at the time of Moses and the Patriarchs the cloud covered the presence of God (cf. Ex 24:16; 40:34-35; 1 Kings 8:10-12). Therefore Mary knows that the Son to whom she gave birth in a virginal manner is precisely that "Holy One," the Son of God, of whom the angel spoke to her.

17.2 During the years of Jesus' hidden life in the house at Nazareth, *Mary's life* too is *"hid with Christ in God"* (cf. Col 3:3) *through faith.* For faith is contact with the mystery of God. Every day Mary is in constant contact with the ineffable mystery of God made man, a mystery that surpasses everything revealed in the Old Covenant. From the moment of the Annunciation, the mind of the Virgin-Mother has been initiated into the radical "newness" of God's self-revelation and has been made aware of the mystery. She is the first of those "little ones" of whom Jesus will say one day: "Father, . . . you have hidden these things from the wise and understanding and revealed them to babes" (Mt 11:25). For "no one knows the Son except the Father" (Mt 11:27). If this is the case, how can Mary "know the Son"? Of course she does not know him as the Father does; and yet she is *the first of those to whom the Father "has chosen to reveal him"* (cf. Mt 11:26-27; 1 Cor 2:11). If though, from the moment of the

Annunciation, the Son — whom only the Father knows completely, as the one who begets him in the eternal "today" (cf. Ps 2:7) — was revealed to Mary, she, his Mother, is in contact with the truth about her Son only in faith and through faith! She is therefore blessed, because "she has believed," and continues to *believe day after day* amidst all the trials and the adversities of Jesus' infancy and then during the years of the hidden life at Nazareth, where he "was obedient to them" (Lk 2:51). He was obedient both to Mary and also to Joseph, since Joseph took the place of his father in people's eyes; for this reason, the Son of Mary was regarded by the people as "the carpenter's son" (Mt 13:55).

17.3 The Mother of *that Son*, therefore, mindful of what has been told her at the Annunciation and in subsequent events, bears within herself the radical "newness" of faith: *the beginning of the New Covenant*. This is the beginning of the Gospel, the joyful Good News. However, it is not difficult to see in that beginning *a particular heaviness of heart*, linked with a sort of "night of faith" — to use the words of Saint John of the Cross — a kind of "veil" through which one has to draw near to the Invisible One and to live in intimacy with the mystery.[36] And this is the way that Mary, for many years, *lived in intimacy with the mystery of her Son*, and went forward in her "pilgrimage of faith," while Jesus "increased in wisdom . . . and in favor with God and man" (Lk 2:52). God's predilection for him was manifested ever more clearly to people's eyes. The first human creature thus permitted to discover Christ was Mary, who lived with Joseph in the same house at Nazareth.

17.4 However, when he had been found in the Temple, and his Mother asked him, "Son, why have you treated us so?" *the twelve-year-old Jesus* answered: "Did you not know that I must be in my Father's house?" And the Evangelist adds: "*And they* (Joseph and Mary) *did not understand* the saying which he spoke to them" (Lk 2:48-50). Jesus was aware that "no one knows the Son except the Father" (cf. Mt 11:27); thus even his Mother, to whom had been revealed most completely the mystery of his divine sonship, lived in intimacy with this mystery only through faith! Living side by side with her Son under the same roof, and faithfully persevering "in her union with her Son," she *"advanced in her pilgrimage of faith,"* as the Council emphasizes.[37] And so it was during Christ's public life too (cf. Mk 3:21-35) that day by day there was fulfilled in her the blessing uttered by Elizabeth at the Visitation: "Blessed is she who believed."

18.1 This blessing reaches its full meaning *when Mary stands beneath the Cross* of her Son (cf. Jn 19:25). The Council says that this happened "not

[36] Cf. *The Ascent of Mount Carmel*, Book II, Chapter 3, 4-6.
[37] Cf. Dogmatic Constitution on the Church *Lumen Gentium*, 58.

without a divine plan": by "suffering deeply with her only-begotten Son and joining herself with her maternal spirit to his sacrifice, lovingly consenting to the immolation of the victim to whom she had given birth," in this way Mary "faithfully preserved her union with her Son even to the Cross."[38] It is a union through faith — the same faith with which she had received the angel's revelation at the Annunciation. At that moment she had also heard the words: "He will be great ... and *the Lord God* will give to him the throne of his father David, and he will reign over the house of Jacob for ever; and of his Kingdom there will be no end" (Lk 1:32-33).

18.2 And now, standing at the foot of the Cross, Mary is the witness, humanly speaking, of the complete *negation of these words*. On that wood of the Cross her Son hangs in agony as one condemned. "He was despised and rejected by men; a man of sorrows ... he was despised, and we esteemed him not": as one destroyed (cf. Is 53:3-5). How great, how heroic then is the *obedience of faith* shown by Mary in the face of God's "unsearchable judgments"! How completely she "abandons herself to God" without reserve, "offering the full assent of the intellect and the will"[39] to him whose "ways are inscrutable" (cf. Rom 11:33)! And how powerful too is the action of grace in her soul, how all-pervading is the influence of the Holy Spirit and of his light and power!

18.3 *Through this faith Mary is perfectly united with Christ in his self- emptying*. For "Christ Jesus, who, though he was in the form of God, did not count equality with God a thing to be grasped, but emptied himself, taking the form of a servant, being born in the likeness of men": precisely on Golgotha "humbled himself and became obedient unto death, even death on a Cross" (cf. Phil 2:5-8). At the foot of the Cross Mary shares through faith in the shocking mystery of this self-emptying. This is perhaps the deepest *"kenosis" of faith* in human history. Through faith the Mother shares in the death of her Son, in his redeeming death; but in contrast with the faith of the disciples who fled, hers was far more enlightened. On Golgotha, Jesus through the Cross definitively confirmed that he was the "sign of contradiction" foretold by Simeon. At the same time, there were also fulfilled on Golgotha the words which Simeon had addressed to Mary: "and a sword will pierce through your own soul also."[40]

19.1 Yes, truly "blessed is she who believed"! These words, spoken by Elizabeth after the Annunciation, here at the foot of the Cross seem to reecho with

---

[38] Ibid., 58.

[39] Cf. Dogmatic Constitution on Divine Revelation *Dei Verbum*, 5.

[40] Concerning Mary's participation or "compassion" in the death of Christ, cf. Saint Bernard, *In Dominica infra octavam Assumptionis Sermo*, 14: *Sancti Bernardi Opera*, V, 1968, 273.

supreme eloquence, and the power contained within them becomes something penetrating. From the Cross, that is to say from the very heart of the mystery of Redemption, there radiates and spreads out the prospect of that blessing of faith. It goes right back to "the beginning," and as a sharing in the sacrifice of Christ — the new Adam — it becomes in a certain sense *the counterpoise to the disobedience and disbelief* embodied in the sin of our first parents. Thus teach the Fathers of the Church and especially Saint Irenaeus, quoted by the Constitution *Lumen Gentium:* "The knot of Eve's disobedience was untied by Mary's obedience; what the virgin Eve bound through her unbelief, the Virgin Mary *loosened by her faith.*"[41] In the light of this comparison with Eve, the Fathers of the Church — as the Council also says — call Mary the "Mother of the living" and often speak of "death through Eve, life through Mary."[42]

19.2 In the expression "Blessed is she who believed," we can therefore rightly find *a kind of "key"* which unlocks for us the innermost reality of Mary, whom the angel hailed as "full of grace." If as "full of grace" she has been eternally present in the mystery of Christ, through faith she became a sharer in that mystery in every extension of her earthly journey. She "advanced in her pilgrimage of faith" and at the same time, in a discreet yet direct and effective way, she made present to humanity *the mystery of Christ.* And she still continues to do so. Through the mystery of Christ, she too is present within mankind. Thus through the mystery of the Son the mystery of the Mother is also made clear.

Behold your Mother

20.1 The *Gospel of Luke* records the moment when "a woman in the crowd raised her voice" and said to Jesus: *"Blessed is the womb that bore you, and the breasts that you sucked!"* (Lk 11:27). These words were an expression of praise of Mary as Jesus' Mother according to the flesh. Probably the Mother of Jesus was not personally known to this woman; in fact, when Jesus began his messianic activity Mary did not accompany him but continued to remain at Nazareth. One could say that the words of that unknown woman in a way brought Mary out of her hiddenness.

20.2 Through these words, there flashed out in the midst of the crowd, at least for an instant, the Gospel of Jesus' infancy. This is the Gospel in which

---

[41] Saint Irenaeus, *Adversus Haereses*, III, 22, 4: SCh 211, 438-444; cf. Dogmatic Constitution on the Church *Lumen Gentium*, 56, Note 6.

[42] Cf. Dogmatic Constitution on the Church *Lumen Gentium*, 56, and the Fathers quoted there in Notes 8 and 9.

Mary is present as the Mother who conceives Jesus in her womb, gives him birth and nurses him: the nursing Mother referred to by the woman in the crowd. *Thanks to this motherhood, Jesus,* the Son of the Most High (cf. Lk 1:32), is a true *son of man.* He is "flesh," like every other man: he is "the Word (who) became flesh" (cf. Jn 1:14). He is of the flesh and blood of Mary![43]

20.3 But to the blessing uttered by that woman upon her who was his Mother according to the flesh, Jesus replies in a significant way: "Blessed rather are *those who hear the word of God and keep it*" (Lk 11:28). He wishes to divert attention from motherhood understood only as a fleshly bond, in order to direct it toward those mysterious bonds of the spirit which develop from hearing and keeping God's word.

20.4 This same shift into the sphere of spiritual values is seen even more clearly in another response of Jesus reported by all the Synoptics. When Jesus is told that "his mother and brothers are standing outside and wish to see him," he replies: *"My mother and my brothers are those who hear the word of God and do it"* (cf. Lk 8:20-21). This he said "looking around on those who sat about him," as we read in Mark (3:34) or, according to Matthew (12:49), "stretching out his hand toward his disciples."

20.5 These statements seem to *fit in with the reply which the twelve-year-old Jesus* gave to Mary and Joseph when he was found after three days in the Temple at Jerusalem.

20.6 Now, when Jesus left Nazareth and began his public life throughout Palestine, *he was completely and exclusively "concerned with his Father's business"* (cf. Lk 2:49). He announced the Kingdom: the "Kingdom of God" and "his Father's business," which add a new dimension and meaning to everything human, and therefore to every human bond, insofar as these things relate to the goals and tasks assigned to every human being. Within this new dimension, also a bond such as that of "brotherhood" means something different from "brotherhood according to the flesh" deriving from a common origin from the same set of parents. *"Motherhood,"* too, *in the dimension of the Kingdom of God and in the radius of the fatherhood of God himself, takes on another meaning.* In the words reported by Luke, Jesus teaches precisely this new meaning of motherhood.

20.7 Is Jesus thereby distancing himself from his Mother according to the flesh? Does he perhaps wish to leave her in the hidden obscurity which she herself has chosen? If this seems to be the case from the tone of those words, one must nevertheless note that the new and different motherhood which

---

[43] "Christ is truth, Christ is flesh: Christ is truth in the mind of Mary, Christ is flesh in the womb of Mary": Saint Augustine, *Sermo* 25 (*Sermones inediti*), 7: *PL* 46, 938.

Jesus speaks of to his disciples refers precisely to Mary in a very special way. Is not Mary *the first of "those who hear the word of God and do it"*? And therefore does not the blessing uttered by Jesus in response to the woman in the crowd refer primarily to her? Without any doubt, Mary is worthy of blessing by the very fact that she became the Mother of Jesus according to the flesh ("Blessed is the womb that bore you, and the breasts that you sucked"), but also and especially because already at the Annunciation she accepted the word of God, because she believed it, *because she was obedient to God,* and because she "kept" the word and "pondered it in her heart" (cf. Lk 1:38, 45; 2:19, 51) and by means of her whole life accomplished it. Thus we can say that the blessing proclaimed by Jesus is not in opposition, despite appearances, to the blessing uttered by the unknown woman, but rather coincides with that blessing in the person of this Virgin Mother, who called herself only "the handmaid of the Lord" (Lk 1:38). If it is true that "all generations will call her blessed" (cf. Lk 1:48), then it can be said that the unnamed woman was the first to confirm unwittingly that prophetic phrase of Mary's *Magnificat* and to begin the *Magnificat* of the ages.

20.8 If through faith Mary became the bearer of the Son given to her by the Father through the power of the Holy Spirit, while preserving her virginity intact, in that same faith she *discovered and accepted the other dimension of motherhood* revealed by Jesus during his messianic mission. One can say that this dimension of motherhood belonged to Mary from the beginning, that is to say from the moment of the conception and birth of her Son. From that time she was "the one who believed." But as the messianic mission of her Son grew clearer to her eyes and spirit, she herself as a mother became ever more open *to that new dimension of motherhood* which was to constitute her "part" beside her Son. Had she not said from the very beginning: "Behold, I am the handmaid of the Lord; let it be to me according to your word" (Lk 1:38)? Through faith Mary continued to hear and to ponder that word, in which there became ever clearer, in a way "which surpasses knowledge" (Eph 3:19), the self-revelation of the living God. Thus *in a sense* Mary as Mother became *the first "disciple" of her Son,* the first to whom he seemed to say: "Follow me," even before he addressed this call to the Apostles or to anyone else (cf. Jn 1:43).

21.1 From this point of view, particularly eloquent is the passage in the *Gospel of John* which presents Mary at the wedding feast of Cana. She appears there as the Mother of Jesus at the beginning of his public life: "There was a *marriage at Cana in Galilee,* and the mother of Jesus was there; Jesus also was invited to the marriage, with his disciples" (Jn 2:1-2). From the text it appears that Jesus and his disciples were invited together with Mary, as if by reason of her presence at the celebration: the Son seems to have been invited because of his Mother. We are familiar with the sequence of events which resulted from that invitation, that "beginning of the signs" wrought by Jesus — the water changed into wine — which prompts the Evangelist to say that Jesus "manifested his glory; and his disciples believed in him" (Jn 2:11).

21.2 Mary is present at Cana in Galilee as the *Mother of Jesus,* and in a significant way she *contributes* to that "beginning of the signs" which reveal the messianic power of her Son. We read: "When the wine gave out, the mother of Jesus said to him, 'They have no wine.' And Jesus said to her, 'O woman, what have you to do with me? My hour has not yet come'" (Jn 2:3-4). In John's Gospel that "hour" means the time appointed by the Father when the Son accomplishes his task and is to be glorified (cf. Jn 7:30; 8:20; 12:23, 27; 13:1; 17:1; 19:27). Even though Jesus' reply to his Mother sounds like a refusal (especially if we consider the blunt statement "My hour has not yet come" rather than the question), Mary nevertheless turns to the servants and says to them: "Do whatever he tells you" (Jn 2:5). Then Jesus orders the servants to fill the stone jars with water, and the water becomes wine, better than the wine which has previously been served to the wedding guests.

21.3 What deep understanding existed between Jesus and his Mother? How can we probe the mystery of their intimate spiritual union? But the fact speaks for itself. It is certain that that event already quite clearly outlines *the new dimension,* the new meaning *of Mary's motherhood.* Her motherhood has a significance which is not exclusively contained in the words of Jesus and in the various episodes reported by the Synoptics (Lk 11:27-28 and Lk 8:19-21; Mt 12:46-50; Mk 3:31-35). In these texts Jesus means above all to contrast the motherhood resulting from the fact of birth with what this "motherhood" (and also "brotherhood") is to be in the dimension of the Kingdom of God, in the salvific radius of God's fatherhood. In John's text on the other hand, the description of the Cana event outlines what is actually manifested as a new kind of motherhood according to the spirit and not just according to the flesh, that is to say *Mary's solicitude for human beings,* her coming to them in the wide variety of their wants and needs. At Cana in Galilee there is shown only one concrete aspect of human need, apparently a small one of little importance ("They have no wine"). But it has a symbolic value: this coming to the aid of human needs means, at the same time, bringing those needs within the radius of Christ's messianic mission and salvific power. Thus there is a mediation: Mary places herself between her Son and mankind in the reality of their wants, needs and sufferings. *She puts herself "in the middle,"* that is to say *she acts as a mediatrix not as an outsider, but in her position as Mother.* She knows that as such she can point out to her Son the needs of mankind, and in fact, she "has the right" to do so. Her mediation is thus in the nature of intercession: Mary "intercedes" for mankind. And that is not all. As a Mother she also *wishes the messianic power of her Son to be manifested,* that salvific power of his which is meant to help man in his misfortunes, to free him from the evil which in various forms and degrees weighs heavily upon his life. Precisely as the Prophet Isaiah had foretold about the Messiah in the famous passage which Jesus quoted before his fellow townsfolk in Nazareth: "To preach good news to the poor . . . to proclaim release to the captives and recovering of sight to the blind. . ." (cf. Lk 4:18).

21.4 Another essential element of Mary's maternal task is found in her words to the servants: "Do whatever he tells you." *The Mother* of Christ presents herself as the *spokeswoman of her Son's will,* pointing out those things which must be done so that the salvific power of the Messiah may be manifested. At Cana, thanks to the intercession of Mary and the obedience of the servants, Jesus begins "his hour." At Cana Mary appears as *believing in Jesus.* Her faith evokes his first "sign" and helps to kindle the faith of the disciples.

22.1 We can therefore say that in this passage of John's Gospel we find as it were a first manifestation of the truth concerning Mary's maternal care. This truth has also found expression *in the teaching of the Second Vatican Council.* It is important to note how the Council illustrates Mary's maternal role as it relates to the mediation of Christ. Thus we read: "Mary's maternal function toward mankind in no way obscures or diminishes the unique mediation of Christ, but rather shows its efficacy," because "there is one mediator between God and men, the man Christ Jesus" (1 Tim 2:5). This maternal role of Mary flows, according to God's good pleasure, "from the superabundance of the merits of Christ; it is founded on his mediation, absolutely depends on it, and draws all its efficacy from it."[44] It is precisely in this sense that the episode at Cana in Galilee offers us *a sort of first announcement of Mary's mediation,* wholly oriented toward Christ and tending to the revelation of his salvific power.

22.2 From the *text of John* it is evident that it is a mediation which is maternal. As the Council proclaims: Mary became "a Mother to us in the order of grace." This motherhood in the order of grace flows from her divine motherhood. Because she was, by the design of divine Providence, the Mother who nourished the divine Redeemer, Mary became "an associate of unique nobil-

---

[44] Dogmatic Constitution on the Church *Lumen Gentium,* 60.

ity, and the Lord's humble handmaid," who "cooperated by her obedience, faith, hope and burning charity in the Savior's work of restoring supernatural life to souls."[45] And "this *maternity of Mary in the order of grace* . . . will last without interruption until the eternal fulfillment of all the elect."[46]

23.1 If John's description of the event at Cana presents Mary's caring motherhood at the beginning of Christ's messianic activity, another passage from the same Gospel confirms this motherhood in the salvific economy of grace at its crowning moment, namely when Christ's sacrifice on the Cross, his Paschal Mystery, is accomplished. John's description is concise: "*Standing by the cross of Jesus* were his mother, and his mother's sister, Mary the wife of Clopas, and Mary Magdalene. When Jesus saw his mother, and the disciple whom he loved standing near, he said to his mother: 'Woman, behold your son!' Then he said to the disciple, 'Behold, your mother!' And from that hour the disciple took her to his own home" (Jn 19:25-27).

23.2 Undoubtedly, we find here an expression of the Son's particular solicitude for his Mother, whom he is leaving in such great sorrow. And yet the "testament of Christ's Cross" says more. Jesus highlights a new relationship between Mother and Son, the whole truth and reality of which he solemnly confirms. One can say that if Mary's motherhood of the human race had already been outlined, now it is clearly stated and established. It *emerges* from the definitive accomplishment of *the Redeemer's Paschal Mystery*. The Mother of Christ, who stands at the very center of this mystery — a mystery which embraces each individual and all humanity — is given as Mother to every single individual and all mankind. The man at the foot of the Cross is John, "the disciple whom he loved."[47] But it is not he alone. Following tradition, the Council does not hesitate to call Mary *"the Mother of Christ and Mother of mankind":* since she "belongs to the offspring of Adam she is one with all human beings. . . . Indeed she is 'clearly the Mother of the members of Christ . . . since she cooperated out of love so that there might be born in the Church the faithful.' "[48]

---

[45] Ibid., 61.

[46] Ibid., 62.

[47] There is a well-known passage of Origen on the presence of Mary and John on Calvary: "The Gospels are the first fruits of all Scripture and the Gospel of John is the first of the Gospels: no one can grasp its meaning without having leaned his head on Jesus' breast and having received from Jesus Mary as Mother": *Commentarium in Ioannem*, I, 6: *PG* 14, 31; cf. Saint Ambrose, *Expositio Evangelii secundum Lucam*, X, 129-131: *CSEL* 32/4, 504-505.

[48] Dogmatic Constitution on the Church *Lumen Gentium*, 54 and 53; the latter text quotes Saint Augustine, *De Sancta Virginitate*, VI, 6: *PL* 40, 399.

23.3 And so this "new motherhood of Mary," generated by faith, is *the fruit of the "new" love* which came to definitive maturity in her at the foot of the Cross, through her sharing in the redemptive love of her Son.

24.1 Thus we find ourselves at the very center of the fulfillment of the promise contained in the Protogospel: the "seed of the woman . . . will crush the head of the serpent" (cf. Gen 3:15). By his redemptive death Jesus Christ conquers the evil of sin and death at its very roots. It is significant that, as he speaks to his Mother from the Cross, he calls her "woman" and says to her: "Woman, behold your son!" Moreover, he had addressed her by the same term at Cana too (cf. Jn 2:4). How can one doubt that especially now, on Golgotha, this expression goes to the very heart of the mystery of Mary, and indicates the unique *place* which she occupies *in the whole economy of salvation?* As the Council teaches, in Mary "the exalted Daughter of Sion, and after a long expectation of the promise, the times were at length fulfilled and the new dispensation established. All this oc-curred when the Son of God took a human nature from her, that he might in the mysteries of his flesh free man from sin."[49]

24.2 The words uttered by Jesus from the Cross signify that *the mother-hood* of her who bore Christ finds a "new" continuation *in the Church and through the Church,* symbolized and represented by John. In this way, she who as the one "full of grace" was brought into the mystery of Christ in order to be his Mother and thus *the Holy Mother of God,* through the Church re-mains in that mystery as *"the woman"* spoken of by the *Book of Genesis* (3:15) at the beginning and by the *Apocalypse* (12:1) at the end of the history of salvation. In accordance with the eternal plan of Providence, Mary's divine motherhood is to be poured out upon the Church, as indicated by statements of Tradition, according to which Mary's "motherhood" of the Church is the reflection and extension of her motherhood of the Son of God.[50]

24.3 According to the Council, the very moment of the Church's birth and full manifestation to the world enables us to glimpse this continuity of Mary's motherhood: "Since it pleased God not to manifest solemnly the mystery of the salvation of the human race until he poured forth the Spirit promised by Christ, we see the *Apostles* before the day of Pentecost 'continuing with one mind *in prayer* with the women and *Mary the mother of Jesus,* and with his brethren' (Acts 1:14). We see Mary prayerfully imploring the gift of the Spirit, who had already overshadowed her in the Annunciation."[51]

---

[49] Dogmatic Constitution on the Church *Lumen Gentium,* 55.
[50] Cf. Saint Leo the Great, *Tractatus 26, De Natale Domini,* 2: CCL 138, 126.
[51] Dogmatic Constitution on the Church *Lumen Gentium,* 59.

24.4 And so, in the redemptive economy of grace, brought about through the action of the Holy Spirit, there is a unique correspondence between the moment of the Incarnation of the Word and the moment of the birth of the Church. The person who links these two moments is Mary: *Mary at Nazareth* and *Mary in the Upper Room at Jerusalem.* In both cases her discreet yet essential presence indicates the path of "birth from the Holy Spirit." Thus she who is present in the mystery of Christ as Mother becomes — by the will of the Son and the power of the Holy Spirit — present in the mystery of the Church. In the Church too she continues to be *a maternal presence,* as is shown by the words spoken from the Cross: "Woman, behold your son!"; "Behold, your mother."

II

The Mother of God at the Center of the Pilgrim Church

The Church, the People of God present in all the nations of the earth

25.1 "The Church 'like a pilgrim in a foreign land, presses forward amid the persecutions of the world and the consolations of God,'[52] announcing the Cross and death of the Lord until he comes (cf. 1 Cor 11:26)."[53] "Israel according to the flesh, which wandered as an exile in the desert, was already called the Church of God (cf. Neh 13:1; Num 20:4; Dt 23:1ff.). Likewise the new Israel . . . is also called the Church of Christ (cf. Mt 16:18). For he has bought it for himself with his blood (Acts 20:28), has filled it with his Spirit, and provided it with those means which befit it as a visible and social unity. *God has gathered together as one all those who in faith look upon Jesus* as the author of salvation and the source of unity and peace, and has established them as Church, that for each and all she may be the visible sacrament of this saving unity."[54]

25.2 The Second Vatican Council speaks of the pilgrim Church, establishing an analogy with the Israel of the Old Covenant journeying through the desert. The journey also has an *external character,* visible in the time and space in which it historically takes place. For the Church "is destined to ex-

---

[52] Saint Augustine, *De Civitate Dei*, XVIII, 51: *CCL* 48, 650.

[53] Second Vatican Ecumenical Council, Dogmatic Constitution on the Church *Lumen Gentium*, 8.

[54] Ibid., 9.

tend to all regions of the earth and so to enter into the history of mankind," but at the same time "she transcends all limits of time and of space."[55] And yet the essential *character* of her pilgrimage is *interior:* it is a question of a *pilgrimage through faith,* by "the power of the risen Lord,"[56] a pilgrimage in the Holy Spirit, given to the Church as the invisible Comforter (*parákletos*) (cf. Jn 14:26, 15:26, 16:7): "Moving forward through trial and tribulation, the Church is strengthened by the power of God's grace promised to her by the Lord, so that . . . moved by the Holy Spirit, she may never cease to renew herself, until through the Cross she arrives at the light which knows no setting."[57]

25.3 It is precisely *in this ecclesial journey or pilgrimage* through space and time, and even more through the history of souls, that *Mary is present,* as the one who is "blessed because she believed," as the one who advanced on the pilgrimage of faith, sharing unlike any other creature in the mystery of Christ. The Council further says that "Mary figured profoundly in the history of salvation and in a certain way unites and mirrors within herself the central truths of the faith."[58] Among all believers she is *like a "mirror"* in which are reflected in the most profound and limpid way "the mighty works of God" (Acts 2:11).

26.1 Built by Christ upon the Apostles, the Church became fully aware of these mighty works of God *on the day of Pentecost,* when those gathered together in the Upper Room "were all filled with the Holy Spirit and began to speak in other tongues, as the Spirit gave them utterance" (Acts 2:4). From that moment there also *begins* that journey of faith, *the Church's pilgrimage* through the history of individuals and peoples. We know that at the beginning of this journey Mary is present. We see her in the midst of the Apostles in the Upper Room, "prayerfully imploring the gift of the Spirit."[59]

26.2 In a sense her journey of faith is longer. The Holy Spirit had already come down upon her, and she became his faithful spouse *at the Annunciation,* welcoming the Word of the true God, offering "the full submission of intellect and will . . . and freely assenting to the truth revealed by him," indeed abandoning herself totally to God through "the obedience of faith,"[60] whereby she replied to the angel: "Behold, I am the handmaid of the Lord; let it be to me

---

[55] Ibid., 9.

[56] Ibid., 8.

[57] Ibid., 9.

[58] Ibid., 65.

[59] Ibid., 59.

[60] Cf. Second Vatican Ecumenical Council, Dogmatic Constitution on Divine Revelation *Dei Verbum,* 5.

according to your word." The journey of faith made by Mary, whom we see praying in the Upper Room, is thus longer than that of the others gathered there: Mary "goes before them," "leads the way" for them.[61] *The moment of Pentecost* in Jerusalem had been prepared for by the *moment of the Annunciation* in Nazareth, as well as by the Cross. In the Upper Room Mary's journey meets the Church's journey of faith. In what way?

26.3 Among those who devoted themselves to prayer in the Upper Room, preparing to go "into the whole world" after receiving the Spirit, some *had been called by Jesus* gradually from the beginning of his mission in Israel. Eleven of them *had been made Apostles,* and to them Jesus had passed on the mission which he himself had received from the Father. "As the Father has sent me, even so I send you" (Jn 20:21), he had said to the Apostles after the Resurrection. And forty days later, before returning to the Father, he had added: "when the Holy Spirit has come upon you . . . *you shall be my witnesses . . .* to the end of the earth" (cf. Acts 1:8). This mission of the Apostles began the moment they left the Upper Room in Jerusalem. The Church is born and then grows through the testimony that Peter and the Apostles bear to the crucified and risen Christ (cf. Acts 2:31-34, 3:15-18, 4:10-12, 5:30-32).

26.4 *Mary did not directly receive this apostolic mission.* She was not among those whom Jesus sent "to the whole world to teach all nations" (cf. Mt 28:19) when he conferred this mission on them. But she was in the Upper Room, where the Apostles were preparing to take up this mission with the coming of the Spirit of truth: she was present with them. In their midst Mary was "devoted to prayer" as the "Mother of Jesus" (cf. Acts 1:13-14), of the crucified and risen Christ. And that first group of those who in faith looked "upon Jesus as the author of salvation,"[62] knew that Jesus was the Son of Mary, and that she was his Mother, and that as such she was from the moment of his conception and birth a unique witness to *the mystery of Jesus,* that mystery which before their eyes had been disclosed and confirmed in the Cross and Resurrection. Thus, from the very first moment, the Church "looked at" Mary through Jesus, just as she "looked at" Jesus through Mary. For the Church of that time and of every time Mary is a singular witness to the years of Jesus' infancy and hidden life at Nazareth, when she "kept all these things, pondering them in her heart" (Lk 2:19, cf. Lk 2:51).

26.5 But above all, in the Church of that time and of every time Mary was

---

[61] Cf. Second Vatican Ecumenical Council, Dogmatic Constitution on the Church *Lumen Gentium,* 63.

[62] Cf. ibid., 9.

and is the one who is "blessed because she believed"; *she was the first to believe.* From the moment of the Annunciation and conception, from the moment of his birth in the stable at Bethlehem, Mary followed Jesus step by step in her maternal pilgrimage of faith. She followed him during the years of his hidden life at Nazareth; she followed him also during the time after he left home, when he began "to do and to teach" (cf. Acts 1:1) in the midst of Israel. Above all she followed him in the tragic experience of Golgotha. Now, while Mary was with the Apostles in the Upper Room in Jerusalem at the dawn of the Church, *her faith, born from the words of the Annunciation, found confirmation.* The angel had said to her then: "You will conceive in your womb and bear a son, and you shall call his name Jesus. He will be great . . . and he will reign over the house of Jacob for ever; and of his Kingdom there will be no end." The recent events on Calvary had shrouded that promise in darkness, yet not even beneath the Cross did Mary's faith fail. She had still remained the one who, like Abraham, "in hope believed against hope" (Rom 4:18). But it is only after the Resurrection that hope had shown its true face and *the promise had begun to be transformed into reality.* For Jesus, before returning to the Father, had said to the Apostles: "Go therefore and make disciples of all nations . . . lo, I am with you always, to the close of the age" (cf. Mt 28:19-20). Thus had spoken the one who by his Resurrection had revealed himself as the conqueror of death, as the one who possessed the kingdom of which, as the angel said, "there will be no end."

27.1 Now, at the first dawn of the Church, at the beginning of the long journey through faith which began at Pentecost in Jerusalem, Mary was with all those who were the seed of the "new Israel." She was present among them as an exceptional witness to the mystery of Christ. And the Church was assiduous in prayer together with her, and at the same time *"contemplated her in the light of the Word made man."* It was always to be so. For when the Church "enters more intimately into the supreme mystery of the Incarnation," she thinks of the Mother of Christ with profound reverence and devotion.[63] Mary belongs indissolubly to the mystery of Christ, and she belongs also to the mystery of the Church from the beginning, from the day of the Church's birth. At the basis of what the Church has been from the beginning, and of what she must continually become from generation to generation, in the midst of all the nations of the earth, we find the one "who believed that there would be a fulfillment of what was spoken to her from the Lord" (Lk 1:45). It is precisely Mary's faith which marks the beginning of the new and eternal Cov-

[63] Cf. ibid., 65.

enant of God with man in Jesus Christ; this heroic *faith* of hers *"precedes"* the apostolic *witness* of the Church, and ever remains in the Church's heart hidden like a special heritage of God's revelation. All those who from generation to generation accept the apostolic witness of the Church share in that mysterious inheritance, and *in a sense share in Mary's faith.*

27.2 Elizabeth's words "Blessed is she who believed" continue to accompany the Virgin also at Pentecost; they accompany her from age to age, wherever knowledge of Christ's salvific mystery spreads, through the Church's apostolic witness and service. Thus is fulfilled the prophecy of the *Magnificat:* *"All generations will call me blessed;* for he who is mighty has done great things for me, and holy is his name" (Lk 1:48-49). For knowledge of the mystery of Christ leads us to bless his Mother, in the form of special veneration for the *Theotókos.* But this veneration always includes a blessing of her faith, for the Virgin of Nazareth became blessed above all through this faith, in accordance with Elizabeth's words. Those who from generation to generation among the different peoples and nations of the earth accept with faith the mystery of Christ, the Incarnate Word and Redeemer of the world, not only turn with veneration to Mary and confidently have recourse to her as his Mother, but also *seek in her faith support for their own.* And it is precisely this lively sharing in Mary's faith that determines her special place in the Church's pilgrimage as the new People of God throughout the earth.

28.1 As the Council says, "Mary figured profoundly in the history of salvation. . . . Hence when she is being preached and venerated, she summons the faithful to her Son and his sacrifice, and to love for the Father."[64] For this reason, Mary's faith, according to the Church's apostolic witness, in some way continues to become the faith of the pilgrim People of God: the faith of individuals and communities, of places and gatherings, and of the various groups existing in the Church. It is a faith that is passed on simultaneously through both the mind and the heart. It is gained or regained continually through prayer. Therefore, *"the Church* in her apostolic work also *rightly looks to her who brought forth Christ,* conceived by the Holy Spirit and born of the Virgin, so that through the Church Christ *may be born and increase in the hearts of the faithful also."*[65]

28.2 Today, as on this pilgrimage of faith we draw near to the end of the second Christian millennium, the Church, through the teaching of the Second Vatican Council, calls our attention to her vision of herself, as the "one People

[64] Ibid., 65.
[65] Ibid., 65.

of God . . . among all the nations of the earth." And she reminds us of that truth according to which all the faithful, though "scattered throughout the world, are in communion with each other in the Holy Spirit."[66] We can therefore say that in this union the mystery of Pentecost is continually being accomplished. At the same time, the Lord's Apostles and disciples, in all the nations of the earth, "devote themselves to prayer *together with Mary, the mother of Jesus*" (Acts 1:14). As they constitute from generation to generation the "sign of the Kingdom" which is not of his world,[67] they are also aware that in the midst of this world they must *gather around that King* to whom the nations have been given in heritage (cf. Ps 2:8), to whom the Father has given "the throne of David his father," so that he "will reign over the house of Jacob for ever, and of his Kingdom there will be no end."

28.3 During this time of vigil, Mary, through the same faith which made her blessed, especially from the moment of the Annunciation, is *present* in the Church's mission, present in the Church's work of introducing into the world *the Kingdom of her Son*.[68]

28.4 This presence of Mary finds many different expressions in our day, just as it did throughout the Church's history. It also has a wide field of action: through the faith and piety of individual believers; through the traditions of Christian families or "domestic churches," of parish and missionary communities, religious institutes and Dioceses; through the radiance and attraction of the great shrines where not only individuals or local groups, but sometimes whole nations and societies, even whole continents, seek to meet the Mother of the Lord, the one who is blessed because she believed, is the first among believers and therefore became the Mother of Emmanuel. This is the message of the Land of Palestine, the spiritual homeland of all Christians because it was the homeland of the Savior of the world and of his Mother. This is the message of the many churches in Rome and throughout the world which have been raised up in the course of the centuries by the faith of Christians. This is the message of centers like Guadalupe, Lourdes, Fatima and the others situated in the various countries. Among them how could I fail to mention the one in my own native land, Jasna Góra? One could perhaps speak of a specific "geography" of faith and Marian devotion, which includes all these special places of pilgrimage where the People of God seek to meet the Mother of God in order to find, within the radius of the maternal presence of her "who be-

[66] Cf. ibid., 13.
[67] Cf. ibid., 13.
[68] Cf. ibid., 13.

lieved," a strengthening of their own faith. For *in Mary's faith*, first at the Annunciation and then fully at the foot of the Cross, an *interior space* was reopened within humanity which the eternal Father can fill "with every spiritual blessing." It is the space "of the new and everlasting Covenant,"[69] and it continues to exist in the Church, which in Christ is "a kind of sacrament or sign of intimate union with God, and of the unity of all mankind."[70]

28.5 In the faith which Mary professed at the Annunciation as the "handmaid of the Lord" and in which she constantly "precedes" the pilgrim People of God throughout the earth, the *Church "strives* energetically and constantly *to bring* all *humanity . . . back to Christ its Head* in the unity of his Spirit."[71]

The Church's journey and the unity of all Christians

29.1 "In all of Christ's disciples the Spirit arouses the desire to be peacefully *united,* in the manner determined by Christ, as one flock *under one shepherd.*"[72] The journey of the Church, especially in our own time, is marked by the sign of ecumenism: Christians are seeking ways to restore that unity which Christ implored from the Father for his disciples on the day before his Passion: "*That they may all be one;* even as you, Father, are in me, and I in you, that they also may be in us, so that the world *may believe* that you have sent me" (Jn 17:21). The unity of Christ's disciples, therefore, is a great sign given in order to kindle faith in the world while their division constitutes a scandal.[73]

29.2 The ecumenical movement, on the basis of a clearer and more widespread awareness of the urgent need to achieve the unity of all Christians, has found on the part of the Catholic Church its culminating expression in the work of the Second Vatican Council: Christians must deepen in themselves and each of their communities that "obedience of faith" of which Mary is the first and brightest example. And since she "shines forth on earth, . . . as a sign of sure hope and solace for the pilgrim People of God," "it gives great joy and comfort to this most holy Synod that *among the divided brethren,* too, there are those who give due honor to the Mother of our Lord and Savior. This is especially so among the Easterners."[74]

[69] Cf. Roman Missal, formula of the Consecration of the Chalice in the Eucharistic Prayers.

[70] Second Vatican Ecumenical Council, Dogmatic Constitution on the Church *Lumen Gentium,* 1.

[71] Ibid., 13.

[72] Ibid., 15.

[73] Cf. Second Vatican Ecumenical Council, Decree on Ecumenism *Unitatis Redintegratio,* 1.

[74] Dogmatic Constitution on the Church *Lumen Gentium,* 68, 69. On Mary Most Holy, promoter of Christian unity, and on the cult of Mary in the East, cf. Leo XIII, Encyclical Epistle *Adiutricem Populi* (September 5, 1885): *Leonis XIII P. M. Acta,* XV, Rome, 1896, 300-312.

30.1 Christians know that their unity will be truly rediscovered only if it is based on the unity of their faith. They must resolve considerable discrepancies of doctrine concerning the mystery and ministry of the Church, and sometimes also concerning the role of Mary in the work of salvation.[75] The dialogues begun by the Catholic Church with the Churches and Ecclesial Communities of the West[76] are steadily converging upon these *two inseparable aspects* of the same mystery of salvation. If the mystery of the Word made flesh enables us to glimpse the mystery of the divine motherhood and if, in turn, contemplation of the Mother of God brings us to a more profound understanding of the mystery of the Incarnation, then the same must be said for the mystery of the Church and Mary's role in the work of salvation. By a more profound study of both Mary and the Church, clarifying each by the light of the other, Christians who are eager to do what Jesus tells them — as their Mother recommends (cf. Jn 2:5) — will be able to go forward together on this "pilgrimage of faith." Mary, who is still the model of this pilgrimage, is to lead them to the unity which is willed by their one Lord and so much desired by those who are attentively listening to what "the Spirit is saying to the Churches" today (Rev 2:7, 11, 17).

30.2 Meanwhile, it is a hopeful sign that these Churches and Ecclesial Communities are finding agreement with the Catholic Church on fundamental points of Christian belief, including matters relating to the Virgin Mary. For they recognize her as the Mother of the Lord and hold that this forms part of our faith in Christ, true God and true man. They look to her who at the foot of the Cross accepts as her son the beloved disciple, the one who in his turn accepts her as his Mother.

30.3 Therefore, why should we not all together look to her as *our common Mother,* who prays for the unity of God's family and who "precedes" us all at the head of the long line of witnesses of faith in the one Lord, the Son of God, who was conceived in her virginal womb by the power of the Holy Spirit?

31.1 On the other hand, I wish to emphasize how profoundly the Catholic Church, the Orthodox Church and the ancient Churches of the East feel united by love and praise of the *Theotókos.* Not only "basic dogmas of the Christian faith concerning the Trinity and God's Word made flesh of the Virgin Mary were defined in Ecumenical Councils held in the East,"[77] but also in their

---

[75] Cf. Second Vatican Ecumenical Council, Decree on Ecumenism *Unitatis Redintegratio,* 20.

[76] Cf. ibid., 19.

[77] Ibid., 14.

liturgical worship "the Orientals pay high tribute, in very beautiful hymns, to Mary ever Virgin . . . God's Most Holy Mother."[78]

31.2 The brethren of these Churches have experienced a complex history, but it is one that has always been marked by an intense desire for Christian commitment and apostolic activity, despite frequent persecution, even to the point of bloodshed. It is a history of fidelity to the Lord, an authentic "pilgrimage of faith" in space and time, during which Eastern Christians have always looked with boundless trust to the Mother of the Lord, celebrated her with praise and invoked her with unceasing prayer. In the difficult moments of their troubled Christian existence, "they have taken refuge under her protection,"[79] conscious of having in her a powerful aid. The Churches which profess the doctrine of Ephesus proclaim the Virgin as "true Mother of God," since "our Lord Jesus Christ, born of the Father before time began according to his divinity, in the last days he himself, for our sake and for our salvation, was begotten of Mary, the Virgin Mother of God according to his humanity."[80] The Greek Fathers and the Byzantine tradition, contemplating the Virgin in the light of the Word made flesh, have sought to penetrate the depth of that bond which unites Mary, as the Mother of God, to Christ and the Church: the Virgin is a permanent presence in the whole reality of the salvific mystery.

31.3 The Coptic and Ethiopian traditions were introduced to this contemplation of the mystery of Mary by Saint Cyril of Alexandria, and in their turn they have celebrated it with a profuse poetic blossoming.[81] The poetic genius of Saint Ephrem the Syrian, called "the lyre of the Holy Spirit," tirelessly sang of Mary, leaving a still living mark on the whole tradition of the Syriac Church.[82]

31.4 In his panegyric of the *Theotókos,* Saint Gregory of Narek, one of the outstanding glories of Armenia, with powerful poetic inspiration ponders the different aspects of the mystery of the Incarnation, and each of them is for him an occasion to sing and extol the extraordinary dignity and magnificent beauty of the Virgin Mary, Mother of the Word made flesh.[83]

---

[78] Ibid., 15.

[79] Second Vatican Ecumenical Council, Dogmatic Constitution on the Church *Lumen Gentium,* 66.

[80] Ecumenical Council of Chalcedon, *Definitio fidei: Conciliorum Oecumenicorum Decreta,* Ed. Istituto per le Scienze Religiose, 3rd ed., Bologna, 1973, 86 (*DS* 301).

[81] Cf. the *Weddâsê Mâryâm* (*Praises of Mary*), which follows the Ethiopian Psalter and contains hymns and prayers to Mary for each day of the week. Cf. also the *Matshafa Kidâna Mehrat* (*Book of the Pact of Mercy*); the importance given to Mary in the Ethiopian hymnology and liturgy deserves to be emphasized.

[82] Cf. Saint Ephrem, *Hymni de Nativitate: Scriptores Syri,* 82, CSCO, 186.

[83] Cf. Saint Gregory of Narek, *Le livre de prières: SCh* 78, 160-163, 428-432.

31.5 It does not surprise us therefore that Mary occupies a privileged place in the worship of the ancient Oriental Churches with an incomparable abundance of feasts and hymns.

32.1 In the Byzantine liturgy, in all the hours of the Divine Office, praise of the Mother is linked with praise of her Son and with the praise which, through the Son, is offered up to the Father in the Holy Spirit. In the Anaphora or Eucharistic Prayer of Saint John Chrysostom, immediately after the epiclesis the assembled community sings in honor of the Mother of God: "It is truly just to proclaim you blessed, O Mother of God, who are most blessed, all pure and Mother of our God. We magnify you who are more honorable than the Cherubim and incomparably more glorious than the Seraphim. You who, without losing your virginity, gave birth to the Word of God. You who are truly the Mother of God."

32.2 These praises, which in every celebration of the Eucharistic Liturgy are offered to Mary, have molded the faith, piety and prayer of the faithful. In the course of the centuries they have permeated their whole spiritual outlook, fostering in them a profound devotion to the "All Holy Mother of God."

33.1 This year there occurs the twelfth centenary of the Second Ecumenical Council of Nicaea (787). Putting an end to the well-known controversy about the cult of sacred images, this Council defined that, according to the teaching of the holy Fathers and the universal Tradition of the Church, there could be exposed for the veneration of the faithful, together with the Cross, also images of the Mother of God, of the angels and of the saints, in churches and houses and at the roadside.[84] This custom has been maintained in the whole of the East and also in the West. Images of the Virgin have a place of honor in churches and houses. In them Mary is represented in a number of ways: as the throne of God carrying the Lord and giving him to humanity (*Theotókos*); as the way that leads to Christ and manifests him (*Hodegetria*); as a praying figure in an attitude of intercession and as a sign of the divine presence on the journey of the faithful until the day of the Lord (*Deësis*); as the protectress who stretches out her mantle over the peoples (*Pokrov*), or as the merciful Virgin of tenderness (*Eleousa*). She is usually represented with her Son, the child Jesus, in her arms: it is the relationship with the Son which glorifies the Mother. Sometimes she embraces him with tenderness (*Glykophilousa*); at other times

---

[84] Second Ecumenical Council of Nicaea: *Conciliorum Oecumenicorum Decreta*, Ed. Istituto per le Scienze Religiose, 3rd ed., Bologna, 1973, 135-138 (*DS* 600-609).

she is a hieratic figure, apparently rapt in contemplation of him who is the Lord of history (cf. Rev 5:9-14).[85]

33.2 It is also appropriate to mention the icon of Our Lady of Vladimir, which continually accompanied the pilgrimage of faith of the peoples of ancient Rus'. The first millennium of the conversion of those noble lands to Christianity is approaching: lands of humble folk, of thinkers and of saints. The icons are still venerated in the Ukraine, in Byelorussia and in Russia under various titles. They are images which witness to the faith and spirit of prayer of that people, who sense the presence and protection of the Mother of God. In these icons the Virgin shines as the image of divine beauty, the abode of Eternal Wisdom, the figure of the one who prays, the prototype of contemplation, the image of glory: she who even in her earthly life possessed the spiritual knowledge inaccessible to human reasoning and who attained through faith the most sublime knowledge. I also recall the icon of the Virgin of the Cenacle, praying with the Apostles as they awaited the Holy Spirit: could she not become the sign of hope for all those who, in fraternal dialogue, wish to deepen their obedience of faith?

34 Such a wealth of praise, built up by the different forms of the Church's great Tradition, could help us to hasten the day when the Church can begin once more to breathe fully with her "two lungs," the East and the West. As I have often said, this is more than ever necessary today. It would be an effective aid in furthering the progress of the dialogue already taking place between the Catholic Church and the Churches and Ecclesial Communities of the West.[86] It would also be the way for the pilgrim Church to sing and to live more perfectly her *"Magnificat."*

The "Magnificat" of the pilgrim Church

35.1 At the present stage of her journey, therefore, the Church seeks to rediscover the unity of all who profess their faith in Christ, in order to show obedience to her Lord, who prayed for this unity before his Passion. "Like a pilgrim in a foreign land, the Church presses forward amid the persecutions of the world and the consolations of God, announcing the Cross and death of the Lord until he comes."[87] "Moving forward through trial and tribulation, *the*

---

[85] Cf. Second Vatican Ecumenical Council, Dogmatic Constitution on the Church *Lumen Gentium*, 59.

[86] Cf. Second Vatican Ecumenical Council, Decree on Ecumenism *Unitatis Redintegratio*, 19.

[87] Second Vatican Ecumenical Council, Dogmatic Constitution on the Church *Lumen Gentium*, 8.

Church is strengthened by the power of God's grace promised to her by the Lord, so that in the weakness of the flesh she may not waver from perfect fidelity, but remain a bride worthy of her Lord; that moved by the Holy Spirit she may never cease to renew herself, until through the Cross she arrives at the light which knows no setting."[88]

35.2 The Virgin Mother is constantly present on this journey of faith of the People of God toward the light. This is shown in a special way by *the canticle of the "Magnificat," which, having welled up from the depths of Mary's faith* at the Visitation, ceaselessly reechoes in the heart of the Church down the centuries. This is proved by its daily recitation in the liturgy of Vespers and at many other moments of both personal and communal devotion.

"My soul magnifies the Lord,
and my spirit rejoices in God my Savior,
for he has looked on his servant in her lowliness.
For behold, henceforth all generations will call me blessed;
for he who is mighty has done great things for me,
and holy is his name:
And his mercy is from age to age
on those who fear him.
He has shown strength with his arm;
he has scattered the proud-hearted,
he has cast down the mighty from their thrones,
and lifted up the lowly;
he has filled the hungry with good things,
sent the rich away empty.
He has helped his servant Israel,
remembering his mercy,
as he spoke to our fathers,
to Abraham and to his posterity for ever" (Lk 1:46-55).

36.1 When Elizabeth greeted her young kinswoman coming from Nazareth, *Mary replied with the Magnificat.* In her greeting, Elizabeth first called Mary "blessed" because of "the fruit of her womb," and then she called her "blessed" because of her faith (cf. Lk 1:42, 45). These two blessings referred directly to the Annunciation. Now, at the Visitation, when Elizabeth's greeting bears witness to that culminating moment, Mary's faith acquires a new consciousness and a new expression. That which remained hidden in the depths of the "obedience of faith" at the Annunciation can now be said to spring forth like a clear

[88] Ibid., 9.

and life-giving flame of the spirit. The words used by Mary on the threshold of Elizabeth's house are *an inspired profession of her faith,* in which *her response to the revealed word* is expressed with the religious and poetical exultation of her whole being toward God. In these sublime words, which are simultaneously very simple and wholly inspired by the sacred texts of the people of Israel,[89] Mary's personal experience, the ecstasy of her heart, shines forth. In them shines a ray of the mystery of God, the glory of his ineffable holiness, the eternal *love which, as an irrevocable gift, enters into human history.*

36.2 Mary is the first to share in this new revelation of God and, within the same, in this new "self-giving" of God. Therefore she proclaims: "For he who is mighty has done great things for me, and holy is his name." Her words reflect a joy of spirit which is difficult to express: "My spirit rejoices in God my Savior." Indeed, "the deepest truth about God and the salvation of man is made clear to us in Christ, who is at the same time the mediator and the fullness of all revelation."[90] In her exultation Mary confesses that she finds herself *in the very heart of this fullness* of Christ. She is conscious that the promise made to the fathers, first of all "to Abraham and to his posterity for ever," is being fulfilled in herself. She is thus aware that concentrated within herself as the Mother of Christ is *the whole salvific economy,* in which "from age to age" is manifested he who, as the God of the Covenant, "remembers his mercy."

37.1 The Church, which from the beginning has modeled her earthly jour-ney on that of the Mother of God, constantly repeats after her the words of the *Magnificat.* From the depths of the Virgin's faith at the Annunciation and the Visitation, the Church derives the truth about the God of the Covenant: the God who is Almighty and does "great things" for man: "holy is his name." In the *Magnificat* the Church sees uprooted that sin which is found at the outset of the earthly history of man and woman, the sin of disbelief and of "little faith" in God. In contrast with the "suspicion" which the "father of lies" sowed in the heart of Eve the first woman, Mary, whom tradition is wont to call the "new Eve"[91] and the true "Mother of the living,"[92] boldly proclaims the *un-*

---

[89] As is well known, the words of the Magnificat contain or echo numerous passages of the Old Testament.

[90] Second Vatican Ecumenical Council, Dogmatic Constitution on Divine Revelation *Dei Verbum,* 2.

[91] Cf., for example, Saint Justin, *Dialogus cum Tryphone Iudaeo,* 100: Otto II, 358; Saint Irenaeus, *Adversus Haereses,* III, 22, 4: SCh 211, 439-445; Tertullian, *De Carne Christi,* 17, 4-6: CCL 2, 904-905.

[92] Cf. Saint Epiphanius, *Panarion,* III, 2; *Haer.* 78, 18: PG 42, 727-730.

dimmed truth about God: the holy and almighty God, who from the beginning is *the source of all gifts,* he who "has done great things" in her, as well as in the whole universe. In the act of creation God gives existence to all that is. In creating man, God gives him the dignity of the image and likeness of himself in a special way as compared with all earthly creatures. Moreover, in his desire to give, *God gives himself in the Son,* notwithstanding man's sin: "He so loved the world that he gave his only Son" (Jn 3:16). Mary is the first witness of this marvelous truth, which will be fully accomplished through "the works and words" (cf. Acts 1:1) of her Son and definitively through his Cross and Resurrection.

37.2 The Church, which even "amid trials and tribulations" does not cease repeating with Mary the words of the *Magnificat,* is sustained by the power of God's truth, proclaimed on that occasion with such extraordinary simplicity. At the same time, *by means of this truth about God,* the Church *desires to shed light upon* the difficult and sometimes tangled paths of man's earthly existence. The Church's journey, therefore, near the end of the second Christian millennium, involves a renewed commitment to her mission. Following him who said of himself: "(God) has anointed me *to preach good news to the poor*" (cf. Lk 4:18), the Church has sought from generation to generation and still seeks today to accomplish that same mission.

37.3 The Church's *love of preference for the poor* is wonderfully inscribed in Mary's *Magnificat.* The God of the Covenant, celebrated in the exultation of her spirit by the Virgin of Nazareth, is also he who "has cast down the mighty from their thrones, and lifted up the lowly, . . . filled the hungry with good things, sent the rich away empty, . . . scattered the proud-hearted . . . and his mercy is from age to age on those who fear him." Mary is deeply imbued with the spirit of the "poor of Yahweh," who in the prayer of the Psalms awaited from God their salvation, placing all their trust in him (cf. Ps 25, 31, 35, 55). Mary truly proclaims the coming of the "Messiah of the poor" (cf. Is 11:4, 61:1). Drawing from Mary's heart, from the depth of her faith expressed in the words of the *Magnificat,* the Church renews ever more effectively in herself the awareness that *the truth about God who saves,* the truth about God who is the source of every gift, *cannot be separated from the manifestation of his love of preference for the poor and humble,* that love which, celebrated in the *Magnificat,* is later expressed in the words and works of Jesus.

37.4 The Church is thus aware — and at the present time this awareness is particularly vivid — not only that these two elements of the message contained in the *Magnificat* cannot be separated, but also that there is a duty to safeguard carefully the importance of "the poor" and of "the option in favor of the poor" in the word of the living God. These are matters and questions intimately connected with the *Christian meaning of freedom and liberation.* "Mary is totally dependent upon God and completely directed toward him, and at the side of her Son, she is *the most perfect image of freedom and of the liberation* of humanity and of the universe. It is to her as Mother and Model that the Church must look in order to understand in its completeness the meaning of her own mission."[93]

III

Maternal Mediation

Mary, the Handmaid of the Lord

38.1 The Church knows and teaches with Saint Paul that *there is only one mediator:* "For there is one God, and there is one mediator between God and men, the man Christ Jesus, who gave himself as a ransom for all" (1 Tim 2:5-6). "The maternal role of Mary toward people in no way obscures or diminishes the unique mediation of Christ, but rather shows its power":[94] it is mediation in Christ.

38.2 The Church knows and teaches that "all *the saving influences of the Blessed Virgin* on mankind originate . . . from the divine pleasure. They flow forth *from the superabundance of the merits of Christ,* rest on his mediation, depend entirely on it, and draw all their power from it. In no way do they impede the immediate union of the faithful with Christ. Rather, they foster this union."[95] This saving influence is sustained by the Holy Spirit, who, just as he overshadowed the Virgin Mary when he began in her the divine motherhood, in a similar way constantly sustains her solicitude for the brothers and sisters of her Son.

38.3 In effect, Mary's mediation *is intimately linked with her motherhood.* It possesses a specifically maternal character, which distinguishes it from the mediation of the other creatures who in various and always subordinate ways share in the one mediation of Christ, although her own mediation is also a shared mediation.[96] In fact, while it is true that "no creature could ever be

[93] Congregation for the Doctrine of the Faith, Instruction on Christian Freedom and Liberation *Libertatis Conscientia* (March 22, 1986), 97.

[94] Second Vatican Ecumenical Council, Dogmatic Constitution on the Church *Lumen Gentium,* 60.

[95] Ibid., 60.

[96] Cf. the formula of mediatrix "ad Mediatorem" of Saint Bernard, *In Dominica infra octavam Assumptionis Sermo,* 2: *Sancti Bernardi Opera,* V, 1968, 263. Mary as a pure mirror sends back to her Son all the glory and honor which she receives: Saint Bernard, *In Nativitate Beatae Mariae Sermo, De Aquaeductu,* 12: loc. cit., 283.

classed with the Incarnate Word and Redeemer," at the same time "the unique mediation of the Redeemer does not exclude but rather gives rise among creatures to *a manifold cooperation* which is but a sharing in this unique source." And thus "the one goodness of God is in reality communicated diversely to his creatures."[97]

38.4 The teaching of the Second Vatican Council presents the truth of Mary's mediation as *"a sharing in the one unique source that is the mediation of Christ himself."* Thus we read: "The Church does not hesitate to profess this subordinate role of Mary. She experiences it continuously and commends it to the hearts of the faithful, so that, encouraged by this maternal help, they may more closely adhere to the Mediator and Redeemer."[98] This role is at the same time *special and extraordinary.* It flows from her divine motherhood and can be understood and lived in faith only on the basis of the full truth of this motherhood. Since by virtue of divine election Mary is the earthly Mother of the Father's consubstantial Son and his "generous companion" in the work of Redemption, "she is a Mother to us in the order of grace."[99] This role constitutes a real dimension of her presence in the saving mystery of Christ and the Church.

39.1 From this point of view we must consider once more the fundamental event in the economy of salvation, namely the Incarnation of the Word at the moment of the Annunciation. It is significant that Mary, recognizing in the words of the divine messenger the will of the Most High and submitting to his power, says: *"Behold, I am the handmaid of the Lord; let it be to me according to your word"* (Lk 1:38). The first moment of submission to the one mediation "between God and men" — the mediation of Jesus Christ — is the Virgin of Nazareth's acceptance of motherhood. Mary consents to God's choice, in order to become through the power of the Holy Spirit the Mother of the Son of God. It can be said that this *consent to motherhood* is above all *a result of her total self-giving to God in virginity.* Mary accepted her election as Mother of the Son of God, guided by spousal love, the love which totally "consecrates" a human being to God. By virtue of this love, Mary wished to be always and in all things "given to God," living in virginity. The words "Behold, I am the handmaid of the Lord" express the fact that from the outset she accepted and understood her own motherhood as a total *gift of self,* a gift of her person to

---

[97] Second Vatican Ecumenical Council, Dogmatic Constitution on the Church *Lumen Gentium,* 62.

[98] Ibid., 62.

[99] Ibid., 61.

the service of the saving plans of the Most High. And to the very end she lived her entire maternal sharing in the life of Jesus Christ, her Son, in a way that matched her vocation to virginity.

39.2 Mary's motherhood, completely pervaded by her spousal attitude as the "handmaid of the Lord," constitutes the first and fundamental dimension of that mediation which the Church confesses and proclaims in her regard[100] and continually "commends to the hearts of the faithful," since the Church has great trust in her. For it must be recognized that before anyone else it was God himself, the Eternal Father, *who entrusted himself to the Virgin of Nazareth,* giving her his own Son in the mystery of the Incarnation. Her election to the supreme office and dignity of Mother of the Son of God refers, on the ontological level, to the very reality of the union of the two natures in the person of the Word (*hypostatic union*). This basic fact of being the Mother of the Son of God is from the very beginning a complete openness to the person of Christ, to his whole work, to his whole mission. The words "Behold, I am the handmaid of the Lord" testify to Mary's openness of spirit: she perfectly unites in herself the love proper to virginity and the love characteristic of motherhood, which are joined and, as it were, fused together.

39.3 For this reason Mary became not only the "nursing mother" of the Son of Man but also the "associate of unique nobility"[101] of the Messiah and Redeemer. As I have already said, she advanced in her pilgrimage of faith, and in this *pilgrimage* to the foot of the Cross there was simultaneously accomplished her maternal *cooperation* with the Savior's whole mission through her actions and sufferings. Along the path of this collaboration with the work of her Son, the Redeemer, Mary's motherhood itself underwent a singular transformation, becoming ever more imbued with "burning charity" toward all those to whom Christ's mission was directed. Through this "burning charity," which sought to achieve, in union with Christ, the restoration of "supernatural life to souls,"[102] Mary *entered, in a way all her own, into the one mediation* "between God and men" *which is the mediation of the man Christ Jesus.* If she was the first to experience within herself the supernatural consequences of this one mediation — in the Annunciation she had been greeted as "full of grace" — then we must say that through this fullness of grace and supernatural life she was especially predisposed to cooperation with Christ, the one Mediator of human salvation. *And such cooperation is precisely this mediation subordinated* to the mediation of Christ.

---

[100] Ibid., 62.
[101] Ibid., 61.
[102] Ibid., 61.

39.4 In Mary's case we have a special and exceptional mediation, based upon her "fullness of grace," which was expressed in the complete willingness of the "handmaid of the Lord." In response to this interior willingness of his Mother, *Jesus Christ prepared her* ever more completely to become for all people their "Mother in the order of grace." This is indicated, at least indirectly, by certain details noted by the Synoptics (cf. Lk 11:28, 8:20-21; Mk 3:32-35; Mt 12:47-50) and still more so by the Gospel of John (cf. 2:1-12, 19:25-27), which I have already mentioned. Particularly eloquent in this regard are the words spoken by Jesus on the Cross to Mary and John.

40.1 After the events of the Resurrection and Ascension, Mary entered the Upper Room together with the Apostles to await Pentecost, and was present there as the Mother of the glorified Lord. She was not only the one who "advanced in her pilgrimage of faith" and loyally persevered in her union with her Son "unto the Cross," *but she was also the "handmaid of the Lord," left by her Son as Mother in the midst of the infant Church:* "Behold your mother." Thus there began to develop a special bond between this Mother and the Church. For the infant Church was the fruit of the Cross and Resurrection of her Son. Mary, who from the beginning had given herself without reserve to the person and work of her Son, could not but pour out upon the Church, from the very beginning, her maternal self-giving. After her Son's departure, her motherhood remains in the Church as maternal mediation: interceding for all her children, the Mother cooperates in the saving work of her Son, the Redeemer of the world. In fact the Council teaches that the "motherhood of Mary in the order of grace . . . *will last without interruption* until the eternal fulfillment of all the elect."[103] With the redeeming death of her Son, the maternal mediation of the handmaid of the Lord took on a universal dimension, for the work of Redemption embraces the whole of humanity. Thus there is manifested in a singular way the efficacy of the one and universal mediation of Christ "between God and men." Mary's cooperation shares, in its subordinate character, *in the universality of the mediation of the Redeemer,* the one Mediator. This is clearly indicated by the Council in the words quoted above.

40.2 "For," the text goes on, "taken up to heaven, she did not lay aside this saving role, but by her manifold acts of intercession continues to win for us gifts of eternal salvation."[104] With this character of "intercession," first manifested at Cana in Galilee, Mary's mediation continues in the history of the Church and the world. We read that Mary "by her maternal charity, cares for

[103] Ibid., 62.
[104] Ibid., 62.

the brethren of her Son who still journey on earth surrounded by dangers and difficulties, until they are led to their happy homeland."[105] In this way Mary's motherhood continues unceasingly in the Church as the mediation which intercedes, and the Church expresses her faith in this truth by invoking Mary "under the titles of Advocate, Auxiliatrix, Adjutrix and Mediatrix."[106]

41.1 Through her mediation, subordinate to that of the Redeemer, Mary contributes *in a special way to the union of the pilgrim Church* on earth with the eschatological and heavenly *reality* of the Communion of Saints, since she has already been "assumed into heaven."[107] The truth of the Assumption, defined by Pius XII, is reaffirmed by the Second Vatican Council, which thus expresses the Church's faith: "Preserved free from all guilt of original sin, the Immaculate Virgin *was taken up body and soul into heavenly glory* upon the completion of her earthly sojourn. She was *exalted* by the Lord *as Queen of the Universe,* in order that she might be the more thoroughly conformed to her Son, the Lord of lords (cf. Rev 19:16) and the conqueror of sin and death."[108] In this teaching Pius XII was in continuity with Tradition, which has found many different expressions in the history of the Church, both in the East and in the West.

41.2 By the mystery of the Assumption into heaven there were definitively accomplished in Mary all the effects of the one mediation of *Christ the Redeemer of the world* and *risen Lord:* "In Christ shall all be made alive. But each in his own order: Christ the first fruits, then at his coming those who belong to Christ" (1 Cor 15:22-23). In the mystery of the Assumption is expressed the faith of the Church, according to which Mary is "united by a close and indissoluble bond" to Christ, for, if as Virgin and Mother she was singularly united with him *in his first coming,* so through her continued collaboration with him she will also be united with him in expectation of the second; "redeemed in an

---

[105] Ibid., 62; in her prayer too the Church recognizes and celebrates Mary's "maternal role": it is a role "of intercession and forgiveness, petition and grace, reconciliation and peace" (cf. Preface of the Mass of the Blessed Virgin Mary, Mother and Mediatrix of Grace, in *Collectio Missarum de Beata Maria Virgine,* editio typica, 1987, I, 120).

[106] Ibid., 62.

[107] Ibid., 62; cf. Saint John Damascene, *Homilia in Dormitionem,* I, 11; II, 2; II, 14; III, 2: SCh 80, 111-112; 127-131; 157-161; 181-185; Saint Bernard, *In Assumptione Beatae Mariae Sermo,* 1-2: *Sancti Bernardi Opera,* V, 1968, 228-238.

[108] Dogmatic Constitution on the Church *Lumen Gentium,* 59; cf. Pius XII, Apostolic Constitution *Munificentissimus Deus* (November 1, 1950): *AAS* 42 (1950), 769-771; Saint Bernard presents Mary immersed in the splendor of the Son's glory: *In Dominica infra octavam Assumptionis Sermo,* 3; *Sancti Bernardi Opera,* V, 1968, 263-264.

especially sublime manner by reason of the merits of her Son,"[109] she also has that specifically maternal role of mediatrix of mercy *at his final coming,* when all those who belong to Christ "shall be made alive," when "the last enemy to be destroyed is death" (1 Cor 15:26).[110]

41.3 Connected with this exaltation of the noble "Daughter of Sion"[111] through her Assumption into heaven is the mystery of her eternal glory. For the Mother of Christ is glorified as "Queen of the Universe."[112] She who at the Annunciation called herself the "handmaid of the Lord" remained throughout her earthly life faithful to what this name expresses. In this she confirmed that she was a true "disciple" of Christ, who strongly emphasized that his mission was one of service: the Son of Man "came not to be served but to serve, and to give his life as a ransom for many" (Mt 20:28). In this way Mary became the first of those who, "serving Christ also in others, with humility and patience lead their brothers and sisters to that King whom to serve is to reign,"[113] and she fully obtained that "state of royal freedom" proper to Christ's disciples: to serve means to reign!

41.4 "Christ obeyed even at the cost of death, and was therefore raised up by the Father (cf. Phil 2:8-9). Thus he entered into the glory of his Kingdom. To him all things are made subject until he subjects himself and all created things to the Father, that God may be all in all (cf. 1 Cor 15:27-28)."[114] Mary, the handmaid of the Lord, has a share in this Kingdom of the Son.[115] The *glory of serving* does not cease to be her royal exaltation: assumed into heaven, she does not cease her saving service, which expresses her maternal mediation "until the eternal fulfillment of all the elect."[116] Thus, she who here on earth "loyally preserved in her union with her Son unto the Cross," continues to remain united with him, while now *"all things are subjected to him, until he*

---

[109] Dogmatic Constitution on the Church *Lumen Gentium,* 53.

[110] On this particular aspect of Mary's mediation as implorer of clemency from the "Son as Judge," cf. Saint Bernard, *In Dominica infra octavam Assumptionis Sermo,* 1-2: *Sancti Bernardi Opera,* V, 1968, 262-263; Leo XIII, Encyclical Epistle *Octobri Mense* (September 22, 1891): *Leonis XIII P. M. Acta,* XI, Rome, 1892, 299-315.

[111] Second Vatican Ecumenical Council, Dogmatic Constitution on the Church *Lumen Gentium,* 55.

[112] Ibid., 59.

[113] Ibid., 36.

[114] Ibid., 36.

[115] With regard to Mary as Queen, cf. Saint John Damascene, *Homilia in Nativitatem,* 6; 12; *Homilia in Dormitionem,* I, 2, 12, 14; II, 11; III, 4: *SCh* 80, 59-60, 77-78; 83-84, 113-114, 117; 151-152; 189-193.

[116] Second Vatican Ecumenical Council, Dogmatic Constitution on the Church *Lumen Gentium,* 62.

subjects to the Father himself and all things." Thus in her Assumption into heaven, Mary is as it were clothed by the whole reality of the Communion of Saints, and her very union with the Son in glory is wholly oriented toward the definitive fullness of the Kingdom, *when "God will be all in all."*

41.5 In this phase too Mary's maternal mediation does not cease to be subordinate to him who is the one Mediator, *until the final realization of "the fullness of time,"* that is to say until "all things are united in Christ" (cf. Eph 1:10).

Mary in the life of the Church and of every Christian

42.1 Linking itself with Tradition, the Second Vatican Council brought new light to bear on the role of the Mother of Christ in the life of the Church. "Through the gift . . . of divine motherhood, Mary is united with her Son, the Redeemer, and with his singular graces and offices. By these, the Blessed Virgin is also intimately united with the Church: *the Mother of God is a figure of the Church* in the matter of faith, charity and perfect union with Christ."[117] We have already noted how, from the beginning, Mary remains with the Apostles in expectation of Pentecost and how, as "the blessed one who believed," she is present in the midst of the pilgrim Church from generation to generation through faith and as the model of the hope which does not disappoint (cf. Rom 5:5).

42.2 Mary believed in the fulfillment of what had been said to her by the Lord. As Virgin, she believed that she would conceive and bear a son: the "Holy One," who bears the name of "Son of God," the name "Jesus" (= God who saves). As handmaid of the Lord, she remained in perfect fidelity to the person and mission of this Son. As Mother, "*believing and obeying . . .* she brought forth on earth the *Father's Son.* This she did, knowing not man but overshadowed by the Holy Spirit."[118]

42.3 For these reasons Mary is honored in the Church "with special reverence. Indeed, from most ancient times the Blessed Virgin Mary has been venerated under the title of 'God-bearer.' In all perils and needs, the faithful have fled prayerfully to her protection."[119] This cult is altogether special: it bears in itself and *expresses* the profound *link* which exists *between the Mother of Christ and the Church.*[120] As Virgin and Mother, Mary remains for the Church

---

[117] Ibid., 63.

[118] Ibid., 63.

[119] Ibid., 66.

[120] Cf. Saint Ambrose, *De Institutione Virginis,* XIV, 88-89: *PL* 16, 341; Saint Augustine, *Sermo* 215, 4: *PL* 38, 1074; *De Sancta Virginitate,* II, 2; V, 5; VI, 6: *PL* 40, 397; 398-399, 399; *Sermo* 191, II, 3: *PL* 38, 1010-1011.

a "permanent model." It can therefore be said that especially under this aspect, namely as a model, or rather as a "figure," Mary, present in the mystery of Christ, remains constantly present also in the mystery of the Church. For the Church too is "called mother and virgin," and these names have a profound biblical and theological justification.[121]

43.1 The Church "*becomes* herself *a mother* by accepting God's word with fidelity."[122] Like Mary, who first believed by accepting the word of God revealed to her at the Annunciation and by remaining faithful to that word in all her trials even unto the Cross, so too the Church becomes a mother when, *accepting with fidelity the word of God*, "by her preaching and by Baptism *she brings forth to a new and immortal life children* who are conceived *of the Holy Spirit* and born of God."[123] This "maternal" characteristic of the Church was expressed in a particularly vivid way by the Apostle to the Gentiles when he wrote: "My little children, with whom I am again in travail until Christ be formed in you!" (Gal 4:19) These words of Saint Paul contain an interesting sign of the early Church's awareness of her own motherhood, linked to her apostolic service to mankind. This awareness enabled and still enables the Church to see the mystery of her life and mission modeled *upon the example of the Mother of the Son*, who is "the first-born among many brethren" (Rom 8:29).

43.2 It can be said that from Mary the Church also learns her own motherhood: she recognizes the maternal dimension of her vocation, which is essentially bound to her sacramental nature, in "contemplating Mary's mysterious sanctity, imitating her charity and faithfully fulfilling the Father's will."[124] If the Church is the sign and instrument of intimate union with God, she is so by reason of her motherhood, because, receiving life from the Spirit, she "generates" sons and daughters of the human race to a new life in Christ. For, just as *Mary is at the service of the mystery of the Incarnation, so the Church is always at the service of the mystery of adoption to sonship* through grace.

43.3 Likewise, following the example of Mary, the Church remains the virgin faithful to her Spouse: "The Church herself is a virgin who keeps whole and pure the fidelity she has pledged to her Spouse."[125] For the Church is the

---

[121] Cf. Second Vatican Ecumenical Council, Dogmatic Constitution on the Church *Lumen Gentium*, 63.

[122] Ibid., 64.

[123] Ibid., 64.

[124] Ibid., 64.

[125] Ibid., 64.

spouse of Christ, as is clear from the Pauline Letters (cf. Eph 5:21-33; 2 Cor 11:2), and from the title found in John: "bride of the Lamb" (Rev 21:9). If *the Church* as spouse "keeps the fidelity she *has pledged* to Christ," this fidelity, even though in the Apostle's teaching it has become an image of marriage (cf. Eph 5:23-33), also has value as a model of total self-giving to God in celibacy "for the Kingdom of heaven," *in virginity consecrated to God* (cf. Mt 19:11-12; 2 Cor 11:2). Precisely such virginity, after the example of the Virgin of Nazareth, is the source of a special spiritual fruitfulness: *it is the source of motherhood in the Holy Spirit.*

43.4 But *the Church* also preserves the faith *received from* Christ. Following the example of Mary, who kept and pondered in her heart everything relating to her divine Son (cf. Lk 2:19, 51), the Church is committed to preserving the word of God and investigating its riches with discernment and prudence, in order to bear faithful witness to it before all mankind in every age.[126]

44.1 Given Mary's relationship to the Church as an exemplar, the Church is close to her and seeks to become like her: "Imitating the Mother of her Lord, and by the power of the Holy Spirit, she preserves with virginal purity an integral faith, a firm hope, and a sincere charity."[127] Mary is thus present in the mystery of the Church as a *model.* But the Church's mystery also consists in generating people to a new and immortal life: this is her motherhood in the Holy Spirit. And here Mary is not only the model and figure of the Church; she is much more. For *"with maternal love she cooperates in the birth and development"* of the sons and daughters of Mother Church. The Church's motherhood is accomplished not only according to the model and figure of the Mother of God but also with her "cooperation." The Church *draws* abundantly from this cooperation, that is to say from the maternal mediation which is characteristic of Mary, insofar as already on earth she cooperated in the rebirth and development of the Church's sons and daughters, as the Mother of that Son whom the Father "placed as the first-born among many brethren."[128]

44.2 She cooperated, as the Second Vatican Council teaches, with a maternal love.[129] Here we perceive the real value of the words spoken by Jesus to

---

[126] Cf. Second Vatican Ecumenical Council, Dogmatic Constitution on Divine Revelation *Dei Verbum*, 8; Saint Bonaventure, *Commentarium in Evangelium Sancti Lucae: Ad Claras Aquas*, VII, 53, No. 40; 68, No. 109.

[127] Second Vatican Ecumenical Council, Dogmatic Constitution on the Church *Lumen Gentium*, 64.

[128] Ibid., 63.

[129] Cf. ibid., 63.

his Mother at the hour of the Cross: "Woman, behold your son" and to the disciple: "Behold your mother" (Jn 19:26-27). They are words which determine *Mary's place in the life of Christ's disciples* and they express — as I have already said — the new motherhood of the Mother of the Redeemer: a spiritual motherhood, born from the heart of the Paschal Mystery of the Redeemer of the world. It is a motherhood in the order of grace, for it implores the gift of the Spirit, who raises up the new children of God, redeemed through the sacrifice of Christ: that Spirit whom together with the Church Mary too received on the day of Pentecost.

44.3 Her motherhood is particularly noted and experienced by the Christian people at the *Sacred Banquet* — the liturgical celebration of the mystery of the Redemption — at which Christ, his *true body born of the Virgin Mary,* becomes present.

44.4 The piety of the Christian people has always very rightly sensed a *profound link* between devotion to the Blessed Virgin and worship of the Eucharist: this is a fact that can be seen in the liturgy of both the West and the East, in the traditions of the Religious Families, in the modern movements of spirituality, including those for youth, and in the pastoral practice of the Marian Shrines. *Mary guides the faithful to the Eucharist.*

45.1 Of the essence of motherhood is the fact that it concerns the person. Motherhood always establishes *a unique and unrepeatable relationship* between two people: *between mother and child* and *between child and mother.* Even when the same woman is the mother of many children, her personal relationship with each one of them is of the very essence of motherhood. For each child is generated in a unique and unrepeatable way, and this is true both for the mother and for the child. Each child is surrounded in the same way by that maternal love on which are based the child's development and coming to maturity as a human being.

45.2 It can be said that motherhood "in the order of grace" preserves the analogy with what "in the order of nature" characterizes the union between mother and child. In the light of this fact it becomes easier to understand why in Christ's testament on Golgotha his Mother's new motherhood is expressed in the singular, in reference to one man: "Behold your son."

45.3 lt can also be said that these same words fully show the reason *for the Marian dimension of the life of Christ's disciples*. This is true not only of John, who at that hour stood at the foot of the Cross together with his Master's Mother, but it is also true of every disciple of Christ, of every Christian. The Redeemer entrusts his Mother to the disciple, and at the same time he gives her to him as his Mother. Mary's motherhood, which becomes man's inheritance, is a gift: *a gift which Christ himself makes* personally to every individual. The Redeemer entrusts Mary to John because he entrusts John to Mary. At the foot of the Cross there begins that special *entrusting of humanity to the Mother of Christ,* which in the history of the Church has been practiced and expressed in different ways. The same Apostle and Evangelist, after reporting the words addressed by Jesus on the Cross to his Mother and to himself, adds: "And from that hour the disciple took her to his own home" (Jn 19:27). This statement certainly means that the role of son was attributed to the disciple and that he assumed responsibility for the Mother of his beloved Master. And since Mary was given as a Mother to him personally, the statement indicates, even though indirectly, everything expressed by the intimate relationship of a child with its mother. And all of this can be included in the word "entrusting." Such entrusting is *the response* to a person's love, and in particular *to the love of a mother.*

45.4 The Marian dimension of the life of a disciple of Christ is expressed in a special way precisely through this filial entrusting to the Mother of Christ, which began with the testament of the Redeemer on Golgotha. Entrusting himself to Mary in a filial manner, the Christian, like the Apostle John, "welcomes" the Mother of Christ "into his own home"[130] and brings her into everything that makes up his inner life, that is to say into his human and Christian "I": he *"took her to his own home."* Thus the Christian seeks to be taken into that "maternal charity" with which the Redeemer's Mother "cares for the brethren of her Son,"[131] "in whose birth and development she cooperates"[132] in the measure of the gift proper to each one through the power of Christ's Spirit. Thus also is exercised that motherhood in the Spirit which became Mary's role at the foot of the Cross and in the Upper Room.

46.1 This filial relationship, this self-entrusting of a child to its mother, not only has its *beginning in Christ* but can also be said to be *definitively directed toward him.* Mary can be said to continue to say to each individual the words which she spoke at Cana in Galilee: "Do whatever he tells you." For he, Christ,

---

[130] Clearly, in the Greek text the expression *"eis ta idia"* goes beyond the mere acceptance of Mary by the disciple in the sense of material lodging and hospitality in his house; it indicates rather a *communion of life* established between the two as a result of the words of the dying Christ; cf. Saint Augustine, *In Ioannis Evangelium Tractatus,* 119, 3: *CCL* 36, 659: "He took her to himself, not into his own property, for he possessed nothing of his own, but among his own duties, which he attended to with dedication."

[131] Second Vatican Ecumenical Council, Dogmatic Constitution on the Church *Lumen Gentium,* 62.

[132] Ibid., 63.

is the one Mediator between God and mankind; he is "the way, and the truth, and the life" (Jn 14:6); it is he whom the Father has given to the world, so that man "should not perish but have eternal life" (Jn 3:16). The Virgin of Nazareth became the first "witness" of this saving love of the Father, and she also wishes *to remain* its *humble handmaid always and everywhere*. For every Christian, for every human being, Mary is the one who first "believed," and precisely with her faith as Spouse and Mother she wishes to act upon all those who entrust themselves to her as her children. And it is well known that the more her children persevere and progress in this attitude, the nearer Mary leads them to the "unsearchable riches of Christ" (Eph 3:8). And to the same degree they recognize more and more clearly the dignity of man in all its fullness and the definitive meaning of his vocation, for "Christ . . . fully reveals man to man himself."[133]

46.2 This Marian dimension of Christian life takes on special importance in relation to women and their status. In fact, femininity has a *unique relationship* with the Mother of the Redeemer, a subject which can be studied in greater depth elsewhere. Here I simply wish to note that the figure of Mary of Nazareth sheds light on *womanhood as such* by the very fact that God, in the sublime event of the Incarnation of his Son, entrusted himself to the ministry, the free and active ministry, of a woman. It can thus be said that women, by looking to Mary, find in her the secret of living their femininity with dignity and of achieving their own true advancement. In the light of Mary, the Church sees in the face of women the reflection of a beauty which mirrors the loftiest sentiments of which the human heart is capable: the self-offering totality of love; the strength that is capable of bearing the greatest sorrows; limitless fidelity and tireless devotion to work; the ability to combine penetrating intuition with words of support and encouragement.

47.1 At the Council, Paul VI solemnly proclaimed that *Mary is the Mother of the Church*, "that is, Mother of the entire Christian people, both faithful and Pastors."[134] Later, in 1968, in the Profession of Faith known as the "Credo of the People of God," he restated this truth in an even more forceful way in these words: "We believe that the Most Holy Mother of God, the new Eve, the Mother of the Church, carries on in heaven her maternal role with regard to the mem-

---

[133] Second Vatican Ecumenical Council, Pastoral Constitution on the Church in the Modern World *Gaudium et Spes*, 22.

[134] Cf. Paul VI, Address at the Closing of the Third Session of the Second Vatican Ecumenical Council (November 21, 1964): *AAS* 56 (1964), 1015.

bers of Christ, cooperating in the birth and development of divine life in the souls of the redeemed."[135]

47.2 The Council's teaching emphasized that the truth concerning the Blessed Virgin, Mother of Christ, is an effective aid in exploring more deeply the truth concerning the Church. When speaking of the Constitution *Lumen Gentium,* which had just been approved by the Council, Paul VI said: "Knowledge of the true Catholic doctrine regarding the Blessed Virgin Mary will always be a key to *the exact understanding of the mystery of Christ and of the Church.*"[136] Mary is present in the Church as the Mother of Christ, and at the same time as that Mother whom Christ, in the mystery of the Redemption, gave to humanity in the person of the Apostle John. Thus, in her new motherhood in the Spirit, Mary embraces each and every one *in* the Church, and embraces each and every one *through* the Church. In this sense Mary, Mother of the Church, is also the Church's model. Indeed, as Paul VI hopes and asks, the Church must draw "from the Virgin Mother of God the most authentic form of perfect imitation of Christ."[137]

47.3 Thanks to this special bond linking the Mother of Christ with the Church, there is further *clarified the mystery of that "woman"* who, from the first chapters of the *Book of Genesis* until the *Book of Revelation,* accompanies the revelation of God's salvific plan for humanity. For Mary, present in the Church as the Mother of the Redeemer, takes part, as a mother, in that "monumental struggle against the powers of darkness"[138] which continues throughout human history. And by her ecclesial identification as the "woman clothed with the sun" (Rev 12:1),[139] it can be said that "in the Most Holy Virgin the Church has already reached that perfection whereby she exists without spot or wrinkle." Hence, as Christians raise their eyes with faith to Mary in the course of their earthly pilgrimage, they "strive to increase in holiness."[140] Mary, the exalted Daughter of Sion, helps all her children, wherever they may be and whatever their condition, *to find in Christ the path to the Father's house.*

47.4 Thus, the Church throughout her life maintains with the Mother of

---

[135] Paul VI, Solemn Profession of Faith (June 30, 1968), 15: *AAS* 60 (1968), 438-439.

[136] Paul VI, Address at the Closing of the Third Session of the Second Vatican Ecumenical Council (November 21, 1964): *AAS* 56 (1964), 1015.

[137] Ibid., 1016.

[138] Cf. Second Vatican Ecumenical Council, Pastoral Constitution on the Church in the Modern World *Gaudium et Spes,* 37.

[139] Cf. Saint Bernard, *In Dominica infra octavam Assumptionis Sermo: Sancti Bernardi Opera,* V, 1968, 262-274.

[140] Second Vatican Ecumenical Council, Dogmatic Constitution on the Church *Lumen Gentium,* 65.

God a link which embraces, in the saving mystery, the past, the present and the future, and venerates her as the spiritual Mother of humanity and the Advocate of grace.

The meaning of the Marian Year

48.1 It is precisely the special bond between humanity and this Mother which has led me to proclaim a Marian Year in the Church, in this period before the end of the second millennium since Christ's birth. A similar initiative was taken in the past, when Pius XII proclaimed 1954 as a Marian Year, in order to highlight the exceptional holiness of the Mother of Christ as expressed in the mysteries of her Immaculate Conception (defined exactly a century before) and of her Assumption into heaven.[141]

48.2 Now, following the line of the Second Vatican Council, I wish to emphasize the *special presence* of the Mother of God in the mystery of Christ and his Church. For this is a fundamental dimension emerging from the Mariology of the Council, the end of which is now more than twenty years behind us. The Extraordinary Synod of Bishops held in 1985 exhorted everyone to follow faithfully the teaching and guidelines of the Council. We can say that these two events — the Council and the Synod — embody what the Holy Spirit himself wishes "to say to the Church" in the present phase of history.

48.3 In this context, the Marian Year is meant to promote a new and more careful reading of what the Council said about the Blessed Virgin Mary, Mother of God, in the mystery of Christ and of the Church, the topic to which the contents of this Encyclical are devoted. Here we speak not only of *the doctrine of faith* but also of *the life of faith,* and thus of authentic "Marian spirituality," seen in the light of Tradition, and especially the spirituality to which the Council exhorts us.[142] Furthermore, Marian *spirituality,* like its corresponding *devotion,* finds a very rich source in the historical experience of individuals and of the various Christian communities present among the different peoples and nations of the world. In this regard, I would like to recall, among the many witnesses and teachers of this

---

[141] Cf. Encyclical Letter *Fulgens Corona* (September 8, 1953): *AAS* 45 (1953), 577-592. Pius X with his Encyclical Letter *Ad Diem Illum* (February 2, 1904), on the occasion of the fiftieth anniversary of the dogmatic definition of the Immaculate Conception of the Blessed Virgin Mary, had proclaimed an Extraordinary Jubilee of a few months: *Pii X P. M. Acta,* I, 147-166.

[142] Cf. Dogmatic Constitution on the Church *Lumen Gentium,* 66-67.

spirituality, the figure of Saint Louis Marie Grignion de Montfort,[143] who proposes consecration to Christ through the hands of Mary, as an effective means for Christians to live faithfully their baptismal commitments. I am pleased to note that in our own time too, new manifestations of this spirituality and devotion are not lacking.

48.4 There thus exist solid points of reference to look to and follow in the context of this Marian Year.

49.1 This Marian Year *will begin on the Solemnity of Pentecost, on June 7 next.* For it is a question not only of recalling that Mary "preceded" the entry of Christ the Lord into the history of the human family, but also of emphasizing, in the light of Mary, that from the moment when the mystery of the Incarnation was accomplished, human history entered "the fullness of time," and that the Church is the sign of this fullness. As the People of God, the Church makes her pilgrim way toward eternity through faith, in the midst of all the peoples and nations, beginning from the day of Pentecost. *Christ's Mother,* who was present at the beginning of "the time of the Church," when in expectation of the coming of the Holy Spirit she devoted herself to prayer in the midst of the Apostles and her Son's disciples, constantly "precedes" *the Church* in her *journey* through human history. She is also the one who, precisely as the "handmaid of the Lord," cooperates unceasingly with the work of salvation accomplished by Christ, her Son.

49.2 Thus by means of this Marian Year *the Church is called* not only to remember everything in her past that testifies to the special maternal cooperation of the Mother of God in the work of salvation in Christ the Lord, but also, on her own part, *to prepare* for the future the paths of this cooperation. For the end of the second Christian millennium opens up as a new prospect.

50.1. As has already been mentioned, also among our divided brethren many honor and celebrate the Mother of the Lord, especially among the Orientals. It is a Marian light cast upon ecumenism. In particular, I wish to mention once more that during the Marian Year there will occur the *millennium of the Baptism* of Saint Vladimir, Grand Duke of Kiev (988). This marked the beginning of Christianity in the territories of what was then called Rus', and subsequently in other territories of Eastern Europe. In this way, through the work of evangelization, Christianity spread beyond Europe, as far as the

---

[143] Saint Louis Marie Grignion de Montfort, *True Devotion to the Blessed Virgin Mary.* This Saint can rightly be linked with the figure of Saint Alphonsus Liguori, the second centenary of whose death occurs this year; cf. among his works *The Glories of Mary.*

northern territories of the Asian continent. We would therefore like, especially during this Year, to join in prayer with all those who are celebrating the millennium of this Baptism, both Orthodox and Catholics, repeating and confirming with the Council those sentiments of joy and comfort that "the Easterners . . . with ardent emotion and devout mind concur in reverencing the Mother of God, ever Virgin."[144] Even though we are still experiencing the painful effects of the separation which took place some decades later (1054), we can say that *in the presence of the Mother of Christ we feel that we are true brothers and sisters* within that messianic People, which is called to be the one family of God on earth. As I announced at the beginning of the New Year: "We desire to reconfirm this universal inheritance of all the sons and daughters of this earth."[145]

50.2 In announcing the Year of Mary, I also indicated that it will end next year on *the Solemnity of the Assumption of the Blessed Virgin into Heaven*, in order to emphasize the "great sign in heaven" spoken of by the *Apocalypse*. In this way we also wish to respond to the exhortation of the Council, which looks to Mary as "a sign of sure hope and solace for the pilgrim People of God." And the Council expresses this exhortation in the following words: "Let the entire body of the faithful pour forth persevering prayer to the Mother of God and Mother of mankind. Let them implore that she who aided the beginning of the Church by her prayers may now, exalted as she is in heaven above all the saints and angels, intercede with her Son in the fellowship of all the saints. May she do so until all the peoples of the human family, whether they are honored with the name of Christian or whether they still do not know their Savior, are happily gathered together in peace and harmony into the one People of God, for the glory of the Most Holy and Undivided Trinity."[146]

Conclusion

51.1 At the end of the daily Liturgy of the Hours, among the invocations addressed to Mary by the Church is the following:
"Loving Mother of the Redeemer,
gate of heaven, star of the sea,
assist your people who have fallen yet strive to rise again.
To the wonderment of nature you bore your Creator!"

---

[144] Dogmatic Constitution on the Church *Lumen Gentium*, 69.
[145] Homily (January 1, 1987), 4: *AAS* 79 (1987), 1148.
[146] Dogmatic Constitution on the Church *Lumen Gentium*, 69.

51.2 "To the wonderment of nature!" These words of the antiphon express that *wonderment of faith* which accompanies the mystery of Mary's divine motherhood. In a sense, it does so in the heart of the whole of creation, and, directly, in the heart of the whole People of God, in the heart of the Church. How wonderfully far God has gone, the Creator and Lord of all things, in the "revelation of himself" to man![147] How clearly he has bridged all the spaces of that infinite "distance" which separates the Creator from the creature! If in himself he remains *ineffable and unsearchable,* still more *ineffable and unsearchable is he in the reality of the Incarnation* of the Word, who became man through the Virgin of Nazareth.

51.3 If he has eternally willed to call man to share in the divine nature (cf. 2 Pet 1:4), it can be said that he has matched the "divinization" of man to humanity's historical conditions, so that even after sin he is ready to restore at a great price the eternal plan of his love through the "humanization" of his Son, who is of the same being as himself. The whole of creation, and more directly man himself, cannot fail to be amazed at this gift in which he has become a sharer, in the Holy Spirit: "God so loved the world that he gave his only Son" (Jn 3:16).

51.4 *At the center of this mystery,* in the midst of this wonderment of faith, stands Mary. As the loving Mother of the Redeemer, she was the first to experience it: "To the wonderment of nature you bore your Creator!"

52.1 The words of this liturgical antiphon also express *the truth of the "great transformation"* which the mystery of the Incarnation establishes for man. It is a transformation which belongs to his entire history, from that beginning which is revealed to us in the first chapters of *Genesis* until the final end, in the perspective of the end of the world, of which Jesus has revealed to us "neither the day nor the hour" (Mt 25:13). It is an unending and continuous transformation between falling and rising again, between the man of sin and the man of grace and justice. The Advent liturgy in particular is at the very heart of this transformation and captures its unceasing "here and now" when it exclaims: "Assist your people who have fallen yet strive to rise again!"

52.2 These words apply to every individual, every community, to nations and peoples, and to the generations and epochs of human history, to our own

---

[147] Cf. Second Vatican Ecumenical Council, Dogmatic Constitution on Divine Revelation *Dei Verbum,* 2: "Through this revelation . . . the invisible God . . . out of the abundance of his love speaks to men as friends . . . and lives among them. . . , so that he may invite and take them into fellowship with himself."

epoch, to these years of the millennium which is drawing to a close: "Assist, yes assist, your people who have fallen!"

52.3 This is the invocation addressed to Mary, the "loving Mother of the Redeemer," the invocation addressed to Christ, who through Mary entered human history. Year after year the antiphon rises to Mary, evoking that moment which saw the accomplishment of this essential historical transformation, which irreversibly continues: the transformation from "falling" to "rising."

52.4 Mankind has made wonderful discoveries and achieved extraordinary results in the fields of science and technology. It has made great advances along the path of progress and civilization, and in recent times one could say that it has succeeded in speeding up the pace of history. But the fundamental transformation, the one which can be called "original," constantly accompanies man's journey, and through all the events of history accompanies each and every individual. It is the transformation from "falling" to "rising," from death to life. It is also *a constant challenge* to people's consciences, a challenge to man's whole historical awareness: the challenge to follow the path of "not falling" in ways that are ever old and ever new, and of "rising again" if a fall has occurred.

52.5 As she goes forward with the whole of humanity toward the frontier between the two millennia, the Church, for her part, with the whole community of believers and in union with all men and women of good will, takes up the great challenge contained in these words of the Marian antiphon: "the people who have fallen yet strive to rise again," and she addresses both the Redeemer and his Mother with the plea: "Assist us." For, as this prayer attests, the Church sees the Blessed Mother of God in the saving mystery of Christ and in her own mystery. She sees Mary deeply rooted in humanity's history, in man's eternal vocation according to the providential plan which God has made for him from eternity. She sees Mary maternally present and sharing in the many complicated problems which *today* beset the lives of individuals, families and nations; she sees her helping the Christian people in the constant struggle between good and evil, to ensure that it "does not fall," or, if it has fallen, that it "rises again."

52.6 I hope with all my heart that the reflections contained in the present Encyclical will also serve to renew this vision in the hearts of all believers.

52.7 As Bishop of Rome, I send to all those to whom these thoughts are addressed the kiss of peace, my greeting and my blessing in our Lord Jesus Christ. Amen.

Given in Rome, at Saint Peter's, on March 25, the Solemnity of the Annunciation of the Lord, in the year 1987, the ninth of my Pontificate.

Sollicitudo Rei Socialis

Editor's Introduction

Although signed on December 30, 1987, Pope John Paul II's encyclical "on social concern" was not officially published until February 19, 1988.[1] Like *Laborem Exercens* (1981), this second social encyclical commemorates a previous papal document. *Sollicitudo Rei Socialis* marks the twentieth anniversary of Paul VI's *Populorum Progressio* (1967). But more than merely recalling the relevance and doctrine of Pope Paul's encyclical, it highlights new themes and responds to the problems of development in the Third World which had emerged in the intervening twenty years.

John Paul writes as a teacher, explaining why the proclamation of the Church's social doctrine belongs to her evangelizing mission. He also writes as an informed witness to the increasing injustice and poverty in the world. Lastly, he writes as a defender of human dignity and inalienable rights, and of every person's transcendent vocation to communion with the Triune God.

In some ways *Sollicitudo Rei Socialis* echoes *Laborem Exercens* (1981). John Paul's use of Sacred Scripture, for example, is similar in that he frequently quotes from the opening chapters of Genesis. The differences between the two social encyclicals, however, are noteworthy. Whereas in *Laborem Exercens* (1981) the Pope never directly cites *Rerum Novarum* (1891), the encyclical of Leo XIII which it commemorates, throughout *Sollicitudo Rei Socialis* John Paul quotes or refers to *Populorum Progressio* more than forty times. It is his constant point of reference. Second, to support his presentation, the Pope marshals statements taken from earlier writings and discourses of his own pontificate, as well as the social teaching of the Second Vatican Council expressed in *Gaudium et Spes*. Third, more than in any other encyclical, John Paul makes use of documents published by the Roman Curia. Especially notable are his six references to the *Instruction on Christian Freedom and Liberation* (1986) issued by the Congregation for the Doctrine of the Faith. He also cites two publications of the Pontifical Commission "Iustitia et Pax": *At the Service of the Human Community: An Ethical Approach to the International Debt Question* (1986) and *The Church and the Housing Problem* (1987).

While *Sollicitudo Rei Socialis* perceptively analyzes the economic, political, social, and cultural dimensions of world development, its perspective is primarily ethical and theological. John Paul rereads *Populorum Progressio* through

---

[1] *Acta Apostolicae Sedis*, 80 (1988), 513-586.

a moral-spiritual lens. His main concern is to form the consciences of individual men and women, to help them in their task of promoting authentic development "in the light of faith and of the Church's Tradition" (§41.7).

Summary

Including the introduction and conclusion, *Sollicitudo Rei Socialis* is divided into seven chapters. In the introduction (§§1-4), the Pope says that, in light of *Populorum Progressio,* he wishes to confirm the patrimony of the Church's social doctrine and to make his own contribution to its renewal. Chapter two, "Originality of the Encyclical *Populorum Progressio*" (§§5-10), discusses the innovative aspects of Paul VI's encyclical, which applied the teachings of the Second Vatican Council to questions of development. Chapter three, "Survey of the Contemporary World" (§§11-26), describes the most striking characteristics of present-day underdevelopment and its underlying political causes. In chapter four, "Authentic Human Development" (§§27-34), John Paul explains the nature of true development, insisting on its moral dimension. He continues this discussion in chapter five, "A Theological Reading of Modern Problems" (§§35-40), in which he analyzes the moral obstacles to development. Chapter six, "Some Particular Guidelines" (§§41-45), affirms once more the importance of the Church's social doctrine and indicates some urgently needed reforms if development is to make progress. The conclusion (§§46-49) explores the relationship between development and liberation, in view of the contemporary relevance of this theme, and ends with a pressing appeal for greater commitment on the part of everyone to the development of peoples.

The encyclical's structure reflects the particular method which the Pope uses in his social Magisterium. He first analyzes the specific situation in the light of the signs of the times. Then he interprets his analysis from an ethical-theological perspective. Finally, he makes some specific policy recommendations which embody the principles enunciated. This procedure follows the classical method of "seeing, judging, and acting" frequently proposed in magisterial documents dealing with questions of social justice.

In the introduction, John Paul refers to the Church's social doctrine as an "updated doctrinal 'corpus'" which is constantly being enriched by applying the Gospel to new situations (§1.2). Then he sets out the two principal objectives of his encyclical: to pay homage to the "historic document of Paul VI and to its teaching," and "to reaffirm the *continuity* of the social doctrine [of his predecessors] as well as its constant *renewal*" (§3.1). From a theological perspective, the Pope intends to emphasize "the need for a fuller and more nuanced concept of development" and to indicate "some ways of putting it into effect" (§4.4).

Novel contributions of Populorum Progressio

Chapter two focuses on the originality of *Populorum Progressio*. In that encyclical, Paul VI applied the social teachings of the Second Vatican Council "to the specific problem of the *development* and the *underdevelopment of peoples*" (§7.3). John Paul singles out three major contributions which his predecessor's encyclical made to the Church's social doctrine.

First, the Pope praises Paul VI for his emphasis on "the *ethical* and *cultural character*" of development as well as for his insistence on "the legitimacy and necessity" of the Church's intervention in this area (§8.3). Second, John Paul recalls *Populorum Progressio*'s broad perspective: its affirmation that "the social question has acquired a worldwide dimension" which goes beyond regional boundaries and national frontiers (§9.2). Third, Pope Paul's encyclical has made a lasting contribution to social doctrine by explaining why peace can be achieved only if there is respect for justice. Here John Paul cites Paul VI's well known maxim: "Development is the new name for peace" (§10.1).

Signs and causes of underdevelopment

In chapter three, the Pope surveys the state of development in the contemporary world. Compared to the hopeful outlook of 1967, today's situation "offers a *rather negative* impression" (§13.1).

John Paul reaches this pessimistic conclusion based on his reading of the signs of the times. First, the economic and social indicators of development show "the persistence and often the widening of the gap" between North and South (§14.1). The former is the developed First and Second Worlds, the West and East, while the latter is the developing Third and Fourth Worlds. This growing abyss between haves and have-nots is characterized by the unequal distribution of wealth, which is increasingly concentrated in the hands of a few nations. Second, the Pope points to the equally negative and indeed even more disturbing cultural factors which characterize the present situation: illiteracy, lack of participation in national life, exploitation, discrimination, and the denial of economic initiative and of other basic human rights. No doubt having both Marxist and authoritarian regimes in mind, John Paul insists on the need to foster a new kind of society built on different principles. Such a society, he observes, would promote "the spirit of initiative, that is to say *the creative subjectivity of the citizen*" (§15.2). The widespread underdevelopment found in many areas of the world is therefore measured not only by economic considerations but also by cultural, political, and human factors.

What are the root causes of this worsening situation? The Pope singles out three reasons: the lack of effective international solidarity, the rivalry between East and West, and the production and selling of arms.

Responsibility for the ever widening gap between rich and poor countries lies in part with the "grave instances of omissions on the part of the developing nations themselves" (§16.2). Moreover, the wealthy countries of the developed North, whether of the Eastern or Western bloc, furnish inadequate assistance to the Third World. According to John Paul, the West is abandoning itself to a "growing and selfish isolationism" (§23.5). As for the East, it ignores "its duty to cooperate in the task of alleviating human misery" (§23.5). Instead of producing shared prosperity, the growth in interdependence among nations has led to an even greater disparity in wealth and to increased exploitation.

Despite the importance of economic factors as a cause of underdevelopment, the most crucial factor responsible for impeding the pace of development in the South is political: the opposition between the Marxist East and capitalist West. This division between East and West is rooted in ideology: each has its own idea of development; each has its own vision of how to organize society and exercise power. For the Pope, both concepts of the development of individuals and peoples are "imperfect and in need of radical correction" (§21.1). Unfortunately, these are the models being exported from the North to the South.

John Paul faults both collectivism and capitalism for harboring "a tendency toward *imperialism*, as it is usually called, or toward forms of neo-colonialism" (§22.3). Ideological conflicts between East and West are transferred to the poorer countries of the South, sometimes provoking internal strife. Instead of maturing as autonomous nations which concentrate their energies on their own development, all too often the developing nations have become merely cogs on a gigantic wheel turned by others. John Paul judges the post-Second World War era harshly: "The present division of the world is a *direct obstacle* to the real transformation of the conditions of underdevelopment in the developing and less advanced countries" (§22.5). East-West rivalry in the North distorts or delays development in the South.

A third obstacle to the development of the Third World is the high level of arms production and trade fostered by the First and Second Worlds. Resources and investments from both blocs are diverted from genuine assistance programs to the manufacture and sale of weapons. Competition between the superpowers is being played out in the poorer nations, which are drawn into conflicts that they can ill afford. In many ways the North aggravates this situation, enticing the South to purchase armaments from capital made available to it. John Paul also notes the "strange phenomenon" that "while economic aid and development plans meet with the obstacle of insuperable ideological barriers, and with tariff and trade barriers, *arms* of whatever origin circulate with almost total freedom all over the world" (§24.1). The burden of the international debt is thereby increased without stimulating local economic development.

In spite of this gloomy panorama, chapter three closes on an optimistic note. The Pope lists some of the positive factors in the world situation which have emerged since 1967, values which "testify to a new moral concern" (§26.11). Among these he includes people's growing awareness of human dignity and "the more *lively concern* that *human rights should be respected*" (§26.2). John Paul also points to the widespread conviction that *de facto* global interdependence should be complemented by effective international solidarity. Lastly, he mentions the upsurge in a genuine concern for life, peace, ecology, and volunteer programs. These positive signs show that "the heavenly Father's Providence lovingly watches over even our daily cares" (§26.11).

Authentic human development

Before describing the true nature of development, John Paul eliminates conceptions of it which he regards as false. Development is not to be confused with mechanistic progress, as if it were inevitable and limitless. This Enlightenment notion has been replaced today, he writes, "by a well-founded anxiety for the fate of humanity" (§27.2). Moreover, development is not "the *mere accumulation* of goods and services" (§28.1). When it is conceived in this way, the perversion of "superdevelopment" results. This "*excessive* availability of every kind of material goods for the benefit of certain social groups" (§28.2) easily makes people slaves to possessions and immediate gratification, and it is contrary to their true welfare and happiness. While respecting its economic component, development is not limited to that dimension. The Pope insists that it is more important for people to "be" rather than to "have" (cf. §28.4).

Genuine development must be integral; it takes into account human beings in the totality of their bodily and spiritual existence. The specific nature of the person determines the true meaning of development. Precisely because man and woman are created in God's image and likeness (cf. Gen 1:26-27), they are to exercise "dominion" over creation (cf. Gen 1:28). This obligation to stewardship, and therefore to the development of the earth, stems from God's command. Working for development is the necessary response, the Pope writes, to "the divine vocation given from the beginning to man and to woman" (§30.5). The duty for everyone to work for the full development of the whole person and of every person comes from the Creator.

The Incarnation adds a fresh perspective to God's mandate to exercise dominion over the earth. John Paul sees development as part of "the divine plan which is meant to order all things to the fullness which dwells in Christ" (§31.5). Authentic human achievements have a lasting value to the extent that they are brought into the mystery of Redemption. Even so, temporal advancements cannot simply be identified with the coming of God's Kingdom. Rather, says the Pope, "all such achievements simply *reflect* and in a sense *anticipate* the glory of the Kingdom" (§48.1).

In the process of development preeminent attention must be paid to its moral dimensions. In particular, the Pope points out that true development entails "a lively *awareness* of the *value* of the rights of all and of each person" (§33.5). Of special significance in this regard are those rights which further a person's transcendent vocation to communion with God, especially the right to religious freedom. The moral character of true development is ultimately "based on the *love of God and neighbor*, and must help to promote the relationships between individuals and society" (§33.8). John Paul ends chapter four with a reminder that the dominion which God gives to humanity is not an absolute power over the earth. It is evident, he writes, "that development, the planning which governs it, and the way in which its resources are used must include respect for moral demands" (§34.5).

Overcoming obstacles to true development

The Pope's discussion of the ways to surmount underdevelopment is forthright. "Precisely because of the essentially moral character of development," he says, "the *obstacles* to development likewise have a moral character" (§35.1). Here John Paul once more betrays his ever-present attention to the human subject. He believes that "the main obstacles to development will be overcome only by means of *essentially moral decisions*" (§35.3). For believers, these ethical decisions will be inspired by their faith.

"Structures of sin" are at the foundation of the division of the world into two blocs governed by "rigid ideologies" which foster an imperialistic attitude toward the developing countries (cf. §36.1). These sinful institutional factors hinder working for the universal common good, especially that of the poorer nations. Nevertheless, the reality of personal sin is at the root of all such situations, mechanisms, or collective behavior of social groups or blocs. These webs of complicity are "always linked to the *concrete acts* of individuals who introduce these structures, consolidate them and make them difficult to re-move" (§36.2). Moral evil, which in this area is the fruit of many sins, hampers the development of peoples. John Paul singles out two particular attitudes which contribute to the structures of sin impeding development: the *"all-con-suming desire for profit"* at any cost and *"the thirst for power* with the intention of imposing one's will upon others" (§37.1).

Any solution to underdevelopment must address ethical questions. Conse-quently, the Pope sees an urgent need "to *change* the *spiritual attitudes* which define each individual's relationship with self, with neighbor, with even the remotest human communities, and with nature itself" (§38.3). For Christians, this change of mentality and behavior, the conquering of sin by goodness, is the gift of grace called "conversion." Only if the Holy Spirit transforms "hearts of stone" into "hearts of flesh" will the deep-seated moral obstacles to develop-ment be eliminated.

Structures of sin can be dismantled by cultivating attitudes opposed to the desire for profit and the thirst for power. At this point, the Pope introduces his idea of solidarity. The practice of this virtue is the path to peace and develop-ment. He concludes that "the 'evil mechanisms' and 'structures of sin' . . . can be overcome only through the exercise of the human and Christian solidarity to which the Church calls us and which she tirelessly promotes" (§40.4).

Urgently needed reforms

In chapter six, John Paul gives "some particular guidelines" for resolving the crisis of underdevelopment. He first recalls that to bring about true devel-opment the Church neither offers technical solutions nor proposes specific economic or political programs. Her contribution is on another plane. The Church proclaims "the truth about Christ, about herself and about man, ap-plying this truth to a concrete situation" (§41.4). Her social doctrine, as part of moral theology, belongs intrinsically to the Gospel she announces. Social teach-ing includes the prophetic condemnation of injustice, but it is primarily di-rected toward guiding people's behavior, by fostering a change of heart. It should lead the faithful to embrace " 'a commitment to justice,' according to each individual's role, vocation and circumstances" (§41.8).

Among the themes of the Church's social doctrine which have emerged most vigorously in recent years is the love of preference for the poor. John Paul defines this preference as "a *special form* of primacy in the exercise of Christian charity" (42.2). It entails a love which obliges individuals and even whole societies to promote justice. To make this love of preference for "the Lord's poor" effective at a global level, the Pope recommends the reform of the system of international trade, the world monetary and financial system, and the exchange of technology between countries. Furthermore, he urges individuals and nations to foster a culture of initiative and the reform of political life. A necessary condition and guarantee of development, he says, is "the free and responsible participation of all citizens in public affairs, in the rule of law and in respect for the promotion of human rights" (§44.5).

Liberation and development

The encyclical's concluding chapter incorporates some ideas and terminology of the theology of liberation which has emerged in recent years. John Paul reaffirms that "the aspiration to freedom from all forms of slavery affecting the individual and society is something *noble* and *legitimate*" (§46.3). Christian liberation should therefore encompass the cultural, transcendent, and religious spheres. The Pope believes that, despite the often tragic conditions of the present, the Church must express her confidence that "true liberation" is possible (cf. §47.1). To meet this challenge, he urges all those who believe in God to commit themselves to actions inspired by solidarity and a love of preference for the poor.

Key Themes

John Paul II warmly praises Paul VI for the originality of *Populorum Progressio.* Can we point to any original contributions to the Church's social doctrine made by John Paul II in *Sollicitudo Rei Socialis?* I would suggest three. Most striking is the Pope's repeated insistence that, because of its ethical and religious dimensions, the question of development belongs to the Church's social Magisterium. Second, John Paul's emphasis on solidarity is innovative. In fact, this idea emerges as a principal hermeneutical key of his social teaching. Third, his analysis of the Church's position with respect to Marxism and capitalism is original.

Social doctrine, evangelization, and development

Throughout *Sollicitudo Rei Socialis* John Paul staunchly defends the Church's right to speak out on issues which touch on the development of peoples. His defense ultimately rests on the Church's duty to safeguard and promote human dignity. At every turn the Pope repeats that "the teaching and spreading of her social doctrine are part of the Church's evangelizing mission" (§41.8, cf. §§1.2, 3.2, 8.3, 14.6, 31.5, 33.8, 47.4).

The doctrinal principles in the Church's social teaching belong to the deposit of faith. They have a "vital link with the Gospel of the Lord" (§3.2), applying "the word of God to people's lives and the life of society" (§8.4). An essential element of this corpus is the dignity of the human person both as an individual and social being. When the Church teaches in the area of development she does so in fidelity to a divine mandate. Her proclamation of the fundamental principles of social doctrine is therefore an integral dimension of the Gospel message.

It is the Church's special responsibility to draw attention to the ethical and religious dimensions of development: How do specific models of development either help or hinder people's response to their transcendent vocation? The Pope constantly points out that the soul of development is the human being in the totality of his *"interior dimension"* (§29.1).

For John Paul II, the commitment to development follows both from being created in God's image and receiving the mandate to subdue the earth, and from being redeemed by Christ. To help people carry out their vocation of restoring all things in Christ, the Church must "concern herself with the problems of development" (§31.5). The Church shines the light of faith on the meaning of authentic development. In denouncing the structures of sin which thwart it, she defends human dignity and the rights which flow from that dignity. Thus, she names moral evil as the root cause of all underdevelopment. According to *Sollicitudo Rei Socialis,* the Church's prophetic role includes the *"condemnation* of evils and injustices" as part of her *"ministry of evangelization"* (§41.9).

Drawing on the Gospel, the Pope also proposes that conversion from the sin embodied in certain structures or institutions is the only path to authentic development. In addressing the nature, conditions, requirements, and aims of integral development, the Church fulfills her mission to evangelize. John Paul maintains that no complete solution to the problems of underdevelopment is possible without the revealed truth of the Gospel. The Church enunciates theological and moral principles, rightly called "doctrinal," with the highest authority.

The Pope is also convinced that ecclesial teaching authority has no specific competence to make practical judgments about how to bring about an integral development worthy of the human person. Even so, he offers some "guidelines" with respect to the concrete application of principles, as a stimulus to the thought and action of others. Here the preeminent role belongs to the laity. Their task, he says, is "to animate temporal realities with Christian commitment" (§47.6). John Paul does not intend, for example, that his views concerning the stabilization of exchange and interest rates should be interpreted as passing a definitive judgment on the world financial system (cf.

§43.3). The distinction between the enunciation of moral principles, which the Pope proposes with the Petrine authority belonging to his papal ministry, and the recommendation of specific policies, which he suggests as a spur to action, must always be kept in mind.

Solidarity

Undoubtedly one of John Paul II's principal contributions to social doctrine is his popularization of the term "solidarity." In *Populorum Progressio,* Paul VI referred to people's "duty to solidarity" in the international arena (§48), and John Paul already spoke about "worker solidarity" in *Laborem Exercens* (1981). In *Sollicitudo Rei Socialis,* however, solidarity moves to the forefront as an idea with profound theological implications. The concept summarizes what the Pope regards as the way to overcome today's individualistic mentality and the structures of sin which hinder genuine development.

Among the positive signs in the contemporary world which the encyclical records is the growing sense among people of the unity of the human race. Sadly, this unity is seriously compromised in practice by the widening gap between North and South. According to John Paul, the increasing interdependence of nations in the global village is far too frequently unaccompanied by ethical considerations. Authentic development requires that "either *all* the nations of the world participate, or it will not be true development" (§17.1).

What is needed, writes the Pope, is "a solidarity which will take up interdependence and transfer it to the moral plane" (§26.5). All people must commit themselves to the task, if the conviction that the world has a common destiny is to have any practical effect. "Collaboration in the development of the whole person and of every human being," he says, "is in fact a duty *of all toward all,* and must be shared by the four parts of the world: East and West, North and South" (§32.2).

The recognition of the economic, political, cultural, and religious factors of interdependence on a worldwide level is a first step to practicing solidarity. The second step is the acknowledgement of the moral ramifications of this interdependence. When people recognize this ethical dimension, the Pope calls their response "solidarity." He then defines this attitude: "[Solidarity] is not a feeling of vague compassion or shallow distress at the misfortunes of many people, both near and far. On the contrary, it is *a firm and persevering determination* to commit oneself to the *common good*; that is to say, the good of all and of each individual, because we are all really responsible *for all*" (§38.6). Solidarity entails a sense of moral responsibility that helps us "to see the 'other' — whether a *person, people or nation* — . . . as our 'neighbor,' a 'helper' (cf. Gen 2:18-20)," as one called "to be made a sharer, on a par with ourselves, in the banquet of life to which all are equally invited by God" (§39.5). Solidarity begins in the family, then reaches out to the community, encompasses the nation and, finally, embraces the whole world.

Lest solidarity be misinterpreted as mere humanitarianism, the Pope emphasizes that it is "undoubtedly a *Christian virtue*" (§40.1). Solidarity is more than an appreciation for the strong natural bonds uniting humanity. It is illuminated by the light of faith. This faith reveals that the unity of the human race, which inspires solidarity, has its deepest roots in the unity and communion of the divine Persons in the Trinity. Solidarity manifests this Trinitarian unity in communion which is "the *soul* of the Church's vocation to be a 'sacrament'" (§40.3). Thus, solidarity is more than just cooperation in a common project. It is based on the love of neighbor, the distinguishing mark of Christ's followers, by which they love as they have been loved (cf. Jn 15:12). For the believer, "solidarity seeks to go beyond itself, to take on the *specifically Christian* dimension of total gratuity, forgiveness and reconciliation" (§40.2).

When practiced by the influential and the wealthy, solidarity leads to a sense of responsibility toward the marginalized and the needy. It looks for ways to help them. When practiced by the weak and poor, solidarity discourages passivity and hopelessness. It animates everyone to contribute, in whatever ways are possible, to the good of all. John Paul sums up the importance he attributes to this virtue when he writes: "The process of *development* and *liberation* takes concrete shape in the exercise of *solidarity*, that is to say in the love and service of neighbor, especially of the poorest" (§46.6).

Collectivism, capitalism, and superpower rivalry

One of the liveliest debates sparked by *Sollicitudo Rei Socialis* stems from the Pope's treatment of the two dominant ideological blocs: the Marxist East and the capitalist West. Commentators argue about whether or not he envisions a kind of "moral equivalence" between them. Does the Pope place himself equidistant from both, proposing a third way between capitalism and collectivism?

When John Paul introduces his discussion of the two blocs, his interest focuses on how each of them conceives the development of individuals and peoples. Without at first specifying any differences between them, he considers each of them to be seriously flawed. Both East and West harm the Third World because each in its own way widens the gap between the more developed and the less developed countries. This is a major reason, the Pope says, "why the Church's social doctrine adopts a critical attitude toward both liberal capitalism and Marxist collectivism" (§21.2).

The rigid ideology of each bloc gives rise to a spirit of imperialism and neocolonialism, rather than to one of interdependence and solidarity. But John Paul never asserts a moral equivalence between East and West. Furthermore, when dealing explicitly with the question whether the Church's social teaching supports any specific political or economic system, the Pope does not take sides. The Church, he affirms, "does not propose economic and political systems or programs, nor does she show preference for one or the other" (§41.1). Catholic social doctrine is "*not* a 'third way' between *liberal capitalism* and *Marxist collectivism* . . . it constitutes a *category of its own*" (§41.7). It is beholden to neither.

When John Paul relies on the rich heritage of the Church's prophetic teaching, he views from "outside" the competing blocs of East and West. He challenges both of them to examine the degree to which their policies enshrine genuine moral values and foster the authentic development of peoples. As far as John Paul II is concerned, the question of "moral equivalence" is a redherring. He neither suggests nor denies such equivalence. The encyclical neither condones nor condemns one bloc at the expense of the other. Papal teaching is a tool of neither. John Paul's main objective in *Sollicitudo Rei Socialis* is to show everyone the urgent need for solidarity, so that the integral development of all people can become a reality.

The Church's social teaching brings to the politics and economics of development a unique perspective: it draws attention to the moral implications of all models of development. Since social doctrine belongs to Church teaching, it is neither an ideology nor a system. It aims instead at pointing out the features of development that are most worthy of human dignity.

In the light of faith and the Church's Tradition, social doctrine interprets human realities. It judges "their conformity with or divergence from the lines of the Gospel teaching on man and his vocation, a vocation which is at once earthly and transcendent" (§41.7). As an "expert in humanity" (§7.2, cf. §41.2), the Church must defend human dignity. Her social teaching belongs to her evangelizing mission. Fulfilling a prophetic role, social doctrine challenges ideologies and systems in proclaiming justice and condemning injustice.

The Pope ends *Sollicitudo Rei Socialis* with a prayer in which he entrusts to Mary and her intercession "this *difficult moment* of the modern world, and the efforts that are being made and will be made, often with great suffering, in order to contribute to the true development of peoples" (§49.1).

* * *

Selected Bibliography

Baum, Gregory. "The Anti-Cold War Encyclical." *The Ecumenist,* 26 (1988), 65-74.

Baum, Gregory, and Ellsberg, Robert, eds. *The Logic of Solidarity: Commentaries on Pope John Paul II's Encyclical "On Social Concern."* Maryknoll: Orbis Books, 1989.

Bowe, Paul. "*Sollicitudo Rei Socialis:* A Commentary on the Encyclical." *Doctrine and Life,* 38 (1988), 227-233.

Byron, William J. "Solidarity: Path to Development and Peace." *America,* 158 (1988), 445-446.

Caldecott, Stratford. "Cosmology, Eschatology, Ecology: Some Reflections on *Sollicitudo Rei Socialis.*" *Communio,* 15 (1988), 305-318.

Calvez, Jean-Yves. "*Sollicitudo Rei Socialis.*" In *The New Dictionary of Catholic Social Thought.* Edited by Judith A. Dwyer. Collegeville: Liturgical Press, 1994. 912-917.

Etchegaray, Roger. Presentation at the Press Conference for the Publication of *Sollicitudo Rei Socialis. L'Osservatore Romano,* 9 (1988), 14.

Faley, Roland James. "Pope as Prophet: The New Social Encyclical." *America,* 158 (1988), 447-450.

Finnis, John. "Goods Are Meant for Everyone." *L'Osservatore Romano,* 12 (1988), 11.

Fonseca, Aloysius J. "Reflections on the Encyclical Letter *Sollicitudo Rei Socialis.*" *Gregorianum,* 70 (1989), 5-24.

Habiger, Matthew. "Situating *Sollicitudo Rei Socialis* in Catholic Social Teaching." *Social Justice Review,* 79 (1988), 138-144.

Heir, J. Bryan. "Taking on the Super-Rivals: Reactions to the Pope's Latest Encyclical." *Commonweal,* 115 (1988), 169-170.

Kiliroor, Matthew. "Social Doctrine in *Sollicitudo Rei Socialis.*" *The Month,* 21 (1988), 711-714.

McGurn, William. "*Sollicitudo Rei Socialis.*" In *A Century of Catholic Social Thought.* Edited by George Weigel and Robert Royal. Lanham: University Press of America, 1991. 163-176.

Mahony, Roger M. "Perspectives for Viewing the Social Concerns Encyclical." *Origins,* 18 (1988), 69-72.

Morneau, Robert F. "The Church's Social Concerns: Ten Lessons." *Emmanuel,* 95 (1989), 70-73.

Myers, Kenneth A., ed. *Aspiring to Freedom: Commentaries on John Paul II's Encyclical "The Social Concerns of the Church."* Grand Rapids: Eerdmans, 1988.

O'Connor, Dennis A. "An Economic Evaluation of John Paul II's Encyclical On Social Concerns." *Social Justice Review,* 79 (1988), 131-137.

Preston, Ronald. "Twenty Years after *Populorum Progressio:* An Appraisal of Pope John Paul's Commemorative Encyclical." *Theology,* 92 (1989), 519-525.

Seminar on Pope John Paul II's Encyclical *Sollicitudo Rei Socialis. L'Osservatore Romano,* 45 (1988), Supplement, i-viii.

"The Solidarity Encyclical." Editorial. *America,* 158 (1988), 251.

"*Sollicitudo Rei Socialis.*" Editorial. *Commonweal,* 115 (1988), 131-132.

Suro, Roberto. "The Writing of *Sollicitudo Rei Socialis:* A Behind-the-Scenes Account." *Critic,* 6 (May 1988), 13-18.

White, Robert Edward. "Blaming the Villains, not the Victim: John Paul II and the Superpowers." *Commonweal,* 115 (1988), 555-559.

Williams, Oliver F., and Houck, John W., eds. *The Making of an Economic Vision: John Paul II's "On Social Concern."* Lanham: University Press of America, 1991).

ENCYCLICAL LETTER
SOLLICITUDO REI SOCIALIS
OF THE SUPREME PONTIFF
JOHN PAUL II
FOR THE TWENTIETH ANNIVERSARY OF
POPULORUM PROGRESSIO

Sollicitudo Rei Socialis

Venerable Brothers and
Dear Sons and Daughters,
Health and the Apostolic Blessing!

I

Introduction

1.1 The social concern of the Church, directed toward an authentic development of man and society which would respect and promote all the dimensions of the human person, has always expressed itself in the most varied ways. In recent years, one of the special means of intervention has been the Magisterium of the Roman Pontiffs which, beginning with the Encyclical *Rerum Novarum* of Leo XIII as a point of reference,[1] has frequently dealt with the question and has sometimes made the dates of publication of the various social documents coincide with the anniversaries of that first document.[2]

1.2 The Popes have not failed to throw fresh light by means of those messages upon new aspects of the social doctrine of the Church. As a result, this doctrine, beginning with the outstanding contribution of Leo XIII and enriched by the successive contributions of the Magisterium, has now become an updated doctrinal "corpus." It builds up gradually, as the Church, in the fullness of the word revealed by Christ Jesus[3] and with the assistance of the Holy Spirit (cf. Jn 14:16, 26; 16:13-15), reads events as they unfold in the course of history. She thus seeks to lead people to respond, with the support also of rational reflection and of the human sciences, to their vocation as responsible builders of earthly society.

---

[1] Leo XIII, Encyclical Letter *Rerum Novarum* (May 15, 1891): *Leonis XIII P. M. Acta*, XI, Rome, 1892, 97-144.

[2] Pius XI, Encyclical Letter *Quadragesimo Anno* (May 15, 1931): *AAS* 23 (1931), 177-228; John XXIII, Encyclical Letter *Mater et Magistra* (May 15, 1961): *AAS* 53 (1961), 401-464; Paul VI, Apostolic Letter *Octogesima Adveniens* (May 14, 1971): *AAS* 63 (1971), 401-441; John Paul II, Encyclical Letter *Laborem Exercens* (September 14, 1981): *AAS* 73 (1981), 577-647. Pius XII also delivered a radio message for the fiftieth anniversary of the Encyclical of Leo XIII (June 1, 1941): *AAS* 33 (1941), 195-205.

[3] Cf. Second Vatican Ecumenical Council, Dogmatic Constitution on Divine Revelation *Dei Verbum*, 4.

2.1 Part of this large body of social teaching is the distinguished Encyclical *Populorum Progressio*[4] which my esteemed Predecessor Paul VI published on March 26, 1967.

2.2 The enduring relevance of this Encyclical is easily recognized if we note the series of commemorations which took place during 1987 in various forms and in many parts of the ecclesiastical and civil world. For this same purpose, the Pontifical Commission "Iustitia et Pax" sent a circular letter to the Synods of the Oriental Catholic Churches and to the Episcopal Conferences, asking for ideas and suggestions on the best way to celebrate the Encyclical's anniversary, to enrich its teachings and, if need be, to update them. At the time of the twentieth anniversary, the same Commission organized a solemn commemoration in which I myself took part and gave the concluding address.[5] And now, also taking into account the replies to the above mentioned circular letter, I consider it appropriate, at the close of the year 1987, to devote an Encyclical to the theme of *Populorum Progressio*.

3.1 In this way I wish principally to achieve *two objectives* of no little importance: on the one hand, to pay homage to this historic document of Paul VI and to its teaching; on the other hand, following in the footsteps of my esteemed Predecessors in the See of Peter, to reaffirm the *continuity* of the social doctrine as well as its constant *renewal*. In effect, continuity and renewal are a proof of the *perennial value* of the teaching of the Church.

3.2 This twofold dimension is typical of her teaching in the social sphere. On the one hand it is *constant*, for it remains identical in its fundamental inspiration, in its "principles of reflection," in its "criteria of judgment," in its basic "directives for action,"[6] and above all in its vital link with the Gospel of the Lord. On the other hand, it is ever *new*, because it is subject to the necessary and opportune adaptations suggested by the changes in historical conditions and by the unceasing flow of the events which are the setting of the life of people and society.

4.1 I am convinced that the teachings of the Encyclical *Populorum Progressio*, addressed to the people and the society of the sixties, retain all their force as

---

[4] Paul VI, Encyclical Letter *Populorum Progressio* (March 26, 1967): *AAS* 59 (1967), 257-299.

[5] Cf. (March 25, 1987): *Insegnamenti* X/1 (1987), 669-677.

[6] Cf. Congregation for the Doctrine of the Faith, Instruction on Christian Freedom and Liberation *Libertatis Conscientia* (March 22, 1986), 72: *AAS* 79 (1987), 586; Paul VI, Apostolic Letter *Octogesima Adveniens* (May 14, 1971), 4: *AAS* 63 (1971), 403-404.

an appeal to conscience today in the last part of the eighties, in an effort to trace the major lines of the present world always within the context of the aim and inspiration of the "development of peoples," which are still very far from being exhausted. I therefore propose to extend the impact of that message by bringing it to bear, with its possible applications, upon the present historical moment, which is no less dramatic than that of twenty years ago.

4.2 As we well know, time maintains a constant and unchanging rhythm. Today however we have the impression that it is passing *ever more quickly,* especially by reason of the multiplication and complexity of the phenomena in the midst of which we live. Consequently, *the configuration of the world* in the course of the last twenty years, while preserving certain fundamental constants, has undergone notable changes and presents some totally new aspects.

4.3 The present period of time, on the eve of the third Christian millennium, is characterized by a widespread expectancy, rather like a new "Advent,"[7] which to some extent touches everyone. It offers an opportunity to study the teachings of the Encyclical in greater detail and to see their possible future developments.

4.4 The aim of the present *reflection* is to emphasize, through a theological investigation of the present world, the need for a fuller and more nuanced concept of development, according to the suggestions contained in the Encyclical. Its aim is also to indicate some ways of putting it into effect.

II

Originality of the Encyclical
Populorum Progressio

5.1 As soon as it appeared, the document of Pope Paul VI captured the attention of public opinion by reason of its *originality.* In a concrete manner and with great clarity, it was possible to identify the above-mentioned characteristics of *continuity* and *renewal* within the Church's social doctrine. The intention of rediscovering numerous aspects of this teaching, through a careful rereading of the Encyclical, will therefore constitute the main thread of the present reflections.

5.2 But first I wish to say a few words about the *date* of publication: the year 1967. The very fact that Pope Paul VI chose to publish a *social Encyclical*

---

[7] Cf. Encyclical Letter *Redemptoris Mater* (March 25, 1987), 3: *AAS* 79 (1987), 363-364; Homily at Mass (January 1, 1987): *AAS* 79 (1987), 1146-1150.

in that year invites us to consider the document in relationship to the Second Vatican Ecumenical Council, which had ended on December 8, 1965.

6.1 We should see something more in this than simple chronological *proximity*. The Encyclical *Populorum Progressio* presents itself, in a certain way, as *a document which applies the teachings of the Council*. It not only makes continual reference to the texts of the Council,[8] but it also flows from the same concern of the Church which inspired the whole effort of the Council — and in a particular way the Pastoral Constitution *Gaudium et Spes* — to coordinate and develop a number of themes of her social teaching.

6.2 We can therefore affirm that the Encyclical *Populorum Progressio* is a kind of response to the *Council's appeal* with which the Constitution *Gaudium et Spes* begins: "The joys and the hopes, the griefs and the anxieties of the people of this age, especially those who are poor or in any way afflicted, these too are the joys and hopes, the griefs and anxieties of the followers of Christ. Indeed, nothing genuinely human fails to raise an echo in their hearts."[9] These words express the *fundamental motive* inspiring the great document of the Council, which begins by noting the situation of *poverty* and of *underdevelopment* in which millions of human beings live.

6.3 This *poverty* and *underdevelopment* are, under another name, the "griefs and the anxieties" of today, of "especially those who are poor." Before this vast panorama of pain and suffering the Council wished to suggest horizons of joy and hope. The Encyclical of Paul VI has the same purpose, in full fidelity to the inspiration of the Council.

7.1 There is also the *theme* of the Encyclical which, in keeping with the great tradition of the Church's social teaching, takes up again in a direct manner the *new exposition* and *rich synthesis* which the Council produced, notably in the Constitution *Gaudium et Spes*.

7.2 With regard to the content and themes once again set forth by the Encyclical, the following should be emphasized: the awareness of the duty of the Church, as "an expert in humanity," "to scrutinize the signs of the times and to interpret them in the light of the Gospel,"[10] the awareness, equally profound, of her mission of "service," a mission distinct from the function of

---

[8] The Encyclical Letter *Populorum Progressio* cites the documents of the Second Vatican Ecumenical Council nineteen times, and sixteen of the references are to the Pastoral Constitution on the Church in the Modern World *Gaudium et Spes*.

[9] *Gaudium et Spes*, 1.

[10] *Gaudium et Spes*, 4; cf. *Populorum Progressio*, 13: loc. cit., 263, 264.

the State, even when she is concerned with people's concrete situation;[11] the reference to the notorious inequalities in the situations of those same people;[12] the confirmation of the Council's teaching, a faithful echo of the centuries-old tradition of the Church regarding the "universal purpose of goods";[13] the appreciation of the culture and the technological civilization which contribute to human liberation,[14] without failing to recognize their limits;[15] finally, on the specific theme of development, which is precisely the theme of the Encyclical, the insistence on the "most serious duty" incumbent on the more developed nations "to help the developing countries."[16] The same idea of development proposed by the Encyclical flows directly from the approach which the Pastoral Constitution takes to this problem.[17]

7.3 These and other explicit references to the Pastoral Constitution lead one to conclude that the Encyclical presents itself as an *application* of the Council's teaching in social matters to the specific problem of the *development* and the *underdevelopment of peoples*.

8.1 This brief analysis helps us to appreciate better the *originality* of the Encyclical, which can be stated in *three* points.

8.2 The *first* is constituted by the *very fact* of a document, issued by the highest authority of the Catholic Church and addressed both to the Church herself and "to all people of good will,"[18] on a matter which at first sight is solely *economic* and *social:* the *development* of peoples. The term "development" is taken from the vocabulary of the social and economic sciences. From this point of view, the Encyclical *Populorum Progressio* follows directly in the line of the Encyclical *Rerum Novarum*, which deals with the "condition of the workers."[19] Considered superficially, both themes could seem extraneous to the legitimate concern of the Church seen as a *religious institution* — and "development" even more so than the "condition of the workers."

8.3 In continuity with the Encyclical of Leo XIII, it must be recognized that the document of Paul VI possesses the merit of having emphasized the *ethical*

---

[11] Cf. *Gaudium et Spes,* 3; *Populorum Progressio,* 13: loc. cit., 264.

[12] Cf. *Gaudium et Spes,* 63; *Populorum Progressio,* 9: loc. cit., 269.

[13] Cf. *Gaudium et Spes,* 69; *Populorum Progressio,* 22: loc. cit., 269.

[14] Cf. *Gaudium et Spes,* 57; *Populorum Progressio,* 41: loc. cit., 277.

[15] Cf. *Gaudium et Spes,* 19; *Populorum Progressio,* 41: loc. cit., 277-278.

[16] Cf. *Gaudium et Spes,* 86; *Populorum Progressio,* 48: loc. cit., 281.

[17] Cf. *Gaudium et Spes,* 69; *Populorum Progressio,* 14-21: loc. cit., 264-268.

[18] Cf. the *inscriptio* of the Encyclical Letter *Populorum Progressio:* loc. cit., 257.

[19] The Encyclical Letter *Rerum Novarum* of Leo XIII has as its principal subject "the condition of the workers": *Leonis XIII P. M. Acta,* XI, Rome, 1892, 97.

and *cultural character* of the problems connected with development, and likewise the legitimacy and necessity of the Church's intervention in this field.

8.4 In addition, the social doctrine of the Church has once more demonstrated its character as an *application* of the word of God to people's lives and the life of society, as well as to the earthly realities connected with them, offering "principles for reflection," "criteria of judgment" and "directives for action."[20] Here, in the document of Paul VI, one finds these three elements with a prevalently practical orientation, that is, directed toward *moral conduct.*

8.5 In consequence, when the Church concerns herself with the "development of peoples," she cannot be accused of going outside her own specific field of competence and, still less, outside the mandate received from the Lord.

9.1 The *second* point of *originality* of *Populorum Progressio* is shown by the *breadth of outlook* open to what is commonly called the "social question."

9.2 In fact, the Encyclical *Mater et Magistra* of Pope John XXIII had already entered into this wider outlook[21] and the Council had echoed the same in the Constitution *Gaudium et Spes.*[22] However, the social teaching of the Church had not yet reached the point of affirming with such clarity that the social question has acquired a worldwide dimension,[23] nor had this affirmation and the accompanying analysis yet been made into a "directive for action," as Paul VI did in his Encyclical.

9.3 Such an explicit taking up of a position offers a *great wealth* of content, which it is appropriate to point out.

9.4 In the first place a *possible misunderstanding* has to be eliminated. Recognition that the "social question" has assumed a worldwide dimension does not at all mean that it has lost its *incisiveness* or its national and local importance. On the contrary, it means that the problems in industrial enterprises or in the workers' and union movements of a particular country or region are not to be considered as isolated cases with no connection. On the contrary they depend more and more on the influence of factors beyond regional boundaries and national frontiers.

[20] Cf. Congregation for the Doctrine of the Faith, Instruction on Christian Freedom and Liberation *Libertatis Conscientia* (March 22, 1986), 72: *AAS* 79 (1987), 586; Paul VI, Apostolic Letter *Octogesima Adveniens* (May 14, 1971), 4: *AAS* 63 (1971), 403-404.

[21] Cf. Encyclical Letter *Mater et Magistra* (May 15, 1961), III: *AAS* 53 (1961), 440.

[22] *Gaudium et Spes,* 63.

[23] Cf. Encyclical Letter *Populorum Progressio,* 3: loc. cit., 258; cf. also ibid., 9: loc. cit., 261.

9.5 Unfortunately, from the economic point of view, the developing countries are much more numerous than the developed ones; the multitudes of human beings who lack the goods and services offered by development are *much more numerous* than those who possess them.

9.6 We are therefore faced with a serious problem of *unequal distribution* of the means of subsistence originally meant for everybody, and thus also an unequal distribution of the benefits deriving from them. And this happens not through the *fault* of the needy people, and even less through a sort of *inevitability* dependent on natural conditions or circumstances as a whole.

9.7 The Encyclical of Paul VI, in declaring that the social question has acquired worldwide dimensions, first of all points out a *moral fact,* one which has its foundation in an objective analysis of reality. In the words of the Encyclical itself, "each one must be conscious" of this fact,[24] precisely because it directly concerns the conscience, which is the source of moral decisions.

9.8 In this framework, the *originality* of the Encyclical consists not so much in the affirmation, historical in character, of the universality of the social question, but rather in the *moral evaluation* of this reality. Therefore political leaders, and citizens of rich countries considered as individuals, especially if they are Christians, have *the moral obligation,* according to the degree of each one's responsibility, to *take into consideration,* in personal decisions and decisions of government, this relationship of universality, this interdependence which exists between their conduct and the poverty and underdevelopment of so many millions of people. Pope Paul's Encyclical translates more succinctly the moral obligation as the "duty of solidarity";[25] and this affirmation, even though many situations have changed in the world, has the same force and validity today as when it was written.

9.9 On the other hand, without departing from the lines of this moral vision, the *originality* of the Encyclical also consists in the basic insight that the *very concept* of development, if considered in the perspective of universal interdependence, changes notably. True development cannot consist in the simple accumulation of wealth and in the greater availability of goods and services, if this is gained at the expense of the development of the masses, and without due consideration for the social, cultural and spiritual dimensions of the human being.[26]

---

[24] Cf. ibid., 3: loc. cit., 258.

[25] Ibid., 48: loc. cit., 281.

[26] Cf. ibid., 14: loc. cit., 264: "Development cannot be limited to mere economic growth. In order to be authentic, it must be complete: integral, that is, it has to promote the good of every man and of the whole man."

10.1 As a *third point*, the Encyclical provides a very original contribution to the social doctrine of the Church in its totality and to the very concept of development. This originality is recognizable in a phrase of the document's concluding paragraph and which can be considered as its summary, as well as its historic label: "Development is the new name for peace."[27]

10.2 In fact, if the social question has acquired a worldwide dimension, this is because *the demand for justice* can only be satisfied on that level. To ignore this demand could encourage the temptation among the victims of injustice to respond with violence, as happens at the origin of many wars. Peoples excluded from the fair distribution of the goods originally destined for all could ask themselves: why not respond with violence to those who first treat us with violence? And if the situation is examined in the light of the division of the world into ideological blocs — a division already existing in 1967— and in the light of the subsequent economic and political repercussions and dependencies, the danger is seen to be much greater.

10.3 The first consideration of the striking content of the Encyclical's historic phrase may be supplemented by a second consideration to which the document itself alludes:[28] how can one justify the fact that *huge sums of money*, which could and should be used for increasing the development of peoples, are instead utilized for the enrichment of individuals or groups, or assigned to the increase of stockpiles of weapons, both in developed countries and in the developing ones, thereby upsetting the real priorities? This is even more serious given the difficulties which often hinder the direct transfer of capital set aside for helping needy countries. If "development is the new name for peace," war and military preparations are the major enemy of the integral development of peoples.

10.4 In the light of this expression of Pope Paul VI, we are thus invited to reexamine the *concept of development*. This of course is not limited to merely satisfying material necessities through an increase of goods, while ignoring the sufferings of the many and making the selfishness of individuals and nations the principal motivation. As the Letter of Saint James pointedly reminds us: "What causes wars, and what causes fightings among you? Is it not your passions that are at war in your members? You desire and do not have" (Jas 4:1-2).

10.5 On the contrary, in a different world, ruled by concern for the *common good* of all humanity, or by concern for the "spiritual and human devel-

[27] Ibid., 87: loc. cit., 299.
[28] Cf. ibid., 53: loc. cit., 283.

opment of all" instead of by the quest for individual profit, peace would be *possible* as the result of a "more perfect justice among people."[29]

10.6 Also this new element of the Encyclical has a *permanent and contemporary value,* in view of the modern attitude which is so sensitive to the close link between respect for justice and the establishment of real peace.

III
Survey of the Contemporary World

11 In its own time *the fundamental teaching* of the Encyclical *Populorum Progressio* received great acclaim for its novel character. The social context in which we live today cannot be said to be completely *identical* to that of twenty years ago. For this reason, I now wish to conduct a brief review of some of the characteristics of today's world, in order to develop the teaching of Paul VI's Encyclical, once again from the point of view of the "development of peoples."

12.1 The *first fact* to note is that the *hopes for development,* at that time so lively, today appear very far from being realized.

12.2 In this regard, the Encyclical had no illusions. Its language, grave and at times dramatic, limited itself to stressing the seriousness of the situation and to bringing before the conscience of all the urgent obligation of contributing to its solution. In those years there was a *certain* widespread *optimism* about the possibility of overcoming, without excessive efforts, the economic backwardness of the poorer peoples, of providing them with infrastructures and assisting them in the process of industrialization.

12.3 In that historical context, over and above the efforts of each country, the United Nations Organization promoted consecutively *two decades of development.*[30] In fact, some measures, bilateral and multilateral, were taken with the aim of helping many nations, some of which had already been independent for some time, and others — the majority — being States just born from the process of decolonization. For her part, the Church felt the duty to deepen her understanding of the problems posed by the new situation, in the hope of supporting these efforts with her religious and human inspiration, in order to give them a "soul" and an effective impulse.

---

[29] Cf. ibid., 76: loc. cit., 295.

[30] The decades referred to are the years 1960-1970 and 1970-1980; the present decade is the third (1980-1990).

13.1 It cannot be said that these various religious, human, economic and technical initiatives have been in vain, for they have succeeded in achieving certain results. But in general, taking into account the various factors, one cannot deny that the present situation of the world, from the point of view of development, offers a *rather negative* impression.

13.2 For this reason, I wish to call attention to a number of *general indicators*, without excluding other specific ones. Without going into an analysis of figures and statistics, it is sufficient to face squarely the reality of an *innumerable multitude of people* — children, adults and the elderly — in other words, real and unique human persons, who are suffering under the intolerable burden of poverty. There are many millions who are deprived of hope due to the fact that, in many parts of the world, their situation has noticeably worsened. Before these tragedies of total indigence and need, in which so many of our *brothers and sisters* are living, it is the Lord Jesus himself who comes to question us (cf. Mt 25:31-46).

14.1 The first *negative observation* to make is the persistence and often the widening of the gap between the areas of the so-called developed North and the developing South. This geographical terminology is only indicative, since one cannot ignore the fact that the frontiers of wealth and poverty intersect within the societies themselves, whether developed or developing. In fact, just as social inequalities down to the level of poverty exist in rich countries, so, in parallel fashion, in the less developed countries one often sees manifestations of selfishness and a flaunting of wealth which is as disconcerting as it is scandalous.

14.2 The abundance of goods and services available in some parts of the world, particularly in the developed North, is matched in the South by an unacceptable delay, and it is precisely in this geopolitical area that the major part of the human race lives.

14.3 Looking at all the various sectors — the production and distribution of foodstuffs, hygiene, health and housing, availability of drinking water, working conditions (especially for women), life expectancy and other economic and social indicators — the general picture is a disappointing one, both considered in itself and in relation to the corresponding data of the more developed countries. The word "gap" returns spontaneously to mind.

14.4 Perhaps this is not the appropriate word for indicating the true reality, since it could give the impression of a *stationary* phenomenon. This is not the case. The *pace of progress* in the developed and developing countries in recent years has differed, and this serves to widen the distances. Thus the developing countries, especially the poorest of them, find themselves in a situation of very serious delay.

14.5 We must also add the *differences of culture* and *value systems* between the various population groups, differences which do not always match the degree of *economic development,* but which help to create distances. These are elements and aspects which render *the social question much more complex,* precisely because this question has assumed a universal dimension.

14.6 As we observe the various parts of the world separated by this widening gap, and note that each of these parts seems to follow its own path with its own achievements, we can understand the current usage which speaks of different worlds within our *one world:* the First World, the Second World, the Third World and at times the Fourth World.[31] Such expressions, which obviously do not claim to classify exhaustively all countries, are significant: they are a sign of a widespread sense that the *unity of the world,* that is, *the unity of the human race,* is seriously compromised. Such phraseology, beyond its more or less objective value, undoubtedly conceals a *moral content,* before which the Church, which is a "sacrament or sign and instrument . . . of the unity of the whole human race,"[32] cannot remain indifferent.

15.1 However, the picture just given would be incomplete if one failed to add to the "economic and social indices" of underdevelopment other indices which are equally negative and indeed even more disturbing, beginning with the cultural level. These are *illiteracy,* the difficulty or impossibility of obtaining *higher education,* the inability to share in the *building of one's own nation,* the *various forms of exploitation* and of economic, social, political and even religious *oppression* of the individual and his other rights, *discrimination of every type,* especially the exceptionally odious form based on difference of race. If some of these scourges are noted with regret in areas of the more developed North, they are undoubtedly more frequent, more lasting and more difficult to root out in the developing and less advanced countries.

15.2 It should be noted that in today's world, among other rights, *the right of economic initiative* is often suppressed. Yet it is a right which is important not only for the individual but also for the common good. Experience shows us that the denial of this right, or its limitation in the name of an alleged

---

[31] The expression "Fourth World" is used not just occasionally for the so-called less advanced countries, but also and especially for the bands of great or extreme poverty in countries of medium and high income.

[32] Second Vatican Ecumenical Council, Dogmatic Constitution on the Church *Lumen Gentium,* 1.

"equality" of everyone in society, diminishes, or in practice absolutely destroys the spirit of initiative, that is to say *the creative subjectivity of the citizen*. As a consequence, there arises, not so much a true equality, as a "leveling down." In the place of creative initiative there appears passivity, dependence and submission to the bureaucratic apparatus which, as the only "ordering" and "decision-making" body — if not also the "owner" — of the entire totality of goods and the means of production, puts everyone in a position of almost absolute dependence, which is similar to the traditional dependence of the worker-proletarian in capitalism. This provokes a sense of frustration or desperation and predisposes people to opt out of national life, impelling many to emigrate and also favoring a form of "psychological" emigration.

15.3 Such a situation has its consequences also from the point of view of the "rights of individual nations." In fact, it often happens that a nation is deprived of its subjectivity, that is to say the "sovereignty" which is its right, in its economic, political-social and in a certain way cultural significance, since in a national community all these dimensions of life are bound together.

15.4 It must also be restated that no social group, for example a political party, has the right to usurp the role of sole leader, since this brings about the destruction of the true subjectivity of society and of the individual citizens, as happens in every form of totalitarianism. In this situation the individual and the people become "objects," in spite of all declarations to the contrary and verbal assurances.

15.5 We should add here that in today's world there are many other *forms of poverty*. For are there not certain privations or deprivations which deserve this name? The denial or the limitation of human rights — as for example the right to religious freedom, the right to share in the building of society, the freedom to organize and to form unions, or to take initiatives in economic matters — do these not impoverish the human person as much as, if not more than, the deprivation of material goods? And is development which does not take into account the full affirmation of these rights really development on the human level?

15.6 In brief, modern underdevelopment is not only economic but also cultural, political and simply human, as was indicated twenty years ago by the Encyclical *Populorum Progressio*. Hence at this point we have to ask ourselves if the sad reality of today might not be, at least in part, the result of a *too narrow idea* of development, that is, a mainly economic one.

16.1 It should be noted that in spite of the praiseworthy efforts made in the last two decades by the more developed or developing nations and the

International Organizations to find a way out of the situation, or at least to remedy some of its symptoms, the conditions have become *notably worse.*

16.2 Responsibility for this deterioration is due to various causes. Notable among them are undoubtedly grave instances of omissions on the part of the developing nations themselves, and especially on the part of those holding economic and political power. Nor can we pretend not to see the responsibility of the developed nations, which have not always, at least in due measure, felt the duty to help countries separated from the affluent world to which they themselves belong.

16.3 Moreover, one must denounce the existence of economic, financial and social *mechanisms* which, although they are manipulated by people, often function almost automatically, thus accentuating the situation of wealth for some and poverty for the rest. These mechanisms, which are maneuvered directly or indirectly by the more developed countries, by their very functioning favor the interests of the people manipulating them. But in the end they suffocate or condition the economies of the less developed countries. Later on these mechanisms will have to be subjected to a careful analysis under the ethical-moral aspect.

16.4 *Populorum Progressio* already foresaw the possibility that under such systems the wealth of the rich would increase and the poverty of the poor would remain.[33] A proof of this forecast has been the appearance of the so-called Fourth World.

17.1 However much society worldwide shows signs of fragmentation, expressed in the conventional names First, Second, Third, and even Fourth World, their interdependence remains close. When this *interdependence* is separated from its ethical requirements, it has *disastrous consequences* for the weakest. Indeed, as a result of a sort of internal dynamic and under the impulse of mechanisms which can only be called perverse, this *interdependence* triggers *negative effects* even in the rich countries. It is precisely within these countries that one encounters, though on a lesser scale, the *more specific manifestations* of underdevelopment. Thus it should be obvious that development either becomes shared in *common* by every part of the world or it undergoes a *process of regression* even in zones marked by constant progress. This tells us a great deal about the nature of *authentic* development: either *all the* nations of the world participate, or it will not be true development.

17.2 Among the *specific signs* of underdevelopment which increasingly

---

[33] Encyclical Letter *Populorum Progressio,* 33: loc. cit., 273.

affect the developed countries also, there are two in particular that reveal a tragic situation. The *first* is the *housing crisis.* During this International Year of the Homeless proclaimed by the United Nations, attention is focused on the millions of human beings lacking adequate housing or with no housing at all, in order to awaken everyone's conscience and to find a solution to this serious problem with its negative consequences for the individual, the family and society.[34]

17.3 The lack of housing is being experienced *universally* and is due in large measure to the growing phenomenon of urbanization.[35] Even the most highly developed peoples present the sad spectacle of individuals and families literally struggling to survive, without a *roof* over their heads or with a roof *so inadequate* as to constitute no roof at all.

17.4 The lack of housing, an extremely serious problem in itself, should be seen as a sign and summing-up of a whole series of shortcomings, economic, social, cultural or simply human in nature. Given the extent of the problem, we should need little convincing of how far we are from an authentic development of peoples.

18.1 *Another indicator* common to the vast majority of nations is the phenomenon of *unemployment* and *underemployment.*

18.2 Everyone recognizes the *reality* and *growing seriousness* of this problem in the industrialized countries.[36] While it is alarming in the developing countries, with their high rate of population growth and their large numbers of young people, in the countries of high economic development the *sources of work* seem to be shrinking, and thus the opportunities for employment are decreasing rather than increasing.

18.3 This phenomenon too, with its series of negative consequences for individuals and for society, ranging from humiliation to the loss of that self-respect which every man and woman should have, prompts us to question seriously the type of development which has been followed over the past twenty

---

[34] It should be noted that the Holy See associated itself with the celebration of this International Year with a special document issued by the Pontifical Commission "Iustitia et Pax" entitled *"What Have You Done to Your Homeless Brother?" The Church and the Housing Problem* (December 27, 1987).

[35] Cf. Paul VI, Apostolic Letter *Octogesima Adveniens* (May 14, 1971), 8-9: AAS 63 (1971), 406-408.

[36] A recent United Nations publication entitled *World Economic Survey 1987* provides the most recent data (cf. pp. 8-9). The percentage of unemployed in the developed countries with a market economy jumped from 3% of the work force in 1970 to 8% in 1986. It now amounts to 29 million people.

years. Here the words of the Encyclical *Laborem Exercens* are extremely appropriate: "It must be stressed that the constitutive element in this *progress* and also the most adequate *way to verify it* in a spirit of justice and peace, which the Church proclaims and for which she does not cease to pray . . . is *the continual reappraisal of man's work,* both in the aspect of its objective finality and in the aspect of the dignity of the subject of all work, that is to say, man." On the other hand, "we cannot fail to be struck by *a disconcerting fact* of immense proportions: the fact that . . . there are huge numbers of people who are unemployed . . . a fact that without any doubt demonstrates that both within the individual political communities and in their relationships on the continental and world level there is something wrong with the organization of work and employment, precisely at the most critical and socially most important points."[37]

18.4 This second phenomenon, like the previous one, because it is *universal* in character and tends to *proliferate,* is a very telling negative sign of the state and the quality of the development of peoples which we see today.

19.1 A *third phenomenon,* likewise characteristic of the most recent period, even though it is not met with everywhere, is without doubt equally indicative of the *interdependence* between developed and less developed countries. It is the question of the *international debt,* concerning which the Pontifical Commission "Iustitia et Pax" has issued a document.[38]

19.2 At this point one cannot ignore the *close connection* between a problem of this kind — the growing seriousness of which was already foreseen in *Populorum Progressio*[39] — and the question of the development of peoples.

19.3 The reason which prompted the developing peoples to accept the offer of abundantly available capital was the hope of being able to invest it in development projects. Thus the availability of capital and the fact of accepting it as a loan can be considered a contribution to development, something desirable and legitimate in itself, even though perhaps imprudent and occasionally hasty.

19.4 Circumstances having changed, both within the debtor nations and

---

[37] Encyclical Letter *Laborem Exercens* (September 14, 1981), 18: *AAS* 73 (1981), 624-625.

[38] *At the Service of the Human Community: An Ethical Approach to the International Debt Question* (December 27, 1986).

[39] Encyclical Letter *Populorum Progressio,* 54: loc. cit., 283-284: "Developing countries will thus no longer risk being overwhelmed by debts whose repayment swallows up the greater part of their gains. Rates of interest and time for repayment of the loan could be so arranged as not to be too great a burden on either party, taking into account free gifts, interest-free or low-interest loans, and the time needed for liquidating the debts."

in the international financial market, the instrument chosen to make a contribution to development has turned into a *counter-productive mechanism*. This is because the debtor nations, in order to service their debt, find themselves obliged to export the capital needed for improving or at least maintaining their standard of living. It is also because, for the same reason, they are unable to obtain new and equally essential financing.

19.5 Through this mechanism, the means intended for the development of peoples has turned into a *brake* upon development instead, and indeed in some cases has even *aggravated underdevelopment*.

19.6 As the recent document of the Pontifical Commission "Iustitia et Pax" states,[40] these observations should make us reflect on the *ethical character* of the interdependence of peoples. And along similar lines, they should make us reflect on the requirements and conditions, equally inspired by ethical principles, for cooperation in development.

20.1 If at this point we examine the *reasons* for this serious delay in the process of development, a delay which has occurred contrary to the indications of the Encyclical *Populorum Progressio*, which had raised such great hopes, our attention is especially drawn to the *political* causes of today's situation.

20.2 Faced with a combination of factors which are undoubtedly complex, we cannot hope to achieve a comprehensive analysis here. However, we cannot ignore a striking fact about the *political picture* since the Second World War, a fact which has considerable impact on the forward movement of the development of peoples.

20.3 I am referring to the *existence of two opposing blocs*, commonly known as the East and the West. The reason for this description is not purely political but is also, as the expression goes, *geopolitical.* Each of the two blocs tends to assimilate or gather around it other countries or groups of countries, to different degrees of adherence or participation.

20.4 The opposition is first of all *political*, inasmuch as each bloc identifies itself with a system of organizing society and exercising power which presents itself as an alternative to the other. The political opposition, in turn, takes its origin from a deeper opposition which is *ideological* in nature.

20.5 In the West there exists a system which is historically inspired by the principles of the *liberal capitalism* which developed with industrialization during the last century. In the East there exists a system inspired by the *Marxist*

---

[40] Cf. Presentation of the document *At the Service of the Human Community: An Ethical Approach to the International Debt Question* (December 27, 1986).

collectivism which sprang from an interpretation of the condition of the proletarian classes made in the light of a particular reading of history. Each of the two ideologies, on the basis of two very different visions of man and of his freedom and social role, has proposed and still promotes, on the economic level, antithetical forms of the organization of labor and of the structures of ownership, especially with regard to the so-called means of production.

20.6 It was inevitable that by developing antagonistic systems and centers of power, each with its own forms of propaganda and indoctrination, the *ideological opposition* should evolve into a growing *military opposition* and give rise to two blocs of armed forces, each suspicious and fearful of the other's domination.

20.7 International relations, in turn, could not fail to feel the effects of this "logic of blocs" and of the respective "spheres of influence." The tension between the two blocs which began at the end of the Second World War has dominated the whole of the subsequent forty years. Sometimes it has taken the form of *"cold war,"* sometimes of *"wars by proxy,"* through the manipulation of local conflicts, and sometimes it has kept people's minds in suspense and anguish by the threat of an *open and total* war.

20.8 Although at the present time this danger seems to have receded, yet without completely disappearing, and even though an initial agreement has been reached on the destruction of one type of nuclear weapon, the existence and opposition of the blocs continue to be a real and worrying fact which still colors the world picture.

21.1 This happens with particularly negative effects in the international relations which concern the developing countries. For as we know the tension *between East and West* is not in itself an opposition between two different *levels* of development but rather between two *concepts* of the development of individuals and peoples, both concepts being imperfect and in need of radical correction. This opposition is transferred to the developing countries themselves, and thus helps to widen the gap already existing on the economic level between *North and South* and which results from the distance between the two *worlds:* the more developed one and the less developed one.

21.2 This is one of the reasons why the Church's social doctrine adopts a critical attitude toward both liberal capitalism and Marxist collectivism. For from the point of view of development the question naturally arises: in what way and to what extent are these two systems capable of changes and updatings such as to favor or promote a true and integral development of individuals and peoples in modern society? In fact, these changes and updatings are urgent and essential for the cause of a development common to all.

21.3 Countries which have recently achieved independence, and which are trying to establish a cultural and political identity of their own, and need effective and impartial aid from all the richer and more developed countries, find themselves involved in, and sometimes overwhelmed by, ideological conflicts, which inevitably create internal divisions, to the extent in some cases of provoking full civil war. This is also because investments and aid for development are often diverted from their proper purpose and used to sustain conflicts, apart from and in opposition to the interests of the countries which ought to benefit from them. Many of these countries are becoming more and more aware of the danger of falling victim to a form of neocolonialism and are trying to escape from it. It is this awareness which in spite of difficulties, uncertainties and at times contradictions gave rise to the *International Movement of Non-Aligned Nations*, which, in its positive aspect, would like to affirm in an effective way the right of every people to its own identity, independence and security, as well as the right to share, on a basis of equality and solidarity, in the goods intended for all.

22.1 In the light of these considerations, we easily arrive at a clearer picture of the last twenty years and a better understanding of the conflicts in the northern hemisphere, namely between East and West, as an important cause of the retardation or stagnation of the South.

22.2 The developing countries, instead of becoming *autonomous nations* concerned with their own progress toward a just sharing in the goods and services meant for all, become parts of a machine, cogs on a gigantic wheel. This is often true also in the field of social communications, which, being run by centers mostly in the northern hemisphere, do not always give due consideration to the priorities and problems of such countries or respect their cultural make-up. They frequently impose a distorted vision of life and of man, and thus fail to respond to the demands of true development.

22.3 Each of the two *blocs* harbors in its own way a tendency toward *imperialism*, as it is usually called, or toward forms of neocolonialism: an easy temptation to which they frequently succumb, as history, including recent history, teaches.

22.4 It is this abnormal situation, the result of a war and of an unacceptably exaggerated concern for *security*, which deadens the impulse toward united cooperation by all for the common good of the human race, to the detriment especially of peaceful peoples who are impeded from their rightful access to the goods meant for all.

22.5 Seen in this way, the present division of the world is a *direct obstacle* to the real transformation of the conditions of underdevelopment in the developing and less advanced countries. However, peoples do not always resign themselves to their fate. Furthermore, the very needs of an economy stifled by military expenditure and by bureaucracy and intrinsic inefficiency now seem to favor processes which might mitigate the existing opposition and make it easier to begin a fruitful dialogue and genuine collaboration for peace.

23.1 The statement in the Encyclical *Populorum Progressio* that the resources and investments devoted to arms production ought to be used to alleviate the misery of impoverished peoples[41] makes more urgent the appeal to overcome the opposition between the two blocs.

23.2 Today, the reality is that these resources are used to enable each of the two blocs to overtake the other and thus guarantee its own security. Nations which historically, economically and politically have the possibility of playing a leadership role are prevented by this fundamentally flawed distortion from adequately fulfilling their duty of solidarity for the benefit of peoples which aspire to full development.

23.3 It is timely to mention — and it is no exaggeration — that a leadership role among nations can only be justified by the possibility and willingness to contribute widely and generously to the common good.

23.4 If a nation were to succumb more or less deliberately to the temptation to close in upon itself and failed to meet the responsibilities following from its superior position in the community of nations, it *would fall seriously short* of its clear ethical duty. This is readily apparent in the circumstances of history, where believers discern the dispositions of divine Providence, ready to make use of the nations for the realization of its plans, so as to render "vain the designs of the peoples" (cf. Ps 33:10).

23.5 When the West gives the impression of abandoning itself to forms of growing and selfish isolation, and the East in its turn seems to ignore for questionable reasons its duty to cooperate in the task of alleviating human misery, then we are up against not only a betrayal of humanity's legitimate expectations — a betrayal that is a harbinger of unforeseeable consequences — but also a real desertion of a moral obligation.

24.1 If arms production is a serious disorder in the present world with regard to true human needs and the employment of the means capable of

---

[41] Cf. Encyclical Letter *Populorum Progressio*, 53: loc. cit., 283.

satisfying those needs, *the arms trade* is equally to blame. Indeed, with reference to the latter it must be added that the *moral judgment is even more severe.* As we all know, this is a trade without frontiers, capable of crossing even the barriers of the blocs. It knows how to overcome the division between East and West, and above all the one between North and South, to the point — and this is more serious — of pushing its way into the *different sections* which make up the southern hemisphere. We are thus confronted with a strange phenomenon: while economic aid and development plans meet with the obstacle of insuperable ideological barriers, and with tariff and trade barriers, *arms* of whatever origin circulate with almost total freedom all over the world. And as the recent document of the Pontifical Commission "Iustitia et Pax" on the international debt points out,[42] everyone knows that in certain cases the capital lent by the developed world has been used in the underdeveloped world to buy weapons.

24.2 If to all this we add the *tremendous* and universally acknowledged *danger* represented by *atomic weapons* stockpiled on an incredible scale, the logical conclusion seems to be this: in today's world, including the world of economics, the prevailing picture is one destined to lead us more quickly *toward death* rather than one of concern for *true development* which would lead all toward a "more human" life, as envisaged by the Encyclical *Populorum Progressio.*[43]

24.3 The consequences of this state of affairs are to be seen in the festering of a *wound* which typifies and reveals the imbalances and conflicts of the modern world: *the millions of refugees* whom war, natural calamities, persecution and discrimination of every kind have deprived of home, employment, family and homeland. The tragedy of these multitudes is reflected in the hopeless faces of men, women and children who can no longer find a home in a divided and inhospitable world.

24.4 Nor may we close our eyes to another painful wound in today's world: the phenomenon of *terrorism,* understood as the intention to kill people and destroy property indiscriminately, and to create a climate of terror and insecurity, often including the taking of hostages. Even when some ideology or the desire to create a better society is adduced as the motivation for this inhuman behavior, acts of terrorism are never justifiable. Even less so when, as happens today, such decisions and such actions, which at times lead to real

---

[42] *At the Service of the Human Community: An Ethical Approach to the International Debt Question* (December 27, 1986), III, 2, 1.

[43] Cf. Encyclical Letter *Populorum Progressio,* 20-21: loc. cit., 267-268.

massacres and to the abduction of innocent people who have nothing to do with the conflicts, claim to have a propaganda purpose for furthering a cause. It is still worse when they are an end in themselves, so that murder is committed merely for the sake of killing. In the face of such horror and suffering, the words I spoke some years ago are still true, and I wish to repeat them again: "What Christianity forbids is to seek solutions . . . by the ways of hatred, by the murdering of defenseless people, by the methods of terrorism."[44]

25.1 At this point something must be said about the *demographic problem* and the way it is spoken of today, following what Paul VI said in his Encyclical[45] and what I myself stated at length in the Apostolic Exhortation *Familiaris Consortio.*[46]

25.2 One cannot deny the existence, especially in the southern hemisphere, of a demographic problem which creates difficulties for development. One must immediately add that in the northern hemisphere the nature of this problem is reversed: here, the cause for concern is the *drop in the birthrate,* with repercussions on the aging of the population, unable even to renew itself biologically. In itself, this is a phenomenon capable of hindering development. Just as it is incorrect to say that such difficulties stem solely from demographic growth, neither is it proved that *all* demographic growth is incompatible with orderly development.

25.3 On the other hand, it is very alarming to see governments in many countries launching *systematic campaigns* against birth, contrary not only to the cultural and religious identity of the countries themselves but also contrary to the nature of true development. It often happens that these campaigns are the result of pressure and financing coming from abroad, and in some cases they are made a condition for the granting of financial and economic aid and assistance. In any event, there is an *absolute lack of respect* for the freedom of choice of the parties involved, men and women often subjected to intolerable pressures, including economic ones, in order to force them to submit to this new form of oppression. It is the poorest populations which suffer such mistreatment, and this sometimes leads to a tendency toward a form of racism, or the promotion of certain equally racist forms of eugenics.

[44] Address at Drogheda, Ireland (September 29, 1979), 5: *AAS* 71 (1979), 1079.

[45] Cf. Encyclical Letter *Populorum Progressio,* 37: loc. cit., 275-276.

[46] Cf. Apostolic Exhortation *Familiaris Consortio* (November 22, 1981), especially in 30: *AAS* 74 (1982), 115-117.

25.4 This fact too, which deserves the most forceful condemnation, is a *sign* of an erroneous and perverse *idea* of true human development.

26.1 This mainly negative overview of the *actual situation* of development in the contemporary world would be incomplete without a mention of the coexistence of *positive aspects.*

26.2 The *first* positive note is the *full awareness* among large numbers of men and women of their own dignity and of that of every human being. This awareness is expressed, for example, in the more *lively concern* that *human rights should be respected,* and in the more vigorous rejection of their violation. One sign of this is the number of recently established private associations, some worldwide in membership, almost all of them devoted to monitoring with great care and commendable objectivity what is happening *internationally* in this sensitive field.

26.3 At this level one must acknowledge the *influence* exercised by the *Declaration of Human Rights,* promulgated some forty years ago by the United Nations Organization. Its very existence and gradual acceptance by the international community are signs of a growing awareness. The same is to be said, still in the field of human rights, of other juridical instruments issued by the United Nations Organization or other International Organizations.[47]

26.4 The awareness under discussion applies not only to *individuals* but also to *nations* and *peoples,* which, as entities having a specific cultural identity, are particularly sensitive to the preservation, free exercise and promotion of their precious heritage.

26.5 At the same time, in a world divided and beset by every type of conflict, the *conviction* is growing of a radical *interdependence* and consequently of the need for a solidarity which will take up interdependence and transfer it to the moral plane. Today perhaps more than in the past, people are realizing that they are linked together by a *common destiny,* which is to be constructed together, if catastrophe for all is to be avoided. From the depth of anguish, fear and escapist phenomena like drugs, *typical of the contemporary world,* the idea is slowly emerging that the good to which we are all called and the happiness to which we aspire cannot be obtained without an *effort and commitment on the part of all,* nobody excluded, and the consequent renouncing of personal selfishness.

26.6 Also to be mentioned here, as a sign of *respect for life* — despite all the temptations to destroy it by abortion and euthanasia — is a *concomitant*

---

[47] Cf. *Human Rights: Collection of International Instruments,* United Nations, New York, 1983; John Paul II, Encyclical Letter *Redemptor Hominis* (March 4, 1979), 17: *AAS* 71 (1979), 296.

concern for peace, together with an awareness that peace is *indivisible*. It is either *for all* or *for none*. It demands an ever greater degree of rigorous respect for justice and consequently a fair distribution of the results of true development.[48]

26.7 Among today's *positive signs* we must also mention a greater realization of the limits of available resources, and of the need to respect the integrity and the cycles of nature and to take them into account when planning for development, rather than sacrificing them to certain demagogic ideas about the latter. Today this is called *ecological concern*.

26.8 It is also right to acknowledge the generous commitment of statesmen, politicians, economists, trade unionists, people of science and international officials — many of them inspired by religious faith — who at no small personal sacrifice try to resolve the world's ills and who give of themselves in every way so as to ensure that an ever increasing number of people may enjoy the benefits of peace and a quality of life worthy of the name.

26.9 The great *International Organizations* and a number of the Regional Organizations, *contribute* to this *in no small measure*. Their united efforts make possible more effective action.

26.10 It is also through these contributions that some Third World countries, despite the burden of many negative factors, have succeeded in reaching a *certain self-sufficiency in food*, or a degree of industrialization which makes it possible to survive with dignity and to guarantee sources of employment for the active population.

26.11 Thus, *all is not negative* in the contemporary world, nor could it be, for the heavenly Father's Providence lovingly watches over even our daily cares (cf. Mt 6:25-32, 10:23-31; Lk 12:6-7, 22-30). Indeed, the positive values which we have mentioned testify to a new moral concern, particularly with respect to the great human problems such as development and peace.

26.12 This fact prompts me to turn my thoughts to the *true nature* of the development of peoples, along the lines of the Encyclical which we are commemorating, and as a mark of respect for its teaching.

---

[48] Cf. Second Vatican Ecumenical Council, Pastoral Constitution on the Church in the Modern World *Gaudium et Spes*, 78; Paul VI, Encyclical Letter *Populorum Progressio*, 76: loc. cit., 294-295: "To wage war on misery and to struggle against injustice is to promote, along with improved conditions, the human and spiritual progress of all men, and therefore the common good of humanity. . . . peace is something that is built up day after day, in the pursuit of an order intended by God, which implies a more perfect form of justice among men."

IV

Authentic Human Development

27.1 The examination which the Encyclical invites us to make of the contemporary world leads us to note in the first place that development *is not* a straightforward process, *as it were automatic* and *in itself limitless*, as though, given certain conditions, the human race were able to progress rapidly toward an undefined perfection of some kind.[49]

27.2 Such an idea — linked to a notion of "progress" with philosophical connotations deriving from the Enlightenment, rather than to the notion of "development"[50] which is used in a specifically economic and social sense — now seems to be seriously called into doubt, particularly since the tragic experience of the two world wars, the planned and partly achieved destruction of whole peoples, and the looming atomic peril. A naive *mechanistic optimism* has been replaced by a well-founded anxiety for the fate of humanity.

28.1 At the same time, however, the *"economic"* concept itself, linked to the word development, has entered into crisis. In fact there is a better understanding today that the *mere accumulation* of goods and services, even for the benefit of the majority, is not enough for the realization of human happiness. Nor, in consequence, does the availability of the many *real benefits* provided in recent times by science and technology, including the computer sciences, bring freedom from every form of slavery. On the contrary, the experience of recent years shows that unless all the considerable body of resources and potential at man's disposal is guided by a *moral understanding* and by an orientation toward the true good of the human race, it easily turns against man to oppress him.

28.2 A *disconcerting conclusion* about the most recent period should serve to enlighten us: side by side with the miseries of underdevelopment, themselves unacceptable, we find ourselves up against a form of *superdevelopment*, equally inadmissible, because like the former it is contrary to what is good and to true happiness. This superdevelopment, which consists in an *excessive* availability of every kind of material goods for the benefit of certain social

---

[49] Cf. Apostolic Exhortation *Familiaris Consortio* (November 22, 1981), 6: *AAS* 74 (1982), 88: "[H]istory is not simply a fixed progression toward what is better, but rather an event of freedom, and even a struggle between freedoms."

[50] For this reason the word "development" was used in the Encyclical rather than the word "progress," but with an attempt to give the word "development" its fullest meaning.

groups, easily makes people slaves of "possession" and of immediate gratification, with no other horizon than the multiplication or continual replacement of the things already owned with others still better. This is the so-called civilization of "consumption" or "consumerism," which involves so much "throwing-away" and "waste." An object already owned but now superseded by something better is discarded, with no thought of its possible lasting value in itself, nor of some other human being who is poorer.

28.3 All of us experience firsthand the sad effects of this blind submission to pure consumerism: in the first place a crass materialism, and at the same time a *radical dissatisfaction*, because one quickly learns — unless one is shielded from the flood of publicity and the ceaseless and tempting offers of products — that the more one possesses the more one wants, while deeper aspirations remain unsatisfied and perhaps even stifled.

28.4 The Encyclical of Pope Paul VI pointed out the difference, so often emphasized today, between "having" and "being,"[51] which had been expressed earlier in precise words by the Second Vatican Council.[52] To "have" objects and goods does not in itself perfect the human subject, unless it contributes to the maturing and enrichment of that subject's "being," that is to say unless it contributes to the realization of the human vocation as such.

28.5 Of course, the difference between "being" and "having," the danger inherent in a mere multiplication or replacement of things possessed compared to the value of "being," need not turn into a *contradiction*. One of the greatest injustices in the contemporary world consists precisely in this: that the ones who possess much are relatively *few* and those who possess almost nothing are *many*. It is the injustice of the poor distribution of the goods and services originally intended for all.

28.6 This then is the picture: there are some people — the few who possess much — who do not really succeed in "being" because, through a reversal of the hierarchy of values, they are hindered by the cult of "having"; and there are others — the many who have little or nothing — who do not succeed in realizing their basic human vocation because they are deprived of essential goods.

[51] Encyclical Letter *Populorum Progressio*, 19, loc. cit., 266-267: "Increased possession is not the ultimate goal of nations or of individuals. All growth is ambivalent. . . . The exclusive pursuit of possessions thus becomes an obstacle to individual fulfilment and to man's true greatness. Both for nations and for individual men, avarice is the most evident form of moral underdevelopment"; cf. also Paul VI, Apostolic Letter *Octogesima Adveniens* (May 14, 1971), 9: *AAS* 63 (1971), 407-408.

[52] Cf. Pastoral Constitution on the Church in the Modern World *Gaudium et Spes*, 35: Paul VI, Address to the Diplomatic Corps (January 7, 1965): *AAS* 57 (1965), 232.

28.7 The evil does not consist in "having" as such, but in possessing without regard for the *quality* and the *ordered hierarchy* of the goods one has. *Quality and hierarchy* arise from the subordination of goods and their availability to man's "being" and his true vocation.

28.8 This shows that although *development* has a *necessary economic dimension,* since it must supply the greatest possible number of the world's inhabitants with an availability of goods essential for them "to be," it is not limited to that dimension. If it is limited to this, then it turns against those whom it is meant to benefit.

28.9 The characteristics of full development, one which is "more human" and able to sustain itself at the level of the true vocation of men and women without denying economic requirements, were described by Paul VI.[53]

29.1 Development which is not only economic must be measured and oriented according to the reality and vocation of man seen in his totality, namely, according to his *interior dimension.* There is no doubt that he needs created goods and the products of industry, which is constantly being enriched by scientific and technological progress. And the ever greater availability of material goods not only meets needs but also opens new horizons. The danger of the misuse of material goods and the appearance of artificial needs should in no way hinder the regard we have for the new goods and resources placed at our disposal and the use we make of them. On the contrary, we must see them as a gift from God and as a response to the human vocation, which is fully realized in Christ.

29.2 However, in trying to achieve true development we must never lose sight of that *dimension* which is in the *specific nature* of man, who has been created by God in his image and likeness (cf. Gen 1:26). It is a bodily and a spiritual nature, symbolized in the second creation account by the two elements: the *earth,* from which God forms man's body, and the *breath of life* which he breathes into man's nostrils (cf. Gen 2:7).

29.3 Thus man comes to have a certain affinity with other creatures: he is called to use them, and to be involved with them. As the Genesis account says (cf. Gen 2:15), he is placed in the garden with the duty of cultivating and watching over it, being superior to the other creatures placed by God under his dominion (cf. Gen 1:25-26). But at the same time man must remain subject to the will of God, who imposes limits upon his use and dominion over things (cf. Gen 2:16-17), just as he promises him immortality (cf. Gen 2:9; Wis 2:23). Thus man, being the image of God, has a true affinity with him too.

[53] Cf. Encyclical Letter *Populorum Progressio,* 20-21: loc. cit., 267-268.

29.4 On the basis of this teaching, development cannot consist only in the use, dominion over and *indiscriminate* possession of created things and the products of human industry, but rather in *subordinating* the possession, dominion and use to man's divine likeness and to his vocation to immortality. This is the *transcendent reality* of the human being, a reality which is seen to be shared from the beginning by a couple, a man and a woman (cf. Gen 1:27), and is therefore fundamentally social.

30.1 According to Sacred Scripture therefore, the notion of development is not only "lay" or "profane," but is also seen to be, while having a socioeconomic dimension of its own, the *modern expression* of an essential dimension of man's vocation.

30.2 The fact is that man was not created, so to speak, immobile and static. The first portrayal of him, as given in the Bible, certainly presents him as a *creature* and *image, defined* in his deepest reality by the *origin* and *affinity* that constitute him. But all this plants within the human being — man and woman — the seed and the *requirement* of a special task to be accomplished by each individually and by them as a couple. The task is "to have dominion" over the other created beings, "to cultivate the garden." This is to be accomplished within the framework of *obedience* to the divine law and therefore with respect for the image received, the image which is the clear foundation of the power of dominion recognized as belonging to man as the means to his perfection (cf. Gen 1:26-30, 2:15-16; Wis 9:2-3).

30.3 When man disobeys God and refuses to submit to his rule, nature rebels against him and no longer recognizes him as its "master," for he has tarnished the divine image in himself. The claim to ownership and use of created things remains still valid, but after sin its exercise becomes difficult and full of suffering (cf. Gen 3:17-19).

30.4 In fact, the following chapter of Genesis shows us that the descendants of Cain build "a city," engage in sheep farming, practice the arts (music) and technical skills (metallurgy); while at the same time people began to "call upon the name of the Lord" (cf. Gen 4:17-26).

30.5 The story of the human race described by Sacred Scripture is, even after the fall into sin, a story of *constant achievements*, which, although always called into question and threatened by sin, are nonetheless repeated, increased and extended in response to the divine vocation given from the beginning to man and to woman (cf. Gen 1:26-28) and inscribed in the image which they received.

30.6 It is logical to conclude, at least on the part of those who believe in the word of God, that today's "development" is to be seen as a moment in the story which began at creation, a story which is constantly endangered by reason of infidelity to the Creator's will, and especially by the temptation to idolatry. But this "development" fundamentally corresponds to the first premises. Anyone wishing to renounce the *difficult yet noble task* of improving the lot of man in his totality, and of all people, with the excuse that the struggle is difficult and that constant effort is required, or simply because of the experience of defeat and the need to begin again, that person would be betraying the will of God the Creator. In this regard, in the Encyclical *Laborem Exercens* I referred to man's vocation to work, in order to emphasize the idea that it is always man who is the protagonist of development.[54]

30.7 Indeed, the Lord Jesus himself, in the parable of the talents, emphasizes the severe treatment given to the man who dared to hide the gift received: "You wicked and slothful servant! You knew that I reap where I have not sowed and gather where I have not winnowed? . . . So take the talent from him, and give it to him who has the ten talents" (Mt 25:26-28). It falls to us, who receive the gifts of God in order to make them fruitful, to "sow" and "reap." If we do not, even what we have will be taken away from us.

30.8 A deeper study of these harsh words will make us commit ourselves more resolutely to the *duty*, which is urgent for everyone today, to work together for the full development of others: "development of the whole human being and of all people."[55]

31.1 *Faith in Christ the Redeemer*, while it illuminates from within the nature of development, also guides us in the task of collaboration. In the Letter of Saint Paul to the Colossians, we read that Christ is "the firstborn of all creation," and that "all things were created through him" and for him (1:15-16). In fact, "all things hold together in him," since "in him all the fullness of God was pleased to dwell, and through him to reconcile to himself all things (1:20).

31.2 A part of this divine plan, which begins from eternity in Christ, the perfect "image" of the Father, and which culminates in him, "the firstborn from the dead" (Col 1:18), *is our own history*, marked by our personal and collective effort to raise up the human condition and to overcome the obstacles which are continually arising along our way. It thus prepares us to share in the fullness which "dwells in the Lord" and which he communicates

---

[54] Cf. Encyclical Letter *Laborem Exercens* (September 14, 1981), 4: *AAS* 73 (1981), 584-585; Paul VI, Encyclical Letter *Populorum Progressio*, 15: loc. cit., 265.

[55] Encyclical Letter *Populorum Progressio*, 42: loc. cit., 278.

"to his body, which is the Church" (Col 1:18; cf. Eph 1:22-23). At the same time sin, which is always attempting to trap us and which jeopardizes our human achievements, is conquered and redeemed by the "reconciliation" accomplished by Christ (cf. Col 1:20).

31.3 Here the perspectives widen. The dream of "unlimited progress" reappears, radically transformed by the *new outlook* created by Christian faith, assuring us that progress is possible only because God the Father has decided from the beginning to make man a sharer of his glory in Jesus Christ risen from the dead, in whom "we have redemption through his blood . . . the forgiveness of our trespasses" (Eph 1:7). In him God wished to conquer sin and make it serve our greater good,[56] which infinitely surpasses what progress could achieve.

31.4 We can say therefore — as we struggle amidst the obscurities and deficiencies of *underdevelopment* and *superdevelopment* — that one day this corruptible body will put on incorruptibility, this mortal body immortality (cf. 1 Cor 15:54), when the Lord "delivers the Kingdom to God the Father" (1 Cor 15:24) and all the works and actions that are worthy of man will be redeemed.

31.5 Furthermore, the concept of faith makes quite clear the reasons which impel the *Church* to concern herself with the problems of development, to consider them a *duty of her pastoral ministry,* and to urge all to think about the nature and characteristics of authentic human development. Through her commitment she desires, on the one hand, to place herself at the service of the divine plan which is meant to order all things to the fullness which dwells in Christ (cf. Col 1:19) and which he communicated to his body; and on the other hand she desires to respond to her fundamental vocation of being a "sacrament," that is to say "a sign and instrument of intimate union with God and of the unity of the whole human race."[57]

31.6 Some Fathers of the Church were inspired by this idea to develop in original ways a concept of the *meaning of history* and of *human work,* directed toward a goal which surpasses this meaning and which is always defined by its relationship to the work of Christ. In other words, one can find in the teaching of the Fathers an *optimistic vision* of history and work, that is to say of the *perennial value* of authentic human achievements,

---

[56] Cf. *Praeconium Paschale, Missale Romanum,* editio typica altera, 1975, 272: "O certe necessarium Adae peccatum, quod Christi morte deletum est! O felix culpa, quae talem ac tantum meruit habere Redemptorem!"

[57] Second Vatican Ecumenical Council, Dogmatic Constitution on the Church *Lumen Gentium,* 1.

inasmuch as they are redeemed by Christ and destined for the promised Kingdom.[58]

31.7 Thus, part of the *teaching* and most ancient *practice* of the Church is her conviction that she is obliged by her vocation — she herself, her ministers and each of her members — to relieve the misery of the suffering, both far and near, not only out of her "abundance" but also out of her "necessities." Faced by cases of need, one cannot ignore them in favor of superfluous church ornaments and costly furnishings for divine worship; on the contrary it could be obligatory to sell these goods in order to provide food, drink, clothing and shelter for those who lack these things.[59] As has been already noted, here we are shown a *"hierarchy of values"* — in the framework of the right to property — between "having" and "being," especially when the "having" of a few can be to the detriment of the "being" of many others.

31.8 In his Encyclical Pope Paul VI stands in the line of this teaching, taking his inspiration from the Pastoral Constitution *Gaudium et Spes*.[60] For my own part, I wish to insist once more on the seriousness and urgency of that teaching, and I ask the Lord to give all Christians the strength to put it faithfully into practice.

32.1 The obligation to commit oneself to the development of peoples is not just an *individual* duty, and still less an *individualistic* one, as if it were possible to achieve this development through the isolated efforts of each individual. It is an imperative which obliges *each and every* man and woman, as well as societies and nations. In particular, it obliges the Catholic Church and the other Churches and Ecclesial Communities, with which we are completely willing to collaborate in this field. In this sense, just as we Catholics invite our Christian brethren to share in our initiatives, so too we declare that we are ready to collaborate in theirs, and we welcome the invitations presented to us.

---

[58] Cf., for example, Saint Basil the Great, *Regulae Fusius Tractatae, Interrogatio* XXXVII, 1-2: *PG* 31, 1009-1012; Theodoret of Cyr, *De Providentia, Oratio* VII: *PG* 83, 665-686; Saint Augustine, *De Civitate Dei*, XIX, 17: *CCL* 48, 683-685.

[59] Cf., for example, Saint John Chrysostom, *In Matthaeum*, Homily 50, 3-4: *PG* 58, 508-510; Saint Ambrose, *De Officiis Ministrorum*, Book II, XXVIII, 136-140: *PL* 16, 139-141; Saint Possidius, *Vita Sancti Augustini Episcopi*, XXIV: *PL* 32, 53-54.

[60] Encyclical Letter *Populorum Progressio*, 23: loc. cit., 268: " 'If someone who has the riches of this world sees his brother in need and closes his heart to him, how does the love of God abide in him?' (1 Jn 3:17). It is well known how strong were the words used by the Fathers of the Church to describe the proper attitude of persons who possess anything toward persons in need." In the previous number, the Pope had cited No. 69 of the Pastoral Constitution *Gaudium et Spes* of the Second Vatican Ecumenical Council.

In this pursuit of integral human development we can also do much with the members of other religions, as in fact is being done in various places.

32.2 Collaboration in the development of the whole person and of every human being is in fact a duty *of all toward all,* and must be shared by the four parts of the world: East and West, North and South; or, as we say today, by the different "worlds." If, on the contrary, people try to achieve it in only one part, or in only one world, they do so at the expense of the others; and, precisely because the others are ignored, their own development becomes exaggerated and misdirected.

32.3 *Peoples* or *nations* too have a right to their own full development, which while including — as already said — the economic and social aspects should also include individual cultural identity and openness to the transcendent. Not even the need for development can be used as an excuse for imposing on others one's own way of life or own religious belief.

33.1 Nor would a type of development which did not respect and promote *human rights* — personal and social, economic and political, including the *rights of nations and of peoples* — be really *worthy of man.*

33.2 Today, perhaps more than in the past, the *intrinsic contradiction* of a development limited *only* to its economic element is seen more clearly. Such development easily subjects the human person and his deepest needs to the demands of economic planning and selfish profit.

33.3 The *intrinsic connection* between authentic development and respect for human rights once again reveals the *moral* character of development: the true elevation of man, in conformity with the natural and historical vocation of each individual, is not attained *only* by exploiting the abundance of goods and services, or by having available perfect infrastructures.

33.4 When individuals and communities do not see a rigorous respect for the moral, cultural and spiritual requirements, based on the dignity of the person and on the proper identity of each community, beginning with the family and religious societies, then all the rest — availability of goods, abundance of technical resources applied to daily life, a certain level of material well-being — will prove unsatisfying and in the end contemptible. The Lord clearly says this in the Gospel, when he calls the attention of all to the true hierarchy of values: "For what will it profit a man, if he gains the whole world and forfeits his life?" (Mt 16:26).

33.5 True development, in keeping with the *specific* needs of the human being — man or woman, child, adult or old person — implies, especially for those who actively share in this process and are responsible for it, a lively *awareness* of the *value* of the rights of all and of each person. It likewise implies a lively awareness of the need to respect the right of every individual to the full use of the benefits offered by science and technology.

33.6 On the *internal level* of every nation, respect for all rights takes on great importance, especially: the right to life at every stage of its existence; the rights of the family, as the basic social community, or "cell of society"; justice in employment relationships; the rights inherent in the life of the political community as such; the rights based on the *transcendent vocation* of the human being, beginning with the right of freedom to profess and practice one's own religious belief.

33.7 On the *international level*, that is, the level of relations between States or, in present-day usage, between the different "worlds," there must be complete *respect* for the identity of each people, with its own historical and cultural characteristics. It is likewise essential, as the Encyclical *Populorum Progressio* already asked, to recognize each people's equal right "to be seated at the table of the common banquet,"[61] instead of lying outside the door like Lazarus, while "the dogs come and lick his sores" (cf. Lk 16:21). Both peoples and individuals must enjoy the *fundamental equality*[62] which is the basis, for example, of the Charter of the United Nations Organization: the equality which is the basis of the right of all to share in the process of full development.

33.8 In order to be genuine, development must be achieved within the framework of *solidarity* and *freedom*, without ever sacrificing either of them under whatever pretext. The moral character of development and its necessary promotion are emphasized when the most rigorous respect is given to all the demands deriving from the order of *truth* and *good* proper to the human person. Furthermore the Christian who is taught to see that man is the image of God, called to share in the truth and the good which is *God himself*, does not understand a commitment to development and its application which excludes regard and respect for the unique dignity of this "image." In other words, true development must be based on the *love of God and neighbor*, and must help to promote the relationships between individuals and society. This is the "civilization of love" of which Paul VI often spoke.

---

[61] Cf. Encyclical Letter *Populorum Progressio*, 47: "[A] world where freedom is not an empty word and where the poor man Lazarus can sit down at the same table with the rich man."

[62] Cf. ibid., 47: "It is a question, rather, of building a world where every man, no matter what his race, religion or nationality, can live a fully human life, freed from servitude imposed on him by other men"; cf. also Second Vatican Ecumenical Council, Pastoral Constitution on the Church in the Modern World *Gaudium et Spes*, 29. Such fundamental equality is one of the basic reasons why the Church has always been opposed to every form of racism.

34.1 Nor can the moral character of development exclude respect *for the beings which constitute* the natural world, which the ancient Greeks — alluding precisely to the *order* which distinguishes it — called the "cosmos." Such realities also demand respect, by virtue of a threefold consideration which it is useful to reflect upon carefully.

34.2 The *first* consideration is the appropriateness of acquiring a *growing awareness* of the fact that one cannot use with impunity the different categories of beings, whether living or inanimate — animals, plants, the natural elements — simply as one wishes, according to one's own economic needs. On the contrary, one must take into account *the nature of each being* and of its *mutual connection* in an ordered system, which is precisely the "cosmos."

34.3 The *second consideration* is based on the realization — which is perhaps more urgent — that *natural resources* are limited; some are not, as it is said, *renewable*. Using them as if they were inexhaustible, with *absolute dominion*, seriously endangers their availability not only for the present generation but above all for generations to come.

34.4 The *third consideration* refers directly to the consequences of a certain type of development on the *quality of life* in the industrialized zones. We all know that the direct or indirect result of industrialization is, ever more frequently, the pollution of the environment, with serious consequences for the health of the population.

34.5 Once again it is evident that development, the planning which governs it, and the way in which resources are used must include respect for moral demands. One of the latter undoubtedly imposes limits on the use of the natural world. The dominion granted to man by the Creator is not an absolute power, nor can one speak of a freedom to "use and misuse," or to dispose of things as one pleases. The limitation imposed from the beginning by the Creator himself and expressed symbolically by the prohibition not to "eat of the fruit of the tree" (cf. Gen 2:16-17) shows clearly enough that, when it comes to the natural world, we are subject not only to biological laws but also to moral ones, which cannot be violated with impunity.

34.6 A true concept of development cannot ignore the use of the elements of nature, the renewability of resources and the consequences of haphazard industrialization — three considerations which alert our consciences to the *moral dimension* of development.[63]

---

[63] Cf. Homily, Val Visdende (July 12, 1987), 5: *AAS* 80 (1988), 49-50; Paul VI, Apostolic Letter *Octogesima Adveniens* (May 14, 1971), 21: *AAS* 63 (1971), 416-417.

V

A Theological Reading of Modern Problems

35.1 Precisely because of the essentially moral character of development, it is clear that the *obstacles* to development likewise have a moral character. If in the years since the publication of Pope Paul's Encyclical there has been no development or very little, irregular, or even contradictory development the reasons are not only economic. As has already been said, political motives also enter in. For the decisions which either accelerate or slow down the development of peoples are really political in character. In order to overcome the misguided mechanisms mentioned earlier and to replace them with new ones which will be more just and in conformity with the common good of humanity, an effective political will is needed. Unfortunately, after analyzing the situation we have to conclude that this political will has been insufficient.

35.2 In a document of a pastoral nature such as this, an analysis limited exclusively to the economic and political causes of underdevelopment (and, *mutatis mutandis*, of so-called superdevelopment) would be incomplete. It is therefore necessary to single out the *moral* causes which, with respect to the behavior of *individuals* considered as *responsible persons*, interfere in such a way as to slow down the course of development and hinder its full achievement.

35.3 Similarly, when the scientific and technical resources are available which, with the necessary concrete political decisions, ought to help lead peoples to true development, the main obstacles to development will be overcome only by means of *essentially moral decisions*. For believers, and especially for Christians, these decisions will take their inspiration from the principles of faith, with the help of divine grace.

36.1 It is important to note therefore that a world which is divided into blocs, sustained by rigid ideologies, and in which instead of interdependence and solidarity different forms of imperialism hold sway, can only be a world subject to structures of sin. The sum total of the negative factors working against a true awareness of the universal *common good*, and the need to further it, gives the impression of creating, in persons and institutions, an obstacle which is difficult to overcome.[64]

[64] Cf. Second Vatican Ecumenical Council, Pastoral Constitution on the Church in the Modern World *Gaudium et Spes*, 25.

36.2 If the present situation can be attributed to difficulties of various kinds, it is not out of place to speak of "structures of sin," which, as I stated in my Apostolic Exhortation *Reconciliatio et Paenitentia,* are rooted in personal sin, and thus always linked to the *concrete acts* of individuals who introduce these structures, consolidate them and make them difficult to remove.[65] And thus they grow stronger, spread, and become the source of other sins, and so influence people's behavior.

36.3 "Sin" and "structures of sin" are categories which are seldom applied to the situation of the contemporary world. However, one cannot easily gain a profound understanding of the reality that confronts us unless we give a name to the root of the evils which afflict us.

36.4 One can certainly speak of "selfishness" and of "shortsightedness," of "mistaken political calculations" and "imprudent economic decisions." And in each of these evaluations one hears an echo of an ethical and moral nature. Man's condition is such that a more profound analysis of individuals' actions and omissions cannot be achieved without implying, in one way or another, judgments or references of an ethical nature.

36.5 This evaluation is in itself *positive,* especially if it is completely consistent and if it is based on faith in God and on his law, which commands what is good and forbids evil.

36.6 In this consists the difference between sociopolitical analysis and formal reference to "sin" and the "structures of sin." According to this latter viewpoint, there enter in the will of the Triune God, his plan for humanity, his justice and his mercy. The God who is *rich in mercy, the Redeemer of man, the Lord and giver of life,* requires from people clear-cut attitudes which express themselves also in actions or omissions toward one's neighbor. We have here a reference to the "second tablet" of the Ten Commandments (cf. Ex 20:12-17;

---

[65] Post-Synodal Apostolic Exhortation *Reconciliatio et Paenitentia* (December 2, 1984), 16: *AAS* 77 (1985), 217: "Whenever the Church speaks of situations of sin, or when she condemns as social sins certain situations or the collective behavior of certain social groups, big or small, or even of whole nations and blocs of nations, she knows and she proclaims that such cases of social sin are the result of the accumulation and concentration of many personal sins. It is a case of the very personal sins of those who cause or support evil or who exploit it; of those who are in a position to avoid, eliminate or at least limit certain social evils but who fail to do so out of laziness, fear or the conspiracy of silence, through secret complicity or indifference; of those who take refuge in the supposed impossibility of changing the world, and also of those who sidestep the effort and sacrifice required, producing specious reasons of a higher order. The real responsibility, then, lies with individuals. A situation — or likewise an institution, a structure, society itself — is not in itself the subject of moral acts. Hence a situation cannot in itself be good or bad."

Dt 5:16-21). Not to observe these is to offend God and hurt one's neighbor, and to introduce into the world influences and obstacles which go far beyond the actions and the brief lifespan of an individual. This also involves interference in the process of the development of peoples, the delay or slowness of which must be judged also in this light.

37.1 This *general analysis*, which is religious in nature, can be supplemented by *a number of particular considerations* to demonstrate that among the actions and attitudes opposed to the will of God, the good of neighbor and the "structures" created by them, two are very typical: on the one hand, the *all-consuming desire for profit*, and on the other, *the thirst for power*, with the intention of imposing one's will upon others. In order to characterize better each of these attitudes, one can add the expression: "at any price." In other words, we are faced with the *absolutizing* of human attitudes with all its possible consequences.

37.2 Since these attitudes can exist independently of each other, they can be separated; however, in today's world both are *indissolubly united*, with one or the other predominating.

37.3 Obviously, not only individuals fall victim to this double attitude of sin; nations and blocs can do so too. And this favors even more the introduction of the "structures of sin" of which I have spoken. If certain forms of modern "imperialism" were considered in the light of these moral criteria, we would see that hidden behind certain decisions, apparently inspired only by economics or politics, are real forms of idolatry: of money, ideology, class, technology.

37.4 I have wished to introduce this type of analysis above all in order to point out the true *nature* of the evil which faces us with respect to the development of peoples: it is a question of a *moral evil*, the fruit of *many sins* which lead to "structures of sin." To diagnose the evil in this way is to identify precisely, on the level of human conduct, *the path to be followed* in order *to overcome it*.

38.1 This path is *long and complex*, and what is more it is constantly threatened because of the intrinsic frailty of human resolutions and achievements, and because of the *mutability* of very unpredictable external circumstances. Nevertheless, one must have the courage to set out on this path, and, where some steps have been taken or a part of the journey made, the courage to go on to the end.

38.2 In the context of these reflections the decision to set out or to continue the journey involves, above all, a *moral* value which men and women of faith recognize as a demand of God's will, the only true foundation of an absolutely binding ethic.

38.3 One would hope that also men and women without an explicit faith would be convinced that the obstacles to integral development are not only economic but rest on *more profound attitudes* which human beings can make into absolute values. Thus one would hope that all those who, to some degree or other, are responsible for ensuring a "more human life" for their fellow human beings, whether or not they are inspired by a religious faith, will become fully aware of the urgent need to *change* the *spiritual attitudes* which define each individual's relationship with self, with neighbor, with even the remotest human communities, and with nature itself; and all of this in view of higher values such as the *common good* or, to quote the felicitous expression of the Encyclical *Populorum Progressio*, the full development "of the whole individual and of all people."[66]

38.4 For *Christians*, as for all who recognize the precise theological meaning of the word "sin," a change of behavior or mentality or mode of existence is called "conversion," to use the language of the Bible (cf. Mk 13:3, 5; Is 30:15). This conversion specifically entails a relationship to God, and to the sin committed, to its consequences and hence to one's neighbor, either an individual or a community. It is God, in "whose hands are the hearts of the powerful"[67] and the hearts of all, who according to his own promise and by the power of his Spirit can transform "hearts of stone" into "hearts of flesh" (cf. Ezek 36:26).

38.5 On the path toward the desired conversion, toward the overcoming of the moral obstacles to development, it is already possible to point to the *positive* and *moral value* of the growing awareness of *interdependence* among individuals and nations. The fact that men and women in various parts of the world feel personally affected by the injustices and violations of human rights committed in distant countries, countries which perhaps they will never visit, is a further sign of a reality transformed into *awareness*, thus acquiring a *moral* connotation.

38.6 It is above all a question of *interdependence*, sensed as a *system determining* relationships in the contemporary world, in its economic, cultural, political and religious elements, and accepted as a *moral category*. When interdependence becomes recognized in this way, the correlative response as a moral and social attitude, as a "virtue," is *solidarity*. This then is not a feeling of vague compassion or shallow distress at the misfortunes of so many people, both near and far. On the contrary, it is *a firm and persevering determination* to commit oneself to the *common good;* that is to say to the good of all and of each indi-

---

[66] Encyclical Letter *Populorum Progressio*, 42: loc. cit., 278.
[67] Cf. Liturgy of the Hours, Wednesday, Week 3 of Ordinary Time, Intercessions at Evening Prayer.

vidual, because we are *all* really responsible *for all.* This determination is based on the solid conviction that what is hindering full development is that desire for profit and that thirst for power already mentioned. These attitudes and "structures of sin" are only conquered — presupposing the help of divine grace — by a *diametrically opposed attitude:* a commitment to the good of one's neighbor with the readiness, in the Gospel sense, to "lose oneself" for the sake of the other instead of exploiting him, and to "serve him" instead of oppressing him for one's own advantage (cf. Mt 10:40-42, 20:25; Mk 10:42-45; Lk 22:25-27).

39.1 The exercise of solidarity *within each society* is valid when its members recognize one another as persons. Those who are more influential, because they have a greater share of goods and common services, should feel *responsible* for the weaker and be ready to share with them all they possess. Those who are weaker, for their part, in the same spirit of *solidarity,* should not adopt a purely *passive* attitude or one that is *destructive* of the social fabric, but, while claiming their legitimate rights, should do what they can for the good of all. The intermediate groups, in their turn, should not selfishly insist on their particular interests, but respect the interests of others.

39.2 Positive signs in the contemporary world are the *growing awareness* of the solidarity of the poor among themselves, their *efforts to support one another,* and their *public demonstrations* on the social scene which, without recourse to violence, present their own needs and rights in the face of the inefficiency or corruption of the public authorities. By virtue of her own evangelical duty the Church feels called to take her stand beside the poor, to discern the justice of their requests, and to help satisfy them, without losing sight of the good of groups in the context of the common good.

39.3 The same criterion is applied by analogy in international relationships. Interdependence must be transformed into *solidarity,* based upon the principle that the goods of creation *are meant for all.* That which human industry produces through the processing of raw materials, with the contribution of work, must serve equally for the good of all.

39.4 Surmounting every type of *imperialism* and determination to preserve their *own hegemony,* the stronger and richer nations must have a sense of moral *responsibility* for the other nations, so that a *real international system* may be established which will rest on the foundation of the *equality* of all peoples and on the necessary respect for their legitimate differences. The economically weaker countries, or those still at subsistence level, must be enabled, with the assistance of other peoples and of the international community, to make a contribution of their own to the common good with their treasures of *humanity* and *culture*, which otherwise would be lost forever.

39.5 *Solidarity* helps us to see the "other" — whether a *person, people or nation* — not just as some kind of instrument, with a work capacity and physical strength to be exploited at low cost and then discarded when no longer useful, but as our "neighbor," a "helper" (cf. Gen 2:18-20), to be made a sharer, on a par with ourselves, in the banquet of life to which all are equally invited by God. Hence the importance of reawakening the *religious awareness* of individuals and peoples.

39.6 Thus the exploitation, oppression and annihilation of others are excluded. These facts, in the present division of the world into opposing blocs, combine to produce the *danger of war* and an excessive preoccupation with personal security, often to the detriment of the autonomy, freedom of decision, and even the territorial integrity of the weaker nations situated within the so-called "areas of influence" or "safety belts."

39.7 The "structures of sin" and the sins which they produce are likewise radically opposed to *peace and development*, for development, in the familiar expression of Pope Paul's Encyclical, is "the new name for peace."[68]

39.8 In this way, the solidarity which we propose is the *path to peace and at the same time to development*. For world peace is inconceivable unless the world's leaders come to recognize that *interdependence* in itself demands the abandonment of the politics of blocs, the sacrifice of all forms of economic, military or political imperialism, and the transformation of mutual distrust into *collaboration*. This is precisely the *act proper* to solidarity among individuals and nations.

39.9 The motto of the Pontificate of my esteemed Predecessor Pius XII was *Opus iustitiae pax*, peace as the fruit of justice. Today one could say, with the same exactness and the same power of biblical inspiration (cf. Is 32:17; Jas 3:18): *Opus solidaritatis pax*, peace as the fruit of solidarity.

39.10 The goal of peace, so desired by everyone, will certainly be achieved through the putting into effect of social and international justice, but also through the practice of the virtues which favor togetherness, and which teach us to live in unity, so as to build in unity, by giving and receiving, a new society and a better world.

40.1 *Solidarity* is undoubtedly a *Christian virtue*. In what has been said so far it has been possible to identify many points of contact between solidarity and *charity*, which is the distinguishing mark of Christ's disciples (cf. Jn 13:35)

---

[68] Encyclical Letter *Populorum Progressio*, 87: loc. cit., 299.

40.2 In the light of faith, solidarity seeks to go beyond itself, to take on the *specifically Christian* dimensions of total gratuity, forgiveness and reconciliation. One's neighbor is then not only a human being with his or her own rights and a fundamental equality with everyone else, but becomes the *living image* of God the Father, redeemed by the blood of Jesus Christ and placed under the permanent action of the Holy Spirit. One's neighbor must therefore be loved, even if an enemy, with the same love with which the Lord loves him or her; and for that person's sake one must be ready for sacrifice, even the ultimate one: to lay down one's life for the brethren (cf. 1 Jn 3:16).

40.3 At that point, awareness of the common fatherhood of God, of the brotherhood of all in Christ — "children in the Son" — and of the presence and life-giving action of the Holy Spirit will bring to our vision of the world *a new criterion* for interpreting it. Beyond human and natural bonds, already so close and strong, there is discerned in the light of faith a new *model* of the *unity* of the human race, which must ultimately inspire our *solidarity*. This supreme *model of unity*, which is a reflection of the intimate life of God, one God in three Persons, is what we Christians mean by the word *"communion."* This specifically Christian communion, jealously preserved, extended and enriched with the Lord's help, is the *soul* of the Church's vocation to be a "sacrament," in the sense already indicated.

40.4 Solidarity therefore must play its part in the realization of this divine plan, both on the level of individuals and on the level of national and international society. The "evil mechanisms" and "structures of sin" of which we have spoken can be overcome only through the exercise of the human and Christian solidarity to which the Church calls us and which she tirelessly promotes. Only in this way can such positive energies be fully released for the benefit of development and peace.

40.5 Many of the Church's canonized saints offer *a wonderful witness* of such solidarity and can serve as examples in the present difficult circumstances. Among them I wish to recall Saint Peter Claver and his service to the slaves at Cartagena de Indias, and Saint Maximilian Maria Kolbe who offered his life in place of a prisoner unknown to him in the concentration camp at Auschwitz.

VI

Some Particular Guidelines

41.1 The Church does not have *technical solutions* to offer for the problem of underdevelopment as such, as Pope Paul VI already affirmed in his Encyclical.[69] For the Church does not propose economic and political systems or programs, nor does she show preference for one or the other, provided that human dignity is properly respected and promoted, and provided she herself is allowed the room she needs to exercise her ministry in the world.

41.2 But the Church is an "expert in humanity,"[70] and this leads her necessarily to extend her religious mission to the various fields in which men and women expend their efforts in search of the always relative happiness which is possible in this world, in line with their dignity as persons.

41.3 Following the example of my Predecessors, I must repeat that whatever affects the dignity of individuals and peoples, such as authentic development, cannot be reduced to a "technical" problem. If reduced in this way, development would be emptied of its true content, and this would be an act of *betrayal* of the individuals and peoples whom development is meant to serve.

41.4 This is why the Church has *something to say* today, just as twenty years ago, and also in the future, about the nature, conditions, requirements and aims of authentic development, and also about the obstacles which stand in its way. In doing so the Church fulfills her mission to *evangelize,* for she offers her *first* contribution to the solution of the urgent problem of development when she proclaims the truth about Christ, about herself and about man, applying this truth to a concrete situation.[71]

41.5 As her *instrument* for reaching this goal, the Church uses her *social doctrine.* In today's difficult situation, a *more exact awareness and a wider diffusion* of the "set of principles for reflection, criteria for judgment and directives for action" proposed by the Church's teaching[72] would be of great help in promoting both the correct definition of the problems being faced and the best solution to them.

41.6 It will thus be seen at once that the questions facing us are above all moral questions; and that neither the analysis of the problem of development as such nor the means to overcome the present difficulties can ignore this essential dimension.

41.7 The Church's social doctrine *is not* a "third way" between *liberal capi-*

---

[69] Cf. ibid., 13, 81: loc. cit., 263-264, 296-297.

[70] Cf. ibid., 13: loc. cit., 263.

[71] Cf. Address at the Opening of the Third General Conference of the Latin American Bishops (January 28, 1979): *AAS* 71 (1979), 189-196.

[72] Congregation for the Doctrine of the Faith, Instruction on Christian Freedom and Liberation *Libertatis Conscientia* (March 22, 1986), 72: *AAS* 79 (1987), 586; Paul VI, Apostolic Letter *Octogesima Adveniens* (May 14, 1971), 4: *AAS* 63 (1971), 403-404.

talism and *Marxist collectivism,* nor even a possible alternative to other solutions less radically opposed to one another: rather, it constitutes a *category of its own.* Nor is it an *ideology,* but rather the *accurate formulation* of the results of a careful reflection on the complex realities of human existence, in society and in the international order, in the light of faith and of the Church's Tradition. Its main aim is to *interpret* these realities, determining their conformity with or divergence from the lines of the Gospel teaching on man and his vocation, a vocation which is at once earthly and transcendent; its aim is thus *to guide* Christian behavior. It therefore belongs to the field, not of *ideology,* but of *theology* and particularly of moral theology.

41.8 The teaching and spreading of her social doctrine are part of the Church's evangelizing mission. And since it is a doctrine aimed at guiding *people's behavior,* it consequently gives rise to a "commitment to justice," according to each individual's role, vocation and circumstances.

41.9 The *condemnation* of evils and injustices is also part of that *ministry of evangelization* in the social field which is an aspect of the Church's *prophetic role.* But it should be made clear that *proclamation* is always more important than *condemnation,* and the latter cannot ignore the former, which gives it true solidity and the force of higher motivation.

42.1 Today more than in the past, the Church's social doctrine must be open to an *international outlook,* in line with the Second Vatican Council,[73] the most recent Encyclicals,[74] and particularly in line with the Encyclical which we are commemorating.[75] It will not be superfluous therefore to reexamine and further clarify in this light the characteristic themes and guidelines dealt with by the Magisterium in recent years.

42.2 Here I would like to indicate one of them: the *option* or *love of preference* for the poor. This is an option, or a *special form* of primacy in the exercise of Christian charity, to which the whole Tradition of the Church bears witness. It affects the life of each Christian inasmuch as he or she seeks to imitate the life of Christ, but it applies equally to our *social responsibilities* and hence to our manner of living, and to the logical decisions to be made concerning the ownership and use of goods.

---

[73] Cf. Pastoral Constitution on the Church in the Modern World *Gaudium et Spes,* Part II, Chapter V, Section 2, Numbers 83-90: "Building up the International Community."

[74] Cf. John XXIII, Encyclical Letter *Mater et Magistra* (May 15, 1961), III: *AAS* 53 (1961), 440; Encyclical Letter *Pacem in Terris* (April 11, 1963), IV: *AAS* 55 (1963), 291-296; Paul VI, Apostolic Letter *Octogesima Adveniens* (May 14, 1971), 2-4: *AAS* 63 (1971), 402-404.

[75] Cf. Encyclical Letter *Populorum Progressio,* 3, 9: loc. cit., 258, 261.

42.3 Today, furthermore, given the worldwide dimension which the social question has assumed,[76] this love of the preference for the poor, and the decisions which it inspires in us, cannot but embrace the immense multitudes of the hungry, the needy, the homeless, those without medical care and, above all, those without hope of a better future. It is impossible not to take account of the existence of these realities. To ignore them would mean becoming like the "rich man" who pretended not to know the beggar Lazarus lying at his gate (cf. Lk 16:19-31).[77]

42.4 Our *daily life* as well as our decisions in the political and economic fields must be marked by these realities. Likewise the *leaders* of nations and the heads of *international bodies,* while they are obliged always to keep in mind the true human dimension as a priority in their development plans, should not forget to give precedence to the phenomenon of growing poverty. Unfortunately, instead of becoming fewer the poor are becoming more numerous, not only in less developed countries but — and this seems no less scandalous — in the more developed ones too.

42.5 It is necessary to state once more the characteristic principle of Christian social doctrine: the goods of this world are *originally meant for all.*[78] The right to private property is *valid and necessary,* but it does not nullify the value of this principle. Private property, in fact, is under a "social mortgage,"[79] which means that it has an intrinsically social function, based upon and justified precisely by the principle of the universal destination of goods. Likewise, in this concern for the poor, one must not overlook that *special form of poverty* which consists in being deprived of fundamental human rights, in particular the right to religious freedom and also the right to freedom of economic initiative.

---

[76] Ibid., 3: loc. cit., 258.

[77] Encyclical Letter *Populorum Progressio,* 47: loc. cit., 280; Congregation for the Doctrine of the Faith, Instruction on Christian Freedom and Liberation *Libertatis Conscientia* (March 22, 1986), 68: AAS 79 (1987), 583-584.

[78] Cf. Second Vatican Ecumenical Council, Pastoral Constitution on the Church in the Modern World *Gaudium et Spes,* 69; Paul VI, Encyclical Letter *Populorum Progressio,* 22: loc. cit., 268; Congregation for the Doctrine of the Faith, Instruction on Christian Freedom and Liberation *Libertatis Conscientia* (March 22, 1986), 90: AAS 79 (1987), 594; Saint Thomas Aquinas, *Summa Theologiae,* II-II, q. 66, a. 2.

[79] Cf. Address at the Opening of the Third General Conference of the Latin American Bishops (January 28, 1979): AAS 71 (1979), 189-196; Address to a Group of Polish Bishops on Their *ad Limina* Visit (December 17, 1987), 6: AAS 80 (1988), 1012-1013.

43.1 The motivating concern for the poor — who are, in the very meaningful term, "the Lord's poor"[80] — must be translated at all levels into concrete actions, until it decisively attains a series of necessary reforms. Each local situation will show what reforms are most urgent and how they can be achieved. But those demanded by the situation of international imbalance, as already described, must not be forgotten.

43.2 In this respect I wish to mention specifically: the *reform of the international trade system*, which is mortgaged to protectionism and increasing bilateralism; the *reform of the world monetary and financial system*, today recognized as inadequate; the *question of technological exchanges* and their proper use; the need for a *review of the structure of the existing International Organizations*, in the framework of an international juridical order.

43.3 The *international trade system* today frequently discriminates against the products of the young industries of the developing countries and discourages the producers of raw materials. There exists, too, a kind of *international division of labor*, whereby the low-cost products of certain countries which lack effective labor laws or which are too weak to apply them are sold in other parts of the world at considerable profit for the companies engaged in this form of production, which knows no frontiers.

43.4 The world *monetary and financial system* is marked by an excessive fluctuation of exchange rates and interest rates, to the detriment of the balance of payments and the debt situation of the poorer countries.

43.5 *Forms of technology and their transfer* constitute today one of the major problems of international exchange and of the grave damage deriving therefrom. There are quite frequent cases of developing countries being denied needed forms of technology or sent useless ones.

43.6 In the opinion of many, the *International Organizations* seem to be at a stage of their existence when their operating methods, operating costs and effectiveness need careful review and possible correction. Obviously, such a delicate process cannot be put into effect without the collaboration of all. This presupposes the overcoming of political rivalries and the renouncing of all desire to manipulate these Organizations, which exist solely *for the common good.*

43.7 The existing Institutions and Organizations have worked well for the benefit of peoples. Nevertheless, humanity today is in a new and more difficult phase of its genuine development. It needs a *greater degree of international ordering*, at the service of the societies, economies and cultures of the whole world.

---

[80] Because the Lord wished to identify himself with them (Mt 25:31-46) and takes special care of them (cf. Ps 12:6; Lk 1:52-53).

44.1 Development demands above all a spirit of initiative on the part of the countries which need it.[81] Each of them must act in accordance with its own responsibilities, *not expecting everything* from the more favored countries, and acting in collaboration with others in the same situation. Each must discover and use to the best advantage its *own area of freedom*. Each must make itself capable of initiatives responding to its own needs as a society. Each must likewise realize its true needs as well as the rights and duties which oblige it to respond to them. The development of peoples begins and is most appropriately accomplished in the dedication of each people to its own development, in collaboration with others.

44.2 It is important then that as far as possible *the developing nations themselves* should favor the *self-affirmation* of each citizen, through access to a wider culture and a free flow of information. Whatever promotes *literacy* and the *basic education* which completes and deepens it is a direct contribution to true development, as the Encyclical *Populorum Progressio* proposed.[82] These goals are still far from being reached in so many parts of the world.

44.3 In order to take this path, *the nations themselves* will have to identify their own *priorities* and clearly recognize their own needs, according to the particular conditions of their people, their geographical setting and their cultural traditions.

44.4 Some nations will have to increase *food production*, in order to have always available what is needed for subsistence and daily life. In the modern world — where starvation claims so many victims, especially among the very young — there are examples of not particularly developed nations which have nevertheless achieved the goal of *food self-sufficiency* and have even become food exporters.

44.5 Other nations need to reform certain unjust structures, and in particular their *political institutions*, in order to replace corrupt, dictatorial and authoritarian forms of government by *democratic* and *participatory* ones. This is a process which we hope will spread and grow stronger. For the "health" of a political community — as expressed in the free and responsible participation of all citizens in public affairs, in the rule of law and in respect for and promotion of human rights — is the *necessary con-*

---

[81] Encyclical Letter *Populorum Progressio*, 55: loc. cit., 284: "These are the men and women that need to be helped, that need to be convinced to take into their own hands their development, gradually acquiring the means"; cf. Second Vatican Ecumenical Council, Pastoral Constitution on the Church in the Modern World *Gaudium et Spes*, 86.

[82] Encyclical Letter *Populorum Progressio*, 35: loc. cit., 274: "Basic education is the first objective of a plan of development."

dition and sure guarantee of the development of "the whole individual and of all people."

45.1 None of what has been said can be achieved *without the collaboration of all* — especially the international community — in the framework of a *solidarity* which includes everyone, beginning with the most neglected. But the developing nations themselves have the duty to practice *solidarity among themselves* and with the neediest countries of the world.

45.2 It is desirable, for example, that nations of the *same geographical area* should establish *forms of cooperation* which will make them less dependent on more powerful producers; they should open their frontiers to the products of the area; they should examine how their products might complement one another; they should combine in order to set up those services which each one separately is incapable of providing; they should extend cooperation to the monetary and financial sector.

45.3 *Interdependence* is already a reality in many of these countries. To acknowledge it, in such a way as to make it more operative, represents an alternative to excessive dependence on richer and more powerful nations, as part of the hoped-for development, without opposing anyone, but discovering and making the best use of the country's *own potential.* The developing countries belonging to one geographical area, especially those included in the term "South," can and ought to set up *new regional organizations* inspired by criteria of *equality, freedom and participation* in the community of nations — as is already happening with promising results.

45.4 An essential condition for global *solidarity* is autonomy and free self-determination, also within associations such as those indicated. But at the same time solidarity demands a readiness to accept the sacrifices necessary for the good of the whole world community.

VII

Conclusion

46.1 Peoples and individuals aspire to be free: their search for full development signals their desire to overcome the many obstacles preventing them from enjoying a "more human life."

46.2 Recently, in the period following the publication of the Encyclical *Populorum Progressio,* a new way of confronting the problems of poverty and underdevelopment has spread in some areas of the world, especially in Latin

America. This approach makes *liberation* the fundamental category and the first principle of action. The positive values, as well as the deviations and risks of deviation, which are damaging to the faith and are connected with this form of theological reflection and method, have been appropriately pointed out by the Church's Magisterium.[83]

46.3 It is fitting to add that the aspiration to freedom from all forms of slavery affecting the individual and society is something *noble* and *legitimate*. This in fact is the purpose of development, or rather liberation and development, taking into account the intimate connection between the two.

46.4 Development which is merely economic is incapable of setting man free; on the contrary, it will end by enslaving him further. Development that does not include the *cultural, transcendent and religious dimensions* of man and society, to the extent that it does not recognize the existence of such dimensions and does not endeavor to direct its goals and priorities toward the same, is even less conducive to authentic liberation. Human beings are totally free only when they are completely *themselves*, in the fullness of their rights and duties. The same can be said about society as a whole.

46.5 The principal obstacle to be overcome on the way to authentic liberation is *sin* and the *structures* produced by sin as it multiplies and spreads.[84]

46.6 The freedom with which Christ has set us free (cf. Gal 5:1) encourages us to become the *servants* of all. Thus the process of *development* and *liberation* takes concrete shape in the exercise of *solidarity*, that is to say in the love and service of neighbor, especially of the poorest: "For where truth and love are missing, the process of liberation results in the death of a freedom which will have lost all support."[85]

47.1 In the context of the *sad experiences* of recent years and of the *mainly negative picture* of the present moment, the Church must strongly affirm the *possibility* of overcoming the obstacles which, by excess or by defect, stand in the way of development. And she must affirm her confidence in a *true liberation*. Ultimately, this confidence and this possibility are based on the *Church's*

[83] Cf. Congregation for the Doctrine of the Faith, Instruction on Certain Aspects of the "Theology of Liberation" *Libertatis Nuntius* (August 6, 1984), Introduction: *AAS* 76 (1984), 876-877.

[84] Cf. Post-Synodal Apostolic Exhortation *Reconciliatio et Paenitentia* (December 2, 1984), 16: *AAS* 77 (1985), 213-217; Congregation for the Doctrine of the Faith, Instruction on Christian Freedom and Liberation *Libertatis Conscientia* (March 22, 1986), 38, 42: *AAS* 79 (1987), 569, 571.

[85] Congregation for the Doctrine of the Faith, Instruction on Christian Freedom and Liberation *Libertatis Conscientia* (March 22, 1986), 24: *AAS* 79 (1987), 564.

awareness of the divine promise guaranteeing that our present history does not remain closed in upon itself but is open to the Kingdom of God.

47.2 The Church has *confidence also in man*, though she knows the evil of which he is capable. For she well knows that — in spite of the heritage of sin, and the sin which each one is capable of committing — there exist in the human person sufficient qualities and energies, a fundamental "goodness" (cf. Gen 1:31), because he is the image of the Creator, placed under the redemptive influence of Christ, who "united himself in some fashion with every man,"[86] and because the efficacious action of the Holy Spirit "fills the earth" (Wis 1:7).

47.3 There is no justification then for despair or pessimism or inertia. Though it be with sorrow, it must be said that just as one may sin through selfishness and the desire for excessive profit and power, *one may also be found wanting* with regard to the urgent needs of multitudes of human beings submerged in conditions of underdevelopment, through *fear, indecision* and, basically, through *cowardice*. We are *all* called, indeed *obliged*, to face the *tremendous challenge* of the last decade of the second millennium, also because the present dangers threaten everyone: a world economic crisis, a war without frontiers, without winners or losers. In the face of such a threat, the distinction between rich individuals and countries and poor individuals and countries *will have little value*, except that a greater responsibility rests on those who have more and can do more.

47.4 This is not however the *sole motive or even the most important one*. At stake is the *dignity of the human person*, whose *defense* and *promotion* have been entrusted to us by the Creator, and to whom the men and women at every moment of history are strictly and responsibly *in debt*. As many people are already more or less clearly aware, the present situation *does not seem to correspond to* this dignity. *Every individual* is called upon to play his or her part in this *peaceful* campaign, a campaign to be conducted by *peaceful* means, in order to secure *development in peace*, in order to safeguard nature itself and the world about us. The Church too feels profoundly involved in this enterprise, and she hopes for its ultimate success.

47.5 Consequently, following the example of Pope Paul VI with his Encyclical *Populorum Progressio*,[87] I wish *to appeal* with simplicity and humility to *everyone*, to all men and women without exception. I wish to ask them to be

---

[86] Cf. Second Vatican Ecumenical Council, Pastoral Constitution on the Church in the Modern World *Gaudium et Spes*, 22; John Paul II, Encyclical Letter *Redemptor Hominis* (March 4, 1979), 8: *AAS* 71 (1979), 272.

[87] Encyclical Letter *Populorum Progressio*, 5: loc. cit., 259: "We believe that all men of good will, together with our Catholic sons and daughters and our Christian brethren, can and should agree on this program"; cf. also 81-83, 87: loc. cit., 296-298, 299.

convinced of the seriousness of the present moment and of each one's individual responsibility, and to implement — by the way they live as individuals and as families, by the use of their resources, by their civic activity, by contributing to economic and political decisions and by personal commitment to national and international undertakings — the *measures* inspired by solidarity and love of preference for the poor. This is what is demanded by the present moment and above all by the very dignity of the human person, the indestructible image of God the Creator, which is *identical* in each one of us.

47.6 In this commitment, the sons and daughters of the Church must serve as examples and guides, for they are called upon, in conformity with the program announced by Jesus himself in the synagogue at Nazareth, to "preach good news to the poor . . . to proclaim release to the captives and recovering of sight to the blind, to set at liberty those who are oppressed, to proclaim the acceptable year of the Lord" (Lk 4:18-19). It is appropriate to emphasize the *preeminent role* that belongs to the *laity*, both men and women, as was reaffirmed in the recent Assembly of the Synod. It is their task to animate temporal realities with Christian commitment, by which they show that they are witnesses and agents of peace and justice.

47.7 I wish to address especially those who, through the Sacrament of Baptism and the profession of the same Creed, *share* a *real*, though imperfect, *communion* with us. I am certain that the concern expressed in this Encyclical as well as the motives inspiring it *will be familiar to them*, for these motives are inspired by the Gospel of Jesus Christ. We can find here a new invitation *to bear witness together* to our *common convictions* concerning the dignity of man, created by God, redeemed by Christ, made holy by the Spirit and called upon in this world to live a life in conformity with this dignity.

47.8 I *likewise address* this appeal to the Jewish people, who share with us the inheritance of Abraham, "our father in faith" (cf. Rom 4:11-12),[88] and the tradition of the Old Testament, as well as to the Muslims who, like us, believe in the just and merciful God. And I extend it to all the followers of *the world's great religions*.

47.9 The meeting held last October 27 in Assisi, the city of Saint Francis, in order to pray for and commit ourselves to *peace* — each one in fidelity to his own religious profession — showed how much peace and, as its necessary condition, the development of the whole person and of all peoples, are also a *matter of religion*, and how the full achievement of both the one and the other

---

[88] Cf. Second Vatican Ecumenical Council, Declaration on the Relationship of the Church to Non-Christian Religions *Nostra Aetate*, 4.

depends on our *fidelity* to our vocation as men and women of faith. For it depends, above all, *on God.*

48.1 The Church well knows that *no temporal achievement* is to be identified with the Kingdom of God, but that all such achievements simply *reflect* and in a sense *anticipate* the glory of the Kingdom, the Kingdom which we await at the end of history, when the Lord will come again. But that expectation can never be an excuse for lack of concern for people in their concrete personal situations and in their social, national and international life, since the former is conditioned by the latter, especially today.

48.2 However imperfect and temporary are all the things that can and ought to be done through the combined efforts of everyone and through divine grace, at a given moment of history, in order to make people's lives "more human," nothing will be *lost* or *will have been in vain.* This is the teaching of the Second Vatican Council, in an enlightening passage of the Pastoral Constitution *Gaudium et Spes:* "When we have spread on earth the fruits of our nature and our enterprise — human dignity, fraternal communion, and freedom — according to the command of the Lord and in his Spirit, we will find them once again, cleansed this time from the stain of sin, illumined and transfigured, when Christ presents to his Father an eternal and universal Kingdom. Here on earth that Kingdom is already present in mystery."[89]

48.3 The Kingdom of God becomes *present* above all in the celebration of the *Sacrament of the Eucharist,* which is the Lord's Sacrifice. In that celebration the fruits of the earth and the work of human hands — the bread and wine — are transformed mysteriously, but really and substantially, through the power of the Holy Spirit and the words of the minister, *into the Body and Blood* of the Lord Jesus Christ, the Son of God and Son of Mary, through whom the *Kingdom of the Father* has been made present in our midst.

48.4 The goods of this world and the work of our hands — the bread and wine — serve for the coming of the *definitive Kingdom,* since the Lord, through his Spirit, takes them up into himself in order to offer himself to the Father and to offer us with himself in the renewal of his one Sacrifice, which anticipates God's Kingdom and proclaims its final coming.

48.5 Thus the Lord *unites us with himself* through the Eucharist — Sacrament and Sacrifice — and he *unites us with himself and with one another* by a bond stronger than any natural union; and thus united, *he sends us* into the whole world to bear witness, through faith and works, to God's love, prepar-

---

[89] *Gaudium et Spes,* 39.

ing the coming of his Kingdom and anticipating it, though in the obscurity of the present time.

48.6 All of us who take part in the Eucharist are called to discover, through this Sacrament, the profound *meaning* of our actions in the world in favor of development and peace; and to receive from it the strength to commit ourselves ever more generously, following the example of Christ, who in this Sacrament lays down his life for his friends (cf. Jn 15:13). Our personal commitment, like Christ's and in union with his, will not be in vain but certainly fruitful.

49.1 I have called the current *Marian Year* in order that the Catholic faithful may look more and more to Mary, who goes before us on the pilgrimage of faith[90] and with maternal care intercedes for us before her Son, our Redeemer. I wish to *entrust to her* and to *her intercession* this *difficult moment* of the modern world, and the efforts that are being made and will be made, often with great suffering, in order to contribute to the true development of peoples proposed and proclaimed by my Predecessor Paul VI.

49.2 In keeping with Christian piety through the ages, we present to the Blessed Virgin difficult individual situations, so that she may place them before her Son, asking that he *alleviate and change* them. But we also present to her *social situations* and *the international crisis* itself, in their worrying aspects of poverty, unemployment, shortage of food, the arms race, contempt for human rights, and situations or dangers of conflict, partial or total. In a filial spirit we wish to place all this before her "eyes of mercy," repeating once more with faith and hope the ancient antiphon: "Holy Mother of God, despise not our petitions in our necessities, but deliver us always from all dangers, O glorious and blessed Virgin."

49.3 Mary most holy, our Mother and Queen, is the one who turns to her Son and says: "They have no more wine" (Jn 2:3). She is also the one who praises God the Father, because "he has put down the mighty from their thrones and exalted those of low degree; he has filled the hungry with good things, and the rich he has sent empty away" (Lk 1:52-53). Her maternal concern extends to the *personal* and *social* aspects of people's life on earth.[91]

---

[90] Cf. Second Vatican Ecumenical Council, Dogmatic Constitution on the Church *Lumen Gentium*, 58; John Paul II, Encyclical Letter *Redemptoris Mater* (March 25, 1987), 5-6: *AAS* 79 (1987), 365-367.

[91] Cf. Paul VI, Apostolic Exhortation *Marialis Cultus* (February 2, 1974), 37: *AAS* 66 (1974), 148-149; John Paul II, Homily at the Shrine of Our Lady of Zapopan, Mexico (January 30, 1979), 4: *AAS* 71 (1979), 230.

49.4 Before the Most Blessed Trinity, I entrust to Mary all that I have written in this Encyclical, and I invite all to reflect and actively commit themselves to promoting the true development of peoples, as the prayer of the Mass for this intention states so well: "Father, you have given all peoples one common origin, and your will is to gather them as one family in yourself. Fill the hearts of all with the fire of your love, and the desire to ensure justice for all their brothers and sisters. By sharing the good things you give us, may we secure justice and equality for every human being, an end to all division and a human society built on love and peace."[92]

49.5 This, in conclusion, is what I ask in the name of all my brothers and sisters, to whom I send a special blessing as a sign of greeting and good wishes.

Given in Rome, at Saint Peter's, on December 30 of the year 1987, the tenth of my Pontificate.

---

[92] Collect of the Mass "For the Development of Peoples": *Missale Romanum*, editio typica altera, 1975, 820.

Redemptoris Missio

Editor's Introduction

In order to celebrate the twenty-fifth anniversary of the Second Vatican Council's Decree on the Church's Missionary Activity, *Ad Gentes,* John Paul II signed his eighth encyclical on December 7, 1990.[1] It is a clarion call to every sector in the Church to renew its commitment to evangelize the world, especially those who have not yet heard the Good News. With an impassioned sense of duty, John Paul repeats, in the name of the whole Church, the cry of Saint Paul: "Woe to me if I do not preach the Gospel" (1 Cor 9:16).

Because the percentage of the world's Christians is declining, the encyclical betrays a tone of urgency, but also one of hope. Looking with confidence toward the third millennium, John Paul dares to say that "God is preparing a great springtime for Christianity" (§86.1). In order to bring about this springtime, the Pope believes that, at the present time, "God is opening before the Church the horizons of a humanity more fully prepared for the sowing of the Gospel" (§3.4). *Redemptoris Missio* presents a theology of mission and a pastoral vision designed to direct the Church's energies to a new evangelization and the mission "to the nations" (*ad gentes*).

At the time of the Second Vatican Council, a certain crisis could already be discerned in discussions about missionary activity, a questioning which challenged the purpose and method of the Church's mission *ad gentes*. This debate intensified in the post-conciliar years. Some proposed that, because evangelization exported a "foreign" religion from one cultural setting to another, it threatened peaceful coexistence among nations. This attitude was abetted by those who maintained that missionary activity chiefly entailed the defense of the religious heritage of non-Christians, thereby casting doubt on the Church's duty to proclaim the Gospel to them. They viewed mission work chiefly as the promotion of interreligious dialogue or human development. According to John Paul II, however, these positions are based on a faulty theology; namely, "a religious relativism which leads to the belief that 'one religion is as good as another' " (§37.1). Besides these theoretical considerations contesting the need for the evangelization of non-Christians, the Pope lists other reasons for the decline of missionary zeal. He particularly notes "past and present divisions among

[1] *Acta Apostolicae Sedis,* 83 (1991), 249-340.

Christians, de-christianization within Christian countries, the decrease of vocations to the apostolate, and the counter-witness of believers and Christian communities" (§36.1).

Despite these negative tendencies, John Paul warmly applauds the fruits of the missionary activity which have in fact been reaped in the years following the Second Vatican Council. Among the developments since then which he praises are the exceptional growth in the number of local churches with native hierarchies and structures, the Church's presence in almost every nation on earth, the increased exchange of gifts among the various communities, and the new awareness that all Christians, especially the laity, have an indispensable role to play in evangelization.

At the same time the Pope is aware of a waning in missionary fervor and activity. He carefully examines the causes of this diminished enthusiasm, with an eye to clearing up "doubts and ambiguities regarding missionary activity *ad gentes*" (§2.5). In a word, the Pope wishes to put an end to the post-conciliar hesitancy regarding evangelization by dispelling errors and confusion about the Church's missionary nature. He also recognizes that by encouraging missionary enthusiasm the Church's faith will be renewed and her identity revitalized: *"Faith is strengthened when it is given to others"* (§2.3).

Redemptoris Missio is the first major document of John Paul II which deals at length with an explicitly ecclesiological theme: the mission of the Church as an aspect of her catholicity. Even so, the encyclical is firmly rooted in the Trinitarian mystery portrayed in *Redemptor Hominis* (1979), *Dives in Misericordia* (1980), and *Dominum et Vivificantem* (1986) which preceded it. All ecclesial mission has its source in the Trinity: "Salvation consists in believing and accepting the mystery of the Father and of his love, made manifest and freely given in Jesus through the Spirit" (§12.1).

The encyclical's sources, besides making abundant use of the classic mission texts from Scripture, show a decided preference for the documents of the Second Vatican Council. In addition to his customary reliance on *Lumen Gentium* and *Gaudium et Spes*, the Pope repeatedly cites *Ad Gentes*, the Council's Decree on the Church's Missionary Activity (1965). As well, he frequently incorporates into his text selections from discourses and homilies delivered during his pastoral visits to mission countries around the world. Very prominent, too, is the contribution of Paul VI's apostolic exhortation on evangelization, *Evangelium Nuntiandi* (1975), a landmark document which John Paul refers to more than twenty times.

In this encyclical the Pope addresses all Catholics: the bishops who are his "venerable brothers" and the "beloved sons and daughters" of the Church. He reiterates for them his Christocentric vision first outlined in *Redemptor Hominis*. There he wrote that the Church's "fundamental function" is "to direct man's gaze, to point the awareness and experience of the whole of humanity toward the mystery of Christ" (§4.1).

Summary

Besides its introduction and conclusion, *Redemptoris Missio* contains eight chapters. Not all of them are of equal doctrinal significance. The first three lay the foundation for John Paul's missiology, and the last five deal with the strategies, structure, agents, and spirituality of evangelization. Chapter one, "Jesus Christ, the Only Savior" (§§4-11), reaffirms that all salvation is mediated through Christ and is communicated to humanity by the Holy Spirit. In chapter two, "The Kingdom of God" (§§12-20), the Pope describes the relationship of the Kingdom to Christ and the Church, while in chapter three, "The Holy Spirit, the Principal Agent of Mission" (§§21-30), he outlines the Spirit's role as the chief protagonist of all evangelization. Chapter four, "The Vast Horizons of the Mission *Ad Gentes*" (§§31-40), discusses the particular groups of people and specific areas of the world to be evangelized, and chapter five, "The Paths of Mission" (§§41-60), takes up some of the theological and practical steps involved in evangelizing. In chapter six, "Leaders and Workers in the Missionary Apostolate" (§§61-76), John Paul addresses the duty of different sectors to evangelize the world, a theme which he continues in chapter seven, "Cooperation in Missionary Activity" (§§77-86). Chapter eight, "Missionary Spirituality" (§§87-91), summarizes the distinct spirituality of those called to be missionaries.

In the introduction, the Pope expresses his conviction that today's decline in missionary activity is at variance both with Christ's command and the directives of the Second Vatican Council. Judging the loss of missionary drive as "a sign of a crisis of faith" (§2.2), he feels impelled to give a boost to evangelization *ad gentes*. His reason is straightforward: "Missionary evangelization . . . is the primary service which the Church can render to every individual and to all humanity in the modern world" (§2.4). Wishing to offset any negative trends about the value of mission work, John Paul hopes that the Church will take advantage of the new world situation which, after the collapse of many totalitarian regimes, now favors renewed efforts of evangelization. He therefore encourages everyone to take part in this endeavor: "No believer in Christ, no institution of the Church can avoid this supreme duty: to proclaim Christ to all peoples" (§3.4).

Doctrinal concerns

In chapters one and two, the Pope indirectly replies to the theological ambiguities which have sapped the strength of missionary vitality in recent years. Consequently, he tackles what he considers to be an inadequate theology of the Trinity, of Christ, and of the Church. Nevertheless, he avoids explicit debate with the post-conciliar theologies of religion. Instead, the Pope develops a missiology that takes traditional teaching as its point of departure. It follows from his approach, however, that some theological positions in Trinitarian theology, Christology, and ecclesiology fail to conform to the mind of the Church.

Without developing the theme at length, the Pope reaffirms the central importance of Trinitarian doctrine to every theology of mission. He rules out any initiatives of evangelization which would ignore or minimize the Trinity, a tactic sometimes taken by those who wish to emphasize a theocentric, non-Trinitarian approach to the divine Mystery. By presenting the Kingdom of God theocentrically, without stressing its link with Christ, they hope to find "common ground in the one divine reality" (§17.3). But, says the Pope, this "is not the Kingdom of God as we know it from revelation" (§18.1).

John Paul also excludes as contrary to Catholic teaching any Christology which denies or obscures that Jesus is the definitive self-revelation of God and the only one capable of revealing him fully. Jesus Christ is not merely one more spiritual master in religious history. The Pope repeatedly affirms that "God's revelation becomes definitive and complete through his only-begotten Son" (§5.3). Moreover, in reply to those who propose that Jesus Christ is just one of the many possible manifestations of the Word in history, John Paul asserts: "Jesus is the Incarnate Word — a single and indivisible person. One cannot separate Jesus from the Christ. . . . Christ is none other than Jesus of Nazareth" (§6.1).

According to the Pope, precisely because Jesus Christ is unique, the only beloved Son of the Father, he has "an absolute and universal significance" (§6.1). Christ is "the Savior of all, the only one able to reveal God and lead to God" (§5.1). There is no parallel way of salvation, no rival savior. John Paul affirms that "for all people — Jews and Gentiles alike — salvation can only come from Jesus Christ" (§5.1). This, he maintains, is the teaching asserted throughout the New Testament (cf. Jn 1:9, 14:6; Acts 4:12; 1 Tim 2:5-7). Christ's one, universal mediation is absolutely fundamental to the Catholic faith. The Pope concludes that "no one, therefore, can enter into communion with God except through Christ, by the working of the Holy Spirit" (§5.4).

The mission of the Church is closely linked to the unique and necessary mediation of Christ as the instrument by which God has chosen to save the world. Sound Christology and ecclesiology go hand in hand. Those who try to sever the relation between Christ and the visible community of the Church, or between Christ and the Kingdom of God, are on the wrong path. The Church, writes the Pope, is Christ's "co-worker in the salvation of the world" (§9.1). As taught by Vatican II, she is "the universal sacrament of salvation" (§9.2). God has a single saving plan for all humanity, a plan in which both Christ and the Church are necessary. The grace by which every person is offered salvation "comes from Christ," a grace which, in turn, always has "a mysterious relationship to the Church" (§10.1).

Chapter three analyzes at length the meaning of the Kingdom of God. The encyclical treats this theme because certain reductionist theologians subordinate both Christ and the Church to the Kingdom. Their only purpose, it is said, is to serve the Kingdom, which alone is primary in God's plan.

After describing how Christ makes the Kingdom present and outlining its specific characteristics and demands, the Pope concludes: "Nowadays the Kingdom is much spoken of, but not always in a way consonant with the thinking of the Church" (§17.1). He specifically mentions two views that are doctrinally erroneous. First, there is a secular interpretation of the Kingdom, one which easily translates it into "one more ideology of purely earthly progress" (§17.1). Mission, then, would be aimed at promoting human development rather than leading people to conversion and Baptism. Second, there is a mistaken theocentric understanding, which fails to see that the Kingdom is "not a concept, a doctrine, or a program subject to free interpretation, but is before all else *a person* with the face and name of Jesus of Nazareth" (§18.2). Above all, the Pope wishes to emphasize that the Kingdom cannot be separated from Christ or the Church; it is indissolubly united to both.

The principal agent of evangelization

Before treating the human agents and structures of evangelization, John Paul considers the role of the Holy Spirit in the Church's mission *ad gentes*. All evangelizing activity is born from the Trinitarian missions: the sending of the Son by the Father, and the sending of the Spirit by the Father and the Son. "Christ sends his own into the world, just as the Father has sent him," writes the Pope, "and to this end he gives them the Spirit" (§22.2). Each account of the missionary mandate recorded in the four Gospels (cf. Mt 28:18-20; Mk 16:15-18; Lk 24:46-49; Jn 20:21-23) insists on two truths: that preaching the Gospel has a "universal dimension," and that the Apostles "will not be alone in this task" (§23.1).

The driving force of evangelization is the Spirit of the risen Lord. As the history of the early Church in the Acts of the Apostles records, he is the "principal agent of the whole of the Church's mission" (§21.2), the source of the impetus to a truly universal outreach. He makes the Apostles witnesses to Christ, enabling them to preach the Gospel with boldness and to bring people together for hearing the word, prayer, and a life of fraternal communion. "It is the Spirit who is the source of the drive to press on, not only geographically but also beyond the frontiers of race and religion, for a truly universal mission" (§25.2). According to John Paul, the same Spirit who is vitally active in the Church is also "at work in the heart of every person, through the 'seeds of the Word,' to be found in human initiatives — including religious ones — and in man's efforts to attain truth, goodness and God himself" (§28.1).

Who is to be evangelized?

The Church has the sole mission of bringing every individual into communion with the divine Persons. In chapter four, the Pope distinguishes three different spheres in which this mission is carried out: the pastoral care of the faithful, the new evangelization, and the mission *ad gentes*. In communities "with adequate and solid ecclesial structures," where people are "fervent in their faith and in Christian living," the Church discharges her normal activity of pastoral care (§33.3). While such communities must be converted ever more profoundly to the Gospel, they consist of believers who already bear witness to Christ. Increasingly, however, especially in places where the Church was formerly strong, there are now many people who "have lost a living sense of the faith, or even no longer consider themselves members of the Church" (§33.4). Here the Church's missionary activity entails what the Pope calls the "new evangelization" or "re-evangelization" of traditionally Christian countries or societies.

Important as mission is in these two situations, the encyclical concentrates on "peoples, groups and sociocultural contexts in which Christ and his Gospel are not known, or which lack Christian communities sufficiently mature to be able to incarnate the faith in their own environment and proclaim it to other groups" (§33.2). Lest it be neglected, this specific and permanent mission to non-Christians needs to be distinguished from other forms of evangelization. Indeed, it is "the first task of the Church, which has been sent forth to all peoples and to the very ends of the earth" (§34.2).

In describing the "horizons" of the mission *ad gentes*, the Pope indicates three different areas where it is to be carried out. First, he draws attention to countries and geographical areas which either lack indigenous ecclesial communities or where the Church has little impact on a local culture. Because the majority of humanity has not yet heard the Gospel, he affirms that "the mission *ad gentes* is still in its infancy" (§40.2). This situation leads him to propose that the Church should concentrate on the evangelization of the South and East of the globe, particularly emphasizing Asia, "toward which the Church's mission *ad gentes* ought to be chiefly directed" (§37.5). Second, the encyclical recommends that the evangelization of non-Christians should also concentrate on big cities, youth, and migrants and refugees in traditional Christian societies. Third, and here the Pope is especially innovative, he calls attention to *"the modern equivalents of the Areopagus"* (§37.11), the new culture created by modern social communications, a world which needs to be evangelized.

How evangelization is carried out

Chapter five discusses the various steps involved in bringing the Gospel to non-Christians. The objective of the mission *ad gentes* is "to found Christian communities and develop Churches to their full maturity" (§48.2). This task is completed when a particular church is firmly established in a local setting. In many parts of the world this work of the *plantatio Ecclesiae* is just beginning.

Because people are attracted to the truth more by example than by word, "the witness of Christian life is the first and irreplaceable form of mission" (§42.1). Even so, such testimony must be completed by the explicit preaching of the Good News "which all peoples have a right to hear" (§44.3). "The subject of proclamation," writes the Pope, "is Christ who was crucified, died and is risen" (§44.3).

While careful to propose but not impose, this proclamation ultimately aims at conversion, at stirring up the response of faith and the acceptance of Baptism. Once again the Pope turns his attention to a theological error. To those who "tend to separate conversion to Christ from Baptism, regarding Baptism as unnecessary" (§47.3), he recalls that Christ himself willed this sacrament as the means of entering into the fullness of new life.

John Paul also considers some practical ways in which the evangelization of peoples can be carried out more forcefully. He first draws attention to the need to work for Christian unity, so that missionary activity will be more effective. Second, the Pope encourages ecclesial basic communities, which he considers as a sign of vitality within the Church and as "a means of evangelization and of the initial proclamation of the Gospel" (§51.2). Third, he affirms that the process of incarnating Christianity in peoples' cultures must go ahead. "Through inculturation," he writes, "the Church makes the Gospel incarnate in different cultures and at the same time introduces peoples, together with their cultures, into her own community" (§52.3). This process is gradual, and it needs supervision and encouragement. Above all, "inculturation must be guided by two principles: 'compatibility with the Gospel and communion with the universal Church'" (§54.1). Fourth, the Pope takes up the important role that interreligious dialogue plays in the accomplishment of the Church's mission.

An examination of the relation between evangelization and the promotion of integral human development concludes chapter five. The Church's principal contribution to the development of peoples is not technical expertise or works of charity but the formation of consciences. Her mission, John Paul says, "consists essentially in offering people an opportunity not to 'have more' but to 'be more,' by awaking their consciences through the Gospel" (58.2). The Church is a force for true human liberation because she fosters the conversion of mind and heart, stimulates the recognition of human dignity, and encourages solidarity among peoples and nations.

Agents of evangelization

Chapter six contains the Pope's appeal to the various agents of evangelization, especially those who are leaders and workers in the missionary apostolate. He recalls their duties and exhorts them to fulfill them. John Paul outlines the concrete tasks of bishops, religious communities, diocesan priests, lay people, and the Congregation for the Evangelization of Peoples.

Responsibility for the world's evangelization "rests primarily with the College of Bishops, headed by the Successor of Peter" (§63.1). The Pope supervises missionary activity mainly through the Congregation for the Evangelization of Peoples. This office of the Roman Curia "has the authority necessary to plan and direct missionary activity and cooperation worldwide" (§75.3). In order to relaunch the mission *ad gentes,* there must be an "authentic reciprocity" among all local churches, a give-and-take overseen by the Bishop of Rome. Each one gives, and each one receives. At the national and regional levels, episcopal conferences play an essential role in supervising and coordinating evangelization.

John Paul warmly encourages men and women who have dedicated their lives totally to evangelization *ad gentes.* "The special vocation of missionaries *'for life'* retains all its validity: it is the model of the Church's missionary commitment" (§66.3). He invites contemplative religious communities to establish foundations in the young churches, and asks active institutes to examine "how willing and able they are to broaden their action in order to extend God's Kingdom" (§69.3). Diocesan priests, too, should be formed in a missionary spirit and urged to commit some years of their ministry to the mission *ad gentes*.

After recalling that some churches owe their origins to the activity of lay missionaries, the Pope emphasizes that, in virtue of Baptism, the laity make their own contribution to evangelization. They fulfill this duty by taking part in missionary associations, volunteer organizations, and ecclesial movements. Among the laity who are evangelizers, "catechists have a place of honor" (§73.1). In order for them to carry out their work effectively, they require careful doctrinal, spiritual, and pedagogical training, as well as just remuneration.

Missionary cooperation and spirituality

In chapters seven and eight, the Pope is more exhortatory, wishing to inspire the Church to take up the challenge of bringing the Gospel to all people. He sees "the dawning of a new missionary age, which will become a radiant day bearing an abundant harvest, if all Christians, and missionaries and young churches in particular, respond with generosity and holiness to the calls and challenges of our time" (§92.1).

How do Christians share in the work of evangelization? According to John Paul, cooperation is rooted in personal union with Christ. "Through holiness of life," he writes, "every Christian can become a fruitful part of the Church's mission" (§77.2). In addition to the witness of a holy life, everyone can take part in the mission *ad gentes* through prayer and sacrifice. The faithful can promote missionary vocations, especially in the family, and they can give generously to help the missions. New forms of missionary cooperation are being opened up for Christians: giving witness to Christ in foreign lands when there as tourists or workers, visiting the foreign missions and lending a hand, even if only temporarily, and offering hospitality at home to non-Christian immigrants and refugees. John Paul warns against any kind of ecclesial isolationism. Older churches, involved as they must be in the new evangelization of their own culture, must not for that reason slacken their outreach to the non-Christian world. For their part, young churches must "willingly accept missionaries and support from other Churches, and do likewise throughout the world" (§85.4).

The mission *ad gentes* "demands a specific spirituality" (§87.1). Such a spirituality is expressed by docility to the Spirit, a contemplative attitude, discernment, hope, courage, and poverty of spirit. It also requires that missionaries be zealous for souls and have a profound love for others, for Christ, and for the Church. The dynamism of future missionary work depends on "a new 'ardor for holiness' among Christians and throughout the Christian community" (§90.3).

Key Themes

While *Redemptoris Missio* is an impassioned appeal to Catholics to respond vigorously to the "great springtime for Christianity" that God is preparing for the Church (§86.1), it is also rich in doctrine. Among the encyclical's major theological emphases are those on the Church's missionary nature, the necessity of Christ and the Church for salvation, and the importance of interreligious dialogue to evangelization.

The Church as missionary

Faithful to the teaching of the Second Vatican Council, John Paul II repeatedly underscores the Church's essentially missionary nature, a nature which originates in the Trinitarian missions: the sending of the Son by the Father, and the sending of the Spirit by the Father and the Son. Jesus' command to preach the Gospel to the nations, so enthusiastically obeyed by the early Church, remains valid and urgent today, "essential and never-ending" (§31.2). This is so because "*the Church is missionary by her very nature*, for Christ's mandate is not something contingent or external, but reaches the very heart of the Church" (§62.1, cf. §§1.3, 5.3). Such a mandate has, as the encyclical's subtitle states, a "permanent validity."

It is, however, more than obedience to the Lord's command that animates the Church's mission. Evangelization is primarily inspired by faith and love, both of which derive "from the profound demands of God's life within us" (§11.5). Christ's love impels individuals and communities to share the truth revealed in "the unsearchable riches of Christ" (Eph 3:8). By proclaiming the Gospel, Christians lend their hand to the satisfying of that yearning for the fullness of life and truth which God has implanted in all people. Indeed, "every person has the right to hear the 'Good News' of the God who reveals and gives himself in Christ" (§46.4). In order for people to hear that Gospel, it must be preached to them (cf. Rom 10:14-18).

Mission is not just one of the Church's tasks. Rather, as the Pope declares, evangelization is "the primary service" she renders to humanity (§2.4) and is "situated at the center of her life" (§32.3). Preaching the Gospel and establishing Christian communities is "the first task of the Church. . . . Without the mission *ad gentes,* the Church's very missionary dimension would be deprived of its essential meaning" (§34.2).

In keeping with the importance given to diocesan churches at Vatican II,

Redemptoris Missio points out that from the beginning of Christianity evangelization has been "a responsibility of the local Church, which needs 'missionaries' in order to push forward toward new frontiers" (§27.1). Because mission is an essential mark of the Church, the Pope insists that every Christian community, especially the particular church gathered around its bishop, must be missionary. "Every Church," he writes, "even one made up of recent converts, is missionary by its very nature, and is both evangelized and evangelizing" (§49.2).

The mediation of Christ and the Church

The encyclical in no way restricts the gift of salvation only to Christians. At the same time, however, it forcefully reaffirms the necessary role of Christ and the Church in enabling people "to share in the communion which exists between the Father and the Son" (§23.3). Both the Bridegroom and the Bride play an indispensable role in the salvation of believers and non-believers alike.

John Paul repeats what he had already said in *Redemptor Hominis:* "for each one is included in the mystery of the Redemption and with each one Christ has united himself forever through this mystery" (§4.2). The Pope is unequivocal: Christ is "the one Savior of all" (§5.1), "the one mediator between God and men" (1 Tim 2:5). God's saving will, which embraces all people, is always realized "in Christ" and never apart from him. For John Paul there is only one path to salvation, and that is through "Christ's one, universal mediation" (§5.4). While non-Christian religions can in some way "mediate" salvation for their adherents, such forms of mediation "acquire meaning and value *only* from Christ's own mediation, and they cannot be understood as parallel or complementary to his" (§5.4). All saving grace, which is necessary for salvation, "comes from Christ; it is the result of his Sacrifice and is communicated by the Holy Spirit. It enables each person to attain salvation through his or her free cooperation" (§10.1). While non-Christians are subjectively unaware of Christ's mediation, it is nonetheless through him, because they share in the Paschal Mystery in a way known to God alone, that they can reach the fullness of life.

In accomplishing the Redemption, Christ is indissolubly related to his Body, the Church. Not only is the Church *the ordinary means of salvation*" and the sole possessor of the "fullness of the means of salvation" (§55.3), she is also Christ's "co-worker in the salvation of the world" (§9.1). He carries out his mission first *for* her and then *through* her. Two complementary truths must be professed at one and the same time. As the Pope points out: "It is necessary to keep these two truths together, namely, the real possibility of salvation in Christ for all mankind and the necessity of the Church for salvation" (§9.2).

John Paul does not believe that eternal salvation depends on incorporation into the visible Church. Indeed, he readily admits that Christ and the Spirit are present and active outside her visible boundaries. Nonetheless, without any fear of an "ecclesiocentrism" which would make the Church more important than Christ, he contends that the Church has a "specific and necessary role" in God's saving plan (§18.3). She is both the universal "sign" and the universal "instrument" of salvation. As a sacrament, the Church effects what she signifies: the divine life of grace. Without indicating how, the Pope affirms that, in the power of the Spirit, Christ carries out his saving mission to all people using the Church as his instrument. "The universal activity of the Spirit," he affirms, "is not to be separated from his particular activity within the Body of Christ" (§29.3). Whatever spiritual fruit the Spirit brings to maturity outside the visible Church is oriented toward its fulfillment in Christ, head of the Church. In a real but hidden way, the salvation made possible by the Redemption necessarily involves "a mysterious relationship to the Church" (§10.1).

Evangelization and interreligious dialogue

Redemptoris Missio furnishes the Pope with an occasion to explain the theological foundations of interreligious dialogue and to give some practical guidelines for how to engage in it. Dialogue with non-Christian religions belongs to the Church's evangelizing mission *ad gentes*. "It has," he writes, "special links with that mission and is one of its expressions" (§55.1).

John Paul scrupulously assures non-Christians that the Church's evangelizing mission is not the arm of any foreign social, political, economic, or cultural imperialism. He tells public authorities in missionary countries that evangelization "has but one purpose: to serve man by revealing to him the love of God made manifest in Jesus Christ" (§2.5). While the Church has a divinely given right to preach the Gospel to all people, she is always to respect their freedom of conscience when she proclaims her message. As the Pope says, "*the Church proposes; she imposes nothing*. She respects individuals and cultures, and she honors the sanctuary of conscience" (§39.2, cf. §46.4). In no way does the Gospel detract from an individual's freedom or from the esteem "owed to every culture and to whatever is good in each religion" (§3.1).

The Pope's attitude to non-Christian religions is shaped by his belief that "God loves all people and grants them the possibility of being saved" (§9.2, cf. §10.1). The special Covenant established with Israel, for example, did not abrogate the earlier covenants that God had already made with creation and with all people (cf. Gen 9:17). Furthermore, the Holy Spirit, not limited by time or space, can work everywhere and in everyone. "The Spirit's presence and activity affect not only individuals but also society and history, peoples, cultures and religions" (§28.3, cf. §29.1). Catholics, then, should broaden their vision in order to ponder the activity of the Spirit throughout the whole of creation.

Non-Christian religions contain the "seeds of the Word" which prepare them for coming to full maturity in the light of Christ's revelation. These seeds of truth and holiness "can only be understood in reference to Christ" (§29.2). For her part, the Church must discover these divine seeds in non-Christian religions and be ready to receive them through dialogue. Genuine interreligious dialogue is based on a positive evaluation of what is true and holy in other religious traditions.

Because the Spirit of Christ is present in non-Christian people "through their spiritual riches, of which their religions are the main and essential expression" (§55.1), Catholics approach interreligious dialogue with "deep respect for everything that has been brought about in human beings by the Spirit who blows where he wills" (§56.1). Non-Christian religions challenge Christians to see God's work among all peoples, to examine their own beliefs more deeply and intelligently, and to bear witness to the fullness of revelation in Christ.

Respect and dialogue do not, however, dispense the Church from proclaiming the Gospel. Instead, they contribute to the inner purification of the Church, greater mutual understanding among peoples, and the elimination of prejudice and intolerance. According to the Pope, interreligious dialogue should be conducted with the conviction that "*the Church is the ordinary means of salvation* and that *she alone* possesses the fullness of the means of salvation" (§55.3).

Pope John Paul II is convinced that on the brink of the third Christian millennium the Church has an extraordinary opportunity to bring "the Gospel, by witness and word, to all people and nations" (§92.1). The heart of her proclamation is Jesus Christ, who is himself the Good News. "All missionary activity," he says, "is directed to the proclamation of his mystery" (§44.2).

* * *

Selected Bibliography

Boyaxhiu, Mother Teresa. "Charity: The Soul of Missionary Activity." *L'Osservatore Romano*, 14 (1991), 5.

Braaten, Carl E. "A Papal Letter on the Church's Missionary Mandate." *Dialog*, 30 (1991), 182-183.

Burrows, William R., ed. *Redemption and Dialogue: Reading "Redemptoris Missio" and Dialogue and Proclamation.* Maryknoll: Orbis, 1993.

Colombo, Domenico. "Mission and the Kingdom." *L'Osservatore Romano,* 17 (1991), 6.

Cordeiro, Joseph. "The Necessity of the Church." *L'Osservatore Romano,* 14 (1991), 7.

Dominic, A. Paul. "Mission before Mission: God's Mission within Us." *Review for Religious,* 52 (1992), 119-130.

Dorr, Donal. "*Redemptoris Missio:* Reflections on the Encyclical." *The Furrow,* 42 (1991), 339-347.

D'Souza, Henry Sebastian. "Pope John Paul's New Challenge to Asia." *L'Osservatore Romano,* 14 (1991), 6.

Gheddo, Piero. "Gospel and Development." *L'Osservatore Romano,* 11 (1991), 5.

Giardini, F. "Trinitarian Communion and Christian Mission in *Redemptoris Missio.*" *Euntes,* 47 (1994), 151-166.

Kroeger, James H. "Rekindling Mission Enthusiasm." *The Priest,* 48 (January, 1992), 32-36.

Lopez-Gay, Jesús. "Spirit, Salvation and Mission." *L'Osservatore Romano,* 9 (1991), 6.

Neuhaus, Richard John. "Reviving the Missionary Mandate." *First Things,* 16 (1991), 61-64.

O'Donnell, Timothy. "The Crisis of Faith and the Theology of Mission: A Reflection on *Redemptoris Missio.*" *Faith and Reason,* 18:3 (1992), 5-13.

Saward, John. *Christ is the Answer: The Christ-Centered Teaching of Pope John Paul II.* Edinburgh: T&T Clark, 1995. 27-43.

Stransky, Thomas F. "From Vatican II to *Redemptoris Missio:* A Development in the Theology of Mission." In *The Good News of the Kingdom: Mission Theology for the Third Millennium.* Edited by Charles Van Engen, Dean S. Gilliland, and Paul E. Pierson. Maryknoll: Orbis, 1993. 137-147.

Teissier, Henri. "Ours Is Not a Silent Witness to Muslims." *L'Osservatore Romano,* 38 (1992), 7.

Tomko, Jozef. Presentation at the Press Conference for the Publication of *Redemptoris Missio. L'Osservatore Romano,* 4 (1991), 1, 21.

Ureña, Manuel. "The Missionary Impulse in the Church according to *Redemptoris Missio.*" *Communio,* 19 (1992), 94-102.

Zago, Marcello. "Church's Mission: Is It One or Many?" *L'Osservatore Romano,* 9 (1991), 7, 9.

ENCYCLICAL LETTER
REDEMPTORIS MISSIO
OF THE SUPREME PONTIFF
JOHN PAUL II
ON THE
PERMANENT VALIDITY
OF THE
CHURCH'S MISSIONARY MANDATE

Redemptoris Missio

Venerable Brothers,
Beloved Sons and Daughters,
Health and the Apostolic Blessing!

Introduction

1.1 The mission of Christ the Redeemer, which is entrusted to the Church, is still very far from completion. As the second millennium after Christ's coming draws to an end, an overall view of the human race shows that this mission is still only beginning and that we must commit ourselves wholeheartedly to its service. It is the Spirit who impels us to proclaim the great works of God: "For if I preach the Gospel, that gives me no ground for boasting. For necessity is laid upon me. Woe to me if I do not preach the Gospel!" (1 Cor 9:16).

1.2 In the name of the whole Church, I sense an urgent duty to repeat this cry of Saint Paul. From the beginning of my Pontificate I have chosen to travel to the ends of the earth in order to show this missionary concern. My direct contact with peoples who do not know Christ has convinced me even more of the *urgency of missionary activity,* a subject to which I am devoting the present Encyclical.

1.3 The Second Vatican Council sought to renew the Church's life and activity in the light of the needs of the contemporary world. The Council emphasized the Church's "missionary nature," basing it in a dynamic way on the Trinitarian mission itself. The missionary thrust therefore belongs to the very nature of the Christian life, and is also the inspiration behind ecumenism: "that they may all be one . . . so that the world may believe that you have sent me" (Jn 17:21).

2.1 The Council has already borne much fruit in the realm of missionary activity. There has been an increase of local Churches with their own Bishops, clergy and workers in the apostolate. The presence of Christian communities is more evident in the life of nations, and communion between the Churches has led to a lively exchange of spiritual benefits and gifts. The commitment of the laity to the work of evangelization is changing ecclesial life, while particular Churches are more willing to meet with the members of other Christian Churches and other religions, and to enter into dialogue and cooperation with them. Above all, there is a new awareness that *missionary activity is a matter for all Christians*, for all Dioceses and parishes, Church institutions and associations.

2.2 Nevertheless, in this "new springtime" of Christianity there is an undeniable negative tendency, and the present Document is meant to help overcome it. Missionary activity specifically directed "to the nations" (*ad gentes*) appears to be waning, and this tendency is certainly not in line with the directives of the Council and of subsequent statements of the Magisterium. Difficulties both internal and external have weakened the Church's missionary thrust toward non-Christians, a fact which must arouse concern among all who believe in Christ. For in the Church's history, missionary drive has always been a sign of vitality, just as its lessening is a sign of a crisis of faith.[1]

2.3 Twenty-five years after the conclusion of the Council and the publication of the Decree on Missionary Activity *Ad Gentes*, fifteen years after the Apostolic Exhortation *Evangelii Nuntiandi* issued by Pope Paul VI, and in continuity with the magisterial teaching of my Predecessors,[2] I wish to invite the Church to *renew her missionary commitment.* The present Document has as its goal an interior renewal of faith and Christian life. For missionary activity renews the Church, revitalizes faith and Christian identity, and offers fresh enthusiasm and new incentive. *Faith is strengthened when it is given to others!* It is in commitment to the Church's universal mission that the new evangelization of Christian peoples will find inspiration and support.

2.4 But what moves me even more strongly to proclaim the urgency of missionary evangelization is the fact that it is the primary service which the Church can render to every individual and to all humanity in the modern world, a world which has experienced marvelous achievements but which seems to have lost its sense of ultimate realities and of existence itself. "Christ the Redeemer," I wrote in my first Encyclical, "fully reveals man to himself. . . . The man who wishes to understand himself thoroughly . . . must . . . draw near to Christ. . . . [The] Redemption that took place

[1] Cf. Paul VI, Message for the 1972 World Mission Day: *Insegnamenti* X (1972), 522: "How many internal tensions, which weaken and divide certain local Churches and institutions, would disappear before the firm conviction that the salvation of local communities is procured through cooperation in work for the spread of the Gospel to the farthest bounds of the earth!"

[2] Cf. Benedict XV, Apostolic Letter *Maximum Illud* (November 30, 1919): *AAS* 11 (1919), 440-455; Pius XI, Encyclical Letter *Rerum Ecclesiae* (February 28, 1926): *AAS* 18 (1926), 65-83; Pius XII, Encyclical Letter *Evangelii Praecones* (June 2, 1951): *AAS* 43 (1951), 497-528; Encyclical Letter *Fidei Donum* (April 21, 1957): *AAS* 49 (1957), 225-248; John XXIII, Encyclical Letter *Princeps Pastorum* (November 28, 1959): *AAS* 51 (1959), 833-864.

through the Cross has definitively restored to man his dignity and given back meaning to his life in the world."[3]

2.5 I also have other reasons and aims: to respond to the many requests for a Document of this kind; to clear up doubts and ambiguities regarding missionary activity *ad gentes*, and to confirm in their commitment those exemplary brothers and sisters dedicated to missionary activity and all those who assist them; to foster missionary vocations; to encourage theologians to explore and expound systematically the various aspects of missionary activity; to give a fresh impulse to missionary activity by fostering the commitment of the particular Churches — especially those of recent origin — to send forth and receive missionaries; and to assure non-Christians, and particularly the authorities of countries to which missionary activity is being directed, that all of this has but one purpose: to serve man by revealing to him the love of God made manifest in Jesus Christ.

3.1 *Peoples everywhere, open the doors to Christ!* His Gospel in no way detracts from man's freedom, from the respect that is owed to every culture and to whatever is good in each religion. By accepting Christ, you open yourselves to the definitive Word of God, to the One in whom God has made himself fully known and has shown us the path to himself.

3.2 The number of those who do not know Christ and do not belong to the Church is constantly on the increase. Indeed, since the end of the Council it has almost doubled. When we consider this immense portion of humanity which is loved by the Father and for whom he sent his Son, the urgency of the Church's mission is obvious.

3.3 On the other hand, our own times offer the Church new opportunities in this field: we have witnessed the collapse of oppressive ideologies and political systems; the opening of frontiers and the formation of a more united world due to an increase in communications; the affirmation among peoples of the Gospel values which Jesus made incarnate in his own life (peace, justice, brotherhood, concern for the needy); and a kind of soulless economic and technical development which only stimulates the search for the truth about God, about man and about the meaning of life itself.

3.4 God is opening before the Church the horizons of a humanity more fully prepared for the sowing of the Gospel. I sense that the moment has come to commit all of the Church's energies to a new evangelization and to the mission *ad gentes*. No believer in Christ, no institution of the Church can avoid this supreme duty: to proclaim Christ to all peoples.

---

[3] Encyclical Letter *Redemptor Hominis* (March 4, 1979), 10: *AAS* 71 (1979), 274-275.

I

Jesus Christ, the Only Savior

4.1 In my first Encyclical, in which I set forth the program of my Pontificate, I said that "the Church's fundamental function in every age, and particularly in ours, is to direct man's gaze, to point the awareness and experience of the whole of humanity toward the mystery of Christ."[4]

4.2 The Church's universal mission is born of faith in Jesus Christ, as is stated in our Trinitarian profession of faith: "I believe in one Lord, Jesus Christ, the only Son of God, eternally begotten of the Father. . . . For us men and for our salvation he came down from heaven: by the power of the Holy Spirit he became incarnate from the Virgin Mary, and was made man."[5] The Redemption event brings salvation to all, "for each one is included in the mystery of the Redemption and with each one Christ has united himself forever through this mystery."[6] It is only in faith that the Church's mission can be understood and only in faith that it finds its basis.

4.3 Nevertheless, also as a result of the changes which have taken place in modern times and the spread of new theological ideas, some people wonder: *Is missionary work among non-Christians still relevant?* Has it not been replaced by interreligious dialogue? Is not human development an adequate goal of the Church's mission? Does not respect for conscience and for freedom exclude all efforts at conversion? Is it not possible to attain salvation in any religion? *Why then should there be missionary activity?*

"No one comes to the Father, but by me" (Jn 14:6)

5.1 If we go back to the beginnings of the Church, we find a clear affirmation that Christ is the one Savior of all, the only one able to reveal God and lead to God. In reply to the Jewish religious authorities who question the Apostles about the healing of the lame man, Peter says: "By the name of Jesus Christ of Nazareth whom you crucified, whom God raised from the dead, by him this man is standing before you well. . . . And there is salvation in no one else, for there is no other name under heaven given among men by which we must be saved" (Acts 4:10, 12). This statement, which was made to the Sanhedrin, has a universal value, since for all

---

[4] Ibid.: loc. cit., 275.

[5] Nicene-Constantinopolitan Creed: *DS* 150.

[6] Encyclical Letter *Redemptor Hominis* (March 4, 1979), 13: *AAS* 71 (1979), 283.

people — Jews and Gentiles alike — salvation can only come from Jesus Christ.

5.2 The universality of this salvation in Christ is asserted throughout the New Testament. Saint Paul acknowledges the risen Christ as the Lord. He writes: "Although there may be so-called gods in heaven or on earth — as indeed there are many 'gods' and many 'lords' — yet for us there is one God, the Father, from whom are all things and for whom we exist, and one Lord, Jesus Christ, through whom are all things and through whom we exist" (1 Cor 8:5-6). One God and one Lord are asserted by way of contrast to the multitude of "gods" and "lords" commonly accepted. Paul reacts against the polytheism of the religious environment of his time and emphasizes what is characteristic of the Christian faith: belief in one God and in one Lord sent by God.

5.3 In the Gospel of Saint John, this salvific universality of Christ embraces all the aspects of his mission of grace, truth and revelation: the Word is "the true light that enlightens every man" (Jn 1:9). And again, "no one has ever seen God; the only Son, who is in the bosom of the Father, he has made him known" (Jn 1:18; cf. Mt 11:27). God's revelation becomes definitive and complete through his only-begotten Son: "In many and various ways God spoke of old to our fathers by the prophets; but in these last days he has spoken to us by a Son, whom he appointed the heir of all things, through whom he also created the world" (Heb 1:1-2; cf. Jn 14:6). In this definitive Word of his revelation, God has made himself known in the fullest possible way. He has revealed to mankind *who he is*. This definitive self-revelation of God is the fundamental reason why the Church is missionary by her very nature. She cannot do other than proclaim the Gospel, that is, the fullness of the truth which God has enabled us to know about himself.

5.4 Christ is the one mediator between God and mankind: "For there is one God, and there is one mediator between God and men, the man Christ Jesus, who gave himself as a ransom for all, the testimony to which was borne at the proper time. For this I was appointed a preacher and apostle (I am telling the truth, I am not lying), a teacher of the Gentiles in faith and truth" (1 Tim 2:5-7; cf. Heb 4:14-16). No one, therefore, can enter into communion with God except through Christ, by the working of the Holy Spirit. Christ's one, universal mediation, far from being an obstacle on the journey toward God, is the way established by God himself, a fact of which Christ is fully aware. Although participated forms of mediation of different kinds and degrees are not excluded, they acquire meaning and value only from Christ's own mediation, and they cannot be understood as parallel or complementary to his.

6.1 To introduce any sort of separation between the Word and Jesus Christ is contrary to the Christian faith. Saint John clearly states that the Word, who "was in the beginning with God," is the very one who "became flesh" (Jn 1:2, 14). Jesus is the Incarnate Word — a single and indivisible person. One cannot separate Jesus from the Christ or speak of a "Jesus of history" who would differ from the "Christ of faith." The Church acknowledges and confesses Jesus as "the Christ, the Son of the living God" (Mt 16:16): Christ is none other than Jesus of Nazareth; he is the Word of God made man for the salvation of all. In Christ "the whole fullness of deity dwells bodily" (Col 2:9) and "from his fullness have we all received" (Jn 1:16). The "only Son, who is the bosom of the Father" (Jn 1:18) is "the beloved Son, in whom we have redemption. . . , For in him all the fullness of God was pleased to dwell, and through him to reconcile to himself all things, whether on earth or in heaven, making peace by the blood of his Cross" (Col 1:13-14, 19-20). It is precisely this uniqueness of Christ which gives him an absolute and universal significance, whereby, while belonging to history, he remains history's center and goal:[7] "I am the Alpha and the Omega, the first and the last, the beginning and the end" (Rev 22:13).

6.2 Thus, although it is legitimate and helpful to consider the various aspects of the mystery of Christ, we must never lose sight of its unity. In the process of discovering and appreciating the manifold gifts — especially the spiritual treasures — that God has bestowed on every people, we cannot separate those gifts from Jesus Christ, who is at the center of God's plan of salvation. Just as "by his Incarnation the Son of God united himself in some sense with every human being," so too "we are obliged to hold that the Holy Spirit offers everyone the possibility of sharing in the Paschal Mystery in a manner known to God."[8] God's plan is "to unite all things in Christ, things in heaven and things on earth" (Eph 1:10).

Faith in Christ is directed to man's freedom

7.1 The urgency of missionary activity derives from the *radical newness of life* brought by Christ and lived by his followers. This new life is a gift from God, and people are asked to accept and develop it, if they wish to realize the

---

[7] Cf. Second Vatican Ecumenical Council, Pastoral Constitution on the Church in the Modern World *Gaudium et Spes,* 2.

[8] Ibid., 22.

fullness of their vocation in conformity to Christ. The whole New Testament is a hymn to the new life of those who believe in Christ and live in his Church. Salvation in Christ, as witnessed to and proclaimed by the Church, is God's self-communication: "It is love which not only creates the good, but also grants participation in the very life of God: Father, Son and Holy Spirit. For he who loves desires to give himself."[9]

7.2 God offers mankind this newness of life. "Can one reject Christ and everything that he has brought about in the history of mankind? Of course one can. Man is free. He can say 'no' to God. He can say 'no' to Christ. But the fundamental question remains: Is it legitimate to do this? And what would make it legitimate?"[10]

8.1 In the modern world there is a tendency to reduce man to his horizontal dimension alone. But without an openness to the Absolute, what does man become? The answer to this question is found in the experience of every individual, but it is also written in the history of humanity with the blood shed in the name of ideologies or by political regimes which have sought to build a "new humanity" without God.[11]

8.2 Moreover, the Second Vatican Council replies to those concerned with safeguarding freedom of conscience: "The human person has a right to religious freedom. . . . All should have such immunity from coercion by individuals, or by groups, or by any human power, that no one should be forced to act against his conscience in religious matters, nor prevented from acting according to his conscience, whether in private or in public, whether alone or in association with others, within due limits."[12]

8.3 Proclaiming Christ and bearing witness to him, when done in a way that respects consciences, does not violate freedom. Faith demands a free adherence on the part of man, but at the same time faith must also be offered to him, because the "multitudes have the right to know the riches of the mystery of Christ — riches in which we believe that the whole of humanity can find, in unsuspected fullness, everything that it is gropingly searching for concerning God, man and his destiny, life and death, and truth. . . . This is why the Church keeps her missionary spirit alive, and

---

[9] Encyclical Letter *Dives in Misericordia* (November 30, 1980), 7: *AAS* 72 (1980), 1202.

[10] Homily at the Celebration of the Eucharist, Krakow (June 10, 1979): *AAS* 71 (1979), 873.

[11] Cf. John XXIII, Encyclical Letter *Mater et Magistra* (May 15, 1961), IV: *AAS* 53 (1961), 453.

[12] Declaration on Religious Freedom *Dignitatis Humanae*, 2.

even wishes to intensify it in the moment of history in which we are living."[13] But it must also be stated, again with the Council, that "in accordance with their dignity as persons, equipped with reason and free will and endowed with personal responsibility, all are impelled by their own nature and are bound by a moral obligation to seek truth, above all religious truth. They are further bound to hold to the truth once it is known, and to regulate their whole lives by its demands."[14]

The Church as sign and instrument of salvation

9.1 The first beneficiary of salvation is the Church. Christ won the Church for himself at the price of his own blood and made the Church his co-worker in the salvation of the world. Indeed, Christ dwells within the Church. She is his Bride. It is he who causes her to grow. He carries out his mission through her.

9.2 The Council makes frequent reference to the Church's role in the salvation of mankind. While acknowledging that God loves all people and grants them the possibility of being saved (cf. 1 Tim 2:4),[15] the Church believes that God has established Christ as the one mediator and that she herself has been established as the universal sacrament of salvation.[16] "To this catholic unity of the People of God, therefore, . . . all are called, and they belong to it or are ordered to it in various ways, whether they be Catholic faithful or others who believe in Christ or finally all people everywhere who by the grace of God are called to salvation."[17] It is necessary to keep these two truths together, namely, the real possibility of salvation in Christ for all mankind and the necessity of the Church for salvation. Both these truths help us to understand the *one mystery of salvation*, so that we can come to know God's mercy and our own responsibility. Salvation, which always remains a gift of the Holy Spirit, requires man's cooperation, both to save himself and to save others. This is God's will, and this is why he established the Church and made her a part of his plan of salvation. Referring to "this

---

[13] Paul VI, Apostolic Exhortation *Evangelii Nuntiandi* (December 8, 1975), 53: *AAS* 68 (1976), 42.

[14] Declaration on Religious Freedom *Dignitatis Humanae*, 2.

[15] Cf. Dogmatic Constitution on the Church *Lumen Gentium*, 14-17; Decree on the Church's Missionary Activity *Ad Gentes*, 3.

[16] Cf. Dogmatic Constitution on the Church *Lumen Gentium*, 48; Pastoral Constitution on the Church in the Modern World *Gaudium et Spes*, 43; Decree on the Church's Missionary Activity *Ad Gentes*, 7, 21.

[17] Dogmatic Constitution on the Church *Lumen Gentium*, 13.

messianic people," the Council says: "It has been set up by Christ as a communion of life, love and truth; by him too it is taken up as the instrument of salvation for all, and sent on a mission to the whole world as the light of the world and the salt of the earth."[18]

Salvation in Christ is offered to all

10.1 The universality of salvation means that it is granted not only to those who explicitly believe in Christ and have entered the Church. Since salvation is offered to all, it must be made concretely available to all. But it is clear that today, as in the past, many people do not have an opportunity to come to know or accept the Gospel revelation or to enter the Church. The social and cultural conditions in which they live do not permit this, and frequently they have been brought up in other religious traditions. For such people salvation in Christ is accessible by virtue of a grace which, while having a mysterious relationship to the Church, does not make them formally part of the Church but enlightens them in a way which is accommodated to their spiritual and material situation. This grace comes from Christ; it is the result of his Sacrifice and is communicated by the Holy Spirit. It enables each person to attain salvation through his or her free cooperation.

10.2 For this reason the Council, after affirming the centrality of the Paschal Mystery, went on to declare that "this applies not only to Christians but to all people of good will in whose hearts grace is secretly at work. Since Christ died for everyone, and since the ultimate calling of each of us comes from God and is therefore a universal one, we are obliged to hold that the Holy Spirit offers everyone the possibility of sharing in this Paschal Mystery in a manner known to God."[19]

"We cannot but speak" (Acts 4:20)

11.1 What then should be said of the objections already mentioned regarding the mission *ad gentes*? While respecting the beliefs and sensitivities of all, we must first clearly affirm our faith in Christ, the one Savior of mankind, a faith we have received as a gift from on high, not as a result of any merit of our own. We say with Paul, "I am not ashamed of the Gospel: it is the power of God for salvation to everyone who has faith" (Rom 1:16). Christian martyrs of all times — including our own — have given and continue to give their lives in order to bear witness to this faith, in the conviction that every

---

[18] Ibid., 9.

[19] Pastoral Constitution on the Church in the Modern World *Gaudium et Spes*, 22.

human being needs Jesus Christ, who has conquered sin and death and reconciled mankind to God.

11.2 Confirming his words by miracles and by his Resurrection from the dead, Christ proclaimed himself to be the Son of God dwelling in intimate union with the Father, and was recognized as such by his disciples. The Church offers mankind the Gospel, that prophetic message which responds to the needs and aspirations of the human heart and always remains "Good News." The Church cannot fail to proclaim that Jesus came to reveal the face of God and to merit salvation for all mankind by his Cross and Resurrection.

11.3 To the question *"why mission?"* we reply with the Church's faith and experience that true liberation consists in opening oneself to the love of Christ. In him, and only in him, are we set free from all alienation and doubt, from slavery to the power of sin and death. Christ is truly "our peace" (Eph 2:14); "the love of Christ impels us" (2 Cor 5:14), giving meaning and joy to our life. *Mission is an issue of faith*, an accurate indicator of our faith in Christ and his love for us.

11.4 The temptation today is to reduce Christianity to merely human wisdom, a pseudo-science of well-being. In our heavily secularized world a "gradual secularization of salvation" has taken place, so that people strive for the good of man, but man who is truncated, reduced to his merely horizontal dimension. We know, however, that Jesus came to bring integral salvation, one which embraces the whole person and all mankind, and opens up the wondrous prospect of divine filiation. *Why mission?* Because to us, as to Saint Paul, "this grace was given, to preach to the Gentiles the unsearchable riches of Christ" (Eph 3:8). Newness of life in him is the "Good News" for men and women of every age: all are called to it and destined for it. Indeed, all people are searching for it, albeit at times in a confused way, and have a right to know the value of this gift and to approach it freely. The Church, and every individual Christian within her, may not keep hidden or monopolize this newness and richness which has been received from God's bounty in order to be communicated to all mankind.

11.5 This is why the Church's mission derives not only from the Lord's mandate but also from the profound demands of God's life within us. Those who are incorporated in the Catholic Church ought to sense their privilege and for that very reason their greater obligation of *bearing witness to the faith and to the Christian life* as a service to their brothers and sisters and as a fitting response to God. They should be ever mindful that "they owe their distinguished status not to their own merits but to Christ's special grace; and if they fail to respond to this grace in thought, word and deed, not only will they not be saved, they will be judged more severely."[20]

II

The Kingdom of God

12.1 "It is 'God, who is rich in mercy' whom Jesus Christ has revealed to us as Father: it is his very Son who, in himself, has manifested him and made him known to us."[21] I wrote this at the beginning of my Encyclical *Dives in Misericordia*, to show that Christ is the revelation and incarnation of the Father's mercy. Salvation consists in believing and accepting the mystery of the Father and of his love, made manifest and freely given in Jesus through the Spirit. In this way the Kingdom of God comes to be fulfilled: the Kingdom prepared for in the Old Testament, brought about by Christ and in Christ, and proclaimed to all peoples by the Church, which works and prays for its perfect and definitive realization.

12.2 The Old Testament attests that God chose and formed a people for himself, in order to reveal and carry out his loving plan. But at the same time God is the Creator and Father of all people; he cares and provides for them, extending his blessing to all (cf. Gen 12:3); he has established a covenant with all of them (cf. Gen 9:1-17). Israel experiences a personal and saving God (cf. Dt 4:37, 7:6-8; Is 43:1-7) and becomes his witness and interpreter among the nations. In the course of her history, Israel comes to realize that her election has a universal meaning (cf. for example Is 2:2-5, 25:6-8, 60:1-6; Jer 3:17, 16:19).

Christ makes the Kingdom present

13.1 Jesus of Nazareth brings God's plan to fulfillment. After receiving the Holy Spirit at his baptism, Jesus makes clear his messianic calling: he goes about Galilee "preaching the Gospel of God and saying: 'The time is fulfilled, and the Kingdom of God is at hand; repent and believe in the Gospel' " (Mk 1:14-15; cf. Mt 4:17; Lk 4:43). The proclamation and establishment of God's Kingdom are the purpose of his mission: "I was sent for this purpose" (Lk 4:43). But that is not all. Jesus himself is the "Good News," as he declares at

---

[20] Second Vatican Ecumenical Council, Dogmatic Constitution on the Church *Lumen Gentium*, 14.

[21] Encyclical Letter *Dives in Misericordia* (November 30, 1980), 1: *AAS* 72 (1980), 1177.

the very beginning of his mission in the synagogue at Nazareth, when he applies to himself the words of Isaiah about the Anointed One sent by the Spirit of the Lord (cf. Lk 4:14-21). Since the "Good News" is Christ, there is an identity between the message and the messenger, between saying, doing and being. His power, the secret of the effectiveness of his actions, lies in his total identification with the message he announces; he proclaims the "Good News" not just by what he says or does, but by what he is.

13.2 The ministry of Jesus is described in the context of his journeys within his homeland. Before Easter, the scope of his mission was focused on Israel. Nevertheless, Jesus offers a new element of extreme importance. The eschatological reality is not relegated to a remote "end of the world," but is already close and at work in our midst. The Kingdom of God is at hand (cf. Mk 1:15); its coming is to be prayed for (cf. Mt 6:10); faith can glimpse it already at work in signs such as miracles (cf. Mt 11:4-5) and exorcisms (cf. Mt 12:25-28), in the choosing of the Twelve (cf. Mk 3:13-19), and in the proclamation of the Good News to the poor (cf. Lk 4:18). Jesus' encounters with Gentiles make it clear that entry into the Kingdom comes through faith and conversion (cf. Mk 1:15), and not merely by reason of ethnic background.

13.3 The Kingdom which Jesus inaugurates is the Kingdom of God. Jesus himself reveals who this God is, the One whom he addresses by the intimate term "Abba," Father (cf. Mk 14:36). God, as revealed above all in the parables (cf. Lk 15:3-32; Mt 20:1-16), is sensitive to the needs and sufferings of every human being: he is a Father filled with love and compassion, who grants forgiveness and freely bestows the favors asked of him.

13.4 Saint John tells us that "God is love" (1 Jn 4:8, 16). Every person therefore is invited to "repent" and to "believe" in God's merciful love. The Kingdom will grow insofar as every person learns to turn to God in the intimacy of prayer as to a Father (cf. Lk 11:2; Mt 23:9) and strives to do his will (cf. Mt 7:21).

Characteristics of the Kingdom and its demands

14.1 Jesus gradually reveals the characteristics and demands of the Kingdom through his words, his actions and his own person.

14.2 The Kingdom of God is meant for all mankind, and all people are called to become members of it. To emphasize this fact, Jesus drew especially near to those on the margins of society, and showed them special favor in announcing the Good News. At the beginning of his ministry he proclaimed that he was "anointed . . . to preach good news to the poor" (Lk 4:18). To all who are victims of rejection and contempt Jesus declares: "Blessed are you poor" (Lk 6:20). What is more, he enables such individuals to experience liberation even now, by being close to them, going to eat in their homes (cf. Lk 5:30, 15:2), treating them as equals and friends (cf. Lk 7:34), and making them feel loved by God, thus revealing his tender care for the needy and for sinners (cf. Lk 15:1-32).

14.3 The liberation and salvation brought by the Kingdom of God come to the human person both in his physical and spiritual dimensions. Two gestures are characteristic of Jesus' mission: healing and forgiving. Jesus' many healings clearly show his great compassion in the face of human distress, but they also signify that in the Kingdom there will no longer be sickness or suffering, and that his mission, from the very beginning, is meant to free people from these evils. In Jesus' eyes, healings are also a sign of spiritual salvation, namely liberation from sin. By performing acts of healing, he invites people to faith, conversion and the desire for forgiveness (cf. Lk 5:24). Once there is faith, healing is an encouragement to go further: it leads to salvation (cf. Lk 18:42-43). The acts of liberation from demonic possession — that supreme evil and symbol of sin and rebellion against God — are signs that indeed "the Kingdom of God has come upon you" (Mt 12:28).

15.1 The Kingdom aims at transforming human relationships; it grows gradually as people slowly learn to love, forgive and serve one another. Jesus sums up the whole Law, focusing it on the commandment of love (cf. Mt 22:34-40; Lk 10:25-28). Before leaving his disciples, he gives them a "new commandment": "Love one another; even as I have loved you" (Jn 13:34, cf. 15:12). Jesus' love for the world finds its highest expression in the gift of his life for mankind (cf. Jn 15:13), which manifests the love which the Father has for the world (cf. Jn 3:16). The Kingdom's nature, therefore, is one of communion among all human beings — with one another and with God.

15.2 The Kingdom is the concern of everyone: individuals, society, and the world. Working for the Kingdom means acknowledging and promoting God's activity, which is present in human history and transforms it. Building the Kingdom means working for liberation from evil in all its forms. In a word, the Kingdom of God is the manifestation and the realization of God's plan of salvation in all its fullness.

In the risen Christ God's Kingdom is fulfilled and proclaimed

16.1 By raising Jesus from the dead, God has conquered death, and in Jesus he has definitely inaugurated his Kingdom. During his earthly life, Jesus was the prophet of the Kingdom; after his Passion, Resurrection and Ascension into heaven he shares in God's power and in his dominion over the world (cf. Mt 28:18; Acts 2:36; Eph 1:18-21). The Resurrection gives a universal scope to Christ's message, his actions and whole mission. The disciples recognize that the Kingdom is already present in the person of Jesus and is slowly being established within man and the world through a mysterious connection with him.

16.2 Indeed, after the Resurrection, the disciples preach the Kingdom by proclaiming Jesus crucified and risen from the dead. In Samaria, Philip "preached good news about the Kingdom of God and the name of Jesus Christ" (Acts 8:12). In Rome, we find Paul "preaching the Kingdom of God and teaching about the Lord Jesus Christ" (Acts 28:31). The first Christians also proclaim "the Kingdom of Christ and of God" (Eph 5:5; cf. Rev 11:15; 12:10), or "the Kingdom of our Lord and Savior Jesus Christ" (2 Pet 1:11). The preaching of the early Church was centered on the proclamation of Jesus Christ, with whom the Kingdom was identified. Now, as then, there is a need to unite *the proclamation of the Kingdom of God* (the content of Jesus' own "kerygma") and *the proclamation of the Christ-event* (the "kerygma" of the Apostles). The two proclamations are complementary; each throws light on the other.

The Kingdom in relation to Christ and the Church

17.1 Nowadays the Kingdom is much spoken of, but not always in a way consonant with the thinking of the Church. In fact, there are ideas about salvation and mission which can be called "anthropocentric" in the reductive sense of the word, inasmuch as they are focused on man's earthly needs. In this view, the Kingdom tends to become something completely human and secularized; what counts are programs and struggles for a liberation which is socioeconomic, political and even cultural, but within a horizon that is closed to the transcendent. Without denying that on this level too there are values to be promoted, such a notion nevertheless remains within the confines of a kingdom of man, deprived of its authentic and profound dimensions. Such a view easily translates into one more ideology of purely earthly progress. The Kingdom of God, however, "is not of this world . . . is not from the world" (Jn 18:36).

17.2 There are also conceptions which deliberately emphasize the Kingdom and which describe themselves as "Kingdom-centered." They stress the image of a Church which is not concerned about herself, but which is totally concerned with bearing witness to and serving the Kingdom. It is a "Church for others" just as Christ is the "man for others." The Church's task is described as though it had to proceed in two directions: on the one hand promoting such "values of the Kingdom" as peace, justice, freedom, brotherhood, etc., while on the other hand fostering dialogue between peoples, cultures and religions, so that through a mutual enrichment they might help the world to be renewed and to journey ever closer toward the Kingdom.

17.3 Together with positive aspects, these conceptions often reveal negative aspects as well. First, they are silent about Christ: the Kingdom of which they speak is "theocentrically" based, since, according to them, Christ cannot be understood by those who lack Christian faith, whereas different peoples, cultures and religions are capable of finding common ground in the one divine reality, by whatever name it is called. For the same reason they put great stress on the mystery of creation, which is reflected in the diversity of cultures and beliefs, but they keep silent about the mystery of Redemption. Furthermore, the Kingdom, as they understand it, ends up either leaving very little room for the Church or undervaluing the Church in reaction to a presumed "ecclesiocentrism" of the past, and because they consider the Church herself only a sign, for that matter a sign not without ambiguity.

18.1 This is not the Kingdom of God as we know it from revelation. The Kingdom cannot be detached either from Christ or from the Church.

18.2 As has already been said, Christ not only proclaimed the Kingdom, but in him the Kingdom itself became present and was fulfilled. This happened not only through his words and his deeds: "Above all, . . . the Kingdom is made manifest in the very person of Christ, Son of God and Son of Man, who came 'to serve and to give his life as a ransom for many' (Mk 10:45)."[22] The Kingdom of God is not a concept, a doctrine, or a program subject to free interpretation, but it is before all else *a person* with the face and name of Jesus of Nazareth, the image of the invisible God.[23] If the Kingdom is separated from Jesus, it is no longer the Kingdom of God which he revealed. The result is a distortion of the meaning of the Kingdom, which runs the risk of being transformed into a purely human or ideological goal, and a distortion of the identity of Christ, who no longer appears as the Lord to whom everything must one day be subjected (cf. 1 Cor 15:27).

[22] Second Vatican Ecumenical Council, Dogmatic Constitution on the Church *Lumen Gentium,* 5.

[23] Cf. Second Vatican Ecumenical Council, Pastoral Constitution on the Church in the Modern World *Gaudium et Spes,* 22.

18.3 Likewise, one may not separate the Kingdom from the Church. It is true that the Church is not an end unto herself, since she is ordered toward the Kingdom of God of which she is the seed, sign and instrument. Yet, while remaining distinct from Christ and the Kingdom, the Church is indissolubly united to both. Christ endowed the Church, his Body, with the fullness of the benefits and means of salvation. The Holy Spirit dwells in her, enlivens her with his gifts and charisms, sanctifies, guides and constantly renews her.[24] The result is a unique and special relationship which, while not excluding the action of Christ and the Spirit outside the Church's visible boundaries, confers upon her a specific and necessary role; hence the Church's special connection with the Kingdom of God and of Christ, which she has "the mission of announcing and inaugurating among all peoples."[25]

19 It is within this overall perspective that the reality of the Kingdom is understood. Certainly, the Kingdom demands the promotion of human values, as well as those which can properly be called "evangelical," since they are intimately bound up with the "Good News." But this sort of promotion, which is at the heart of the Church, must not be detached from or opposed to other fundamental tasks, such as proclaiming Christ and his Gospel, and establishing and building up communities which make present and active within mankind the living image of the Kingdom. One need not fear falling thereby into a form of "ecclesiocentrism." Pope Paul VI, who affirmed the existence of "a profound link between Christ, the Church and evangelization,"[26] also said that the Church "is not an end unto herself, but rather is fervently concerned to be completely of Christ, in Christ and for Christ, as well as completely of men, among men and for men."[27]

The Church at the service of the Kingdom

20.1 The Church is effectively and concretely at the service of the Kingdom. This is seen especially in her preaching, which is a call to conversion. Preaching constitutes the Church's first and fundamental way of serving the coming of the Kingdom in individuals and in human society. Eschatological

---

[24] Cf. Second Vatican Ecumenical Council, Dogmatic Constitution on the Church *Lumen Gentium*, 4.

[25] Ibid., 5.

[26] Apostolic Exhortation *Evangelii Nuntiandi* (December 8, 1975), 16: *AAS* 68 (1976), 15.

[27] Address at the Opening of the Third Session of the Second Vatican Ecumenical Council (September 14, 1964): *AAS* 56 (1964), 810.

salvation begins even now in newness of life in Christ: "To all who believed in him, who believed in his name, he gave power to become children of God" (Jn 1:12).

20.2 The Church, then, serves the Kingdom by establishing communities and founding new particular Churches, and by guiding them to mature faith and charity in openness toward others, in service to individuals and society, and in understanding and esteem for human institutions.

20.3 The Church serves the Kingdom by spreading throughout the world the "Gospel values" which are an expression of the Kingdom and which help people to accept God's plan. It is true that the inchoate reality of the Kingdom can also be found beyond the confines of the Church among peoples everywhere, to the extent that they live "Gospel values" and are open to the working of the Spirit who breathes when and where he wills (cf. Jn 3:8). But it must immediately be added that this temporal dimension of the Kingdom remains incomplete unless it is related to the Kingdom of Christ present in the Church and straining toward eschatological fullness.[28]

20.4 The many dimensions of the Kingdom of God[29] do not weaken the foundations and purposes of missionary activity, but rather strengthen and extend them. The Church is the sacrament of salvation for all mankind, and her activity is not limited only to those who accept her message. She is a dynamic force in mankind's journey toward the eschatological Kingdom, and is the sign and promoter of Gospel values.[30] The Church contributes to mankind's pilgrimage of conversion to God's plan through her witness and through such activities as dialogue, human promotion, commitment to justice and peace, education and the care of the sick, and aid to the poor and to children. In carrying on these activities, however, she never loses sight of the priority of the transcendent and spiritual realities which are premises of eschatological salvation.

20.5 Finally, the Church serves the Kingdom by her intercession, since the Kingdom by its very nature is God's gift and work, as we are reminded by the Gospel parables and by the prayer which Jesus taught us. We must ask for the Kingdom, welcome it and make it grow within us; but we must also work together so that it will be welcomed and will grow among all people, until the

---

[28] Cf. Paul VI, Apostolic Exhortation *Evangelii Nuntiandi* (December 8, 1975), 34: *AAS* 68 (1976), 28.

[29] Cf. International Theological Commission, *Select Themes of Ecclesiology on the Occasion of the Twentieth Anniversary of the Closing of the Second Vatican Council* (October 7, 1985), 10: "The Eschatological Character of the Church: Kingdom and Church."

[30] Cf. Second Vatican Ecumenical Council, Pastoral Constitution on the Church in the Modern World *Gaudium et Spes*, 39.

time when Christ "delivers the Kingdom to God the Father" and "God will be everything to everyone" (cf. 1 Cor 15:24, 28).

III

The Holy Spirit, the Principal Agent of Mission

21.1 "At the climax of Jesus' messianic mission, the Holy Spirit becomes present in the Paschal Mystery in all of his divine subjectivity: as the one who is now to continue the salvific work rooted in the sacrifice of the Cross. Of course Jesus entrusts this work to human beings: to the Apostles, to the Church. Nevertheless, in and through them the Holy Spirit remains the transcendent and principal agent for the accomplishment of this work in the human spirit and in the history of the world."[31]

21.2 The Holy Spirit is indeed the principal agent of the whole of the Church's mission. His action is preeminent in the mission *ad gentes*, as can clearly be seen in the early Church: in the conversion of Cornelius (cf. Acts 10), in the decisions made about emerging problems (cf. Acts 15) and in the choice of regions and peoples to be evangelized (cf. Acts 16:6ff). The Spirit worked through the Apostles, but at the same time he was also at work in those who heard them: "Through his action the Good News takes shape in human minds and hearts and extends through history. In all of this it is the Holy Spirit who gives life."[32]

Sent forth "to the end of the earth" (Acts 1:8)

22.1 All the Evangelists, when they describe the risen Christ's meeting with his Apostles, conclude with the "missionary mandate": "All authority in heaven and on earth has been given to me. Go therefore and make disciples of all nations, . . . and lo, I am with you always, to the close of the age" (Mt 28:18-20; cf. Mk 16:15-18; Lk 24:46-49; Jn 20:21-23).

22.2 This is *a sending forth in the Spirit*, as is clearly apparent in the Gospel of John: Christ sends his own into the world, just as the Father has sent him, and to this end he gives them the Spirit. Luke, for his part, closely links the witness the Apostles are to give to Christ with the working of the Spirit, who will enable them to fulfill the mandate they have received.

---

[31] Encyclical Letter *Dominum et Vivificantem* (May 18, 1986), 42: *AAS* 78 (1986), 857.
[32] Ibid., 64: loc. cit., 892.

23.1 The different versions of the "missionary mandate" contain common elements as well as characteristics proper to each. Two elements, however, are found in all the versions. First, there is the universal dimension of the task entrusted to the Apostles, who are sent to "all nations" (Mt 28:19); "into all the world and . . . to the whole creation" (Mk 16:15); to "all nations" (Lk 24:47); "to the end of the earth" (Acts 1:8). Secondly, there is the assurance given to the Apostles by the Lord that they will not be alone in the task, but will receive the strength and the means necessary to carry out their mission. The reference here is to the presence and power of the Spirit and the help of Jesus himself: "And they went forth and preached everywhere, while the Lord worked with them" (Mk 16:20).

23.2 As for the different emphases found in each version, Mark presents mission as proclamation or kerygma: "Preach the Gospel" (Mk 16:15). His aim is to lead his readers to repeat Peter's profession of faith: "You are the Christ" (Mk 8:29), and to say with the Roman centurion who stood before the body of Jesus on the Cross: "Truly this man was the Son of God!" (Mk 15:39). In Matthew, the missionary emphasis is placed on the foundation of the Church and on her teaching (cf. Mt 28:19-20, 16:18). According to him, the mandate shows that the proclamation of the Gospel must be completed by a specific ecclesial and sacramental catechesis. In Luke, mission is presented as witness (cf. Lk 24:48; Acts 1:8), centered especially on the Resurrection (cf. Acts 1:22). The missionary is invited to believe in the transforming power of the Gospel and to proclaim what Luke presents so well, that is, conversion to God's love and mercy, the experience of a complete liberation which goes to the root of all evil, namely sin.

23.3 John is the only Evangelist to speak explicitly of a "mandate," a word equivalent to "mission." He directly links the mission which Jesus entrusts to his disciples with the mission which he himself has received from the Father: "As the Father has sent me, even so I send you" (Jn 20:21). Addressing the Father, Jesus says: "As you sent me into the world, so I have sent them into the world" (Jn 17:18). The entire missionary sense of John's Gospel is expressed in the "priestly prayer": "This is eternal life, that they know you, the only true God, and Jesus Christ whom you have sent" (Jn 17:3). The ultimate purpose of mission is to enable people to share in the communion which exists between the Father and the Son. The disciples are to live in unity with one another, remaining in the Father and the Son, so that the world may know and believe (cf. Jn 17:21-23). This is a very important missionary text. It makes us understand that we are missionaries above all because of *what we are* as a Church whose innermost life is unity in love, even before we become missionaries *in word or deed.*

23.4 The four Gospels therefore bear witness to a certain pluralism within the fundamental unity of the same mission, a pluralism which reflects different experiences and situations within the first Christian communities. It is also the result of the driving force of the Spirit himself; it encourages us to pay heed to the variety of missionary charisms and to the diversity of circumstances and peoples. Nevertheless, all the Evangelists stress that the mission of the disciples is to cooperate in the mission of Christ: "Lo, I am with you always, to the close of the age" (Mt 28:20). Mission, then, is based not on human abilities but on the power of the risen Lord.

The Spirit directs the Church's mission

24.1 The mission of the Church, like that of Jesus, is God's work or, as Luke often puts it, the work of the Spirit. After the Resurrection and Ascension of Jesus, the Apostles have a powerful experience which completely transforms them: the experience of Pentecost. The coming of the Holy Spirit makes them *witnesses* and *prophets* (cf. Acts 1:8, 2:17-18). It fills them with a serene courage which impels them to pass on to others their experience of Jesus and the hope which motivates them. The Spirit gives them the ability to bear witness to Jesus with "boldness."[33]

24.2 When the first evangelizers go down from Jerusalem, the Spirit becomes even more of a "guide," helping them to choose both those to whom they are to go and the places to which their missionary journey is to take them. The working of the Spirit is manifested particularly in the impetus given to the mission which, in accordance with Christ's words, spreads out from Jerusalem to all of Judea and Samaria, and to the farthest ends of the earth.

24.3 The Acts of the Apostles records six summaries of the "missionary discourses" which were addressed to the Jews during the Church's infancy (cf. Acts 2:22-39, 3:12-26, 4:9-12, 5:29-32, 10:34-43, 13:16-41). These model speeches, delivered by Peter and by Paul, proclaim Jesus and invite those listening to "be converted," that is, to accept Jesus in faith and to let themselves be transformed in him by the Spirit.

24.4 Paul and Barnabas are impelled by the Spirit to go to the Gentiles (cf. Acts 13:46-48), a development not without certain tensions and problems. How are these converted Gentiles to live their faith in Jesus? Are they bound by the traditions of Judaism and the law of circumcision? At the first Council,

---

[33] The Greek word *parrhesia* also means enthusiasm or energy; cf. Acts 2:29; 4:13, 29, 31; 9:27-28; 13:46; 14:3; 18:26; 19:8, 26; 28:31.

which gathers the members of the different Churches together with the Apostles in Jerusalem, a decision is taken which is acknowledged as coming from the Spirit: it is not necessary for a Gentile to submit to the Jewish Law in order to become a Christian (cf. Acts 15:5-11, 28). From now on the Church opens her doors and becomes the house which all may enter, and in which all can feel at home, while keeping their own culture and traditions, provided that these are not contrary to the Gospel.

25.1 The missionaries continued along this path, taking into account people's hopes and expectations, their anguish and sufferings, as well as their culture, in order to proclaim to them salvation in Christ. The speeches in Lystra and Athens (cf. Acts 14:15-17, 17:22-31) are acknowledged as models for the evangelization of the Gentiles. In these speeches Paul enters into "dialogue" with the cultural and religious values of different peoples. To the Lycaonians, who practiced a cosmic religion, he speaks of religious experiences related to the cosmos. With the Greeks he discusses philosophy and quotes their own poets (cf. Acts 17:18, 26-28). The God whom Paul wishes to reveal is already present in their lives; indeed, this God has created them and mysteriously guides nations and history. But if they are to recognize the true God, they must abandon the false gods which they themselves have made and open themselves to the One whom God has sent to remedy their ignorance and satisfy the longings of their hearts. These are speeches which offer an example of the inculturation of the Gospel.

25.2 Under the impulse of the Spirit, the Christian faith is decisively opened to the "nations." Witness to Christ spreads to the most important centers of the eastern Mediterranean and then to Rome and the far regions of the West. It is the Spirit who is the source of the drive to press on, not only geographically but also beyond the frontiers of race and religion, for a truly universal mission.

The Holy Spirit makes the whole Church missionary

26.1 The Spirit leads the company of believers to "form a community," to be the Church. After Peter's first proclamation on the day of Pentecost and the conversions that followed, the first community takes shape (cf. Acts 2:42-47, 4:32-35).

26.2 One of the central purposes of mission is to bring people together in hearing the Gospel, in fraternal communion, in prayer and in the Eucharist. To live in "fraternal communion" (*koinonia*) means to be "of one heart and soul" (Acts 4:32), establishing fellowship from every point of view: human, spiritual and material. Indeed, a true Christian community is also committed to distributing earthly goods, so that no one is in want, and all can receive such goods "as they need" (cf. Acts 2:45, 4:35). The first communities, made up of "glad and generous hearts" (Acts 2:46), were open and missionary: they enjoyed "favor with all the people" (Acts 2:47). Even before activity, mission means witness and a way of life that shines out to others.[34]

27.1 The Acts of the Apostles indicates that the mission which was directed first to Israel and then to the Gentiles develops on many levels. First and foremost, there is the group of the Twelve which as a single body, led by Peter, proclaims the Good News. Then there is the community of believers, which in its way of life and its activity bears witness to the Lord and converts the Gentiles (cf. Acts 2:46-47). Then there are the special envoys sent out to proclaim the Gospel. Thus the Christian community at Antioch sends its members forth on mission; having fasted, prayed and celebrated the Eucharist, the community recognizes that the Spirit has chosen Paul and Barnabas to be "sent forth" (cf. Acts 13:1-4). In its origins, then, mission is seen as a community commitment, a responsibility of the local Church, which needs "missionaries" in order to push forward toward new frontiers. Side by side with those who had been sent forth, there were also others, who bore spontaneous witness to the newness which had transformed their lives, and who subsequently provided a link between the emerging communities and the apostolic Church.

27.2 Reading the Acts of the Apostles helps us to realize that at the beginning of the Church the mission *ad gentes*, while it had missionaries dedicated "for life" by a special vocation, was in fact considered the normal outcome of Christian living, to which every believer was committed through the witness of personal conduct and through explicit proclamation whenever possible.

The Spirit is present and active in every time and place

28.1 The Spirit manifests himself in a special way in the Church and in her members. Nevertheless, his presence and activity are universal, limited neither by space nor time.[35] The Second Vatican Council recalls that the Spirit

---

[34] Cf. Paul VI, Apostolic Exhortation *Evangelii Nuntiandi* (December 8, 1975), 41-42: *AAS* 68 (1976), 31-33.

[35] Cf. Encyclical Letter *Dominum et Vivificantem* (May 18, 1986), 53: *AAS* 78 (1986), 874-875.

is at work in the heart of every person, through the "seeds of the Word," to be found in human initiatives — including religious ones — and in mankind's efforts to attain truth, goodness and God himself.[36]

28.2 The Spirit offers the human race "the light and strength to respond to its highest calling"; through the Spirit, "mankind attains in faith to the contemplation and savoring of the mystery of God's design"; indeed, "we are obliged to hold that the Holy Spirit offers everyone the possibility of sharing in the Paschal Mystery in a manner known to God."[37] The Church "is aware that humanity is being continually stirred by the Spirit of God and can therefore never be completely indifferent to the problems of religion" and that "people will always . . . want to know what meaning to give their life, their activity and their death."[38] The Spirit, therefore, is at the very source of man's existential and religious questioning, a questioning which is occasioned not only by contingent situations but by the very structure of his being.[39]

28.3 The Spirit's presence and activity affect not only the individuals but also society and history, peoples, cultures and religions. Indeed, the Spirit is at the origin of the noble ideals and undertakings which benefit humanity on its journey through history: "The Spirit of God with marvelous foresight directs the course of the ages and renews the face of the earth."[40] The risen Christ "is now at work in human hearts through the strength of his Spirit, not only instilling a desire for the world to come but also thereby animating, purifying and reinforcing the noble aspirations which drive the human family to make its life one that is more human and to direct the whole earth to this end."[41] Again, it is the Spirit who sows the "seeds of the Word" present in various customs and cultures, preparing them for full maturity in Christ.[42]

---

[36] Cf. Second Vatican Ecumenical Council, Decree on the Church's Missionary Activity *Ad Gentes*, 3, 11, 15; Pastoral Constitution on the Church in the Modern World *Gaudium et Spes*, 10-11, 22, 26, 38, 41, 92-93.

[37] Second Vatican Ecumenical Council, Pastoral Constitution on the Church in the Modern World *Gaudium et Spes*, 10, 15, 22.

[38] Ibid., 41.

[39] Cf. Encyclical Letter *Dominum et Vivificantem* (May 18, 1986), 54: *AAS* 78 (1986), 875-876.

[40] Second Vatican Ecumenical Council, Pastoral Constitution on the Church in the Modern World *Gaudium et Spes*, 26.

[41] Ibid., 38, cf. 93.

[42] Cf. Second Vatican Ecumenical Council, Dogmatic Constitution on the Church *Lumen Gentium*, 17; Decree on the Church's Missionary Activity *Ad Gentes*, 3, 15.

29.1 Thus the Spirit, who "blows where he wills" (cf. Jn 3:8), who "was already at work in the world before Christ was glorified,"[43] and who "has filled the world, . . . holds all things together [and] knows what is said" (Wis 1:7), leads us to broaden our vision in order to ponder his activity in every time and place.[44] I have repeatedly called this fact to mind, and it has guided me in my meetings with a wide variety of peoples. The Church's relationship with other religions is dictated by a twofold respect: "Respect for man in his quest for answers to the deepest questions of his life, and respect for the action of the Spirit in man."[45] Excluding any mistaken interpretation, the interreligious meeting held in Assisi was meant to confirm my conviction that "every authentic prayer is prompted by the Holy Spirit, who is mysteriously present in every human heart."[46]

29.2 This is the same Spirit who was at work in the Incarnation and in the life, death and Resurrection of Jesus, and who is at work in the Church. He is therefore not an alternative to Christ, nor does he fill a sort of void which is sometimes suggested as existing between Christ and the Logos. Whatever the Spirit brings about in human hearts and in the history of peoples, in cultures and religions serves as a preparation for the Gospel[47] and can only be understood in reference to Christ, the Word who took flesh by the power of the Spirit "so that as perfectly human he would save all human beings and sum up all things."[48]

29.3 Moreover, the universal activity of the Spirit is not to be separated from his particular activity within the Body of Christ, which is the Church. Indeed, it is always the Spirit who is at work, both when he gives life to the Church and impels her to proclaim Christ, and when he implants and develops his gifts in all individuals and peoples, guiding the Church to discover these gifts, to foster them and to receive them through dialogue. Every form of

---

[43] Second Vatican Ecumenical Council, Decree on the Church's Missionary Activity *Ad Gentes*, 4.

[44] Cf. Encyclical Letter *Dominum et Vivificantem* (May 18, 1986), 53: *AAS* 78 (1986), 874.

[45] Address to Representatives of Non-Christian Religions, Madras (February 5, 1986): *AAS* 78 (1986), 767; cf. Message to the Peoples of Asia, Manila (February 21, 1981), 2-4: *AAS* 73 (1981), 392-393; Address to Representatives of Other Religions, Tokyo (February 24, 1981), 3-4: *Insegnamenti* IV/1 (1981), 507-508.

[46] Address to the Cardinals and the Roman Curia (December 22, 1986), 11: *AAS* 79 (1987), 1089.

[47] Cf. Second Vatican Ecumenical Council, Dogmatic Constitution on the Church *Lumen Gentium*, 16.

[48] Second Vatican Ecumenical Council, Pastoral Constitution on the Church in the Modern World *Gaudium et Spes*, 45; cf. Encyclical Letter *Dominum et Vivificantem* (May 18, 1986), 54: *AAS* 78 (1986), 876.

the Spirit's presence is to be welcomed with respect and gratitude, but the discernment of this presence is the responsibility of the Church, to which Christ gave his Spirit in order to guide her into all the truth (cf. Jn 16:13).

Missionary activity is only beginning

30.1 Our own time, with humanity on the move and in continual search, demands *a resurgence of the Church's missionary activity*. The horizons and possibilities for mission are growing ever wider, and we Christians are called to an apostolic courage based upon trust in the Spirit. *He is the principal agent of mission!*

30.2 The history of humanity has known many major turning points which have encouraged missionary outreach, and the Church, guided by the Spirit, has always responded to them with generosity and farsightedness. Results have not been lacking. Not long ago we celebrated the millennium of the evangelization of Rus' and the Slav peoples, and we are now preparing to celebrate the five hundredth anniversary of the evangelization of the Americas. Similarly, there have been recent commemorations of the centenaries of the first missions in various countries of Asia, Africa and Oceania. Today the Church must face other challenges and push forward to new frontiers, both in the initial mission *ad gentes* and in the new evangelization of those peoples who have already heard Christ proclaimed. Today all Christians, the particular Churches and the universal Church, are called to have the same courage that inspired the missionaries of the past, and the same readiness to listen to the voice of the Spirit.

IV

The Vast Horizons of the Mission *Ad Gentes*

31.1 The Lord Jesus sent his Apostles to every person, people and place on earth. In the Apostles, the Church received a universal mission — one which knows no boundaries — which involves the communication of salvation in its integrity according to that fullness of life which Christ came to bring (cf. Jn 10:10). The Church was "sent by Christ to reveal and communicate the love of God to all people and nations."[49]

31.2 This mission is one and undivided, having one origin and one final purpose; but within it, there are different tasks and kinds of activity. First,

---

[49] Second Vatican Ecumenical Council, Decree on the Church's Missionary Activity *Ad Gentes*, 10.

there is the missionary activity which we call *mission ad gentes*, in reference to the opening words of the Council's Decree on this subject. This is one of the Church's fundamental activities: it is essential and never-ending. The Church, in fact, "cannot withdraw from her *permanent mission of bringing the Gospel* to the multitudes — the millions and millions of men and women — who as yet do not know Christ the Redeemer of humanity. In a specific way this is the missionary work which Jesus entrusted and still entrusts each day to his Church."[50]

A complex and ever-changing religious picture

32.1 Today we face a religious situation which is extremely varied and changing. Peoples are on the move; social and religious realities which were once clear and well defined are today increasingly complex. We need only think of certain phenomena such as urbanization, mass migration, the flood of refugees, the de-Christianization of countries with ancient Christian traditions, the increasing influence of the Gospel and its values in overwhelmingly non-Christian countries, and the proliferation of messianic cults and religious sects. Religious and social upheaval makes it difficult to apply in practice certain ecclesial distinctions and categories to which we have become accustomed. Even before the Council it was said that some Christian cities and countries had become "mission territories"; the situation has certainly not improved in the years since then.

32.2 On the other hand, missionary work has been very fruitful throughout the world, so that there are now well-established Churches, sometimes so sound and mature that they are able to provide for the needs of their own communities and even send personnel to evangelize in other Churches and territories. This is in contrast to some traditionally Christian areas which are in need of re-evangelization. As a result, some are questioning whether it is still appropriate to speak of *specific missionary activity* or specifically "missionary" areas, or whether we should speak instead of a *single missionary situation*, with one single mission, the same everywhere. The difficulty of relating this complex and changing reality to the mandate of evangelization is apparent in the "language of mission." For example, there is a certain hesitation to use the terms "mission" and "missionaries," which are considered obsolete and as having negative historical connotations. People prefer to use instead the noun "mission" in the singular and the adjective "missionary" to describe all the Church's activities.

[50] Post-Synodal Apostolic Exhortation *Christifideles Laici* (December 30, 1988), 35: *AAS* 81 (1989), 457.

32.3 This uneasiness denotes a real change, one which has certain positive aspects. The so-called return or "repatriation" of the *missions* into the Church's mission, the insertion of *missiology* into *ecclesiology*, and the integration of both areas into the Trinitarian plan of salvation have given a fresh impetus to missionary activity itself, which is not considered a marginal task for the Church but is situated at the center of her life, as a fundamental commitment of the whole People of God. Nevertheless, care must be taken to avoid the risk of putting very different situations on the same level and of reducing, or even eliminating, the Church's mission and missionaries *ad gentes*. To say that the whole Church is missionary does not preclude the existence of a specific mission *ad gentes*, just as saying that all Catholics must be missionaries not only does not exclude, but actually requires that there be persons who have a specific vocation to be "life-long missionaries *ad gentes*."

Mission "ad gentes" retains its value

33.1 The fact that there is a diversity of activities *in the Church's one mission* is not intrinsic to that mission, but arises from the variety of circumstances in which that mission is carried out.[51] Looking at today's world from the viewpoint of evangelization, we can distinguish *three situations*.

33.2 First, there is the situation which the Church's missionary activity addresses: peoples, groups, and sociocultural contexts in which Christ and his Gospel are not known, or which lack Christian communities sufficiently mature to be able to incarnate the faith in their own environment and proclaim it to other groups. This is mission *ad gentes* in the proper sense of the term.[52]

33.3 Secondly, there are Christian communities with adequate and solid ecclesial structures. They are fervent in their faith and in Christian living. They bear witness to the Gospel in their surroundings and have a sense of commitment to the universal mission. In these communities the Church carries out her activity and pastoral care.

33.4 Thirdly, there is an intermediate situation, particularly in countries with ancient Christian roots, and occasionally in the younger Churches as well, where entire groups of the baptized have lost a living sense of the faith, or even no longer consider themselves members of the Church, and live a life far removed from Christ and his Gospel. In this case what is needed is a "new evangelization" or a "re-evangelization."

---

[51] Cf. Second Vatican Ecumenical Council, Decree on the Church's Missionary Activity *Ad Gentes*, 6.

[52] Cf. ibid., 6.

34.1 Missionary activity proper, namely the mission *ad gentes*, is directed to "peoples or groups who do not yet believe in Christ," "who are far from Christ," in whom the Church "has not yet taken root"[53] and whose culture has not yet been influenced by the Gospel.[54] It is distinct from other ecclesial activities inasmuch as it is addressed to groups and settings which are non-Christian because the preaching of the Gospel and the presence of the Church are either absent or insufficient. It can thus be characterized as the work of proclaiming Christ and his Gospel, building up the local Church and promoting the values of the Kingdom. The specific nature of this mission *ad gentes* consists in its being addressed to "non-Christians." It is therefore necessary to ensure that this specifically "missionary work that Jesus entrusted and still entrusts each day to his Church"[55] does not become an indistinguishable part of the overall mission of the whole People of God and as a result become neglected or forgotten.

34.2 On the other hand, the boundaries between *pastoral care of the faithful, new evangelization* and *specific missionary activity* are not clearly definable, and it is unthinkable to create barriers between them or to put them into watertight compartments. Nevertheless, there must be no lessening of the impetus to preach the Gospel and to establish new Churches among peoples or communities where they do not yet exist, for this is the first task of the Church, which has been sent forth to all peoples and to the very ends of the earth. Without the mission *ad gentes*, the Church's very missionary dimension would be deprived of its essential meaning and of the very activity that exemplifies it.

34.3 Also to be noted is the real and growing *interdependence* which exists between these various saving activities of the Church. Each of them influences, stimulates and assists the others. The missionary thrust fosters exchanges between the Churches and directs them toward the larger world, with positive influences in every direction. The Churches in traditionally Christian countries, for example, involved as they are in the challenging task of new evangelization, are coming to understand more clearly that they cannot be missionaries to non-Christians in other countries and continents unless they are seriously concerned about the non-Christians at home. Hence missionary activity *ad intra* is a credible sign and a stimulus for missionary activity *ad extra*, and vice versa.

---

[53] Cf. ibid., 6, 23, 27.

[54] Cf. Paul VI, Apostolic Exhortation *Evangelii Nuntiandi* (December 8, 1975), 18-20: *AAS* 68 (1976), 17-19.

[55] Post-Synodal Apostolic Exhortation *Christifideles Laici* (December 30, 1988), 35: *AAS* 81 (1989), 457.

To all peoples, in spite of difficulties

35.1 The mission *ad gentes* faces an enormous task, which is in no way disappearing. Indeed, both from the numerical standpoint of demographic increase and from the sociocultural standpoint of the appearance of new relationships, contacts and changing situations, the mission seems destined to have ever wider horizons. The task of proclaiming Jesus Christ to all peoples appears to be immense and out of all proportion to the Church's human resources.

35.2 *The difficulties* seem insurmountable and could easily lead to discouragement, if it were a question of a merely human enterprise. In certain countries missionaries are refused entry. In others, not only is evangelization forbidden but conversion as well, and even Christian worship. Elsewhere the obstacles are of a cultural nature: passing on the Gospel message seems irrelevant or incomprehensible, and conversion is seen as a rejection of one's own people and culture.

36.1 Nor are *difficulties* lacking *within* the People of God; indeed these difficulties are the most painful of all. As the first of these difficulties Pope Paul VI pointed to "the lack of fervor (which) is all the more serious because it comes from within. It is manifested in fatigue, disenchantment, compromise, lack of interest and above all lack of joy and hope."[56] Other great obstacles to the Church's missionary work include past and present divisions among Christians,[57] de-christianization within Christian countries, the decrease of vocations to the apostolate, and the counter-witness of believers and Christian communities failing to follow the model of Christ in their lives. But one of the most serious reasons for the lack of interest in the missionary task is a widespread indifferentism, which, sad to say, is found also among Christians. It is based on incorrect theological perspectives and is characterized by a religious relativism which leads to the belief that "one religion is as good as another." We can add, using the words of Pope Paul VI, that there are also certain "excuses which would impede evangelization. The most insidious of these excuses are certainly the ones which people claim to find support for in such and such a teaching of the Council."[58]

36.2 In this regard, I earnestly ask theologians and professional Christian journalists to intensify the service they render to the Church's mission in

---

[56] Apostolic Exhortation *Evangelii Nuntiandi* (December 8, 1975), 80: *AAS* 68 (1976), 73.

[57] Cf. Second Vatican Ecumenical Council, Decree on the Church's Missionary Activity *Ad Gentes*, 6.

[58] Apostolic Exhortation *Evangelii Nuntiandi* (December 8, 1975), 80: *AAS* 68 (1976), 73.

order to discover the deep meaning of their work, along the sure path of "thinking with the Church" (*sentire cum Ecclesia*).

36.3 Internal and external difficulties must not make us pessimistic or inactive. What counts, here as in every area of Christian life, is the confidence that comes from faith, from the certainty that it is not we who are the principal agents of the Church's mission, but Jesus Christ and his Spirit. We are only co-workers, and when we have done all that we can, we must say: "We are unworthy servants; we have only done what was our duty" (Lk 17:10).

Parameters of the Church's mission "ad gentes"

37.1 By virtue of Christ's universal mandate, the mission *ad gentes* knows no boundaries. Still, it is possible to determine certain parameters within which that mission is exercised, in order to gain a real grasp of the situation.

37.2 (a) *Territorial limits*. Missionary activity has normally been defined in terms of specific territories. The Second Vatican Council acknowledged the territorial dimension of the mission *ad gentes*,[59] a dimension which even today remains important for determining responsibilities, competencies and the geographical limits of missionary activity. Certainly, a universal mission implies a universal perspective. Indeed, the Church refuses to allow her missionary presence to be hindered by geographical boundaries or political barriers. But it is also true that missionary activity *ad gentes*, being different from the pastoral care of the faithful and the new evangelization of the non-practicing, is exercised within well-defined territories and groups of people.

37.3 The growth in the number of new Churches in recent times should not deceive us. Within the territories entrusted to these Churches — particularly in Asia, but also in Africa, Latin America and Oceania — there remain vast regions still to be evangelized. In many nations entire peoples and cultural areas of great importance have not yet been reached by the proclamation of the Gospel and the presence of the local Church.[60] Even in traditionally Christian countries there are regions that are under the special structures of the mission *ad gentes*, with groups and areas not yet evangelized. Thus, in these countries too there is a need not only for a new evangelization, but also, in some cases, for an initial evangelization.[61]

37.4 Situations are not, however, the same everywhere. While acknowledging that statements about the missionary responsibility of the Church are

---

[59] Cf. Decree on the Church's Missionary Activity *Ad Gentes*, 6.

[60] Cf. ibid., 20.

[61] Cf. Address to the Members of the Symposium of the Council of the European Episcopal Conferences (October 11, 1985): *AAS* 78 (1986), 178-189.

not credible unless they are backed up by a serious commitment to a new evangelization in the traditionally Christian countries, it does not seem justified to regard as identical the situation of a people which has never known Jesus Christ and that of a people which has known him, accepted him and then rejected him, while continuing to live in a culture which in large part has absorbed Gospel principles and values. These are two basically different situations with regard to the faith.

37.5 Thus the criterion of geography, although somewhat imprecise and always provisional, is still a valid indicator of the frontiers toward which missionary activity must be directed. There are countries and geographical and cultural areas which lack indigenous Christian communities. In other places, these communities are so small as not to be a clear sign of a Christian presence; or they lack the dynamism to evangelize their societies, or belong to a minority population not integrated into the dominant culture of the nation. Particularly in Asia, toward which the Church's mission *ad gentes* ought to be chiefly directed, Christians are a small minority, even though sometimes there are significant numbers of converts and outstanding examples of Christian presence.

37.6 (b) *New worlds and new social phenomena.* The rapid and profound transformations which characterize today's world, especially in the southern hemisphere, are having a powerful effect on the overall missionary picture. Where before there were stable human and social situations, today everything is in flux. One thinks, for example, of urbanization and the massive growth of cities, especially where demographic pressure is greatest. In not a few countries, over half the population already lives in a few "megalopolises," where human problems are often aggravated by the feeling of anonymity experienced by masses of people.

37.7 In the modern age, missionary activity has been carried out especially in isolated regions which are far from centers of civilization and which are hard to penetrate because of difficulties of communication, language or climate. Today the image of mission *ad gentes* is perhaps changing: efforts should be concentrated on the big cities, where new customs and styles of living arise together with new forms of culture and communication, which then influence the wider population. It is true that the "option for the neediest" means that we should not overlook the most abandoned and isolated human groups, but it is also true that individual or small groups cannot be evangelized if we neglect the centers where a new humanity, so to speak, is emerging, and where new models of development are taking shape. The future of the younger nations is being shaped in the cities.

37.8 Speaking of the future, we cannot forget the young, who in many countries comprise more than half the population. How do we bring the message of Christ to non-Christian young people who represent the future of entire continents? Clearly, the ordinary means of pastoral work are not sufficient: what are needed are associations, institutions, special centers and groups, and cultural and social initiatives for young people. This is a field where modern ecclesial movements have ample room for involvement.

37.9 Among the great changes taking place in the contemporary world, migration has produced a new phenomenon: non-Christians are becoming very numerous in traditionally Christian countries, creating fresh opportunities for contacts and cultural exchanges, and calling the Church to hospitality, dialogue, assistance and, in a word, fraternity. Among migrants, refugees occupy a very special place and deserve the greatest attention. Today there are many millions of refugees in the world and their number is constantly increasing. They have fled from conditions of political oppression and inhuman misery, from famine and drought of catastrophic proportions. The Church must make them part of her overall apostolic concern.

37.10 Finally, we may mention the situations of poverty — often on an intolerable scale — which have been created in not a few countries, and which are often the cause of mass migration. The community of believers in Christ is challenged by these inhuman situations: the proclamation of Christ and the Kingdom of God must become the means for restoring the human dignity of these people.

37.11 (c) *Cultural sectors: the modern equivalents of the Areopagus.* After preaching in a number of places, Saint Paul arrived in Athens, where he went to the Areopagus and proclaimed the Gospel in language appropriate to and understandable in those surroundings (cf. Acts 17:22-31). At that time the Areopagus represented the cultural center of the learned people of Athens, and today it can be taken as a symbol of the new sectors in which the Gospel must be proclaimed.

37.12 The first Areopagus of the modern age is the *world of communications,* which is unifying humanity and turning it into what is known as a "global village." The means of social communication have become so important as to be for many the chief means of information and education, of guidance and inspiration in their behavior as individuals, families and within society at large. In particular, the younger generation is growing up in a world conditioned by the mass media. To some degree perhaps this Areopagus has been neglected. Generally, preference has been given to other means of preaching the Gospel and of Christian education, while the mass media are left to the initiative of individuals or small groups and enter into pastoral planning only in a secondary way. Involvement in the mass media, however, is not meant merely to strengthen the preaching of the Gospel. There is a deeper reality involved here: since the very evangelization of modern culture depends to a great extent on the influence of the media, it is not enough to use the media simply to spread the Christian message and the Church's authentic teaching. It is also necessary to integrate that message into the "new culture" created by modern communications. This is a complex issue, since the "new culture" originates not just from whatever content is eventually expressed, but from the very fact that there exist new ways of communicating, with new languages, new techniques and a new psychology. Pope Paul VI said that "the split between the Gospel and culture is undoubtedly the tragedy of our time,"[62] and the field of communications fully confirms this judgment.

37.13 There are many other forms of the "Areopagus" in the modern world toward which the Church's missionary activity ought to be directed; for example, commitment to peace, development and the liberation of peoples; the rights of individuals and peoples, especially those of minorities; the advancement of women and children; safeguarding the created world. These too are areas which need to be illuminated with the light of the Gospel.

37.14 We must also mention the immense "Areopagus" of culture, scientific research, and international relations which promote dialogue and open up new possibilities. We would do well to be attentive to these modern areas of activity and to be involved in them. People sense that they are, as it were, traveling together across life's sea, and that they are called to ever greater unity and solidarity. Solutions to pressing problems must be studied, discussed and worked out with the involvement of all. That is why International Organizations and meetings are proving increasingly important in many sectors of human life, from culture to politics, from the economy to research. Christians who live and work in this international sphere must always remember their duty to bear witness to the Gospel.

38 Our times are both momentous and fascinating. While on the one hand people seem to be pursuing material prosperity and to be sinking ever deeper into consumerism and materialism, on the other hand we are witnessing a desperate search for meaning, the need for an inner life, and a desire to learn new forms and methods of meditation and prayer. Not only in cultures with strong religious elements, but also in secularized societies, the spiritual dimension of life is being sought after as an antidote to dehumanization. This

---

[62] Apostolic Exhortation *Evangelii Nuntiandi* (December 8, 1975), 20: *AAS* 68 (1976), 19.

phenomenon — the so-called "religious revival" — is not without ambiguity, but it also represents an opportunity. The Church has an immense spiritual patrimony to offer mankind, a heritage in Christ, who called himself "the way, and the truth, and the life" (Jn 14:6): it is the Christian path to meeting God, to prayer, to asceticism, and to the search for life's meaning. Here too there is an "Areopagus" to be evangelized.

Fidelity to Christ and the promotion of human freedom

39.1 All forms of missionary activity are marked by an awareness that one is furthering human freedom by proclaiming Jesus Christ. The Church must be faithful to Christ, whose Body she is, and whose mission she continues. She must necessarily "go the same road that Christ went — namely a road of poverty, obedience, service and self-sacrifice even unto death, from which he emerged a victor through his Resurrection."[63] The Church is thus obliged to do everything possible to carry out her mission in the world and to reach all peoples. And she has the right to do this, a right given her by God for the accomplishment of his plan. Religious freedom, which is still at times limited or restricted, remains the premise and guarantee of all the freedoms that ensure the common good of individuals and peoples. It is to be hoped that authentic religious freedom will be granted to all people everywhere. The Church strives for this in all countries, especially in those with a Catholic majority, where she has greater influence. But it is not a question of the religion of the majority or the minority, but of an inalienable right of each and every human person.

39.2 On her part, the Church addresses people with full respect for their freedom.[64] Her mission does not restrict freedom but rather promotes it. *The Church proposes; she imposes nothing.* She respects individuals and cultures, and she honors the sanctuary of conscience. To those who for various reasons oppose missionary activity, the Church repeats: *Open the doors to Christ!*

39.3 Here I wish to address all the particular Churches, both young and old. The world is steadily growing more united, and the Gospel spirit must lead us to overcome cultural and nationalistic barriers, avoiding all isolationism. Pope Benedict XV already cautioned the missionaries of his time lest they "forget their proper dignity and think more of their earthly homeland than of

---

[63] Second Vatican Ecumenical Council, Decree on the Church's Missionary Activity *Ad Gentes,* 5; cf. Dogmatic Constitution on the Church *Lumen Gentium,* 8.

[64] Cf. Second Vatican Ecumenical Council, Declaration on Religious Freedom *Dignitatis Humanae,* 3-4; Paul VI, Apostolic Exhortation *Evangelii Nuntiandi* (December 8, 1975), 79-80: AAS 68 (1976), 71-75; John Paul II, Encyclical Letter *Redemptor Hominis* (March 4, 1979), 12: AAS 71 (1979), 278-281.

their heavenly one."[65] This same advice is valid today for the particular Churches: Open the doors to missionaries, for "each individual Church that would voluntarily cut itself off from the universal Church would lose its relationship to God's plan and would be impoverished in its ecclesial mission."[66]

Directing attention toward the South and the East

40.1 Today missionary activity still represents the greatest challenge for the Church. As the end of the second millennium of the Redemption draws near, it is clear that the peoples who have not yet received an initial proclamation of Christ constitute the majority of mankind. The results of missionary activity in modern times are certainly positive. The Church has been established on every continent; indeed today the majority of believers and particular Churches is to be found no longer in Europe but on the continents which missionaries have opened up to the faith.

40.2 The fact remains, however, that the "ends of the earth" to which the Gospel must be brought are growing ever more distant. Tertullian's saying, that the Gospel has been proclaimed to all the earth and to all peoples,[67] is still very far from being a reality. The mission *ad gentes* is still in its infancy. New peoples appear on the world scene, and they too have a right to receive the proclamation of salvation. Population growth in non-Christian countries of the South and the East is constantly increasing the number of people who remain unaware of Christ's Redemption.

40.3 We need therefore to direct our attention toward those geographical areas and cultural settings which still remain uninfluenced by the Gospel. All who believe in Christ should feel, as an integral part of their faith, an apostolic concern to pass on to others its light and joy. This concern must become, as it were, a hunger and thirst to make the Lord known, given the vastness of the non-Christian world.

V

The Paths of Mission

41.1 "Missionary activity is nothing other and nothing less than the manifestation or epiphany of God's plan and its fulfillment in the world and in history; in this history God, by means of missions, clearly accomplishes the

---

[65] Apostolic Letter *Maximum Illud* (November 30, 1919): *AAS* 11 (1919), 446.

[66] Paul VI, Apostolic Exhortation *Evangelii Nuntiandi* (December 8, 1975), 62: *AAS* 68 (1976), 52.

[67] Cf. *De Praescriptione Haereticorum*, XX: *CCL* I, 201-202.

history of salvation."[68] What paths does the Church follow in order to achieve this goal?

41.2 Mission is a single but complex reality, and it develops in a variety of ways. Among these ways, some have particular importance in the present situation of the Church and the world.

The first form of evangelization is witness

42.1 People today put more trust in witnesses than in teachers,[69] in experience than in teaching, and in life and action than in theories. The witness of a Christian life is the first and irreplaceable form of mission: Christ, whose mission we continue, is the "witness" *par excellence* (Rev 1:5, 3:14) and the model of all Christian witness. The Holy Spirit accompanies the Church along her way and associates her with the witness he gives to Christ (cf. Jn 15:26-27).

42.2 The first form of witness is *the very life of the missionary, of the Christian family*, and *of the ecclesial community*, which reveal a new way of living. The missionary who, despite all his or her human limitations and defects, lives a simple life, taking Christ as the model, is a sign of God and of transcendent realities. But everyone in the Church, striving to imitate the Divine Master, can and must bear this kind of witness;[70] in many cases it is the only possible way of being a missionary.

42.3 The evangelical witness which the world finds most appealing is that of concern for people, and of charity toward the poor, the weak and those who suffer. The complete generosity underlying this attitude and these actions stands in marked contrast to human selfishness. It raises precise questions which lead to God and to the Gospel. A commitment to peace, justice, human rights and human promotion is also a witness to the Gospel when it is a sign of concern for persons and is directed toward integral human development.[71]

43.1 Christians and Christian communities are very much a part of the life of their respective nations and can be a sign of the Gospel in their fidelity to their native land, people and national culture, while always preserving the

---

[68] Second Vatican Ecumenical Council, Decree on the Church's Missionary Activity *Ad Gentes*, 9, cf. 10-18.

[69] Cf. Paul VI, Apostolic Exhortation *Evangelii Nuntiandi* (December 8, 1975), 41: *AAS* 68 (1976), 31-32.

[70] Cf. Second Vatican Ecumenical Council, Dogmatic Constitution on the Church *Lumen Gentium*, 28, 35, 38; Pastoral Constitution on the Church in the Modern World *Gaudium et Spes*, 43; Decree on the Church's Missionary Activity *Ad Gentes*, 11-12.

[71] Cf. Paul VI, Encyclical Letter *Populorum Progressio* (March 26, 1967), 21, 42: *AAS* 59 (1967), 267-268, 278.

freedom brought by Christ. Christianity is open to universal brotherhood, for all men and women are sons and daughters of the same Father and brothers and sisters in Christ.

43.2 The Church is called to bear witness to Christ by taking courageous and prophetic stands in the face of the corruption of political or economic power; by not seeking her own glory and material wealth; by using her resources to serve the poorest of the poor and by imitating Christ's own simplicity of life. The Church and her missionaries must also bear the witness of humility, above all with regard to themselves — a humility which allows them to make a personal and communal examination of conscience in order to correct in their behavior whatever is contrary to the Gospel and disfigures the face of Christ.

The initial proclamation of Christ the Savior

44.1 Proclamation is the permanent priority of mission. The Church cannot elude Christ's explicit mandate, nor deprive men and women of the "Good News" about their being loved and saved by God. "Evangelization will always contain — as the foundation, center and at the same time the summit of its dynamism — a clear proclamation that, in Jesus Christ . . . salvation is offered to all people, as a gift of God's grace and mercy."[72] All forms of missionary activity are directed to this proclamation, which reveals and gives access to the mystery hidden for ages and made known in Christ (cf. Eph 3:3-9; Col 1:25-29), the mystery which lies at the heart of the Church's mission and life, as the hinge on which all evangelization turns.

44.2 In the complex reality of mission, initial proclamation has a central and irreplaceable role, since it introduces man "into the mystery of the love of God, who invites him to enter into a personal relationship with himself in Christ"[73] and opens the way to conversion. Faith is born of preaching, and every ecclesial community draws its origin and life from the personal response of each believer to that preaching.[74] Just as the whole economy of salvation has its center in Christ, so too all missionary activity is directed to the proclamation of his mystery.

44.3 The subject of proclamation is Christ, who was crucified, died and is

---

[72] Paul VI, Apostolic Exhortation *Evangelii Nuntiandi* (December 8, 1975), 27: *AAS* 68 (1976), 23.

[73] Second Vatican Ecumenical Council, Decree on the Church's Missionary Activity *Ad Gentes*, 13.

[74] Cf. Paul VI, Apostolic Exhortation *Evangelii Nuntiandi* (December 8, 1975), 15: *AAS* 68 (1976), 13-15; Second Vatican Ecumenical Council, Decree on the Church's Missionary Activity *Ad Gentes*, 13-14.

risen: through him is accomplished our full and authentic liberation from evil, sin and death; through him God bestows "new life" that is divine and eternal. This is the "Good News" which changes man and his history, and which all peoples have a right to hear. This proclamation is to be made within the context of the lives of the individuals and peoples who receive it. It is to be made with an attitude of love and esteem toward those who hear it, in language which is practical and adapted to the situation. In this proclamation the Spirit is at work and establishes a communion between the missionary and his hearers, a communion which is possible inasmuch as both enter into communion with God the Father through Christ.[75]

45.1 Proclamation, because it is made in union with the entire ecclesial community, is never a merely personal act. The missionary is present and carries out his work by virtue of a mandate he has received; even if he finds himself alone, he remains joined by invisible but profound bonds to the evangelizing activity of the whole Church.[76] Sooner or later, his hearers come to recognize in him the community which sent him and which supports him.

45.2 Proclamation is inspired by faith, which gives rise to enthusiasm and fervor in the missionary. As already mentioned, the Acts of the Apostles uses the word *parrhesia* to describe this attitude, a word which means to speak frankly and with courage. This term is found also in Saint Paul: "We had courage in our God to declare to you the Gospel of God in the face of great opposition" (1 Thess 2:2); "Pray . . . also for me, that utterance may be given me in opening my mouth boldly to proclaim the mystery of the Gospel for which I am an ambassador in chains; that I may declare it boldly, as I ought to speak" (Eph 6:18-20).

45.3 In proclaiming Christ to non-Christians, the missionary is convinced that, through the working of the Spirit, there already exists in individuals and peoples an expectation, even if an unconscious one, of knowing the truth about God, about man, and about how we are to be set free from sin and death. The missionary's enthusiasm in proclaiming Christ comes from the conviction that he is responding to that expectation, and so he does not become discouraged or cease his witness even when he is called to manifest his faith in an environment that is hostile or indifferent. He knows that the Spirit of the Father is speaking through him (cf. Mt 10:17-20; Lk 12:11-12) and he can say with the Apostles: "We are witnesses to these things, and so is the

---

[75] Cf. Encyclical Letter *Dominum et Vivificantem* (May 18, 1986), 42, 64: *AAS* 78 (1986), 857-859, 892-894.

[76] Cf. Paul VI, Apostolic Exhortation *Evangelii Nuntiandi* (December 8, 1975), 60: *AAS* 68 (1976), 50-51.

Holy Spirit" (Acts 5:32). He knows that he is not proclaiming a human truth, but the "word of God," which has an intrinsic and mysterious power of its own (cf. Rom 1:16).

45.4 The supreme test is the giving of one's life, to the point of accepting death in order to bear witness to one's faith in Jesus Christ. Throughout Christian history, martyrs, that is, "witnesses," have always been numerous and indispensable to the spread of the Gospel. In our own age, there are many: Bishops, priests, men and women religious, lay people — often unknown heroes who give their lives to bear witness to the faith. They are *par excellence* the heralds and witnesses of the faith.

Conversion and Baptism

46.1 The proclamation of the word of God has *Christian conversion* as its aim: a complete and sincere adherence to Christ and his Gospel through faith. Conversion is a gift of God, a work of the Blessed Trinity. It is the Spirit who opens people's hearts so that they can believe in Christ and "confess him" (cf. 1 Cor 12:3); of those who draw near to him through faith Jesus says: "No one can come to me unless the Father who sent me draws him" (Jn 6:44).

46.2 From the outset, conversion is expressed in faith which is total and radical, and which neither limits nor hinders God's gift. At the same time, it gives rise to a dynamic and lifelong process which demands a continual turning away from "life according to the flesh" to "life according to the Spirit" (cf. Rom 8:3-13). Conversion means accepting, by a personal decision, the saving sovereignty of Christ and becoming his disciple.

46.3 The Church calls all people to this conversion, following the example of John the Baptist, who prepared the way for Christ by "preaching a baptism of repentance for the forgiveness of sins" (Mk 1:4), as well as the example of Christ himself, who "after John was arrested, . . . came into Galilee preaching the Gospel of God and saying: 'The time is fulfilled, and the Kingdom of God is at hand; repent and believe in the Gospel'" (Mk 1:14-15).

46.4 Nowadays the call to conversion which missionaries address to non-Christians is put into question or passed over in silence. It is seen as an act of "proselytizing"; it is claimed that it is enough to help people to become more human or more faithful to their own religion, that it is enough to build communities capable of working for justice, freedom, peace and solidarity. What is overlooked is that every person has the right to hear the "Good News" of the God who reveals and gives himself in Christ, so that each one can live out in its fullness his or her proper calling. This lofty reality is expressed in the words of Jesus to the Samaritan woman: "If you knew the gift of God," and in the unconscious but ardent desire of the woman: "Sir, give me this water, that I may not thirst" (Jn 4:10, 15).

47.1 The Apostles, prompted by the Spirit, invited all to change their lives, to be converted and to be baptized. Immediately after the event of Pentecost, Peter spoke convincingly to the crowd: "When they heard this, they were cut to the heart, and said to Peter and the rest of the Apostles, 'Brethren, what shall we do?' And Peter said to them, 'Repent, and be baptized every one of you in the name of Jesus Christ for the forgiveness of your sins; and you shall receive the gift of the Holy Spirit' " (Acts 2:37-38). That very day some three thousand persons were baptized. And again, after the healing of the lame man, Peter spoke to the crowd and repeated: "Repent therefore, and turn again, that your sins may be blotted out!" (Acts 3:19).

47.2 Conversion to Christ is joined to Baptism not only because of the Church's practice, but also by the will of Christ himself, who sent the Apostles to make disciples of all nations and to baptize them (cf. Mt 28:19). Conversion is also joined to Baptism because of the intrinsic need to receive the fullness of new life in Christ. As Jesus says to Nicodemus: "Truly, truly, I say to you, unless one is born of water and the Spirit, he cannot enter the Kingdom of God" (Jn 3:5). In Baptism, in fact, we are born anew to the life of God's children, united to Jesus Christ and anointed in the Holy Spirit. Baptism is not simply a seal of conversion, and a kind of external sign indicating conversion and attesting to it. Rather, it is the sacrament which signifies and effects rebirth from the Spirit, establishes real and unbreakable bonds with the Blessed Trinity, and makes us members of the Body of Christ, which is the Church.

47.3 All this needs to be said, since not a few people, precisely in those areas involved in the mission ad gentes, tend to separate conversion to Christ from Baptism, regarding Baptism as unnecessary. It is true that in some places sociological considerations associated with Baptism obscure its genuine meaning as an act of faith. This is due to a variety of historical and cultural factors which must be removed where they still exist, so that the sacrament of spiritual rebirth can be seen for what it truly is. Local ecclesial communities must devote themselves to this task. It is also true that many profess an interior commitment to Christ and his message yet do not wish to be committed sacramentally, since, owing to prejudice or because of the failings of Christians, they find it difficult to grasp the true nature of the Church as a mystery of faith and love.[77] I wish to encourage such people to be fully open to Christ,

---

[77] Cf. Second Vatican Ecumenical Council, Dogmatic Constitution on the Church Lumen Gentium, 6-9.

and to remind them that, if they feel drawn to Christ, it was he himself who desired that the Church should be the "place" where they would in fact find him. At the same time, I invite the Christian faithful, both individually and as communities, to bear authentic witness to Christ through the new life they have received.

47.4 Certainly, every convert is a gift to the Church and represents a serious responsibility for her, not only because converts have to be prepared for Baptism through the catechumenate and then be guided by religious instruction, but also because — especially in the case of adults — such converts bring with them a kind of new energy, an enthusiasm for the faith, and a desire to see the Gospel lived out in the Church. They would be greatly disappointed if, having entered the ecclesial community, they were to find a life lacking fervor and without signs of renewal! We cannot preach conversion unless we ourselves are converted anew every day.

Forming local Churches

48.1 Conversion and Baptism give entry into a Church already in existence or require the establishment of new communities which confess Jesus as Savior and Lord. This is part of God's plan, for it pleases him "to call human beings to share in his own life not merely as individuals, without any unifying bond between them, but rather to make them into a people in which his children, who had been widely scattered, might be gathered together in unity."[78]

48.2 The mission *ad gentes* has this objective: to found Christian communities and develop Churches to their full maturity. This is a central and determining goal of missionary activity, so much so that the mission is not completed until it succeeds in building a new particular Church which functions normally in its local setting. The Decree *Ad Gentes* deals with this subject at length,[79] and since the Council, a line of theological reflection has developed which emphasizes that the whole mystery of the Church is contained in each particular Church, provided it does not isolate itself but remains in communion with the universal Church and becomes missionary in its own turn. Here we are speaking of a great and lengthy process, in which it is hard to identify the precise stage at which missionary activity properly so-called comes to an end and is replaced by pastoral activity. Even so, certain points must remain clear.

---

[78] Second Vatican Ecumenical Council, Decree on the Church's Missionary Activity *Ad Gentes*, 2; cf. Dogmatic Constitution on the Church *Lumen Gentium*, 9.

[79] Cf. Decree on the Church's Missionary Activity *Ad Gentes*, 19-22.

49.1 It is necessary first and foremost to strive to establish Christian communities everywhere, communities which are "a sign of the presence of God in the world"[80] and which grow until they become Churches. Notwithstanding the high number of Dioceses, there are still very large areas where there are no local Churches or where their number is insufficient in relation to the vastness of the territory and the density of the population. There is still much to be done in implanting and developing the Church. This phase of ecclesial history, called the *plantatio Ecclesiae,* has not reached its end; indeed, for much of the human race it has yet to begin.

49.2 Responsibility for this task belongs to the universal Church and to the particular Churches, to the whole People of God and to all its missionary forces. Every Church, even one made up of recent converts, is missionary by its very nature, and is both evangelized and evangelizing. Faith must always be presented as a gift of God to be lived out in community (families, parishes, associations), and to be extended to others through witness in word and deed. The evangelizing activity of the Christian community, first in its own locality, and then elsewhere as part of the Church's universal mission, is the clearest sign of a mature faith. A radical conversion in thinking is required in order to become missionary, and this holds true both for individuals and entire communities. The Lord is always calling us to come out of ourselves and to share with others the goods we possess, starting with the most precious gift of all — our faith. The effectiveness of the Church's organizations, movements, parishes and apostolic works must be measured in the light of this missionary imperative. Only by becoming missionary will the Christian community be able to overcome its internal divisions and tensions, and rediscover its unity and its strength of faith.

49.3 Missionary personnel coming from other Churches and countries must work in communion with their local counterparts for the development of the Christian community. In particular, it falls to missionary personnel — in accordance with the directives of the Bishops and in cooperation with those responsible at the local level — to foster the spread of the faith and the expansion of the Church in non-Christian environments and among non-Christian groups, and to encourage a missionary sense within the particular Churches, so that pastoral concern will always be combined with concern for the mission *ad gentes.* In this way, every Church will make its own the solicitude of Christ the Good Shepherd, who fully devotes himself to his flock, but at the same time is mindful of the "other sheep that are not of this fold" (Jn 10:16).

[80] Ibid., 15.

50.1 This solicitude will serve as a motivation and stimulus for a renewed commitment to ecumenism. The relationship between *ecumenical activity* and *missionary activity* makes it necessary to consider two closely associated factors. On the one hand, we must recognize that "the division among Christians damages the holy work of preaching the Gospel to every creature and is a barrier for many in their approach to the faith."[81] The fact that the Good News of reconciliation is preached by Christians who are divided among themselves weakens their witness. It is thus urgent to work for the unity of Christians, so that missionary activity can be more effective. At the same time we must not forget that efforts toward unity are themselves a sign of the work of reconciliation which God is bringing about in our midst.

50.2 On the other hand, it is true that some kind of communion, though imperfect, exists among all those who have received Baptism in Christ. On this basis the Council established the principle that "while all appearance of indifferentism and confusion is ruled out, as well as any appearance of unhealthy rivalry, Catholics should collaborate in a spirit of fellowship with their separated brothers and sisters in accordance with the norms of the Decree on Ecumenism: by a common profession of faith in God and in Jesus Christ before the nations — to the extent that this is possible — and by their cooperation in social and technical as well as in cultural and religious matters."[82]

50.3 Ecumenical activity and harmonious witness to Jesus Christ by Christians who belong to different Churches and Ecclesial Communities has already borne abundant fruit. But it is ever more urgent that they work and bear witness together at this time when Christian and para-Christian sects are sowing confusion by their activity. The expansion of these sects represents a threat for the Catholic Church and for all the Ecclesial Communities with which she is engaged in dialogue. Wherever possible, and in the light of local circumstances, the response of Christians can itself be an ecumenical one.

"Ecclesial basic communities" as a force for evangelization

51.1 A rapidly growing phenomenon in the young Churches — one sometimes fostered by the Bishops and their Conferences as a pastoral priority — is that of "ecclesial basic communities" (also known by other names) which are proving to be good centers for Christian formation and missionary outreach. These are groups of Christians who, at the level of the family or in a similarly restricted setting, come together for prayer, Scripture reading,

---

[81] Ibid., 6.
[82] Ibid., 15; cf. Decree on Ecumenism *Unitatis Redintegratio*, 3.

catechesis, and discussion on human and ecclesial problems with a view to a common commitment. These communities are a sign of vitality within the Church, an instrument of formation and evangelization, and a solid starting point for a new society based on a "civilization of love."

51.2 These communities decentralize and organize the parish community, to which they always remain united. They take root in less privileged and rural areas, and become a leaven of Christian life, of care for the poor and neglected, and of commitment to the transformation of society. Within them, the individual Christian experiences community and therefore senses that he or she is playing an active role and is encouraged to share in the common task. Thus, these communities become a means of evangelization and of the initial proclamation of the Gospel, and a source of new ministries. At the same time, by being imbued with Christ's love, they also show how divisions, tribalism and racism can be overcome.

51.3 Every community, if it is to be Christian, must be founded on Christ and live in him, as it listens to the word of God, focuses its prayer on the Eucharist, lives in a communion marked by oneness of heart and soul, and shares according to the needs of its members (cf. Acts 2:42-47). As Pope Paul VI recalled, every community must live in union with the particular and the universal Church, in heartfelt communion with the Church's Pastors and the Magisterium, with a commitment to missionary outreach and without yielding to isolationism or ideological exploitation.[83] And the Synod of Bishops stated: "Because the Church is communion, the new 'basic communities,' if they truly live in unity with the Church, are a true expression of communion and a means for the construction of a more profound communion. They are thus cause for great hope for the life of the Church."[84]

Incarnating the Gospel in peoples' culture

52.1 As she carries out missionary activity among the nations, the Church encounters different cultures and becomes involved in the process of inculturation. The need for such involvement has marked the Church's pilgrimage throughout her history, but today it is particularly urgent.

52.2 The process of the Church's insertion into peoples' cultures is a lengthy one. It is not a matter of purely external adaptation, for inculturation "means the intimate transformation of authentic cultural values through their integration in Christianity and the insertion of Christianity in the various human

[83] Cf. Apostolic Exhortation *Evangelii Nuntiandi* (December 8, 1975), 58: *AAS* 68 (1976), 46-49.

[84] Second Extraordinary Assembly (December 7, 1985), Final Report, II, C, 6.

cultures."[85] The process is thus a profound and all-embracing one, which involves the Christian message and also the Church's reflection and practice. But at the same time it is a difficult process, for it must in no way compromise the distinctiveness and integrity of the Christian faith.

52.3 Through inculturation the Church makes the Gospel incarnate in different cultures and at the same time introduces peoples, together with their cultures, into her own community.[86] She transmits to them her own values, at the same time taking the good elements that already exist in them and renewing them from within.[87] Through inculturation the Church, for her part, becomes a more intelligible sign of what she is, and a more effective instrument of mission.

52.4 Thanks to this action within the local Churches, the universal Church herself is enriched with forms of expression and values in the various sectors of Christian life, such as evangelization, worship, theology and charitable works. She comes to know and to express better the mystery of Christ, all the while being motivated to continual renewal. During my Pastoral Visits to the young Churches I have repeatedly dealt with these themes, which are present in the Council and the subsequent Magisterium.[88]

52.5 Inculturation is a slow journey which accompanies the whole of missionary life. It involves those working in the Church's mission *ad gentes*, the Christian communities as they develop, and the Bishops, who have the task of providing discernment and encouragement for its implementation.[89]

53.1 Missionaries, who come from other Churches and countries, must immerse themselves in the cultural milieu of those to whom they are sent, moving beyond their own cultural limitations. Hence they must learn the language of the place in which they work, become familiar with the most important expressions of the local culture, and discover its values through direct

---

[85] Ibid., II, D, 4.

[86] Cf. Apostolic Exhortation *Catechesi Tradendae* (October 16, 1979), 53: *AAS* 71 (1979), 1320; Encyclical Epistle *Slavorum Apostoli* (June 2, 1985), 21: *AAS* 77 (1985), 802-803.

[87] Cf. Paul VI, Apostolic Exhortation *Evangelii Nuntiandi* (December 8, 1975), 20: *AAS* 68 (1976), 18-19.

[88] Cf. Address to the Bishops of Zaire, Kinshasa (May 3, 1980), 4-6: *AAS* 72 (1980), 432-435; Address to the Bishops of Kenya, Nairobi (May 7, 1980), 6: *AAS* 72 (1980), 497; Address to the Bishops of India, Delhi (February 1, 1986), 5: *AAS* 78 (1986), 748-749; Homily, Cartagena (July 6, 1986), 7-8: *AAS* 79 (1987), 105-106; cf. also Encyclical Epistle *Slavorum Apostoli* (June 2, 1985), 21-22: *AAS* 77 (1985), 802-804.

[89] Cf. Second Vatican Ecumenical Council, Decree on the Church's Missionary Activity *Ad Gentes*, 22.

experience. Only if they have this kind of awareness will they be able to bring to people the knowledge of the hidden mystery (cf. Rom 16:25-27; Eph 3:5) in a credible and fruitful way. It is not of course a matter of missionaries renouncing their own cultural identity, but of understanding, appreciating, fostering and evangelizing the culture of the environment in which they are working, and therefore of equipping themselves to communicate effectively with it, adopting a manner of living which is a sign of Gospel witness and of solidarity with the people.

53.2 Developing ecclesial communities, inspired by the Gospel, will gradually be able to express their Christian experience in original ways and forms that are consonant with their own cultural traditions, provided that those traditions are in harmony with the objective requirements of the faith itself. To this end, especially in the more delicate areas of inculturation, particular Churches of the same region should work in communion with each other[90] and with the whole Church, convinced that only through attention both to the universal Church and to the particular Churches will they be capable of translating the treasure of faith into a legitimate variety of expressions.[91] Groups which have been evangelized will thus provide the elements for a "translation" of the Gospel message,[92] keeping in mind the positive elements acquired down the centuries from Christianity's contact with different cultures and not forgetting the dangers of alterations which have sometimes occurred.[93]

54.1 In this regard, certain guidelines remain basic. Properly applied, inculturation must be guided by two principles: "compatibility with the Gospel and communion with the universal Church."[94] Bishops, as guardians of the "deposit of faith," will take care to ensure fidelity and, in particular, to provide discernment,[95] for which a deeply balanced approach is required. In

---

[90] Cf. ibid., 22.

[91] Cf. Paul VI, Apostolic Exhortation *Evangelii Nuntiandi* (December 8, 1975), 64: *AAS* 68 (1976), 55.

[92] Ibid., 63: loc. cit., 53: Particular Churches "have the task of assimilating the essence of the Gospel message and of transposing it, without the slightest betrayal of its essential truth, into the language that these people understand, then of proclaiming it in this language. . . . And the word 'language' should be understood here less in the semantic or literary sense than in the sense which one may call anthropological or cultural."

[93] Cf. Address at General Audience (April 13, 1988): *Insegnamenti* XI/1 (1988), 877-881.

[94] Apostolic Exhortation *Familiaris Consortio* (November 22, 1981), 10: *AAS* 74 (1982), 91, which speaks of inculturation "in the context of marriage and the family."

[95] Cf. Paul VI, Apostolic Exhortation *Evangelii Nuntiandi* (December 8, 1975), 63-65: *AAS* 68 (1976), 53-56.

fact there is a risk of passing uncritically from a form of alienation from culture to an overestimation of culture. Since culture is a human creation and is therefore marked by sin, it too needs to be "healed, ennobled and perfected."[96]

54.2 This kind of process needs to take place gradually, in such a way that it really is an expression of the community's Christian experience. As Pope Paul VI said in Kampala: "It will require an incubation of the Christian 'mystery' in the genius of your people in order that its native voice, more clearly and frankly, may then be raised harmoniously in the chorus of other voices in the universal Church."[97] In effect, inculturation must involve the whole People of God, and not just a few experts, since the people reflect the authentic "sensus fidei" which must never be lost sight of. Inculturation needs to be guided and encouraged, but not forced, lest it give rise to negative reactions among Christians. It must be an expression of the community's life, one which must mature within the community itself, and not be exclusively the result of erudite research. The safeguarding of traditional values is the work of a mature faith.

Dialogue with our brothers and sisters of other religions

55.1 Interreligious dialogue is a part of the Church's evangelizing mission. Understood as a method and means of mutual knowledge and enrichment, dialogue is not in opposition to the mission *ad gentes;* indeed, it has special links with that mission and is one of its expressions. This mission, in fact, is addressed to those who do not know Christ and his Gospel, and who belong for the most part to other religions. In Christ, God calls all peoples to himself and he wishes to share with them the fullness of his revelation and love. He does not fail to make himself present in many ways, not only to individuals but also to entire peoples through their spiritual riches, of which their religions are the main and essential expression, even when they contain "gaps, insufficiencies and errors."[98] All of this has been given ample emphasis by the Council and the subsequent

[96] Second Vatican Ecumenical Council, Dogmatic Constitution on the Church *Lumen Gentium,* 17.

[97] Address to Those Participating in the Symposium of African Bishops, Kampala (July 31, 1969), 2: *AAS* 61 (1969), 577.

[98] Paul VI, Address at the Opening of the Second Session of the Second Vatican Ecumenical Council (September 29, 1963): *AAS* 55 (1963), 858; cf. Second Vatican Ecumenical Council, Declaration on the Relationship of the Church to Non-Christian Religions *Nostra Aetate,* 2; Dogmatic Constitution on the Church *Lumen Gentium,* 16; Decree on the Church's Missionary Activity *Ad Gentes,* 9; Paul VI, Apostolic Exhortation *Evangelii Nuntiandi* (December 8, 1975), 53: *AAS* 68 (1976), 41-42.

Magisterium, without detracting in any way from the fact that *salvation comes from Christ and that dialogue does not dispense from evangelization*.[99]

55.2 In the light of the economy of salvation, the Church sees no conflict between proclaiming Christ and engaging in interreligious dialogue. Instead, she feels the need to link the two in the context of her mission *ad gentes*. These two elements must maintain both their intimate connection and their distinctiveness; therefore they should not be confused, manipulated or regarded as identical, as though they were interchangeable.

55.3 I recently wrote to the Bishops of Asia: "Although the Church gladly acknowledges whatever is true and holy in the religious traditions of Buddhism, Hinduism and Islam as a reflection of that truth which enlightens all people, this does not lessen her duty and resolve to proclaim without fail Jesus Christ who is 'the way, and the truth and the life.' . . . The fact that the followers of other religions can receive God's grace and be saved by Christ apart from the ordinary means which he has established does not thereby cancel the call to faith and Baptism which God wills for all people."[100] Indeed Christ himself "while expressly insisting on the need for faith and Baptism, at the same time confirmed *the need for the Church,* into which people enter through Baptism as through a door."[101] Dialogue should be conducted and implemented with the conviction that *the Church is the ordinary means of salvation* and that *she alone* possesses the fullness of the means of salvation.[102]

56.1 Dialogue does not originate from tactical concerns or self-interest, but is an activity with its own guiding principles, requirements and dignity. It is demanded by deep respect for everything that has been brought about in human beings by the Spirit who blows where he wills.[103] Through dialogue,

---

[99] Cf. Paul VI, Encyclical Letter *Ecclesiam Suam* (August 6, 1964): *AAS* 56 (1964), 609-659; Second Vatican Ecumenical Council, Decree on the Church's Missionary Activity *Ad Gentes,* 11, 41; Secretariat for Non-Christians, *The Attitude of the Church toward the Followers of Other Religions: Reflections and Orientations on Dialogue and Mission* (June 10, 1984): *AAS* 76 (1984), 816-828.

[100] Letter to the Fifth Plenary Assembly of Asian Bishops' Conferences (June 23, 1990), 4: *AAS* 83 (1991), 101-102.

[101] Second Vatican Ecumenical Council, Dogmatic Constitution on the Church *Lumen Gentium,* 14; cf. Decree on the Church's Missionary Activity *Ad Gentes,* 7.

[102] Cf. Second Vatican Ecumenical Council, Decree on Ecumenism *Unitatis Redintegratio,* 3; Decree on the Church's Missionary Activity *Ad Gentes,* 7.

[103] Cf. Encyclical Letter *Redemptor Hominis* (March 4, 1979), 12: *AAS* 71 (1979), 279.

the Church seeks to uncover the "seeds of the Word,"[104] a "ray of that truth which enlightens all men";[105] these are found in individuals and in the religious traditions of mankind. Dialogue is based on hope and love, and will bear fruit in the Spirit. Other religions constitute a positive challenge for the Church: they stimulate her both to discover and acknowledge the signs of Christ's presence and of the working of the Spirit, as well as to examine more deeply her own identity and to bear witness to the fullness of revelation which she has received for the good of all.

56.2 This gives rise to the spirit which must enliven dialogue in the context of mission. Those engaged in this dialogue must be consistent with their own religious traditions and convictions, and be open to understanding those of the other party without pretense or close-mindedness, but with truth, humility and frankness, knowing that dialogue can enrich each side. There must be no abandonment of principles nor false irenicism, but instead a witness given and received for mutual advancement on the road of religious inquiry and experience, and at the same time for the elimination of prejudice, intolerance and misunderstandings. Dialogue leads to inner purification and conversion which, if pursued with docility to the Holy Spirit, will be spiritually fruitful.

57.1 A vast field lies open to dialogue, which can assume many forms and expressions: from exchanges between experts in religious traditions or official representatives of those traditions to cooperation for integral development and the safeguarding of religious values; and from a sharing of their respective spiritual experiences to the so-called "dialogue of life," through which believers of different religions bear witness before each other in daily life to their own human and spiritual values, and help each other to live according to those values in order to build a more just and fraternal society.

57.2 Each member of the faithful and all Christian communities are called to practice dialogue, although not always to the same degree or in the same way. The contribution of the laity is indispensable in this area, for they "can favor the relations which ought to be established with the followers of various religions through their example in the situations in which they live and in

---

[104] Second Vatican Ecumenical Council, Decree on the Church's Missionary Activity *Ad Gentes*, 11, 15.

[105] Second Vatican Ecumenical Council, Declaration on the Relationship of the Church to Non-Christian Religions *Nostra Aetate*, 2.

their activities."[106] Some of them also will be able to make a contribution through research and study.[107]

57.3 I am well aware that many missionaries and Christian communities find in the difficult and often misunderstood path of dialogue their only way of bearing sincere witness to Christ and offering generous service to others. I wish to encourage them to persevere with faith and love, even in places where their efforts are not well received. Dialogue is a path toward the Kingdom and will certainly bear fruit, even if the times and seasons are known only to the Father (cf. Acts 1:7).

Promoting development by forming consciences

58.1 The mission *ad gentes* is still being carried out today, for the most part in the southern regions of the world, where action on behalf of integral development and liberation from all forms of oppression is most urgently needed. The Church has always been able to generate among the peoples she evangelizes a drive toward progress. Today, more than in the past, missionaries are being recognized as *promoters of development* by governments and international experts who are impressed at the remarkable results achieved with scanty means.

58.2 In the Encyclical *Sollicitudo Rei Socialis,* I stated that "the Church does not have technical solutions to offer for the problem of underdevelopment as such," but "offers her first contribution to the solution of the urgent problem of development when she proclaims the truth about Christ, about herself and about man, applying this truth to a concrete situation."[108] The Conference of Latin American Bishops at Puebla stated that "the best service we can offer to our brother is evangelization, which helps him to live and act as a son of God, sets him free from injustices and assists his overall development."[109] It is not the Church's mission to work directly on the economic, technical or political levels, or to contribute materially to development. Rather, her mission consists essentially in offering people an opportunity not to "have more" but to "be more," by awakening their consciences through the Gospel.

---

[106] Post-Synodal Apostolic Exhortation *Christifideles Laici* (December 30, 1988), 35: *AAS* 81 (1989), 458.

[107] Cf. Second Vatican Ecumenical Council, Decree on the Church's Missionary Activity *Ad Gentes,* 41.

[108] Encyclical Letter *Sollicitudo Rei Socialis* (December 30, 1987), 41: *AAS* 80 (1988), 570-571.

[109] Documents of the Third General Conference of Latin American Bishops, Puebla (1979), 3760 (1145).

"Authentic human development must be rooted in an ever deeper evangelization."[110]

58.3 The Church and her missionaries also promote development through schools, hospitals, printing presses, universities and experimental farms. But a people's development does not derive primarily from money, material assistance or technological means, but from the formation of consciences and the gradual maturing of ways of thinking and patterns of behavior. *Man is the principal agent of development,* not money or technology. The Church forms consciences by revealing to peoples the God whom they seek and do not yet know, the grandeur of man created in God's image and loved by him, the equality of all men and women as God's sons and daughters, the mastery of man over nature created by God and placed at man's service, and the obligation to work for the development of the whole person and of all mankind.

59.1 Through the Gospel message, the Church offers a force for liberation which promotes development precisely because it leads to conversion of heart and of ways of thinking, fosters the recognition of each person's dignity, encourages solidarity, commitment and service of one's neighbor, and gives everyone a place in God's plan, which is the building of his Kingdom of peace and justice, beginning already in this life. This is the biblical perspective of the "new heavens and a new earth" (cf. Is 65:17; 2 Pet 3:13; Rev 21:1), which has been the stimulus and goal for mankind's advancement in history. Man's development derives from God, and from the model of Jesus — God and man — and must lead back to God.[111] That is why there is a close connection between the proclamation of the Gospel and human promotion.

59.2 The contribution of the Church and of evangelization to the development of peoples concerns not only the struggle against material poverty and underdevelopment in the South of the world, but also concerns the North, which is prone to a moral and spiritual poverty caused by "overdevelopment."[112] A certain way of thinking, uninfluenced by a religious outlook and widespread in some parts of today's world, is based on the idea that increasing wealth and the promotion of economic and technical growth is enough for people to de-

---

[110] Address to Clergy and Religious, Jakarta (October 10, 1989), 5: *Insegnamenti* XII/2 (1989), 845.

[111] Cf. Paul VI, Encyclical Letter *Populorum Progressio* (March 26, 1967), 14-21, 40-42: *AAS* 59 (1967), 264-268, 277-278; John Paul II, Encyclical Letter *Sollicitudo Rei Socialis* (December 30, 1987), 27-41: *AAS* 80 (1988), 547-572.

[112] Cf. Encyclical Letter *Sollicitudo Rei Socialis* (December 30, 1987), 28: *AAS* 80 (1988), 548-550.

velop on the human level. But a soulless development cannot suffice for human beings, and an excess of affluence is as harmful as excessive poverty. This is a "development model" which the North has constructed and is now spreading to the South, where a sense of religion as well as human values is in danger of being overwhelmed by a wave of consumerism.

59.3 "Fight hunger by changing your lifestyle" is a motto which has appeared in Church circles and which shows the people of the rich nations how to become brothers and sisters of the poor. We need to turn to a more austere way of life which will favor a new model of development that gives attention to ethical and religious values. To the poor, *missionary activity* brings light and an impulse toward true development, while a new evangelization ought to create among the wealthy a realization that the time has arrived for them to become true brothers and sisters of the poor through the conversion of all to an "integral development" open to the Absolute.[113]

Charity: source and criterion of mission

60.1 As I said during my Pastoral Visit to Brazil: "The Church all over the world wishes to be the Church of the poor . . . she wishes to draw out all the truth contained in the Beatitudes of Christ, and especially in the first one: 'Blessed are the poor in spirit.' . . . She wishes to teach this truth and she wishes to put it into practice, just as Jesus came to do and to teach."[114]

60.2 The young Churches, which for the most part are to be found among peoples suffering from widespread poverty, often give voice to this concern as an integral part of their mission. The Conference of Latin American Bishops at Puebla, after recalling the example of Jesus, wrote that "the poor deserve preferential attention, whatever their moral or personal situation. They have been made in the image and likeness of God to be his children, but this image has been obscured and even violated. For this reason, God has become their defender and loves them. It follows that the poor are those to whom the mission is first addressed, and their evangelization is *par excellence* the sign and proof of the mission of Jesus."[115]

60.3 In fidelity to the spirit of the Beatitudes, the Church is called to be on the side of those who are poor and oppressed in any way. I therefore exhort

---

[113] Cf. ibid., 27-34: loc. cit., 547-560; Paul VI, Encyclical Letter *Populorum Progressio* (March 26, 1967), 19-21, 41-42: *AAS* 59 (1967), 266-268, 277-278.

[114] Address to the Residents of "Favela Vidigal," Rio de Janeiro (July 2, 1980), 4: *AAS* 72 (1980), 854.

[115] Documents of the Third General Conference of Latin American Bishops, Puebla (1979), 3757 (1142).

the disciples of Christ and all Christian communities — from families to Dioceses, from parishes to Religious Institutes — to carry out a sincere review of their lives regarding their solidarity with the poor. At the same time, I express gratitude to the missionaries who, by their loving presence and humble service to people, are working for the integral development of individuals and of society through schools, health-care centers, leprosaria, homes for the handicapped and the elderly, projects for the promotion of women and other similar apostolates. I thank the priests, religious Brothers and Sisters, and members of the laity for their dedication, and I also encourage the volunteers from non-governmental organizations who in ever increasing numbers are devoting themselves to works of charity and human promotion.

60.4 It is in fact these "works of charity" that reveal the soul of all missionary activity: *love*, which has been and remains *the driving force of mission*, and is also "the sole criterion for judging what is to be done or not done, changed or not changed. It is the principle which must direct every action, and the end to which that action must be directed. When we act with a view to charity, or are inspired by charity, nothing is unseemly and everything is good."[116]

VI

Leaders and Workers in the Missionary Apostolate

61.1 Without witnesses there can be no witness, just as without missionaries there can be no missionary activity. Jesus chooses and sends people forth to be his witnesses and apostles, so that they may share in his mission and continue in his saving work: "You shall be my witnesses in Jerusalem and in all Judea and Samaria and to the end of the earth" (Acts 1:8).

61.2 The Twelve are the first to work in the Church's universal mission. They constitute a "collegial subject" of that mission, having been chosen by Jesus to be with him and to be sent forth "to the lost sheep of the house of Israel" (Mt 10:6). This collegiality does not prevent certain figures from assuming prominence within the group, such as James, John and above all Peter, who is so prominent as to justify the expression: "Peter and the other Apostles" (Acts 2:14, 37). It was thanks to Peter that the horizons of the Church's universal mission were expanded, and the way was prepared for the out-

---

[116] Blessed Isaac of Stella, *Sermon* 31: *PL* 194, 1793.

standing missionary work of Paul, who by God's will was called and sent forth to the nations (cf. Gal 1:15-16).

61.3 In the early Church's missionary expansion, we find alongside the Apostles other lesser figures who should not be overlooked. These include individuals, groups and communities. A typical example is the local Church at Antioch which, after being evangelized, becomes an evangelizing community which sends missionaries to others (cf. Acts 13:2-3). The early Church experiences her mission as a community task, while acknowledging in her midst certain "special envoys" or "missionaries devoted to the Gentiles," such as Paul and Barnabas.

62.1 What was done at the beginning of Christianity to further its universal mission remains valid and urgent today. *The Church is missionary by her very nature*, for Christ's mandate is not something contingent or external, but reaches the very heart of the Church. It follows that the universal Church and each individual Church is sent forth to the nations. Precisely "so that this missionary zeal may flourish among the people of their own country," it is highly appropriate that young Churches should "share as soon as possible in the universal missionary work of the Church. They should themselves send missionaries to proclaim the Gospel all over the world, even though they are suffering from a shortage of clergy."[117] Many are already doing so, and I strongly encourage them to continue.

62.2 In this essential bond between the universal Church and the particular Churches the authentic and full missionary nature of the Church finds practical expression: "In a world where the lessening of distance makes the world increasingly smaller, the Church's communities ought to be connected with each other, exchange vital energies and resources, and commit themselves as a group to the one and common mission of proclaiming and living the Gospel. . . . So-called younger Churches have need of the strength of the older Churches and the older ones need the witness and the impulse of the younger, so that each Church can draw on the riches of the other Churches."[118]

Those primarily responsible for missionary activity

63.1 Just as the risen Lord gave the universal missionary mandate to the College of the Apostles with Peter as its head, so this same responsibility now rests primarily with the College of Bishops, headed by the Successor of Pe-

---

[117] Second Vatican Ecumenical Council, Decree on the Church's Missionary Activity *Ad Gentes*, 20.

[118] Post-Synodal Apostolic Exhortation *Christifideles Laici* (December 30, 1988), 35: *AAS* 81 (1989), 458.

ter.[119] Conscious of this responsibility, I feel the duty to give expression to it in my meetings with the Bishops, both with regard to new evangelization and the universal mission. I have traveled all over the world in order "to proclaim the Gospel, to 'strengthen the brothers' in the faith, to console the Church, to meet people. They are journeys of faith . . . they are likewise opportunities for traveling catechesis, for evangelical proclamation in spreading the Gospel and the apostolic Magisterium to the full extent of the world."[120]

63.2 My brother Bishops are directly responsible, together with me, for the evangelization of the world, both as members of the College of Bishops and as Pastors of the particular Churches. In this regard the Council states: "The charge of announcing the Gospel throughout the world belongs to the body of shepherds, to all of whom in common Christ gave the command."[121] It also stated that the Bishops "have been consecrated not only for a particular Diocese but for the salvation of the entire world."[122] This collegial responsibility has certain practical consequences. Thus, "the Synod of Bishops . . . should, among the concerns of general importance, pay special attention to missionary activity, the greatest and holiest duty of the Church."[123] The same responsibility is reflected to varying degrees in Episcopal Conferences and their organisms at a continental level, which must make their own contribution to the missionary task.[124]

63.3 Each Bishop too, as the Pastor of a particular Church, has a wide-ranging missionary duty. It falls to him "as the ruler and center of unity in the diocesan apostolate, to promote missionary activity, to direct and coordinate it. . . . Let him also see to it that apostolic activity is not limited only to those who are already converted, but that a fair share both of personnel and funds be devoted to the evangelization of non-Christians."[125]

64.1 Each particular Church must be generous and open to the needs of the other Churches. Cooperation between the Churches, in an authentic reciprocity that prepares them both to give and to receive, is a source of enrichment for all of them and touches the various spheres of ecclesial life. In this respect, the declaration of the Bishops at Puebla is exemplary: "The hour has

---

[119] Cf. Second Vatican Ecumenical Council, Decree on the Church's Missionary Activity *Ad Gentes*, 38.

[120] Address to the Cardinals and Those Associated in the Work of the Roman Curia, Vatican City and the Vicariate of Rome (June 28, 1980), 10: *Insegnamenti* III/1 (1980), 1887.

[121] Dogmatic Constitution on the Church *Lumen Gentium*, 23.

[122] Decree on the Church's Missionary Activity *Ad Gentes*, 38.

[123] Ibid., 29.

[124] Cf. ibid., 38.

[125] Ibid., 30.

finally come for Latin America . . . to be projected beyond her frontiers, *ad gentes*. Certainly we have need of missionaries ourselves, nevertheless we must give from our own poverty."[126]

64.2 In the same spirit, I exhort Bishops and Episcopal Conferences to act generously in implementing the provisions of the *Norms* which the Congregation for the Clergy issued regarding cooperation between particular Churches and especially regarding the better distribution of clergy in the world.[127]

64.3 The Church's mission is wider than the "communion among the Churches"; it ought to be directed not only to aiding re-evangelization but also and primarily to missionary activity as such. I appeal to all the Churches, young and old alike, to share in this concern of mine by seeking to overcome the various obstacles and increase missionary vocations.

Missionaries and Religious Institutes "ad gentes"

65.1 Now, as in the past, among those involved in the missionary apostolate a place of fundamental importance is held by the persons and institutions to whom the Decree *Ad Gentes* devotes the special chapter entitled "Missionaries."[128] This requires careful reflection, especially on the part of missionaries themselves, who may be led, as a result of changes occurring within the missionary field, no longer to understand the meaning of their vocation and no longer to know exactly what the Church expects of them today.

65.2 The following words of the Council are a point of reference: "Although the task of spreading the faith, to the best of one's ability, falls to each disciple of Christ, the Lord always calls from the number of his disciples those whom he wishes, so that they may be with him and that he may send them to preach to the nations. Accordingly, through the Holy Spirit, who distributes his gifts as he wishes for the good of all, Christ stirs up a missionary vocation in the hearts of individuals, and at the same time raises up in the Church those Institutes which undertake the duty of evangelization, which is the responsibility of the whole Church, as their special task."[129]

65.3 What is involved, therefore, is a "special vocation," patterned on that of the Apostles. It is manifested in a total commitment to evangelization, a

---

[126] Documents of the Third General Conference of Latin American Bishops, Puebla (1979), 2941 (368).

[127] Cf. Norms for the Cooperation of the Local Churches among Themselves and Especially for a Better Distribution of the Clergy in the World *Postquam Apostoli* (March 25, 1980): *AAS* 72 (1980), 343-364.

[128] Cf. Decree on the Church's Missionary Activity *Ad Gentes*, 23-27.

[129] Ibid., 23.

commitment which involves the missionary's whole person and life, and demands a self-giving without limits of energy or time. Those who have received this vocation, "sent by legitimate authority, go out, in faith and obedience, to those who are far from Christ, set aside for the work to which they have been called as ministers of the Gospel."[130] Missionaries must always meditate on the response demanded by the gift they have received, and continually keep their doctrinal and apostolic formation up to date.

66.1 Missionary Institutes, drawing from their experience and creativity while remaining faithful to their founding charism, must employ all means necessary to ensure the adequate preparation of candidates and the renewal of their members' spiritual, moral and physical energies.[131] They should sense that they are a vital part of the ecclesial community and should carry out their work in communion with it. Indeed, "every Institute exists for the Church and must enrich her with its distinctive characteristics, according to a particular spirit and a specific mission"; the guardians of this fidelity to the founding charism are the Bishops themselves.[132]

66.2 In general, Missionary Institutes came into being in Churches located in traditionally Christian countries, and historically they have been the means employed by the Congregation of *Propaganda Fide* for the spread of the faith and the founding of new Churches. Today, these Institutes are receiving more and more candidates from the young Churches which they founded, while new Missionary Institutes have arisen in countries which previously only received missionaries, but are now also sending them. This is a praiseworthy trend which demonstrates the continuing validity and relevance of the specific missionary vocation of these Institutes. They remain "absolutely necessary,"[133] not only for missionary activity *ad gentes,* in keeping with their tradition, but also for stirring up missionary fervor both in the Churches of traditionally Christian countries and in the younger Churches.

66.3 The special vocation of missionaries *"for life"* retains all its validity: it is the model of the Church's missionary commitment, which always stands in need of radical and total self-giving, of new and bold endeavors. Therefore the

---

[130] Ibid., 23.

[131] Ibid., 23, 27.

[132] Cf. Sacred Congregation for Religious and Secular Institutes and Sacred Congregation for Bishops, Directives for Mutual Relations between Bishops and Religious in the Church *Mutuae Relationes* (May 14, 1978), 14b: AAS 70 (1978), 482; cf. 28: loc. cit., 490.

[133] Second Vatican Ecumenical Council, Decree on the Church's Missionary Activity *Ad Gentes,* 27.

men and women missionaries who have devoted their whole lives to bearing witness to the risen Lord among the nations must not allow themselves to be daunted by doubts, misunderstanding, rejection or persecution. They should revive the grace of their specific charism and courageously press on, prefer-ring — in a spirit of faith, obedience and communion with their Pastors — to seek the lowliest and most demanding places.

Diocesan priests for the universal mission

67.1 As co-workers of the Bishops, priests are called by virtue of the Sacra-ment of Orders to share in concern for the Church's mission: "The spiritual gift that priests have received in ordination prepares them, not for any narrow and limited mission, but for *the most universal and all-embracing mission of salvation* 'to the end of the earth.' For every priestly ministry shares in the universal scope of the mission that Christ entrusted to his Apostles."[134] For this reason, the for-mation of candidates to the priesthood must aim at giving them "*the true Catholic spirit*, whereby they will learn to transcend the bounds of their own Diocese, country or rite, and come to the aid of the whole Church, in readiness to preach the Gospel anywhere."[135] All priests must have the mind and the heart of mis-sionaries — open to the needs of the Church and the world, with concern for those farthest away, and especially for the non-Christian groups in their own area. They should have at heart, in their prayers and particularly at the Eucha-ristic Sacrifice, the concern of the whole Church for all of humanity.

67.2 Especially in those areas where Christians are a minority, priests must be filled with special missionary zeal and commitment. The Lord en-trusts to them not only the pastoral care of the Christian community, but also and above all the evangelization of those of their fellow citizens who do not belong to Christ's flock. Priests will "not fail to make themselves readily avail-able to the Holy Spirit and the Bishop, to be sent to preach the Gospel beyond the borders of their country. This will demand of them not only maturity in their vocation, but also an uncommon readiness to detach themselves from their own homeland, culture and family, and a special ability to adapt to other cultures, with understanding and respect for them."[136]

---

[134] Second Vatican Ecumenical Council, Decree on the Ministry and Life of Priests *Presbyterorum Ordinis*, 10; cf. Decree on the Church's Missionary Activity *Ad Gentes*, 39.

[135] Second Vatican Ecumenical Council, Decree on Priestly Formation *Optatam Totius*, 20: cf. *Guide de la vie pastorale pour les prêtres diocésains des Eglises qui dépendent de la Congrégation pour l'Evangélisation des Peuples*, Rome, 1989.

[136] Address to the Plenary Assembly of the Congregation for the Evangelization of Peoples (April 14, 1989), 4: *AAS* 81 (1989), 1140.

68 In his Encyclical *Fidei Donum,* Pope Pius XII, with prophetic insight, encouraged Bishops to offer some of their priests for temporary service in the Churches of Africa, and gave his approval to projects already existing for that purpose. Twenty-five years later, I pointed out the striking newness of that Encyclical, which "surmounted the territorial dimension of priestly service in order to direct it toward the entire Church."[137] Today it is clear how effective and fruitful this experience has been. Indeed, *Fidei Donum* priests are a unique sign of the bond of communion existing among the Churches. They make a valuable contribution to the growth of needy ecclesial communities, while drawing from them freshness and liveliness of faith. Of course, the missionary service of the diocesan priest must conform to certain criteria and conditioning. The priests to be sent should be selected from among the most suitable candidates, and should be duly prepared for the particular work that awaits them.[138] With an open and fraternal attitude, they should become part of the new setting of the Church which welcomes them, and form one presbyterate with the local priests, under the authority of the Bishop.[139] I hope that a spirit of service will increase among the priests of the long-established Churches, and that it will be fostered among priests of the Churches of more recent origin.

The missionary fruitfulness of consecrated life

69.1 From the inexhaustible and manifold richness of the Spirit come the vocations of the *Institutes of Consecrated Life,* whose members, "because of the dedication to the service of the Church deriving from their very consecration, have an obligation to play a special part in missionary activity, in a manner appropriate to their Institute."[140] History witnesses to the outstanding service rendered by Religious Families in the spread of the faith and the formation of new Churches: from the ancient monastic institutions, to the medieval Orders, up to the more recent Congregations.

69.2 (a) Echoing the Council, I invite *Institutes of Contemplative Life* to establish communities in the young Churches, so as to "bear glorious witness

---

[137] Message for the 1982 World Mission Day: *Insegnamenti* V/2 (1982), 1879.

[138] Cf. Second Vatican Ecumenical Council, Decree on the Church's Missionary Activity *Ad Gentes,* 38; Sacred Congregation for the Clergy, Norms for the Cooperation of the Local Churches among Themselves and Especially for a Better Distribution of the Clergy in the World *Postquam Apostoli* (March 25, 1980), 24-25: *AAS* 72 (1980), 361.

[139] Cf. Sacred Congregation for the Clergy, Norms for the Cooperation of the Local Churches among Themselves and Especially for a Better Distribution of the Clergy in the World *Postquam Apostoli* (March 25, 1980), 29: *AAS* 72 (1980), 362-363; Second Vatican Ecumenical Council, Decree on the Church's Missionary Activity *Ad Gentes,* 20.

[140] *Code of Canon Law,* Canon 783.

among non-Christians to the majesty and love of God, as well as to unity in Christ."[141] This presence is beneficial throughout the non-Christian world, especially in those areas where religious traditions hold the contemplative life in great esteem for its asceticism and its search for the Absolute.

69.3 (b) To *Institutes of Active Life,* I would recommend the immense opportunities for works of charity, for the proclamation of the Gospel, for Christian education, cultural endeavors and solidarity with the poor and those suffering from discrimination, abandonment and oppression. Whether they pursue a strictly missionary goal or not, such Institutes should ask themselves how willing and able they are to broaden their action in order to extend God's Kingdom. In recent times many Institutes have responded to this request, which I hope will be given even greater consideration and implementation for a more authentic service. The Church needs to make known the great Gospel values of which she is the bearer. No one witnesses more effectively to these values than those who profess the consecrated life in chastity, poverty and obedience, in a total gift of self to God and in complete readiness to serve humanity and society after the example of Christ.[142]

70 I extend a special word of appreciation to the missionary Religious Sisters, in whom virginity for the sake of the Kingdom is transformed into a motherhood in the spirit that is rich and fruitful. It is precisely the mission *ad gentes* that offers them vast scope for "the gift of self with love in a total and undivided manner."[143] The example and activity of women who through virginity are consecrated to love of God and neighbor, especially the very poor, are an indispensable evangelical sign among those peoples and cultures where women still have far to go on the way toward human promotion and liberation. It is my hope that many young Christian women will be attracted to giving themselves generously to Christ, and will draw strength and joy from their consecration in order to bear witness to him among the peoples who do not know him.

All the laity are missionaries by Baptism

71.1 Recent Popes have stressed the importance of the role of the laity in missionary activity.[144] In the Exhortation *Christifideles Laici,* I spoke explicitly

---

[141] Decree on the Church's Missionary Activity *Ad Gentes,* 40.

[142] Cf. Paul VI, Apostolic Exhortation *Evangelii Nuntiandi* (December 8, 1975), 69: *AAS* 68 (1976), 58-59.

[143] Apostolic Letter *Mulieris Dignitatem* (August 15, 1988), 20: *AAS* 80 (1988), 1703.

[144] Cf. Pius XII, Encyclical Letter *Evangelii Praecones* (June 2, 1951): *AAS* 43 (1951), 510ff.; Encyclical Letter *Fidei Donum* (April 21, 1957): *AAS* 49 (1957), 228ff.; John XXIII Encyclical Letter *Princeps Pastorum* (November 28, 1959): *AAS* 51 (1959), 855ff.; Paul VI, Apostolic Exhortation *Evangelii Nuntiandi* (December 8, 1975), 70-73: *AAS* 68 (1976), 59-63.

of the Church's "permanent mission of bringing the Gospel to the multitudes — the millions and millions of men and women — who as yet do not know Christ the Redeemer of humanity,"[145] and of the responsibility of the lay faithful in this regard. The mission *ad gentes* is incumbent upon the entire People of God. Whereas the foundation of a new Church requires the Eucharist and hence the priestly ministry, missionary activity, which is carried out in a wide variety of ways, is the task of all the Christian faithful.

71.2 It is clear that from the very origins of Christianity, the laity — as individuals, families, and entire communities — shared in spreading the faith. Pope Pius XII recalled this fact in his first Encyclical on the missions,[146] in which he pointed out some instances of lay missions. In modern times, this active participation of lay men and women missionaries has not been lacking. How can we forget the important role played by women: their work in the family, in schools, in political, social and cultural life, and especially their teaching of Christian doctrine? Indeed, it is necessary to recognize — and it is a title of honor — that some Churches owe their origins to the activity of lay men and women missionaries.

71.3 The Second Vatican Council confirmed this tradition in its description of the missionary character of the entire People of God and of the apostolate of the laity in particular,[147] emphasizing the specific contribution to missionary activity which they are called to make.[148] The need for all the faithful to share in this responsibility is not merely a matter of making the apostolate more effective, it is a right and duty based on their baptismal dignity, whereby "the faithful participate, for their part, in the threefold mission of Christ as priest, prophet and king."[149] Therefore, "they are bound by the general obligation and they have the right, whether as individuals or in associations, to strive so that the divine message of salvation may be known and accepted by all people throughout the world. This obligation is all the more insistent in circumstances in which only through them are people able to hear the Gospel and to know Christ."[150]

---

[145] Post-Synodal Apostolic Exhortation *Christifideles Laici* (December 30, 1988), 35: *AAS* 81 (1989), 457.

[146] Cf. Encyclical Letter *Evangelii Praecones* (June 2, 1951): *AAS* 43 (1951), 510-514.

[147] Cf. Dogmatic Constitution on the Church *Lumen Gentium*, 17, 33-38.

[148] Cf. Decree on the Church's Missionary Activity *Ad Gentes*, 35-36, 41.

[149] Post-Synodal Apostolic Exhortation *Christifideles Laici* (December 30, 1988), 14: *AAS* 81 (1989), 410.

[150] *Code of Canon Law*, Canon 225 §1; cf. Second Vatican Ecumenical Council, Decree on the Apostolate of the Laity *Apostolicam Actuositatem*, 6, 13.

Furthermore, because of their secular character, they especially are called "to seek the Kingdom of God by engaging in temporal affairs and ordering these in accordance with the will of God."[151]

72.1 The sphere in which lay people are present and active as missionaries is very extensive. "Their own field . . . is the vast and complicated world of politics, society and economics. . ."[152] on the local, national and international levels. Within the Church, there are various types of services, functions, ministries and ways of promoting the Christian life. I call to mind, as a new development occurring in many Churches in recent times, the rapid growth of "ecclesial movements" filled with missionary dynamism. When these movements humbly seek to become part of the life of local Churches and are welcomed by Bishops and priests within diocesan and parish structures, they represent a true gift of God both for new evangelization and for missionary activity properly so-called. I therefore recommend that they be spread, and that they be used to give fresh energy, especially among young people, to the Christian life and to evangelization, within a pluralistic view of the ways in which Christians can associate and express themselves.

72.2 Within missionary activity, the different forms of the lay apostolate should be held in esteem, with respect for their nature and aims. Lay missionary associations, international Christian volunteer organizations, ecclesial movements, groups and sodalities of different kinds — all these should be involved in the mission *ad gentes* as cooperators with the local Churches. In this way the growth of a mature and responsible laity will be fostered, a laity whom the younger Churches are recognizing as "an essential and undeniable element in the *"plantatio Ecclesiae."*[153]

The work of catechists and the variety of ministries

73.1 Among the laity who become evangelizers, catechists have a place of honor. The Decree on the Church's Missionary Activity speaks of them as "that army of catechists, both men and women, worthy of praise, to whom missionary work among the nations owes so much. Imbued with the apostolic

---

[151] Second Vatican Ecumenical Council, Dogmatic Constitution on the Church *Lumen Gentium*, 31; cf. *Code of Canon Law*, Canon 225 §2.

[152] Paul VI, Apostolic Exhortation *Evangelii Nuntiandi* (December 8, 1975), 70: *AAS* 68 (1976), 60.

[153] Post-Synodal Apostolic Exhortation *Christifideles Laici* (December 30, 1988), 35: *AAS* 81 (1989), 458.

spirit, they make a singular and absolutely necessary contribution to the spread of the faith and of the Church by their strenuous efforts."[154] It is with good reason that the older and established Churches, committed to a new evangelization, have increased the numbers of their catechists and intensified catechetical activity. But "the term 'catechists' belongs above all to the catechists in mission lands. . . . Churches that are flourishing today would not have been built up without them."[155]

73.2 Even with the extension of the services rendered by lay people both within and outside the Church, there is always need for the ministry of catechists, a ministry with its own characteristics. Catechists are specialists, direct witnesses and irreplaceable evangelizers who, as I have often stated and experienced during my missionary journeys, represent the basic strength of Christian communities, especially in the young Churches. The new Code of Canon Law acknowledges the tasks, qualities and qualifications of catechists.[156]

73.3 However, it must not be forgotten that the work of catechists is becoming more and more difficult and demanding as a result of ecclesial and cultural changes. What the Council suggested is still valid today: a more careful doctrinal and pedagogical training, continuing spiritual and apostolic renewal, and the need to provide "a decent standard of living and social security."[157] It is also important to make efforts to establish and support schools for catechists, which are to be approved by the Episcopal Conferences and confer diplomas officially recognized by the latter.[158]

74 Besides catechists, mention must also be made of other ways of serving the Church and her mission; namely, other Church personnel: leaders of prayer, song and liturgy; leaders of basic ecclesial communities and Bible study groups; those in charge of charitable works; administrators of Church resources; leaders in the various forms of the apostolate; religion teachers in schools. All the members of the laity ought to devote a part of their time to the Church, living their faith authentically.

---

[154] Second Vatican Ecumenical Council, Decree on the Church's Missionary Activity *Ad Gentes*, 17.

[155] Apostolic Exhortation *Catechesi Tradendae* (October 16, 1979), 66: *AAS* 71 (1979), 1331.

[156] Cf. Canon 785 §1.

[157] Decree on the Church's Missionary Activity *Ad Gentes*, 17.

[158] Cf. Plenary Assembly of the Sacred Congregation for the Evangelization of Peoples on catechists (1969), and the related "Instruction" (April 1970): *Bibliographia Missionaria* 34 (1970), 197-212, and *S. C. de Propaganda Fide Memoria Rerum*, III/2 (1976), 821-831.

The Congregation for the Evangelization of Peoples and other structures for missionary activity

75.1 Leaders and agents of missionary pastoral activity should sense their unity within the communion which characterizes the Mystical Body. Christ prayed for this at the Last Supper when he said: "Even as you, Father, are in me, and I in you, that they also may be in us, so that the world may believe that you have sent me" (Jn 17:21). The fruitfulness of missionary activity is to be found in this communion.

75.2 But since the Church is also a communion which is visible and organic, her mission requires an external and ordered union between the various responsibilities and functions involved, in such a way that all the members "may in harmony spend their energies for the building up of the Church."[159]

75.3 To the Congregation responsible for missionary activity it falls "to direct and coordinate throughout the world the work of evangelizing peoples and of missionary cooperation, with due regard for the competence of the Congregation for the Oriental Churches."[160] Hence, its task is to "recruit missionaries and distribute them in accordance with the more urgent needs of various regions . . . draw up an ordered plan of action, issue norms and directives, as well as principles which are appropriate for the work of evangelization, and assist in the initial stages of their work."[161] I can only confirm these wise directives. In order to relaunch the mission *ad gentes*, a center of outreach, direction and coordination is needed, namely, the Congregation for the Evangelization of Peoples. I invite the Episcopal Conferences and their various bodies, the major superiors of Orders, Congregations and Institutes, as well as lay organizations involved in missionary activity, to cooperate faithfully with this Dicastery, which has the authority necessary to plan and direct missionary activity and cooperation worldwide.

75.4 The same Congregation, which has behind it a long and illustrious history, is called to play a role of primary importance with regard to reflection and programs of action which the Church needs in order to be more decisively oriented toward the mission in its various forms. To this end, the Congregation should maintain close relations with the other Dicasteries of the Holy

---

[159] Second Vatican Ecumenical Council, Decree on the Church's Missionary Activity *Ad Gentes*, 28.

[160] John Paul II, Apostolic Constitution *Pastor Bonus* (June 28, 1988), 85: *AAS* 80 (1988), 881; cf. Second Vatican Ecumenical Council, Decree on the Church's Missionary Activity *Ad Gentes*, 29.

[161] Second Vatican Ecumenical Council, Decree on the Church's Missionary Activity *Ad Gentes*, 29: cf. John Paul II, Apostolic Constitution *Pastor Bonus* (June 28, 1988), 86: *AAS* 80 (1988), 882.

See, with the local Churches and the various missionary forces. In an ecclesiology of communion in which the entire Church is missionary, but in which specific vocations and institutions for missionary work *ad gentes* remains indispensable, the guiding and coordinating role of the Congregation for the Evangelization of Peoples remains very important in order to ensure a united effort in confronting great questions of common concern, with due regard for the competence proper to each authority and structure.

76.1 Episcopal Conferences and their various groupings have great importance in directing and coordinating missionary activity on the national and regional levels. The Council asks them to "confer together in dealing with more important questions and urgent problems, without, however, overlooking local differences,"[162] and to consider the complex issue of inculturation. In fact, large-scale and regular activity is already taking place in this area, with visible results. It is an activity which must be intensified and better coordinated with that of other bodies of the same Conferences, so that missionary concern will not be left to the care of only one sector or body, but will be shared by all.

76.2 The bodies and institutions involved in missionary activity should join forces and initiatives as opportunity suggests. Conferences of Major Superiors should have this same concern in their own sphere, maintaining contact with Episcopal Conferences in accordance with established directives and norms,[163] and also having recourse to mixed commissions.[164] Also desirable are meetings and other forms of cooperation between the various missionary institutions, both in formation and study,[165] as well as in the actual apostolate.

VII

Cooperation in Missionary Activity

77.1 Since they are members of the Church by virtue of their Baptism, all Christians share responsibility for missionary activity. "Missionary coopera-

---

[162] Decree on the Church's Missionary Activity *Ad Gentes*, 31.
[163] Cf. ibid., 33.
[164] Cf. Paul VI, Apostolic Letter Motu Proprio *Ecclesiae Sanctae* (August 6, 1966), II, 43: *AAS* 58 (1966), 782.
[165] Cf. Second Vatican Ecumenical Council, Decree on the Church's Missionary Activity *Ad Gentes*, 34; Paul VI, Apostolic Letter Motu Proprio *Ecclesiae Sanctae* (August 6, 1966), III, 22: *AAS* 58 (1966), 787.

tion" is the expression used to describe the sharing by communities and individual Christians in this right and duty.

77.2 Missionary cooperation is rooted and lived, above all, in personal union with Christ. Only if we are united to him as the branches to the vine (cf. Jn 15:5) can we produce good fruit. Through holiness of life every Christian can become a fruitful part of the Church's mission. The Second Vatican Council invited all "to a profound interior renewal, so that having a lively awareness of their personal responsibility for the spreading of the Gospel, they may play their part in missionary work among the nations."[166]

77.3 Sharing in the universal mission therefore is not limited to certain specific activities, but is the sign of maturity in faith and of a Christian life that bears fruit. In this way, individual believers extend the reach of their charity and show concern for those both far and near. They pray for the missions and missionary vocations. They help missionaries and follow their work with interest. And when missionaries return, they welcome them with the same joy with which the first Christian communities heard from the Apostles the marvelous things which God had wrought through their preaching (cf. Acts 14:27).

Prayer and sacrifice for missionaries

78 Among the forms of sharing, first place goes to spiritual cooperation through prayer, sacrifice and the witness of Christian life. Prayer should accompany the journey of missionaries so that the proclamation of the word will be effective through God's grace. In his letters, Saint Paul often asks the faithful to pray for him so that he might proclaim the Gospel with confidence and conviction. Prayer needs to be accompanied by sacrifice. The redemptive value of suffering, accepted and offered to God with love, derives from the sacrifice of Christ himself, who calls the members of his Mystical Body to share in his sufferings, to complete them in their own flesh (cf. Col 1:24). The sacrifice of missionaries should be shared and accompanied by the sacrifices of all the faithful. I therefore urge those engaged in the pastoral care of the sick to teach them about the efficacy of suffering, and to encourage them to offer their sufferings to God for missionaries. By making such an offering, the sick themselves become missionaries, as emphasized by a number of movements which have sprung up among them and for them. The solemnity of Pentecost — the beginning of the Church's mission — is celebrated in some communities as a "Day of Suffering for the Missions."

---

[166] Second Vatican Ecumenical Council, Decree on the Church's Missionary Activity *Ad Gentes*, 35; cf. *Code of Canon Law*, Canons 211, 781.

"Here I am, Lord! I am ready! Send me!" (cf. Is 6:8)

79.1 Cooperation is expressed above all by promoting missionary vocations. While acknowledging the validity of various ways of being involved in missionary activity, it is necessary at the same time to reaffirm that *a full and lifelong commitment to the work of the missions holds pride of place*, especially in Missionary Institutes and Congregations. Promoting such vocations is at the heart of missionary cooperation. Preaching the Gospel requires preachers; the harvest needs laborers. The mission is carried out above all by men and women who are consecrated for life to the work of the Gospel and are prepared to go forth into the whole world to bring salvation.

79.2 I wish to call to mind and to recommend this *concern for missionary vocations*. Conscious of the overall responsibility of Christians to contribute to missionary activity and to the development of poorer peoples, we must ask ourselves how it is that in some countries, while monetary contributions are on the increase, missionary vocations, which are the real measure of self-giving to one's brothers and sisters, are in danger of disappearing. Vocations to the priesthood and the consecrated life are a sure sign of the vitality of a Church.

80.1 As I think of this serious problem, I appeal with great confidence and affection to families and to young people. Families, especially parents, should be conscious that they ought to "offer a special contribution to the missionary cause of the Church by fostering missionary vocations among their sons and daughters."[167]

80.2 An intense prayer life, a genuine sense of service to one's neighbor and a generous participation in Church activities provide families with conditions that favor vocations among young people. When parents are ready to allow one of their children to leave for the missions, when they have sought this grace from the Lord, he will repay them, in joy, on the day that their son or daughter hears his call.

80.3 I ask young people themselves to listen to Christ's words as he says to them what he once said to Simon Peter and to Andrew at the lakeside: "Follow me, and I will make you fishers of men" (Mt 4:19). May they have the courage to reply as Isaiah did: "Here am I, Lord! I am ready! Send me!" (cf. Is 6:8). They will have a wonderful life ahead of them, and they will know the genuine joy of proclaiming the "Good News" to brothers and sisters whom they will lead on the way of salvation.

---

[167] Apostolic Exhortation *Familiaris Consortio* (November 22, 1981), 54: *AAS* 74 (1982), 147.

"It is more blessed to give than to receive" (Acts 20:35)

81.1 The material and financial needs of the missions are many: not only to set up the Church with minimal structures (chapels, schools for catechists and seminarians, housing), but also to support works of charity, education and human promotion — a vast field of action especially in poor countries. The missionary Church gives what she receives, and distributes to the poor the material goods that her materially richer sons and daughters generously put at her disposal. Here I wish to thank all those who make sacrifices and contribute to the work of the missions. Their sacrifices and sharing are indispensable for building up the Church and for showing love.

81.2 In the matter of material help, it is important to consider the spirit in which donations are made. For this we should reassess our own way of living: the missions ask not only for a contribution but for a sharing in the work of preaching and charity toward the poor. All that we have received from God — life itself as well as material goods — does not belong to us but is given to us for our use. Generosity in giving must always be enlightened and inspired by faith: then we will truly be more blessed in giving than in receiving.

81.3 *World Mission Day*, which seeks to heighten awareness of the missions, as well as to collect funds for them, is an important date in the life of the Church, because it teaches how to give: as an offering made to God, *in* the Eucharistic celebration and *for* all the missions of the world.

New forms of missionary cooperation

82.1 Today, cooperation includes new forms — not only economic assistance, but also direct participation. New situations connected with the phenomenon of mobility demand from Christians an authentic missionary spirit.

82.2 International tourism has now become a mass phenomenon. This is a positive development if tourists maintain an attitude of respect and a desire for mutual cultural enrichment, avoiding ostentation and waste, and seeking contact with other people. But Christians are expected above all to be aware of their obligation to bear witness always to their faith and love of Christ. Firsthand knowledge of the missionary life and of new Christian communities also can be an enriching experience and can strengthen one's faith. Visiting the missions is commendable, especially on the part of young people who go there to serve and to gain an intense experience of the Christian life.

82.3 Reasons of work nowadays bring many Christians from young communities to areas where Christianity is unknown and at times prohibited or persecuted. The same is true of members of the faithful from traditionally Christian countries who work for a time in non-Christian countries. These circumstances are certainly an opportunity to live the faith and to bear witness to it. In the early centuries, Christianity spread because Christians, traveling to or settling in regions where Christ had not yet been proclaimed, bore courageous witness to their faith and founded the first communities there.

82.4 More numerous are the citizens of mission countries and followers of non-Christian religions who settle in other nations for reasons of study or work, or are forced to do so because of the political or economic situations in their native lands. The presence of these brothers and sisters in traditionally Christian countries is a challenge for the ecclesial communities, and a stimulus to hospitality, dialogue, service, sharing, witness and direct proclamation. In Christian countries, communities and cultural groups are also forming which call for the mission *ad gentes*, and the local Churches, with the help of personnel from the immigrants' own countries and of returning missionaries, should respond generously to these situations.

82.5 Missionary cooperation can also involve leaders in politics, economics, culture and journalism, as well as experts of the various international bodies. In the modern world it is becoming increasingly difficult to determine geographical or cultural boundaries. There is an increasing interdependence between peoples, and this constitutes a stimulus for Christian witness and evangelization.

Missionary promotion and formation among the People of God

83.1 Missionary formation is the task of the local Church, assisted by missionaries and their Institutes, and by personnel from the young Churches. This work must be seen not as peripheral but as central to the Christian life. Even for the "new evangelization" of Christian countries the theme of the missions can prove very helpful: the witness of missionaries retains its appeal even for the non-practicing and non-believers, and it communicates Christian values. Particular Churches should therefore make the promotion of the missions a key element in the normal pastoral activity of parishes, associations and groups, especially youth groups.

83.2 With this end in view, it is necessary to spread information through missionary publications and audiovisual aids. These play an important role in making known the life of the universal Church and in voicing the experiences of missionaries and of the local Churches in which they work. In those younger Churches which are still not able to have a press and other means of their own, it is important that Missionary Institutes devote personnel and resources to these undertakings.

83.3 Such formation is entrusted to priests and their associates, to educators and teachers, and to theologians, particularly those who teach in seminaries and centers for the laity. Theological training cannot and should not ignore the Church's universal mission, ecumenism, the study of the great religions and missiology. I recommend that such studies be undertaken especially in seminaries and in houses of formation for men and women Religious, ensuring that some priests or other students specialize in the different fields of missiology.

83.4 Activities aimed at promoting interest in the missions must always be geared to these specific goals; namely, informing and forming the People of God to share in the Church's universal mission, promoting vocations *ad gentes* and encouraging cooperation in the work of evangelization. It is not right to give an incomplete picture of missionary activity, as if it consisted principally in helping the poor, contributing to the liberation of the oppressed, promoting development or defending human rights. The missionary Church is certainly involved on these fronts but her primary task lies elsewhere: the poor are hungry for God, not just for bread and freedom. Missionary activity must first of all bear witness to and proclaim salvation in Christ, and establish local Churches which then become means of liberation in every sense.

The primary responsibility of the Pontifical Mission Societies

84.1 The leading role in this work of promotion belongs to the Pontifical Mission Societies, as I have often pointed out in my Messages for World Mission Day. The four Societies — Propagation of the Faith, Saint Peter the Apostle, Holy Childhood and the Missionary Union — have the common purpose of fostering a universal missionary spirit among the People of God. The Missionary Union has as its immediate and specific purpose the promotion of missionary consciousness and formation among priests and men and women Religious, who in turn will provide this consciousness and formation within the Christian communities. In addition, the Missionary Union seeks to promote the other Societies, of which it is the "soul."[168] "This must be our motto: All the Churches united for the conversion of the whole world."[169]

84.2 Because they are under the auspices of the Pope and of the College of Bishops, these Societies, also within the boundaries of the particular Churches, rightly have "the first place . . . since they are the means by which Catholics from their very infancy are imbued with a genuinely universal and missionary

---

[168] Cf. Paul VI, Apostolic Letter *Graves et Increscentes* (September 5, 1966): *AAS* 58 (1966), 750-756.

[169] P. Manna, *Le nostre "Chiese" e la propagazione del Vangelo*, 2nd ed., Trentola Ducenta, 1952, 35.

spirit; they are also the means which ensure an effective collection of resources for the good of all the missions, in accordance with the needs of each one."[170] Another purpose of the Missionary Societies is the fostering of lifelong vocations *ad gentes*, in both the older and younger Churches. I earnestly recommend that their promotional work be increasingly directed to this goal.

84.3 In their activities, these Societies depend at the worldwide level on the Congregation for the Evangelization of Peoples; at the local level they depend on the Episcopal Conferences and the Bishops of individual Churches, in collaboration with existing promotional centers. They bring to the Catholic world that spirit of universality and of service to the Church's mission, without which authentic cooperation does not exist.

Not only giving to the missions but receiving from them as well

85.1 Cooperating in missionary activity means not just giving but also receiving. All the particular Churches, both young and old, are called to give and to receive in the context of the universal mission, and none should be closed to the needs of others. The Council states: "By virtue of . . . catholicity, the individual parts bring their own gifts to the other parts and to the whole Church, in such a way that the whole and individual parts grow greater through the mutual communication of all and their united efforts toward fullness in unity. . . . Between the different parts of the Church there are bonds of intimate communion with regard to spiritual riches, apostolic workers and temporal assistance."[171]

85.2 I exhort all the Churches, and the Bishops, priests, Religious and members of the laity, to *be open to the Church's universality,* and to avoid every form of provincialism or exclusiveness, or feelings of self-sufficiency. Local Churches, although rooted in their own people and their own culture, must always maintain an effective sense of the universality of the faith, giving and receiving spiritual gifts, experiences of pastoral work in evangelization and initial proclamation, as well as personnel for the apostolate and material resources.

85.3 The temptation to become isolated can be a strong one. The older Churches, involved in new evangelization, may think that their mission is now at home, and thus they may risk slackening their drive toward the non-Christian world, begrudgingly conceding vocations to Missionary Institutes, Religious Congregations or other particular Churches. But it is by giving generously of what we have that we will receive. Already the young Churches, many

---

[170] Second Vatican Ecumenical Council, Decree on the Church's Missionary Activity *Ad Gentes,* 38.

[171] Dogmatic Constitution on the Church *Lumen Gentium,* 13.

of which are blessed with an abundance of vocations, are in a position to send priests and men and women Religious to the older Churches.

85.4 On the other hand, the young Churches are concerned about their own identity, about inculturation, and about their freedom to grow independently of external influences, with the possible result that they close their doors to missionaries. To these Churches I say: Do not isolate yourselves; willingly accept missionaries and support from other Churches, and do likewise throughout the world. Precisely because of the problems that concern you, you need to be in continuous contact with your brothers and sisters in the faith. With every legitimate means, seek to ensure recognition of the freedom to which you have a right, remembering that Christ's disciples must "obey God rather than men" (Acts 5:29).

God is preparing a new springtime for the Gospel

86.1 If we look at today's world, we are struck by many negative factors that can lead to pessimism. But this feeling is unjustified: we have faith in God our Father and Lord, in his goodness and mercy. As the third millennium of the Redemption draws near, God is preparing a great springtime for Christianity, and we can already see its first signs. In fact, both in the non-Christian world and in the traditionally Christian world, people are gradually drawing closer to Gospel ideals and values, a development which the Church seeks to encourage. Today in fact there is a new consensus among peoples about these values: the rejection of violence and war; respect for the human person and for human rights; the desire for freedom, justice and brotherhood; the surmounting of different forms of racism and nationalism; the affirmation of the dignity and role of women.

86.2 Christian hope sustains us in committing ourselves fully to the new evangelization and to the worldwide mission, and leads us to pray as Jesus taught us: "Thy Kingdom come. Thy will be done, on earth as it is in heaven" (Mt 6:10).

86.3 The number of those awaiting Christ is still immense: the human and cultural groups not yet reached by the Gospel, or for whom the Church is scarcely present, are so widespread as to require the uniting of all the Church's resources. As she prepares to celebrate the Jubilee of the year 2000, the whole Church is even more committed to a new missionary advent. We must increase our apostolic zeal to pass on to others the light and joy of the faith, and to this high ideal the whole People of God must be educated.

86.4 We cannot be content when we consider the millions of our brothers and sisters, who like us have been redeemed by the blood of Christ, but who live in ignorance of the love of God. For each believer, as for the entire Church, the missionary task must remain foremost, for it concerns the eternal destiny of humanity and corresponds to God's mysterious and merciful plan.

VIII

Missionary Spirituality

87.1 Missionary activity demands a specific spirituality, which applies in particular to all those whom God has called to be missionaries.

Being led by the Spirit

87.2 This spirituality is expressed first of all by a life of complete docility to the Spirit. It commits us to being molded from within by the Spirit, so that we may become ever more like Christ. It is not possible to bear witness to Christ without reflecting his image, which is made alive in us by grace and the power of the Spirit. This docility then commits us to receive the gifts of fortitude and discernment, which are essential elements of missionary spirituality.

87.3 An example of this is found with the Apostles during the Master's public life. Despite their love for him and their generous response to his call, they proved to be incapable of understanding his words and reluctant to follow him along the path of suffering and humiliation. The Spirit transformed them into courageous witnesses to Christ and enlightened heralds of his word. It was the Spirit himself who guided them along the difficult and new paths of mission.

87.4 Today, as in the past, that mission is difficult and complex, and demands the courage and light of the Spirit. We often experience the dramatic situation of the first Christian community which witnessed unbelieving and hostile forces "gathered together against the Lord and his Anointed" (Acts 4:26). Now, as then, we must pray that God will grant us boldness in preaching the Gospel; we must ponder the mysterious ways of the Spirit and allow ourselves to be led by him into all the truth (cf. Jn 16:13).

Living the mystery of Christ, "the One who was sent"

88.1 An essential characteristic of missionary spirituality is intimate communion with Christ. We cannot understand or carry out the mission unless we refer it to Christ as the one who was sent to evangelize. Saint Paul describes Christ's attitude: "Have this mind among yourselves, which is yours in Christ Jesus, who, though he was in the form of God, did not count equality with God a thing to be grasped, but emptied himself, taking the form of a servant, being born in the likeness of men. And being found in human form he humbled himself and became obedient unto death, even death on a Cross" (Phil 2:5-8).

88.2 The mystery of the Incarnation and Redemption is thus described as a total self-emptying which leads Christ to experience fully the human condition and to accept totally the Father's plan. This is an emptying of self which is permeated by love and expresses love. The mission follows this same path and leads to the foot of the Cross.

88.3 The missionary is required to "renounce himself and everything that up to this point he considered as his own, and to make himself everything to everyone."[172] This he does by a poverty which sets him free for the Gospel, overcoming attachment to the people and things about him, so that he may become a brother to those to whom he is sent and thus bring them Christ the Savior. This is the goal of missionary spirituality: "To the weak I became weak. . . ; I have become all things to all men, that I might by all means save some. I do it all for the sake of the Gospel. . ." (1 Cor 9:22-23).

88.4 It is precisely because he is "sent" that the missionary experiences the consoling presence of Christ, who is with him at every moment of life — "Do not be afraid . . . for I am with you" (Acts 18:9-10) — and who awaits him in the heart of every person.

Loving the Church and humanity as Jesus did

89.1 Missionary spirituality is also marked by apostolic charity, the charity of Christ who came "to gather into one the children of God who are scattered abroad" (Jn 11:52), of the Good Shepherd who knows his sheep, who searches them out and offers his life for them (cf. Jn 10). Those who have the missionary spirit feel Christ's burning love for souls, and love the Church as Christ did.

89.2 The missionary is urged on by "zeal for souls," a zeal inspired by Christ's own charity, which takes the form of concern, tenderness, compassion, openness, availability and interest in people's problems. Jesus' love is very deep: he who "knew what was in man" (Jn 2:25) loved everyone by offering them redemption and suffered when it was rejected.

89.3 The missionary is a person of charity. In order to proclaim to all his brothers and sisters that they are loved by God and are capable of loving, he must show love toward all, giving his life for his neighbor. The missionary is the "universal brother," bearing in himself the Church's spirit, her openness to and interest in all peoples and individuals, especially the least and poorest

---

[172] Second Vatican Ecumenical Council, Decree on the Church's Missionary Activity *Ad Gentes*, 24.

of his brethren. As such, he overcomes barriers and divisions of race, caste or ideology. He is a sign of God's love in the world — a love without exclusion or partiality.

89.4 Finally, like Christ he must love the Church: "Christ loved the Church and gave himself up for her" (Eph 5:25). This love, even to the point of giving one's life, is a focal point for him. Only profound love for the Church can sustain the missionary's zeal. His daily pressure, as Saint Paul says, is "anxiety for all the Churches" (2 Cor 11:28). For every missionary "fidelity to Christ cannot be separated from fidelity to the Church."[173]

The true missionary is the saint

90.1 The call to mission derives, of its nature, from the call to holiness. A missionary is really such only if he commits himself to the way of holiness: "Holiness must be called a fundamental presupposition and an irreplaceable condition for everyone in fulfilling the mission of salvation in the Church."[174]

90.2 *The universal call to holiness* is closely linked to the *universal call to mission.* Every member of the faithful is called to holiness and to mission. This was the earnest desire of the Council, which hoped to be able "to enlighten all people with the brightness of Christ, which gleams over the face of the Church, by preaching the Gospel to every creature."[175] The Church's missionary spirituality is a journey toward holiness.

90.3 The renewed impulse to the mission *ad gentes* demands holy missionaries. It is not enough to update pastoral techniques, organize and coordinate ecclesial resources, or delve more deeply into the biblical and theological foundations of faith. What is needed is the encouragement of a new "ardor for holiness" among missionaries and throughout the Christian community, especially among those who work most closely with missionaries.[176]

90.4 Dear brothers and sisters: let us remember the missionary enthusiasm of the first Christian communities. Despite the limited means of travel and communication in those times, the proclamation of the Gospel quickly reached the ends of the earth. And this was the religion of the Son of Man,

---

[173] Second Vatican Ecumenical Council, Decree on the Ministry and Life of Priests *Presbyterorum Ordinis,* 14.

[174] Post-Synodal Apostolic Exhortation *Christifideles Laici* (December 30, 1988), 17: *AAS* 81 (1989), 419.

[175] Dogmatic Constitution on the Church *Lumen Gentium,* 1.

[176] Cf. Address at CELAM Meeting, Port-au-Prince (March 9, 1983): *AAS* 75 (1983), 771-779; Homily for the Opening of the "Novena of Years" promoted by CELAM, Santo Domingo (October 12, 1984): *Insegnamenti* VII/2 (1984), 885-897.

who had died on a Cross, "a stumbling block to Jews and folly to Gentiles!" (1 Cor 1:23). Underlying this missionary dynamism was the holiness of the first Christians and the first communities.

91.1 I therefore address myself to the recently baptized members of the young communities and young Churches. Today, you are the hope of this two-thousand-year-old Church of ours: being young in faith, you must be like the first Christians and radiate enthusiasm and courage, in generous devotion to God and neighbor. In a word, you must set yourselves on the path of holiness. Only thus can you be a sign of God in the world and relive in your own countries the missionary epic of the early Church. You will also be a leaven of missionary spirit for the older Churches.

91.2 For their part, missionaries should reflect on the duty of holiness required of them by the gift of their vocation, renew themselves in spirit day by day, and strive to update their doctrinal and pastoral formation. The missionary must be a "contemplative in action." He finds answers to problems in the light of God's word and in personal and community prayer. My contact with representatives of the non-Christian spiritual traditions, particularly those of Asia, has confirmed me in the view that the future of mission depends to a great extent on contemplation. Unless the missionary is a contemplative, he cannot proclaim Christ in a credible way. He is a witness to the experience of God, and must be able to say with the Apostles: "that which we have looked upon . . . concerning the word of life, . . . we proclaim also to you" (1 Jn 1:1-3).

91.3 The missionary is a person of the Beatitudes. Before sending out the Twelve to evangelize, Jesus, in his "missionary discourse" (cf. Mt 10), teaches them the paths of mission: poverty, meekness, acceptance of suffering and persecution, the desire for justice and peace, charity — in other words, the Beatitudes, lived out in the apostolic life (cf. Mt 5:1-12). By living the Beatitudes, the missionary experiences and shows concretely that the Kingdom of God has already come, and that he has accepted it. The characteristic of every authentic missionary life is the inner joy that comes from faith. In a world tormented and oppressed by so many problems, a world tempted to pessimism, the one who proclaims the "Good News" must be a person who has found true hope in Christ.

Conclusion

92.1 Today, as never before, the Church has the opportunity of bringing the Gospel, by witness and word, to all people and nations. I see the dawning of a new missionary age, which will become a radiant day bearing an abundant harvest, if all Christians, and missionaries and young Churches in particular, respond with generosity and holiness to the calls and challenges of our time.

92.2 Like the Apostles after Christ's Ascension, the Church must gather in the Upper Room "together with Mary, the Mother of Jesus" (Acts 1:14), in order to pray for the Spirit and to gain strength and courage to carry out the missionary mandate. We too, like the Apostles, need to be transformed and guided by the Spirit.

92.3 On the eve of the third millennium the whole Church is invited to live more intensely the mystery of Christ by gratefully cooperating in the work of salvation. The Church does this together with Mary and following the example of Mary, the Church's Mother and model: Mary is the model of that maternal love which should inspire all who cooperate in the Church's apostolic mission for the rebirth of humanity. Therefore, "strengthened by the presence of Christ, the Church journeys through time toward the consummation of the ages and goes to meet the Lord who comes. But on this journey . . . she proceeds along *the path* already trodden by the Virgin Mary."[177]

92.4 To "Mary's mediation, wholly oriented toward Christ and tending to the revelation of his salvific power,"[178] I entrust the Church and, in particular, those who commit themselves to carrying out the missionary mandate in today's world. As Christ sent forth his Apostles in the name of the Father and of the Son and of the Holy Spirit, so too, renewing that same mandate, I extend to all of you my Apostolic Blessing, in the name of the same Most Holy Trinity. Amen.

Given in Rome, at Saint Peter's, on December 7, the twenty-fifth anniversary of the conciliar Decree *Ad Gentes,* in the year 1990, the thirteenth of my Pontificate.

[177] Encyclical Letter *Redemptoris Mater* (March 25, 1987), 2: *AAS* 79 (1987), 362-363.
[178] Ibid., 22: loc. cit., 390.

Centesimus Annus

Editor's Introduction

Pope John Paul II issued his ninth encyclical, *Centesimus Annus*, on May 1, 1991.[1] Not surprisingly, the Pope chose to mark the centenary of Leo XIII's *Rerum Novarum* (1891) with a document of his own. In the four years since the signing of *Sollicitudo Rei Socialis* (1987) the Berlin Wall had collapsed, and in the light of this event John Paul offers his "rereading" of *Rerum Novarum*. His purpose is twofold. He wishes to recall Leo's contribution to the development of the Church's social teaching and to honor the Popes who drew upon the encyclical's "vital energies" in their social teaching.

Centesimus Annus has some interesting peculiarities. First, among all John Paul's encyclicals, it relies the least on citing Sacred Scripture. Its few biblical references are primarily exhortatory or illustrative. For his sources the Pope depends mostly on *Rerum Novarum* and on the social encyclicals of his predecessors, as well as on earlier documents and discourses of his own Magisterium. Second, much of the encyclical's content is conditioned by current geopolitical affairs. Indeed, the encyclical reads as if the Pope had *Rerum Novarum* in one hand and a diary of the 1989 events sweeping eastern Europe in the other.

Despite the opinions of some commentators, John Paul's primary interest is not to pass judgment on either failed socialism or contemporary capitalism. Above all, in keeping with his desire to articulate a Christian anthropology, he recalls the need for Catholic social doctrine to have a "*correct view of the human person* and of his unique value" (§11.3). Without such a view, he believes, it is impossible to solve today's social, economic, and political problems. The Church's distinctive contribution to meeting these challenges is her vision of the transcendent dignity of the human person created in God's image and redeemed by Christ's blood.

The Pope's rereading of Leo XIII encompasses three time frames: "looking back" at *Rerum Novarum* itself, "looking around" at the contemporary situation, and "looking to the future" (§3.1). In looking back, John Paul confirms the enduring principles of Leo's encyclical, principles that belong to the Church's doctrinal inheritance. His "pastoral solicitude" also impels the Pope to analyze recent political events from the perspective of the Gospel "in order to discern the new requirements of evangelization" (§3.5).

[1] *Acta Apostolicae Sedis*, 83 (1991), 793-867.

Even more clearly than in his two previous social encyclicals, *Laborem Exercens* (1981) and *Sollicitudo Rei Socialis* (1987), John Paul clearly distinguishes the authentic doctrine contained in the Church's social teaching from the analysis of contingent historical events. This analysis, he states, "is not meant to pass definitive judgments, since this does not fall *per se* within the Magisterium's specific domain" (§3.5). Whatever comes within the doctrinal sphere, however, "pertains to the Church's evangelizing mission and is an essential part of the Christian message" (§5.5).

Summary

The encyclical is composed of an introduction and six chapters. The introduction (§§1-3) sets out the encyclical's purpose: to show the fruitfulness of the principles enunciated by Leo XIII and to apply them to the requirements of the new evangelization. In chapter one, "Characteristics of *Rerum Novarum*" (§§4-11), John Paul "looks back" to Pope Leo in order to discover the seeds of the themes he takes up in his document. The next four chapters "look around," nuancing and updating Leo's social teaching. Chapter two, "Toward the 'New Things' of Today" (§§12-21), continues his rereading of *Rerum Novarum* and then describes the global situation after the Second World War. In chapter three, "The Year 1989" (§§22-29), the Pope discusses the causes and consequences of the fall of Marxism in central and eastern Europe. The following two chapters develop his thought on economic and political life: chapter four, "Private Property and the Universal Destination of Material Goods" (§§30-43), and chapter five, "State and Culture" (§§44-52). The encyclical ends by "looking to the future" in the chapter entitled "Man Is the Way of the Church" (§§53-62).

The "new things" of Leo XIII

Chapter one focuses on how *Rerum Novarum* responded, in the light of Catholic teaching, to the conception of society and the State that was emerging at the end of the nineteenth century. Here, and throughout *Centesimus Annus,* the Pope uses Leo's encyclical as a springboard in order to develop his own reflections on social doctrine.

In the sphere of nineteenth-century economics a new form of property appeared, capital; and a new form of work, labor for wages. These innovations led to the conflict between labor and capital, and to the division of society into opposing classes. When Leo XIII intervened to defend the rights of workers, he invoked the authority of his "apostolic office" (§5.3). His teaching, says John Paul II, "created a lasting paradigm for the Church" (§5.4). Given a great impetus by the initiative of Leo XIII, the Church has developed a genuine social doctrine to apply to individual and communal, as well as to national and international, situations. This teaching is "a *corpus* which enables her to analyze social realities, to make judgments about them and to indicate directions for the just resolution of the problems involved" (§5.4).

Rerum Novarum's principal themes include the dignity of work, the right to private property, the right to form private associations, including trade unions, the right to a just wage, and the right to practice one's religion freely. *Centesimus Annus* likewise treats each of these points. John Paul also mentions two other subjects of continuing relevance raised by Leo's encyclical: the social and economic systems of socialism and liberalism, and the basic principles regarding the role of the state, especially in the regulation of economic life.

The "new things" of today

The Pope begins chapter two with a review of Leo's critique of socialism, and then describes the world situation in the forty years since the Second World War. John Paul "looks around," considering the reasons for the demise of socialism in eastern Europe. The events of 1989 confirmed Leo XIII's judgment about the evil of socialism and his "surprisingly accurate" prognosis about its collapse (§12.1). Proposed as a way to right the conditions of workers, socialism proved to be a remedy that was "worse than the sickness" (§12.3).

According to the encyclical, "the fundamental error of socialism is anthropological in nature" (§13.1); it compromises the dignity of the human person. How? First, socialism, as a State system such as that which existed in the eastern bloc, treats the individual as "a molecule within the social organism" and subordinates his good to "the functioning of the socioeconomic mechanism" (§13.1). Second, real socialism robs human beings of personal responsibility in the choice between good and evil; it suppresses "the concept of the person as the autonomous subject of moral decision" (§13.1). Free choice disappears. So, too, does the "subjectivity" or uniquely personal nature of the individual and society.

Real socialism's faulty view of human nature is ultimately rooted in atheism. The denial of God deprives individuals of their moorings. Moreover, it leads to a social order "without reference to the person's dignity and responsibility" (§13.3). With its origins in Enlightenment rationalism, atheism rejects the truth that a human being's true greatness lies in the capacity to transcend earthly realities. Because of its atheistic basis, socialism encourages violent class struggle as a means for achieving its goal. When cut loose from an objective moral order, conflict is unrestrained by ethical or juridical considerations.

According to the Pope, if human freedom is detached from "obedience to the truth" (§17.1), then the absolute duty to respect the rights of others vanishes.

Before introducing his discussion of the collapse of socialism, John Paul briefly sketches four different economic-political systems which grew up after the Second World War. He first describes "the spread of Communist totalitarianism over more than half of Europe and over other parts of the world" (§19.1). Then he mentions three alternative responses to Marxism: liberal democracies, national security States, and consumer societies. The democratic societies inspired by social justice and free market mechanisms attempted "to deliver work from the mere condition of 'a commodity,' and to guarantee its dignity" (§19.2). National security States, in trying to protect their citizens from Communism, ran "the grave risk of destroying the freedom and values of the person" (§19.3). For their part, consumer societies seek "to defeat Marxism on the level of pure materialism by showing how a free-market society can achieve a greater satisfaction of material human needs than Communism" (§19.4). Ironically, like Marxism, consumer societies treat people under the one-dimensional optic of practical materialism.

Causes and consequences of the collapse of Marxism in 1989

The encyclical's third chapter outlines John Paul's interpretation of the nonviolent events which brought an end to real socialism in Europe and to many dictatorial regimes in Africa, Asia, and Latin America. The Pope's conviction that the religious and moral message of Christianity was decisive in this turn of events comes through with extraordinary clarity. To be sure, all political commentators recognize that the Church's commitment to defend and promote human rights, guided by John Paul II, significantly contributed to the fall of the socialist bloc.

The Pope's line of thought is straightforward. After explaining the three main reasons why the oppressive regimes of eastern Europe fell, he discusses the positive and negative consequences of the end of totalitarianism.

The first factor responsible for the overthrow of the Marxist governments of central and eastern Europe was the stimulus provided by the workers' resentment that their rights were being violated. Beginning with the Solidarity movement in Poland, workers began to protest, "using only the weapons of truth and justice" (§23.2). This peaceful protest disarmed the oppressors. Second, the Pope mentions the decisive role played by the inefficiency of real socialism. It was unable to produce sufficient goods or to provide adequate services for the people. This situation was caused by the "violation of the human rights to private initiative, to ownership of property and to freedom in the economic sector" (§24.1). Third and most important, the "true cause" for the overthrow of real socialism was "the spiritual void brought about by atheism" (§24.2). Especially the young, deprived of direction and searching for the meaning of life, rediscovered "the religious roots of their national cultures" (§24.2). Because cultures coalesce around religious beliefs, many began to question the worldview imposed by atheistic governments.

In the events of 1989 John Paul sees "an example of the success of willingness to negotiate and of the Gospel spirit" (§25.1) when dealing with unscrupulous adversaries. The people's struggle was born in prayer, carried out in union with Christ's sufferings, and nourished by the desire for true freedom.

While the overthrow of totalitarianism in 1989 was largely a European affair, John Paul also describes the global implications of these events. On the positive side, the alliance of the workers' movement with Marxism was finally broken in many countries. During the struggles for freedom, the Church actively supported the workers' demands for justice. Now, says the Pope, the workers' movement, "far from opposing the Catholic Church, looks to her with interest" (§26.3).

On the negative side, the new situation left open the possibility that strife could again break out. Communism built up much hatred and ill-will. The Pope expresses the fear, later verified, that there is "a real danger that these will reexplode after the collapse of dictatorship, provoking serious conflicts and casualties" (§27.1). This challenge can be met, he believes, by keeping alive the moral commitment and conscious striving to bear witness to truth which inspired the overthrow of totalitarianism. Also needed, John Paul adds, are "international structures capable of intervening through appropriate arbitration" in order to resolve any conflicts which arise (§27.2).

The downfall of the eastern bloc highlights the fact of interdependence among all people. More than ever, the Pope says, peace and prosperity are to be viewed as "goods which belong to the whole human race" (§27.3). A new era of development must begin. On the one hand, citizens in the nations of newly won freedom must be "the primary agents of their own development" (§28.1). On the other hand, assistance from other countries is needed so that authentic development will take place. More than merely economic, the development sought must enhance "every individual's dignity and creativity, as well as his capacity to respond to his personal vocation, and thus to God's call" (§29).

Economic life and the market economy

The longest, most complex, and most commented on section of *Centesimus Annus* is chapter four. After discussing Leo's views on private property, John

Paul winds his way through several themes: the universal destination of created goods, the person as the decisive resource in economic life, and the strengths and weaknesses of a free market economy. As always, the Pope is primarily concerned with the factors which promote human dignity and rights.

Centesimus Annus confirms the Church's traditional teaching on the natural right to private property. It is an extension of human freedom, necessary "for the autonomy and development of the person" (§30.1). At the same time, the encyclical reasserts that "God gave the earth to the whole human race for the sustenance of all its members" (§31.2). Property, therefore, also has an intrinsic social character.

Another point emphasized by John Paul is that "*human work* is becoming increasingly important as the productive factor of non-material and of material wealth" (§31.3). Thus, men and women are humanity's principal resource, especially insofar as they possess technological and scientific knowledge. Such knowledge, especially in the Third World, is unfortunately far too scarce. In many countries this scarcity of expertise is creating a new situation of marginalization and exploitation, one reminiscent of the ruthless capitalism of the first phase of industrialization.

John Paul's assessment of the strengths and weaknesses of the free market is the theme that ties chapter four together. He formulates the key question: "Can it perhaps be said that, after the failure of Communism, capitalism is the victorious social system, and that capitalism should be the goal of the countries now making efforts to rebuild their economy and society?" (§42.1). Here he has in mind not the unbridled capitalism of the past, which he roundly condemns, but the "new" capitalism or market economy of the developed western nations.

In various ways the Pope points out the strengths of free market economies. First, they are based on private ownership of the means of production, with all that this implies for the exercise of freedom and creativity. Second, he praises the disciplined work and creative initiatives which market economies make available. Economic freedom, when directed to "being" more rather than merely "having" more, is an essential aspect of human freedom. Third, the market economy makes more goods available for widespread distribution. John Paul judges that both within and among nations "*the free market* is the most efficient instrument for utilizing resources and effectively responding to needs" (§34.1).

Despite its listing of these positive factors, *Centesimus Annus* pays more attention to the dangers and weaknesses inherent in the free market than to its advantages. It warns of the "risk of an 'idolatry' of the market" (§40.2). This idolatry "ignores the existence of goods which by their nature are not and cannot be mere commodities" (§40.2). Many human needs are unable to be satisfied by recourse to market mechanisms. In fact, the Pope maintains that the State must provide for "the defense and preservation of common goods such as the natural and human environments" (§40.1).

The encyclical also asserts that the profitability of an enterprise should not be viewed as the sole indicator of its success. "It is possible," says *Centesimus Annus,* "for the financial accounts to be in order, and yet for the people — who make up the firm's most valuable asset — to be humiliated and their dignity offended" (§35.3). Businesses must also consider human and moral factors in making decisions, and accept their responsibility to form a community of persons in the workplace.

John Paul then takes up three dangers inherent in present-day advanced economies. What is wrong, he says, is that they frequently promote the idea that a style of life "is presumed to be better when it is directed toward 'having' rather than 'being'" (§36.4). According to the Pope, the consumerism of wealthy societies produces a new form of "alienation." It ensnares people "in a web of false and superficial gratifications" rather than helping them "to experience their personhood in an authentic and concrete way" (§41.2). Second, he mentions the negative ecological consequences that accompany a consumerism which plunders the earth's resources "in an excessive and disordered way" (§37.1). Third, the Pope contends that without a strong ethical and cultural underpinning the social fabric is weakened, and the production of goods and services alone becomes paramount. This upsets the "human ecology" or moral conditions necessary for all forms of human flourishing.

Centesimus Annus points out, moreover, that the negative factors found in advanced capitalist societies have a common root: the failure to put the economy at the service of "the value and grandeur of the human person" (§41.3). John Paul therefore excludes a certain kind of capitalism as a legitimate moral option. What is ethically unacceptable, he affirms, is "a system in which freedom in the economic sector is not circumscribed within a strong juridical framework which places it at the service of human freedom in its totality" (§42.2).

Political life and democracy

Chapter five of the encyclical considers the second major change provoked by the events of 1989: the end of totalitarianism and the resurgence of democratic governments in many countries. After assessing the inadequacy of the totalitarian theory of the State, the Pope explains the moral foundations of authentic democracy. For the good of the political order the Church contributes "her vision of the dignity of the person revealed in all its fullness in the mystery of the Incarnate Word" (§47.3).

Totalitarianism, writes the Pope, "arises out of a denial of truth in the objective sense" (§44.2). It disavows the individual's transcendent dignity and the rights inherent in that dignity. By doing so, a totalitarian regime rejects "the affirmation of an *objective criterion of good and evil* beyond the will of those in power" (§45.1). If objective truth does not guide political activity, then such activity can easily be manipulated. Because the Church insists so strongly on the objectivity of the moral norms founded on the natural law, she testifies to a higher authority that rules human affairs. Consequently, totalitarian States always try to destroy the Church or force her into submission.

More clearly than any previous magisterial documents have ever done, *Centesimus Annus* argues in favor of "authentic democracy" as the political system most likely to foster human dignity. For a democracy to fulfill its purpose, it must rest on a "correct conception of the human person" (§46.2). According to the Pope, the Church values the democratic system because it enables the practice of, though it does not guarantee, two principles of Catholic social doctrine: subsidiarity and solidarity.

Democracy favors "the 'subjectivity' of society through the creation of structures of participation and shared responsibility" (§46.2). According to the principle of subsidiarity, a community of a higher order should not deprive a community of a lower order of its proper competencies but should support and coordinate its activities with other groups. This is the Catholic version of "small is beautiful." The Church's social doctrine insists on the rights of intermediate organizations and associations in society. Acting as a buffer between the individual and the State, families, local communities, and unions are social subjects responsible for carrying out their particular functions on their own. These intermediate communities "personalize" society (cf. §49.3).

True democracies also foster solidarity within societies and between countries. Society's intermediate communities, especially the family, "give life to specific networks of solidarity" (§49.3) and, when necessary, are to be assisted in their tasks by higher communities. The State, furthermore, has the obligation to respect the inviolable right to the "open search for truth" (§50.1) which expresses itself in a people's culture. At the international level, a firm commitment to solidarity fosters collective responsibility for the peaceful resolution of conflicts and the promotion of development in less advanced nations.

The person as the way of the Church

John Paul's concluding chapter reaffirms that today the Church's social doctrine focuses especially on the person who is "involved in a complex network of relationships within modern societies" (§54.1). Receiving the meaning of the human person from divine revelation, the Church bears witness that "man's true identity is only fully revealed to him through faith, and it is precisely from faith that the Church's social teaching begins" (§54.1). Only the perspective of faith can ultimately solve present-day social, economic, and political problems. By proclaiming God's gift of salvation to humanity, the Church "contributes to the enrichment of human dignity" (§55.3).

In all her social teaching the Church insists on the need for spiritual and religious values: she preaches that the world's goods are meant for all; and she teaches that societies should be based on a spirit of cooperation and solidarity. Above all, the Pope recalls that the Gospel's social message, which is an integral element in all evangelization, is not merely a theory. Rather, it is "a basis and a motivation for action" (§57.1). Furthermore, social doctrine becomes credible primarily by the witness of action: by love for the poor and the promotion of justice.

Key Themes

Centesimus Annus contains three themes that are vital to the social and moral teaching of John Paul II. In one way or another he has dealt with all of them in earlier encyclicals, and will do so again in future documents. These themes can be summarized in three couplets which form the encyclical's backbone: truth and freedom, human dignity and human rights, and participation and subsidiarity.

Truth and freedom

"You will know the truth, and the truth will make you free" (Jn 8:32). For John Paul, these words of Christ reveal that knowing and living the truth is a condition for authentic freedom. As a divine gift, "freedom attains its full development only by accepting the truth" (§46.4). No genuine freedom exists apart from or in opposition to the truth. This truth about God, the human person, and social life is made known to humanity through the twofold mystery of creation and Redemption.

As a being "who seeks the truth and strives to live in that truth" (§49.3), a person must obey whatever truth is open to him. Freedom, then, is not simply an absence of tyranny or a warrant to do as one pleases. It is bound to the truth which God makes available. Dire consequences result when freedom is detached from objective truth. In private life it degenerates into license, and in social life into the raw exercise of power. "If there is no transcendent truth, in obedience to which man achieves his full dignity," the Pope writes, "then there is no sure principle for guaranteeing just relations between people" (§44.2).

John Paul cautions his readers about the negative repercussions in economic and social life when the essential bond between freedom and truth is severed. Freedom in the economic sphere, he holds, is neither unlimited nor without specific responsibilities. Economic freedom is bound to truth. John Paul issues a warning: "A person who is concerned solely or primarily with possessing and enjoying, who is no longer able to control his instincts and passions, or to subordinate them by obedience to the truth, cannot be free: *obedience to the truth* about God and man is the first condition of freedom, making it possible for a person to order his needs and desires and to choose the means of satisfying them according to a correct scale of values" (§41.4).

Just as freedom in the marketplace ends in the alienation and oppression of people if it is detached from truth, the same holds true in political life. When freedom no longer recognizes its necessary connection with truth, then it is impossible to establish human rights on a solid foundation. Indeed, a new tyranny can emerge. "If there is no ultimate truth to guide and direct political activity," the Pope affirms, "then ideas and convictions can easily be manipulated for reasons of power" (§46.2). An alliance between a deformed democracy and ethical relativism undermines the moral foundation of political and social life.

Human dignity and human rights

In *Centesimus Annus*, John Paul II praises Leo XIII for speaking out in defense of the human person, a duty to which the Church wishes to remain faithful. Indeed, as the Pope remarks, "after the Second World War, she put the dignity of the person at the center of her social messages" (§61.1). The transcendent dignity of the human person is the heart of Catholic social teaching.

The Church's contribution to the political, economic, social, and cultural order is her particular vision of human dignity. "This, and this alone," writes the Pope, "is the principle which inspires the Church's social doctrine" (§53.2). Time and again John Paul recalls that only divine revelation can reveal the full meaning of human dignity and establish an indestructible foundation for human rights. A person's identity is "only fully revealed to him through faith" (§54.1). By shedding the Gospel's light on the meaning of the person, the Church contributes to solving present-day problems.

Recognition of human dignity entails acceptance of the truth that all people have a supernatural vocation which transcends earthly realities. The Pope sees this capacity for transcendence as the basis of making "the free gift of self" to others and to God (cf. §41.3). Consequently, the Church must carefully guard this transcendence in her service to humanity.

Human dignity belongs inherently to every human being. "Man receives from God his essential dignity" (§38.2), writes the Pope. Never earned, it can only be received as a gift. Because people possess a transcendent dignity, they are subjects of rights "which no one may violate — no individual, group, class, nation or State" (§44.2). As visible bearers of the divine image, everyone deserves respect, enjoying those rights "which flow from his essential dignity as a person" (§11.3). Since they are grounded in human dignity, these rights precede one's incorporation into society. They are inherent, universal, and inviolable.

What are these rights? Catholic social teaching has attempted to identify them in every major area of life. In *Centesimus Annus,* John Paul provides his own list, though without claiming that it is exhaustive. The most important of these rights include: "the right to life, an integral part of which is the right of the child to develop in the mother's womb from the moment of conception; the right to live in a united family and a moral environment conducive to the growth of the child's personality; the right to develop one's intelligence and freedom in seeking and knowing the truth; the right to share in the work which makes wise use of the earth's material resources, and to derive from that work the means to support oneself and one's dependents; and the right freely to establish a family, to have and to rear children through the responsible exercise of one's sexuality. In a certain sense, the source and synthesis of these rights is religious freedom, understood as the right to live in the truth of one's faith and in conformity with one's transcendent dignity as a person" (§47.1).

Subsidiarity and participation

For John Paul, the just ordering of society requires that the principle of subsidiarity be respected in economic and political life: "a community of a higher order should not interfere in the internal life of a community of a lower order, depriving the latter of its functions, but rather should support it in case of need and help to coordinate its activity with the activities of the rest of society, always with a view to the common good" (§48.4). Subsidiarity attempts to regulate how institutions with different, though interlocking, spheres of responsibilities relate to one another.

Of particular concern in *Centesimus Annus* are the State's competencies regarding the economic and political life of a nation. The principle of subsidiarity favors decentralization, individual responsibility, and the promotion of free associations. These intermediate organizations include the family, as well as economic, social, political, and cultural groups. According to John Paul II, they "stem from human nature itself and have their own autonomy, always with a view to the common good" (§13.2). These intermediate groups make an indispensable contribution to building a culture of freedom.

At the heart of the Pope's social doctrine is his view that persons have a right to participate in economic and political life. The guarantee of the right to private property is one means to this end. Important as this right is, John Paul pays more attention to the right of workers "to share in a fully human way in the life of their place of employment" (§15.4). Work is "with" others and "for" others; it allows individuals "to make an active contribution to the common good of humanity" (§34.1). Besides securing benefits for its members, unions should "enable workers to participate more fully and honorably in the life of their nation" (§35.1). As for political life, the Pope favors democracy, insofar as "it ensures the participation of citizens in making political choices" (§46.1).

True participation is fostered when the principle of subsidiarity is put into practice. Abuses occur when communities of a higher order, usually the State in one form or another, either absorb or neglect society's intermediate groups. On the one hand, socialist societies fail to respect the rightful autonomy of these intermediate sectors, reducing citizens "to being a 'cog' in the State machine" (§15.1). On the other hand, the "Welfare State" also undermines genuine participation. John Paul clearly points out its weakness: the Welfare State "leads to a loss of human energies and an inordinate increase of public agencies, which are dominated more by bureaucratic ways of thinking than by concern for serving their clients" (§48.5). Opposed to any State that would jeopardize an individual's authentic subjectivity, John Paul encourages individual responsibility, creativity, and entrepreneurial skills as the basis of free societies.

Does subsidiarity therefore exclude all State intervention in economic, political, and social life? Not according to the Pope. Like Leo XIII, John Paul II favors State intervention to the extent that it promotes the common good and ensures everyone's participation in all aspects of society's life.

Rerum Novarum, however, frequently insisted on the "necessary limits to the State's intervention and on its instrumental character" (§11.2). The individual, the family, and society exist prior to the State. The State exists to protect their rights, not to stifle them. Respect for subsidiarity involves assuming certain moral responsibilities. The State has the function of protecting human rights and promoting justice and solidarity among its citizens. According to John Paul, it carries out this role in four ways.

First, the State has "the task of determining the juridical framework within which economic affairs are to be conducted, and thus of safeguarding the prerequisites of a free economy" (§15.1). This role, the Pope adds, "presumes a certain equality between the parties, such that one party would not be so powerful as practically to reduce the other to subservience" (§15.1). Second, the State has the responsibility "of overseeing and directing the exercise of human rights in the economic sector" (§48.2). Nonetheless, even here the primary responsibility belongs to individuals and the various groups and associations which make up society. Third, the State is to provide for "the defense and preservation of common goods such as the natural and human environments, which cannot be safeguarded simply by market forces" (§40.1). Fourth, besides creating favorable conditions for the free exercise of economic activity, the State is to foster solidarity by defending the weakest in society. John Paul II endorses Leo XIII's principle expressed in *Rerum Novarum:* "the more that individuals are defenseless within a given society, the more they require the care and concern of others, and in particular the intervention of governmental authority" (§10.2).

The Church's social doctrine is ultimately aimed at "helping man on the path of salvation" (§54.1). By proclaiming the truth about God, the human person, and society, it sheds light on human dignity and rights, and the proper ordering of economic, political, social, and cultural life. The teaching of *Centesimus Annus* marks one further step on the path of the Church's preparation for the new millennium. It is John Paul's prayer that "in the third millennium too, the Church will be faithful *in making man's way her own,* knowing that she does not walk alone, but with Christ her Lord" (§62.3).

* * *

Selected Bibliography

Acts of the United Nations Seminar on Centesimus Annus: John Paul II's Latest Social Encyclical. *L'Osservatore Romano,* 47 (1991), Supplement, i-xii.

Baum, Gregory. "Capitalism *ex cathedra.*" *Health Progress,* 73 (April 1992), 44-48.

Bayer, Richard C. "Christian Personalism and Democratic Capitalism." *Horizons,* 21 (1994), 313-331.

Bowe, Paul. "*Centesimus Annus.*" *Doctrine and Life,* 41 (1991), 312-318, 324-331.

Buttiglione, Rocco. "Behind *Centesimus Annus.*" *Crisis,* 9 (June 1991), 8-9.

Etchegary, Roger. Presentation at the Press Conference for the Publication of *Centesimus Annus. L'Osservatore Romano,* 18 (1991), 1, 4.

Fortin, Ernest L. "Free Markets Have Their Limits: Two Cheers for Capitalism." *Crisis,* 10 (November 1992), 20-25.

Habiger, Matthew. "Reflections on *Centesimus Annus.*" *Social Justice Review,* 82 (1991), 139-142.

Hauerwas, Stanley. "In Praise of *Centesimus Annus.*" In *To Do Justice and Right Upon Earth.* Edited by Mary E. Stamps. Collegeville: Liturgical Press, 1993. 63-83.

Hittinger, Russell. "The Pope and the Liberal State." *First Things,* 28 (1992), 33-41.

Hollenbach, David. "Christian Social Ethics after the Cold War." *Theological Studies,* 53 (1992), 75-95.

Hollenbach, David. "The Pope and Capitalism." *America,* 164 (1991), 590-591.

Loades, Ann L., ed. "On *Centesimus Annus.*" *Theology,* 95 (1992), 405-432.

Lynn, Thomas D. "Of Politics, Catholics and the Social Doctrine." *Social Justice Review,* 84 (1993), 18-21.

McCormick, Patrick. "*Centesimus Annus.*" In *The New Dictionary of Catholic Social Thought.* Edited by Judith A. Dwyer. Collegeville: Liturgical Press, 1994. 132-143.

McCormick, Patrick. "That They May Converse: Voices of Catholic Social Thought." *Cross Currents,* 42 (Winter 1992), 521-527.

Mahony, Roger. "The Teaching of Revelation." *L'Osservatore Romano,* 32/33 (1991), 9.

Martini, Marco. "Gospel Is Basis for Action." *L'Osservatore Romano,* 29 (1991), 9.

Naughton, Michael J. "The Virtuous Manager and *Centesimus Annus.*" *Social Justice Review,* 85 (1994), 150-152.

Neuhaus, Richard John. *Doing Well and Doing Good: The Challenge to the Christian Capitalist.* New York: Doubleday, 1992.

Neuhaus, Richard John. "John Paul's 'Second Thoughts' on Capitalism." *First Things,* 41 (1994), 65-67.

Preston, R. H. "*Centesimus Annus:* An Appraisal." *Theology,* 95 (1992), 405-416.

Schall, James V. "The Teaching of *Centesimus Annus.*" *Gregorianum,* 74 (1993), 17-43.

Selling, Joseph A. "The Theological Presuppositions of *Centesimus Annus*." *Louvain Studies*, 17 (Spring 1992), 35-47.

Symposium on *Centesimus Annus*. *The Pope Speaks*, 37 (1992), 80-82.

Torre, Joseph M. de la. "John Paul II's Stubborn Humanism." *Homiletic and Pastoral Review*, 92 (February 1992), 56-59.

Tucker, Jeffrey A. "Papal Economics 101: The Catholic Ethic and the Spirit of Capitalism." *Crisis*, 9 (June 1991), 16-21.

Turner, Frank. "John Paul II's Social Analysis." *The Month*, 24 (1991), 344-349.

Utz, Arthur F. "*Centesimus Annus* Gives Us a Profoundly Ethical View of Social and Economic Politics." *L'Osservatore Romano*, 28 (1991), 8, 10.

Weigel, George A., ed. *A New Worldly Order: John Paul II and Human Freedom*. Washington: Ethics and Public Policy Center, 1992.

Wright, Clive. "Work, Life-style and Gospel." *The Way*, 34 (April 1994), 126-137.

ENCYCLICAL LETTER

CENTESIMUS ANNUS

ADDRESSED BY THE SUPREME PONTIFF

JOHN PAUL II

TO HIS VENERABLE BROTHERS

IN THE EPISCOPATE

THE PRIESTS AND DEACONS

FAMILIES OF MEN AND WOMEN RELIGIOUS

ALL THE CHRISTIAN FAITHFUL

AND TO ALL MEN AND WOMEN OF GOOD WILL

ON THE HUNDREDTH ANNIVERSARY

OF *RERUM NOVARUM*

Centesimus Annus

Venerable Brothers,
Beloved Sons and Daughters,
Health and the Apostolic Blessing!

Introduction

1.1 The centenary of the promulgation of the Encyclical which begins with the words *"Rerum Novarum,"*[1] by my Predecessor of venerable memory Pope Leo XIII, is an occasion of great importance for the present history of the Church and for my own Pontificate. It is an Encyclical that has the distinction of having been commemorated by solemn papal documents from its fortieth anniversary to its ninetieth. It may be said that its path through history has been marked by other documents which paid tribute to it and applied it to the circumstances of the day.[2]

1.2 In doing likewise for the hundredth anniversary, in response to requests from many Bishops, Church institutions, and study centers, as well as business leaders and workers, both individually and as members of associations, I wish first and foremost to satisfy the debt of gratitude which the whole Church owes to this great Pope and his "immortal document."[3] I also mean to show that *the vital energies* rising from that root have not been spent with the passing of the years, but rather *have increased even more.* This is evident from the various initiatives which have preceded, and which are to accompany and follow the celebration, initiatives promoted by Episcopal Conferences, by international agencies, universities and academic institutes, by professional associations and by other institutions and individuals in many parts of the world.

2.1 The present Encyclical is part of these celebrations, which are meant to thank God — the origin of "every good endowment and every perfect gift"

---

[1] Leo XIII, Encyclical Letter *Rerum Novarum* (May 15, 1891): *Leonis XIII P. M. Acta,* XI, Rome, 1892, 97-144.

[2] Pius XI, Encyclical Letter *Quadragesimo Anno* (May 15, 1931): *AAS* 23 (1931), 177-228; Pius XII, Radio Message (June 1, 1941): *AAS* 33 (1941), 195-205; John XXIII, Encyclical Letter *Mater et Magistra* (May 15, 1961): *AAS* 53 (1961), 401-464; Paul VI, Apostolic Letter *Octogesima Adveniens* (May 14, 1971): *AAS* 63 (1971), 401-441.

[3] Cf. Pius XI, Encyclical Letter *Quadragesimo Anno* (May 15, 1931), III: *AAS* 23 (1931), 228.

(Jas 1:17) — for having used a document published a century ago by the See of Peter to achieve so much good and to radiate so much light in the Church and in the world. Although the commemoration at hand is meant to honor *Rerum Novarum*, it also honors those Encyclicals and other documents of my Predecessors which have helped to make Pope Leo's Encyclical present and alive in history, thus constituting what would come to be called the Church's "social doctrine," "social teaching" or even "social Magisterium."

2.2 The validity of this teaching has already been pointed out in two Encyclicals published during my Pontificate: *Laborem Exercens* on human work, and *Sollicitudo Rei Socialis* on current problems regarding the development of individuals and peoples.[4]

3.1 I now wish to propose a "rereading" of Pope Leo's Encyclical by issuing an invitation to "look back" at the text itself in order to discover anew the richness of the fundamental principles which it formulated for dealing with the question of the condition of workers. But this is also an invitation to "look around" at the "new things" which surround us and in which we find ourselves caught up, very different from the "new things" which characterized the final decade of the last century. Finally, it is an invitation to "look to the future" at a time when we can already glimpse the third millennium of the Christian era, so filled with uncertainties but also with promises — uncertainties and promises which appeal to our imagination and creativity, and which reawaken our responsibility, as disciples of the "one teacher" (cf. Mt 23:8), to show the way, to proclaim the truth and to communicate the life which is Christ (cf. Jn 14:6).

3.2 A rereading of this kind will not only confirm *the permanent value of such teaching*, but will also manifest *the true meaning of the Church's Tradition* which, being ever living and vital, builds upon the foundation laid by our fathers in the faith, and particularly upon what "the Apostles passed down to the Church"[5] in the name of Jesus Christ, who is her irreplaceable foundation (cf. 1 Cor 3:11).

3.3 It was out of an awareness of his mission as the Successor of Peter that Pope Leo XIII proposed to speak out, and Peter's Successor today is moved by that same awareness. Like Pope Leo and the Popes before and after him, I take my inspiration from the Gospel image of "the scribe who has been trained

---

[4] Encyclical Letter *Laborem Exercens* (September 14, 1981): *AAS* 73 (1981), 577-647; Encyclical Letter *Sollicitudo Rei Socialis* (December 30, 1987): *AAS* 80 (1988), 513-586.

[5] Cf. Saint Irenaeus, *Adversus Haereses*, I, 10, 1; III, 4, 1: *PG* 7, 549-550; 855-856; *SCh* 264, 154-155; *SCh* 211, 44-46.

for the Kingdom of heaven," whom the Lord compares to "a householder who brings out of his treasure what is new and what is old" (Mt 13:52). The treasure is the great outpouring of the Church's Tradition, which contains "what is old" — received and passed on from the very beginning — and which enables us to interpret the "new things" in the midst of which the life of the Church and the world unfolds.

3.4 Among the things which become "old" as a result of being incorporated into Tradition, and which offer opportunities and material for enriching both Tradition and the life of faith, there is the fruitful activity of many millions of people, who, spurred on by the social Magisterium, have sought to make that teaching the inspiration for their involvement in the world. Acting either as individuals or joined together in various groups, associations and organizations, these people represent a *great movement for the defense of the human person* and the safeguarding of human dignity. Amid changing historical circumstances, this movement has contributed to the building up of a more just society or at least to the curbing of injustice.

3.5 The present Encyclical seeks to show the fruitfulness of the principles enunciated by Leo XIII, which belong to the Church's doctrinal patrimony and, as such, involve the exercise of her teaching authority. But pastoral solicitude also prompts me to propose *an analysis of some events of recent history*. It goes without saying that part of the responsibility of Pastors is to give careful consideration to current events in order to discern the new requirements of evangelization. However, such an analysis is not meant to pass definitive judgments, since this does not fall *per se* within the Magisterium's specific domain.

I

Characteristics of *Rerum Novarum*

4.1 Toward the end of the last century the Church found herself facing an historical process which had already been taking place for some time, but which was by then reaching a critical point. The determining factor in this process was a combination of radical changes which had taken place in the political, economic and social fields, and in the areas of science and technology, to say nothing of the wide influence of the prevailing ideologies. In the sphere of politics, the result of these changes was a *new conception of society and of the State*, and consequently *of authority itself*. A traditional society was passing away and another was beginning to be formed — one which brought the hope of new freedoms but also the threat of new forms of injustice and servitude.

4.2 In the sphere of economics, in which scientific discoveries and their practical application come together, new structures for the production of consumer goods had progressively taken shape. A *new form of property* had appeared — capital; and a *new form of labor* — labor for wages, characterized by high rates of production which lacked due regard for sex, age or family situation, and were determined solely by efficiency, with a view to increasing profits.

4.3 In this way labor became a commodity to be freely bought and sold on the market, its price determined by the law of supply and demand, without taking into account the bare minimum required for the support of the individual and his family. Moreover, the worker was not even sure of being able to sell "his own commodity," continually threatened as he was by unemployment, which, in the absence of any kind of social security, meant the specter of death by starvation.

4.4 The result of this transformation was a society "divided into two classes, separated by a deep chasm."[6] This situation was linked to the marked change taking place in the political order already mentioned. Thus the prevailing political theory of the time sought to promote total economic freedom by appropriate laws, or, conversely, by a deliberate lack of any intervention. At the same time, another conception of property and economic life was beginning to appear in an organized and often violent form, one which implied a new political and social structure.

4.5 At the height of this clash, when people finally began to realize fully the very grave injustice of social realities in many places and the danger of a revolution fanned by ideals which were then called "socialist," Pope Leo XIII intervened with a document which dealt in a systematic way with the "condition of the workers." The Encyclical had been preceded by others devoted to teachings of a political character; still others would appear later.[7] Here, particular mention must be made of the Encyclical *Libertas Praestantissimum*,

---

[6] Leo XIII, Encyclical Letter *Rerum Novarum* (May 15, 1891): *Leonis XIII P. M. Acta*, XI, Rome, 1892, 132.

[7] Cf., for example, Leo XIII, Encyclical Epistle *Arcanum Divinae Sapientiae* (February 10, 1880): *Leonis XIII P. M. Acta*, II, Rome, 1882, 10-40; Encyclical Epistle *Diuturnum Illud* (June 29, 1881): *Leonis XIII P. M. Acta*, II, Rome, 1882, 269-287; Encyclical Letter *Libertas Praestantissimum* (June 20, 1888): *Leonis XIII P. M. Acta*, VIII, Rome, 1889, 212-246; Encyclical Epistle *Graves de Communi* (January 18, 1901): *Leonis XIII P. M. Acta*, XXI, Rome, 1902, 3-20.

which called attention to the essential bond between human freedom and truth, so that freedom which refused to be bound to the truth would fall into arbitrariness and end up submitting itself to the vilest of passions, to the point of self-destruction. Indeed, what is the origin of all the evils to which *Rerum Novarum* wished to respond, if not a kind of freedom which, in the area of economic and social activity, cuts itself off from the truth about man?

4.6 The Pope also drew inspiration from the teaching of his Predecessors, as well as from the many documents issued by Bishops, from scientific studies promoted by members of the laity, from the work of Catholic movements and associations, and from the Church's practical achievements in the social field during the second half of the nineteenth century.

5.1 The "new things" to which the Pope devoted his attention were anything but positive. The first paragraph of the Encyclical describes in strong terms the "new things" (*rerum novarum*) which gave it its name: "That *the spirit of revolutionary change* which has long been disturbing the nations of the world should have passed beyond the sphere of politics and made its influence felt in the related sphere of practical economics is not surprising. Progress in industry, the development of new trades, the changing relationship between employers and workers, the enormous wealth of a few as opposed to the poverty of the many, the increasing self-reliance of the workers and their closer association with each other, as well as a notable decline in morality: all these elements have led to the conflict now taking place."[8]

5.2 The Pope and the Church with him were confronted, as was the civil community, by a society which was torn by a conflict all the more harsh and inhumane because it knew no rule or regulation. It was *the conflict between capital and labor,* or — as the Encyclical puts it — the worker question. It is precisely about this conflict, in the very pointed terms in which it then appeared, that the Pope did not hesitate to speak.

5.3 Here we find the first reflection for our times as suggested by the Encyclical. In the face of a conflict which set man against man, almost as if they were "wolves," a conflict between the extremes of mere physical survival on the one side and opulence on the other, the Pope did not hesitate lo intervene by virtue of his "apostolic office,"[9] that is, on the basis of the mission received from Jesus Christ himself to "feed his lambs and tend his sheep" (cf. Jn 21:15-17), and to "bind and loose" on earth for the Kingdom of heaven (cf. Mt 16:19).

---

[8] Encyclical Letter *Rerum Novarum* (May 15, 1891): *Leonis XIII P. M. Acta,* XI, Rome, 1892, 97.

[9] Ibid.: loc. cit., 98.

The Pope's intention was certainly to restore peace, and the present-day reader cannot fail to note his severe condemnation, in no uncertain terms, of the class struggle.[10] However, the Pope was very much aware that *peace is built on the foundation of justice:* what was essential to the Encyclical was precisely its proclamation of the fundamental conditions for justice in the economic and social situation of the time.[11]

5.4 In this way, Pope Leo XIII, in the footsteps of his Predecessors, created a lasting paradigm for the Church. The Church, in fact, has something to say about specific human situations, both individual and communal, national and international. She formulates a genuine doctrine for these situations, a *corpus* which enables her to analyze social realities, to make judgments about them and to indicate directions to be taken for the just resolution of the problems involved.

5.5 In Pope Leo XIII's time such a concept of the Church's right and duty was far from being commonly admitted. Indeed, a twofold approach prevailed: one directed to this world and this life, to which faith ought to remain extraneous; the other directed toward a purely other-worldly salvation, which neither enlightens nor directs existence on earth. The Pope's approach in publishing *Rerum Novarum* gave the Church "citizenship status" as it were, amid the changing realities of public life, and this standing would be more fully confirmed later on. In effect, to teach and to spread her social doctrine pertains to the Church's evangelizing mission and is an essential part of the Christian message, since this doctrine points out the direct consequences of that message in the life of society and situates daily work and struggles for justice in the context of bearing witness to Christ the Savior. This doctrine is likewise a source of unity and peace in dealing with the conflicts which inevitably arise in social and economic life. Thus it is possible to meet these new situations without degrading the human person's transcendent dignity, either in oneself or in one's adversaries, and to direct those situations toward just solutions.

5.6 Today, at a distance of a hundred years, the validity of this approach affords me the opportunity to contribute to the development of Christian social doctrine. The "new evangelization," which the modern world urgently needs and which I have emphasized many times, must include among its essential elements *a proclamation of the Church's social doctrine.* As in the days of Pope Leo XIII, this doctrine is still suitable for indicating the right way to respond to the great challenges of today, when ideologies are being increasingly discred-

[10] Cf. ibid.: loc. cit., 109-110.
[11] Cf. ibid.: description of working conditions; anti-Christian workers' associations: loc. cit., 110-111, 136-137.

ited. Now, as then, we need to repeat that there can be *no genuine solution of the "social question" apart from the Gospel,* and that the "new things" can find in the Gospel the context for their correct understanding and the proper moral perspective for judgment on them.

6.1 With the intention of shedding light on the *conflict* which had arisen between capital and labor, Pope Leo XIII affirmed the fundamental rights of workers. Indeed, the key to reading the Encyclical is the *dignity of the worker* as such, and, for the same reason, the *dignity of work,* which is defined as follows: "to exert oneself for the sake of procuring what is necessary for the various purposes of life, and first of all for self-preservation."[12] The Pope describes work as "personal, inasmuch as the energy expended is bound up with the personality and is the exclusive property of him who acts, and, furthermore, was given to him for his advantage."[13] Work thus belongs to the vocation of every person; indeed, man expresses and fulfills himself by working. At the same time, work has a "social" dimension through its intimate relationship not only to the family, but also to the common good, since "it may truly be said that it is only by the labor of working-men that States grow rich."[14] These are themes that I have taken up and developed in my Encyclical *Laborem Exercens.*[15]

6.2 Another important principle is undoubtedly that of the *right to "private property."*[16] The amount of space devoted to this subject in the Encyclical shows the importance attached to it. The Pope is well aware that private property is not an absolute value, nor does he fail to proclaim the necessary complementary principles, such as the *universal destination of the earth's goods.*[17]

6.3 On the other hand, it is certainly true that the type of private property which Leo XIII mainly considers is land ownership.[18] But this does not mean that the reasons adduced to safeguard private property or to affirm the right to possess the things necessary for one's personal development and the development of one's family, whatever the concrete form which that right may assume, are not still valid today. This is something which must be affirmed once

---

[12] Ibid.: loc. cit., 130; cf. also 114-115.

[13] Ibid.: loc. cit., 130.

[14] Ibid.: loc. cit., 123.

[15] Cf. Encyclical Letter *Laborem Exercens* (September 14, 1981), 1-2, 6: *AAS* 73 (1981), 578-583, 589-592.

[16] Cf. Encyclical Letter *Rerum Novarum* (May 15, 1891): *Leonis XIII P. M. Acta,* XI, Rome, 1892, 99-107.

[17] Cf. ibid.: loc. cit., 102-103.

[18] Cf. ibid.: loc. cit., 101-104.

more in the face of the changes we are witnessing in systems formerly dominated by collective ownership of the means of production, as well as in the face of the increasing instances of poverty or, more precisely, of hindrances to private ownership in many parts of the world, including those where systems predominate which are based on an affirmation of the right to private property. As a result of these changes and of the persistence of poverty, a deeper analysis of the problem is called for, an analysis which will be developed later in this document.

7.1 In close connection with the right to private property, Pope Leo XIII's Encyclical also affirms *other rights* as inalienable and proper to the human person. Prominent among these, because of the space which the Pope devotes to it and the importance which he attaches to it, is the "natural human right" to form private associations. This means above all *the right to establish professional associations* of employers and workers, or of workers alone.[19] Here we find the reason for the Church's defense and approval of the establishment of what are commonly called trade unions: certainly not because of ideological prejudices or in order to surrender to a class mentality, but because the right of association is a natural right of the human being, which therefore precedes his or her incorporation into political society. Indeed, the formation of unions "cannot . . . be prohibited by the State," because "the State is bound to protect natural rights, not to destroy them; and if it forbids its citizens to form associations, it contradicts the very principle of its own existence."[20]

7.2 Together with this right, which — it must be stressed — the Pope explicitly acknowledges as belonging to workers, or, using his own language, to "the working class," the Encyclical affirms just as clearly the right to the "limitation of working hours," the right to legitimate rest and the right of children and women[21] to be treated differently with regard to the type and duration of work.

7.3 If we keep in mind what history tells us about the practices permitted or at least not excluded by law regarding the way in which workers were employed, without any guarantees as to working hours or the hygienic conditions of the workplace, or even regarding the age and sex of apprentices, we can appreciate the Pope's severe statement: "It is neither just nor human so to grind men down with excessive labor as to stupefy their minds and wear out their bodies." And referring to the "contract" aimed at putting into effect "labor

---

[19] Cf. ibid.: loc. cit., 134-135, 137-138.

[20] Ibid.: loc. cit., 135.

[21] Cf. ibid.: loc. cit., 128-129.

relations" of this sort, he affirms with greater precision that "in all agreements between employers and workers there is always the condition expressed or understood" that proper rest be allowed, proportionate to "the wear and tear of one's strength." He then concludes: "To agree in any other sense would be against what is right and just."[22]

8.1 The Pope immediately adds *another right* which the worker has as a person. This is the right to a "just wage," which cannot be left to the "free consent of the parties, so that the employer, having paid what was agreed upon, has done his part and seemingly is not called upon to do anything beyond."[23] It was said at the time that the State does not have the power to intervene in the terms of these contracts, except to ensure the fulfillment of what had been explicitly agreed upon. This concept of relations between employers and employees, purely pragmatic and inspired by a thoroughgoing individualism, is severely censured in the Encyclical as contrary to the two-fold nature of work as a personal and necessary reality. For if work *as something personal* belongs to the sphere of the individual's free use of his own abilities and energy, *as something necessary* it is governed by the grave obligation of every individual to ensure "the preservation of life." "It necessarily follows," the Pope concludes, "that every individual has a natural right to procure what is required to live; and the poor can procure that in no other way than by what they can earn through their work."[24]

8.2 A workman's wages should be sufficient to enable him to support himself, his wife and his children. "If through necessity or fear of a worse evil the workman accepts harder conditions because an employer or contractor will afford no better, he is made the victim of force and injustice."[25]

8.3 Would that these words, written at a time when what has been called "unbridled capitalism" was pressing forward, should not have to be repeated today with the same severity. Unfortunately, even today one finds instances of contracts between employers and employees which lack reference to the most elementary justice regarding the employment of children or women, working hours, the hygienic condition of the workplace and fair pay; and this is the case despite the *International Declarations* and *Conventions* on the subject[26] and the *internal laws* of States. The Pope attributed to the "public authority"

---

[22] Ibid.: loc. cit., 129.
[23] Ibid.: loc. cit., 129.
[24] Ibid.: loc. cit., 130-131.
[25] Ibid.: loc. cit., 131.
[26] Cf. Universal Declaration of Human Rights (1948).

the "strict duty" of providing properly for the welfare of the workers, because a failure to do so violates justice; indeed, he did not hesitate to speak of "distributive justice."[27]

9.1 To these rights Pope Leo XIII adds another right regarding the condition of the working class, one which I wish to mention because of its importance: namely, the right to discharge freely one's religious duties. The Pope wished to proclaim this right within the context of the other rights and duties of workers, notwithstanding the general opinion, even in his day, that such questions pertained exclusively to an individual's private life. He affirms the need for Sunday rest so that people may turn their thoughts to heavenly things and to the worship which they owe to Almighty God.[28] No one can take away this human right, which is based on a commandment; in the words of the Pope: "no man may with impunity violate that human dignity which God himself treats with great reverence," and consequently, the State must guarantee to the worker the exercise of this freedom.[29]

9.2 It would not be mistaken to see in this clear statement a springboard for the principle of the right to religious freedom, which was to become the subject of many solemn *International Declarations* and *Conventions,*[30] as well as of the Second Vatican Council's well-known *Declaration* and of my own repeated teaching.[31] In this regard, one may ask whether existing laws and the practice of industrialized societies effectively ensure in our own day the exercise of this basic right to Sunday rest.

10.1 Another important aspect, which has many applications to our own day, is the concept of the relationship between the State and its citizens. *Rerum Novarum* criticizes two social and economic systems: socialism and liberalism. The opening section, in which the right to private property is reaffirmed, is devoted to socialism. Liberalism is not the subject of a special section, but it is worth noting that criticisms of it are raised in the treatment of

[27] Cf. Encyclical Letter *Rerum Novarum* (May 15, 1891): *Leonis XIII P. M. Acta*, XI, Rome, 1892, 121-123.

[28] Cf. ibid.: loc. cit., 127.

[29] Ibid.: loc. cit., 126-127.

[30] Cf. Universal Declaration of Human Rights (1948); Declaration on the elimination of every form of intolerance and discrimination based on religion or convictions.

[31] Cf. Second Vatican Ecumenical Council, Declaration on Religious Freedom *Dignitatis Humanae;* John Paul II, Letter to Heads of State (September 1, 1980): *AAS* 72 (1980), 1252-1260; Message for the 1988 World Day of Peace (January 1, 1988): *AAS* 80 (1988), 278-286.

the duties of the State.[32] The State cannot limit itself to "favoring one portion of the citizens," namely the rich and prosperous, nor can it "neglect the other," which clearly represents the majority of society. Otherwise, there would be a violation of that law of justice which ordains that every person should receive his due. "When there is question of defending the rights of individuals, the defenseless and the poor have a claim to special consideration. The richer class has many ways of shielding itself, and stands less in need of help from the State; whereas the mass of the poor have no resources of their own to fall back on, and must chiefly depend on the assistance of the State. It is for this reason that wage-earners, since they mostly belong to the latter class, should be specially cared for and protected by the government."[33]

10.2 These passages are relevant today, especially in the face of the new forms of poverty in the world, and also because they are affirmations which do not depend on a specific notion of the State or on a particular political theory. Leo XIII is repeating an elementary principle of sound political organization, namely, the more that individuals are defenseless within a given society, the more they require the care and concern of others, and in particular the intervention of governmental authority.

10.3 In this way what we nowadays call the principle of solidarity, the validity of which both in the internal order of each nation and in the international order I have discussed in the Encyclical *Sollicitudo Rei Socialis*,[34] is clearly seen to be one of the fundamental principles of the Christian view of social and political organization. This principle is frequently stated by Pope Leo XIII, who uses the term "friendship," a concept already found in Greek philosophy. Pope Pius XI refers to it with the equally meaningful term "social charity." Pope Paul VI, expanding the concept to cover the many modern aspects of the social question, speaks of a "civilization of love."[35]

11.1 Rereading the Encyclical in the light of contemporary realities enables us to appreciate *the Church's constant concern for and dedication to*

---

[32] Cf. Encyclical Letter *Rerum Novarum* (May 15, 1891): *Leonis XIII P. M. Acta,* XI, Rome, 1892, 99-105, 130-131, 135.

[33] Ibid.: loc. cit., 125.

[34] Cf. Encyclical Letter *Sollicitudo Rei Socialis* (December 30, 1987), 38-40: *AAS* 80 (1988), 564-569; cf. also John XXIII, Encyclical Letter *Mater et Magistra* (May 15, 1961), I: *AAS* 53 (1961), 407.

[35] Cf. Leo XIII, Encyclical Letter *Rerum Novarum* (May 15, 1891): *Leonis XIII P. M. Acta,* XI, Rome, 1892, 114-116; Pius XI, Encyclical Letter *Quadragesimo Anno* (May 15, 1931), III: *AAS* 23 (1931), 208; Paul VI, Homily for the Closing of the Holy Year (December 25, 1975): *AAS* 68 (1976), 145; Message for the 1977 World Day of Peace (January 1, 1977): *AAS* 68 (1976), 709.

categories of people who are especially beloved to the Lord Jesus. The content of the text is an excellent testimony to the continuity within the Church of the so-called "preferential option for the poor," an option which I defined as a "special form of primacy in the exercise of Christian charity."[36] Pope Leo's Encyclical on the "condition of the workers" is thus an Encyclical on the poor and on the terrible conditions to which the new and often violent process of industrialization had reduced great multitudes of people. Today, in many parts of the world, similar processes of economic, social and political transformation are creating the same evils.

11.2 If Pope Leo XIII calls upon the State to remedy the condition of the poor in accordance with justice, he does so because of his timely awareness that the State has the duty of watching over the common good and of ensuring that every sector of social life, not excluding the economic one, contributes to achieving that good, while respecting the rightful autonomy of each sector. This should not however lead us to think that Pope Leo expected the State to solve every social problem. On the contrary, he frequently insists on necessary limits to the State's intervention and on its instrumental character, inasmuch as the individual, the family and society are prior to the State, and inasmuch as the State exists in order to protect their rights and not stifle them.[37]

11.3 The relevance of these reflections for our own day is inescapable. It will be useful to return later to this important subject of the limits inherent in the nature of the State. For now the points which have been emphasized (certainly not the only ones in the Encyclical) are situated in continuity with the Church's social teaching, and in the light of a sound view of private property, work, the economic process, the reality of the State and, above all, of man himself. Other themes will be mentioned later when we examine certain aspects of the contemporary situation. From this point forward it will be necessary to keep in mind that the main thread and, in a certain sense, the guiding principle of Pope Leo's Encyclical, and of all of the Church's social doctrine, is a *correct view of the human person* and of his unique value, inasmuch as man ". . . is the only creature on earth which God willed for itself."[38] God has imprinted his own image and likeness on man (cf. Gen 1:26), conferring upon him an incomparable dignity, as the Encyclical frequently insists. In effect,

---

[36] Encyclical Letter *Sollicitudo Rei Socialis* (December 30, 1987), 42: *AAS* 80 (1988), 572.

[37] Cf. Encyclical Letter *Rerum Novarum* (May 15, 1891): *Leonis XIII P. M. Acta*, XI, Rome, 1892, 101-102, 104-105, 130-131, 136.

[38] Second Vatican Ecumenical Council, Pastoral Constitution on the Church in the Modern World *Gaudium et Spes*, 24.

beyond the rights which man acquires by his own work, there exist rights which do not correspond to any work he performs, but which flow from his essential dignity as a person.

II
Toward the "New Things" of Today

12.1 The commemoration of *Rerum Novarum* would be incomplete unless reference were also made to the situation of the world today. The document lends itself to such a reference, because the historical picture and the prognosis which it suggests have proved to be surprisingly accurate in the light of what has happened since then.

12.2 This is especially confirmed by the events which took place near the end of 1989 and at the beginning of 1990. These events, and the radical transformations which followed, can only be explained by the preceding situations which, to a certain extent, crystallized or institutionalized Leo XIII's predictions and the increasingly disturbing signs noted by his Successors. Pope Leo foresaw the negative consequences — political, social and economic — of the social order proposed by "socialism," which at that time was still only a social philosophy and not yet a fully structured movement. It may seem surprising that "socialism" appeared at the beginning of the Pope's critique of solutions to the "question of the working class" at a time when "socialism" was not yet in the form of a strong and powerful State, with all the resources which that implies, as was later to happen. However, he correctly judged the danger posed to the masses by the attractive presentation of this simple and radical solution to the "question of the working class" of the time — all the more so when one considers the terrible situation of injustice in which the working classes of the recently industrialized nations found themselves.

12.3 Two things must be emphasized here: first, the great clarity in perceiving, in all its harshness, the actual condition of the working class — men, women and children; secondly, equal clarity in recognizing the evil of a solution which, by appearing to reverse the positions of the poor and the rich, was in reality detrimental to the very people whom it was meant to help. The remedy would prove worse than the sickness. By defining the nature of the socialism of his day as the suppression of private property, Leo XIII arrived at the crux of the problem.

12.4 His words deserve to be reread attentively: "To remedy these wrongs (the unjust distribution of wealth and the poverty of the workers), the socialists encourage the poor man's envy of the rich and strive to do away with private property, contending that individual possessions should become the common property of all. . . ; but their contentions are so clearly powerless to end the controversy that, were they carried into effect, the working man himself would be among the first to suffer. They are moreover emphatically unjust, for they would rob the lawful possessor, distort the functions of the State, and create utter confusion in the community."[39] The evils caused by the setting up of this type of socialism as a State system — which would later be called "Real Socialism" — could not be better expressed.

13.1 Continuing our reflections, and referring also to what has been said in the Encyclicals *Laborem Exercens* and *Sollicitudo Rei Socialis*, we have to add that the fundamental error of socialism is anthropological in nature. Socialism considers the individual person simply as an element, a molecule within the social organism, so that the good of the individual is completely subordinated to the functioning of the socioeconomic mechanism. Socialism likewise maintains that the good of the individual can be realized without reference to his free choice, to the unique and exclusive responsibility which he exercises in the face of good or evil. Man is thus reduced to a series of social relationships, and the concept of the person as the autonomous subject of moral decision disappears, the very subject whose decisions build the social order. From this mistaken conception of the person there arise both a distortion of law, which defines the sphere of the exercise of freedom, and an opposition to private property. A person who is deprived of something he can call "his own," and of the possibility of earning a living through his own initiative, comes to depend on the social machine and on those who control it. This makes it much more difficult for him to recognize his dignity as a person, and hinders progress toward the building up of an authentic human community.

13.2 In contrast, from the Christian vision of the human person there necessarily follows a correct picture of society. According to *Rerum Novarum* and the whole social doctrine of the Church, the social nature of man is not completely fulfilled in the State, but is realized in various intermediary groups, beginning with the family and including economic, social, political and cultural groups which stem from human nature itself and have their own autonomy, always with a view to the common good. This is what I have called the

[39] Encyclical Letter *Rerum Novarum* (May 15, 1891): *Leonis XIII P. M. Acta*, XI, Rome, 1892, 99.

"subjectivity" of society which, together with the subjectivity of the individual, was canceled out by "Real Socialism."[40]

13.3 If we then inquire as to the source of this mistaken concept of the nature of the person and the "subjectivity" of society, we must reply that its first cause is atheism. It is by responding to the call of God contained in the being of things that man became aware of his transcendent dignity. Every individual must give this response, which constitutes the apex of his humanity, and no social mechanism or collective subject can substitute for it. The denial of God deprives the person of his foundation, and consequently leads to a reorganization of the social order without reference to the person's dignity and responsibility.

13.4 The atheism of which we are speaking is also closely connected with the rationalism of the Enlightenment, which views human and social reality in a mechanistic way. Thus there is a denial of the supreme insight concerning man's true greatness, his transcendence in respect to earthly realities, the contradiction in his heart between the desire for the fullness of what is good and his own inability to attain it and, above all, the need for salvation which results from this situation.

14.1 From the same atheistic source, socialism also derives its choice of the means of action condemned in *Rerum Novarum*, namely, class struggle. The Pope does not, of course, intend to condemn every possible form of social conflict. The Church is well aware that in the course of history conflicts of interest between different social groups inevitably arise, and that in the face of such conflicts Christians must often take a position, honestly and decisively. The Encyclical *Laborem Exercens* moreover clearly recognized the positive role of conflict when it takes the form of a "struggle for social justice";[41] *Quadragesimo Anno* had already stated that "if the class struggle abstains from enmities and mutual hatred, it gradually changes into an honest discussion of differences founded on a desire for justice."[42]

14.2 However, what is condemned in class struggle is the idea that conflict is not restrained by ethical or juridical considerations, or by respect for the dignity of others (and consequently of oneself); a reasonable compromise is

[40] Cf. Encyclical Letter *Sollicitudo Rei Socialis* (December 30, 1987), 15, 28: *AAS* 80 (1988), 530, 548-550.

[41] Cf. Encyclical Letter *Laborem Exercens* (September 14, 1981), 11-15: *AAS* 73 (1981), 602-618.

[42] Pius XI, Encyclical Letter *Quadragesimo Anno* (May 15, 1931), III: *AAS* 23 (1931), 213.

thus excluded, and what is pursued is not the general good of society, but a partisan interest which replaces the common good and sets out to destroy whatever stands in its way. In a word, it is a question of transferring to the sphere of internal conflict between social groups the doctrine of "total war," which the militarism and imperialism of that time brought to bear on international relations. As a result of this doctrine, the search for a proper balance between the interests of the various nations was replaced by attempts to impose the absolute domination of one's own side through the destruction of the other side's capacity to resist, using every possible means, not excluding the use of lies, terror tactics against citizens, and weapons of utter destruction (which precisely in those years were beginning to be designed). Therefore class struggle in the Marxist sense and militarism have the same root, namely, atheism and contempt for the human person, which place the principle of force above that of reason and law.

15.1 *Rerum Novarum* is opposed to State control of the means of production, which would reduce every citizen to being a "cog" in the State machine. It is no less forceful in criticizing a concept of the State which completely excludes the economic sector from the State's range of interest and action. There is certainly a legitimate sphere of autonomy in economic life which the State should not enter. The State, however, has the task of determining the juridical framework within which economic affairs are to be conducted, and thus of safeguarding the prerequisites of a free economy, which presumes a certain equality between the parties, such that one party would not be so powerful as practically to reduce the other to subservience.[43]

15.2 In this regard, *Rerum Novarum* points the way to just reforms which can restore dignity to work as the free activity of man. These reforms imply that society and the State will both assume responsibility, especially for protecting the worker from the nightmare of unemployment. Historically, this has happened in two converging ways: either through economic policies aimed at ensuring balanced growth and full employment, or through unemployment insurance and retraining programs capable of ensuring a smooth transfer of workers from crisis sectors to those in expansion.

15.3 Furthermore, society and the State must ensure wage levels adequate for the maintenance of the worker and his family, including a certain amount for savings. This requires a continuous effort to improve workers' training and capability so that their work will be more skilled and productive, as well as

---

[43] Cf. Encyclical Letter *Rerum Novarum* (May 15, 1891): *Leonis XIII P. M. Acta*, XI, Rome, 1892, 121-125.

careful controls and adequate legislative measures to block shameful forms of exploitation, especially to the disadvantage of the most vulnerable workers, of immigrants and of those on the margins of society. The role of trade unions in negotiating minimum salaries and working conditions is decisive in this area.

15.4 Finally, "humane" working hours and adequate free-time need to be guaranteed, as well as the right to express one's own personality at the workplace without suffering any affront to one's conscience or personal dignity. This is the place to mention once more the role of trade unions, not only in negotiating contracts, but also as "places" where workers can express themselves. They serve the development of an authentic culture of work and help workers to share in a fully human way in the life of their place of employment.[44]

15.5 The State must contribute to the achievement of these goals both directly and indirectly. Indirectly and according to the *principle of subsidiarity*, by creating favorable conditions for the free exercise of economic activity, which will lead to abundant opportunities for employment and sources of wealth. Directly and according to the *principle of solidarity*, by defending the weakest, by placing certain limits on the autonomy of the parties who determine working conditions, and by ensuring in every case the necessary minimum support for the unemployed worker.[45]

15.6 The Encyclical and the related social teaching of the Church had far-reaching influence in the years bridging the nineteenth and twentieth centuries. This influence is evident in the numerous reforms which were introduced in the areas of social security, pensions, health insurance and compensation in the case of accidents, within the framework of greater respect for the rights of workers.[46]

16.1 These reforms were carried out in part by States, but in the struggle to achieve them *the role of the workers' movement* was an important one. This movement, which began as a response of moral conscience to unjust and harmful situations, conducted a widespread campaign for reform, far removed from vague ideology and closer to the daily needs of workers. In this context

---

[44] Cf. Encyclical Letter *Laborem Exercens* (September 14, 1981), 20: *AAS* 73 (1981), 629-632; Address to the International Labor Organization (ILO), Geneva (June 15, 1982): *Insegnamenti* V/2 (1982), 2250-2266; Paul VI, Address to the International Labor Organization (June 10, 1969): *AAS* 61 (1969), 491-502.

[45] Cf. Encyclical Letter *Laborem Exercens* (September 14, 1981), 8: *AAS* 73 (1981), 594-598.

[46] Cf. Pius XI, Encyclical Letter *Quadragesimo Anno* (May 15, 1931), I: *AAS* 23 (1931), 178-181.

its efforts were often joined to those of Christians in order to improve workers' living conditions. Later on, this movement was dominated to a certain extent by the Marxist ideology against which *Rerum Novarum* had spoken.

16.2 These same reforms were also partly the result of *an open process by which society organized itself* through the establishment of effective instruments of solidarity, which were capable of sustaining an economic growth more respectful of the values of the person. Here we should remember the numerous efforts to which Christians made a notable contribution in establishing producers', consumers' and credit cooperatives, in promoting general education and professional training, in experimenting with various forms of participation in the life of the workplace and in the life of society in general.

16.3 Thus, as we look at the past, there is good reason to thank God that the great Encyclical was not without an echo in human hearts and indeed led to a generous response on the practical level. Still, we must acknowledge that its prophetic message was not fully accepted by people at the time. Precisely for this reason there ensued some very serious tragedies.

17.1 Reading the Encyclical within the context of Pope Leo's whole Magisterium,[47] we see how it points essentially to the socioeconomic consequences of an error which has even greater implications. As has been mentioned, this error consists in an understanding of human freedom which detaches it from obedience to the truth, and consequently from the duty to respect the rights of others. The essence of freedom then becomes self-love carried to the point of contempt for God and neighbor, a self-love which leads to an unbridled affirmation of self-interest and which refuses to be limited by any demand of justice.[48]

17.2 This very error had extreme consequences in the tragic series of wars which ravaged Europe and the world between 1914 and 1945. Some of these resulted from militarism and exaggerated nationalism, and from related forms of totalitarianism; some derived from the class struggle; still others were civil wars or wars of an ideological nature. Without the terrible burden of hatred

[47] Cf. Encyclical Epistle *Arcanum Divinae Sapientiae* (February 10, 1880): *Leonis XIII P. M. Acta*, II, Rome, 1882, 10-40; Encyclical Epistle *Diuturnum Illud* (June 29, 1881): *Leonis XIII P. M. Acta*, II, Rome, 1882, 269-287; Encyclical Epistle *Immortale Dei* (November 1, 1885): *Leonis XIII P. M. Acta*, V, Rome, 1886, 118-150; Encyclical Letter *Sapientiae Christianae* (January 10, 1890): *Leonis XIII P. M. Acta*, X, Rome, 1891, 10-41; Encyclical Epistle *Quod Apostolici Muneris* (December 28, 1878): *Leonis XIII P. M. Acta*, I, Rome, 1881, 170-183; Encyclical Letter *Libertas Praestantissimum* (June 20, 1888): *Leonis XIII P. M. Acta*, VIII, Rome, 1889, 212-246.

[48] Cf. Leo XIII, Encyclical Letter *Libertas Praestantissimum* (June 20, 1888), 10: *Leonis XIII P. M. Acta*, VIII, Rome, 1889, 224-226.

and resentment which had built up as a result of so many injustices both on the international level and within individual States, such cruel wars would not have been possible, in which great nations invested their energies and in which there was no hesitation to violate the most sacred human rights, with the extermination of entire peoples and social groups being planned and carried out. Here we recall the Jewish people in particular, whose terrible fate has become a symbol of the aberration of which man is capable when he turns against God.

17.3 However, it is only when hatred and injustice are sanctioned and organized by the ideologies based on them, rather than on the truth about man, that they take possession of entire nations and drive them to act.[49] *Rerum Novarum* opposed ideologies of hatred and showed how violence and resentment could be overcome by justice. May the memory of those terrible events guide the actions of everyone, particularly the leaders of nations in our own time, when other forms of injustice are fueling new hatreds and when new ideologies which exalt violence are appearing on the horizon.

18.1 While it is true that since 1945 weapons have been silent on the European continent, it must be remembered that true peace is never simply the result of military victory, but rather implies both the removal of the causes of war and genuine reconciliation between peoples. For many years there has been in Europe and the world a situation of non-war rather than genuine peace. Half of the continent fell under the domination of a Communist dictatorship, while the other half organized itself in defense against this threat. Many peoples lost the ability to control their own destiny and were enclosed within the suffocating boundaries of an empire in which efforts were made to destroy their historical memory and the centuries-old roots of their culture. As a result of this violent division of Europe, enormous masses of people were compelled to leave their homeland or were forcibly deported.

18.2 An insane arms race swallowed up the resources needed for the development of national economies and for assistance to the less developed nations. Scientific and technological progress, which should have contributed to man's well-being, was transformed into an instrument of war: science and technology were directed to the production of ever more efficient and destructive weapons. Meanwhile, an ideology, a perversion of authentic philosophy,

---

[49] Cf. Message for the 1980 World Day of Peace (January 1, 1980): *AAS* 71 (1979), 1572-1580.

was called upon to provide doctrinal justification for the new war. And this war was not simply expected and prepared for, but was actually fought with enormous bloodshed in various parts of the world. The logic of power blocs or empires, denounced in various Church documents and recently in the Encyclical *Sollicitudo Rei Socialis*,[50] led to a situation in which controversies and disagreements among Third World countries were systematically aggravated and exploited in order to create difficulties for the adversary.

18.3 Extremist groups, seeking to resolve such controversies through the use of arms, found ready political and military support and were equipped and trained for war; those who tried to find peaceful and humane solutions, with respect for the legitimate interests of all parties, remained isolated and often fell victim to their opponents. In addition, the precariousness of the peace which followed the Second World War was one of the principal causes of the militarization of many Third World countries and the fratricidal conflicts which afflicted them, as well as of the spread of terrorism and of increasingly barbaric means of political and military conflict. Moreover, the whole world was oppressed by the threat of an atomic war capable of leading to the extinction of humanity. Science used for military purposes had placed this decisive instrument at the disposal of hatred, strengthened by ideology. But if war can end without winners or losers in a suicide of humanity, then we must repudiate the logic which leads to it: the idea that the effort to destroy the enemy, confrontation and war itself are factors of progress and historical advancement.[51] When the need for this repudiation is understood, the concepts of "total war" and "class struggle" must necessarily be called into question.

19.1 At the end of the Second World War, however, such a development was still being formed in people's consciences. What received attention was the spread of Communist totalitarianism over more than half of Europe and over other parts of the world. The war, which should have reestablished freedom and restored the right of nations, ended without having attained these goals. Indeed, in a way, for many peoples, especially those which had suffered most during the war, it openly contradicted these goals. It may be said that the situation which arose has evoked different responses.

19.2 Following the destruction caused by the war, we see in some coun-

---

[50] Cf. Encyclical Letter *Sollicitudo Rei Socialis* (December 30, 1987), 20: *AAS* 80 (1988), 536-537.

[51] Cf. John XXIII, Encyclical Letter *Pacem in Terris* (April 11, 1963), III: *AAS* 55 (1963), 286-289.

tries and under certain aspects a positive effort to rebuild a democratic society inspired by social justice, so as to deprive Communism of the revolutionary potential represented by masses of people subjected to exploitation and oppression. In general, such attempts endeavor to preserve free market mechanisms, ensuring, by means of a stable currency and the harmony of social relations, the conditions for steady and healthy economic growth in which people through their own work can build a better future for themselves and their families. At the same time, these attempts try to avoid making market mechanisms the only point of reference for social life, and they tend to subject them to public control which upholds the principle of the common destination of material goods. In this context, an abundance of work opportunities, a solid system of social security and professional training, the freedom to join trade unions and the effective action of unions, the assistance provided in cases of unemployment, the opportunities for democratic participation in the life of society — all these are meant to deliver work from the mere condition of "a commodity," and to guarantee its dignity.

19.3 Then there are the other social forces and ideological movements which oppose Marxism by setting up systems of "national security," aimed at controlling the whole of society in a systematic way, in order to make Marxist infiltration impossible. By emphasizing and increasing the power of the State, they wish to protect their people from Communism, but in doing so they run the grave risk of destroying the freedom and values of the person, the very things for whose sake it is necessary to oppose Communism.

19.4 Another kind of response, practical in nature, is represented by the affluent society or the consumer society. It seeks to defeat Marxism on the level of pure materialism by showing how a free market society can achieve a greater satisfaction of material human needs than Communism, while equally excluding spiritual values. In reality, while on the one hand it is true that this social model shows the failure of Marxism to contribute to a humane and better society, on the other hand, insofar as it denies an autonomous existence and value to morality, law, culture and religion, it agrees with Marxism, in the sense that it totally reduces man to the sphere of economics and the satisfaction of material needs.

20.1 During the same period a widespread process of "decolonization" occurred, by which many countries gained or regained their independence and the right freely to determine their own destiny. With the formal reacquisition of State sovereignty, however, these countries often find themselves merely at the beginning of the journey toward the construction of genuine independence. Decisive sectors of the economy still remain *de facto* in the hands of large foreign companies which are unwilling to commit themselves to the long-term development of the host country. Political life itself is controlled by foreign powers, while within the national boundaries there are tribal groups not yet amalgamated into a genuine national community. Also lacking is a class of competent professional people capable of running the State apparatus in an honest and just way, nor are there qualified personnel for managing the economy in an efficient and responsible manner.

20.2 Given this situation, many think that Marxism can offer a sort of shortcut for building up the nation and the State; thus many variants of socialism emerge with specific national characteristics. Legitimate demands for national recovery, forms of nationalism and also of militarism, principles drawn from ancient popular traditions (which are sometimes in harmony with Christian social doctrine) and Marxist-Leninist concepts and ideas — all these mingle in the many ideologies which take shape in ways that differ from case to case.

21.1 Lastly, it should be remembered that after the Second World War, and in reaction to its horrors, there arose a more lively sense of human rights, which found recognition in a number of *International Documents*[52] and, one might say, in the drawing up of a new "right of nations," to which the Holy See has constantly contributed. The focal point of this evolution has been the United Nations Organization. Not only has there been a development in awareness of the rights of individuals, but also in awareness of the rights of nations, as well as a clearer realization of the need to act in order to remedy the grave imbalances that exist between the various geographical areas of the world. In a certain sense, these imbalances have shifted the center of the social question from the national to the international level.[53]

21.2 While noting this process with satisfaction, nevertheless one cannot ignore the fact that the overall balance of the various policies of aid for development has not always been positive. The United Nations, moreover, has not yet succeeded in establishing, as alternatives to war, effective means for the

---

[52] Cf. Universal Declaration of Human Rights, issued in 1948; John XXIII, Encyclical Letter *Pacem in Terris* (April 11, 1963), IV: *AAS* 55 (1963), 291-296; "Final Act" of the Conference on Cooperation and Security in Europe, Helsinki, 1975.

[53] Cf. Paul VI, Encyclical Letter *Populorum Progressio* (March 26, 1967), 61-65: *AAS* 59 (1967), 287-289.

resolution of international conflicts. This seems to be the most urgent problem which the international community has yet to resolve.

III
The Year 1989

22.1 It is on the basis of the world situation just described, and already elaborated in the Encyclical *Sollicitudo Rei Socialis*, that the unexpected and promising significance of the events of recent years can be understood. Although they certainly reached their climax in 1989 in the countries of Central and Eastern Europe, they embrace a longer period of time and a wider geographical area. In the course of the '80s, certain dictatorial and oppressive regimes fell one by one in some countries of Latin America and also of Africa and Asia. In other cases there began a difficult but productive transition toward more participatory and more just political structures. An important, even decisive, contribution was made by *the Church's commitment to defend and promote human rights*. In situations strongly influenced by ideology, in which polarization obscured the awareness of a human dignity common to all, the Church affirmed clearly and forcefully that every individual —whatever his or her personal convictions — bears the image of God and therefore deserves respect. Often, the vast majority of people identified themselves with this kind of affirmation, and this led to a search for forms of protest and for political solutions more respectful of the dignity of the person.

22.2 From this historical process new forms of democracy have emerged which offer a hope for change in fragile political and social structures weighed down by a painful series of injustices and resentments, as well as by a heavily damaged economy and serious social conflicts. Together with the whole Church, I thank God for the often heroic witness borne in such difficult circumstances by many Pastors, entire Christian communities, individual members of the faithful, and other people of good will; at the same time I pray that he will sustain the efforts being made by everyone to build a better future. This is, in fact, a responsibility which falls not only to the citizens of the countries in question, but to all Christians and people of good will. It is a question of showing that the complex problems faced by those peoples can be resolved through dialogue and solidarity, rather than by a struggle to destroy the enemy through war.

23.1 Among the many factors involved in the fall of oppressive regimes, some deserve special mention. Certainly, the decisive factor which gave rise to the changes was the violation of the rights of workers. It cannot be forgotten that the fundamental crisis of systems claiming to express the rule and indeed the dictatorship of the working class began with the great upheavals which took place in Poland in the name of solidarity. It was the throngs of working people which foreswore the ideology which presumed to speak in their name. On the basis of a hard, lived experience of work and of oppression, it was they who recovered and, in a sense, rediscovered the content and principles of the Church's social doctrine.

23.2 Also worthy of emphasis is the fact that the fall of this kind of "bloc" or empire was accomplished almost everywhere by means of peaceful protest, using only the weapons of truth and justice. While Marxism held that only by exacerbating social conflicts was it possible to resolve them through violent confrontation, the protests which led to the collapse of Marxism tenaciously insisted on trying every avenue of negotiation, dialogue, and witness to the truth, appealing to the conscience of the adversary and seeking to reawaken in him a sense of shared human dignity.

23.3 It seemed that the European order resulting from the Second World War and sanctioned by the *Yalta Agreements* could only be overturned by another war. Instead, it has been overcome by the non-violent commitment of people who, while always refusing to yield to the force of power, succeeded time after time in finding effective ways of bearing witness to the truth. This disarmed the adversary, since violence always needs to justify itself through deceit, and to appear, however falsely, to be defending a right or responding to a threat posed by others.[54] Once again I thank God for having sustained people's hearts amid difficult trials, and I pray that this example will prevail in other places and other circumstances. May people learn to fight for justice without violence, renouncing class struggle in their internal disputes, and war in international ones.

24.1 The second factor in the crisis was certainly the inefficiency of the economic system, which is not to be considered simply as a technical problem, but rather a consequence of the violation of the human rights to private initiative, to ownership of property and to freedom in the economic sector. To this must be added the cultural and national dimension: it is not possible to understand man on the basis of economics alone, nor to define him simply on

---

[54] Cf. Message for the 1980 World Day of Peace (January 1, 1980): *AAS* 71 (1979), 1572-1580.

the basis of class membership. Man is understood in a more complete way when he is situated within the sphere of culture through his language, history, and the position he takes toward the fundamental events of life, such as birth, love, work and death. At the heart of every culture lies the attitude man takes to the greatest mystery: the mystery of God. Different cultures are basically different ways of facing the question of the meaning of personal existence. When this question is eliminated, the culture and moral life of nations are corrupted. For this reason the struggle to defend work was spontaneously linked to the struggle for culture and for national rights.

24.2 But the true cause of the new developments was the spiritual void brought about by atheism, which deprived the younger generations of a sense of direction and in many cases led them, in the irrepressible search for personal identity and for the meaning of life, to rediscover the religious roots of their national cultures, and to rediscover the person of Christ himself as the existentially adequate response to the desire in every human heart for goodness, truth and life. This search was supported by the witness of those who, in difficult circumstances and under persecution, remained faithful to God. Marxism had promised to uproot the need for God from the human heart, but the results have shown that it is not possible to succeed in this without throwing the heart into turmoil.

25.1 The events of 1989 are an example of the success of willingness to negotiate and of the Gospel spirit in the face of an adversary determined not to be bound by moral principles. These events are a warning to those who, in the name of political realism, wish to banish law and morality from the political arena. Undoubtedly, the struggle which led to the changes of 1989 called for clarity, moderation, suffering and sacrifice. In a certain sense, it was a struggle born of prayer, and it would have been unthinkable without immense trust in God, the Lord of history, who carries the human heart in his hands. It is by uniting their own sufferings, for the sake of truth and freedom, to the sufferings of Christ on the Cross that man is able to accomplish the miracle of peace and is in a position to discern the often narrow path between the cowardice which gives in to evil and the violence which, under the illusion of fighting evil, only makes it worse.

25.2 Nevertheless, it cannot be forgotten that the manner in which the individual exercises his freedom is conditioned in innumerable ways. While these certainly have an influence on freedom, they do not determine it; they make the exercise of freedom more difficult or less difficult, but they cannot destroy it. Not only is it wrong from the ethical point of view to disregard human nature, which is made for freedom, but in practice it is impossible to do so. Where society is so organized as to reduce arbitrarily or even suppress the sphere in which freedom is legitimately exercised, the result is that the life of society becomes progressively disorganized and goes into decline.

25.3 Moreover, man, who was created for freedom, bears within himself the wound of original sin, which constantly draws him toward evil and puts him in need of redemption. Not only is *this doctrine an integral part of Christian revelation,* it also has great hermeneutical value insofar as it helps one to understand human reality. Man tends toward good, but he is also capable of evil. He can transcend his immediate interest and still remain bound to it. The social order will be all the more stable, the more it takes this fact into account and does not place in opposition personal interest and the interests of society as a whole, but rather seeks ways to bring them into fruitful harmony. In fact, where self-interest is violently suppressed, it is replaced by a burdensome system of bureaucratic control which dries up the wellsprings of initiative and creativity. When people think they possess the secret of a perfect social organization which makes evil impossible, they also think that they can use any means, including violence and deceit, in order to bring that organization into being. Politics then becomes a "secular religion" which operates under the illusion of creating paradise in this world. But no political society — which possesses its own autonomy and laws[55] — can ever be confused with the Kingdom of God. The Gospel parable of the weeds among the wheat (cf. Mt 13:24-30; 36-43) teaches that it is for God alone to separate the subjects of the Kingdom from the subjects of the Evil One, and that this judgment will take place at the end of time. By presuming to anticipate judgment here and now, man puts himself in the place of God and sets himself against the patience of God.

25.4 Through Christ's sacrifice on the Cross, the victory of the Kingdom of God has been achieved once and for all. Nevertheless, the Christian life involves a struggle against temptation and the forces of evil. Only at the end of history will the Lord return in glory for the final judgment (cf. Mt 25:31) with the establishment of a new heaven and a new earth (cf. 2 Pet 3:13; Rev 21:1); but as long as time lasts, the struggle between good and evil continues even in the human heart itself.

25.5 What Sacred Scripture teaches us about the prospects of the Kingdom of God is not without consequences for the life of temporal societies, which, as the adjective indicates, belong to the realm of time, with all that this

---

[55] Cf. Second Vatican Ecumenical Council, Pastoral Constitution on the Church in the Modern World *Gaudium et Spes,* 36, 39.

implies of imperfection and impermanence. The Kingdom of God, being *in* the world without being *of* the world, throws light on the order of human society, while the power of grace penetrates that order and gives it life. In this way the requirements of a society worthy of man are better perceived, deviations are corrected, the courage to work for what is good is reinforced. In union with all people of good will, Christians, especially the laity, are called to this task of imbuing human realities with the Gospel.[56]

26.1 The events of 1989 took place principally in the countries of Eastern and Central Europe. However, they have worldwide importance because they have positive and negative consequences which concern the whole human family. These consequences are not mechanistic or fatalistic in character, but rather are opportunities for human freedom to cooperate with the merciful plan of God who acts within history.

26.2 The first consequence was *an encounter* in some countries *between the Church and the workers' movement,* which came about as a result of an ethical and explicitly Christian reaction against a widespread situation of injustice. For about a century the workers' movement had fallen in part under the dominance of Marxism, in the conviction that the working class, in order to struggle effectively against oppression, had to appropriate its economic and materialistic theories.

26.3 In the crisis of Marxism, the natural dictates of the consciences of workers have reemerged in a demand for justice and a recognition of the dignity of work, in conformity with the social doctrine of the Church.[57] The workers' movement is part of a more general movement among workers and other people of good will for the liberation of the human person and for the affirmation of human rights. It is a movement which today has spread to many countries, and which, far from opposing the Catholic Church, looks to her with interest.

26.4 The crisis of Marxism does not rid the world of the situations of injustice and oppression which Marxism itself exploited and on which it fed. To those who are searching today for a new and authentic theory and praxis of liberation, the Church offers not only her social doctrine and, in general, her teaching about the human person redeemed in Christ, but also her concrete commitment and material assistance in the struggle against marginalization and suffering.

[56] Cf. Post-Synodal Apostolic Exhortation *Christifideles Laici* (December 30, 1988), 32-44: *AAS* 81 (1989), 451-481.

[57] Cf. Encyclical Letter *Laborem Exercens* (September 14, 1981), 20: *AAS* 73 (1981), 629-632.

26.5 In the recent past, the sincere desire to be on the side of the oppressed and not to be cut off from the course of history has led many believers to seek in various ways an impossible compromise between Marxism and Christianity. Moving beyond all that was short-lived in these attempts, present circumstances are leading to a reaffirmation of the positive value of an authentic theology of integral human liberation.[58] Considered from this point of view, the events of 1989 are proving to be important also for the countries of the Third World, which are searching for their own path to development, just as they were important for the countries of Central and Eastern Europe.

27.1 The second consequence concerns the peoples of Europe themselves. Many individual, social, regional and national injustices were committed during and prior to the years in which Communism dominated; much hatred and ill will have accumulated. There is a real danger that these will reexplode after the collapse of dictatorship, provoking serious conflicts and casualties, should there be a lessening of the moral commitment and conscious striving to bear witness to the truth which were the inspiration for past efforts. It is to be hoped that hatred and violence will not triumph in people's hearts, especially among those who are struggling for justice, and that all people will grow in the spirit of peace and forgiveness.

27.2 What is needed are concrete steps to create or consolidate international structures capable of intervening through appropriate arbitration in the conflicts which arise between nations, so that each nation can uphold its own rights and reach a just agreement and peaceful settlement vis-à-vis the rights of others. This is especially needed for the nations of Europe, which are closely united in a bond of common culture and an age-old history. A great effort is needed to rebuild morally and economically the countries which have abandoned Communism. For a long time the most elementary economic relationships were distorted, and basic virtues of economic life, such as truthfulness, trustworthiness and hard work were denigrated. A patient material and moral reconstruction is needed, even as people, exhausted by longstanding privation, are asking their governments for tangible and immediate results in the form of material benefits and an adequate fulfillment of their legitimate aspirations.

27.3 The fall of Marxism has naturally had a great impact on the division of the planet into worlds which are closed to one another and in jealous competition. It has further highlighted the reality of interdependence among peoples,

---

[58] Cf. Congregation for the Doctrine of the Faith, Instruction on Christian Freedom and Liberation *Libertatis Conscientia* (March 22, 1986): *AAS* 79 (1987), 554-599.

as well as the fact that human work, by its nature, is meant to unite peoples, not divide them. Peace and prosperity, in fact, are goods which belong to the whole human race: it is not possible to enjoy them in a proper and lasting way if they are achieved and maintained at the cost of other peoples and nations, by violating their rights or excluding them from the sources of well-being.

28.1 In a sense, for some countries of Europe the real post-war period is just beginning. The radical reordering of economic systems, hitherto collectivized, entails problems and sacrifices comparable to those which the countries of Western Europe had to face in order to rebuild after the Second World War. It is right that in the present difficulties the formerly Communist countries should be aided by the united effort of other nations. Obviously they themselves must be the primary agents of their own development, but they must also be given a reasonable opportunity to accomplish this goal, something that cannot happen without the help of other countries. Moreover, their present condition, marked by difficulties and shortages, is the result of an historical process in which the formerly Communist countries were often objects and not subjects. Thus they find themselves in the present situation not as a result of free choice or mistakes which were made, but as a consequence of tragic historical events which were violently imposed on them, and which prevented them from following the path of economic and social development.

28.2 Assistance from other countries, especially the countries of Europe which were part of that history and which bear responsibility for it, represents a debt in justice. But it also corresponds to the interest and welfare of Europe as a whole, since Europe cannot live in peace if the various conflicts which have arisen as a result of the past are to become more acute because of a situation of economic disorder, spiritual dissatisfaction and desperation.

28.3 This need, however, must not lead to a slackening of efforts to sustain and assist the countries of the Third World, which often suffer even more serious conditions of poverty and want.[59] What is called for is a special effort to mobilize resources, which are not lacking in the world as a whole, for the purpose of economic growth and common development, redefining the priorities and hierarchies of values on the basis of which economic and political choices are made. Enormous resources can be made available by disarming the huge military machines which were constructed for the conflict between East and West. These resources could become even more abundant if, in place

---

[59] Cf. Address at the Headquarters of the Economic Community of Western Africa on the Occasion of the Tenth Anniversary of the "Appeal for the Sahel," Ouagadougou, Burkina Faso (January 29, 1990): *AAS* 82 (1990), 816-821.

of war, reliable procedures for the resolution of conflicts could be set up, with the resulting spread of the principle of arms control and arms reduction, also in the countries of the Third World, through the adoption of appropriate measures against the arms trade.[60] But it will be necessary above all to abandon a mentality in which the poor — as individuals and as peoples — are considered a burden, as irksome intruders trying to consume what others have produced. The poor ask for the right to share in enjoying material goods and to make good use of their capacity for work, thus creating a world that is more just and prosperous for all. The advancement of the poor constitutes a great opportunity for the moral, cultural and even economic growth of all humanity.

29.1 Finally, development must not be understood solely in economic terms, but in a way that is fully human.[61] It is not only a question of raising all peoples to the level currently enjoyed by the richest countries, but rather of building up a more decent life through united labor, of concretely enhancing every individual's dignity and creativity, as well as his capacity to respond to his personal vocation, and thus to God's call. The apex of development is the exercise of the right and duty to seek God, to know him and to live in accordance with that knowledge.[62] In the totalitarian and authoritarian regimes, the principle that force predominates over reason was carried to the extreme. Man was compelled to submit to a conception of reality imposed on him by coercion, and not reached by virtue of his own reason and the exercise of his own freedom. This principle must be overturned and total recognition must be given to *the rights of the human conscience,* which is bound only to the truth, both natural and revealed. The recognition of these rights represents the primary foundation of every authentically free political order.[63] It is important to reaffirm this latter principle for several reasons:

29.2 a) because the old forms of totalitarianism and authoritarianism are not yet completely vanquished; indeed there is a risk that they will regain their strength. This demands renewed efforts of cooperation and solidarity between all countries;

---

[60] Cf. John XXIII, Encyclical Letter *Pacem in Terris* (April 11, 1963), III: *AAS* 55 (1963), 286-288.

[61] Cf. Encyclical Letter *Sollicitudo Rei Socialis* (December 30, 1987), 27-28: *AAS* 80 (1988), 547-550; Paul VI, Encyclical Letter *Populorum Progressio* (March 26, 1967), 43-44: *AAS* 59 (1967), 278-279.

[62] Cf. Encyclical Letter *Sollicitudo Rei Socialis* (December 30, 1987), 29-31: *AAS* 80 (1988), 550-556.

[63] Cf. Helsinki Final Act and Vienna Accord; Leo XIII, Encyclical Letter *Libertas Praestantissimum* (June 20, 1888), 5: *Leonis XIII P. M. Acta,* VIII, Rome, 1889, 215-217.

29.3 b) because in the developed countries there is sometimes an excessive promotion of purely utilitarian values, with an appeal to the appetites and inclinations toward immediate gratification, making it difficult to recognize and respect the hierarchy of the true values of human existence;

29.4 c) because in some countries new forms of religious fundamentalism are emerging which covertly, or even openly, deny to citizens of faiths other than that of the majority the full exercise of their civil and religious rights, preventing them from taking part in the cultural process, and restricting both the Church's right to preach the Gospel and the rights of those who hear this preaching to accept it and to be converted to Christ. No authentic progress is possible without respect for the natural and fundamental right to know the truth and live according to that truth. The exercise and development of this right includes the right to discover and freely to accept Jesus Christ, who is man's true good.[64]

IV

Private Property and the Universal Destination of Material Goods

30.1 In *Rerum Novarum,* Leo XIII strongly affirmed the natural character of the right to private property, using various arguments against the socialism of his time.[65] This right, which is fundamental for the autonomy and development of the person, has always been defended by the Church up to our own day. At the same time, the Church teaches that the possession of material goods is not an absolute right, and that its limits are inscribed in its very nature as a human right.

30.2 While the Pope proclaimed the right to private ownership, he affirmed with equal clarity that the "use" of goods, while marked by freedom, is subordinated to their original common destination as created goods, as well as to the will of Jesus Christ as expressed in the Gospel. Pope Leo wrote: "those whom fortune favors are admonished . . . that they should tremble at the warnings of Jesus Christ . . . and that a most strict account must be given to the Supreme Judge for the use of all they possess"; and quoting Saint Thomas

---

[64] Cf. Encyclical Letter *Redemptoris Missio* (December 7, 1990), 7: *AAS* 83 (1991), 255-256.

[65] Cf. Encyclical Letter *Rerum Novarum* (May 15, 1891): *Leonis XIII P. M. Acta,* XI, Rome, 1892, 99-107, 131-133.

Aquinas, he added: "But if the question be asked, how must one's possessions be used? the Church replies without hesitation that man should not consider his material possessions as his own, but as common to all. . . ," because "above the laws and judgments of men stands the law, the judgment of Christ."[66]

30.3 The Successors of Leo XIII have repeated this twofold affirmation: the necessity and therefore the legitimacy of private ownership, as well as the limits which are imposed on it. [67] The Second Vatican Council likewise clearly restated the traditional doctrine in words which bear repeating: "In making use of the exterior things we lawfully possess, we ought to regard them not just as our own but also as common, in the sense that they can profit not only the owners but others too"; and a little later we read: "Private property or some ownership of external goods affords each person the scope needed for personal and family autonomy, and should be regarded as an extension of human freedom. . . . Of its nature private property also has a social function which is based on the law of the *common purpose of goods*."[68] I have returned to this same doctrine, first in my address to the Third Conference of the Latin American Bishops at Puebla, and later in the Encyclicals *Laborem Exercens* and *Sollicitudo Rei Socialis.*[69]

31.1 Rereading this teaching on the right to property and the common destination of material wealth as it applies to the present time, the question can be raised concerning the origin of the material goods which sustain human life, satisfy people's needs and are an object of their rights.

31.2 The original source of all that is good is the very act of God, who created both the earth and man, and who gave the earth to man, so that he might have dominion over it by his work and enjoy its fruits (Gen 1:28). God gave the earth to the whole human race for the sustenance of all its members, without excluding or favoring anyone. This is *the foundation of the universal destination of the earth's goods*. The earth, by reason of its fruitfulness and its

---

[66] Ibid.: loc. cit., 111, 113-114.

[67] Cf. Pius XI, Encyclical Letter *Quadragesimo Anno* (May 15, 1931), II: *AAS* 23 (1931), 191; Pius XII, Radio Message (June 1, 1941): *AAS* 33 (1941), 199; John XXIII, Encyclical Letter *Mater et Magistra* (May 15, 1961), II: *AAS* 53 (1961), 428-429; Paul VI, Encyclical Letter *Populorum Progressio* (March 26, 1967), 22-24: *AAS* 59 (1967), 268-269.

[68] Second Vatican Ecumenical Council, Pastoral Constitution on the Church in the Modern World *Gaudium et Spes,* 69, 71.

[69] Cf. Address at the Opening of the Third General Conference of the Latin American Bishops (January 28, 1979), III, 4: *AAS* 71 (1979), 199-201; Encyclical Letter *Laborem Exercens* (September 14, 1981), 14: *AAS* 73 (1981), 612-616; Encyclical Letter *Sollicitudo Rei Socialis* (December 30, 1987), 42: *AAS* 80 (1988), 572-574.

capacity to satisfy human needs, is God's first gift for the sustenance of human life. But the earth does not yield its fruits without a particular human response to God's gift, that is to say, without work. It is through work that man, using his intelligence and exercising his freedom, succeeds in dominating the earth and making it a fitting home. In this way, he makes part of the earth his own, precisely the part which he has acquired through work; this is *the origin of individual property*. Obviously, he also has the responsibility not to hinder others from having their own part of God's gift; indeed, one must cooperate with others so that together all can dominate the earth.

31.3 In history, these two factors — *work* and *the land* — are to be found at the beginning of every human society. However, they do not always stand in the same relationship to each other. At one time *the natural fruitfulness of the earth* appeared to be, and was in fact, the primary factor of wealth, while work was, as it were, the help and support for this fruitfulness. In our time, *the role of human work* is becoming increasingly important as the productive factor both of nonmaterial and of material wealth. Moreover, it is becoming clearer how a person's work is naturally interrelated with the work of others. More than ever, work is *work with others* and *work for others:* it is a matter of doing something for someone else. Work becomes ever more fruitful and productive to the extent that people become more knowledgeable of the productive potentialities of the earth and more profoundly cognizant of the needs of those for whom their work is done.

32.1 In our time, in particular, there exists another form of ownership which is becoming no less important than land: *the possession of know-how, technology and skill*. The wealth of the industrialized nations is based much more on this kind of ownership than on natural resources.

32.2 Mention has just been made of the fact that *people work with each other*, sharing in a "community of work" which embraces ever widening circles. A person who produces something other than for his own use generally does so in order that others may use it after they have paid a just price, mutually agreed upon through free bargaining. It is precisely the ability to foresee both the needs of others and the combinations of productive factors most adapted to satisfying those needs that constitutes another important source of wealth in modern society. Besides, many goods cannot be adequately produced through the work of an isolated individual; they require the cooperation of many people in working toward a common goal. Organizing such a productive effort, planning its duration in time, making sure that it corresponds in a positive way to the demands which it must satisfy, and taking the necessary risks — all this too is a source of wealth in today's society. In this way, the *role* of disciplined and creative *human work* and, as an essential part of that work, *initiative and entrepreneurial ability* becomes increasingly evident and decisive.[70]

32.3 This process, which throws practical light on a truth about the person which Christianity has constantly affirmed, should be viewed carefully and favorably. Indeed, besides the earth, man's principal resource is *man himself*. His intelligence enables him to discover the earth's productive potential and the many different ways in which human needs can be satisfied. It is his disciplined work in close collaboration with others that makes possible the creation of ever more extensive *working communities* which can be relied upon to transform man's natural and human environments. Important virtues are involved in this process, such as diligence, industriousness, prudence in undertaking reasonable risks, reliability and fidelity in interpersonal relationships, as well as courage in carrying out decisions which are difficult and painful but necessary, both for the overall working of a business and in meeting possible setbacks.

32.4 The modern *business economy* has positive aspects. Its basis is human freedom exercised in the economic field, just as it is exercised in many other fields. Economic activity is indeed but one sector in a great variety of human activities, and like every other sector, it includes the right to freedom, as well as the duty of making responsible use of freedom. But it is important to note that there are specific differences between the trends of modern society and those of the past, even the recent past. Whereas at one time the decisive factor of production was *the land,* and later capital — understood as a total complex of the instruments of production — today the decisive factor is increasingly *man himself,* that is, his knowledge, especially his scientific knowledge, his capacity for interrelated and compact organization, as well as his ability to perceive the needs of others and to satisfy them.

33.1 However, the risks and problems connected with this kind of process should be pointed out. The fact is that many people, perhaps the majority today, do not have the means which would enable them to take their place in an effective and humanly dignified way within a productive system in which work is truly central. They have no possibility of acquiring the basic knowledge which would enable them to express their creativity and develop their potential. They have no way of entering the network of knowledge and inter-

[70] Cf. Encyclical Letter *Sollicitudo Rei Socialis* (December 30, 1987), 15: *AAS* 80 (1988), 528-531.

communication which would enable them to see their qualities appreciated and utilized. Thus, if not actually exploited, they are to a great extent marginalized; economic development takes place over their heads, so to speak, when it does not actually reduce the already narrow scope of their old subsistence economies. They are unable to compete against the goods which are produced in ways which are new and which properly respond to needs, needs which they had previously been accustomed to meeting through traditional forms of organization. Allured by the dazzle of an opulence which is beyond their reach, and at the same time driven by necessity, these people crowd the cities of the Third World where they are often without cultural roots, and where they are exposed to situations of violent uncertainty, without the possibility of becoming integrated. Their dignity is not acknowledged in any real way, and sometimes there are even attempts to eliminate them from history through coercive forms of demographic control which are contrary to human dignity.

33.2 Many other people, while not completely marginalized, live in situations in which the struggle for a bare minimum is uppermost. These are situations in which the rules of the earliest period of capitalism still flourish in conditions of "ruthlessness" in no way inferior to the darkest moments of the first phase of industrialization. In other cases the land is still the central element in the economic process, but those who cultivate it are excluded from ownership and are reduced to a state of quasi-servitude.[71] In these cases, it is still possible today, as in the days of *Rerum Novarum*, to speak of inhuman exploitation. In spite of the great changes which have taken place in the more advanced societies, the human inadequacies of capitalism and the resulting domination of things over people are far from disappearing. In fact, for the poor, to the lack of material goods has been added a lack of knowledge and training which prevents them from escaping their state of humiliating subjection.

33.3 Unfortunately, the great majority of people in the Third World still live in such conditions. It would be a mistake, however, to understand this *"world"* in purely geographic terms. In some regions and in some social sectors of that world, development programs have been set up which are centered on the use not so much of the material resources available but of the "human resources."

33.4 Even in recent years it was thought that the poorest countries would develop by isolating themselves from the world market and by depending only on their own resources. Recent experience has shown that countries which

---

[71] Cf. Encyclical Letter *Laborem Exercens* (September 14, 1981), 21: *AAS* 73 (1981), 632-634.

did this have suffered stagnation and recession, while the countries which experienced development were those which succeeded in taking part in the general interrelated economic activities at the international level. It seems therefore that the chief problem is that of gaining fair access to the international market, based not on the unilateral principle of the exploitation of the natural resources of these countries but on the proper use of human resources.[72]

33.5 However, aspects typical of the Third World also appear in developed countries, where the constant transformation of the methods of production and consumption devalues certain acquired skills and professional expertise, and thus requires a continual effort of retraining and updating. Those who fail to keep up with the times can easily be marginalized, as can the elderly, the young people who are incapable of finding their place in the life of society and, in general, those who are weakest or part of the so-called Fourth World. The situation of women too is far from easy in these conditions.

34.1 It would appear that, on the level of individual nations and of international relations, *the free market* is the most efficient instrument for utilizing resources and effectively responding to needs. But this is true only for those needs which are "solvent," insofar as they are endowed with purchasing power, and for those resources which are "marketable" insofar as they are capable of obtaining a satisfactory price. But there are many human needs which find no place on the market. It is a strict duty of justice and truth not to allow fundamental human needs to remain unsatisfied, and not to allow those burdened by such needs to perish. It is also necessary to help these needy people to acquire expertise, to enter the circle of exchange, and to develop their skills in order to make the best use of their capacities and resources. Even prior to the logic of a fair exchange of goods and the forms of justice appropriate to it, there exists *something which is due to man because he is man*, by reason of his lofty dignity. Inseparable from that required "something" is the possibility to survive and, at the same time, to make an active contribution to the common good of humanity.

34.2 In Third World contexts, certain objectives stated by *Rerum Novarum* remain valid, and, in some cases, still constitute a goal yet to be reached, if a man's work and his very being are not to be reduced to the level of a mere commodity. These objectives include a sufficient wage for the support of the

---

[72] Cf. Paul VI, Encyclical Letter *Populorum Progressio* (March 26, 1967), 33-42: *AAS* 59 (1967), 273-278.

family, social insurance for old age and unemployment, and adequate protection for the conditions of employment.

35.1 Here we find a wide range of *opportunities for commitment and effort* in the name of justice on the part of trade unions and other workers' organizations. These defend workers' rights and protect their interests as persons, while fulfilling a vital cultural role, so as to enable workers to participate more fully and honorably in the life of their nation and to assist them along the path of development.

35.2 In this sense, it is right to speak of a struggle against an economic system, if the latter is understood as a method of upholding the absolute predominance of capital, the possession of the means of production and of the land, in contrast to the free and personal nature of human work.[73] In the struggle against such a system, what is being proposed as an alternative is not the socialist system, which in fact turns out to be State capitalism, but rather *a society of free work, of enterprise and of participation.* Such a society is not directed against the market, but demands that the market be appropriately controlled by the forces of society and by the State, so as to guarantee that the basic needs of the whole of society are satisfied.

35.3 The Church acknowledges the legitimate *role of profit* as an indication that a business is functioning well. When a firm makes a profit, this means that productive factors have been properly employed and corresponding human needs have been duly satisfied. But profitability is not the only indicator of a firm's condition. It is possible for the financial accounts to be in order, and yet for the people — who make up the firm's most valuable asset — to be humiliated and their dignity offended. Besides being morally inadmissible, this will eventually have negative repercussions on the firm's economic efficiency. In fact, the purpose of a business firm is not simply to make a profit, but is to be found in its very existence as a *community of persons* who in various ways are endeavoring to satisfy their basic needs, and who form a particular group at the service of the whole of society. Profit is a regulator of the life of a business, but it is not the only one; *other human and moral factors* must also be considered which, in the long term, are at least equally important for the life of a business.

35.4 We have seen that it is unacceptable to say that the defeat of so-called "Real Socialism" leaves capitalism as the only model of economic organization. It is necessary to break down the barriers and monopolies which leave so

---

[73] Cf. Encyclical Letter *Laborem Exercens* (September 14, 1981), 7: *AAS* 73 (1981), 592-594.

many countries on the margins of development, and to provide all individuals and nations with the basic conditions which will enable them to share in development. This goal calls for programmed and responsible efforts on the part of the entire international community. Stronger nations must offer weaker ones opportunities for taking their place in international life, and the latter must learn how to use these opportunities by making the necessary efforts and sacrifices and by ensuring political and economic stability, the certainty of better prospects for the future, the improvement of workers' skills, and the training of competent business leaders who are conscious of their responsibilities.[74]

35.5 At present, the positive efforts which have been made along these lines are being affected by the still largely unsolved problem of the foreign debt of the poorer countries. The principle that debts must be paid is certainly just. However, it is not right to demand or expect payment when the effect would be the imposition of political choices leading to hunger and despair for entire peoples. It cannot be expected that the debts which have been contracted should be paid at the price of unbearable sacrifices. In such cases it is necessary to find — as in fact is partly happening — ways to lighten, defer or even cancel the debt, compatible with the fundamental right of peoples to subsistence and progress.

36.1 It would now be helpful to direct our attention to the specific problems and threats emerging within the more advanced economies and which are related to their particular characteristics. In earlier stages of development, man always lived under the weight of necessity. His needs were few and were determined, to a degree, by the objective structures of his physical make-up. Economic activity was directed toward satisfying these needs. It is clear that today the problem is not only one of supplying people with a sufficient quantity of goods, but also of responding to *a demand for quality:* the quality of the goods to be produced and consumed, the quality of the services to be enjoyed, the quality of the environment and of life in general.

36.2 To call for an existence which is qualitatively more satisfying is of itself legitimate, but one cannot fail to draw attention to the new responsibilities and dangers connected with this phase of history. The manner in which new needs arise and are defined is always marked by a more or less appropriate concept of man and of his true good. A given culture reveals its overall understanding of life through the choices it makes in production and consumption. It is here that *the phenomenon of consumerism* arises. In singling

---

[74] Cf. ibid., 8: loc. cit., 594-598.

out new needs and new means to meet them, one must be guided by a comprehensive picture of man which respects all the dimensions of his being and which subordinates his material and instinctive dimensions to his interior and spiritual ones. If, on the contrary, a direct appeal is made to human instincts — while ignoring in various ways the reality of the person as intelligent and free — then *consumer attitudes* and *lifestyles* can be created which are objectively improper and often damaging to the person's physical and spiritual health. Of itself, an economic system does not possess criteria for correctly distinguishing new and higher forms of satisfying human needs from artificial new needs which hinder the formation of a mature personality. *Thus a great deal of educational and cultural work* is urgently needed, including the education of consumers in the responsible use of their power of choice, the formation of a strong sense of responsibility among producers and among people in the mass media in particular, as well as the necessary intervention by public authorities.

36.3 A striking example of artificial consumption contrary to the health and dignity of the human person, and certainly not easy to control, is the use of drugs. Widespread drug use is a sign of a serious malfunction in the social system; it also implies a materialistic and, in a certain sense, destructive "reading" of human needs. In this way the innovative capacity of a free economy is brought to a one-sided and inadequate conclusion. Drugs, as well as pornography and other forms of consumerism which exploit the frailty of the weak, tend to fill the resulting spiritual void.

36.4 It is not wrong to want to live better; what is wrong is a style of life which is presumed to be better when it is directed toward "having" rather than "being," and which wants to have more, not in order to be more but in order to spend life in enjoyment as an end in itself.[75] It is therefore necessary to create lifestyles in which the quest for truth, beauty, goodness and communion with others for the sake of common growth are the factors which determine consumer choices, savings and investments. In this regard, it is not a matter of the duty of charity alone, that is, the duty to give from one's "abundance," and sometimes even out of one's needs, in order to provide what is essential for the life of a poor person. I am referring to the fact that even the decision to invest in one place rather than another, in one productive sector rather than another, is always *a moral and cultural choice.* Given the utter necessity of certain economic conditions and of political stability, the decision to invest, that

[75] Cf. Second Vatican Ecumenical Council, Pastoral Constitution on the Church in the Modern World *Gaudium et Spes,* 35; Paul VI, Encyclical Letter *Populorum Progressio* (March 26, 1967), 19: *AAS* 59 (1967), 266-267.

is, to offer people an opportunity to make good use of their own labor, is also determined by an attitude of human sympathy and trust in Providence, which reveal the human quality of the person making such decisions.

37.1 Equally worrying is *the ecological question* which accompanies the problem of consumerism and which is closely connected to it. In his desire to have and to enjoy rather than to be and to grow, man consumes the resources of the earth and his own life in an excessive and disordered way. At the root of the senseless destruction of the natural environment lies an anthropological error, which unfortunately is widespread in our day. Man, who discovers his capacity to transform and in a certain sense create the world through his own work, forgets that this is always based on God's prior and original gift of the things that are. Man thinks that he can make arbitrary use of the earth, subjecting it without restraint to his will, as though the earth did not have its own requisites and a prior God-given purpose, which man can indeed develop but must not betray. Instead of carrying out his role as a cooperator with God in the work of creation, man sets himself up in place of God and thus ends up provoking a rebellion on the part of nature, which is more tyrannized than governed by him.[76]

37.2 In all this, one notes first the poverty or narrowness of man's outlook, motivated as he is by a desire to possess things rather than to relate them to the truth, and lacking that disinterested, unselfish and aesthetic attitude that is born of wonder in the presence of being and of the beauty which enables one to see in visible things the message of the invisible God who created them. In this regard, humanity today must be conscious of its duties and obligations toward future generations.

38.1 In addition to the irrational destruction of the natural environment, we must also mention the more serious destruction of the *human environment,* something which is by no means receiving the attention it deserves. Although people are rightly worried — though much less than they should be — about preserving the natural habitats of the various animal species threatened with extinction, because they realize that each of these species makes its particular contribution to the balance of nature in general, too little effort is made to *safeguard the moral conditions for an authentic "human ecology."* Not only has God given the earth to man, who must use it with respect for the

---

[76] Cf. Encyclical Letter *Sollicitudo Rei Socialis* (December 30, 1987), 34: *AAS* 80 (1988), 559-560; Message for the 1990 World Day of Peace (January 1, 1990): *AAS* 82 (1990), 147-156.

original good purpose for which it was given, but man too is God's gift to man. He must therefore respect the natural and moral structure with which he has been endowed. In this context, mention should be made of the serious problems of modern urbanization, of the need for urban planning which is concerned with how people are to live, and of the attention which should be given to a "social ecology" of work.

38.2 Man receives from God his essential dignity and with it the capacity to transcend every social order so as to move toward truth and goodness. But he is also conditioned by the social structure in which he lives, by the education he has received and by his environment. These elements can either help or hinder his living in accordance with the truth. The decisions which create a human environment can give rise to specific structures of sin which impede the full realization of those who are in any way oppressed by them. To destroy such structures and replace them with more authentic forms of living in community is a task which demands courage and patience.[77]

39.1 The first and fundamental structure for "human ecology" is *the family*, in which man receives his first formative ideas about truth and goodness, and learns what it means to love and to be loved, and thus what it actually means to be a person. Here we mean the *family founded on marriage*, in which the mutual gift of self by husband and wife creates an environment in which children can be born and develop their potentialities, become aware of their dignity and prepare to face their unique and individual destiny. But it often happens that people are discouraged from creating the proper conditions for human reproduction and are led to consider themselves and their lives as a series of sensations to be experienced rather than as a work to be accomplished. The result is a lack of freedom, which causes a person to reject a commitment to enter into a stable relationship with another person and to bring children into the world, or which leads people to consider children as one of the many "things" which an individual can have or not have, according to taste, and which compete with other possibilities.

39.2 It is necessary to go back to seeing the family as the *sanctuary of life*. The family is indeed sacred: it is the place in which life — the gift of God — can be properly welcomed and protected against the many attacks to which it is exposed, and can develop in accordance with what constitutes authentic

---

[77] Cf. Post-Synodal Apostolic Exhortation *Reconciliatio et Paenitentia* (December 2, 1984), 16: *AAS* 77 (1985), 213-217; Pius XI, Encyclical Letter *Quadragesimo Anno* (May 15, 1931), III: *AAS* 23 (1931), 219.

human growth. In the face of the so-called culture of death, the family is the heart of the culture of life.

39.3 Human ingenuity seems to be directed more toward limiting, suppressing or destroying the sources of life — including recourse to abortion, which unfortunately is so widespread in the world — than toward defending and opening up the possibilities of life. The Encyclical *Sollicitudo Rei Socialis* denounced systematic anti-childbearing campaigns which, on the basis of a distorted view of the demographic problem and in a climate of "absolute lack of respect for the freedom of choice of the parties involved," often subject them "to intolerable pressures . . . in order to force them to submit to this new form of oppression."[78] These policies are extending their field of action by the use of new techniques, to the point of poisoning the lives of millions of defenseless human beings, as if in a form of "chemical warfare."

39.4 These criticisms are directed not so much against an economic system as against an ethical and cultural system. The economy in fact is only one aspect and one dimension of the whole of human activity. If economic life is absolutized, if the production and consumption of goods become the center of social life and society's only value, not subject to any other value, the reason is to be found not so much in the economic system itself as in the fact that the entire sociocultural system, by ignoring the ethical and religious dimension, has been weakened, and ends by limiting itself to the production of goods and services alone.[79]

39.5 All of this can be summed up by repeating once more that economic freedom is only one element of human freedom. When it becomes autonomous, when man is seen more as a producer or consumer of goods than as a subject who produces and consumes in order to live, then economic freedom loses its necessary relationship to the human person and ends up by alienating and oppressing him.[80]

40.1 It is the task of the State to provide for the defense and preservation of common goods such as the natural and human environments, which cannot be safeguarded simply by market forces. Just as in the time of primitive capitalism the State had the duty of defending the basic rights of workers, so now, with the new capitalism, the State and all of society have the duty of *defending those collective goods* which, among others, constitute the essential framework for the legitimate pursuit of personal goals on the part of each individual.

---

[78] Encyclical Letter *Sollicitudo Rei Socialis* (December 30, 1987), 25: *AAS* 80 (1988), 544.
[79] Cf. ibid., 34: loc. cit., 559-560.
[80] Cf. Encyclical Letter *Redemptor Hominis* (March 4, 1979), 15: *AAS* 71 (1979), 286-289.

40.2 Here we find a new limit on the market: there are collective and qualitative needs which cannot be satisfied by market mechanisms. There are important human needs which escape its logic. There are goods which by their very nature cannot and must not be bought or sold. Certainly the mechanisms of the market offer secure advantages: they help to utilize resources better; they promote the exchange of products; above all they give central place to the person's desires and preferences, which, in a contract, meet the desires and preferences of another person. Nevertheless, these mechanisms carry the risk of an "idolatry" of the market, an idolatry which ignores the existence of goods which by their nature are not and cannot be mere commodities.

41.1 Marxism criticized capitalist bourgeois societies, blaming them for the commercialization and alienation of human existence. This rebuke is of course based on a mistaken and inadequate idea of alienation, derived solely from the sphere of relationships of production and ownership, that is, giving them a materialistic foundation and moreover denying the legitimacy and positive value of market relationships even in their own sphere. Marxism thus ends up by affirming that only in a collective society can alienation be eliminated. However, the historical experience of socialist countries has sadly demonstrated that collectivism does not do away with alienation but rather increases it, adding to it a lack of basic necessities and economic inefficiency.

41.2 The historical experience of the West, for its part, shows that even if the Marxist analysis and its foundation of alienation are false, nevertheless alienation — and the loss of the authentic meaning of life — is a reality in Western societies too. This happens in consumerism, when people are ensnared in a web of false and superficial gratifications rather than being helped to experience their personhood in an authentic and concrete way. Alienation is found also in work, when it is organized so as to ensure maximum returns and profits with no concern whether the worker, through his own labor, grows or diminishes as a person, either through increased sharing in a genuinely supportive community or through increased isolation in a maze of relationships marked by destructive competitiveness and estrangement, in which he is considered only a means and not an end.

41.3 The concept of alienation needs to be led back to the Christian vision of reality, by recognizing in alienation a reversal of means and ends. When man does not recognize in himself and in others the value and grandeur of the human person, he effectively deprives himself of the possibility of benefitting from his humanity and of entering into that relationship of solidarity and communion with others for which God created him. Indeed, it is through the free gift of self that one truly finds oneself.[81] This gift is made possible by the human person's essential "capacity for transcendence." Man cannot give himself to a purely human plan for reality, to an abstract ideal or to a false utopia. As a person, he can give himself to another person or to other persons, and ultimately to God, who is the author of our being and who alone can fully accept our gift.[82] Man is alienated if he refuses to transcend himself and to live the experience of self-giving and of the formation of an authentic human community oriented toward his final destiny, which is God. A society is alienated if its forms of social organization, production and consumption make it more difficult to offer this gift of self and to establish this solidarity between people.

41.4 Exploitation, at least in the forms analyzed and described by Karl Marx, has been overcome in Western society. Alienation, however, has not been overcome as it exists in various forms of exploitation, when people use one another, and when they seek an ever more refined satisfaction of their individual and secondary needs, while ignoring the principal and authentic needs which ought to regulate the manner of satisfying the other ones too.[83] A person who is concerned solely or primarily with possessing and enjoying, who is no longer able to control his instincts and passions, or to subordinate them by obedience to the truth, cannot be free: *obedience to the truth* about God and man is the first condition of freedom, making it possible for a person to order his needs and desires and to choose the means of satisfying them according to a correct scale of values, so that the ownership of things may become an occasion of personal growth. This growth can be hindered as a result of manipulation by the means of mass communication, which impose fashions and trends of opinion through carefully orchestrated repetition, without its being possible to subject to critical scrutiny the premises on which these fashions and trends are based.

42.1 Returning now to the initial question: can it perhaps be said that, after the failure of Communism, capitalism is the victorious social system, and that capitalism should be the goal of the countries now making efforts to rebuild their economy and society? Is this the model which ought to be proposed to the countries of the Third World which are searching for the path to true economic and civil progress?

---

[81] Cf. Second Vatican Ecumenical Council, Pastoral Constitution on the Church in the Modern World *Gaudium et Spes*, 24.

[82] Cf. ibid., 41.

[83] Cf. ibid., 26.

42.2 The answer is obviously complex. If by "capitalism" is meant an economic system which recognizes the fundamental and positive role of business, the market, private property and the resulting responsibility for the means of production, as well as free human creativity in the economic sector, then the answer is certainly in the affirmative, even though it would perhaps be more appropriate to speak of a "business economy," "market economy" or simply "free economy." But if by "capitalism" is meant a system in which freedom in the economic sector is not circumscribed within a strong juridical framework which places it at the service of human freedom in its totality and sees it as a particular aspect of that freedom, the core of which is ethical and religious, then the reply is certainly negative.

42.3 The Marxist solution has failed, but the realities of marginalization and exploitation remain in the world, especially the Third World, as does the reality of human alienation, especially in the more advanced countries. Against these phenomena the Church strongly raises her voice. Vast multitudes are still living in conditions of great material and moral poverty. The collapse of the Communist system in so many countries certainly removes an obstacle to facing these problems in an appropriate and realistic way, but it is not enough to bring about their solution. Indeed, there is a risk that a radical capitalistic ideology could spread which refuses even to consider these problems, in the *a priori* belief that any attempt to solve them is doomed to failure, and which blindly entrusts their solution to the free development of market forces.

43.1 The Church has no models to present; models that are real and truly effective can only arise within the framework of different historical situations, through the efforts of all those who responsibly confront concrete problems in all their social, economic, political and cultural aspects, as these interact with one another.[84] For such a task the Church offers her social teaching as *an indispensable and ideal orientation*, a teaching which, as already mentioned, recognizes the positive value of the market and of enterprise, but which at the same time points out that these need to be oriented toward the common good. This teaching also recognizes the legitimacy of workers' efforts to obtain full respect for their dignity and to gain broader areas of participation in the life of industrial enterprises so that, while cooperating with others and under the direction of others, they can

---

[84] Cf. Second Vatican Ecumenical Council, Pastoral Constitution on the Church in the Modern World *Gaudium et Spes*, 36; Paul VI, Apostolic Letter *Octogesima Adveniens* (May 14, 1971), 2-5: *AAS* 63 (1971), 402-405.

in a certain sense "work for themselves"[85] through the exercise of their intelligence and freedom.

43.2 The integral development of the human person through work does not impede but rather promotes the greater productivity and efficiency of work itself, even though it may weaken consolidated power structures. A business cannot be considered only as a "society of capital goods"; it is also a "society of persons" in which people participate in different ways and with specific responsibilities, whether they supply the necessary capital for the company's activities or take part in such activities through their labor. To achieve these goals there is still need for a broad associated workers' movement, directed toward the liberation and promotion of the whole person.

43.3 In the light of today's "new things," we have reread *the relationship between individual or private property and the universal destination of material wealth*. Man fulfills himself by using his intelligence and freedom. In so doing he utilizes the things of this world as objects and instruments and makes them his own. The foundation of the right to private initiative and ownership is to be found in this activity. By means of his work man commits himself, not only for his own sake but also *for others* and *with others*. Each person collaborates in the work of others and for their good. Man works in order to provide for the needs of his family, his community, his nation, and ultimately all humanity.[86] Moreover, a person collaborates in the work of his fellow employees, as well as in the work of suppliers and in the customers' use of goods, in a progressively expanding chain of solidarity. Ownership of the means of production, whether in industry or agriculture, is just and legitimate if it serves useful work. It becomes illegitimate, however, when it is not utilized or when it serves to impede the work of others, in an effort to gain a profit which is not the result of the overall expansion of work and the wealth of society, but rather is the result of curbing them or of illicit exploitation, speculation or the breaking of solidarity among working people.[87] Ownership of this kind has no justification, and represents an abuse in the sight of God and man.

43.4 The obligation to earn one's bread by the sweat of one's brow also presumes the right to do so. A society in which this right is systematically denied, in which economic policies do not allow workers to reach satisfactory levels of employment, cannot be justified from an ethical point of view, nor

---

[85] Cf. Encyclical Letter *Laborem Exercens* (September 14, 1981), 15: *AAS* 73 (1981), 616-618.

[86] Cf. ibid., 10: loc. cit., 600-602.

[87] Ibid., 14: loc. cit., 612-616.

can that society attain social peace.[88] Just as the person fully realizes himself in the free gift of self, so too ownership morally justifies itself in the creation, at the proper time and in the proper way, of opportunities for work and human growth for all.

V

State and Culture

44.1 Pope Leo XIII was aware of the need for a sound *theory of the State* in order to ensure the normal development of man's spiritual and temporal activities, both of which are indispensable.[89] For this reason, in one passage of *Rerum Novarum* he presents the organization of society according to the three powers — legislative, executive and judicial — something which at the time represented a novelty in Church teaching.[90] Such an ordering reflects a realistic vision of man's social nature, which calls for legislation capable of protecting the freedom of all. To that end, it is preferable that each power be balanced by other powers and by other spheres of responsibility which keep it within proper bounds. This is the principle of the "rule of law," in which the law is sovereign, and not the arbitrary will of individuals.

44.2 In modern times, this concept has been opposed by totalitarianism, which, in its Marxist-Leninist form, maintains that some people, by virtue of a deeper knowledge of the laws of the development of society, or through membership of a particular class or through contact with the deeper sources of the collective consciousness, are exempt from error and can therefore arrogate to themselves the exercise of absolute power. It must be added that totalitarianism arises out of a denial of truth in the objective sense. If there is no transcendent truth, in obedience to which man achieves his full identity, then there is no sure principle for guaranteeing just relations between people. Their self-interest as a class, group or nation would inevitably set them in opposition to one another. If one does not acknowledge transcendent truth, then the force of power takes over, and each person tends to make full use of the means at his disposal in order to impose his own interests or his own opinion, with no regard for the rights of others. People are then respected only to the extent that they can be exploited for selfish ends.

---

[88] Cf. ibid., 18: loc. cit., 622-625.

[89] Cf. Encyclical Letter *Rerum Novarum* (May 15, 1891): *Leonis XIII P. M. Acta*, XI, Rome, 1892, 126-128.

[90] Ibid.: loc. cit., 121-122.

Thus, the root of modern totalitarianism is to be found in the denial of the transcendent dignity of the human person who, as the visible image of the invisible God, is therefore by his very nature the subject of rights which no one may violate — no individual, group, class, nation or State. Not even the majority of a social body may violate these rights, by going against the minority, by isolating, oppressing, or exploiting it, or by attempting to annihilate it.[91]

45.1 The culture and praxis of totalitarianism also involve a rejection of the Church. The State or the party which claims to be able to lead history toward perfect goodness, and which sets itself above all values, cannot tolerate the affirmation of *an objective criterion of good and evil* beyond the will of those in power, since such a criterion, in given circumstances, could be used to judge their actions. This explains why totalitarianism attempts to destroy the Church, or at least to reduce her to submission, making her an instrument of its own ideological apparatus.[92]

45.2 Furthermore, the totalitarian State tends to absorb within itself the nation, society, the family, religious groups and individuals themselves. In defending her own freedom, the Church is also defending the human person, who must obey God rather than men (cf. Acts 5:29), as well as defending the family, the various social organizations and nations — all of which enjoy their own spheres of autonomy and sovereignty.

46.1 The Church values the democratic system inasmuch as it ensures the participation of citizens in making political choices, guarantees to the governed the possibility both of electing and holding accountable those who govern them, and of replacing them through peaceful means when appropriate.[93] Thus she cannot encourage the formation of narrow ruling groups which usurp the power of the State for individual interests or for ideological ends.

46.2 Authentic democracy is possible only in a State ruled by law, and on the basis of a correct conception of the human person. It requires that the necessary conditions be present for the advancement both of the individual through education and formation in true ideals, and of the "subjectivity" of

[91] Cf. Leo XIII, Encyclical Letter *Libertas Praestantissimum* (June 20, 1888): *Leonis XIII P. M. Acta*, VIII, Rome, 1889, 224-226.

[92] Cf. Second Vatican Ecumenical Council, Pastoral Constitution on the Church in the Modern World *Gaudium et Spes*, 76.

[93] Cf. ibid., 29; Pius XII, Christmas Radio Message (December 24, 1944): *AAS* 37 (1945), 10-20.

society through the creation of structures of participation and shared responsibility. Nowadays there is a tendency to claim that agnosticism and skeptical relativism are the philosophy and the basic attitude which correspond to democratic forms of political life. Those who are convinced that they know the truth and firmly adhere to it are considered unreliable from a democratic point of view, since they do not accept that truth is determined by the majority, or that it is subject to variation according to different political trends. It must be observed in this regard that if there is no ultimate truth to guide and direct political activity, then ideas and convictions can easily be manipulated for reasons of power. As history demonstrates, a democracy without values easily turns into open or thinly disguised totalitarianism.

46.3 Nor does the Church close her eyes to the danger of fanaticism or fundamentalism among those who, in the name of an ideology which purports to be scientific or religious, claim the right to impose on others their own concept of what is true and good. *Christian truth* is not of this kind. Since it is not an ideology, the Christian faith does not presume to imprison changing sociopolitical realities in a rigid schema, and it recognizes that human life is realized in history in conditions that are diverse and imperfect. Furthermore, in constantly reaffirming the transcendent dignity of the person, the Church's method is always that of respect for freedom.[94]

46.4 But freedom attains its full development only by accepting the truth. In a world without truth, freedom loses its foundation and man is exposed to the violence of passion and to manipulation, both open and hidden. The Christian upholds freedom and serves it, constantly offering to others the truth which he has known (cf. Jn 8:31-32), in accordance with the missionary nature of his vocation. While paying heed to every fragment of truth which he encounters in the life experience and in the culture of individuals and of nations, he will not fail to affirm in dialogue with others all that his faith and the correct use of reason have enabled him to understand.[95]

47.1 Following the collapse of Communist totalitarianism and of many other totalitarian and "national security" regimes, today we are witnessing a predominance, not without signs of opposition, of the democratic ideal, together with lively attention to and concern for human rights. But for this very reason it is necessary for peoples in the process of reforming their

---

[94] Cf. Second Vatican Ecumenical Council, Declaration on Religious Freedom *Dignitatis Humanae*.

[95] Cf. Encyclical Letter *Redemptoris Missio* (December 7, 1990), 11: *AAS* 83 (1991), 259-260.

systems to give democracy an authentic and solid foundation through the explicit recognition of those rights.[96] Among the most important of these rights, mention must be made of the right to life, an integral part of which is the right of the child to develop in the mother's womb from the moment of conception; the right to live in a united family and in a moral environment conducive to the growth of the child's personality; the right to develop one's intelligence and freedom in seeking and knowing the truth; the right to share in the work which makes wise use of the earth's material resources, and to derive from that work the means to support oneself and one's dependents; and the right freely to establish a family, to have and to rear children through the responsible exercise of one's sexuality. In a certain sense, the source and synthesis of these rights is religious freedom, understood as the right to live in the truth of one's faith and in conformity with one's transcendent dignity as a person.[97]

47.2 Even in countries with democratic forms of government, these rights are not always fully respected. Here we are referring not only to the scandal of abortion, but also to different aspects of a crisis within democracies themselves, which seem at times to have lost the ability to make decisions aimed at the common good. Certain demands which arise within society are sometimes not examined in accordance with criteria of justice and morality, but rather on the basis of the electoral or financial power of the groups promoting them. With time, such distortions of political conduct create distrust and apathy, with a subsequent decline in the political participation and civic spirit of the general population, which feels abused and disillusioned. As a result, there is a growing inability to situate particular interests within the framework of a coherent vision of the common good. The latter is not simply the sum total of particular interests; rather it involves an assessment and integration of those interests on the basis of a balanced hierarchy of values; ultimately, it demands a correct understanding of the dignity and the rights of the person.[98]

47.3 The Church respects *the legitimate autonomy of the democratic order* and is not entitled to express preferences for this or that institutional or constitutional solution. Her contribution to the political order is precisely her

---

[96] Cf. Encyclical Letter *Redemptor Hominis* (March 4, 1979), 17: AAS 71 (1979), 270-272.

[97] Cf. Message for the 1988 World Day of Peace (January 1, 1988): AAS 80 (1988), 1572-1580; Message for the 1991 World Day of Peace (January 1, 1991): AAS 83 (1991), 410-421; Second Vatican Ecumenical Council, Declaration on Religious Freedom *Dignitatis Humanae*, 1-2.

[98] Cf. Second Vatican Ecumenical Council, Pastoral Constitution on the Church in the Modern World *Gaudium et Spes*, 26.

vision of the dignity of the person revealed in all its fullness in the mystery of the Incarnate Word.[99]

48.1 These general observations also apply to *the role of the State in the economic sector*. Economic activity, especially the activity of a market economy, cannot be conducted in an institutional, juridical or political vacuum. On the contrary, it presupposes sure guarantees of individual freedom and private property, as well as a stable currency and efficient public services. Hence the principal task of the State is to guarantee this security, so that those who work and produce can enjoy the fruits of their labors and thus feel encouraged to work efficiently and honestly. The absence of stability, together with the corruption of public officials and the spread of improper sources of growing rich and of easy profits deriving from illegal or purely speculative activities, constitutes one of the chief obstacles to development and to the economic order.

48.2 Another task of the State is that of overseeing and directing the exercise of human rights in the economic sector. However, primary responsibility in this area belongs not to the State but to individuals and to the various groups and associations which make up society. The State could not directly ensure the right to work for all its citizens unless it controlled every aspect of economic life and restricted the free initiative of individuals. This does not mean, however, that the State has no competence in this domain, as was claimed by those who argued against any rules in the economic sphere. Rather, the State has a duty to sustain business activities by creating conditions which will ensure job opportunities, by stimulating those activities where they are lacking or by supporting them in moments of crisis.

48.3 The State has the further right to intervene when particular monopolies create delays or obstacles to development. In addition to the tasks of harmonizing and guiding development, in exceptional circumstances the State can also exercise a *substitute function*, when social sectors or business systems are too weak or are just getting under way, and are not equal to the task at hand. Such supplementary interventions, which are justified by urgent reasons touching the common good, must be as brief as possible, so as to avoid removing permanently from society and business systems the functions which are properly theirs, and so as to avoid enlarging excessively the sphere of State intervention to the detriment of both economic and civil freedom.

48.4 In recent years the range of such intervention has vastly expanded, to the point of creating a new type of State, the so-called "Welfare State." This

---

[99] Cf. ibid., 22.

has happened in some countries in order to respond better to many needs and demands, by remedying forms of poverty and deprivation unworthy of the human person. However, excesses and abuses, especially in recent years, have provoked very harsh criticisms of the Welfare State, dubbed the "Social Assistance State." Malfunctions and defects in the Social Assistance State are the result of an inadequate understanding of the tasks proper to the State. Here again *the principle of subsidiarity* must be respected: a community of a higher order should not interfere in the internal life of a community of a lower order, depriving the latter of its functions, but rather should support it in case of need and help to coordinate its activity with the activities of the rest of society, always with a view to the common good.[100]

48.5 By intervening directly and depriving society of its responsibility, the Social Assistance State leads to a loss of human energies and an inordinate increase of public agencies, which are dominated more by bureaucratic ways of thinking than by concern for serving their clients, and which are accompanied by an enormous increase in spending. In fact, it would appear that needs are best understood and satisfied by people who are closest to them and who act as neighbors to those in need. It should be added that certain kinds of demands often call for a response which is not simply material but which is capable of perceiving the deeper human need. One thinks of the condition of refugees, immigrants, the elderly, the sick, and all those in circumstances which call for assistance, such as drug abusers: all these people can be helped effectively only by those who offer them genuine fraternal support, in addition to the necessary care.

49.1 Faithful to the mission received from Christ her Founder, the Church has always been present and active among the needy, offering them material assistance in ways that neither humiliate nor reduce them to mere objects of assistance, but which help them to escape their precarious situation by promoting their dignity as persons. With heartfelt gratitude to God it must be pointed out that active charity has never ceased to be practiced in the Church; indeed, today it is showing a manifold and gratifying increase. In this regard, special mention must be made of *volunteer work*, which the Church favors and promotes by urging everyone to cooperate in supporting and encouraging its undertakings.

49.2 In order to overcome today's widespread individualistic mentality, what is required is *a concrete commitment to solidarity and charity*, beginning

[100] Cf. Pius XI, Encyclical Letter *Quadragesimo Anno* (May 15, 1931), I: *AAS* 23 (1931), 184-186.

in the family with the mutual support of husband and wife and the care which the different generations give to one another. In this sense the family too can be called a community of work and solidarity. It can happen, however, that when a family does decide to live up fully to its vocation, it finds itself without the necessary support from the State and without sufficient resources. It is urgent therefore to promote not only family policies, but also those social policies which have the family as their principal object, policies which assist the family by providing adequate resources and efficient means of support, both for bringing up children and for looking after the elderly, so as to avoid distancing the latter from the family unit and in order to strengthen relations between generations.[101]

49.3 Apart from the family, other intermediate communities exercise primary functions and give life to specific networks of solidarity. These develop as real communities of persons and strengthen the social fabric, preventing society from becoming an anonymous and impersonal mass, as unfortunately often happens today. It is in interrelationships on many levels that a person lives, and that society becomes more "personalized." The individual today is often suffocated between two poles represented by the State and the marketplace. At times it seems as though he exists only as a producer and consumer of goods, or as an object of State administration. People lose sight of the fact that life in society has neither the market nor the State as its final purpose, since life itself has a unique value which the State and the market must serve. Man remains above all a being who seeks the truth and strives to live in that truth, deepening his understanding of it through a dialogue which involves past and future generations.[102]

50.1 From this open search for truth, which is renewed in every generation, *the culture of a nation* derives its character. Indeed, the heritage of values which has been received and handed down is always challenged by the young. To challenge does not necessarily mean to destroy or reject *a priori*, but above all to put these values to test in one's own life, and through this existential verification to make them more real, relevant and personal, distinguishing the valid elements in the tradition from false and erroneous ones, or from obsolete forms which can be usefully replaced by others more suited to the times.

50.2 In this context, it is appropriate *to recall that evangelization too plays*

---

[101] Cf. Apostolic Exhortation *Familiaris Consortio* (November 22, 1981), 45: *AAS* 74 (1982), 136-137.

[102] Cf. Address to UNESCO (June 2, 1980): *AAS* 72 (1980), 735-752.

a role in the culture of the various nations, sustaining culture in its progress toward the truth, and assisting in the work of its purification and enrichment.[103] However, when a culture becomes inward-looking, and tries to perpetuate obsolete ways of living by rejecting any exchange or debate with regard to the truth about man, then it becomes sterile and is heading for decadence.

51.1 All human activity takes place within a culture and interacts with culture. For an adequate formation of a culture, the involvement of the whole man is required, whereby he exercises his creativity, intelligence, and knowledge of the world and of people. Furthermore, he displays his capacity for self-control, personal sacrifice, solidarity and readiness to promote the common good. Thus the first and most important task is accomplished within man's heart. The way in which he is involved in building his own future depends on the understanding he has of himself and of his own destiny. It is on this level that *the Church's specific and decisive contribution to true culture* is to be found. The Church promotes those aspects of human behavior which favor a true culture of peace, as opposed to models in which the individual is lost in the crowd, in which the role of his initiative and freedom is neglected, and in which his greatness is posited in the arts of conflict and war. The Church renders this service to human society *by preaching the truth about the creation of the world*, which God has placed in human hands so that people may make it fruitful and more perfect through their work; and *by preaching the truth about the* Redemption, whereby the Son of God has saved mankind and at the same time has united all people, making them responsible for one another. Sacred Scripture continually speaks to us of an active commitment to our neighbor and demands of us a shared responsibility for all of humanity.

51.2 This duty is not limited to one's own family, nation or State, but extends progressively to all mankind, since no one can consider himself extraneous or indifferent to the lot of another member of the human family. No one can say that he is not responsible for the well-being of his brother or sister (cf. Gen 4:9; Lk 10:29-37; Mt 25:31-46). Attentive and pressing concern for one's neighbor in a moment of need — made easier today because of the new means of communication which have brought people closer together — is especially important with regard to the search for ways of resolving international conflicts other than by war. It is not hard to see that the terrifying power of the means of destruction — to which even medium and small-sized coun-

---

[103] Cf. Encyclical Letter *Redemptoris Missio* (December 7, 1990), 39, 52: *AAS* 83 (1991), 286-287, 299-300.

tries have access — and the ever closer links between the peoples of the whole world make it very difficult or practically impossible to limit the consequences of a conflict.

52.1 Pope Benedict XV and his successors clearly understood this danger.[104] I myself, on the occasion of the recent tragic war in the Persian Gulf, repeated the cry: "War — never again!" No, never again war, which destroys the lives of innocent people, teaches how to kill, throws into upheaval even the lives of those who do the killing and leaves behind a trail of resentment and hatred, thus making it all the more difficult to find a just solution of the very problems which provoked the war. Just as the time has finally come when in individual States a system of private vendetta and reprisal has given way to the rule of law, so too a similar step forward is now urgently needed in the international community. Furthermore, it must not be forgotten that at the root of war there are usually real and serious grievances: injustices suffered, legitimate aspirations frustrated, poverty, and the exploitation of multitudes of desperate people who see no real possibility of improving their lot by peaceful means.

52.2 For this reason, another name for peace is *development*.[105] Just as there is a collective responsibility for avoiding war, so too there is a collective responsibility for promoting development. Just as within individual societies it is possible and right to organize a solid economy which will direct the functioning of the market to the common good, so too there is a similar need for adequate interventions on the international level. For this to happen, *a great effort must be made to enhance mutual understanding and knowledge, and to increase the sensitivity of consciences.* This is the culture which is hoped for, one which fosters trust in the human potential of the poor, and consequently in their ability to improve their condition through work or to make a positive contribution to economic prosperity. But to accomplish this, the poor — be they individuals or nations — need to be provided with realistic opportunities. Creating such conditions calls for a *concerted worldwide effort to promote development*, an effort which

[104] Cf. Benedict XV, Exhortation *Ubi Primum* (September 8, 1914): *AAS* 6 (1914), 501-502; Pius XI, Radio Message to the Catholic Faithful and to the Entire World (September 29, 1938): *AAS* 30 (1938), 309-310; Pius XII, Radio Message to the Entire World (August 24, 1939): *AAS* 31 (1939), 333-335; John XXIII, Encyclical Letter *Pacem in Terris* (April 11, 1963), III: *AAS* 55 (1963), 285-289; Paul VI, Address to the General Assembly of the United Nations (October 4, 1965): *AAS* 57 (1965), 877-885.

[105] Cf. Paul VI, Encyclical Letter *Populorum Progressio* (March 26, 1967), 76-77: *AAS* 59 (1967), 294-295.

also involves sacrificing the positions of income and of power enjoyed by the more developed economies.[106]

52.3 This may mean making important changes in established lifestyles, in order to limit the waste of environmental and human resources, thus enabling every individual and all the peoples of the earth to have a sufficient share of those resources. In addition, the new material and spiritual resources must be utilized which are the result of the work and culture of peoples who today are on the margins of the international community, so as to obtain an overall human enrichment of the family of nations.

VI

Man Is the Way of the Church

53.1 Faced with the poverty of the working class, Pope Leo XIII wrote: "We approach this subject with confidence, and in the exercise of the rights which manifestly pertain to us. . . . By keeping silence we would seem to neglect the duty incumbent on us."[107] During the last hundred years the Church has repeatedly expressed her thinking, while closely following the continuing development of the social question. She has certainly not done this in order to recover former privileges or to impose her own vision. Her sole purpose has been *care and responsibility* for man, who has been entrusted to her by Christ himself: for *this man,* whom, as the Second Vatican Council recalls, is the only creature on earth which God willed for its own sake, and for which God has his plan, that is, a share in eternal salvation. We are not dealing here with man in the "abstract," but with the real, "concrete," "historical" man. We are dealing with *each individual,* since each one is included in the mystery of Redemption, and through this mystery Christ has united himself with each one forever.[108] It follows that the Church cannot abandon man, and that "*this man* is the primary route that the Church must travel in fulfilling her mission . . . the way traced out by Christ himself, the way that leads invariably through the mystery of the Incarnation and the Redemption."[109]

---

[106] Cf. Apostolic Exhortation *Familiaris Consortio* (November 22, 1981), 48: *AAS* 74 (1982), 139-140.

[107] Encyclical Letter *Rerum Novarum* (May 15, 1891): *Leonis XIII P. M. Acta,* XI, Rome, 1892, 107.

[108] Cf. Encyclical Letter *Redemptor Hominis* (March 4, 1979), 13: *AAS* 71 (1979), 283.

[109] Ibid., 14: loc. cit., 284-285.

53.2 This, and this alone, is the principle which inspires the Church's social doctrine. The Church has gradually developed that doctrine in a systematic way, above all in the century that has followed the date we are commemorating, precisely because the horizon of the Church's whole wealth of doctrine is man in his concrete reality as sinful and righteous.

54.1 Today, the Church's social doctrine focuses especially *on man* as he is involved in a complex network of relationships within modern societies. The human sciences and philosophy are helpful for interpreting *man's central place within society* and for enabling him to understand himself better as a "social being." However, a man's true identity is only fully revealed to him through faith, and it is precisely from faith that the Church's social teaching begins. While drawing upon all the contributions made by the sciences and philosophy, her social teaching is aimed at helping everyone on the path of salvation.

54.2 The Encyclical *Rerum Novarum* can be read as a valid contribution to socioeconomic analysis at the end of the nineteenth century, but its specific value derives from the fact that it is a document of the Magisterium and is fully a part of the Church's evangelizing mission, together with many other documents of this nature. Thus the Church's *social teaching* is itself a valid *instrument of evangelization*. As such, it proclaims God and his mystery of salvation in Christ to every human being, and for that very reason reveals man to himself. In this light, and only in this light, does it concern itself with everything else: the human rights of the individual, and in particular of the "working class," the family and education, the duties of the State, the ordering of national and international society, economic life, culture, war and peace, and respect for life from the moment of conception until death.

55.1 The Church receives "the meaning of man" from divine revelation. "In order to know man, authentic man, man in his fullness, one must know God," said Pope Paul VI, and he went on to quote Saint Catherine of Siena, who, in prayer, expressed the same idea: "In your nature, O eternal Godhead, I shall know my own nature."[110]

55.2 Christian anthropology therefore is really a chapter of theology, and for this reason, the Church's social doctrine, by its concern for man and by its interest in him and in the way he conducts himself in the world, "belongs to the field . . . of theology and particularly of moral theology."[111] The theological

---

[110] Paul VI, Homily at the Final Public Session of the Second Vatican Ecumenical Council (December 7, 1965): *AAS* 58 (1966), 58.

[111] Encyclical Letter *Sollicitudo Rei Socialis* (December 30, 1987), 41: *AAS* 80 (1988), 571.

dimension is needed both for interpreting and solving present-day problems in human society. It is worth noting that this is true in contrast both to the "atheistic" solution, which deprives man of one of his basic dimensions, namely the spiritual one, and to permissive and consumerist solutions, which under various pretexts seek to convince man that he is free from every law and from God himself, thus imprisoning him within a selfishness which ultimately harms both him and others.

55.3 When the Church proclaims God's salvation *to man*, when she offers and communicates the life of God through the sacraments, when she gives direction to human life through the commandments of love of God and neighbor, she contributes to the enrichment of human dignity. But just as the Church can never abandon her religious and transcendent mission on behalf of man, so too she is aware that today her activity meets with particular difficulties and obstacles. That is why she devotes herself with ever new energies and methods to an evangelization which promotes the whole human being. Even on the eve of the third millennium she continues to be "a sign and safeguard of the transcendence of the human person,"[112] as indeed she has always sought to be from the beginning of her existence, walking together with man through history. The Encyclical *Rerum Novarum* itself is a significant sign of this.

56.1 On the hundredth anniversary of that Encyclical I wish to thank all those who have devoted themselves to studying, expounding and making better known Christian social teaching. To this end, the cooperation of the local Churches is indispensable, and I would hope that the present anniversary will be a source of fresh enthusiasm for studying, spreading and applying that teaching in various contexts.

56.2 In particular, I wish this teaching to be made known and applied in the countries which, following the collapse of "Real Socialism," are experiencing a serious lack of direction in the work of rebuilding. The Western countries, in turn, run the risk of seeing this collapse as a one-sided victory of their own economic system, and thereby failing to make necessary corrections in that system. Meanwhile, the countries of the Third World are experiencing more than ever the tragedy of underdevelopment, which is becoming more serious with each passing day.

56.3 After formulating principles and guidelines for the solution of the worker question, Pope Leo XIII made this incisive statement: "Everyone should

---

[112] Second Vatican Ecumenical Council, Pastoral Constitution on the Church in the Modern World *Gaudium et Spes*, 76; cf. John Paul II, Encyclical Letter *Redemptor Hominis* (March 4, 1979), 13: *AAS* 71 (1979), 283.

put his hand to the work which falls to his share, and that at once and straight-way, lest the evil which is already so great become through delay absolutely beyond remedy," and he added, "in regard to the Church, her cooperation will never be found lacking."[113]

57.1 As far as the Church is concerned, the social message of the Gospel must not be considered a theory, but above all else a basis and a motivation for action. Inspired by this message, some of the first Christians distributed their goods to the poor, bearing witness to the fact that, despite different so-cial origins, it was possible for people to live together in peace and harmony. Through the power of the Gospel, down the centuries monks tilled the land, men and women Religious founded hospitals and shelters for the poor, Con-fraternities as well as individual men and women of all states of life devoted themselves to the needy and to those on the margins of society, convinced as they were that Christ's words "as you did it to one of the least of these my brethren, you did it to me" (Mt 25:40) were not intended to remain a pious wish, but were meant to become a concrete life commitment.

57.2 Today more than ever, the Church is aware that her social message will gain credibility more immediately from the *witness of actions* than as a result of its internal logic and consistency. This awareness is also a source of her preferential option for the poor, which is never exclusive or discriminatory toward other groups. This option is not limited to material poverty, since it is well known that there are many other forms of poverty, especially in modern society — not only economic but cultural and spiritual poverty as well. The Church's love for the poor, which is essential for her and a part of her con-stant tradition, impels her to give attention to a world in which poverty is threatening to assume massive proportions in spite of technological and eco-nomic progress. In the countries of the West, different forms of poverty are being experienced by groups which live on the margins of society, by the eld-erly and the sick, by the victims of consumerism, and even more immediately by so many refugees and migrants. In the developing countries, tragic crises loom on the horizon unless internationally coordinated measures are taken before it is too late.

58 Love for others, and in the first place love for the poor, in whom the Church sees Christ himself, is made concrete in the *promotion of justice*. Jus-tice will never be fully attained unless people see in the poor person, who is

---

[113] Encyclical Letter *Rerum Novarum* (May 15, 1891): *Leonis XIII P. M. Acta*, XI, Rome, 1892, 143.

asking for help in order to survive, not an annoyance or a burden, but an opportunity for showing kindness and a chance for greater enrichment. Only such an awareness can give the courage needed to face the risk and the change involved in every authentic attempt to come to the aid of another. It is not merely a matter of "giving from one's surplus," but of helping entire peoples which are presently excluded or marginalized to enter into the sphere of economic and human development. For this to happen, it is not enough to draw on the surplus goods which in fact our world abundantly produces; it requires above all a change of lifestyles, of models of production and consumption, and of the established structures of power which today govern societies. Nor is it a matter of eliminating instruments of social organization which have proved useful, but rather of orienting them according to an adequate notion of the common good in relation to the whole human family. Today we are facing the so-called "globalization" of the economy, a phenomenon which is not to be dismissed, since it can create unusual opportunities for greater prosperity. There is a growing feeling, however, that this increasing internationalization of the economy ought to be accompanied by effective international agencies which will oversee and direct the economy to the common good, something that an individual State, even if it were the most powerful on earth, would not be in a position to do. In order to achieve this result, it is necessary that there be increased coordination among the more powerful countries, and that in international agencies the interests of the whole human family be equally represented. It is also necessary that in evaluating the consequences of their decisions, these agencies always give sufficient consideration to peoples and countries which have little weight in the international market, but which are burdened by the most acute and desperate needs, and are thus more dependent on support for their development. Much remains to be done in this area.

59.1 Therefore, in order that the demands of justice may be met, and attempts to achieve this goal may succeed, what is needed is *the gift of grace*, a gift which comes from God. Grace, in cooperation with human freedom, constitutes that mysterious presence of God in history which is Providence.

59.2 The newness which is experienced in following Christ demands to be communicated to other people in their concrete difficulties, struggles, problems and challenges, so that these can then be illuminated and made more human in the light of faith. Faith not only helps people to find solutions; it makes even situations of suffering humanly bearable, so that in these situations people will not become lost or forget their dignity and vocation.

59.3 In addition, the Church's social teaching has an important interdisciplinary dimension. In order better to incarnate the one truth about man in different and constantly changing social, economic and political contexts, this teaching enters into dialogue with the various disciplines concerned with man. It assimilates what these disciplines have to contribute, and helps them to open themselves to a broader horizon, aimed at serving the individual person who is acknowledged and loved in the fullness of his or her vocation.

59.4 Parallel with the interdisciplinary aspect, mention should also be made of the practical and as it were experiential dimension of this teaching, which is to be found at the crossroads where Christian life and conscience come into contact with the real world. This teaching is seen in the efforts of individuals, families, people involved in cultural and social life, as well as politicians and statesmen, to give it a concrete form and application in history.

60.1 In proclaiming the principles for a solution of the worker question, Pope Leo XIII wrote: "This most serious question demands the attention and the efforts of others."[114] He was convinced that the grave problems caused by industrial society could be solved only by cooperation between all forces. This affirmation has become a permanent element of the Church's social teaching, and also explains why Pope John XXIII addressed his Encyclical on peace to "all people of good will."

60.2 Pope Leo, however, acknowledged with sorrow that the ideologies of his time, especially Liberalism and Marxism, rejected such cooperation. Since then, many things have changed, especially in recent years. The world today is ever more aware that solving serious national and international problems is not just a matter of economic production or of juridical or social organization, but also calls for specific ethical and religious values, as well as changes of mentality, behavior and structures. The Church feels a particular responsibility to offer this contribution and, as I have written in the Encyclical *Sollicitudo Rei Socialis*, there is a reasonable hope that the many people who profess no religion will also contribute to providing the social question with the necessary ethical foundation.[115]

60.3 In that same Encyclical I also addressed an appeal to the Christian Churches and to all the great world religions, inviting them to offer the unanimous witness of our common convictions regarding the dignity of man, created by God.[116] In fact I am convinced that the various religions, now and in

---

[114] Ibid.: loc. cit., 107.

[115] Cf. Encyclical Letter *Sollicitudo Rei Socialis* (December 30, 1987), 38: *AAS* 80 (1988), 564-566.

[116] Ibid., 47: loc. cit., 582.

the future, will have a preeminent role in preserving peace and in building a society worthy of man.

60.4 Indeed, openness to dialogue and to cooperation is required of all people of good will, and in particular of individuals and groups with specific responsibilities in the areas of politics, economics and social life, at both the national and international levels.

61.1 At the beginning of industrialized society, it was "a yoke little better than that of slavery itself" which led my Predecessor to speak out *in defense of man*. Over the past hundred years the Church has remained faithful to this duty. Indeed, she intervened in the turbulent period of class struggle after the First World War in order to defend people from economic exploitation and from the tyranny of the totalitarian systems. After the Second World War, she put the dignity of the person at the center of her social messages, insisting that material goods were meant for all, and that the social order ought to be free of oppression and based on a spirit of cooperation and solidarity. The Church has constantly repeated that the person and society need not only material goods but spiritual and religious values as well. Furthermore, as she has become more aware of the fact that too many people live, not in the prosperity of the Western world, but in the poverty of the developing countries amid conditions which are still "a yoke little better than that of slavery itself," she has felt and continues to feel obliged to denounce this fact with absolute clarity and frankness, although she knows that her call will not always win favor with everyone.

61.2 One hundred years after the publication of *Rerum Novarum*, the Church finds herself still facing "new things" and new challenges. The centenary celebration should therefore confirm the commitment of all people of good will and of believers in particular.

62.1 The present Encyclical has looked at the past, but above all it is directed to the future. Like *Rerum Novarum*, it comes almost at the threshold of a new century, and its intention, with God's help, is to prepare for that moment.

62.2 In every age the true and perennial "newness of things" comes from the infinite power of God, who says: "Behold, I make all things new" (Rev 21:5). These words refer to the fulfillment of history, when Christ "delivers the Kingdom to God the Father . . . that God may be everything to everyone" (1 Cor 15:24, 28). But the Christian well knows that the newness which we await in its fullness at the Lord's second coming has been present since the creation of the world, and in a special way since the time when God became man in Jesus Christ and brought about a "new creation" with him and through him (2 Cor 5:17; Gal 6:15).

62.3 In concluding this Encyclical I again give thanks to Almighty God, who has granted his Church the light and strength to accompany humanity on its earthly journey toward its eternal destiny. In the third millennium too, the Church will be faithful *in making man's way her own*, knowing that she does not walk alone, but with Christ her Lord. It is Christ who made man's way his own, and who guides him, even when he is unaware of it.

62.4 Mary, the Mother of the Redeemer, constantly remained beside Christ in his journey toward the human family and in its midst, and she goes before the Church on the pilgrimage of faith. May her maternal intercession accompany humanity toward the next millennium, in fidelity to him who "is the same yesterday and today and for ever" (cf. Heb 13:8), Jesus Christ our Lord, in whose name I cordially impart my blessing to all.

Given in Rome, at Saint Peter's, on May 1, the Memorial of Saint Joseph the Worker, in the year 1991, the thirteenth of my Pontificate.

Veritatis Splendor

Editor's Introduction

On August 6, 1993, John Paul II signed his tenth encyclical, *Veritatis Splendor*, regarding certain fundamental truths of the Church's moral teaching.[1] Undoubtedly it is the Pope's most complex and most discussed document. Since its publication, the encyclical has generated a great deal of comment in the media and among theologians. This is not surprising, since *Veritatis Splendor* is the first-ever papal document on the theological and philosophical foundations of Catholic moral teaching. In this encyclical the Pope affirms that divine revelation contains "a specific and determined moral content, universally valid and permanent" (§37.1), which the Magisterium has the competence to interpret and teach.

Six years before, in the apostolic letter *Spiritus Domini* (1987), John Paul had publicly announced his intention to publish a document which would treat "more fully and more deeply the issues regarding the very foundations of moral theology" (§5.1). For several reasons the encyclical's preparation took longer than was first anticipated. First, the Pope widely consulted bishops and theologians throughout the world, and various drafts were drawn up. Second, he thought that it was fitting for the encyclical "to be preceded by the *Catechism of the Catholic Church*, which contains a complete and systematic exposition of Christian moral teaching" (§5.3). The *Catechism*, published in 1992, gives a full presentation of the Church's moral doctrine, including that on particular questions, and expounds it in a positive way. *Veritatis Splendor*, on the other hand, limits itself to dealing with the fundamental principles underlying all moral teaching.

But why does John Paul think that an encyclical on moral issues will serve the Church and the world on the threshold of the third millennium? According to him, reflection on the ethical implications of Christian faith, lived from the beginning as the "way" (Acts 22:4), belongs to the full proclamation of the Gospel. Moreover, he is convinced that society is in the throes of a *"crisis of truth"* (§32.2). This crisis has the "most serious implications for the moral life of the faithful and for communion in the Church, as well as for a just and fraternal social life" (§5.2).

The dechristianization of many cultures involves not only a loss of faith but also *"a decline or obscuring of the moral sense"* (§106.2). This new moral

---

[1] *Acta Apostolicae Sedis*, 85 (1993), 1133-1228.

situation brings with it "the *confusion between good and evil*, which makes it impossible to build up and to preserve the moral order" (§93.1). The ethical bewilderment of some Catholics has led to "the spread of numerous doubts and objections of a human and psychological, social and cultural, religious and even properly theological nature, with regard to the Church's moral teachings" (§4.2). In an increasingly secular world, believers are "making judgments and decisions [that] often appear extraneous or even contrary to those of the Gospel" (§88.2). Moreover, dissent from Catholic moral teaching often entails "an overall and systematic calling into question of traditional moral doctrine" (§4.2). Thus, as a service to the ethical and spiritual welfare of individuals and cultures, John Paul addresses the basic moral principles handed down by the Christian Tradition.

In order to meet his goal, the Pope responds in a constructive way to the contemporary moral crisis by proclaiming "the splendor of the truth." When he announced the forthcoming publication of *Veritatis Splendor,* he described the encyclical's purpose: "It reaffirms the dignity of the human person, created in God's image, and proposes anew the genuine concept of human freedom, showing its essential and constitutive relationship with the truth in accordance with Christ's words: 'The truth will make you free!' (Jn 8:32)."[2] On another occasion, John Paul said that he intended the encyclical to be "a proclamation of truth and a hymn to freedom: values felt strongly by contemporary man and deeply respected by the Church."[3] His primary aim, then, is not to censure specific dissident moral opinions but to proclaim that Christ is "the true and final answer to the problem of morality" (§85).

John Paul sets several specific objectives for the encyclical. First, he wishes "*to reflect on the whole of the Church's moral teaching*, with the precise goal of recalling certain fundamental truths of Catholic doctrine which, in the present circumstances, risk being distorted or denied" (§4.2, cf. §30.1). Second, he aims to show the faithful "the inviting splendor of that truth which is Jesus Christ himself" (§83.2). Christ alone is the answer to humanity's questions, "the only response fully capable of satisfying the desire of the human heart" (§7.1). Third, if the present crisis is to be successfully resolved, the Magisterium must authoritatively discern "*interpretations of Christian morality which are not consistent with 'sound teaching' (2 Tim 4:3)*" (§29.4, cf. §27.4). This pastoral discernment of the Pope and bishops is necessary as a way of assuring "*the right of the faithful* to receive Catholic doctrine in its purity and integrity" (§113.2).

[2] Angelus, October 3, 1993, *L'Osservatore Romano,* 40 (1993), 1.
[3] Angelus, October 17, 1993, *L'Osservatore Romano,* 42 (1993), 1.

The Pope addresses *Veritatis Splendor* specifically to his brother bishops. He intends them to be the first, but not exclusive, recipients of the encyclical. John Paul reminds them of their responsibility to safeguard and find "ever new ways of speaking with love and mercy" about *"the path of the moral life"* (§3.1,2).

John Paul II's training in ethics and moral theology is clearly evident in *Veritatis Splendor.* The encyclical's exposition is sometimes highly technical, especially in its analyses and responses to opinions contrary to Church teaching. While some commentators have voiced disagreement about the accuracy of the Pope's descriptions of the ethical positions with which he disagrees, they respect his desire to be fair-minded. As we shall see, whenever John Paul deals with an opinion he disagrees with, he first takes great pains to point out what is positive in the view. Only after doing this does he then examine its weaknesses. When unmasking theological and philosophical ideas incompatible with revealed truth, he scrupulously avoids imposing "any particular theological system, still less a philosophical one" (§29.4).

Throughout the encyclical the Pope repeatedly draws inspiration from the Bible. Chapter one, structured around the encounter of Jesus with the rich young man (Mt 19:16-21), establishes a biblical foundation for fundamental moral principles. In this chapter the Pope wishes to apply the theological method proposed by the Second Vatican Council: "Sacred Scripture remains the living and fruitful source of the Church's moral doctrine" (§28.2, cf. §5.3). Chapter two, on the other hand, uses Scripture chiefly to corroborate positions advanced on the basis of the natural moral law. The beginning of chapter three returns to a more biblical approach; it discusses discipleship in terms of the Paschal Mystery and of martyrdom as the supreme expression of following Christ.

More so than in his other encyclicals, in *Veritatis Splendor* John Paul relies considerably on the teaching of Saint Thomas Aquinas, referring to him directly at least twenty times, and on the teaching of Saint Augustine, citing him sixteen times. The Pope also mines extensively the documents of Vatican II, especially *Gaudium et Spes,* which he cites more than twenty-five times. Except for one reference to Saint Alphonsus Liguori and a single direct citation of John Henry Newman, the Pope mentions no moral philosopher or theologian after the Middle Ages.

Summary

Besides the introduction and conclusion, the encyclical contains three main chapters. Each begins with a scriptural text and is followed by a heading giving its principal theme. Many of the subheadings are also biblical citations or references. Chapter one, "Christ and the Answer to the Question about Morality" (§§6-27), is a biblical meditation on the essential elements of Christian morality. Chapter two, "The Church and the Discernment of Certain Tendencies in Present-Day Moral Theology" (§§28-83), is longer, more doctrinal, and considerably more technical. In the light of the Church's living Tradition, especially the Second Vatican Council, it discerns faulty trends in contemporary moral theology. Because of its length, chapter two is subdivided into four major sections: freedom and law, conscience and truth, fundamental choice and specific kinds of behavior, and the moral act. Chapter three, "Moral Good for the Life of the Church and of the World" (§§84-117), is more pastoral. It highlights the need for moral renewal in personal and communal life if the Church and society are to flourish. By presenting all men and women with the beauty of living in the truth, this chapter confirms that *Veritatis Splendor* is not primarily directed to quelling moral controversy.

Christ and the moral life

Chapter one is a prolonged commentary on the question that the rich young man asked Jesus: "Teacher, what good must I do to have eternal life?" (Mt 19:16). This religious query, which echoes in the heart of everyone, is "not so much about rules to be followed, but *about the full meaning of life*," about the search for happiness (§7.1).

In his reply to the young man, Jesus expresses the nucleus and spirit of Christian morality. Through this dialogue Christ reveals "the essential elements of revelation in the Old and New Testament with regard to moral action" (§28.1). The answer to the question about moral goodness and its connection to eternal life can be found only in God. One cannot know what is good without knowing goodness itself. For the believer, God is "the One who 'alone is good'; the One who despite man's sin remains the 'model' for moral action" (§10.2). To become good is to become like God. People need to turn to Christ; they receive from him *"the answer to their question about what is good and what is evil"* (§8.2). Essential to all morality is the recognition of God's sovereignty over the moral order: *"acknowledging the Lord as God is the very core, the heart of the Law"* (§11.1). The first truth of the moral life is that human beings are God's creatures.

John Paul also calls attention to Christ's teaching on the close connection *"between eternal life and obedience to God's commandments"* (§12.2). Jesus corroborates the young man's assumption that attaining " 'eternal life,' which is a participation in the very life of God" (§12.2), requires right action: "If you wish to enter life, keep the commandments" (Mt 19:17). God's first revelation about what is good for human beings comes from creation, when he inscribes a law in their hearts (cf. Rom 2:15). Later, when God gives the Decalogue on Sinai, he reaffirms that creation teaches people about what is good, clarifies truths obscured by sin, and points to the future perfection of the Law in his Son. With the Incarnation, Jesus "*brings God's commandments to fulfillment*, particularly the commandment of love of neighbor, *by interiorizing their demands and by bringing out their fullest meaning*" (§15.2). He confirms the commandments, assimilating them to his new law of love and revealing them as the path of life.

Lastly, the Pope's biblical meditation affirms that the moral life consists in discipleship, in an interpersonal relationship with Jesus. The following of Christ "touches man at the very depths of his being. . . . [It] means *becoming conformed to him* who became a servant even to giving himself on the Cross" (§21.1). More than accepting him merely as the teacher of commandments, disciples hold fast "*to the very person of Jesus*, partaking of his life and his destiny" (§19.3). They imitate Jesus' love, loving others as he has loved them (cf. Jn 15:12). Doing this entails more than observing the golden rule. It means following Jesus, who made "the sacrificial gift of his life on the Cross, as the witness to a love 'to the end' (Jn 13:1)" (§20.2).

Lest anyone should think, mistakenly, that discipleship rests only on human efforts, John Paul affirms that communion with Christ is "the *effect of grace*, of the active presence of the Holy Spirit in us" (§21.1). Disciples can imitate Christ's love "*only by virtue of a gift received*" (§22.3). Through this gift of the Spirit, they are "enabled to interiorize the law, to receive it and live it as the motivating force of true personal freedom" (§83.2). The Gospel's new law, which is the grace of the Holy Spirit, enlightens the mind, instills love for the truth, and makes possible the living of the truth.

With God's constant help, disciples can imitate Jesus "*along the path of love, a love which gives itself completely to the brethren out of love for God*" (§20.1). The Pope assures his readers that, even if the keeping of God's law is sometimes extremely difficult, obedience to it is always possible. "It is in the saving Cross of Christ, in the gift of the Holy Spirit, in the Sacraments which flow forth from the pierced side of the Redeemer (cf. Jn 19:34)," he writes, "that believers find the grace and the strength always to keep God's holy law, even amid the gravest of hardships" (§103.2).

Freedom and law

In chapter two, John Paul offers incisive critiques of some contemporary trends in moral theology. He does not provide thorough summaries of these opinions but instead calls attention to specific ways in which they fail to respect the intimate link between freedom and truth. Where possible, the Pope draws from these trends insights which are helpful to the renewal of moral theology, despite the fact they he finds many of the views deficient. When dealing with opinions contrary to Catholic teaching, John Paul follows the same pattern as that of Saint Thomas Aquinas: he first presents contemporary objections to the position he wishes to defend, and then answers them. Because the Pope bases his criticism on his understanding of the relationship between freedom and truth, it is important to grasp his teaching on this point.

While praising today's "strong sense of freedom" (§31.2), which has often been accompanied by an increased appreciation of human dignity, John Paul also deplores how freedom is frequently misunderstood. On the one hand, some exalt freedom to such an extent *that it becomes an absolute, which would then be the source of values* (§32.1). On the other hand, others so emphasize the psychological and social factors which condition human freedom that they question the very existence of that freedom. These opinions, like all mistaken views about freedom, "are at one in lessening or even denying *the dependence of freedom on truth*" (§34.2).

The Pope's teaching on the connection between freedom and law is simple. No contradiction exists between exercising human freedom and accepting the truth expressed by the moral law. Each has the same purpose: the fostering of human dignity. Citing a previous address of his, the Pope writes: "According to Christian faith and the Church's teaching, 'only the freedom which submits to the Truth leads the human person to his true good. The good of the person is to be in the Truth and to *do* the Truth'" (§84.2). Human beings are free precisely when they submit to the truth.

Freedom to choose is an essential characteristic of the moral life. What matters more, however, is choosing rightly. In order to make the right choices, people must know what is true about the human condition and, consequently, what is good for it. They discover this truth in the moral law. This law is neither arbitrary, aimed at something contrary to human nature, nor imposed on people. Rather, "God, who alone is good, knows perfectly well what is good for man, and by virtue of his very love proposes this good to man in the commandments" (§35.2). The moral law is "an expression of divine wisdom: by submitting to the law, freedom submits to the truth of creation" (§41.2). The perfection of freedom, then, does not consist in the right to determine what is good and evil, but in the choice of living in the truth. Obedience to objective truth is the foundation of right action.

According to John Paul, the role of human reason is to discover and apply the moral law which has its source in God. It does not itself create moral norms. Human beings do not make things to be good. They discover them to be good.

Natural moral law

In the section on freedom and law, the Pope also explains Catholic teaching on the natural law, especially as it was formulated by Saint Thomas Aquinas. For John Paul, the foundation of an "objective" morality is the natural law. According to his teaching, natural law is "the participation of the practical reason in the wisdom of the divine Creator and Lawgiver" (§40, cf. §12.1). It is the light of reason inscribed by the Creator in the heart of everyone (cf. Rom 2:15). By means of the natural moral law, human beings can know what they must do and what they must avoid.

John Paul considers three contemporary objections to the Church's teaching on the natural law. First, he mentions ethicists who attempt to establish norms based on "the results of a statistical study of concrete human behavior patterns and the opinions about morality encountered in the majority of people" (§46.1). But statistics, he reminds us, tell only what people do, not what they should do. Second, the Pope takes up the *objections of physicalism and naturalism*" (§47) leveled against the traditional Catholic view of the natural law. Those who hold such positions think that people are free to manipulate nature in whatever way they choose, and that they can disregard the moral relevance of any natural inclinations of the body. John Paul points out that these criticisms often depend on a moral theory which reduces "the human person to a 'spiritual' and purely formal freedom" (§49). Such a theory contradicts Church teaching on "the 'nature of the human person,' which is *the person himself in the unity of body and soul*" (§50.1). Third, against those who maintain that all norms are totally conditioned by history and culture, the Pope defends the universality and immutability of the natural law. Its authority "extends to all mankind" (§51.3), and its negative precepts "are universally valid," obliging "always and under all circumstances" (§52.1, 2). Not the prisoner of any culture, the human person's transcendent nature is the measure of all culture.

The natural law, therefore, entails universality: "Inasmuch as it is inscribed in the rational nature of the person, it makes itself felt to all beings endowed with reason and living in history" (§51.2). For this reason, the Pope affirms that "it is precisely *on the path of the moral life that the way of salvation is open to all*" (§3.2). The natural law is, he believes, fully compatible with, though not identical to, the moral principles taught by the Church. Her fruitful dialogue with modern culture is rooted in "the rational — and thus universally understandable and communicable — character of moral norms belonging to the sphere of the natural moral law" (§36.2). If such a law did not exist, rational discourse, without an explicit appeal to faith, would be impossible.

Conscience and truth

In eleven paragraphs (§§54-64), the encyclical treats the moral conscience in light of the relationship between freedom and truth. It closely follows the teaching of the Second Vatican Council which describes the conscience as man's "sanctuary" (*Gaudium et Spes*, §16). In the moral conscience echoes the voice of God, calling individuals to do good and avoid evil.

The Pope first affirms that the "heightened sense . . . of the respect due to the journey of conscience [toward truth] certainly represents one of the positive achievements of modern culture" (§31.3). But he also warns against cultural trends which set freedom of conscience against the Church's moral teaching. At the basis of these errors is a mistaken notion of conscience, one that understands it as an infallible tribunal which excludes appeal to any other authority. An individual's conscience, it is held, is itself the source of truth and values.

According to John Paul, these cultural trends betray "a *'creative' understanding of moral conscience*, which diverges from the teaching of the Church's tradition and her Magisterium" (54.2). Those who hold such a view maintain that the actions of conscience are autonomous "decisions" and that, when made maturely, they can dispense from obedience to law and the truth. Indeed, freedom and law are set in opposition to each other. Ultimately, then, it is the individual conscience "which would in fact make the final decision about what is good and what is evil" (§56.1). Thus, the moral conscience could "permit one to do in practice and in good conscience what is qualified as intrinsically evil by the moral law" (§56.1).

In replying to these contemporary moral theorists, the Pope asserts that conscience is an act of practical judgment; it "makes known what man must do or not do," according to objective norms (§59.2). Conscience, then, is not a tribunal that creates the good by a "creative" individual decision, but is "*the witness of God himself*, whose voice and judgment penetrate the depths of man's soul," calling him to obedience (§58). The judgment of conscience does not establish the moral law, but applies it to a particular case. It formulates obligation in light of "the 'divine law,' *the universal and objective norm of morality*" (§60). The Pope also points out that knowledge of God's law, while necessary, is not sufficient for making true judgments of conscience. True judgments depend on "the 'heart' converted to the Lord and to the love of what is good . . . what is essential is a sort of *'connaturality' between man and the true good*" (§64.1).

Like all people, Christians must follow their consciences; however, they are also obliged to form them in the light of the truth to which Church teaching bears witness. "The Church seeks, with great love, to help all the faithful to form a moral conscience which will make judgments and lead to decisions in accordance with the truth" (§85).

The true good of human beings requires that they recognize their constant need for divine mercy. Rather than adapt moral norms to their own capacities, they should acknowledge the "disproportion" between the law and their ability to fulfill it. This recognition opens the gate to forgiveness. "What is unacceptable," the Pope writes, "is the attitude of one who makes his own weakness the criterion of the truth about the good, so that he can feel self-justified, without even the need to have recourse to God and his mercy" (§104.1). Self-justification is not only spiritually perilous for the individual but also corrupts society by confusing good and evil.

Fundamental option

The third section of chapter two deals with the relationship of individual moral acts to what some contemporary moralists call the "fundamental option," or basic moral direction of a person's life. In this section the encyclical also confirms the Church's teaching on mortal sin.

According to some moralists, the fundamental option is "brought about by that fundamental freedom whereby the person makes an overall self-determination, not through a specific and conscious decision on the level of reflection, but in a 'transcendental' and 'athematic' way" (§65.2). It is the choice by which an individual directs his whole self either toward God or against God. Particular moral acts which flow from this option only partially express a person's basic stance. The fundamental option itself, some argue, thus remains untouched by specific moral choices.

John Paul recognizes that "Christian moral teaching, even in its biblical roots, acknowledges the specific importance of a fundamental choice which qualifies the moral life and engages freedom on a radical level before God" (§66.1). He rejects, however, that the fundamental option can be separated from specific acts. Morality is not restricted to a consideration of the individual's fundamental option, "prescinding in whole or in part from his choice of particular actions" (§65.3). The Pope fears serious pastoral consequences when concrete actions are viewed in this way. For those who hold this theory, an individual could still be in the state of grace, "even if certain of his specific kinds of behavior were deliberately and gravely contrary to God's commandments as set forth by the Church" (§68.1). The proponents of the theory measure the gravity of sin by the degree of engagement of an individual's freedom rather than by the act freely chosen.

On the other hand, John Paul states that "to separate the fundamental option from concrete kinds of behavior means to contradict the substantial integrity or personal unity of the moral agent in his body and in his soul" (§67.2). In fact, it is always through particular choices that individuals make or change their fundamental option. If even a single free choice entails morally grave matter, he teaches, then one's fundamental option for God is revoked.

Veritatis Splendor also reaffirms Catholic teaching on "the importance and permanent validity of the distinction between mortal and venial sins, in accordance with the Church's Tradition" (§70.1). It restates this doctrine because some moralists have suggested that mortal sin should be restricted to the reversal of an individual's fundamental option, a reversal which involves the explicit rejection of God. But, according to the encyclical, mortal sin is committed whenever a person freely chooses something gravely disordered. Particular acts can indeed radically change one's fundamental option.

The moral act

In this complex and decisive section, John Paul II deals with the criteria to be used in the moral evaluation of human acts. His treatment is a response to the contemporary ethical theories of consequentialism and proportionalism, "which call for careful discernment on the part of the Church's Magisterium" (§74.2). The Pope summarizes these trends of thought with broad strokes; he makes no claim to be addressing the views of any particular ethicist or moral theologian.

According to *Veritatis Splendor,* both consequentialism and proportionalism deny that there are some moral norms which apply always and without exception. Consequentialists argue that a particular act can be described as immoral only after its foreseeable consequences have been weighed. In evaluating the morality of an act, proportionalists consider a wider set of factors. They focus "on the proportion acknowledged between the good and bad effects of that choice, with a view to the 'greater good' or 'lesser evil' actually possible in a particular situation" (§75.1). Despite their differences, both consequentialists and proportionalists hold that the morality of an act is determined by weighing the good and evil consequences of an action, and then choosing the one whose foreseeable results are the most positive. For the Pope, both positions lead to justifying, on occasion, the doing of evil so that good may come of it.

John Paul acknowledges that an ethically responsible person, when evaluating the morality of an act, must consider its intentions and consequences. But these considerations are "not sufficient for judging the moral quality of a concrete choice" (§77.1). Following the analysis of Saint Thomas, the Pope holds that *"the morality of the human act depends primarily and fundamentally on the 'object' rationally chosen by the deliberate will"* (§78.1). The object of a moral act is, therefore, not the physical happening alone, but what one freely chooses. The "object" of an act of adultery, for example, is not sexual relations but the free choice to have intercourse with someone other than one's spouse.

Contrary to both consequentialists and proportionalists, the Pope maintains that the object of the human act is "the primary and decisive element for moral judgment" (§79.2). This object, what one freely and willingly chooses to do, determines whether an act *"is capable of being ordered to the good and to the ultimate end, which is God"* (§79.2). "Acting is morally good," John Paul writes, "when the choices of freedom are *in conformity with man's true good* and thus express the voluntary ordering of the person toward his ultimate end: God himself" (§72.1).

Some acts are incapable of being ordered to God, "because they radically contradict the good of the person made in his image" (§80.1). These acts, which of their nature directly contradict a person's orientation to God, can never be justified. Neither a calculation of foreseeable positive consequences nor a good intention can morally justify acts which are intrinsically evil. Such acts are such always evil "on account of their very object, and quite apart from the ulterior intentions of the one acting and the circumstances" (§80.1, cf. §81.2). Here the Pope confirms the Catholic moral tradition that it is never morally permissible, even for the best of reasons, to do evil that good may come of it (cf. Rom 3:8).

Morality and social renewal

Chapter three integrates the insights of the first two chapters in order to describe the contribution that Catholic moral teaching can make to the renewal of the Church and society. "A comparison between the Church's teaching and today's social and cultural situation," the encyclical states, "immediately makes clear the urgent need *for the Church herself to develop an intense pastoral effort*" (§84.3). She has the responsibility to proclaim moral truth in the face of the relativism and individualism that threaten the foundations of human dignity and social life.

Because of her "love for the person, for his true good, for his authentic freedom" (§95.2), the Church is bound to propose moral truth clearly to all people of good will. A primary way in which she carries out this mission is by defending "the universal and permanent validity of the precepts prohibiting intrinsically evil acts" (§95.1, cf. §96.1). This defense of moral absolutes fosters the good of both individuals and the community.

First, the Church reminds everyone, believer and non-believer alike, that "only by obedience to universal moral norms does man find full confirmation of his personal uniqueness and the possibility of authentic moral growth" (§96.2). Absolute moral norms are necessary to protect the inviolable personal dignity of every human being. Regardless of one's good intentions or the seemingly extenuating circumstances, no one is ever free to violate basic and inalienable human rights.

Second, the Church's insistence on universal moral norms serves society as a whole. These norms are "the unshakable foundation and solid guarantee of a just and peaceful human coexistence" (§96.2). The negative moral precepts, those contained in the second tablet of the Decalogue, "constitute the indispensable rules of all social life" (§97.1). John Paul is also convinced that a renewed society must be built upon the truth about God, Creator and Redeemer, and the truth about the human person, created and redeemed by him. Thus, a morality founded upon truth and open to authentic freedom "renders a primordial, indispensable and immensely valuable service . . . for society and its genuine development" (§101.2). Whenever moral acts are divorced from truth, the way is open to political, economic, and cultural totalitarianism. A stable and just society, if it is to survive and flourish, must be based on objective moral norms concerning what is right and wrong.

Prophetic mission of moral theologians and bishops

Chapter three concludes with a reminder to moral theologians and bishops of their specific responsibilities to the Church and to social life when questions of moral doctrine are at stake.

Moral theology is "a scientific reflection on the *Gospel as the gift and commandment of new life*" (§110.1). It should be carried out *in* and *for* the Church as a community of faith. Moral theologians have the task of developing a deeper understanding of the reasons underlying the Church's moral teaching, and of expounding "the validity and obligatory nature of the precepts it proposes" (§110.2). They should clarify "ever more fully the biblical foundations, the ethical significance and the anthropological concerns which underlie the moral doctrine and the vision of man set forth by the Church" (§110.2). The behavioral sciences can help moral theologians in their task, but the encyclical also mentions that these sciences are limited: their empirical methodology cannot lead to the affirmation of moral principles. Moral theology, for its part, must consider "first and foremost *the spiritual dimension of the human heart and its vocation to divine love*" (§112.1).

The Pope warns moral theologians to be alert to the dangers of relativism, pragmatism, and positivism. He also emphasizes that they have the grave duty of helping the faithful "to be committed to the true good and to have confident recourse to God's grace" (§113.1). Public dissent, especially when vented in the media, is *"opposed to ecclesial communion and to a correct understanding of the hierarchical constitution of the People of God"* (§113.2). John Paul encourages moral theologians to cooperate with the bishops in teaching the faithful the fullness of the Catholic moral doctrine to which they have a right.

Like the Apostles, bishops must be *"vigilant over the right conduct of Christians,"* just as they are "vigilant for the purity of the faith" (§26.1, cf. §§27.1, 110.1). It falls to the bishops, "by the assistance of the Holy Spirit and in communion *cum Petro et sub Petro*" (§116.1), to protect their flocks from unsound moral teaching (cf. 2 Tim 4:3).

The teaching of the bishops should not, however, be merely negative. The Pope reminds his fellow pastors that in proclaiming morality they "must first of all show the inviting splendor of that truth which is Jesus Christ himself" (§83.2). In replying to people's moral questions, bishops are to answer with *"the Church's reply* [which] *contains the voice of Jesus Christ, the voice of the truth about good and evil"* (§117.2).

Key Themes

Among the many decisive themes in *Veritatis Splendor,* three are especially significant: the relationship between freedom and truth, the inseparable link between faith and morality, and the Church's teaching on moral absolutes. Throughout the encyclical John Paul repeatedly returns to these fundamental ideas.

Obedience of freedom to truth

The intrinsic connection between freedom and truth is a theme not only in *Veritatis Splendor* but also in many of the Pope's writings. Freedom, he insists, is bound to the truth. Everyone has the strict moral obligation "to seek the truth and to adhere to it once it is known" (§34.1).

Today, unfortunately, the relationship between freedom and truth is widely misconstrued. At the root of ethical theories which challenge the Church's moral doctrine are "currents of thought which end by detaching human freedom from its essential and constitutive relationship to the truth" (§4.2, cf. §§34.2, 99.2). These opinions are reflected in slogans such as "I decide what is true for me," or "everyone must create his own values to live by."

Obedience to the truth, which involves the making of choices that direct a person to God, enhances human freedom. "Patterned on God's freedom," writes John Paul, "man's freedom is not negated by his obedience to the divine law; indeed, only through this obedience does it abide in the truth and conform to human dignity" (§42.1). Genuine freedom is far more than freedom from physical or psychological constraint. It reaches its fulfillment when it attains what is truly good for the human person, ultimately the infinite good: God, who alone can fully satisfy the heart. Obedience to the truth of the moral law enables people to be truly free by acting out of love for goodness. As the Pope says: "*Human freedom and God's law meet and are called to intersect* . . . human reason and human will participate in God's wisdom and providence" (§41.1, 2). On the other hand, to act against the truth erodes human freedom and enslaves the person.

For John Paul, the authentic meaning of freedom is disclosed by the crucified Christ, the personification of perfect freedom: "*he lives it fully in the total gift of himself* and calls his disciples to share in his freedom" (§85). Through his preaching, Jesus proclaims that "the frank and open acceptance of truth is the condition for authentic freedom" (§87.1): "You will know the truth, and the truth will set you free" (Jn 8:32). Through his actions, Christ also reveals that "freedom is acquired in *love*, that is, in the *gift of self* . . . in service to God and one's brethren" (§87.2): "Greater love has no man than this, that a man lay down his life for his friends" (Jn 15:13).

Morality and faith

The separation of faith from morality confronts the Church's mission of evangelization with a great challenge. This *"serious and destructive dichotomy"* (§88.1) is characteristic of a secularism which puts religion into a compartment isolated from other areas of life. Secularism creates an autonomous morality, which separates morality from faith.

John Paul, however, insists on the "intrinsic and unbreakable bond between faith and morality" (§4.3). Faith, he maintains, "possesses a moral content . . . and calls for a consistent life commitment" (§89.1). It is a decision involving a person's whole existence. More than the acceptance of propositions, faith "is a lived knowledge of Christ, a living remembrance of his commandments, and *a truth to be lived out*" (§88.4). The connection between faith and morality is so inseparable that "*the unity of the Church* is damaged not only by Christians who reject or distort the truths of faith but also by those who disregard the moral obligations to which they are called by the Gospel" (§26.2). The new evangelization of secular societies must be founded on the proclamation of Saint Paul: "Do not be conformed to this world" (Rom 12:2).

From the beginning of Christianity, the following of Jesus has entailed a distinct way of living. The first disciples differed from others "not only in their faith and their liturgy but also in the witness of their moral conduct, which was inspired by the New Law" (§26.1). By their actions Christians are to live out their fidelity to the gift of new life received from God. The Church therefore carries out her mission of evangelization "through the gift not only of the word proclaimed but also of the word lived" (§107.2).

By means of the moral life, faith becomes witness before the world as well as confession of the truth. People bear testimony to moral truth by making the gift of self to God and others. The supreme witness to moral truth is martyrdom. According to John Paul, martyrdom, "accepted as an affirmation of the inviolability of the moral order, bears splendid witness both to the holiness of God's law and to the inviolability of the personal dignity of man" (§92.1). Susanna in the Old Testament, John the Baptist at the dawn of the New Testament, and the countless Christian martyrs down the ages confirm that "the love of God entails the obligation to respect his commandments, even in the most dire of circumstances, and the refusal to betray those commandments, even for the sake of saving one's life" (§91.4). By freely laying down their lives, martyrs testify to the splendor of divine truth and to the perfection of human freedom.

Moral absolutes

At numerous points *Veritatis Splendor* reaffirms the teaching that some acts are always morally evil because of the object freely chosen. According to John Paul, "the *negative precepts* of the natural law are universally valid. They oblige each and every individual, always and in every circumstance" (§52.1, cf. §80.1). Negative moral precepts, which forbid certain acts, apply to everyone without exception.

The moral norms forbidding intrinsically evil acts are rooted in reason and revelation. Despite the circumstances or the good end one hopes to achieve, such acts may never be done. In fact, the Pope's chief criticism of consequentialist and proportionalist ethics is directed against their denial of Catholic teaching on intrinsically evil acts (cf. §§75.2, 82.2). These theories, he says, "are not faithful to the Church's teaching, when they believe they can justify, as morally good, deliberate choices of kinds of behavior contrary to the commandments of the divine and natural law" (§76.2). While a good intention or particular circumstances can diminish the evil of disordered acts, a consideration of noteworthy pastoral significance, "they remain 'irremediably' evil acts; *per se* and in themselves they are not capable of being ordered to God and to the good of the person" (§81.2). Intrinsically evil acts are not wrong because they are prohibited; they are prohibited because they are wrong.

The Pope relies on *Gaudium et Spes*, §27, for examples of moral absolutes. It cites acts such as homicide, genocide, abortion, euthanasia, and suicide, which are "hostile to life itself"; acts such as mutilation and torture, which violate "the integrity of the human person"; and acts such as slavery, prostitution, and the treatment of workers as mere instruments of profit, which are "offensive to human dignity" (§80.1).

Negative moral absolutes are both universal and immutable. They are universal in the sense that they are specific actions which are always and everywhere gravely wrong because of their object. They allow for no exceptions. John Paul asserts: "The Church has always taught that one may never choose kinds of behavior prohibited by the moral commandments expressed in negative form in the Old and New Testaments" (§52.3, cf. §§67.2, 115.3). When pointing out that universal and unchanging moral norms are at the service of the person and society, he notes that "*there are no privileges or exceptions for anyone. . . .* Before the demands of morality we are all absolutely equal" (§96.2).

Because of the contemporary view that culture is historically conditioned, some ethicists deny the existence of objective moral norms which are valid for the past, present, and future. The Pope, however, maintains that human nature transcends all cultures; it is "the condition ensuring that man does not become the prisoner of any of his cultures" (§53.2). Moral absolutes are immutable through time, since they express the nature which all human beings have shared from "the beginning" (cf. Mt 19:1-9). Citing *Gaudium et Spes*, §10, John Paul affirms that this immutability is "*ultimately founded upon Christ*, who is the same yesterday and today and forever" (§53.2). At the same time, in the light of different historical and cultural contexts, universal and permanent moral norms need to be constantly reformulated. In every age the norms expressing the truth of the moral law require a formulation "capable of ceaselessly expressing their historical relevance, of making them understood and of authentically interpreting their truth" (§53.3).

In the conclusion of *Veritatis Splendor* the Pope turns to Mary, Mother of Mercy, "the radiant sign and inviting model of the moral life" (§120.2). Her intercession, which obtains mercy, enables people to live a morally good life. John Paul recalls the profound simplicity of Christian morality; it consists "in *following Jesus Christ*, in abandoning oneself to him, in letting oneself be transformed by his grace and renewed by his mercy, gifts which come to us in the communion of his Church" (§119). The splendor of truth is the splendor of freedom in Christ.

* * *

Selected Bibliography

Albacete, Lorenzo. "The Pope against Moralism and Legalism." *Anthropos*, 10 (1994), 81-86.

Allsopp, Michael E., and O'Keefe, John J., eds. *Veritatis Splendor: American Responses*. Kansas City: Sheed & Ward, 1995.

Anderson, Carl A. "*Veritatis Splendor* and the New Evangelization." *Anthropos*, 10 (1994), 61-74.

Bruguès, Jean-Louis. "Man Comes from beyond Himself Since He Is Created in God's Image." *L'Osservatore Romano*, 15 (1994), 10-11.

Cahill, Lisa Sowle. "The Lasting Contribution of *Veritatis Splendor*." *Commonweal*, 120 (1993), 15-16.

Cessario, Romanus. "Moral Absolutes in the Civilization of Love." *Crisis*, 13 (May 1995), 18-23.

Chapelle, Albert. "Encyclical's Clarifications Develop Catechism's Treatment of Morality." *L'Osservatore Romano*, 18 (1994), 21-22.

Cottier, Georges. "Morality of a Human Act Depends Primarily on Object Chosen by Will." *L'Osservatore Romano*, 6 (1994), 11.

"A Coup for the Pope." Editorial. *The Tablet*, 247 (1993), 1251-1252.

Dulles, Avery. "John Paul II and the Truth about Freedom." *First Things*, 55 (1995), 36-41.

Ernst, Wilhelm. "Theology Is Essentially an Ecclesial Science That Must Serve the Church." *L'Osservatore Romano*, 16 (1994), 6.

Fedoryka, Damian P. "The Gift of *Veritatis Splendor*." *Social Justice Review*, 85 (1994), 140-150.

Finnis, John. "Beyond the Encyclical." *The Tablet*, 248 (1994), 9-10.

Finnis, John, and Grisez, Germain. "Negative Moral Precepts Protect the Dignity of the Human Person." *L'Osservatore Romano,* 8 (1994), 6-7.

Fraling, Bernhard. "Freedom Is Not Abolished by God's Law, but Is Protected and Promoted." *L'Osservatore Romano,* 3 (1994), 9-10.

Fuchs, Joseph. "Good Acts and Good Persons." *The Tablet,* 247 (1993), 1444-1445.

Grisez, Germain. "*Veritatis Splendor:* Revealed Truth versus Dissent." *Homiletic and Pastoral Review,* 94 (March 1994), 8-17.

Hauerwas, Stanley Martin. "*Veritatis Splendor* Is Unique." *Commonweal,* 120 (1993), 16-18.

Hausman, Noëlle. "Moral Theologians Are Obliged To Teach Authentic Church Doctrine." *L'Osservatore Romano,* 12 (1994), 10-11.

Healy, Jack. "*Veritatis Splendor* and the Human Person." *The Linacre Quarterly,* 61 (November 1994), 16-36.

Hittinger, Russell. "Law and Liberty in *Veritatis Splendor.*" *Crisis,* 13 (May 1995), 13-17.

Hittinger, Russell. "Natural Law as 'Law': Reflections on the occasion of *Veritatis Splendor.*" *The American Journal of Jurisprudence,* 39 (1995), 1-32.

Hittinger, Russell. "The Pope and the Theorists: The Oneness of Truth." *Crisis,* 11 (December 1993), 31-36.

Janssens, Louis, and Selling, Joseph A. "Teleology and Proportionality: Thoughts about the Encyclical *Veritatis Splendor.*" *Bijdragen,* 55 (1994), 118-132.

Johnstone, Brian V. "The Catholic Moral Tradition and *Veritatis Splendor.*" *Studia Moralia,* 31 (1993), 283-306.

Johnstone, Brian V. "The Encyclical *Veritatis Splendor.*" *The Ecumenical Review,* 48 (1996), 164-172.

Johnstone, Brian V. "Sin Is Healed by Grace, but Church Must Help Sinner Acknowledge Guilt." *L'Osservatore Romano,* 5 (1994), 10.

Keating, James. "An Ethic of Prayerful Listening: *Veritatis Splendor.*" *Emmanuel,* 100 (1994), 345-350.

Kennedy, Terrence. " 'Fundamental Option' Can Radically Change as Result of Particular Acts." *L'Osservatore Romano,* 4 (1994), 10.

Kiely, Bartholomew. "Humble Admission of Limitations Allows Person to Grow in Freedom." *L'Osservatore Romano,* 9 (1994), 11.

Kmiec, Douglas W. "Behind the 'Empty Cloud' of Autonomous Reason — Or Why It Doesn't Matter if the Natural Law of *Veritatis Splendor* Is 'Real Law.' " *The American Journal of Jurisprudence,* 39 (1995), 37-46.

McCabe, Herbert. "Manuals and Rule Books." *The Tablet,* 247 (1993), 1583-1585.

McCormick, Richard A. "Some Early Reactions to *Veritatis Splendor*." *Theological Studies*, 55 (1994), 481-506. Reply by Richard John Neuhaus. "Moral Theology and Its Pique." *First Things*, 49 (1995), 88-92.

McCormick, Richard A. "*Veritatis Splendor* and Moral Theology." *America*, 169 (October 30, 1993), 8-11.

McHugh, James T. "Bishops Must See that the Church's Moral Doctrine Is Faithfully Taught." *L'Osservatore Romano*, 17 (1994), 22.

McInerny, Ralph. "Locating Right and Wrong: *Veritatis Splendor* versus Muddled Moralizing." *Crisis*, 11 (December 1993), 37-40.

MacIntyre, Alasdair. "How Can We Learn What *Veritatis Splendor* Has To Teach?" *The Thomist*, 58 (1994), 171-195.

McQuillen, Michael P. "The Tarnished Splendor of Autonomy." *Linacre Quarterly*, 62 (Fall 1995), 49-51.

Martin, Francis X. "The Integrity of Christian Moral Activity: The First Letter of John and *Veritatis Splendor*." *Communio*, 21 (1994), 265-285.

May, William E. "Moral Theologians and *Veritatis Splendor*." *Homiletic and Pastoral Review*, 95 (December 1994), 7-16.

May, William E. "*The Splendor of Accuracy*: How Accurate?" *The Thomist*, 59 (1995), 465-483.

May, William E. "Theologians and Theologies in the Encyclical." *Anthropos*, 10 (1994), 39-60.

May, William E. "*Veritatis Splendor*: An Overview of the Encyclical." *Communio*, 21 (1994), 228-251.

Maestri, William F. *A Guide for the Study of "Veritatis Splendor."* Boston: St. Paul Books and Media, 1993.

Melina, Livio. "Conscience Witnesses to a Truth that Precedes It and Surpasses It." *L'Osservatore Romano*, 2 (1994), 10-11.

Merecki, Jaroslaw, and Styczen, Tadeusz. "The Splendor of Human Freedom Must Be Seen in Relation to Truth." *L'Osservatore Romano*, 49 (1993), 10-11.

Moynihan, Robert. "Truth Is Ecumenical, Says Ratzinger: Letter from Rome." *Crisis*, 11 (November 1993), 25-27.

Mudge, Lewis S. "*Veritatis Splendor* and Today's Ecumenical Conversation." *The Ecumenical Review*, 48 (1996), 158-163.

Nash, Nicholas. "Teaching in Crisis." *The Tablet*, 247 (1993), 1480-1482.

Neuhaus, Richard John, ed. "The Splendor of Truth: A Symposium." *First Things*, 39 (1994), 14-29.

"The New Encyclical." Editorial. *America*, 169 (October 23, 1993), 3.

Novak, Michael. "The Hope of Splendor." *Crisis*, 11 (December 1993), 4-5.

Novak, Michael. "The Pope Strikes Again." *Crisis*, 11 (November 1993), 5-7.

O'Donovan, Oliver. "A Summons to Reality." *The Tablet*, 247 (1993), 1550-1552.

Petrà, B. "God's Laws Are Not Impossible, for Divine Grace Enables Man to Obey." *L'Osservatore Romano*, 11 (1994), 10-11.

Pinckaers, Servais. "The Use of Scripture and the Renewal of Moral Theology: The Catechism and *Veritatis Splendor*." *The Thomist*, 59 (1995), 1-19.

Pinckaers, Servais. "We Are Capable of Living Christ's Love by Saving Grace of His Spirit." *L'Osservatore Romano*, 47 (1993), 11.

Porter, Jean. "Moral Reasoning, Authority, and Community in *Veritatis Splendor*." *Annual of the Society of Christian Ethics*, 15 (1995), 201-219.

Potterie, Ignace de la. "Believers Should Live and Act in Light of Christ's Life and Example." *L'Osservatore Romano*, 46 (1993), 10.

Ratzinger, Joseph. "Christian Faith as 'the Way': An Introduction to *Veritatis Splendor*." *Communio*, 21 (1994), 109-207.

"The Resplendence of Truth." Editorial. *The Tablet*, 247 (1993), 999-1000.

Rhonheimer, Martin. "Given His Creaturely Status, Man's Autonomy Is Essentially Theonomy." *L'Osservatore Romano*, 51/52 (1993), 8-9.

Rhonheimer, Martin. "Intrinsically Evil Acts and the Moral Viewpoint: Clarifying a Central Teaching of *Veritatis Splendor*." *The Thomist*, 58 (1994), 1-39.

Rodríguez Luño, Angel. "Decisions Contrary to Law of God Are Not Justified by 'Good Intention.' " *L'Osservatore Romano*, 7 (1994), 10-11.

Saward, John. *Christ Is the Answer: The Christ-Centered Teaching of Pope John Paul II*. Edinburgh: T&T Clark, 1995. 91-100.

Schooyans, Michel. "Man Can Misuse His Will, Claiming a Sovereignty That Is Not His Own." *L'Osservatore Romano*, 10 (1994), 10-11.

Scola, Angelo. "Following Christ: On John Paul II's Encyclical *Veritatis Splendor*." *Communio*, 20 (1993), 724-727.

Scola, Angelo. "In Christ Man Learns That Freedom and the Moral Law Are Not Opposed." *L'Osservatore Romano*, 44 (1993), 10.

Segalla, Giuseppe. "In His Life and Teaching Jesus Fulfills the Law and Reveals the Will of God." *L'Osservatore Romano*, 48 (1993), 10-11.

Selling, Joseph A. "Ideological Differences: Some Background Considerations for Understanding *Veritatis Splendor*." *The Month*, 27 (1994), 12-14.

Selling, Joseph A., and Jans, Jan, eds. *The Splendor of Accuracy: An Examination of the Assertions Made by "Veritatis Splendor."* Grand Rapids: Eerdmans, 1994.

Smith, Janet. "Natural Law Is a Guide to Morality for Christians and Non-Christians." *L'Osservatore Romano*, 1 (1994), 10.

Smith, Russell E. "*Veritatis Splendor* Teaches the Splendor of the Truth." *Faith & Reason*, 21 (1995), 55-75.

Smith, William B. "*Veritatis Splendor* Is a Moral Masterpiece: No Truth, No Freedom." *Crisis*, 11 (November 1993), 28-31.

Spaemann, Robert. "Even the Best of Intentions Does Not Justify the Use of Evil Means." *L'Osservatore Romano*, 50 (1993), 11.

Stafford, James Francis. "Reflections on *Veritatis Splendor*." *Communio*, 21 (1994), 363-366.

Stravopoulos, Alexandre M. "*Veritatis Splendor:* An Orthodox Reaction." *The Ecumenical Review*, 48 (1996), 155-157.

Szostek, Andrzej. "Man's Fundamental Option Can Be Radically Altered by Individual Acts." *L'Osservatore Romano*, 16 (1994), 14.

Tettamanzi, Dionigi. "The Call to Freedom Lived in Truth Is Heart of the New Evangelization." *L'Osservatore Romano*, 13 (1994), 9-10.

Tremblay, Réal. "Grace of Christ's Presence Heals and Transforms the Human Heart." *L'Osservatore Romano*, 45 (1993), 10.

Tuck, Mary. "A Message in Season." *The Tablet*, 247 (1993), 1583-1585.

Vree, Dale. "The Splendor of Truth and the Squalor of Sin." *New Oxford Review*, 60 (December 1993), 2-8.

Wilkins, John, ed. *Considering Veritatis Splendor*. Cleveland: The Pilgrims Press, 1994.

Zieba, Maciej. "Truth and Freedom in the Thought of Pope John Paul." *The Tablet*, 247 (1993), 1510-1512.

ENCYCLICAL LETTER

VERITATIS SPLENDOR

ADDRESSED BY THE SUPREME PONTIFF

JOHN PAUL II

TO ALL THE BISHOPS

OF THE CATHOLIC CHURCH

REGARDING CERTAIN

FUNDAMENTAL QUESTIONS

OF THE CHURCH'S MORAL TEACHING

Veritatis Splendor

Venerable Brothers
in the Episcopate,
Health and the Apostolic Blessing!

The splendor of truth shines forth in the works of the Creator and, in a special way, in man, created in the image and likeness of God (cf. Gen 1:26). Truth enlightens man's intelligence and shapes his freedom, leading him to know and love the Lord. Hence the Psalmist prays: "Let the light of your face shine on us, O Lord" (Ps 4:6).

Introduction

Jesus Christ, the true light that enlightens everyone

1.1 Called to salvation through faith in Jesus Christ, "the true light that enlightens everyone" (Jn 1:9), people become "light in the Lord" and "children of light" (Eph 5:8), and are made holy by "obedience to the truth" (1 Pet 1:22).

1.2 This obedience is not always easy. As a result of that mysterious original sin, committed at the prompting of Satan, the one who is "a liar and the father of lies" (Jn 8:44), man is constantly tempted to turn his gaze away from the living and true God in order to direct it toward idols (cf. 1 Thess 1:9), exchanging "the truth about God for a lie" (Rom 1:25). Man's capacity to know the truth is also darkened, and his will to submit to it is weakened. Thus, giving himself over to relativism and skepticism (cf. Jn 18:38), he goes off in search of an illusory freedom apart from truth itself.

1.3 But no darkness of error or of sin can totally take away from man the light of God the Creator. In the depths of his heart there always remains a yearning for absolute truth and a thirst to attain full knowledge of it. This is eloquently proved by man's tireless search for knowledge in all fields. It is proved even more by his search for *the meaning of life.* The development of science and technology, this splendid testimony of the human capacity for understanding and for perseverance, does not free humanity from the obligation to ask the ultimate religious questions. Rather, it spurs us on to face the most painful and decisive of struggles, those of the heart and of the moral conscience.

2.1 No one can escape from the fundamental questions: *What must I do? How do I distinguish good from evil?* The answer is only possible thanks to the splendor of the truth which shines forth deep within the human spirit, as the Psalmist bears witness: "There are many who say: 'O that we might see some good! Let the light of your face shine on us, O Lord'" (Ps 4:6).

2.2 The light of God's face shines in all its beauty on the countenance of Jesus Christ, "the image of the invisible God" (Col 1:15), the "reflection of God's glory" (Heb 1:3), "full of grace and truth" (Jn 1:14). Christ is "the way, and the truth, and the life" (Jn 14:6). Consequently the decisive answer to every one of man's questions, his religious and moral questions in particular, is given by Jesus Christ, or rather is Jesus Christ himself, as the Second Vatican Council recalls: "In fact, *it is only in the mystery of the Word Incarnate that light is shed on the mystery of man.* For Adam, the first man, was a figure of the future man, namely, of Christ the Lord. It is Christ, the last Adam, who fully discloses man to himself and unfolds his noble calling by revealing the mystery of the Father and the Father's love."[1]

2.3 Jesus Christ, the "light of the nations," shines upon the face of his Church, which he sends forth to the whole world to proclaim the Gospel to every creature (cf. Mk 16:15).[2] Hence the Church, as the People of God among the nations,[3] while attentive to the new challenges of history and to mankind's efforts to discover the meaning of life, offers to everyone the answer which comes from the truth about Jesus Christ and his Gospel. The Church remains deeply conscious of her "duty in every age of examining the signs of the times and interpreting them in the light of the Gospel, so that she can offer in a manner appropriate to each generation replies to the continual human questionings on the meaning of this life and the life to come and on how they are related."[4]

3.1 The Church's Pastors, in communion with the Successor of Peter, are close to the faithful in this effort; they guide and accompany them by their authoritative teaching, finding ever new ways of speaking with love and mercy not only to believers but to all people of good will. The Second Vatican Council remains an extraordinary witness of this attitude on the part of the Church

---

[1] Pastoral Constitution on the Church in the Modern World *Gaudium et Spes*, 22.

[2] Cf. Second Vatican Ecumenical Council, Dogmatic Constitution on the Church *Lumen Gentium*, 1.

[3] Cf. ibid., 9.

[4] Second Vatican Ecumenical Council, Pastoral Constitution on the Church in the Modern World *Gaudium et Spes*, 4.

which, as an "expert in humanity,"[5] places herself at the service of every individual and of the whole world.[6]

3.2 The Church knows that the issue of morality is one which deeply touches every person; it involves all people, even those who do not know Christ and his Gospel or God himself. She knows that it is precisely *on the path of the moral life that the way of salvation is open to all*. The Second Vatican Council clearly recalled this when it stated that "those who without any fault do not know anything about Christ or his Church, yet who search for God with a sincere heart and under the influence of grace, try to put into effect the will of God as known to them through the dictate of conscience . . . can obtain eternal salvation." The Council added: "Nor does divine Providence deny the helps that are necessary for salvation to those who, through no fault of their own, have not yet attained to the express recognition of God, yet who strive, not without divine grace, to lead an upright life. For whatever goodness and truth is found in them is considered by the Church as a preparation for the Gospel and bestowed by him who enlightens everyone that they may in the end have life."[7]

The purpose of the present Encyclical

4.1 At all times, but particularly in the last two centuries, the Popes, whether individually or together with the College of Bishops, have developed and proposed a moral teaching regarding the *many different spheres of human life*. In Christ's name and with his authority they have exhorted, passed judgment and explained. In their efforts on behalf of humanity, in fidelity to their mission, they have confirmed, supported and consoled. With the guarantee of assistance from the Spirit of truth they have contributed to a better understanding of moral demands in the areas of human sexuality, the family, and social, economic and political life. In the tradition of the Church and in the history of humanity, their teaching represents a constant deepening of knowledge with regard to morality.[8]

4.2 Today, however, it seems necessary *to reflect on the whole of the Church's moral teaching*, with the precise goal of recalling certain fundamental truths of

---

[5] Paul VI, Address to the General Assembly of the United Nations (October 4, 1965), 1: *AAS* 57 (1965), 878; cf. Encyclical Letter *Populorum Progressio* (March 26, 1967), 13: *AAS* 59 (1967), 263-264.

[6] Cf. Second Vatican Ecumenical Council, Pastoral Constitution on the Church in the Modern World *Gaudium et Spes*, 33.

[7] Dogmatic Constitution on the Church *Lumen Gentium*, 16.

[8] Pius XII had already pointed out this doctrinal development: cf. Radio Message for the Fiftieth Anniversary of the Encyclical Letter *Rerum Novarum* of Leo XIII (June 1, 1941): *AAS* 33 (1941), 195-205. Also John XXIII, Encyclical Letter *Mater et Magistra* (May 15, 1961), I: *AAS* 53 (1961), 410-413.

Catholic doctrine which, in the present circumstances, risk being distorted or denied. In fact, a new situation has come about *within the Christian community itself*, which has experienced the spread of numerous doubts and objections of a human and psychological, social and cultural, religious and even properly theological nature, with regard to the Church's moral teachings. It is no longer a matter of limited and occasional dissent, but of an overall and systematic calling into question of traditional moral doctrine, on the basis of certain anthropological and ethical presuppositions. At the root of these presuppositions is the more or less obvious influence of currents of thought which end by detaching human freedom from its essential and constitutive relationship to truth. Thus the traditional doctrine regarding the natural law, and the universality and the permanent validity of its precepts, is rejected; certain of the Church's moral teachings are found simply unacceptable; and the Magisterium itself is considered capable of intervening in matters of morality only in order to "exhort consciences" and to "propose values," in the light of which each individual will independently make his or her decisions and life choices.

4.3 In particular, note should be taken of the *lack of harmony between the traditional response of the Church and certain theological positions*, encountered even in seminaries and in faculties of theology, *with regard to questions of the greatest importance* for the Church and for the life of faith of Christians, as well as for the life of society itself. In particular, the question is asked: do the commandments of God, which are written on the human heart and are part of the Covenant, really have the capacity to clarify the daily decisions of individuals and entire societies? Is it possible to obey God and thus love God and neighbor, without respecting these commandments in all circumstances? Also, an opinion is frequently heard which questions the intrinsic and unbreakable bond between faith and morality, as if membership in the Church and her internal unity were to be decided on the basis of faith alone, while in the sphere of morality a pluralism of opinions and of kinds of behavior could be tolerated, these being left to the judgment of the individual subjective conscience or to the diversity of social and cultural contexts.

5.1 Given these circumstances, which still exist, I came to the decision — as I announced in my Apostolic Letter *Spiritus Domini,* issued on August 1, 1987, on the second centenary of the death of Saint Alphonsus Maria de Liguori — to write an Encyclical with the aim of treating "more fully and more deeply the issues regarding the very foundations of moral theology,"[9] foundations which are being undermined by certain present-day tendencies.

[9] Apostolic Letter *Spiritus Domini* (August 1, 1987): *AAS* 79 (1987), 1374.

5.2 I address myself to you, Venerable Brothers in the Episcopate, who share with me the responsibility of safeguarding "sound teaching" (2 Tim 4:3), with the intention of *clearly setting forth certain aspects of doctrine which are of crucial importance in facing what is certainly a genuine crisis*, since the difficulties which it engenders have most serious implications for the moral life of the faithful and for communion in the Church, as well as for a just and fraternal social life.

5.3 If this Encyclical, so long awaited, is being published only now, one of the reasons is that it seemed fitting for it to be preceded by the *Catechism of the Catholic Church*, which contains a complete and systematic exposition of Christian moral teaching. The Catechism presents the moral life of believers in its fundamental elements and in its many aspects as the life of the "children of God": "Recognizing in the faith their new dignity, Christians are called to lead henceforth a life 'worthy of the Gospel of Christ' (Phil 1:27). Through the sacraments and prayer they receive the grace of Christ and the gifts of his Spirit which make them capable of such a life."[10] Consequently, while referring to the Catechism "as a sure and authentic reference text for teaching Catholic doctrine,"[11] the Encyclical will limit itself to dealing with *certain fundamental questions regarding the Church's moral teaching*, taking the form of a necessary discernment about issues being debated by ethicists and moral theologians. The specific purpose of the present Encyclical is this: to set forth, with regard to the problems being discussed, the principles of a moral teaching based upon Sacred Scripture and the living Apostolic Tradition,[12] and at the same time to shed light on the presuppositions and consequences of the dissent which that teaching has met.

I

"Teacher, What Good Must I Do. . . ?" (Mt 19:16)

Christ and the Answer to the Question about Morality

"Someone came to him. . . ." (Mt 19:16)

6 *The dialogue of Jesus with the rich young man*, related in the nineteenth chapter of Saint Matthew's Gospel, can serve as a useful guide *for listening*

---

[10] *Catechism of the Catholic Church*, No. 1692.

[11] Apostolic Constitution *Fidei Depositum* (October 11, 1992), 4: *AAS* 86 (1994), 117.

[12] Cf. Second Vatican Ecumenical Council, Dogmatic Constitution on Divine Revelation *Dei Verbum*, 10.

once more in a lively and direct way to his moral teaching: "Then someone came to him and said, 'Teacher, what good must I do to have eternal life?' And he said to him, 'Why do you ask me about what is good? There is only one who is good. If you wish to enter into life, keep the commandments.' He said to him, 'Which ones?' And Jesus said, 'You shall not murder; You shall not commit adultery; You shall not steal; You shall not bear false witness; Honor your father and mother; also, You shall love your neighbor as yourself.' The young man said to him, 'I have kept all these; what do I still lack?' Jesus said to him, 'If you wish to be perfect, go, sell your possessions and give the money to the poor, and you will have treasure in heaven; then come, follow me'" (Mt 19:16-21).[13]

7.1 *"Then someone came to him..."* In the young man, whom Matthew's Gospel does not name, we can recognize every person who, consciously or not, *approaches Christ the Redeemer of man and questions him about morality.* For the young man, the question is not so much about rules to be followed, but *about the full meaning of life.* This is in fact the aspiration at the heart of every human decision and action, the quiet searching and interior prompting which sets freedom in motion. This question is ultimately an appeal to the absolute Good which attracts us and beckons us; it is the echo of a call from God who is the origin and goal of man's life. Precisely in this perspective the Second Vatican Council called for a renewal of moral theology, so that its teaching would display the lofty vocation which the faithful have received in Christ,[14] the only response fully capable of satisfying the desire of the human heart.

7.2 *In order to make this "encounter" with Christ possible, God willed his Church.* Indeed, the Church "wishes to serve this single end: that each person may be able to find Christ, in order that Christ may walk with each person the path of life."[15]

"Teacher, what good must I do to have eternal life?" (Mt 19:16)

8.1 The question which the rich young man puts to Jesus of Nazareth is one which rises from the depths of his heart. It is *an essential and unavoidable question for the life of every man,* for it is about the moral good which must be done, and about eternal life. The young man senses that there is a

---

[13] Cf. Apostolic Letter to the Young People of the World on the Occasion of the International Year of Youth *Parati Semper* (March 31, 1985), 2-8: *AAS* 77 (1985), 581-600.

[14] Cf. Decree on Priestly Formation *Optatam Totius,* 16.

[15] Encyclical Letter *Redemptor Hominis* (March 4, 1979), 13: *AAS* 71 (1979), 282.

connection between moral good and the fulfillment of his own destiny. He is a devout Israelite, raised as it were in the shadow of the Law of the Lord. If he asks Jesus this question, we can presume that it is not because he is ignorant of the answer contained in the Law. It is more likely that the attractiveness of the person of Jesus had prompted within him new questions about moral good. He feels the need to draw near to the One who had begun his preaching with this new and decisive proclamation: "The time is fulfilled and the Kingdom of God is at hand; repent, and believe in the Gospel" (Mk 1:15).

8.2 *People today need to turn to Christ once again in order to receive from him the answer to their questions about what is good and what is evil.* Christ is the Teacher, the Risen One who has life in himself and who is always present in his Church and in the world. It is he who opens up to the faithful the book of the Scriptures and, by fully revealing the Father's will, teaches the truth about moral action. At the source and summit of the economy of salvation, as the Alpha and the Omega of human history (cf. Rev 1:8, 21:6, 22:13), Christ sheds light on man's condition and his integral vocation. Consequently, "the man who wishes to understand himself thoroughly — and not just in accordance with immediate, partial, often superficial, and even illusory standards and measures of his being — must, with his unrest, uncertainty and even his weakness and sinfulness, with his life and death, draw near to Christ. He must, so to speak, enter into him with all his own self, he must 'appropriate' and assimilate the whole of the reality of the Incarnation and Redemption in order to find himself. If this profound process takes place within him, he then bears fruit not only of adoration of God but also of deeper wonder at himself."[16]

8.3 If we therefore wish to go to the heart of the Gospel's moral teaching and grasp its profound and unchanging content, we must carefully inquire into the meaning of the question asked by the rich young man in the Gospel and, even more, the meaning of Jesus' reply, allowing ourselves to be guided by him. Jesus, as a patient and sensitive teacher, answers the young man by taking him, as it were, by the hand, and leading him step by step to the full truth.

"There is only one who is good" (Mt 19:17)

9.1 Jesus says: "Why do you ask me about what is good? There is only one who is good. If you wish to enter into life, keep the commandments" (Mt 19:17). In the versions of the Evangelists Mark and Luke the question is phrased in this way: "Why do you call me good? No one is good but God alone" (Mk 10:18; cf. Lk 18:19).

---

[16] Ibid., 10: loc. cit., 274.

9.2 Before answering the question, Jesus wishes the young man to have a clear idea of why he asked his question. The "Good Teacher" points out to him — and to all of us — that the answer to the question, "What good must I do to have eternal life?" can only be found by turning one's mind and heart to the "One" who is good: "No one is good but God alone" (Mk 10:18; cf. Lk 18:19). *Only God can answer the question about what is good, because he is the Good itself.*

9.3 *To ask about the good,* in fact, *ultimately means to turn toward God,* the fullness of goodness. Jesus shows that the young man's question is really a *religious question,* and that the goodness that attracts and at the same time obliges man has its source in God, and indeed is God himself. God alone is worthy of being loved "with all one's heart, and with all one's soul, and with all one's mind" (Mt 22:37). He is the source of man's happiness. Jesus brings the question about morally good action back to its religious foundations, to the acknowledgment of God, who alone is goodness, fullness of life, the final end of human activity, and perfect happiness.

10.1 The Church, instructed by the Teacher's words, believes that man, made in the image of the Creator, redeemed by the blood of Christ and made holy by the presence of the Holy Spirit, has as the *ultimate purpose* of his life *to live "for the praise of God's glory"* (cf. Eph 1:12), striving to make each of his actions reflect the splendor of that glory. "Know, then, O beautiful soul, that you are *the image of God,*" writes Saint Ambrose. "Know that you are *the glory of God* (1 Cor 11:7). Hear how you are his glory. The Prophet says: *Your knowledge has become too wonderful for me* (cf. Ps 138:6, Vulgate). That is to say, in my work your majesty has become more wonderful; in the counsels of men your wisdom is exalted. When I consider myself, such as I am known to you in my secret thoughts and deepest emotions, the mysteries of your knowledge are disclosed to me. Know then, O man, your greatness, and be vigilant."[17]

10.2 *What man is and what he must do becomes clear as soon as God reveals himself.* The Decalogue is based on these words: "I am the Lord your God, who brought you out of the land of Egypt, out of the house of bondage" (Ex 20:2-3). In the "ten words" of the Covenant with Israel, and in the whole Law, God makes himself known and acknowledged as the One who "alone is good"; the One who, despite man's sin, remains the "model" for moral action in accordance with his command, "You shall be holy; for I the Lord your God am holy" (Lev 19:2); as the One who, faithful to his love for man, gives him his

---

[17] *Exameron,* Dies VI, *Sermo* IX, 8, 50: *CSEL* 32, 24.

Law (cf. Ex 19:9-24 and 20:18-21) in order to restore man's original and peaceful harmony with the Creator and with all creation, and, what is more, to draw him into his divine love: "I will walk among you, and will be your God, and you shall be my people" (Lev 26:12).

10.3 *The moral life presents itself as the response* due to the many gratuitous initiatives taken by God out of love for man. It is a response of love, according to the statement made in Deuteronomy about the fundamental commandment: "Hear, O Israel: The Lord our God is one Lord; and you shall love the Lord your God with all your heart, and with all your soul, and with all your might. And these words which I command you this day shall be upon your heart; and you shall teach them diligently to your children" (Dt 6:4-7). Thus the moral life, caught up in the gratuitousness of God's love, is called to reflect his glory: "For the one who loves God it is enough to be pleasing to the One whom he loves: for no greater reward should be sought than that love itself; charity in fact is of God in such a way that God himself is charity."[18]

11.1 The statement that "There is only one who is good" thus brings us back to the "first tablet" of the commandments, which calls us to acknowledge God as the one Lord of all and to worship him alone for his infinite holiness (cf. Ex 20:2-11). *The good is belonging to God, obeying him,* walking humbly with him in doing justice and in loving kindness (cf. Mic 6:8). *Acknowledging the Lord as God is the very core, the heart of the Law,* from which the particular precepts flow and toward which they are ordered. In the morality of the commandments the fact that the people of Israel belong to the Lord is made evident, because God alone is the One who is good. Such is the witness of Sacred Scripture, imbued in every one of its pages with a lively perception of God's absolute holiness: "Holy, holy, holy is the Lord of hosts" (Is 6:3).

11.2 But if God alone is the Good, no human effort, not even the most rigorous observance of the commandments, succeeds in "fulfilling" the Law, that is, acknowledging the Lord as God and rendering him the worship due to him alone (cf. Mt 4:10). *This "fulfillment" can come only from a gift of God:* the offer of a share in the divine Goodness revealed and communicated in Jesus, the one whom the rich young man addresses with the words "Good Teacher" (Mk 10:17; Lk 18:18). What the young man now perhaps only dimly perceives will, in the end, be fully revealed by Jesus himself in the invitation: "Come, follow me" (Mt 19:21).

[18] Saint Leo the Great, *Sermo XCII,* Chapter III: *PL* 54, 454.

"If you wish to enter into life, keep the commandments" (Mt 19:17)

12.1 Only God can answer the question about the good, because he is the Good. But God has already given an answer to this question: he did so *by creating man and ordering him* with wisdom and love to his final end, through the law which is inscribed in his heart (cf. Rom 2:15), the "natural law." The latter "is nothing other than the light of understanding infused in us by God, whereby we understand what must be done and what must be avoided. God gave this light and this law to man at creation."[19] He also did so *in the history of Israel,* particularly in the "ten words," *the commandments of Sinai,* whereby he brought into existence the people of the Covenant (cf. Ex 24) and called them to be his "own possession among all peoples," "a holy nation" (Ex 19:5-6), which would radiate his holiness to all peoples (cf. Wis 18:4; Ezek 20:41). The gift of the Decalogue was a promise and sign of the *New Covenant,* in which the law would be written in a new and definitive way upon the human heart (cf. Jer 31:31-34), replacing the law of sin which had disfigured that heart (cf. Jer 17:1). In those days, "a new heart" would be given, for in it would dwell "a new spirit," the Spirit of God (cf. Ezek 36:24-28).[20]

12.2 Consequently, after making the important clarification, "There is only one who is good," Jesus tells the young man: "If you wish to enter into life, keep the commandments" (Mt 19:17). In this way, a close connection is made *between eternal life and obedience to God's commandments:* God's commandments show man the path of life and they lead to it. From the very lips of Jesus, the new Moses, man is once again given the commandments of the Decalogue. Jesus himself definitively confirms them and proposes them to us as the way and condition of salvation. *The commandments are linked to a promise.* In the Old Covenant the object of the promise was the possession of a land where the people would be able to live in freedom and in accordance with righteousness (cf. Dt 6:20-25). In the New Covenant the object of the promise is the "Kingdom of heaven," as Jesus declares at the beginning of the "Sermon on the Mount" — a sermon which contains the fullest and most complete formulation of the New Law (cf. Mt 5-7), clearly linked to the Decalogue entrusted by God to Moses on Mount Sinai. This same reality of the Kingdom is referred to in the expression "eternal life," which is a participation in the very life of God. It is attained in its perfection only after death, but in faith it is

---

[19] Saint Thomas Aquinas, *In Duo Praecepta Caritatis et in Decem Legis Praecepta, Prologus: Opuscula Theologica,* 11, No. 1129, Turin, 1954, 245; cf. *Summa Theologiae,* I-II, q. 91, a. 2; *Catechism of the Catholic Church,* No. 1955.

[20] Cf. Saint Maximus the Confessor, *Quaestiones ad Thalassium,* q. 64: *PG* 90, 723-728.

even now a light of truth, a source of meaning for life, an inchoate share in the full following of Christ. Indeed, Jesus says to his disciples after speaking to the rich young man: "Every one who has left houses or brothers or sisters or father or mother or children or lands, for my name's sake, will receive a hundredfold and inherit eternal life" (Mt 19:29).

13.1 Jesus' answer is not enough for the young man, who continues by asking the Teacher about the commandments which must be kept: "He said to him, 'Which ones?' " (Mt 19:18). He asks what he must do in life in order to show that he acknowledges God's holiness. After directing the young man's gaze toward God, Jesus reminds him of the commandments of the Decalogue regarding one's neighbor: "Jesus said: 'You shall not murder; You shall not commit adultery; You shall not bear false witness; Honor your father and mother; also, You shall love your neighbor as yourself' " (Mt 19:18-19).

13.2 From the context of the conversation, and especially from a comparison of Matthew's text with the parallel passages in Mark and Luke, it is clear that Jesus does not intend to list each and every one of the commandments required in order to "enter into life," but rather wishes to draw the young man's attention to the *"centrality" of the Decalogue* with regard to every other precept, inasmuch as it is the interpretation of what the words "I am the Lord your God" mean for man. Nevertheless we cannot fail to notice which commandments of the Law the Lord recalls to the young man. They are some of the commandments belonging to the so-called "second tablet" of the Decalogue, the summary (cf. Rom 13:8-10) and foundation of which is *the commandment of love of neighbor:* "You shall love your neighbor as yourself" (Mt 19:19; cf. Mk 12:31). In this commandment we find a precise expression of *the singular dignity of the human person,* "the only creature that God has wanted for its own sake."[21] The different commandments of the Decalogue are really only so many reflections of the one commandment about the good of the person, at the level of the many different goods which characterize his identity as a spiritual and bodily being in relationship with God, with his neighbor and with the material world. As we read in the *Catechism of the Catholic Church,* "the ten commandments are part of God's revelation. At the same time, they teach us man's true humanity. They shed light on the essential duties, and so indirectly on the fundamental rights, inherent in the nature of the human person."[22]

[21] Second Vatican Ecumenical Council, Pastoral Constitution on the Church in the Modern World *Gaudium et Spes,* 24.

[22] *Catechism of the Catholic Church,* No. 2070.

13.3 The commandments of which Jesus reminds the young man are meant to safeguard *the good* of the person, the image of God, by protecting his *goods*. "You shall not murder; You shall not commit adultery; You shall not steal; You shall not bear false witness" are moral rules formulated in terms of prohibitions. These negative precepts express with particular force the ever urgent need to protect human life, the communion of persons in marriage, private property, truthfulness and people's good name.

13.4 The commandments thus represent the basic condition for love of neighbor; at the same time they are the proof of that love. They are the *first necessary step on the journey toward freedom*, its starting-point. "The beginning of freedom," Saint Augustine writes, "is to be free from crimes . . . such as murder, adultery, fornication, theft, fraud, sacrilege and so forth. Once one is without these crimes (and every Christian should be without them), one begins to lift up one's head toward freedom. But this is only the beginning of freedom, not perfect freedom . . ."[23]

14.1 This certainly does not mean that Christ wishes to put the love of neighbor higher than, or even to set it apart from, the love of God. This is evident from his conversation with the teacher of the Law, who asked him a question very much like the one asked by the young man. Jesus refers him to *the two commandments of love of God and love of neighbor* (cf. Lk 10:25-27), and reminds him that only by observing them will he have eternal life: "Do this, and you will live" (Lk 10:28). Nonetheless it is significant that it is precisely the second of these commandments which arouses the curiosity of the teacher of the Law, who asks him: "And who is my neighbor?" (Lk 10:29). The Teacher replies with the parable of the Good Samaritan, which is critical for fully understanding the commandment of love of neighbor (cf. Lk 10:30-37).

14.2 These two commandments, on which "depend all the Law and the Prophets" (Mt 22:40), are profoundly connected and mutually related. *Their inseparable unity* is attested to by Christ in his words and by his very life: his mission culminates in the Cross of our Redemption (cf. Jn 3:14-15), the sign of his indivisible love for the Father and for humanity (cf. Jn 13:1).

14.3 Both the Old and the New Testaments explicitly affirm that *without love of neighbor*, made concrete in keeping the commandments, *genuine love for God is not possible*. Saint John makes the point with extraordinary forcefulness: "If anyone says, 'I love God,' and hates his brother, he is a liar; for he who does not love his brother whom he has seen, cannot love God whom he has not seen" (1 Jn 4:20). The Evangelist echoes the moral preaching of Christ,

---

[23] *In Iohannis Evangelium Tractatus*, 41, 10: CCL 36, 363.

expressed in a wonderful and unambiguous way in the parable of the Good Samaritan (cf. Lk 10:30-37) and in his words about the final judgment (cf. Mt 25:31-46).

15.1 In the "Sermon on the Mount," the magna charta of Gospel moral-ity,[24] Jesus says: "Do not think that I have come to abolish the Law and the Prophets; I have come not to abolish them but to fulfill them" (Mt 5:17). Christ is the key to the Scriptures: "You search the Scriptures. . . ; and it is they that bear witness to me" (Jn 5:39). Christ is the center of the economy of salvation, the recapitulation of the Old and New Testaments, of the promises of the Law and of their fulfillment in the Gospel; he is the living and eternal link between the Old and the New Covenants. Commenting on Paul's statement that "Christ is the end of the law" (Rom 10:4), Saint Ambrose writes: "end not in the sense of a deficiency, but in the sense of the fullness of the Law: a fullness which is achieved in Christ (*plenitudo legis in Christo est*), since he came not to abolish the Law but to bring it to fulfillment. In the same way that there is an Old Testament, but all truth is in the New Testament, so it is for the Law: what was given through Moses is a figure of the true law. Therefore, the Mosaic Law is an image of the truth."[25]

15.2 *Jesus brings God's commandments to fulfillment*, particularly the com-mandment of love of neighbor, *by interiorizing their demands and by bringing out their fullest meaning.* Love of neighbor springs from *a loving heart* which, precisely because it loves, is ready to live out *the loftiest challenges.* Jesus shows that the commandments must not be understood as a minimum limit not to be gone beyond, but rather as a path involving a moral and spiritual journey toward perfection, at the heart of which is love (cf. Col 3:14). Thus the commandment "You shall not murder" becomes a call to an attentive love which protects and promotes the life of one's neighbor. The precept prohibit-ing adultery becomes an invitation to a pure way of looking at others, capable of respecting the spousal meaning of the body: "You have heard that it was said to the men of old, '*You shall not kill; and whoever kills shall be liable to judgment.*' *But I say to you* that every one who is angry with his brother shall be liable to judgment. . . . You have heard that it was said, '*You shall not com-mit adultery.*' *But I say to you* that every one who looks at a woman lustfully has already committed adultery with her in his heart" (Mt 5:21-22, 27-28). *Jesus himself is the living "fulfillment" of the Law* inasmuch as he fulfills its

---

[24] Cf. Saint Augustine, *De Sermone Domini in Monte*, I, 1, 1: *CCL* 35, 1-2.

[25] *In Psalmum CXVIII Expositio, Sermo* 18, 37: *PL* 15, 1541; cf. Saint Chromatius of Aquileia, *Tractatus in Matthaeum*, XX, I, 1-4: *CCL* 9/A, 291-292.

authentic meaning by the total gift of himself: *he himself becomes a living and personal Law*, who invites people to follow him; through the Spirit, he gives the grace to share his own life and love and provides the strength to bear witness to that love in personal choices and actions (cf. Jn 13:34-35).

"If you wish to be perfect" (Mt 19:21)

16.1 The answer he receives about the commandments does not satisfy the young man, who asks Jesus a further question. "I have kept all these; *what do I still lack?*" (Mt 19:20). It is not easy to say with a clear conscience "I have kept all these," if one has any understanding of the real meaning of the demands contained in God's Law. And yet, even though he is able to make this reply, even though he has followed the moral ideal seriously and generously from childhood, the rich young man knows that he is still far from the goal: before the person of Jesus he realizes that he is still lacking something. It is his awareness of this insufficiency that Jesus addresses in his final answer. Conscious of *the young man's yearning for something greater, which would transcend a legalistic interpretation of the commandments*, the Good Teacher invites him to enter upon the path of perfection: "If you wish to be perfect, go, sell your possessions and give the money to the poor, and you will have treasure in heaven; then come, follow me" (Mt 19:21).

16.2 Like the earlier part of Jesus' answer, this part too must be read and interpreted in the context of the whole moral message of the Gospel, and in particular in the context of the Sermon on the Mount, the Beatitudes (cf. Mt 5:3-12), the first of which is precisely the Beatitude of the poor, the "poor in spirit" as Saint Matthew makes clear (Mt 5:3), the humble. In this sense it can be said that the Beatitudes are also relevant to the answer given by Jesus to the young man's question: "What good must I do to have eternal life?" Indeed, each of the Beatitudes promises, from a particular viewpoint, that very "good" which opens man up to eternal life, and indeed is eternal life.

16.3 *The Beatitudes* are not specifically concerned with certain particular rules of behavior. Rather, they speak of basic attitudes and dispositions in life and therefore they *do not coincide exactly with the commandments*. On the other hand, *there is no separation or opposition* between the Beatitudes and the commandments: both refer to the good, to eternal life. The Sermon on the Mount begins with the proclamation of the Beatitudes, but also refers to the commandments (cf. Mt 5:20-48). At the same time, the Sermon on the Mount demonstrates the openness of the commandments and their orientation toward the horizon of the perfection proper to the Beatitudes. These latter are above all *promises*, from which there also indirectly flow *normative indications* for the moral life. In their originality and profundity they are a sort of *self-portrait of Christ*, and for this very reason are *invitations to discipleship and communion of life with Christ.*[26]

17.1 We do not know how clearly the young man in the Gospel understood the profound and challenging import of Jesus' first reply: "If you wish to enter into life, keep the commandments." But it is certain that the young man's commitment to respect all the moral demands of the commandments represents the absolutely essential ground in which the desire for perfection can take root and mature, the desire, that is, for the meaning of the commandments to be completely fulfilled in following Christ. Jesus' conversation with the young man helps us to grasp *the conditions for the moral growth of man, who has been called to perfection:* the young man, having observed all the commandments, shows that he is incapable of taking the next step by himself alone. To do so requires mature human freedom ("If you wish to be perfect") and God's gift of grace ("Come, follow me").

17.2 *Perfection demands that maturity in self-giving to which human freedom is called.* Jesus points out to the young man that the commandments are the first and indispensable condition for having eternal life; on the other hand, for the young man to give up all he possesses and to follow the Lord is presented as an invitation: "If you wish. . . ." These words of Jesus reveal the particular dynamic of freedom's growth toward maturity, and at the same time *they bear witness to the fundamental relationship between freedom and divine law.* Human freedom and God's Law are not in opposition; on the contrary, they appeal one to the other. The follower of Christ knows that his vocation is to freedom. "You were called to freedom, brethren" (Gal 5:13), proclaims the Apostle Paul with joy and pride. But he immediately adds: "only do not use your freedom as an opportunity for the flesh, but through love be servants of one another" (ibid.). The firmness with which the Apostle opposes those who believe that they are justified by the Law has nothing to do with man's "liberation" from precepts. On the contrary, the latter are at the service of the practice of love: "For he who loves his neighbor has fulfilled the Law. The commandments, *'You shall not commit adultery; You shall not murder; You shall not steal; You shall not covet,'* and any other commandment, are summed up in this sentence, *'You shall love your neighbor as yourself'* " (Rom 13:8-9). Saint Augustine, after speaking of the observance of the commandments as being a kind of incipient, imperfect freedom, goes on to say: "Why, someone will ask, is it not yet perfect? Because 'I see in my members

[26] Cf. *Catechism of the Catholic Church,* No. 1717.

another law at war with the law of my reason.' . . . In part freedom, in part sla-very: not yet complete freedom, not yet pure, not yet whole, because we are not yet in eternity. In part we retain our weakness and in part we have attained freedom. All our sins were destroyed in Baptism, but does it follow that no weak-ness remained after iniquity was destroyed? Had none remained, we would live without sin in this life. But who would dare to say this except someone who is proud, someone unworthy of the mercy of our deliverer? . . . Therefore, since some weakness has remained in us, I dare to say that to the extent to which we serve God we are free, while to the extent that we follow the law of sin, we are still slaves."[27]

18.1 Those who live "by the flesh" experience God's law as a burden, and indeed as a denial or at least a restriction of their own freedom. On the other hand, those who are impelled by love and "walk by the Spirit" (Gal 5:16), and who desire to serve others, find in God's Law the fundamental and necessary way in which to practice love as something freely chosen and freely lived out. Indeed, they feel an interior urge — a genuine "necessity" and no longer a form of coercion — not to stop at the minimum demands of the Law, but to live them in their "fullness." This is a still uncertain and fragile journey as long as we are on earth, but it is one made possible by grace, which enables us to possess the full freedom of the children of God (cf. Rom 8:21) and thus to live our moral life in a way worthy of our sublime vocation as "sons in the Son."

18.2 This vocation to perfect love is not restricted to a small group of indi-viduals. *The invitation* "go, sell your possessions and give the money to the poor," and the promise "you will have treasure in heaven," *are meant for everyone*, because they bring out the full meaning of the commandment of love for neigh-bor, just as the invitation which follows, "Come, follow me," is the new, specific form of the commandment of love of God. Both the commandments and Jesus' invitation to the rich young man stand at the service of a single and indivisible charity, which spontaneously tends toward that perfection whose measure is God alone: "You, therefore, must be perfect, as your heavenly Father is perfect" (Mt 5:48). In the Gospel of Luke, Jesus makes even clearer the meaning of this perfection: "Be merciful, even as your Father is merciful" (Lk 6:36).

"Come, follow me" (Mt 19:21)

19.1 The way and at the same time the content of this perfection consists in the following of Jesus, *sequela Christi*, once one has given up one's own wealth and very self. This is precisely the conclusion of Jesus' conversation

---

[27] *In Iohannis Evangelium Tractatus*, 41, 10: CCL 36, 363.

with the young man: "Come, follow me" (Mt 19:21). It is an invitation the marvelous grandeur of which will be fully perceived by the disciples after Christ's Resurrection, when the Holy Spirit leads them to all truth (cf. Jn 16:13).

19.2 It is Jesus himself who takes the initiative and calls people to follow him. His call is addressed first to those to whom he entrusts a particular mission, beginning with the Twelve; but it is also clear that every believer is called to be a follower of Christ (cf. Acts 6:1). *Following Christ is thus the essential and primordial foundation of Christian morality:* just as the people of Israel followed God, who led them through the desert toward the Promised Land (cf. Ex 13:21), so every disciple must follow Jesus, toward whom he is drawn by the Father himself (cf. Jn 6:44).

19.3 This is not a matter only of disposing oneself to hear a teaching and obediently accepting a commandment. More radically, it involves *holding fast to the very person of Jesus,* partaking of his life and his destiny, sharing in his free and loving obedience to the will of the Father. By responding in faith and following the one who is Incarnate Wisdom, the disciple of Jesus truly becomes a disciple of God (cf. Jn 6:45). Jesus is indeed the light of the world, the light of life (cf. Jn 8:12). He is the shepherd who leads his sheep and feeds them (cf. Jn 10:11-16); he is the way, and the truth, and the life (cf. Jn 14:6). It is Jesus who leads to the Father, so much so that to see him, the Son, is to see the Father (cf. Jn 14:6-10). And thus to imitate the Son, "the image of the invisible God" (Col 1:15), means to imitate the Father.

20.1 *Jesus asks us to follow him and to imitate him along the path of love, a love which gives itself completely to the brethren out of love for God:* "This is my commandment, that you love one another as I have loved you" (Jn 15:12). The word "as" requires imitation of Jesus and of his love, of which the washing of feet is a sign: "If I then, your Lord and Teacher, have washed your feet, you also ought to wash one another's feet. For I have given you an example, that you should do as I have done to you" (Jn 13:14-15). Jesus' way of acting and his words, his deeds and his precepts constitute the moral rule of Christian life. Indeed, his actions, and in particular his Passion and death on the Cross, are the living revelation of his love for the Father and for others. This is exactly the love that Jesus wishes to be imitated by all who follow him. It is the *"new" commandment:* "A new commandment I give to you, that you love one another; even as I have loved you, that you also love one another. By this all men will know that you are my disciples, if you have love for one another" (Jn 13:34-35).

20.2 The word "as" also indicates the *degree* of Jesus' love, and of the love with which his disciples are called to love one another. After saying, "This is my commandment, that you love one another as I have loved you" (Jn 15:12), Jesus continues with words which indicate the sacrificial gift of his life on the Cross, as the witness to a love "to the end" (Jn 13:1): "Greater love has no man than this, that a man lay down his life for his friends" (Jn 15:13).

20.3 As he calls the young man to follow him along the way of perfection, Jesus asks him to be perfect in the command of love, in "his" commandment: to become part of the unfolding of his complete giving, to imitate and rekindle the very love of the "Good" Teacher, the one who loved "to the end." This is what Jesus asks of everyone who wishes to follow him: "If any man would come after me, let him deny himself and take up his cross and follow me" (Mt 16:24).

21.1 *Following Christ* is not an outward imitation, since it touches man at the very depths of his being. Being a follower of Christ means *becoming conformed to him* who became a servant even to giving himself on the Cross (cf. Phil 2:5-8). Christ dwells by faith in the heart of the believer (cf. Eph 3:17), and thus the disciple is conformed to the Lord. This is the *effect of grace*, of the active presence of the Holy Spirit in us.

21.2 Having become one with Christ, the Christian *becomes a member of his Body, which is the Church* (cf. 1 Cor 12:13, 27). By the work of the Spirit, Baptism radically configures the faithful to Christ in the Paschal Mystery of death and resurrection; it "clothes him" in Christ (cf. Gal 3:27): "Let us rejoice and give thanks," exclaims Saint Augustine speaking to the baptized, "for we have become not only Christians, but Christ. . . . Marvel and rejoice: we have become Christ!"[28] Having died to sin, those who are baptized receive new life (cf. Rom 6:3-11): alive for God in Christ Jesus, they are called to walk by the Spirit and to manifest the Spirit's fruits in their lives (cf. Gal 5:16-25). Sharing in the *Eucharist*, the Sacrament of the New Covenant (cf. 1 Cor 11:23-29), is the culmination of our assimilation to Christ, the source of "eternal life" (cf. Jn 6:51-58), the source and power of that complete gift of self, which Jesus — according to the testimony handed on by Paul — commands us to commemorate in liturgy and in life: "As often as you eat this bread and drink the cup, you proclaim the Lord's death until he comes" (1 Cor 11:26).

"With God all things are possible" (Mt 19:26)

22.1 The conclusion of Jesus' conversation with the rich young man is very poignant: "When the young man heard this, he went away sorrowful, for

---

[28] *In Iohannis Evangelium Tractatus*, 21, 8: *CCL* 36, 216.

he had many possessions" (Mt 19:22). Not only the rich man but the disciples themselves are taken aback by Jesus' call to discipleship, the demands of which transcend human aspirations and abilities: "When the disciples heard this, they were greatly astounded and said, 'Then who can be saved?'" (Mt 1-9:25). *But the Master refers them to God's power:* "With men this is impossible, but with God all things are possible" (Mt 19:26).

22.2 In the same chapter of Matthew's Gospel (19:3-10), Jesus, interpreting the Mosaic Law on marriage, rejects the right to divorce, appealing to a "beginning" more fundamental and more authoritative than the Law of Moses: God's original plan for mankind, a plan which man after sin has no longer been able to live up to: "For your hardness of heart Moses allowed you to divorce your wives, but from the beginning it was not so" (Mt 19:8). Jesus' appeal to the "beginning" dismays the disciples, who remark: "If such is the case of a man with his wife, it is not expedient to marry" (Mt 19:10). And Jesus, referring specifically to the charism of celibacy "for the Kingdom of heaven" (Mt 19:12), but stating a general rule, indicates the new and surprising possibility opened up to man by God's grace. "He said to them: 'Not everyone can accept this saying, but only those to whom it is given'" (Mt 19:11).

22.3 To imitate and live out the love of Christ is not possible for man by his own strength alone. *He becomes capable of this love only by virtue of a gift received.* As the Lord Jesus receives the love of his Father, so he in turn freely communicates that love to his disciples: "As the Father has loved me, so have I loved you; abide in my love" (Jn 15:9). *Christ's gift is his Spirit,* whose first "fruit" (cf. Gal 5:22) is charity: "God's love has been poured into our hearts through the Holy Spirit which has been given to us" (Rom 5:5). Saint Augustine asks: "Does love bring about the keeping of the commandments, or does the keeping of the commandments bring about love?" And he answers: "But who can doubt that love comes first? For the one who does not love has no reason for keeping the commandments."[29]

23.1 "The law of the Spirit of life in Christ Jesus has set me free from the law of sin and death" (Rom 8:2). With these words the Apostle Paul invites us to consider in the perspective of the history of salvation, which reaches its fulfillment in Christ, *the relationship between the* (Old) *Law and grace* (the New Law). He recognizes the pedagogic function of the Law, which, by enabling sinful man to take stock of his own powerlessness and by stripping him of the presumption of his self-sufficiency, leads him to ask for and to receive "life in the Spirit." Only in this new life is it possible to carry out God's

---

[29] Ibid., 82, 3: *CCL* 36, 533.

commandments. Indeed, it is through faith in Christ that we have been made righteous (cf. Rom 3:28): the "righteousness" which the Law demands, but is unable to give, is found by every believer to be revealed and granted by the Lord Jesus. Once again it is Saint Augustine who admirably sums up this Pauline dialectic of law and grace: "The law was given that grace might be sought; and grace was given, that the law might be fulfilled."[30]

23.2 Love and life according to the Gospel cannot be thought of first and foremost as a kind of precept, because what they demand is beyond man's abilities. They are possible only as a result of a gift of God who heals, restores and transforms the human heart by his grace: "For the law was given through Moses; grace and truth came through Jesus Christ" (Jn 1:17). The promise of eternal life is thus linked to the gift of grace, and the gift of the Spirit which we have received is even now the "guarantee of our inheritance" (Eph 1:14).

24.1 And so we find revealed the authentic and original aspect of the commandment of love and of the perfection to which it is ordered: we are speaking of a *possibility opened up to man exclusively by grace,* by the gift of God, by his love. On the other hand, precisely the awareness of having received the gift, of possessing in Jesus Christ the love of God, generates and sustains *the free response* of a full love for God and the brethren, as the Apostle John insistently reminds us in his First Letter: "Beloved, let us love one another; for love is of God and knows God. He who does not love does not know God; for God is love. . . . Beloved, if God so loved us, we ought also to love one another. . . . We love, because he first loved us" (1 Jn 4:7-8, 11, 19).

24.2 This inseparable connection between the Lord's grace and human freedom, between gift and task, has been expressed in simple yet profound words by Saint Augustine in his prayer: *"Da quod iubes et iube quod vis"* (grant what you command and command what you will).[31]

24.3 *The gift does not lessen but reinforces the moral demands of love:* "This is his commandment, that we should believe in the name of his Son Jesus Christ and love one another, just as he has commanded us" (1 Jn 3:23). One can "abide" in love only by keeping the commandments, as Jesus states: "If you keep my commandments, you will abide in my love, just as I have kept my Father's commandments and abide in his love" (Jn 15:10).

24.4 Going to the heart of the moral message of Jesus and the preaching of the Apostles, and summing up in a remarkable way the great tradition of the

---

[30] *De Spiritu et Littera,* 19, 34: *CSEL* 60, 187.
[31] *Confessiones,* X, 29, 40: *CCL* 27, 176; cf. *De Gratia et Libero Arbitrio,* XV: *PL* 44, 899.

Fathers of the East and West, and of Saint Augustine in particular,[32] Saint Thomas was able to write that *the New Law is the grace of the Holy Spirit given through faith in Christ.*[33] The external precepts also mentioned in the Gospel dispose one for this grace or produce its effects in one's life. Indeed, the New Law is not content to say what must be done, but also gives the power to "do what is true" (cf. Jn 3:21). Saint John Chrysostom likewise observed that the New Law was promulgated at the descent of the Holy Spirit from heaven on the day of Pentecost, and that the Apostles "did not come down from the mountain carrying, like Moses, tablets of stone in their hands; but they came down carrying the Holy Spirit in their hearts . . . having become by his grace a living law, a living book."[34]

"Lo, I am with you always, to the close of the age" (Mt 28:20)

25.1 Jesus' conversation with the rich young man continues, in a sense, *in every period of history, including our own.* The question "Teacher, what good must I do to have eternal life?" arises in the heart of every individual, and it is Christ alone who is capable of giving the full and definitive answer. The Teacher who expounds God's commandments, who invites others to follow him and gives the grace for a new life, is always present and at work in our midst, as he himself promised: "Lo, I am with you always, to the close of the age" (Mt 28:20). *Christ's relevance for people of all times is shown forth in his Body, which is the Church.* For this reason the Lord promised his disciples the Holy Spirit, who would "bring to their remembrance" and teach them to understand his commandments (cf. Jn 14:26), and who would be the principal and constant source of a new life in the world (cf. Jn 3:5-8; Rom 8:1-13).

25.2 The moral prescriptions which God imparted in the Old Covenant, and which attained their perfection in the New and Eternal Covenant in the very person of the Son of God made man, must be *faithfully kept and continually put into practice* in the various different cultures throughout the course of history. The task of interpreting these prescriptions was entrusted by Jesus to the Apostles and their successors, with the special assistance of the Spirit of truth: "He who hears you hears me" (Lk 10:16). By the light and the strength of this Spirit the Apostles carried out their mission of preaching the Gospel and of pointing out the "way" of the Lord

---

[32] Cf. *De Spiritu et Littera*, 21, 36; 26, 46: *CSEL* 60, 189-190; 200-201.
[33] Cf. *Summa Theologiae*, I-II, q. 106, a. 1 *corpus* and ad 2.
[34] *In Matthaeum*, Homily, I, 1: *PG* 57, 15.

(cf. Acts 18:25), teaching above all how to follow and imitate Christ: "For to me to live is Christ" (Phil 1:21).

26.1 In the *moral catechesis of the Apostles*, besides exhortations and directions connected to specific historical and cultural situations, we find an ethical teaching with precise rules of behavior. This is seen in their Letters, which contain the interpretation, made under the guidance of the Holy Spirit, of the Lord's precepts as they are to be lived in different cultural circumstances (cf. Rom 12-15; 1 Cor 11-14; Gal 5-6; Eph 4-6; Col 3-4; 1 Pet and Jas). From the Church's beginnings, the Apostles, by virtue of their pastoral responsibility to preach the Gospel, *were vigilant over the right conduct of Christians*,[35] just as they were vigilant for the purity of the faith and the handing down of the divine gifts in the sacraments.[36] The first Christians, coming both from the Jewish people and from the Gentiles, differed from the pagans not only in their faith and their liturgy but also in the witness of their moral conduct, which was inspired by the New Law.[37] The Church is in fact a communion both of faith and of life; her rule of life is "faith working through love" (Gal 5:6).

26.2 No damage must be done to the *harmony between faith and life: the unity of the Church* is damaged not only by Christians who reject or distort the truths of faith but also by those who disregard the moral obligations to which they are called by the Gospel (cf. 1 Cor 5:9-13). The Apostles decisively rejected any separation between the commitment of the heart and the actions which express or prove it (cf. 1 Jn 2:3-6). And ever since Apostolic times the Church's Pastors have unambiguously condemned the behavior of those who fostered division by their teaching or by their actions.[38]

27.1 Within the unity of the Church, promoting and preserving the faith and the moral life is the task entrusted by Jesus to the Apostles (cf. Mt 28:19-20), a task which continues in the ministry of their successors. This is apparent from the *living Tradition*, whereby — as the Second Vatican Council teaches

---

[35] Cf. Saint Irenaeus, *Adversus Haereses*, IV, 26, 2-5: *SCh* 100/2, 718-729.

[36] Cf. Saint Justin, *Apologia*, I, 66: *PG* 6, 427-430.

[37] Cf. 2 Pet 1:12ff.; cf. *Didache*, II, 2: *Patres Apostolici*, ed. F. X. Funk, I, 6-9; Clement of Alexandria, *Paedagogus*, I, 10; II, 10: *PG* 8, 355-364; 497-536; Tertullian, *Apologeticum*, IX, 8: *CSEL* 69, 24.

[38] Cf. Saint Ignatius of Antioch, *Epistula ad Magnesios*, VI, 1-2: *Patres Apostolici*, ed. F. X. Funk, I, 234-235; Saint Irenaeus, *Adversus Haereses*, IV, 33, 1; IV, 33, 6; IV, 33, 7: *SCh* 100/2, 802-805; 814-815; 816-819.

— "the Church, in her teaching, life and worship, perpetuates and hands on to every generation all that she is and all that she believes. This Tradition which comes from the Apostles, progresses in the Church under the assistance of the Holy Spirit."[39] In the Holy Spirit, the Church receives and hands down the Scripture as the witness to the "great things" which God has done in history (cf. Lk 1:49); she professes by the lips of her Fathers and Doctors the truth of the Word made flesh, puts his precepts and love into practice in the lives of her saints and in the sacrifice of her martyrs, and celebrates her hope in him in the liturgy. By this same Tradition Christians receive "the living voice of the Gospel,"[40] as the faithful expression of God's wisdom and will.

27.2 Within Tradition, *the authentic interpretation* of the Lord's law develops, with the help of the Holy Spirit. The same Spirit who is at the origin of the revelation of Jesus' commandments and teachings, guarantees that they will be reverently preserved, faithfully expounded and correctly applied in different times and places. This constant "putting into practice" of the commandments is the sign and fruit of a deeper insight into revelation and of an understanding in the light of faith of new historical and cultural situations. Nevertheless, it can only confirm the permanent validity of revelation and follow in the line of the interpretation given to it by the great Tradition of the Church's teaching and life, as witnessed by the teaching of the Fathers, the lives of the saints, the Church's liturgy and the teaching of the Magisterium.

27.3 In particular, as the Council affirms, *"the task of authentically interpreting the word of God, whether in its written form or in that of Tradition, has been entrusted only to those charged with the Church's living Magisterium, whose authority is exercised in the name of Jesus Christ."*[41] The Church, in her life and teaching, is thus revealed as "the pillar and bulwark of the truth" (1 Tim 3:15), including the truth regarding moral action. Indeed, "the Church has the right always and everywhere to proclaim moral principles, even in respect of the social order, and to make judgments about any human matter insofar as this is required by fundamental human rights or the salvation of souls."[42]

27.4 Precisely on the questions frequently debated in moral theology today and with regard to which new tendencies and theories have developed, the Magisterium, in fidelity to Jesus Christ and in continuity with the Church's Tradition, senses more urgently the duty to offer its own discernment and teaching, in order to help man in his journey toward truth and freedom.

---

[39] Dogmatic Constitution on Divine Revelation *Dei Verbum*, 8.
[40] Cf. ibid., 8.
[41] Ibid., 10.
[42] *Code of Canon Law*, Canon 747 §2.

II

"Do Not Be Conformed to This World" (Rom 12:2)

The Church and the Discernment of Certain Tendencies in Present-Day Moral Theology

Teaching what befits sound doctrine (cf. Tit 2:1)

28.1 Our meditation on the dialogue between Jesus and the rich young man has enabled us to bring together the essential elements of revelation in the Old and New Testament with regard to moral action. These are: the *subordination of man and his activity to God,* the One who "alone is good"; the *relationship between the moral good,* clearly indicated in the divine commandments, of human acts *and eternal life; Christian discipleship,* which opens up before man the perspective of perfect love; and finally the *gift of the Holy Spirit,* source and means of the moral life of the "new creation" (cf. 2 Cor 5:17).

28.2 In her reflection on morality, *the Church* has always kept in mind the words of Jesus to the rich young man. Indeed, Sacred Scripture remains the living and fruitful source of the Church's moral doctrine; as the Second Vatican Council recalled, the Gospel is "the source of all saving truth and moral teaching."[43] The Church has faithfully preserved what the word of God teaches not only about truths which must be believed but also about moral action, action pleasing to God (cf. 1 Thess 4:1); she has achieved a *doctrinal development* analogous to that which has taken place in the realm of the truths of faith. Assisted by the Holy Spirit who leads her into all the truth (cf. Jn 16:13), the Church has not ceased, nor can she ever cease, to contemplate the "mystery of the Word Incarnate," in whom "light is shed on the mystery of man."[44]

29.1 The Church's moral reflection, always conducted in the light of Christ, the "Good Teacher," has also developed in the specific form of the theological science called *"moral theology,"* a science which accepts and examines divine revelation while at the same time responding to the demands of human reason. Moral theology is a reflection concerned with "morality," with the good

---

[43] Dogmatic Constitution on Divine Revelation *Dei Verbum,* 7.

[44] Second Vatican Ecumenical Council, Pastoral Constitution on the Church in the Modern World *Gaudium et Spes,* 22.

and the evil of human acts and of the person who performs them; in this sense it is accessible to all people. But it is also "theology," inasmuch as it acknowledges that the origin and end of moral action are found in the One who "alone is good" and who, by giving himself to man in Christ, offers him the happiness of divine life.

29.2 The Second Vatican Council invited scholars to take *"special care for the renewal of moral theology"* in such a way that "its scientific presentation, increasingly based on the teaching of Scripture, will cast light on the exalted vocation of the faithful in Christ and on their obligation to bear fruit in charity for the life of the world."[45] The Council also encouraged theologians, "while respecting the methods and requirements of theological science, to look for *a more appropriate way of communicating* doctrine to the people of their time; since there is a difference between the deposit or the truths of faith and the manner in which they are expressed, keeping the same meaning and the same judgment."[46] This led to a further invitation, one extended to all the faithful, but addressed to theologians in particular: "The faithful should live in the closest contact with others of their time, and should work for a perfect understanding of their modes of thought and feelings as expressed in their culture."[47]

29.3 The work of many theologians who found support in the Council's encouragement has already borne fruit in interesting and helpful reflections about the truths of faith to be believed and applied in life, reflections offered in a form better suited to the sensitivities and questions of our contemporaries. The Church, and particularly the Bishops, to whom Jesus Christ primarily entrusted the ministry of teaching, are deeply appreciative of this work, and encourage theologians to continue their efforts, inspired by that profound and authentic "fear of the Lord, which is the beginning of wisdom" (cf. Prov 1:7).

29.4 At the same time, however, within the context of the theological debates which followed the Council, there have developed *certain interpretations of Christian morality which are not consistent with "sound teaching"* (2 Tim 4:3). Certainly the Church's Magisterium does not intend to impose upon the faithful any particular theological system, still less a philosophical one. Nevertheless, in order to "reverently preserve and faithfully expound" the word of God, [48] the Magisterium has the duty to state that some trends of theological

---

[45] Decree on Priestly Formation *Optatam Totius*, 16.

[46] Pastoral Constitution on the Church in the Modern World *Gaudium et Spes*, 62.

[47] Ibid., 62.

[48] Cf. Second Vatican Ecumenical Council, Dogmatic Constitution on Divine Revelation *Dei Verbum*, 10.

thinking and certain philosophical affirmations are incompatible with revealed truth.[49]

30.1 In addressing this Encyclical to you, my Brother Bishops, it is my intention to state *the principles necessary for discerning what is contrary to "sound doctrine,"* drawing attention to those elements of the Church's moral teaching which today appear particularly exposed to error, ambiguity or neglect. Yet these are the very elements on which there depends "the answer to the obscure riddles of the human condition which today also, as in the past, profoundly disturb the human heart. What is man? What is the meaning and purpose of our life? What is good and what is sin? What origin and purpose do sufferings have? What is the way to attain true happiness? What are death, judgment and retribution after death? Lastly, what is that final, unutterable mystery which embraces our lives and from which we take our origin and toward which we tend?"[50] These and other questions, such as: what is freedom and what is its relationship to the truth contained in God's law? what is the role of conscience in man's moral development? how do we determine, in accordance with the truth about the good, the specific rights and duties of the human person? — can all be summed up in the fundamental question which the young man in the Gospel put to Jesus: "Teacher, what good must I do to have eternal life?" Because the Church has been sent by Jesus to preach the Gospel and to "make disciples of all nations. . . , teaching them to observe all" that he has commanded (cf. Mt 28:19-20), *she today once more puts forward the Master's reply,* a reply that possesses a light and a power capable of answering even the most controversial and complex questions. This light and power also impel the Church constantly to carry out not only her dogmatic but also her moral reflection within an interdisciplinary context, which is especially necessary in facing new issues.[51]

30.2 It is in the same light and power that *the Church's Magisterium continues to carry out its task of discernment,* accepting and living out the admonition addressed by the Apostle Paul to Timothy: "I charge you in the

---

[49] Cf. First Vatican Ecumenical Council, Dogmatic Constitution on the Catholic Faith *Dei Filius,* Chapter 4: *DS* 3018.

[50] Second Vatican Ecumenical Council, Declaration on the Relationship of the Church to Non-Christian Religions *Nostra Aetate,* 1.

[51] Cf. Second Vatican Ecumenical Council, Pastoral Constitution on the Church in the Modern World *Gaudium et Spes,* 43-44.

presence of God and of Christ Jesus who is to judge the living and the dead, and by his appearing and his Kingdom: preach the word, be urgent in season and out of season, convince, rebuke, and exhort, be unfailing in patience and in teaching. For the time will come when people will not endure sound teaching, but having itching ears they will accumulate for themselves teachers to suit their own likings, and will turn away from listening to the truth and wander into myths. As for you, always be steady, endure suffering, do the work of an evangelist, fulfill your ministry" (2 Tim 4:1-5; cf. Tit 1:10,13-14).

"You will know the truth, and the truth will make you free" (Jn 8:32)

31.1 The human issues most frequently debated and differently resolved in contemporary moral reflection are all closely related, albeit in various ways, to a crucial issue: *human freedom.*

31.2 Certainly people today have a particularly strong sense of freedom. As the Council's Declaration on Religious Freedom *Dignitatis Humanae* had already observed, "the dignity of the human person is a concern of which people of our time are becoming increasingly more aware."[52] Hence the insistent demand that people be permitted to "enjoy the use of their own responsible judgment and freedom, and decide on their actions on grounds of duty and conscience, without external pressure or coercion."[53] In particular, the right to religious freedom and to respect for conscience on its journey toward the truth is increasingly perceived as the foundation of the cumulative rights of the person.[54]

31.3 This heightened sense of the dignity of the human person and of his or her uniqueness, and of the respect due to the journey of conscience, certainly represents one of the positive achievements of modern culture. This perception, authentic as it is, has been expressed in a number of more or less adequate ways, some of which however diverge from

[52] Declaration on Religious Freedom *Dignitatis Humanae*, 1, referring to John XXIII, Encyclical Letter *Pacem in Terris* (April 11, 1963), II: *AAS* 55 (1963), 279; ibid., I: loc. cit., 265, and to Pius XII, Christmas Radio Message (December 24, 1944): *AAS* 37 (1945), 14.

[53] Declaration on Religious Freedom *Dignitatis Humanae*, 1.

[54] Cf. Encyclical Letter *Redemptor Hominis* (March 4, 1979), 17: *AAS* 71 (1979), 295-300; Address to Those Taking Part in the Fifth International Colloquium of Juridical Studies (March 10, 1984), 4: *Insegnamenti* VII/1 (1984), 656; Congregation for the Doctrine of the Faith, Instruction on Christian Freedom and Liberation *Libertatis Conscientia* (March 22, 1986), 19: *AAS* 79 (1987), 561.

the truth about man as a creature and the image of God, and thus need to be corrected and purified in the light of faith.[55]

32.1 Certain currents of modern thought have gone so far as to *exalt freedom to such an extent that it becomes an absolute, which would then be the source of values*. This is the direction taken by doctrines which have lost the sense of the transcendent or which are explicitly atheistic. The individual conscience is accorded the status of a supreme tribunal of moral judgment which hands down categorical and infallible decisions about good and evil. To the affirmation that one has a duty to follow one's conscience is unduly added the affirmation that one's moral judgment is true merely by the fact that it has its origin in conscience. But in this way the inescapable claims of truth disappear, yielding their place to a criterion of sincerity, authenticity and "being at peace with oneself," so much so that some have come to adopt a radically subjectivistic conception of moral judgment.

32.2 As is immediately evident, *the crisis of truth* is not unconnected with this development. Once the idea of a universal truth about the good, knowable by human reason, is lost, inevitably the notion of conscience also changes. Conscience is no longer considered in its primordial reality as an act of a person's intelligence, the function of which is to apply the universal knowledge of the good in a specific situation and thus to express a judgment about the right conduct to be chosen here and now. Instead, there is a tendency to grant to the individual conscience the prerogative of independently determining the criteria of good and evil and then acting accordingly. Such an outlook is quite congenial to an individualistic ethic, wherein each individual is faced with his own truth, different from the truth of others. Taken to its extreme consequences, this individualism leads to a denial of the very idea of human nature.

32.3 These different notions are at the origin of currents of thought which posit a radical opposition between moral law and conscience, and between nature and freedom.

33.1 *Side by side* with its exaltation of freedom, yet oddly in contrast with it, *modern culture radically questions the very existence of this freedom*. A number of disciplines, grouped under the name of the "behavioral sciences," have rightly drawn attention to the many kinds of psychological and social condi-

---

[55] Cf. Second Vatican Ecumenical Council, Pastoral Constitution on the Church in the Modern World *Gaudium et Spes,* 11.

tioning which influence the exercise of human freedom. Knowledge of these conditionings and the study they have received represent important achievements which have found application in various areas, for example in pedagogy or the administration of justice. But some people, going beyond the conclusions which can be legitimately drawn from these observations, have come to question or even deny the very reality of human freedom.

33.2 Mention should also be made here of theories which misuse scientific research about the human person. Arguing from the great variety of customs, behavior patterns and institutions present in humanity, these theories end up, if not with an outright denial of universal human values, at least with a relativistic conception of morality.

34.1 *"Teacher, what good must I do to have eternal life?" The question of morality,* to which Christ provides the answer, *cannot prescind from the issue of freedom. Indeed, it considers that issue central,* for there can be no morality without freedom: "It is only in freedom that man can turn to what is good."[56] *But what sort of freedom?* The Council, considering our contemporaries who "highly regard" freedom and "assiduously pursue" it, but who "often cultivate it in wrong ways as a license to do anything they please, even evil," speaks of *"genuine" freedom:* "Genuine freedom is an outstanding manifestation of the divine image in man. For God willed to leave man 'in the power of his own counsel' (cf. Sir 15:14), so that he would seek his Creator of his own accord and would freely arrive at full and blessed perfection by cleaving to God."[57] Although each individual has a right to be respected in his own journey in search of the truth, there exists a prior moral obligation, and a grave one at that, to seek the truth and to adhere to it once it is known.[58] As Cardinal John Henry Newman, that outstanding defender of the rights of conscience, forcefully put it: "Conscience has rights because it has duties."[59]

34.2 Certain tendencies in contemporary moral theology, under the influ-

---

[56] Ibid., 17.

[57] Ibid., 17.

[58] Cf. Second Vatican Ecumenical Council, Declaration on Religious Freedom *Dignitatis Humanae,* 2; cf. also Gregory XVI, Encyclical Epistle *Mirari Vos Arbitramur* (August 15, 1832): *Acta Gregorii Papae XVI,* I, 169-174; Pius IX, Encyclical Epistle *Quanta Cura* (December 8, 1864): *Pii IX P. M. Acta,* I, 3, 687-700; Leo XIII, Encyclical Letter *Libertas Praestantissimum* (June 20, 1888): *Leonis XIII P. M. Acta,* VIII, Rome, 1889, 212-246.

[59] *A Letter Addressed to His Grace the Duke of Norfolk: Certain Difficulties Felt by Anglicans in Catholic Teaching* (Uniform Edition: Longman, Green and Company, London, 1868-1881), vol. 2, 250.

ence of the currents of subjectivism and individualism just mentioned, involve novel interpretations of the relationship of freedom to the moral law, human nature and conscience, and propose novel criteria for the moral evaluation of acts. Despite their variety, these tendencies are at one in lessening or even denying *the dependence of freedom on truth.*

34.3 If we wish to undertake a critical discernment of these tendencies — a discernment capable of acknowledging what is legitimate, useful and of value in them, while at the same time pointing out their ambiguities, dangers and errors — we must examine them in the light of the fundamental dependence of freedom upon truth, a dependence which has found its clearest and most authoritative expression in the words of Christ: "You will know the truth, and the truth will set you free" (Jn 8:32).

I. FREEDOM AND LAW

"Of the tree of the knowledge of good and evil you shall not eat" *(Gen 2:17)*

35.1 In the Book of Genesis we read: "The Lord God commanded the man, saying, 'You may eat freely of every tree of the garden; but of the tree of the knowledge of good and evil you shall not eat, for in the day that you eat of it you shall die' " (Gen 2:16-17).

35.2 With this imagery, revelation teaches that *the power to decide what is good and what is evil does not belong to man, but to God alone.* The man is certainly free, inasmuch as he can understand and accept God's commands. And he possesses an extremely far-reaching freedom, since he can eat "of every tree of the garden." But his freedom is not unlimited: it must halt before the "tree of the knowledge of good and evil," for it is called to accept the moral law given by God. In fact, human freedom finds its authentic and complete fulfillment precisely in the acceptance of that law. God, who alone is good, knows perfectly what is good for man, and by virtue of his very love proposes this good to man in the commandments.

35.3 God's law does not reduce, much less do away with human freedom; rather, it protects and promotes that freedom. In contrast, however, some present-day cultural tendencies have given rise to several currents of thought in ethics which center upon *an alleged conflict between freedom and law.* These doctrines would grant to individuals or social groups the right *to determine what is good or evil.* Human freedom would thus be able to "create values" and would enjoy a primacy over truth, to the point that truth itself would be considered a creation of freedom. Freedom would thus lay claim to a *moral autonomy* which would actually amount to an *absolute sovereignty*.

36.1 The modern concern for the claims of autonomy has not failed to exercise an *influence* also *in the sphere of Catholic moral theology*. While the latter has certainly never attempted to set human freedom against the divine law or to question the existence of an ultimate religious foundation for moral norms, it has, nonetheless, been led to undertake a profound rethinking about the role of reason and of faith in identifying moral norms with reference to specific "inner-worldly" kinds of behavior involving oneself, others and the material world.

36.2 It must be acknowledged that underlying this work of rethinking there are *certain positive concerns* which to a great extent belong to the best tradition of Catholic thought. In response to the encouragement of the Second Vatican Council,[60] there has been a desire to foster dialogue with modern culture, emphasizing the rational — and thus universally understandable and communicable — character of moral norms belonging to the sphere of the natural moral law.[61] There has also been an attempt to reaffirm the interior character of the ethical requirements deriving from that law, requirements which create an obligation for the will only because such an obligation was previously acknowledged by human reason and, concretely, by personal conscience.

36.3 Some people, however, disregarding the dependence of human reason on divine wisdom and the need, given the present state of fallen nature, for divine revelation as an effective means for knowing moral truths, even those of the natural order,[62] have actually posited a *complete sovereignty of reason* in the domain of moral norms regarding the right ordering of life in this world. Such norms would constitute the boundaries for a merely "human" morality; they would be the expression of a law which man in an autonomous manner lays down for himself and which has its source exclusively in human reason. In no way could God be considered the Author of this law, except in the sense that human reason exercises its autonomy in setting down laws by virtue of a primordial and total mandate given to man by God. These trends of thought have led to a denial, in

---

[60] Cf. Pastoral Constitution on the Church in the Modern World *Gaudium et Spes*, 40, 43.

[61] Cf. Saint Thomas Aquinas, *Summa Theologiae*, I-II, q. 71, a. 6; see also ad 5.

[62] Cf. Pius XII, Encyclical Letter *Humani Generis* (August 12, 1950): *AAS* 42 (1950), 561-562.

opposition to Sacred Scripture (cf. Mt 15:3-6) and the Church's constant teaching, of the fact that the natural moral law has God as its Author, and that man, by the use of reason, participates in the eternal law, which it is not for him to establish.

37.1 In their desire, however, to keep the moral life in a Christian context, certain moral theologians have introduced a sharp distinction, contrary to Catholic doctrine,[63] between *an ethical order,* which would be human in origin and of value for *this world* alone, and an *order of salvation,* for which only certain intentions and interior attitudes regarding God and neighbor would be significant. This has then led to an actual denial that there exists, in divine revelation, a specific and determined moral content, universally valid and permanent. The word of God would be limited to proposing an exhortation, a generic paraenesis, which the autonomous reason alone would then have the task of completing with normative directives which are truly "objective," that is, adapted to the concrete historical situation. Naturally, an autonomy conceived in this way also involves the denial of a specific doctrinal competence on the part of the Church and her Magisterium with regard to particular moral norms which deal with the so-called "human good." Such norms would not be part of the proper content of revelation, and would not in themselves be relevant for salvation.

37.2 No one can fail to see that such an interpretation of the autonomy of human reason involves positions incompatible with Catholic teaching.

37.3 In such a context it is absolutely necessary to clarify, in the light of the word of God and the living Tradition of the Church, the fundamental notions of human freedom and of the moral law, as well as their profound and intimate relationship. Only thus will it be possible to respond to the rightful claims of human reason in a way which accepts the valid elements present in certain currents of contemporary moral theology without compromising the Church's heritage of moral teaching with ideas derived from an erroneous concept of autonomy.

"God left man in the power of his own counsel" (Sir 15:14)

38.1 Taking up the words of Sirach, the Second Vatican Council explains the meaning of that "genuine freedom" which is "an outstanding manifestation of the divine image" in man: "God willed to leave man in the power of his own counsel, so that he would seek his Creator of his own accord and would

---

[63] Cf. Ecumenical Council of Trent, Session VI, Decree on Justification *Cum Hoc Tempore,* Canons 19-21: *DS* 1569-1571.

freely arrive at full and blessed perfection by cleaving to God."[64] These words indicate the wonderful depth of the *sharing in God's dominion* to which man has been called: they indicate that man's dominion extends in a certain sense over man himself. This has been a constantly recurring theme in theological reflection on human freedom, which is described as a form of kingship. For example, Saint Gregory of Nyssa writes: "The soul shows its royal and exalted character . . . in that it is free and self-governed, swayed autonomously by its own will. Of whom else can this be said, save a king? . . . Thus human nature, created to rule other creatures, was by its likeness to the King of the universe made as it were a living image, partaking with the Archetype both in dignity and in name."[65]

38.2 *The exercise of dominion over the world* represents a great and responsible task for man, one which involves his freedom in obedience to the Creator's command: "Fill the earth and subdue it" (Gen 1:28). In view of this, a rightful autonomy is due to every man, as well as to the human community, a fact to which the Council's Constitution *Gaudium et Spes* calls special attention. This is the autonomy of earthly realities, which means that "created things have their own laws and values which are to be gradually discovered, utilized and ordered by man."[66]

39.1 Not only the world, however, but also *man himself* has been *entrusted to his own care and responsibility*. God left man "in the power of his own counsel" (Sir 15:14), that he might seek his Creator and freely attain perfection. Attaining such perfection means *personally building up that perfection in himself*. Indeed, just as man in exercising his dominion over the world shapes it in accordance with his own intelligence and will, so too in performing morally good acts, man strengthens, develops and consolidates within himself his likeness to God.

39.2 Even so, the Council warns against a false concept of the autonomy of earthly realities, one which would maintain that "created things are not dependent on God and that man can use them without reference to their Creator."[67] With regard to man himself, such a concept of autonomy produces particularly baneful effects, and eventually leads to atheism: "Without its Creator the creature simply disappears. . . . If God is ignored the creature itself is impoverished."[68]

---

[64] Pastoral Constitution on the Church in the Modern World *Gaudium et Spes*, 17.

[65] *De Hominis Opificio*, Chapter 4: *PG* 44, 135-136.

[66] Pastoral Constitution on the Church in the Modern World *Gaudium et Spes*, 36.

[67] Ibid., 36.

[68] Ibid., 36.

40 The teaching of the Council emphasizes, on the one hand, *the role of human reason* in discovering and applying the moral law: the moral life calls for that creativity and originality typical of the person, the source and cause of his own deliberate acts. On the other hand, reason draws its own truth and authority from the eternal law, which is none other than divine wisdom itself.[69] At the heart of the moral life we thus find the principle of a "rightful autonomy"[70] of man, the personal subject of his actions. *The moral law has its origin in God and always finds its source in him:* at the same time, by virtue of natural reason, which derives from divine wisdom, it is *a properly human law.* Indeed, as we have seen, the natural law "is nothing other than the light of understanding infused in us by God, whereby we understand what must be done and what must be avoided. God gave this light and this law to man at creation."[71] The rightful autonomy of the practical reason means that man possesses in himself his own law, received from the Creator. Nevertheless, *the autonomy of reason cannot mean* that reason itself *creates values and moral norms.*[72] Were this autonomy to imply a denial of the participation of the practical reason in the wisdom of the divine Creator and Lawgiver, or were it to suggest a freedom which creates moral norms, on the basis of historical contingencies or the diversity of societies and cultures, this sort of alleged autonomy would contradict the Church's teaching on the truth about man.[73] It would be the death of true freedom: "But of the tree of the knowledge of good and evil you shall not eat, for in the day that you eat of it you shall die" (Gen 2:17).

41.1 Man's *genuine moral autonomy* in no way means the rejection but rather the acceptance of the moral law, of God's command: "The Lord God gave this command to the man. . ." (Gen 2:16). *Human freedom and God's law meet and are called to intersect,* in the sense of man's free obedience to God and of God's completely gratuitous benevolence toward man. Hence obedience to God is not, as some would believe, a *heteronomy,* as if the moral life

---

[69] Cf. Saint Thomas Aquinas, *Summa Theologiae,* I-II, q. 93, a. 3, ad 2; cited by John XXIII, Encyclical Letter *Pacem in Terris* (April 11, 1963), II: *AAS* 55 (1963), 271.

[70] Second Vatican Ecumenical Council, Pastoral Constitution on the Church in the Modern World *Gaudium et Spes,* 41.

[71] Saint Thomas Aquinas, *In Duo Praecepta Caritatis et in Decem Legis Praecepta, Prologus: Opuscula Theologica,* 11, No. 1129, Turin, 1954, 245.

[72] Cf. Address to a Group of Bishops from the United States on Their *ad Limina* Visit (October 15, 1988), 6: *Insegnamenti* XI/3 (1988), 1228.

[73] Cf. Second Vatican Ecumenical Council, Pastoral Constitution on the Church in the Modern World *Gaudium et Spes,* 47.

were subject to the will of something all-powerful, absolute, extraneous to man and intolerant of his freedom. If in fact a heteronomy of morality were to mean a denial of man's self-determination or the imposition of norms unrelated to his good, this would be in contradiction to the revelation of the Covenant and of the redemptive Incarnation. Such a heteronomy would be nothing but a form of alienation, contrary to divine wisdom and to the dignity of the human person.

41.2 Others speak, and rightly so, of *theonomy,* or *participated theonomy,* since man's free obedience to God's law effectively implies that human reason and human will participate in God's wisdom and providence. By forbidding man to "eat of the tree of the knowledge of good and evil," God makes it clear that man does not originally possess such "knowledge" as something properly his own, but only participates in it by the light of natural reason and of divine revelation, which manifest to him the requirements and the promptings of eternal wisdom. Law must therefore be considered an expression of divine wisdom: by submitting to the law, freedom submits to the truth of creation. Consequently one must acknowledge in the freedom of the human person the image and the nearness of God, who is present in all (cf. Eph 4:6). But one must likewise acknowledge the majesty of the God of the universe and revere the holiness of the law of God, who is infinitely transcendent: *Deus semper maior.*[74]

Blessed is the man who takes delight in the law of the Lord (cf. Ps 1:1-2)

42.1 Patterned on God's freedom, man's freedom is not negated by his obedience to the divine law; indeed, only through this obedience does it abide in the truth and conform to human dignity. This is clearly stated by the Council: "Human dignity requires man to act through conscious and free choice, as motivated and prompted personally from within, and not through blind internal impulse or merely external pressure. Man achieves such dignity when he frees himself from all subservience to his feelings, and in a free choice of the good, pursues his own end by effectively and assiduously marshaling the appropriate means."[75]

42.2 In his journey toward God, the One who "alone is good," man must freely do good and avoid evil. But in order to accomplish this he must *be able to distinguish good from evil.* And this takes place above all *thanks to the light of natural reason,* the reflection in man of the splendor of God's countenance.

[74] Cf. Saint Augustine, *Enarratio in Psalmum LXII,* 16: *CCL* 39, 804.
[75] Pastoral Constitution on the Church in the Modern World *Gaudium et Spes,* 17.

Thus Saint Thomas, commenting on a verse of Psalm 4, writes: "After saying: Offer right sacrifices (Ps 4:5), as if some had then asked him what right works were, the Psalmist adds: *There are many who say: Who will make us see good?* And in reply to the question he says: *The light of your face, Lord, is signed upon us*, thereby implying that the light of natural reason whereby we discern good from evil, which is the function of the natural law, is nothing else but an imprint on us of the divine light."[76] It also becomes clear why this law is called the natural law: it receives this name not because it refers to the nature of irrational beings but because the reason which promulgates it is proper to human nature.[77]

43.1 The Second Vatican Council points out that the "supreme rule of life is the divine law itself, the eternal, objective and universal law by which God out of his wisdom and love arranges, directs and governs the whole world and the paths of the human community. God has enabled man to share in this divine law, and hence man is able under the gentle guidance of God's providence increasingly to recognize the unchanging truth."[78]

43.2 The Council refers to the classic teaching on *God's eternal law*. Saint Augustine defines this as "the reason or the will of God, who commands us to respect the natural order and forbids us to disturb it."[79] Saint Thomas identifies it with "the type of the divine wisdom as moving all things to their due end."[80] And God's wisdom is providence, a love which cares. God himself loves and cares, in the most literal and basic sense, for all creation (cf. Wis 7:22, 8:11). But God provides for man differently from the way in which he provides for beings which are not persons. He cares for man not "from without," through the laws of physical nature, but "from within," through reason, which, by its natural knowledge of God's eternal law, is consequently able to show man the right direction to take in his free actions.[81] In this way God calls man to participate in his own providence, since he desires to guide the world — not only the world of nature but also the world of human persons — through man himself, through man's reasonable and responsible care. The natural law enters here as the human expression of God's eternal law. Saint Thomas writes: "Among all others, the rational creature is subject to divine Providence in the most excellent way, insofar as it partakes of a share of providence, being

---

[76] *Summa Theologiae*, I-II, q. 91, a. 2.
[77] Cf. *Catechism of the Catholic Church*, No. 1955.
[78] Declaration on Religious Freedom *Dignitatis Humanae*, 3.
[79] *Contra Faustum*, Book 22, Chapter 27: *PL* 42, 418.
[80] *Summa Theologiae*, I-II, q. 93, a. 1.
[81] Cf. ibid., I-II, q. 90, a. 4, ad 1.

provident both for itself and for others. Thus it has a share of the eternal Reason, whereby it has a natural inclination to its proper act and end. This participation of the eternal law in the rational creature is called natural law."[82]

44.1 The Church has often made reference to the Thomistic doctrine of natural law, including it in her own teaching on morality. Thus my Venerable Predecessor Leo XIII emphasized *the essential subordination of reason and human law to the Wisdom of God and to his law.* After stating that "the natural law is written and engraved in the heart of each and every man, since it is none other than human reason itself which commands us to do good and counsels us not to sin," Leo XIII appealed to the "higher reason" of the divine Lawgiver: "But this prescription of human reason could not have the force of law unless it were the voice and the interpreter of some higher reason to which our spirit and our freedom must be subject." Indeed, the force of law consists in its authority to impose duties, to confer rights and to sanction certain behavior: "Now all of this, clearly, could not exist in man if, as his own supreme legislator, he gave himself the rule of his own actions." And he concluded: "It follows that the natural law is *itself the eternal law,* implanted in beings endowed with reason, and inclining them *toward their right action and end;* it is none other than the eternal reason of the Creator and Ruler of the universe."[83]

44.2 Man is able to recognize good and evil thanks to that discernment of good from evil which he himself carries out by his *reason, in particular by his reason enlightened by divine revelation and by faith,* through the law which God gave to the Chosen People, beginning with the commandments on Sinai. Israel was called to accept and to live out *God's law as a particular gift and sign of its election and of the divine Covenant,* and also as a pledge of God's blessing. Thus Moses could address the children of Israel and ask them: "What great nation is there that has a god so near to it as the Lord our God is to us, whenever we call upon him? And what great nation is there that has statutes and ordinances so righteous as all this law which I set before you this day?" (Dt 4:7-8). In the Psalms we encounter the sentiments of praise, gratitude and veneration which the Chosen People is called to show toward God's law, together with an exhortation to know it, ponder it and translate it into life. "Blessed is the man who walks not in the counsel of the wicked, nor stands in the way of sinners, nor sits in the seat of scoffers, but his delight is in the law

[82] Ibid., I-II, q. 91, a. 2.
[83] Encyclical Letter *Libertas Praestantissimum* (June 20, 1888): *Leonis XIII P. M. Acta,* VIII, Rome, 1889, 219.

of the Lord and on his law he meditates day and night" (Ps 1:1-2). "The law of the Lord is perfect, reviving the soul; the testimony of the Lord is sure, making wise the simple; the precepts of the Lord are right, rejoicing the heart; the commandment of the Lord is pure, enlightening the eyes" (Ps 18:8-9).

45.1 The Church gratefully accepts and lovingly preserves the entire deposit of revelation, treating it with religious respect and fulfilling her mission of authentically interpreting God's law in the light of the Gospel. In addition, the Church receives the gift of the New Law, which is the "fulfillment" of God's law in Jesus Christ and in his Spirit. This is an "interior" law (cf. Jer 31:31-33), "written not with ink but with the Spirit of the living God, not on tablets of stone but on tablets of human hearts" (2 Cor 3:3); a law of perfection and of freedom (cf. 2 Cor 3:17); "the law of the Spirit of life in Christ Jesus" (Rom 8:2). Saint Thomas writes that this law "can be called law in two ways. First, the law of the spirit is the Holy Spirit . . . who, dwelling in the soul, not only teaches what it is necessary to do by enlightening the intellect on the things to be done, but also inclines the affections to act with uprightness. . . . Second, the law of the spirit can be called the proper effect of the Holy Spirit, and thus faith working through love (cf. Gal 5:6), which teaches inwardly about the things to be done . . . and inclines the affections to act."[84]

45.2 Even if moral-theological reflection usually distinguishes between the positive or revealed law of God and the natural law, and, within the economy of salvation, between the "Old" and the "New" Law, it must not be forgotten that these and other useful distinctions always refer to that law whose author is the one and the same God and which is always meant for man. The different ways in which God, acting in history, cares for the world and for mankind are not mutually exclusive; on the contrary, they support each other and intersect. They have their origin and goal in the eternal, wise and loving counsel whereby God predestines men and women "to be conformed to the image of his Son" (Rom 8:29). God's plan poses no threat to man's genuine freedom; on the contrary, the acceptance of God's plan is the only way to affirm that freedom.

"What the law requires is written on their hearts" (Rom 2:15)

46.1 The alleged conflict between freedom and law is forcefully brought up once again today with regard to the natural law, and particularly with regard to nature. *Debates about nature and freedom* have always marked the history of moral reflection; they grew especially heated at the time of the Renaissance

---

[84] *In Epistulam ad Romanos*, c. VIII, lect. 1.

and the Reformation, as can be seen from the teaching of the Council of Trent.[85] Our own age is marked, though in a different sense, by a similar tension. The penchant for empirical observation, the procedures of scientific objectification, technological progress and certain forms of liberalism have led to these two terms being set in opposition, as if a dialectic, if not an absolute conflict, between freedom and nature were characteristic of the structure of human history. At other periods, it seemed that "nature" subjected man totally to its own dynamics and even its own unbreakable laws. Today too, the situation of the world of the senses within space and time, physio-chemical constants, bodily processes, psychological impulses and forms of social conditioning seem to many people the only really decisive factors of human reality. In this context even moral facts, despite their specificity, are frequently treated as if they were statistically verifiable data, patterns of behavior which can be subject to observation or explained exclusively in categories of psychosocial processes. As a result, *some ethicists*, professionally engaged in the study of human realities and behavior, can be tempted to take as the standard for their discipline and even for its operative norms the results of a statistical study of concrete human behavior patterns and the opinions about morality encountered in the majority of people.

46.2 *Other moralists*, however, in their concern to stress the importance of values, remain sensitive to the dignity of freedom, but they frequently conceive of freedom as somehow in opposition to or in conflict with material and biological nature, over which it must progressively assert itself. Here various approaches are at one in overlooking the created dimension of nature and in misunderstanding its integrity. *For some*, "nature" becomes reduced to raw material for human activity and for its power: thus nature needs to be profoundly transformed, and indeed overcome by freedom, inasmuch as it represents a limitation and denial of freedom. *For others*, it is in the untrammeled advancement of man's power, or of his freedom, that economic, cultural, social and even moral values are established: nature would thus come to mean everything found in man and the world apart from freedom. In such an understanding, nature would include in the first place the human body, its make-up and its processes: against this physical datum would be opposed whatever is "constructed," in other words "culture," seen as the product and result of freedom. Human nature, understood in this way, could be reduced to and treated as a readily available biological or social material. This ultimately means making freedom self-defining and a phenomenon creative of itself and its values. Indeed, when all is said and done man would not even have a

---

[85] Cf. Session VI, Decree on Justification *Cum Hoc Tempore*, Chapter 1: *DS* 1521.

nature; he would be his own personal life-project. Man would be nothing more than his own freedom!

47 In this context, *objections of physicalism and naturalism* have been leveled against the traditional conception of *the natural law*, which is accused of presenting as moral laws what are in themselves mere biological laws. Consequently, in too superficial a way, a permanent and unchanging character would be attributed to certain kinds of human behavior, and, on the basis of this, an attempt would be made to formulate universally valid moral norms. According to certain theologians, this kind of "biologistic or naturalistic argumentation" would even be present in certain documents of the Church's Magisterium, particularly those dealing with the area of sexual and conjugal ethics. It was, they maintain, on the basis of a naturalistic understanding of the sexual act that contraception, direct sterilization, autoeroticism, premarital sexual relations, homosexual relations and artificial insemination were condemned as morally unacceptable. In the opinion of these same theologians, a morally negative evaluation of such acts fails to take into adequate consideration both man's character as a rational and free being and the cultural conditioning of all moral norms. In their view, man, as a rational being, not only can but actually *must freely determine the meaning* of his behavior. This process of "determining the meaning" would obviously have to take into account the many limitations of the human being, as existing in a body and in history. Furthermore, it would have to take into consideration the behavioral models and the meanings which the latter acquire in any given culture. Above all, it would have to respect the fundamental commandment of love of God and neighbor. Still, they continue, God made man as a rationally free being; he left him "in the power of his own counsel" and he expects him to shape his life in a personal and rational way. Love of neighbor would mean above all and even exclusively respect for his freedom to make his own decisions. The workings of typically human behavior, as well as the so-called "natural inclinations," would establish at the most — so they say — a general orientation toward correct behavior, but they cannot determine the moral assessment of individual human acts, so complex from the viewpoint of situations.

48.1 Faced with this theory, one has to consider carefully the correct relationship existing between freedom and human nature, and in particular *the place of the human body in questions of natural law*.

48.2 A freedom which claims to be absolute ends up treating the human body as a raw datum, devoid of any meaning and moral values until freedom has shaped it in accordance with its design. Consequently, human nature and the body appear as *presuppositions or preambles,* materially *necessary,* for freedom to make its choice, yet extrinsic to the person, the subject and the human act. Their functions would not be able to constitute reference points for moral decisions, because the finalities of these inclinations would be merely *"physical"* goods, called by some "pre-moral." To refer to them, in order to find in them rational indications with regard to the order of morality, would be to expose oneself to the accusation of physicalism or biologism. In this way of thinking, the tension between freedom and a nature conceived of in a reductive way is resolved by a division within man himself.

48.3 This moral theory does not correspond to the truth about man and his freedom. It contradicts the *Church's teachings on the unity of the human person,* whose rational soul is *per se et essentialiter* the form of his body.[86] The spiritual and immortal soul is the principle of unity of the human being, whereby it exists as a whole — *corpore et anima unus*[87] — as a person. These definitions not only point out that the body, which has been promised the resurrection, will also share in glory. They also remind us that reason and free will are linked with all the bodily and sense faculties. *The person, including the body, is completely entrusted to himself, and it is in the unity of body and soul that the person is the subject of his own moral acts.* The person, by the light of reason and the support of virtue, discovers in the body the anticipatory signs, the expression and the promise of the gift of self, in conformity with the wise plan of the Creator. It is in the light of the dignity of the human person — dignity which must be affirmed for its own sake — that reason grasps the specific moral value of certain goods toward which the person is naturally inclined. And since the human person cannot be reduced to a freedom which is self-designing, but entails a particular spiritual and bodily structure, the primordial moral requirement of loving and respecting the person as an end and never as a mere means also implies, by its very nature, respect for certain fundamental goods, without which one would fall into relativism and arbitrariness.

49 *A doctrine which dissociates the moral act from the bodily dimensions of its exercise is contrary to the teaching of Scripture and Tradition.* Such a doctrine revives, in new forms, certain ancient errors which have always been

---

[86] Cf. Ecumenical Council of Vienne, Constitution *Fidei Catholicae: DS* 902; Fifth Lateran Ecumenical Council, Bull *Apostolici Regiminis: DS* 1440.

[87] Cf. Second Vatican Ecumenical Council, Pastoral Constitution on the Church in the Modern World *Gaudium et Spes,* 14.

opposed by the Church, inasmuch as they reduce the human person to a "spiritual" and purely formal freedom. This reduction misunderstands the moral meaning of the body and of kinds of behavior involving it (cf. 1 Cor 6:19). Saint Paul declares that "the immoral, idolaters, adulterers, sexual perverts, thieves, the greedy, drunkards, revilers, robbers" are excluded from the Kingdom of God (cf. 1 Cor 6:9-10). This condemnation — repeated by the Council of Trent[88] — lists as "mortal sins" or "immoral practices" certain specific kinds of behavior the willful acceptance of which prevents believers from sharing in the inheritance promised to them. In fact, *body and soul are inseparable:* in the person, in the willing agent and in the deliberate act, *they stand or fall together.*

50.1 At this point the true meaning of the natural law can be understood: it refers to man's proper and primordial nature, the "nature of the human person,"[89] which is *the person himself in the unity of soul and body,* in the unity of his spiritual and biological inclinations and of all the other specific characteristics necessary for the pursuit of his end. "The natural moral law expresses and lays down the purposes, rights and duties which are based upon the bodily and spiritual nature of the human person. Therefore this law cannot be thought of as simply a set of norms on the biological level; rather it must be defined as the rational order whereby man is called by the Creator to direct and regulate his life and actions and in particular to make use of his own body."[90] To give an example, the origin and the foundation of the duty of absolute respect for human life are to be found in the dignity proper to the person and not simply in the natural inclination to preserve one's own physical life. Human life, even though it is a fundamental good of man, thus acquires a moral significance in reference to the good of the person, who must always be affirmed for his own sake. While it is always morally illicit to kill an innocent human being, it can be licit, praiseworthy or even imperative to give

---

[88] Cf. Session VI, Decree on Justification *Cum Hoc Tempore*, Chapter 15: *DS* 1544. The Post-Synodal Apostolic Exhortation on Reconciliation and Penance in the Mission of the Church Today cites other texts of the Old and New Testaments which condemn as mortal sins certain modes of conduct involving the body: cf. *Reconciliatio et Paenitentia* (December 2, 1984), 17: *AAS* 77 (1985), 218-223.

[89] Second Vatican Ecumenical Council, Pastoral Constitution on the Church in the Modern World *Gaudium et Spes*, 51.

[90] Congregation for the Doctrine of the Faith, Instruction on Respect for Human Life in Its Origin and on the Dignity of Procreation *Donum Vitae* (February 22, 1987), Introduction, 3: *AAS* 80 (1988), 74; cf. Paul VI, Encyclical Letter *Humanae Vitae* (July 25, 1968), 10: *AAS* 60 (1968), 487-488.

up one's own life (cf. Jn 15:13) out of love of neighbor or as a witness to the truth. Only in reference to the human person in his "unified totality" that is, as "a soul which expresses itself in a body and a body informed by an immortal spirit,"[91] can the specifically human meaning of the body be grasped. Indeed, natural inclinations take on moral relevance only insofar as they refer to the human person and his authentic fulfillment, a fulfillment which for that matter can take place always and only in human nature. By rejecting all manipulations of corporeity which alter its human meaning, the Church serves man and shows him the path of true love, the only path on which he can find the true God.

50.2 The natural law thus understood does not allow for any division between freedom and nature. Indeed, these two realities are harmoniously bound together, and each is intimately linked to the other.

"From the beginning it was not so" (Mt 19:8)

51.1 The alleged conflict between freedom and nature also has repercussions on the interpretation of certain specific aspects of the natural law, especially its *universality and immutability*. "Where then are these rules written," Saint Augustine wondered, "except in the book of that light which is called truth? From thence every just law is transcribed and transferred to the heart of the man who works justice, not by wandering but by being, as it were, impressed upon it, just as the image from the ring passes over to the wax, and yet does not leave the ring."[92]

51.2 Precisely because of this "truth" *the natural law involves universality*. Inasmuch as it is inscribed in the rational nature of the person, it makes itself felt to all beings endowed with reason and living in history. In order to perfect himself in his specific order, the person must do good and avoid evil, be concerned for the transmission and preservation of life, refine and develop the riches of the material world, cultivate social life, seek truth, practice good and contemplate beauty.[93]

51.3 The separation which some have posited between the freedom of individuals and the nature which all have in common — as it emerges from certain philosophical theories which are highly influential in present-day culture — obscures the perception of the universality of the moral law on the part of reason. But inasmuch as the natural law expresses the dignity of the human person and lays the foundation for his fundamental rights and duties, it is

---

[91] Apostolic Exhortation *Familiaris Consortio* (November 22, 1981), 11: *AAS* 74 (1982), 92.
[92] *De Trinitate*, XIV, 15, 21: *CCL* 50/A, 451.
[93] Cf. Saint Thomas Aquinas, *Summa Theologiae*, I-II, q. 94, a. 2.

universal in its precepts and its authority extends to all mankind. *This universality does not ignore the individuality of human beings,* nor is it opposed to the absolute uniqueness of each person. On the contrary, it embraces at its root each of the person's free acts, which are meant to bear witness to the universality of the true good. By submitting to the common law, our acts build up the true communion of persons and by God's grace, practice charity, "which binds everything together in perfect harmony" (Col 3:14). When on the contrary they disregard the law, or even are merely ignorant of it, whether culpably or not, our acts damage the communion of persons, to the detriment of each.

52.1 It is right and just, always and for everyone, to serve God, to render him the worship which is his due and to honor one's parents as they deserve. Positive precepts such as these, which order us to perform certain actions and to cultivate certain dispositions, are universally binding; they are "unchanging."[94] They unite in the same common good all people of every period of history, created for "the same divine calling and destiny."[95] These universal and permanent laws correspond to things known by the practical reason and are applied to particular acts through the judgment of conscience. The acting subject personally assimilates the truth contained in the law. He appropriates this truth of his being and makes it his own by his acts and the corresponding virtues. The *negative precepts* of the natural law are universally valid. They oblige each and every individual, always and in every circumstance. It is a matter of prohibitions which forbid a given action *semper et pro semper,* without exception, because the choice of this kind of behavior is in no case compatible with the goodness of the will of the acting person, with his vocation to life with God and to communion with his neighbor. It is prohibited — to everyone and in every case — to violate these precepts. They oblige everyone, regardless of the cost, never to offend in anyone, beginning with oneself, the personal dignity common to all.

52.2 On the other hand, the fact that only the negative commandments

[94] Cf. Second Vatican Ecumenical Council, Pastoral Constitution on the Church in the Modern World *Gaudium et Spes,* 10; Sacred Congregation for the Doctrine of the Faith, Declaration on Certain Questions Concerning Sexual Ethics *Persona Humana* (December 29, 1975), 4: *AAS* 68 (1976), 80: "But in fact, divine revelation and, in its own proper order, philosophical wisdom, emphasize the authentic exigencies of human nature. They thereby necessarily manifest the existence of immutable laws inscribed in the constitutive elements of human nature and which are revealed to be identical in all beings endowed with reason."

[95] Second Vatican Ecumenical Council, Pastoral Constitution on the Church in the Modern World *Gaudium et Spes,* 29.

oblige always and under all circumstances does not mean that in the moral life prohibitions are more important than the obligation to do good indicated by the positive commandments. The reason is this: the commandment of love of God and neighbor does not have in its dynamic any higher limit, but it does have a lower limit, beneath which the commandment is broken. Furthermore, what must be done in any given situation depends on the circumstances, not all of which can be foreseen; on the other hand there are kinds of behavior which can never, in any situation, be a proper response — a response which is in conformity with the dignity of the person. Finally, it is always possible that man, as the result of coercion or other circumstances, can be hindered from doing certain good actions; but he can never be hindered from not doing certain actions, especially if he is prepared to die rather than to do evil.

52.3 The Church has always taught that one may never choose kinds of behavior prohibited by the moral commandments expressed in negative form in the Old and New Testaments. As we have seen, Jesus himself reaffirms that these prohibitions allow no exceptions: "If you wish to enter into life, keep the commandments. . . . You shall not murder, You shall not commit adultery, You shall not steal, You shall not bear false witness" (Mt 19:17-18).

53.1 The great concern of our contemporaries for historicity and for culture has led some to call into question *the immutability of the natural law itself,* and thus the existence of "objective norms of morality"[96] valid for all people of the present and the future, as for those of the past. Is it ever possible, they ask, to consider as universally valid and always binding certain rational determinations established in the past, when no one knew the progress humanity would make in the future?

53.2 It must certainly be admitted that man always exists in a particular culture, but it must also be admitted that man is not exhaustively defined by that same culture. Moreover, the very progress of cultures demonstrates that there is something in man which transcends those cultures. This "something" is precisely human nature: this nature is itself the measure of culture and the condition ensuring that man does not become the prisoner of any of his cultures, but asserts his personal dignity by living in accordance with the profound truth of his being. To call into question the permanent structural elements of man which are connected with his own bodily dimension would not only conflict with common experience, but would render meaningless *Jesus' reference to the "beginning,"* precisely where the social and cultural context of the time had distorted the primordial meaning and the role of certain moral

---

[96] Cf. ibid., 16.

norms (cf. Mt 19:1-9). This is the reason why "the Church affirms that under-lying so many changes there are some things which do not change and are *ultimately founded upon Christ, who is the same yesterday and today and forever."* [97] Christ is the "Beginning" who, having taken on human nature, definitively illumines it in its constitutive elements and in its dynamism of charity toward God and neighbor.[98]

53.3 Certainly there is a need to seek out and to discover *the most adequate formulation* for universal and permanent moral norms in the light of different cultural contexts, a formulation most capable of ceaselessly expressing their historical relevance, of making them understood and of authentically interpreting their truth. This truth of the moral law — like that of the "deposit of faith" — unfolds down the centuries: the norms expressing that truth remain valid in their substance, but must be specified and determined *"eodem sensu eademque sententia"*[99] in the light of historical circumstances by the Church's Magisterium, whose decision is preceded and accompanied by the work of interpretation and formulation characteristic of the reason of individual believers and of theological reflection.[100]

II. CONSCIENCE AND TRUTH

Man's sanctuary

54.1 The relationship between man's freedom and God's law is most deeply lived out in the "heart" of the person, in his moral conscience. As the Second Vatican Council observed: "In the depths of his conscience man detects a law which he does not impose on himself, but which holds him to obedience. Always summoning him to love good and avoid evil, the voice of this law can

[97] Ibid., 10.

[98] Cf. Saint Thomas Aquinas, *Summa Theologiae,* I-II, q. 108, a. 1. Saint Thomas bases the fact that moral norms, even in the context of the New Law, are not merely formal in character but have a determined content, upon the assumption of human nature by the Word.

[99] Saint Vincent of Lerins, *Commonitorium Primum,* 23: *PL* 50, 668.

[100] The development of the Church's moral doctrine is similar to that of the doctrine of the faith (cf. First Vatican Ecumenical Council, Dogmatic Constitution on the Catholic Faith *Dei Filius,* Chapter 4: *DS* 3020; and Canon 4: *DS* 3024). The words spoken by John XXIII at the opening of the Second Vatican Ecumenical Council can also be applied to moral doctrine: "This certain and unchanging teaching [that is, Christian doctrine in its completeness], to which the faithful owe obedience, needs to be more deeply understood and set forth in a way adapted to the needs of our time. Indeed, this deposit of the faith, the truths contained in our time-honored teaching, is one thing; the manner in which these truths are set forth (with their meaning preserved intact) is something else": *AAS* 54 (1962), 792; cf. *L'Osservatore Romano,* October 12, 1962, 2.

when necessary speak to his heart more specifically: 'do this, shun that.' For man has in his heart a law written by God. To obey it is the very dignity of man; according to it he will be judged (cf. Rom 2:14-16)."[101]

54.2 The way in which one conceives the relationship between freedom and law is thus intimately bound up with one's understanding of the moral conscience. Here the cultural tendencies referred to above — in which freedom and law are set in opposition to each another and kept apart, and freedom is exalted almost to the point of idolatry — lead to a *"creative" understanding of moral conscience*, which diverges from the teaching of the Church's Tradition and her Magisterium.

55.1 According to the opinion of some theologians, the function of conscience had been reduced, at least at a certain period in the past, to a simple application of general moral norms to individual cases in the life of the person. But those norms, they continue, cannot be expected to foresee and to respect all the individual concrete acts of the person in all their uniqueness and particularity. While such norms might somehow be useful for a correct *assessment* of the situation, they cannot replace the individual personal *decision* on how to act in particular cases. The critique already mentioned of the traditional understanding of human nature and of its importance for the moral life has even led certain authors to state that these norms are not so much a binding objective criterion for judgments of conscience, but a *general perspective* which helps man tentatively to put order into his personal and social life. These authors also stress the *complexity* typical of the phenomenon of conscience, a complexity profoundly related to the whole sphere of psychology and the emotions, and to the numerous influences exerted by the individual's social and cultural environment. On the other hand, they give maximum attention to the value of conscience, which the Council itself defined as "the sanctuary of man, where he is alone with God whose voice echoes within him."[102] This voice, it is said, leads man not so much to a meticulous observance of universal norms as to a creative and responsible acceptance of the personal tasks entrusted to him by God.

55.2 In their desire to emphasize the "creative" character of conscience, certain authors no longer call its actions "judgments" but "decisions": only by making these decisions "autonomously" would man be able to attain moral maturity. Some even hold that this process of maturing is inhibited by the

---

[101] Pastoral Constitution on the Church in the Modern World *Gaudium et Spes*, 16.
[102] Ibid., 16.

excessively categorical position adopted by the Church's Magisterium in many moral questions; for them, the Church's interventions are the cause of unnecessary *conflicts of conscience.*

56.1 In order to justify these positions, some authors have proposed a kind of double status of moral truth. Beyond the doctrinal and abstract level, one would have to acknowledge the priority of a certain more concrete existential consideration. The latter, by taking account of circumstances and the situation, could legitimately be the basis of certain *exceptions to the general rule* and thus permit one to do in practice and in good conscience what is qualified as intrinsically evil by the moral law. A separation, or even an opposition, is thus established in some cases between the teaching of the precept, which is valid in general, and the norm of the individual conscience, which would in fact make the final decision about what is good and what is evil. On this basis, an attempt is made to legitimize so-called "pastoral" solutions contrary to the teaching of the Magisterium, and to justify a "creative" hermeneutic according to which the moral conscience is in no way obliged, in every case, by a particular negative precept.

56.2 No one can fail to realize that these approaches pose a challenge to the *very identity of the moral conscience* in relation to human freedom and God's law. Only the clarification made earlier with regard to the relationship, based on truth, between freedom and law makes possible a *discernment* concerning this "creative" understanding of conscience.

The judgment of conscience

57.1 The text of the Letter to the Romans which has helped us to grasp the essence of the natural law also indicates *the biblical understanding of conscience,* especially *in its specific connection with the law:* "When Gentiles who have not the law do by nature what the law requires, they are a law unto themselves, even though they do not have the law. They show that what the law requires is written on their hearts, while their conscience also bears witness and their conflicting thoughts accuse or perhaps excuse them" (Rom 2:14-15).

57.2 According to Saint Paul, conscience in a certain sense confronts man with the law, and thus becomes a *"witness" for man:* a witness of his own faithfulness or unfaithfulness with regard to the law, of his essential moral rectitude or iniquity. Conscience is the *only* witness, since what takes place in the heart of the person is hidden from the eyes of everyone outside. Conscience makes its witness known only to the person himself. And, in turn, only the person himself knows what his own response is to the voice of conscience.

58 The importance of this interior *dialogue of man with himself* can never be adequately appreciated. But it is also a *dialogue of man with God*, the author of the law, the primordial image and final end of man. Saint Bonaventure teaches that "conscience is like God's herald and messenger; it does not command things on its own authority, but commands them as coming from God's authority, like a herald when he proclaims the edict of the king. This is why conscience has binding force."[103] Thus it can be said that conscience bears witness to man's own rectitude or iniquity to man himself but, together with this and indeed even beforehand, conscience is *the witness of God himself,* whose voice and judgment penetrate the depths of man's soul, calling him *fortiter et suaviter* to obedience. "Moral conscience does not close man within an insurmountable and impenetrable solitude, but opens him to the call, to the voice of God. In this, and not in anything else, lies the entire mystery and the dignity of the moral conscience: in being the place, the sacred place where God speaks to man."[104]

59.1 Saint Paul does not merely acknowledge that conscience acts as a "witness"; he also reveals the way in which conscience performs that function. He speaks of "conflicting thoughts" which accuse or excuse the Gentiles with regard to their behavior (cf. Rom 2:15). The term "conflicting thoughts" clarifies the precise nature of conscience: it is a *moral judgment about man and his actions,* a judgment either of acquittal or of condemnation, according as human acts are in conformity or not with the law of God written on the heart. In the same text the Apostle clearly speaks of the judgment of actions, the judgment of their author and the moment when that judgment will be definitively rendered: "(This will take place) on that day when, according to my Gospel, God judges the secrets of men by Christ Jesus" (Rom 2:16).

59.2 The judgment of conscience is a *practical judgment,* a judgment which makes known what man must do or not do, or which assesses an act already performed by him. It is a judgment which applies to a concrete situation the rational conviction that one must love and do good and avoid evil. This first principle of practical reason is part of the natural law, indeed it constitutes the very foundation of the natural law, inasmuch as it expresses that primordial insight about good and evil, that reflection of God's creative wisdom which,

---

[103] *In II Librum Sententiarum,* dist. 39, a. 1, q. 3, conclusion: Ad Claras Aquas, II, 907b.
[104] Address at General Audience (August 17, 1983), 2: *Insegnamenti* VI/2 (1983), 256.

like an imperishable spark (*scintilla animae*), shines in the heart of every man. But whereas the natural law discloses the objective and universal demands of the moral good, conscience is the application of the law to a particular case; this application of the law thus becomes an inner dictate for the individual, a summons to do what is good in this particular situation. Conscience thus formulates *moral obligation* in the light of the natural law: it is the obligation to do what the individual, through the workings of his conscience, *knows* to be a good he is called to do *here and now*. The universality of the law and its obligation are acknowledged, not suppressed, once reason has established the law's application in concrete present circumstances. The judgment of conscience states "in an ultimate way" whether a certain particular kind of behavior is in conformity with the law; it formulates the proximate norm of the morality of a voluntary act, "applying the objective law to a particular case."[105]

60 Like the natural law itself and all practical knowledge, the judgment of conscience also has an imperative character: man must act in accordance with it. If man acts against this judgment or, in a case where he lacks certainty about the rightness and goodness of a determined act, still performs that act, he stands condemned by his own conscience, *the proximate norm of personal morality*. The dignity of this rational forum and the authority of its voice and judgments derive from the truth about moral good and evil, which it is called to listen to and to express. This truth is indicated by the "divine law," *the universal and objective norm of morality.* The judgment of conscience does not establish the law; rather it bears witness to the authority of the natural law and of the practical reason with reference to the supreme good, whose attractiveness the human person perceives and whose commandments he accepts. "Conscience is not an independent and exclusive capacity to decide what is good and what is evil. Rather there is profoundly imprinted upon it a principle of obedience vis-à-vis the objective norm which establishes and conditions the correspondence of its decisions with the commands and prohibitions which are at the basis of human behavior."[106]

61.1 The truth about moral good, as that truth is declared in the law of reason, is practically and concretely recognized by the judgment of conscience,

---

[105] Supreme Sacred Congregation of the Holy Office, Instruction on "Situation Ethics" *Contra Doctrinam* (February 2, 1956): *AAS* 48 (1956), 144.

[106] Encyclical Letter *Dominum et Vivificantem* (May 18, 1986), 43: *AAS* 78 (1986), 859; cf. Second Vatican Ecumenical Council, Pastoral Constitution on the Church in the Modern World *Gaudium et Spes*, 16; Declaration on Religious Freedom *Dignitatis Humanae*, 3.

which leads one to take responsibility for the good or the evil one has done. If man does evil, the just judgment of his conscience remains within him as a witness to the universal truth of the good, as well as to the malice of his particular choice. But the verdict of conscience remains in him also as a pledge of hope and mercy: while bearing witness to the evil he has done, it also reminds him of his need, with the help of God's grace, to ask forgiveness, to do good and to cultivate virtue constantly.

61.2 Consequently *in the practical judgment of conscience,* which imposes on the person the obligation to perform a given act, *the link between freedom and truth is made manifest.* Precisely for this reason conscience expresses itself in acts of "judgment" which reflect the truth about the good, and not in arbitrary "decisions." The maturity and responsibility of these judgments — and, when all is said and done, of the individual who is their subject — are not measured by the liberation of the conscience from objective truth, in favor of an alleged autonomy in personal decisions, but, on the contrary, by an insistent search for truth and by allowing oneself to be guided by that truth in one's actions.

Seeking what is true and good

62.1 Conscience, as the judgment of an act, is not exempt from the possibility of error. As the Council puts it, "not infrequently conscience can be mistaken as a result of invincible ignorance, although it does not on that account forfeit its dignity; but this cannot be said when a man shows little concern for seeking what is true and good, and conscience gradually becomes almost blind from being accustomed to sin."[107] In these brief words the Council sums up the doctrine which the Church down the centuries has developed with regard to the *erroneous conscience.*

62.2 Certainly, in order to have a "good conscience" (1 Tim 1:5), man must seek the truth and must make judgments in accordance with that same truth. As the Apostle Paul says, the conscience must be "confirmed by the Holy Spirit" (cf. Rom 9:1); it must be "clear" (2 Tim 1:3); it must not "practice cunning and tamper with God's word," but "openly state the truth" (cf. 2 Cor 4:2). On the other hand, the Apostle also warns Christians: "Do not be conformed to this world but be transformed by the renewal of your mind, that you may prove what is the will of God, what is good and acceptable and perfect" (Rom 12:2).

62.3 Paul's admonition urges us to be watchful, warning us that in the

---

[107] Second Vatican Ecumenical Council, Pastoral Constitution on the Church in the Modern World *Gaudium et Spes,* 16.

judgments of our conscience the possibility of error is always present. Conscience *is not an infallible judge;* it can make mistakes. However, error of conscience can be the result of an *invincible ignorance,* an ignorance of which the subject is not aware and which he is unable to overcome by himself.

62.4 The Council reminds us that in cases where such invincible ignorance is not culpable, conscience does not lose its dignity, because even when it directs us to act in a way not in conformity with the objective moral order, it continues to speak in the name of that truth about the good which the subject is called to seek sincerely.

63.1 In any event, it is always from the truth that the dignity of conscience derives. In the case of the correct conscience, it is a question of the *objective truth* received by man; in the case of the erroneous conscience, it is a question of what man, mistakenly, *subjectively* considers to be true. It is never acceptable to confuse a "subjective" error about moral good with the "objective" truth rationally proposed to man in virtue of his end, or to make the moral value of an act performed with a true and correct conscience equivalent to the moral value of an act performed by following the judgment of an erroneous conscience.[108] It is possible that the evil done as the result of invincible ignorance or a non-culpable error of judgment may not be imputable to the agent; but even in this case it does not cease to be an evil, a disorder in relation to the truth about the good. Furthermore, a good act which is not recognized as such does not contribute to the moral growth of the person who performs it; it does not perfect him and it does not help to dispose him for the supreme good. Thus, before feeling easily justified in the name of our conscience, we should reflect on the words of the Psalm: "Who can discern his errors? Clear me from hidden faults" (Ps 19:12). There are faults which we fail to see but which nevertheless remain faults, because we have refused to walk toward the light (cf. Jn 9:39-41).

63.2 Conscience, as the ultimate concrete judgment, compromises its dignity when it is *culpably erroneous,* that is to say, "when man shows little concern for seeking what is true and good, and conscience gradually becomes almost blind from being accustomed to sin."[109] Jesus alludes to the danger of the conscience being deformed when he warns: "The eye is the lamp of the body. So if your eye is sound, your whole body will be full of light; but if your

---

[108] Cf. Saint Thomas Aquinas, *De Veritate,* q. 17, a. 4.

[109] Second Vatican Ecumenical Council, Pastoral Constitution on the Church in the Modern World *Gaudium et Spes,* 16.

eye is not sound, your whole body will be full of darkness. If then the light in you is darkness, how great is the darkness!" (Mt 6:22-23).

64.1 The words of Jesus just quoted also represent a call to *form our conscience*, to make it the object of a continuous conversion to what is true and to what is good. In the same vein, Saint Paul exhorts us not to be conformed to the mentality of this world, but to be transformed by the renewal of our mind (cf. Rom 12:2). It is the "heart" converted to the Lord and to the love of what is good which is really the source of *true* judgments of conscience. Indeed, in order to "prove what is the will of God, what is good and acceptable and perfect" (Rom 12:2), knowledge of God's law in general is certainly necessary, but it is not sufficient: what is essential is a sort of *"connaturality" between man and the true good.*[110] Such a connaturality is rooted in and develops through the virtuous attitudes of the individual himself: prudence and the other cardinal virtues, and even before these the theological virtues of faith, hope and charity. This is the meaning of Jesus' saying: "He who does what is true comes to the light" (Jn 3:21).

64.2 Christians have a great help for the formation of conscience *in the Church and her Magisterium.* As the Council affirms: "In forming their consciences the Christian faithful must give careful attention to the sacred and certain teaching of the Church. For the Catholic Church is by the will of Christ the teacher of truth. Her charge is to announce and teach authentically that truth which is Christ, and at the same time with her authority to declare and confirm the principles of the moral order which derive from human nature itself."[111] It follows that the authority of the Church, when she pronounces on moral questions, in no way undermines the freedom of conscience of Christians. This is so not only because freedom of conscience is never freedom "from" the truth but always and only freedom "in" the truth, but also because the Magisterium does not bring to the Christian conscience truths which are extraneous to it; rather it brings to light the truths which it ought already to possess, developing them from the starting point of the primordial act of faith. The Church puts herself always and only at the *service of conscience*, helping it to avoid being tossed to and fro by every wind of doctrine proposed by human deceit (cf. Eph 4:14), and helping it not to swerve from the truth about the good of man, but rather, especially in more difficult questions, to attain the truth with certainty and to abide in it.

---

[110] Cf. Saint Thomas Aquinas, *Summa Theologiae*, II-II, q. 45, a. 2.
[111] Declaration on Religious Freedom *Dignitatis Humanae*, 14.

III. FUNDAMENTAL CHOICE AND SPECIFIC KINDS OF BEHAVIOR

"Only do not use your freedom as an opportunity for the flesh" (Gal 5:13)

65.1 The heightened concern for freedom in our own day has led many students of the behavioral and the theological sciences to develop a more penetrating analysis of its nature and of its dynamics. It has been rightly pointed out that freedom is not only the choice for one or another particular action; it is also, within that choice, a *decision about oneself* and a setting of one's own life for or against the Good, for or against the Truth, and ultimately for or against God. Emphasis has rightly been placed on the importance of certain choices which "shape" a person's entire moral life, and which serve as bounds within which other particular everyday choices can be situated and allowed to develop.

65.2 Some authors, however, have proposed an even more radical revision of the *relationship between person and acts*. They speak of a "fundamental freedom," deeper than and different from freedom of choice, which needs to be considered if human actions are to be correctly understood and evaluated. According to these authors, the *key role in the moral life* is to be attributed to a "fundamental option," brought about by that fundamental freedom whereby the person makes an overall self-determination, not through a specific and conscious decision on the level of reflection, but in a "transcendental" and "athematic" way. *Particular acts* which flow from this option would constitute only partial and never definitive attempts to give it expression; they would only be its "signs" or symptoms. The immediate object of such acts would not be absolute Good (before which the freedom of the person would be expressed on a transcendental level), but particular (also termed "categorical") goods. In the opinion of some theologians, none of these goods, which by their nature are partial, could determine the freedom of man as a person in his totality, even though it is only by bringing them about or refusing to do so that man is able to express his own fundamental option.

65.3 A *distinction* thus comes to be introduced *between the fundamental option and deliberate choices of a concrete kind of behavior*. In some authors this division tends to become a *separation*, when they expressly limit moral "good" and "evil" to the transcendental dimension proper to the fundamental option, and describe as "right" or "wrong" the choices of particular "inner-worldly" kinds of behavior: those, in other words, concerning man's relationship with himself, with others and with the material world. There thus appears to be established within human acting a clear disjunction between two levels of morality: on the one hand the order of good and evil, which is dependent on the will, and on the other hand specific kinds of behavior, which are judged to be morally right or wrong only on the basis of a technical calculation of the proportion between the "pre-moral" or "physical" goods and evils which actually result from the action. This is pushed to the point where a concrete kind of behavior, even one freely chosen, comes to be considered as a merely physical process, and not according to the criteria proper to a human act. The conclusion to which this eventually leads is that the properly moral assessment of the person is reserved to his fundamental option, prescinding in whole or in part from his choice of particular actions, of concrete kinds of behavior.

66.1 There is no doubt that Christian moral teaching, even in its biblical roots, acknowledges the specific importance of a fundamental choice which qualifies the moral life and engages freedom on a radical level before God. It is a question of the decision of faith, of the *obedience of faith* (cf. Rom 16:26) "by which man makes a total and free self-commitment to God, offering 'the full submission of intellect and will to God as he reveals.' "[112] This faith, which works through love (cf. Gal 5:6), comes from the core of man, from his "heart" (cf. Rom 10:10), whence it is called to bear fruit in works (cf. Mt 12:33-35; Lk 6:43-45; Rom 8:5-10; Gal 5:22). In the Decalogue, one finds, as an introduction to the various commandments, the basic clause: "I am the Lord your God. . ." (Ex 20:2), which, by impressing upon the numerous and varied particular prescriptions their primordial meaning, gives the morality of the Covenant its aspect of completeness, unity and profundity. Israel's fundamental decision, then, is about the fundamental commandment (cf. Jos 24:14-25; Ex 19:3-8; Mic 6:8). The morality of the New Covenant is similarly dominated by the fundamental call of Jesus to follow him — thus he also says to the young man: "If you wish to be perfect . . . then come, follow me" (Mt 19:21); to this call the disciple must respond with a radical decision and choice. The Gospel parables of the treasure and the pearl of great price, for which one sells all one's possessions, are eloquent and effective images of the radical and unconditional nature of the decision demanded by the Kingdom of God. The radical nature of the decision to follow Jesus is admirably expressed in his own words: "Whoever would save his life will lose it; and whoever loses his life for my sake and the Gospel's will save it" (Mk 8:35).

---

[112] Second Vatican Ecumenical Council, Dogmatic Constitution on Divine Revelation *Dei Verbum*, 5; cf. First Vatican Ecumenical Council, Dogmatic Constitution on the Catholic Faith *Dei Filius*, Chapter 3: *DS* 3008.

66.2 Jesus' call to "come, follow me" marks the greatest possible exaltation of human freedom, yet at the same time it witnesses to the truth and to the obligation of acts of faith and of decisions which can be described as involving a fundamental option. We find a similar exaltation of human freedom in the words of Saint Paul: "You were called to freedom, brethren" (Gal 5:13). But the Apostle immediately adds a grave warning: "Only do not use your freedom as an opportunity for the flesh." This warning echoes his earlier words: "For freedom Christ has set us free; stand fast therefore, and do not submit again to a yoke of slavery" (Gal 5:1). Paul encourages us to be watchful, because freedom is always threatened by slavery. And this is precisely the case when an act of faith — in the sense of a fundamental option — becomes separated from the choice of particular acts, as in the tendencies mentioned above.

67.1 These tendencies are therefore contrary to the teaching of Scripture itself, which sees the fundamental option as a genuine choice of freedom and links that choice profoundly to particular acts. By his fundamental choice, man is capable of giving his life direction and of progressing, with the help of grace, toward his end, following God's call. But this capacity is actually exercised in the particular choices of specific actions, through which man deliberately conforms himself to God's will, wisdom and law. It thus needs to be stated that *the so-called fundamental option, to the extent that it is distinct from a generic intention* and hence one not yet determined in such a way that freedom is obligated, *is always brought into play through conscious and free decisions.* Precisely for this reason, *it is revoked when man engages his freedom in conscious decisions to the contrary, with regard to morally grave matter.*

67.2 To separate the fundamental option from concrete kinds of behavior means to contradict the substantial integrity or personal unity of the moral agent in his body and in his soul. A fundamental option understood without explicit consideration of the potentialities which it puts into effect and the determinations which express it does not do justice to the rational finality immanent in man's acting and in each of his deliberate decisions. In point of fact, the morality of human acts is not deduced only from one's intention, orientation or fundamental option, understood as an intention devoid of a clearly determined binding content or as an intention with no corresponding positive effort to fulfill the different obligations of the moral life. Judgments about morality cannot be made without taking into consideration whether or not the deliberate choice of a specific kind of behavior is in conformity with the dignity and integral vocation of the human person. Every choice always implies a reference by the deliberate will to the goods and evils indicated by the natural law as goods to be pursued and evils to be avoided. In the case of the positive moral precepts, prudence always has the task of verifying that they apply in a specific situation, for example, in view of other duties which may be more important or urgent. But the negative moral precepts, those prohibiting certain concrete actions or kinds of behavior as intrinsically evil, do not allow for any legitimate exception. They do not leave room, in any morally acceptable way, for the "creativity" of any contrary determination whatsoever. Once the moral species of an action prohibited by a universal rule is concretely recognized, the only morally good act is that of obeying the moral law and of refraining from the action which it forbids.

68.1 Here an important pastoral consideration must be added. According to the logic of the positions mentioned above, an individual could, by virtue of a fundamental option, remain faithful to God independently of whether or not certain of his choices and his acts are in conformity with specific moral norms or rules. By virtue of a primordial option for charity, that individual could continue to be morally good, persevere in God's grace and attain salvation, even if certain of his specific kinds of behavior were deliberately and gravely contrary to God's commandments as set forth by the Church.

68.2 In point of fact, man does not suffer perdition only by being unfaithful to that fundamental option whereby he has made "a free self-commitment to God."[113] With every freely committed mortal sin, he offends God as the giver of the law and as a result becomes guilty with regard to the entire law (cf. Jas 2:8-11); even if he perseveres in faith, he loses "sanctifying grace," "charity" and "eternal happiness."[114] As the Council of Trent teaches, "the grace of justification once received is lost not only by apostasy, by which faith itself is lost, but also by any other mortal sin."[115]

Mortal and venial sin

69 As we have just seen, reflection on the fundamental option has also led some theologians to undertake a basic revision of the traditional distinction

---

[113] Second Vatican Ecumenical Council, Dogmatic Constitution on Divine Revelation *Dei Verbum*, 5; cf. Sacred Congregation for the Doctrine of the Faith, Declaration on Certain Questions Concerning Sexual Ethics *Persona Humana* (December 29, 1975), 10: *AAS* 68 (1976), 88-90.

[114] Cf. Post-Synodal Apostolic Exhortation *Reconciliatio et Paenitentia* (December 2, 1984), 17: *AAS* 77 (1985), 218-223.

[115] Session VI, Decree on Justification *Cum Hoc Tempore*, Chapter 15: *DS* 1544; Canon 19: *DS* 1569.

between *mortal* sins and *venial* sins. They insist that the opposition to God's law which causes the loss of sanctifying grace — and eternal damnation, when one dies in such a state of sin — could only be the result of an act which engages the person in his totality: in other words, an act of fundamental option. According to these theologians, mortal sin, which separates man from God, only exists in the rejection of God, carried out at a level of freedom which is neither to be identified with an act of choice nor capable of becoming the object of conscious awareness. Consequently, they go on to say, it is difficult, at least psychologically, to accept the fact that a Christian, who wishes to remain united to Jesus Christ and to his Church, could so easily and repeatedly commit mortal sins, as the "matter" itself of his actions would sometimes indicate. Likewise, it would be hard to accept that man is able, in a brief lapse of time, to sever radically the bond of communion with God and afterwards be converted to him by sincere repentance. The gravity of sin, they maintain, ought to be measured by the degree of engagement of the freedom of the person performing an act, rather than by the matter of that act.

70.1 The Post-Synodal Apostolic Exhortation *Reconciliatio et Paenitentia* reaffirmed the importance and permanent validity of the distinction between mortal and venial sins, in accordance with the Church's Tradition. And the 1983 Synod of Bishops, from which that Exhortation emerged, "not only reaffirmed the teaching of the Council of Trent concerning the existence and nature of mortal and venial sins, but it also recalled that mortal sin is sin whose object is grave matter and which is also committed with full knowledge and deliberate consent."[116]

70.2 The statement of the Council of Trent does not only consider the "grave matter" of mortal sin; it also recalls that its necessary condition is "full awareness and deliberate consent." In any event, both in moral theology and in pastoral practice one is familiar with cases in which an act which is grave by reason of its matter does not constitute a mortal sin because of a lack of full awareness or deliberate consent on the part of the person performing it. Even so, "care will have to be taken not to reduce mortal sin to an act of *'fundamental option'* — as is commonly said today — against God," seen either as an explicit and formal rejection of God and neighbor or as an implicit and unconscious rejection of love. "For mortal sin exists also when a person knowingly and willingly, for whatever reason, chooses something gravely disordered. In fact, such a choice already includes contempt for the divine law, a

---

[116] Post-Synodal Apostolic Exhortation *Reconciliatio et Paenitentia* (December 2, 1984), 17: *AAS* 77 (1985), 221.

rejection of God's love for humanity and the whole of creation: the person turns away from God and loses charity. Consequently, *the fundamental orientation can be radically changed by particular acts.* Clearly situations can occur which are very complex and obscure from a psychological viewpoint, and which influence the sinner's subjective imputability. But from a consideration of the psychological sphere one cannot proceed to create a theological category, which is precisely what the 'fundamental option' is, understanding it in such a way that it objectively changes or casts doubt upon the traditional concept of mortal sin."[117]

70.3 The separation of fundamental option from deliberate choices of particular kinds of behavior, disordered in themselves or in their circumstances, which would not engage that option, thus involves a denial of Catholic doctrine on *mortal sin:* "With the whole Tradition of the Church, we call mortal sin the act by which man freely and consciously rejects God, his law, the covenant of love that God offers, preferring to turn in on himself or to some created and finite reality, something contrary to the divine will (*conversio ad creaturam*). This can occur in a direct and formal way, in the sins of idolatry, apostasy and atheism; or in an equivalent way, as in every act of disobedience to God's commandments in a grave matter."[118]

IV. THE MORAL ACT

Teleology and teleologism

71.1 The relationship between man's freedom and God's law, which has its intimate and living center in the moral conscience, is manifested and realized in human acts. It is precisely through his acts that man attains perfection as man, as one who is called to seek his Creator of his own accord and freely to arrive at full and blessed perfection by cleaving to him.[119]

71.2 Human acts are moral acts because they express and determine the goodness or evil of the individual who performs them.[120] They do not produce a change merely in the state of affairs outside of man but, to the extent that they are deliberate choices, they give moral definition to the very person who performs them, determining his *profound spiritual traits.* This was percep-

---

[117] Ibid.: loc. cit., 223.

[118] Ibid.: loc. cit., 222.

[119] Cf. Second Vatican Ecumenical Council, Pastoral Constitution on the Church in the Modern World *Gaudium et Spes,* 17.

[120] Cf. Saint Thomas Aquinas, *Summa Theologiae,* I-II, q. 1, a. 3: "Idem sunt actus morales et actus humani."

tively noted by Saint Gregory of Nyssa: "All things subject to change and to becoming never remain constant, but continually pass from one state to another, for better or worse. . . . Now, human life is always subject to change; it needs to be born ever anew . . . but here birth does not come about by a foreign intervention, as is the case with bodily beings. . . ; it is the result of a free choice. Thus *we are* in a certain way our own parents, creating ourselves as we will, by our decisions."[121]

72.1 The *morality of acts* is defined by the relationship of man's freedom with the authentic good. This good is established, as the eternal law, by divine wisdom which orders every being toward its end: this eternal law is known both by man's natural reason (hence it is "natural law"), and — in an integral and perfect way — by God's supernatural revelation (hence it is called divine law). Acting is morally good when the choices of freedom are *in conformity with man's true good* and thus express the voluntary ordering of the person toward his ultimate end: God himself, the supreme good in whom man finds his full and perfect happiness. The first question in the young man's conversation with Jesus: "What good must I do to have eternal life?" (Mt 19:6) immediately brings out *the essential connection between the moral value of an act and man's final end.* Jesus, in his reply, confirms the young man's conviction: the performance of good acts, commanded by the One who "alone is good," constitutes the indispensable condition of and path to eternal blessedness: "If you wish to enter into life, keep the commandments" (Mt 19:17). Jesus' answer and his reference to the commandments also make it clear that the path to that end is marked by respect for the divine laws which safeguard human good. *Only the act in conformity with the good can be a path that leads to life.*

72.2 The rational ordering of the human act to the good in its truth and the voluntary pursuit of that good, known by reason, constitute morality. Hence human activity cannot be judged as morally good merely because it is a means for attaining one or another of its goals, or simply because the subject's intention is good.[122] Activity is morally good when it attests to and expresses the voluntary ordering of the person to his ultimate end and the conformity of a concrete action with the human good as it is acknowledged in its truth by reason. If the object of the concrete action is not in harmony with the true good of the person, the choice of that action makes our will and ourselves morally evil, thus putting us in conflict with our ultimate end, the supreme good, God himself.

[121] *De Vita Moysis*, II, 2-3: *PG* 44, 327-328.
[122] Cf. Saint Thomas Aquinas, *Summa Theologiae*, II-II, q. 148, a. 3.

73.1 The Christian, thanks to God's revelation and to faith, is aware of the "newness" which characterizes the morality of his actions: these actions are called to show either consistency or inconsistency with that dignity and vocation which have been bestowed on him by grace. In Jesus Christ and in his Spirit, the Christian is a "new creation," a child of God; by his actions he shows his likeness or unlikeness to the image of the Son who is the first-born among many brethren (cf. Rom 8:29), he lives out his fidelity or infidelity to the gift of the Spirit, and he opens or closes himself to eternal life, to the communion of vision, love and happiness with God the Father, Son and Holy Spirit.[123] As Saint Cyril of Alexandria writes, Christ "forms us according to his image, in such a way that the traits of his divine nature shine forth in us through sanctification and justice and the life which is good and in conformity with virtue. . . . The beauty of this image shines forth in us who are in Christ, when we show ourselves to be good in our works."[124]

73.2 Consequently the moral life has an essential *"teleological" character*, since it consists in the deliberate ordering of human acts to God, the supreme good and ultimate end (*telos*) of man. This is attested to once more by the question posed by the young man to Jesus: "What good must I do to have eternal life?" But this ordering to one's ultimate end is not something subjective, dependent solely upon one's intention. It presupposes that such acts are in themselves capable of being ordered to this end, insofar as they are in conformity with the authentic moral good of man, safeguarded by the commandments. This is what Jesus himself points out in his reply to the young man: "If you wish to enter into life, keep the commandments" (Mt 19:17).

73.3 Clearly such an ordering must be rational and free, conscious and deliberate, by virtue of which man is "responsible" for his actions and subject to the judgment of God, the just and good judge who, as the Apostle Paul reminds us, rewards good and punishes evil: "We must all appear before the judgment

---

[123] The Second Vatican Ecumenical Council, in the Pastoral Constitution on the Church in the Modern World *Gaudium et Spes*, 22, makes this clear: "This applies not only to Christians but to all men of good will in whose hearts grace is secretly at work. Since Christ died for all and since man's ultimate calling comes from God and is therefore a universal one, we are obliged to hold that the Holy Spirit offers to all the possibility of sharing in this Paschal Mystery in a manner known to God."

[124] *Tractatus ad Tiberium Diaconum Sociosque, II. Responsiones ad Tiberium Diaconum Sociosque:* Saint Cyril of Alexandria, *In Divi Johannis Evangelium*, vol. III, ed. Philip Edward Pusey, Brussels, Culture et Civilisation (1965), 590.

seat of Christ, so that each one may receive good or evil, according to what he has done in the body" (2 Cor 5:10).

74.1 But on what does the moral assessment of man's free acts depend? What is it that ensures this *ordering of human acts to God?* Is it the *intention* of the acting subject, the *circumstances* — and in particular the consequences — of his action, or the *object* itself of his act?

74.2 This is what is traditionally called the problem of the "sources of morality." Precisely with regard to this problem there have emerged in the last few decades new or newly-revived theological and cultural trends which call for careful discernment on the part of the Church's Magisterium.

74.3 Certain *ethical theories*, called *"teleological,"* claim to be concerned for the conformity of human acts with the ends pursued by the agent and with the values intended by him. The criteria for evaluating the moral rightness of an action are drawn from the *weighing of the non-moral or pre-moral goods* to be gained and the corresponding non-moral or pre-moral values to be respected. For some, concrete behavior would be right or wrong according as whether or not it is capable of producing a better state of affairs for all concerned. Right conduct would be the one capable of "maximizing" goods and "minimizing" evils.

74.4 Many of the Catholic moralists who follow in this direction seek to distance themselves from utilitarianism and pragmatism, where the morality of human acts would be judged without any reference to the man's true ultimate end. They rightly recognize the need to find ever more consistent rational arguments in order to justify the requirements and to provide a foundation for the norms of the moral life. This kind of investigation is legitimate and necessary, since the moral order, as established by the natural law, is in principle accessible to human reason. Furthermore, such investigation is well-suited to meeting the demands of dialogue and cooperation with non-Catholics and non-believers, especially in pluralistic societies.

75.1 But as part of the effort to work out such a rational morality (for this reason it is sometimes called an "autonomous morality") there exist *false solutions, linked in particular to an inadequate understanding of the object of moral action. Some authors* do not take into sufficient consideration the fact that the will is involved in the concrete choices which it makes: these choices are a condition of its moral goodness and its being ordered to the ultimate end of the person. *Others* are inspired by a notion of freedom which prescinds from the actual conditions of its exercise, from its objective reference to the truth about the good, and from its determination through choices of concrete kinds of behavior. According to these theories, free will would neither be morally subjected to specific obligations nor shaped by its choices, while nonetheless still remaining responsible for its own acts and for their consequences. This *"teleologism,"* as a method for discovering the moral norm, can thus be called — according to terminology and approaches imported from different currents of thought — *"consequentialism"* or *"proportionalism."* The former claims to draw the criteria of the rightness of a given way of acting solely from a calculation of foreseeable consequences deriving from a given choice. The latter, by weighing the various values and goods being sought, focuses rather on the proportion acknowledged between the good and bad effects of that choice, with a view to the "greater good" or "lesser evil" actually possible in a particular situation.

75.2 The *teleological ethical theories (proportionalism, consequentialism),* while acknowledging that moral values are indicated by reason and by revelation, maintain that it is never possible to formulate an absolute prohibition of particular kinds of behavior which would be in conflict, in every circumstance and in every culture, with those values. The acting subject would indeed be responsible for attaining the values pursued, but in two ways: the values or goods involved in a human act would be, from one viewpoint, *of the moral order* (in relation to properly moral values, such as love of God and neighbor, justice, etc.) and, from another viewpoint, *of the pre-moral order,* which some term non-moral, physical or ontic (in relation to the advantages and disadvantages accruing both to the agent and to all other persons possibly involved, such as, for example, health or its endangerment, physical integrity, life, death, loss of material goods, etc.). In a world where goodness is always mixed with evil, and every good effect linked to other evil effects, the morality of an act would be judged in two different ways: its moral "goodness" would be judged on the basis of the subject's intention in reference to moral goods, and its "rightness" on the basis of a consideration of its foreseeable effects or consequences and of their proportion. Consequently, concrete kinds of behavior could be described as "right" or "wrong," without it being thereby possible to judge as morally "good" or "bad" the will of the person choosing them. In this way, an act which, by contradicting a universal negative norm, directly violates goods considered as "pre-moral" could be qualified as morally acceptable if the intention of the subject is focused, in accordance with a "responsible" assessment of the goods involved in the concrete action, on the moral value judged to be decisive in the situation.

75.3 The evaluation of the consequences of the action, based on the proportion between the act and its effects and between the effects themselves, would regard only the pre-moral order. The moral specificity of acts, that is their goodness or evil, would be determined exclusively by the faithfulness of the person to the highest values of charity and prudence, without this faithfulness necessarily being incompatible with choices contrary to certain particular moral precepts. Even when grave matter is concerned, these precepts should be considered as operative norms which are always relative and open to exceptions.

75.4 In this view, deliberate consent to certain kinds of behavior declared illicit by traditional moral theology would not imply an objective moral evil.

The object of the deliberate act

76.1 These theories can gain a certain persuasive force from their affinity to the scientific mentality, which is rightly concerned with ordering technical and economic activities on the basis of a calculation of resources and profits, procedures and their effects. They seek to provide liberation from the constraints of a voluntaristic and arbitrary morality of obligation which would ultimately be dehumanizing.

76.2 Such theories however are not faithful to the Church's teaching, when they believe they can justify, as morally good, deliberate choices of kinds of behavior contrary to the commandments of the divine and natural law. These theories cannot claim to be grounded in the Catholic moral tradition. Although the latter did witness the development of a casuistry which tried to assess the best ways to achieve the good in certain concrete situations, it is nonetheless true that this casuistry concerned only cases in which the law was uncertain, and thus the absolute validity of negative moral precepts, which oblige without exception, was not called into question. The faithful are obliged to acknowledge and respect the specific moral precepts declared and taught by the Church in the name of God, the Creator and Lord.[125] When the Apostle Paul sums up the fulfillment of the law in the precept of love of neighbor as oneself (cf. Rom 13:8-10), he is not weakening the commandments but reinforcing them, since he is revealing their requirements and their gravity. *Love of God and of one's neighbor cannot be separated from the observance of the commandments of the Covenant* renewed in the blood of Jesus Christ and in the gift of the Spirit. It is an honor characteristic of Christians to obey God rather than men (cf. Acts 4:19, 5:29) and to accept even martyrdom as a conse-

---

[125] Cf. Ecumenical Council of Trent, Session VI, Decree on Justification *Cum Hoc Tempore,* Canon 19: *DS* 1569. See also Clement XI, Constitution against the Errors of Paschasius Quesnel *Unigenitus Dei Filius* (September 8, 1713), 53-56: *DS* 2453-2456.

quence, like the holy men and women of the Old and New Testaments, who are considered such because they gave their lives rather than perform this or that particular act contrary to faith or virtue.

77.1 In order to offer rational criteria for a right moral decision, the theories mentioned above take account of the intention and *consequences* of human action. Certainly there is need to take into account both the intention — as Jesus forcefully insisted in clear disagreement with the scribes and Pharisees, who prescribed in great detail certain outward practices without paying attention to the heart (cf. Mk 7:20-21; Mt 15:19) — and the goods obtained and the evils avoided as a result of a particular act. Responsibility demands as much. But the consideration of these consequences, and also of intentions, is not sufficient for judging the moral quality of a concrete choice. The weighing of the goods and evils foreseeable as the consequence of an action is not an adequate method for determining whether the choice of that concrete kind of behavior is "according to its species," or "in itself," morally good or bad, licit or illicit. The foreseeable consequences are part of those circumstances of the act, which, while capable of lessening the gravity of an evil act, nonetheless cannot alter its moral species.

77.2 Moreover, everyone recognizes the difficulty, or rather the impossibility, of evaluating all the good and evil consequences and effects — defined as pre-moral — of one's own acts: an exhaustive rational calculation is not possible. How then can one go about establishing proportions which depend on a measuring, the criteria of which remain obscure? How could an absolute obligation be justified on the basis of such debatable calculations?

78.1 *The morality of the human act depends primarily and fundamentally on the "object" rationally chosen by the deliberate will,* as is borne out by the insightful analysis, still valid today, made by Saint Thomas.[126] In order to be able to grasp the object of an act which specifies that act morally, it is therefore necessary to place oneself *in the perspective of the acting person.* The object of the act of willing is in fact a freely chosen kind of behavior. To the extent that it is in conformity with the order of reason, it is the cause of the goodness of the will; it perfects us morally, and disposes us to recognize our ultimate end in the perfect good, primordial love. By the object of a given moral act, then, one cannot mean a process or an event of the merely physical order, to be assessed on the basis of its ability to bring about a given state of affairs in the outside world. Rather, that object is the proximate end of a

---

[126] Cf. *Summa Theologiae,* I-II, q. 18, a. 6.

deliberate decision which determines the act of willing on the part of the act-ing person. Consequently, as the *Catechism of the Catholic Church* teaches, "there are certain specific kinds of behavior that are always wrong to choose, because choosing them involves a disorder of the will, that is, a moral evil."[127] And Saint Thomas observes that "it often happens that man acts with a good intention, but without spiritual gain, because he lacks a good will. Let us say that someone robs in order to feed the poor: in this case, even though the intention is good, the uprightness of the will is lacking. Consequently, no evil done with a good intention can be excused. 'There are those who say: And why not do evil that good may come? Their condemnation is just' (Rom 3:8)."[128]

78.2 The reason why a good intention is not itself sufficient, but a correct choice of actions is also needed, is that the human act depends on its object, whether that object is *capable or not of being ordered* to God, to the One who "alone is good," and thus brings about the perfection of the person. An act is therefore good if its object is in conformity with the good of the person with respect for the goods morally relevant for him. Christian ethics, which pays particular attention to the moral object, does not refuse to consider the inner "teleology" of acting, inasmuch as it is directed to promoting the true good of the person; but it recognizes that it is really pursued only when the essential elements of human nature are respected. The human act, good according to its object, is also *capable of being ordered* to its ultimate end. That same act then attains its ultimate and decisive perfection when the will *actually does order* it to God through charity. As the Patron of moral theologians and con-fessors teaches: "It is not enough to do good works; they need to be done well. For our works to be good and perfect, they must be done for the sole purpose of pleasing God."[129]

"Intrinsic evil": it is not licit to do evil that good may come of it (cf. Rom 3:8)

79.1 *One must therefore reject the thesis*, characteristic of teleological and proportionalist theories, *which holds that it is impossible to qualify as morally evil according to its species* — its "object" — *the deliberate choice of certain kinds of behavior or specific acts, apart from a consideration of the intention for which the choice is made or the totality of the foreseeable consequences of that act for all persons concerned.*

[127] *Catechism of the Catholic Church*, No. 1761.

[128] *In Duo Praecepta Caritatis et in Decem Legis Praecepta, De Dilectione Dei: Opuscula Theologica*, II, No. 1168, Turin, 1954, 250.

[129] Saint Alphonsus Liguori, *Pratica di amar Gesù Cristo*, VII, 3.

79.2 The primary and decisive element for moral judgment is the object of the human act, which establishes whether it is *capable of being ordered to the good and to the ultimate end, which is God*. This capability is grasped by reason in the very being of man, considered in his integral truth, and therefore in his natural inclinations, his motivations and his finalities, which always have a spiritual dimension as well. It is precisely these which are the contents of the natural law and hence that ordered complex of "personal goods" which serve the "good of the person": the good which is the person himself and his perfection. These are the goods safeguarded by the commandments, which, according to Saint Thomas, contain the whole natural law.[130]

80.1 Reason attests that there are objects of the human act which are by their nature "incapable of being ordered" to God, because they radically contradict the good of the person made in his image. These are the acts which, in the Church's moral tradition, have been termed "intrinsically evil" (*intrinsece malum*): they are such *always and per se*, in other words, on account of their very object, and quite apart from the ulterior intentions of the one acting and the circumstances. Consequently, without in the least denying the influence on morality exercised by circumstances and especially by intentions, the Church teaches that "there exist acts which *per se* and in themselves, independently of circumstances, are always seriously wrong by reason of their object."[131] The Second Vatican Council itself, in discussing the respect due to the human person, gives a number of examples of such acts: "Whatever is hostile to life itself, such as any kind of homicide, genocide, abortion, euthanasia and voluntary suicide; whatever violates the integrity of the human person, such as mutilation, physical and mental torture and attempts to coerce the spirit; whatever is offensive to human dignity, such as subhuman living conditions, arbitrary imprisonment, deportation, slavery, prostitution and trafficking in women and children; degrading conditions of work which treat laborers as mere instruments of profit, and not as free responsible persons: all

---

[130] Cf. *Summa Theologiae*, I-II, q. 100, a. 1.

[131] Post-Synodal Apostolic Exhortation *Reconciliatio et Paenitentia* (December 2, 1984), 17: *AAS* 77 (1985), 221; cf. Paul VI, Address to Members of the Congregation of the Most Holy Redeemer (September 22, 1967): *AAS* 59 (1967), 962: "Far be it from Christians to be led to embrace another opinion, as if the Council taught that nowadays some things are permitted which the Church had previously declared intrinsically evil. Who does not see in this the rise of a depraved moral relativism, one that clearly endangers the Church's entire doctrinal heritage?"

these and the like are a disgrace, and so long as they infect human civilization they contaminate those who inflict them more than those who suffer injustice, and they are a negation of the honor due to the Creator." [132]

80.2 With regard to intrinsically evil acts, and in reference to contraceptive practices whereby the conjugal act is intentionally rendered infertile, Pope Paul VI teaches: "Though it is true that sometimes it is lawful to tolerate a lesser moral evil in order to avoid a greater evil or in order to promote a greater good, it is never lawful, even for the gravest reasons, to do evil that good may come of it (cf. Rom 3:8) — in other words, to intend directly something which of its very nature contradicts the moral order, and which must therefore be judged unworthy of man, even though the intention is to protect or promote the welfare of an individual, of a family or of society in general." [133]

81.1 In teaching the existence of intrinsically evil acts, the Church accepts the teaching of Sacred Scripture. The Apostle Paul emphatically states: "Do not be deceived: neither the immoral, nor idolaters, nor adulterers, nor sexual perverts, nor thieves, nor the greedy, nor drunkards, nor revilers, nor robbers will inherit the Kingdom of God" (1 Cor 6:9-10).

81.2 If acts are intrinsically evil, a good intention or particular circumstances can diminish their evil, but they cannot remove it. They remain "irremediably" evil acts; *per se* and in themselves they are not capable of being ordered to God and to the good of the person. "As for acts which are themselves sins (*cum iam opera ipsa peccata sunt*)," Saint Augustine writes, "like theft, fornication, blasphemy, who would dare affirm that, by doing them for good motives (*causis bonis*), they would no longer be sins, or, what is even more absurd, that they would be sins that are justified?" [134]

81.3 Consequently, circumstances or intentions can never transform an act intrinsically evil by virtue of its object into an act "subjectively" good or defensible as a choice.

82.1 Furthermore, an intention is good when it has as its aim the true good of the person in view of his ultimate end. But acts whose object is "not capable of being ordered" to God and "unworthy of the human person" are always and in every case in conflict with that good. Consequently, respect for

---

[132] Pastoral Constitution on the Church in the Modern World *Gaudium et Spes*, 27.

[133] Encyclical Letter *Humanae Vitae* (July 25, 1968), 14: *AAS* 60 (1968), 490-491.

[134] *Contra Mendacium*, VII, 18: *PL* 40, 528; cf. Saint Thomas Aquinas, *Quaestiones Quodlibetales*, IX, q. 7, a. 2; *Catechism of the Catholic Church*, Nos. 1753-1755.

norms which prohibit such acts and oblige *semper et pro semper,* that is, without any exception, not only does not inhibit a good intention, but actually represents its basic expression.

82.2 The doctrine of the object as a source of morality represents an authentic explication of the biblical morality of the Covenant and of the commandments, of charity and of the virtues. The moral quality of human acting is dependent on this fidelity to the commandments, as an expression of obedience and of love. For this reason — we repeat — the opinion must be rejected as erroneous which maintains that it is impossible to qualify as morally evil according to its species the deliberate choice of certain kinds of behavior or specific acts, without taking into account the intention for which the choice was made or the totality of the foreseeable consequences of that act for all persons concerned. Without the *rational determination of the morality of human acting* as stated above, it would be impossible to affirm the existence of an "objective moral order"[135] and to establish any particular norm the content of which would be binding without exception. This would be to the detriment of human fraternity and the truth about the good, and would be injurious to ecclesial communion as well.

83.1 As is evident, in the question of the morality of human acts, and in particular the question of whether there exist intrinsically evil acts, we find ourselves faced with *the question of man himself,* of his *truth* and of the moral consequences flowing from that truth. By acknowledging and teaching the existence of intrinsic evil in given human acts, the Church remains faithful to the integral truth about man; she thus respects and promotes man in his dignity and vocation. Consequently, she must reject the theories set forth above, which contradict this truth.

83.2 Dear Brothers in the Episcopate, we must not be content merely to warn the faithful about the errors and dangers of certain ethical theories. We must first of all show the inviting splendor of that truth which is Jesus Christ himself. In him, who is the Truth (cf. Jn 14:6), man can understand fully and live perfectly, through his good actions, his vocation to freedom in obedience to the divine law summarized in the commandment of love of God and neighbor. And this is what takes place through the gift of the Holy Spirit, the Spirit of truth, of freedom and of love: in him we are enabled to interiorize the law, to receive it and to live it as the motivating force of true personal freedom: "the perfect law, the law of liberty" (Jas 1:25).

[135] Second Vatican Ecumenical Council, Declaration on Religious Freedom *Dignitatis Humanae,* 7.

III

"Lest the Cross of Christ Be Emptied of Its Power" (1 Cor 1:17)

Moral Good for the Life of the Church and of the World

"For freedom Christ has set us free" (Gal 5:1)

84.1 The *fundamental question* which the moral theories mentioned above pose in a particularly forceful way is that of the relationship of man's freedom to God's law; it is ultimately the question of the *relationship between freedom and truth.*

84.2 According to Christian faith and the Church's teaching, "only the freedom which submits to the truth leads the human person to his true good. The good of the person is to be in the truth and to *do* the truth."[136]

84.3 A comparison between the Church's teaching and today's social and cultural situation immediately makes clear the urgent need *for the Church herself to develop an intense pastoral effort precisely with regard to this fundamental question.* "This essential bond between truth, the good and freedom has been largely lost sight of by present-day culture. As a result, helping man to rediscover it represents nowadays one of the specific requirements of the Church's mission, for the salvation of the world. Pilate's question: 'What is truth?' reflects the distressing perplexity of a man who often no longer knows *who he is, whence* he comes and *where* he is going. Hence we not infrequently witness the fearful plunging of the human person into situations of gradual self-destruction. According to some, it appears that one no longer need acknowledge the enduring absoluteness of any moral value. All around us we encounter contempt for human life after conception and before birth; the ongoing violation of basic rights of the person; the unjust destruction of goods minimally necessary for a human life. Indeed, something more serious has happened: man is no longer convinced that only in the truth can he find salvation. The saving power of the truth is contested, and freedom alone, uprooted from any objectivity, is left to decide by itself what is good and what is evil. This relativism becomes, in the field of theology, a lack of trust in the wisdom of God, who guides man with the moral law. Concrete situations are unfavorably contrasted with the precepts of the moral law, nor is it any longer

---

[136] Address to Those Taking Part in the International Congress of Moral Theology (April 10, 1986), 1: *Insegnamenti* IX/1 (1986), 970.

maintained that, when all is said and done, the law of God is always the one true good of man."[137]

85 The discernment which the Church carries out with regard to these ethical theories is not simply limited to denouncing and refuting them. In a positive way, the Church seeks, with great love, to help all the faithful to form a moral conscience which will make judgments and lead to decisions in accordance with the truth, following the exhortation of the Apostle Paul: "Do not be conformed to this world but be transformed by the renewal of your mind, that you may prove what is the will of God, what is good and acceptable and perfect" (Rom 12:2). This effort by the Church finds its support — the "secret" of its educative power — not so much in doctrinal statements and pastoral appeals to vigilance, as in *constantly looking to the Lord Jesus.* Each day the Church looks to Christ with unfailing love, fully aware that the true and final answer to the problem of morality lies in him alone. In a particular way, it is *in the crucified Christ* that *the Church finds the answer* to the question troubling so many people today: how can obedience to universal and unchanging moral norms respect the uniqueness and individuality of the person, and not represent a threat to his freedom and dignity? The Church makes her own the Apostle Paul's awareness of the mission he had received: "Christ . . . sent me . . . to preach the Gospel, and not with eloquent wisdom, lest the cross of Christ be emptied of its power. . . . We preach Christ crucified, a stumbling block to Jews and folly to Gentiles, but to those who are called, both Jews and Greeks, Christ the power of God and the wisdom of God" (1 Cor 1:17, 23-24). *The crucified Christ reveals the authentic meaning of freedom; he lives it fully in the total gift of himself* and calls his disciples to share in his freedom.

86.1 Rational reflection and daily experience demonstrate the weakness which marks man's freedom. That freedom is real but limited: its absolute and unconditional origin is not in itself, but in the life within which it is situated and which represents for it, at one and the same time, both a limitation and a possibility. Human freedom belongs to us as creatures; it is a freedom which is given as a gift, one to be received like a seed and to be cultivated responsibly. It is an essential part of that creaturely image which is the basis of the dignity of the person. Within that freedom there is an echo of the primordial vocation whereby the Creator calls man to the true Good, and even more, through Christ's revelation, to become his friend and to share his own divine life. It is at once inalienable self-possession and openness to all that

---

[137] Ibid., 2: loc. cit., 970-971.

exists, in passing beyond self to knowledge and love of the other.[138] Freedom then is rooted in the truth about man, and it is ultimately directed toward communion.

86.2 Reason and experience not only confirm the weakness of human freedom; they also confirm its tragic aspects. Man comes to realize that his freedom is in some mysterious way inclined to betray this openness to the True and the Good, and that all too often he actually prefers to choose finite, limited and ephemeral goods. What is more, within his errors and negative decisions, man glimpses the source of a deep rebellion, which leads him to reject the Truth and the Good in order to set himself up as an absolute principle unto himself: "You will be like God" (Gen 3:5). Consequently, *freedom itself needs to be set free. It is Christ who sets it free:* he "has set us free for freedom" (cf. Gal 5:1).

87.1 Christ reveals, first and foremost, that the frank and open acceptance of truth is the condition for authentic freedom: "You will know the truth, and the truth will set you free" (Jn 8:32).[139] This is truth which sets one free in the face of worldly power and which gives the strength to endure martyrdom. So it was with Jesus before Pilate: "For this I was born, and for this I have come into the world, to bear witness to the truth" (Jn 18:37). The true worshipers of God must thus worship him "in spirit and truth" (Jn 4:23): *in this worship they become free.* Worship of God and a relationship with truth are revealed in Jesus Christ as the deepest foundation of freedom.

87.2 Furthermore, Jesus reveals by his whole life, and not only by his words, that freedom is acquired in *love*, that is, in the *gift of self.* The one who says, "Greater love has no man than this, that a man lay down his life for his friends" (Jn 15:13), freely goes out to meet his Passion (cf. Mt 26:46), and in obedience to the Father gives his life on the Cross for all men (cf. Phil 2:6-11). Contemplation of Jesus crucified is thus the high road which the Church must tread every day if she wishes to understand the full meaning of freedom: the gift of self in *service to God and one's brethren.* Communion with the crucified and risen Lord is the never-ending source from which the Church draws unceasingly in order to live in freedom, to give of herself and to serve. Commenting on the verse in Psalm 100, "Serve the Lord with gladness," Saint Augustine says: "In the house of the Lord, slavery is free. It is free because it serves not out of necessity, but out of charity. . . . Charity should make you a

---

[138] Cf. Second Vatican Ecumenical Council, Pastoral Constitution on the Church in the Modern World *Gaudium et Spes,* 24.

[139] Cf. Encyclical Letter *Redemptor Hominis* (March 4, 1979), 12: AAS 71 (1979), 280-281.

servant, just as truth has made you free . . . you are at once both a servant and free: a servant, because you have become such; free, because you are loved by God your Creator; indeed, you have also been enabled to love your Creator. . . . You are a servant of the Lord and you are a freedman of the Lord. Do not go looking for a liberation which will lead you far from the house of your liberator!"[140]

87.3 The Church, and each of her members, is thus called to share in the *munus regale* of the crucified Christ (cf. Jn 12:32), to share in the grace and in the responsibility of the Son of man who came "not to be served but to serve, and to give his life as a ransom for many" (Mt 20:28).[141]

87.4 Jesus, then, is the living, personal summation of perfect freedom in total obedience to the will of God. His crucified flesh fully reveals the unbreakable bond between freedom and truth, just as his Resurrection from the dead is the supreme exaltation of the fruitfulness and saving power of a freedom lived out in truth.

Walking in the light (cf. 1 Jn 1:7)

88.1 The attempt to set freedom in opposition to truth, and indeed to separate them radically, is the consequence, manifestation and consummation of *another more serious and destructive dichotomy, that which separates faith from morality.*

88.2 This separation represents one of the most acute pastoral concerns of the Church amid today's growing secularism, wherein many, indeed too many, people think and live "as if God did not exist." We are speaking of a mentality which affects, often in a profound, extensive and all-embracing way, even the attitudes and behavior of Christians, whose faith is weakened and loses its character as a new and original criterion for thinking and acting in personal, family and social life. In a widely dechristianized culture, the criteria employed by believers themselves in making judgments and decisions often appear extraneous or even contrary to those of the Gospel.

88.3 It is urgent then that Christians should rediscover *the newness of the faith and its power to judge* a prevalent and all-intrusive culture. As the Apostle Paul admonishes us: "Once you were darkness, but now you are light in the Lord; walk as children of the light (for the fruit of the light is found in all that is good and right and true), and try to learn what is pleasing to the Lord. Take no

---

[140] *Enarratio in Psalmum XCIX*, 7: *CCL* 39, 1397.

[141] Cf. Second Vatican Ecumenical Council, Dogmatic Constitution on the Church *Lumen Gentium*, 36; cf. Encyclical Letter *Redemptor Hominis* (March 4, 1979), 21: *AAS* 71 (1979), 316-317.

part in the unfruitful works of darkness, but instead expose them. . . . Look carefully then how you walk, not as unwise men but as wise, making the most of the time, because the days are evil" (Eph 5:8-11, 15-16; cf. 1 Thess 5:4-8).

88.4 It is urgent to rediscover and to set forth once more the authentic reality of the Christian faith, which is not simply a set of propositions to be accepted with intellectual assent. Rather, faith is a lived knowledge of Christ, a living remembrance of his commandments, and a *truth to be lived out.* A word, in any event, is not truly received until it passes into action, until it is put into practice. Faith is a decision involving one's whole existence. It is an encounter, a dialogue, a communion of love and of life between the believer and Jesus Christ, the way, and the truth, and the life (cf. Jn 14:6). It entails an act of trusting abandonment to Christ, which enables us to live as he lived (cf. Gal 2:20), in profound love of God and of our brothers and sisters.

89.1 Faith also possesses a moral content. It gives rise to and calls for a consistent life commitment; it entails and brings to perfection the acceptance and observance of God's commandments. As Saint John writes, "God is light and in him is no darkness at all. If we say we have fellowship with him while we walk in darkness, we lie and do not live according to the truth. . . . And by this we may be sure that we know him, if we keep his commandments. He who says 'I know him' but disobeys his commandments is a liar, and the truth is not in him; but whoever keeps his word, in him truly love for God is perfected. By this we may be sure that we are in him: he who says he abides in him ought to walk in the same way in which he walked" (1 Jn 1:5-6, 2:3-6).

89.2 Through the moral life, faith becomes "confession," not only before God but also before men: it becomes *witness.* "You are the light of the world," said Jesus; "a city set on a hill cannot be hid. Nor do men light a lamp and put it under a bushel, but on a stand, and it gives light to all in the house. Let your light so shine before men, that they may see your good works and give glory to your Father who is in heaven" (Mt 5:14-16). These works are above all those of charity (cf. Mt 25:31-46) and of the authentic freedom which is manifested and lived in the gift of self, *even to the total gift of self,* like that of Jesus, who on the Cross "loved the Church and gave himself up for her" (Eph 5:25). Christ's witness is the source, model and means for the witness of his disciples, who are called to walk on the same road: "If any man would come after me, let him deny himself and take up his cross daily and follow me" (Lk 9:23). Charity, in conformity with the radical demands of the Gospel, can lead the believer to the supreme witness of *martyrdom.* Once again this means imitating Jesus who died on the Cross: "Be imitators of God, as beloved children,"

Paul writes to the Christians of Ephesus, "and walk in love, as Christ loved us and gave himself up for us, a fragrant offering and sacrifice to God" (Eph 5:1-2).

Martyrdom, the exaltation of the inviolable holiness of God's law

90.1 The relationship between faith and morality shines forth with all its brilliance in the *unconditional respect due to the insistent demands of the personal dignity of every man*, demands protected by those moral norms which prohibit without exception actions which are intrinsically evil. The universality and the immutability of the moral norm make manifest and at the same time serve to protect the personal dignity and inviolability of man, on whose face is reflected the splendor of God (cf. Gen 9:5-6).

90.2 The unacceptability of "teleological," "consequentialist" and "proportionalist" ethical theories, which deny the existence of negative moral norms regarding specific kinds of behavior, norms which are valid without exception, is confirmed in a particularly eloquent way by Christian martyrdom, which has always accompanied and continues to accompany the life of the Church even today.

91.1 In the Old Testament we already find admirable witnesses of fidelity to the holy law of God even to the point of a voluntary acceptance of death. A prime example is the story of Susanna: in reply to the two unjust judges who threatened to have her condemned to death if she refused to yield to their sinful passion, she says: "I am hemmed in on every side. For if I do this thing, it is death for me; and if I do not, I shall not escape your hands. I choose not to do it and to fall into your hands, rather than to sin in the sight of the Lord!" (Dan 13:22-23). Susanna, preferring to "fall innocent" into the hands of the judges, bears witness not only to her faith and trust in God but also to her obedience to the truth and to the absoluteness of the moral order. By her readiness to die a martyr, she proclaims that it is not right to do what God's law qualifies as evil in order to draw some good from it. Susanna chose for herself the "better part": hers was a perfectly clear witness, without any compromise, to the truth about the good and to the God of Israel. By her acts, she revealed the holiness of God.

91.2 At the dawn of the New Testament, *John the Baptist*, unable to refrain from speaking of the law of the Lord and rejecting any compromise with evil, "gave his life in witness to truth and justice,"[142] and thus also became the

---

[142] Roman Missal, Prayer for the Memorial of the Beheading of John the Baptist, Martyr, August 29.

forerunner of the Messiah in the way he died (cf. Mk 6:17-29). "The one who came to bear witness to the light and who deserved to be called by that same light, which is Christ, a burning and shining lamp, was cast into the darkness of prison. . . . The one to whom it was granted to baptize the Redeemer of the world was thus baptized in his own blood."[143]

91.3 In the New Testament we find many examples of *followers of Christ*, beginning with the deacon Stephen (cf. Acts 6:8-7:60) and the Apostle James (cf. Acts 12:1-2), who died as martyrs in order to profess their faith and their love for Christ, unwilling to deny him. In this they followed the Lord Jesus who "made the good confession" (1 Tim 6:13) before Caiaphas and Pilate, confirming the truth of his message at the cost of his life. Countless other martyrs accepted persecution and death rather than perform the idolatrous act of burning incense before the statue of the Emperor (cf. Rev 13:7-10). They even refused to feign such worship, thereby giving an example of the duty to refrain from performing even a single concrete act contrary to God's love and the witness of faith. Like Christ himself, they obediently trusted and handed over their lives to the Father, the one who could free them from death (cf. Heb 5:7).

91.4 The Church proposes the example of numerous saints who bore witness to and defended moral truth even to the point of enduring martyrdom, or who preferred death to a single mortal sin. In raising them to the honor of the altars, the Church has canonized their witness and declared the truth of their judgment, according to which the love of God entails the obligation to respect his commandments, even in the most dire of circumstances, and the refusal to betray those commandments, even for the sake of saving one's own life.

92.1 Martyrdom, accepted as an affirmation of the inviolability of the moral order, bears splendid witness both to the holiness of God's law and to the inviolability of the personal dignity of man, created in God's image and likeness. This dignity may never be disparaged or called into question, even with good intentions, whatever the difficulties involved. Jesus warns us most sternly: "What does it profit a man, to gain the whole world and forfeit his life?" (Mk 8:36).

92.2 Martyrdom rejects as false and illusory whatever "human meaning" one might claim to attribute, even in "exceptional" conditions, to an act morally evil in itself. Indeed, it even more clearly unmasks the true face of such an act: *it is a violation of man's "humanity,"* in the one perpetrating it even before

---

[143] Saint Bede the Venerable, *Homeliarum Evangelii Libri*, II, 23: CCL 122, 556-557.

the one enduring it.[144] Hence martyrdom is also the exaltation of a person's perfect "humanity" and of true "life," as is attested by Saint Ignatius of Antioch, addressing the Christians of Rome, the place of his own martyrdom: "Have mercy on me, brethren: do not hold me back from living; do not wish that I die. . . . Let me arrive at the pure light; once there *I will be truly a man.* Let me imitate the passion of my God."[145]

93.1 Finally, martyrdom is an *outstanding sign of the holiness of the Church.* Fidelity to God's holy law, witnessed to by death, is a solemn proclamation and missionary commitment *usque ad sanguinem,* so that the splendor of moral truth may be undimmed in the behavior and thinking of individuals and society. This witness makes an extraordinarily valuable contribution to warding off, in civil society and within the ecclesial communities themselves, a headlong plunge into the most dangerous crisis which can afflict man: the *confusion between good and evil,* which makes it impossible to build up and to preserve the moral order of individuals and communities. By their eloquent and attractive example of a life completely transfigured by the splendor of moral truth, the martyrs and, in general, all the Church's saints, light up every period of history by reawakening its moral sense. By witnessing fully to the good, they are a living reproof to those who transgress the law (cf. Wis 2:12), and they make the words of the Prophet echo ever afresh: "Woe to those who call evil good and good evil, who put darkness for light and light for darkness, who put bitter for sweet and sweet for bitter!" (Is 5:20).

93.2 Although martyrdom represents the high point of the witness to moral truth, and one to which relatively few people are called, there is nonetheless a consistent witness which all Christians must daily be ready to make, even at the cost of suffering and grave sacrifice. Indeed, faced with the many difficulties which fidelity to the moral order can demand, even in the most ordinary circumstances, the Christian is called, with the grace of God invoked in prayer, to a sometimes heroic commitment. In this he or she is sustained by the virtue of fortitude, whereby — as Gregory the Great teaches — one can actually "love the difficulties of this world for the sake of eternal rewards."[146]

94 In this witness to the absoluteness of the moral good *Christians are not alone:* they are supported by the moral sense present in peoples and by the

---

[144] Cf. Second Vatican Ecumenical Council, Pastoral Constitution on the Church in the Modern World *Gaudium et Spes,* 27.

[145] *Epistula ad Romanos,* VI, 2-3: *Patres Apostolici,* ed. F. X. Funk, I, 260-261.

[146] *Moralia in Job,* VII, 21, 24: *PL* 75, 778: "huius mundi aspera pro aeternis praemiis amare."

great religious and sapiential traditions of East and West, from which the interior and mysterious workings of God's Spirit are not absent. The words of the Latin poet Juvenal apply to all: "Consider it the greatest of crimes to prefer survival to honor and, out of love of physical life, to lose the very reason for living."[147] The voice of conscience has always clearly recalled that there are truths and moral values for which one must be prepared to give up one's life. In an individual's words and above all in the sacrifice of his life for a moral value, the Church sees a single testimony to that truth which, already present in creation, shines forth in its fullness on the face of Christ. As Saint Justin put it, "the Stoics, at least in their teachings on ethics, demonstrated wisdom, thanks to the seed of the Word present in all peoples, and we know that those who followed their doctrines met with hatred and were killed."[148]

Universal and unchanging moral norms at the service of the person and of society

95.1 The Church's teaching, and in particular her firmness in defending the universal and permanent validity of the precepts prohibiting intrinsically evil acts, is not infrequently seen as the sign of an intolerable intransigence, particularly with regard to the enormously complex and conflict-filled situations present in the moral life of individuals and of society today; this intransigence is said to be in contrast with the Church's motherhood. The Church, one hears, is lacking in understanding and compassion. But the Church's motherhood can never in fact be separated from her teaching mission, which she must always carry out as the faithful Bride of Christ, who is the Truth in person. "As Teacher, she never tires of proclaiming the moral norm. . . . The Church is in no way the author or the arbiter of this norm. In obedience to the truth which is Christ, whose image is reflected in the nature and dignity of the human person, the Church interprets the moral norm and proposes it to all people of good will, without concealing its demands of radicalness and perfection."[149]

95.2 In fact, genuine understanding and compassion must mean love for the person, for his true good, for his authentic freedom. And this does not result, certainly, from concealing or weakening moral truth, but rather from proposing it in its most profound meaning as an outpouring of God's eternal

---

[147] *Satirae*, VIII, 83-84: "Summum crede nefas animam praeferre pudori et propter vitam vivendi perdere causas."

[148] *Apologia*, II, 8: *PG* 6, 457-458.

[149] Apostolic Exhortation *Familiaris Consortio* (November 22, 1981), 33: *AAS* 74 (1982), 120.

Wisdom, which we have received in Christ, and as a service to man, to the growth of his freedom and to the attainment of his happiness.[150]

95.3 Still, a clear and forceful presentation of moral truth can never be separated from a profound and heartfelt respect, born of that patient and trusting love which man always needs along his moral journey, a journey frequently wearisome on account of difficulties, weakness and painful situations. The Church can never renounce "the principle of truth and consistency, whereby she does not agree to call good evil and evil good";[151] she must always be careful not to break the bruised reed or to quench the dimly burning wick (cf. Is 42:3). As Paul VI wrote: "While it is an outstanding manifestation of charity toward souls to omit nothing from the saving doctrine of Christ, this must always be joined with tolerance and charity, as Christ himself showed by his conversations and dealings with men. Having come not to judge the world but to save it, he was uncompromisingly stern toward sin, but patient and rich in mercy toward sinners."[152]

96.1 The Church's firmness in defending the universal and unchanging moral norms is not demeaning at all. Its only purpose is to serve man's true freedom. Because there can be no freedom apart from or in opposition to the truth, the categorical — unyielding and uncompromising — defense of the absolutely essential demands of man's personal dignity must be considered the way and the condition for the very existence of freedom.

96.2 This service is directed to *every man,* considered in the uniqueness and singularity of his being and existence: only by obedience to universal moral norms does man find full confirmation of his personal uniqueness and the possibility of authentic moral growth. For this very reason, this service is also directed to *all mankind:* it is not only for individuals but also for the community, for society as such. These norms in fact represent the unshakable foundation and solid guarantee of a just and peaceful human coexistence, and hence of genuine democracy, which can come into being and develop only on the basis of the equality of all its members, who possess common rights and duties. *When it is a matter of the moral norms prohibiting intrinsic evil, there are no privileges or exceptions for anyone.* It makes no difference whether one is the master of the world or the "poorest of the poor" on

---

[150] Cf. ibid., 34: loc. cit., 123-125.

[151] Post-Synodal Apostolic Exhortation *Reconciliatio et Paenitentia* (December 2, 1984), 34: *AAS* 77 (1985), 272.

[152] Encyclical Letter *Humanae Vitae* (July 25, 1968), 29: *AAS* 60 (1968), 501.

the face of the earth. Before the demands of morality we are all absolutely equal.

97.1 In this way, moral norms, and primarily the negative ones, those prohibiting evil, manifest their *meaning and force, both personal and social.* By protecting the inviolable personal dignity of every human being they help to preserve the human social fabric and its proper and fruitful development. The commandments of the second tablet of the Decalogue in particular — those which Jesus quoted to the young man of the Gospel (cf. Mt 19:19) — constitute the indispensable rules of all social life.

97.2 These commandments are formulated in general terms. But the very fact that "the origin, the subject and the purpose of all social institutions is and should be the human person"[153] allows for them to be specified and made more explicit in a detailed code of behavior. The fundamental moral rules of social life thus entail *specific demands* to which both public authorities and citizens are required to pay heed. Even though intentions may sometimes be good, and circumstances frequently difficult, civil authorities and particular individuals never have authority to violate the fundamental and inalienable rights of the human person. In the end, only a morality which acknowledges certain norms as valid always and for everyone, with no exception, can guarantee the ethical foundation of social coexistence, both on the national and international levels.

Morality and the renewal of social and political life

98.1 In the face of serious forms of social and economic injustice and political corruption affecting entire peoples and nations, there is a growing reaction of indignation on the part of very many people whose fundamental human rights have been trampled upon and held in contempt, as well as an ever more widespread and acute sense of *the need for a radical* personal and social *renewal* capable of ensuring justice, solidarity, honesty and openness.

98.2 Certainly there is a long and difficult road ahead; bringing about such a renewal will require enormous effort, especially on account of the number and the gravity of the causes giving rise to and aggravating the situations of injustice present in the world today. But, as history and personal experience show, it is not difficult to discover at the bottom of these situations causes which are properly "cultural," linked to particular ways of looking at

---

[153] Second Vatican Ecumenical Council, Pastoral Constitution on the Church in the Modern World *Gaudium et Spes*, 25.

man, society and the world. Indeed, at the heart of the issue of culture we find the *moral sense,* which is in turn rooted and fulfilled in the *religious sense.*[154]

99.1 Only God, the Supreme Good, constitutes the unshakable foundation and essential condition of morality, and thus of the commandments, particularly those negative commandments which always and in every case prohibit behavior and actions incompatible with the personal dignity of every man. The Supreme Good and the moral good meet in *truth:* the truth of God, the Creator and Redeemer, and the truth of man created and redeemed by him. Only upon this truth is it possible to construct a renewed society and to solve the complex and weighty problems affecting it, above all the problem of overcoming the various forms of totalitarianism, so as to make way for the authentic *freedom* of the person. "Totalitarianism arises out of a denial of truth in the objective sense. If there is no transcendent truth, in obedience to which man achieves his full identity, then there is no sure principle for guaranteeing just relations between people. Their self-interest as a class, group or nation would inevitably set them in opposition to one another. If one does not acknowledge transcendent truth, then the force of power takes over, and each person tends to make full use of the means at his disposal in order to impose his own interests or his own opinion, with no regard for the rights of others. . . . Thus, the root of modern totalitarianism is to be found in the denial of the transcendent dignity of the human person who, as the visible image of the invisible God, is therefore by his very nature the subject of rights which no one may violate — no individual, group, class, nation or State. Not even the majority of a social body may violate these rights, by going against the minority, by isolating, oppressing, or exploiting it, or by attempting to annihilate it."[155]

99.2 Consequently, the inseparable connection between truth and freedom — which expresses the essential bond between God's wisdom and will — is extremely significant for the life of persons in the socioeconomic and sociopolitical sphere. This is clearly seen in the Church's social teaching — which "belongs to the field . . . of theology and particularly of moral theology"[156] — and from her presentation of commandments governing social, economic and political life, not only with regard to general attitudes but also to precise and specific kinds of behavior and concrete acts.

---

[154] Cf. Encyclical Letter *Centesimus Annus* (May 1, 1991), 24: *AAS* 83 (1991), 821-822.

[155] Ibid., 44: loc. cit., 848-849; cf. Leo XIII, Encyclical Letter *Libertas Praestantissimum* (June 20, 1888), *Leonis XIII P. M. Acta,* VIII, Rome, 1889, 224-226.

[156] Encyclical Letter *Sollicitudo Rei Socialis* (December 30, 1987), 41: *AAS* 80 (1988), 571.

100 The *Catechism of the Catholic Church* affirms that "in economic matters, respect for human dignity requires the practice of the virtue of *temperance*, to moderate our attachment to the goods of this world; of the virtue of *justice*, to preserve our neighbor's rights and to render what is his or her due; and of *solidarity*, following the Golden Rule and in keeping with the generosity of the Lord, who 'though he was rich, yet for your sake . . . became poor, so that by his poverty you might become rich' (2 Cor 8:9)."[157] The Catechism goes on to present a series of kinds of behavior and actions contrary to human dignity: theft, deliberate retention of goods lent or objects lost, business fraud (cf. Dt 25:13-16), unjust wages (cf. Dt 24:14-15), forcing up prices by trading on the ignorance or hardship of another (cf. Amos 8:4-6), the misappropriation and private use of the corporate property of an enterprise, work badly done, tax fraud, forgery of checks and invoices, excessive expenses, waste, etc.[158] It continues: "The seventh commandment prohibits actions or enterprises which for any reason — selfish or ideological, commercial or totalitarian — lead to the *enslavement of human beings*, disregard for their personal dignity, buying or selling or exchanging them like merchandise. Reducing persons by violence to use-value or a source of profit is a sin against their dignity as persons and their fundamental rights. Saint Paul set a Christian master right about treating his Christian slave 'no longer as a slave but . . . as a brother . . . in the Lord' (Philem 16)."[159]

101.1 In the political sphere, it must be noted that truthfulness in the relations between those governing and those governed, openness in public administration, impartiality in the service of the body politic, respect for the rights of political adversaries, safeguarding the rights of the accused against summary trials and convictions, the just and honest use of public funds, the rejection of equivocal or illicit means in order to gain, preserve or increase power at any cost — all these are principles which are primarily rooted in, and in fact derive their singular urgency from, the transcendent value of the person and the objective moral demands of the functioning of States.[160] When these principles are not observed, the very basis of political coexistence is weakened and the life of society itself is gradually jeopardized, threatened and doomed to decay (cf. Ps 14:3-4; Rev 18:2-3, 9-24). Today, when many

---

[157] *Catechism of the Catholic Church*, No. 2407.

[158] Cf. ibid., Nos. 2408-2413.

[159] Ibid., No. 2414.

[160] Cf. Post-Synodal Apostolic Exhortation *Christifideles Laici* (December 30, 1988), 42: *AAS* 81 (1989), 472-476.

countries have seen the fall of ideologies which bound politics to a totalitarian conception of the world — Marxism being the foremost of these — there is no less grave a danger that the fundamental rights of the human person will be denied and that the religious yearnings which arise in the heart of every human being will be absorbed once again into politics. This is *the risk of an alliance between democracy and ethical relativism,* which would remove any sure moral reference point from political and social life, and on a deeper level make the acknowledgment of truth impossible. Indeed, "if there is no ultimate truth to guide and direct political activity, then ideas and convictions can easily be manipulated for reasons of power. As history demonstrates, a democracy without values easily turns into open or thinly disguised totalitarianism."[161]

101.2 Thus, in every sphere of personal, family, social and political life, morality — founded upon truth and open in truth to authentic freedom — renders a primordial, indispensable and immensely valuable service not only for the individual person and his growth in the good, but also for society and its genuine development.

Grace and obedience to God's law

102.1 Even in the most difficult situations man must respect the norm of morality so that he can be obedient to God's holy commandment and consistent with his own dignity as a person. Certainly, maintaining a harmony between freedom and truth occasionally demands uncommon sacrifices, and must be won at a high price: it can even involve martyrdom. But, as universal and daily experience demonstrates, man is tempted to break that harmony: "I do not do what I want, but I do the very thing I hate. . . . I do not do the good I want, but the evil I do not want" (Rom 7:15, 19).

102.2 What is the ultimate source of this inner division of man? His history of sin begins when he no longer acknowledges the Lord as his Creator and himself wishes to be the one who determines, with complete independence, what is good and what is evil. "You will be like God, knowing good and evil" (Gen 3:5): this was the first temptation, and it is echoed in all the other temptations to which man is more easily inclined to yield as a result of the original Fall.

102.3 But temptations can be overcome, sins can be avoided, because together with the commandments the Lord gives us the possibility of keeping them: "His eyes are on those who fear him, and he knows every deed of man. He has not commanded any one to be ungodly, and he has not given anyone

---

[161] Encyclical Letter *Centesimus Annus* (May 1, 1991), 46: *AAS* 83 (1991), 850.

permission to sin" (Sir 15:19-20). Keeping God's law in particular situations can be difficult, extremely difficult, but it is never impossible. This is the constant teaching of the Church's Tradition, and was expressed by the Council of Trent: "But no one, however much justified, ought to consider himself exempt from the observance of the commandments, nor should he employ that rash statement, forbidden by the Fathers under anathema, that the commandments of God are impossible of observance by one who is justified. For God does not command the impossible, but in commanding he admonishes you to do what you can and to pray for what you cannot, and he gives his aid to enable you. His commandments are not burdensome (cf. 1 Jn 5:3); his yoke is easy and his burden light (cf. Mt 11:30)."[162]

103.1 Man always has before him the spiritual horizon of hope, thanks to the *help of divine grace* and with *the cooperation of human freedom.*

103.2 It is in the saving Cross of Jesus, in the gift of the Holy Spirit, in the sacraments which flow forth from the pierced side of the Redeemer (cf. Jn 19:34), that believers find the grace and the strength always to keep God's holy law, even amid the gravest of hardships. As Saint Andrew of Crete observes, the law itself "was enlivened by grace and made to serve it in a harmonious and fruitful combination. Each element preserved its characteristics without change or confusion. In a divine manner, he turned what could be burdensome and tyrannical into what is easy to bear and a source of freedom."[163]

103.3 *Only in the mystery of Christ's Redemption do we discover the "concrete" possibilities of man.* "It would be a very serious error to conclude . . . that the Church's teaching is essentially only an 'ideal' which must then be adapted, proportioned, graduated to the so-called concrete possibilities of man, according to a 'balancing of the goods in question.' But what are the 'concrete possibilities of man'? And of *which* man are we speaking? Of man *dominated* by lust or of man *redeemed by Christ?* This is what is at stake: the *reality* of Christ's Redemption. *Christ has redeemed us!* This means that he has given us the possibility of realizing *the entire* truth of our being; he has set our freedom free from the *domination* of concupiscence. And if redeemed man still sins, this is not due to an imperfection of Christ's redemptive act, but to man's will not to avail himself of the grace which flows from that act. God's command is of course proportioned to man's capabilities; but to the capabili-

---

[162] Session VI, Decree on Justification *Cum Hoc Tempore*, Chapter 11: *DS* 1536; cf. Canon 18: *DS* 1568. The celebrated text from Saint Augustine, which the Council cites, is found in *De Natura et Gratia*, 43, 50: *CSEL* 60, 270.

[163] *Oratio* I: *PG* 97, 805-806.

ties of the man to whom the Holy Spirit has been given; of the man who, though he has fallen into sin, can always obtain pardon and enjoy the presence of the Holy Spirit."[164]

104.1 In this context, appropriate allowance is made both for *God's mercy* toward the sinner who converts and for the *understanding of human weakness*. Such understanding never means compromising and falsifying the standard of good and evil in order to adapt it to particular circumstances. It is quite human for the sinner to acknowledge his weakness and to ask mercy for his failings; what is unacceptable is the attitude of one who makes his own weakness the criterion of the truth about the good, so that he can feel self-justified, without even the need to have recourse to God and his mercy. An attitude of this sort corrupts the morality of society as a whole, since it encourages doubt about the objectivity of the moral law in general and a rejection of the absoluteness of moral prohibitions regarding specific human acts, and it ends up by confusing all judgments about values.

104.2 Instead, we should take to heart the *message of the Gospel parable of the Pharisee and the tax collector* (cf. Lk 18:9-14). The tax collector might possibly have had some justification for the sins he committed, such as to diminish his responsibility. But his prayer does not dwell on such justifications, but rather on his own unworthiness before God's infinite holiness: "God, be merciful to me a sinner!" (Lk 18:13). The Pharisee, on the other hand, is self-justified, finding some excuse for each of his failings. Here we encounter two different attitudes of the moral conscience of man in every age. The tax collector represents a "repentant" conscience, fully aware of the frailty of its own nature and seeing in its own failings, whatever their subjective justifications, a confirmation of its need for redemption. The Pharisee represents a "self-satisfied" conscience, under the illusion that it is able to observe the law without the help of grace and convinced that it does not need mercy.

105.1 All people must take great care not to allow themselves to be tainted by the attitude of the Pharisee, which would seek to eliminate awareness of one's own limits and of one's own sin. In our own day this attitude is expressed particularly in the attempt to adapt the moral norm to one's own capacities and personal interests, and even in the rejection of the very idea of

---

[164] Address to Those Taking Part in a Course on "Responsible Parenthood" (March 1, 1984), 4: *Insegnamenti* VII/1 (1984), 583.

a norm. Accepting, on the other hand, the "disproportion" between the law and human ability (that is, the capacity of the moral forces of man left to himself) kindles the desire for grace and prepares one to receive it. "Who will deliver me from this body of death?" asks the Apostle Paul. And in an outburst of joy and gratitude he replies: "Thanks be to God through Jesus Christ our Lord!" (Rom 7:24-25).

105.2 We find the same awareness in the following prayer of Saint Ambrose of Milan: "What then is man, if you do not visit him? Remember, Lord, that you have made me as one who is weak, that you formed me from dust. How can I stand, if you do not constantly look upon me, to strengthen this clay, so that my strength may proceed from your face? *When you hide your face, all grows weak* (Ps 104:29); if you turn to look at me, woe is me! You have nothing to see in me but the stain of my crimes; there is no gain either in being abandoned or in being seen, because when we are seen, we offend you. Still, we can imagine that God does not reject those he sees, because he purifies those upon whom he gazes. Before him burns a fire capable of consuming our guilt (cf. Joel 2:3)."[165]

Morality and new evangelization

106.1 Evangelization is the most powerful and stirring challenge which the Church has been called to face from her very beginning. Indeed, this challenge is posed not so much by the social and cultural milieux which she encounters in the course of history, as by the mandate of the risen Christ, who defines the very reason for the Church's existence: "Go into all the world and preach the Gospel to the whole creation" (Mk 16:15).

106.2 At least for many peoples, however, the present time is instead marked by a formidable challenge to undertake a "new evangelization," a proclamation of the Gospel which is always new and always the bearer of new things, an evangelization which must be "new in its ardor, methods and expression."[166] Dechristianization, which weighs heavily upon entire peoples and communities once rich in faith and Christian life, involves not only the loss of faith or in any event its becoming irrelevant for everyday life, but also, and of necessity, *a decline or obscuring of the moral sense.* This comes about both as a result of a loss of awareness of the originality of Gospel morality and as a result of an eclipse of fundamental principles and ethical values themselves. Today's widespread tendencies toward subjectivism, utilitarianism and relativism appear

---

[165] *De Interpellatione David,* IV, 6, 22: *CSEL* 32/2, 283-284.
[166] Address to the Bishops of CELAM (March 9, 1983), III: *Insegnamenti* VI/1 (1983), 698.

not merely as pragmatic attitudes or patterns of behavior, but rather as approaches having a basis in theory and claiming full cultural and social legitimacy.

107.1 *Evangelization — and therefore the "new evangelization" — also involves the proclamation and presentation of morality.* Jesus himself, even as he preached the Kingdom of God and its saving love, called people to faith and conversion (cf. Mk 1:15). And when Peter, with the other Apostles, proclaimed the Resurrection of Jesus of Nazareth from the dead, he held out a new life to be lived, a "way" to be followed, for those who would be disciples of the Risen One (cf. Acts 2:37-41, 3:17-20).

107.2 Just as it does in proclaiming the truths of faith, and even more so in presenting the foundations and content of Christian morality, the new evangelization will show its authenticity and unleash all its missionary force when it is carried out through the gift not only of the word proclaimed but also of the word lived. In particular, *the life of holiness* which is resplendent in so many members of the People of God, humble and often unseen, constitutes the simplest and most attractive way to perceive at once the beauty of truth, the liberating force of God's love, and the value of unconditional fidelity to all the demands of the Lord's law, even in the most difficult situations. For this reason, the Church, as a wise teacher of morality, has always invited believers to seek and to find in the saints, and above all in the Virgin Mother of God "full of grace" and "all-holy," the model, the strength and the joy needed to live a life in accordance with God's commandments and the Beatitudes of the Gospel.

107.3 The lives of the saints, as a reflection of the goodness of God — the One who "alone is good" — constitute not only a genuine profession of faith and an incentive for sharing it with others, but also a glorification of God and his infinite holiness. The life of holiness thus brings to full expression and effectiveness the threefold and unitary *munus propheticum, sacerdotale et regale* which every Christian receives as a gift by being born again "of water and the Spirit" (Jn 3:5) in Baptism. His moral life has the value of a "spiritual worship" (Rom 12:1; cf. Phil 3:3), flowing from and nourished by that inexhaustible source of holiness and glorification of God which is found in the sacraments, especially in the Eucharist: by sharing in the sacrifice of the Cross, the Christian partakes of Christ's self-giving love and is equipped and committed to live this same charity in all his thoughts and deeds. In the moral life the Christian's royal service is also made evident and effective: with the help of grace, the more one obeys the new law of the Holy Spirit, the more one grows in the freedom to which he or she is called by the service of truth, charity and justice.

108.1 At the heart of the new evangelization and of the new moral life which it proposes and awakens by its fruits of holiness and missionary zeal, there is *the Spirit of Christ,* the principle and strength of the fruitfulness of Holy Mother Church. As Pope Paul VI reminded us: "Evangelization will never be possible without the action of the Holy Spirit."[167] The Spirit of Jesus, received by the humble and docile heart of the believer, brings about the flourishing of Christian moral life and the witness of holiness amid the great variety of vocations, gifts, responsibilities, conditions and life situations. As Novatian once pointed out — here expressing the authentic faith of the Church — it is the Holy Spirit "who confirmed the hearts and minds of the disciples, who revealed the mysteries of the Gospel, who shed upon them the light of things divine. Strengthened by his gift, they did not fear either prisons or chains for the name of the Lord; indeed they even trampled upon the powers and torments of the world, armed and strengthened by him, having in themselves the gifts which this same Spirit bestows and directs like jewels to the Church, the Bride of Christ. It is in fact he who raises up prophets in the Church, instructs teachers, guides tongues, works wonders and healings, accomplishes miracles, grants the discernment of spirits, assigns governance, inspires counsels, distributes and harmonizes every other charismatic gift. In this way he completes and perfects the Lord's Church everywhere and in all things."[168]

108.2 In the living context of this new evangelization, aimed at generating and nourishing "the faith which works through love" (cf. Gal 5:6), and in relation to the work of the Holy Spirit, we can now understand the proper place which *continuing theological reflection about the moral life* holds in the Church, the community of believers. We can likewise speak of the mission and the responsibility proper to moral theologians.

The service of moral theologians

109.1 The whole Church is called to evangelization and to the witness of a life of faith, by the fact that she has been made a sharer in the *munus propheticum* of the Lord Jesus through the gift of his Spirit. Thanks to the permanent presence of the Spirit of truth in the Church (cf. Jn 14:16-17), "the universal body of the faithful who have received the anointing of the holy one

---

[167] Apostolic Exhortation *Evangelii Nuntiandi* (December 8, 1975), 75: *AAS* 68 (1976), 64.
[168] *De Trinitate*, XXIX, 9-10: *CCL* 4, 70.

(cf. 1 Jn 2:20, 27) cannot be mistaken in belief. It displays this particular quality through a supernatural sense of the faith in the whole people when, 'from the Bishops to the last of the lay faithful,' it expresses the consensus of all in matters of faith and morals."[169]

109.2 In order to carry out her prophetic mission, the Church must constantly reawaken or "rekindle" her own life of faith (cf. 2 Tim 1:6), particularly through an ever deeper reflection, under the guidance of the Holy Spirit, upon the content of faith itself. *The "vocation" of the theologian in the Church* is specifically at the service of this "believing effort to understand the faith." As the Instruction *Donum Veritatis* teaches: "Among the vocations awakened by the Spirit in the Church is that of the theologian. His role is to pursue in a particular way an ever deeper understanding of the word of God found in the inspired Scriptures and handed on by the living Tradition of the Church. He does this in communion with the Magisterium, which has been charged with the responsibility of preserving the deposit of faith. By its nature, faith appeals to reason because it reveals to man the truth of his destiny and the way to attain it. Revealed truth, to be sure, surpasses our telling. All our concepts fall short of its ultimately unfathomable grandeur (cf. Eph 3:19). Nonetheless, revealed truth beckons reason — God's gift fashioned for the assimilation of truth — to enter into its light and thereby come to understand in a certain measure what it has believed. Theological science responds to the invitation of truth as it seeks to understand the faith. It thereby aids the People of God in fulfilling the Apostle's command (cf. 1 Pet 3:15) to give an accounting for their hope to those who ask it."[170]

109.3 It is fundamental for defining the very identity of theology, and consequently for theology to carry out its proper mission, to recognize its *profound and vital connection with the Church, her mystery, her life and her mission:* "Theology is an ecclesial science because it grows in the Church and works on the Church. . . . It is a service to the Church and therefore ought to feel itself actively involved in the mission of the Church, particularly in its prophetic mission."[171] By its very nature and procedures, authentic theology can flourish and develop only through a committed and responsible participa-

---

[169] Second Vatican Ecumenical Council, Dogmatic Constitution on the Church *Lumen Gentium,* 12.

[170] Congregation for the Doctrine of the Faith, Instruction on the Ecclesial Vocation of the Theologian *Donum Veritatis* (May 24, 1990), 6: *AAS* 82 (1990), 1552.

[171] Address to the Professors and Students of the Pontifical Gregorian University (December 15, 1979), 6: *Insegnamenti* II/2 (1979), 1424.

tion in and "belonging" to the Church as a "community of faith." In turn, the fruits of theological research and deeper insight become a source of enrichment for the Church and her life of faith.

110.1 All that has been said about theology in general can and must also be said for *moral theology,* seen in its specific nature as a scientific reflection on the *Gospel as the gift and commandment of new life,* a reflection on the life which "professes the truth in love" (cf. Eph 4:15) and on the Church's life of holiness, in which there shines forth the truth about the good brought to its perfection. The Church's Magisterium intervenes not only in the sphere of faith, but also, and inseparably so, in the sphere of morals. It has the task of "discerning, by means of judgments normative for the consciences of believers, those acts which in themselves conform to the demands of faith and foster their expression in life and those which, on the contrary, because intrinsically evil, are incompatible with such demands."[172] In proclaiming the commandments of God and the charity of Christ, the Church's Magisterium also teaches the faithful specific particular precepts and requires that they consider them in conscience as morally binding. In addition, the Magisterium carries out an important work of vigilance, warning the faithful of the presence of possible errors, even merely implicit ones, when their consciences fail to acknowledge the correctness and the truth of the moral norms, which the Magisterium teaches.

110.2 This is the point at which to consider the specific task of all those who by mandate of their legitimate Pastors teach moral theology in seminaries and faculties of theology. They have the grave duty to instruct the faithful — especially future Pastors — about all those commandments and practical norms authoritatively declared by the Church.[173] While recognizing the possible limitations of the human arguments employed by the Magisterium, moral theologians are called to develop a deeper understanding of the reasons underlying its teachings and to expound the validity and obligatory nature of the precepts it proposes, demonstrating their connection with one another and their relation with man's ultimate end.[174] Moral theologians are to set forth the Church's teaching and to give, in the exercise of their ministry, the example of a loyal assent, both internal and external, to the Magisterium's teaching in

---

[172] Congregation for the Doctrine of the Faith, Instruction on the Ecclesial Vocation of the Theologian *Donum Veritatis* (May 24, 1990), 16: *AAS* 82 (1990), 1557.

[173] Cf. *Code of Canon Law,* Canons 252 §1, 659 §3.

[174] Cf. First Vatican Ecumenical Council, Dogmatic Constitution on the Catholic Faith *Dei Filius,* Chapter 4: *DS* 3016.

the areas of both dogma and morality.[175] Working together in cooperation with the hierarchical Magisterium, theologians will be deeply concerned to clarify ever more fully the biblical foundations, the ethical significance and the anthropological concerns which underlie the moral doctrine and the vision of man set forth by the Church.

111.1 The service which moral theologians are called to provide at the present time is of the utmost importance, not only for the Church's life and mission, but also for human society and culture. Moral theologians have the task, in close and vital connection with biblical and dogmatic theology, to highlight through their scientific reflection "that dynamic aspect which will elicit the response that man must give to the divine call which comes in the process of his growth in love, within a community of salvation. In this way, moral theology will acquire an inner spiritual dimension in response to the need to develop fully the *imago Dei* present in man, and in response to the laws of spiritual development described by Christian ascetical and mystical theology."[176]

111.2 Certainly moral theology and its teaching are meeting with particular difficulty today. Because the Church's morality necessarily involves a *normative* dimension, moral theology cannot be reduced to a body of knowledge worked out purely in the context of the so-called *behavioral sciences*. The latter are concerned with the phenomenon of morality as a historical and social fact; moral theology, however, while needing to make use of the behavioral and natural sciences, does not rely on the results of formal empirical observation or phenomenological understanding alone. Indeed, the relevance of the behavioral sciences for moral theology must always be measured against the primordial question: *What is good or evil? What must be done to have eternal life?*

112.1 The moral theologian must therefore exercise careful discernment in the context of today's prevalently scientific and technical culture, exposed as it is to the dangers of relativism, pragmatism and positivism. From the theological viewpoint, moral principles are not dependent upon the historical moment in which they are discovered. Moreover, the fact that some believers act without following the teachings of the Magisterium, or erroneously con-

---

[175] Cf. Paul VI, Encyclical Letter *Humanae Vitae* (July 25, 1968), 28: *AAS* 60 (1968), 501.

[176] Sacred Congregation for Catholic Education, *The Theological Formation of Future Priests* (February 22, 1976), 100. See Nos. 95-101, which present the prospects and conditions for a fruitful renewal of moral theology.

sider as morally correct a kind of behavior declared by their Pastors as contrary to the law of God, cannot be a valid argument for rejecting the truth of the moral norms taught by the Church. The affirmation of moral principles is not within the competence of formal empirical methods. While not denying the validity of such methods, but at the same time not restricting its viewpoint to them, moral theology, faithful to the supernatural sense of the faith, takes into account first and foremost *the spiritual dimension of the human heart and its vocation to divine love.*

112.2 In fact, while the behavioral sciences, like all experimental sciences, develop an empirical and statistical concept of "normality," faith teaches that this normality itself bears the traces of a fall from man's original situation — in other words, it is affected by sin. Only Christian faith points out to man the way to return to "the beginning" (cf. Mt 19:8), a way which is often quite different from that of empirical normality. Hence the behavioral sciences, despite the great value of the information which they provide, cannot be considered decisive indications of moral norms. It is the Gospel which reveals the full truth about man and his moral journey, and thus enlightens and admonishes sinners; it proclaims to them God's mercy, which is constantly at work to preserve them both from despair at their inability fully to know and keep God's law and from the presumption that they can be saved without merit. God also reminds sinners of the joy of forgiveness, which alone grants the strength to see in the moral law a liberating truth, a grace-filled source of hope, a path of life.

113.1 Teaching moral doctrine involves the conscious acceptance of these intellectual, spiritual and pastoral responsibilities. Moral theologians, who have accepted the charge of teaching the Church's doctrine, thus have a grave duty to train the faithful to make this moral discernment, to be committed to the true good and to have confident recourse to God's grace.

113.2 While exchanges and conflicts of opinion may constitute normal expressions of public life in a representative democracy, moral teaching certainly cannot depend simply upon respect for a process: indeed, it is in no way established by following the rules and deliberative procedures typical of a democracy. *Dissent,* in the form of carefully orchestrated protests and polemics carried on in the media, *is opposed to ecclesial communion and to a correct understanding of the hierarchical constitution of the People of God.* Opposition to the teaching of the Church's Pastors cannot be seen as a legitimate expression either of Christian freedom or of the diversity of the Spirit's gifts. When this happens, the Church's Pastors have the duty to act in conformity with their apostolic mission, insisting that *the right of the faithful* to receive Catholic doctrine in its purity and integrity must always be respected. "Never forgetting that he too is a member of the People of God, the theologian must be respectful of them, and be committed to offering them a teaching which in no way does harm to the doctrine of the faith."[177]

Our own responsibilities as Pastors

114.1 As the Second Vatican Council reminds us, responsibility for the faith and the life of faith of the People of God is particularly incumbent upon the Church's Pastors: "Among the principal tasks of Bishops the preaching of the Gospel is preeminent. For the Bishops are the heralds of the faith who bring new disciples to Christ. They are authentic teachers, that is, teachers endowed with the authority of Christ, who preach to the people entrusted to them the faith to be believed and put into practice; they illustrate this faith in the light of the Holy Spirit, drawing out of the treasury of revelation things old and new (cf. Mt 13:52); they make it bear fruit and they vigilantly ward off errors that are threatening their flock (cf. 2 Tim 4:1-4)."[178]

114.2 It is our common duty, and even before that our common grace, as Pastors and Bishops of the Church, to teach the faithful the things which lead them to God, just as the Lord Jesus did with the young man in the Gospel. Replying to the question: "What good must I do to have eternal life?" Jesus referred the young man to God, the Lord of creation and of the Covenant. He reminded him of the moral commandments already revealed in the Old Testament and he indicated their spirit and deepest meaning by inviting the young man to follow him in poverty, humility and love: "Come, follow me!" The truth of this teaching was sealed on the Cross in the blood of Christ: in the Holy Spirit, it has become the new law of the Church and of every Christian.

114.3 This "answer" to the question about morality has been entrusted by Jesus Christ in a particular way to us, the Pastors of the Church; we have been called to make it the object of our preaching, in the fulfillment of our *munus propheticum.* At the same time, our responsibility as Pastors with regard to Christian moral teaching must also be exercised as part of the *munus sacerdotale:* this happens when we dispense to the faithful the gifts of grace and sanctification as an effective means for obeying God's holy law, and when with our constant and confident prayers we support believers in their efforts

---

[177] Congregation for the Doctrine of the Faith, Instruction on the Ecclesial Vocation of the Theologian *Donum Veritatis* (May 24, 1990), 11: *AAS* 82 (1990), 1554; cf. ibid., in particular Nos. 32-39, devoted to the problem of dissent: loc. cit., 1562-1568.

[178] Dogmatic Constitution on the Church *Lumen Gentium*, 25.

to be faithful to the demands of the faith and to live in accordance with the Gospel (cf. Col 1:9-12). Especially today, Christian moral teaching must be one of the chief areas in which we exercise our pastoral vigilance, in carrying out our *munus regale.*

115.1 This is the first time, in fact, that the Magisterium of the Church has set forth in detail the fundamental elements of this teaching, and presented the principles for the pastoral discernment necessary in practical and cultural situations which are complex and even crucial.

115.2 In the light of revelation and of the Church's constant teaching, especially that of the Second Vatican Council, I have briefly recalled the essential characteristics of freedom, as well as the fundamental values connected with the dignity of the person and the truth of his acts, so as to be able to discern in obedience to the moral law a grace and a sign of our adoption in the one Son (cf. Eph 1:4-6). Specifically, this Encyclical has evaluated certain trends in moral theology today. I now pass this evaluation on to you, in obedience to the word of the Lord who entrusted to Peter the task of strengthening his brethren (cf. Lk 22:32), in order to clarify and aid our common discernment.

115.3 Each of us knows how important is the teaching which represents the central theme of this Encyclical and which is today being restated with the authority of the Successor of Peter. Each of us can see the seriousness of what is involved, not only for individuals but also for the whole of society, with the *reaffirmation of the universality and immutability of the moral commandments,* particularly those which prohibit always and without exception *intrinsically evil acts.*

115.4 In acknowledging these commandments, Christian hearts and our pastoral charity listen to the call of the One who "first loved us" (1 Jn 4:19). God asks us to be holy as he is holy (cf. Lev 19:2), to be — in Christ — perfect as he is perfect (cf. Mt 5:48). The unwavering demands of that commandment are based upon God's infinitely merciful love (cf. Lk 6:36), and the purpose of that commandment is to lead us, by the grace of Christ, on the path of that fullness of life proper to the children of God.

116.1 We have the duty, as Bishops, to *be vigilant that the word of God is faithfully taught.* My Brothers in the Episcopate, it is part of our pastoral ministry to see to it that this moral teaching is faithfully handed down and to have recourse to appropriate measures to ensure that the faithful are guarded from every doctrine and theory contrary to it. In carrying out this task we are all assisted by theologians; even so, theological opinions constitute neither the rule nor the norm of our teaching. Its authority is derived, by the assistance of the Holy Spirit and in communion *cum Petro et sub Petro,* from our fidelity to the Catholic faith which comes from the Apostles. As Bishops, we have the "grave obligation" to be *personally* vigilant that the "sound doctrine" (1 Tim 1:10) of faith and morals is taught in our Dioceses.

116.2 A particular responsibility is incumbent upon Bishops with regard to *Catholic institutions.* Whether these are agencies for the pastoral care of the family or for social work, or institutions dedicated to teaching or health care, Bishops can canonically erect and recognize these structures and delegate certain responsibilities to them. Nevertheless, Bishops are never relieved of their own personal obligations. It falls to them, in communion with the Holy See, both to grant the title "Catholic" to Church-related schools,[179] universities,[180] health-care facilities and counseling services, and, in cases of a serious failure to live up to that title, to take it away.

117.1 In the heart of every Christian, in the inmost depths of each person, there is always an echo of the question which the young man in the Gospel once asked Jesus: "Teacher, what good must I do to have eternal life?" (Mt 19:16). Everyone, however, needs to address this question to the "Good Teacher," since he is the only one who can answer in the fullness of truth, in all situations, in the most varied of circumstances. And when Christians ask him the question which rises from their conscience, the Lord replies in the words of the New Covenant which have been entrusted to his Church. As the Apostle Paul said of himself, we have been sent "to preach the Gospel, and not with eloquent wisdom, lest the Cross of Christ be emptied of its power" (1 Cor 1.17). The Church's answer to man's question contains the wisdom and power of Christ crucified, the Truth which gives of itself.

117.2 *When people ask the Church the questions raised by their consciences,* when the faithful in the Church turn to their Bishops and Pastors, *the Church's reply contains the voice of Jesus Christ, the voice of the truth about good and evil.* In the words spoken by the Church there resounds, in people's inmost being, the voice of God who "alone is good" (cf. Mt 19:17), who alone "is love" (1 Jn 4:8, 16).

117.3 Through the *anointing of the Spirit* this gentle but challenging word becomes light and life for man. Again the Apostle Paul invites us to have confidence, because "our competence is from God, who has made us compe-

---

[179] Cf. *Code of Canon Law,* Canon 803 §3.
[180] Cf. *Code of Canon Law,* Canon 808.

tent to be ministers of a new covenant, not in a written code but in the Spirit. . . . The Lord is the Spirit, and where the Spirit of the Lord is, there is freedom. And all of us, with unveiled faces, reflecting the glory of the Lord, are being changed into his likeness from one degree of glory to another; for this comes from the Lord, the Spirit" (2 Cor 3:5-6, 17-18).

Conclusion

Mary, Mother of Mercy

118.1 At the end of these considerations, let us entrust ourselves, the sufferings and the joys of our life, the moral life of believers and people of good will, and the research of moralists, to Mary, Mother of God and Mother of Mercy.

118.2 Mary is Mother of Mercy because her Son, Jesus Christ, was sent by the Father as the revelation of God's mercy (cf. Jn 3:16-18). Christ came not to condemn but to forgive, to show mercy (cf. Mt 9:13). And the greatest mercy of all is found in his being in our midst and calling us to meet him and to confess with Peter, that he is "the Son of the living God" (Mt 16:16). No human sin can erase the mercy of God, or prevent him from unleashing all his triumphant power, if we only call upon him. Indeed, sin itself makes even more radiant the love of the Father who, in order to ransom a slave, sacrificed his Son:[181] his mercy toward us is Redemption. This mercy reaches its fullness in the gift of the Spirit who bestows new life and demands that it be lived. No matter how many and great the obstacles put in his way by human frailty and sin, the Spirit, who renews the face of the earth (cf. Ps 104:30), makes possible the miracle of the perfect accomplishment of the good. This renewal, which gives the ability to do what is good, noble, beautiful, pleasing to God and in conformity with his will, is in some way the flowering of the gift of mercy, which offers liberation from the slavery of evil and gives the strength to sin no more. Through the gift of new life, Jesus makes us sharers in his love and leads us to the Father in the Spirit.

119 Such is the consoling certainty of Christian faith, the source of its profound humanity and *extraordinary simplicity*. At times, in the discussions about new and complex moral problems, it can seem that Christian morality is in itself too demanding, difficult to understand and almost impossible to

---

[181] "O inaestimabilis dilectio caritatis: ut servum redimeres, Filium tradidisti!": *Missale Romanum, In Resurrectione Domini, Praeconium Paschale.*

practice. This is untrue, since Christian morality consists, in the simplicity of the Gospel, in *following Jesus Christ,* in abandoning oneself to him, in letting oneself be transformed by his grace and renewed by his mercy, gifts which come to us in the living communion of his Church. Saint Augustine reminds us that "he who would live has a place to live, and has everything needed to live. Let him draw near, let him believe, let him become part of the body, that he may have life. Let him not shrink from the unity of the members."[182] By the light of the Holy Spirit, the living essence of Christian morality can be understood by everyone, even the least learned, but particularly those who are able to preserve an "undivided heart" (Ps 86:11). On the other hand, this evangelical simplicity does not exempt one from facing reality in its complexity; rather it can lead to a more genuine understanding of reality, inasmuch as following Christ will gradually bring out the distinctive character of authentic Christian morality, while providing the vital energy needed to carry it out. It is the task of the Church's Magisterium to see that the dynamic process of following Christ develops in an organic manner, without the falsification or obscuring of its moral demands, with all their consequences. The one who loves Christ keeps his commandments (cf. Jn 14:15).

120.1 Mary is also Mother of Mercy because it is to her that Jesus entrusts his Church and all humanity. At the foot of the Cross, when she accepts John as her son, when she asks, together with Christ, forgiveness from the Father for those who do not know what they do (cf. Lk 23:34), Mary experiences, in perfect docility to the Spirit, the richness and the universality of God's love, which opens her heart and enables it to embrace the entire human race. Thus Mary becomes Mother of each and every one of us, the Mother who obtains for us divine mercy.

120.2 Mary is the radiant sign and inviting model of the moral life. As Saint Ambrose put it, "The life of this one person can serve as a model for everyone"[183] and while speaking specifically to virgins but within a context open to all, he affirmed: "The first stimulus to learning is the nobility of the teacher. Who can be more noble than the Mother of God? Who can be more glorious than the one chosen by Glory itself?"[184] Mary lived and exercised her freedom precisely by giving herself to God and accepting God's gift within herself. Until the time of his birth, she sheltered in her womb the Son of God who became man; she raised him and enabled him to grow, and she accompa-

---

[182] *In Iohannis Evangelium Tractatus,* 26, 13: *CCL* 36, 266.

[183] *De Virginibus,* Book II, Chapter II, 15: *PL* 16, 222.

[184] Ibid., Book II, Chapter II, 7: *PL* 16, 220.

nied him in that supreme act of freedom which is the complete sacrifice of his own life. By the gift of herself, Mary entered fully into the plan of God who gives himself to the world. By accepting and pondering in her heart events which she did not always understand (cf. Lk 2:19), she became the model of all those who hear the word of God and keep it (cf. Lk 11:28), and merited the title of "Seat of Wisdom." This Wisdom is Jesus Christ himself, the Eternal Word of God, who perfectly reveals and accomplishes the will of the Father (cf. Heb 10:5-10). Mary invites everyone to accept this Wisdom. To us too she addresses the command she gave to the servants at Cana in Galilee during the marriage feast: "Do whatever he tells you" (Jn 2:5).

120.3 Mary shares our human condition, but in complete openness to the grace of God. Not having known sin, she is able to have compassion on every kind of weakness. She understands sinful man and loves him with a Mother's love. Precisely for this reason she is on the side of truth and shares the Church's burden in recalling always and to everyone the demands of morality. Nor does she permit sinful man to be deceived by those who claim to love him by justifying his sin, for she knows that the sacrifice of Christ her Son would thus be emptied of its power. No absolution offered by beguiling doctrines, even in the areas of philosophy and theology, can make man truly happy: only the Cross and the glory of the risen Christ can grant peace to his conscience and salvation to his life.

120.4 O Mary,
Mother of Mercy,
watch over all people,
that the Cross of Christ
may not be emptied of its power,
that man may not stray
from the path of the good
or become blind to sin,
but may put his hope ever more fully in God
who is "rich in mercy" (Eph 2:4).
May he carry out the good works
prepared by God beforehand (cf. Eph 2:10)
and so live completely
"for the praise of his glory" (Eph 1:12).

Given in Rome, at Saint Peter's, on August 6, Feast of the Transfiguration of the Lord, in the year 1993, the fifteenth of my Pontificate.

Evangelium Vitae

Editor's Introduction

"The *Gospel of life* is at the heart of Jesus' message" (§1.1). With these words Pope John Paul II begins his eleventh encyclical, *Evangelium Vitae*, published on March 25, 1995.[1] He aptly chose the feast of the Annunciation, which celebrates Mary's welcoming of the Son of God who took flesh in her womb, to issue a document dedicated to the value and inviolability of human life. By taking up the cause of the "great multitude of weak and defenseless human beings" (§5.4), especially unborn children and those at the end of life, the Pope continues the defense of human dignity dealt with in his three social encyclicals. *Evangelium Vitae* is an anguished and vigorous response to *"scientifically and systematically programmed threats"* against life (§17.2), assaults which have repercussions on Church teaching, touching upon "the core of her faith in the redemptive Incarnation of the Son of God" (§3.1).

For John Paul, the cause of life is the cause of the Gospel entrusted to the Church, which is duty-bound to raise her voice in the defense of life. His encyclical is a "pressing appeal addressed to each and every person, in the name of God: *respect, protect, love and serve life, every human life!*" (§5.5).

Preparations for the encyclical began in April 1991, when the Pope called a special meeting in Rome of the College of Cardinals to discuss current threats to human life. After their deliberations, the cardinals asked him "to reaffirm with the authority of the Successor of Peter the value of human life and its inviolability" (§5.1). As a first response to their request, the Pope wrote a personal letter to every bishop, seeking contributions to the planned document. They replied with valuable suggestions, and he incorporated many of their proposals into the encyclical. *Evangelium Vitae*, then, is the fruit of genuine episcopal collegiality. By taking an active part in its preparation, the bishops "bore witness to their unanimous desire to share in the doctrinal and pastoral mission of the Church with regard to the *Gospel of life*" (§5.2).

Unlike *Veritatis Splendor*, which was directed primarily to bishops, John Paul intends *Evangelium Vitae* to be read also by the lay faithful, indeed by all people of good will. Concern for the sacredness of human life is not just a

[1] *Acta Apostolicae Sedis*, 87 (1995), 401-522.

matter for Catholics. "The value at stake," writes the Pope, "is one which every human being can grasp by the light of reason" (§101.2). The essential truths of the Gospel of life "are written in the heart of every man and woman," echoing in every human conscience "from the time of creation itself" (§29.3). He insists that anyone who is sincerely open to truth and goodness can discover "the sacred value of human life from its very beginning until its end, and can affirm the right of every human being to have this primary good respected to the highest degree" (§2.2).

The encyclical's style is typically Wojtylan. It intersperses rigorous analysis with prayers and exhortations. As can be seen from the more than three hundred biblical quotations and references, Scripture accompanies the Pope's presentation from start to finish, giving *Evangelium Vitae* an inspirational tone and familiar style. He also relies heavily on the Church Fathers. The eighteen patristic quotations that appear in the encyclical reinforce the truths that God is the origin of life, that human beings share in divine life, and that Jesus gave his life so that others might live. As is customary, John Paul frequently cites the documents of the Second Vatican Council — here, more than twenty-five times. He also makes use of the *Catechism of the Catholic Church*, citing it on ten occasions.

Of particular significance in *Evangelium Vitae* are the Pope's three authoritative doctrinal pronouncements: on the direct and voluntary killing of innocent human life (cf. §57.4), on abortion (cf. §62.3), and on euthanasia (cf. §65.3). In each of these formal statements John Paul recalls, through his ordinary magisterium, that a specific proposition is taught infallibly by the ordinary and universal Magisterium of the College of Bishops in communion with the Successor of Peter. He does not, therefore, call upon the charism which belongs to the Petrine ministry to teach infallibly, as this was defined at the First Vatican Council (1870). Rather, the Pope "confirms" or "declares" (as in the case of abortion) a doctrine already taught by the bishops as belonging to the Catholic faith. Thus, there is nothing "new" in the Pope's affirmations, but merely the reiteration of teaching about which a consensus exists in the Episcopal College.

Summary

After its introduction (§§1-6), the 48,000 word encyclical unfolds in four chapters. In chapter one, "Present-Day Threats to Human Life" (§§7-28), the Pope analyzes the lights and the shadows of the contemporary situation, concentrating on the threats which are signs of a "culture of death." In chapter two, "The Christian Message concerning Life" (§§29-51), he reflects meditatively on the biblical message of life as a divine gift. Chapter three, "God's Holy Law" (§§52-77), discusses the commandment, "You shall not kill," and applies it to the unprecedented ways in which life is being imperiled today. Besides authoritatively confirming the Church's teaching on innocent human life, abortion, and euthanasia, this chapter also examines the relation between moral and civil law. Chapter four, "For a New Culture of Human Life" (§§78-101), launches the challenge of building a civilization at the service of life, an enormous effort involving all sectors of the Church and society. In the conclusion (§§102-105), the Pope invokes Mary as the model of how life should be welcomed and cared for.

The culture of death

Chapter one of *Evangelium Vitae* soberly describes the dark shadows cast over today's world by threats to life. These attacks, both more serious and more numerous than in the past, entail a "*war of the powerful against the weak . . .* [a] *'conspiracy against life'* " (§12, cf. §17.2). According to John Paul, "we are facing an enormous and dramatic clash between good and evil, death and life, the 'culture of death' and the 'culture of life' " (§28.1, cf. §§50.2, 104.3). At times, it even appears as if the forces of death have the upper hand. Tragically, the biblical story of Cain's murder of Abel (cf. Gen 4:2-16) is "a page rewritten daily, with inexorable and degrading frequency, in the book of human history" (§7.3). This book contains pages which recount the unjust distribution of resources among peoples and social classes, the misery of untold millions, fratricidal wars, trading in arms, drug trafficking, reckless tampering with the world's ecological balance, and sexual risk-taking.

In addition to these perils, John Paul notes grave threats to human life at its very beginning. First, enormous sums of money are now being spent to fund research and promote drugs that make it possible to kill unborn children. Second, babies born with serious handicaps or diseases are sometimes denied the most basic care in order to hasten their death, a situation which marks the return to "a state of barbarism which one hoped had been left behind forever" (§14.3). Third, techniques of artificial procreation have a high rate of failure, thus exposing many embryos to the risk of death. Moreover, these methods produce "spare embryos" that are frequently either destroyed or used for research. Under the cover of scientific or medical progress, life is treated as if it were "simple 'biological material' to be freely disposed of" (§14.1).

Today the incurably sick and the dying are also exposed to serious risks. More and more people are succumbing to the temptation "*to resolve the problem of suffering by eliminating it at the root*, by hastening death so that it occurs at the moment considered most suitable" (§15.1). In some nations, causing the death of the severely handicapped or terminally ill is, if not legalized, at least benignly tolerated.

Biblical teaching on life

Chapter two of *Evangelium Vitae* describes the scriptural message concerning the goodness of human life which comes from God as his gift and is destined for fulfillment in communion with him. "*The Gospel of life* is something concrete and personal," writes the Pope, "for it consists in the proclamation of *the very person of Jesus*" (§29.2). Divine revelation makes known "*the complete truth* concerning the value of human life" (§29.3). This disclosure begins in the Old Testament and is brought to perfection in the New Testament.

Through its experience of God's gentle and intense love, Israel gradually came to appreciate that "life is always a good" (§34.1). In the Decalogue, God expressly reveals the truth about the sacred value of life. At the center of the Covenant is the commandment "You shall not kill" (Ex 20:13). This negative precept is "the beginning and the first necessary stage of the journey toward freedom" (§75.2). As well as prohibiting murder, the fifth commandment forbids, as Israel's later legislation makes clear, any personal injury inflicted on another person. The Law's high regard for the physical life of each individual reaches its summit in the Old Testament precept "You shall love your neighbor as yourself" (Lev 19:18).

For the Pope, the incomparable value of every person's life is forcefully confirmed by the very fact of the Incarnation. In becoming man, the Son receives life from the Father and shares this life with his followers, giving their existence an unsurpassable value. Now his disciples know for sure that their lives are "a gift carefully guarded in the hands of the Father" (§32.2). Through his teaching, Christ vigorously confirms the commandment "You shall not kill." But he also expands its scope. In the Sermon on the Mount, Jesus demands from his disciples a respect for life more exacting than what was previously known (cf. Mt 5:21-22). The profound meaning of the fifth commandment emerges in its full clarity as the "*requirement to show reverence and love for every person and the life of every person*" (§41.4).

In addition to preaching about life, Christ proclaims its value by making a total gift of his own life for the sake of others. Through his death, "*Jesus reveals all the splendor and value of life*" (§33.2); the Cross is "the fulfillment and the complete revelation of the whole Gospel of life" (§50.1). By offering himself at Calvary, Jesus becomes the source of new life for everyone. The

Redemption therefore confirms *"how precious man is in God's eyes and how priceless the value of his life"* (§25.3).

Innocent human life

Chapter three presents the doctrinal core of *Evangelium Vitae*. Here John Paul confronts the challenge posed by the "progressive weakening in individual consciences and in society of the sense of the absolute and grave moral illicitness of the direct taking of all innocent human life, especially at its beginning and at its end" (§57.3).

The Pope begins by reaffirming a traditional moral principle: "The commandment 'You shall not kill' has absolute value when it refers to the *innocent person*" (§57.1). While the right to life is always precious, he mentions two instances when it is not absolute. First, he repeats the Church's common teaching on the right to legitimate self-defense, a right based on "the intrinsic value of life and the duty to love oneself no less than others" (§55.1). Second, he allows for the possibility of morally legitimate capital punishment. But John Paul foresees extremely few instances when capital punishment can in fact be justified: "Today . . . as a result of steady improvements in the organization of the penal system, such cases are very rare, if not practically non-existent" (§56.2).

Because of the gravity of the present-day attacks on life, the Pope authoritatively reasserts Catholic doctrine on the inviolability of innocent human life: *"I confirm that the direct and voluntary killing of an innocent human being is always gravely immoral"* (§57.4). This teaching, he continues, is "based upon that unwritten law which man, in the light of reason, finds in his own heart (cf. Rom 2:14-15), is reaffirmed by Sacred Scripture, transmitted by the Tradition of the Church and taught by the ordinary and universal Magisterium" (§57.4). Even if done with the intention of helping another, the killing of an innocent human being is always "an absolutely unacceptable act" (§63.2).

Abortion

Procured abortion is the deliberate and direct killing of a human being, by whatever means it is carried out, at any time between conception and birth. It includes the killing of human embryos "produced" for medical experiments or for tissue used to treat certain diseases. Abortion is a "particularly serious and deplorable" crime (§58.1).

All those who directly or indirectly influence a woman to have an abortion bear moral responsibility for the deed. The child's father is to blame if he exerts pressure on the mother to have an abortion or leaves her to face the pregnancy alone. Similarly, guilt for the sin can extend to other family members and friends: to all those who subject the mother "to such strong pressure that she feels psychologically forced to have an abortion" (§59.1). Doctors and medical personnel are likewise guilty, if "they place at the service of death skills which were acquired for promoting life" (§59.1). Complicity in the evil of abortion also involves legislators, international organizations, and those who in any way encourage sexual permissiveness, a lack of esteem for motherhood, or systematic campaigns for the legalization and spread of abortion.

Evangelium Vitae recognizes that Sacred Scripture contains "no direct and explicit calls to protect human life at its very beginning, specifically life not yet born" (§44.1). But the encyclical also points out that the mere possibility of threatening unborn life is "completely foreign to the religious and cultural way of thinking of the People of God" (§44.1). Moreover, many scriptural passages refer with awe and love to the conception, growth, and birth of a child. The Bible affirms that *"the life of every individual, from its very beginning, is part of God's plan"* (§44.3): "Before I formed you in the womb I knew you, and before you were born I consecrated you" (Jer 1:15).

Given the contemporary moral climate, the Pope believes that the Church's teaching on abortion must be authoritatively restated. Once again invoking "the authority which Christ conferred upon Peter and his Successors, in communion with the Bishops," John Paul writes: *"I declare that direct abortion, that is, abortion willed as an end or as a means, always constitutes a grave moral disorder,* since it is the deliberate killing of an innocent human being" (§62.3). Procured abortion is invariably an intrinsically evil act which can never be justified.

Since the Pope also wants to persuade men and women of good will who do not accept Church authority that abortion is evil, he answers two arguments which they routinely put forward to justify it. First, some argue that in cases such as rape and incest the fetus can be considered as an "unjust aggressor." Because the unborn child is conceived by an act of violence, they maintain that it is not "innocent." Abortion could then be allowed as a form of legitimate self-defense on the mother's part. John Paul writes, however, that "no one more absolutely *innocent* could be imagined" (§58.3). Despite the tragic circumstances, an unborn child is never an aggressor, but always an innocent human being with the inviolable right to life.

Second, others defend abortion on the grounds that the embryo, at least for the first few weeks, does not yet enjoy the rights of a human person. To justify this position they sometimes invoke medieval theories on "ensoulment," which was commonly held to occur a few weeks after conception, depending on the child's sex. Consequently, in their view, it is morally permissible to terminate the pregnancy prior to ensoulment. The Pope, however, insists that the fetus must be treated as a human person from the moment of conception. To defend his position, he draws on an established tenet of modern biology: from the time that the ovum is fertilized, a distinct human life exists which is separate from that of the mother. For this reason, "the Church has always taught and continues to teach that the result of human procreation, from the first moment of its existence, must be guaranteed that unconditional respect which is morally due to the human being" (§60.2). An "individual" conceived by his or her mother is always a "person" with the absolute right to life.

Euthanasia

After treating abortion, John Paul turns his attention to the deliberate taking of life in its final stages. He defines euthanasia as "an action or omission which of itself and by intention causes death, with the purpose of eliminating all suffering" (§65.1). Like abortion, euthanasia can have accomplices. Anyone who shares the intention of a person who chooses to end his life or aids him in bringing it about is guilty of euthanasia.

The Pope carefully points out, however, that a sick person's decision to forgo extraordinary medical treatment is different from euthanasia. When death is clearly imminent and inevitable, there is no moral obligation to resort to "aggressive medical treatment." Procedures "which no longer correspond to the real situation of the patient, either because they are by now disproportionate to any expected results or because they impose an excessive burden on the patient and his family," need not be undergone (§65.2). "To forgo extraordinary or disproportionate means is not," John Paul writes, "the equivalent of suicide or euthanasia; it rather expresses acceptance of the human condition in the face of death" (§65.2).

Depending on the circumstances, euthanasia involves the moral evil of either suicide or murder. When individuals will to cause their own death, this choice entails the malice of suicide. Taking one's own life is a gravely immoral act: "It involves the rejection of love of self and the renunciation of the obligation of justice and charity toward one's neighbor, toward the communities to which one belongs, and toward society as a whole" (§66.1). Assisted suicide may be motivated by a concern to alleviate another's suffering, but John Paul refers to this complicity in causing death as a *false mercy,* and indeed a disturbing 'perversion' of mercy" (§66.2). True compassion leads to sharing pain, not killing someone whose suffering seems to be unbearable.

Euthanasia is even more evil when it takes the form of murder. This occurs when family members, medical personnel, or State authorities cause the death of a person who has neither requested it nor consented to it. A particularly nefarious form of euthanasia is that practiced "in order to increase the availability of organs for transplants . . . without respecting objective and adequate criteria which verify the death of the donor" (§15.3). When euthanasia entails murder, the Pope sees the temptation of Eden reenacted in modern dress: individuals or institutions claim the right to decide who should live and who should die. This arrogance, says John Paul, is "the height of arbitrariness and injustice" (§66.3).

In chapter two, the Pope considers the biblical foundations for the Church's teaching on euthanasia. The Old Testament does not explicitly condemn attempts to end the life of the sick or the aged. There is no need for it to do so, since "the cultural and religious context of the Bible is in no way touched by such temptations" (§46.1). While the New Testament fails to mention euthanasia by name, it teaches that no one "can arbitrarily choose whether to live or die; the absolute master of such a decision is the Creator alone" (§47.3).

Unfortunately, large segments of contemporary society fail to show the reverence for life that emerges from the biblical tradition. *Evangelium Vitae* gives three reasons why the cultural climate in many parts of the world increasingly favors euthanasia. First, society rejects suffering as an evil "always and in every way to be avoided" (§23.2). When its avoidance is impossible, "then life appears to have lost all meaning and the temptation grows in man to claim the right to suppress it" (§23.2). Insofar as people value life only to the extent that it can bring pleasure, the door is open to "mercy killing." Second, when efficient production and consumption are society's guiding principles, then it seems that "a hopelessly impaired life no longer has any value" (§64.3). Especially in prosperous countries, the elderly, the incurably ill, and mentally and physically handicapped persons are all too often viewed, and are made to feel, as if they are an onus on themselves or others. Third, the encyclical mentions the "utilitarian motive of avoiding costs which bring no return and weigh heavily on society" as an attitude which fosters euthanasia (§15.3).

In order to remove any possible doubt concerning what the Church believes about euthanasia, John Paul authoritatively reaffirms her teaching: "In harmony with the Magisterium of my Predecessors and in communion with the Bishops of the Catholic Church, *I confirm that euthanasia is a grave violation of the law of God*, since it is the deliberate and morally unacceptable killing of a human person. This doctrine is based upon the natural law and upon the written word of God, is transmitted by the Church's Tradition and taught by the ordinary and universal Magisterium" (§65.4). The Church's rejection of euthanasia is, therefore, unequivocal. Catholics are to accept this teaching as a truth taught definitively by the bishops in union with the Pope.

Moral foundation of civil law

In the closing sections of chapter three, John Paul examines the relationship between civil and moral law in matters that touch upon human life. According to Catholic teaching, civil law should acknowledge, defend, and promote the authentic moral values which can be known from reason; that is, civil law should mirror the natural moral law. "The doctrine on the necessary *conformity of civil law with the moral law*," observes the Pope, "is in continuity with the whole tradition of the Church" (§72.1). Legislation must therefore assure "respect for certain fundamental rights which innately belong to the person, rights which every positive law must recognize and guarantee" (§71.3). Foremost among these rights is the right to life of every innocent human being.

The Pope also recalls that the moral value of democracy depends on its "conformity to the moral law to which it, like every other form of human behavior, must be subject" (§70.4). When democracy is misunderstood as the purely formal rule of the majority, it has no objective moral anchor and readily "moves toward a form of totalitarianism" (§20.2).

John Paul recognizes that civil law cannot take the place of conscience or dictate moral norms; rather, it has the specific role of "ensuring the common good of people through the recognition and defense of their fundamental rights, and the promotion of peace and of public morality" (§71.3). Thus, civil law may never legitimize the actions of individuals who disregard the right to life. Laws which permit abortion and euthanasia — practices which are radically opposed to justice, the common good, and the fundamental rights of human beings — lack juridical validity and are not binding. The Pope insists that "in the case of an intrinsically unjust law, such as a law permitting abortion or euthanasia, it is therefore never licit to obey it, or to 'take part in a propaganda campaign in favor of such a law, or vote for it' " (§73.2). In order to fulfill their duty to protect innocent human life, Catholics are to oppose unjust laws by conscientious objection.

People of life and for life

In chapter four of *Evangelium Vitae*, the Pope points out that the Gospel of life is at the heart of the evangelizing mission of the Church, which must proclaim Jesus, the "word of life" (1 Jn 1:1). He invites all her members to testify before the world that they are a *"people of life and for life"* (§78.3). They are people *of* life because God has saved them through the Cross, the source of all life. Through their new birth, they are empowered to become a people *for* life. Both as individuals and as a Church community, God entrusts people with the threefold responsibility of proclaiming, celebrating, and serving the Gospel of life; they are "to make unconditional respect for human life the foundation of a renewed society" (§77.3).

Everyone in the Church is to announce by word and deed the good news that human life is sacred and inviolable. This proclamation demands *"the renewal of a culture of life within Christian communities themselves"* (§95.3). All Catholics, including bishops, priests, parents, theologians, catechists, and teachers, have a role to play in carrying out this *prophetic* mission. With gratitude for the beauty and grandeur of *"the God of life, the God who gives life"* (§84.1), the people for life fulfill their *priestly* mission above all by adopting *"a contemplative outlook."* "It is the outlook," the Pope says, "of those who do not presume to take possession of reality but instead accept it as a gift, discovering in all things the reflection of the Creator and seeing in every person his living image" (§83.2). As sharers in Christ's *royal* mission, people foster life through works of charity. Individual acts of mercy, volunteer work, social activity, and political commitment are ways of showing care for *"all life and for the life of everyone"* (§87.3). The Pope appeals to individuals, families, movements, and associations to share the task of building "a society in which the dignity of each person is recognized and protected and the lives of all are defended and enhanced" (§90.2).

John Paul II makes a pressing appeal for "a *general mobilization of consciences* and a *united ethical effort* to activate a *great campaign in support of life. All together, we must build a new culture of life"* (§95.2). Every family, parish, and Church institution must incorporate the Gospel of life into its mission. The Pope singles out six groups as the principal artisans of the hoped-for civilization of love: the family, women, educators, health-care professionals, intellectuals, and media personnel.

Evangelium Vitae closes with a trusting invocation of Mary, "who accepted 'Life' in the name of all and for the sake of all" (§102.2). Portrayed in Revelation as the "woman" engaged in combat with the "great red dragon" (12:1-3), she "helps the Church to *realize that life is always at the center of a great struggle* between good and evil, between light and darkness" (§104.3). In Mary's motherhood of all men and women, the Church finds "a sign of sure hope and solace" (§105.3).

Key Themes

As well as clearly setting out the Church's teaching on innocent human life, abortion, and euthanasia, *Evangelium Vitae* reflects other major concerns of John Paul II. Two can be mentioned here: the roots of the culture of death and the relationship between civil and moral law in matters concerned with human life.

Roots of the culture of death

John Paul singles out four main factors which foster the culture of death: a misunderstanding of the person as a "subject," a false idea of freedom, loss of the sense of God, and the obscuring of the moral conscience.

The Pope places a high premium on the individual as a being who enjoys freedom and responsibility. Whether unborn, handicapped, weak, defenseless, or terminally ill, all people, whatever their condition, enjoy dignity and rights as human subjects. This affirmation leads him to warn against the distorted and limited idea which "recognizes as a subject of rights only the person who enjoys full or at least incipient autonomy and who emerges from a state of total dependence on others" (§19.2). He then adds: "It is clear that on the basis of these presuppositions there is no place in the world for anyone who, like the unborn or the dying, is a weak element in the social structure, or for anyone who appears completely at the mercy of others" (§19.2). According to the Pope, basic rights are not acquired or merited: all people enjoy inalienable rights because they are created in God's image and redeemed by his Son.

Second, in *Evangelium Vitae* John Paul reaffirms what he discussed at length in *Veritatis Splendor* (1993): "Freedom negates and destroys itself, and becomes a factor leading to the destruction of others, when it no longer recognizes and respects *its essential link with the truth*" (§19.5, cf. §96.1). Those with an individualistic idea of freedom determine their moral choices by "subjective and changeable opinion or . . . selfish interest and whim" (§19.5). This so-called freedom is untethered from the objective truth about what is truly good and evil.

When this view of freedom takes hold, which understands it as the right to make arbitrary decisions, "to do your own thing," social life is governed by "the shifting sands of complete relativism" (§20.1). In this case, convention, not truth, determines what moral decisions and civil laws are made. *"Everything is negotiable, everything is open to bargaining,"* the Pope laments, "even the first of the fundamental rights, the right to life" (§20.1).

If freedom is interpreted as absolute personal autonomy, the right to do as you please, conflict inevitably results. This sinister caricature of true freedom "leads to the breakdown of a genuinely human coexistence" (§20.2). According to the Pope, "to claim the right to abortion, infanticide and euthanasia, and to recognize that right in law means to attribute to human freedom a *perverse and evil significance:* that of an *absolute power over others and against others*" (§20.3, cf. §18.2). Society becomes an agglomeration of individuals without mutual bonds. Solidarity and concern for others are neglected, and people are put "at the mercy of the unrestrained will of individuals or the oppressive totalitarianism of public authority" (§96.2).

To the extent that solidarity with other people is spurned, the meaning of authentic freedom is undermined. Genuine freedom accepts that God has entrusted men and women to one another. They are free in order to serve and love others: to be their "brother's keeper" (Gen 4:10). John Paul affirms that "there is no true freedom where life is not welcomed and loved; and there is no fullness of life except in freedom" (§96.1).

Third, the roots of the culture of death also lie in "*the eclipse of the sense of God and of man*, typical of a social and cultural climate dominated by secularism" (§21.1). This eclipse of the transcendent, according to John Paul, leads to practical materialism, which breeds individualism, utilitarianism, hedonism, the censoring of suffering, the denigration of the body, and the depersonalization of sexuality (cf. §23). It leaves the door open to the forces of evil to sabotage reverence for life in novel and ingenious ways. Because of their "Promethean attitude" (§15.3), people are willing to ratify Cain's sin. Claiming to be the total masters of their own fate and accountable to no one higher than themselves, human beings set themselves against God or ignore his existence. Men and women dare to assume that they "can control life and death by taking the decisions about them into their own hands" (§15.3). But the Pope believes that human life is something which does not belong to them, "because it is the property and gift of God the Creator and Father" (§40.1).

John Paul could not be more forthright: "Where God is denied and people live as though he did not exist, or his commandments are not taken into account, the dignity of the human person and the inviolability of human life also end up being rejected or compromised" (§96.3). The decline in religious faith that accompanies secularism influences how human life is regarded. "When *God* is not acknowledged *as God*," says the Pope, "the profound meaning of man is betrayed and communion between people is compromised" (§36.1). Indifference to religion leads people to regard individuals as "things" instead of "persons." Life is no longer recognized as God's gift: a sacred reality entrusted to human veneration and responsibility. Rather, life becomes man's "exclusive property, completely subject to his control and manipulation" (§22.1). Without God, contempt for life inevitably results.

Lastly, the darkening of the moral conscience also contributes to an anti-life culture. Contemporary women and men are finding it "increasingly difficult to distinguish between good and evil in what concerns the basic value of human life" (§4.3). When people are confused about whether life is truly good, they often make choices which desecrate its dignity. In turn, this violation of the moral law "produces a kind of progressive darkening of the capacity to discern God's living and saving presence" (§21.1). Moral conscience, whether of an individual or of society as a whole, becomes more and more obscure. This darkened conscience tolerates, and even promotes, anti-life attitudes and behavior, thus "creating and consolidating actual 'structures of sin' which go against life" (§24.1). In the Pope's mind, confusion between good and evil brought on by the eclipse of conscience presents an *"extremely serious and mortal danger"* to personal and social life (§24.1).

Human life and the law

John Paul II is disconcerted because legislation in many countries no longer punishes attacks on innocent life but has made them legal. This is "a disturbing symptom and a significant cause of grave moral decline" (§4.2). Instead of condemning such assaults as "crimes," people claim them as "rights." This situation, the Pope points out, contains a *"surprising contradiction"* (§18.3). On the one hand, no previous generation has spoken so insistently about inalienable human rights. On the other hand, the right to life is often trampled upon in practice as a consequence of anti-life laws.

Tragically, the very right to life has become the object of legislative debate. Instead of being accepted as given by creation, this right is now often viewed as granted by the State. The Pope insists, however, that the State is the guardian of inalienable human rights; it has no power to modify or abolish them. Attempts to do so are, he says, a "tragic caricature of legality" (§20.2). Indeed, "the value of democracy stands or falls with the values which it embodies and promotes" (§70.4). If a government's laws fail to defend life, it is "transformed into a *tyrant State*, which arrogates to itself the right to dispose of the life of the weakest and most defenseless members" (§20.2).

John Paul describes the two different views concerning the relation of civil law to moral law which are proposed by those who favor abortion, euthanasia, and other anti-life practices. On the one hand, some argue that, with regard to life questions, every individual has the right to make whatever "private" choices he or she wants. Thus, their argument runs, "people should be allowed complete freedom to dispose of their own lives as well as of the lives of the unborn" (§68.4). The only limitation which they admit is that of not infringing on the freedom or rights of others. According to them, therefore, the

State should not legislate in this sphere; it should neither adopt nor approve any specific ethical position on life issues.

On the other hand, other advocates of anti-life practices recognize the need for legislation in these areas and lobby for permissive laws. In fact, they are often successful in securing a legal justification for attacks on human life, "as if they were rights which the State, at least under certain conditions, must acknowledge as belonging to citizens" (§68.1). Laws concerning life should express what "the majority itself considers moral and actually practices" (§69.1). Only this practical relativism, they claim, can guarantee freedom and social harmony in a pluralistic society. To insist on objective moral norms as the foundation of law would lead to the authoritarianism of one group imposing its will on another.

The Pope, however, rejects both of these positions. First, the protection of life cannot be left to the whim of personal choice. The State, which exists to serve the common good and the good of each individual, has the duty of defending and promoting human life, dignity, and rights. Thus, it must recognize and defend the principle of "unconditional respect for the right to life of every innocent person — from conception to natural death" (§101.3). Second, authentic moral norms cannot be founded on changeable majority opinion. Public authority, writes the Pope, "can never presume to legitimize as a right of individuals — even if they are the majority of the members of society — an offense against other persons caused by the disregard of so fundamental a right as the right to life" (§71.3). Majorities have no right to deny the natural law written in the human heart. If they do, they are guilty of "making a 'tyrannical' decision with regard to the weakest and most defenseless human beings" (§70.3). True democracy is built on the acknowledgment of every person's dignity and rights.

In the face of laws which allow the direct killing of innocent human beings, the encyclical restates a firm principle of Catholic teaching: "A civil law authorizing abortion or euthanasia ceases by that very fact to be a true, morally binding civil law" (§72.2). Laws which embody an injustice are inherently unjust and therefore lack all moral authority. With this principle in mind, John Paul takes up the practical question about how Catholics in the areas of politics and health care should deal with anti-life legislation.

Many political leaders, including some who are Catholics, maintain that they must "clearly separate the realm of private conscience from that of public conduct" (§69.1). When legislating, they are willing to lay aside their personal convictions about the inviolability of human life in deference to other people's freedom of choice. In this case, as the Pope observes, "individual responsibility is thus turned over to the civil law, with a renouncing of personal conscience, at least in the public sphere" (§69.2). He affirms, on the contrary, that a politician cannot renounce personal responsibility for public decisions, "especially when he or she has a legislative or decision-making mandate, which calls that person to answer to God, to his or her own conscience and to the whole of society for choices which may be contrary to the common good" (§90.3). If an individual is personally opposed to a proposed unjust law, he or she must not vote for it and, if passed, must work to change it. Furthermore, Catholics may never campaign or vote to introduce anti-life legislation. "This cooperation," writes John Paul, "can never be justified" (§74.2).

While Catholics can never support the legalization of intrinsically evil acts such as abortion and euthanasia, the delicate question arises whether they can ever vote for a law which aims to restrict, but not eliminate, abortion. Today some countries are beginning to rethink their permissive abortion laws. The Pope addresses the situation when there is no real possibility of passing legislation which outlaws all direct abortion. Does voting for a restrictive proposal involve the approval of evil?

In carefully chosen words, John Paul answers: "When it is not possible to overturn or completely abrogate a pro-abortion law, an elected official, whose absolute personal opposition to procured abortion was well known, could licitly support proposals aimed at *limiting the harm* done by such a law and at lessening its negative consequences at the level of general opinion and public morality" (§73.3). In these circumstances, the Pope recognizes the legitimacy of political compromise. Voting for a more restrictive law "does not in fact represent an illicit cooperation with an unjust law, but rather a legitimate and proper attempt to limit its evil aspects" (§73.3).

Besides politicians and voters, those in the health and allied professions who have to work in situations where unjust laws are in force also face acute moral dilemmas. To what extent can they cooperate in a practice such as abortion which, though legal, is contrary to the natural and revealed law?

Evangelium Vitae leaves no room for ambiguity. "There is no obligation in conscience to obey such laws; instead there is a *grave and clear obligation to oppose them by conscientious objection*" (§73.1). The encyclical gives two reasons for this position. First, no one has a "right" to kill innocent human life. Second, the morality of an act is not determined by what civil law permits but by the dictates of the moral law: "We must obey God rather than men" (Acts 5:29). "Christians, like all people of good will," says John Paul, "are called upon under grave obligation of conscience not to cooperate formally in practices which, even if permitted by civil legislation, are contrary to God's law"

(§74.2). The refusal to take part in attacks on innocent human life is, therefore, an absolute moral imperative.

The Pope also makes a plea expressly aimed at legislators in countries which have legalized anti-life practices. When abortion laws are on the books, civil law should guarantee the right of conscientious objection to those in positions where unjust laws impinge upon the practice of their profession. According to him, everyone has a basic human right to refuse to take part in any consultation, preparation, or carrying out of an act against life. The reason is clear. No State which respects true human dignity and freedom can force a person "to perform an action intrinsically incompatible with human dignity" (§74.3). Furthermore, in such cases legislation should protect conscientious objectors from punitive disciplinary, professional, and financial measures.

To build a new culture of life, John Paul is convinced that "*a great prayer for life is urgently needed*, a prayer which will rise up throughout the world" (§100.2). Every believer, association, and Church community should commit itself to prayer and fasting "so that power from on high will break down the walls of lies and deceit: the walls which conceal from the sight of so many of our brothers and sisters the evil of practices and laws which are hostile to life" (§100.2). Despite his dire warnings about the ravages of the culture of death, the Pope's chief concern in *Evangelium Vitae* is to ignite a new passion for the cause of life, and he enlists Mary in this noble cause. "As a living word of comfort for the Church in her struggle against death" (§105.1), the Virgin Mother assures us that her Son has already defeated the forces of death. And so, with confidence, the Pope prays:

"O Mary,
bright dawn of the new world,
Mother of the living,
to you do we entrust the *cause of life*" (§105.4).

* * *

Selected Bibliography

Anderson, Carl A. "Gospel Offers Man the Opportunity To Regain His Authentic Personhood." *L'Osservatore Romano*, 26 (1995), 10.

Basso, Domingo. "Encyclical Is Meant Vigorously To Arouse the Conscience of Society." *L'Osservatore Romano*, 36 (1995), 6.

Caffarra, Carlo. "Death of God's Only Son Revealed Dignity and Value of All Human Life." *L'Osservatore Romano*, 21 (1995), 10.

Callam, Daniel. "The Gospel of Life." *The Canadian Catholic Review*, 13 (June 1995), 2-3.

Carrasco de Paula, Ignacio. "Church's Moral Teaching Shows Man the Way to Eternal Salvation." *L'Osservatore Romano*, 32/33 (1995), 6.

Casini, Carlo. "When Sense of God Is Lost, There Is Tendency to Lose Sense of Man." *L'Osservatore Romano*, 18 (1995), 6.

Ciccione, Lino. "Acceptance of Contraception Leads to Promotion of Abortion." *L'Osservatore Romano*, 24 (1995), 10.

Cole, Basil. "The New Sins against Faith and *Evangelium Vitae*." *Angelicum*, 73 (1996), 3-19.

Colombo, Roberto. "Discoveries of Science Support Prohibition of Killing Human Embryo." *L'Osservatore Romano*, 42 (1995), 10-11.

Cottier, Georges. "Distorted Concept of Subjectivity Contradicts Dignity of the Person." *L'Osservatore Romano*, 43 (1995), 10.

Curley, Terence P. "*Evangelium Vitae* and Our Culture." *The Priest*, 51 (October 1995), 18-20.

Devaux, Michaël. "The Truth of Love, the Lie of Death." *Communio* 23 (1996), 110-121.

Figueiredo, Fernando A. "Human Beings Are Merely Stewards and Not Lords Who Can Dispose of Life at Will." *L'Osservatore Romano*, 46 (1995), 10.

Haas, John. " 'The Gospel of Life' and the Death of Penalty." *Crisis*, 13 (July/August 1995), 20-23.

Hehir, J. Bryan. "Get a (Culture of) Life: The Pope's Moral Vision." *Commonweal*, 122 (1995), 8-9.

Herranz, Gonzalo. "The Respect and Care of All Human Beings Is Part of Doctor's Charism." *L'Osservatore Romano*, 30 (1995), 10.

Herranz, Julián. "Conversion of the Offender Is Goal of Canonical Sanction for Abortion." *L'Osservatore Romano*, 25 (1995), 10.

Hickey, James A. "The Path to Spiritual Healing after Abortion Is through Reconciliation." *L'Osservatore Romano*, 40 (1995), 6.

Hume, Basil. "Introducing the Encyclical *Evangelium Vitae*." *Briefing*, 25 (April 1995), 3-8.

Johnstone, Brian V. "Life in a Culture of Death." *Priests & People*, 9 (November 1995), 409-413.

Lobato, Abelardo. "Technological Man Has Neglected Moral Sense That Underlies Culture." *L'Osservatore Romano*, 20 (1995), 10-11.

López Trujillo, Alfonso. "Church Believes That Human Life, However Weak, Is Gift from God." *L'Osservatore Romano*, 17 (1995), 9-10.

McCormick, Richard A. "The Gospel of Life." *America,* 172 (1995), 10-17.

Marthaler, Berard L. "The Gospel of Life." *Living Light,* 32 (Fall 1995), 6-45.

May, William E. "Evangelium Vitae." *Linacre Quarterly* (February 1996), 87-96.

Medina Estévez, Jorge. "Communion with God Gives Truth and Joy to Every Expression of Life." *L'Osservatore Romano,* 23 (1995), 10-11.

Melady, Thomas. "Public Catholicism and *Evangelium Vitae.*" *Crisis,* 13 (June 1995), 16.

Melina, Livio. "Lack of Objective Moral Anchor Leads to Abuse of Political Power." *L'Osservatore Romano,* 19 (1995), 10-11.

Merecki, Jaroslaw, and Styczen, Tadeusz. "Denying Legal Protection to Weakest Undermines the State Itself." *L'Osservatore Romano,* 44 (1995), 10.

Neuhaus, Richard John. "The Prophetic Humanism of *Evangelium Vitae.*" *Crisis,* 14 (May 1996), 22-26.

Novak, Michael. "The Gospel of Life." *Crisis,* 13 (June 1995), 6-7.

O'Connor, John J. "Holy Father Warns Us That We Face an Objective 'Conspiracy against Life.' " *L'Osservatore Romano,* 27 (1995), 10.

Ratzinger, Joseph. Presentation at the Press Conference for the Publication of *Evangelium Vitae. L'Osservatore Romano,* 14 (1995), 1-2.

Roth, Gottfried. "Life Must Awaken in the Physician a Reverential Awe of the Lord's Gift." *L'Osservatore Romano,* 37 (1995), 6.

"The Sacredness of Human Life." Editorial. *The Tablet,* 249 (1995), 411.

Schambeck, Herbert. "State Cannot Create Human Values, but Only Respect and Promote Them." *L'Osservatore Romano,* 35 (1995), 6.

Schindler, David L. "Christological Aesthetics and *Evangelium Vitae.*" *Communio,* 22 (1995), 193-224.

Sgreccia, Elio. "New Connection Emerges between Safeguarding Life and Environment." *L'Osservatore Romano,* 29 (1995), 10-11.

Sullivan, Francis A. "The Doctrinal Weight of *Evangelium Vitae.*" *Theological Studies,* 56 (1995), 560-565.

Symposium on *Evangelium Vitae. The Human Life Review,* 21 (Summer 1995), 25-72.

"The Vatican's Summary of *Evangelium Vitae.*" *Origins,* 24 (1995), 728-730.

Vial Correra, Juan de Dios. "Objective Forms of Evil Aimed at Weakest Have No Justification." *L'Osservatore Romano,* 31 (1995), 6.

Woodrow, Alain. "The Pope's Challenge to Western Democracy." *The Tablet,* 249 (1995), 448-449.

ENCYCLICAL LETTER

EVANGELIUM VITAE

ADDRESSED BY THE SUPREME PONTIFF

JOHN PAUL II

TO THE BISHOPS

PRIESTS AND DEACONS

MEN AND WOMEN RELIGIOUS

LAY FAITHFUL

AND ALL PEOPLE OF GOOD WILL

ON THE VALUE AND INVIOLABILITY

OF HUMAN LIFE

Evangelium Vitae

Introduction

1.1 The *Gospel of life* is at the heart of Jesus' message. Lovingly received day after day by the Church, it is to be preached with dauntless fidelity as "good news" to the people of every age and culture.

1.2 At the dawn of salvation, it is the birth of a child which is proclaimed as joyful news: "I bring you good news of a great joy which will come to all the people; for to you is born this day in the city of David a Savior, who is Christ the Lord" (Lk 2:10-11). The source of this "great joy" is the birth of the Savior; but Christmas also reveals the full meaning of every human birth, and the joy which accompanies the birth of the Messiah is thus seen to be the foundation and fulfillment of joy at every child born into the world (cf. Jn 16:21).

1.3 When he presents the heart of his redemptive mission, Jesus says: "I came that they may have life, and have it abundantly" (Jn 10:10). In truth, he is referring to that "new" and "eternal" life which consists in communion with the Father, to which every person is freely called in the Son by the power of the Sanctifying Spirit. It is precisely in this "life" that all the aspects and stages of human life achieve their full significance.

The incomparable worth of the human person

2.1 Man is called to a fullness of life which far exceeds the dimensions of his earthly existence because it consists in sharing the very life of God. The loftiness of this supernatural vocation reveals the *greatness* and the *inestimable value* of human life even in its temporal phase. Life in time, in fact, is the fundamental condition, the initial stage and an integral part of the entire unified process of human existence. It is a process which, unexpectedly and undeservedly, is enlightened by the promise and renewed by the gift of divine life, which will reach its full realization in eternity (cf. 1 Jn 3:1-2). At the same time, it is precisely this supernatural calling which highlights the *relative character* of each individual's earthly life. After all, life on earth is not an "ultimate" but a "penultimate" reality; even so, it remains a *sacred reality* entrusted to us, to be preserved with a sense of responsibility and brought to perfection in love and in the gift of ourselves to God and to our brothers and sisters.

2.2 The Church knows that this *Gospel of life*, which she has received from

[handwritten marginalia, left and bottom margins:] Since this life of God is undeserved, it must not belong to the notion of person as such. Hence, since the supernatural vocation reveals the value of human life (since human life is a pre-condition for the divine life) it must be that the intrinsic worth of the person is enhanced and increased by the possibility of sharing the life of God. ∴ The person is lovable insofar as he is able to partake of such a good (i.e., the divine life), not vice versa. Hence, the primacy of the common good over the personal / individual good.

her Lord,[1] has a profound and persuasive echo in the heart of every person — believer and nonbeliever alike — because it marvelously fulfills all the heart's expectations while infinitely surpassing them. Even in the midst of difficulties and uncertainties, every person sincerely open to truth and goodness can, by the light of reason and the hidden action of grace, come to recognize in the natural law written in the heart (cf. Rom 2:14-15) the sacred value of human life from its very beginning until its end, and can affirm the right of every human being to have this primary good respected to the highest degree. Upon the recognition of this right, every human community and the political community itself are founded.

2.3 In a special way, believers in Christ must defend and promote this right, aware as they are of the wonderful truth recalled by the Second Vatican Council: "By his Incarnation the Son of God has united himself in some fashion with every human being."[2] This saving event reveals to humanity not only the boundless love of God, who "so loved the world that he gave his only Son" (Jn 3:16), but also the *incomparable value of every human person.*

2.4 The Church, faithfully contemplating the mystery of the Redemption, acknowledges this value with ever new wonder.[3] She feels called to proclaim to the people of all times this "Gospel," the source of invincible hope and true joy for every period of history. *The Gospel of God's love for man, the Gospel of the dignity of the person and the Gospel of life are a single and indivisible Gospel.*

2.5 For this reason, man — living man — represents the primary and fundamental way for the Church.[4]

New threats to human life

3.1 Every individual, precisely by reason of the mystery of the Word of God who was made flesh (cf. Jn 1:14), is entrusted to the maternal care of the Church. Therefore every threat to human dignity and life must necessarily be felt in the Church's very heart; it cannot but affect her at the core of her faith in the redemptive Incarnation of the Son of God, and engage her in her mission of proclaiming the *Gospel of life* in all the world and to every creature (cf. Mk 16:15).

3.2 Today this proclamation is especially pressing because of the extra-

---

[1] The expression "Gospel of life" is not found as such in Sacred Scripture. But it does correspond to an essential dimension of the biblical message.

[2] Pastoral Constitution on the Church in the Modern World *Gaudium et Spes,* 22.

[3] Cf. John Paul II, Encyclical Letter *Redemptor Hominis* (March 4, 1979), 10: *AAS* 71 (1979), 275.

[4] Cf. ibid., 14: loc. cit., 285.

ordinary increase and gravity of threats to the life of individuals and peoples, especially where life is weak and defenseless. In addition to the ancient scourges of poverty, hunger, endemic diseases, violence and war, new threats are emerging on an alarmingly vast scale.

3.3 The Second Vatican Council, in a passage which retains all its relevance today, forcefully condemned a number of crimes and attacks against human life. Thirty years later, taking up the words of the Council and with the same forcefulness, I repeat that condemnation in the name of the whole Church, certain that I am interpreting the genuine sentiment of every upright conscience: "Whatever is opposed to life itself such as any type of murder, genocide, abortion, euthanasia or willful self-destruction; whatever violates the integrity of the human person such as mutilation, torments inflicted on body or mind, attempts to coerce the will itself; whatever insults human dignity such as subhuman living conditions, arbitrary imprisonment, deportation, slavery, prostitution, the selling of women and children; as well as disgraceful working conditions, where people are treated as mere instruments of gain rather than as free and responsible persons; all these things and others like them are infamies indeed. They poison human society, and they do more harm to those who practice them than to those who suffer from the injury. Moreover, they are a supreme dishonor to the Creator."[5]

4.1 Unfortunately, this disturbing state of affairs, far from decreasing, is expanding: with the new prospects opened up by scientific and technological progress there arise new forms of attacks on the dignity of the human being. At the same time a new cultural climate is developing and taking hold which gives crimes against life a *new and — if possible — even more sinister character,* giving rise to further grave concern: broad sectors of public opinion justify certain crimes against life in the name of the rights of individual freedom, and on this basis they claim not only exemption from punishment but even authorization by the State, so that these things can be done with total freedom and indeed with the free assistance of health-care systems.

4.2 All this is causing a profound change in the way in which life and relationships between people are considered. The fact that legislation in many countries, perhaps even departing from basic principles of their constitutions, has determined not to punish these practices against life, and even to make them altogether legal, is both a disturbing symptom and a significant cause of grave moral decline. Choices once unanimously considered criminal and rejected by the common moral sense are gradually becoming socially accept-

[5] Pastoral Constitution on the Church in the Modern World *Gaudium et Spes,* 27.

able. Even certain sectors of the medical profession, which by its calling is directed to the defense and care of human life, are increasingly willing to carry out these acts against the person. In this way the very nature of the medical profession is distorted and contradicted, and the dignity of those who practice it is degraded. In such a cultural and legislative situation, the serious demographic, social and family problems which weigh upon many of the world's peoples and which require responsible and effective attention from national and international bodies are left open to false and deceptive solutions, opposed to the truth and the good of persons and nations.

4.3 The end result of this is tragic: not only is the fact of the destruction of so many human lives still to be born or in their final stage extremely grave and disturbing, but no less grave and disturbing is the fact that conscience itself, darkened as it were by such widespread conditioning, is finding it increasingly difficult to distinguish between good and evil in what concerns the basic value of human life.

In communion with all the Bishops of the world

5.1 The *Extraordinary Consistory* of Cardinals held in Rome on April 4-7, 1991, was devoted to the problem of the threats to human life in our day. After a thorough and detailed discussion of the problem and of the challenges it poses to the entire human family and in particular to the Christian community, the Cardinals unanimously asked me to reaffirm with the authority of the Successor of Peter the value of human life and its inviolability, in the light of present circumstances and attacks threatening it today.

5.2 In response to this request, at Pentecost in 1991 I wrote a *personal letter* to each of my Brother Bishops asking them, in the spirit of episcopal collegiality, to offer me their cooperation in drawing up a specific document.[6] I am deeply grateful to all the Bishops who replied and provided me with valuable facts, suggestions and proposals. In so doing they bore witness to their unanimous desire to share in the doctrinal and pastoral mission of the Church with regard to the *Gospel of life*.

5.3 In that same letter, written shortly after the celebration of the centenary of the Encyclical *Rerum Novarum,* I drew everyone's attention to this striking analogy: "Just as a century ago it was the working classes which were oppressed in their fundamental rights, and the Church very courageously came to their defense by proclaiming the sacrosanct rights of the worker as a person, so now, when another category of persons is being oppressed in the

---

[6] Cf. Letter to All My Brothers in the Episcopate regarding the "Gospel of Life" (May 19, 1991): *Insegnamenti* XIV/1 (1991), 1293-1296.

fundamental right to life, the Church feels in duty bound to speak out with the same courage on behalf of those who have no voice. Hers is always the evangelical cry in defense of the world's poor, those who are threatened and despised and whose human rights are violated."[7]

5.4 Today there exists a great multitude of weak and defenseless human beings, unborn children in particular, whose fundamental right to life is being trampled upon. If, at the end of the last century, the Church could not be silent about the injustices of those times, still less can she be silent today when the social injustices of the past, unfortunately not yet overcome, are being compounded in many regions of the world by still more grievous forms of injustice and oppression, even if these are being presented as elements of progress in view of a new world order.

5.5 The present Encyclical, the fruit of the cooperation of the Episcopate of every country of the world, is therefore meant to be a *precise and vigorous reaffirmation of the value of human life and its inviolability,* and at the same time a pressing appeal addressed to each and every person in the name of God: *respect, protect, love and serve life, every human life!* Only in this direction will you find justice, development, true freedom, peace and happiness!

5.6 May these words reach all the sons and daughters of the Church! May they reach all people of good will who are concerned for the good of every man and woman and for the destiny of the whole of society!

6.1 In profound communion with all my brothers and sisters in the faith and inspired by genuine friendship toward all, I wish to *meditate once more upon and proclaim the Gospel of life,* the splendor of truth which enlightens consciences, the clear light which corrects the darkened gaze, and the unfailing source of faithfulness and steadfastness in facing the ever new challenges which we meet along our path.

6.2 As I recall the powerful experience of the Year of the Family, as if to complete the *Letter* which I wrote "to every particular family in every part of the world,"[8] I look with renewed confidence to every household and I pray that at every level a general commitment to support the family will reappear and be strengthened, so that today too — even amid so many difficulties and serious threats — the family will always remain, in accordance with God's plan, the "sanctuary of life."[9]

6.3 To all the members of the Church, *the people of life and for life,* I make

---

[7] Ibid.: loc. cit., 1294.

[8] Letter to Families *Gratissimam Sane* (February 2, 1994), 4: *AAS* 86 (1994), 871.

[9] John Paul II, Encyclical Letter *Centesimus Annus* (May 1, 1991), 39: *AAS* 83 (1991), 842.

this most urgent appeal, that together we may offer this world of ours new signs of hope and work to ensure that justice and solidarity will increase and that a new culture of human life will be affirmed, for the building of an authentic civilization of truth and love.

I

The Voice of Your Brother's Blood
Cries to Me from the Ground

Present-Day Threats to Human Life

"Cain rose up against his brother Abel and killed him" (Gen 4:8): the roots of violence against life

7.1 "God did not make death, and he does not delight in the death of the living. For he has created all things that they might exist. . . . *God created man for incorruption* and made him in the image of his own eternity, but through the devil's envy *death entered the world,* and those who belong to his party experience it" (Wis 1:13-14, 2:23-24).

7.2 The *Gospel of life,* proclaimed in the beginning when man was created in the image of God for a destiny of full and perfect life (cf. Gen 2:7; Wis 9:2-3), is contradicted by the painful experience of *death which enters the world* and casts its shadow of meaninglessness over man's entire existence. Death came into the world as a result of the devil's envy (cf. Gen 3:1, 4-5) and the sin of our first parents (cf. Gen 2:17, 3:17-19). And death entered it in a violent way, *through the killing of Abel by his brother Cain:* "And when they were in the field, Cain rose up against his brother Abel, and killed him" (Gen 4:8).

7.3 This first murder is presented with singular eloquence in a page of the Book of Genesis which has universal significance: it is a page rewritten daily, with inexorable and degrading frequency, in the book of human history.

7.4 Let us reread together this biblical account which, despite its archaic structure and its extreme simplicity, has much to teach us.

"Now Abel was a keeper of sheep, and Cain a tiller of the ground. In the course of time Cain brought to the Lord an offering of the fruit of the ground, and Abel brought of the firstlings of his flock and of their fat portions. And the Lord had regard for Abel and his offering, but for Cain and his offering he had not regard. So Cain was very angry, and his countenance fell. The Lord said to Cain, 'Why are you angry and why has your countenance fallen? If you do

well, will you not be accepted? And if you do not do well, sin is crouching at the door; its desire is for you, but you must master it.'

"Cain said to Abel his brother, 'Let us go out to the field.' And when they were in the field, Cain rose up against his brother Abel, and killed him. Then the Lord said to Cain, 'Where is Abel your brother?' He said, 'I do not know; am I my brother's keeper?' And the Lord said, 'What have you done? The voice of your brother's blood is crying to me from the ground. And now you are cursed from the ground, which has opened its mouth to receive your brother's blood from your hand. When you till the ground, it shall no longer yield to you its strength; you shall be a fugitive and a wanderer on the earth.' Cain said to the Lord, 'My punishment is greater than I can bear. Behold, you have driven me this day away from the ground; and from your face I shall be hidden; and I shall be a fugitive and a wanderer on the earth, and whoever finds me will slay me.' Then the Lord said to him, 'Not so! If anyone slays Cain, vengeance shall be taken on him sevenfold.' And the Lord put a mark on Cain, lest any who came upon him should kill him. Then Cain went away from the presence of the Lord, and dwelt in the land of Nod, east of Eden" (Gen 4:2-16).

8.1 Cain was "very angry" and his countenance "fell" because "the Lord had regard for Abel and his offering" (Gen 4:4-5). The biblical text does not reveal the reason why God prefers Abel's sacrifice to Cain's. It clearly shows, however, that God, although preferring Abel's gift, *does not interrupt his dialogue with Cain.* He admonishes him, *reminding him of his freedom in the face of evil:* man is in no way predestined to evil. Certainly, like Adam, he is tempted by the malevolent force of sin which, like a wild beast, lies in wait at the door of his heart, ready to leap on its prey. But Cain remains free in the face of sin. He can and must overcome it: "Its desire is for you, but you must master it" (Gen 4:7).

8.2 *Envy and anger* have the upper hand over the Lord's warning, and so Cain attacks his own brother and kills him. As we read in the *Catechism of the Catholic Church:* "In the account of Abel's murder by his brother Cain, Scripture reveals the presence of anger and envy in man, consequences of original sin, from the beginning of human history. Man has become the enemy of his fellow man."[10]

8.3 *Brother kills brother.* Like the first fratricide, every murder is a violation of the *"spiritual" kinship* uniting mankind in one great family,[11] in which all share the same fundamental good: equal personal dignity. Not infrequently

[10] No. 2259.
[11] Cf. Saint Ambrose, *De Noe*, 26, 94-96: *CSEL* 32, 480-481.

the *kinship "of flesh and blood"* is also violated; for example when threats to life arise within the relationship between parents and children such as happens in abortion or when, in the wider context of family or kinship, euthanasia is encouraged or practiced.

8.4 At the root of every act of violence against one's neighbor there is *a concession to the "thinking" of the evil one,* the one who "was a murderer from the beginning" (Jn 8:44). As the Apostle John reminds us: "For this is the message which you have heard from the beginning, that we should love one another, and not be like Cain who was of the evil one and murdered his brother" (1 Jn 3:11-12). Cain's killing of his brother at the very dawn of history is thus a sad witness of how evil spreads with amazing speed: man's revolt against God in the earthly paradise is followed by the deadly combat of man against man.

8.5 After the crime, *God intervenes to avenge the one killed.* Before God, who asks him about the fate of Abel, Cain, instead of showing remorse and apologizing, arrogantly eludes the question: "I do not know; am I my brother's keeper?" (Gen 4:9). *"I do not know":* Cain tries to cover up his crime with a lie. This was and still is the case, when all kinds of ideologies try to justify and disguise the most atrocious crimes against human beings. *"Am I my brother's keeper?":* Cain does not wish to think about his brother and refuses to accept the responsibility which every person has toward others. We cannot but think of today's tendency for people to refuse to accept responsibility for their brothers and sisters. Symptoms of this trend include the lack of solidarity toward society's weakest members — such as the elderly, the infirm, immigrants, children — and the indifference frequently found in relations between the world's peoples even when basic values such as survival, freedom and peace are involved.

9.1 But *God cannot leave the crime unpunished:* from the ground on which it has been spilt, the blood of the one murdered demands that God should render justice (cf. Gen 37:26; Is 26:21; Ezek 24:7-8). From this text the Church has taken the name of the "sins which cry to God for justice," and first among them she has included willful murder.[12] For the Jewish people, as for many peoples of antiquity, blood is the source of life. Indeed "the blood is the life" (Dt 12:23), and life, especially human life, belongs only to God: for this reason *whoever attacks human life, in some way attacks God himself.*

9.2 Cain is cursed by God and also by the earth, which will deny him its fruit (cf. Gen 4:11-12). *He is punished:* he will live in the wilderness and the

---

[12] Cf. *Catechism of the Catholic Church,* Nos. 1867 and 2268.

desert. Murderous violence profoundly changes man's environment. From being the "garden of Eden" (Gen 2:15), a place of plenty, of harmonious interpersonal relationships and of friendship with God, the earth becomes "the land of Nod" (Gen 4:16), a place of scarcity, loneliness and separation from God. Cain will be "a fugitive and a wanderer on the earth" (Gen 4:14): uncertainty and restlessness will follow him forever.

9.3 And yet God, who is always merciful even when he punishes, "*put a mark on Cain,* lest any who came upon him should kill him" (Gen 4:15). He thus gave him a distinctive sign, not to condemn him to the hatred of others, but to protect and defend him from those wishing to kill him, even out of a desire to avenge Abel's death. *Not even a murderer loses his personal dignity,* and God himself pledges to guarantee this. And it is precisely here that the *paradoxical mystery of the merciful justice of God* is shown forth. As Saint Ambrose writes: "Once the crime is admitted at the very inception of this sinful act of parricide, then the divine law of God's mercy should be immediately extended. If punishment is forthwith inflicted on the accused, then men in the exercise of justice would in no way observe patience and moderation, but would straightaway condemn the defendant to punishment. . . . God drove Cain out of his presence and sent him into exile far away from his native land, so that he passed from a life of human kindness to one which was more akin to the rude existence of a wild beast. God, who preferred the correction rather than the death of a sinner, did not desire that a homicide be punished by the exaction of another act of homicide."[13]

"What have you done?" (Gen 4:10): the eclipse of the value of life

10.1 The Lord said to Cain: "What have you done? The voice of your brother's blood is crying to me from the ground" (Gen 4:10). *The voice of the blood shed by men continues to cry out* from generation to generation in ever new and different ways.

10.2 The Lord's question, "What have you done?" which Cain cannot escape, is addressed also to the people of today, to make them realize the extent and gravity of the attacks against life which continue to mark human history; to make them discover what causes these attacks and feeds them; and to make them ponder seriously the consequences which derive from these attacks for the existence of individuals and peoples.

10.3 Some threats come from nature itself, but they are made worse by the culpable indifference and negligence of those who could in some cases remedy them. Others are the result of situations of violence, hatred and conflict-

---

[13] *De Cain et Abel*, II, 10, 38: *CSEL* 32, 408.

ing interests, which lead people to attack others through murder, war, slaughter and genocide.

10.4 And how can we fail to consider the violence against life done to millions of human beings, especially children, who are forced into poverty, malnutrition and hunger because of an unjust distribution of resources between peoples and between social classes? And what of the violence inherent not only in wars as such, but in the scandalous arms trade, which spawns the many armed conflicts which stain our world with blood? What of the spreading of death caused by reckless tampering with the world's ecological balance, by the criminal spread of drugs or by the promotion of certain kinds of sexual activity which, besides being morally unacceptable, also involve grave risks to life? It is impossible to catalog completely the vast array of threats to human life, so many are the forms, whether explicit or hidden, in which they appear today!

11.1 Here though we shall concentrate particular attention on *another category of attacks* affecting life in its earliest and in its final stages, attacks which present *new characteristics with respect to the past and which raise questions of extraordinary seriousness*. It is not only that in generalized opinion these attacks tend no longer to be considered as "crimes"; paradoxically they assume the nature of "rights," to the point that the State is called upon to give them *legal recognition and to make them available through the free services of health-care personnel*. Such attacks strike human life at the time of its greatest frailty, when it lacks any means of self-defense. Even more serious is the fact that, most often, those attacks are carried out in the very heart of and with the complicity of the family — the family, which by its nature is called to be the "sanctuary of life."

11.2 How did such a situation come about? Many different factors have to be taken into account. In the background there is the profound crisis of culture, which generates skepticism in relation to the very foundations of knowledge and ethics, and which makes it increasingly difficult to grasp clearly the meaning of what man is, the meaning of his rights and his duties. Then there are all kinds of existential and interpersonal difficulties, made worse by the complexity of a society in which individuals, couples and families are often left alone with their problems. There are situations of acute poverty, anxiety or frustration in which the struggle to make ends meet, the presence of unbearable pain or instances of violence, especially against women, make the choice to defend and promote life so demanding as sometimes to reach the point of heroism.

11.3 All this explains, at least in part, how the value of life can today undergo a kind of "eclipse," even though conscience does not cease to point to it as a sacred and inviolable value, as is evident in the tendency to disguise certain crimes against life in its early or final stages by using innocuous medical terms which distract attention from the fact that what is involved is the right to life of an actual human person.

12 In fact, while the climate of widespread moral uncertainty can in some way be explained by the multiplicity and gravity of today's social problems, and these can sometimes mitigate the subjective responsibility of individuals, it is no less true that we are confronted by an even larger reality, which can be described as a veritable *structure of sin*. This reality is characterized by the emergence of a culture which denies solidarity and in many cases takes the form of a veritable "culture of death." This culture is actively fostered by powerful cultural, economic and political currents which encourage an idea of society excessively concerned with efficiency. Looking at the situation from this point of view, it is possible to speak in a certain sense of a *war of the powerful against the weak:* a life which would require greater acceptance, love and care is considered useless or held to be an intolerable burden, and is therefore rejected in one way or another. A person who, because of illness, handicap or, more simply, just by existing, compromises the well-being or life-style of those who are more favored tends to be looked upon as an enemy to be resisted or eliminated. In this way a kind of *"conspiracy against life"* is unleashed. This conspiracy involves not only individuals in their personal, family or group relationships, but goes far beyond, to the point of damaging and distorting at the international level relations between peoples and States.

13.1 In order to facilitate the spread of *abortion,* enormous sums of money have been invested and continue to be invested in the production of pharmaceutical products which make it possible to kill the fetus in the mother's womb without recourse to medical assistance. On this point, scientific research itself seems to be almost exclusively preoccupied with developing products which are ever more simple and effective in suppressing life and which at the same time are capable of removing abortion from any kind of control or social responsibility.

13.2 It is frequently asserted that *contraception,* if made safe and available to all, is the most effective remedy against abortion. The Catholic Church is then accused of actually promoting abortion because she obstinately continues to teach the moral unlawfulness of contraception. When looked at carefully, this objection is clearly unfounded. It may be that many people use contraception with a view to excluding the subsequent temptation of abortion. But the negative values inherent in the "contraceptive mentality" — which is very different from responsible parenthood lived in respect for the full truth of the conjugal act — are such that they in fact strengthen this temptation when an unwanted life is conceived. Indeed, the pro-abortion culture is especially strong precisely where the Church's teaching on contraception is rejected. Certainly, from the moral point of view contraception and abortion are *specifically different* evils: the former contradicts the full truth of the sexual act as the proper expression of conjugal love, while the latter destroys the life of a human being; the former is opposed to the virtue of chastity in marriage, the latter is opposed to the virtue of justice and directly violates the divine commandment "You shall not kill."

13.3 But despite their differences of nature and moral gravity, contraception and abortion are often closely connected, as fruits of the same tree. It is true that in many cases contraception and even abortion are practiced under the pressure of real-life difficulties, which nonetheless can never exonerate from striving to observe God's law fully. Still, in very many other instances such practices are rooted in a hedonistic mentality unwilling to accept responsibility in matters of sexuality, and they imply a self-centered concept of freedom, which regards procreation as an obstacle to personal fulfillment. The life which could result from a sexual encounter thus becomes an enemy to be avoided at all costs, and abortion becomes the only possible decisive response to failed contraception.

13.4 The close connection which exists in mentality between the practice of contraception and that of abortion is becoming increasingly obvious. It is being demonstrated in an alarming way by the development of chemical products, intrauterine devices and vaccines which, distributed with the same ease as contraceptives, really act as abortifacients in the very early stages of the development of the life of the new human being.

14.1 The various *techniques of artificial reproduction*, which would seem to be at the service of life and which are frequently used with this intention, actually open the door to new threats against life. Apart from the fact that they are morally unacceptable since they separate procreation from the fully human context of the conjugal act,[14] these techniques have a high rate of failure: not just failure in relation to fertilization, but with regard to the subse-

---

[14] Cf. Congregation for the Doctrine of the Faith, Instruction on Respect for Human Life in Its Origin and on the Dignity of Procreation *Donum Vitae* (February 22, 1987): *AAS* 80 (1988), 70-102.

quent development of the embryo, which is exposed to the risk of death, generally within a very short space of time. Furthermore, the number of embryos produced is often greater than that needed for implantation in the woman's womb, and these so-called "spare embryos" are then destroyed or used for research which, under the pretext of scientific or medical progress, in fact reduces human life to the level of simple "biological material" to be freely disposed of.

14.2 *Prenatal diagnosis*, which presents no moral objections if carried out in order to identify the medical treatment which may be needed by the child in the womb, all too often becomes an opportunity for proposing and procuring an abortion. This is eugenic abortion, justified in public opinion on the basis of a mentality — mistakenly held to be consistent with the demands of "therapeutic interventions" — which accepts life only under certain conditions and rejects it when it is affected by any limitation, handicap or illness.

14.3 Following this same logic, the point has been reached where the most basic care, even nourishment, is denied to babies born with serious handicaps or illnesses. The contemporary scene, moreover, is becoming even more alarming by reason of the proposals advanced here and there to justify even *infanticide*, following the same arguments used to justify the right to abortion. In this way we revert to a state of barbarism which one hoped had been left behind forever.

15.1 Threats which are no less serious hang over the *incurably ill* and the *dying*. In a social and cultural context which makes it more difficult to face and accept suffering, the *temptation* becomes all the greater *to resolve the problem of suffering by eliminating it at the root*, by hastening death so that it occurs at the moment considered most suitable.

15.2 Various considerations usually contribute to such a decision, all of which converge in the same terrible outcome. In the sick person the sense of anguish, of severe discomfort and even of desperation brought on by intense and prolonged suffering can be a decisive factor. Such a situation can threaten the already fragile equilibrium of an individual's personal and family life, with the result that, on the one hand, the sick person, despite the help of increasingly effective medical and social assistance, risks feeling overwhelmed by his or her own frailty; and on the other hand, those close to the sick person can be moved by an understandable, even if misplaced, compassion. All this is aggravated by a cultural climate which fails to perceive any meaning or value in suffering, but rather considers suffering the epitome of evil, to be eliminated at all costs. This is especially the case in the absence of a religious outlook which could help to provide a positive understanding of the mystery of suffering.

15.3 On a more general level, there exists in contemporary culture a certain Promethean attitude which leads people to think that they can control life and death by taking the decisions about them into their own hands. What really happens in this case is that the individual is overcome and crushed by a death deprived of any prospect of meaning or hope. We see a tragic expression of all this in the spread of *euthanasia* — disguised and surreptitious or practiced openly and even legally. As well as for reasons of a misguided pity at the sight of the patient's suffering, euthanasia is sometimes justified by the utilitarian motive of avoiding costs which bring no return and which weigh heavily on society. Thus it is proposed to eliminate malformed babies, the severely handicapped, the disabled, the elderly, especially when they are not self-sufficient, and the terminally ill. Nor can we remain silent in the face of other more furtive, but no less serious and real forms of euthanasia. These could occur for example when, in order to increase the availability of organs for transplants, organs are removed without respecting objective and adequate criteria which verify the death of the donor.

16.1 Another present-day *phenomenon*, frequently used to justify threats and attacks against life, is the *demographic* question. This question arises in different ways in different parts of the world. In the rich and developed countries there is a disturbing decline or collapse of the birthrate. The poorer countries, on the other hand, generally have a high rate of population growth, difficult to sustain in the context of low economic and social development, and especially where there is extreme underdevelopment. In the face of over-population in the poorer countries, instead of forms of global intervention at the international level — serious family and social policies, programs of cultural development and of fair production and distribution of resources — anti-birth policies continue to be enacted.

16.2 Contraception, sterilization and abortion are certainly part of the reason why in some cases there is a sharp decline in the birthrate. It is not difficult to be tempted to use the same methods and attacks against life also where there is a situation of "demographic explosion."

16.3 The Pharaoh of old, haunted by the presence and increase of the children of Israel, submitted them to every kind of oppression and ordered that every male child born of the Hebrew women was to be killed (cf. Ex 1:7-22). Today not a few of the powerful of the earth act in the same way. They too are haunted by the current demographic growth and fear that the most prolific and poorest peoples represent a threat for the well-being and peace of their own countries. Consequently, rather than wishing to face and solve these serious problems with respect for the dignity of individuals and families and for every person's inviolable right to life, they prefer to promote and impose by whatever means a massive program of birth control. Even the economic help which they would be ready to give is unjustly made conditional on the acceptance of an anti-birth policy.

17.1 Humanity today offers us a truly alarming spectacle if we consider not only how extensively attacks on life are spreading, but also their unheard-of numerical proportion and the fact that they receive widespread and powerful support from a broad consensus on the part of society, from widespread legal approval and the involvement of certain sectors of health-care personnel.

17.2 As I emphatically stated at Denver, on the occasion of the Eighth World Youth Day, "with time the threats against life have not grown weaker. They are taking on vast proportions. They are not only threats coming from the outside, from the forces of nature or the 'Cains' who kill the 'Abels'; no, they are *scientifically and systematically programmed threats*. The twentieth century will have been an era of massive attacks on life, an endless series of wars and a continual taking of innocent human life. False prophets and false teachers have had the greatest success."[15] Aside from intentions, which can be varied and perhaps can seem convincing at times, especially if presented in the name of solidarity, we are in fact faced by an objective *"conspiracy against life,"* involving even international institutions engaged in encouraging and carrying out actual campaigns to make contraception, sterilization and abortion widely available. Nor can it be denied that the mass media are often implicated in this conspiracy, by lending credit to that culture which presents recourse to contraception, sterilization, abortion and even euthanasia as a mark of progress and a victory of freedom, while depicting as enemies of freedom and progress those positions which are unreservedly pro-life.

"Am I my brother's keeper?" (Gen 4:9): a perverse idea of freedom

18.1 The panorama described needs to be understood not only in terms of the phenomena of death which characterize it, but also in the *variety of causes* which determine it. The Lord's question, "What have you done?" (Gen 4:10),

---

[15] Address during the Prayer Vigil for the Eighth World Youth Day, Denver (August 14, 1993), II, 3: *AAS* 86 (1994), 419.

seems almost like an invitation addressed to Cain to go beyond the material dimension of his murderous gesture in order to recognize in it all the gravity of the *motives* which occasioned it and the *consequences* which result from it.

18.2 Decisions that go against life sometimes arise from difficult or even tragic situations of profound suffering, loneliness, a total lack of economic prospects, depression and anxiety about the future. Such circumstances can mitigate even to a notable degree subjective responsibility and the consequent culpability of those who make these choices, which in themselves are evil. But today the problem goes far beyond the necessary recognition of these personal situations. It is a problem which exists at the cultural, social and political level, where it reveals its more sinister and disturbing aspect in the tendency, ever more widely shared, to interpret the above crimes against life as *legitimate expressions of individual freedom, to be acknowledged and protected as actual rights.*

18.3 In this way, and with tragic consequences, a long historical process is reaching a turning point. The process which once led to discovering the idea of "human rights" — rights inherent in every person and prior to any constitution and State legislation — is today marked by a *surprising contradiction.* Precisely in an age when the inviolable rights of the person are solemnly proclaimed and the value of life is publicly affirmed, the very right to life is being denied or trampled upon, especially at the more significant moments of existence: the moment of birth and the moment of death.

18.4 On the one hand, the various declarations of human rights and the many initiatives inspired by these declarations show that at the global level there is a growing moral sensitivity more alert to acknowledging the value and dignity of every individual as a human being, without any distinction of race, nationality, religion, political opinion or social class.

18.5 On the other hand, these noble proclamations are unfortunately contradicted by a tragic repudiation of them in practice. This denial is still more distressing, indeed more scandalous, precisely because it is occurring in a society which makes the affirmation and protection of human rights its primary objective and its boast. How can these repeated affirmations of principle be reconciled with the continual increase and widespread justification of attacks on human life? How can we reconcile these declarations with the refusal to accept those who are weak and needy, or elderly, or those who have just been conceived? These attacks go directly against respect for life, and they represent a *direct threat to the entire culture of human rights.* It is a threat capable in the end of jeopardizing the very meaning of democratic coexistence: *rather than societies of "people living together," our cities risk becoming societies of people who are rejected,* marginalized, uprooted and oppressed. If we then look at the wider worldwide perspective, how can we fail to think that the very affirmation of the rights of individuals and peoples made in distinguished international assemblies is a merely futile exercise of rhetoric, if we fail to unmask the selfishness of the rich countries, which exclude poorer countries from access to development or make such access dependent on arbitrary prohibitions against procreation, setting up an opposition between development and man himself? Should we not question the very economic models often adopted by States which, also as a result of international pressures and forms of conditioning, cause and aggravate situations of injustice and violence in which the life of whole peoples is degraded and trampled upon?

19.1 What are *the roots of this remarkable contradiction?*

19.2 We can find them in an overall assessment of a cultural and moral nature, beginning with the mentality which *carries the concept of subjectivity to an extreme* and even distorts it, and recognizes as a subject of rights only the person who enjoys full or at least incipient autonomy and who emerges from a state of total dependence on others. But how can we reconcile this approach with *the exaltation of man as a being who is "not to be used"?* The theory of human rights is based precisely on the affirmation that the human person, unlike animals and things, cannot be subjected to domination by others. We must also mention the mentality which tends to *equate personal dignity with the capacity for verbal and explicit,* or at least perceptible, *communication.* It is clear that on the basis of these presuppositions there is no place in the world for anyone who, like the unborn or the dying, is a weak element in the social structure, or for anyone who appears completely at the mercy of others and radically dependent on them, and can only communicate through the silent language of a profound sharing of affection. In this case it is force which becomes the criterion for choice and action in interpersonal relations and in social life. But this is the exact opposite of what a State ruled by law, as a community in which the "reasons of force" are replaced by the "force of reason," historically intended to affirm.

19.3 At another level, the roots of the contradiction between the solemn affirmation of human rights and their tragic denial in practice lie in a *notion of freedom* which exalts the isolated individual in an absolute way and gives no place to solidarity, to openness to others and service of them. While it is true that the taking of life not yet born or in its final stages is sometimes marked by a mistaken sense of altruism and human compassion, it cannot be denied that such a culture of death, taken as a whole, betrays a completely individualistic concept of freedom, which ends up by becoming the freedom of "the strong" against the weak who have no choice but to submit.

19.4 It is precisely in this sense that Cain's answer to the Lord's question "Where is Abel your brother?" can be interpreted: "I do not know; *am I my brother's keeper?*" (Gen 4:9). Yes, every man is his "brother's keeper," because God entrusts us to one another. And it is also in view of this entrusting that God gives everyone freedom, a freedom which possesses an *inherently relational dimension.* This is a great gift of the Creator, placed as it is at the service of the person and of his fulfillment through the gift of self and openness to others; but when freedom is made absolute in an individualistic way, it is emptied of its original content, and its very meaning and dignity are contradicted.

19.5 There is an even more profound aspect which needs to be emphasized: freedom negates and destroys itself and becomes a factor leading to the destruction of others, when it no longer recognizes and respects *its essential link with the truth.* When freedom, out of a desire to emancipate itself from all forms of tradition and authority, shuts out even the most obvious evidence of an objective and universal truth, which is the foundation of personal and social life, then the person ends up by no longer taking as the sole and indisputable point of reference for his own choices the truth about good and evil, but only his subjective and changeable opinion or, indeed, his selfish interest and whim.

20.1 This view of freedom *leads to a serious distortion of life in society.* If the promotion of the self is understood in terms of absolute autonomy, people inevitably reach the point of rejecting one another. Everyone else is considered an enemy from whom one has to defend oneself. Thus society becomes a mass of individuals placed side by side, but without any mutual bonds. Each one wishes to assert himself independently of the other and in fact intends to make his own interests prevail. Still, in the face of other people's analogous interests, some kind of compromise must be found if one wants a society in which the maximum possible freedom is guaranteed to each individual. In this way, any reference to common values and to a truth absolutely binding on everyone is lost, and social life ventures on to the shifting sands of complete relativism. At that point, *everything is negotiable, everything is open to bargaining:* even the first of the fundamental rights, the right to life.

20.2 This is what is happening also at the level of politics and government: the original and inalienable right to life is questioned or denied on the basis of a parliamentary vote or the will of one part of the people — even if it is the majority. This is the sinister result of a relativism which reigns unopposed: the "right" ceases to be such, because it is no longer firmly founded on the inviolable dignity of the person, but is made subject to the will of the stronger part. In this way democracy, contradicting its own principles, effectively moves toward a form of totalitarianism. The State is no longer the "common home" where all can live together on the basis of principles of fundamental equality, but is transformed into a *tyrant State* which arrogates to itself the right to dispose of the life of the weakest and most defenseless members, from the unborn child to the elderly, in the name of a public interest which is really nothing but the interest of one part. The appearance of the strictest respect for legality is maintained, at least when the laws permitting abortion and euthanasia are the result of a ballot in accordance with what are generally seen as the rules of democracy. Really, what we have here is only the tragic caricature of legality; the democratic ideal, which is only truly such when it acknowledges and safeguards the dignity of every human person, *is betrayed in its very foundations:* "How is it still possible to speak of the dignity of every human person when the killing of the weakest and most innocent is permitted? In the name of what justice is the most unjust of discriminations practiced: some individuals are held to be deserving of defense and others are denied that dignity?"[16] When this happens, the process leading to the breakdown of a genuinely human coexistence and the disintegration of the State itself has already begun.

20.3 To claim the right to abortion, infanticide and euthanasia, and to recognize that right in law, means to attribute to human freedom a *perverse and evil significance*: that of an *absolute power over others and against others*. This is the death of true freedom: "Truly, truly, I say to you, everyone who commits sin is a slave to sin" (Jn 8:34).

"And from your face I shall be hidden" (Gen 4:14): the eclipse of the sense of God and of man

21.1 In seeking the deepest roots of the struggle between the "culture of life" and the "culture of death," we cannot restrict ourselves to the perverse idea of freedom mentioned above. We have to go to the heart of the tragedy being experienced by modern man: *the eclipse of the sense of God and of man,* typical of a social and cultural climate dominated by secularism, which, with its ubiquitous tentacles, succeeds at times in putting Christian communities themselves to the test. Those who allow themselves to be influenced by this

---

[16] John Paul II, Address to the Participants at the Study Conference on "The Right to Life and Europe" (December 18, 1987), 2: *Insegnamenti* X/3 (1987), 1446-1447.

climate easily fall into a sad, vicious circle: *when the sense of God is lost, there is also a tendency to lose the sense of man,* of his dignity and his life; in turn, the systematic violation of the moral law, especially in the serious matter of respect for human life and its dignity, produces a kind of progressive darkening of the capacity to discern God's living and saving presence.

21.2 Once again we can gain insight from the story of Abel's murder by his brother. After the curse imposed on him by God, Cain thus addresses the Lord: "My punishment is greater than I can bear. Behold, you have driven me this day away from the ground; and *from your face I shall be hidden,* and I shall be a fugitive and wanderer on the earth, and whoever finds me will slay me" (Gen 4:13-14). Cain is convinced that his sin will not obtain pardon from the Lord and that his inescapable destiny will be to have to "hide his face" from him. If Cain is capable of confessing that his fault is "greater than he can bear," it is because he is conscious of being in the presence of God and before God's just judgment. It is really only before the Lord that man can admit his sin and recognize its full seriousness. Such was the experience of David who, after "having committed evil in the sight of the Lord," and being rebuked by the Prophet Nathan, exclaimed: "My offenses truly I know them; my sin is always before me. Against you, you alone, have I sinned; what is evil in your sight I have done" (Ps 51:5-6).

22.1 Consequently, when the sense of God is lost, the sense of man is also threatened and poisoned, as the Second Vatican Council concisely states: "Without the Creator, the creature would disappear. . . . But when God is forgotten, the creature itself grows unintelligible."[17] Man is no longer able to see himself as "mysteriously different" from other earthly creatures; he regards himself merely as one more living being, as an organism which, at most, has reached a very high stage of perfection. Enclosed in the narrow horizon of his physical nature, he is somehow reduced to being "a thing," and no longer grasps the "transcendent" character of his "existence as man." He no longer considers life as a splendid gift of God, something "sacred" entrusted to his responsibility and thus also to his loving care and "veneration." Life itself becomes a mere "thing," which man claims as his exclusive property, completely subject to his control and manipulation.

22.2 Thus, in relation to life at birth or at death, man is no longer capable of posing the question of the truest meaning of his own existence, nor can he assimilate with genuine freedom these crucial moments of his own history. He is concerned only with "doing," and, using all kinds of technology, he busies himself with programming, controlling and dominating birth and death. Birth

---

[17] Pastoral Constitution on the Church in the Modern World *Gaudium et Spes,* 36.

and death, instead of being primary experiences demanding to be "lived," become things to be merely "possessed" or "rejected."

22.3 Moreover, once all reference to God has been removed, it is not surprising that the meaning of everything else becomes profoundly distorted. Nature itself, from being *"mater"* (mother), is now reduced to being "matter," and is subjected to every kind of manipulation. This is the direction in which a certain technical and scientific way of thinking, prevalent in present-day culture, appears to be leading when it rejects the very idea that there is a truth of creation which must be acknowledged, or a plan of God for life which must be respected. Something similar happens when concern about the consequences of such a "freedom without law" leads some people to the opposite position of a "law without freedom," as for example in ideologies which consider it unlawful to interfere in any way with nature, practically "divinizing" it. Again, this is a misunderstanding of nature's dependence on the plan of the Creator. Thus it is clear that the loss of contact with God's wise design is the deepest root of modern man's confusion, both when this loss leads to a freedom without rules and when it leaves man in "fear" of his freedom.

22.4 By living "as if God did not exist," man not only loses sight of the mystery of God, but also of the mystery of the world and the mystery of his own being.

23.1 The eclipse of the sense of God and of man inevitably leads to a *practical materialism,* which breeds individualism, utilitarianism and hedonism. Here too we see the permanent validity of the words of the Apostle: "And since they did not see fit to acknowledge God, God gave them up to a base mind and to improper conduct" (Rom 1:28). The values of *being* are replaced by those of *having.* The only goal which counts is the pursuit of one's own material well-being. The so-called "quality of life" is interpreted primarily or exclusively as economic efficiency, inordinate consumerism, physical beauty and pleasure, to the neglect of the more profound dimensions — interpersonal, spiritual and religious — of existence.

23.2 In such a context *suffering,* an inescapable burden of human existence but also a factor of possible personal growth, is "censored," rejected as useless, indeed opposed as an evil always and in every way to be avoided. When it cannot be avoided and the prospect of even some future well-being vanishes, then life appears to have lost all meaning and the temptation grows in man to claim the right to suppress it.

23.3 Within this same cultural climate, the *body* is no longer perceived as a properly personal reality, a sign and place of relations with others, with God and with the world. It is reduced to pure materiality: it is simply a complex of organs, functions and energies to be used according to the sole criteria of pleasure and efficiency. Consequently, *sexuality* too is depersonalized and exploited: from being the sign, place and language of love, that is, of the gift of self and acceptance of another in all the other's richness as a person, it increasingly becomes the occasion and instrument for self-assertion and the selfish satisfaction of personal desires and instincts. Thus the original import of human sexuality is distorted and falsified, and the two meanings, unitive and procreative, inherent in the very nature of the conjugal act, are artificially separated: in this way the marriage union is betrayed and its fruitfulness is subjected to the caprice of the couple. *Procreation* then becomes the "enemy" to be avoided in sexual activity: if it is welcomed, this is only because it expresses a desire, or indeed the intention, to have a child "at all costs," and not because it signifies the complete acceptance of the other and therefore an openness to the richness of life which the child represents.

23.4 In the materialistic perspective described so far, *interpersonal relations are seriously impoverished.* The first to be harmed are women, children, the sick or suffering, and the elderly. The criterion of personal dignity — which demands respect, generosity and service — is replaced by the criterion of efficiency, functionality and usefulness: others are considered not for what they "are," but for what they "have, do and produce." This is the supremacy of the strong over the weak.

24.1 *It is at the heart of the moral conscience* that the eclipse of the sense of God and of man, with all its various and deadly consequences for life, is taking place. It is a question, above all, of the *individual* conscience as it stands before God in its singleness and uniqueness.[18] But it is also a question, in a certain sense, of the "moral conscience" *of society:* in a way it too is responsible, not only because it tolerates or fosters behavior contrary to life, but also because it encourages the "culture of death," creating and consolidating actual "structures of sin" which go against life. The moral conscience, both individual and social, is today subjected, also as a result of the penetrating influence of the media, to an *extremely serious and mortal danger:* that of *confusion between good and evil,* precisely in relation to the fundamental right to life. A large part of contemporary society looks sadly like that humanity which Paul describes in his Letter to the Romans. It is composed "of men who by their wickedness suppress the truth" (1:18): having denied God and believing that they can build the earthly city without him, "they became futile in

---

[18] Cf. ibid., 16.

their thinking" so that "their senseless minds were darkened" (1:21); "claiming to be wise, they became fools" (1:22), carrying out works deserving of death, and "they not only do them but approve those who practice them" (1:32). When conscience, this bright lamp of the soul (cf. Mt 6:22-23), calls "evil good and good evil" (Is 5:20), it is already on the path to the most alarming corruption and the darkest moral blindness.

24.2 And yet all the conditioning and efforts to enforce silence fail to stifle the voice of the Lord echoing in the conscience of every individual: it is always from this intimate sanctuary of the conscience that a new journey of love, openness and service to human life can begin.

"You have come to the sprinkled blood" (cf. Heb 12:22, 24): signs of hope and invitation to commitment

25.1 "The voice of your brother's blood is crying to me from the ground" (Gen 4:10). It is not only the voice of the blood of Abel, the first innocent man to be murdered, which cries to God, the source and defender of life. The blood of every other human being who has been killed since Abel is also a voice raised to the Lord. In an absolutely singular way, as the author of the Letter to the Hebrews reminds us, *the voice of the blood of Christ*, of whom Abel in his innocence is a prophetic figure, cries out to God: "You have come to Mount Zion and to the city of the living God . . . to the mediator of a new covenant, and to the sprinkled blood that speaks more graciously than the blood of Abel" (12:22, 24).

25.2 It is *the sprinkled blood*. A symbol and prophetic sign of it had been the blood of the sacrifices of the Old Covenant, whereby God expressed his will to communicate his own life to men, purifying and consecrating them (cf. Ex 24:8; Lev 17:11). Now all of this is fulfilled and comes true in Christ: his is the sprinkled blood which redeems, purifies and saves; it is the blood of the Mediator of the New Covenant "poured out for many for the forgiveness of sins" (Mt 26:28). This blood, which flows from the pierced side of Christ on the Cross (cf. Jn 19:34), "speaks more graciously" than the blood of Abel; indeed it expresses and requires a more radical "justice," and above all it implores mercy,[19] it makes intercession for the brethren before the Father (cf. Heb 7:25), and it is the source of perfect redemption and the gift of new life.

25.3 The blood of Christ, while it reveals the grandeur of the Father's love, *shows how precious man is in God's eyes and how priceless the value of his life*. The Apostle Peter reminds us of this: "You know that you were ransomed from the futile ways inherited from your fathers, not with perishable things such as silver or gold, but with the precious blood of Christ, like that of a lamb

---

[19] Cf. Saint Gregory the Great, *Moralia in Job*, 13, 23: *CCL* 143A, 683.

without blemish or spot" (1 Pet 1:18-19). Precisely by contemplating the precious blood of Christ, the sign of his self-giving love (cf. Jn 13:1), the believer learns to recognize and appreciate the almost divine dignity of every human being and can exclaim with ever renewed and grateful wonder: "How precious must man be in the eyes of the Creator, if he 'gained so great a Redeemer' (*Exsultet* of the Easter Vigil), and if God 'gave his only Son' in order that man 'should not perish but have eternal life' (cf. Jn 3:16)!"[20]

25.4 Furthermore, Christ's blood reveals to man that his greatness, and therefore his vocation, consists in *the sincere gift of self.* Precisely because it is poured out as the gift of life, the blood of Christ is no longer a sign of death, of definitive separation from the brethren, but the instrument of a communion which is richness of life for all. Whoever in the Sacrament of the Eucharist drinks this blood and abides in Jesus (cf. Jn 6:56) is drawn into the dynamism of his love and gift of life, in order to bring to its fullness the original vocation to love which belongs to everyone (cf. Gen 1:27, 2:18-24).

25.5 It is from the blood of Christ that all draw *the strength to commit themselves to promoting life.* It is precisely this blood that is *the most powerful source of hope, indeed it is the foundation of the absolute certitude that in God's plan life will be victorious.* "And death shall be no more," exclaims the powerful voice which comes from the throne of God in the heavenly Jerusalem (Rev 21:4). And Saint Paul assures us that the present victory over sin is a sign and anticipation of the definitive victory over death, when there "shall come to pass the saying that is written: 'Death is swallowed up in victory.' 'O death, where is your victory? O death, where is your sting?' " (1 Cor 15:54-55).

26.1 In effect, signs which point to this victory are not lacking in our societies and cultures, strongly marked though they are by the "culture of death." It would therefore be to give a one-sided picture, which could lead to sterile discouragement, if the condemnation of the threats to life were not accompanied by the presentation of the *positive signs* at work in humanity's present situation.

26.2 Unfortunately, it is often hard to see and recognize these positive signs, perhaps also because they do not receive sufficient attention in the communications media. Yet how many initiatives of help and support for people who are weak and defenseless have sprung up and continue to spring up in the Christian community and in civil society at the local, national and international level through the efforts of individuals, groups, movements and organizations of various kinds!

[20] John Paul II, Encyclical Letter *Redemptor Hominis* (March 4, 1979), 10: *AAS* 71 (1979), 274.

26.3 There are still many *married couples* who, with a generous sense of responsibility, are ready to accept children as "the supreme gift of marriage."[21] Nor is there a lack of *families* which, over and above their everyday service to life, are willing to accept abandoned children, boys and girls and teenagers in difficulty, handicapped persons, elderly men and women who have been left alone. Many *centers in support of life*, or similar institutions, are sponsored by individuals and groups which, with admirable dedication and sacrifice, offer moral and material support to mothers who are in difficulty and are tempted to have recourse to abortion. Increasingly, there are appearing in many places *groups of volunteers* prepared to offer hospitality to persons without a family, who find themselves in conditions of particular distress or who need a supportive environment to help them to overcome destructive habits and discover anew the meaning of life.

26.4 *Medical science*, thanks to the committed efforts of researchers and practitioners, continues in its efforts to discover ever more effective remedies: treatments which were once inconceivable but which now offer much promise for the future are today being developed for the unborn, the suffering and those in an acute or terminal stage of sickness. Various agencies and organizations are mobilizing their efforts to bring the benefits of the most advanced medicine to countries most afflicted by poverty and endemic diseases. In a similar way national and international associations of physicians are being organized to bring quick relief to peoples affected by natural disasters, epidemics or wars. Even if a just international distribution of medical resources is still far from being a reality, how can we not recognize in the steps taken so far the sign of a growing solidarity among peoples, a praiseworthy human and moral sensitivity and a greater respect for life?

27.1 In view of laws which permit abortion and in view of efforts, which here and there have been successful, to legalize euthanasia, *movements and initiatives to raise social awareness in defense of life* have sprung up in many parts of the world. When, in accordance with their principles, such movements act resolutely but without resorting to violence, they promote a wider and more profound consciousness of the value of life, and evoke and bring about a more determined commitment to its defense.

27.2 Furthermore, how can we fail to mention *all those daily gestures of openness, sacrifice and unselfish care* which countless people lovingly make in families, hospitals, orphanages, homes for the elderly and other centers or

[21] Second Vatican Ecumenical Council, Pastoral Constitution on the Church in the Modern World *Gaudium et Spes*, 50.

communities which defend life? Allowing herself to be guided by the example of Jesus the "Good Samaritan" (cf. Lk 10:29-37) and upheld by his strength, the Church has always been in the front line in providing charitable help: so many of her sons and daughters, especially men and women Religious, in traditional and ever new forms, have consecrated and continue to consecrate their lives to God, freely giving of themselves out of love for their neighbor, especially for the weak and needy. These deeds strengthen the bases of the "civilization of love and life," without which the life of individuals and of society itself loses its most genuinely human quality. Even if they go unnoticed and remain hidden to most people, faith assures us that the Father "who sees in secret" (Mt 6:6) not only will reward these actions but already here and now makes them produce lasting fruit for the good of all.

27.3 Among the signs of hope we should also count the spread at many levels of public opinion of *a new sensitivity ever more opposed to war* as an instrument for the resolution of conflicts between peoples and increasingly oriented to finding effective but "non-violent" means to counter the armed aggressor. In the same perspective there is evidence of a *growing public opposition to the death penalty,* even when such a penalty is seen as a kind of "legitimate defense" on the part of society. Modern society in fact has the means of effectively suppressing crime by rendering criminals harmless without definitively denying them the chance to reform.

27.4 Another welcome sign is the growing attention being paid to the *quality of life* and to *ecology,* especially in more developed societies, where people's expectations are no longer concentrated so much on problems of survival as on the search for an overall improvement of living conditions. Especially significant is the reawakening of an ethical reflection on issues affecting life. The emergence and ever more widespread development of *bioethics* is promoting more reflection and dialogue — between believers and non-believers, as well as between followers of different religions — on ethical problems, including fundamental issues pertaining to human life.

28.1 This situation, with its lights and shadows, ought to make us all fully aware that we are facing an enormous and dramatic clash between good and evil, death and life, the "culture of death" and the "culture of life." We find ourselves not only "faced with" but necessarily "in the midst of" this conflict: we are all involved and we all share in it, with the inescapable responsibility of *choosing to be unconditionally pro-life.*

28.2 For us too Moses' invitation rings out loud and clear: "See, I have set before you this day life and good, death and evil. . . . I have set before you life and death, blessing and curse; *therefore choose life, that you and your descendants may live*" (Dt 30:15,19). This invitation is very appropriate for us who are called day by day to the duty of choosing between the "culture of life" and the "culture of death." But the call of Deuteronomy goes even deeper, for it urges us to make a choice which is properly religious and moral. It is a question of giving our own existence a basic orientation and living the law of the Lord faithfully and consistently: "If you obey the commandments of the Lord your God which I command you this day, by *loving the Lord your God,* by *walking in his ways,* and by *keeping his commandments* and his statutes and his ordinances, then you shall live. . . . Therefore choose life, that you and your descendants may live, loving the Lord your God, obeying his voice, and cleaving to him; *for that means life to you and length of days*" (30:16,19-20).

28.3 The unconditional choice for life reaches its full religious and moral meaning when it flows from, is formed by and nourished by *faith in Christ.* Nothing helps us so much to face positively the conflict between death and life in which we are engaged as faith in the Son of God who became man and dwelt among men so "that they may have life, and have it abundantly" (Jn 10:10). It is a matter of *faith in the risen Lord, who has conquered death;* faith in the blood of Christ "that speaks more graciously than the blood of Abel" (Heb 12:24).

28.4 With the light and strength of this faith, therefore, in facing the challenges of the present situation, the Church is becoming more aware of the grace and responsibility which come to her from her Lord of proclaiming, celebrating and serving the *Gospel of life.*

II

I Came That They May Have Life

The Christian Message concerning Life

"The life was made manifest, and we saw it" (1 Jn 1:2): with our gaze fixed on Christ, "the Word of life"

29.1 Faced with the countless grave threats to life present in the modern world, one could feel overwhelmed by sheer powerlessness: good can never be powerful enough to triumph over evil!

29.2 At such times the People of God, and this includes every believer, is called to profess with humility and courage its faith in Jesus Christ, "the Word of life" (1 Jn 1:1). The *Gospel of life* is not simply a reflection, however new and profound, on human life. Nor is it merely a commandment aimed at raising awareness and bringing about significant changes in society. Still less is it an illusory promise of a better future. The *Gospel of life* is something concrete and personal, for it consists in the proclamation of *the very person of Jesus.* Jesus made himself known to the Apostle Thomas, and in him to every person, with the words: "I am the way, and the truth, and the life" (Jn 14:6). This is also how he spoke of himself to Martha, the sister of Lazarus: "I am the resurrection and the life; he who believes in me, though he die, yet shall he live, and whoever lives and believes in me shall never die" (Jn 11:25-26). Jesus is the Son who from all eternity receives life from the Father (cf. Jn 5:26), and who has come among men to make them sharers in this gift: "I came that they may have life, and have it abundantly" (Jn 10:10).

29.3 Through the words, the actions and the very person of Jesus, man is given the possibility of "knowing" *the complete truth* concerning the value of human life. From this "source" he receives, in particular, the capacity to "accomplish" this truth perfectly (cf. Jn 3:21), that is, to accept and fulfill completely the responsibility of loving and serving, of defending and promoting human life. In Christ, the *Gospel of life* is definitively proclaimed and fully given. This is the Gospel which, already present in the revelation of the Old Testament and indeed written in the heart of every man and woman, has echoed in every conscience "from the beginning," from the time of creation itself, in such a way that, despite the negative consequences of sin, *it can also be known in its essential traits by human reason.* As the Second Vatican Council teaches, Christ "perfected revelation by fulfilling it through his whole work of making himself present and manifesting himself; through his words and deeds, his signs and wonders, but especially through his death and glorious Resurrection from the dead and final sending of the Spirit of truth. Moreover, he confirmed with divine testimony what revelation proclaimed: that God is with us to free us from the darkness of sin and death, and to raise us up to life eternal."[22]

30.1 Hence, with our attention fixed on the Lord Jesus, we wish to hear from him once again "the words of God" (Jn 3:34) and meditate anew on the *Gospel of life.* The deepest and most original meaning of this meditation on what revelation tells us about human life was taken up by the Apostle John in the opening words of his First Letter: "That which was from the beginning, which we have heard, which we have seen with our eyes, which we have looked

---

[22] Dogmatic Constitution on Divine Revelation *Dei Verbum,* 4.

upon and touched with our hands, concerning the Word of life — the life was made manifest, and we saw it, and testify to it, and proclaim to you the eternal life which was with the Father and was made manifest to us — that which we have seen and heard we proclaim also to you, so that you may have fellowship with us" (1:1-3).

30.2 In Jesus, the "Word of life," God's eternal life is thus proclaimed and given. Thanks to this proclamation and gift, our physical and spiritual life, also in its earthly phase, acquires its full value and meaning, for God's eternal life is in fact the end to which our living in this world is directed and called. In this way the *Gospel of life* includes everything that human experience and reason tell us about the value of human life, accepting it, purifying it, exalting it and bringing it to fulfillment.

"The Lord is my strength and my song, and he has become my salvation" (Ex 15:2): life is always a good

31.1 The fullness of the Gospel message about life was prepared for in the Old Testament. Especially in the events of the Exodus, the center of the Old Testament faith experience, Israel discovered the preciousness of its life in the eyes of God. When it seemed doomed to extermination because of the threat of death hanging over all its newborn males (cf. Ex 1:15-22), the Lord revealed himself to Israel as its Savior, with the power to ensure a future to those without hope. Israel thus comes to know clearly that *its existence* is not at the mercy of a Pharaoh who can exploit it at his despotic whim. On the contrary, Israel's life is *the object of God's gentle and intense love.*

31.2 Freedom from slavery meant the gift of an identity, the recognition of an indestructible dignity and *the beginning of a new history,* in which the discovery of God and discovery of self go hand in hand. The Exodus was a foundational experience and a model for the future. Through it, Israel comes to learn that whenever its existence is threatened it need only turn to God with renewed trust in order to find in him effective help: "I formed you, you are my servant; O Israel, you will not be forgotten by me" (Is 44:21).

31.3 Thus, in coming to know the value of its own existence as a people, Israel also grows in its *perception of the meaning and value of life itself.* This reflection is developed more specifically in the Wisdom Literature, on the basis of daily experience of the precariousness of life and awareness of the threats which assail it. Faced with the contradictions of life, faith is challenged to respond.

31.4 More than anything else, it is the problem of suffering which challenges faith and puts it to the test. How can we fail to appreciate the universal anguish of man when we meditate on the Book of Job? The innocent man overwhelmed by suffering is understandably led to wonder: "Why is light given to him that is in misery, and life to the bitter in soul, who long for death, but it comes not, and dig for it more than for hid treasures?" (3:20-21). But even when the darkness is deepest, faith points to a trusting and adoring acknowledgment of the "mystery": "I know that you can do all things, and that no purpose of yours can be thwarted" (Job 42:2).

31.5 Revelation progressively allows the first notion of immortal life planted by the Creator in the human heart to be grasped with ever greater clarity: "He has made everything beautiful in its time; also he has put eternity into man's mind" (Eccles 3:11). This *first notion of totality and fullness* is waiting to be manifested in love and brought to perfection, by God's free gift, through sharing in his eternal life.

"The name of Jesus . . . has made this man strong" (Acts 3:16): in the uncertainties of human life, Jesus brings life's meaning to fulfillment

32.1 The experience of the people of the Covenant is renewed in the experience of all the "poor" who meet Jesus of Nazareth. Just as God who "loves the living" (cf. Wis 11:26) had reassured Israel in the midst of danger, so now the Son of God proclaims to all who feel threatened and hindered that their lives too are a good to which the Father's love gives meaning and value.

32.2 "The blind receive their sight, the lame walk, lepers are cleansed, and the deaf hear, the dead are raised up, the poor have good news preached to them" (Lk 7:22). With these words of the Prophet Isaiah (35:5-6, 61:1), Jesus sets forth the meaning of his own mission: all who suffer because their lives are in some way "diminished" thus hear from him the "good news" of God's concern for them, and they know for certain that their lives too are a gift carefully guarded in the hands of the Father (cf. Mt 6:25-34).

32.3 It is above all the "poor" to whom Jesus speaks in his preaching and actions. The crowds of the sick and the outcasts who follow him and seek him out (cf. Mt 4:23-25) find in his words and actions a revelation of the great value of their lives and of how their hope of salvation is well-founded.

32.4 The same thing has taken place in the Church's mission from the beginning. When the Church proclaims Christ as the one who "went about doing good and healing all that were oppressed by the devil, for God was with him" (Acts 10:38), she is conscious of being the bearer of a message of salvation which resounds in all its newness precisely amid the hardships and poverty of human life. Peter cured the cripple who daily sought alms at the "Beautiful Gate" of the Temple in Jerusalem, saying: "I have no silver and gold, but I give you what I have; in the name of Jesus Christ of Nazareth, walk" (Acts 3:6). By faith in Jesus, "the Author of life" (Acts 3:15), life which lies abandoned and cries out for help regains self-esteem and full dignity.

32.5 The words and deeds of Jesus and those of his Church are not meant only for those who are sick or suffering or in some way neglected by society. On a deeper level they affect *the very meaning of every person's life in its moral and spiritual dimensions*. Only those who recognize that their life is marked by the evil of sin can discover in an encounter with Jesus the Savior the truth and the authenticity of their own existence. Jesus himself says as much: "Those who are well have no need of a physician, but those who are sick; I have not come to call the righteous, but sinners to repentance" (Lk 5:31-32).

32.6 But the person who, like the rich landowner in the Gospel parable, thinks that he can make his life secure by the possession of material goods alone, is deluding himself. Life is slipping away from him, and very soon he will find himself bereft of it without ever having appreciated its real meaning: "Fool! This night your soul is required of you; and the things you have prepared, whose will they be?" (Lk 12:20).

33.1 In Jesus' own life, from beginning to end, we find a singular "dialectic" between the experience of the uncertainty of human life and the affirmation of its value. Jesus' life is marked by uncertainty from the very moment of his birth. He is certainly *accepted* by the righteous, who echo Mary's immediate and joyful "yes" (cf. Lk 1:38). But there is also, from the start, *rejection* on the part of a world which grows hostile and looks for the child in order "to destroy him" (Mt 2:13); a world which remains indifferent and unconcerned about the fulfillment of the mystery of this life entering the world: "there was no place for them in the inn" (Lk 2:7). In this contrast between threats and insecurity on the one hand and the power of God's gift on the other, there shines forth all the more clearly the glory which radiates from the house at Nazareth and from the manger at Bethlehem: this life which is born is salvation for all humanity (cf. Lk 2:11).

33.2 Life's contradictions and risks were fully accepted by Jesus: "though he was rich, yet for your sake he became poor, so that by his poverty you might become rich" (2 Cor 8:9). The poverty of which Paul speaks is not only a stripping of divine privileges, but also a sharing in the lowliest and most vulnerable conditions of human life (cf. Phil 2:6-7). Jesus lived this poverty throughout his life until the culminating moment of the Cross: "He humbled himself and became obedient unto death, even death on a cross. Therefore

God has highly exalted him and bestowed on him the name which is above every name" (Phil 2:8-9). It is precisely *by his death* that Jesus *reveals all the splendor and value of life,* inasmuch as his self-oblation on the Cross becomes the source of new life for all people (cf. Jn 12:32). In his journeying amid contradictions and in the very loss of his life, Jesus is guided by the certainty that his life is in the hands of the Father. Consequently, on the Cross he can say to him: "Father, into your hands I commend my spirit!" (Lk 23:46), that is, my life. Truly great must be the value of human life if the Son of God has taken it up and made it the instrument of the salvation of all humanity!

"Called . . . to be conformed to the image of his Son" (Rom 8:28-29): God's glory shines on the face of man

34.1 Life is always a good. This is an instinctive perception and a fact of experience, and man is called to grasp the profound reason why this is so.

34.2 *Why is life a good?* This question is found everywhere in the Bible, and from the very first pages it receives a powerful and amazing answer. The life which God gives man is quite different from the life of all other living creatures, inasmuch as man, although formed from the dust of the earth (cf. Gen 2:7, 3:19; Job 34:15; Ps 103:14, 104:29), *is a manifestation of God in the world, a sign of his presence, a trace of his glory* (cf. Gen 1:26-27; Ps 8:6). This is what Saint Irenaeus of Lyons wanted to emphasize in his celebrated definition: "Man, living man, is the glory of God."[23] Man has been given *a sublime dignity* based on the intimate bond which unites him to his Creator: in man there shines forth a reflection of God himself.

34.3 The Book of Genesis affirms this when, in the first account of creation, it places man at the summit of God's creative activity, as its crown, at the culmination of a process which leads from indistinct chaos to the most perfect of creatures. *Everything in creation is ordered to man, and everything is made subject to him:* "Fill the earth and subdue it; and have dominion over . . . every living thing" (1:28); this is God's command to the man and the woman. A similar message is found also in the other account of creation: "The Lord God took the man and put him in the garden of Eden to till it and keep it" (Gen 2:15). We see here a clear affirmation of the primacy of man over things; these are made subject to him and entrusted to his responsible care, whereas for no reason can he be made subject to other men and almost reduced to the level of a thing.

34.4 In the biblical narrative, the difference between man and other creatures is shown above all by the fact that only the creation of man is presented

---

[23] "Gloria Dei vivens homo": *Adversus Haereses,* IV, 20, 7: *SCh* 100/2, 648-649.

as the result of a special decision on the part of God, a deliberation to estab-lish *a particular and specific bond with the Creator:* "Let us make man in our image, after our likeness" (Gen 1:26). *The life* which God offers to man *is a gift by which God shares something of himself with his creature.*

34.5 Israel would ponder at length the meaning of this particular bond between man and God. The Book of Sirach too recognizes that God, in creat-ing human beings, "endowed them with strength like his own, and made them in his own image" (17:3). The biblical author sees as part of this image not only man's dominion over the world but also *those spiritual faculties which are distinctively human,* such as reason, discernment between good and evil, and free will: "He filled them with knowledge and understanding, and showed them good and evil" (Sir 17:7). *The ability to attain truth and freedom are human prerogatives* inasmuch as man is created in the image of his Creator, God who is true and just (cf. Dt 32:4). Man alone, among all visible creatures, is "capable of knowing and loving his Creator."[24] The life which God bestows upon man is much more than mere existence in time. It is a drive toward fullness of life; *it is the seed of an existence which transcends the very limits of time:* "For God created man for incorruption, and made him in the image of his own eternity" (Wis 2:23).

35.1 The Yahwist account of creation expresses the same conviction. This ancient narrative speaks of *a divine breath* which *is breathed into man* so that he may come to life: "The Lord God formed man of dust from the ground, and breathed into his nostrils the breath of life; and man became a living being" (Gen 2:7).

35.2 The divine origin of this spirit of life explains the perennial dissatis-faction which man feels throughout his days on earth. Because he is made by God and bears within himself an indelible imprint of God, man is naturally drawn to God. When he heeds the deepest yearnings of the heart, every man must make his own the words of truth expressed by Saint Augustine: "You have made us for yourself, O Lord, and our hearts are restless until they rest in you."[25]

35.3 How very significant is the dissatisfaction which marks man's life in Eden as long as his sole point of reference is the world of plants and animals (cf. Gen 2:20). Only the appearance of the woman, a being who is flesh of his flesh and bone of his bones (cf. Gen 2:23), and in whom the spirit of God the

---

[24] Second Vatican Ecumenical Council, Pastoral Constitution on the Church in the Modern World *Gaudium et Spes,* 12.

[25] *Confessions,* I, 1: CCL 27, 1.

Creator is also alive, can satisfy the need for interpersonal dialogue, so vital for human existence. In the other, whether man or woman, there is a reflection of God himself, the definitive goal and fulfillment of every person.

35.4 "What is man that you are mindful of him, and the son of man that you care for him?" the Psalmist wonders (Ps 8:4). Compared to the immensity of the universe, man is very small, and yet this very contrast reveals his greatness: "You have made him little less than a god, and crown him with glory and honor" (Ps 8:5). *The glory of God shines on the face of man.* In man the Creator finds his rest, as Saint Ambrose comments with a sense of awe: "The sixth day is finished and the creation of the world ends with the formation of that masterpiece which is man, who exercises dominion over all living creatures and is as it were the crown of the universe and the supreme beauty of every created being. Truly we should maintain a reverential silence, since the Lord rested from every work he had undertaken in the world. He rested then in the depths of man, he rested in man's mind and in his thought; after all, he had created man endowed with reason, capable of imitating him, of emulating his virtue, of hungering for heavenly graces. In these his gifts God reposes, who has said: 'Upon whom shall I rest, if not upon the one who is humble, contrite in spirit and trembles at my word?' (Is 66:1-2). I thank the Lord our God who has created so wonderful a work in which to take his rest."[26]

36.1 Unfortunately, God's marvelous plan was marred by the appearance of sin in history. Through sin, man rebels against his Creator and ends up by *worshiping creatures:* "They exchanged the truth about God for a lie and worshiped and served the creature rather than the Creator" (Rom 1:25). As a result man not only deforms the image of God in his own person, but is tempted to offenses against it in others as well, replacing relationships of communion by attitudes of distrust, indifference, hostility and even murderous hatred. When *God* is not acknowledged *as God,* the profound meaning of man is betrayed and communion between people is compromised.

36.2 In the life of man, God's image shines forth anew and is again revealed in all its fullness at the coming of the Son of God in human flesh. "Christ is the image of the invisible God" (Col 1:15); he "reflects the glory of God and bears the very stamp of his nature" (Heb 1:3). He is the perfect image of the Father.

36.3 The plan of life given to the first Adam finds at last its fulfillment in Christ. Whereas the disobedience of Adam had ruined and marred God's plan for human life and introduced death into the world, the redemptive obedience

---

[26] *Exameron,* VI, 75-76: *CSEL* 32, 260-261.

of Christ is the source of grace poured out upon the human race, opening wide to everyone the gates of the Kingdom of life (cf. Rom 5:12-21). As the Apostle Paul states: "The first man Adam became a living being; the last Adam became a life-giving spirit" (1 Cor 15:45).

36.4 All who commit themselves to following Christ are given the fullness of life: the divine image is restored, renewed and brought to perfection in them. God's plan for human beings is this, that they should "be conformed to the image of his Son" (Rom 8:29). Only thus, in the splendor of this image, can man be freed from the slavery of idolatry, rebuild lost fellowship and rediscover his true identity.

"Whoever lives and believes in me shall never die" (Jn 11:26): the gift of eternal life

37.1 The life which the Son of God came to give to human beings cannot be reduced to mere existence in time. The life which was always "in him" and which is the "light of men" (Jn 1:4) *consists in being begotten of God and sharing in the fullness of his love:* "To all who received him, who believed in his name, he gave power to become children of God; who were born, not of blood nor of the will of the flesh nor of the will of man, but of God" (Jn 1:12-13).

37.2 Sometimes Jesus refers to this life which he came to give simply as "life," and he presents being born of God as a necessary condition if man is to attain the end for which God has created him: "Unless one is born anew, he cannot see the kingdom of God" (Jn 3:3). To give this life is the real object of Jesus' mission: he is the one who "comes down from heaven, and gives life to the world" (Jn 6:33). Thus can he truly say: "He who follows me . . . will have the light of life" (Jn 8:12).

37.3 At other times, Jesus speaks of "eternal life." Here the adjective does more than merely evoke a perspective which is beyond time. The life which Jesus promises and gives is "eternal" because it is a full participation in the life of the "Eternal One." Whoever believes in Jesus and enters into communion with him has eternal life (cf. Jn 3:15, 6:40) because he hears from Jesus the only words which reveal and communicate to his existence the fullness of life. These are the "words of eternal life" which Peter acknowledges in his confession of faith: "Lord, to whom shall we go? You have the words of eternal life; and we have believed, and have come to know, that you are the Holy One of God" (Jn 6:68-69). Jesus himself, addressing the Father in the great priestly prayer, declares what eternal life consists in: "This is eternal life, that they may know you, the only true God, and Jesus Christ, whom you have sent" (Jn 17:3). To know God and his Son is to accept the mystery of the loving communion of the Father, the Son and the Holy Spirit into one's own life, which *even now* is open to eternal life because it *shares in the life of God.*

38.1 Eternal life is therefore the life of God himself and at the same time the *life of the children of God.* As they ponder this unexpected and inexpressible truth which comes to us from God in Christ, believers cannot fail to be filled with ever new wonder and unbounded gratitude. They can say in the words of the Apostle John: "See what love the Father has given us, that we should be called children of God; and so we are. . . . Beloved, we are God's children now; it does not yet appear what we shall be, but we know that when he appears we shall be like him, for we shall see him as he is" (1 Jn 3:1-2).

38.2 *Here the Christian truth about life becomes most sublime.* The dignity of this life is linked not only to its beginning, to the fact that it comes from God, but also to its final end, to its destiny of fellowship with God in knowledge and love of him. In the light of this truth Saint Irenaeus qualifies and completes his praise of man: "The glory of God" is indeed, "man, living man," but "the life of man consists in the vision of God."[27]

38.3 Immediate consequences arise from this for human life in its *earthly state,* in which, for that matter, eternal life already springs forth and begins to grow. Although man instinctively loves life because it is a good, this love will find further inspiration and strength, and new breadth and depth, in the divine dimensions of this good. Similarly, the love which every human being has for life cannot be reduced simply to a desire to have sufficient space for self-expression and for entering into relationships with others; rather, it develops in a joyous awareness that life can become the "place" where God manifests himself, where we meet him and enter into communion with him. The life which Jesus gives in no way lessens the value of our existence in time; it takes it and directs it to its final destiny: "I am the resurrection and the life . . . whoever lives and believes in me shall never die" (Jn 11:25-26).

"From man in regard to his fellow man I will demand an accounting" (Gen 9:5): reverence and love for every human life

39.1 Man's life comes from God; it is his gift, his image and imprint, a sharing in his breath of life. *God* therefore *is the sole Lord of this life:* man cannot do with it as he wills. God himself makes this clear to Noah after the flood: "For your own lifeblood, too, I will demand an accounting . . . and from man in regard to his fellow man I will demand an accounting for human life" (Gen 9:5). The biblical text is concerned to emphasize how the sacredness of

---

[27] "Vita autem hominis visio Dei": *Adversus Haereses,* IV, 20, 7: *SCh* 100/2, 648-649.

life has its foundation in God and in his creative activity: "For God made man in his own image" (Gen 9:6).

39.2 Human life and death are thus in the hands of God, in his power: "In his hand is the life of every living thing and the breath of all mankind," exclaims Job (12:10). "The Lord brings to death and brings to life; he brings down to Sheol and raises up" (1 Sam 2:6). He alone can say: "It is I who bring both death and life" (Dt 32:39).

39.3 But God does not exercise this power in an arbitrary and threatening way, but rather as part of his *care and loving concern for his creatures*. If it is true that human life is in the hands of God, it is no less true that these are loving hands, like those of a mother who accepts, nurtures and takes care of her child: "I have calmed and quieted my soul like a child quieted at its mother's breast; like a child that is quieted is my soul" (Ps 131:2; cf. Is 49:15, 66:12-13; Hos 11:4). Thus Israel does not see in the history of peoples and in the destiny of individuals the outcome of mere chance or of blind fate, but rather the results of a loving plan by which God brings together all the possibilities of life and opposes the powers of death arising from sin: "God did not make death, and he does not delight in the death of the living. For he created all things that they might exist" (Wis 1:13-14).

40.1 The sacredness of life gives rise to its *inviolability, written from the beginning in man's heart*, in his conscience. The question "What have you done?" (Gen 4:10), which God addresses to Cain after he has killed his brother Abel, interprets the experience of every person: in the depths of his conscience, man is always reminded of the inviolability of life — his own life and that of others — as something which does not belong to him, because it is the property and gift of God the Creator and Father.

40.2 The commandment regarding the inviolability of human life reverberates *at the heart of the "ten words" in the Covenant of Sinai* (cf. Ex 34:28). In the first place that commandment prohibits murder: "You shall not kill" (Ex 20:13); "do not slay the innocent and righteous" (Ex 23:7). But, as is brought out in Israel's later legislation, it also prohibits all personal injury inflicted on another (cf. Ex 21:12-27). Of course we must recognize that in the Old Testament this sense of the value of life, though already quite marked, does not yet reach the refinement found in the Sermon on the Mount. This is apparent in some aspects of the current penal legislation, which provided for severe forms of corporal punishment and even the death penalty. But the overall message, which the New Testament will bring to perfection, is a forceful appeal for respect for the inviolability of physical life and the integrity of the person. It culminates in the positive commandment which obliges us to be responsible for our neighbor as for ourselves: "You shall love your neighbor as yourself" (Lev 19:18).

41.1 The commandment "You shall not kill," included and more fully expressed in the positive command of love for one's neighbor, is *reaffirmed in all its force by the Lord Jesus.* To the rich young man who asks him, "Teacher, what good deed must I do to have eternal life?" Jesus replies, "If you would enter life, keep the commandments" (Mt 19:16, 17). And he quotes, as the first of these, "You shall not kill" (Mt 19:18). In the Sermon on the Mount, Jesus demands from his disciples a *righteousness which surpasses* that of the scribes and Pharisees, also with regard to respect for life: "You have heard that it was said to the men of old, 'You shall not kill; and whoever kills shall be liable to judgment.' But I say to you that every one who is angry with his brother shall be liable to judgment" (Mt 5:21-22).

41.2 By his words and actions Jesus further unveils the positive requirements of the commandment regarding the inviolability of life. These requirements were already present in the Old Testament, where legislation dealt with protecting and defending life when it was weak and threatened: in the case of foreigners, widows, orphans, the sick and the poor in general, including children in the womb (cf. Ex 21:22, 22:20-26). With Jesus these positive requirements assume new force and urgency, and are revealed in all their breadth and depth: they range from caring for the life of one's *brother* (whether a blood brother, someone belonging to the same people, or a foreigner living in the land of Israel) to showing concern for the *stranger,* even to the point of loving one's *enemy.*

41.3 A stranger is no longer a stranger for the person who must *become a neighbor* to someone in need, to the point of accepting responsibility for his life, as the parable of the Good Samaritan shows so clearly (cf. Lk 10:25-37). Even an enemy ceases to be an enemy for the person who is obliged to love him (cf. Mt 5:38-48; Lk 6:27-35), to "do good" to him (cf. Lk 6:27, 33, 35) and to respond to his immediate needs promptly and with no expectation of repayment (cf. Lk 6:34-35). The height of this love is to pray for one's enemy. By so doing we achieve harmony with the providential love of God: "But I say to you, love your enemies and pray for those who persecute you, so that you may be children of your Father who is in heaven; for he makes his sun rise on the evil and on the good and sends rain on the just and on the unjust" (Mt 5:44-45; cf. Lk 6:28, 35).

41.4 Thus the deepest element of God's commandment to protect human life is the *requirement to show reverence and love* for every person and the life of every person. This is the teaching which the Apostle Paul, echoing the words of Jesus, addresses to the Christians in Rome: "The commandments, 'You shall not commit adultery, You shall not kill, You shall not steal, You shall not covet,' and any other commandment, are summed up in this sentence, *'You shall love your neighbor as yourself.'* Love does no wrong to a neighbor; therefore love is the fulfilling of the law" (Rom 13:9-10).

"Be fruitful and multiply, and fill the earth and subdue it" (Gen 1:28): man's responsibility for life

42.1 To defend and promote life, to show reverence and love for it, is a task which God entrusts to every man, calling him as his living image to share in his own lordship over the world: "God blessed them, and God said to them, 'Be fruitful and multiply, and fill the earth and subdue it; and have dominion over the fish of the sea and over the birds of the air and over every living thing that moves upon the earth' " (Gen 1:28).

42.2 The biblical text clearly shows the breadth and depth of the lordship which God bestows on man. It is a matter first of all of *dominion over the earth and over every living creature,* as the Book of Wisdom makes clear: "O God of my fathers and Lord of mercy. . . . By your wisdom you have formed man, to have dominion over the creatures you have made, and rule the world in holiness and righteousness" (Wis 9:1-3). The Psalmist too extols the dominion given to man as a sign of glory and honor from his Creator: "You have given him dominion over the works of your hands; you have put all things under his feet, all sheep and oxen, and also the beasts of the field, the birds of the air, and the fish of the sea, whatever passes along the paths of the sea" (Ps 8:6-8).

42.3 As one called to till and look after the garden of the world (cf. Gen 2:15), man has a specific responsibility toward *the environment in which he lives,* toward the creation which God has put at the service of his personal dignity, of his life, not only for the present but also for future generations. It is the *ecological question* — ranging from the preservation of the natural habitats of the different species of animals and of other forms of life to "human ecology" properly speaking[28] — which finds in the Bible clear and strong ethical direction leading to a solution which respects the great good of life, of every life. In fact, "the dominion granted to man by the Creator is not an absolute power, nor can one speak of a freedom to 'use and misuse,' or to dispose of things as one pleases. The limitation imposed from the beginning by the Creator himself and expressed symbolically by the prohibition not to

---

[28] Cf. John Paul II, Encyclical Letter *Centesimus Annus* (May 1, 1991), 38: *AAS* 83 (1991), 840-841.

'eat of the fruit of the tree' (cf. Gen 2:16-17) shows clearly enough that, when it comes to the natural world, we are subject not only to biological laws but also to moral ones, which cannot be violated with impunity."[29]

43.1 A certain sharing by man in God's lordship is also evident in the *specific responsibility* which he is given *for human life as such*. It is a responsibility which reaches its highest point in the giving of life *through procreation* by man and woman in marriage. As the Second Vatican Council teaches: "God himself who said, 'It is not good for man to be alone' (Gen 2:18) and 'who made man from the beginning male and female' (Mt 19:4), wished to share with man a certain special participation in his own creative work. Thus he blessed male and female, saying: 'Increase and multiply' (Gen 1:28)."[30]

43.2 By speaking of "a certain special participation" of man and woman in the "creative work" of God, the Council wishes to point out that having a child is an event which is deeply human and full of religious meaning, insofar as it involves both the spouses, who form "one flesh" (Gen 2:24), and God who makes himself present. As I wrote in my *Letter to Families:* "When a new person is born of the conjugal union of the two, he brings with him into the world a particular image and likeness of God himself: *the genealogy of the person is inscribed in the very biology of generation.* In affirming that the spouses, as parents, cooperate with God the Creator in conceiving and giving birth to a new human being, we are not speaking merely with reference to the laws of biology. Instead, we wish to emphasize that *God himself is present in human fatherhood and motherhood* quite differently than he is present in all other instances of begetting 'on earth.' Indeed, God alone is the source of that 'image and likeness' which is proper to the human being, as it was received at creation. Begetting is the continuation of creation."[31]

43.3 This is what the Bible teaches in direct and eloquent language when it reports the joyful cry of the first woman, "the mother of all the living" (Gen 3:20). Aware that God has intervened, Eve exclaims: "I have begotten a man with the help of the Lord" (Gen 4:1). In procreation therefore, through the communication of life from parents to child, God's own image and likeness is transmitted, thanks to the creation of the immortal soul.[32] The beginning of

[29] John Paul II, Encyclical Letter *Sollicitudo Rei Socialis* (December 30, 1987), 34: *AAS* 80 (1988), 560.

[30] Pastoral Constitution on the Church in the Modern World *Gaudium et Spes,* 50.

[31] Letter to Families *Gratissimam Sane* (February 2, 1994), 9: *AAS* 86 (1994), 878; cf. Pius XII, Encyclical Letter *Humani Generis* (August 12, 1950): *AAS* 42 (1950), 574.

[32] "Anima enim a Deo immediate creari catholica fides nos retinere iubet": Pius XII, Encyclical Letter *Humani Generis* (August 12, 1950): *AAS* 42 (1950), 575.

the "book of the genealogy of Adam" expresses it in this way: "When God created man, he made him in the likeness of God. Male and female he created them, and he blessed them and called them man when they were created. When Adam had lived a hundred and thirty years, he became the father of a son in his own likeness, after his image, and named him Seth" (Gen 5:1-3). It is precisely in their role as co-workers with God *who transmits his image to the new creature* that we see the greatness of couples who are ready "to cooperate with the love of the Creator and the Savior, who through them will enlarge and enrich his own family day by day."[33] This is why the Bishop Amphilochius extolled "holy matrimony, chosen and elevated above all other earthly gifts" as "the begetter of humanity, the creator of images of God."[34]

43.4 Thus, a man and woman joined in matrimony become partners in a divine undertaking: through the act of procreation, God's gift is accepted and a new life opens to the future.

43.5 But over and above the specific mission of parents, *the task of accepting and serving life involves everyone; and this task must be fulfilled above all toward life when it is at its weakest.* It is Christ himself who reminds us of this when he asks to be loved and served in his brothers and sisters who are suffering in any way: the hungry, the thirsty, the foreigner, the naked, the sick, the imprisoned. . . . Whatever is done to each of them is done to Christ himself (cf. Mt 25:31-46).

"For you formed my inmost being" (Ps 139:13): the dignity of the unborn child

44.1 Human life finds itself most vulnerable when it enters the world and when it leaves the realm of time to embark upon eternity. The word of God frequently repeats the call to show care and respect, above all where life is undermined by sickness and old age. Although there are no direct and explicit calls to protect human life at its very beginning, specifically life not yet born and life nearing its end, this can easily be explained by the fact that the mere possibility of harming, attacking or actually denying life in these circumstances is completely foreign to the religious and cultural way of thinking of the People of God.

44.2 In the Old Testament, sterility is dreaded as a curse, while numerous offspring are viewed as a blessing: "Sons are a heritage from the Lord, the

---

[33] Second Vatican Ecumenical Council, Pastoral Constitution on the Church in the Modern World *Gaudium et Spes*, 50; cf. John Paul II, Apostolic Exhortation *Familiaris Consortio* (November 22, 1981), 28: *AAS* 74 (1982), 114.

[34] *Homilies*, II, 1; *CCSG* 3, 39.

fruit of the womb a reward" (Ps 127:3; cf. Ps 128:3-4). This belief is also based on Israel's awareness of being the people of the Covenant, called to increase in accordance with the promise made to Abraham: "Look toward heaven, and number the stars, if you are able to number them . . . so shall your descendants be" (Gen 15:5). But more than anything else, at work here is the certainty that the life which parents transmit has its origins in God. We see this attested in the many biblical passages which respectfully and lovingly speak of conception, of the forming of life in the mother's womb, of giving birth and of the intimate connection between the initial moment of life and the action of God the Creator.

44.3 "Before I formed you in the womb I knew you, and before you were born I consecrated you" (Jer 1:5): *the life of every individual, from its very beginning, is part of God's plan.* Job, from the depth of his pain, stops to contemplate the work of God, who miraculously formed his body in his mother's womb. Here he finds reason for trust, and he expresses his belief that there is a divine plan for his life: "You have fashioned and made me; will you then turn and destroy me? Remember that you have made me of clay; and will you turn me to dust again? Did you not pour me out like milk and curdle me like cheese? You clothed me with skin and flesh, and knit me together with bones and sinews. You have granted me life and steadfast love; and your care has preserved my spirit" (Job 10:8-12). Expressions of awe and wonder at God's intervention in the life of a child in its mother's womb occur again and again in the Psalms.[35]

44.4 How can anyone think that even a single moment of this marvelous process of the unfolding of life could be separated from the wise and loving work of the Creator, and left prey to human caprice? Certainly the mother of the seven brothers did not think so; she professes her faith in God, both the source and guarantee of life from its very conception, and the foundation of the hope of new life beyond death: "I do not know how you came into being in my womb. It was not I who gave you life and breath, nor I who set in order the elements within each of you. Therefore the Creator of the world, who shaped the beginning of man and devised the origin of all things, will in his mercy give life and breath back to you again, since you now forget yourselves for the sake of his laws" (2 Mac 7:22-23).

45 The New Testament revelation confirms the *indisputable recognition of the value of life from its very beginning.* The exaltation of fruitfulness and the eager expectation of life resound in the words with which Elizabeth rejoices in

---

[35] See, for example, Psalms 22:10-11, 71:6, 139:13-14.

her pregnancy: "The Lord has looked on me . . . to take away my reproach among men" (Lk 1:25). And even more so, the value of the person from the moment of conception is celebrated in the meeting between the Virgin Mary and Elizabeth, and between the two children whom they are carrying in the womb. It is precisely the children who reveal the advent of the messianic age: in their meeting, the redemptive power of the presence of the Son of God among men first becomes operative. As Saint Ambrose writes: "The arrival of Mary and the blessings of the Lord's presence are also speedily declared. . . . Elizabeth was the first to hear the voice; but John was the first to experience grace. She heard according to the order of nature; he leaped because of the mystery. She recognized the arrival of Mary; he the arrival of the Lord. The woman recognized the woman's arrival; the child, that of the child. The women speak of grace; the babies make it effective from within to the advantage of their mothers who, by a double miracle, prophesy under the inspiration of their children. The infant leaped, the mother was filled with the Spirit. The mother was not filled before the son, but after the son was filled with the Holy Spirit, he filled his mother too."[36]

"I kept my faith even when I said, 'I am greatly afflicted' " (Ps 116:10): life in old age and at times of suffering

46.1 With regard to the last moments of life too, it would be anachronistic to expect biblical revelation to make express reference to present-day issues concerning respect for elderly and sick persons, or to condemn explicitly attempts to hasten their end by force. The cultural and religious context of the Bible is in no way touched by such temptations; indeed, in that context the wisdom and experience of the elderly are recognized as a unique source of enrichment for the family and for society.

46.2 *Old age is characterized by dignity and surrounded with reverence* (cf. 2 Mac 6:23). The just man does not seek to be delivered from old age and its burden; on the contrary his prayer is this: "You, O Lord, are my hope, my trust, O Lord, from my youth . . . so even to old age and gray hairs, O God, do not forsake me, till I proclaim your might to all the generations to come" (Ps 71:5, 18). The ideal of the messianic age is presented as a time when "no more shall there be . . . an old man who does not fill out his days" (Is 65:20).

46.3 In old age, how should one face the inevitable decline of life? *How should one act in the face of death? The believer knows that his life is in the hands of God:* "You, O Lord, hold my lot" (cf. Ps 16:5), and he accepts from God the need to die: "This is the decree from the Lord for all flesh, and how can you reject the good

---

[36] *Expositio Evangelii secundum Lucam,* II, 22-23: *CCL* 14, 40-41.

pleasure of the Most High?" (Sir 41:3-4). Man is not the master of life nor is he the master of death. In life and in death, he has to entrust himself completely to the "good pleasure of the Most High," to his loving plan.

46.4 In moments of *sickness* too, man is called to have the same trust in the Lord and to renew his fundamental faith in the One who "heals all your diseases" (cf. Ps 103:3). When every hope of good health seems to fade before a person's eyes — so as to make him cry out, "My days are like an evening shadow; I wither away like grass" (Ps 102:11) — even then the believer is sustained by an unshakable faith in God's life-giving power. Illness does not drive such a person to despair and to seek death, but makes him cry out in hope: "I kept my faith, even when I said, 'I am greatly afflicted'" (Ps 116:10); "O Lord my God, I cried to you for help, and you have healed me. O Lord, you have brought up my soul from Sheol, restored me to life from among those gone down to the pit" (Ps 30:2-3).

47.1 The mission of Jesus, with the many healings he performed, shows *God's great concern even for man's bodily life*. Jesus, as "the physician of the body and of the spirit,"[37] was sent by the Father to proclaim the good news to the poor and to heal the brokenhearted (cf. Lk 4:18; Is 61:1). Later, when he sends his disciples into the world, he gives them a mission, a mission in which healing the sick goes hand in hand with the proclamation of the Gospel: "And preach as you go, saying, 'The kingdom of heaven is at hand.' Heal the sick, raise the dead, cleanse lepers, cast out demons" (Mt 10:7-8; cf. Mk 6:13, 16:18).

47.2 Certainly *the life of the body in its earthly state is not an absolute good* for the believer, especially as he may be asked to give up his life for a greater good. As Jesus says: "Whoever would save his life will lose it; and whoever loses his life for my sake and the gospel's will save it" (Mk 8:35). The New Testament gives many different examples of this. Jesus does not hesitate to sacrifice himself, and he freely makes of his life an offering to the Father (cf. Jn 10:17) and to those who belong to him (cf. Jn 10:15). The death of John the Baptist, precursor of the Savior, also testifies that earthly existence is not an absolute good; what is more important is remaining faithful to the word of the Lord even at the risk of one's life (cf. Mk 6:17-29). Stephen, losing his earthly life because of his faithful witness to the Lord's Resurrection, follows in the Master's footsteps and meets those who are stoning him with words of forgiveness (cf. Acts 7:59-60), thus becoming the first of a countless host of martyrs whom the Church has venerated since the very beginning.

---

[37] Saint Ignatius of Antioch, *Letter to the Ephesians*, 7, 2: *Patres Apostolici*, ed. F. X. Funk, II, 82.

47.3 No one, however, can arbitrarily choose whether to live or die; the absolute master of such a decision is the Creator alone, in whom "we live and move and have our being" (Acts 17:28).

"All who hold her fast will live" (Bar 4:1): from the Law of Sinai to the gift of the Spirit

48.1 Life is indelibly marked by a *truth of its own.* By accepting God's gift, man is obliged to *maintain life in this truth,* which is essential to it. To detach oneself from this truth is to condemn oneself to meaninglessness and unhappiness, and possibly to become a threat to the existence of others, since the barriers guaranteeing respect for life and the defense of life in every circumstance have been broken down.

48.2 *The truth of life is revealed by God's commandment.* The word of the Lord shows concretely the course which life must follow if it is to respect its own truth and to preserve its own dignity. The protection of life is not only ensured by the specific commandment "You shall not kill" (Ex 20:13; Dt 5:17); *the entire Law of the Lord* serves to protect life, because it reveals that truth in which life finds its full meaning.

48.3 It is not surprising, therefore, that God's Covenant with his people is so closely linked to the perspective of life, also in its bodily dimension. In that Covenant, God's *commandment* is offered as *the path of life:* "I have set before you this day life and good, death and evil. If you obey the commandments of the Lord your God which I command you this day, by loving the Lord your God, by walking in his ways, and by keeping his commandments and his statutes and his ordinances, then you shall live and multiply, and the Lord your God will bless you in the land which you are entering to take possession of" (Dt 30:15-16). What is at stake is not only the land of Canaan and the existence of the people of Israel, but also the world of today and of the future, and the existence of all humanity. In fact, it is altogether impossible for life to remain authentic and complete once it is detached from the good; and the good, in its turn, is essentially bound to the commandments of the Lord, that is, to the "law of life" (Sir 17:11). The good to be done is not added to life as a burden which weighs on it, since the very purpose of life is that good and only by doing it can life be built up.

48.4 It is thus *the Law as a whole* which fully protects human life. This explains why it is so hard to remain faithful to the commandment "You shall not kill" when the other "words of life" (cf. Acts 7:38) with which this commandment is bound up are not observed. Detached from this wider framework, the commandment is destined to become nothing more than an obligation imposed from without, and very soon we begin to look for its limits and try to find mitigating factors and exceptions. Only when people are open to the fullness of the truth about God, man and history will the words "You shall not kill" shine forth once more as a good for man in himself and in his relations with others. In such a perspective we can grasp the full truth of the passage of the Book of Deuteronomy which Jesus repeats in reply to the first temptation: "Man does not live by bread alone, but . . . by everything that proceeds out of the mouth of the Lord" (Dt 8:3; cf. Mt 4:4).

48.5 It is by listening to the word of the Lord that we are able to live in dignity and justice. It is by observing the Law of God that we are able to bring forth fruits of life and happiness: "All who hold her fast will live, and those who forsake her will die" (Bar 4:1).

49.1 The history of Israel shows how *difficult it is to remain faithful to the law of life* which God has inscribed in human hearts and which he gave on Sinai to the people of the Covenant. When the people look for ways of living which ignore God's plan, it is the Prophets in particular who forcefully remind them that the Lord alone is the authentic source of life. Thus Jeremiah writes: "My people have committed two evils: they have forsaken me, the fountain of living waters, and hewed out cisterns for themselves, broken cisterns, that can hold no water" (2:13). The Prophets point an accusing finger at those who show contempt for life and violate people's rights: "They trample the head of the poor into the dust of the earth" (Amos 2:7); "they have filled this place with the blood of innocents" (Jer 19:4). Among them, the Prophet Ezekiel frequently condemns the city of Jerusalem, calling it "the bloody city" (22:2; 24:6, 9), the "city that sheds blood in her own midst" (22:3).

49.2 But while the Prophets condemn offenses against life, they are concerned above all to awaken *hope for a new principle of life*, capable of bringing about a renewed relationship with God and with others, and of opening up new and extraordinary possibilities for understanding and carrying out all the demands inherent in the *Gospel of life*. This will only be possible thanks to the gift of God who purifies and renews: "I will sprinkle clean water upon you, and you shall be clean from all your uncleannesses, and from all your idols I will cleanse you. A new heart I will give you, and a new spirit I will put within you" (Ezek 36:25-26; cf. Jer 31:34). This "new heart" will make it possible to appreciate and achieve the deepest and most authentic meaning of life: namely, that of being *a gift which is fully realized in the giving of self*. This is the splendid message about the value of life which comes to us from the figure of the Servant of the Lord: "When he makes himself an offering for sin, he shall see his offspring, he shall prolong his life . . . he shall see the fruit of the travail of his soul and be satisfied" (Is 53:10,11).

49.3 It is in the coming of Jesus of Nazareth that the Law is fulfilled and that a new heart is given through his Spirit. Jesus does not deny the Law but brings it to fulfillment (cf. Mt 5:17): the Law and the Prophets are summed up in the golden rule of mutual love (cf. Mt 7:12). In Jesus the Law becomes once and for all the "Gospel," the good news of God's lordship over the world, which brings all life back to its roots and its original purpose. This is the *New Law*, "the law of the Spirit of life in Christ Jesus" (Rom 8:2), and its fundamental expression, following the example of the Lord who gave his life for his friends (cf. Jn 15:13), is *the gift of self in love for one's brothers and sisters*: "We know that we have passed out of death into life, because we love the brethren" (1 Jn 3:14). This is the law of freedom, joy and blessedness.

"They shall look on him whom they have pierced" (Jn 19:37): the Gospel of life is brought to fulfillment on the tree of the Cross

50.1 At the end of this chapter, in which we have reflected on the Christian message about life, I would like to pause with each one of you to *contemplate the One who was pierced* and who draws all people to himself (cf. Jn 19:37, 12:32). Looking at "the spectacle" of the Cross (cf. Lk 23:48) we shall discover in this glorious tree the fulfillment and the complete revelation of the whole *Gospel of life*.

50.2 In the early afternoon of Good Friday, "there was darkness over the whole land . . . while the sun's light failed; and the curtain of the temple was torn in two" (Lk 23:44, 45). This is the symbol of a great cosmic disturbance and a massive conflict between the forces of good and the forces of evil, between life and death. Today we too find ourselves in the midst of a dramatic conflict between the "culture of death" and the "culture of life." But the glory of the Cross is not overcome by this darkness; rather, it shines forth ever more radiantly and brightly, and is revealed as the center, meaning and goal of all history and of every human life.

50.3 Jesus is nailed to the Cross and is lifted up from the earth. He experiences the moment of his greatest "powerlessness," and his life seems completely delivered to the derision of his adversaries and into the hands of his executioners: he is mocked, jeered at, insulted (cf. Mk 15:24-36). And yet, precisely amid all this, having seen him breathe his last, the Roman centurion exclaims: "Truly this man was the Son of God!" (Mk 15:39). It is thus, at the moment of his greatest weakness, that the Son of God is revealed for who he is: *on the Cross his glory is made manifest.*

50.4 By his death, Jesus sheds light on the meaning of the life and death of every human being. Before he dies, Jesus prays to the Father, asking forgiveness for his persecutors (cf. Lk 23:34), and to the criminal who asks him to remember him in his Kingdom he replies: "Truly, I say to you, today you will be with me in paradise" (Lk 23:43). After his death, "the tombs also were opened, and many bodies of the saints who had fallen asleep were raised" (Mt 27:52). The salvation wrought by Jesus is the bestowal of life and resurrection. Throughout his earthly life, Jesus had indeed bestowed salvation by healing and doing good to all (cf. Acts 10:38). But his miracles, healings and even his raising of the dead were signs of another salvation, a salvation which consists in the forgiveness of sins, that is, in setting man free from his greatest sickness and in raising him to the very life of God.

50.5 On the Cross, the miracle of the serpent lifted up by Moses in the desert (Jn 3:14-15; cf. Num 21:8-9) is renewed and brought to full and definitive perfection. Today too, by looking upon the one who was pierced, every person whose life is threatened encounters the sure hope of finding freedom and redemption.

51.1 But there is yet another particular event which moves me deeply when I consider it. "When Jesus had received the vinegar, he said, 'It is finished'; and he bowed his head and gave up his spirit" (Jn 19:30). Afterward, the Roman soldier "pierced his side with a spear, and at once there came out blood and water" (Jn 19:34).

51.2 Everything has now reached its complete fulfillment. The "giving up" of the spirit describes Jesus' death, a death like that of every other human being, but it also seems to allude to the "gift of the Spirit," by which Jesus ransoms us from death and opens before us a new life.

51.3 It is the very life of God which is now shared with man. It is the life which through the sacraments of the Church — symbolized by the blood and water flowing from Christ's side — is continually given to God's children, making them the people of the New Covenant. *From the Cross, the source of life, the "people of life" is born and increases.*

51.4 The contemplation of the Cross thus brings us to the very heart of all that has taken place. Jesus, who upon entering into the world said, "I have come, O God, to do your will" (cf. Heb 10:9), made himself obedient to the Father in everything and, "having loved his own who were in the world, he loved them to the end" (Jn 13:1), giving himself completely for them.

51.5 He who had come "not to be served but to serve, and to give his life as a ransom for many" (Mk 10:45), attains on the Cross the heights of love:

"Greater love has no man than this, that a man lay down his life for his friends" (Jn 15:13). And he died for us while we were yet sinners (cf. Rom 5:8).

51.6 In this way Jesus proclaims that *life finds its center, its meaning and its fulfillment when it is given up.*

51.7 At this point our meditation becomes praise and thanksgiving, and at the same time urges us to imitate Christ and follow in his footsteps (cf. 1 Pet 2:21).

51.8 We too are called to give our lives for our brothers and sisters, and thus to realize in the fullness of truth the meaning and destiny of our existence.

51.9 We shall be able to do this because you, O Lord, have given us the example and have bestowed on us the power of your Spirit. We shall be able to do this if every day, with you and like you, we are obedient to the Father and do his will.

51.10 Grant, therefore, that we may listen with open and generous hearts to every word which proceeds from the mouth of God. Thus we shall learn not only to obey the commandment not to kill human life, but also to revere life, to love it and to foster it.

III

You Shall Not Kill

God's Holy Law

"If you would enter life, keep the commandments" (Mt 19:17): Gospel and commandment

52.1 "And behold, one came up to him, saying, 'Teacher, what good deed must I do, to have eternal life?' " (Mt 19:6). Jesus replied, "If you would enter life, keep the commandments" (Mt 19:17). The Teacher is speaking about eternal life, that is, a sharing in the life of God himself. This life is attained through the observance of the Lord's commandments, including the commandment "You shall not kill." This is the first precept from the Decalogue which Jesus quotes to the young man who asks him what commandments he should observe: "Jesus said, 'You shall not kill, you shall not commit adultery, you shall not steal' " (Mt 19:18).

52.2 *God's commandment is never detached from his love:* it is always a gift meant for man's growth and joy. As such, it represents an essential and indispensable aspect of the Gospel, actually becoming "gospel" itself: joyful good news. The *Gospel of life* is both a great gift of God and an exacting task for humanity. It gives rise to amazement and gratitude in the person graced with freedom, and it asks to be welcomed, preserved and esteemed, with a deep sense of responsibility. In giving life to man, God *demands* that he love, respect and promote life. *The gift* thus *becomes a commandment, and the commandment is itself a gift.*

52.3 Man, as the living image of God, is willed by his Creator to be ruler and lord. Saint Gregory of Nyssa writes that "God made man capable of carrying out his role as king of the earth. . . . Man was created in the image of the One who governs the universe. Everything demonstrates that from the beginning man's nature was marked by royalty. . . . Man is a king. Created to exercise dominion over the world, he was given a likeness to the king of the universe; he is the living image who participates by his dignity in the perfection of the divine archetype."[38] Called to be fruitful and multiply, to subdue the earth and to exercise dominion over other lesser creatures (cf. Gen 1:28), man is ruler and lord not only over things but especially over himself,[39] and in a certain sense, over the life which he has received and which he is able to transmit through procreation, carried out with love and respect for God's plan. Man's *lordship* however is not absolute, but *ministerial:* it is a real reflection of the unique and infinite lordship of God. Hence man must exercise it with *wisdom and love,* sharing in the boundless wisdom and love of God. And this comes about through obedience to God's holy Law: a free and joyful obedience (cf. Ps 119) born of and fostered by an awareness that the precepts of the Lord are a gift of grace entrusted to man always and solely for his good, for the preservation of his personal dignity and the pursuit of his happiness.

52.4 With regard to things, but even more with regard to life, man is not the absolute master and final judge, but rather — and this is where his incomparable greatness lies — he is the "minister of God's plan."[40]

52.5 Life is entrusted to man as a treasure which must not be squandered, as a talent which must be used well. Man must render an account of it to his Master (cf. Mt 25:14-30; Lk 19:12-27).

"From man in regard to his fellow man I will demand an accounting for human life" (Gen 9:5): human life is sacred and inviolable

53.1 "Human life is sacred because from its beginning it involves 'the creative action of God,' and it remains forever in a special relationship with the

---

[38] *De Hominis Opificio,* 4: *PG* 44, 136.

[39] Cf. Saint John Damascene, *De Fide Orthodoxa,* 2, 12: *PG* 920; quoted in Saint Thomas Aquinas, *Summa Theologiae,* I-II, Prologue.

[40] Paul VI, Encyclical Letter *Humanae Vitae* (July 25, 1968), 13: *AAS* 60 (1968), 489.

Creator, who is its sole end. God alone is the Lord of life from its beginning until its end: no one can, in any circumstance, claim for himself the right to destroy directly an innocent human being."[41] With these words the Instruction *Donum Vitae* sets forth the central content of God's revelation on the sacredness and inviolability of human life.

53.2 *Sacred Scripture* in fact presents the precept "You shall not kill" as a divine commandment (Ex 20:13; Dt 5:17). As I have already emphasized, this commandment is found in the Decalogue, at the heart of the Covenant which the Lord makes with his chosen people; but it was already contained in the original covenant between God and humanity after the purifying punishment of the flood, caused by the spread of sin and violence (cf. Gen 9:5-6).

53.3 God proclaims that he is absolute Lord of the life of man, who is formed in his image and likeness (cf. Gen 1:26-28). Human life is thus given a sacred and inviolable character, which reflects the inviolability of the Creator himself. Precisely for this reason God will severely judge every violation of the commandment "You shall not kill," the commandment which is at the basis of all life together in society. He is the *"goel,"* the defender of the innocent (cf. Gen 4:9-15; Is 41:14; Jer 50:34; Ps 19:14). God thus shows that he does not delight in the death of the living (cf. Wis 1:13). Only Satan can delight therein: for through his envy death entered the world (cf. Wis 2:24). He who is "a murderer from the beginning," is also "a liar and the father of lies" (Jn 8:44). By deceiving man he leads him to projects of sin and death, making them appear as goals and fruits of life.

54.1 As explicitly formulated, the precept "You shall not kill" is strongly negative: it indicates the extreme limit which can never be exceeded. Implicitly, however, it encourages a positive attitude of absolute respect for life; it leads to the promotion of life and to progress along the way of a love which gives, receives and serves. The people of the Covenant, although slowly and with some contradictions, progressively matured in this way of thinking and thus prepared for the great proclamation of Jesus that the commandment to love one's neighbor is like the commandment to love God: "On these two commandments depend all the Law and the Prophets" (cf. Mt 22:36-40). Saint Paul emphasizes that "the commandment . . . you shall not kill . . . and any other commandment, are summed up in this phrase: 'You shall love your neighbor as yourself'" (Rom 13:9; cf. Gal 5:14). Taken up and brought to

---

[41] Congregation for the Doctrine of the Faith, Instruction on Respect for Human Life in Its Origin and on the Dignity of Procreation *Donum Vitae* (February 22, 1987), Introduction, 5: AAS 80 (1988), 76-77; cf. *Catechism of the Catholic Church*, No. 2258.

fulfillment in the New Law, the commandment "You shall not kill" stands as an indispensable condition for being able "to enter life" (cf. Mt 19:16-19). In this same perspective, the words of the Apostle John have a categorical ring: "Anyone who hates his brother is a murderer, and you know that no murderer has eternal life abiding in him" (1 Jn 3:15).

54.2 From the beginning, the *living Tradition of the Church* — as shown by the *Didache*, the most ancient non-biblical Christian writing — categorically repeated the commandment "You shall not kill": "There are two ways, a way of life and a way of death; there is a great difference between them. . . . In accordance with the precept of the teaching: You shall not kill . . . you shall not put a child to death by abortion nor kill it once it is born. . . . The way of death is this: . . . they show no compassion for the poor, they do not suffer with the suffering, they do not acknowledge their Creator, they kill their children and by abortion cause God's creatures to perish; they drive away the needy, oppress the suffering, they are advocates of the rich and unjust judges of the poor; they are filled with every sin. May you be able to stay ever apart, O children, from all these sins!"[42]

54.3 As time passed, the Church's Tradition has always consistently taught the absolute and unchanging value of the commandment "You shall not kill." It is a known fact that in the first centuries murder was put among the three most serious sins — along with apostasy and adultery — and required a particularly heavy and lengthy public penance before the repentant murderer could be granted forgiveness and readmission to the ecclesial community.

55.1 This should not cause surprise: to kill a human being, in whom the image of God is present, is a particularly serious sin. *Only God is the master of life!* Yet from the beginning, faced with the many and often tragic cases which occur in the life of individuals and society, Christian reflection has sought a fuller and deeper understanding of what God's commandment prohibits and prescribes.[43] There are in fact situations in which values proposed by God's Law seem to involve a genuine paradox. This happens for example in the case of *legitimate defense*, in which the right to protect one's own life and the duty not to harm someone else's life are difficult to reconcile in practice. Certainly, the intrinsic value of life and the duty to love oneself no less than others are the basis of *a true right* to self-defense. The demanding commandment of love

---

[42] *Didache*, I, 1; II, 1-2; V, 1 and 3: *Patres Apostolici*, ed. F. X. Funk, I, 2-3; 6-9; 14-17; cf. *Letter of Pseudo-Barnabas*, XIX, 5: loc. cit., 90-93.

[43] Cf. *Catechism of the Catholic Church*, Nos. 2263-2269; cf. also *Catechism of the Council of Trent*, III, §§327-332.

of neighbor, set forth in the Old Testament and confirmed by Jesus, itself presupposes love of oneself as the basis of comparison: "You shall love your neighbor *as yourself*" (Mk 12:31). Consequently, no one can renounce the right to self-defense out of lack of love for life or for self. This can only be done in virtue of a heroic love which deepens and transfigures the love of self into a radical self-offering, according to the spirit of the Gospel Beatitudes (cf. Mt 5:38-40). The sublime example of this self-offering is the Lord Jesus himself.

55.2 Moreover, "legitimate defense can be not only a right but a grave duty for someone responsible for another's life, the common good of the family or of the State."[44] Unfortunately, it happens that the need to render the aggressor incapable of causing harm sometimes involves taking his life. In this case, the fatal outcome is attributable to the aggressor whose action brought it about, even though he may not be morally responsible because of a lack of the use of reason.[45]

56.1 This is the context in which to place the problem of the *death penalty*. On this matter there is a growing tendency, both in the Church and in civil society, to demand that it be applied in a very limited way or even that it be abolished completely. The problem must be viewed in the context of a system of penal justice ever more in line with human dignity and thus, in the end, with God's plan for man and society. The primary purpose of the punishment which society inflicts is "to redress the disorder caused by the offense."[46] Public authority must redress the violation of personal and social rights by imposing on the offender an adequate punishment for the crime, as a condition for the offender to regain the exercise of his or her freedom. In this way authority also fulfills the purpose of defending public order and ensuring people's safety, while at the same time offering the offender an incentive and help to change his or her behavior and be rehabilitated.[47]

56.2 It is clear that for these purposes to be achieved, *the nature and extent of the punishment* must be carefully evaluated and decided upon, and ought not go to the extreme of executing the offender except in cases of absolute necessity: in other words, when it would not be possible otherwise to defend society. Today, however, as a result of steady improvements in the organization of the penal system, such cases are very rare, if not practically nonexistent.

[44] *Catechism of the Catholic Church*, No. 2265.

[45] Cf. Saint Thomas Aquinas, *Summa Theologiae*, II-II, q. 64, a. 7; Saint Alphonsus Liguori, *Theologia Moralis*, Book III, tr. 4, c. 1, dub. 3.

[46] *Catechism of the Catholic Church*, No. 2266.

[47] Cf. ibid., No. 2266.

56.3 In any event, the principle set forth in the new *Catechism of the Catholic Church* remains valid: "If bloodless means are sufficient to defend human lives against an aggressor and to protect public order and the safety of persons, public authority must limit itself to such means, because they better correspond to the concrete conditions of the common good and are more in conformity to the dignity of the human person."[48]

57.1 If such great care must be taken to respect every life, even that of criminals and unjust aggressors, the commandment "You shall not kill" has absolute value when it refers to the *innocent person*. And all the more so in the case of weak and defenseless human beings, who find their ultimate defense against the arrogance and caprice of others only in the absolute binding force of God's commandment.

57.2 In effect, the absolute inviolability of innocent human life is a moral truth clearly taught by Sacred Scripture, constantly upheld in the Church's Tradition and consistently proposed by her Magisterium. This consistent teaching is the evident result of that "supernatural sense of the faith" which, inspired and sustained by the Holy Spirit, safeguards the People of God from error when "it shows universal agreement in matters of faith and morals."[49]

57.3 Faced with the progressive weakening in individual consciences and in society of the sense of the absolute and grave moral illicitness of the direct taking of all innocent human life, especially at its beginning and at its end, *the Church's Magisterium* has spoken out with increasing frequency in defense of the sacredness and inviolability of human life. The papal Magisterium, particularly insistent in this regard, has always been seconded by that of the Bishops, with numerous and comprehensive doctrinal and pastoral documents issued either by Episcopal Conferences or by individual Bishops. The Second Vatican Council also addressed the matter forcefully in a brief but incisive passage.[50]

57.4 Therefore, by the authority which Christ conferred upon Peter and his Successors, and in communion with the Bishops of the Catholic Church, *I confirm that the direct and voluntary killing of an innocent human being is always gravely immoral.* This doctrine, based upon that unwritten law which man, in the light of reason, finds in his own heart (cf. Rom 2:14-15), is re-

[48] Ibid., No. 2267.

[49] Second Vatican Ecumenical Council, Dogmatic Constitution on the Church *Lumen Gentium*, 12.

[50] Cf. Second Vatican Ecumenical Council, Pastoral Constitution on the Church in the Modern World *Gaudium et Spes*, 27.

affirmed by Sacred Scripture, transmitted by the Tradition of the Church and taught by the ordinary and universal Magisterium.[51]

57.5 The deliberate decision to deprive an innocent human being of his life is always morally evil and can never be licit either as an end in itself or as a means to a good end. It is in fact a grave act of disobedience to the moral law, and indeed to God himself, the author and guarantor of that law; it contradicts the fundamental virtues of justice and charity. "Nothing and no one can in any way permit the killing of an innocent human being, whether a fetus or an embryo, an infant or an adult, an old person, or one suffering from an incurable disease or a person who is dying. Furthermore, no one is permitted to ask for this act of killing, either for himself or herself or for another person entrusted to his or her care, nor can he or she consent to it, either explicitly or implicitly. Nor can any authority legitimately recommend or permit such an action."[52]

57.6 As far as the right to life is concerned, every innocent human being is absolutely equal to all others. This equality is the basis of all authentic social relationships which, to be truly such, can only be founded on truth and justice, recognizing and protecting every man and woman as a person and not as an object to be used. Before the moral norm which prohibits the direct taking of the life of an innocent human being "there are no privileges or exceptions for anyone. It makes no difference whether one is the master of the world or the 'poorest of the poor' on the face of the earth. Before the demands of morality we are all absolutely equal."[53]

"Your eyes beheld my unformed substance" (Ps 139:16): the unspeakable crime of abortion

58.1 Among all the crimes which can be committed against life, procured abortion has characteristics making it particularly serious and deplorable. The Second Vatican Council defines abortion, together with infanticide, as an "unspeakable crime."[54]

58.2 But today in many people's consciences the perception of its gravity has become progressively obscured. The acceptance of abortion in the popu-

[51] Cf. Second Vatican Ecumenical Council, Dogmatic Constitution on the Church *Lumen Gentium*, 25.

[52] Congregation for the Doctrine of the Faith, Declaration on Euthanasia *Iura et Bona* (May 5, 1980), II: *AAS* 72 (1980), 546.

[53] John Paul II, Encyclical Letter *Veritatis Splendor* (August 6, 1993), 96: *AAS* 85 (1993), 1209.

[54] Pastoral Constitution on the Church in the Modern World *Gaudium et Spes*, 51: "Abortus necnon infanticidium nefanda sunt crimina."

lar mind, in behavior and even in law itself, is a telling sign of an extremely dangerous crisis of the moral sense, which is becoming more and more incapable of distinguishing between good and evil, even when the fundamental right to life is at stake. Given such a grave situation, we need now more than ever to have the courage to look the truth in the eye and to *call things by their proper name*, without yielding to convenient compromises or to the temptation of self-deception. In this regard the reproach of the Prophet is extremely straightforward: "Woe to those who call evil good and good evil, who put darkness for light and light for darkness" (Is 5:20). Especially in the case of abortion there is a widespread use of ambiguous terminology, such as "interruption of pregnancy," which tends to hide abortion's true nature and to attenuate its seriousness in public opinion. Perhaps this linguistic phenomenon is itself a symptom of an uneasiness of conscience. But no word has the power to change the reality of things: procured abortion is *the deliberate and direct killing, by whatever means it is carried out, of a human being in the initial phase of his or her existence, extending from conception to birth.*

58.3 The moral gravity of procured abortion is apparent in all its truth if we recognize that we are dealing with murder and, in particular, when we consider the specific elements involved. The one eliminated is a human being at the very beginning of life. No one more absolutely *innocent* could be imagined. In no way could this human being ever be considered an aggressor, much less an unjust aggressor! He or she is *weak*, defenseless, even to the point of lacking that minimal form of defense consisting in the poignant power of a newborn baby's cries and tears. The unborn child is *totally entrusted to* the protection and care of the woman carrying him or her in the womb. And yet sometimes it is precisely the mother herself who makes the decision and asks for the child to be eliminated, and who then goes about having it done.

58.4 It is true that the decision to have an abortion is often tragic and painful for the mother, insofar as the decision to rid herself of the fruit of conception is not made for purely selfish reasons or out of convenience, but out of a desire to protect certain important values such as her own health or a decent standard of living for the other members of the family. Sometimes it is feared that the child to be born would live in such conditions that it would be better if the birth did not take place. Nevertheless, these reasons and others like them, however serious and tragic, *can never justify the deliberate killing of an innocent human being.*

59.1 As well as the mother, there are often other people too who decide upon the death of the child in the womb. In the first place, the father of the child may be to blame, not only when he directly pressures the woman to have an abortion, but also when he indirectly encourages such a decision on her part by leaving her alone to face the problems of pregnancy:[55] in this way the family is thus mortally wounded and profaned in its nature as a community of love and in its vocation to be the "sanctuary of life." Nor can one overlook the pressures which sometimes come from the wider family circle and from friends. Sometimes the woman is subjected to such strong pressure that she feels psychologically forced to have an abortion: certainly in this case moral responsibility lies particularly with those who have directly or indirectly obliged her to have an abortion. Doctors and nurses are also responsible, when they place at the service of death skills which were acquired for promoting life.

59.2 But responsibility likewise falls on the legislators who have promoted and approved abortion laws, and, to the extent that they have a say in the matter, on the administrators of the health-care centers where abortions are performed. A general and no less serious responsibility lies with those who have encouraged the spread of an attitude of sexual permissiveness and a lack of esteem for motherhood, and with those who should have ensured — but did not — effective family and social policies in support of families, especially larger families and those with particular financial and educational needs. Finally, one cannot overlook the network of complicity which reaches out to include international institutions, foundations and associations which systematically campaign for the legalization and spread of abortion in the world. In this sense abortion goes beyond the responsibility of individuals and beyond the harm done to them, and takes on a distinctly social dimension. It is a most serious *wound* inflicted on society and its culture by the very people who ought to be society's promoters and defenders. As I wrote in my *Letter to Families,* "we are facing an immense threat to life: not only to the life of individuals but also to that of civilization itself."[56] We are facing what can be called a *"structure of sin" which opposes human life not yet born.*

60.1 Some people try to justify abortion by claiming that the result of conception, at least up to a certain number of days, cannot yet be considered a personal human life. But in fact, "from the time that the ovum is fertilized, a life is begun which is neither that of the father nor the mother; it is rather the life of a new human being with his own growth. It would never be made human if it were not human already. This has always been clear, and . . . modern

---

[55] Cf. John Paul II, Apostolic Letter *Mulieris Dignitatem* (August 15, 1988), 14: *AAS* 80 (1988), 1686.

[56] No. 21: *AAS* 86 (1994), 920.

genetic science offers clear confirmation. It has demonstrated that from the first instant there is established the program of what this living being will be: a person, this individual person with his characteristic aspects already well determined. Right from fertilization the adventure of a human life begins, and each of its capacities requires time — a rather lengthy time — to find its place and to be in a position to act."[57] Even if the presence of a spiritual soul cannot be ascertained by empirical data, the results themselves of scientific research on the human embryo provide "a valuable indication for discerning by the use of reason a personal presence at the moment of the first appearance of a human life: how could a human individual not be a human person?"[58]

60.2 Furthermore, what is at stake is so important that, from the standpoint of moral obligation, the mere probability that a human person is involved would suffice to justify an absolutely clear prohibition of any intervention aimed at killing a human embryo. Precisely for this reason, over and above all scientific debates and those philosophical affirmations to which the Magisterium has not expressly committed itself, the Church has always taught and continues to teach that the result of human procreation, from the first moment of its existence, must be guaranteed that unconditional respect which is morally due to the human being in his or her totality and unity as body and spirit: *"The human being is to be respected and treated as a person from the moment of conception;* and therefore from that same moment his rights as a person must be recognized, among which in the first place is the inviolable right of every innocent human being to life."[59]

61.1 The texts of *Sacred Scripture* never address the question of deliberate abortion and so do not directly and specifically condemn it. But they show such great respect for the human being in the mother's womb that they require as a logical consequence that God's commandment "You shall not kill" be extended to the unborn child as well.

61.2 Human life is sacred and inviolable at every moment of existence, including the initial phase which precedes birth. All human beings, from their mothers' womb, belong to God who searches them and knows them, who forms them and knits them together with his own hands, who gazes on them

---

[57] Congregation for the Doctrine of the Faith, Declaration on Procured Abortion (November 18, 1974), 12-13: *AAS* 66 (1974), 738.

[58] Congregation for the Doctrine of the Faith, Instruction on Respect for Human Life in Its Origin and on the Dignity of Procreation *Donum Vitae* (February 22, 1987), I, 1: *AAS* 80 (1988), 78-79.

[59] Ibid.: loc. cit., 79.

when they are tiny shapeless embryos and already sees in them the adults of tomorrow whose days are numbered and whose vocation is even now written in the "book of life" (cf. Ps 139:1, 13-16). There too, when they are still in their mothers' womb — as many passages of the Bible bear witness[60] — they are the personal objects of God's loving and fatherly providence.

61.3 *Christian Tradition* — as the *Declaration* issued by the Congregation for the Doctrine of the Faith points out so well[61] — is clear and unanimous, from the beginning up to our own day, in describing abortion as a particularly grave moral disorder. From its first contacts with the Greco-Roman world, where abortion and infanticide were widely practiced, the first Christian community, by its teaching and practice, radically opposed the customs rampant in that society, as is clearly shown by the *Didache* mentioned earlier.[62] Among the Greek ecclesiastical writers, Athenagoras records that Christians consider as murderesses women who have recourse to abortifacient medicines, because children, even if they are still in their mother's womb, "are already under the protection of divine Providence."[63] Among the Latin authors, Tertullian affirms: "It is anticipated murder to prevent someone from being born; it makes little difference whether one kills a soul already born or puts it to death at birth. He who will one day be a man is a man already."[64]

61.4 Throughout Christianity's two-thousand-year history, this same doctrine has been constantly taught by the Fathers of the Church and by her Pastors and Doctors. Even scientific and philosophical discussions about the precise moment of the infusion of the spiritual soul have never given rise to any hesitation about the moral condemnation of abortion.

62.1 The more recent *papal Magisterium* has vigorously reaffirmed this common doctrine. Pius XI in particular, in his Encyclical *Casti Connubii*, re-

---

[60] Hence the Prophet Jeremiah: "The word of the Lord came to me saying: 'Before I formed you in the womb I knew you, and before you were born I consecrated you; I appointed you a prophet to the nations'" (1:4-5). The Psalmist, for his part, addresses the Lord in these words: "Upon you I have leaned from my birth; you are he who took me from my mother's womb" (Ps 71:6; cf. Is 46:3; Job 10:8-12; Ps 22:10-11). So too the Evangelist Luke — in the magnificent episode of the meeting of the two mothers, Elizabeth and Mary, and their two sons, John the Baptist and Jesus, still hidden in their mothers' wombs (cf. 1:39-45) — emphasizes how even before their birth the two little ones are able to communicate: the child recognizes the coming of the Child and leaps for joy.

[61] Cf. Declaration on Procured Abortion (November 18, 1974), 7: *AAS* 66 (1974), 740-747.

[62] "You shall not put to death the child by abortion nor shall you kill it after it is born": V, 2: *Patres Apostolici*, ed. F. X. Funk, I, 17.

[63] *Apologia on Behalf of the Christians*, 35: *PG* 6, 969.

[64] *Apologeticum*, IX, 8: *CSEL* 69, 24.

jected the specious justifications of abortion.[65] Pius XII excluded all direct abortion, that is, every act tending directly to destroy human life in the womb, "whether such destruction is intended as an end or only as a means to an end."[66] John XXIII reaffirmed that human life is sacred because "from its very beginning it directly involves God's creative activity."[67] The Second Vatican Council, as mentioned earlier, sternly condemned abortion: "From the moment of its conception life must be guarded with the greatest care, while abortion and infanticide are unspeakable crimes."[68]

62.2 The *Church's canonical discipline*, from the earliest centuries, has inflicted penal sanctions on those guilty of abortion. This practice, with more or less severe penalties, has been confirmed in various periods of history. The 1917 *Code of Canon Law* punished abortion with excommunication.[69] The revised canonical legislation continues this tradition when it decrees that "a person who actually procures an abortion incurs automatic (*latae sententiae*) excommunication."[70] The excommunication affects all those who commit this crime with knowledge of the penalty attached, and thus includes those accomplices without whose help the crime would not have been committed.[71] By this reiterated sanction, the Church makes clear that abortion is a most serious and dangerous crime, thereby encouraging those who commit it to seek without delay the path of conversion. In the Church the purpose of the penalty of excommunication is to make an individual fully aware of the gravity of a certain sin and then to foster genuine conversion and repentance.

62.3 Given such unanimity in the doctrinal and disciplinary tradition of the Church, Paul VI was able to declare that this tradition is unchanged and unchangeable.[72] Therefore, by the authority which Christ conferred upon Peter and his Successors, in communion with the Bishops — who on various occasions have condemned abortion and who in the aforementioned consul-

---

[65] Cf. Encyclical Letter *Casti Connubii* (December 31, 1930), II: *AAS* 22 (1930), 562-592.

[66] Address to the Biomedical Association "San Luca" (November 12, 1944): *Discorsi e Radiomessaggi* VI (1944-1945), 191; cf. Address to the Italian Catholic Union of Midwives (October 29, 1951), 2: *AAS* 43 (1951), 838.

[67] Encyclical Letter *Mater et Magistra* (May 15, 1961), III: *AAS* 53 (1961), 447.

[68] Pastoral Constitution on the Church in the Modern World *Gaudium et Spes*, 51.

[69] Canon 2350 §1.

[70] *Code of Canon Law*, Canon 1398; cf. *Code of Canons of the Eastern Churches*, Canon 1450 §2.

[71] Cf. *Code of Canon Law*, Canon 1329; *Code of Canons of the Eastern Churches*, Canon 1417.

[72] Cf. Address to the National Congress of Italian Jurists (December 9, 1972): *AAS* 64 (1972), 777; Encyclical Letter *Humanae Vitae* (July 25, 1968), 14: *AAS* 60 (1968), 490.

tation, albeit dispersed throughout the world, have shown unanimous agreement concerning this doctrine — *I declare that direct abortion, that is, abortion willed as an end or as a means, always constitutes a grave moral disorder,* since it is the deliberate killing of an innocent human being. This doctrine is based upon the natural law and upon the written word of God, is transmitted by the Church's Tradition and taught by the ordinary and universal Magisterium.[73]

62.4 No circumstance, no purpose, no law whatsoever can ever make licit an act which is intrinsically illicit, since it is contrary to the law of God which is written in every human heart, knowable by reason itself and proclaimed by the Church.

63.1 This evaluation of the morality of abortion is to be applied also to the recent forms of *intervention on human embryos* which, although carried out for purposes legitimate in themselves, inevitably involve the killing of those embryos. This is the case with *experimentation on embryos,* which is becoming increasingly widespread in the field of biomedical research and is legally permitted in some countries. Although "one must uphold as licit procedures carried out on the human embryo which respect the life and integrity of the embryo and do not involve disproportionate risks for it, but rather are directed to its healing, the improvement of its condition of health or its individual survival,"[74] it must nonetheless be stated that the use of human embryos or fetuses as an object of experimentation constitutes a crime against their dignity as human beings who have a right to the same respect owed to a child once born, just as to every person.[75]

63.2 This moral condemnation also regards procedures that exploit living human embryos and fetuses — sometimes specifically "produced" for this purpose by *in vitro* fertilization — either to be used as "biological material" or as *providers of organs or tissue for transplants* in the treatment of certain diseases. The killing of innocent human creatures, even if carried out to help others, constitutes an absolutely unacceptable act.

63.3 Special attention must be given to evaluating the morality of *prenatal diagnostic techniques* which enable the early detection of possible anomalies in the unborn child. In view of the complexity of these techniques, an accurate

[73] Cf. Second Vatican Ecumenical Council, Dogmatic Constitution on the Church *Lumen Gentium,* 25.

[74] Congregation for the Doctrine of the Faith, Instruction on Respect for Human Life in Its Origin and on the Dignity of Procreation *Donum Vitae* (February 22, 1987), I, 3: *AAS* 80 (1988), 80.

[75] Cf. Charter of the Rights of the Family (October 22, 1983), 4b: Vatican Polyglot Press, 1983.

and systematic moral judgment is necessary. When they do not involve disproportionate risks for the child and the mother, and are meant to make possible early therapy or even to favor a serene and informed acceptance of the child not yet born, these techniques are morally licit. But since the possibilities of prenatal therapy are today still limited, it not infrequently happens that these techniques are used with a eugenic intention which accepts selective abortion in order to prevent the birth of children affected by various types of anomalies. Such an attitude is shameful and utterly reprehensible, since it presumes to measure the value of a human life only within the parameters of "normality" and physical well-being, thus opening the way to legitimizing infanticide and euthanasia as well.

63.4 And yet the courage and the serenity with which so many of our brothers and sisters suffering from serious disabilities lead their lives when they are shown acceptance and love bears eloquent witness to what gives authentic value to life, and makes it, even in difficult conditions, something precious for them and for others. The Church is close to those married couples who, with great anguish and suffering, willingly accept gravely handicapped children. She is also grateful to all those families which, through adoption, welcome children abandoned by their parents because of disabilities or illnesses.

"It is I who bring both death and life" (Dt 32:39): the tragedy of euthanasia

64.1 At the other end of life's spectrum, men and women find themselves facing the mystery of death. Today, as a result of advances in medicine and in a cultural context frequently closed to the transcendent, the experience of dying is marked by new features. When the prevailing tendency is to value life only to the extent that it brings pleasure and well-being, suffering seems like an unbearable setback, something from which one must be freed at all costs. Death is considered "senseless" if it suddenly interrupts a life still open to a future of new and interesting experiences. But it becomes a "rightful liberation" once life is held to be no longer meaningful because it is filled with pain and inexorably doomed to even greater suffering.

64.2 Furthermore, when he denies or neglects his fundamental relationship to God, man thinks he is his own rule and measure, with the right to demand that society should guarantee him the ways and means of deciding what to do with his life in full and complete autonomy. It is especially people in the developed countries who act in this way: they feel encouraged to do so also by the constant progress of medicine and its ever more advanced techniques. By using highly sophisticated systems and equipment, science and medical practice today are able not only to attend to cases formerly considered untreatable and to reduce or eliminate pain, but also to sustain and prolong life even in situations of extreme frailty, to resuscitate artificially patients whose basic biological functions have undergone sudden collapse, and to use special procedures to make organs available for transplanting.

64.3 In this context the temptation grows to have recourse to *euthanasia*, that is, *to take control of death and bring it about before its time*, "gently" ending one's own life or the life of others. In reality what might seem logical and humane, when looked at more closely, is seen to be *senseless and inhumane*. Here we are faced with one of the more alarming symptoms of the "culture of death," which is advancing above all in prosperous societies, marked by an attitude of excessive preoccupation with efficiency, and which sees the growing number of elderly and disabled people as intolerable and too burdensome. These people are very often isolated by their families and by society, which are organized almost exclusively on the basis of criteria of productive efficiency, according to which a hopelessly impaired life no longer has any value.

65.1 For a correct moral judgment on euthanasia, in the first place a clear definition is required. *Euthanasia in the strict sense* is understood to be an action or omission which of itself and by intention causes death, with the purpose of eliminating all suffering. "Euthanasia's terms of reference, therefore, are to be found in the intention of the will and in the methods used."[76]

65.2 Euthanasia must be distinguished from the decision to forgo so-called "aggressive medical treatment," in other words, medical procedures which no longer correspond to the real situation of the patient either because they are by now disproportionate to any expected results or because they impose an excessive burden on the patient and his family. In such situations, when death is clearly imminent and inevitable, one can in conscience "refuse forms of treatment that would only secure a precarious and burdensome prolongation of life, so long as the normal care due to the sick person in similar cases is not interrupted."[77] Certainly there is a moral obligation to care for oneself and to allow oneself to be cared for, but this duty must take account of concrete circumstances. It needs to be determined whether the means of treatment available are objectively proportionate to the prospects for improvement. To forgo extraordinary or disproportionate means is not the equivalent of suicide

---

[76] Congregation for the Doctrine of the Faith, Declaration on Euthanasia *Iura et Bona* (May 5, 1980), II: *AAS* 72 (1980), 546.

[77] Ibid., IV: loc. cit., 551.

or euthanasia; it rather expresses acceptance of the human condition in the face of death.[78]

65.3 In modern medicine, increased attention is being given to what are called "methods of palliative care," which seek to make suffering more bearable in the final stages of illness and to ensure that the patient is supported and accompanied in his or her ordeal. Among the questions which arise in this context is that of the licitness of using various types of painkillers and sedatives for relieving the patient's pain when this involves the risk of shortening life. While praise may be due to the person who voluntarily accepts suffering by forgoing treatment with painkillers in order to remain fully lucid and, if a believer, to share consciously in the Lord's Passion, such "heroic" behavior cannot be considered the duty of everyone. Pius XII affirmed that it is licit to relieve pain by narcotics, even when the result is decreased consciousness and a shortening of life, "if no other means exist, and if, in the given circumstances, this does not prevent the carrying out of other religious and moral duties."[79] In such a case, death is not willed or sought, even though for reasonable motives one runs the risk of it: there is simply a desire to ease pain effectively by using the analgesics which medicine provides. All the same, "it is not right to deprive the dying person of consciousness without a serious reason":[80] as they approach death people ought to be able to satisfy their moral and family duties, and above all they ought to be able to prepare in a fully conscious way for their definitive meeting with God.

65.4 Taking into account these distinctions, in harmony with the Magisterium of my Predecessors[81] and in communion with the Bishops of the Catholic Church, *I confirm that euthanasia is a grave violation of the law of God*, since it is the deliberate and morally unacceptable killing of a human person. This doctrine is based upon the natural law and upon the written

---

[78] Cf. ibid.

[79] Pius XII, Address to an International Group of Physicians (February 24, 1957), III: *AAS* 49 (1957), 147; cf. Congregation for the Doctrine of the Faith, Declaration on Euthanasia *Iura et Bona* (May 5, 1980), III: *AAS* 72 (1980), 547-548.

[80] Pius XII, Address to an International Group of Physicians (February 24, 1957), III: *AAS* 49 (1957), 145.

[81] Cf. Pius XII, Address to an International Group of Physicians (February 24, 1957): loc. cit., 129-147; Supreme Sacred Congregation of the Holy Office, *Decretum de directa insontium occisione* (December 2, 1940): *AAS* 32 (1940), 553-554; Paul VI, Message to French Television (January 27, 1971): "Every life is sacred": *Insegnamenti* IX (1971), 57-58; Address to the International College of Surgeons (June 1, 1972): *AAS* 64 (1972), 432-436; Second Vatican Ecumenical Council, Pastoral Constitution on the Church in the Modern World *Gaudium et Spes*, 27.

word of God, is transmitted by the Church's Tradition and taught by the ordinary and universal Magisterium.[82]

65.5 Depending on the circumstances, this practice involves the malice proper to suicide or murder.

66.1 Suicide is always as morally objectionable as murder. The Church's tradition has always rejected it as a gravely evil choice.[83] Even though a certain psychological, cultural and social conditioning may induce a person to carry out an action which so radically contradicts the innate inclination to life, thus lessening or removing subjective responsibility, *suicide*, when viewed objectively, is a gravely immoral act. In fact, it involves the rejection of love of self and the renunciation of the obligation of justice and charity toward one's neighbor, toward the communities to which one belongs and toward society as a whole.[84] In its deepest reality, suicide represents a rejection of God's absolute sovereignty over life and death as proclaimed in the prayer of the ancient sage of Israel: "You have power over life and death; you lead men down to the gates of Hades and back again" (Wis 16:13; cf. Tob 13:2).

66.2 To concur with the intention of another person to commit suicide and to help in carrying it out through so-called "assisted suicide" means to cooperate in, and at times to be the actual perpetrator of, an injustice which can never be excused even if it is requested. In a remarkably relevant passage, Saint Augustine writes that "it is never licit to kill another: even if he should wish it, indeed if he request it because, hanging between life and death, he begs for help in freeing the soul struggling against the bonds of the body and longing to be released; nor is it licit even when a sick person is no longer able to live."[85] Even when not motivated by a selfish refusal to be burdened with the life of someone who is suffering, euthanasia must be called a *false mercy*, and indeed a disturbing "perversion" of mercy. True "compassion" leads to sharing another's pain; it does not kill the person whose suffering we cannot bear. Moreover, the act of euthanasia appears all the more perverse if it is carried out by those, like relatives, who are supposed to treat a family member with patience and love, or by those, such as doctors, who by virtue of their

---

[82] Cf. Second Vatican Ecumenical Council, Dogmatic Constitution on the Church *Lumen Gentium*, 25.

[83] Cf. Saint Augustine, *De Civitate Dei*, I, 20: CCL 47, 22; Saint Thomas Aquinas, *Summa Theologiae*, II-II, q. 6, a. 5.

[84] Congregation for the Doctrine of the Faith, Declaration on Euthanasia *Iura et Bona* (May 5, 1980), I: AAS 72 (1980), 545; *Catechism of the Catholic Church*, Nos. 2281-2283.

[85] *Epistula* 204, 5: CSEL 57, 320.

specific profession are supposed to care for the sick person even in the most painful terminal stages.

66.3 The choice of euthanasia becomes more serious when it takes the form of a *murder* committed by others on a person who has in no way requested it and who has never consented to it. The height of arbitrariness and injustice is reached when certain people, such as physicians or legislators, arrogate to themselves the power to decide who ought to live and who ought to die. Once again we find ourselves before the temptation of Eden: to become like God, who "knows good and evil" (cf. Gen 3:5). God alone has the power over life and death: "It is I who bring both death and life" (Dt 32:39; cf. 2 Kings 5:7; 1 Sam 2:6). But he only exercises this power in accordance with a plan of wisdom and love. When man usurps this power, being enslaved by a foolish and selfish way of thinking, he inevitably uses it for injustice and death. Thus the life of the person who is weak is put into the hands of the one who is strong; in society the sense of justice is lost, and mutual trust, the basis of every authentic interpersonal relationship, is undermined at its root.

67.1 Quite different from this is the *way of love and true mercy*, which our common humanity calls for, and upon which faith in Christ the Redeemer, who died and rose again, sheds ever new light. The request which arises from the human heart in the supreme confrontation with suffering and death, especially when faced with the temptation to give up in utter desperation, is above all a request for companionship, sympathy and support in the time of trial. It is a plea for help to keep on hoping when all human hopes fail. As the Second Vatican Council reminds us: "It is in the face of death that the riddle of human existence becomes most acute" and yet "man rightly follows the intuition of his heart when he abhors and repudiates the absolute ruin and total disappearance of his own person. Man rebels against death because he bears in himself an eternal seed which cannot be reduced to mere matter."[86]

67.2 This natural aversion to death and this incipient hope of immortality are illumined and brought to fulfillment by Christian faith, which both promises and offers a share in the victory of the risen Christ: it is the victory of the one who by his redemptive death has set man free from death, "the wages of sin" (Rom 6:23), and has given him the Spirit, the pledge of resurrection and of life (cf. Rom 8:11). The certainty of future immortality and *hope in the promised resurrection* cast new light on the mystery of suffering and death, and fill the believer with an extraordinary capacity to trust fully in the plan of God.

67.3 The Apostle Paul expressed this newness in terms of belonging com-

---

[86] Pastoral Constitution on the Church in the Modern World *Gaudium et Spes*, 18.

pletely to the Lord who embraces every human condition: "None of us lives to himself, and none of us dies to himself. If we live, we live to the Lord, and if we die, we die to the Lord; so then, whether we live or whether we die, we are the Lord's" (Rom 14:7-8). *Dying to the Lord* means experiencing one's death as the supreme act of obedience to the Father (cf. Phil 2:8), being ready to meet death at the "hour" willed and chosen by him (cf. Jn 13:1), which can only mean when one's earthly pilgrimage is completed. *Living to the Lord* also means recognizing that suffering, while still an evil and a trial in itself, can always become a source of good. It becomes such if it is experienced for love and with love through sharing, by God's gracious gift and one's own personal and free choice, in the suffering of Christ crucified. In this way the person who lives his suffering in the Lord grows more fully conformed to him (cf. Phil 3:10; 1 Pet 2:21) and more closely associated with his redemptive work on behalf of the Church and humanity.[87] This was the experience of Saint Paul, which every person who suffers is called to relive: "I rejoice in my sufferings for your sake, and in my flesh I complete what is lacking in Christ's afflictions for the sake of his Body, that is, the Church" (Col 1:24).

"We must obey God rather than men" (Acts 5:29): civil law and the moral law

68.1 One of the specific characteristics of present-day attacks on human life — as has already been said several times — consists in the trend to demand a *legal justification* for them, as if they were rights which the State, at least under certain conditions, must acknowledge as belonging to citizens. Consequently, there is a tendency to claim that it should be possible to exercise these rights with the safe and free assistance of doctors and medical personnel.

68.2 It is often claimed that the life of an unborn child or a seriously disabled person is only a relative good: according to a proportionalist approach or one of sheer calculation, this good should be compared with and balanced against other goods. It is even maintained that only someone present and personally involved in a concrete situation can correctly judge the goods at stake: consequently, only that person would be able to decide on the morality of his choice. The State, therefore, in the interest of civil coexistence and social harmony, should respect this choice, even to the point of permitting abortion and euthanasia.

68.3 At other times, it is claimed that civil law cannot demand that all

---

[87] Cf. John Paul II, Apostolic Letter *Salvifici Doloris* (February 11, 1984), 14-24: *AAS* 76 (1984), 214-234.

citizens should live according to moral standards higher than what all citizens themselves acknowledge and share. Hence the law should always express the opinion and will of the majority of citizens and recognize that they have, at least in certain extreme cases, the right even to abortion and euthanasia. Moreover the prohibition and the punishment of abortion and euthanasia in these cases would inevitably lead — so it is said — to an increase of illegal practices: and these would not be subject to necessary control by society and would be carried out in a medically unsafe way. The question is also raised whether supporting a law which in practice cannot be enforced would not ultimately undermine the authority of all laws.

68.4 Finally, the more radical views go so far as to maintain that in a modern and pluralistic society people should be allowed complete freedom to dispose of their own lives as well as of the lives of the unborn: it is asserted that it is not the task of the law to choose between different moral opinions, and still less can the law claim to impose one particular opinion to the detriment of others.

69.1 In any case, in the democratic culture of our time it is commonly held that the legal system of any society should limit itself to taking account of and accepting the convictions of the majority. It should therefore be based solely upon what the majority itself considers moral and actually practices. Furthermore, if it is believed that an objective truth shared by all is *de facto* unattainable, then respect for the freedom of the citizens — who in a democratic system are considered the true rulers — would require that on the legislative level the autonomy of individual consciences be acknowledged. Consequently, when establishing those norms which are absolutely necessary for social coexistence, the only determining factor should be the will of the majority, whatever this may be. Hence every politician, in his or her activity, should clearly separate the realm of private conscience from that of public conduct.

69.2 As a result we have what appear to be two diametrically opposed tendencies. On the one hand, individuals claim for themselves in the moral sphere the most complete freedom of choice and demand that the State should not adopt or impose any ethical position but limit itself to guaranteeing maximum space for the freedom of each individual, with the sole limitation of not infringing on the freedom and rights of any other citizen. On the other hand, it is held that, in the exercise of public and professional duties, respect for other people's freedom of choice requires that each one should set aside his or her own convictions in order to satisfy every demand of the citizens which is recognized and guaranteed by law; in carrying out one's duties, the only moral criterion should be what is laid down by the law itself. Individual responsibility is thus turned over to the civil law, with a renouncing of personal conscience, at least in the public sphere.

70.1 At the basis of all these tendencies lies the *ethical relativism* which characterizes much of present-day culture. There are those who consider such relativism an essential condition of democracy, inasmuch as it alone is held to guarantee tolerance, mutual respect between people and acceptance of the decisions of the majority, whereas moral norms considered to be objective and binding are held to lead to authoritarianism and intolerance.

70.2 But it is precisely the issue of respect for life which shows what misunderstandings and contradictions, accompanied by terrible practical consequences, are concealed in this position.

70.3 It is true that history has known cases where crimes have been committed in the name of "truth." But equally grave crimes and radical denials of freedom have also been committed and are still being committed in the name of "ethical relativism." When a parliamentary or social majority decrees that it is legal, at least under certain conditions, to kill unborn human life, is it not really making a "tyrannical" decision with regard to the weakest and most defenseless of human beings? Everyone's conscience rightly rejects those crimes against humanity of which our century has had such sad experience. But would these crimes cease to be crimes if, instead of being committed by unscrupulous tyrants, they were legitimated by popular consensus?

70.4 Democracy cannot be idolized to the point of making it a substitute for morality or a panacea for immorality. Fundamentally, democracy is a "system" and as such is a means and not an end. Its "moral" value is not automatic, but depends on conformity to the moral law to which it, like every other form of human behavior, must be subject: in other words, its morality depends on the morality of the ends which it pursues and of the means which it employs. If today we see an almost universal consensus with regard to the value of democracy, this is to be considered a positive "sign of the times," as the Church's Magisterium has frequently noted.[88] But the value of democracy stands or falls with the values which it embodies and promotes. Of course, values such as the dignity of every human person, respect for inviolable and inalienable human rights, and the adoption of the "common good" as the end and criterion regulating political life are certainly fundamental and not to be ignored.

[88] Cf. John Paul II, Encyclical Letter *Centesimus Annus* (May 1, 1991), 46: *AAS* 83 (1991), 850; Pius XII, Christmas Radio Message (December 24, 1944): *AAS* 37 (1945), 10-20.

70.5 The basis of these values cannot be provisional and changeable "major-ity" opinions, but only the acknowledgment of an objective moral law which, as the "natural law" written in the human heart, is the obligatory point of reference for civil law itself. If, as a result of a tragic obscuring of the collective conscience, an attitude of skepticism were to succeed in bringing into question even the fundamental principles of the moral law, the democratic system itself would be shaken in its foundations and would be reduced to a mere mechanism for regu-lating different and opposing interests on a purely empirical basis.[89]

70.6 Some might think that even this function, in the absence of anything better, should be valued for the sake of peace in society. While one acknowl-edges some element of truth in this point of view, it is easy to see that without an objective moral grounding not even democracy is capable of ensuring a stable peace, especially since peace which is not built upon the values of the dignity of every individual and of solidarity between all people frequently proves to be illusory. Even in participatory systems of government, the regulation of interests often occurs to the advantage of the most powerful, since they are the ones most capable of maneuvering not only the levers of power but also of shaping the formation of consensus. In such a situation, democracy easily becomes an empty word.

71.1 It is therefore urgently necessary, for the future of society and the development of a sound democracy, to rediscover those essential and innate human and moral values which flow from the very truth of the human being and express and safeguard the dignity of the person: values which no indi-vidual, no majority and no State can ever create, modify or destroy, but must only acknowledge, respect and promote.

71.2 Consequently, there is a need to recover the *basic elements of a vision of the relationship between civil law and moral law,* which are put forward by the Church, but which are also part of the patrimony of the great juridical traditions of humanity.

71.3 Certainly *the purpose of civil law* is different and more limited in scope than that of the moral law. But "in no sphere of life can the civil law take the place of conscience or dictate norms concerning things which are outside its competence,"[90] which is that of ensuring the common good of people through

---

[89] Cf. John Paul II, Encyclical Letter *Veritatis Splendor* (August 6, 1993), 97, 99: *AAS* 85 (1993), 1209-1211.

[90] Congregation for the Doctrine of the Faith, Instruction on Respect for Human Life in Its Origin and on the Dignity of Procreation *Donum Vitae* (February 22, 1987), III: *AAS* 80 (1988), 98.

the recognition and defense of their fundamental rights, and the promotion of peace and of public morality.[91] The real purpose of civil law is to guarantee an ordered social coexistence in true justice, so that all may "lead a quiet and peaceable life, godly and respectful in every way" (1 Tim 2:2). Precisely for this reason, civil law must ensure that all members of society enjoy respect for certain fundamental rights which innately belong to the person, rights which every positive law must recognize and guarantee. First and fundamental among these is the inviolable right to life of every innocent human being. While public authority can sometimes choose not to put a stop to something which — were it prohibited — would cause more serious harm,[92] it can never presume to legitimize as a right of individuals — even if they are the majority of the members of society — an offense against other persons caused by the disregard of so fundamental a right as the right to life. The legal toleration of abortion or of euthanasia can in no way claim to be based on respect for the conscience of others, precisely because society has the right and the duty to protect itself against the abuses which can occur in the name of conscience and under the pretext of freedom.[93]

71.4 In the Encyclical *Pacem in Terris,* John XXIII pointed out that "it is generally accepted today that the common good is best safeguarded when personal rights and duties are guaranteed. The chief concern of civil authorities must therefore be to ensure that these rights are recognized, respected, coordinated, defended and promoted, and that each individual is enabled to perform his duties more easily. For 'to safeguard the inviolable rights of the human person and to facilitate the performance of his duties is the principal duty of every public authority.' Thus any government which refused to recognize human rights or acted in violation of them would not only fail in its duty; its decrees would be wholly lacking in binding force."[94]

72.1 The doctrine on the necessary *conformity of civil law with the moral law* is in continuity with the whole tradition of the Church. This is clear once more from John XXIII's Encyclical: "Authority is a postulate of the moral order

---

[91] Cf. Second Vatican Ecumenical Council, Declaration on Religious Freedom *Dignitatis Humanae,* 7.

[92] Cf. Saint Thomas Aquinas, *Summa Theologiae,* I-II, q. 96, a. 2.

[93] Cf. Second Vatican Ecumenical Council, Declaration on Religious Freedom *Dignitatis Humanae,* 7.

[94] Encyclical Letter *Pacem in Terris* (April 11, 1963), II: *AAS* 55 (1963), 273-274. The internal quote is from Pius XII, Radio Message of Pentecost (June 1, 1941): *AAS* 33 (1941), 200. On this topic the Encyclical cites: Pius XI, Encyclical Letter *Mit brennender Sorge* (March 14, 1937): *AAS* 29 (1937), 159; Encyclical Letter *Divini Redemptoris* (March 19, 1937), III: *AAS* 29 (1937), 79; Pius XII, Christmas Radio Message (December 24, 1942): *AAS* 35 (1943), 9-24.

and derives from God. Consequently, laws and decrees enacted in contravention of the moral order, and hence of the divine will, can have no binding force in conscience. . . ; indeed, the passing of such laws undermines the very nature of authority and results in shameful abuse."[95] This is the clear teaching of Saint Thomas Aquinas, who writes that "human law is law inasmuch as it is in conformity with right reason and thus derives from the eternal law. But when a law is contrary to reason, it is called an unjust law; but in this case it ceases to be a law and becomes instead an act of violence."[96] And again: "Every law made by man can be called a law insofar as it derives from the natural law. But if it is somehow opposed to the natural law, then it is not really a law but rather a corruption of the law."[97]

72.2 Now the first and most immediate application of this teaching concerns a human law which disregards the fundamental right and source of all other rights which is the right to life, a right belonging to every individual. Consequently, laws which legitimize the direct killing of innocent human beings through abortion or euthanasia are in complete opposition to the inviolable right to life proper to every individual; they thus deny the equality of everyone before the law. It might be objected that such is not the case in euthanasia, when it is requested with full awareness by the person involved. But any State which made such a request legitimate and authorized it to be carried out would be legalizing a case of suicide-murder, contrary to the fundamental principles of absolute respect for life and of the protection of every innocent life. In this way the State contributes to lessening respect for life and opens the door to ways of acting which are destructive of trust in relations between people. Laws which authorize and promote abortion and euthanasia are therefore radically opposed not only to the good of the individual but also to the common good; as such they are completely lacking in authentic juridical validity. Disregard for the right to life, precisely because it leads to the killing of the person whom society exists to serve, is what most directly conflicts with the possibility of achieving the common good. Consequently, a civil law authorizing abortion or euthanasia ceases by that very fact to be a true, morally binding civil law.

73.1 Abortion and euthanasia are thus crimes which no human law can claim to legitimize. There is no obligation in conscience to obey such laws;

---

[95] Encyclical Letter *Pacem in Terris* (April 11, 1963), II: *AAS* 55 (1963), 271.

[96] *Summa Theologiae*, I-II, q. 93, a. 3, ad 2.

[97] Ibid., I-II, q. 95, a. 2. Aquinas quotes Saint Augustine: "non videtur esse lex, quae iusta non fuerit": *De Libero Arbitrio*, I, 5, 11: *PL* 32, 1227.

instead there is a *grave and clear obligation to oppose them by conscientious objection.* From the very beginnings of the Church, the apostolic preaching reminded Christians of their duty to obey legitimately constituted public authorities (cf. Rom 13:1-7; 1 Pet 2:13-14), but at the same time it firmly warned that "we must obey God rather than men" (Acts 5:29). In the Old Testament, precisely in regard to threats against life, we find a significant example of resistance to the unjust command of those in authority. After Pharaoh ordered the killing of all newborn males, the Hebrew midwives refused. "They did not do as the king of Egypt commanded them, but let the male children live" (Ex 1:17). But the ultimate reason for their action should be noted: *"the midwives feared God"* (ibid.). It is precisely from obedience to God — to whom alone is due that fear which is acknowledgment of his absolute sovereignty — that the strength and the courage to resist unjust human laws are born. It is the strength and the courage of those prepared even to be imprisoned or put to the sword, in the certainty that this is what makes for "the endurance and faith of the saints" (Rev 13:10).

73.2 In the case of an intrinsically unjust law, such as a law permitting abortion or euthanasia, it is therefore never licit to obey it, or to "take part in a propaganda campaign in favor of such a law or vote for it."[98]

73.3 A particular problem of conscience can arise in cases where a legislative vote would be decisive for the passage of a more restrictive law, aimed at limiting the number of authorized abortions, in place of a more permissive law already passed or ready to be voted on. Such cases are not infrequent. It is a fact that while in some parts of the world there continue to be campaigns to introduce laws favoring abortion, often supported by powerful international organizations, in other nations — particularly those which have already experienced the bitter fruits of such permissive legislation — there are growing signs of a rethinking in this matter. In a case like the one just mentioned, when it is not possible to overturn or completely abrogate a pro-abortion law, an elected official, whose absolute personal opposition to procured abortion was well known, could licitly support proposals aimed at *limiting the harm* done by such a law and at lessening its negative consequences at the level of general opinion and public morality. This does not in fact represent an illicit cooperation with an unjust law, but rather a legitimate and proper attempt to limit its evil aspects.

---

[98] Congregation for the Doctrine of the Faith, Declaration on Procured Abortion (November 18, 1974), 22: *AAS* 66 (1974), 744.

74.1 The passing of unjust laws often raises difficult problems of conscience for morally upright people with regard to the issue of cooperation, since they have a right to demand not to be forced to take part in morally evil actions. Sometimes the choices which have to be made are difficult; they may require the sacrifice of prestigious professional positions or the relinquishing of reasonable hopes of career advancement. In other cases, it can happen that carrying out certain actions, which are provided for by legislation that overall is unjust but which in themselves are indifferent or even positive, can serve to protect human lives under threat. There may be reason to fear, however, that willingness to carry out such actions will not only cause scandal and weaken the necessary opposition to attacks on life, but will gradually lead to further capitulation to a mentality of permissiveness.

74.2 In order to shed light on this difficult question, it is necessary to recall the general principles concerning *cooperation in evil actions*. Christians, like all people of good will, are called upon under grave obligation of conscience not to cooperate formally in practices which, even if permitted by civil legislation, are contrary to God's law. Indeed, from the moral standpoint, it is never licit to cooperate formally in evil. Such cooperation occurs when an action, either by its very nature or by the form it takes in a concrete situation, can be defined as a direct participation in an act against innocent human life or a sharing in the immoral intention of the person committing it. This cooperation can never be justified either by invoking respect for the freedom of others or by appealing to the fact that civil law permits it or requires it. Each individual in fact has moral responsibility for the acts which he personally performs; no one can be exempted from this responsibility, and on the basis of it everyone will be judged by God himself (cf. Rom 2:6, 14:12).

74.3 To refuse to take part in committing an injustice is not only a moral duty; it is also a basic human right. Were this not so, the human person would be forced to perform an action intrinsically incompatible with human dignity, and in this way human freedom itself, the authentic meaning and purpose of which are found in its orientation to the true and the good, would be radically compromised. What is at stake therefore is an essential right which, precisely as such, should be acknowledged and protected by civil law. In this sense, the opportunity to refuse to take part in the phases of consultation, preparation and execution of these acts against life should be guaranteed to physicians, health-care personnel and directors of hospitals, clinics and convalescent facilities. Those who have recourse to conscientious objection must be protected not only from legal penalties, but also from any negative effects on the legal, disciplinary, financial and professional plane.

"You shall love your neighbor as yourself" (Lk 10:27): "promote" life

75.1 God's commandments teach us the way of life. *The negative moral precepts*, which declare that the choice of certain actions is morally unacceptable, have an absolute value for human freedom: they are valid always and everywhere, without exception. They make it clear that the choice of certain ways of acting is radically incompatible with the love of God and with the dignity of the person created in his image. Such choices cannot be redeemed by the goodness of any intention or of any consequence; they are irrevocably opposed to the bond between persons; they contradict the fundamental decision to direct one's life to God.[99]

75.2 In this sense, the negative moral precepts have an extremely important positive function. The "no" which they unconditionally require makes clear the absolute limit beneath which free individuals cannot lower themselves. At the same time they indicate the minimum which they must respect and from which they must start out in order to say "yes" over and over again, a "yes" which will gradually embrace the *entire horizon of the good* (cf. Mt 5:48). The commandments, in particular the negative moral precepts, are the beginning and the first necessary stage of the journey toward freedom. As Saint Augustine writes, "The beginning of freedom is to be free from crimes . . . like murder, adultery, fornication, theft, fraud, sacrilege and so forth. Only when one stops committing these crimes (and no Christian should commit them), one begins to lift up one's head toward freedom. But this is only the beginning of freedom, not perfect freedom."[100]

76.1 The commandment "You shall not kill" thus establishes the point of departure for the start of true freedom. It leads us to promote life actively, and to develop particular ways of thinking and acting which serve life. In this way we exercise our responsibility toward the persons entrusted to us and we show, in deeds and in truth, our gratitude to God for the great gift of life (cf. Ps 139:13-14).

---

[99] Cf. *Catechism of the Catholic Church*, Nos. 1753-1755; John Paul II, Encyclical Letter *Veritatis Splendor* (August 6, 1993), 81-82: *AAS* 85 (1993), 1198-1199.

[100] *In Iohannis Evangelium Tractatus*, 41, 10: *CCL* 36, 363; cf. John Paul II, Encyclical Letter *Veritatis Splendor* (August 6, 1993), 13: *AAS* 85 (1993), 1144.

76.2 The Creator has entrusted man's life to his responsible concern, not to make arbitrary use of it, but to preserve it with wisdom and to care for it with loving fidelity. The God of the Covenant has entrusted the life of every individual to his or her fellow human beings, brothers and sisters, according to the law of reciprocity in giving and receiving, of self-giving and of the acceptance of others. In the fullness of time, by taking flesh and giving his life for us, the Son of God showed what heights and depths this law of reciprocity can reach. With the gift of his Spirit, Christ gives new content and meaning to the law of reciprocity, to our being entrusted to one another. The Spirit who builds up communion in love creates between us a new fraternity and solidarity, a true reflection of the mystery of mutual self-giving and receiving proper to the Most Holy Trinity. The Spirit becomes the new law which gives strength to believers and awakens in them a responsibility for sharing the gift of self and for accepting others, as a sharing in the boundless love of Jesus Christ himself.

77.1 This new law also gives spirit and shape to the commandment "You shall not kill." For the Christian it involves an absolute imperative to respect, love and promote the life of every brother and sister, in accordance with the requirements of God's bountiful love in Jesus Christ. "He laid down his life for us; and we ought to lay down our lives for the brethren" (1 Jn 3:16).

77.2 The commandment "You shall not kill," even in its more positive aspects of respecting, loving and promoting human life, is binding on every individual human being. It resounds in the moral conscience of everyone as an irrepressible echo of the original covenant of God the Creator with mankind. It can be recognized by everyone through the light of reason, and it can be observed thanks to the mysterious working of the Spirit who, blowing where he wills (cf. Jn 3:8), comes to and involves every person living in this world.

77.3 It is therefore a service of love which we are all committed to ensure to our neighbor, that his or her life may be always defended and promoted, especially when it is weak or threatened. It is not only a personal but a social concern which we must all foster: a concern to make unconditional respect for human life the foundation of a renewed society.

77.4 We are asked to love and honor the life of every man and woman and to work with perseverance and courage so that our time, marked by all too many signs of death, may at last witness the establishment of a new culture of life, the fruit of the culture of truth and of love.

IV

You Did It to Me

For a New Culture of Human Life

"You are God's own people, that you may declare the wonderful deeds of him who called you out of darkness into his marvelous light" (1 Pet 2:9): a people of life and for life

78.1 The Church has received the Gospel as a proclamation and a source of joy and salvation. She has received it as a gift from Jesus, sent by the Father "to preach good news to the poor" (Lk 4:18). She has received it through the Apostles, sent by Christ to the whole world (cf. Mk 16:15; Mt 28:19-20). Born from this evangelizing activity, the Church hears every day the echo of Saint Paul's words of warning: "Woe to me if I do not preach the Gospel!" (1 Cor 9:16). As Paul VI wrote, *"evangelization is the grace and vocation proper to the Church, her deepest identity. She exists in order to evangelize."*[101]

78.2 Evangelization is an all-embracing progressive activity through which the Church participates in the prophetic, priestly and royal mission of the Lord Jesus. It is therefore inextricably linked to *preaching, celebration and the service of charity*. Evangelization is a *profoundly ecclesial act*, which calls all the various workers of the Gospel to action, according to their individual charisms and ministry.

78.3 This is also the case with regard to the proclamation of the *Gospel of life*, an integral part of that Gospel which is Jesus Christ himself. We are at the service of this Gospel, sustained by the awareness that we have received it as a gift and are sent to preach it to all humanity, "to the end of the earth" (Acts 1:8). With humility and gratitude we know that we are the *people of life and for life*, and this is how we present ourselves to everyone.

79.1 We are the *people of life* because God, in his unconditional love, has given us the *Gospel of life* and by this same Gospel we have been transformed and saved. We have been ransomed by the "Author of life" (Acts 3:15) at the price of his precious blood (cf. 1 Cor 6:20, 7:23; 1 Pet 1:19). Through the waters of Baptism we have been made a part of him (cf. Rom 6:4-5; Col 2:12), as branches which draw nourishment and fruitfulness from the one tree (cf.

---

[101] Apostolic Exhortation *Evangelii Nuntiandi* (December 8, 1975), 14: *AAS* 68 (1976), 13.

Jn 15:5). Interiorly renewed by the grace of the Spirit, "who is the Lord and giver of life," we have become a *people for life* and we are called to act accordingly.

79.2 *We have been sent.* For us, being at the service of life is not a boast but rather a duty born of our awareness of being "God's own people, that we may declare the wonderful deeds of him who called us out of darkness into his marvelous light" (cf. 1 Pet 2:9). On our journey *we are guided and sustained by the law of love:* a love which has as its source and model the Son of God made man, who "by dying gave life to the world."[102]

79.3 *We have been sent as a people.* Everyone has an obligation to be at the service of life. This is a properly "ecclesial" responsibility, which requires concerted and generous action by all the members and by all sectors of the Christian community. This community commitment does not however eliminate or lessen the responsibility of each *individual*, called by the Lord to "become the neighbor" of everyone: "Go and do likewise" (Lk 10:37).

79.4 Together we all sense our duty to *preach the Gospel of life*, to *celebrate it* in the liturgy and in our whole existence, and to *serve it* with the various programs and structures which support and promote life.

"That which we have seen and heard we proclaim also to you" (1 Jn 1:3): proclaiming the Gospel of life

80.1 "That which was from the beginning, which we have heard, which we have seen with our eyes, which we have looked upon and touched with our hands, concerning the Word of life. . . . We proclaim also to you, so that you may have fellowship with us" (1 Jn 1:1, 3). *Jesus is the only Gospel:* we have nothing further to say or any other witness to bear.

80.2 *To proclaim Jesus is itself to proclaim life.* For Jesus is "the Word of life" (1 Jn 1:1). In him "life was made manifest" (1 Jn 1:2); he himself is "the eternal life which was with the Father and was made manifest to us" (1 Jn 1:2). By the gift of the Spirit, this same life has been bestowed on us. It is in being destined to life in its fullness, to "eternal life," that every person's earthly life acquires its full meaning.

80.3 Enlightened by this *Gospel of life*, we feel a need to proclaim it and to bear witness to it in all its marvelous newness. Since it is one with Jesus himself, who makes all things new[103] and conquers the "oldness" which comes

---

[102] Cf. Roman Missal, prayer of the celebrant before Communion.

[103] Cf. Saint Irenaeus: "Omnem novitatem attulit, semetipsum afferens, qui fuerat annuntiatus": *Adversus Haereses*, IV, 34, 1: *SCh* 100/2, 846-847.

from sin and leads to death,[104] this Gospel exceeds every human expectation and reveals the sublime heights to which the dignity of the human person is raised through grace. This is how Saint Gregory of Nyssa understands it: "Man, as a being, is of no account; he is dust, grass, vanity. But once he is adopted by the God of the universe as a son, he becomes part of the family of that Being, whose excellence and greatness no one can see, hear or understand. What words, thoughts or flight of the spirit can praise the superabundance of this grace? Man surpasses his nature: mortal, he becomes immortal; perishable, he becomes imperishable; fleeting, he becomes eternal; human, he becomes divine."[105]

80.4 Gratitude and joy at the incomparable dignity of man impel us to share this message with everyone: "That which we have seen and heard we proclaim also to you, so that you may have fellowship with us" (1 Jn 1:3). We need to bring the *Gospel of life* to the heart of every man and woman and to make it penetrate every part of society.

81.1 This involves above all proclaiming *the core* of this Gospel. It is the proclamation of a living God who is close to us, who calls us to profound communion with himself and awakens in us the certain hope of eternal life. It is the affirmation of the inseparable connection between the person, his life and his bodiliness. It is the presentation of human life as a life of relationship, a gift of God, the fruit and sign of his love. It is the proclamation that Jesus has a unique relationship with every person, which enables us to see in every human face the face of Christ. It is the call for a "sincere gift of self" as the fullest way to realize our personal freedom.

81.2 It also involves making clear all *the consequences* of this Gospel. These can be summed up as follows: human life, as a gift of God, is sacred and inviolable. For this reason procured abortion and euthanasia are absolutely unacceptable. Not only must human life not be taken, but it must be protected with loving concern. The meaning of life is found in giving and receiving love, and in this light human sexuality and procreation reach their true and full significance. Love also gives meaning to suffering and death; despite the mystery which surrounds them, they can become saving events. Respect for life requires that science and technology should always be at the service of man and his integral development. Society as a whole must respect, defend and promote the dignity

---

[104] Cf. Saint Thomas Aquinas: "Peccator inveterascit, recedens a novitate Christi": *In Psalmos Davidis Lectura*, 6, 5.

[105] *De Beatitudinibus, Oratio* VII: *PG* 44, 1280.

of every human person, at every moment and in every condition of that person's life.

82.1 To be truly a people at the service of life we must propose these truths constantly and courageously from the very first proclamation of the Gospel, and thereafter *in catechesis, in the various forms of preaching, in personal dialogue and in all educational activity.* Teachers, catechists and theologians have the task of emphasizing the *anthropological reasons* upon which respect for every human life is based. In this way, by making the newness of the *Gospel of life* shine forth, we can also help everyone discover in the light of reason and of personal experience how the Christian message fully reveals what man is and the meaning of his being and existence. We shall find important points of contact and dialogue also with non-believers, in our common commitment to the establishment of a new culture of life.

82.2 Faced with so many opposing points of view and a widespread rejection of sound doctrine concerning human life, we can feel that Paul's entreaty to Timothy is also addressed to us: "Preach the word, be urgent in season and out of season, convince, rebuke and exhort, be unfailing in patience and in teaching" (2 Tim 4:2). This exhortation should resound with special force in the hearts of those members of the Church who directly share in different ways in her mission as "teacher" of the truth. May it resound above all for us who are *Bishops:* we are the first ones called to be untiring preachers of the *Gospel of life.* We are also entrusted with the task of ensuring that the doctrine which is once again being set forth in this Encyclical is faithfully handed on in its integrity. We must use appropriate means to defend the faithful from all teaching which is contrary to it. We need to make sure that in theological faculties, seminaries and Catholic institutions sound doctrine is taught, explained and more fully investigated.[106] May Paul's exhortation strike a chord in all *theologians, pastors, teachers* and in all those responsible for *catechesis and the formation of consciences.* Aware of their specific role, may they never be so grievously irresponsible as to betray the truth and their own mission by proposing personal ideas contrary to the *Gospel of life* as faithfully presented and interpreted by the Magisterium.

82.3 In the proclamation of this Gospel we must not fear hostility or unpopularity, and we must refuse any compromise or ambiguity which might conform us to the world's way of thinking (cf. Rom 12:2). We must be *in the world* but not *of the world* (cf. Jn 15:19, 17:16), drawing our strength from

---

[106] Cf. John Paul II, Encyclical Letter *Veritatis Splendor* (August 6, 1993), 116: *AAS* 85 (1993), 1224.

Christ, who by his death and Resurrection has overcome the world (cf. Jn 16:33).

"I give you thanks that I am fearfully, wonderfully made" (Ps 139:14): celebrating the Gospel of life

83.1 Because we have been sent into the world as a "people for life," our proclamation must also become *a genuine celebration of the Gospel of life*. This celebration, with the evocative power of its gestures, symbols and rites, should become a precious and significant setting in which the beauty and grandeur of this Gospel is handed on.

83.2 For this to happen, we need first of all to *foster* in ourselves and in others *a contemplative outlook*.[107] Such an outlook arises from faith in the God of life, who has created every individual as a "wonder" (cf. Ps 139:14). It is the outlook of those who see life in its deeper meaning, who grasp its utter gratuitousness, its beauty and its invitation to freedom and responsibility. It is the outlook of those who do not presume to take possession of reality, but instead accept it as a gift, discovering in all things the reflection of the Creator and seeing in every person his living image (cf. Gen 1:27; Ps 8:5). This outlook does not give in to discouragement when confronted by those who are sick, suffering, outcast or at death's door. Instead, in all these situations it feels challenged to find meaning, and precisely in these circumstances it is open to perceiving in the face of every person a call to encounter, dialogue and solidarity.

83.3 It is time for all of us to adopt this outlook and with deep religious awe to rediscover the ability to *revere and honor every person*, as Paul VI invited us to do in one of his first Christmas messages.[108] Inspired by this contemplative outlook, the new people of the redeemed cannot but respond with *songs of joy, praise and thanksgiving for the priceless gift of life*, for the mystery of every individual's call to share through Christ in the life of grace and in an existence of unending communion with God our Creator and Father.

84.1 *To celebrate the Gospel of life means to celebrate the God of life, the God who gives life:* "We must celebrate eternal Life, from which every other life proceeds. From this, in proportion to its capacities, every being which in any way participates in life, receives life. This divine Life, which is above every other life, gives and preserves life. Every life and every living movement pro-

---

[107] Cf. John Paul II, Encyclical Letter *Centesimus Annus* (May 1, 1991), 37: *AAS* 83 (1991), 840.

[108] Cf. Message for Christmas 1967: *AAS* 60 (1968), 40.

ceed from this Life, which transcends all life and every principle of life. It is to this that souls owe their incorruptibility; and because of this all animals and plants live, which receive only the faintest glimmer of life. To men, beings made of spirit and matter, Life grants life. Even if we should abandon Life, because of its overflowing love for man, it converts us and calls us back to itself. Not only this: it promises to bring us, soul and body, to perfect life, to immortality. It is too little to say that this Life is alive: it is the principle of life, the cause and sole wellspring of life. Every living thing must contemplate it and give it praise: it is Life which overflows with life."[109]

84.2 Like the Psalmist, we too, in our *daily prayer* as individuals and as a community praise and bless God our Father, who knitted us together in our mother's womb, and saw and loved us while we were still without form (cf. Ps 139:13, 15-16). We exclaim with overwhelming joy: "I give you thanks that I am fearfully, wonderfully made; wonderful are your works. You know me through and through" (Ps 139:14). Indeed, "despite its hardships, its hidden mysteries, its suffering and its inevitable frailty, this mortal life is a most beautiful thing, a marvel ever new and moving, an event worthy of being exalted in joy and glory."[110] Moreover, man and his life appear to us not only as one of the greatest marvels of creation: for God has granted to man a dignity which is near to divine (Ps 8:5-6). In every child which is born and in every person who lives or dies we see the image of God's glory. We celebrate this glory in every human being, a sign of the living God, an icon of Jesus Christ.

84.3 We are called to express wonder and gratitude for the gift of life and to welcome, savor and share the *Gospel of life* not only in our personal and community prayer, but above all in the *celebrations of the liturgical year*. Particularly important in this regard are the *sacraments*, the efficacious signs of the presence and saving action of the Lord Jesus in Christian life. The sacraments make us sharers in divine life and provide the spiritual strength necessary to experience life, suffering and death in their fullest meaning. Thanks to a genuine rediscovery and a better appreciation of the significance of these rites, our liturgical celebrations, especially celebrations of the sacraments, will be ever more capable of expressing the full truth about birth, life, suffering and death, and will help us to live these moments as a participation in the Paschal Mystery of the crucified and risen Christ.

85.1 In celebrating the *Gospel of life* we also need to *appreciate and make good use of the wealth of gestures and symbols present in the traditions and*

---

[109] Pseudo-Dionysius the Areopagite, *On the Divine Names*, 6, 1-3: *PG* 3, 856-857.
[110] Paul VI, *Pensiero alla morte*, Istituto Paolo VI, Brescia, 1988, 24.

customs of different cultures and peoples. There are special times and ways in which the peoples of different nations and cultures express joy for a newborn life, respect for and protection of individual human lives, care for the suffering or needy, closeness to the elderly and the dying, participation in the sorrow of those who mourn, and hope and desire for immortality.

85.2 In view of this and following the suggestion made by the Cardinals in the Consistory of 1991, I propose that a *Day for Life* be celebrated each year in every country, as already established by some Episcopal Conferences. The celebration of this Day should be planned and carried out with the active participation of all sectors of the local Church. Its primary purpose should be to foster in individual consciences, in families, in the Church and in civil society a recognition of the meaning and value of human life at every stage and in every condition. Particular attention should be drawn to the seriousness of abortion and euthanasia, without neglecting other aspects of life which from time to time deserve to be given careful consideration as occasion and circumstances demand.

86.1 As part of the spiritual worship acceptable to God (cf. Rom 12:1), the *Gospel of life* is to be celebrated above all in *daily living*, which should be filled with self-giving love for others. In this way, our lives will become a genuine and responsible acceptance of the gift of life and a heartfelt song of praise and gratitude to God, who has given us this gift. This is already happening in the many different acts of selfless generosity, often humble and hidden, carried out by men and women, children and adults, the young and the old, the healthy and the sick.

86.2 It is in this context, so humanly rich and filled with love, that *heroic actions* too are born. These are *the most solemn celebration of the Gospel of life*, for they proclaim it *by the total gift of self*. They are the radiant manifestation of the highest degree of love, which is to give one's life for the person loved (cf. Jn 15:13). They are a sharing in the mystery of the Cross, in which Jesus reveals the value of every person and how life attains its fullness in the sincere gift of self. Over and above such outstanding moments, there is an everyday heroism made up of gestures of sharing, big or small, which build up an authentic culture of life. A particularly praiseworthy example of such gestures is the donation of organs, performed in an ethically acceptable manner, with a view to offering a chance of health and even of life itself to the sick who sometimes have no other hope.

86.3 Part of this daily heroism is also the silent but effective and eloquent witness of all those "brave mothers who devote themselves to their own family without reserve, who suffer in giving birth to their children and who are ready to make any effort, to face any sacrifice, in order to pass on to them the best of themselves."[111] In living out their mission "these heroic women do not always find support in the world around them. On the contrary, the cultural models frequently promoted and broadcast by the media do not encourage motherhood. In the name of progress and modernity the values of fidelity, chastity, sacrifice, to which a host of Christian wives and mothers have borne and continue to bear outstanding witness, are presented as obsolete. . . . We thank you, heroic mothers, for your invincible love! We thank you for your intrepid trust in God and in his love. We thank you for the sacrifice of your life. . . . In the Paschal Mystery, Christ restores to you the gift you gave him. Indeed, he has the power to give you back the life you gave him as an offering."[112]

"What does it profit, my brethren, if a man says he has faith but has not works?" (Jas 2:14): serving the Gospel of life

87.1 By virtue of our sharing in Christ's royal mission, our support and promotion of human life must be accomplished through the *service of charity,* which finds expression in personal witness, various forms of volunteer work, social activity and political commitment. This is a *particularly pressing need at the present time,* when the "culture of death" so forcefully opposes the "culture of life" and often seems to have the upper hand. But even before that it is a need which springs from "faith working through love" (Gal 5:6). As the Letter of James admonishes us: "What does it profit, my brethren, if a man says he has faith but has not works? Can his faith save him? If a brother or sister is ill-clad and in lack of daily food, and one of you says to them, 'Go in peace, be warmed and filled,' without giving them the things needed for the body, what does it profit? So faith by itself, if it has no works, is dead" (2:14-17).

87.2 In our service of charity, *we must be inspired and distinguished by a specific attitude:* we must care for the other as a person for whom God has made us responsible. As disciples of Jesus, we are called to become neighbors to everyone (cf. Lk 10:29-37), and to show special favor to those who are poorest, most alone and most in need. In helping the hungry, the thirsty, the foreigner, the naked, the sick, the imprisoned — as well as the child in the womb and the old person who is suffering or near death — we have the opportunity to serve Jesus. He himself said: "As you did it to one of the least of these

[111] John Paul II, Homily for the Beatification of Isidore Bakanja, Elisabetta Canori Mora and Gianna Beretta Molla (April 24, 1994): *AAS* 87 (1995), 167.

[112] Ibid.

my brethren, you did it to me" (Mt 25:40). Hence we cannot but feel called to account and judged by the ever relevant words of Saint John Chrysostom: "Do you wish to honor the body of Christ? Do not neglect it when you find it naked. Do not do it homage here in the church with silk fabrics only to neglect it outside where it suffers cold and nakedness."[113]

87.3 *Where life is involved, the service of charity must be profoundly consistent.* It cannot tolerate bias and discrimination, for human life is sacred and inviolable at every stage and in every situation; it is an indivisible good. We need then to *"show care" for all life and for the life of everyone.* Indeed, at an even deeper level, we need to go to the very roots of life and love.

87.4 It is this deep love for every man and woman which has given rise down the centuries to an *outstanding history of charity,* a history which has brought into being in the Church and society many forms of service to life which evoke admiration from all unbiased observers. Every Christian community, with a renewed sense of responsibility, must continue to write this history through various kinds of pastoral and social activity. To this end, appropriate and effective programs of *support for new life* must be implemented, with special closeness to mothers who, even without the help of the father, are not afraid to bring their child into the world and to raise it. Similar care must be shown for the life of the marginalized or suffering, especially in its final phases.

88.1 All of this involves a patient and fearless *work of education* aimed at encouraging one and all to bear each other's burdens (cf. Gal 6:2). It requires a continuous promotion of *vocations to service,* particularly among the young. It involves the implementation of long-term practical *projects and initiatives* inspired by the Gospel.

88.2 Many are the *means* toward this end which *need to be developed* with skill and serious commitment. At the first stage of life, *centers for natural methods of regulating fertility* should be promoted as a valuable help to responsible parenthood, in which all individuals, and in the first place the child, are recognized and respected in their own right, and where every decision is guided by the ideal of the sincere gift of self. *Marriage and family counseling agencies* by their specific work of guidance and prevention, carried out in accordance with an anthropology consistent with the Christian vision of the person, of the couple and of sexuality, also offer valuable help in rediscovering the meaning of love and life, and in supporting and accompanying every family in its mission as the "sanctuary of life." Newborn life is also served by

---

[113] *In Matthaeum,* Homily, 50, 3: *PG* 58, 508.

centers of assistance and homes or centers where new life receives a welcome. Thanks to the work of such centers, many unmarried mothers and couples in difficulty discover new hope and find assistance and support in overcoming hardship and the fear of accepting a newly conceived life or life which has just come into the world.

88.3 When life is challenged by conditions of hardship, maladjustment, sickness or rejection, other programs — such as *communities for treating drug addiction, residential communities for minors or the mentally ill, care and relief centers for AIDS patients, associations for solidarity especially toward the disabled* — are eloquent expressions of what charity is able to devise in order to give everyone new reasons for hope and practical possibilities for life.

88.4 And when earthly existence draws to a close, it is again charity which finds the most appropriate means for enabling the *elderly,* especially those who can no longer look after themselves, and the *terminally ill* to enjoy genuinely humane assistance and to receive an adequate response to their needs, in particular their anxiety and their loneliness. In these cases the role of families is indispensable; yet families can receive much help from social welfare agencies and, if necessary, from recourse to *palliative care,* taking advantage of suitable medical and social services available in public institutions or in the home.

88.5 In particular, the role of *hospitals, clinics* and *convalescent homes* needs to be reconsidered. These should not merely be institutions where care is provided for the sick or the dying. Above all they should be places where suffering, pain and death are acknowledged and understood in their human and specifically Christian meaning. This must be especially evident and effective in institutes *staffed by Religious or in any way connected with the Church.*

89.1 Agencies and centers of service to life, and all other initiatives of support and solidarity which circumstances may from time to time suggest, need to be directed by *people who are generous in their involvement and fully aware* of the importance of the *Gospel of life* for the good of individuals and society.

89.2 *A unique responsibility belongs to health-care personnel: doctors, pharmacists, nurses, chaplains, men and women Religious, administrators and volunteers.* Their profession calls for them to be guardians and servants of human life. In today's cultural and social context, in which science and the practice of medicine risk losing sight of their inherent ethical dimension, health-care professionals can be strongly tempted at times to become manipulators of life or even agents of death. In the face of this temptation their responsibility today is greatly increased. Its deepest inspiration and strongest support lie in the intrinsic and undeniable ethical dimension of the health-care profession, something already recognized by the ancient and still relevant *Hippocratic Oath*, which requires every doctor to commit himself to absolute respect for human life and its sacredness.

89.3 Absolute respect for every innocent human life also requires the *exercise of conscientious objection* in relation to procured abortion and euthanasia. "Causing death" can never be considered a form of medical treatment, even when the intention is solely to comply with the patient's request. Rather, it runs completely counter to the health-care profession, which is meant to be an impassioned and unflinching affirmation of life. Biomedical research too, a field which promises great benefits for humanity, must always reject experimentation, research or applications which disregard the inviolable dignity of the human being, and thus cease to be at the service of people and become instead means which, under the guise of helping people, actually harm them.

90.1 *Volunteer workers* have a specific role to play: they make a valuable contribution to the service of life when they combine professional ability and generous, selfless love. The *Gospel of life* inspires them to lift their feelings of good will toward others to the heights of Christ's charity; to renew every day, amid hard work and weariness, their awareness of the dignity of every person; to search out people's needs and, when necessary, to set out on new paths where needs are greater but care and support weaker.

90.2 If charity is to be realistic and effective, it demands that the *Gospel of life* be implemented also by means of certain *forms of social activity and commitment in the political field,* as a way of defending and promoting the value of life in our ever more complex and pluralistic societies. *Individuals, families, groups and associations,* albeit for different reasons and in different ways, all have a responsibility for shaping society and developing cultural, economic, political and legislative projects which, with respect for all and in keeping with democratic principles, will contribute to the building of a society in which the dignity of each person is recognized and protected and the lives of all are defended and enhanced.

90.3 This task is the particular responsibility of *civil leaders.* Called to serve the people and the common good, they have a duty to make courageous choices in support of life, especially through *legislative measures.* In a democratic system, where laws and decisions are made on the basis of the consensus of many, the sense of personal responsibility in the consciences of individuals invested with authority may be weakened. But no one can ever renounce this responsibility, especially when he or she has a legislative or decision-making mandate, which calls that person to answer to God, to his or her own conscience and to the whole of society for choices which may be contrary to the common good. Although laws are not the only means of protecting human life, nevertheless they do play a very important and sometimes decisive role in influencing patterns of thought and behavior. I repeat once more that a law which violates an innocent person's natural right to life is unjust and, as such, is not valid as a law. For this reason I urgently appeal once more to all political leaders not to pass laws which, by disregarding the dignity of the person, undermine the very fabric of society.

90.4 The Church well knows that it is difficult to mount an effective legal defense of life in pluralistic democracies, because of the presence of strong cultural currents with differing outlooks. At the same time, certain that moral truth cannot fail to make its presence deeply felt in every conscience, the Church encourages political leaders, starting with those who are Christians, not to give in, but to make those choices which, taking into account what is realistically attainable, will lead to the reestablishment of a just order in the defense and promotion of the value of life. Here it must be noted that it is not enough to remove unjust laws. The underlying causes of attacks on life have to be eliminated, especially by ensuring proper support for families and motherhood. A *family policy must be the basis and driving force of all social policies.* For this reason there need to be set in place social and political initiatives capable of guaranteeing conditions of true freedom of choice in matters of parenthood. It is also necessary to rethink labor, urban, residential and social service policies so as to harmonize working schedules with time available for the family, so that it becomes effectively possible to take care of children and the elderly.

91.1 Today an important part of policies which favor life is the *issue of population growth.* Certainly public authorities have a responsibility to "intervene to orient the demography of the population."[114] But such interventions must always take into account and respect the primary and inalienable responsibility of married couples and families, and cannot employ methods which fail to respect the person and fundamental human rights, beginning with the right to life of every innocent human being. It is therefore morally unacceptable to encourage, let alone impose, the use of methods such as contraception, sterilization and abortion in order to regulate births. The ways of solving the population problem are quite different. Governments and the various in-

---

[114] *Catechism of the Catholic Church,* No. 2372.

ternational agencies must above all strive to create economic, social, public health and cultural conditions which will enable married couples to make their choices about procreation in full freedom and with genuine responsibility. They must then make efforts to ensure "greater opportunities and a fairer distribution of wealth so that everyone can share equitably in the goods of creation. Solutions must be sought on the global level by establishing a true *economy of communion and sharing of goods*, in both the national and international order."[115] This is the only way to respect the dignity of persons and families as well as the authentic cultural patrimony of peoples.

91.2 Service of the *Gospel of life* is thus an immense and complex task. This service increasingly appears as a valuable and fruitful area for positive cooperation with our brothers and sisters of other Churches and Ecclesial Communities, in accordance with the *practical ecumenism* which the Second Vatican Council authoritatively encouraged.[116] It also appears as a providential area for dialogue and joint efforts with the followers of other religions and with all people of good will. *No single person or group has a monopoly on the defense and promotion of life. These are everyone's task and responsibility.* On the eve of the third millennium, the challenge facing us is an arduous one: only the concerted efforts of all those who believe in the value of life can prevent a setback of unforeseeable consequences for civilization.

"Your children will be like olive shoots around your table" (Ps 128:3): the family as the "sanctuary of life"

92.1 Within the "people of life and the people for life," *the family has a decisive responsibility.* This responsibility flows from its very nature as a community of life and love, founded upon marriage, and from its mission to "guard, reveal and communicate love."[117] Here it is a matter of God's own love, of which parents are co-workers and as it were interpreters when they transmit life and raise it according to his fatherly plan.[118] This is the love that becomes selflessness, receptiveness and gift. Within the family each member is accepted, respected and honored precisely because he or she is a person; and if

---

[115] John Paul II, Address to the Fourth General Conference of Latin American Bishops, Santo Domingo (October 12, 1992), 15: *AAS* 85 (1993), 819.

[116] Cf. Decree on Ecumenism *Unitatis Redintegratio*, 12; Pastoral Constitution on the Church in the Modern World *Gaudium et Spes*, 90.

[117] John Paul II, Apostolic Exhortation *Familiaris Consortio* (November 22, 1981), 17: *AAS* 74 (1982), 100.

[118] Cf. Second Vatican Ecumenical Council, Pastoral Constitution on the Church in the Modern World *Gaudium et Spes*, 50.

any family member is in greater need, the care which he or she receives is all the more intense and attentive.

92.2 The family has a special role to play throughout the life of its members, from birth to death. It is truly "the *sanctuary of life:* the place in which life — the gift of God — can be properly welcomed and protected against the many attacks to which it is exposed, and can develop in accordance with what constitutes authentic human growth."[119] Consequently the role of the family in building a culture of life is *decisive and irreplaceable.*

92.3 As the *domestic church,* the family is summoned to proclaim, celebrate and serve the *Gospel of life.* This is a responsibility which first concerns married couples, called to be givers of life, on the basis of an ever greater *awareness of the meaning of procreation* as a unique event which clearly reveals that *human life is a gift received in order then to be given as a gift.* In giving origin to a new life, parents recognize that the child, "as the fruit of their mutual gift of love, is, in turn, a gift for both of them, a gift which flows from them."[120]

92.4 It is above all in *raising children* that the family fulfills its mission to proclaim the *Gospel of life.* By word and example, in the daily round of relations and choices, and through concrete actions and signs, parents lead their children to authentic freedom, actualized in the sincere gift of self, and they cultivate in them respect for others, a sense of justice, cordial openness, dialogue, generous service, solidarity and all the other values which help people to live life as a gift. In raising children, Christian parents must be concerned about their children's faith and help them to fulfill the vocation God has given them. The parents' mission as educators also includes teaching and giving their children an example of the true meaning of suffering and death. They will be able to do this if they are sensitive to all kinds of suffering around them and, even more, if they succeed in fostering attitudes of closeness, assistance and sharing toward sick or elderly members of the family.

93.1 The family *celebrates the Gospel of life* through *daily prayer,* both individual prayer and family prayer. The family prays in order to glorify and

---

[119] John Paul II, Encyclical Letter *Centesimus Annus* (May 1, 1991), 39: *AAS* 83 (1991), 842.

[120] John Paul II, Address to Participants in the Seventh Symposium of European Bishops on the Theme of "Contemporary Attitudes toward Life and Death: A Challenge for Evangelization" (October 17, 1989), 5: *Insegnamenti* XII/2 (1989), 945. Children are presented in the biblical tradition precisely as God's gift (cf. Ps 127:3) and as a sign of his blessing on those who walk in the ways of God (cf. Ps 128:3-4).

give thanks to God for the gift of life, and implores his light and strength in order to face times of difficulty and suffering without losing hope. But the celebration which gives meaning to every other form of prayer and worship is found in *the family's actual daily life together,* if it is a life of love and self-giving.

93.2 This celebration thus becomes a *service to the Gospel of life,* expressed through *solidarity* as experienced within and around the family in the form of concerned, attentive and loving care shown in the humble, ordinary events of each day. A particularly significant expression of solidarity between families is a willingness to *adopt* or *take in* children abandoned by their parents or in situations of serious hardship. True parental love is ready to go beyond the bonds of flesh and blood in order to accept children from other families, offering them whatever is necessary for their well-being and full development. Among the various forms of adoption, consideration should be given to *adoption-at-a-distance,* preferable in cases where the only reason for giving up the child is the extreme poverty of the child's family. Through this type of adoption, parents are given the help needed to support and raise their children, without their being uprooted from their natural environment.

93.3 As "a firm and persevering determination to commit oneself to the common good,"[121] solidarity also needs to be practiced through *participation in social and political life.* Serving the *Gospel of life* thus means that the family, particularly through its membership in family associations, works to ensure that the laws and institutions of the State in no way violate the right to life, from conception to natural death, but rather protect and promote it.

94.1 Special attention must be given to the *elderly.* While in some cultures older people remain a part of the family with an important and active role, in others the elderly are regarded as a useless burden and are left to themselves. Here the temptation to resort to euthanasia can more easily arise.

94.2 Neglect of the elderly or their outright rejection is intolerable. Their presence in the family, or at least their closeness to the family in cases where limited living space or other reasons make this impossible, is of fundamental importance in creating a climate of mutual interaction and enriching communication between the different age groups. It is therefore important to preserve, or to reestablish where it has been lost, a sort of "covenant" between generations. In this way parents, in their later years, can receive from their children the acceptance and solidarity which they themselves gave to their

[121] John Paul II, Encyclical Letter *Sollicitudo Rei Socialis* (December 30, 1987), 38: *AAS* 80 (1988), 565-566.

children when they brought them into the world. This is required by obedience to the divine commandment to honor one's father and mother (cf. Ex 20:12; Lev 19:3). But there is more. The elderly are not only to be considered the object of our concern, closeness and service. They themselves have a valuable contribution to make to the *Gospel of life*. Thanks to the rich treasury of experiences they have acquired through the years, the elderly can and must *be sources of wisdom and witnesses of hope and love.*

94.3 Although it is true that "the future of humanity passes by way of the family,"[122] it must be admitted that modern social, economic and cultural conditions make the family's task of serving life more difficult and demanding. In order to fulfill its vocation as the "sanctuary of life," as the cell of a society which loves and welcomes life, *the family urgently needs to be helped and supported.* Communities and States must guarantee all the support, including economic support, which families need in order to meet their problems in a truly human way. For her part, the Church must untiringly promote a plan of pastoral care for families, capable of making every family rediscover and live with joy and courage its mission to further the *Gospel of life.*

"Walk as children of light" (Eph 5:8): bringing about a transformation of culture

95.1 "Walk as children of light . . . and try to learn what is pleasing to the Lord. Take no part in the unfruitful works of darkness" (Eph 5:8, 10-11). In our present social context, marked by a dramatic struggle between the "culture of life" and the "culture of death," there is need to *develop a deep critical sense,* capable of discerning true values and authentic needs.

95.2 What is urgently called for is a *general mobilization of consciences* and a *united ethical effort* to activate a *great campaign in support of life. All together, we must build a new culture of life:* new, because it will be able to confront and solve today's unprecedented problems affecting human life; new, because it will be adopted with deeper and more dynamic conviction by all Christians; new, because it will be capable of bringing about a serious and courageous cultural dialogue among all parties. While the urgent need for such a cultural transformation is linked to the present historical situation, it is also rooted in the Church's mission of evangelization. The purpose of the Gospel, in fact, is "to transform humanity from within and to make it new."[123]

---

[122] John Paul II, Apostolic Exhortation *Familiaris Consortio* (November 22, 1981), 86: *AAS* 74 (1982), 188.

[123] Paul VI, Apostolic Exhortation *Evangelii Nuntiandi* (December 8, 1975), 18: *AAS* 68 (1976), 17.

Like the yeast which leavens the whole measure of dough (cf. Mt 13:33), the Gospel is meant to permeate all cultures and give them life from within,[124] so that they may express the full truth about the human person and about human life.

95.3 We need to begin with *the renewal of a culture of life within Christian communities themselves.* Too often it happens that believers, even those who take an active part in the life of the Church, end up by separating their Christian faith from its ethical requirements concerning life, and thus fall into moral subjectivism and certain objectionable ways of acting. With great openness and courage, we need to question how widespread is the culture of life today among individual Christians, families, groups and communities in our Dioceses. With equal clarity and determination, we must identify the steps we are called to take in order to serve life in all its truth. At the same time, we need to promote a serious and in-depth exchange about basic issues of human life with everyone, including non-believers, in intellectual circles, in the various professional spheres and at the level of people's everyday life.

96.1 The first and fundamental step toward this cultural transformation consists in *forming consciences* with regard to the incomparable and inviolable worth of every human life. It is of the greatest importance *to reestablish the essential connection between life and freedom.* These are inseparable goods: where one is violated, the other also ends up being violated. There is no true freedom where life is not welcomed and loved; and there is no fullness of life except in freedom. Both realities have something inherent and specific which links them inextricably: the vocation to love. Love, as a sincere gift of self,[125] is what gives the life and freedom of the person their truest meaning.

96.2 No less critical in the formation of conscience is *the recovery of the necessary link between freedom and truth.* As I have frequently stated, when freedom is detached from objective truth it becomes impossible to establish personal rights on a firm rational basis; and the ground is laid for society to be at the mercy of the unrestrained will of individuals or the oppressive totalitarianism of public authority.[126]

96.3 It is therefore essential that man should acknowledge his inherent condition as a creature to whom God has granted being and life as a gift and

---

[124] Cf. ibid., 20: loc. cit., 18.

[125] Cf. Second Vatican Ecumenical Council, Pastoral Constitution on the Church in the Modern World *Gaudium et Spes*, 24.

[126] Cf. John Paul II, Encyclical Letter *Centesimus Annus* (May 1, 1991), 17: *AAS* 83 (1991), 814; Encyclical Letter *Veritatis Splendor* (August 6, 1993), 95-101: *AAS* 85 (1993), 1208-1213.

a duty. Only by admitting his innate dependence can man live and use his freedom to the full, and at the same time respect the life and freedom of every other person. Here especially one sees that "at the heart of every culture lies the attitude man takes to the greatest mystery: the mystery of God."[127] Where God is denied and people live as though he did not exist, or his commandments are not taken into account, the dignity of the human person and the inviolability of human life also end up being rejected or compromised.

97.1 Closely connected with the formation of conscience is the *work of education*, which helps individuals to be ever more human, leads them ever more fully to the truth, instills in them growing respect for life, and trains them in right interpersonal relationships.

97.2 In particular, there is a need for education about the value of life *from its very origins*. It is an illusion to think that we can build a true culture of human life if we do not help the young to accept and experience sexuality and love and the whole of life according to their true meaning and in their close interconnection. Sexuality, which enriches the whole person, "manifests its inmost meaning in leading the person to the gift of self in love."[128] The trivialization of sexuality is among the principal factors which have led to contempt for new life. Only a true love is able to protect life. There can be no avoiding the duty to offer, especially to adolescents and young adults, an authentic *education in sexuality and in love*, an education which involves *training in chastity* as a virtue which fosters personal maturity and makes one capable of respecting the "spousal" meaning of the body.

97.3 The work of educating in the service of life involves the *training of married couples in responsible procreation*. In its true meaning, responsible procreation requires couples to be obedient to the Lord's call and to act as faithful interpreters of his plan. This happens when the family is generously open to new lives, and when couples maintain an attitude of openness and service to life, even if, for serious reasons and in respect for the moral law, they choose to avoid a new birth for the time being or indefinitely. The moral law obliges them in every case to control the impulse of instinct and passion, and to respect the biological laws inscribed in their person. It is precisely this respect which makes legitimate, at the service of responsible procreation, the *use of natural methods of regulating fertility*. From the scientific point of view,

[127] John Paul II, Encyclical Letter *Centesimus Annus* (May 1, 1991), 24: *AAS* 83 (1991), 822.

[128] John Paul II, Apostolic Exhortation *Familiaris Consortio* (November 22, 1981), 37: *AAS* 74 (1982), 128.

these methods are becoming more and more accurate and make it possible in practice to make choices in harmony with moral values. An honest appraisal of their effectiveness should dispel certain prejudices which are still widely held, and should convince married couples, as well as health-care and social workers, of the importance of proper training in this area. The Church is grateful to those who, with personal sacrifice and often unacknowledged dedication, devote themselves to the study and spread of these methods, as well to the promotion of education in the moral values which they presuppose.

97.4 *The work of education cannot avoid a consideration of suffering and death.* These are a part of human existence, and it is futile, not to say misleading, to try to hide them or ignore them. On the contrary, people must be helped to understand their profound mystery in all its harsh reality. Even pain and suffering have meaning and value when they are experienced in close connection with love received and given. In this regard, I have called for the yearly celebration of the *World Day of the Sick,* emphasizing "the salvific nature of the offering up of suffering which, experienced in communion with Christ, belongs to the very essence of the Redemption."[129] Death itself is anything but an event without hope. It is the door which opens wide on eternity and, for those who live in Christ, an experience of participation in the mystery of his death and Resurrection.

98.1 In a word, we can say that the cultural change which we are calling for demands from everyone the courage to *adopt a new lifestyle,* consisting in making practical choices — at the personal, family, social and international level — on the basis of a correct scale of values: *the primacy of being over having,*[130] *of the person over things.*[131] This renewed lifestyle involves a passing *from indifference to concern for others, from rejection to acceptance of them.* Other people are not rivals from whom we must defend ourselves, but brothers and sisters to be supported. They are to be loved for their own sakes, and they enrich us by their very presence.

98.2 In this mobilization for a new culture of life no one must feel excluded: *everyone has an important role to play.* Together with the family, *teach-*

---

[129] Letter establishing the World Day of the Sick (May 13, 1992), 2: *Insegnamenti* XV/1 (1992), 1410.

[130] Cf. Second Vatican Ecumenical Council, Pastoral Constitution on the Church in the Modern World *Gaudium et Spes,* 35; Paul VI, Encyclical Letter *Populorum Progressio* (March 26, 1967), 15: *AAS* 59 (1967), 265.

[131] Cf. John Paul II, Letter to Families *Gratissimam Sane* (February 2, 1994), 13: *AAS* 86 (1994), 892.

ers and *educators* have a particularly valuable contribution to make. Much will depend on them if young people, trained in true freedom, are to be able to preserve for themselves and make known to others new, authentic ideals of life, and if they are to grow in respect for and service to every other person, in the family and in society.

98.3 *Intellectuals* can also do much to build a new culture of human life. A special task falls to *Catholic* intellectuals, who are called to be present and active in the leading centers where culture is formed in schools and universities, in places of scientific and technological research, of artistic creativity and of the study of man. Allowing their talents and activity to be nourished by the living force of the Gospel, they ought to place themselves at the service of a new culture of life by offering serious and well-documented contributions, capable of commanding general respect and interest by reason of their merit. It was precisely for this purpose that I established the *Pontifical Academy for Life,* assigning it the task of "studying and providing information and training about the principal problems of law and biomedicine pertaining to the promotion of life, especially in the direct relationship they have with Christian morality and the directives of the Church's Magisterium."[132] A specific contribution will also have to come from *universities*, particularly from *Catholic universities*, and from *centers, institutes and committees of bioethics.*

98.4 An important and serious responsibility belongs to *those involved in the mass media,* who are called to ensure that the messages which they so effectively transmit will support the culture of life. They need to present noble models of life and make room for instances of people's positive and sometimes heroic love for others. With great respect they should also present the positive values of sexuality and human love, and not insist on what defiles and cheapens human dignity. In their interpretation of things, they should refrain from emphasizing anything that suggests or fosters feelings or attitudes of indifference, contempt or rejection in relation to life. With scrupulous concern for factual truth, they are called to combine freedom of information with respect for every person and a profound sense of humanity.

99.1 In transforming culture so that it supports life, *women* occupy a place in thought and action which is unique and decisive. It depends on them to promote a "new feminism" which rejects the temptation of imitating models of "male domination," in order to acknowledge and affirm the true genius of

---

[132] John Paul II, Motu Proprio *Vitae Mysterium* (February 11, 1994), 4: *AAS* 86 (1994), 386-387.

women in every aspect of the life of society, and overcome all discrimination, violence and exploitation.

99.2 Making my own the words of the concluding message of the Second Vatican Council, I address to women this urgent appeal: *"Reconcile people with life."*[133] You are called to *bear witness to the meaning of genuine love,* of that gift of self and of that acceptance of others which are present in a special way in the relationship of husband and wife, but which ought also to be at the heart of every other interpersonal relationship. The experience of mother-hood makes you acutely aware of the other person and, at the same time, confers on you a particular task: "Motherhood involves a special communion with the mystery of life, as it develops in the woman's womb. . . . This unique contact with the new human being developing within her gives rise to an attitude toward human beings — not only toward her own child, but every human being — which profoundly marks the woman's personality."[134] A mother welcomes and carries in herself another human being, enabling it to grow inside her, giving it room, respecting it in its otherness. Women first learn and then teach others that human relations are authentic if they are open to accepting the other person: a person who is recognized and loved because of the dignity which comes from being a person and not from other consider-ations, such as usefulness, strength, intelligence, beauty or health. This is the fundamental contribution which the Church and humanity expect from women. And it is the indispensable prerequisite for an authentic cultural change.

99.3 I would now like to say a special word to *women who have had an abortion.* The Church is aware of the many factors which may have influenced your decision, and she does not doubt that in many cases it was a painful and even shattering decision. The wound in your heart may not yet have healed. Certainly what happened was and remains terribly wrong. But do not give in to discouragement and do not lose hope. Try rather to understand what hap-pened and face it honestly. If you have not already done so, give yourselves over with humility and trust to repentance. The Father of mercies is ready to give you his forgiveness and his peace in the Sacrament of Reconciliation. To the same Father and to his mercy you can with sure hope entrust your child. With the friendly and expert help and advice of other people, and as a result of your own painful experience, you can be among the most eloquent defenders of everyone's right to life. Through your commitment to life, whether by ac-

[133] Closing Messages of the Council (December 8, 1965): To Women.
[134] John Paul II, Apostolic Letter *Mulieris Dignitatem* (August 15, 1988), 18: *AAS* 80 (1988), 1696.

cepting the birth of other children or by welcoming and caring for those most in need of someone to be close to them, you will become promoters of a new way of looking at human life.

100.1 In this great endeavor to create a new culture of life we are *inspired and sustained by the confidence* that comes from knowing that the *Gospel of life*, like the Kingdom of God itself, is growing and producing abundant fruit (cf. Mk 4:26-29). There is certainly an enormous disparity between the powerful resources available to the forces promoting the "culture of death" and the means at the disposal of those working for a "culture of life and love." But we know that we can rely on the help of God, for whom nothing is impossible (cf. Mt 19:26).

100.2 Filled with this certainty, and moved by profound concern for the destiny of every man and woman, I repeat what I said to those families who carry out their challenging mission amid so many difficulties:[135] *a great prayer for life is urgently needed*, a prayer which will rise up throughout the world. Through special initiatives and in daily prayer, may an impassioned plea rise to God, the Creator and lover of life, from every Christian community, from every group and association, from every family and from the heart of every believer. Jesus himself has shown us by his own example that prayer and fasting are the first and most effective weapons against the forces of evil (cf. Mt 4:1-11). As he taught his disciples, some demons cannot be driven out except in this way (cf. Mk 9:29). Let us therefore discover anew the humility and the courage to *pray and fast* so that power from on high will break down the walls of lies and deceit: the walls which conceal from the sight of so many of our brothers and sisters the evil of practices and laws which are hostile to life. May this same power turn their hearts to resolutions and goals inspired by the civilization of life and love.

"We are writing this that our joy may be complete" (1 Jn 1:4): the Gospel of life is for the whole of human society

101.1 "We are writing you this that our joy may be complete" (1 Jn 1:4). The revelation of the *Gospel of life* is given to us as a good to be shared with all people: so that all men and women may have fellowship with us and with the Trinity (cf. 1 Jn 1:3). Our own joy would not be complete if we failed to share this Gospel with others but kept it only for ourselves.

101.2 The *Gospel of life* is not for believers alone: *it is for everyone*. The

---

[135] Cf. John Paul II, Letter to Families *Gratissimam Sane* (February 2, 1994), 5: *AAS* 86 (1994), 872.

issue of life and its defense and promotion is not a concern of Christians alone. Although faith provides special light and strength, this question arises in every human conscience which seeks the truth and which cares about the future of humanity. Life certainly has a sacred and religious value, but in no way is that value a concern only of believers. The value at stake is one which every human being can grasp by the light of reason; thus it necessarily concerns everyone.

101.3 Consequently, all that we do as the "people of life and for life" should be interpreted correctly and welcomed with favor. When the Church declares that unconditional respect for the right to life of every innocent person — from conception to natural death — is one of the pillars on which every civil society stands, she "wants simply *to promote a human State. A State which recognizes the defense of the fundamental rights of the human person, especially of the weakest, as its primary duty.*"[136]

101.4 The *Gospel of life* is for the whole of human society. To be actively pro-life is to contribute to the *renewal of society* through the promotion of the common good. It is impossible to further the common good without acknowledging and defending the right to life, upon which all the other inalienable rights of individuals are founded and from which they develop. A society lacks solid foundations when, on the one hand, it asserts values such as the dignity of the person, justice and peace, but then, on the other hand, radically acts to the contrary by allowing or tolerating a variety of ways in which human life is devalued and violated, especially where it is weak or marginalized. Only respect for life can be the foundation and guarantee of the most precious and essential goods of society, such as democracy and peace.

101.5 There can be no *true democracy* without a recognition of every person's dignity and without respect for his or her rights.

101.6 Nor can there be *true peace* unless *life is defended and promoted.* As Paul VI pointed out: "Every crime against life is an attack on peace, especially if it strikes at the moral conduct of people. . . . But where human rights are truly professed and publicly recognized and defended, peace becomes the joyful and operative climate of life in society."[137]

101.7 The "people of life" rejoice in being able to share their commitment with so many others. Thus may the "people for life" constantly grow in number and may a new culture of love and solidarity develop for the true good of the whole of human society.

---

[136] John Paul II, Address to the Participants at the Study Conference on "The Right to Life and Europe" (December 18, 1987), 1: *Insegnamenti* X/3 (1987), 1446.

[137] Message for the 1977 World Day of Peace (January 1, 1977): *AAS* 68 (1976), 711-712.

Conclusion

102.1 At the end of this Encyclical, we naturally look again to the Lord Jesus, "the child born for us" (cf. Is 9:6), that in him we may contemplate "the Life" which "was made manifest" (1 Jn 1:2). In the mystery of Christ's birth, the encounter of God with man takes place, and the earthly journey of the Son of God begins, a journey which will culminate in the gift of his life on the Cross. By his death, Christ will conquer death and become for all humanity the source of new life.

102.2 The one who accepted "Life" in the name of all and for the sake of all was Mary, the Virgin Mother; she is thus most closely and personally associated with the *Gospel of life*. Mary's consent at the Annunciation and her motherhood stand at the very beginning of the mystery of life which Christ came to bestow on humanity (cf. Jn 10:10). Through her acceptance and loving care for the life of the Incarnate Word, human life has been rescued from condemnation to final and eternal death.

102.3 For this reason, Mary, "like the Church of which she is the type, is a Mother of all who are reborn to life. She is in fact the Mother of the Life by which everyone lives, and when she brought it forth from herself she in some way brought to rebirth all those who were to live by that Life."[138]

102.4 As the Church contemplates Mary's motherhood, she discovers the meaning of her own motherhood and the way in which she is called to express it. At the same time, the Church's experience of motherhood leads to a most profound understanding of Mary's experience as the *incomparable model of how life should be welcomed and cared for.*

"A great portent appeared in heaven, a woman clothed with the sun" (Rev 12:1): the motherhood of Mary and of the Church

103.1 The mutual relationship between the mystery of the Church and Mary appears clearly in the "great portent" described in the Book of Revelation: "A great portent appeared in heaven, a woman clothed with the sun, with the moon under her feet, and on her head a crown of twelve stars" (12:1). In this sign the Church recognizes an image of her own mystery: present in history, she knows that she transcends history, inasmuch as she constitutes on earth the "seed and beginning" of the Kingdom of God.[139] The Church sees this

---

[138] Blessed Guerric of Igny, *In Assumptione Beatae Mariae*, Sermo I, 2: *PL* 185, 188.

[139] Second Vatican Ecumenical Council, Dogmatic Constitution on the Church *Lumen Gentium*, 5.

mystery fulfilled in complete and exemplary fashion in Mary. She is the woman of glory in whom God's plan could be carried out with supreme perfection.

103.2 The "woman clothed with the sun" — the Book of Revelation tells us — "was with child" (12:2). The Church is fully aware that she bears within herself the Savior of the world, Christ the Lord. She is aware that she is called to offer Christ to the world, giving men and women new birth into God's own life. But the Church cannot forget that her mission was made possible by the motherhood of Mary, who conceived and bore the One who is "God from God," "true God from true God." Mary is truly the Mother of God, the *Theotókos*, in whose motherhood the vocation to motherhood bestowed by God on every woman is raised to its highest level. Thus Mary becomes the model of the Church, called to be the "new Eve," the Mother of believers, the Mother of the "living" (cf. Gen 3:20).

103.3 The Church's spiritual motherhood is only achieved — the Church knows this too — through the pangs and "the labor" of childbirth (cf. Rev 12:2), that is to say, in constant tension with the forces of evil which still roam the world and affect human hearts, offering resistance to Christ: "In him was life, and the life was the light of men. The light shines in the darkness, and the darkness has not overcome it" (Jn 1:4-5).

103.4 Like the Church, Mary too had to live her motherhood amid suffering: "This child is set . . . for a sign that is spoken against — and a sword will pierce through your own soul also — that thoughts out of many hearts may be revealed" (Lk 2:34-35). The words which Simeon addresses to Mary at the very beginning of the Savior's earthly life sum up and prefigure the rejection of Jesus, and with him of Mary, a rejection which will reach its culmination on Calvary. "Standing by the cross of Jesus" (Jn 19:25), Mary shares in the gift which the Son makes of himself: she offers Jesus, gives him over, and begets him to the end for our sake. The "yes" spoken on the day of the Annunciation reaches full maturity on the day of the Cross, when the time comes for Mary to receive and beget as her children all those who become disciples, pouring out upon them the saving love of her Son: "When Jesus saw his Mother and the disciple whom he loved standing near, he said to his Mother, 'Woman, behold, your son!' " (Jn 19:26).

"And the dragon stood before the woman . . . that he might devour her child when she brought it forth" (Rev 12:4): life menaced by the forces of evil

104.1 In the Book of Revelation, the "great portent" of the "woman" (12:1) is accompanied by "another portent which appeared in heaven": "a great red dragon" (Rev 12:3), which represents Satan, the personal power of evil, as well as all the powers of evil at work in history and opposing the Church's mission.

104.2 Here too Mary sheds light on the community of believers. The hostility of the powers of evil is, in fact, an insidious opposition which, before affecting the disciples of Jesus, is directed against his Mother. To save the life of her Son from those who fear him as a dangerous threat, Mary has to flee with Joseph and the child into Egypt (cf. Mt 2:13-15).

104.3 Mary thus helps the Church to *realize that life is always at the center of a great struggle* between good and evil, between light and darkness. The dragon wishes to devour "the child brought forth" (cf. Rev 12:4), a figure of Christ, whom Mary brought forth "in the fullness of time" (Gal 4:4) and whom the Church must unceasingly offer to people in every age. But in a way that child is also a figure of every person, every child, especially every helpless baby whose life is threatened, because — as the Council reminds us — "by his Incarnation the Son of God has united himself in some fashion with every person."[140] It is precisely in the "flesh" of every person that Christ continues to reveal himself and to enter into fellowship with us, so that *rejection of human life*, in whatever form that rejection takes, *is really a rejection of Christ*. This is the fascinating but also demanding truth which Christ reveals to us and which his Church continues untiringly to proclaim: "Whoever receives one such child in my name receives me" (Mt 18:5); "Truly, I say to you, as you did it to one of the least of these my brethren, you did it to me" (Mt 25:40).

"Death shall be no more" (Rev 21:4): the splendor of the Resurrection

105.1 The angel's Annunciation to Mary is framed by these reassuring words: "Do not be afraid, Mary" and "with God nothing will be impossible" (Lk 1:30, 37). The whole of the Virgin Mother's life is in fact pervaded by the certainty that God is near to her and that he accompanies her with his providential care. The same is true of the Church, which finds "a place prepared by God" (Rev 12:6) in the desert, the place of trial but also of the manifestation of God's love for his people (cf. Hos 2:16). Mary is a living word of comfort for the Church in her struggle against death. Showing us the Son, the Church assures us that in him the forces of death have already been defeated: "Death with life contended: combat strangely ended! Life's own champion, slain, yet lives to reign."[141]

105.2 *The Lamb who was slain* is alive, bearing the marks of his Passion in the splendor of the Resurrection. He alone is master of all the events of history: he opens its "seals" (cf. Rev 5:1-10) and proclaims, in time and be-

---

[140] Pastoral Constitution on the Church in the Modern World *Gaudium et Spes*, 22.
[141] Roman Missal, Sequence for Easter Sunday.

yond, *the power of life over death*. In the "new Jerusalem," that new world toward which human history is traveling, "*death shall be no more*, neither shall there be mourning nor crying nor pain anymore, for the former things have passed away" (Rev 21:4).

105.3 And as we, the pilgrim people, the people of life and for life, make our way in confidence toward "a new heaven and a new earth" (Rev 21:1), we look to her who is for us "a sign of sure hope and solace."[142]

> 105.4 O Mary,
> bright dawn of the new world,
> Mother of the living,
> to you do we entrust the *cause of life:*
> Look down, O Mother,
> upon the vast numbers
> of babies not allowed to be born,
> of the poor whose lives are made difficult,
> of men and women who are
> victims of brutal violence,
> of the elderly and the sick killed
> by indifference or out of misguided mercy.
> Grant that all who believe in your Son
> may *proclaim the Gospel of life*
> with honesty and love
> to the people of our time.
> Obtain for them the grace
> to *accept that Gospel*
> as a gift ever new,
> the joy *of celebrating* it with gratitude
> throughout their lives
> and the courage to *bear witness to it*
> resolutely, in order to build,
> together with all people of good will,
> the civilization of truth and love,
> to the praise and glory of God,
> the Creator and lover of life.

Given in Rome, at Saint Peter's, on March 25, the Solemnity of the Annunciation of the Lord, in the year 1995, the seventeeth of my Pontificate.

---

[142] Second Vatican Ecumenical Council, Dogmatic Constitution on the Church *Lumen Gentium*, 68.

Ut Unum Sint

Editor's Introduction

"That they may all be one!" (Jn 17:21). In the opening words of his twelfth encyclical, dedicated to the Church's commitment to ecumenism and signed on May 25, 1995,[1] John Paul II repeats with impassioned intensity Christ's prayer for the unity of his disciples. In *Ut Unum Sint,* the Pope praises God for the progress toward unity achieved since the Second Vatican Council and, on the threshold of the third millennium, renews the Church's commitment to work for the full, visible communion of Christians.

Present-day concerns of the ecumenical movement are in the background. Some lament the lukewarm efforts of recent years, referring to an "ecumenical winter." Others point to the increasing tensions between Orthodox and Catholics concerning proselytism and questions of jurisdiction in eastern Europe. To these pessimistic views John Paul vigorously replies with a positive evaluation of the efforts made by the ecumenical movement in the last thirty years. By means of this encyclical he wishes to dispel "a halfhearted commitment to unity and, even more, a prejudicial opposition or a defeatism which tends to see everything in negative terms" (§79.2).

Strains of thanksgiving, joy, and optimism run through *Ut Unum Sint.* The encyclical abounds with thanks for the steps already taken toward the reestablishment of Christian unity. For the Pope, these achievements are "truly an immense gift of God, one which deserves all our gratitude" (§41.1, cf. §§71.1, 102.3). He also expresses satisfaction at the deepening awareness of the unity which already exists among Christians. It is a cause of "deep joy" for him that "an imperfect but real communion is preserved and is growing at many levels of ecclesial life" (§84.1, cf. §2.2). The Pope's unshakable confidence in God's plan for the future of ecumenism is evident throughout the encyclical. "There is no doubt," he writes, "that the Holy Spirit is accomplishing this endeavor and that he is leading the Church to the full realization of the Father's plan, in conformity with the will of Christ" (§100.2).

Repeatedly John Paul insists that the Church is irreversibly committed to ecumenism; it "*is not just some sort of 'appendix'* which is added to the Church's traditional activity. Rather, ecumenism is an organic part of her life and work, and consequently must pervade all that she is and does; it must be like the fruit borne by a healthy and flourishing tree which grows to its full stature"

[1] *Acta Apostolicae Sedis,* 87 (1995), 921-982.

(§20.1). The quest for unity is, therefore, "a duty which springs from the very nature of the Christian community" (§49.2).

The Pope gives three reasons for renewing this commitment to the unity of Christians. First, the Church must be obedient to Christ's prayer that his disciples may be one, "a living communion" (§6). Unity is essential to their community of faith and life: "God wills the Church, because he wills unity, and unity is an expression of the whole depth of his *agape*" (§9.1). Thus, all Christians "should be inspired by and submissive to Christ's prayer for unity" (§33). Quite simply, as John Paul states, "to believe in Christ means to desire unity; to desire unity means to desire the Church; to desire the Church means to desire the communion of grace which corresponds to the Father's plan from all eternity" (§9.2).

Second, the Catholic Church's obligation to pursue Christian unity stems from an explicit mandate of the Second Vatican Council. As a result of the Council's reading of the signs of the times, "the Catholic Church committed herself *irrevocably* to following the path of the ecumenical venture" (§3.1, cf. §17.2). More than merely a point of departure for this endeavor, Vatican II "remains a powerful source of incentive and orientation" for stimulating ecumenical activity (§49.1). Through the publication of *Ut Unum Sint,* John Paul sets his seal of approval on the Catholic Church's participation in the ecumenical movement.

Third, the effective evangelization of the world depends on the united witness of Christians. It is an "imperative of charity" for Christians to make every effort to overcome "the grave obstacle which the lack of unity represents for the proclamation of the Gospel" (§99, cf. §§2.1, 23.1, 98.1). Division among Christian believers seriously damages the credibility of their testimony before the world: "When non-believers meet missionaries who do not agree among themselves, even though they all appeal to Christ, will they be in a position to receive the true message?" (§98.2).

Given the gravity of the Church's duty to foster Christian unity, John Paul declares that "the ecumenical task is 'one of the pastoral priorities' of my Pontificate" (§99). *Ut Unum Sint* is proof of his concern "to encourage the efforts of all who work for the cause of unity" (§3.3).

Unlike other papal encyclicals, *Ut Unum Sint* has no opening salutation specifying its audience. Only in the last paragraph does the Pope indicate to whom he is writing: "to you, the faithful of the Catholic Church, and to you, my brothers and sisters of the other Churches and Ecclesial Communities" (§103.1). Furthermore, since Christian unity has as its goal "that the world may believe" (Jn 17:21), he also intends this encyclical to be read by all men and women of good will.

Because the Second Vatican Council marks a watershed in the Catholic Church's commitment to ecumenism, in *Ut Unum Sint* John Paul draws very heavily upon conciliar teaching. Among the documents he cites most often are the Dogmatic Constitution on the Church, *Lumen Gentium,* and the Declaration on Religious Freedom, *Dignitatis Humanae.* Above all, however, he relies on the Council's Decree on Ecumenism, *Unitatis Redintegratio,* which forms the structural backbone of *Ut Unum Sint;* 70 of the encyclical's 162 footnotes refer to it. Indeed, in this encyclical John Paul furnishes an authoritative commentary on this Decree, showing the extent to which it has been "received" by Catholics and other Christians in the last thirty years. On several occasions he also cites the *Directory for the Application of Principles and Norms on Ecumenism,* published in 1993 by the Pontifical Council for Promoting Christian Unity, documents of the Faith and Order Commission of the World Council of Churches, and reports of various bilateral ecumenical dialogues.

Ut Unum Sint is highly readable, because it is written with passion and a sense of urgency. "Essentially pastoral in character" (§3.3), it is the most personal of all John Paul's encyclicals. He weaves together theological reflection and spiritual insights with detailed accounts of the key events of the post-conciliar ecumenical movement. At various points the Pope interjects prayers of thanksgiving or adds his own comments on meetings and liturgies with other Christian leaders.

Summary

Ut Unum Sint is divided into three parts, along with an introduction and closing exhortation. In the introduction (§§1-4) John Paul, with serene determination, explains his resolve to heal the deplorable divisions among Christians. Chapter one, "The Catholic Church's Commitment to Ecumenism" (§§5-40), develops the basic principles of ecumenical activity and describes the spiritual, doctrinal, and practical ways to promote Christian unity. In chapter two, "The Fruits of Dialogue" (§§41-76), the Pope discusses the ecumenical movement since the Second Vatican Council, first in a general way, and then with specific reference to the churches of the East, and the churches and ecclesial communities of the West. Chapter three, *"Quanta Est Nobis Via?"* or "How Much Further Must We Travel?" (§§77-99), recommends a future agenda for ecumenism, including a reflection on the papal ministry. In the closing exhortation (§§100-103), John Paul recalls the obligation of Christians to pray for unity, give thanks for what has been accomplished, and have confidence that the Spirit will give men and women the courage to take the steps necessary to restore the full and visible communion of all who believe in Christ.

God's plan for unity

The Church's firm commitment to ecumenism stems from her obedience to the plan of God who wills "the unity of all divided humanity" (§6). The unity of Christians is a sacramental sign which manifests and brings this about. Because of their Baptism, Christians have the duty of giving visible expression to the "fullness of reconciliation and communion" won by Christ's Paschal Mystery (§6). Before describing how communion among Christians can be fostered, the Pope affirms two principles: God's gift of unity has been preserved in the Catholic Church, and authentic ecclesial values are present in other churches and ecclesial communities.

During her two-thousand-year history, the Catholic Church "has been preserved in unity, with all the means with which God wishes to endow his Church" (§11.1). John Paul recalls Vatican II's teaching on this point: "The Constitution *Lumen Gentium*, in a fundamental affirmation echoed by the Decree *Unitatis Redintegratio*, states that the one Church of Christ subsists in the Catholic Church. The Decree on Ecumenism emphasizes the presence in her of the fullness (*plenitudo*) of the means of salvation" (§86). Despite the often severe crises which have shaken the Church, her original unity established at Pentecost has never been substantially compromised.

The existence of divisions among Christians attests that the perfect, visible unity of Christians is yet to be achieved. "Full unity will come about," the Pope states, "when all share in the fullness of the means of salvation entrusted by Christ to his Church" (§86). But, even now, the other churches and ecclesial communities share in "a certain, though imperfect communion" with the Catholic Church because of "the elements of sanctification and truth" present in them (§11.2-3, cf. §§12.1, 13.3). Indeed, some aspects of the Christian mystery have at times been more effectively emphasized and lived outside the visible limits of the Catholic Church. These positive elements, the foremost of which is Baptism, "bear within themselves a tendency toward unity, having their fullness in that unity" (§14). They are also "by their nature a force for the reestablishment of unity" (§49.2). Ecumenism's goal, therefore, is to make "the partial communion existing between Christians grow toward full communion in truth and charity" (§14). The sign of this unity will be the common celebration of the Eucharist.

Spiritual ecumenism

Spiritual renewal is the key to ecumenism. The interior conversion and persevering prayer of all Christians are the chief instruments for fostering full unity: "The commitment to ecumenism must be based upon the conversion of hearts and upon prayer, which will also lead to the *necessary purification of past memories*" (§2.3).

Relying on the Council's teaching, John Paul recalls the need for both personal and communal conversion if Christian unity is to be achieved. For individuals, a radical conversion to the Gospel is required, a renewal of mind and heart. The Pope is no exception to this rule: "The Bishop of Rome himself must fervently make his own Christ's prayer for that conversion which is indispensable for 'Peter' to be able to serve his brethren" (§4.2). For every community, the desire for unity "goes hand in hand with its fidelity to the Gospel" (§15.2). The interior conversion of individuals and communities is the indispensable spiritual foundation of all true ecumenism. *Ut Unum Sint* confirms the teaching of *Unitatis Redintegratio*, §7: "*There can be no ecumenism worthy of the name without a change of heart*" (§15.1).

Conversion requires repentance for sins committed against the Church's unity: "Not only personal sins must be forgiven and left behind," writes John Paul, "but also social sins, which is to say the sinful 'structures' themselves which have contributed and can still contribute to division and to the reinforcing of division" (§34). On the one hand, "each individual must recognize his own faults, confess his sins, and place himself in the hands of the One who is our Intercessor before the Father, Jesus Christ" (§82.1). On the other hand, communities must repent "of certain exclusions which seriously harm fraternal charity, of certain refusals to forgive, of a certain pride, of an unevangelical insistence on condemning the 'other side,' of a disdain born of an unhealthy presumption" (§15.3, cf. §§3.1, 34). For ecumenism to make progress, Christians need to be purified from all that is erroneous, limited, and imperfect in their understanding of the unity of the Church.

Prayer is the preeminent means for restoring full Christian unity: "In this journey which we are undertaking with other Christians toward the new millennium, prayer must occupy the first place" (§102.2). Above all, the joint prayer of Christians is necessary, prayer specifically for unity but also for other intentions. The encyclical refers to three ecumenical benefits of this prayer in common. First, it helps believers to "grow in awareness of how little divides them in comparison to what unites them" (§22.2, cf. §26.1). Second, prayer together inspires Christians "to gain the courage to face all the painful human reality of their divisions" (§22.2). Third, "*fellowship in prayer leads people to look at the Church and Christianity in a new way*" (§23.1, cf. §26.2).

John Paul also mentions occasions when common prayer suitably takes place: at ecumenical gatherings, during the Week of Prayer for Christian Unity, and in the course of his meetings with Christian leaders and people both in

Rome and abroad. Commenting on his pastoral visits around the world, the Pope says that they "have almost always included an ecumenical meeting and *common prayer with our brothers and sisters who seek unity in Christ and in his Church*" (§24).

Dialogue in truth and charity

If prayer is "the 'soul' of ecumenical renewal," theological dialogue is the privileged instrument for bringing it about. In the light of "today's *personalist way of thinking*," dialogue is "an indispensable step along the path *toward human self-realization*" which involves "an exchange of gifts" between communities (§28.1, 2). Besides fostering this horizontal reciprocity, dialogue also has a vertical thrust directed to God. Before the Lord, Christians acknowledge their sinfulness. By doing so, they create "that interior space where Christ, the source of the Church's unity, can effectively act, with all the power of his Spirit" (§35).

How is ecumenical dialogue to be carried out? First, the participants in any dialogue must appreciate "the degree of communion already present" among them (§49.3). Because of this solid foundation, John Paul says that "*each side must presuppose in the other a desire for reconciliation, for unity in truth. For this to happen, any display of mutual opposition must disappear*" (§29). The laying to rest of former polemics requires a mutual spirit of conversion to the Gospel, a spirit nourished by an examination of conscience regarding sins that contributed to divisions among Christians. Furthermore, authentic dialogue must be marked "by a common quest for truth" (§33). Inevitably, genuine disagreements in matters of faith will emerge. When this occurs, the dialogue partners should face them "in a sincere spirit of fraternal charity, of respect for the demands of one's own conscience and of the conscience of the other part, with profound humility and love for the truth" (§39).

Progress in ecumenism since Vatican II

Chapter two begins with a lengthy catalog of the positive results of the ecumenical movement since Vatican II. John Paul is profoundly thankful that "the 'universal brotherhood of Christians' has become a firm ecumenical conviction" (§42.1). He associates the growth in communion which has taken place since the Council with several factors: a shift in ecumenical vocabulary, recognition of the oneness of Baptism, a growing convergence regarding Scripture and liturgy, deeper appreciation of the common witness of holiness, and practical cooperation.

The terminology used by Catholics to refer to other Christians has changed in recent years. "Separated brethren," the term that was common in the first stages of ecumenism, has been replaced by expressions such as "other Christians," "others who have received Baptism," or "Christians of other Communities." John Paul believes that this new terminology more readily evokes "the deep communion — linked to the baptismal character — which the Spirit fosters in spite of historical and canonical divisions" (§42.1). It reflects what unites Christians rather than what divides them.

Christian brotherhood is not founded on what the Pope calls "a large-hearted philanthropy or a vague family spirit." Instead, it is rooted "in recognition of the oneness of Baptism and the subsequent duty to glorify God in his work" (§42.3, cf. §66.6). Because Baptism establishes a sacramental bond of unity among all those reborn by water and the Spirit, it is the ultimate foundation of all ecumenical endeavors.

John Paul also notes that ecumenical translations of the Bible and liturgical practices shared by all Christians are signs of increasing communion. Modern liturgical renewal, for example, has not been restricted to the Catholic Church. Many communities in the West have begun to prize liturgical signs, to celebrate the Lord's Supper more frequently, and to use cycles of liturgical readings common to other Christians in their worship. The encyclical also mentions the possibility, when the necessary conditions are met, of Christians not in full communion with the Catholic Church receiving the sacraments of Eucharist, Penance, and Anointing of the Sick. For their part, Catholics "can request these same sacraments from ministers of Churches in which these sacraments are valid" (§46).

More direct and frequent contact between Catholics and other Christians has also fostered a deeper awareness of the fact that the mutual witness of holiness "has an ecumenical potential extraordinarily rich in grace" (§48.2). This potential manifests itself in a joint martyrology shared by all Christians. "Despite the tragedy of our divisions," the Pope writes, "these brothers and sisters have preserved an attachment to Christ and to the Father so radical and absolute as to lead even to the shedding of blood" (§83). The common heritage of Christians is found "first and foremost [in] this reality of holiness" (§84.3).

Lastly, the Pope describes how relations among Christians are increasingly marked by working together in the service of the world. This, too, manifests the communion which already exists among the baptized. Not merely humanitarian action, such ecumenical cooperation draws its inspiration from the Gospel and takes place at pastoral, cultural, and social levels. This practical ecumenism is especially concerned with the defense of human dignity, social justice, and peace. For the Pope, these shared practical efforts represent "a true school of ecumenism, a dynamic road to unity. Unity of action leads to the full unity of faith" (§40.3, cf. §75.4). Common Christian testimony in the service of humanity "has the clear value of a joint witness to the name of the Lord. It is also a form of proclamation, since it reveals the face of Christ" (§75.2).

Churches of the East

Throughout his pontificate John Paul has devoted considerable attention to the churches of the East. In *Ut Unum Sint* he repeats his conviction that "the Church must breathe with her two lungs!": East and West (§54.2). With respect to the churches of the East, the Pope confirms Vatican II's teaching on "their ecclesial nature and the real bonds of communion linking them with the Catholic Church" (§50.2). He also reviews significant post-conciliar developments which have deepened communion between the churches of the East and the West.

John Paul happily recalls the lifting of the mutual excommunications between Catholics and Orthodox by Pope Paul VI and Patriarch Athenagoras I in 1965. This act was, he says, "at once a healing of historical memories, a mutual forgiveness, and a firm commitment to strive for communion" (§52.1, cf. §56.1). Among the regular contacts now established between East and West, he mentions his meetings with Patriarch Dimitrios I, the mutual exchange of delegations for great feasts, and the setting up in 1979 of the Joint International Commission for the Theological Dialogue between the Catholic Church and the Orthodox Church. The Pope also takes note of the ecumenical significance of the 1984 Jubilee commemorating the evangelizing activity of Saints Cyril and Methodius, and the celebration of the millennium of the Baptism of Rus' in 1988.

Ut Unum Sint confirms two theological ideas suggested in *Unitatis Redintegratio* which could prove helpful in restoring full communion: the inspiration of the first millennium as a model for the future (treated below) and the concept of "sister churches." Local Orthodox churches, each one gathered around its Bishop, rightly deserve to be called "sister Churches" (§§56.1, 57.1). Indeed, mutual acceptance of this designation is the doctrinal foundation for fostering dialogue between Catholics and Orthodox.

Since the Council, fraternal relations have likewise been restored with many ancient churches of the East, which rejected the Christological formulations of the Councils of Ephesus (431) and Chalcedon (451). In recent years, the Pope has joined the Patriarchs of some of these churches "in declaring our common faith in Jesus Christ, true God and true man" (§62.2). Thus, ecumenical contacts have clarified long-standing controversies about Christology and opened the way to resolving other disputed theological questions.

Churches and ecclesial communities of the West

With respect to the churches and ecclesial communities which "have their origins in the Reformation" (§65.1), John Paul ratifies the teaching of the Second Vatican Council and evaluates the growth toward unity since then. While these churches and ecclesial communities are "Western," the bonds of communion between post-Reformation Christians and Catholics are weaker than those between the Orthodox and Catholics. Even so, the Pope affirms that common Baptism has profound "theological, pastoral and ecumenical implications" (§66.6). The "communion of faith" already existing between Catholics and other Christians of the West provides "a solid foundation" for joint action in the religious and social spheres (§75.3).

To the doctrinal disagreements which emerged at the time of the Reformation regarding the Church, sacraments, and ordained ministry, ethical questions can be added today: "there is much room for dialogue concerning the moral principles of the Gospel and their implications" (§68.3). John Paul also observes that bilateral and multilateral dialogues with different churches and ecclesial communities have been "fruitful and full of promise" (§69.3).

As he does for the East, the Pope also recounts the encounters, common prayer, and practical initiatives which "attest to progress on the path to unity" in the West (§71.1). He specifically remarks that some of his pastoral visits have had "a precise ecumenical 'priority' " (§71.2), especially those to the United Kingdom, the Scandinavian and Nordic countries, the United States, and Canada. The Pope also praises the many programs and endeavors undertaken by local Catholic churches which further the cause of unity.

The future agenda

In chapter three, John Paul looks to the future, asking how much farther the Church "must travel until that blessed day when full unity in faith will be attained and we can celebrate together in peace the Holy Eucharist of the Lord" (§77.1). The "affective and effective growth of communion" among Christians since the Second Vatican Council still needs to be perfected by the reestablishment of full, visible unity among all the baptized (§77.1, cf. §78.4). The Pope then recommends that Christians take four steps to advance further on their ecumenical journey together: they should continue theological dialogue, "receive" the results achieved, renew their commitment to prayer and interior conversion, and jointly reassess how the Bishop of Rome can best exercise his ministry of unity.

Because theological dialogue must take account of "all the demands of revealed truth" (§79.3), some questions require additional study before a consensus of faith can be reached. John Paul mentions the following five issues: the relationship between Scripture and Tradition; the Eucharist as the real presence of Christ and as a sacrificial memorial; Ordination as a sacrament, and the threefold ministry of the episcopate, presbyterate, and diaconate; the Magisterium of the Pope and bishops; and the role of Mary in salvation history (cf. §79.1).

With respect to the theological dialogues already concluded, the Pope indicates that "a new task lies before us: that of receiving the results already achieved" (§80.1). Churches and ecclesial communities must find ways of officially expressing their agreement, when this is the case, with the statements of bilateral dialogues. In this way their results will not remain the conclusions of commissions but will become a common heritage. Today no structures exist through which this can be done. Consequently, a procedure needs to be established which "analyzes the results and rigorously tests their consistency with the Tradition of faith received from the Apostles and lived out in the community of believers gathered around the Bishop, their legitimate Pastor" (§80.2). This process should involve the whole community, and competent persons must be designated to make the results of reception known. For Catholics, "the Church's teaching authority is responsible for expressing a definitive judgment" in this regard (§81.2).

In his third suggestion for the future ecumenical agenda, John Paul returns to the role of spiritual ecumenism and of bearing common witness to holiness. He encourages individuals and communities to examine their consciences and thus engage in a "dialogue of conversion": the confession of their sins against unity and the acceptance of God's demand to deepen the bonds of communion among them. In this way God draws "the Christian Communities into this completely interior spiritual space in which Christ, by the power of the Spirit, leads them all, without exception, to examine themselves before the Father and to ask themselves whether they have been faithful to his plan for the Church" (§82.3, cf. §35). John Paul also invites his readers to look to the impressive witness of Christian holiness to inspire their ecumenical efforts. The saints and martyrs, who come from all churches and ecclesial communities, testify to the power of divine grace. As such, they are a source of hope for those seeking unity: "God will do for them [Christians] what he did for their saints" (§84.5). According to the Pope, the martyrs are "the most powerful proof that every factor of division can be transcended and overcome in the total gift of self for the sake of the Gospel" (§1.2, cf. §84.4).

Lastly, John Paul recognizes that, for most Christians, the papal ministry is an obstacle to the restoration of full communion: the papacy's "memory is marked by certain painful recollections" (§88). To the extent that the Catholic Church is responsible for this situation, the Pope asks forgiveness. Fortunately, the ecumenical climate has changed in recent years. "After centuries of bitter controversies," he writes, "the other Churches and Ecclesial Communities are more and more taking a fresh look at this ministry of unity" (§89, cf. §97.2). Indeed, many of their members express the need for such a ministry at the service of the universal Church, and John Paul wishes to contribute personally to an ecumenical dialogue on papal primacy.

The Pope is thus willing to join others in rethinking how his ministry of unity can be more effectively exercised for the good of all Christians. He accepts the challenge that he should try to "find a way of exercising the primacy which, while in no way renouncing what is essential to its mission, is nonetheless open to a new situation" (§95.2). Since he cannot carry out this reassessment alone, he asks leaders and theologians from other churches and ecclesial communities to propose innovative ways in which the Petrine ministry could fulfill its specific charge. John Paul hopes that together they will engage "in a patient and fraternal dialogue on this subject, a dialogue in which, leaving useless controversies behind, we could listen to one another, keeping before us only the will of Christ for his Church" (§96).

Key Themes

Among the themes interwoven in *Ut Unum Sint*, three are of particular significance in the Catholic Church's initiatives to restore Christian unity: the ecclesiology of communion, the appreciation expressed for unity in diversity, and the possibility of exercising the Petrine ministry in a different way.

Ecclesiology of communion

John Paul constantly depicts the relationship of the Catholic Church to other churches and ecclesial communities in terms of "communion." The Holy Spirit animates the whole Body of Christ: "It is not that beyond the boundaries of the Catholic community there is an ecclesial vacuum" (§13.3). Unfortunately, however, all Christians are "not in full communion" (§§1.2, 21.2, 35). At present, theirs is a communion which is "real although not yet full" (§45.2); it is still "partial" (§14) and "imperfect" (§§84.1, 96). The goal of the ecumenical movement is the reestablishment of full communion: "From this basic but partial unity it is now necessary to advance toward the visible unity which is required and sufficient and which is manifested in a real and concrete way, so that the Churches may truly become a sign of that full communion in the one, holy, catholic and apostolic Church which will be expressed in the common celebration of the Eucharist" (§78.4).

Communion among the baptized entails more than the enjoyment of close ties of horizontal brotherhood. Above all, it is a vertical, spiritual reality: "the *communion* of Christians is none other than the manifestation in them of the grace by which God makes them sharers in his own *communion*, which is his eternal life" (§9.2). God wills the visible communion of Christians, "which is both praise of his glory and service of his plan of salvation" (§84.5). In the Pope's words, "the bonds of fraternal *koinonia* must be forged before God and in Christ Jesus" (§82.2). These ties of perfect communion already exist as a common heritage among those living in glory. For those still on their earthly pilgrimage, however, this communion is imperfect. Even so, it "is truly and solidly grounded in the full communion of the saints . . . [who] come from all the Churches and Ecclesial Communities which gave them entrance into the communion of salvation" (§84.2).

But God's will requires that the invisible communion of grace must also be manifested by the visible unity of Christians. This visible communion entails "a unity constituted by the bonds of the profession of faith, the sacraments and hierarchical communion" (§9.2). Each of these bonds sheds light on the conditions necessary for the restoration of full communion among Christians.

First, the unity that Christ wills for his Church "can be attained only by the adherence of all to the content of revealed faith in its entirety. In matters of faith, compromise is a contradiction with God who is Truth" (§18, cf. §70.1). While the Pope accepts the legitimacy of complementary formulations of dogma, he insists that full communion "will have to come about through the acceptance of the whole truth into which the Holy Spirit guides Christ's disciples" (§36.4). Christian unity must be "founded on the unity of faith, following in the footsteps and experience of the ancient Church" (§59, cf. §77.1).

Communion in the sacraments is a second bond of unity. Through the one Baptism which they share, all Christians belong to Christ (cf. §§42.1, 42.2, 66.6). The communion signified by this sacrament is oriented to its full expression, which is manifested by Eucharistic communion. While common celebration of the Eucharist is not yet possible, the Pope remarks that "we do have a burning desire to join in celebrating the one Eucharist" (§45.2). Catholics and Orthodox already share the same sacraments, even though they do not yet celebrate a common Eucharist. With the churches and ecclesial communities stemming from the Reformation, which for the most part celebrate only Baptism and the Lord's Supper, the sacramental bonds are less strong.

Third, visible Christian unity also requires communion in ministry, both among bishops as heads of particular churches, and between them and the Pope. John Paul affirms that full unity demands that every bishop must be in communion with the Successor of Peter: "All the Churches are in full and visible communion, because all the Pastors are in communion with Peter and therefore united in Christ" (§94.1). With the churches of the East, the Catholic Church shares the episcopal ministry rooted in the apostolic succession. But, because their particular churches are not in communion with the Roman See, perfect, visible communion is impaired. With the churches and ecclesial communities of the West, not only is this hierarchical communion wanting, but there is also a lack of agreement about the validity of their ministry.

Unity in diversity

According to John Paul II, "the quest for Christian unity is not a matter of choice or expediency, but a duty which springs from the very nature of the Christian community" (§49.2). The effective pursuit of this goal requires that ecclesial unity be correctly understood. In *Ut Unum Sint* the Pope explains his understanding of the unity willed by Christ in such a way that it cannot be confused with uniformity. First, he proposes that the unity which existed in the first millennium can serve as a model of restored unity; second, he is convinced that unity in faith is compatible with diversity in expression. Both of his ideas are founded on a fundamental principle of ecumenism: "one must not impose any burden beyond that which is strictly necessary" (§78.5).

Primarily interested in improving ecumenical relations with the East, the Pope appeals to "the unity which, in spite of everything, was experienced in the first millennium and in a certain sense now serves as a kind of model" (§55.1). The Catholic Church, he says, finds inspiration for full communion in the "structures of unity which existed before the separation" (§56.2, cf. §61). Ecclesial structures in both East and West evolved from the same apostolic heritage and, for a millennium, they maintained the pattern established by Christ: the bishops were in communion with the Bishop of Rome. At the same time, as stated in *Unitatis Redintegratio*, §14, "if disagreements in belief and discipline arose among them, the Roman See acted by common consent as moderator" (§95.2). These ancient structures are "a heritage of experience that guides our common path toward the reestablishment of full communion" (§56.2, cf. §61). For John Paul, "it is to that unity, thus structured, which we must look" (§55.1).

Some ecumenists think that the restoration of visible unity among Christians might entail a stifling sameness. To allay these fears, the Pope states that "the vision of the full communion to be sought is that of unity in legitimate diversity" (§54.2, cf. §57.1). Many local churches have preserved their own manner of living the faith in ways that have aptly inculturated the Gospel. These traditions and disciplines are not divisive, but authentically express the one Church of Christ. John Paul confirms Vatican II's teaching that "legitimate diversity is in no way opposed to the Church's unity, but rather enhances her splendor and contributes greatly to the fulfillment of her mission" (§50.3). The Pope, then, does not just tolerate diversity but judges it fruitful for fostering communion, since it encourages "the exchange of gifts between the Churches" (§57.4).

The encyclical applies the same principle of unity in diversity to questions involving the formulation of dogma. Like John XXIII, John Paul II believes that "the distinction between the deposit of faith and the formulation in which it is expressed" is a fundamental principle of ecumenical dialogue (§81.3). Sadly, in the past, "intolerant polemics and controversies have made incompatible assertions out of what was really the result of two different ways of looking at the same reality" (§38.2). However, when Christians engage in frank dialogue today, they "help one another to look at themselves together in the light of the Apostolic Tradition" (§16.2). This joint scrutiny leads them to welcome different formulations of dogma and fosters new ones. Nonetheless, in the Pope's mind, this common undertaking is not license for "altering the deposit of faith, changing the meaning of dogmas, eliminating essential words from them, accommodating truth to the preferences of a particular age, or suppressing certain articles of the *Creed*" (§18). Instead, complementary formulations of dogmatic truth prove that the content of the faith can truly speak to all cultures. "The element which determines communion in truth is *the meaning of truth*," John Paul writes. "The expression of truth can take different forms" (§19.1).

The ministry of unity

In *Ut Unum Sint*, John Paul II's spiritual and theological reflection on the papal ministry is extraordinarily personal. It culminates, as we have seen, in his bold invitation to all Christians, including himself, to take a fresh look at how the Petrine ministry is exercised. This endeavor, he writes, is "an immense task which we cannot refuse and which I cannot carry out by myself" (§96). While the Pope believes that his office is a divine gift for building up the Church, he recognizes that it has also been an obstacle to the full, visible communion of Christians. To escape this dilemma, John Paul offers some suggestions for ways in which the ministry of unity could be carried out in the future.

The Pope reaffirms that, among the Apostles, Jesus entrusted Peter with a "special mission in the Church" (§4.1). The place assigned to Peter "is based on the words of Christ himself, as they are recorded in the Gospel traditions" (§90.2). Petrine primacy is, therefore, divinely instituted.

By God's design, the ministry of Peter "must continue in the Church so that under her sole Head, who is Jesus Christ, she may be visibly present in the world as the communion of all his disciples" (§97.1). God wills that there should always be a Successor of Peter; and that Successor is now the Bishop of Rome, "the heir to the mission of Peter in the Church" (§92.2). Therefore, the papal office "corresponds to the will of Christ" (§95.1); it is an "essential good" of the Church (§88). According to *Ut Unum Sint,* the communion of all bishops with the Bishop of Rome belongs to God's plan and is "an essential requisite of full and visible communion" (§97.1). Obedience to the divine will requires that all Christians recognize the ministry of unity discharged by the Pope.

Throughout the encyclical, John Paul constantly refers to himself as "the Bishop of Rome," a significant detail, especially considering the East's under-standing that the Petrine ministry is essentially an episcopal responsibility. Moreover, he emphasizes the fittingness of Peter's Successor being "the Bishop of the Church which preserves the mark of the martyrdom of Peter and of Paul" (§90.1). The Petrine office is thus historically and spiritually linked to the Roman See, "which has been made fruitful by the blood of the Princes of the Apostles" (§92.1) — Peter *and* Paul. Paul is therefore intimately associated with the origin of the ministry of unity held by the Bishop of Rome (cf. §§90.1, 91.2). Furthermore, John Paul stresses that the weakness of both Peter and Paul "shows that the Church is founded upon the infinite power of grace" (§91.2). This Pauline accent points out that the ministry of the Bishop of Rome is necessarily collegial and is exercised from within a particular church.

In keeping with the ecclesiological tone of the encyclical, the Pope chooses to describe the relationship of the Bishop of Rome with other bishops in terms of "communion" rather than "collegiality." Indeed, his ministry is to "ensure the communion of all the Churches" (§94.2, cf. §§24, 94.1). With his eye on the structures of unity in the first millennium, John Paul holds that "the mission of the Bishop of Rome [is] within the College of all the Pastors" (§94.1). Moreover, he insists that the Catholic Church "does not separate this office [of the Bishop of Rome] from the mission entrusted to the whole body of Bishops"

(§95.1). To make his point even more forcefully, John Paul affirms that the ministry of unity must "always" be carried out "in communion" (§95.1).

The Pope's specific ministry to ecclesial communion is to be "the first servant of unity" (§94.2). Peter's Successor is "the visible sign and guarantor of unity" (§88) within the College of Bishops and thus for the whole Church, including the churches and ecclesial communities lacking full communion with the Roman See. In John Paul's words, "whatever relates to the unity of all Christian communities clearly forms part of the concerns of the primacy" (§95.2).

While refraining from presenting the whole of Catholic teaching on the papacy as it was defined at the First Vatican Council (1870), John Paul II nonetheless offers some thoughts on papal jurisdiction and teaching authority.

As a matter of fact, the Pope never uses the term "jurisdiction" to describe the authority of his office. Instead, he stresses that his ministry as the "servant of the servants of God" is a gift of God's mercy. The purpose of its service is not that of "exercising power over the people" (§94.1), but of ensuring the communion of all the churches. For John Paul, "the authority proper to this ministry is completely at the service of God's merciful plan and it must always be seen in this perspective" (§92.2). Among his duties — those which Vatican I assigned to the Pope's full, supreme, ordinary, immediate, episcopal, and universal jurisdiction — John Paul mentions "vigilance over the handing down of the Word, the celebration of the liturgy and the sacraments, the Church's mission, discipline and the Christian life" (§94.2). Because of his responsibility to the common good of the Church, the Bishop of Rome also has the task of cautioning and admonishing other bishops and the faithful at large.

In order to explain the Pope's teaching role, John Paul invokes Peter as a model. Peter is the "spokesman of the Apostolic College" (§90.2, cf. §55.1) and "the one who speaks in the name of the apostolic group" (§97.1). Similarly, the Successor of Peter must teach "in the name of all the Pastors in communion with him" (§94.2). The Pope has the duty of "keeping watch (*episkopein*), like a sentinel, so that, through the efforts of the Pastors, the true voice of Christ the Shepherd may be heard in all the particular Churches" (§94.1). The encyclical also mentions that the Pope can bear witness to truth, under the conditions laid down at Vatican I, by declaring "*ex cathedra* that a certain doctrine belongs to the deposit of faith" (§94.2).

Ut Unum Sint not only recounts the remarkable progress made toward Christian unity since the Second Vatican Council but also gives ecumenism a fresh impetus. At the dawn of the new millennium, Pope John Paul II invites all Christians to renew their commitment of striving for the unity for which Christ prayed. The Pope is convinced that the grace of full communion will be obtained through prayer and docility to the Holy Spirit who is guiding the ecumenical journey. "And should we ask if all this is possible, the answer will always be yes. It is the same answer which Mary of Nazareth heard: with God nothing is impossible" (§102.5).

* * *

Selected Bibliography

"An Offer from the Pope." *The Tablet,* 249 (1995), 694-695.

"Applause for the Pope's Unity Call — with Reservations." *The Tablet,* 249 (1995), 714.

Bouboutsis, E. K. "Toward Unity with Diversity and Equality." *Ecumenical Trends,* 25 (1996), 10-12.

Cassidy, Edward Idris. "*Ut Unum Sint* and the Great Jubilee Year 2000." *Bulletin* [Centro Pro Unione], 49 (Spring 1996), 3-8.

Cassidy, Edward Idris, and Fortino, Eleuterio F. "Comment on the Encyclical Letter *Ut Unum Sint* of the Holy Father Pope John Paul II on Commitment to Ecumenism." *Information Service* [Pontifical Council for Promoting Christian Unity], 89 (1995), 83-87.

Clément, Olivier. "Some Orthodox Reflections on Recent Papal Encyclicals." *One in Christ,* 31 (1995), 273-280.

Crow, P. A. "One the Most Powerful Witnesses in Recent Times." *Inside the Oikoumene,* 9 (1995), 6-8.

Mcfarlane, R. "An Anglican Response to the Encyclical *Ut Unum Sint.*" *Ecumenical Trends,* 25 (1996), 12-14.

Neuhaus, Richard John. " 'That They May All Be One': The Pope's Twelfth Encyclical." *Crisis,* 13 (September 1995), 25-27.

Nilson, J. "The Challenges of *Ut Unum Sint.*" *Ecumenical Trends,* 25 (1996), 8-10.

"Reactions to *Ut Unum Sint* from Protestant Churches around the World." *Catholic International,* 6 (1995), 397-398.

Reardon, Ruth. " 'A Source of Joy': *Ut Unum Sint* and Interchurch Families." *One in Christ,* 31 (1995), 280-286.

Strong, R. "An Anglican Response to the Papal Encyclical *Ut Unum Sint.*" *Unity Digest,* 13 (1995), 7-12.

Tillard, Jean-Marie. "Catholic Church Is at the Heart of *Communio.*" *L'Osservatore Romano,* 43 (1995), 8-9.

Zago, Marcello. "The Missionary Importance of the Encyclical *Ut Unum Sint.*" *Omnis Terra,* 29 (1995), 488-494.

ENCYCLICAL LETTER
UT UNUM SINT
OF THE HOLY FATHER
JOHN PAUL II
ON COMMITMENT
TO ECUMENISM

Ut Unum Sint

Introduction

1.1 *"Ut unum sint!"* The call for Christian unity made by the Second Vatican Ecumenical Council with such impassioned commitment is finding an ever greater echo in the hearts of believers, especially as the year 2000 approaches, a year which Christians will celebrate as a sacred Jubilee, the commemoration of the Incarnation of the Son of God, who became man in order to save humanity.

1.2 The courageous witness of so many martyrs of our century, including members of Churches and Ecclesial Communities not in full communion with the Catholic Church, gives new vigor to the Council's call and reminds us of our duty to listen to and put into practice its exhortation. These brothers and sisters of ours, united in the selfless offering of their lives for the Kingdom of God, are the most powerful proof that every factor of division can be transcended and overcome in the total gift of self for the sake of the Gospel.

1.3 *Christ calls all his disciples to unity.* My earnest desire is to renew this call today, to propose it once more with determination, repeating what I said at the Roman Colosseum on Good Friday 1994, at the end of the meditation on the *Via Crucis* prepared by my Venerable Brother Bartholomew, the Ecumenical Patriarch of Constantinople. There I stated that believers in Christ, united in following in the footsteps of the martyrs, cannot remain divided. If they wish truly and effectively to oppose the world's tendency to reduce to powerlessness the mystery of Redemption, they must *profess together the same truth about the Cross.*[1] The Cross! An anti-Christian outlook seeks to minimize the Cross, to empty it of its meaning, and to deny that in it man has the source of his new life. It claims that the Cross is unable to provide either vision or hope. Man, it says, is nothing but an earthly being, who must live as if God did not exist.

2.1 No one is unaware of the challenge which all this poses to believers. They cannot fail to meet this challenge. Indeed, how could they refuse to do everything possible, with God's help, to break down the walls of division and distrust, to overcome obstacles and prejudices which thwart the proclamation

---

[1] Cf. Address following the Way of the Cross on Good Friday (April 1, 1994), 3: *AAS* 87 (1995), 88.

of the Gospel of salvation in the Cross of Jesus, the one Redeemer of man, of every individual?

2.2 I thank the Lord that he has led us to make progress along the path of unity and communion between Christians, a path difficult but so full of joy. Interconfessional dialogues at the theological level have produced positive and tangible results: this encourages us to move forward.

2.3 Nevertheless, besides the doctrinal differences needing to be resolved, Christians cannot underestimate the burden of *long-standing misgivings* inherited from the past, and of mutual *misunderstandings* and *prejudices*. *Complacency, indifference* and *insufficient knowledge of one another* often make this situation worse. Consequently, the commitment to ecumenism must be based upon the conversion of hearts and upon prayer, which will also lead to the necessary purification of past memories. With the grace of the Holy Spirit, the Lord's disciples, inspired by love, by the power of the truth and by a sincere desire for mutual forgiveness and reconciliation, are called to *reexamine together their painful past* and the hurt which that past regrettably continues to provoke even today. All together, they are invited by the ever fresh power of the Gospel to acknowledge with sincere and total objectivity the mistakes made and the contingent factors at work at the origins of their deplorable divisions. *What is needed is a calm, clear-sighted and truthful vision of things*, a vision enlivened by divine mercy and capable of freeing people's minds and of inspiring in everyone a renewed willingness, precisely with a view to proclaiming the Gospel to the men and women of every people and nation.

3.1 At the Second Vatican Council, the Catholic Church committed herself *irrevocably* to following the path of the ecumenical venture, thus heeding the Spirit of the Lord, who teaches people to interpret carefully the "signs of the times." The experiences of these years have made the Church even more profoundly aware of her identity and her mission in history. The Catholic Church acknowledges and confesses *the weaknesses of her members*, conscious that their sins are so many betrayals of and obstacles to the accomplishment of the Savior's plan. Because she feels herself constantly called to be renewed in the spirit of the Gospel, she does not cease to do penance. At the same time, she acknowledges and exalts still more *the power of the Lord*, who fills her with the gift of holiness, leads her forward, and conforms her to his Passion and Resurrection.

3.2 Taught by the events of her history, the Church is committed to freeing herself from every purely human support, in order to live in depth the Gospel law of the Beatitudes. Conscious that the truth does not impose itself except "by virtue of its own truth, as it makes its entrance into the mind at once quietly and with power,"[2] she seeks nothing for herself but the freedom to proclaim the Gospel. Indeed, her authority is exercised in the service of truth and charity.

3.3 I myself intend *to promote every suitable initiative* aimed at making the witness of the entire Catholic community understood in its full purity and consistency, especially considering the engagement which awaits the Church at the threshold of the new millennium. That will be an exceptional occasion, in view of which she asks the Lord to increase the unity of all Christians until they reach full communion.[3] The present Encyclical Letter is meant as a contribution to this most noble goal. Essentially pastoral in character, it seeks to encourage the efforts of all who work for the cause of unity.

4.1 This is a specific duty of the Bishop of Rome as the Successor of the Apostle Peter. I carry out this duty with the profound conviction that I am obeying the Lord, and with a clear sense of my own human frailty. Indeed, if Christ himself gave Peter this special mission in the Church and exhorted him to strengthen his brethren, he also made clear to him his human weakness and his special need of conversion: "And when you have turned again, strengthen your brethren" (Lk 22:32). It is precisely in Peter's human weakness that it becomes fully clear that the Pope, in order to carry out this special ministry in the Church, depends totally on the Lord's grace and prayer: "I have prayed for you that your faith may not fail" (Lk 22:32). The conversion of Peter and that of his Successors is upheld by the very prayer of the Redeemer, and the Church constantly makes this petition her own. In our ecumenical age, marked by the Second Vatican Council, the mission of the Bishop of Rome is particularly directed to recalling the need for full communion among Christ's disciples.

4.2 The Bishop of Rome himself must fervently make his own Christ's prayer for that conversion which is indispensable for "Peter" to be able to serve his brethren. I earnestly invite the faithful of the Catholic Church and all Christians to share in this prayer. May all join me in praying for this conversion!

4.3 We know that during her earthly pilgrimage the Church has suffered

[2] Second Vatican Ecumenical Council, Declaration on Religious Freedom *Dignitatis Humanae*, 1.

[3] Cf. Apostolic Letter *Tertio Millennio Adveniente* (November 10, 1994), 16: *AAS* 87 (1995), 15.

and will continue to suffer opposition and persecution. But the hope which sustains her is unshakable, just as the joy which flows from this hope is indestructible. In effect, the firm and enduring rock upon which she is founded is Jesus Christ, her Lord.

I
The Catholic Church's Commitment to Ecumenism

God's plan and communion

5.1 Together with all Christ's disciples, the Catholic Church bases upon God's plan her ecumenical commitment to gather all Christians into unity. Indeed, "the Church is not a reality closed in on herself. Rather, she is permanently open to missionary and ecumenical endeavor, for she is sent to the world to announce and witness, to make present and spread the mystery of communion which is essential to her, and to gather all people and all things into Christ, so as to be for all an 'inseparable sacrament of unity.' "[4]

5.2 Already in the Old Testament, the Prophet Ezekiel, referring to the situation of God's People at that time and using the simple sign of two broken sticks which are first divided and then joined together, expressed the divine will to "gather from all sides" the members of his scattered people. "I will be their God, and they shall be my people. Then the nations will know that I the Lord sanctify Israel" (cf. 37:16-28). The Gospel of John, for its part, considering the situation of the People of God at the time it was written, sees in Jesus' death the reason for the unity of God's children: "Jesus would die for the nation, and not for the nation only, but to gather into one the children of God who are scattered abroad" (11:51-52). Indeed, as the Letter to the Ephesians explains, Jesus "broke down the dividing wall of hostility . . . through the Cross, thereby bringing the hostility to an end"; in place of what was divided he brought about unity (cf. 2:14-16).

6 The unity of all divided humanity is the will of God. For this reason he sent his Son, so that by dying and rising for us he might bestow on us the Spirit of love. On the eve of his sacrifice on the Cross, Jesus himself prayed to

---

[4] Congregation for the Doctrine of the Faith, Letter to the Bishops of the Catholic Church on Some Aspects of the Church Understood as Communion *Communionis Notio* (May 28, 1992), 4: *AAS* 85 (1993), 840.

the Father for his disciples and for all those who believe in him, that they *might be one*, a living communion. This is the basis not only of the duty, but also of the responsibility before God and his plan, which falls to those who through Baptism become members of the Body of Christ, a Body in which the fullness of reconciliation and communion must be made present. How is it possible to remain divided, if we have been "buried" through Baptism in the Lord's death, in the very act by which God, through the death of his Son, has broken down the walls of division? Division "openly contradicts the will of Christ, provides a stumbling block to the world, and inflicts damage on the most holy cause of proclaiming the Good News to every creature."[5]

The way of ecumenism: the way of the Church

7 "The Lord of the ages wisely and patiently follows out the plan of his grace on behalf of us sinners. In recent times he has begun to bestow more generously upon divided Christians remorse over their divisions and a longing for unity. Everywhere, large numbers have felt the impulse of this grace, and among our separated brethren also *there increases from day to day a movement*, fostered by the grace of the Holy Spirit, *for the restoration of unity among all Christians*. Taking part in this movement, which is called ecumenical, are those who invoke the Triune God and confess Jesus as Lord and Savior. They join in not merely as individuals but also as members of the corporate groups in which they have heard the Gospel, and which each regards as his Church and, indeed, God's. And yet almost everyone, though in different ways, *longs that there may be one visible Church of God*, a Church truly universal and sent forth to the whole world that the world may be converted to the Gospel and so be saved, to the glory of God."[6]

8.1 This statement of the Decree *Unitatis Redintegratio* is to be read in the context of the complete teaching of the Second Vatican Council. The Council expresses the Church's decision to take up the ecumenical task of working for Christian unity and to propose it with conviction and vigor: "This sacred Synod exhorts all the Catholic faithful to recognize the signs of the times and to participate actively in the work of ecumenism."[7]

8.2 In indicating the Catholic principles of ecumenism, the Decree *Unitatis Redintegratio* recalls above all the teaching on the Church set forth in the

---

[5] Second Vatican Ecumenical Council, Decree on Ecumenism *Unitatis Redintegratio*, 1.
[6] Ibid., 1.
[7] Ibid., 4.

Dogmatic Constitution *Lumen Gentium* in its chapter on the People of God.[8] At the same time, it takes into account everything affirmed in the Council's Declaration on Religious Freedom *Dignitatis Humanae*.[9]

8.3 The Catholic Church embraces with hope the commitment to ecumenism as a duty of the Christian conscience enlightened by faith and guided by love. Here too we can apply the words of Saint Paul to the first Christians of Rome: "God's love has been poured into our hearts through the Holy Spirit"; thus our "hope does not disappoint us" (Rom 5:5). This is the hope of Christian unity, which has its divine source in the Trinitarian unity of the Father, the Son and the Holy Spirit.

9.1 Jesus himself, at the hour of his Passion, prayed "that they may all be one" (Jn 17:21). This unity, which the Lord has bestowed on his Church and in which he wishes to embrace all people, is not something added on, but stands at the very heart of Christ's mission. Nor is it some secondary attribute of the community of his disciples. Rather, it belongs to the very essence of this community. God wills the Church, because he wills unity, and unity is an expression of the whole depth of his *agape*.

9.2 In effect, this unity bestowed by the Holy Spirit does not merely consist in the gathering of people as a collection of individuals. It is a unity constituted by the bonds of the profession of faith, the sacraments and hierarchical communion.[10] The faithful are *one* because, in the Spirit, they are in *communion* with the Son and, in him, share in his *communion* with the Father: "Our *fellowship* is with the Father and with his Son Jesus Christ" (1 Jn 1:3). For the Catholic Church, then, the *communion* of Christians is none other than the manifestation in them of the grace by which God makes them sharers in his own *communion*, which is his eternal life. Christ's words "that they may be one" are thus his prayer to the Father that the Father's plan may be fully accomplished, in such a way that everyone may clearly see "what is the plan of the mystery hidden for ages in God who created all things" (Eph 3:9). To believe in Christ means to desire unity; to desire unity means to desire the Church; to desire the Church means to desire the communion of grace which corresponds to the Father's plan from all eternity. Such is the meaning of Christ's prayer: *"Ut unum sint."*

---

[8] Cf. Second Vatican Ecumenical Council, Dogmatic Constitution on the Church *Lumen Gentium*, 14.

[9] Cf. Second Vatican Ecumenical Council, Declaration on Religious Freedom *Dignitatis Humanae*, 1, 2.

[10] Cf. Second Vatican Ecumenical Council, Dogmatic Constitution on the Church *Lumen Gentium*, 14.

10.1 In the present situation of the lack of unity among Christians and of the confident quest for full communion, the Catholic faithful are conscious of being deeply challenged by the Lord of the Church. The Second Vatican Council strengthened their commitment with a clear ecclesiological vision, open to all the ecclesial values present among other Christians. The Catholic faithful face the ecumenical question in a spirit of faith.

10.2 The Council states that the Church of Christ "subsists in the Catholic Church, which is governed by the Successor of Peter and by the Bishops in communion with him," and at the same time acknowledges that "many elements of sanctification and of truth can be found outside her visible structure. These elements, however, as gifts properly belonging to the Church of Christ, possess an inner dynamism toward Catholic unity."[11]

10.3 "It follows that these separated Churches and Communities, though we believe that they suffer from defects, have by no means been deprived of significance and value in the mystery of salvation. For the Spirit of Christ has not refrained from using them as means of salvation which derive their efficacy from the very fullness of grace and truth entrusted to the Catholic Church."[12]

11.1 The Catholic Church thus affirms that during the two thousand years of her history she has been preserved in unity, with all the means with which God wishes to endow his Church, and this despite the often grave crises which have shaken her, the infidelity of some of her ministers, and the faults into which her members daily fall. The Catholic Church knows that, by virtue of the strength which comes to her from the Spirit, the weaknesses, mediocrity, sins and at times the betrayals of some of her children cannot destroy what God has bestowed on her as part of his plan of grace. Moreover, "the powers of death shall not prevail against it" (Mt 16:18). Even so, the Catholic Church does not forget that many among her members cause God's plan to be discernible only with difficulty. Speaking of the lack of unity among Christians, the Decree on Ecumenism does not ignore the fact that "people of both sides were to blame,"[13] and acknowledges that responsibility cannot be attributed only to the "other side." By God's grace, however, neither what belongs to the structure of the Church of Christ nor that communion which still exists with the other Churches and Ecclesial Communities has been destroyed.

11.2 Indeed, the elements of sanctification and truth present in the other

---

[11] Ibid., 8.
[12] Second Vatican Ecumenical Council, Decree on Ecumenism *Unitatis Redintegratio*, 3.
[13] Ibid., 3.

Christian Communities, in a degree which varies from one to the other, constitute the objective basis of the communion, albeit imperfect, which exists between them and the Catholic Church.

11.3 To the extent that these elements are found in other Christian Communities, the one Church of Christ is effectively present in them. For this reason the Second Vatican Council speaks of a certain, though imperfect communion. The Dogmatic Constitution *Lumen Gentium* stresses that the Catholic Church "recognizes that in many ways she is linked"[14] with these Communities by a true union in the Holy Spirit.

12.1 The same Dogmatic Constitution listed at length "the elements of sanctification and truth" which in various ways are present and operative beyond the visible boundaries of the Catholic Church: "For there are many who honor Sacred Scripture, taking it as a norm of belief and of action, and who show a true religious zeal. They lovingly believe in God the Father Almighty and in Christ, Son of God and Savior. They are consecrated by Baptism, through which they are united with Christ. They also recognize and receive other sacraments within their own Churches or Ecclesial Communities. Many of them rejoice in the episcopate, celebrate the Holy Eucharist, and cultivate devotion toward the Virgin Mother of God. They also share with us in prayer and other spiritual benefits. Likewise, we can say that in some real way they are joined with us in the Holy Spirit, for to them also he gives his gifts and graces, and is thereby operative among them with his sanctifying power. Some indeed he has strengthened to the extent of the shedding of their blood. In all of Christ's disciples the Spirit arouses the desire to be peacefully united, in the manner determined by Christ, as one flock under one shepherd."[15]

12.2 The Council's Decree on Ecumenism, referring to the Orthodox Churches, went so far as to declare that "through the celebration of the Eucharist of the Lord in each of these Churches, the Church of God is built up and grows in stature."[16] Truth demands that all this be recognized.

13.1 The same Document carefully draws out the doctrinal implications of this situation. Speaking of the members of these Communities, it declares: "All those justified by faith through Baptism are incorporated into Christ. They therefore have a right to be honored by the title of Christian, and are

[14] No. 15.
[15] Ibid., 15.
[16] Second Vatican Ecumenical Council, Decree on Ecumenism *Unitatis Redintegratio*, 15.

properly regarded as brothers and sisters in the Lord by the sons and daughters of the Catholic Church."[17]

13.2 With reference to the many positive elements present in the other Churches and Ecclesial Communities, the Decree adds: "All of these, which come from Christ and lead back to him, belong by right to the one Church of Christ. The separated brethren also carry out many of the sacred actions of the Christian religion. Undoubtedly, in many ways that vary according to the condition of each Church or community, these actions can truly engender a life of grace and can be rightly described as capable of providing access to the community of salvation."[18]

13.3 These are extremely important texts for ecumenism. It is not that beyond the boundaries of the Catholic community there is an ecclesial vacuum. Many elements of great value (*eximia*), which in the Catholic Church are part of the fullness of the means of salvation and of the gifts of grace which make up the Church, are also found in the other Christian Communities.

14 All these elements bear within themselves a tendency toward unity, having their fullness in that unity. It is not a matter of adding together all the riches scattered throughout the various Christian Communities in order to arrive at a Church which God has in mind for the future. In accordance with the great Tradition, attested to by the Fathers of the East and of the West, the Catholic Church believes that in the Pentecost event God has *already* manifested the Church in her eschatological reality, which he had prepared "from the time of Abel, the just one."[19] This reality is something already given. Consequently we are even now in the last times. The elements of this already-given Church exist, found in their fullness in the Catholic Church and, without this fullness, in the other Communities,[20] where certain features of the Christian mystery have at times been more effectively emphasized. Ecumenism is directed precisely to making the partial communion existing between Christians grow toward full communion in truth and charity.

Renewal and conversion

15.1 Passing from principles, from the obligations of the Christian conscience, to the actual practice of the ecumenical journey toward unity, the

---

[17] Ibid., 3.

[18] Ibid., 3.

[19] Saint Gregory the Great, *Homilies on the Gospel*, 19, 1: *PL* 76, 1154; quoted in Second Vatican Ecumenical Council, Dogmatic Constitution on the Church *Lumen Gentium*, 2.

[20] Cf. Second Vatican Ecumenical Council, Decree on Ecumenism *Unitatis Redintegratio*, 4.

Second Vatican Council emphasizes above all *the need for interior conversion.* The messianic proclamation that "the time is fulfilled, and the Kingdom of God is at hand," and the subsequent call to "repent, and believe in the Gospel" (Mk 1:15) with which Jesus begins his mission, indicate the essential element of every new beginning: the fundamental need for evangelization at every stage of the Church's journey of salvation. This is true in a special way of the process begun by the Second Vatican Council, when it indicated as a dimension of renewal the ecumenical task of uniting divided Christians. *"There can be no ecumenism worthy of the name without a change of heart."*[21]

15.2 The Council calls for personal conversion as well as for communal conversion. The desire of every Christian Community for unity goes hand in hand with its fidelity to the Gospel. In the case of individuals who live their Christian vocation, the Council speaks of interior conversion, of a renewal of mind.[22]

15.3 Each one therefore ought to be more radically converted to the Gospel and, without ever losing sight of God's plan, change his or her way of looking at things. Thanks to ecumenism, our contemplation of "the mighty works of God" *(mirabilia Dei)* has been enriched by new horizons, for which the Triune God calls us to give thanks: the knowledge that the Spirit is at work in other Christian Communities, the discovery of examples of holiness, the experience of the immense riches present in the communion of saints, and contact with unexpected dimensions of Christian commitment. In a corresponding way, there is an increased sense of the need for repentance: an awareness of certain exclusions which seriously harm fraternal charity, of certain refusals to forgive, of a certain pride, of an unevangelical insistence on condemning the "other side," of a disdain born of an unhealthy presumption. Thus, the entire life of Christians is marked by a concern for ecumenism; and they are called to let themselves be shaped, as it were, by that concern.

16.1 In the teaching of the Second Vatican Council there is a clear connection between renewal, conversion and reform. The Council states that "Christ summons the Church, as she goes her pilgrim way, to that continual reformation of which she always has need, insofar as she is an institution of human beings here on earth. Therefore, if the influence of events or of the times has led to deficiencies . . . these should be appropriately rectified at the proper moment."[23] No Christian Community can exempt itself from this call.

---

[21] Ibid., 7.
[22] Cf. ibid., 7.
[23] Ibid., 6.

16.2 By engaging in frank dialogue, Communities help one another to look at themselves together in the light of the Apostolic Tradition. This leads them to ask themselves whether they truly express in an adequate way all that the Holy Spirit has transmitted through the Apostles.[24] With regard to the Catholic Church, I have frequently recalled these obligations and perspectives, as for example on the anniversary of the *Baptism of Kievan Rus'*[25] or in commemorating the eleven hundred years since the evangelizing activity of Saints Cyril and Methodius.[26] More recently, the *Directory for the Application of Principles and Norms on Ecumenism*, issued with my approval by the Pontifical Council for Promoting Christian Unity, has applied them to the pastoral sphere.[27]

17.1 With regard to other Christians, the principal documents of the Commission on *Faith and Order*[28] and the statements of numerous bilateral dialogues have already provided Christian Communities with useful tools for discerning what is necessary to the ecumenical movement and to the conversion which it must inspire. These studies are important from two points of view: they demonstrate the remarkable progress already made, and they are a source of hope inasmuch as they represent a sure foundation for further study.

17.2 The increase of fellowship in a reform which is continuous and carried out in the light of the Apostolic Tradition is certainly, in the present circumstances of Christians, one of the distinctive and most important aspects of ecumenism. Moreover, it is an essential guarantee for its future. The faithful of the Catholic Church cannot forget that the ecumenical thrust of the Second Vatican Council is one consequence of all that the Church at that time committed herself to doing in order to reexamine herself in the light of the Gospel and the great Tradition. My Predecessor, Pope John XXIII, understood this clearly: in calling the Council, he refused to separate renewal from ecumenical openness.[29] At the conclusion of the Council, Pope Paul VI solemnly

---

[24] Cf. Second Vatican Ecumenical Council, Dogmatic Constitution on Divine Revelation *Dei Verbum*, 7.

[25] Cf. Apostolic Letter *Euntes in Mundum* (January 25, 1988): *AAS* 80 (1988), 935-956.

[26] Cf. Encyclical Epistle *Slavorum Apostoli* (June 2, 1985): *AAS* 77 (1985), 779-813.

[27] Cf. *Directory for the Application of Principles and Norms on Ecumenism* (March 25, 1993): *AAS* 85 (1993), 1039-1119.

[28] Cf. in particular, the Lima document: *Baptism, Eucharist, Ministry* (January 1982); and the study of the Joint Working Group between the Catholic Church and the World Council of Churches, *Confessing the "One" Faith* (1991): Document No. 153 of the Commission on Faith and Order, Geneva, 1991.

[29] Cf. Address at the Opening of the Second Vatican Ecumenical Council (October 11, 1962): *AAS* 54 (1962), 793.

sealed the Council's commitment to ecumenism, renewing the dialogue of char-ity with the Churches in communion with the Patriarch of Constantinople, and joining the Patriarch in the concrete and profoundly significant gesture which "condemned to oblivion" and "removed from memory and from the midst of the Church" the excommunications of the past. It is worth recalling that the establishment of a special body for ecumenical matters coincided with the launching of preparations for the Second Vatican Council[30] and that through this body the opinions and judgments of the other Christian Communities played a part in the great debates about revelation, the Church, the nature of ecumenism and religious freedom.

The fundamental importance of doctrine

18 Taking up an idea expressed by Pope John XXIII at the opening of the Council,[31] the Decree on Ecumenism mentions the way of formulating doctrine as one of the elements of a continuing reform.[32] Here it is not a question of altering the deposit of faith, changing the meaning of dogmas, eliminating essential words from them, accommodating truth to the pref-erences of a particular age, or suppressing certain articles of the *Creed* under the false pretext that they are no longer understood today. The unity willed by God can be attained only by the adherence of all to the content of revealed faith in its entirety. In matters of faith, compromise is in contra-diction with God, who is Truth. In the Body of Christ, "the way, and the truth, and the life" (Jn 14:6), who could consider legitimate a reconcilia-tion brought about at the expense of the truth? The Council's Declaration on Religious Freedom *Dignitatis Humanae* attributes to human dignity the quest for truth, "especially in what concerns God and his Church,"[33] and adherence to truth's demands. A "being together" which betrayed the truth

[30] We are speaking of the Secretariat for Promoting Christian Unity, established by Pope John XXIII with the Motu Proprio *Superno Dei Nutu* (June 5, 1960), 9: *AAS* 52 (1960), 436, and confirmed by successive documents: Motu Proprio *Appropinquante Concilio* (August 6, 1962), Chapter III, Article 7, §2.II: *AAS* 54 (1962), 614; cf. Paul VI, Apostolic Constitution *Regimini Ecclesiae Universae* (August 15, 1967), 92-94: *AAS* 59 (1967), 918-919. This dicastery is now called the Pontifical Council for Promoting Christian Unity: cf. John Paul II, Apostolic Consti-tution *Pastor Bonus* (June 28, 1988), V, Articles 135-138: *AAS* 80 (1988), 895-896.

[31] Address at the Opening of the Second Vatican Ecumenical Council (October 11, 1962): *AAS* 54 (1962), 792.

[32] Cf. Second Vatican Ecumenical Council, Decree on Ecumenism *Unitatis Redintegratio*, 6.

[33] Cf. Second Vatican Ecumenical Council, Declaration on Religious Freedom *Dignitatis Humanae*, 1.

would thus be opposed both to the nature of God, who offers his communion, and to the need for truth found in the depths of every human heart.

19.1 Even so, doctrine needs to be presented in a way that makes it understandable to those for whom God himself intends it. In my Encyclical Epistle *Slavorum Apostoli,* I recalled that this was the very reason why Saints Cyril and Methodius labored to translate the ideas of the Bible and the concepts of Greek theology in the context of very different historical experiences and ways of thinking. They wanted the one word of God to be "made accessible in each civilization's own forms of expression."[34] They recognized that they could not therefore "impose on the peoples assigned to their preaching either the undeniable superiority of the Greek language and Byzantine culture, or the customs and way of life of the more advanced society in which they had grown up."[35] Thus they put into practice that "perfect communion in love which preserves the Church from all forms of particularism, ethnic exclusivism or racial prejudice, and from any nationalistic arrogance."[36] In the same spirit, I did not hesitate to say to the Aboriginal Peoples of Australia: "You do not have to be divided into two parts. . . . Jesus calls you to accept his words and his values into your own culture."[37] Because by its nature the content of faith is meant for all humanity, it must be translated into all cultures. Indeed, the element which determines communion in truth is *the meaning of truth*. The expression of truth can take different forms. The renewal of these forms of expression becomes necessary for the sake of transmitting to the people of today the Gospel message in its unchanging meaning.[38]

19.2 "This renewal therefore has notable ecumenical significance."[39] And not only renewal in which the faith is expressed, but also of the very life of faith. It might therefore be asked: who is responsible for doing this? To this question the Council replies clearly: "Concern for restoring unity pertains to the whole Church, faithful and clergy alike. It extends to everyone, according to the ability of each, whether it be exercised in daily Christian living or in theological and historical studies."[40]

[34] Encyclical Epistle *Slavorum Apostoli* (June 2, 1985), 11: *AAS* 77 (1985), 792.

[35] Ibid., 13: loc. cit., 794.

[36] Ibid., 11: loc. cit., 792.

[37] Address to the Indigenous Peoples, Alice Springs (November 29, 1986), 12: *AAS* 79 (1987), 977.

[38] Cf. Saint Vincent of Lerins, *Commonitorium Primum*, 23: *PL* 50, 667-668.

[39] Second Vatican Ecumenical Council, Decree on Ecumenism *Unitatis Redintegratio*, 6.

[40] Ibid., 5.

20.1 All this is extremely important and of fundamental significance for ecumenical activity. Thus it is absolutely clear that ecumenism, the movement promoting Christian unity, *is not just some sort of "appendix"* which is added to the Church's traditional activity. Rather, ecumenism is an organic part of her life and work, and consequently must pervade all that she is and does; it must be like the fruit borne by a healthy and flourishing tree which grows to its full stature.

20.2 This is what Pope John XXIII believed about the unity of the Church and how he saw full Christian unity. With regard to other Christians, to the great Christian family, he observed: "What unites us is much greater than what divides us." The Second Vatican Council for its part exhorts "all Christ's faithful to remember that the more purely they strive to live according to the Gospel, the more they are fostering and even practicing Christian unity. For they can achieve depth and ease in strengthening mutual brotherhood to the degree that they enjoy profound communion with the Father, the Word, and the Holy Spirit."[41]

The primacy of prayer

21.1 "This *change of heart and holiness of life, along with public and private prayer for the unity of Christians,* should be regarded as the soul of the whole ecumenical movement, and can rightly be called 'spiritual ecumenism.' "[42]

21.2 We proceed along the road leading to the conversion of hearts guided by love which is directed to God and, at the same time, to all our brothers and sisters, including those not in full communion with us. Love gives rise to the desire for unity, even in those who have never been aware of the need for it. Love builds communion between individuals and between Communities. If we love one another, we strive to deepen our communion and make it perfect. *Love is given to God* as the perfect source of communion — the unity of Father, Son and Holy Spirit — that we may draw from that source the strength to build communion between individuals and Communities or to reestablish it between Christians still divided. Love is the great undercurrent which gives life and adds vigor to the movement toward unity.

21.3 This love *finds its most complete expression in common prayer.* When brothers and sisters who are not in perfect communion with one another come together to pray, the Second Vatican Council defines their prayer as *the soul of the whole ecumenical movement.* This prayer is "a very effective means of petitioning for the grace of unity," "a *genuine expression of the ties which even*

[41] Ibid., 7.
[42] Ibid., 8.

now bind Catholics to their separated brethren."[43] Even when prayer is not specifically offered for Christian unity, but for other intentions such as peace, it actually becomes an expression and confirmation of unity. The common prayer of Christians is an invitation to Christ himself to visit the community of those who call upon him: "Where two or three are gathered in my name, there am I in the midst of them" (Mt 18:20).

22.1 When Christians pray together, the goal of unity seems closer. The long history of Christians marked by many divisions seems to converge once more because it tends toward that source of its unity which is Jesus Christ. He "is the same yesterday, today and forever!" (Heb 13:8). In the fellowship of prayer Christ is truly present; he prays "in us," "with us" and "for us." It is he who leads our prayer in the Spirit-Consoler whom he promised and then bestowed on his Church in the Upper Room in Jerusalem, when he established her in her original unity.

22.2 Along the ecumenical path to unity, pride of place certainly belongs to *common prayer,* the prayerful union of those who gather together around Christ himself. If Christians, despite their divisions, can grow ever more united in common prayer around Christ, they will grow in the awareness of how little divides them in comparison to what unites them. If they meet more often and more regularly before Christ in prayer, they will be able to gain the courage to face all the painful human reality of their divisions, and they will find themselves together once more in that community of the Church which Christ constantly builds up in the Holy Spirit, in spite of all weaknesses and human limitations.

23.1 Finally, *fellowship in prayer leads people to look at the Church and Christianity in a new way.* It must not be forgotten in fact that the Lord prayed to the Father that his disciples might be one, so that their unity might bear witness to his mission and the world would believe that the Father had sent him (cf. Jn 17:21). It can be said that the ecumenical movement in a certain sense was born out of the negative experience of each one of those who, in proclaiming the one Gospel, appealed to his own Church or Ecclesial Community. This was a contradiction which could not escape those who listened to the message of salvation and found in this fact an obstacle to acceptance of the Gospel. Regrettably, this grave obstacle has not been overcome. It is true that we are not yet in full communion. And yet, despite our divisions, we are on the way toward full unity, that unity which marked the Apostolic Church at its birth and which we sincerely seek. Our common prayer, inspired by

[43] Ibid., 8.

faith, is proof of this. In that prayer, we gather together in the name of Christ who is One. He is our unity.

23.2 *"Ecumenical" prayer is at the service of the Christian mission and its credibility.* It must thus be especially present in the life of the Church and in every activity aimed at fostering Christian unity. It is as if we constantly need to go back and meet in the Upper Room of Holy Thursday, even though our presence together in that place will not be perfect until the obstacles to full ecclesial communion are overcome and all Christians can gather together in the common celebration of the Eucharist.[44]

24 It is a source of joy to see that the many ecumenical meetings almost always include and indeed culminate in prayer. The *Week of Prayer for Christian Unity*, celebrated in January or, in some countries, around Pentecost, has become a widespread and well established tradition. But there are also many other occasions during the year when Christians are led to pray together. In this context I wish to mention the special experience of the *Pope's pilgrimages to the various Churches* in the different continents and countries of the present-day *oikoumene*. I am very conscious that it was the Second Vatican Council which led the Pope to exercise his apostolic ministry in this particular way. Even more can be said. The Council made these visits of the Pope a specific responsibility in carrying out the role of the Bishop of Rome at the service of communion.[45] My visits have almost always included an ecumenical meeting and *common prayer with our brothers and sisters who seek unity in Christ and in his Church*. With profound emotion I remember praying together with the Primate of the Anglican Communion at Canterbury Cathedral (May 29, 1982); in that magnificent edifice, I saw "an eloquent witness *both to our long years of common inheritance and to the sad years of division that followed.*"[46] Nor can I forget the meetings held in the Scandinavian and Nordic countries (June 1-10, 1989), in North and South America and in Africa, and at the headquarters of the World Council of Churches (June 12, 1984), the organization committed to calling its member Churches and Ecclesial Communities "to the goal of visible unity in one faith and in one Eucharistic fellowship expressed in worship and in common life in Christ."[47] And how could I ever forget taking part in the Eucharistic Liturgy in the Church of Saint George at the Ecumenical Pa-

---

[44] Cf. ibid., 4.

[45] Cf. John Paul II, Apostolic Letter *Tertio Millennio Adveniente* (November 10, 1994), 24: *AAS* 87 (1995), 19-20.

[46] Address at Canterbury Cathedral (May 29, 1982), 5: *AAS* 74 (1982), 922.

[47] World Council of Churches, *Constitution and Rules*, III, 1.

triarchate (November 30, 1979), and the service held in Saint Peter's Basilica during the visit to Rome of my Venerable Brother, Patriarch Dimitrios I (December 6, 1987)? On that occasion, at the Altar of the Confession, we recited together the Nicene-Constantinopolitan Creed according to its original Greek text. It is hard to describe in a few words the unique nature of each of these occasions of prayer. Given the differing ways in which each of these meetings was conditioned by past events, each had its own special eloquence. They have all become part of the Church's memory as she is guided by the Paraclete to seek the full unity of all believers in Christ.

25 It is not just the Pope who has become a pilgrim. In recent years, many distinguished leaders of other Churches and Ecclesial Communities have visited me in Rome, and I have been able to join them in prayer, both in public and in private. I have already mentioned the visit of the Ecumenical Patriarch Dimitrios I. I would now like to recall the prayer meeting, also held in Saint Peter's Basilica, at which I joined the Lutheran Archbishops, the Primates of Sweden and Finland, for the celebration of Vespers on the occasion of the sixth centenary of the canonization of Saint Birgitta (October 5, 1991). This is just one example, because awareness of the duty to pray for unity has become an integral part of the Church's life. There is no important or significant event which does not benefit from Christians coming together and praying. It is impossible for me to give a complete list of such meetings, even though each one deserves to be mentioned. Truly the Lord has taken us by the hand and is guiding us. These exchanges and these prayers have already written pages and pages of our "Book of unity," a "Book" which we must constantly return to and reread so as to draw from it new inspiration and hope.

26.1 Prayer, the community at prayer, enables us always to discover anew the evangelical truth of the words: *"You have one Father"* (Mt 23:9), the Father — *Abba* — invoked by Christ himself, the only-begotten and consubstantial Son. And again, *"You have one teacher, and you are all brethren"* (Mt 23:8). "Ecumenical" prayer discloses this fundamental dimension of brotherhood in Christ, who died to gather together the children of God who were scattered, so that in becoming "sons and daughters in the Son" (cf. Eph 1:5) we might show forth more fully both the mysterious reality of God's fatherhood and the truth about the human nature shared by each and every individual.

26.2 "Ecumenical" prayer, as the prayer of brothers and sisters, expresses all this. Precisely because they are separated from one another, they *meet in Christ* with all the more hope, *entrusting to him the future of their unity and their communion.* Here too we can appropriately apply the teaching of the

Council: "The Lord Jesus, when he prayed to the Father *'that all may be one . . . as we are one'* (Jn 17:21-22), opened up vistas closed to human reason. For he implied a certain likeness between the union of the divine persons, and the union of God's children in truth and charity."[48]

26.3 The change of heart which is the essential condition for every authentic search for unity flows from prayer and its realization is guided by prayer: "For it is from newness of attitudes, from self-denial and unstinted love, that yearnings for unity take their rise and grow toward maturity. We should therefore *pray to the divine Spirit* for the grace to be genuinely self-denying, humble, gentle in the service of others, and to have an attitude of brotherly generosity toward them."[49]

27 Praying for unity is not a matter reserved only to those who actually experience the lack of unity among Christians. In the deep personal dialogue which each of us must carry on with the Lord in prayer, concern for unity cannot be absent. Only in this way, in fact, will that concern fully become part of the reality of our life and of the commitments we have taken on in the Church. It was in order to reaffirm this duty that I set before the faithful of the Catholic Church a model which I consider exemplary, the model of a Trappistine sister, *Blessed Maria Gabriella of Unity,* whom I beatified on January 25, 1983.[50] Sister Maria Gabriella, called by her vocation to be apart from the world, devoted her life to meditation and prayer centered on chapter 17 of Saint John's Gospel, and offered her life for Christian unity. This is truly the cornerstone of all prayer: the total and unconditional offering of one's life to the Father, through the Son, in the Holy Spirit. The example of Sister Maria Gabriella is instructive; it helps us to understand that there are no special times, situations or places of prayer for unity. Christ's prayer to the Father is offered as a model for everyone, always and everywhere.

Ecumenical dialogue

28.1 If prayer is the "soul" of ecumenical renewal and of the yearning for unity, it is the basis and support for *everything the Council defines as "dialogue."* This definition is certainly not unrelated to today's *personalist way of*

---

[48] Second Vatican Ecumenical Council, Pastoral Constitution on the Church in the Modern World *Gaudium et Spes,* 24.

[49] Second Vatican Ecumenical Council, Decree on Ecumenism *Unitatis Redintegratio,* 7.

[50] Maria Sagheddu was born at Dorgali (Sardinia) in 1914. At twenty-one years of age she entered the Trappistine monastery in Grottaferrata. Through the apostolic labors of Abbé Paul Couturier, she came to understand the need for prayers and spiritual sacrifices for the unity of Christians. In 1936, at the time of an *Octave for Unity,* she chose to offer her life for the unity of the Church. Following a grave illness, Sister Maria Gabriella died on April 23, 1939.

thinking. The capacity for "dialogue" is rooted in the nature of the person and his dignity. As seen by philosophy, this approach is linked to the Christian truth concerning man as expressed by the Council: man is in fact "the only creature on earth which God willed for itself"; thus he cannot "fully find himself except through a sincere gift of himself."[51] Dialogue is an indispensable step along the path *toward human self-realization,* the self-realization both of *each individual* and *of every human community.* Although the concept of "dialogue" might appear to give priority to the cognitive dimension (*dia-logos*), all dialogue implies a global, existential dimension. It involves the human subject in his or her entirety; dialogue between Communities involves in a particular way the subjectivity of each.

28.2 This truth about dialogue, so profoundly expressed by Pope Paul VI in his Encyclical *Ecclesiam Suam,*[52] was also taken up by the Council in its teaching and ecumenical activity. Dialogue is not simply an exchange of ideas. In some way it is always an "exchange of gifts."[53]

29 For this reason, the Council's Decree on Ecumenism also emphasizes the importance of "every effort to eliminate words, judgments and actions which do not respond to the condition of separated brethren with truth and fairness and so make mutual relations between them more difficult."[54] The Decree approaches the question from the standpoint of the Catholic Church and refers to the criteria which she must apply in relation to other Christians. In all this, however, reciprocity is required. To follow these criteria is a commitment of each of the parties which desire to enter into dialogue, and it is a precondition for starting such dialogue. It is necessary to pass from antagonism and conflict to a situation where each party recognizes the other as a *partner.* When undertaking dialogue, *each side must presuppose in the other a desire for reconciliation,* for *unity in truth.* For this to happen, any display of mutual opposition must disappear. Only thus will dialogue help to overcome division and lead us closer to unity.

30 It can be said, with a sense of lively gratitude to the Spirit of truth, that the Second Vatican Council was a blessed time, during which the

[51] Second Vatican Ecumenical Council, Pastoral Constitution on the Church in the Modern World *Gaudium et Spes,* 24.

[52] Cf. *AAS* 56 (1964), 609-659.

[53] Cf. Second Vatican Ecumenical Council, Dogmatic Constitution on the Church *Lumen Gentium,* 13.

[54] Second Vatican Ecumenical Council, Decree on Ecumenism *Unitatis Redintegratio,* 4.

bases for the Catholic Church's participation in ecumenical dialogue were laid. At the same time, the presence of many observers from various Churches and Ecclesial Communities, their deep involvement in the events of the Council, the many meetings and the common prayer which the Council made possible also helped bring about *the conditions for dialogue with one another.* During the Council the representatives of other Churches and Ecclesial Communities experienced the readiness of the worldwide Catholic episcopate, and in particular of the Apostolic See, to engage in dialogue.

Local structures of dialogue

31 The Church's commitment to ecumenical dialogue, as it has clearly appeared since the Council, far from being the responsibility of the Apostolic See alone, is also the duty of individual local or particular Churches. Special commissions for fostering the ecumenical spirit and ecumenical activity have been set up by the Bishops' Conferences and the Synods of the Eastern Catholic Churches. Suitable structures similar to these are operating in individual Dioceses. These initiatives are a sign of the widespread practical commitment of the Catholic Church to apply the Council's guidelines on ecumenism: this is an essential aspect of the ecumenical movement.[55] Dialogue has not only been undertaken; it *has become an outright necessity, one of the Church's priorities.* As a result, the "methods" of dialogue have been improved, which in turn has helped the spirit of dialogue to grow. In this context mention has to be made in the first place of "dialogue between competent experts from different Churches and Communities. In their meetings, which are organized in a religious spirit, each explains the teaching of his Communion in greater depth and brings out clearly its distinctive features."[56] Moreover, it is useful for all the faithful to be familiar with the method which makes dialogue possible.

32.1 As the Council's Declaration on Religious Freedom affirms: "Truth is to be sought after in a manner proper to the dignity of the human person and his social nature. The inquiry is to be free, carried on with the aid of teaching or instruction, communication and dialogue. In the course of these, people explain to one another the truth they have discovered, or think they have discovered, in order thus to assist one another in the quest for truth. More-

[55] Cf. *Code of Canon Law,* Canon 755; *Code of Canons of the Eastern Churches,* Canons 902-904.

[56] Second Vatican Ecumenical Council, Decree on Ecumenism *Unitatis Redintegratio,* 4.

over, as the truth is discovered, it is by a personal assent that individuals are to adhere to it."[57]

32.2 Ecumenical dialogue is of essential importance. "Through such dialogue everyone gains a truer knowledge and *more just appreciation* of the teaching and religious life of both Communions. In addition, these Communions *cooperate more closely* in whatever projects a Christian conscience demands for the common good. They also come together for common prayer, where that is permitted. Finally, all are led to examine their own faithfulness to Christ's will for the Church and, wherever necessary, undertake with vigor the tasks of renewal and reform."[58]

Dialogue as an examination of conscience

33 In the Council's thinking, ecumenical dialogue is marked by a common quest for truth, particularly concerning the Church. In effect, truth forms consciences and directs efforts to promote unity. At the same time, it demands that the consciences and actions of Christians, as brethren divided from one another, should be inspired by and submissive to Christ's prayer for unity. There is a close relationship between prayer and dialogue. Deeper and more conscious prayer makes dialogue more fruitful. If, on the one hand, dialogue depends on prayer, so, in another sense, prayer also becomes the ever more mature fruit of dialogue.

34 Thanks to ecumenical dialogue we can speak of a greater maturity in our common prayer for one another. This is possible inasmuch as *dialogue also serves as an examination of conscience*. In this context, how can we fail to recall the words of the First Letter of John? "If we say we have no sin, we deceive ourselves, and the truth is not in us. If we confess our sins, God is faithful and just, and will forgive our sins and cleanse us from all unrighteousness" (1:8-9). John even goes so far as to state: "If we say that we have not sinned, we make him a liar, and his word is not in us" (1:10). *Such a radical exhortation to acknowledge our condition as sinners* ought also to mark the spirit which we bring to ecumenical dialogue. If such dialogue does not become an examination of conscience, a kind of "dialogue of consciences," can we count on the assurance which the First Letter of John gives us? "My little children, I am writing this to you so that you may not sin; but if any one does sin, *we have an advocate with the*

[57] Second Vatican Ecumenical Council, Declaration on Religious Freedom *Dignitatis Humanae*, 3.

[58] Second Vatican Ecumenical Council, Decree on Ecumenism *Unitatis Redintegratio*, 4.

Father, Jesus Christ the righteous; and he is the expiation for our sins, and not for ours only but also for the sins of the whole world" (2:1-2). All the sins of the world were gathered up in the saving sacrifice of Christ, including the sins committed against the Church's unity: the sins of Christians, those of the pastors no less than those of the lay faithful. Even after the many sins which have contributed to our historical divisions, *Christian unity is possible,* provided that we are humbly conscious of having sinned against unity and are convinced of our need for conversion. Not only personal sins must be forgiven and left behind, but also social sins, which is to say the sinful "structures" themselves which have contributed and can still contribute to division and to the reinforcing of division.

35 Here once again the Council proves helpful. It can be said that the entire Decree on Ecumenism is permeated by the spirit of conversion.[59] In the document, ecumenical dialogue takes on a specific characteristic; it becomes a *"dialogue of conversion,"* and thus, in the words of Pope Paul VI, an authentic "dialogue of salvation."[60] Dialogue cannot take place merely on a horizontal level, being restricted to meetings, exchanges of points of view or even the sharing of gifts proper to each Community. It has also a primarily vertical thrust, directed toward the One who, as the Redeemer of the world and the Lord of history, is himself our Reconciliation. This vertical aspect of dialogue lies in our acknowledgment, jointly and to each other, that we are men and women who have sinned. It is precisely this acknowledgment which creates in brothers and sisters living in Communities not in full communion with one another that interior space where Christ, the source of the Church's unity, can effectively act, with all the power of his Spirit, the Paraclete.

Dialogue as a means of resolving disagreements

36.1 Dialogue is also a natural instrument for comparing differing points of view and, above all, for examining those disagreements which hinder full communion between Christians. The Decree on Ecumenism dwells in the first place on a description of the attitudes under which doctrinal discussions should take place: "Catholic theologians engaged in ecumenical dialogue, while standing fast by the teaching of the Church and searching together with separated brothers and sisters into the divine mysteries, should act with love for truth, with charity, and with humility."[61]

[59] Cf. ibid., 4.
[60] Encyclical Letter *Ecclesiam Suam* (August 6, 1964), III: *AAS* 56 (1964), 642.
[61] Second Vatican Ecumenical Council, Decree on Ecumenism *Unitatis Redintegratio*, 11.

36.2 Love for the truth is the deepest dimension of any authentic quest for full communion between Christians. Without this love it would be impossible to face the objective theological, cultural, psychological and social difficulties which appear when disagreements are examined. This dimension, which is interior and personal, must be inseparably accompanied by a spirit of charity and humility. There must be charity toward one's partner in dialogue, and humility with regard to the truth which comes to light and which might require a review of assertions and attitudes.

36.3 With regard to the study of areas of disagreement, the Council requires that the whole body of doctrine be clearly presented. At the same time, it asks that the manner and method of expounding the Catholic faith should not be a hindrance to dialogue with our brothers and sisters.[62] Certainly it is possible to profess one's faith and to explain its teaching in a way that is correct, fair and understandable, and which at the same time takes into account both the way of thinking and the actual historical experiences of the other party.

36.4 Full communion of course will have to come about through the acceptance of the whole truth into which the Holy Spirit guides Christ's disciples. Hence all forms of reductionism or facile "agreement" must be absolutely avoided. Serious questions must be resolved, for if not, they will reappear at another time, either in the same terms or in a different guise.

37 The Decree *Unitatis Redintegratio* also indicates a criterion to be followed when Catholics are presenting or comparing doctrines: "They should remember that in Catholic teaching there exists an order or 'hierarchy' of truths, since they vary in their relationship to the foundation of the Christian faith. Thus the way will be opened for this kind of fraternal rivalry to incite all to a deeper realization and a clearer expression of the unfathomable riches of Christ."[63]

38.1 In dialogue, one inevitably comes up against the problem of the different formulations whereby doctrine is expressed in the various Churches and Ecclesial Communities. This has more than one consequence for the work of ecumenism.

38.2 In the first place, with regard to doctrinal formulations which differ from those normally in use in the community to which one belongs, it is certainly right to determine whether the words involved say the same thing. This has been

---

[62] Cf. ibid., 11.

[63] Ibid., 11; cf. Congregation for the Doctrine of the Faith, Declaration in Defense of Catholic Doctrine on the Church *Mysterium Ecclesiae* (June 24, 1973), 4: *AAS* 65 (1973), 402.

ascertained in the case, for example, of the recent common declarations signed by my Predecessors or by myself with the Patriarchs of Churches with which for centuries there have been disputes about Christology. As far as the formulation of revealed truths is concerned, the Declaration *Mysterium Ecclesiae* states: "Even though the truths which the Church intends to teach through her dogmatic formulas are distinct from the changeable conceptions of a given epoch and can be expressed without them, nevertheless it can sometimes happen that these truths may be enunciated by the sacred Magisterium in terms that bear traces of such conceptions. In view of this, it must be stated that the dogmatic *formulas* of the Church's Magisterium were from the very beginning suitable for communicating revealed truth, and that as they are they remain forever suitable for communicating this truth to those who interpret them correctly."[64] In this regard, ecumenical dialogue, which prompts the parties involved to question each other, to understand each other and to explain their positions to each other, makes surprising discoveries possible. Intolerant polemics and controversies have made incompatible assertions out of what was really the result of two different ways of looking at the same reality. Nowadays we need to find the formula which, by capturing the reality in its entirety, will enable us to move beyond partial readings and eliminate false interpretations.

38.3 One of the advantages of ecumenism is that it helps Christian Communities to discover the unfathomable riches of the truth. Here too, everything that the Spirit brings about in "others" can serve for the building up of all Communities[65] and in a certain sense instruct them in the mystery of Christ. Authentic ecumenism is a gift at the service of truth.

39 Finally, dialogue puts before the participants real and genuine disagreements in matters of faith. Above all, these disagreements should be faced in a sincere spirit of fraternal charity, of respect for the demands of one's own conscience and of the conscience of the other party, with profound humility and love for the truth. The examination of such disagreements has two essential points of reference: Sacred Scripture and the great Tradition of the Church. Catholics have the help of the Church's living Magisterium.

Practical cooperation

40.1 Relations between Christians are not aimed merely at mutual knowledge, common prayer and dialogue. They presuppose and from now on call

---

[64] Congregation for the Doctrine of the Faith, Declaration in Defense of Catholic Doctrine on the Church *Mysterium Ecclesiae* (June 24, 1973), 5: *AAS* 65 (1973), 403.

[65] Cf. Second Vatican Ecumenical Council, Decree on Ecumenism *Unitatis Redintegratio*, 4.

for every possible form of practical cooperation at all levels: pastoral, cultural and social, as well as that of witnessing to the Gospel message.[66]

40.2 "Cooperation among all Christians vividly expresses that bond which already unites them, and it sets in clearer relief the features of Christ the servant."[67] This cooperation based on our common faith is not only filled with fraternal communion, but is a manifestation of Christ himself.

40.3 Moreover, ecumenical cooperation is a true school of ecumenism, a dynamic road to unity. Unity of action leads to the full unity of faith: "Through such cooperation, all believers in Christ are able to learn easily how they can understand each other better and esteem each other more, and how the road to the unity of Christians may be made smooth."[68]

40.4 In the eyes of the world, cooperation among Christians becomes a form of common Christian witness and a means of evangelization which benefits all involved.

II

The Fruits of Dialogue

Brotherhood rediscovered

41.1 What has been said above about ecumenical dialogue since the end of the Council inspires us to give thanks to the Spirit of Truth promised by Christ the Lord to the Apostles and the Church (cf. Jn 14:26). It is the first time in history that efforts on behalf of Christian unity have taken on such great proportions and have become so extensive. This is truly an immense gift of God, one which deserves all our gratitude. From the fullness of Christ we receive "grace upon grace" (Jn 1:16). An appreciation of how much God has already given is the condition which disposes us to receive those gifts still indispensable for bringing to completion the ecumenical work of unity.

41.2 An overall view of the last thirty years enables us better to appreciate many of the fruits of this common conversion to the Gospel which the Spirit of God has brought about by means of the ecumenical movement.

42.1 It happens for example that, in the spirit of the Sermon on the Mount, Christians of one confession no longer consider other Christians as enemies

---

[66] Cf. Common Christological Declaration between the Catholic Church and the Assyrian Church of the East (November 11, 1994): *AAS* 87 (1995), 685-687.

[67] Second Vatican Ecumenical Council, Decree on Ecumenism *Unitatis Redintegratio*, 12.

[68] Ibid., 12.

or strangers but see them as brothers and sisters. Again, the very expression *separated brethren* tends to be replaced today by expressions which more readily evoke the deep communion — linked to the baptismal character — which the Spirit fosters in spite of historical and canonical divisions. Today we speak of "other Christians," "others who have received Baptism," and "Christians of other Communities." The *Directory for the Application of Principles and Norms on Ecumenism* refers to the Communities to which these Christians belong as "Churches and Ecclesial Communities that are not in full communion with the Catholic Church."[69] This broadening of vocabulary is indicative of a significant change in attitudes. There is an increased awareness that we all belong to Christ. I have personally been able many times to observe this during the ecumenical celebrations which are an important part of my apostolic visits to various parts of the world, and also in the meetings and ecumenical celebrations which have taken place in Rome. The "universal brotherhood" of Christians has become a firm ecumenical conviction. Consigning to oblivion the excommunications of the past, Communities which were once rivals are now in many cases helping one another: places of worship are sometimes lent out; scholarships are offered for the training of ministers in the Communities most lacking in resources; approaches are made to civil authorities on behalf of other Christians who are unjustly persecuted; and the slander to which certain groups are subjected is shown to be unfounded.

42.2 In a word, Christians have been converted to a fraternal charity which embraces all Christ's disciples. If it happens that, as a result of violent political disturbances, a certain aggressiveness or a spirit of vengeance appears, the leaders of the parties in question generally work to make the "New Law" of the spirit of charity prevail. Unfortunately, this spirit has not been able to transform every situation where brutal conflict rages. In such circumstances those committed to ecumenism are often required to make choices which are truly heroic.

42.3 It needs to be reaffirmed in this regard that acknowledging our brotherhood is not the consequence of a large-hearted philanthropy or a vague family spirit. It is rooted in recognition of the oneness of Baptism and the subsequent duty to glorify God in his work. The *Directory for the Application of Principles and Norms on Ecumenism* expresses the hope that Baptisms will be mutually and officially recognized.[70] This is something much more than an act of ecumenical courtesy; it constitutes a basic ecclesiological statement.

[69] Pontifical Council for Promoting Christian Unity, *Directory for the Application of Principles and Norms on Ecumenism* (March 25, 1993), 5: *AAS* 85 (1993), 1040.

[70] Ibid., 94: loc. cit., 1078.

42.4 It is fitting to recall that the fundamental role of Baptism in building up the Church has been clearly brought out thanks also to multilateral dialogues.[71]

Solidarity in the service of humanity

43.1 It happens more and more often that the leaders of Christian Communities join together in taking a stand in the name of Christ on important problems concerning man's calling and on freedom, justice, peace, and the future of the world. In this way they "communicate" in one of the tasks which constitutes the mission of Christians: that of reminding society of God's will in a realistic manner, warning the authorities and their fellow citizens against taking steps which would lead to the trampling of human rights. It is clear, as experience shows, that in some circumstances the united voice of Christians has more impact than any one isolated voice.

43.2 Nor are the leaders of Communities the only ones joined in the work for unity. Many Christians from all Communities, by reason of their faith, are jointly involved in bold projects aimed at changing the world by inculcating respect for the rights and needs of everyone, especially the poor, the lowly and the defenseless. In my Encyclical Letter *Sollicitudo Rei Socialis*, I was pleased to note this cooperation, stressing that the Catholic Church cannot fail to take part in these efforts.[72] In effect, Christians who once acted independently are now engaged together in the service of this cause, so that God's mercy may triumph.

43.3 This way of thinking and acting is already that of the Gospel. Hence, reaffirming what I wrote in my first Encyclical Letter *Redemptor Hominis*, I have had occasion "to insist on this point and to encourage every effort made in this direction, at all levels where we meet our other brother Christians."[73] I have thanked God "for what he has already accomplished in the other Churches and Ecclesial Communities and through them," as well as through the Catholic Church.[74] Today I see with satisfaction that the already vast network of ecumenical cooperation is constantly growing. Thanks also to the influence of the World Council of Churches, much is being accomplished in this field.

---

[71] Cf. Commission on Faith and Order of the World Council of Churches, *Baptism, Eucharist, Ministry* (January 1982), especially Nos. 1-23.

[72] Cf. Encyclical Letter *Sollicitudo Rei Socialis* (December 30, 1987), 32: *AAS* 80 (1988), 556.

[73] Address to the Cardinals and the Roman Curia (June 28, 1985), 10: *AAS* 77 (1985), 1158; cf. Encyclical Letter *Redemptor Hominis* (March 4, 1979), 11: *AAS* 71 (1979), 277-278.

[74] Address to the Cardinals and the Roman Curia (June 28, 1985), 10: *AAS* 77 (1985), 1158.

Approaching one another through the Word of God and through divine worship

44 Significant progress in ecumenical cooperation has also been made in another area, that of the Word of God. I am thinking above all of the importance for the different language groups of ecumenical translations of the Bible. Following the promulgation by the Second Vatican Council of the Constitution *Dei Verbum*, the Catholic Church could not fail to welcome this development.[75] These translations, prepared by experts, generally offer a solid basis for the prayer and pastoral activity of all Christ's followers. Anyone who recalls how heavily debates about Scripture influenced divisions, especially in the West, can appreciate the significant step forward which these common translations represent.

45.1 Corresponding to the liturgical renewal carried out by the Catholic Church, certain other Ecclesial Communities have made efforts to renew their worship. Some, on the basis of a recommendation expressed at the ecumenical level,[76] have abandoned the custom of celebrating their liturgy of the Lord's Supper only infrequently and have opted for a celebration each Sunday. Again, when the cycles of liturgical readings used by the various Christian Communities in the West are compared, they appear to be essentially the same. Still on the ecumenical level,[77] very special prominence has been given to the liturgy and liturgical signs (images, icons, vestments, light, incense, gestures). Moreover, in schools of theology where future ministers are trained, courses in the history and significance of the liturgy are beginning to be part of the curriculum in response to a newly discovered need.

45.2 These are signs of convergence which regard various aspects of the sacramental life. Certainly, due to disagreements in matters of faith, it is not yet possible to celebrate together the same Eucharistic Liturgy. And yet we do have a burning desire to join in celebrating the one Eucharist of the Lord, and this desire itself is already a common prayer of praise, a single supplication. Together we speak to the Father, and increasingly we do so "with one heart."

[75] Cf. Secretariat for Promoting Christian Unity and the Executive Committee of the United Bible Societies, *Guidelines for Interconfessional Cooperation in Translating the Bible* (1968). This was revised and published by the Secretariat for Promoting Christian Unity, *Information Service* 65 (1987), 140-145.

[76] Cf. Commission on Faith and Order of the World Council of Churches, *Baptism, Eucharist, Ministry* (January 1982).

[77] For example, at the most recent assemblies of the World Council of Churches in Vancouver (1983) and in Canberra (1991), and of the Commission on Faith and Order in Santiago de Compostela (1993).

At times it seems that we are closer to being able finally to seal this "real although not yet full" communion. A century ago who could even have imagined such a thing?

46 In this context, it is a source of joy to note that Catholic ministers are able, in certain particular cases, to administer the Sacraments of the Eucharist, Penance and Anointing of the Sick to Christians who are not in full communion with the Catholic Church but who greatly desire to receive these sacraments, freely request them and manifest the faith which the Catholic Church professes with regard to these sacraments. Conversely, in specific cases and in particular circumstances, Catholics too can request these same sacraments from ministers of Churches in which these sacraments are valid. The conditions for such reciprocal reception have been laid down in specific norms; for the sake of furthering ecumenism these norms must be respected.[78]

Appreciating the endowments present among other Christians

47 Dialogue does not extend exclusively to matters of doctrine but engages the whole person; it is also a dialogue of love. The Council has stated: "Catholics must joyfully acknowledge and esteem the truly Christian endowments from our common heritage which are to be found among our separated brothers and sisters. It is right and salutary to recognize the riches of Christ and virtuous works in the lives of others who are bearing witness to Christ, sometimes even to the shedding of their blood. For God is always wonderful in his works and worthy of admiration."[79]

48.1 The relationships which the members of the Catholic Church have established with other Christians since the Council have enabled us to discover what God is bringing about in the members of other Churches and Ecclesial Communities. This direct contact, at a variety of levels, with pastors and with the members of these Communities has made us aware of the witness which other Christians bear to God and to Christ. A vast new field has thus opened up for the whole ecumenical experience, which

---

[78] Cf. Second Vatican Ecumenical Council, Decree on Ecumenism *Unitatis Redintegratio*, 15; *Code of Canon Law*, Canon 844; *Code of Canons of the Eastern Churches*, Canon 671; Pontifical Council for Promoting Christian Unity, *Directory for the Application of Principles and Norms on Ecumenism* (March 25, 1993), 122-125, 129-131, 123 and 132: *AAS* 85 (1993), 1086-1087, 1088-1089, 1087 and 1089.

[79] Second Vatican Ecumenical Council, Decree on Ecumenism *Unitatis Redintegratio*, 4.

at the same time is the great challenge of our time. Is not the twentieth century a time of great witness, which extends "even to the shedding of blood"? And does not this witness also involve the various Churches and Ecclesial Communities which take their name from Christ, crucified and risen?

48.2 Such a joint witness of holiness, as fidelity to the one Lord, has an ecumenical potential extraordinarily rich in grace. The Second Vatican Council made it clear that elements present among other Christians can contribute to the edification of Catholics: "Nor should we forget that whatever is wrought by the grace of the Holy Spirit in the hearts of our separated brothers and sisters can contribute to our own edification. Whatever is truly Christian never conflicts with the genuine interests of the faith; indeed, it can always result in a more ample realization of the very mystery of Christ and the Church."[80] Ecumenical dialogue, as a true dialogue of salvation, will certainly encourage this process, which has already begun well, to advance toward true and full communion.

The growth of communion

49.1 A valuable result of the contacts between Christians and of the theological dialogue in which they engage is the growth of communion. Both contacts and dialogue have made Christians aware of the elements of faith which they have in common. This has served to consolidate further their commitment to full unity. In all of this, the Second Vatican Council remains a powerful source of incentive and orientation.

49.2 The Dogmatic Constitution *Lumen Gentium* links its teaching on the Catholic Church to an acknowledgment of the saving elements found in other Churches and Ecclesial Communities.[81] It is not a matter of becoming aware of static elements passively present in those Churches and Communities. Insofar as they are elements of the Church of Christ, these are by their nature a force for the reestablishment of unity. Consequently, the quest for Christian unity is not a matter of choice or expediency, but a duty which springs from the very nature of the Christian community.

49.3 In a similar way, the bilateral theological dialogues carried on with the major Christian Communities start from a recognition of the degree of communion already present, in order to go on to discuss specific areas of disagreement. The Lord has made it possible for Christians in our day to reduce the number of matters traditionally in dispute.

[80] Ibid., 4.
[81] Cf. No. 15.

Dialogue with the Churches of the East

50.1 In this regard, it must first be acknowledged, with particular gratitude to divine Providence, that our bonds with the Churches of the East, weakened in the course of the centuries, were strengthened through the Second Vatican Council. The observers from these Churches present at the Council, together with representatives of the Churches and Ecclesial Communities of the West, stated publicly, at that very solemn moment for the Catholic Church, their common willingness to seek the reestablishment of communion.

50.2 The Council, for its part, considered the Churches of the East with objectivity and deep affection, stressing their ecclesial nature and the real bonds of communion linking them with the Catholic Church. The Decree on Ecumenism points out: "Through the celebration of the Eucharist of the Lord in each of these Churches, the Church of God is built up and grows in stature." It adds, as a consequence, that "although these Churches are separated from us, they possess true sacraments, above all — by apostolic succession — the priesthood and the Eucharist, whereby they are still joined to us in a very close relationship."[82]

50.3 Speaking of the Churches of the East, the Council acknowledged their great liturgical and spiritual tradition, the specific nature of their historical development, the disciplines coming from the earliest times and approved by the holy Fathers and Ecumenical Councils, and their own particular way of expressing their teaching. The Council made this acknowledgement in the conviction that legitimate diversity is in no way opposed to the Church's unity, but rather enhances her splendor and contributes greatly to the fulfillment of her mission.

50.4 The Second Vatican Ecumenical Council wished to base dialogue on the communion which already exists, and it draws attention to the noble reality of the Churches of the East: "Therefore, this sacred Synod urges all, but especially those who plan to devote themselves to the work of restoring the full communion that is desired between the Eastern Churches and the Catholic Church, to give due consideration to these special aspects of the origin and growth of the Churches of the East, and to the character of the relations which obtained between them and the Roman See before the separation, and to form for themselves a correct evaluation of these facts."[83]

51.1 The Council's approach has proved fruitful both for the steady maturing of fraternal relations through the dialogue of charity, and for doctrinal

[82] No. 15.
[83] Ibid., 14.

discussion in the framework of the *Joint International Commission for the Theological Dialogue between the Catholic Church and the Orthodox Church*. It has likewise proved most fruitful in relations with the Ancient Churches of the East.

51.2 The process has been slow and arduous, yet a source of great joy; and it has been inspiring, for it has led to the gradual rediscovery of brotherhood.

Resuming contacts

52.1 With regard to the Church of Rome and the Ecumenical Patriarchate of Constantinople, the process which we have just mentioned began thanks to the mutual openness demonstrated by Popes John XXIII and Paul VI, on the one hand, and by the Ecumenical Patriarch Athenagoras I and his successors on the other. The resulting change found its historical expression in the ecclesial act whereby "there was removed from memory and from the midst of the Church"[84] the remembrance of the excommunications which 900 years before, in 1054, had become the symbol of the schism between Rome and Constantinople. That ecclesial event, so filled with ecumenical commitment, took place during the last days of the Council, on December 7, 1965. The Council thus ended with a solemn act which was at once a healing of historical memories, a mutual forgiveness, and a firm commitment to strive for communion.

52.2 This gesture had been preceded by the meeting of Pope Paul VI and Patriarch Athenagoras I in Jerusalem, in January 1964, during the Pope's pilgrimage to the Holy Land. At that time Pope Paul was also able to meet Benedictos, the Orthodox Patriarch of Jerusalem. Later Pope Paul visited Patriarch Athenagoras at the Phanar (Istanbul), on July 25, 1967, and in October of the same year the Patriarch was solemnly received in Rome. These prayer-filled meetings mapped out the path of rapprochement between the Church of the East and the Church of the West, and of the reestablishment of the unity they shared in the first millennium.

52.3 Following the death of Pope Paul VI and the brief Pontificate of Pope John Paul I, when the ministry of Bishop of Rome was entrusted to me, I considered it one of the first duties of my Pontificate to renew personal contact with the Ecumenical Patriarch Dimitrios I, who had meanwhile succeeded Patriarch Athenagoras in the See of Constantinople. During my visit to the Phanar on November 29, 1979, the Patriarch and I were able to decide to

---

[84] Cf. Joint Declaration of Pope Paul VI and the Patriarch of Constantinople Athenagoras I (December 7, 1965): *Tomos Agapis*, Vatican-Phanar (1958-1970), Rome-Istanbul, 1971, 280-281.

begin theological dialogue between the Catholic Church and all the Orthodox Churches in canonical communion with the See of Constantinople. In this regard it would seem important to add that at that time preparations were already under way for the convocation of a future Council of the Orthodox Churches. The quest for harmony between them contributes to the life and vitality of these sister Churches; this is also significant in view of the role they are called to play in the path toward unity. The Ecumenical Patriarch decided to repay my visit, and in December 1987 I had the joy of welcoming him to Rome with deep affection and with the solemnity due to him. It is in this context of ecclesial fraternity that we should mention the practice, which has now been in place for a number of years, of welcoming a delegation from the Ecumenical Patriarchate to Rome for the feast of the holy Apostles Peter and Paul, as well as the custom of sending a delegation of the Holy See to the Phanar for the solemn celebration of Saint Andrew.

53.1 Among other things, these regular contacts permit a direct exchange of information and opinions with a view to fostering fraternal coordination. Furthermore, taking part together in prayer accustoms us once more to living side by side and helps us in accepting and putting into practice the Lord's will for his Church.

53.2 On the path which we have traveled since the Second Vatican Council, at least two particularly telling events of great ecumenical significance for relations between East and West should be mentioned. The first of these was the 1984 Jubilee in commemoration of the eleventh centenary of the evangelizing activity of Saints Cyril and Methodius, an occasion which enabled me to proclaim the two holy Apostles of the Slavs, those heralds of faith, co-patrons of Europe. In 1964, during the Council, Pope Paul VI had already proclaimed Saint Benedict patron of Europe. Associating the two brothers from Thessalonica with the great founder of Western monasticism serves indirectly to highlight that twofold ecclesial and cultural tradition which has proved so significant for the two thousand years of Christianity which mark the history of Europe. Consequently it is worth recalling that Saints Cyril and Methodius came from the background of the Byzantine Church of their day, at a time when the latter was in communion with Rome. In proclaiming them patrons of Europe, together with Saint Benedict, it was my intention not only to reaffirm the historical truth about Christianity in Europe, but also to provide an important topic for the dialogue between East and West which has raised such high hopes in the period since the Council. As in Saint Benedict, so in Saints Cyril and Methodius, Europe can rediscover its spiritual roots. Now, as the second millennium since the birth of Christ draws to a close, they must be venerated *together,* as the patrons of our past and as the saints to whom the Churches and nations of Europe entrust their future.

54.1 The other event which I am pleased to recall is the celebration of the millennium of the Baptism of Rus' (988-1988). The Catholic Church, and this Apostolic See in particular, desired to take part in the Jubilee celebrations and also sought to emphasize that the Baptism conferred on Saint Vladimir in Kiev was a key event in the evangelization of the world. The great Slav nations of Eastern Europe owe their faith to this event, as do the peoples living beyond the Ural Mountains and as far as Alaska.

54.2 In this perspective an expression which I have frequently employed finds its deepest meaning: the Church must breathe with her two lungs! In the first millennium of the history of Christianity, this expression refers primarily to the relationship between Byzantium and Rome. From the time of the Baptism of Rus' it comes to have an even wider application: evangelization spread to a much vaster area, so that it now includes the entire Church. If we then consider that the salvific event which took place on the banks of the Dnieper goes back to a time when the Church in the East and the Church in the West were not divided, we understand clearly that the vision of the full communion to be sought is that of unity in legitimate diversity. This is what I strongly asserted in my Encyclical Letter *Slavorum Apostoli*[85] on Saints Cyril and Methodius and in my Apostolic Letter *Euntes in Mundum*[86] addressed to the faithful of the Catholic Church in commemoration of the millennium of the Baptism of Kievan Rus'.

Sister Churches

55.1 In its historical survey the Council Decree *Unitatis Redintegratio* has in mind the unity which, in spite of everything, was experienced in the first millennium and in a certain sense now serves as a kind of model. "This most sacred Synod gladly reminds all . . . that in the East there flourish many particular or local Churches; among them the patriarchal Churches hold first place; and of these, many glory in taking their origin from the Apostles themselves."[87] The Church's journey began in Jerusalem on the day of Pentecost and its original expansion in the *oikoumene* of that time was centered around Peter and the Eleven (cf. Acts 2:14). The structures of the Church in the East

---

[85] Cf. *AAS* 77 (1985), 779-813.
[86] Cf. *AAS* 80 (1988), 988-997.
[87] Second Vatican Ecumenical Council, Decree on Ecumenism *Unitatis Redintegratio,* 14.

and in the West evolved in reference to that apostolic heritage. Her unity during the first millennium was maintained within those same structures through the Bishops, Successors of the Apostles, in communion with the Bishop of Rome. If today at the end of the second millennium we are seeking to restore full communion, it is to that unity, thus structured, which we must look.

55.2 The Decree on Ecumenism highlights a further distinctive aspect, thanks to which all the particular Churches remained in unity: "an eager desire to perpetuate in a communion of faith and charity those family ties which ought to thrive between local Churches, as between sisters."[88]

56.1 Following the Second Vatican Council, and in the light of earlier tradition, it has again become usual to refer to the particular or local Churches gathered around their Bishop as "sister Churches." In addition, the lifting of the mutual excommunications, by eliminating a painful canonical and psychological obstacle, was a very significant step on the way toward full communion.

56.2 The structures of unity which existed before the separation are a heritage of experience that guides our common path toward the reestablishment of full communion. Obviously, during the second millennium the Lord has not ceased to bestow on his Church abundant fruits of grace and growth. Unfortunately, however, the gradual and mutual estrangement between the Churches of the West and the East deprived them of the benefits of mutual exchanges and cooperation. With the grace of God a great effort must be made to reestablish full communion among them, the source of such good for the Church of Christ. This effort calls for all our good will, humble prayer and a steadfast cooperation which never yields to discouragement. Saint Paul urges us: "Bear one another's burdens" (Gal 6:2). How appropriate and relevant for us is the Apostle's exhortation! The traditional designation of "sister Churches" should ever accompany us along this path.

57.1 In accordance with the hope expressed by Pope Paul VI, our declared purpose is to reestablish together full unity in legitimate diversity: "God has granted us to receive in faith what the Apostles saw, understood, and proclaimed to us. By Baptism 'we are *one in Christ Jesus*' (Gal 3:28). In virtue of the apostolic succession, we are united more closely by the priesthood and the Eucharist. By participating in the gifts of God to his Church we are brought into communion with the Father through the Son in the Holy Spirit. . . . In each local Church this mystery of divine love is enacted, and surely this is the

---

[88] Ibid., 14.

ground of the traditional and very beautiful expression 'sister Churches,' which local Churches were fond of applying to one another (cf. Decree, *Unitatis Redintegratio*, 14). For centuries we lived this life of 'sister Churches,' and together held Ecumenical Councils which guarded the deposit of faith against all corruption. And now, after a long period of division and mutual misunderstanding, the Lord is enabling us to discover ourselves as 'sister Churches' once more, in spite of the obstacles which were once raised between us."[89] If today, on the threshold of the third millennium, we are seeking the reestablishment of full communion, it is for the accomplishment of this reality that we must work and it is to this reality that we must refer.

57.2 Contact with this glorious tradition is most fruitful for the Church. As the Council points out: "From their very origins the Churches of the East have had a treasury from which the Church of the West has amply drawn for its liturgy, spiritual tradition and jurisprudence."[90]

57.3 Part of this "treasury" are also "the riches of those spiritual traditions to which monasticism gives special expression. From the glorious days of the holy Fathers, there flourished in the East that monastic spirituality which later flowed over into the Western world."[91] As I have had the occasion to emphasize in my recent Apostolic Letter *Orientale Lumen*, the Churches of the East have lived with great generosity the commitment shown by monastic life, "starting with evangelization, the highest service that the Christian can offer his brother, followed by many other forms of spiritual and material service. Indeed it can be said that monasticism in antiquity — and at various times in subsequent ages too — has been the privileged means for the evangelization of peoples."[92]

57.4 The Council does not limit itself to emphasizing the elements of similarity between the Churches in the East and in the West. In accord with historical truth, it does not hesitate to say: "It is hardly surprising if sometimes one tradition has come nearer than the other to an apt appreciation of certain aspects of the revealed mystery or has expressed them in a clearer manner. As a result, these various theological formulations are often to be considered as complementary rather than conflicting."[93] Communion is made fruitful by the exchange of gifts between the Churches insofar as they complement each other.

---

[89] Apostolic Brief *Anno Ineunte* (July 25, 1967): *Tomos Agapis*, Vatican-Phanar (1958-1970), Rome-Istanbul, 1971, 388-391.

[90] Second Vatican Ecumenical Council, Decree on Ecumenism *Unitatis Redintegratio*, 14.

[91] Ibid., 15.

[92] No. 14: *AAS* 87 (1995), 760-761.

[93] Second Vatican Ecumenical Council, Decree on Ecumenism *Unitatis Redintegratio*, 17.

58.1 From the reaffirmation of an already existing communion of faith, the Second Vatican Council drew pastoral consequences which are useful for the everyday life of the faithful and for the promotion of the spirit of unity. By reason of the very close sacramental bonds between the Catholic Church and the Orthodox Churches, the Decree on Eastern Catholic Churches *Orientalium Ecclesiarum,* has stated: "Pastoral experience clearly shows that with respect to our Eastern brethren there should and can be taken into consideration various circumstances affecting individuals, wherein the unity of the Church is not jeopardized nor are intolerable risks involved, but in which salvation itself and the spiritual profit of souls are urgently at issue. Hence, in view of special circumstances of time, place and personage, the Catholic Church has often adopted and now adopts a milder policy, offering to all the means of salvation and an example of charity among Christians through participation in the sacraments and in other sacred functions and objects."[94]

58.2 In the light of experience gained in the years following the Council, this theological and pastoral orientation has been incorporated into the two Codes of Canon Law.[95] It has been explicitly treated from the pastoral standpoint in the *Directory for the Application of Principles and Norms on Ecumenism.*[96]

58.3 In so important and sensitive a matter, it is necessary for Pastors to instruct the faithful with care, making them clearly aware of the specific reasons both for this sharing in liturgical worship and for the various regulations which govern it.

58.4 There must never be a loss of appreciation for the ecclesiological implication of sharing in the sacraments, especially in the Holy Eucharist.

Progress in dialogue

59 Since its establishment in 1979, the *Joint International Commission for the Theological Dialogue between the Catholic Church and the Orthodox Church* has worked steadily, directing its study to areas decided upon by mutual agreement, with the purpose of reestablishing full communion between the two Churches. This communion which is founded on the unity of faith, following in the footsteps of the experience and tradition of the ancient Church, will find its fulfillment in the common celebration of the Holy Eucharist. In a

---

[94] No. 26.

[95] Cf. *Code of Canon Law,* Canon 844 §§2 and 3; *Code of Canons of the Eastern Churches,* Canon 671 §§2 and 3.

[96] Pontifical Council for Promoting Christian Unity, *Directory for the Application of Principles and Norms on Ecumenism* (March 25, 1993), 122-128: AAS 85 (1993), 1086-1088.

positive spirit, and on the basis of what we have in common, the Joint Commission has been able to make substantial progress and, as I was able to declare in union with my Venerable Brother, His Holiness Dimitrios I, the Ecumenical Patriarch, it has concluded "that the Catholic Church and the Orthodox Church can already profess together that common faith in the mystery of the Church and the bond between faith and sacraments."[97] The Commission was then able to acknowledge that "in our Churches apostolic succession is fundamental for the sanctification and the unity of the People of God."[98] These are important points of reference for the continuation of the dialogue. Moreover, these joint affirmations represent the basis for Catholics and Orthodox to be able from now on to bear a faithful and united common witness in our time, that the name of the Lord may be proclaimed and glorified.

60.1 More recently, the Joint International Commission took a significant step forward with regard to the very sensitive question of the method to be followed in reestablishing full communion between the Catholic Church and the Orthodox Church, an issue which has frequently embittered relations between Catholics and Orthodox. The Commission has laid the doctrinal foundations for a positive solution to this problem on the basis of the doctrine of sister Churches. Here too it has become evident that the method to be followed toward full communion is the dialogue of truth, fostered and sustained by the dialogue of love. A recognition of the right of the Eastern Catholic Churches to have their own organizational structures and to carry out their own apostolate, as well as the actual involvement of these Churches in the dialogue of charity and in theological dialogue, will not only promote a true and fraternal mutual esteem between Orthodox and Catholics living in the same territory, but will also foster their joint commitment to work for unity.[99] A step forward has been taken. The commitment must continue. Already there are signs of a lessening of tensions, which is making the quest for unity more fruitful.

[97] Declaration by His Holiness Pope John Paul II and the Ecumenical Patriarch Dimitrios I (December 7, 1987): *AAS* 80 (1988), 253.

[98] Joint International Commission for the Theological Dialogue between the Catholic Church and the Orthodox Church, *The Sacrament of Order in the Sacramental Structure of the Church, in Particular the Importance of Apostolic Succession for the Sanctification and Unity of the People of God* (June 26, 1988), 1: *Information Service* 68 (1988), 173.

[99] Cf. John Paul II, Letter to the Bishops of Europe on the Relations between Catholics and Orthodox in the New Situation of Central and Eastern Europe (May 31, 1991), 6: *AAS* 84 (1992), 168.

60.2 With regard to the Eastern Catholic Churches in communion with the Catholic Church, the Council expressed its esteem in these terms: "While thanking God that many Eastern sons of the Catholic Church . . . are already living in full communion with their brethren who follow the tradition of the West, this sacred Synod declares that this entire heritage of spirituality and liturgy, of discipline and theology, in their various traditions, belongs to the full catholic and apostolic character of the Church."[100] Certainly the Eastern Catholic Churches, in the spirit of the Decree on Ecumenism, will play a constructive role in the dialogue of love and in the theological dialogue at both the local and international levels, and thus contribute to mutual understanding and the continuing pursuit of full unity.[101]

61 In view of all this, the Catholic Church desires nothing less than full communion between East and West. She finds inspiration for this in the experience of the first millennium. In that period, indeed, "the development of different experiences of ecclesial life did not prevent Christians, through mutual relations, from continuing to feel certain that they were at home in any Church, because praise of the one Father, through Christ in the Holy Spirit, rose from them all, in a marvelous variety of languages and melodies; all were gathered together to celebrate the Eucharist, the heart and model for the community regarding not only spirituality and the moral life, but also the Church's very structure, in the variety of ministries and services under the leadership of the Bishop, Successor of the Apostles. The first Councils are an eloquent witness to this enduring unity in diversity."[102] How can unity be restored after almost a thousand years? This is the great task which the Catholic Church must accomplish, a task equally incumbent on the Orthodox Church. Thus can be understood the continuing relevance of dialogue, guided by the light and strength of the Holy Spirit.

Relations with the Ancient Churches of the East

62.1 In the period following the Second Vatican Council, the Catholic Church has also, in different ways and with greater or lesser rapidity, restored fraternal relations with the Ancient Churches of the East which rejected the dogmatic formulations of the Councils of Ephesus and Chalcedon. All these Churches sent official observers to the Second Vatican Council; their Patriarchs have honored us by their visits, and the Bishop of Rome has been able

---

[100] Second Vatican Ecumenical Council, Decree on Ecumenism *Unitatis Redintegratio*, 17.
[101] Cf. Apostolic Letter *Orientale Lumen* (May 2, 1995), 24: *AAS* 87 (1995), 771.
[102] Ibid., 18: loc. cit., 764-765.

to converse with them as with brothers who, after a long time, joyfully meet again.

62.2 The return of fraternal relations with the Ancient Churches of the East witnesses to the Christian faith in situations which are often hostile and tragic. This is a concrete sign of how we are united in Christ in spite of historical, political, social and cultural barriers. And precisely in relation to Christology, we have been able to join the Patriarchs of some of these Churches in declaring our common faith in Jesus Christ, true God and true man. Pope Paul VI of venerable memory signed declarations to this effect with His Holiness Shenouda III, the Coptic Orthodox Pope and Patriarch,[103] and with His Beatitude Jacoub III, the Syrian Orthodox Patriarch of Antioch.[104] I myself have been able to confirm this Christological agreement and draw on it for the development of dialogue with Pope Shenouda,[105] and for pastoral cooperation with the Syrian Patriarch of Antioch Mor Ignatius Zakka I Iwas.[106]

62.3 When the Venerable Patriarch of the Ethiopian Church, Abuna Paulos, paid me a visit in Rome on June 11, 1993, together we emphasized the deep communion existing between our two Churches: "We share the faith handed down from the Apostles, as also the same sacraments and the same ministry, rooted in the apostolic succession. . . . Today, moreover, we can affirm that we have the one faith in Christ, even though for a long time this was a source of division between us."[107]

62.4 More recently, the Lord has granted me the great joy of signing a common Christological declaration with the Assyrian Patriarch of the East, His Holiness Mar Dinkha IV, who for this purpose chose to visit me in Rome in November 1994. Taking into account the different theological formulations, we were able to profess together the true faith in Christ.[108] I wish to express

---

[103] Cf. Joint Declaration by His Holiness Pope Paul VI and His Holiness Shenouda III, Pope of Alexandria and Patriarch of the See of Saint Mark of Alexandria (May 10, 1973): *AAS* 65 (1973), 299-301.

[104] Cf. Joint Declaration by His Holiness Pope Paul VI and His Beatitude Mar Ignatius Jacoub III, Patriarch of the Church of Antioch of the Syrians (October 27, 1971): *AAS* 63 (1971), 814-815.

[105] Cf. Address to the Delegates of the Coptic Orthodox Church (June 2, 1979): *AAS* 71 (1979), 1000-1001.

[106] Cf. Joint Declaration of Pope John Paul II and the Syrian-Orthodox Patriarch of Antioch, Moran Mor Ignatius Zakka I Iwas (June 23, 1984): *Insegnamenti* VII/1 (1984), 1902-1906.

[107] Address to His Holiness Abuna Paulos, Patriarch of the Orthodox Church of Ethiopia (June 11, 1993), 2: *Insegnamenti* XVI/1 (1993), 1473.

[108] Cf. Common Christological Declaration between the Catholic Church and the Assyrian Church of the East (November 11, 1994): *AAS* 87 (1995), 685-687.

my joy at all this in the words of the Blessed Virgin: "My soul proclaims the greatness of the Lord" (Lk 1:46).

63 Ecumenical contacts have thus made possible essential clarifications with regard to the traditional controversies concerning Christology, so much so that we have been able to profess together the faith which we have in common. Once again it must be said that this important achievement is truly a fruit of theological investigation and fraternal dialogue. And not only this. It is an encouragement for us: for it shows us that the path followed is the right one and that we can reasonably hope to discover together the solution to other disputed questions.

Dialogue with other Churches and Ecclesial Communities in the West

64.1 In its great plan for the reestablishment of unity among all Christians, the Decree on Ecumenism also speaks of relations with the Churches and Ecclesial Communities of the West. Wishing to create a climate of Christian fraternity and dialogue, the Council situates its guidelines in the context of two general considerations: one of an historical and psychological nature, and the other theological and doctrinal. On the one hand, this Decree affirms: "The Churches and Ecclesial Communities which were separated from the Apostolic See of Rome during the very serious crisis that began in the West at the end of the Middle Ages, or during later times, are bound to the Catholic Church by a special affinity and close relationship in view of the long span of earlier centuries when the Christian people lived in ecclesiastical communion."[109] On the other hand, with equal realism the same Document states: "At the same time one should recognize that between these Churches and Communities on the one hand, and the Catholic Church on the other, there are very weighty differences not only of an historical, sociological, psychological and cultural nature, but especially in the interpretation of revealed truth."[110]

65.1 Common roots and similar, if distinct, considerations have guided the development in the West of the Catholic Church and of the Churches and Communities which have their origins in the Reformation. Consequently these share the fact that they are "Western" in character. Their "diversities," although significant as has been pointed out, do not therefore preclude mutual interaction and complementarity.

[109] Second Vatican Ecumenical Council, Decree on Ecumenism *Unitatis Redintegratio*, 19.
[110] Ibid., 19.

65.2 The ecumenical movement really began within the Churches and Ecclesial Communities of the Reform. At about the same time, in January 1920, the Ecumenical Patriarchate expressed the hope that some kind of co-operation among the Christian Communions could be organized. This fact shows that the weight of cultural background is not the decisive factor. What is essential is the question of faith. The prayer of Christ, our one Lord, Redeemer and Master, speaks to everyone in the same way, both in the East and in the West. That prayer becomes an imperative to leave behind our divisions in order to seek and reestablish unity, as a result also of the bitter experiences of division itself.

66.1 The Second Vatican Council did not attempt to give a "description" of post-Reformation Christianity, since "in origin, teaching and spiritual practice these Churches and Ecclesial Communities differ not only from us but also among themselves to a considerable degree."[111] Furthermore, the Decree observes that the ecumenical movement and the desire for peace with the Catholic Church have not yet taken root everywhere.[112] These circumstances notwithstanding, the Council calls for dialogue.

66.2 The Council Decree then seeks to "propose . . . some considerations which can and ought to serve as a basis and motivation for such dialogue."[113]

66.3 "Our thoughts are concerned . . . with those Christians who openly confess Jesus Christ as God and Lord and as the sole Mediator between God and man unto the glory of the one God, Father, Son and Holy Spirit."[114]

66.4 These brothers and sisters promote love and veneration for the Sacred Scriptures: "Calling upon the Holy Spirit, they seek in these Sacred Scriptures God as he speaks to them in Christ, the one whom the Prophets foretold, God's Word made flesh for us. In the Scriptures they contemplate the life of Christ, as well as the teachings and the actions of the divine Master on behalf of the salvation of all, in particular the mysteries of his Death and Resurrection. . . . They affirm the divine authority of the Sacred Books."[115]

66.5 At the same time, however, they "think differently from us . . . about the relationship between the Scriptures and the Church. In the Church, according to Catholic belief, an authentic teaching office plays a special role in the explanation and proclamation of the written Word of God."[116] Even so, "in

[111] Ibid., 19.
[112] Cf. ibid., 19.
[113] Ibid., 19.
[114] Ibid., 20.
[115] Ibid., 21.
[116] Ibid., 21.

[ecumenical] dialogue itself, the sacred utterances are precious instruments in the mighty hand of God for attaining that unity which the Savior holds out to all."[117]

66.6 Furthermore, the Sacrament of Baptism, which we have in common, represents "a sacramental bond of unity linking all who have been reborn by means of it."[118] The theological, pastoral and ecumenical implications of our common Baptism are many and important. Although this sacrament of itself is "only a beginning, a point of departure," it is "oriented toward a complete profession of faith, a complete incorporation into the system of salvation such as Christ himself willed it to be and, finally, toward a complete participation in Eucharistic communion."[119]

67.1 Doctrinal and historical disagreements at the time of the Reformation emerged with regard to the Church, the sacraments and the ordained ministry. The Council therefore calls for "dialogue to be undertaken concerning the true meaning of the Lord's Supper, the other sacraments and the Church's worship and ministry."[120]

67.2 The Decree *Unitatis Redintegratio*, pointing out that the post-Reformation Communities lack that "fullness of unity with us which should flow from Baptism," observes that "especially because of the lack of the Sacrament of Orders they have not preserved the genuine and total reality of the Eucharistic mystery," even though "when they commemorate the Lord's death and Resurrection in the Holy Supper, they profess that it signifies life in communion with Christ and they await his coming in glory."[121]

68.1 The Decree does not overlook the spiritual life and its moral consequences: "The Christian way of life of these brethren is nourished by faith in Christ. It is strengthened by the grace of Baptism and the hearing of God's Word. This way of life expresses itself in private prayer, in meditation on the Bible, in Christian family life and in services of worship offered by Communities assembled to praise God. Furthermore, their worship sometimes displays notable features of the ancient, common liturgy."[122]

68.2 The Council document moreover does not limit itself to these spiritual, moral and cultural aspects but extends its appreciation to the lively

[117] Ibid., 21.
[118] Ibid., 22.
[119] Ibid., 22.
[120] Ibid., 22; cf. 20.
[121] Ibid., 22.
[122] Ibid., 23.

sense of justice and to the sincere charity toward others which are present among these brothers and sisters. Nor does it overlook their efforts to make social conditions more humane and to promote peace. All this is the result of a sincere desire to be faithful to the Word of Christ as the source of Christian life.

68.3 The text thus raises a series of questions which, in the area of ethics and morality, is becoming ever more urgent in our time: "There are many Christians who do not always understand the Gospel in the same way as Catholics."[123] In this vast area there is much room for dialogue concerning the moral principles of the Gospel and their implications.

69.1 The hopes and invitation expressed by the Second Vatican Council have been acted upon, and bilateral theological dialogue with the various worldwide Churches and Christian Communities in the West has been progressively set in motion.

69.2 Moreover, with regard to multilateral dialogue, as early as 1964 the process of setting up a "Joint Working Group" with the World Council of Churches was begun, and since 1968 Catholic theologians have been admitted as full members of the theological department of the Council, the Commission on Faith and Order.

69.3 This dialogue has been and continues to be fruitful and full of promise. The topics suggested by the Council Decree have already been addressed, or will be in the near future. The reflections of the various bilateral dialogues, conducted with a dedication which deserves the praise of all those committed to ecumenism, have concentrated on many disputed questions such as Baptism, the Eucharist, the ordained ministry, the sacramentality and authority of the Church, and apostolic succession. As a result, unexpected possibilities for resolving these questions have come to light, while at the same time there has been a realization that certain questions need to be studied more deeply.

70.1 This difficult and delicate research, which involves questions of faith and respect for one's own conscience as well as for the consciences of others, has been accompanied and sustained by the prayer of the Catholic Church and of the other Churches and Ecclesial Communities. Prayer for unity, already so deeply rooted in and spread throughout the body of the Church, shows that Christians do indeed see the importance of ecumenism. Precisely because the search for full unity requires believers to question one another in

[123] Ibid., 23.

relation to their faith in the one Lord, prayer is the source of enlightenment concerning the truth which has to be accepted in its entirety.

70.2 Moreover, through prayer the quest for unity, far from being limited to a group of specialists, comes to be shared by all the baptized. Everyone, regardless of their role in the Church or level of education, can make a valuable contribution, in a hidden and profound way.

Ecclesial relations

71.1 We must give thanks to divine Providence also for all the events which attest to progress on the path to unity. Besides theological dialogue, mention should be made of other forms of encounter, common prayer and practical cooperation. Pope Paul VI strongly encouraged this process by his visit to the headquarters of the World Council of Churches in Geneva on June 10, 1969, and by his many meetings with representatives of various Churches and Ecclesial Communities. Such contacts greatly help to improve mutual knowledge and to increase Christian fraternity.

71.2 Pope John Paul I, during his very brief Pontificate, expressed the desire to continue on this path.[124] The Lord has enabled me to carry on this work. In addition to important ecumenical meetings held in Rome, a significant part of my pastoral visits is regularly devoted to fostering Christian unity. Some of my journeys have a precise ecumenical "priority," especially in countries where the Catholic Communities constitute a minority with respect to the post-Reformation Communities or where the latter represent a considerable portion of the believers in Christ in a given society.

72.1 This is true above all for the European countries, in which these divisions first appeared, and for North America. In this regard, without wishing to minimize the other visits, I would especially mention those within Europe which took me twice to Germany, in November 1980 and in April-May 1987; to the United Kingdom (England, Scotland and Wales) in May-June 1982; to Switzerland in June 1984; and to the Scandinavian and Nordic countries (Finland, Sweden, Norway, Denmark and Iceland) in June 1989. In an atmosphere of joy, mutual respect, Christian solidarity and prayer I met so very many brothers and sisters, all making a committed effort to be faithful to the Gospel. Seeing all this has been for me a great source of encouragement. We experienced the Lord's presence among us.

72.2 In this respect I would like to mention one demonstration dictated by fraternal charity and marked by deep clarity of faith which made a profound

---

[124] Cf. Radio Message *Urbi et Orbi* (August 27, 1978): *AAS* 70 (1978), 695-696.

impression on me. I am speaking of the Eucharistic celebrations at which I presided in Finland and Sweden during my journey to the Scandinavian and Nordic countries. At Communion time, the Lutheran Bishops approached the celebrant. They wished, by means of an agreed gesture, to demonstrate their desire for that time when we, Catholics and Lutherans, will be able to share the same Eucharist, and they wished to receive the celebrant's blessing. With love I blessed them. The same gesture, so rich in meaning, was repeated in Rome at the Mass at which I presided in Piazza Farnese, on the sixth centenary of the canonization of Saint Birgitta of Sweden, on October 6, 1991.

72.3 I have encountered similar sentiments on the other side of the ocean also: in Canada, in September 1984; and particularly in September 1987 in the United States, where one notices a great ecumenical openness. This was the case, to give one example, of the ecumenical meeting held at Columbia, South Carolina, on September 11, 1987. The very fact that such meetings regularly take place between the Pope and these brothers and sisters whose Churches and Ecclesial Communities originate in the Reformation is important in itself. I am deeply grateful for the warm reception which I have received both from the leaders of the various Communities and from the Communities as a whole. From this standpoint, I consider significant the ecumenical celebration of the Word held in Columbia on the theme of the family.

73 It is also a source of great joy to observe how in the postconciliar period and in the local Churches many programs and activities on behalf of Christian unity are in place, programs and activities which have a stimulating effect at the level of Episcopal Conferences, individual Dioceses and parishes, and at the level of the various ecclesial organizations and movements.

Achievements of cooperation

74.1 "Not every one who says to me, 'Lord, Lord,' will enter the Kingdom of heaven, but he who does the will of my Father who is in heaven" (Mt 7:21). The consistency and honesty of intentions and of statements of principles are verified by their application to real life. The Council Decree on Ecumenism notes that among other Christians "the faith by which they believe in Christ bears fruit in praise and thanksgiving for the benefits received from the hands of God. Joined to it are a lively sense of justice and a true neighborly charity."[125]

74.2 What has just been outlined is fertile ground not only for dialogue but also for practical cooperation: "Active faith has produced many organizations for the relief of spiritual and bodily distress, the education of youth, the ad-

---

[125] Second Vatican Ecumenical Council, Decree on Ecumenism *Unitatis Redintegratio*, 23.

vancement of humane social conditions and the promotion of peace throughout the world."[126]

74.3 Social and cultural life offers ample opportunities for ecumenical cooperation. With increasing frequency Christians are working together to defend human dignity, to promote peace, to apply the Gospel to social life, to bring the Christian spirit to the world of science and of the arts. They find themselves ever more united in striving to meet the sufferings and the needs of our time: hunger, natural disasters and social injustice.

75.1 For Christians, this cooperation, which draws its inspiration from the Gospel itself, is never mere humanitarian action. It has its reason for being in the Lord's words: "For I was hungry and you gave me food" (Mt 25:35). As I have already emphasized, the cooperation among Christians clearly manifests that degree of communion which already exists among them.[127]

75.2 Before the world, united action in society on the part of Christians has the clear value of a joint witness to the name of the Lord. It is also a form of proclamation, since it reveals the face of Christ.

75.3 The doctrinal disagreements which remain exercise a negative influence and even place limits on cooperation. Still, the communion of faith which already exists between Christians provides a solid foundation for their joint action not only in the social field but also in the religious sphere.

75.4 Such cooperation will facilitate the quest for unity. The Decree on Ecumenism noted that "through such cooperation all believers in Christ are able to learn easily how they can understand each other better and esteem each other more, and how the road to the unity of Christians may be made smooth."[128]

76.1 In this context, how can I fail to mention the ecumenical interest in peace, expressed in prayer and action by ever greater numbers of Christians and with a steadily growing theological inspiration? It could not be otherwise. Do we not believe in Jesus Christ, the Prince of Peace? Christians are becoming ever more united in their rejection of violence, every kind of violence, from wars to social injustice.

76.2 We are called to make ever greater efforts, so that it may be ever more apparent that religious considerations are not the real cause of current conflicts, even though, unfortunately, there is still a risk of religion being exploited for political and polemical purposes.

76.3 In 1986, at Assisi, during the *World Day of Prayer for Peace*, Chris-

---

[126] Ibid., 23.
[127] Cf. ibid., 12.
[128] Ibid., 12.

tians of the various Churches and Ecclesial Communities prayed with one voice to the Lord of history for peace in the world. That same day, in a different but parallel way, Jews and representatives of non-Christian religions also prayed for peace in a harmonious expression of feelings which struck a resonant chord deep in the human spirit.

76.4 Nor do I wish to overlook the *Day of Prayer for Peace in Europe, especially in the Balkans,* which took me back to the town of Saint Francis as a pilgrim on January 9-10, 1993, and the *Mass for Peace in the Balkans and especially in Bosnia-Herzegovina,* which I celebrated on January 23, 1994, in Saint Peter's Basilica during the *Week of Prayer for Unity.*

76.5 When we survey the world, joy fills our hearts. For we note that Christians feel ever more challenged by the issue of peace. They see it as intimately connected with the proclamation of the Gospel and with the coming of God's Kingdom.

III
Quanta Est Nobis Via?

Continuing and deepening dialogue

77.1 We can now ask how much further we must travel until that blessed day when full unity in faith will be attained and we can celebrate together in peace the Holy Eucharist of the Lord. The greater mutual understanding and the doctrinal convergences already achieved between us, which have resulted in an affective and effective growth of communion, cannot suffice for the conscience of Christians who profess that the Church is one, holy, catholic and apostolic. The ultimate goal of the ecumenical movement is to reestablish full visible unity among all the baptized.

77.2 In view of this goal, all the results so far attained are but one stage of the journey, however promising and positive.

78.1 In the ecumenical movement, it is not only the Catholic Church and the Orthodox Churches which hold to this demanding concept of the unity willed by God. The orientation toward such unity is also expressed by others.[129]

---

[129] The steady work of the Commission on Faith and Order has led to a comparable vision adopted by the Seventh Assembly of the World Council of Churches in the Canberra Declaration (February 7-20, 1991); cf. *Signs of the Spirit,* Official Report, Seventh Assembly, WCC, Geneva, 1991, 235-258. This vision was reaffirmed by the World Conference on Faith and Order at Santiago de Compostela (August 3-4, 1993): cf. *Information Service* 85 (1994), 18-37.

78.2 Ecumenism implies that the Christian Communities should help one another so that there may be truly present in them the full content and all the requirements of "the heritage handed down by the Apostles."[130] Without this, full communion will never be possible. This mutual help in the search for truth is a sublime form of evangelical charity.

78.3 The documents of the many International Mixed Commissions of dialogue have expressed this commitment to seeking unity. On the basis of a certain fundamental doctrinal unity, these texts discuss Baptism, Eucharist, ministry and authority.

78.4 From this basic but partial unity it is now necessary to advance toward the visible unity which is required and sufficient, and which is manifested in a real and concrete way, so that the Churches may truly become a sign of that full communion in the one, holy, catholic and apostolic Church which will be expressed in the common celebration of the Eucharist.

78.5 This journey toward the necessary and sufficient visible unity, in the communion of the one Church willed by Christ, continues to require patient and courageous efforts. In this process, one must not impose any burden beyond that which is strictly necessary (cf. Acts 15:28).

79.1 It is already possible to identify the areas in need of fuller study before a true consensus of faith can be achieved: 1) the relationship between Sacred Scripture, as the highest authority in matters of faith, and Sacred Tradition, as indispensable to the interpretation of the Word of God; 2) the Eucharist, as the Sacrament of the Body and Blood of Christ, an offering of praise to the Father, the sacrificial memorial and Real Presence of Christ and the sanctifying outpouring of the Holy Spirit; 3) Ordination, as a sacrament, to the threefold ministry of the episcopate, presbyterate and diaconate; 4) the Magisterium of the Church, entrusted to the Pope and the Bishops in communion with him, understood as a responsibility and an authority exercised in the name of Christ for teaching and safeguarding the faith; 5) the Virgin Mary, as Mother of God and Icon of the Church, the spiritual Mother who intercedes for Christ's disciples and for all humanity.

79.2 In this courageous journey toward unity, the transparency and the prudence of faith require us to avoid both false irenicism and indifference to the Church's ordinances.[131] Conversely, that same transparency and prudence urge us to reject a halfhearted commitment to unity and, even more, a prejudicial opposition or a defeatism which tends to see everything in negative terms.

---

[130] Second Vatican Ecumenical Council, Decree on Ecumenism *Unitatis Redintegratio*, 14.
[131] Cf. ibid., 4 and 11.

79.3 To uphold a vision of unity which takes account of all the demands of revealed truth does not mean to put a brake on the ecumenical movement.[132] On the contrary, it means preventing it from settling for apparent solutions which would lead to no firm and solid results.[133] The obligation to respect the truth is absolute. Is this not the law of the Gospel?

Reception of the results already achieved

80.1 While dialogue continues on new subjects or develops at deeper levels, a new task lies before us: that of receiving the results already achieved. These cannot remain the statements of bilateral commissions but must become a common heritage. For this to come about and for the bonds of communion to be thus strengthened, a serious examination needs to be made, which, by different ways and means and at various levels of responsibility, must involve the whole People of God. We are in fact dealing with issues which frequently are matters of faith, and these require universal consent, extending from the Bishops to the lay faithful, all of whom have received the anointing of the Holy Spirit.[134] It is the same Spirit who assists the Magisterium and awakens the *sensus fidei*.

80.2 Consequently, for the outcome of dialogue to be received, there is needed a broad and precise critical process which analyzes the results and rigorously tests their consistency with the Tradition of faith received from the Apostles and lived out in the community of believers gathered around the Bishop, their legitimate Pastor.

81.1 This process, which must be carried forward with prudence and in a spirit of faith, will be assisted by the Holy Spirit. If it is to be successful, its results must be made known in appropriate ways by competent persons. Significant in this regard is the contribution which theologians and faculties of theology are called to make by exercising their charism in the Church. It is also clear that ecumenical commissions have very specific responsibilities and tasks in this regard.

81.2 The whole process is followed and encouraged by the Bishops and the Holy See. The Church's teaching authority is responsible for expressing a definitive judgment.

---

[132] Cf. Address to the Cardinals and the Roman Curia (June 28, 1985), 6: *AAS* 77 (1985), 1153.

[133] Cf. ibid.

[134] Cf. Second Vatican Ecumenical Council, Dogmatic Constitution on the Church *Lumen Gentium*, 12.

81.3 In all this, it will be of great help methodologically to keep carefully in mind the distinction between the deposit of faith and the formulation in which it is expressed, as Pope John XXIII recommended in his opening address at the Second Vatican Council.[135]

Continuing spiritual ecumenism and bearing witness to holiness

82.1 It is understandable how the seriousness of the commitment to ecumenism presents a deep challenge to the Catholic faithful. The Spirit calls them to make a serious examination of conscience. The Catholic Church must enter into what might be called a "dialogue of conversion," which constitutes the spiritual foundation of ecumenical dialogue. In this dialogue, which takes place before God, each individual must recognize his own faults, confess his sins and place himself in the hands of the One who is our Intercessor before the Father, Jesus Christ.

82.2 Certainly, in this attitude of conversion to the will of the Father and, at the same time, of repentance and absolute trust in the reconciling power of the truth which is Christ, we will find the strength needed to bring to a successful conclusion the long and arduous pilgrimage of ecumenism. The "dialogue of conversion" with the Father on the part of each community, with the full acceptance of all that it demands, is the basis of fraternal relations which will be something more than a mere cordial understanding or external sociability. The bonds of fraternal *koinonia* must be forged before God and in Christ Jesus.

82.3 Only the act of placing ourselves before God can offer a solid basis for that conversion of individual Christians and for that constant reform of the Church, insofar as she is also a human and earthly institution,[136] which represent the preconditions for all ecumenical commitment. One of the first steps in ecumenical dialogue is the effort to draw the Christian Communities into this completely interior spiritual space in which Christ, by the power of the Spirit, leads them all, without exception, to examine themselves before the Father and to ask themselves whether they have been faithful to his plan for the Church.

83 I have mentioned the will of the Father and the spiritual space in which each community hears the call to overcome the obstacles to unity. All Christian Communities know that, thanks to the power given by the Spirit, obeying that will and overcoming those obstacles are not beyond their reach. All of

---

[135] Cf. *AAS* 54 (1962), 792.

[136] Cf. Second Vatican Ecumenical Council, Decree on Ecumenism *Unitatis Redintegratio*, 6.

them in fact have martyrs for the Christian faith.[137] Despite the tragedy of our divisions, these brothers and sisters have preserved an attachment to Christ and to the Father so radical and absolute as to lead even to the shedding of blood. But is not this same attachment at the heart of what I have called a "dialogue of conversion"? Is it not precisely this dialogue which clearly shows the need for an ever more profound experience of the truth if full communion is to be attained?

84.1 In a theocentric vision, we Christians already have a common *martyrology*. This also includes the martyrs of our own century, more numerous than one might think, and it shows how, at a profound level, God preserves communion among the baptized in the supreme demand of faith, manifested in the sacrifice of life itself.[138] The fact that one can die for the faith shows that other demands of the faith can also be met. I have already remarked, and with deep joy, how an imperfect but real communion is preserved and is growing at many levels of ecclesial life. I now add that this communion is already perfect in what we all consider the highest point of the life of grace, *martyria* unto death, the truest communion possible with Christ who shed his blood, and by that sacrifice brings near those who once were far off (cf. Eph 2:13).

84.2 While for all Christian communities the martyrs are the proof of the power of grace, they are not the only ones to bear witness to that power. Albeit in an invisible way, the communion between our Communities, even if still incomplete, is truly and solidly grounded in the full communion of the saints — those who, at the end of a life faithful to grace, are in communion with Christ in glory. These *saints* come from all the Churches and Ecclesial Communities which gave them entrance into the communion of salvation.

84.3 When we speak of a common heritage, we must acknowledge as part of it not only the institutions, rites, means of salvation and the traditions which all the Communities have preserved and by which they have been shaped, but first and foremost this reality of holiness.[139]

84.4 In the radiance of the "heritage of the saints" belonging to all Communities, the "dialogue of conversion" toward full and visible unity thus appears as a source of hope. This universal presence of the saints is in fact a proof of the transcendent power of the Spirit. It is the sign and proof of God's victory

---

[137] Cf. ibid., 4; Paul VI, Homily for the Canonization of the Ugandan Martyrs (October 18, 1964): *AAS* 56 (1964), 906.

[138] Cf. John Paul II, Apostolic Letter *Tertio Millennio Adveniente* (November 10, 1994), 37: *AAS* 87 (1995), 29-30.

[139] Cf. Paul VI, Address at the Shrine in Namugongo, Uganda (August 2, 1969): *AAS* 61 (1969), 590-591.

over the forces of evil which divide humanity. As the liturgies sing: "You are glorified in your saints, for their glory is the crowning of your gifts."[140]

84.5 Where there is a sincere desire to follow Christ, the Spirit is often able to pour out his grace in extraordinary ways. The experience of ecumenism has enabled us to understand this better. If, in the interior spiritual space described above, Communities are able truly to "be converted" to the quest for full and visible communion, God will do for them what he did for their saints. He will overcome the obstacles inherited from the past and will lead Communities along his paths to where he wills: to the visible *koinonia* which is both praise of his glory and service of his plan of salvation.

85 Since God in his infinite mercy can always bring good even out of situations which are an offense to his plan, we can discover that the Spirit has allowed conflicts to serve in some circumstances to make explicit certain aspects of the Christian vocation, as happens in the lives of the saints. In spite of fragmentation, which is an evil from which we need to be healed, there has resulted a kind of rich bestowal of grace which is meant to embellish the *koinonia*. God's grace will be with all those who, following the example of the saints, commit themselves to meeting its demands. How can we hesitate to be converted to the Father's expectations? He is with us.

Contribution of the Catholic Church to the quest for Christian unity

86 The Constitution *Lumen Gentium,* in a fundamental affirmation echoed by the Decree *Unitatis Redintegratio,*[141] states that the one Church of Christ subsists in the Catholic Church.[142] The Decree on Ecumenism emphasizes the presence in her of the fullness (*plenitudo*) of the means of salvation.[143] Full unity will come about when all share in the fullness of the means of salvation entrusted by Christ to his Church.

87 Along the way that leads to full unity, ecumenical dialogue works to awaken a reciprocal fraternal assistance, whereby Communities strive to give in mutual exchange what each one needs in order to grow toward definitive

---

[140] Cf. Roman Missal, Preface of Holy Men and Women I: "Sanctorum coronando merita tua dona coronans."

[141] Cf. Second Vatican Ecumenical Council, Decree on Ecumenism *Unitatis Redintegratio,* 4.

[142] Cf. Second Vatican Ecumenical Council, Dogmatic Constitution on the Church *Lumen Gentium,* 8.

[143] Cf. Second Vatican Ecumenical Council, Decree on Ecumenism *Unitatis Redintegratio,* 3.

fullness in accordance with God's plan (cf. Eph 4:11-13). I have said how we are aware, as the Catholic Church, that we have received much from the witness borne by other Churches and Ecclesial Communities to certain common Christian values, from their study of those values, and even from the way in which they have emphasized and experienced them. Among the achievements of the last thirty years, this reciprocal fraternal influence has had an important place. At the stage which we have now reached,[144] this process of mutual enrichment must be taken seriously into account. Based on the communion which already exists as a result of the ecclesial elements present in the Christian Communities, this process will certainly be a force impelling toward full and visible communion, the desired goal of the journey we are making. Here we have the ecumenical expression of the Gospel law of sharing. This leads me to state once more: "We must take every care to meet the legitimate desires and expectations of our Christian brethren, coming to know their way of thinking and their sensibilities. . . . The talents of each must be developed for the utility and the advantage of all."[145]

Ministry of unity of the Bishop of Rome

88 Among all the Churches and Ecclesial Communities, the Catholic Church is conscious that she has preserved the ministry of the Successor of the Apostle Peter, the Bishop of Rome, whom God established as her "perpetual and visible principle and foundation of unity"[146] and whom the Spirit sustains in order that he may enable all the others to share in this essential good. In the beautiful expression of Pope Saint Gregory the Great, my ministry is that of *servus servorum Dei*. This designation is the best possible safeguard against the risk of separating power (and in particular the primacy) from ministry. Such a separation would contradict the very meaning of power according to the Gospel: "I am among you as one who serves" (Lk 22:27), says our Lord Jesus Christ, the Head of the Church. On the other hand, as I acknowledged on the important occasion of a visit to the World Council of Churches in Geneva on June 12, 1984, the Catholic Church's conviction that in the ministry of the Bishop of Rome she has preserved, in fidelity to the apostolic Tradition and

---

[144] After the Lima Document of the Commission on Faith and Order, *Baptism, Eucharist, Ministry* (January 1982), and in the spirit of the Declaration of the Seventh General Assembly of the World Council of Churches, *The Unity of the Church as "koinonia": Gift and Task*, Canberra (February 7-20, 1991): cf. *Istina* 36 (1991), 389-391.

[145] Address to the Cardinals and the Roman Curia (June 28, 1985), 4: *AAS* 77 (1985), 1151-1152.

[146] Second Vatican Ecumenical Council, Dogmatic Constitution on the Church *Lumen Gentium*, 23.

the faith of the Fathers, the visible sign and guarantor of unity, constitutes a difficulty for most other Christians, whose memory is marked by certain painful recollections. To the extent that we are responsible for these, I join my Predecessor Paul VI in asking forgiveness.[147]

89 It is nonetheless significant and encouraging that the question of the primacy of the Bishop of Rome has now become a subject of study which is already under way or will be in the near future. It is likewise significant and encouraging that this question appears as an essential theme not only in the theological dialogues in which the Catholic Church is engaging with other Churches and Ecclesial Communities, but also more generally in the ecumenical movement as a whole. Recently the delegates to the Fifth World Assembly of the Commission on Faith and Order of the World Council of Churches, held in Santiago de Compostela, recommended that the Commission "begin a new study of the question of a universal ministry of Christian unity."[148] After centuries of bitter controversies, the other Churches and Ecclesial Communities are more and more taking a fresh look at this ministry of unity.[149]

90.1 The Bishop of Rome is the Bishop of the Church which preserves the mark of the martyrdom of Peter and of Paul: "By a mysterious design of Providence it is at Rome that [Peter] concludes his journey in following Jesus, and it is at Rome that he gives his greatest proof of love and fidelity. Likewise Paul, the Apostle of the Gentiles, gives his supreme witness at Rome. In this way the Church of Rome became the Church of Peter and of Paul."[150]

90.2 In the New Testament, the person of Peter has an eminent place. In the first part of the Acts of the Apostles, he appears as the leader and spokesman of the Apostolic College described as "Peter . . . and the Eleven" (2:14, cf.

[147] Cf. Address at the Headquarters of the World Council of Churches, Geneva (June 12, 1984), 2: *Insegnamenti* VII/1 (1984), 1686.

[148] World Conference of the Commission on Faith and Order, Report of the Second Section, Santiago de Compostela (1993): *Confessing the One Faith to God's Glory*, 31, 2, Faith and Order Paper No. 166, World Council of Churches, Geneva, 1994, 243.

[149] To cite only a few examples: Anglican-Roman Catholic International Commission, *Final Report*, ARCIC-I (September 1981); International Commission for Dialogue between the Disciples of Christ and the Roman Catholic Church, *Report* (1981); Roman Catholic/Lutheran Joint Commission, *The Ministry in the Church* (March 13, 1981). The problem takes clear shape in the research conducted by the Joint International Commission for the Theological Dialogue between the Catholic Church and the Orthodox Church.

[150] Address to the Cardinals and the Roman Curia (June 28, 1985), 3: *AAS* 77 (1985), 1150.

2:37, 5:29). The place assigned to Peter is based on the words of Christ himself, as they are recorded in the Gospel traditions.

91.1 The Gospel of Matthew gives a clear outline of the pastoral mission of Peter in the Church: "Blessed are you, Simon Bar-Jona! For flesh and blood has not revealed this to you, but my Father who is in heaven. And I tell you, you are Peter, and on this rock I will build my Church and the powers of death shall not prevail against it. I will give you the keys of the kingdom of heaven, and whatever you bind on earth shall be bound in heaven, and whatever you loose on earth shall be loosed in heaven" (16:17-19). Luke makes clear that Christ urged Peter to strengthen his brethren, while at the same time reminding him of his own human weakness and need of conversion (cf. 22:31-32). It is just as though, against the backdrop of Peter's human weakness, it were made fully evident that his particular ministry in the Church derives altogether from grace. It is as though the Master especially concerned himself with Peter's conversion as a way of preparing him for the task he was about to give him in his Church, and for this reason was very strict with him. This same role of Peter, similarly linked with a realistic affirmation of his weakness, appears again in the Fourth Gospel: "Simon, son of John, do you love me more than these?. . . Feed my sheep" (cf. Jn 21:15-19). It is also significant that according to the First Letter of Paul to the Corinthians the risen Christ appears to Cephas and then to the Twelve (cf. 15:5).

91.2 It is important to note how the weakness of Peter and of Paul clearly shows that the Church is founded upon the infinite power of grace (cf. Mt 16:17; 2 Cor 12:7-10). Peter, immediately after receiving his mission, is rebuked with unusual severity by Christ, who tells him: "You are a hindrance to me" (Mt 16:23). How can we fail to see that the mercy which Peter needs is related to the ministry of that mercy which he is the first to experience? And yet, Peter will deny Jesus three times. The Gospel of John emphasizes that Peter receives the charge of shepherding the flock on the occasion of a threefold profession of love (cf. 21:15-17), which corresponds to his threefold denial (cf. 13:38). Luke, for his part, in the words of Christ already quoted, words which the early tradition will concentrate upon in order to clarify the mission of Peter, insists on the fact that he will have to "strengthen his brethren when he has turned again" (cf. 22:32).

92.1 As for Paul, he is able to end the description of his ministry with the amazing words which he had heard from the Lord himself: "My grace is sufficient for you, for my power is made perfect in weakness"; consequently, he can exclaim: "When I am weak, then I am strong" (2 Cor 12:9-10). This is a basic characteristic of the Christian experience.

92.2 As the heir to the mission of Peter in the Church, which has been made fruitful by the blood of the Princes of the Apostles, the Bishop of Rome exercises a ministry originating in the manifold mercy of God. This mercy converts hearts and pours forth the power of grace where the disciple experiences the bitter taste of his personal weakness and helplessness. The authority proper to this ministry is completely at the service of God's merciful plan, and it must always be seen in this perspective. Its power is explained from this perspective.

93.1 Associating himself with Peter's threefold profession of love, which corresponds to the earlier threefold denial, his Successor knows that he must be a sign of mercy. His is a ministry of mercy, born of an act of Christ's own mercy. This whole lesson of the Gospel must be constantly read anew, so that the exercise of the Petrine ministry may lose nothing of its authenticity and transparency.

93.2 The Church of God is called by Christ to manifest to a world ensnared by its sins and evil designs that, despite everything, God in his mercy can convert hearts to unity and enable them to enter into communion with him.

94.1 This service of unity, rooted in the action of divine mercy, is entrusted within the College of Bishops to one among those who have received from the Spirit the task, not of exercising power over the people — as the rulers of the Gentiles and their great men do (cf. Mt 20:25; Mk 10:42) — but of leading them toward peaceful pastures. This task can require the offering of one's own life (cf. Jn 10:11-18). Saint Augustine, after showing that Christ is "the one Shepherd, in whose unity all are one," goes on to exhort: "May all shepherds thus be one in the one Shepherd; may they let the one voice of the Shepherd be heard; may the sheep hear this voice and follow their Shepherd, not this shepherd or that, but the only one; in him may they all let one voice be heard and not a babble of voices . . . the voice free of all division, purified of all heresy, that the sheep hear."[151] The mission of the Bishop of Rome within the College of all the Pastors consists precisely in "keeping watch" (*episkopein*), like a sentinel, so that, through the efforts of the Pastors, the true voice of Christ the Shepherd may be heard in all the particular Churches. In this way, in each of the particular Churches entrusted to those Pastors, the *una, sancta, catholica et apostolica ecclesia* is made present. All the Churches are in full

---

[151] Sermon XLVI, 30: *CCL* 41, 557.

and visible communion, because all the Pastors are in communion with Peter and therefore united in Christ.

94.2 With the power and the authority without which such an office would be illusory, the Bishop of Rome must ensure the communion of all the Churches. For this reason, he is the first servant of unity. This primacy is exercised on various levels, including vigilance over the handing down of the Word, the celebration of the liturgy and the sacraments, the Church's mission, discipline and the Christian life. It is the responsibility of the Successor of Peter to recall the requirements of the common good of the Church, should anyone be tempted to overlook it in the pursuit of personal interests. He has the duty to admonish, to caution and to declare at times that this or that opinion being circulated is irreconcilable with the unity of faith. When circumstances require it, he speaks in the name of all the Pastors in communion with him. He can also — under very specific conditions clearly laid down by the First Vatican Council — declare *ex cathedra* that a certain doctrine belongs to the deposit of faith.[152] By thus bearing witness to the truth, he serves unity.

95.1 All this, however, must always be done in communion. When the Catholic Church affirms that the office of the Bishop of Rome corresponds to the will of Christ, she does not separate this office from the mission entrusted to the whole body of Bishops, who are also "vicars and ambassadors of Christ."[153] The Bishop of Rome is a member of the "College," and the Bishops are his brothers in the ministry.

95.2 Whatever relates to the unity of all Christian Communities clearly forms part of the concerns of the primacy. As Bishop of Rome I am fully aware, as I have reaffirmed in the present Encyclical Letter, that Christ ardently desires the full and visible communion of all those Communities in which, by virtue of God's faithfulness, his Spirit dwells. I am convinced that I have a particular responsibility in this regard, above all in acknowledging the ecumenical aspirations of the majority of the Christian Communities and in heeding the request made of me to find a way of exercising the primacy which, while in no way renouncing what is essential to its mission, is nonetheless open to a new situation. For a whole millennium Christians were united in "a brotherly fraternal communion of faith and sacramental life. . . . If disagreements in belief and

[152] Cf. First Vatican Ecumenical Council, Dogmatic Constitution on the Church of Christ *Pastor Aeternus*: DS 3074.

[153] Second Vatican Ecumenical Council, Dogmatic Constitution on the Church *Lumen Gentium*, 27.

discipline arose among them, the Roman See acted by common consent as moderator."[154]

95.3 In this way the primacy exercised its office of unity. When addressing the Ecumenical Patriarch His Holiness Dimitrios I, I acknowledged my awareness that "for a great variety of reasons, and against the will of all concerned, what should have been a service sometimes manifested itself in a very different light. But . . . it is out of a desire to obey the will of Christ truly that I recognize that as Bishop of Rome I am called to exercise that ministry. . . . I insistently pray the Holy Spirit to shine his light upon us, enlightening all the Pastors and theologians of our Churches, that we may seek — together, of course — the forms in which this ministry may accomplish a service of love recognized by all concerned."[155]

96 This is an immense task, which we cannot refuse and which I cannot carry out by myself. Could not the real but imperfect communion existing between us persuade Church leaders and their theologians to engage with me in a patient and fraternal dialogue on this subject, a dialogue in which, leaving useless controversies behind, we could listen to one another, keeping before us only the will of Christ for his Church and allowing ourselves to be deeply moved by his plea "that they may all be one . . . so that the world may believe that you have sent me" (Jn 17:21)?

The communion of all particular Churches with the Church of Rome: a necessary condition for unity

97.1 The Catholic Church, both in her *praxis* and in her solemn documents, holds that the communion of the particular Churches with the Church of Rome, and of their Bishops with the Bishop of Rome, is — in God's plan — an essential requisite of full and visible communion. Indeed full communion, of which the Eucharist is the highest sacramental manifestation, needs to be visibly expressed in a ministry in which all the Bishops recognize that they are united in Christ and all the faithful find confirmation for their faith. The first part of the Acts of the Apostles presents Peter as the one who speaks in the name of the apostolic group and who serves the unity of the community — all the while respecting the authority of James, the head of the Church in Jerusalem. This function of Peter must continue in the Church so that under her sole Head, who is Jesus Christ, she may be visibly present in the world as the communion of all his disciples.

[154] Second Vatican Ecumenical Council, Decree on Ecumenism *Unitatis Redintegratio*, 14.

[155] Homily in the Vatican Basilica in the presence of Dimitrios I, Archbishop of Constantinople and Ecumenical Patriarch (December 6, 1987), 3: *AAS* 80 (1988), 714.

97.2 Do not many of those involved in ecumenism today feel a need for such a ministry? A ministry which presides in truth and love so that the ship — that beautiful symbol which the World Council of Churches has chosen as its emblem — will not be buffeted by the storms and will one day reach its haven.

Full unity and evangelization

98.1 The ecumenical movement in our century, more than the ecumenical undertakings of past centuries, the importance of which must not however be underestimated, has been characterized by a missionary outlook. In the verse of John's Gospel which is ecumenism's inspiration and guiding motif — "that they may all be one . . . so that the world may believe that you have sent me" (Jn 17:21) — the phrase *that the world may believe* has been so strongly emphasized that at times we run the risk of forgetting that, in the mind of the Evangelist, unity is above all for the glory of the Father. At the same time it is obvious that the lack of unity among Christians contradicts the Truth which Christians have the mission to spread and, consequently, it gravely damages their witness. This was clearly understood and expressed by my Predecessor Pope Paul VI, in his Apostolic Exhortation *Evangelii Nuntiandi:* "As evangelizers, we must offer Christ's faithful not the image of people divided and separated by unedifying quarrels, but the image of people who are mature in faith and capable of finding a meeting point beyond the real tensions, thanks to a shared, sincere and disinterested search for truth. Yes, the destiny of evangelization is certainly bound up with the witness of unity given by the Church. . . . At this point we wish to emphasize the sign of unity among all Christians as the way and instrument of evangelization. The division among Christians is a serious reality which impedes the very work of Christ."[156]

98.2 How indeed can we proclaim the Gospel of reconciliation without at the same time being committed to working for reconciliation between Christians? However true it is that the Church, by the prompting of the Holy Spirit and with the promise of indefectibility, has preached and still preaches the Gospel to all nations, it is also true that she must face the difficulties which derive from the lack of unity. When non-believers meet missionaries who do not agree among themselves, even though they all appeal to Christ, will they be in a position to receive the true message? Will they not think that the

---

[156] Apostolic Exhortation *Evangelii Nuntiandi* (December 8, 1975), 77: *AAS* 68 (1976), 69; cf. Second Vatican Ecumenical Council, Decree on Ecumenism *Unitatis Redintegratio*, 1; Pontifical Council for Promoting Christian Unity, *Directory for the Application of Principles and Norms on Ecumenism* (March 25, 1993), 205-209: *AAS* 85 (1993), 1112-1114.

Gospel is a cause of division, despite the fact that it is presented as the fundamental law of love?

99 When I say that for me, as Bishop of Rome, the ecumenical task is "one of the pastoral priorities" of my Pontificate,[157] I think of the grave obstacle which the lack of unity represents for the proclamation of the Gospel. A Christian Community which believes in Christ and desires, with Gospel fervor, the salvation of mankind can hardly be closed to the promptings of the Holy Spirit, who leads all Christians toward full and visible unity. Here an imperative of charity is in question, an imperative which admits of no exception. Ecumenism is not only an internal question of the Christian Communities. It is a matter of the love which God has in Jesus Christ for all humanity; to stand in the way of this love is an offense against him and against his plan to gather all people in Christ. As Pope Paul VI wrote to the Ecumenical Patriarch Athenagoras I: "May the Holy Spirit guide us along the way of reconciliation, so that the unity of our Churches may become an ever more radiant sign of hope and consolation for all mankind."[158]

Exhortation

100.1 In my recent letter to the Bishops, clergy and faithful of the Catholic Church indicating the path to be followed toward the celebration of the *great Jubilee of the Holy Year 2000*, I wrote that "the best preparation for the new millennium can only be expressed in a *renewed commitment to apply, as faithfully as possible, the teachings of Vatican II to the life of every individual and of the whole Church.*"[159] The Second Vatican Council is the great beginning — the Advent as it were — of the journey leading us to the threshold of the third millennium. Given the importance which the Council attributed to the work of rebuilding Christian unity, and in this our age of grace for ecumenism, I thought it necessary to reaffirm the fundamental convictions which the Council impressed upon the consciousness of the Catholic Church, recalling them in the light of the progress subsequently made toward the full communion of all the baptized.

100.2 There is no doubt that the Holy Spirit is active in this endeavor and

---

[157] Address to the Cardinals and the Roman Curia (June 28, 1985), 4: *AAS* 77 (1985), 1151.

[158] Letter of January 13, 1970: *Tomos Agapis*, Vatican-Phanar (1958-1970), Rome-Istanbul, 1971, 610-611.

[159] Apostolic Letter *Tertio Millennio Adveniente* (November 10, 1994), 20: *AAS* 87 (1995), 17.

that he is leading the Church to the full realization of the Father's plan, in conformity with the will of Christ. This will was expressed with heartfelt urgency in the prayer which, according to the Fourth Gospel, he uttered at the moment when he entered upon the saving mystery of his Passover. Just as he did then, today too Christ calls everyone to renew their commitment to work for full and visible communion.

101 I therefore exhort my Brothers in the Episcopate to be especially mindful of this commitment. The two *Codes of Canon Law* include among the responsibilities of the Bishop that of promoting the unity of all Christians by supporting all activities or initiatives undertaken for this purpose, in the awareness that the Church has this obligation from the will of Christ himself.[160] This is part of the episcopal mission and it is a duty which derives directly from fidelity to Christ, the Shepherd of the Church. Indeed all the faithful are asked by the Spirit of God to do everything possible to strengthen the bonds of communion between all Christians and to increase cooperation between Christ's followers: "Concern for restoring unity pertains to the whole Church, faithful and clergy alike. It extends to everyone according to the potential of each."[161]

102.1 The power of God's Spirit gives growth and builds up the Church down the centuries. As the Church turns her gaze to the new millennium, she asks the Spirit for the grace to strengthen her own unity and to make it grow toward full communion with other Christians.

102.2 How is the Church to obtain this grace? In the first place, through *prayer*. Prayer should always concern itself with the longing for unity, and as such is one of the basic forms of our love for Christ and for the Father who is rich in mercy. In this journey which we are undertaking with other Christians toward the new millennium, prayer must occupy the first place.

102.3 How is she to obtain this grace? Through *giving thanks*, so that we do not present ourselves empty-handed at the appointed time: "Likewise the Spirit helps us in our weakness . . . [and] intercedes for us with sighs too deep for words" (Rom 8:26), disposing us to ask God for what we need.

102.4 How is she to obtain this grace? Through *hope* in the Spirit, who can banish from us the painful memories of our separation. The Spirit is able to grant us clear-sightedness, strength and courage to take whatever steps are necessary, that our commitment may be ever more authentic.

---

[160] Cf. *Code of Canon Law*, Canon 755; *Code of Canons of the Eastern Churches*, Canon 902.

[161] Second Vatican Ecumenical Council, Decree on Ecumenism *Unitatis Redintegratio*, 5.

102.5 And should we ask if all this is possible, the answer will always be yes. It is the same answer which Mary of Nazareth heard: with God nothing is impossible.

102.6 I am reminded of the words of Saint Cyprian's commentary on *the Lord's Prayer*, the prayer of every Christian: "God does not accept the sacrifice of a sower of disunion, but commands that he depart from the altar so that he may first be reconciled with his brother. For God can be appeased only by prayers that make peace. To God, the better offering is peace, brotherly concord and a people made one in the unity of the Father, Son and Holy Spirit."[162]

102.7 At the dawn of the new millennium, how can we not implore from the Lord, with renewed enthusiasm and a deeper awareness, the grace to prepare ourselves, together, to offer this *sacrifice of unity?*

103 I, John Paul, *servus servorum Dei*, venture to make my own the words of the Apostle Paul, whose martyrdom, together with that of the Apostle Peter, has bequeathed to this See of Rome the splendor of its witness, and I say to you, the faithful of the Catholic Church, and to you, my brothers and sisters of the other Churches and Ecclesial Communities: *"Mend your ways, encourage one another, live in harmony, and the God of love and peace will be with you. . . . The grace of the Lord Jesus Christ and the love of God and the fellowship of the Holy Spirit be with you all"* (2 Cor 13:11, 13).

Given in Rome, at Saint Peter's, on May 25, the Solemnity of the Ascension of the Lord, in the year 1995, the seventeenth of my Pontificate.

---

[162] *On the Lord's Prayer*, 23: *CSEL* 3, 284-285.

Indexes

The references in these indexes are to paragraph numbers in the encyclicals. Their titles are abbreviated in accordance with the list of abbreviations below. References are listed in chronological order, based on the date of the encyclical's publication.

Abbreviations and Chronological Order of Encyclicals

RH   *Redemptor Hominis:* March 4, 1979
DM   *Dives in Misericordia:* November 30, 1980
LE   *Laborem Exercens:* September 14, 1981
SA   *Slavorum Apostoli:* June 2, 1985
DV   *Dominum et Vivificantem:* May 18, 1986
RMA   *Redemptoris Mater:* March 25, 1987
SRS   *Sollicitudo Rei Socialis:* December 30, 1987
RM   *Redemptoris Missio:* December 7, 1990
CA   *Centesimus Annus:* May 1, 1991
VS   *Veritatis Splendor:* August 6, 1993
EV   *Evangelium Vitae:* March 25, 1995
UUS   *Ut Unum Sint:* May 25, 1995

Biblical Index

Subject Index